CINEMA SYMBOLISM 3
THE MYSTERIES OF
OCCULT HOLLYWOOD UNVEILED

© April 2020, March 2021 Robert W. Sullivan IV

CINEMA SYMBOLISM 3
THE MYSTERIES OF OCCULT HOLLYWOOD UNVEILED

by
Robert W. Sullivan IV, Esq.

© April 2020, Robert W. Sullivan IV
Copyright Office, Library of Congress. All rights reserved.
Print ISBN: 978-0-578-80659-4

Front Cover: (Top Left) *Beauty and the Beast*: Belle dances with the Beast; (Top Right) *The Dark Knight Rises*: Catwoman-Selina Kyle; (Bottom Right) *Suspiria*: Susie Bannion dances the witchcraft-styled *Volk*; (Bottom Left) *Metropolis*: C.A. Rotwang and the *Maschinenmensch*; (Left Center) *Joker*: Arthur Fleck-Joker. (Center) The Bates Motel. Back Cover: In *Black Swan*, ballerina Nina Sayers performs alchemy, becoming her shadow; in *The Red Shoes*, crimson ballet slippers terrorize Vicky Page.

Graphic Design: Rebekkah Dreskin

Published by DEADWOOD PUBLISHING, LLC., Baltimore, Maryland, 2020.

Legal Disclaimer: All images (including cover and back cover) which appear in *Cinema Symbolism 3* are either: 1) in the public domain; 2) permitted by the Fair Use Doctrine (text is educational research); 3) and the Nominative Use Doctrine for any trademarks-logos. The author does not maintain ownership over any of the images which appear in this book except the About the Author image. *Rare Fish* by Félicien Rops.

CINEMA SYMBOLISM 3. All rights reserved. No part of this book may be reproduced, stored, or transmitted by any means whether auditory, graphic, mechanical, electronic without written permission of both publisher and author, except in the case of brief excerpts used in critical articles and reviews. Unauthorized reproduction of any part of this work is illegal and punishable by law.

OTHER BOOKS

by Robert W. Sullivan IV

NONFICTION

The Royal Arch of Enoch: The Impact of Masonic Ritual, Philosophy, and Symbolism, 2nd Edition (2016)

Cinema Symbolism: A Guide to Esoteric Imagery in Popular Movies, 2nd Edition (2017)

Cinema Symbolism 2: More Esoteric Imagery in Popular Movies, (2017)

FICTION

A Pact with the Devil: The Witches of Highgate, Vol. I (2017)

WWW.ROBERTWSULLIVANIV.COM

Non hic piscis omnium: This fish is not for everyone

CONTENTS

List of Illustrations I

Preface XIII

Introduction XXIX

Chapter I: Easter Eggs in the Bates Motel 1

Chapter II: Gnostic Hollywood 18

- The Above and Below of Fritz Lang's Metropolis
- Aeons, Archons, and Tuning: The Fallen Strangers of Dark City
- Mad World: Donnie Darko and the Robert W. Sullivan IV Connection
- Basilides' Nothingness in David Cronenberg's eXistenZ
- Splicing Dream and Reality in Vanilla Sky
- The Sword of Exact Zero: Prophetic Visions in the Lego Movie
- Snowpiercer's Deus Ex Machina: We Control the Engine, We Control the World

Chapter III: Archetypes, Alchemy, and Jungian Psychology in Disney's Beauty and the Beast 123

Chapter IV: Give Your Soul to the Dance: Melancholic Horror and Suspense 141

- Desolation and the Resurrected Dead: The Mummy 1932
- A Season in the Abyss: the German Autumn and Suspiria 2018
- History Repeats Itself: the Déjà Vu of Halloween 2018
- Birds of a Feather Flock Together: Chloe Sevigny and Kristen Stewart in Lizzie
- The Astrological Tropes in the House with a Clock in Its Walls

- Bubba Didn't Do It: Shining Light on the Archetypes of Dark Night of the Scarecrow
- Black Phillip Saith I Can Do What I Like: The Triumph of Evil over Good in The Witch
- Hymn to Pan's Labyrinth
- It's just a Spring Clean for the May Queen: Midsommar's Transcendent Gloom

Chapter V: Golem Making in Tinseltown: Blade Runner Revisited and Blade Runner 2049 287

- Blade Runner Revisited
- Blade Runner 2049

Chapter VI: The Mummy, the Golem, and the Automaton Reimagined: Dr. Caligari's Somnambulist 307

Chapter VII: Sable Visionaries: Christopher Nolan's Dark Knight Trilogy and Todd Phillips' Joker 316

- Winged Fear: Batman Begins
- Exploding Fire: The Dark Knight
- Black Ice: The Dark Knight Rises
- Put on a Happy Face: Joker

Chapter VIII: The Dark Side of the Moon: The Uncanny Electricity of the Temptress 360

- The Dance of Death: The Romantic Satanism of The Red Shoes
- Lolita: Kubrick's Occult Impulse
- The Neon Demon: Are We Having a Party or Something?
- The Red Shoes and Hairspray transcend The Shape of Water
- Uncle Toby Sent Me: Red Sparrow vs. Black Swan

Chapter IX: The Star Wars Saga Continues **435**
- The Gnostic Tao of Star Wars: The Force Awakens
- Rogue One: An Estrogen Driven Monomyth
- The Last Jedi's Ancient Religions

Chapter X: Elvis Presley Lights the Morning Sky: The New World's Masonic-Solar-Apollonian God of Music and the Christ Archetype in Film **466**

Chapter XI: Kabbalah and the Biblical Mysteries of Mother! **485**

Chapter XII: Tales from the Black and White Lodges: the Arcane Noir of David Lynch Continues **500**
- Eraserhead's Ironic Gnostic Paradox
- The Duality of Fire: Wild at Heart's Alchemical Wedding
- Twin Peaks Seasons 1 and 2: the Owls are not What They Seem
- Twin Peaks: Fire Walk with Me
- Twin Peaks Season 3: The Return

Chapter XIII: Return to Middle-earth: Bilbo Baggins and the Monomyth **601**
- An Unexpected Journey
- The Desolation of Smaug
- The Battle of the Five Armies

Conclusion **616**
Filmography **620**
Bibliography **649**
Index **675**
About the Author **683**

LIST OF ILLUSTRATIONS

Preface
- Gabriel Albinet's poster for the third Rose Croix salon.
- Frontispiece titled "Only Authentic Portrait of Wilhelm Heinrich Sebastian Von Troomp (From the Oil Painting)"
- Cover of *Baron Trump's Marvellous Underground Journey*
- Barron Trump
- Chris MacNeil on the set of *Crash Course*, *The Exorcist*
- Aleister Crowley making the Sign of Pan
- The logo for Homerun Pizza, *Satanic Panic*
- Operation Latte Thunder, *Fight Club*
- *The Sphere* formerly of the World Trade Center's Plaza
- Beavis and Butt-Head
- Dylan B. Klebold
- Eric D. Harris
- Bart Simpson, "The City of New York vs. Homer Simpson"
- Painting of Notre-Dame Cathedral (or St. Patrick's) engulfed in flames, *Rosemary's Baby*
- Notre-Dame Cathedral in Paris, France becomes an inferno, 15 April 2019
- *The Bridesmaid* painting by John Everett Millais
- Edith Cushing, *Crimson Peak*

Introduction
- Larry Talbot, Gwen Conliffe (Evelyn Ankers, 1918-1985), and the wolf's head cane. From *The Wolf Man*.
- Talbot's wolf's head cane leaning against a wall in Drearcliff House. From *The House of Fear*.
- Eliphas Levi's Baphomet, the Goat of Mendes
- Stanislas de Guaita's Goat Pentagram
- The Tree of the Dead, *Sleepy Hollow*
- The Tree of the Dead, *Alice in Wonderland*
- Pee Wee Herman and Simone, *Pee-wee's Big Adventure*

- Tucker and Esther Cobblepot, *Batman Returns*
- Nina Sayers masturbates in a bathtub, *Black Swan*
- In her bedroom, Nina transmogrifies into a bird, *Black Swan*
- Nina and Lila hit the dancefloor, *Black Swan*
- Edith Cushing and Lady Lucille Sharpe in the park, *Crimson Peak*
- Edith Cushing strolls in the park, *Crimson Peak*
- Victorian era gravestone with clasped hands iconography.
- Suzy Bannion in a taxicab, *Suspiria*
- Elizabeth walks to work, *9 ½ Weeks*
- Tyler Durden's business card, *Fight Club*
- Albus Dumbledore, *Harry Potter and the Half-Blood Prince*
- One-sheet movie poster for the film *Mother!*
- One-sheet movie poster for the film *Häxan: Witchcraft Through the Ages*
- Elizabeth flaunts her black silk stockings, *9 ½ Weeks*
- Elizabeth becomes aroused, *9 ½ Weeks*
- A portrait of a woman touching herself, *9 ½ Weeks*
- Elizabeth drools and sweats profusely while masturbating, *9 ½ Weeks*
- The Triumph of the Shadow: Elizabeth's black silk stockings and black high heels are hoisted high in the air signifying the release of her shadow self, *9 ½ Weeks*
- *L'Idole* by Félicien Rops
- Painting of the *Ars Goetia* demon Bael, *9 ½ Weeks*
- Painting of an *Ars Goetia* demon Paimon, *9 ½ Weeks*
- Conal Cochran, *Halloween III: Season of the Witch*
- SAMHAIN, *Halloween II*
- Jack's green tie, *The Shining*
- Jack's green tie, *The Shining*
- The hedge maze, *The Shining*
- The eight children of the Halloween School Bus Massacre with Mr. Kreeg (Gerald Paetz), *Trick 'r Treat*
- Mr. Wilkins' pumpkin, *Trick 'r Treat*
- Nina Sayers passes her doppelganger on the street, *Black Swan*
- Nina Sayers' reflection comes alive, *Black Swan*
- Two Ninas, *Black Swan*

- Maria Bosic, *Maria's Lovers*
- Superman at a bar, *Superman III*
- Supergirl at a bar, *Supergirl* (TV Series)
- Supergirl at a bar, *Supergirl* (TV Series)
- The chichi Elizabeth McGraw, *9 ½ Weeks*
- Elizabeth gazes into a mirror at the Chelsea Hotel, *9 ½ Weeks*
- A Hispanic prostitute fondles Elizabeth's black silk stockings, *9 ½ Weeks*
- A Hispanic prostitute removes Elizabeth's black silk stockings, *9 ½ Weeks*
- Mouse, *The Matrix*
- Elan Sleazebaggano and Obi-Wan Kenobi, *Star Wars: Attack of the Clones*
- The Woman in Red, *The Matrix*
- Hayde Gofai, *Star Wars: Attack of the Clones*
- Jane Forrester Lodge and her black silk stockings, *The New York Ripper*
- Elizabeth McGraw and her black silk stockings, *9 ½ Weeks*
- Selina Kyle, *The Dark Knight Rises*
- Holly Golightly (Audrey Hepburn) publicity photo for *Breakfast at Tiffany's*
- Wayne Hall, *Joker*
- Billboard for the movie *Ace in the Hole*, *Joker*
- The Deathly Hallows symbol, *Harry Potter and the Deathly Hallows Part 1*
- The symbol for the Philosopher's Stone
- The reverse of the Great Seal of the United States on the back of the one-dollar bill
- Hellfire eyes, or the finality of the *rubedo*, *Black Swan*
- Nina's webbed foot, *Black Swan*
- Embracing darkness, or the pleasure of the *nigredo*, *Black Swan*
- Rosemary Woodhouse receives red roses, *Rosemary's Baby*
- The Devil's eyes, *Rosemary's Baby*
- Rosemary wears a red frock, *Rosemary's Baby*
- Rosemary wears a red suit, *Rosemary's Baby*

- Suzy Bannion with Helena Markos' peacock sculpture, *Suspiria* 1977
- Julian Craster, Vicky Page, and Boris Lermontov, *The Red Shoes*
- Lermontov and a sculpture of a ballet slipper, *The Red Shoes*
- Vicky's crimson ballet slippers, *The Red Shoes*
- Count Mora and Luna, *Mark of the Vampire*
- *Salvatore Mundi* by Leonardo da Vinci

Chapter I

- *Susanna and the Elders* oil painting by either Frans van Mieris the Elder or Willem van Mieris, Frans' youngest son
- Sam Loomis subdues Norman Bates, *Psycho* (1960)
- *The House by the Railroad* oil painting by Edward Hopper
- The Bates Motel and Bates' hilltop house

Chapter II

- Evil from *Time Bandits*
- The Supreme Being from *Time Bandits*
- Oz the Great and Powerful from *The Wizard of Oz*
- Point Within A Circle
- *Metropolis'* New Tower of Babel
- Max Shreck's Corporate Headquarters, *Batman Returns*
- The Strangers, *Dark City*
- The Gentlemen, *Buffy the Vampire Slayer*
- Count Orlock, *Nosferatu*
- Riff Raff, *The Rocky Horror Picture Show*
- The Strangers' Clock, *Dark City*
- Frank the Rabbit, *Donnie Darko*
- Elizabeth Darko as Vivian Darkbloom, *Donnie Darko*
- Vivian Darkbloom and Clare Quilty, *Lolita*
- Allegra Gellar at the Country Gas Station, *eXistenZ*
- The Overlook Movie Theater, *Ready Player One*
- David Aames and Sophia Sorreno, *Vanilla Sky*
- *The Freewheelin' Bob Dylan* Album Cover

- Katie Holmes on the cover of the September 1998 issue of *Rolling Stone*
- President Business wields the Sword of Exact Zero, *The Lego Movie*
- "Here's Johnny!" *The Shining*
- Franco the Elder, *Snowpiercer*

Chapter III

- *Beauty and the Beast* 2017 one-sheet movie poster
- *Maleficent: Mistress of Evil* 2019 one-sheet movie poster
- Maleficent, *Maleficent: Mistress of Evil*
- Erica Sayers, *Black Swan*
- Beth Macintyre, *Black Swan*
- Nina stands before an idol of Rothbart, *Black Swan*
- Nina becomes Odile, the Black Swan, *Black Swan*

Chapter IV

- The mummy of Ramses III
- *The Mummy* 1932 one-sheet movie poster
- Aleister Crowley performing the Sign of Horus, the Enterer
- Susie Bannion unveils the Sign of Horus, the Enterer, *Suspiria* 2018
- Philippine "Pina" Bausch
- Madame Veva Blanc, *Suspiria* 2018
- Susie before a poster advertising the Markos Dance Group, *Suspiria* 2018
- ALL OF THEM WITCHES: Scrabble pieces and the book, *All of the Witches, Rosemary's Baby*
- Susie dreams of herself as a child sleeping in a cupboard, *Suspiria*
- *Self-Portrait (in cupboard)* by Claude Cahun, 1932.
- The Microprosopus
- The sabbath, *Suspiria* 2018
- The Tower, Card XVI of the Major Arcana
- Susie at dinner in *Suspiria* 2018

- Suzy investigates the dance school's hidden corridors in *Suspiria* 1977
- The Sign of Babalon, the Babe of the Abyss, the Attitude of Baphomet
- Susie promotional image imitating the Sign of Babalon, the Babe of the Abyss, the Attitude of Baphomet
- William Shatner/Captain Kirk Don Post Halloween Mask alongside Michael Myers' mask, *Halloween*
- Laurie Strode and her daughter Karen, *Halloween* 2018
- Black lingerie outside a window, *Suspiria* 1977
- The Demon's Eyes, *Suspiria* 1977
- Patricia Hingle attacked, *Suspiria* 1977
- The skulls of Andrew and Abby Borden, Fall River Historical Society
- A Green Lion devouring the Sun, *Rosarium Philosophorum*
- Kristen Stewart and Chloe Sevigny, *Lizzie*
- Alamo Movie Theater, *The House with a Clock in Its Walls*
- *Tales from Space* comic book, *Back to the Future*
- Cronin Mansion, Marshall, Michigan
- The Dark of the Moon, *The House with a Clock in Its Walls*
- The Rites of Lucifer, *The Black Cat*
- 19th-century engraving of John Dee and Edward Kelley performing necromancy
- *The Persistence of Memory* oil painting by Salvador Dali
- Astrological symbol of Taurus
- Astrological fountain, *The House with a Clock in Its Walls*
- Original *TV Guide* ad for *Dark Night of the Scarecrow* (Illinois-Wisconsin edition)
- *Witches' Sabbath* oil painting by Francisco Goya
- The Ace of Cups from the Rider-Waite Tarot deck
- Holda, *Gretel & Hansel: A Grim Fairy Tale*
- The Mysterious and Fulminating Wand, Chapter III, *The Red Dragon*
- Ofelia, *Pan's Labyrinth*
- Mural from Allerdale Hall, *Crimson Peak*
- *Saturn Devouring His Son* by Francisco Goya

- Dani and Terri Ardor's sleeping parents, *Midsommar*
- Terri's corpse, *Midsommar*
- The May Queen Procession, *Midsommar*
- Jayne Mansfield-Sophia Loren wardrobe malfunction photo, April 1957
- Photo of Jayne Mansfield with Anton LaVey
- *Ännu sitter Tuvstarr kvar och ser ner i vattnet* (English: *Still, Tuvstarr sits and gazes down into the water*) by John Bauer
- *Stackars lilla basse!* (English: *Poor little bear!*) by John Bauer
- Dani inside the door of her apartment, *Midsommar*
- *Print Number 23* by Julia Petrova
- *Saint John the Baptist* by da Vinci
- Bunkhouse mural, *Midsommar*
- Dani asleep in the bunkhouse, *Midsommar*
- Danny Torrance playing with his toys in the Overlook Hotel, *The Shining*
- Dani's nightmare featuring her deceased parents and her sister Terri, *Midsommar*
- Mark standing before the Hårga's pyramid, *Midsommar*
- Dani's father, *Midsommar*
- Dani's mother and sister, *Midsommar*
- Mark's skin stuffed with straw, wearing the hat of the fool, *Midsommar*
- Sgt. Howie dressed as Punch-as-the-Fool, *The Wicker Man*
- Mu Pan's untitled *Midsommar* painting, *Midsommar*

Chapter VI

- *Nude Descending a Staircase, No. 2* by Marcel Duchamp
- Dr. Caligari and Cesare, *The Cabinet of Dr. Caligari*
- Gwynplaine, *The Man Who Laughs*

Chapter VII

- Johnny Clay wears a Weary Willie mask, *The Killing*
- The Joker as Pagliacci, wearing a Weary Willie mask, from the episode "The Joker is Wild," from the 1960s television show *Batman*

- The Joker holds up a bank wearing a Weary Willie mask, *The Dark Knight*
- The Joker disguised as a policeman, panel from *Batman* Comic Book #1
- The Joker disguised as a policeman, *The Dark Knight*
- Two-Face, *The Dark Knight*
- *The Dark Knight* one-sheet movie poster
- The World Trade Center (Twin Towers), September 11, 2001
- Arthur Fleck as the Joker, *Joker*
- John Wayne Gacy as Pogo the Clown
- Inside Ha-Has, Arthur puts on his clown makeup, *Joker*
- Sock and Buskin
- Arthur applies white face paint, *Joker*
- Nina, the White Swan, *Black Swan*
- Nina, WHORE, *Black Swan*
- Arthur-as-Joker, *PUT ON A HAPPY FACE*, Joker

Chapter VIII

- Odile de Caray, *Eye of the Devil*
- Nina Sayers, *Black Swan*
- Charles Manson (image from the cover of *Life* magazine, 1969)
- The Dakota Apartment Building, New York City
- Nina masturbates, *Black Swan*
- Nina masturbates, *Black Swan*
- India Stoker licks an ice cream cone, *Stoker*
- India Stoker's saddle shoes, *Stoker*
- India Stoker masturbates, *Stoker*
- *Thérèse Dreaming* by Balthus
- Oil Painting of the luminous all-seeing eye, *9 ½ Weeks*
- Elizabeth mesmerized, *9 ½ Weeks*
- Elizabeth masturbates, *9 ½ Weeks*
- Art gallery buffet with a picked apart fish, *9 ½ Weeks*
- Selina Kyle paints it black, *Batman Returns*
- Catwoman's broken psyche, *Batman Returns*
- Vicky Page's red ballet slippers torture her, *The Red Shoes*
- Vicky Pages red ballet slippers destroy her, *The Red Shoes*

CINEMA SYMBOLISM 3

- Broken Music Box Dancer Figurine, *Black Swan*
- The Moon, Card XVIII of the Major Arcana, Rider-Waite Deck
- Vicky's suffers anxiety, *The Red Shoes*
- Vicky personifies the moon, *The Red Shoes*
- *Lolita* one-sheet movie poster
- Camp Climax, *Lolita*
- Humbert Humbert and Camp Climax's stuffed beaver, *Lolita*
- George Peatty shot in the face, *The Killing*
- Bullet hole to the portrait titled *Mrs. Bryan Cooke* (painted ca. 1787-1791) by George Romney, *Lolita*
- Louise Bourgeois' *The Arch of Hysteria*
- Bondage performance art, *The Neon Demon*
- One of Jeffrey Dahmer's victims
- Ruby and Jesse, *The Neon Demon*
- Elisa with the Amphibian Man, *The Shape of Water*
- Esmeralda and Quasimodo, *The Hunchback of Notre Dame*
- Elisa embraces the Amphibian Man, *The Shape of Water*
- Nina as Odile, *Black Swan*
- Katsushika Hokusai's *The Great Wave off Kanagawa*
- The wall in Elisa's apartment, *The Shape of Water*
- Boris Lermontov's office window, *The Red Shoes*
- Elisa's apartment window, *The Shape of Water*
- Giles' apartment window, *The Shape of Water*
- Nina Sayers, *Black Swan*
- Dominika Egorova, *Red Sparrow*
- The Moon, Card XVIII from the Rider-Waite Tarot deck
- A dog wanders in a snowy Moscow, *Red Sparrow*
- Wheel of Fortune, Card X from the Rider-Waite Tarot deck
- Nina in Leroy's apartment, *Black Swan*
- The symbol of Yale University's Skull and Bones, Order 322, the Brotherhood of Death
- Elizabeth's self-gratification, *9 ½ Weeks*
- Elizabeth's self-gratification, *9 ½ Weeks*
- Elizabeth's black stockings and high heels, *9 ½ Weeks*
- Elizabeth's emotional ruination, *9 ½ Weeks*

Chapter IX

- The game of Dejarik, *Star Wars: A New Hope*
- *Vav* (or *Vau*), the sixth letter of the Hebrew alphabet
- FN-2187, *Star Wars: The Force Awakens*
- The Death Star, *Star Wars*
- The moon Mimas, also known as Saturn I
- Rey's mirror reflections, *The Last Jedi*
- Nina's mirror reflections, *Black Swan*

Chapter X

- Elvis Presley in concert (1974) wearing his Aztec Sun Stone jumpsuit
- Jadis the White Witch, *The Lion, the Witch and the Wardrobe*
- Victor Frankenstein and Fritz graverobbing, *Frankenstein*
- Stained glass window at St. John the Baptist's Anglican Church, New South Wales
- John Coffey, *The Green Mile*

Chapter XI

- The astrological symbol of Pisces
- *Rosemary's Baby* one-sheet movie poster
- Third promotional one-sheet poster for *Mother!*
- *Madonna and Child* by Giovanni Battista Salvi da Sassoferrato
- Sculpture of Isis nursing Horus
- Strength, Card VIII of the Major Arcana, Rider-Waite Deck

Chapter XII

- The Lullaby League, *The Wizard of Oz*
- Mandie, Candie, and Sandie, *Twin Peaks: The Return*
- Renee Madison and Alice Wakefield, *Lost Highway*
- The dinner scene, *Eraserhead*
- Norman Rockwell's *Freedom from Want* (aka *The Thanksgiving Picture*)
- The Lovers, Card VI of the Major Arcana, Rider-Waite Deck
- Glinda the Good Witch of the South, *Wild at Heart*

- Winkie's, *Mulholland Drive*
- The hallway in Henry's apartment, *Eraserhead*
- The Red Room (or Waiting Room), *Twin Peaks*
- The Magician, Card I of the Major Arcana, Rider-Waite Deck
- Holly Golightly, *Breakfast at Tiffany's*
- Evelyn Marsh, *Twin Peaks*
- WALLIES, *Twin Peaks*
- Wally Brando, *Twin Peaks: The Return*
- Laura Palmer in the Red Room, *Twin Peaks*
- Laura's doppelganger in the Red Room, *Twin Peaks*
- Jean-Gaspard Deburau, *Les Enfants du paradis*
- Audrey Horne exchanges her saddles shoes for red high heels, *Twin Peaks*
- The Man from Another Place presents the green ring, *Twin Peaks: Fire Walk with Me*
- The Cigarette Smoking Man, *The X-Files*
- Agent Dana Scully is shown a pack of Morley Cigarettes, *The X-Files*
- A pack of Morley Cigarettes in *Twin Peaks: The Return*
- Dougie Jones, *Twin Peaks: The Return*
- Dougie Jones wearing the green ring, *Twin Peaks: The Return*
- Jade, *Twin Peaks: The Return*

Chapter XIII
- Galadriel's dark side, *The Hobbit: The Battle of the Five Armies*
- Gloin, *The Hobbit: The Battle of the Five Armies*
- Gimli, *The Lord of the Rings*

Conclusion
- The Masturbator Tarot card (00), *Rob's Forbidden Tarot* (Coming Soon)
- The Chaos Magician Tarot card (V), *Rob's Forbidden Tarot*
- The Shrunken Head Tarot card (XVIII), *Rob's Forbidden Tarot*

PREFACE

I shall be watching you with my third eye.
Sherlock Holmes, "The Mazarin Stone,"
The Memoirs of Sherlock Holmes, 1994

Rosebud.
Charles Foster Kane, *Citizen Kane*, 1941

It's almost time kids, the clock is ticking.
Be in front of your TV sets for the Horrorthon,
and remember the Big Giveaway at nine.
Don't miss it. And don't forget to wear your masks.
The clock is ticking. It's almost time.
Silver Shamrock Commercial Narrator,
Halloween III: Season of the Witch, 1982

Only the infinity of the depths of a man's mind can really tell the story.
Dr. Alton, *Glen or Glenda*, 1953

I'm the Swan Queen!
Nina Sayers, *Black Swan*, 2010

Everything's true. God's an astronaut.
Oz is over the rainbow, and Midian's where the monsters live.
And you came to die.
Peloquin, *Nightbreed*, 1990

♫ All the other kids with the pumped up kicks
You'd better run, better run, faster than my bullet ♫
Foster the People, "Pumped Up Kicks," 2010

Put on the red shoes, Vicky, and dance for us again.
Boris Lermontov, *The Red Shoes*, 1948

All Imperial forces have been evacuated,
and I stand ready to destroy the entire moon.
Director Orson Krennic, *Rogue One*, 2016

The dictum of Joséphin Péladan's (1858-1918) final Rose Croix salon (1897) defines Hollywood's methodology in the following century: "Man needs neither pure truth nor perfect realization; Man needs Mystery, not to penetrate it but to experience it," *Ordre de la Rose+Croix du temple et du Graal. VI geste esthétique. Sixième salon, catalogue,* 2-5. Moviemaking is a marvelous art; the audience, entering a theater, goes on a magical mystery tour experiencing realities beyond mundane existence. Led by the hierophant Papus (Gérard Encausse, 1865-1916), late 19th-century Paris was a petri dish culturing Martinism, Theosophy, Rosicrucianism, Freemasonry, theurgy, Hermeticism, black magic, alchemy, and Gnosticism, producing a bouquet of imaginative endeavors, foretelling Tinseltown's cauldron of cinematic occultism. Surely, all Freemasons know the Hermetic maxim is *as above, so below*; dark, cold, and home to supersonic winds, distant Neptune governs the motion picture industry. As the ruler of dreams, it influences Hollywood's mysticism and wizardry; Neptune also impacted France's Third Republic (1870-1940), inspiring its artists, writers, and poets.

La Belle Époque's (1871-1914) *je ne sais quoi* pervades countless movies, clearly visible in the works of James Whale (1889-1957), the Archers, Billy Wilder (1906-2002), Alfred Hitchcock (1899-1980), Stanley Kubrick (1928-1999), Alex Proyas, Roger Corman, Roman Polanski, David Lynch, and Guillermo del Toro, informing Ed Wood's (1924-1978) theatre of the absurd. *Sunset Boulevard*'s (1950) deuteragonist Norma Desmond (Gloria Swanson, 1899-1983) would've have wallowed in its whimsical atmosphere. Like the esoteric celebutantes haunting the City of Lights, the fallen star was open to the uncanny, her pet monkey a symbol of a bygone era. Hammer Horror owes a debt of gratitude to occult Paris, and it's indisputable that *Le Théâtre du Grand-Guignol* (est. 1897) spawned grindhouse and splatter films.

The famous French actress Sarah Bernhardt (1844-1923), one of the first prominent performers to make sound recordings and to act in motion pictures, was a Decadent goddess with a penchant for dark, morbid, and diabolical imagery. Cloaked in Pre-Raphaelite and Symbolist ambiance, she dressed like a Mephisthophelean work of art. Her home was decorated like a funeral parlor. She often slept in a coffin, sharing her abode with a skeleton she named Lazarus. She owned a full-length mirror framed in black velvet; perched on its frame was a stuffed vampire bat, a real one, with its wings

When form becomes actuality: Gabriel Albinet's (1865-1930) fascinating poster for Péladan's third Rose Croix salon (1894) sowed the seeds of one of the greatest hoaxes of the 20th and 21st centuries. It depicts the polymath Leonardo da Vinci (1592-1519) as Joseph of Arimathea, the godfather of the Holy Grail mysteries, and poet Dante Alighieri (ca. 1265-1321) as Hugues de Payens (ca. 1070-1136), Grand Master and cofounder of the Knights Templar. An angel descends with the holy chalice, the sacred feminine, passing its secrets to the initiated few. The advertisement triggered Pierre Plantard (1920-2000) and Philippe de Chérisey's (1923-1985) Priory of Sion *ludibrium* (obviously!): Jesus Christ's bloodline, symbolized by the Grail, was still extant, covertly documented by a Masonic-Rosicrucian secret society, corroborated by the *Dossiers Secrets d'Henri Lobineau*. The Priory claims, among others, da Vinci, mathematician and physicist Isaac Newton (1642-1727), astrologer and occultist Robert Fludd (1574-1637), and composer Claude Debussy (1862-1918) as Grand Masters; the latter having transformed music through Hermetic initiation: the immersion in divine intellect (*nous*) invisible to the world and the worldly. The poster produced the germ that became the book *Holy Blood, Holy Grail* (1982), begetting Dan Brown's puerile *The Da Vinci Code* novel (2003) and movie (2006).

outstretched. Bernhardt's prized possession was a human skull given to her by Victor Hugo (1802-1885), on which he inscribed one of his poems. Her staging of a demonic feminine persona became a way of transgressing traditional womanly behavior, signaling aloofness from societal rules and pious propriety, a modus operandi permeating Hollywood.

The French sage Eliphas Levi (1810-1875) identified Lucifer–the Great Magical Agent–as the driving force behind ingenuity since the Light Bearer is the vehicle of illumination and the receptacle of all forms. Warming, liberating, and vivifying in its prudent use, among the pomp and works of Hell are those illusory images of pleasure, wealth, and glory, which are misdirected by the vertigo of this sublime Light. It follows that if Hermeticism's fundamental tenets are innovation and creativity, enunciated by Hermes Trismegistus in his Gnostic dialogs, then Los Angeles is its visionary, kabalistic capital. Hollywood is its Vatican: a mecca of occult modernity, and its postulants' sole article of faith: the Stanislavski Technique. Since its halcyon days in the early 20th century, this neopagan synagogue has gone back to the future, basking in a Babylonian aura. In 1916, Freemason and occultist extraordinaire, Aleister Crowley (1875-1947), passed through Hollywood, taking note of the natives as "the cinema crowd of cocaine-crazed, sexual lunatics." The remark is hypocritical or made tongue-in-cheek, coming from the self-proclaimed Great Beast 666, sex magick guru, and drug addict. Regardless, the comment speaks volumes regarding Hollywood's creed: art is its godhead, Luciferianism its philosophy, and hedonism its religion with champagne baths for all; scandal, vice, fame, sex, glamor, excess, fortune, and redemption by sin are Tinseltown's way of life.

From Crowley to D.W. Griffith (1875-1948), from one Freemason to another, the Purple Epoch's Masonic maestro started it all with his great *Sun-Play of the Ages*, *Intolerance* (1916), demanding eight giant white elephants, perched atop massive pillars, dominating Belshazzar's Feast. Griffith, filming Babylon's wickedness, was carrying on the European Descendants and Symbolists' tradition; that is, to produce a hierophany: a manifestation of the sacred. And that's what cinema is all about: using art to generate neo-mythologies and egregores, casting necromantic, visual spells some darker than others, getting Apollyon's two thumbs up. Hollywood draws down supernal forces or uses the Acheron's, Lethe's, Styx's, Cocytus', and Phlegethon's hydropower to energize its studios, for La-La Land's enchanters recognize good and evil's interdependence. The Romantic Satanist, William Blake (1757-1827), opined: "Poetry, painting and music, the three powers in man for conversing with paradise that the flood did not sweep away." Add a fourth and fifth to that enumeration: thespianism and moviemaking. Blake's radicalism, occult preoccupations, and reliance on other earlier esoteric traditions challenged his day's religious, socioeconomic, and political institutions. Likewise, Hollywood has a deep interest in the mysterious and the blasphemous, defying orthodoxy by synthesizing sorcery with entertainment to undermine religion and influence the populace, hypnotizing the masses without them even knowing it. Maybe it is the New Jerusalem, the Aquarian Age's shining city on a hill.

Do movies and TV shows predict the future? The mystic, scientist, and rumored Jacobite Freemason Emanuel Swedenborg (1688-1772), after his visionary entry into discarnate realms, was a prolific chronicler of the unseen, the future, auguring Hollywood's eldritch ability to use its art to prophesize, turning out, in some instances, celluloid prognostications. Swedenborg, who accurately predicted the date of his death, was also interested in psychology, influencing the theories of the psychiatrist, Carl Gustav Jung (1875-1961), over two centuries later. Jung should be considered the inheritor of the Swedenborgian mysteries.

CINEMA SYMBOLISM 3

(Left) Frontispiece titled "Only Authentic Portrait of Wilhelm Heinrich Sebastian Von Troomp (From the Oil Painting)" from the book (center) *Baron Trump's Marvellous Underground Journey* (1893). (Right) Real-life Barron Trump bears an eerily similarity to the portrait of Von Troomp, called Little Baron Trump. His adventure begins in Russia under the tutelage of a character named Don, described as a *learned thinker and philosopher*. Believe it or not.

On November 16, 2016, Comedy Central's cartoon, *Legends of Chamberlain Heights*, aired an episode titled "End of Days," featuring basketball superstar Kobe Bryant (1978-2020) dying in a helicopter crash. Fast-forward three years to January 26, 2020, when Kobe perished in a helicopter crash in Calabasas, California, killing all on board. Is it a coincidence that *The China Syndrome*, a film about a nuclear reactor disaster, was released on March 16, 1979, a mere twelve days before the meltdown of reactor 2 at the Three Mile Island Nuclear Generating Station?

What about commercials and books–can they be prophetic? In 2010, New York real-estate magnate Donald Trump appeared in a television ad for Serta Mattresses, featuring sheep standing outside hotel rooms 11 and 9, prophesying his winning the Presidency on November 9, 2016, six years later.[1] Years earlier, as crazy as it sounds, these numbers materialize in *Gremlins 2: The New Batch*, released in June 1990. Two news reporters, with nine and eleven on their microphones, viz. 9/11, interview Daniel Clamp (John Glover), a Donald Trump analog. Going back even further, to 1958, when a television western, *Trackdown* (1957-1959), featured an episode titled "The End of the World" (May 9, 1958), with a snake-oil

---

1 In the United States, Election Day 2016 was Tuesday, November 8; however, Trump wasn't declared President-Elect until the early-morning hours of November 9.

salesman named Walter Trump (Lawrence Dobkin, 1919-2002), promising salvation by building a wall. Funny enough, the episode's title, "The End of the World," anticipated the Democrats' nervous breakdown over the election of 45th President.[2]

And how about Ingersoll Lockwood's (1841-1918) novel, *Baron Trump's Marvellous Underground Journey* (1893), wherein the protagonist, Baron Trump, begins his adventure in Northern Russia, mentored by a scholar named Don Fum. Before voyaging into the unknown, the family's motto, *Per Ardua ad Astra* (English: *The pathway to glory is strewn with pitfalls and dangers*), reminds the young adventurer to beware, to take care. The aphorism foreshadows the Deep State's failed effort to remove the Churchillian President by hook or by crook. But by Lockwood's third novel, *1900: Or; The Last President* (1896), things become even more eerily tied to the present. The story begins in early November, describing a panicked New York City in a state of uproar after the election of a vehemently opposed outsider candidate. "The entire East Side is in a state of uproar," police officers shouted through the streets, warning the city folk to stay indoors for the night. "Mobs of vast size are organizing under the lead of anarchists and socialists, and threaten to plunder and despoil the houses of the rich who have wronged and oppressed them for so many years. The Fifth Avenue Hotel will be the first to feel the fury of the mob," the novel continues, citing an address in New York City where Trump Tower now stands. "Would the troops be in time to save it?"[3] One will have to read the book to find out what happens next; nevertheless, the parallels between Lockwood's story and the post-2016 political reality of the United States are extraordinary.

In a May 16, 2019 video, President Trump (@realDonaldTrump) tweeted that New York City Mayor Bill de Blasio would never be President because he (Trump) is "pretty good at predicting things like that." Granted, one doesn't have to be Nostradamus (1503-1566) to know de Blasio will never be Commander in Chief. But still, one wonders: does Trump's tweet infer time travel? Curiously, the President's uncle, John Trump (1907-1985),

---

2 Generation Snowflake: young misguided brats of the 2010s more prone to taking offense and less resilient than previous generations, or as being too emotionally vulnerable to cope with views that challenge their own.
3 Dan Evon, "Is 'Baron Trump's Marvelous Underground Journey' a Real Book from the 1890s?" *Snopes*, August 1, 2017, https://www.snopes.com/fact-check/baron-trumps-marvelous-underground-journey/ (accessed November 1, 2018).

was an electrical engineer, inventor, physicist, and research chief at MIT. Uncle John was charged with reviewing the notes and research of fellow electric engineer and futurist Nikola Tesla (1856-1943) postmortem. Tesla, of course, is rumored to have flirted with time travel, among other fascinating technologies. What did Uncle John discover and invent? Is the 45th President using Tesla's technology to move forward and backward in time? Or, is this evidence of a parallel universe bleeding through, or merging realities (the Mandela Effect), or the collective unconscious anticipating the future, or is it all just a coincidence?[4] I prefer to let the reader decide.

And what about the CIA's involvement with Hollywood? After graduating from Georgetown University, the author of *The Exorcist* (published 1971), William Peter Blatty (1928-2017), worked in Lebanon in the '50s for the CIA under U.S. Information Agency cover.[5] Later, Blatty returned to Washington D.C. to become a policy branch chief of the Psychological Warfare Division of the U.S. Air Force. His domestic duties involved the military's promotion of popular anti-Communist sentiment akin to McCarthyism while fostering traditional Cold War (1947-1991) foreign policy abroad. The orchestrated exodus of Catholics from North to South Vietnam in the mid-50s exemplified psychological warfare. In collaboration with Dr. Tom Dooley (1927-1961, whom Blatty quotes in his novel) and others, an extensive campaign was carried out by the Catholic Relief Service. Local Catholic leaders and an American psychological warfare team combined to drive peasants south of the DMZ by telling them, "The Virgin Mary has departed from the north [and] Christ has gone to the south." Amateur as this appears now, "The mass flight was admittedly the result of an extensive, well-conducted, and in terms of its objective, very successful American psychological warfare operation." (quotes from *The Indochina Story*, Bantam, 1970).[6]

In the post-60s era, when a majority of youth, both on and off college campuses, displayed frustration with, or abandonment of, traditional political protest activities, movie-going enjoyed a sharp increase. This atmosphere

---

4 During two of his rallies in 2016, would-be attackers of Donald Trump claimed to be time travelers, indicating the President himself might have the ability to move backward and forward through time. This author's recent online search to locate articles discussing the time-traveling element yielded no results, seemingly erased from existence.
5 Georgetown University was where the campus scenes of *The Exorcist* were filmed.
6 "The Exorcist: CIA Script?" *Ann Arbor Sun*, June 28, 1974, https://aadl.org/node/197187 (accessed June 25, 2019).

Chris MacNeil exits her trailer to shoot the student protest scene in *Crash Course*. Later, Chris jokingly describes the movie to her assistant, Sharon (Kitty Winn), as "The Walt Disney version of the Ho Chi Minh story." From *The Exorcist*.

produced a new widespread audience, one without specific political or spiritual direction and, therefore, ripe for suggestion. The covert methods used by Blatty in his terrifying novel were well-honed from his years of implementing cloak-and-dagger psychological warfare techniques for the U.S. Government. During the '50s, these tactics could be foisted on the naïve public, but by the early to mid-70s, a more sophisticated approach was needed to convey critical messages. Accordingly, Blatty used his talent, applying the same subliminal techniques to the horror film spawned by his novel. The movie, directed by William Friedkin, seeks to extinguish the leftover radicalism of the '60s while bringing the occult to the mainstream; remember, Regan MacNeil (Linda Blair) uses Ouija to conjure Captain Howdy *qua* Pazuzu. *The Exorcist*, released December 1973, features an actress, Chris MacNeil (Ellen Burstyn), starring in a film called *Crash Course*. A scene depicts Chris' character, a college professor, determined to shut down a student protest, implying it is a waste of time because any change must be made "within the system." The expulsion of an unruly demon by erudite Jesuits represents the supreme authority of the church over a trouble-making entity, instinctively suggesting the power of the state over the populace, thereby making *The Exorcist* a tool of political reaction and a product of government-sponsored psychological

(Left) The Great Beast, Aleister Crowley, makes the Sign of Pan; emblazoned on his hat is the Eye of Horus also known as the Eye of Providence. Employed by the Freemasons since time immemorial, the Eye in the Triangle symbolizes the godhead, the Supreme Being, appearing on the society's aprons, trestle boards, and medals, among other things. The sigil associates with the Illuminati, signifying their quest to become godlike, ruling humankind from the shadows. In *Satanic Panic*, Homerun Pizza employs the Eye of Horus as its gaudy logo (right), appearing on the t-shirts worn by its delivery guys and gals, including the busking, virginal protagonist, Samantha Craft. The emblem insinuates the coven's overarching desire to rule the world by using witchcraft to become omnipotent, like the Illuminati.

manipulation. For dogmatic religion, activated as a response to a conceived threat–demonic possession–can be a powerful ideological cement to keep the masses submissive and spellbound in a time of social transition, from the revolutionary '60s to the passive and decadent '70s.[7]

Does the Illuminati rule the world, shepherding Hollywood's sorcery? The legendary director, Stanley Kubrick, hints this was the case. The historical Illuminati was founded on Beltane, May 1, 1776, by Professor Adam Weishaupt (1748-1830) of Ingolstadt to achieve absolute political power, restrict governments, and revolutionize religion. Today, the Jesuit-inspired secret society denotes an elite cabal operating on global, political, and socioeconomic levels, using Hollywood to promote a Babylonian agenda, to cause the populace to abandon the Abrahamic Faiths, and traditional values, in

---

7 Ibid. See also George Case, *Here's to My Sweet Satan: How the Occult Haunted Music, Movies, and Pop Culture* (Fresno: Quill Driver Books, 2016), 29.

favor of radical Luciferianism. They destroy all those that stand in their way or threaten to expose their plot and modus operandi. In his Illuminati masterpiece, *Eyes Wide Shut* (1999), the *New York Post* has the headline LUCKY TO BE ALIVE. The protagonist, Bill Hartford (Tom Cruise), buys a copy, reading about the death of Amanda Curran (Julienne Davis), an apparent Illuminati sacrifice. The headline tells it like it is because the Illuminati disposes of all those attempting to reveal its subterfuge; let's ask Jeffrey Epstein (1953-2019), who was about to spill the beans, exposing his globalist sex trafficking ring in a plea deal. He was found hanged in his jailcell–a so-called suicide–inside a federal detention facility, the Metropolitan Correctional Center (MCC New York). Epstein's death makes Kubrick's film feel more like a documentary than a work of fiction. By making *Eyes Wide Shut*, many believe Kubrick was trying to unmask the Illuminati and, in doing so, ended up taking a dirt nap just like Epstein for dead men tell no tales.

Many films like *Escape from New York* (1981), *Fight Club* (1999), *The Matrix* (1999), *The Patriot* (2000), and *The Simpsons* TV episode "The City of New York vs. Homer Simpson" (September 21, 1997) herald the

(Right) *Fight Club*'s Space Monkeys destroy a piece of corporate art, bearing a striking resemblance to *The Sphere* (left) formerly in the Twin Towers' plaza. *Fight Club* was released in theaters in the United States on September 10, 1999, nearly two years to September 11, 2001. *The Simpsons* episode, "New York City vs. Homer Simpson," aired two years earlier, on September 21, 1997, almost four years before 9/11/01. It appears that an unknown occult force synchronizes *The Simpsons* episode, *Fight Club*, and the events of 9/11.

attack on the World Trade Center on September 11, 2001. For example, in *Fight Club*, before the controlled demolition of the financial buildings *qua* World Trade Center, Tyler Durden (Brad Pitt) refers to the site as "ground zero." Known as Operation Latte Thunder, Durden's disciples–the Space Monkeys–are ordered to destroy a piece of corporate art while taking out a franchise coffee bar simultaneously. The sculpture they destroy bears an uncanny resemblance to Fritz Koenig's (1924-2017) *The Sphere* previously at the World Trade Center, presaging Lower Manhattan's destruction and chaos. Even real-life events seem to portend 9/11. On April 20, 1999, a mere two and a half years earlier, Eric Harris (1999-2001) and Dylan Klebold

When the archetypes turn deadly. (Top) Popular in the 1990s, the cartoon characters Beavis (right) and Butt-Head (left), two high school misfits, epitomize the zero card of the Major Arcana, the Fool archetype: a dunce capable–under certain conditions–of becoming an injurious wild card. "Pumped Up Kicks": Beavis and Butt-Head became the murderous duo of Dylan Klebold (bottom left) and Eric Harris (bottom right) who shot and killed 13 people on April 20, 1999, during the Columbine High School massacre. Like Beavis and Butt-Head, they were high school outsiders. Unlike their comical cartoon counterparts, Dylan and Eric became melancholic Death archetypes, embodying the Tarot's 13th card (Major Arcana), which is the number of people they murdered. They epitomize the card's archetypal qualities: corrosive and destructive actions, i.e., alchemy's *nigredo* phase, striking and harming humankind, dark vitality causing drastic change, plaguing others with catastrophe, and victim collection. Like the Grim Reaper, the Saturnian plowman, Dylan and Eric dressed in black, identifying them as death merchants; the Reaper's black robe was their black trench coats, and the Reaper's scythe became their firearms. Psychologically, the pair became a living Tarot trump, awakened from the collective unconscious, hence the macabre fascination with their case.

(1981-1999) tried to blow up the cafeteria (known as the commons) at their school, Columbine High, during the height of lunch hour. When the bombs failed to detonate, they went inside and shot up the school, the library specifically, killing several students and wounding countless others. They modeled their attack after the L.A. Riots (1992) and the bombing of Oklahoma City's Federal Building (1995), attempting to surpass the death tolls in both of those earlier disasters. In Harris' journal, he detailed a plan to hijack an airplane, load it with explosives, and crash it into New York City. Oddly, his partner-in-crime, Klebold, was born on September 11, 1981, the day of the aerial attacks on the Twin Towers twenty years later. The diary entry and birthdate, when combined, anticipate or predict the terrorism of 9/11, becoming a textbook example of Jungian synchronicity.

Maybe the orchestrators of 9/11–often thought to be rogue elements in the United States intelligence and covert-military apparatus–sought inspiration from cinema. According to many conspiracy experts, the Twin Towers and 7 World Trade Center were brought down via explosives in an elaborate controlled demolition. This theory begs the obvious question: how were bombs planted in the buildings without anyone noticing? Believe it or not, a mysterious company–which is now defunct–named the Ace Elevator Company was allowed access to the World Trade Center from January to September 2001, in an extensive elevator renovation project. To this day, the Ace Elevator Company remains a mystery; however, it's undisputed the foremost elevator repair company is the Otis Elevator Company, not Ace. In 1853, Elisha Otis (1811-1861) founded the company in Yonkers, New York. A pioneer in its field, Otis develops, manufactures, installs, repairs, and markets elevators, escalators, moving walkways, and related equipment; it is the world's largest manufacturer of vertical transportation systems. One would think Otis would have been hired to do any repair work or renovations on the elevators in the World Trade Center.

Bart Simpson anticipates the 9/11 terrorist attack in the 1997 *Simpsons* episode "New York City vs. Homer Simpson." Nine-eleven manifests on the magazine cover with the Twin Towers substituting for the number 11.

CINEMA SYMBOLISM 3

The Mystery of the Cathedral: in Polanski's satanic thriller, Rosemary glances at a painting of Notre-Dame Cathedral on fire, seemingly prophesizing the April 15, 2019, inferno that engulfed Notre-Dame (right), destroying most of the Paris church. Rosemary sees the painting as she surreptitiously enters Roman and Minnie's apartment, shortly before discovering her baby, Adrian, the Devil's son. The fire at Notre-Dame Cathedral, having occurred the day after Palm Sunday and during Easter Week, feels like an attack by the Devil himself. "Satan is his father, not Guy. He came up from Hell and begat a son of mortal woman. Satan is his father, and his name is Adrian. He shall overthrow the mighty and lay waste their temples. He shall redeem the despised and wreak vengeance in the name of the burned and the tortured. Hail Adrian! Hail Satan! Hail Satan!" – Roman Castevet, *Rosemary's Baby*. Note: In Levin's novel, the painting of the fiery cathedral is St. Patrick's in New York City. However, the artwork resembles Notre-Dame, which makes sense because of Polanski's European heritage.

Forsooth, the Ace Elevator Company draws forth *Spies Like Us* (1985), in which the Ace Tomato Company, a shell company, secretly performs the wet works and black ops for the U.S. Government. The two companies' names are almost identical; Ace Tomato operates from a secret bunker via a rapidly descending elevator, which only adds to the strangeness. Did the masterminds of 9/11 borrow Ace Tomato Company to create a shadow company, a phony elevator repair business, to gain access to the World Trade Center's elevator shafts? If so, this would have permitted Ace Elevator repairmen unfettered access to the Twin Towers' core, allowing them to plant thermite cutting devices on the support columns and load-bearing members unnoticed and unhindered. The result would have been the controlled demolition of the Twin Towers and 7 WTC. If this is the case, then the shadow organization behind 9/11–whatever that may be–drew inspiration from *Spies Like Us* to execute their evil plan. Life, it seems, does imitate art after all.

On the doctrine of life imitating art and vice versa, nothing could be truer than the case of Elisa Lam (1991-2013). The body of Lam, a student at the University of British Columbia in Vancouver, was recovered from a water tank atop the Cecil Hotel in downtown Los Angeles on February 19, 2013, after she'd been reported missing at the beginning of the month. Hotel maintenance workers discovered the body when investigating guest complaints about problems with the water, indicating it tasted disgustedly sweet, had a strange odor, becoming black when turning on the shower.

Her disappearance was widely reported. Interest increased five days before her body's discovery when the LAPD released a video of her on the date she disappeared, taken by a security camera. In the footage, Lam is seen exiting and re-entering a malfunctioning elevator, pressing its buttons, talking and gesturing in the hallway outside, and sometimes hiding. The video went viral on the Internet, with many viewers reporting they found it unsettling, with explanations ranging from claims of paranormal activity to a Lam's bipolar disorder; it has also been suggested the video was altered before its release. The circumstances of Lam's death, once her corpse was found, also raised questions, especially in light of the Cecil's eldritch history. Numerous suicides have occurred in the hotel, and serial killers Johann "Jack" Unterweger (1950-1994) and Richard "the Night Stalker" Ramirez (1960-2013) stayed there while on the prowl.

Lam's body was discovered naked with most of her clothes and personal effects floating in the water nearby. It took the Los Angeles County Coroner's office four months, after repeated delays, to release the autopsy report, indicating no evidence of physical trauma, stating the manner of death was accidental. While all this was occurring, there was a tuberculous outbreak in the neighborhood around the Cecil Hotel. Believe it or not, since the late '70s, the kit's name, administered to assay people for the disease, is LAM-ELISA.

Making this matter particularly weird, the movie *Dark Water* (2005) predicted many elements from the Lam case eight years earlier. To briefly summarize, a mother and daughter move into an apartment; the daughter's name is Cecilia (Ariel Gade), conjuring the Cecil Hotel. The mother discovers dark water in the bathroom leading her to find the body of a murdered girl in the apartment's water tank, anticipating exactly how Lam's body was found. It concludes with a ghostly visitation in a haunted elevator portending Lam's erratic behavior and final moments depicted in the video. As I've said during podcasts many times, you can't make this stuff up.

* * * * *

When I began outlining this book, I immediately tried to come up with a suitable subtitle, but it was a bit of a struggle. I thought the subtitles of my previous movie books worked well, and I wanted this book to have one, but it had to be considerably different. After all, *Even More Esoteric Imagery in Popular Movies* wasn't going to work–it is repetitive and uninspired. After contemplating for a short time, I came up with *The Mysteries of Occult Hollywood Unveiled*. I believe it to be original, unique, and, most important, it is accurate. For in this third installment, the recherché techniques Hollywood employs will be, once again, presented and analyzed.

These pithy marvels go far beyond occult images hidden in plain sight, although these are critical too. Directors, set designers, and producers employ color schemes, costuming, music, and theatrical artwork like posters; interestingly, actors and actresses are cast to conceal and reveal hidden undercurrents. This latter artistry, which I call *occult casting*, is when a performer is hired to bring their cultural-iconic-cinematic baggage to a film. Like occult symbols and arcane themes, the thespian's appearance is a mnemonic emerging from Giordano Bruno's (1548-1600) magical art of memory, affecting the viewer's subconscious and imagination, energizing the archetypes dwelling within us all. This art seeks to memorize through a technique of impressing places or images on memory. Bruno's efforts were to base memory on celestial images: on archetypal images, divine shadows of ideas, manifesting in the soul of the world, dwelling in human minds, and, thus, to organize the innumerable individuals and all the contents of memory.[8] If symbolism and hidden themes are the bone, then occult casting is the marrow; it is the closest thing I can think of to modern-day sorcery; it is a form of mind control. For if memory, Mnemosyne, was the mother of the Muses, she was also to be the mother of method; art of memory is an elusive human power plunging us into murky waters.[9] With its religious and ethical associations, Bruno's approach was transplanted into his occult systems, steering Renaissance esoteric memory techniques in the direction of secret societies.[10] Not only toward the Rosicrucians, the Freemasons, and the Illuminati but to Hollywood as well.

---

8 Frances Yates, *Giordano Bruno and the Hermetic Tradition* (1964; repr., Chicago: The University of Chicago Press, 1991), 76.
9 Frances Yates, *The Art of Memory* (1966; repr., London: The Bodley Head, 2014), 297.
10 Ibid. See also Eliphas Levi, *The History of Magic*, trans. Arthur Edward Waite (1860/1913; repr., Mansfield Centre, CT: Martino Publishing, 2012), 29-32.

The art world's impact on cinema: the Pre-Raphaelite portrait, *The Bridesmaid* (left, 1831), by John Everett Millais (1829-1896) influenced the costume design and appearance of *Crimson Peak*'s Edith Cushing (right). Del Toro's ghost story is a meditation on Dark Romanticism; its abundant symbolism, intense colors, and complex compositions make Edith–and the villainous Lucille–look like Pre-Raphaelite paintings brought to life.

I have decided to keep the Preface and Introduction relatively short because I intend to define Tinseltown's methodology as the book unfolds rather than condensing it all initially, as I did in my two previous cinema books. Nevertheless, please read the Introduction because it is a roadmap; consider it an esoteric primer. As the reader progresses, the curtain will be pulled back; arcane doctrines will be applied to pop culture, disclosing Hollywood's occult mysteries. The mind's eye is baffled and intrigued; it is open to the depths, and possibly the heights, that had previously been concealed. Don't expect Hollywood's *éminences grises*, the puppet masters of illusion, to impart this secret information because good magicians never reveal their secrets. As a Freemason, I know this to be true.

Robert W. Sullivan IV, Esq.
Candlemas (Imbolc) 2018
Baltimore, Maryland, USA

INTRODUCTION

(13) – The Thirteenth Spirit is called Beleth (or Bileth, or Bilet).
He is a mighty King and terrible. He rideth on a pale horse with
trumpets and other kinds of musical instruments playing before him.
Ars Goetia, The Lesser Key of Solomon the King,
Translated by Samuel Liddell MacGregor Mathers, 1904

I am Criswell. For years, I have told the almost unbelievable,
related the unreal, and showed it to be more than a fact.
Now I tell a tale of the Threshold People,
so astounding that some of you may faint.
This is a story of those in the twilight time. Once human, now monsters,
in a void between the living and the dead. Monsters to be pitied,
monsters to be despised. A night with the ghouls,
the ghouls reborn from the innermost depths of the world.
The Emperor, *Orgy of the Dead*, 1965

Ye black minions! Dost hear that, yolk devils!
Wake! Wake from this! Did ye make some unholy bond with that goat?
William, *The Witch*, 2015

Symbolism comes therefore from God, though it may be formulated by men.
Eliphas Levi, *Transcendental Magic*, 1854

It is time. They have reached the second crucial turning
point in their destiny. Their message is about to reach millions.
But we will change all that. When our mission is successful,
no longer will the world be dominated by the legacy of these two fools!
No longer will we hear this. [*plays air guitar*]
Chuck De Nomolos, *Bill and Ted's Bogus Journey*, 1991

Some people can read *War and Peace* and come away thinking
it's a simple adventure story. Others can read the ingredients
on a chewing gum wrapper, and unlock the secrets of the universe.
Lex Luthor, *Superman*, 1978

Symbolism may be comprehended under two broad classifications: exoteric and esoteric. The former includes the signs, figures, and abbreviations used to express mathematics, chemistry, pharmacy, weights, measures, and meteorology. The latter applies to the concealed expression of occult, spiritual, and philosophical truths; it is the subject of this book.[11] The impetus of all symbolism has its origin in something more than the desire for brevity; instead, its sole purpose is secrecy, message communication, furthering an agenda known to the initiated few.[12] In cinema, occult emblems and undercurrents can be well hidden, while in some movies, it is more noticeable depending on the sophistication of the moviemaker.

Let us now begin to examine Hollywood's powerful magic. Appearances can make quite an impression; take, for instance, *The Exorcist*'s vile demon, having taken possession of Regan, where it intended to stay "Until she rots and lies stinking in the earth," caused some moviegoers to vomit and faint. In *London After Midnight* (1927), director Tod Browning (1880-1962), and its star, Lon "The Man of a Thousand Faces" Chaney (1883-1930), created a horrific visage, remembered for its shark-like dentures. The primitive razor-mouth, superimposed on a ghastly face, evokes a Freudian concept: the devouring, castrating *vagina dentata*. In 1928, Chaney's gruesome makeup inspired brutal murder in London's Hyde Park. The killer claimed to have seen visions of Chaney's frightful face, urging him to slash a woman's throat with a razor. The murder made headlines, adding to the lost movie's dark allure.

At the culmination of *Back to the Future* (1985), Emmett "Doc" Brown (Christopher Lloyd), embodies the scientific zeal of Dr. Benjamin Franklin (1706-1790), the magus drawing lightning from the heavens for the betterment of humankind. The film is a comparative religion study, alluding to the Osirian mysteries; thus, the archetypes have an Egyptian bent, defined by Aleister Crowley's *The Book of Thoth* (1944), applying Qabalism to the traditional deck.[13] Did you know the Smurfs are a cartoon version of

---

[11] George W. Plummer, *Rosicrucian Symbology* (New York: Macoy Publishing and Masonic Supply Co., 1916), 1.
[12] Ibid, 3.
[13] Robert W. Sullivan, *Cinema Symbolism: A Guide to Esoteric Imagery in Popular Movies*, 2nd ed. (Baltimore: Deadwood Publishing, 2017), Chapter IV. *Nota bene*: as I am writing and editing this book, I am also re-editing all my previous tomes. The page numbers and text in the earlier editions are evolving, so I am omitting them altogether when I reference my books. These new, revised editions will include further analyses and information while leaving most of the text intact.

CINEMA SYMBOLISM 3

Karl Marx (1818-1883) and Friedrich Engels' (1820-1895) *Communist Manifesto* (1848)? For more on the Smurfs and this pessimistic paradigm, I refer the reader to my previous works: *Cinema Symbolism* and *Cinema Symbolism 2* (see *CS2* for Smurfette as an alchemical-kabalistic golem, created by Gargamel to sow chaos and discord in the Smurfs' perfected communistic village). But Hollywood isn't infallible: some of its sleight of hand is stupid, pedestrian, so ridiculous it's not even worth discussing. For example, *Mac and Me* (1988), the *Citizen Kane* of wheelchair-bound-paraplegic-kid-going-over-a-cliff movies, is nothing more than an hour-and-a-half McDonald's commercial. The restaurant chain takes a big McBite out of this *E.T.* (1982) rip-off: the subliminal **M**ysterious **A**lien **C**reature, or Mac, alludes to the franchise's tasty Big Mac, even Ronald McDonald (Squire Fridell) makes a cameo at a fast-food dance contest. Currently, it has a zero rating on Rotten Tomatoes.

Sometimes, the imagery occurs because of an inside joke, a monkeyshine, carried out by a production designer or an art director. Such is the case with *The House of Fear* (1945), the Sherlock Holmes murder

♫ I saw Lon Chaney Jr., walking with the Queen, uh! / Doing the werewolves of London ♫. An excellent example of someone in the prop department screwing around. (Left) Larry Talbot's wolf's head cane from *The Wolfman* turns up in the Sherlock Holmes murder mystery *The House of Fear* (right) leaning against a wall in Drearcliff House. Both movies are Universal Pictures, but, other than that, there is no nexus between them.

However, some text will be different, re-edited, and augmented within these new editions. When I cite one of my books, I am omitting the page number(s) because they will change, identifying the citation by Chapter number only.

mystery based on Sir Arthur Conan Doyle's (1859-1930) *The Five Orange Pips* (1891). Inside Drearcliff House's library, next to the bookshelves, Larry Talbot's (Lon Chaney Jr., 1906-1973) wolf's head cane leans against the wall. The MacGuffin first appeared in *The Wolf Man* (1941), a horror classic unrelated to *The House of Fear*. There is no hidden meaning or agenda; instead, someone in the Universal prop department was screwing around, obviously pulling a prank.

What's in a name? Much, depending on the circumstances. Take, for instance, *The Wicker Man* (1973): Sgt. Neil Howie (Edward Woodward, 1930-2009) is searching for Rowan Morrison (Geraldine Cowper), who has gone missing, presumed dead. The girl is named after *Sorbus aucuparia*, also known as the Mountain Ash, a tree long associated with European paganism. On May 1, animals were passed through a large hoop made of rowan to protect them and ensure fertility.[14] Her forename implies Summerisle's scheme, made clear at the May Day celebration: a human sacrifice to the sun to guarantee the apple crops will flourish. Rowan's totem is a hare, an animal linked to heathenism; specifically, rebirth, rejuvenation, and resurrection, signifying her return from the dead, and the sun's renaissance at Beltane.[15]

In *Maleficent* (2014) and *Maleficent: Mistress of Evil* (2019), the Dark Fey's sorcery changes color because she oscillates between good and evil, concealing and revealing her bisexuality simultaneously. When she is in a good mood, her magic is gold, but when she is angry, her magic is green, signifying duality, designating her hermaphroditism, sexual confusion, and frustration.[16] *Nightbreed* (1990) is a Knights Templar-like fable; after persecution by the Inquisition, a misunderstood cabal of monsters go underground to worship Baphomet, paralleling the Templars banishment for allegedly adoring the same pagan deity. While watching *The Witch* (2015), when the goat, Black Phillip, morphs into a humanoid Devil *qua* Lucifer, his left leg remains thin, black, and hairy with a cloven hoof

---

14 Raven Grimassi, *Encyclopedia of Wicca and Witchcraft*, 2nd ed. (Woodbury, MN: Llewellyn Publications, 2019), 350.
15 Ibid, 203.
16 In *Mistress of Evil*, her magic is a mixture of green and gold, signifying the interdependence of good and evil.

epitomizing Baphomet, the Goat of Mendes, Stanislas de Guaita's (1861-1897) Goat of the Witches' Sabbath.[17]

In *Angel Heart* (1987), Louis Cyphre (Robert De Niro) retains the law firm of Winesap & McIntosh to hire private detective Harry Angel (Mickey Rourke) to locate pre-World War II crooner Johnny Favorite. Winesap and McIntosh are apple cultivars conjuring, to the subconscious mind, the forbidden knowledge associated with the wise Luciferian serpent.[18] At its climax, Harry discovers what has been hidden from him; that is, what he's been searching for, costing him his soul. How about this one: *Coming to America's* (1988) royal family, King Jaffe Joffer, played by James Earl Jones, and Queen Aoleon, played by Madge Sinclair, both return as the regal family in *The Lion King* (1994). Jones and Sinclair provide the voices of King Mufasa (Jones) and Queen Sarabi (Sinclair), resurrecting their aristocratic presence. Or, for example, in the *Harry Potter* saga, Azkaban Prison is named after Alcatraz Island, home to the infamous federal prison. It confined the most hardened criminals influencing Azkaban, which imprisons only the worst witches and warlocks.

Did you know *Jacob's Ladder* (1990) illustrates the CIA's MK-Ultra mind-control program; the movie asks epistemological questions: what is real, and what is fantasy? Who is mind-controlled, and who isn't? Pay attention to the gurney's swivel when, in the hospital, Jacob Singer (Tim Robbins) is descending to Hell. The wheel is slightly off the ground–turning and creaking endlessly–to make the viewer anxious, projecting the nebulous vanguard of the CIA's mind-bending agenda. The Hermes Trismegistus (Thrice-Greatest) analog, Louis Denardo (Danny Aiello), speaks to Jacob Singer (Tim Robbins) about the sagacious Meister Eckhart (1260–1328). Like Dante Alighieri, Eckhart saw Hell too; however, all is what not what it seems. Angels and demons are to be interpreted subjectively; their purpose

---

17 Charlie played Black Phillip in goat form, Wahab Chaudhry portrayed Black Phillip as the Devil.
18 That is, applying Gnosticism to the Book of Genesis. In *Angel Heart*, *nota bene*, one can observe a theme suggesting an ouroboros. It begins with a shadowing figure walking casually in an alley, then segues to a corpse lying on the pavement nearby. One can only presume the figure is Cyphre because the person walks with a cane, something Cyphre carries with him throughout the film. The corpse indicates "there is death everywhere," which Cyphre tells Angel/Favorite at the conclusion. Thus, it ends where it begins: with Cyphre and death omnipresent, creating a cinematic ouroboros, signifying Cyphre's serpentine nature. The movie swallows its tail, thereby going back to the beginning at its end. Although *Angel Heart* is more Gnostic than alchemical, one must always bear in mind that medieval alchemists took their philosophies from the Gnostics.

(Left) Eliphas Levi's intaglioed Baphomet, the Goat of Mendes in *Dogme et Rituel de la Haute Magie*, a tome presented in two parts: "The Doctrine of Transcendental Magic" and "The Ritual of Transcendental Magic." Each of these is divided into twenty-two chapters, paralleling the twenty-two cards of the Major Arcana of the Tarot. *Dogme et Rituel de la Haute Magie* was translated into English by the Masonic mystic, Arthur Edward Waite (1857-1942), as *Transcendental Magic, its Doctrine and Ritual* (1896). Baphomet was a deity allegedly worshipped by the Knights Templar, according to confessions extracted by torture during the trials of members of the Order after its condemnation in 1307. The pentagram on Baphomet's forehead is a symbol of light and will, the Pentalpha of Pythagoras, or the Pentangle of Solomon, having five lines and five angles; and is, among the Freemasons, the Blazing Star: an emblem of fellowship. Levi combined elements of the Tarot's Devil Card, and the he-goat adored at witches' sabbaths. Baphomet has a human torso with rounded, female breasts, a caduceus in the midriff, cloven feet, black wings, a goat's head with a torch on top between two horns. These attributes symbolize androgyny, viz. *coincidentia oppositorum*, connotating horror and sin, magic, intelligence, alchemy, universal equilibrium, spirit over matter, and the generative principle. They represent Astral Light, the central concept in Levi's magical synthesis. Its human arms and hands form a sign of occultism–as above, so below–inscribed upon his Emerald Tablet of Hermes Trismegistus. Written on Baphomet's arms are *Solve* (separate), and *Coagula* (dissolve), active principles of alchemical transformation. The white and black crescent moons at the figure's side denote the kabalistic pillars of mercy and severity with Baphomet as the Middle Pillar. (Right) Inspired by Levi's image, poet and mystic Stanislas de Guaita drew the first goat pentagram, with two points (horns) upward, attacking Heaven. The picture appeared in his book, *La Clef de la Magie Noir* (English: *Key of Black Magic*, 1897), and is commonly referred to as the Sabbatic Goat.

is to devest departed souls of their material attachments, freeing them from the hylic world. The demons *qua* angels transmogrify the spirit, placing it on a path to God. Eckhart's complex, negative theology further suggests the soul must undergo a four-stage synthesis, the *unio mysitica*, to achieve the godhead.[19] A comparable alchemical-spiritual modus operandi is the function of *Twin Peaks*' (1990-1991) Black and White Lodges.

---

19 Eckhart von Hochheim, *The Complete Mystical Works of Meister Eckhart*, trans. and ed. Maurice O'C Walshe (New York: The Crossroad Publishing Company, 2009), 4-25, *passim*.

CINEMA SYMBOLISM 3

Hollywood often turns to history for inspiration. In *Star Wars: A New Hope* (1977), Grand Moff Tarkin (Peter Cushing, 1913-1994) announces that the Emperor has dissolved the Imperial Senate, delegating control to the regional governors, authorizing them to rule by fear. The Emperor's plan imitates England's Commonwealth: between August 1655 and January 1657, Great Britain was led by the Major-Generals; after the dissolution of Parliament, there was a period of direct military government during Oliver Cromwell's (1599-1658) Protectorate, running parallel with the Emperor's scheme. Like the Emperor devolving control to the governors, England and Wales were divided into ten regions, each governed by a Major-General who answered directly to the stern Lord Protector.

Walter Hill's *The Warriors* (1979) is lifted from the pages of *Anabasis*, the most famous book of the Ancient Greek professional soldier and writer Xenophon (431-354 BCE). The seven-volume tome was composed around the year 370 BCE, and, in translation, *Anabasis* is rendered as *The March of the Ten Thousand* and as *The March Up Country*. Xenophon accompanied the Ten Thousand, an army of Greek mercenaries hired by Cyrus the Younger (?-401 BCE), who intended to seize the throne of Persia from his brother, Artaxerxes II (453/445-358 BCE). Though Cyrus' mixed army fought to a tactical victory at Cunaxa in Babylon (401 BC), Cyrus was killed, rendering the actions of the Greeks irrelevant and the expedition a failure. Stranded deep in Persia, the Spartan general Clearchus (450-401 BCE) and the other Greek senior officers were then killed or captured by treachery on the part of the Persian satrap Tissaphernes (445-395 BCE). Xenophon, one of three remaining leaders elected by the soldiers, played an instrumental role in encouraging the 10,000 to march north across foodless deserts and snow-filled mountain passes toward the Black Sea and the comparative security of its Greek shoreline cities. Now abandoned in northern Mesopotamia, without supplies other than what they could obtain by force or diplomacy, the 10,000 had to fight their way northwards through Corduene and Armenia, making ad hoc decisions about their leadership, tactics, provender, and destiny.

To make matters worse, Artaxerxes' army, along with hostile natives, barred their way, attacking their flanks. One can see parallels between Xenophon, his men, and the Warriors. For example, after the assassination of Cyrus (Roger Hill, 1948-2014), stuck deep in enemy territory, their war chief, Cleon (Dorsey Wright), is captured or killed. The Warriors have to fight their way back to their turf, having to make spur of the moment decisions to survive. They are surrounded by hostile forces, while Swan (Michael Beck), the de facto war chief, has his leadership challenged by fellow Warrior, Ajax (James Remar).

Although outside the world of the occult, foreshadowing can reveal key cinematic elements, forcing the viewer to recall the movie entirely, evoking Bruno's occult system. In *Mulholland Drive* (2001), when Betty Elms (Naomi Watts) meets Rita (Laura Harring), the former infers the truth about her Hollywood fantasy by saying she's "In this *dream place*." However, the viewer does not discover the line's literal meaning until Diane Selwin (Watts again) wakes up, terminating her buoyant vision, ending Betty's existence. In *Ghostbusters* (1984), when Dana Barrett (Sigourney Weaver) unpacks her groceries, the eggs start cooking on the counter supernaturally. One will notice a bag of Stay-Puft Marshmallows foreshadowing Volguus Zildrohar's form during the apocalypse.[20]

Hollywood sometimes employs the above and below of Hermes Trismegistus when releasing a film. *The Omen* was released on June 24, 1976, midsummer, the Feast of St. John the Baptist–the celebration of the summer solstice–when daylight begins decreasing, anticipating the rise of darkness, the Antichrist.[21] Think I'm stretching this? *Omen III: The Final Conflict* was released on the vernal equinox of 1981 (March 20) to signify the return of divine light, the sun, designating the end of wintery gloom. On that day, sunlight is equal to night; after the vernal equinox, daylight increases while night diminishes. As such, *Omen III* documents the Second Coming of Jesus Christ *qua* the sun to defeat the night, Damien Thorn (Sam Neill), the Antichrist. A confrontation between Damien and a group of assassin-monks on Dartmoor is an art of memory mnemonic, conjuring Conan Doyle's *The Hound of the Baskervilles* (1902) and the devilry lurking on the moors.[22] Damien defeats the monks, and, at least for the time being, evil is triumphant.

---

[20] Volguus Zildrohar, also known as Gozer the Gozerian, was portrayed by Slavitza Jovan and voiced by Paddi Edwards (1931-1999).

[21] In *Rosemary's Baby*, the Antichrist is born on June 25, 1966, when solar light starts to decrease. Christmas–the birth of Jesus on December 25–celebrates the newly birthed sun as the darkness begins to retreat, and daylight is returned.

[22] In Cornwall, Roche Rock and its environs substituted for Dartmoor.

(Top) The Tree of the Dead in Tim Burton's *Sleepy Hollow* turns up in *Alice in Wonderland* (bottom), insinuating the movies inhabit the same universe.

Some filmmakers employ subtleties to forge a link between their films, or earlier movies, producing positive and negative vibrations. For example, in the mid-80s, director Fred Dekker released two movies occupying the same cinematic universe. The first, *The Night of the Creeps* (1986), pays homage to ghoulish, flying saucer movies of the '50s and '60s; even the housemother (Evelyn Smith) watches *Plan 9 from Outer Space* (1959). The second, *The Monster Squad* (1987), is a tribute to the old Universal horror films of the '30s, '40s, and '50s, such as *Dracula* (1931), *Frankenstein* (1931), *The Mummy* (1932), *The Wolfman* (1941), and *The Creature from the Black Lagoon* (1954). In *Night of the Creeps*, when J.C. (Steve Marshall) crawls across the bathroom floor, right before a creepy-crawly jumps into his mouth, one will notice the graffiti on the wall "Go Monster Squad!" forging a nexus between the two movies. They become interwoven, only adding to their mythology, amplifying their eventual cult status. Another example hides in Tim Burton's *Alice in Wonderland* (2010), featuring the Tree of the Dead, alluding to his movie *Sleepy Hollow* (1999), making them parallel fairy tales. Easter egg: when watching *The Monster Squad*, keep an eye out for the armadillo in Dracula's castle, appearing during the opening credits. It is an homage to the armadillos creeping about Dracula's lair in the Universal classic. In *Dracula*, the Armadillos make cameos because the *little armored ones* occasionally dig in cemeteries, leading to the filmmakers' mistaken belief they would dig their way into coffins and eat the corpses.

Burton strikes again with *Pee-wee's Big Adventure* (1985) and *Batman Returns* (1992). In the former, Pee-wee Herman (Paul Reubens) encourages the waitress Simone (Diane Salinger) to pursue her ambitions while she tells him to keep searching for his bike. In the latter, their dreams are shattered: Reubens and Salinger portray Tucker and Esther Cobblepot, the parents of the doomed Oswald Cobblepot, the Penguin (Danny DeVito), whom they dispose of by tossing him–and his crib–down a sewer. To this author, when these interrelated mnemonics are discovered, it reminds us Hollywood is forever generating mythologies, constructing pop culture before our very eyes

In some instances, symbolism can be minute, meticulous, and thus elusive. In the thriller *Atomic Blonde* (2017), MI6 spy Lorraine Broughton (Charlize Theron) drinks Stolichnaya vodka, a well-known Soviet brand, cleverly inferring she may be a double agent working for the KGB, placing her loyalty to the West in doubt. The audience never knows if she is the hero or the villain. There are veiled similarities between *Crimson Peak* (2015) and *The Shining* (1980) because they are both about struggling writers tormented by ghosts; *Crimson Peak*'s director Guillermo del Toro deems *The Shining* "the Mount Everest of haunted-house movies."[23] *The Exorcist* illustrates a Neoplatonic conflict between good and evil represented by the solar warmth and frigid darkness, ascent and descent, and apotheosis contrasted by debasement. A kindred Manichaeism haunts the corridors of Hogwarts School of Witchcraft and Wizardry. The totem of Gryffindor Hall is the lion, denoting the constellation Leo, which governs the sun.

---

23 Russ Fischer, "New Details on Guillermo del Toro's Haunted House Movie 'Crimson Peak,' Plus New 'Pacific Rim' Images," *Slash Film*, February 18, 2013, https://www.slashfilm.com/new-details-on-guillermo-del-toros-haunted-house-movie-crimson-peak-plus-new-pacific-rim-images/ (accessed May 1, 2018).

(Top) In *Pee-wee's Big Adventure*, Pee-wee Herman and Simone are soulmates. (Bottom) Their reality becomes a nightmare in *Batman Returns* when they become the parents of the Penguin, ridding themselves of the deformed child by throwing him and his crib over a bridge, consigning the little monster to Gotham's sewers. This pragmatic paradigm echoes occult casting; by using the same actors but reversing their circumstances, Burton's cinematic sorcery weaves a spell in the subconscious mind; however, a pop culture mythology results when the viewer becomes conscious of this model.

Such symbolism designates the lightning-bolt scarred wizard, Harry Potter (Daniel Radcliffe), as a solar god-man, a heroic archetype, in the vein of Jesus, Horus, Mithras, Samas, and Apollo. Tom Riddle, before he became Lord Voldemort (Ralph Fiennes), was assigned to the house of the serpent, Slytherin Hall, identifying the black magician with the Devil, the Dragon, Set/Typhon, Mercurius, or Python.

Each time this author watches *Black Swan* (2010), an ode to metamorphic masturbation, he observes something fresh. In particular, Nina Sayers (Natalie Portman) and Lily's (Mila Kunis) lesbian scene occurs 69 minutes

CINEMA SYMBOLISM 3

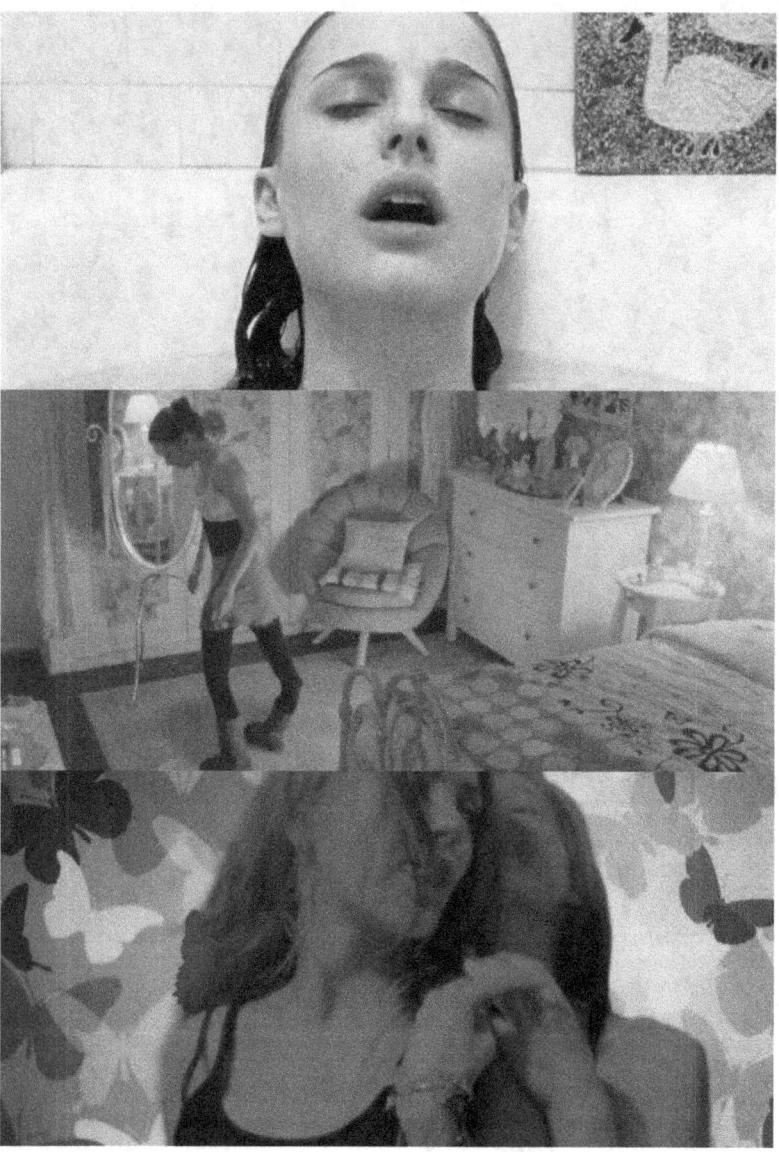

(Top) A conspicuous white swan mosaic rests behind Nina on the bathtub's rim while she caresses herself, signifying her sexual inexperience and innocence; alone and frustrated, she reacquaints herself with onanism, her only solace. (Center) Through chaos magic *qua* Transyuggothian sorcery, Nina perfects alchemy by transmogrifying into a birdlike creature. Her spell is an extreme diet of masochism, humiliation, and self-stimulation; thus, her knees buckle backward like a swan. Her bedroom is an alchemical kitchen; its wallpaper represents the metamorphic process: an endless array of butterflies suggesting transformation from one thing, an innocent White Swan, to another, a seductive Black Swan. (Bottom) Having a hard time seeing the butterflies on the wallpaper? If so, observe when Nina and Lily hit the dancefloor. The butterfly wallpaper flashes behind them ever so briefly–keep an eye for it next time you, the reader, watch *Black Swan*.

into the film. The sexual inference of *69* is crystal clear. However, one could also interpret it as an erotic yin-yang or the psychological-alchemical unification of contradictions: order *qua* Nina merges with chaos *qua* Lily, thereby awakening the former's sable consciousness, equipping her to dance the Black Swan.[24] At breakfast, Nina consumes a grapefruit; it is a symbol of bitterness and mental illness. It symbolizes the love-hate relationship with her mother Erica (Barbara Hershey), presaging Nina's lunacy and sexual deviancies. Furthermore, this author couldn't help but notice the white swan mosaic sitting on Nina's bathtub representing her virginal innocence, her timid White Swan/Odette persona. Moreover, her bedroom's wallpaper is a swarm of kaleidoscopic butterflies suggesting a remaking; the insect begins as a caterpillar, then changes to pupa, finally becoming a beautiful aphid. When Nina and Lily get jiggy with it, keep an eye out for the colorful wallpaper emerging quickly behind them. For Nina, the insect represents her metamorphosis from a pathetic White Swan to a confident, graceful yet grotesque Black Swan, calling her to the footlights, drawing her from the mundane to the elegantly horrific. Darren Aronofsky's use of time-sequencing, the grapefruit, the white swan mosaic, and the wallpaper are masterful; when analyzing films, one critical thing to always keep in mind is the context, the surrounding circumstances, the symbol or theme is presented. In my estimation, context is routinely overlooked by researchers in this field.

Let's continue to analyze the butterfly, a traditional symbol for immortality. The insect represents transformation in *Black Swan*, but something entirely different in *Crimson Peak*. In del Toro's movie, the butterfly denotes the sun, identifying the protagonist, Edith Cushing (Mia Wasikowska), as a solar heroine, the dawn. Edith befriends a toy dog at Allerdale Hall that had previously owned by Enola Sciotti, one of the Sharpes' victims. The small canine is a breed known as Papillon; in French, *papillon* means *butterfly*. The dog tallies with the spectral yarn's Manicheanism: Edith, symbolized by the butterfly, the eternal diurnal orb, the glorious dawn, battles for her life against the forces of darkness personified by the Sharpe siblings, brother and sister, represented by the Stygian moth. The moth, symbolizing an oppressive fiend, appears in Blake's *Albion Rose* (ca. 1795), second slate, featuring the grotesque insect

---

24 *Black Swan* borrows from the 1997 Japanese animated psychological horror-thriller *Perfect Blue*.

(Top) In *Crimson Peak*, Lady Lucille Sharpe gently rubs Edith Cushing's cheek with a butterfly–a symbol of light–imbuing the latter with the solar attributes of the insect. What does an emblem conceal and reveal? (Bottom left) While in the park, Edith wears a belt featuring clasped hands. (Bottom right) During the Victorian era, this was a universal symbol on gravestones, indicating the relationship between the person who had passed away and the loved ones left behind. The belt represents the bond between Edith and her deceased mother, and that mother's ghost is with her. However, do the clasped hands have a more profound symbolism? Was the costume designer, Kate Hawley, trying to convey something else, perhaps something erotic?

as an emblem of the French Revolution's (1789-1799) degeneration into the horrific Terror. Thus, we know, like so many symbols, the butterfly's meaning is multilayered; in both films, the insect's use is discrete and appropriate. Easter egg: Blake's *Albion Rose* was modeled after da Vinci's *Vitruvian Man* (ca. 1490); the name derives from the ancient and mythological name of Britain, Albion. In Blake's cosmology, Albion was the primeval man whose fall and division resulted in the Four Zoas: Urizen, Tharmas, Luvah, and Urthona.

CINEMA SYMBOLISM 3

Hollywood uses rain, or a shower, to connote both rebirth and transformation, depending on the circumstances. In *Suspiria* (1977), when Suzy Bannion (Jessica Harper) arrives in Germany, it is pouring, looking like Noahic flooding. The storm is her baptism, a spiritual purification, giving her the strength and temperance to battle evil: the coven of witches hiding in the *Tanzakademie* (English: dance academy).[25] Rain comes from heaven, the higher powers above, indicating a spiritual cleansing; Suzy's mission is numinous, justified, and right.[26] During the opening credits of *9 ½ Weeks* (1986), Elizabeth McGraw (Kim Basinger) strolls to work through rainwater puddles. For her, the saturated streets and sidewalks denote albification, indicating she embodies alchemy's *albedo* (whiteness, silver, the moon), heralding transmogrification.[27] Elizabeth will attempt a metamorphosis to liberate her shadow self, an erotic persona. Here, the use of rain is proper; Dario Argento, the director of *Susipira*, and Adrian Lyne, the director of *9 ½ Weeks*, know what they are doing.

Thus, the surroundings in which a recondite symbol, theme, or undercurrent is presented is critical to analyzing it; if a token is interpreted out-of-context, then the analysis is worthless. "Garbage in, garbage out," as we attorneys often say. This book describes movie symbolism contextually with supporting analysis and documentation. By stating this, this author is skeptical of the hypothesis that veiled currents are part of a Satanic-Illuminati-Hollywood-Occult-Masonic-Mind-Control agenda; to the rational mind, this theory is unsubstantiated pablum. On the other hand, one must bear in mind the motivations behind using the occult in media. However, in meditating on this subject for over twenty years, at no time have I come to believe the placement of an arcane symbol or thread in a movie was evil.

Au contraire, the use of esoteric symbolism is akin to an architect or city planner incorporating sacred geometry in their blueprint, design, or template. Nevertheless, everything casts a shadow, and there are diabolical forces in this world, toiling as it sleeps. Because of the strange, almost supernatural nature of movie symbolism, it is easy to oscillate between two extremes: demonical conspiratorial agenda and coincidence.

---

25 J. E. Cirlot, *A Dictionary of Symbols* (New York: Philosophical Library, 1962), 259.
26 Ibid.
27 Ibid.

♪ Someone left the cake out in the rain ♪. (Left) In *Suspiria*, Suzy Bannion rides in the back of a taxicab during a rainstorm on her way to the Tanz Dance Academy. (Right) In *9 ½ Weeks*, Elizabeth McGraw walks to work–the Spring Street Art Gallery–passing through rainwater puddles. Rain signifies different things, depending on the surrounding circumstances.

What fascinates this author is the great lengths filmmakers, whether it be the director, producer, writer, or set designer, will go to lace their production with occult undertones. For example, *Fight Club* (1999) veils Gnosticism: rebellion against materialism and commercialism. Durden's Space Monkeys destroy themselves physically to obtain enlightenment–spiritual gnosis–while combating the Demiurge's hylic reality. Durden does not exist; instead, he is an imaginary, an alchemical trickster or juggler (the Magician Tarot card), the Jungian shadow of the protagonist billed as the Narrator (Edward Norton). And Mercury *qua* the trickster is happiest when he or she's at play: fucking around, raising Cain, causing headaches, wrecking worlds, destroying to rebuild. Without Durden, he cannot affect radical change; he is unable to transform society. Concealed deeper within *Fight Club*'s Gnostic matrix is a Masonic undercurrent. Durden, a quasi-Worshipful Master, presides over a male-only secret society, and its first rule is silence; like the passwords and tokens of Masonry, one "does not talk about Fight Club." To be initiated into its mysteries, the candidate must wait outside the dojo for three days without encouragement; the three days represent the degrees of Masonry's Blue Lodge: Entered Apprentice, Fellowcraft, and Master Mason. Initiation is a perspective against the false lights of mysticism; it equips human logic with its relative value and proportional infallibility, connecting it with supreme reason by the chain

Tyler Durden's business card identifies the address of Fight Club's temple of initiation as 537 Paper Street. The number 537 is a veiled allusion to Masonry's 3, 5, and 7, its sanctum of secrecy, and the power of occult philosophies.

of analogies.[28] Hence, the initiate knows no vague hopes, no absurd fears because he has no irrational beliefs; he is acquainted with the extent of his power, and he can be bold without danger.[29]

Initiation prepares the Space Monkeys spiritually, supplying them with a higher understanding, readying them for a cataclysmic eventuality: Project Mayhem. Fight Club's headquarters are located at 537 Paper Street, identified on Durden's business card, furthering the film's Freemasonry. Five, three, and seven, are an allusion to 357; in Masonry proper–explained during the second-degree lecture–there are three great pillars of the Temple: Wisdom, Strength, and Beauty. There are five noble orders of architecture: Roman, Corinthian, Ionic, Doric, and Tuscan. There are seven liberal arts and sciences: Grammar, Rhetoric, Logic, Arithmetic, Geometry, Music, and Astronomy. Three, five, and seven links Fight Club's temple of initiation to Masonry's Sanctum Sanctorum; a Space Monkey, as a postulant, seeks entry to ignite his divine spark. Post-initiation, they are part of a priesthood, questing for both self-enlightenment and destruction, becoming nihilistic hierophants.

A similar exemplar appears in *Harry Potter and the Half-Blood Prince* (2009), depicting Albus Dumbledore (Michael Gambon) conspicuously standing before a billboard advertising *Divine Magic*. As I have explained in my previous cinema books, Dumbledore epitomizes the Hermes Mercurius Trismegistus archetype, the mysterious and powerful god of magic. He knows everything, but choose to dole out his wisdom piecemeal. This figure

---

28 Eliphas Levi, *Transcendental Magic: Its Doctrine and Ritual*, trans. Arthur Edward Waite (1896/1958; repr., Mansfield Centre, CT: Martino Publishing, 2011), 93-94.
29 Ibid, 94.

is often a wizard, a hermit, a sage, a scholar par excellence; usually, he wears a robe and has a distinctive graybeard. His eyes are fixed, and his look is strangely acute. The *Hermetica* (ca. 2nd century CE), the works ascribed Hermes Trismegistus, mentions the Son of God, viz. the Creative Word, in both the *Asclepius* and *The Poimandres* (*Corpus Hermeticum*, *Libellus* I), thereby designating Dumbledore a theurgic hierophant. The Neoplatonic magus protects the Boy Who Lived, the savior of the wizarding world whose white sorcery will thwart Lord Voldemort.[30] In Masonic lore, Hermes relates to *ascensio*: by breaching the Vault of Enoch, then pronouncing the Tetragrammaton correctly, the Thrice-Greatest restores the Seven Liberal Arts and Sciences to humankind. This mystical act, the recovery of God's name, is the backbone of the Royal Arch degree, signifying the transcendence of the sublunary world, spiritual purification, ascension to cabalistic apotheosis.[31] In J.K. Rowling's mythology, Dumbledore is a polymath, the headmaster of Hogwarts, reflecting Masonry's *trivium* and *quadrivium*; in both instances, the white wizard's shrewdness and sagacity are second to none, making him a supreme godly educator.

Hogwarts' Professor Albus Dumbledore is a practitioner of divine magic; of this, there is no doubt. Like Ob-Wan Kenobi (Alec Guinness, 1914-2000), in *Star Wars*, and Gandalf the Grey in *The Hobbit* and *The Lord of the Rings*, Dumbledore is a Hermes Trismegistus analog, a graybeard archetype. Screenshot from *Harry Potter and the Half-Blood Prince*.

---

30 Garth Fowden, *The Egyptian Hermes: A Historical Approach to the Late Pagan Mind* (1986; repr., Princeton: Princeton University Press, 1993), 179-181, discussing the Church Fathers' use of the *Hermetica*, identifying the pagan Mercurius Trismegistus as a prophet of Jesus Christ.
31 Yates, *Giordano Bruno*, 25-27.

Another technique employed by Hollywood is the promotion material, that is to say, posters. These neo-broadsides offer filmmakers a way to tease the hidden iconography in their art, while the posters–especially ones with cool artwork–are highly sought after by collectors. Some posters bring a king's ransom at auction houses such as Sotheby's, Christie's, and eBay, elevating the film's status in pop culture to iconic. Although it was not a box office success, the one-sheet for *Mother!* (2017) offers a subtle glance at its arcana. Jennifer Lawrence *qua* Mother Nature presents her heart, conjuring the devotion to the Sacred Heart, also known as the Most Sacred Heart of Jesus, or *Sacratissimum Cor Iesu*. The symbol is one of the most well-known Roman Catholic devotions, taking Christ's heart as the representation of his love for humanity. In the context of *Mother!*– thoroughly analyzed in Chapter XI–the film's atheistic director, Aronofsky, seeks to rebuff Christianity, especially its Latin version, illustrating the destructiveness of the religion. Mother (Lawrence) is not like Christ at all;

(Left) The first promotional poster for the film, *Mother!*, is imbued with symbolism. (Right) The poster for *Häxan: Witchcraft Through the Ages* features the Devil with an inverted pentagram on his forehead; the two points up is the sign of the cloven hoof symbolizing the Goat of Mendes' horns attacking heaven, the fall of divine light.

instead, she despises humankind, ending the Piscean Age by fire–observe, in the lower right corner, the cigarette lighter with Pisces' astrological symbol. The poster also depicts an eight-sided doorknob and a frog, hinting at its Biblical mysteries. On the other end of the theological spectrum, the demonic poster for *Häxan: Witchcraft through Ages* (1922) correctly depicts an inverted pentagram on the Devil's forehead; one-point up signifies cabalistic white magic, but when the two points are raised, the pentagram becomes an emblem of black magic.

* * * * *

Imagery aside, also contemporaneous on the filmmakers' pallet of esoteric techniques, is music. Melodies, when deployed by the wizards in Hollywood, harmonizes sound and substance; it is powerful, potent, and sensual. They enhance the drama, or even conjure something from an earlier film; this lyrical occultism surfaces in season five of the *Bates Motel* (Chapter I). From one coronation to another, music transfers the potency of divine kingship to an infernal monarch. In *Hereditary* (2018), when Peter Graham (Alex Wolff) ascends into the treehouse, wherein he is crowned Paimon, a King of Hell, the score, "Reborn," by Colin Stetson evokes regal pomp and circumstance. "Reborn" is a somber rendition of *Zadok the Priest* (1727), composed by George Frideric Handel (1685-1759) for the enthroning of King George II (1683-1760), performed at the coronation of every British monarch since its composition. In *Halloween* (1978), the song "Don't Fear the Reaper" (1976) by Blue Oyster Cult blares on the radio when Laurie Strode (Jamie Lee Curtis) and Annie Brackett (Nancy Kyes) drive to their babysitting jobs, presaging Michael Myers' nocturnal killing spree. The song is prophetic: although Michael murders Annie, Laurie survives, suggesting Death, the rider of the pale horse (Revelation 6:8), wasn't interested in claiming her soul that night. In *An American Werewolf in London* (1981), listen attentively to the soundtrack: all the songs have the word *moon* in their title, implying the werewolf's vehicle of transformation. In *9 ½ Weeks*, when the masturbator takes flight, Eurythmics' "This City Never Sleeps" envelops her caresses. The song admonishes Elizabeth that her ephemeral pleasure is "♪ just a feeling ♪" and to not substitute wanton lust for love and affection.

In Hollywood, alchemy is a critical device. Alchemy was the art by which base metals were supposed to be transmuted into gold and silver. While the alchemist's practical techniques were rooted in the banausic skills of the jeweler, the glassmaker, and such like, the theoretical pretensions ultimately touched upon the human soul's relationship to God. An interest in imitating the appearance and color of precious metals evolved gradually into a habit of thinking of metals as composed of a lifeless physical base, or *body*, and an invigorating principle, or *soul*, which imparted character and distinctiveness to the physical base.[32] The material base was the same for all metals, but the *soul* was present in varying degrees of purity; hence, the different characteristics of each metal, and the belief it was possible to transmute base metals into gold by manipulating the *soul*.[33] But the same distinction between the body and soul of metals stimulated in some alchemists another, more analogical line of thought, which used alchemical imagery to describe the purification of the human soul and its ascent to its divine source so that a physical process became a generative symbol of a spiritual experience.[34]

The basic alchemical process involves dissolving natural elements into the abyss from which they arose, separating this indifferent mass into spirit and matter, active and passive, male and female, and then reuniting these opposites: a chemical marriage to synthesize the Philosopher's Stone. As Paracelsus (1493-1541) observes, alchemical dissolution and resolution reenacts God's activities in Genesis, who, alchemically interpreted, separates chaos into distinctions only later to rejoin these antinomies at the marriage feast of Revelation.[35] Paracelsus assumed everything originates from a profound matrix: just as the cosmos emerges from a boundless deep, so inorganic forms arise from the muddy earth and animated ones from liquid wombs.[36] To Jung, alchemy was a psychological operation to attain selfhood. Pop culture synthesizes the alchemy of Paracelsus and Jung, leaving little room for the transmutation of base metal to gold. Rather, alchemical films document the transition of a character from one thing into

---

32 Fowden, *Egyptian Hermes*, 89.
33 Ibid.
34 Ibid, 89-90.
35 Eric Wilson, *The Melancholy Android: On the Psychology of Sacred Machines* (Albany: State University of New York Press, 2006), 73.
36 Ibid.

another; sometimes, the change is physical, but it almost always results in emotional upheaval.

Let's apply philosophic alchemy to *9 ½ Weeks*. Elizabeth's frenzied masturbation is a devilish chimera, attempting an erotic metamorphosis: the release of her passionate shadow. In a penumbra of dimness yet illuminated by the slide projector, Elizabeth touches herself in the glow of the *Sol Niger* (English: Black Sun) as an expression of the *lumen naturae* (English: the light of nature). The Black Sun is an alchemical idea that brightens one's inner darkness, turning saturnine quiddity into luminescence, or, symbolically, lead to gold. This formula facilitates the *albedo*, the moon, the sacred feminine to adapt to the black night of the soul, the *nigredo*, blackening.[37] For the feminine, it is the kind shadow light that heralds a developing consciousness of both sexuality and other nebulous aspects dwelling in the repressed feminine shadow.[38] For the masculine, it represents the emergence of the destroyer, a Mr. Hyde-like personality. *Lumen naturae* can be like a sinister *coincidentia oppositorum*, more akin to an occult formula in which Saturn transforms into *Sol Niger*, the Luciferian sun.[39] To the initiate, male or female, serving Saturn was, therefore, paying homage to the Black Sun, contributing to the *dark brother's* or *sister's* triumphant return, that is, the shadow self.[40] Such a methodology was at the heart and soul of the Romantic Satanists of the 18th and 19th centuries, lionized in the works of Blake, Percy Bysshe Shelley (1792-1822), Voltaire (1694-1778), Lord Byron (1788-1824), Levi, Victor Hugo, Sheridan Le Fanu (1814-1873), and Mary Shelley (1797-1851), taking inspiration from John Milton's (1608-1674) *Paradise Lost* (1667).[41] Romantic Satanists were proponents of sex, magic, political reform, and revolt, commingling Satan with rebels like Cain, Percy Shelley's Cythna (*The Revolt of Islam*, 1818), Prometheus, the Wandering Jew, Carmilla, and even Frankenstein's Monster, expressing themselves darkly through literature, art,

---

37 Stanton Marlan, *The Black Sun: The Alchemy and the Art of Darkness* (College Station: Texas A&M University Press, 2016), 97-98.
38 Ibid, 121.
39 Ruben van Luijk, *Children of Lucifer: The Origins of Modern Religious Satanism* (New York: Oxford University Press, 2016), 302.
40 Ibid.
41 Ruben van Luijk, "The Resurrection of Satan in Nineteenth-Century (Counter) Culture," in *The Devil's Party: Satanism in Modernity*, eds. Per Faxneld and Jesper Aa. Petersen (New York: Oxford University Press, 2013), 41-51, *passim*.

science, and poetry.[42] Within this heterodoxy is an inversion: good is evil, evil is good; infernal fire is life's essence, Heaven is a meager portion of this energy purloined from the abyss. Satan and his host are not evil, but a positive force liberating the body and mind. Easter egg: *The Bride of Frankenstein*'s (1935) prologue shows us the Romantic Satanists at play. The Gothic castle signifies the Brocken, the sinister and strange place where the Devil holds feasts for witches. Mary Shelley (Elsa Lanchester, 1902-1986) is Lucifer, a cast out angel holding captive sway over her attendant demons, the poets Lord Byron (Gavin Gordon, 1901-1983) and Percy Shelley (Douglas Walton, 1909-1961). Bryon remarks he's England's greatest sinner, and the lightning raging outside is meant for him, targeted by an irate Jehovah. But he cannot flatter himself, for the thunder could be applause for Mary because she has "written a tale that sent my blood into icy creeps." Wanting to hear more of Frankenstein and his Monster, and since it's a perfect night for mystery and horror, they gather around her, begging her to open the pits of Hell.

The Dark Angel epitomizes sexual deviancy: by masturbating publicly to the rays of the Black Sun, that is, the slide projector flashing grotesque and demonic images, Elizabeth transgresses womanly decorum, revering Saturn, seeking a seductive transformation. She rebels against her daily doldrums, her prosaic chit-chats with her girlfriends in the art gallery's offices by demolishing her stagnant libido, liberating her suppressed erotic side, birthing her shadow identity, genuflecting before the Prince of Darkness.

But she is not the only Romantic Satanist to grace the silver screen. The urbane Lord Summerisle (Christopher Lee, 1922-2015), an enlightened heathen dwelling in a Christian country, Great Britain, is like a fallen Lucifer: he is out of time and place, living like a cast out, exiled on his remote island. Leading the May Day parade, Summerisle carries a sickle *qua* scythe, identifying him with Saturn, his lord and master. He is more shadow than light: the justice of the peace is ready and willing to perform a human sacrifice–a devoutly Christian police officer–to the sun god to ensure the apple crops return. Anakin Skywalker (Hayden Christensen) falls in love with Padme Amidala (Natalie Portman), then rebels against the Jedi Order, surrendering willingly to the Force's Dark Side, signaling his Romantic Satanism. In *Suspiria* (2018), Madame Blanc's (Tilda Swinton) Neo-expressionist dance, *Volk*, embodies matriarchal disobedience. When

---

42 Ibid.

not rehearsing her dance, honing her witchcraft, Blanc seeks to refine her sapphism with her protégé, Susie Bannion (Dakota Johnson), identifying her, and Susie as saturnine disciples of the Left-Hand Path. Satanism, much like Gnosticism, has a critical dimensional sometimes ignored: at its core, it is a language of resistance to convention, a counter-discourse.[43]

Romantic Satanism is not for the timid, the conformist, or the weak-willed; one must be independent, daring, an erudite libertine. Returning to the erotic alchemy of *9 ½ Weeks*, Saturn's mysterious influence upon Elizabeth results in her fondly embracing weird attributes, tokens of her dark pleasures. Specifically, she cultivates a distinct compulsion for black silk stockings, facilitating her liberation, transforming her into a chic piece of performance art, satisfying her pride, her *body*, yet corrupting her *soul*, her psychology.[44] Silk, signifying wealth, taste, and vanity, sows the seeds of her magic; yet, fixation is a corruption of the supernatural, mystical, and necromantic. Elizabeth's classy hosiery becomes parasitic and destructive, ruining her emotionally; she comes to understand–when it's too late–that her sultry onanism was nothing more than a crass sideshow.[45] Her failure is not surprising: according to kabalistic tradition, the alchemist, or the person seeking transition, was both the vessel of the work and the substance in it. If the alchemist were besieged by materialism, lust, and desire, their mystical undertaking would be futile; dripping from the heavens above, their star-semen, or moon-spittle, would be corrupted, rendered impotent.[46]

Blossoming like she's one of Charles Baudelaire's (1821-1867) *Les Fleurs du mal* (English: *The Flowers of Evil*, 1857), in league with "Satan Trismegistus," Elizabeth embodies the Decadent precept that high art is magic; she is a provocative daughter of Mercurius, a promiscuous voluptuary. As part of her salacious arcanum, she rejects bra and pantyhose because they block her caresses. Her black high heels, stockings, garter belt and straps, and pencil skirt entice masturbation–it's all Isabel Marant's style, 30-years early. Add to the mix her smoky eyes, tousled, blonde wavy hair, candy-apple red lipstick, red fingernail polish, white cashmere-cotton cardigan, and gray slip

---

[43] Per Faxneld, *Satanic Feminism: Lucifer as the Liberator of Women in Nineteenth-Century Culture* (New York: Oxford University Press, 2017), 424.
[44] Her black silk stockings are the devil Mercurius, the agent of her great change. Elizabeth's stockings masturbate her, rousing her repressed erotic side.
[45] Andrew Lang, *Custom and Myth* (New York: Harper & Brothers, 1885), 212-244.
[46] Richard Cavendish, *The Black Arts* (New York: G.P. Putnam's Sons, 1967), 169.

CINEMA SYMBOLISM 3

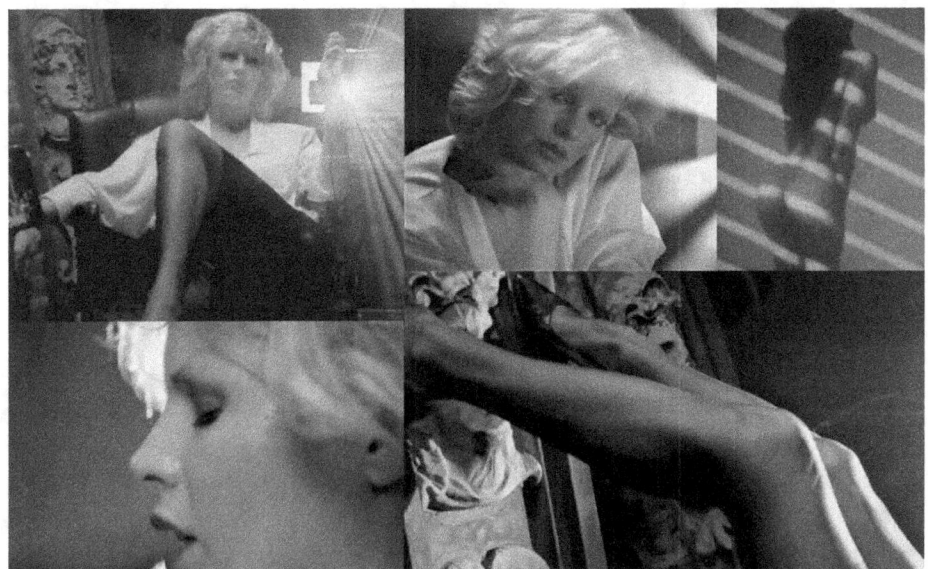

"Conquer every Repulsion in thy self, subdue every Aversion. Assimilate all Poison, for therein only is there Profit. Seek constantly therefore to know what is painful and to cleave thereunto, for by Pain cometh true Pleasure." – Aleister Crowley, *Liber Aleph vel CXI: The Book of Wisdom or Folly*. (Top left) Living Deliciously: in the art gallery's crepuscular basement, *9 ½ Weeks*' Elizabeth proudly flaunts her black silk stockings. They are an alchemical fetish–an erotic talisman–allowing the release of Mercurius, freeing her shadow. (Top center) As Elizabeth views portraits of women touching themselves (top right), her bedroom eyes exude ecstasy, sulfurous fluid her fantasies, seduced by sexy phantasmagoria; hypnotized, her face effuses a puckish, satanic glee. (Bottom left) Masturbating, the luminescence of her skin is a blank canvas; her smudgy black eyeliner and swollen red lips transmogrify her into high art. Her fingers are paintbrushes, soothing her fleshy canvas. Elizabeth is, indeed, Salvador Dali's (1904-1989) *Great Masturbator* (1929) oil painting incarnate. (Bottom right) Deceived by the sensation of silky fabrics against her skin, she turbulently raises her legs in black silk stockings, and feet in black high heels, signifying the shadow's triumph–lascivious darkness reigns! The Eurythmics' song, "This City Never Sleeps," dovetails with her Postmodern onanism perfectly because it both encourages and admonishes the pursuit of sensual pleasures. Although she's a divorcée in her thirties, the scene depicts Elizabeth as a virgin descending into darker, more pleasurable, sexual mysteries. Her volcanic orgasm suggests she has just discovered masturbation, climaxing for the first time like an inexperienced teenager. Earlier, in the art gallery's exhibition area, she is the only one who knows who recognizes the framed chastity belt for what it is, implying she's innocent and the contraption is her own. By placing the belt on exhibit–proudly hanging it on the gallery's wall–Elizabeth is shedding her restraint, prudishness, and self-control. Thus, rid of the chastity belt, she is devoured by vigorous masturbation in the basement, unlocking the flesh's lesser mysteries. Free of the constrictive device, Elizabeth has likewise rejected a bra and pantyhose, replacing the latter with an elegant black garter belt and luxurious black silk stockings, allowing easy access to her erogenous zone. By masturbating, she has performed alchemy, transmuting herself into a living piece of decadent art, an exemplar of earthly delights. As Elizabeth climaxes, the slide projector rapidly fires the images, implying her unfettered rapture. Next, she energetically runs through a puddle of water because she has just gushed like a waterfall, tainting the art gallery with her essence, unabashed by her poetic perversion. She has trashed her ego, guided only by the pleasure principle–the force behind the shadow–regardless of consequence. Perfecting the spagyric art, Elizabeth becomes a lustful exhibit; to best represent *coincidentia oppositorum*, her molten flesh should be displayed next to the inhibitory apparatus.

round out her sexy ensemble, preparing her for her solo flight. By pleasuring herself to demonic artwork, she embodies *nuditas criminalis*, viz. lascivious and vain spectacle, transforming into a cynosure worthy of display in the Spring Street Gallery or any cosmopolitan *kunstkammer*.[47] Ergo, desirous of imitating the artwork she peddles, Elizabeth employs the gallery's caliginous basement as her hedonistic atelier, masturbating as people walk over the apertures above, watching her hot-blooded performance. Garters, stockings, and belts were symbols of grandeur and authority, investing the female sorceress wearing them with magical properties and mystical abilities.[48] These are Elizabeth's lucky charms, and her sex magick is an éclat vacating all notions of prim-and-proper womanhood, making her Lilith in the flesh: a lustful, racy, satanic lady.

Elizabeth's caresses reflect society's twofold attitude toward female masturbation: liberating but abject, ecstatic but humiliating, lyrical but second-rate.[49] These polarities infer *coincidentia oppositorum*; like an alchemist with his athanor, mortar and pestle, Hessian crucible, aludel, retort, and alembic, Elizabeth also has magical paraphernalia. Dressed to the nines, she dons alchemy's colors to create an equilibrium, a juicy synthesis: her black stockings, the *nigredo*; her white blouse, the *albedo*; her gold watch, the *citirinitas*; and her lipstick and nail polish, the *rubedo*. The masturbator's rapture transcends duality, generating saturnine feminine energy that is receptive and transmissive, passive and active, sensual and innocent, producing an erotic force seeking to liberate her suppressed passions. Still, the release is temporary, not permanent.[50]

One could further argue her onanism is a primitive form of priapic worship–the wooden sculpture on her right has a pointy penis-like protrusion. While she pleasures herself, some of the slides she watches are

---

47 Faxneld, *Satanic Feminism*, Chapter 9, "Becoming the Demon Woman," 386-426, analyzing the wicked woman's clothing and jewelry, reinforcing their eccentric behavior. See also Anton LaVey, *The Compleat Witch or What to do When Virtue Fails* (New York: Dodd, Mead, & Company, 1971), 162-172, arguing that stockings and high heels are witchy talismans.
48 Margaret Murray, *The God of the Witches* (London: Sampson Low, Marston & Co., 1933), 37-40; Doreen Valiente, *An ABC of Witchcraft Past & Present* (New York: St. Martin's Press, 1973), 190-192. See also Grimassi, *Encyclopedia*, 47, discussing stockings as magical totems, connected with Befana, a gift-giving witch in Italian folklore.
49 Thomas W. Laqueur, *Solitary Sex: A Cultural History of Masturbation* (Brooklyn, NY: Zone Books, 2004), 406.
50 Grimassi, *Encyclopedia*, 155.

paintings of demons, which, along with hobgoblins, represented the phallus in ancient cultures. Over time, these demons morphed into mythological figures like Robin Goodfellow of English folklore, linking Elizabeth to Devil worship, advancing her Romantic Satanism.[51] By the time *9 ½ Weeks'* end credits roll, it is evident Elizabeth's magical self-gratification has failed. Her lust, alchemical fetishism, and desire have consumed her, corrupting her spirit-soul, torturing her flesh-body, demolishing her vanity. Instead of generating a femme fatale personality, she has become the Tarot's Fool, a simpleton, an archetype, a naïve queen for a day.

Lastly, Elizabeth's sultry event horizon celebrates the engravings of Félicien Rops (1833-1898), a visual artist who emphasized Satan's connection to sensuality and carnal pleasures. A devout anticleric, his illustration of St. Teresa of Ávila (1515-1582) shows the Carmelite nun naked except her veil with a dildo wedged in her vagina; the Spanish reformer and mystic's ecstasy exposed as masturbating to an open Bible. Like Elizabeth, an expression of waggish rapture contorts St. Teresa's features. In 1861, Rops was initiated into the Masonic lodge *La Bonne Amitié* of the Grand Orient of Belgium. Impersonating his art, Rops did his best to look like the Devil: with a nose sharp and brusque, subtle lips, he had a goatee and a sufficient shock of hair resembling two horns. Perseverance created an image: Rops was content to be a living symbol of something people wanted, something Crowley embraced.[52] His notorious engravings depict women's insatiable lust, leading them to Devil worship inevitably, an idea coming from *Malleus Maleficarum* (English: *Hammer of the Witches*, 1487), a treatise endorsing the extermination of witches. For instance, in *L'Idole* (1882, English: *The Idol*), Rops has the satanic woman mount the penis of a laurel-crowned statue of the Devil (or Pan), flanked by two phallic-shaped columns with breasts and goat's hooves at their bases,

---

51 Sanger Brown, *The Sex Worship and Symbolism of Primitive Races* (Boston: Richard G. Badger, 1916), 93-94. cf. John Michael Greer, *The New Encyclopedia of the Occult* (St. Paul: Llewellyn Publications, 2005), 370. Greer contests the antiquity of the phallic religion, writing: "A fixation (and in large part an invention) of eighteenth and nineteenth-century European scholars, phallic religion was the worship of the powers of fertility in the form of the penis…Writings concerning phallic religion played an important role in the evolution of the Romantic image of the witch, and thus in the prehistory of modern Wicca and Neopaganism."
52 Tobias Churton, *Occult Paris: The Lost Magic of the Belle Époque* (Rochester, VT: Inner Traditions, 2016), 35-38.

ejaculating fire from their tips.[53] She gazes awestruck at his satanic majesty, just like Elizabeth is glued to the demonic artwork.[54] A sense of gloomy and mysterious splendor permeates Rops' crepuscular image–owing to the temple-like setting–anticipating the art gallery's basement with its haze, piercing light, and pagan-like faces.[55] As is often the case, Rops inserts a detail–here, the modern, high-heeled shoes worn by the woman (like Elizabeth's black high heels)–to show the scene is not an archaic one, but depicts the female of his time.[56] Even though she is a beautiful, sophisticated, a connoisseur of Neo-expressionist and Postmodern artwork, Elizabeth cannot resist her primal impulses. She succumbs to her lustful desires, liberating her animalistic instincts by masturbating in public,[57] and later has sex in a clock tower, thereby venerating Mephistopheles, cementing her status as a Romantic Satanist.[58] Her dynamic, tantric exhibition would have made her the toast of the 19th-century Decadents and Symbolists. Many artisans showcasing their talents in Joséphin Péladan's Rose-Croix Salons would have admired Elizabeth's ethereal aesthetics, recognizing her as a "Maccabee of Beauty" while a snobby clique would have found it tasteless, snickering behind her back. Sadly, women were prohibited from exhibiting; her titillating swank denied, she would've had to settle with hanging out at Edmond Bailly's (1850-1966) trendy occult bookshop. She could've had a lesbian fling with Liane de Pougy (1869-1950) or, perhaps, drop in on a séance at *chez* Lady Caithness, Duchess of Pomar (Marie Sinclair, 1830-1895), attempting to contact Mary, Queen of Scots (1542-1587).

* * * * *

Numbers and their associated sequences–such as doubles and repetition–are crucial devices used by these celluloid sorcerers. Every number has a specific power not expressed by the figure or symbol employed to denote quantity only.[59] This power rests in an occult connection existing between

---

53 Faxneld, *Satanic Feminism*, 290.
54 Brad Holland painted the artwork cast by the basement's slide projector, his webpage: https://www.bradholland.net/. This author could not find the names or titles of his paintings, only portfolios.
55 Faxneld, *Satanic Feminism*, *supra* note 53.
56 Ibid, 290-291.
57 Brown, *Sex Worship*, 94-95.
58 Van Luijk, "The Resurrection of Satan in Nineteenth-Century (Counter) Culture," 41-51, *passim*.
59 Sepharial, *The Kabalah of Numbers: A Handbook of Interpretation* (London: William Rider and Son, Limited, 1911), 5.

(Left) *L'Idole*, from Rops' *Les Sataniques*, a series of five engravings, retouched heliogravure, 1882, ca. 28 x 21 cm. Elizabeth begins masturbating when this painting (center) is projected on the screen, featuring the *Ars Goetia* demon Bael, the First Principle Spirit, ruling in the East, who "…appeareth in divers shapes, sometimes like a Cat,…and sometimes like a Man." She continues to caress herself, observing this next portrait (right) depicting Paimon, another demon from *Ars Goetia*. Paimon, a Great King of Hell, and very obedient to Lucifer, who "…appeareth in the form of a Man….with a Crown most glorious upon his head." Her gold watch is her lamen-like pendant, awakening her erotic consciousness. The projected paintings are a visual grimoire's pages; by masturbating to them, Elizabeth performs sex magick to consummate alchemy. Next to the screen sits an empty easel because Elizabeth is the piece of artwork; seated, her brushstrokes are her caresses, her viscous sweat is her sticky, passionate oil paints. Center and right images from *9 ½ Weeks*.

the relations of things and the principles in nature of which they are the expressions.[60] The use of numbers is akin to Gematria: a kabalistic method of interpreting the Hebrew scriptures by computing the numerical value of words, based on their constituent letters to convey secret codes. It is artistic magic; through complex calculations and combinations, the magus could depict the world's organization and manipulate the natural forces of earth, air, fire, and water. Numbers do not lie, and filmmakers employ them to forge occult nexuses, provide intrigue, revealing and concealing obscure revelations. In *Poltergeist* (1982), Tobe Hooper (1943-2017) and Steven Spielberg pay homage to Kubrick's Rocky Mountain tale of terror. When Carol Ann Freeling (Heather O'Rourke (1975-1988)) approaches the television, warning her parents, "They're here," notice the time on the set is 2:37 am, referencing the Overlook's room 237. The number links Danny Torrance (Danny Lloyd) to Carol Ann because supernatural forces terrorize both children, investing *Poltergeist* with *The Shining*'s omnipresent dread.

---

60 Ibid.

When *The Exorcist* introduces Father Damien Karras (Jason Miller, 1939-2001), he ascends a subway staircase from 33rd Street. Thirty-three designates his apotheosis; that is, he will become Regan's Christlike savior, ridding her of the demon possessing her.[61] In *Escape from New York*, the kabalistic code name and number for Air Force One is David 14. Matthew 1:17 states: "So all the generations from Abraham to David are fourteen generations; and from David until the carrying away into Babylon are fourteen generations; and from the carrying away into Babylon unto Christ are fourteen generations." Furthermore, fourteen is Hebrew for David (D=4, V=6, D=4; 4+6+4=14); ergo, Air Force One's numeric designation covertly identifies the United States President (Donald Pleasence, 1919-1995) as a Biblical savior, the preserver of Western Civilization, the contents of his briefcase averting the apocalypse. These examples are akin to Bruno's art of memory, illustrating the power of numbers, mnemonics, used today by Hollywood's magi.

Samhain, the eve of November, was a day designating the sun's death, on which a votive sacrifice was owed to evil powers. Though overcome at Moytura, diabolism was ascendant at Samhain. Methods of discovering the spirits' will works better at this time of year naturally; thus, charms and invocations had more power because ghosts were near to help if care was taken not to anger them, and due honors paid.[62] Since the sun is dead, the moon is exalted, presiding over the impending seasonal darkness. In *Halloween III: Season of the Witch* (1982), the newscaster states one of Stonehenge's 19 bluestones is missing, linking the megalithic structure the 19-year Metonic-lunar cycle. However, the full lunar cycle with no intercalations (the Islamic calendar) is 33 years; thus, Stonehenge's Sarsen Circle is 33 meters in diameter, consisting of 30 stones and 30 lintels (*33*), indicating the ancient structure is a lunar-solar-astronomical calendar. The film's antagonist, a reclusive Irishman named Conal Cochran (Dan O'Herlihy, 1919-2005), intends to take advantage of "ancient technology" to quote the Hibernian, by exploiting a supernal alignment. The planetary arrangement, occurring on Samhain/Halloween, facilitates black magic by the sacrifice of millions of children. Cochran is the CEO of Silver Shamrock Novelties; its name conjures the earth's satellite because silver

---

61 Jesus Christ was 33 years old when he was crucified.
62 Ruth E. Kelley, *The Book of Hallowe'en* (Boston: Lothrop, Lee & Shepard Co., 1919), 21-22.

is the moon's color. *Halloween III* forges a nexus between Stonehenge and the moon; thus, 33 is omnipresent, reinforcing this astronomical occultism subconsciously. Conal Cochran's first and last names begin with the letter *C*, the third letter, making his initials *CC*, or *33*. The town of Santa Mira, the home of his company, is on Route 33, and its logo is a three-leafed clover, or trefoil shamrock, while Silver Shamrock manufactures three Halloween masks to get 33. Silver Shamrock Novelties, it seems, is a covert temple to Hecate with Cochran serving as the high priest of this demonic moon cult. Easter egg: Cochran's big three Halloween masks are a witch, skull, and pumpkin, indicative of the tripartite colors of Ireland's flag: green (witch), white (skull), and orange (pumpkin).

Blink, and you'll miss it. (Left) Silver Shamrock Novelties' Chief Executive Officer is the warlock, Conal Cochran, seen here with one of his cursed skull masks. Cochran is an expert in golem making, having crafted an army of humanoid robots that do his bidding without question. Moreover, Cochran's diabolical Big Giveaway, occurring on the evening of Samhain or Halloween, is synchronized with an astronomical alignment. He explains the axiomatic *above and below*, "...Halloween, the festival of Samhain! The last great one took place three thousand years ago when the hills ran red with the blood of animals and children ... it's time again. In the end, we don't decide these things, you know, the planets do. They're in alignment, and it's time again." From *Halloween III*. (Right) *Halloween II* foreshadows Cochran's scheme when Michael Myers (Dick Warlock) wrote *SAMHAIN* in blood on a chalkboard in Haddonfield's elementary school. Underneath the bloody word, Homework Assignment B instructs the class to create an astronomical chart with all the planets in their orbits, anticipating the planetary alignment necessary for Cochran's "Joke on the children," to quote the evil mask maker.

Numbers take up residency at the Overlook Hotel, transcending Kubrick's horror masterpiece, *The Shining*. Kubrick uses numbers, repetition, and doubles as tropes to convey–both to the conscious and subconscious mind–that the resort is a symbolic ouroboros: *Hen to Pan, the all is one*, forever born and reborn. The hotel endlessly swallows (or bites) its tail because it houses a cyclic paradigm–an infinity–destined to

CINEMA SYMBOLISM 3

(Top three images) Kubrick's *The Shining* is sheer repetition; its beginning is its ending, becoming a murderous revolving door signifying the Overlook's never-ending reincarnation cycle. During the interview, Jack wears a green tie, which has a pattern mirroring the hedge maze in which he will freeze to death at the end. Similar symbolism hides in *Trick 'r Treat* (2007). Like *The Shining*, it begins with its ending. When Emma (Leslie Bibb) is taking down the Halloween decorations, observe the eight School Bus Massacre children *qua* living dead on the other side of the street (center, seen here still alive). They leave Mr. Kreeg's (Brian Cox) house after killing him during the closing moments. (Bottom) And keep an eye on Rhonda's (Samm Todd) red wagon with its solitary jack-o'-lantern, which, likewise, opens the Halloween gem–it is the movie's prelude. She crosses the street, causing the werewolves' car to brake suddenly; recognize the lit pumpkin she hauls? "You need a root beer?" It's the jack-o'-lantern Principal Wilkins (Dylan Baker) carves as he sits on his stoop next to Charlie (Brett Kelly), musing about Halloween's mysteries, poisoning the obese miscreant with tainted candy. He gives the pumpkin to Macy (Britt McKillip), which she claims is for a scavenger hunt. In turn, she takes it to the quarry with her fellow tricksters as an offering to the dead, a gift to the eight murdered children. Rhonda survives the ghostly attack, carting the pumpkin off in her wagon, bumping into Sam (Quinn Lord), until it is finally seen at the end, which is the beginning. The jack-o'-lantern ties the stories together, much like *Creepshow*'s (1982) ashtray.

repeat, Delbert Grady (Philip Stone, 1934-2003), Charles Grady, and Jack Torrance (Jack Nicholson) reincarnate over and over and over again. The three men are the same because they are the perpetual caretakers of the Overlook. To project samsara, Kubrick repeats numbers; specifically, he utilizes *42*. First, Danny's (Danny Lloyd) sweatshirt bears the number 42; next, Danny and Wendy (Shelley Duvall) watch *Summer of '42* (1971) while snowed-in at the resort. Finally, Dick Holloran's (Scatman Crothers, 1910-1986) license plate has the number 42, observable when he returns to the hotel in the snowstorm. According to the New Testament, *42* associates with the Antichrist, his evil efforts lasting 42 months. Revelation 11: 1-2 reads, "And there was given me a reed like unto a rod: and the angel stood, saying, Rise, and measure the temple of God, and the altar, and them that worship therein. But the court which is without the temple leave out, and measure it not; for it is given unto the Gentiles: and the holy city shall they tread under foot forty and two months." Then at Revelation 13: 4-5, "And they worshipped the dragon which gave power unto the beast: and they worshipped the beast, saying, who is like unto the beast? Who is able to make war with him? And there was given unto him a mouth speaking great things and blasphemies; and power was given unto him to continue forty and two months." Forty-two appears three times; add 4+2 to get 6, or 666. Kubrick uses 42 to imbue the Overlook with apocalyptic demonism, and the murderous Jack with the Antichrist; in other words, the failed writer has become evil incarnate.[63]

But Kubrick doesn't end the doubles, the repetition, with 42. Wendy wears two bathrobes, the first of which features a light blue hue, observable when the actors' names appear during the opening credits; moreover, the Grady twins' (Lisa and Louise Burns) dresses are the same color blue. Two opposite times of the year surface: the black and white photo is a July 4th celebration, yet Jack seems to attend a New Year's Eve party, generating an epistemological crisis. This dilemma is augmented by Stuart Ullman (Barry Nelson, 1917-2007), who tells Jack, during his interview, the hotel is closed during the winter months. The conundrum questions the fabric

---

[63] Robert W. Sullivan, *Cinema Symbolism 2: More Esoteric Imagery in Popular Movies* (Baltimore: Deadwood Publishing, LLC., 2017), Chapter V. I revealed Jack drinks alcohol at approximately 66 minutes and 6 seconds into the film, further associating him with the devilry of the Antichrist.

of reality, leaving us, like the Torrance family, to wonder what is genuine and what is an illusion.

Jack informs Lloyd the Bartender (Joe Turkel) he has two twenties and two tens in his wallet, mentioning two Portlands: one in Oregon, the other in Maine. There are two mazes: the one outside and the dark labyrinthine hallways of the Overlook. There are two boilers, two tennis balls, and two sets of twins: Grady's daughters and two sisters passing by Ullman on the way to the Torrance family's quarters. The doubles refer to a representation of the ego that can assume various forms, e.g., shadow, reflection, portrait, double, twin, found in primitive animism as a narcissistic extension and guarantee of immortality. But with the withdrawal of narcissism, he becomes a harbinger of death, e.g., Jack's kill-crazy rampage, a source of criticism and persecution. The figure of the double dates back to primitive civilizations, featured in legends, reoccurring in literature and cinema. It was Austrian psychoanalyst Otto Rank (1884-1939), in his essay on the double titled *Der Doppelgänger* (1914), who was the first to develop this idea in psychoanalysis, and Sigmund Freud (1856-1939) quotes him at length in *The Uncanny* (1919). However, the idea of the doubling of consciousness

(Top left) In *Black Swan*, Nina Sayers, dressed in virginal whites with her back to the audience, passes her doppelganger. Her clone is darkly dressed, signifying Nina's shadow self, the unfathomable terror dwelling within. As Nina begins to embrace her dark side, she frees herself from her repressive ego by delighting in masochism, masturbation, drug use, lesbianism, and humiliation to become perfect. She performs alchemy to achieve perfection and become the Black Swan: a confident, graceful, and seductive ballerina. (Bottom left) Nina's alchemy begins to pay off; no longer repressed, her dark side comes alive in a mirror while Nina clings to her lowly White Swan persona's vestiges. (Right) On the dancefloor, Nina splits in half, signifying her mental erosion, her inability to reconcile shadow with ego, reality with fantasy. *Solve et coagula*.

is present in his first texts on hysteria (1893, 1895). Freud introduces the unconscious as another consciousness capable of producing dreams, parapraxes, and so on. The theme of the double is taken up by Freud and integrated into his concept of the uncanny. To Freud, the uncanny is that form of terror leading back to something long known to us, once very familiar, but has become terrifying because it corresponds to something repressed that has returned. "The double," Freud wrote citing German literary critic Heinrich Heine (1797-1856), "has become an image of terror, just as, after the collapse of their religion, the gods turned into demons." Robert Louis Stevenson (1850-1894) had spent years searching for a story that would fit his keen sense of a man's duality when the plot of *Dr. Jekyll and Mr. Hyde* (1886) was suddenly revealed to him in a dream.[64] Now we, as an audience, understand Kubrick's use of doubles: not only do they designate repetition, but they also represent Jack's alchemical metamorphosis, becoming a living nightmare, Mr. Hyde, a terrifying monster.

Certain taboos arise from the double; by seeing their twin, a person criticizes the self by becoming aware of their conscience and desires. When that happens, they become cognizant of what the double represents–the unacceptable part of their conscious ego: the positive attributes relating to identity and intuition. This unsuitable component is what Jung referred to as the *shadow* (Freud's id), or the shadow self: darkness, malevolence, and negativity. Put another way, the conscious ego, or ego, is mainly responsible

Primitive cultures, past and present, believe mirrors reflect the soul, which will be lost or corrupted if one underestimates the mirror's temptations. In *Maria's Lovers* (1984), Maria Bosic (Nastassja Kinski) stands half-naked before a mirror; seduced by her reflection, Maria resorts to fervent onanism to ease her sexual frustration, satisfying her carnal impulses.

---

64 Carl G. Jung, "Approaching the Unconscious," in *Man and his Symbols*, ed. Carl G. Jung (New York: Dell, 1968), 25.

for feelings of identity and continuity according to the reality principle: acting for benefit, not grief. The ego is contrasted by the devious shadow, the unknown, the reservoir of our darkest impulses. Everything and everyone cast shadows; for example, da Vinci, who painted *The Mona Lisa* (1503) and *Madonna of the Rocks* (1483-1486) masterpieces, also drew up blueprints for a tank and a machine gun to kill as many people as possible.

The doppelganger/double usage in cinema gives insight to the narrow threshold between self, ego and shadow, and perception of the other. In terms of self-orientation, the double represents the opposite of what the person perceives. It denotes the aspects of humanity we deny to preserve our self-image or the core aspects of what makes each person unique. The doppelganger is a visual representation of the darker parts of the individual psyche humans deny so they're seen by society in a better way, as opposed to who they truly are at their core. Therefore, in cinema or literature, the doppelganger would signify a person's worst fears or dark desires visualized into something they're scared of becoming.

In *The Empire Strikes Back* (1980), inside a cave on Dagobah, Luke Skywalker (Mark Hamill) duels the dark lord of the Sith, Darth Vader. After Luke defeats Vader with his lightsaber, Vader's mask disappears, revealing Luke's face, his doppelganger. The symbolism is clear: Luke has confronted his inner darkness, acknowledged and integrated it, and is now more equipped to confront the real Lord Vader when the time is right. Unbeknownst to Luke at the time, his encounter with his shadow exposes what he fears the most: transformation into his tyrannical father, falling victim to Emperor Sheev Palpatine/Darth Sidious (Ian McDiarmid) and the Dark Side of the Force, becoming a Sith.

One of the best ways to convey the shadow, the dark side, is via a mirror. The image in the mirror reflects the ego; that is, what the ego does not identify with, thereby used to demonstrate the darker side or shadow self of the person gazing into it. In dreams, a mirror can symbolize the sublime power of the unconscious to imitate the individual objectively, giving a view of him or herself they may never have had before. Only through the unconscious can such a view–which often shocks and upsets the ego–be obtained; look to the Greek myth of the Gorgon, Medusa, whose look turned men to stone, but her evil reflection could be gazed upon in

The dark side lives! (Top) Exposed to a counterfeit piece of Kryptonite in *Superman III*, Superman's (Christopher Reeve, 1952-2004) shadow emerges. Drunk and bellicose, the Man of Steel sits at a bar–before a mirror–firing peanuts at bottles of alcohol. (Bottom, Left and Right). In the television series *Supergirl* ("Falling," airdate March 14, 2016), Kara Danvers *qua* Supergirl (Melissa Benoist), is exposed to corrupting red Kryptonite; sitting at a bar, she belligerently fires peanuts at bottles of alcohol.

a mirror without consequence.[65] In *Suspiria '77*, Suzy solves the riddle of the blue iris by observing its reflection in a mirror; shortly afterward, she unlocks the mystery of the *Tanzakademie* by discovering the evil witches hiding within. In *Evil Dead II: Dead by Dawn* (1987), Ash Williams' (Bruce Campbell) reflection comes alive in a mirror, grabbing him, reminding him he's not *fine*. Ash has dismembered his girlfriend with a chainsaw; it is his shadow acknowledging his ghoulish deed. In *9 ½ Weeks*, Elizabeth, dressed in black, glances at a mirror inside the Chelsea Hotel, anticipating her libertine impulses, surrendering to her sapphic yearnings

---

65 M.-L. von Franz, "The Process of Individuation," in *Man and his Symbols*, ed. Carl G. Jung (New York: Dell, 1968), 218; text accompanying the illustration of Caravaggio's *Medusa*, depicting the Gorgon's severed head reflected in a shield.

with a Hispanic prostitute; she is playing with fire, dangerously adopting the characteristics of the shadow persona. Elizabeth's sexual alchemy has an unseen consequence: the development of a homosexual disposition; she has a diabolical clitoris better suited for women than men.[66]

One method sophisticated filmmakers utilize with notable effect is what I refer to as *occult casting*. This technique is when, briefly explained in

(Left) In *9 ½ Weeks*, Kim Basinger as Elizabeth epitomizes the best of 1980s fashion in the Big Apple. Strolling along the boardwalk at Coney Island, the balloons represent her childlike innocence; she is not prepared for her psychological alchemy. Her hat indicates an unconscious desire to be part of a social class; she wants to transcend the swanky art world. And why not? New York City is a character; the Spring Street Art Gallery, the Chelsea Market, and the Chelsea Hotel reflect the megalopolis when it was bustling with creativity and energy, much like La Belle Époque. (Top Center) Inside the Chelsea Hotel, Elizabeth's reflection anticipates her other self's sable and sensual side. Stripped down to her black lingerie, Elizabeth sits on the edge of a bed (top right) when a Hispanic prostitute unexpectedly begins to caress her black silk stockings and garter straps–Elizabeth's fetish–arousing her so much that her seething flesh emits steam. Elizabeth starts to alchemically transition into her shadow self by welcoming the forbidden pleasures of lesbianism. These are likely the same stockings Elizabeth wore earlier, arousing her, enticing her to masturbate. (Bottom right) Unexpectedly, the Hispanic begins removing Elizabeth's stockings, her idée fixe, stripping her of her dark side allegorically, and, simultaneously, breaking her wanton pride and erotic hubris, destroying her emotionally. In the world of the occult, prophetic dreams, and witchcraft, when a woman loses her stockings is a harbinger of trouble and distress. Her amatory juju has betrayed her; once removed, i.e., discarded, Elizabeth's pleasurable black stockings are now a frigid talisman cursing her with sexual frustration, humiliation, and melancholy. She now knows her earlier experiment–ostentatiously masturbating in public–was vulgar and pathetic; it was not powerful sex magicks, nor was it an exercise in sophisticated aesthetics.

---

66 Faxneld, *Satanic Feminism*, 329.

the Preface, a director or producer casts a particular actress or actor to bring their cultural-cinematic baggage, a cultural valence, from an earlier film(s), creating a mnemonic, perpetuating mythology. The presence of the trouper resurrects a past performance(s) affecting the new movie, transferring thematic imagery from the earlier film implanting it in the viewer's subconscious mind while watching the new one. A fascinating instance of occult casting occurs in *Star Wars: Attack of the Clones* (2002), summoning the Gnosticism of *The Matrix*.

In the Valentinian fable, Mouse, played by Matt Dorin, is one of Morpheus' (Laurence Fishburne) disciples; he has taken the red pill and is part of the *Nebuchadnezzar*'s crew. He knows the Matrix is a false reality; as such, Mouse designs the computer program–the woman in a red dress–played by Fiona Johnson, to warn Neo (Keanu Reeves) that a predatory Agent could be anyone. In *Attack of the Clones*, Dorin cameos as Elan Sleazebaggano, a death-stick dealer in the nightclub, the Outlander. When Obi-Wan Kenobi (Ewan McGregor) and Anakin Skywalker enter the bar in hot pursuit of the bounty hunter Zam Wesell (Leeanna Walsman), Kenobi goes to the bar for a drink and offered death sticks by Sleazebaggano. During the inconsequential scene, a red cocktail sits on the bar before Sleazebaggano while Kenobi sips a blue beverage. By casting Dorin, Lucas is conjuring *The Matrix*'s Gnosticism, suggesting the galaxy of *Star Wars* is, perhaps, a demiurgic mirage. Mouse took the red pill; thus, Sleazebaggano downs a red potation. Red designates Mouse and Sleazebaggano's vitality and consciousness. At the same time, Kenobi guzzles a blue libation, a symbolic blue pill, implying the Jedi Knight is trapped in an illusion, sound asleep, living in nightmarish stasis. This occult paradigm is corroborated minutes later when Anakin passes a female partier named Hayde Gofai portrayed by none other than Fiona Johnson, who played Mouse's woman in red. Her casting implies the *Star Wars* galaxy is a simulation controlled by a Demiurge–think *The Matrix Reloaded*'s (2003) Architect (Helmut Bakaitis)–wherein the Sith and Jedi play a deadly, make-believe game of chess. Such casting is daring; at the very least, it is a way for Lucas to pay homage to the Wachowski siblings and their *Matrix* trilogy, forever altering the way one may perceive the *Star Wars* Universe.[67]

---

[67] Andrew Ziegler, "There's a 'Matrix' Reference in 'Star Wars' That'll Make You Question Everything," *Buzzfeed*, November 29, 2017, https://www.buzzfeed.com/andrewziegler/

(Top left) Mouse in *The Matrix* was played by actor Matt Dorin who also portrayed Elan Sleazebaggono (top right) in *Attack of the Clones*. (Bottom left) Fiona Johnson plays Mouse's computer training program, the woman in red, portraying (lower right) Hayda Gofai in *Attack of the Clones*.

Hollywood uses costuming and color to convey hidden themes, producing allusions often missed by casual moviegoers. In *An American Werewolf in London*, while traveling across the East Proctor moors, David Kessler's (David Naughton) and Jack Goodman's (Griffin Dunne) down jackets and rucksacks make them look like astronauts exploring unfamiliar terrain. They appear like unwelcomed outsiders, men from another planet, when they enter the Slaughtered Lamb, a rustic pub marked with the pentagram. David's red coat is a nod to *Little Red Riding Hood*, a fairy tale about a girl who encounters a lycanthrope on her way to grandma's house. So is Naughty Nina Carter's skimpy red dress seen in the *News of the World* TV commercial just before David's first transformation into the

---

this-link-between-the-matrix-and-star-wars will-bl (accessed April 14, 2018).

titular monster. Scotland Yard's Inspector Villiers (Don McKillop, 1929-2005) arrives at Piccadilly Circus in a red car to investigate the mayhem but the werewolf attacks, biting his head off. And speaking of red: in *Satanic Panic* (2019), Samantha "Sam" Craft's (Hayley Griffith) red Converse shoes summon Dorothy Gale's (Judy Garland, 1922-1969) ruby slippers from *The Wizard of Oz*. Like a bumpkin from Kansas, Sam must navigate an unsettling environment to find her way home, defeating an evil witch along the way. For Dorothy and Sam, their red shoes are protective talismans, helping them traverse mysterious and perilous wonderlands.

Director Adrian Lyne is an expert in this field; in *Fatal Attraction* (1987), Alex Forrest (Glenn Close) wardrobe is either black, white, or black and white, signifying her fractured good girl/bad girl personality.

In *The Dark Knight Rises* (2012), Selina Kyle's (Anne Hathaway) attire comes from the closet of Holly Golightly (Audrey Hepburn, 1929-1993) in *Breakfast at Tiffany's* (1960). Ms. Kyle's clothing gives off an air of

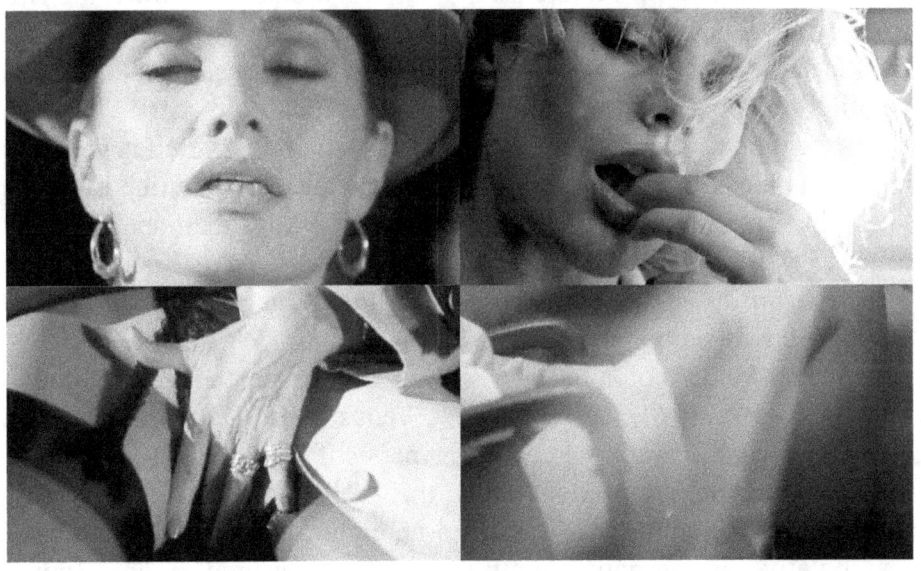

Comparative Cinema: a fixation for black silk stockings. (Left, top and bottom) Adrian Lyne borrows from the grindhouse-*giallo* film *The New York Ripper* (1982). Jane Forrester Lodge (Alexandra Delli Colli) wears black silk stockings to signify and satisfy her dark, lustful yearnings. Jane masturbates in public to erotic performance art, audio recording her orgasm to embarrass herself, relishing her humiliation. (Right, top and bottom) Likewise, in *9 ½ Weeks*, Elizabeth debases herself by masturbating in public to weird artwork while wearing black silk stockings, signifying her shadow self and dark impulses. She fingers her luscious red lips, implying her fingers are busy down below, messaging her swollen clit, her vagina raining on wet, her body swamped with concupiscence. Both women also like candy apple red fingernail polish, heightening their fleshy pleasures, transforming them into erotic avant-garde works of art for public consumption.

mercurial aloofness mingled with leisurely magnetism, dovetailing with her savvy nocturnal persona, Catwoman.

Returning to Edwardian world of *Crimson Peak*, wherein style and substance walk hand-in-hand, Edith dresses in vivid yellow and golden frocks to indicate her solar-butterfly attributes; she embodies the dawn: a progressive heroine battling aristocratic darkness. Later, in Allerdale Hall, Edith dons a thin, pale, skeletal nightgown to represent her unhealthy condition as a result of Lady Lucille's (Jessica Chastain) poisoning. But that's not all. Do *Crimson Peak*'s lavish costumes hide the sexual orientations of the two female leads? In the kitchen, when Lucille discovers Edith and her brother, Sir Thomas (Tom Hiddleston), have finally consummated their marriage, she goes ballistic, attempting to strike Edith with a pot of hot food. Lucille laments how she despises loneliness, while Edith, clearly rattled, says she no longer feels well. This incident, coupled with when Lucille enticed Edith with a pornographic fore-edge book, signals a latent love-hate relationship between the two women; a pang of deep unconscious guilt lingers between them. Does Lucille show Edith the indecent book hoping it arouses her? During this volatile kitchen episode, Edith wears a gray coat with dark blue trim hiding her yellow dress, her natural butterfly-solar color. Sullen gray and midnight blue belong to Lucille, so this could mean by donning Lucille's hues, she is emulating her sister-in-law in more ways than one? Is Edith eager to explore forbidden erotica like lesbianism just as Lucille craves incest? *Crimson Peak*'s costuming infers the sexual orientations of the two women are ambiguous at best.

Green is Venus' color, the eternal consort of Diana, the moon goddess; thus, in *Nerve* (2016), the protagonist, Venus "Vee" Delmonico (Emma Roberts), wears a swanky green dress, personifying a heroine *qua* deity, transcending mere mortals.[68] Only this Venusian-Luciferian beauty, this luminous evening star, is skillful enough to negotiate and defeat a manipulative online game, shutting it down in a modern-day Roman Coliseum during the film's hectic conclusion.

* * * * *

---

68 Manly P. Hall, *The Secret Teachings of All Ages: An Encyclopedic Outline of Masonic, Hermetic, Qabbalistic and Rosicrucian Symbolic Philosophy* (1928; repr., New York: Jeremy P. Tarcher/Penguin, 2003), 629. See also Grimassi, *Encyclopedia*, 260, Cavendish, *Black Arts*, 28, 30.

(Left) In *The Dark Knight Rises*, Selina Kyle's (Anne Hathaway) clothing comes out of Holly Golightly's wardrobe from *Breakfast at Tiffany's*, seen in this publicity photo (right) of Audrey Hepburn as the gadabout.

Believe it or not, movies within movies can reveal the secret motivations and taboo desires of the characters, exposing crucial plot points. This technique produces a psychological, occult manifestation, akin to magic, a visual form echoing narrative content to convey hidden meanings, to energize archetypal imagery buried in the psyche. Again, we think of Bruno's art of memory occult mnemonics. To observe an exemplar of this sorcery, we return to *Halloween* and its 1981 sequel, *Halloween II*. On the night of Samhain, 1978, in Haddonfield, Illinois, a faceless menace, the Shape or Michael Myers (Nick Castle), terrorizes the township, murdering babysitters, butchering all those that cross his path. "Pale tapers glimmer in the sky, the dead and dying leaves go by; Dimly across the faded green, Strange shadows, stranger shades, are seen

– It is the mystic Hallowe'en," so wrote A.F. Murray in *Harper's Weekly*, October 30, 1909, describing the malevolent ambiance of Carpenter's movies to perfection approximately seventy years earlier.[69] During the two films, Dr. Dementia (voiced by Tommy Lee Wallace) hosts a horror film trifecta; they are, in order: *The Thing from Another World* (1951, also known as *The Thing*), *Forbidden Planet* (1956), and *Night of the Living Dead* (1968). The first two are televised in *Halloween*, and the third in *Halloween II*. These three movies are favorites of the director. On the surface, one might conclude Carpenter programmed this marathon for sentimental reasons, as a trip down memory lane; but upon closer examination, a dark psychological undercurrent emerges.

The first, *The Thing*, features a monstrous space alien (James Arness, 1923-2011) terrorizing a USAF team in the Arctic. The alien resembles a man, but it is not human; Arness' organism is, essentially, a vegetable pretending to be a man. The creature parallels Dr. Sam Loomis' (Donald Pleasence) theory that, while Michael Myers may look like a man, he is not; instead, he is pure evil personified, a Shape masquerading as a human. One will observe Dr. Carrington (Robert Cornthwaite, 1917-2006)) is Dr. Loomis' anthesis; while the former wants to communicate with the alien to learn from it, the latter knows everything about Michael, the Shape, understanding its destruction is the only viable solution. The button-downed Laurie Strode (Jamie Lee Curtis) is chaste, a good student, and a responsible babysitter; embodying the ego, she is conscientious and cautious. Underneath his white mask, Michael represents Laurie's shadow, unfettered and on-the-loose animality, killing her friends who express their desires and satisfy their libidos: Annie Brackett (Nancy Kyes) and Lynda van der Klok (P.J. Soles).[70]

Thus, the second movie Dr. Dementia presents is *Forbidden Planet*, wherein the unconscious, nebulous motives of Dr. Edward Morbius (Walter Pidgeon, 1897-1984) manifest physically, threatening to destroy him and his world. Similarly, Laurie is almost demolished by the strength of her

---

69 Poem quoted in Kelley, *Hallowe'en*, 178.
70 Michael Giammarino, "'He's Coming to Get You, Laurie!' What Dr. Dementia's Halloween Horror Movie Marathon Tells Us About Michael Myers And Laurie Strode," *Dread Central*, April 29, 2019, https://www.dreadcentral.com/editorials/293221/hes-coming-to-get-you-laurie-what-dr-dementias-halloween-horror-movie-marathon-tells-us-about-michael-myers-and-laurie-strode/ (accessed October 4, 2019).

repressed, unconscious impulses; as a virgin, she desires a boyfriend–Bennett "Ben" Tramer–and intimacy with the opposite sex. But Laurie's ego suffocates her, making her shy and timid, thus impossible for her to obtain a lover. Moreover, since Laurie ends up babysitting two children, she has zero privacy, so masturbation is out of the question; hence, her battle with Michael is a substitute for pleasure, for copulation. Like Dr. Morbius, the Shape is a manifestation of her dark impulses, only hers are erotic. Denied sensual stimulation, Laurie now suffers a crippling Freudian nightmare, causing her ego and sexuality to collapse into chaos. Unable to suppress her shadow any longer, Laurie becomes a psychological hermaphrodite, donning a symbolic strap-on dildo so she can penetrate Michael. First, Laurie stabs him with a priapic sewing needle. Next, she unwinds a clothes hanger making it long and pointy, poking him in the eye with it. Then, she stabs him with a phallic knife thrusting upward aggressively; for Laurie, this is coitus, unleashing her repressed energy to integrate her shadow, losing her virginity figuratively, fucking him hard, tasting Halloween's forbidden delights. Laurie seems to want more, so she removes Michael's prophylactic–his rubber mask–to continue to their fight *qua* tryst, only to be interrupted by a parental figure–Dr. Loomis–who blasts the boogieman, ending their murderous lovemaking.

Lastly, we have *Night of the Living Dead* featuring Barbra (Judith O'Dea) as a proto-Laurie. Barbra is pent-up, sexually frustrated, mundane, epitomizing the rationalist ego. Her brother, Johnny (Russell Steiner), personifies the shadow, complaining about the drive to the cemetery to pay respects at their father's gravesite, teasing Barbra while she prays. "They're coming to get you, Barbra," Johnny wisecracks, tormenting her. After Johnny's killed in a scuffle with a zombie in the graveyard, Michael and Johnny begin to parallel each other. Johnny becomes a ghoul, an undead thing; later, he finds his sister, vulnerable and trapped in a farmhouse with a mob of other hungry ghouls, finally doing Barbra in. Likewise, in *Halloween II*, Michael has become the living dead, a resurrected zombie after Loomis shoots him six times. Michael's pace is reduced, ever more methodical than earlier in the evening. He lumbers about, taking stairs much slower like a senior citizen, eyes forward and trance-like. Just hours before, he was a bat out of Hell, rushing down the staircase after Laurie in the Wallace residence, then smashing open the closet door to find Laurie hiding inside. Now, like Johnny pursuing his sister Barbra, Michael spends the rest of the Halloween night tracking down his sister, revealed to be Laurie. After she is taken to the hospital and treated for her wounds, Laurie suffers a catatonic reaction to the meds she's been given. Barbra also slips into a stupor, although in her case, she's succumbing to a situational ordeal. The cause may be different, but the outcome is the same. The context is also identical: both women deal with extreme trauma at various points, and both become vacuous, thereby connecting the two characters. Even the wig Jaime Lee Curtis was forced to wear in the sequel is reminiscent of Judith O'Dea *qua* Barbra's boring hairstyle in Romeo's black and white masterpiece.[71]

Dr. Dementia's tripartite horror movie marathon is more than just nostalgia; instead, the films unveil psychological insights into the characters and their motives. Easter egg: in *Halloween*, after the Shape strikes, Laurie tells Lindsey Wallace (Kyle Richards) and Tommy Doyle (Brian Andrews) to "go to the Mackenzies" for help. In *Scream* (1996), when Casey's (Drew Barrymore) parents come home, they suspect something's amiss, so her father (David Booth) tells her mother (Carla Hatley) to "go to the Mackenzies," recalling Carpenter's immortal classic.

* * * * *

Movies are loaded with Jungian archetypal imagery emanating from humankind's collective unconscious. The collective unconscious, a term coined by Jung, refers to structures of the unconscious mind that are shared among beings of the same species. According to the Swiss psychiatrist, the collective unconscious is populated by instincts and by archetypes. Jung considered the collective unconscious to underpin and surround the unconscious mind, distinguishing it from the personal unconscious of Freudian psychoanalysis. He argued the collective unconscious had a profound influence on the lives of individuals, who were living out its symbols and images, clothing them in meaning through their experiences. The psychotherapeutic practice of analytical psychology revolves around examining the patient's relationship to the collective unconscious. Does the collective unconscious hold the key to prophetic cinema? Is the collective unconscious, which Jung based on Plato's (428/427 or 424/423–348/347

---

[71] Ibid.

The psychology of cinema within cinema: two movies, one real, one fictitious, appear in *Joker* (2019). (Left) Charlie Chaplin's (1889-1977) *Modern Times* (1936) plays at Wayne Hall as civil unrest erupts in Gotham City. In the movie, the Tramp is a working-class man, a factory worker, suffering a nervous breakdown, becoming trapped–literally–in the machinery of industrialization. The film anticipates Arthur Fleck's (Joaquin Phoenix) gloomy predicament as a mentally ill man, a loner, chewed and devoured by Gotham City because he is a forgotten member of the lower class. By the end of *Modern Times*, the Tramp has become a popular entertainer, getting applause from an adoring crowd. By the end of *Joker*, Fleck *qua* Joker has become a nefarious media superstar, adored by the proletariat. Subconsciously, *Modern Times* seeks to reinforce *Joker*'s ubiquitous class warfare, demonstrating how inequality can transform a loner into a psychopath. (Right) Contrast this melancholy with the fictitious film, *Ace in the Hole*, advertised on a Gotham billboard. The three-act porno alludes to *The Dark Knight* (2008); captured, the Joker refers to Harvey Dent *qua* Two-Face as his "Ace in the hole," his agent of chaos, paralleling the mayhem Arthur-as-Joker inflicts upon Gotham.

BCE) Theory of Forms, bridged by Bruno's art of memory mnemonics, somehow predictive as well as inherited? Does the creative, cinematic process somehow miraculously project, or fuel, prophetic, or predictive visions buried deep in our unconscious minds, onto the silver screen? Or is there an Illuminati-like Hollywood cabal of puppet masters using black magic to foresee future events, putting these events in movies to further a diabolical agenda?

This sinister paradigm, known as predictive programming, is a crucial component of many conspiracy theories. The theory follows that when these global conspirators–the Illuminati–plan a false flag operation, they hide allusions to it in the popular media before the atrocity takes place. When the event occurs, the public has been softened up, passively accepting it rather than offering resistance. Predictive programming arises from pareidolia and conspiracist paranoia, perceiving reality as an off-kilter, surreal construct with subtle foreshadowing, controlled by sinister global engineers.

Does another of Jung's theorems account for predictive programming? Does he offer a more sober explanation? What some refer to as predictive programming, Jung termed *synchronicity*. Jungian synchronicity is a hypothesis that holds events are *germane coincidences* if they occur with no causal relationship yet seem to be meaningfully related, activated, or linked by archetypal figures or imagery. Jung defined *synchronicity* as an acausal connecting (togetherness) principle, meaningful coincidence, and acausal parallelism. When coincidences pile up in this way, one cannot be helped being impressed by them–for the greater the number of events in such a series, or the more unusual its character, the more improbable it becomes.[72] Synchronicity is a modern differentiation of the obsolete concept of correspondences, sympathy, and harmony. It is based not on philosophical assumptions, but empirical experience and experimentation.[73] Synchronicity, as an explicative theory, applies to phenomena related to parapsychology, mysticism, astrology, and premonitions.

Predating Jung by nearly three millennia, parallel doctrines were documented in the 9th century BCE text *I Ching* or the *Book of Changes*. These credos emerge in *Escape from New York*: an airplane–Air Force One–crashes into lower Manhattan, presaging the tragic events twenty years later, the terrorist attack of 9/11. Yet there is no causal relationship between the two on the surface, a movie set in a dystopia and an actual terrorist attack, but they synch nevertheless. In creating the concept of synchronicity, Jung sketched a way to penetrate deeper the interrelationship or psyche and matter, finding the answer in the supernatural world. Most of the time, examples of synchronicity, such as the nexus between Elvis Presley (1935-1977) and the sun, pass unnoticed because the individual has not yet learned to observe sublime coincidences. He or she has failed to make coincidences meaningful concerning the metaphysical iconography of dreams; unlike the adept, initiate, or the Ipsissimus, the vulgar and profane are unable to forge links between the occult, alchemy, psychology, divination, symbolism, and magic.

---

72 Carl G. Jung, *The Portable Jung*, ed. Joseph Campbell, trans. R.F.C. Hull (New York: Penguin Books, 1976), Chapter 14, "On Synchronicity," 505-518.
73 Ibid.

The collective unconscious, the Theory of Forms, the art of memory, predictive programming, Jungian synchronicity, or a combination thereof; this author will, once again, let the reader render a verdict when it comes to prophetic cinema.

Dwelling in the collective unconscious, the world's soul, are the archetypes:

> Strictly speaking, Jungian archetypes are underlying forms emerging from images and universal motifs such as the mother, the father, the magician *qua* trickster (Mercury), and the wise man *qua* hermit, a mystagogue, a Hermes Trismegistus analog. There's also the crone, temptress, hero (the sun), heroine (the moon, and the dawn), and the villain (the Devil), among many others. It is history, culture, and personal context shaping these manifest representations giving them their specific content; they are embedded in the imagery of Tarot cards, which both conceal and reveal Hermetic, alchemical, astrological, and mystical truths. Since they are unconscious, the existence of archetypes can only be deduced indirectly by examining behavior, images, art, myths, religions, and dreams. They are inherited potentials actualized when they enter consciousness as images or surface in behavior on interaction with the outside world. As such, the collective unconscious does not develop individually; instead, it is inherited.[74]

Other archetypes include Death (Saturn, the Grim Reaper), the child (the Pages from the Tarot's Minor Arcana), the traitor (the Tarot's Hanged Man), the Lovers, the self-destroyer, e.g., the Tower from the Major Arcana, and the most enigmatic of them all, the Fool. They populate Joseph Campbell's (1904-1987) monomyth under a variety of guises. The Tarot pervades *The People Under the Stairs* (1991), an archetypal, haunted house adventure with the protagonist, Poindexter Williams (Brandon Adams), nicknamed "Fool" after the zero card.

According to Jung, the archetypes are alive and well, functioning in our unconscious minds, working with far-reaching effects.[75] Archetypes are typical manners of comprehension, and wherever we meet with uniform and regularly recurring modes of apprehension, we are dealing with an

---

[74] Robert W. Sullivan, *Cinema Symbolism*, Introduction. Sallie Nichols, *Jung and Tarot: An Archetypal Journey* (1984; repr., San Francisco: Weiser Books, 2004), 9-21.
[75] Hill et al., *The Supernatural*, 25.

archetype, no matter whether its mythological character is recognized or not.[76] Just as everybody possesses tendencies, so too does every man and woman have a stockpile of archetypal images.[77] Understanding the power of the archetypes is critical to analyzing movies–they draw us to cinema like a moth to a flame, and filmmakers know this, which is why they are routinely employed. In her hit song "Style" (2014), Taylor Swift sings of the archetypes, about the everlasting bad boy-girl good paradigm. She lyricizes, "♪ You got that James Dean daydream look in your eye / And I got that red lip, classic thing that you like / And when we go crashing down, we come back every time / 'Cause we never go out of style, we never go out of style / You've got that long hair slick back, white t-shirt / And I got that good girl faith and a tight little skirt ♪." And she's right; indeed, they never go *out of style* because they've been with us since time immemorial, and will continue to affect us in the future. Humankind is hardwired to the archetypes, linking past to present, inspiring us throughout the annals of human culture, becoming the images of ritual, mythology, theology, superstition, theater, cultural vision, film, and, thus, popular culture.[78] It is critical to understand that Hollywood's magical apparatus not only relies on archetypes but can generate them. Ask anyone to speak like a vampire, and they'll impersonate Bela Lugosi's Hungarian accent from *Dracula*.

In the hands of a magus or a secret society, the archetypes can be utilized with occult precision. They are powerful, potent, and everlasting, impacting history and culture. The most significant works in the English language, we find the archetypes populating the plays of William Shakespeare (1564-1616), considered to be Francis Bacon (1561-1626), working in tandem with a secret society: the Rosicrucian, the Knights of the Helmut, or both. For example, *The Winter's Tale* (1611) illustrates the solar myth of Demeter and Persephone, the central doctrine of the Eleusinian Mysteries, personified by Perdita, comprehended by the initiated few, implying a secret society influence.[79]

---

76 Jung, *Portable Jung*, 57.
77 Ibid.
78 Joseph Campbell, *The Hero with a Thousand Faces*, 3rd ed. (Novato, CA: New World Library, 2008), 14.
79 W.F.C. Wigston, *Bacon, Shakespeare, and the Rosicrucians* (London: George Redway, 1888), xiii, 142-151

CINEMA SYMBOLISM 3

The myth of Demeter and Persephone, or Ceres and Proserpine, their Roman counterparts, is a changing year allegory, signing the ecliptic, rendering the above as the below, making it archetypal. It is a personified tale of the earth's seasons, documenting a winter-to-summer story. For the loss of Persephone–and her eventual restoration–signifies the earth's waxing and waning transition from spring, summer, autumn, and then to winter, from life to death, returning to life again. Summer's vitality is ushered in by the spring only to be lost in autumn, expiring in winter. The changing seasons were personified by a beautiful maiden who associated with flowers, a May Queen, as it were. She remains six months with her mother the earth, and then she is carried away by Dis or Pluto to the underworld where she resides during winter. She embodies the earth's life, and its spirit, bringing new energy to sleeping nature–Demeter, her sorrowing mother. Demeter, with her yellow tresses veiled in a dark mourning mantle, sought her over land and sea, and learning from the sun her daughter's fate she withdrew in high dudgeon from the gods and took up her abode at Eleusis, where she presented herself to the king's daughters in the guise of an old woman, sitting sadly under an olive tree's shadow beside the Maiden's Well, to which the damsels had come to draw water in bronze pitchers for their father's house.[80] In her wrath at her bereavement, the goddess suffered the seed not to grow in the earth, vowing never to set foot on Olympus and never let the corn sprout till her lost daughter is restored to her.[81]

Art imitates life, or, in this instance, the seasonal cycle: with the loss of beautiful Persephone (who was wooed by Hermes and Apollo), the spring/summer, the earth-as-Demeter falls into the icy image of death or sleep, winter. The allegory of the mother and lost her lost child is microcosmic, signifying the changing seasons. But it is also macrocosmic: the movement of the earth around the sun: the glorious orb is a second, visible god, according to Hermes Trismegistus.

We turn to Perdita in *The Winter's Tale*, wherein she plays the part of a lost child, not only identified with the spring and flowers but invoking the prototypical Persephone whom she resembles. Not only is Perdita introduced in Act IV, Scene IV, as a kind of Flora, but extraordinary emphasis is given

---

80 J.G. Frazer, *The Golden Bough: A Study in Magic and Religion*, Abridged ed. (1922; repr., London: Papermac, 1994), 389.
81 Ibid.

to her speeches, in which she treats of winter and summer. If the poet were presenting us Persephone herself–the spring–with her new spirit and life, how could he make it more evident?[82] Florizel says of Perdita:

> These your unusual weeds to each part of you
> Do give a life: no shepherdess, but Flora
> Peering in April's front.

Note the expression "unusual weeds to each part of you," alluding to winter, thawing to the spring. She identifies with "Flora peering in April's front," or spring itself. And mark the expression, "Do give a life." What gives life to the earth? The answer: the sun, its divine spirit, of course.

Bacon interprets Persephone/Proserpine's solar spirit in his *Wisdom of the Ancients* (1609). He writes: "By Proserpina is meant that ethereal Spirit which, being separated from the upper globe, is shut up and detained under the earth represented by Pluto." Again, "Concerning the six months' custom [the re-finding of Ceres and her rape], it is no other than an elegant description of the division of the year, the spirit mixed with the earth appears above ground in vegetable bodies during the summer months, and in the winter sinks again."[83]

Bacon's analysis is correct, which, in the abstract, is life returning to the dead earth in winter. It is a rebirth, the revelation of nature's immortality by a return of the spirit, a return of the sun at the vernal equinox. The separation of the soul from the body is, therefore, death. For such is the condition of nature during winter: earth, in its northern hemisphere, is deceased because the sun's energy is decreased. By comparing Perdita to winter and summer, the Bard *qua* Bacon gives us evidence he is presenting us with Persephone-as-Perdita. First, she is compared to a goddess:

> Florizel. This your Sheep-shearing
> Is as a meeting of the petty gods,
> And you the queen on 't."

We know Persephone was Queen of the Underworld:

---

[82] Wigston, *Bacon, Shakespeare*, 142-151.
[83] Ibid.

CINEMA SYMBOLISM 3

> Perdita. And me, poor lowly maid,
> Most goddess-like, prank's up.

That the poet is thinking of the gods is most evident from the following passage:

> Florizel.   Apprehend
> Nothing but jollity. The gods themselves,
> Humbling their deities to love, have taken
> The shapes of beasts upon them : Jupiter,
> Became a bull, and bellow'd; the green Neptune
> A ram, and bleated ; and the fire-robed god,
> Golden Apollo, a poor humble swain.
> As I seem now.

Indeed, it seems like Florizel were but a disguise for Apollo or Horus himself, the sun which awakens the spring. Now let us give the flower scenes, so well-known and so beautiful when Perdita presents flowers to suit all her guests:

> Perdita. Give me those flowers there, Dorcas. Reverend sirs,
> For you there's rosemary and rue; these keep
> Seeming and savour all the winter long.

> Polixenes.   Shepherdess, —
> A fair one are you–well you fit our ages
> With flowers of winter.

> Perdita. Sir, the year growing ancient,
> Not yet on summer's death, nor on the birth
> Of trembling winter, the fairest flowers of the season
> Are our carnations and streak'd gillyvors,
> Which some call nature's bastards: of that kind
> Our rustic garden's barren; and I care not
> To get slips of them.

> Polixenes. Wherefore, gentle maiden,

Perdita.   Do you neglect them?

Perdita.   For I have heard it said
There is an art which in their piedness shares
With great creating nature.

If the earth were to be pictured displaying all its seasonal flowers, Perdita would step forward, presenting herself. We see the poet dwelling upon winter and summer, employing their flowers in this scene. And once more, to reiterate, we draw forth the parallel, for the myth of Demeter and Persephone (Ceres and Proserpine) is an archetypal winter and summer story. For what is this story but a retelling of the earth locked in wintery death, seeking for its immortal spirit or life, the lost child–rebirth in the spring. Not only is Perdita allied with the spring and summer, signified by her vernal beauty, but she's an archetype emphasizing the glory of full midsummer; thus, Persephone has often been termed the *summer child* of Ceres.[84]

Finally, we have Perdita's speech on her prototype, Persephone/Proserpine:

Perdita.   O Proserpina!
For the flowers now, that frighted thou let'st fall
From Dis's [sic] waggon! daffodils,
That come before the swallow dares, and take
The winds of March with beauty; violets dim,
But sweeter than the lids of Juno's eyes
Or Cytherea's breath; pale primroses
That die unmarried, ere they can behold
Bight Phoebus in his strength--a malady
Most incident to maids; bold oxlips and
The crown imperial; lilies of all kinds,
The flower-de-luce being one!"

The flower-de-luce is the fleur-de-lis, a solar, Rosicrucian emblem, and the flowers, once again, evokes the seasonal transition from death to life. Only Bacon, aided by the Knights of the Helmut, could produce masterstrokes like

---
84 Ibid.

CINEMA SYMBOLISM 3

A Winter's Tale, fostering a pedagogical plan of pansophic enlightenment via theatre. Easter egg: Rapunzel, in the Brothers Grimm 1812 fairy tale, also embodies Persephone: the life-giving sun. Rapunzel is shut up in the witch's garden, enclosed by high walls, i.e., the earth trapped in the icy arms of winter. The prince reaches her, ascending on the maiden's long golden locks; "For Rapunzel had long and beautiful hair, as fine as spun gold," betokening the rays of the sun, liberated by a vigorous young man at the vernal equinox.[85]

* * * * *

The Rosicrucians of 17th-century Europe were a cabal of mystics; they assembled, studied, and promoted the mystical side of religion, philosophy, and science, which their founder, Christian Rosenkreuz, had learned from Arabian sages. They were in the inheritors of Alexandrian culture. This Egyptian city, a chief emporium of commerce and a center of intellectual learning, flourished before the rise of the imperial power of Rome. The Romans, who, having conquered it, took great pains to destroy the arts and sciences of Egypt. They seemed to have had a terrible fear of those magical arts, which, as tradition had informed them, flourished in the Nile Valley. This same esoteric history is familiar to English people via our acquaintance with the kabalistic Book of Genesis. Within the world of the occult, Genesis' author was taught in Egypt all the arts and sciences he possessed, even as the Bible itself tells us; nevertheless, the orthodox like to slur over this assertion regarding the Old Testament narrative.[86] Calling themselves the Invisibles, the Rosicrucians possessed secret wisdom handed down through secret orders and sects, from one generation to the next. Their teachings were an abnegation, a subduing of all egotism, vanity, or self-seeking, professing doctrines which were dangerous to publish openly.

The Chymical Wedding of Christian Rosenkreutz (1616) veils forbidden alchemical knowledge. The manuscript, attributed to the Rosicrucian Johannes Valentinus Andreae (1586-1654), documents the symbolic marriage of the sun and the moon, featuring both archetypes and paradigmatic imagery, illustrated on Tarot cards, influencing pop cult

---

[85] Charles De. B. Mills, *The Tree of Mythology, It's Growth and Fruitage: Genesis of the Nursery Tale, Saws of Folk-Lore, Etc* (Syracuse: C.W. Bardeen Publishers, 1889), 105.

[86] W. Wynn Westcott, *Christian Rosenkreuz and the Rosicrucians* (London: Theosophical Publishing Society, 1894), 3.

subsequently. For example, one finds parallels between *Chymical Wedding* and the Harry Potter stories, with similarities turning up in the *Star Wars* saga. The Harry Potter novels and movies and *Star Wars* are monomythic, archetypal, and mystical, so drawing comparisons to an equally mysterious Rosicrucian tale only speaks to the power of the collective unconscious, to mnemonics, and underlying forms. For example, *Chymical Wedding* lasts seven days while Harry Potter's adventure lasts seven years. The protagonist, the mystic Christian Rosycross, foretells the boy theurgist in Rowling's narrative, Harry. In *Chymical Wedding*, there is a wonderful castle full of wonders, which becomes Hogwarts; in both strongholds, floating candles illuminate mealtime. Christian Rosycross chooses one of four paths, while Harry chooses one of four houses. In *Chymical Wedding*, there is an Old Man (or warden) in the Tower, morphing into Albus Dumbledore at Hogwarts. Remember, the Major Arcana of the Tarot has both a Hermit and a Tower, reflecting this archetypal imagery.[87] In *Star Wars: A New Hope*, the Old Man in the Tower is the Hermetic knight, Obi-Wan Kenobi, sneaking around the Death Star to deactivate the tractor beam high atop an elevated structure. These examples prove the archetypes are the nuclei of the psyche; they are representations and motifs–instinctive trends–manifesting by our need to create, understood and utilized by groups

(Left) The archetypal symbol of the for the Deathly Hallows (Harry Potter saga) borrows from the alchemical symbol for the Philosopher's Stone (center), indicating the Great Work has been accomplished. (Right) The Magnum Opus finished, the United States created, the symbol for the Elixir (i.e., eternal life, perfection) also manifests in the reverse of the Great Seal of the United States (right), appearing on the back of the one-dollar bill.

---

[87] "Exploring the Spiritual Foundation of Harry Potter: Alchemy," *Harry Potter for Seekers*, n.d., http://www.harrypotterforseekers.com/alchemy/alchemy.php (accessed September 7, 2019). This online article suggests the Harry Potter stories are based upon *The Chymical Wedding*. I believe the Potter tales and *The Chymical Wedding* are archetypal and monomythic hence their similarities.

like the Knights Templar, Rosicrucians, Freemasons, Jesuits, Kabbalists, Sufis, the Illuminati, and, thus, Hollywood.

Other occult dogmas arise in cinema to be more thoroughly fleshed out as this tome unfolds, such as alchemy, black and white magic, the monomyth or the hero's journey, and ancient doctrines like Neoplatonism and heresies like Gnosticism. We are introduced to magical creations such as golems, automatons (moving mechanical devices made in imitation of a human) and robots, a somnambulist and a mummy, and tulpas, the latter specific to David Lynch's *Twin Peaks: The Return* (2017). These doctrines exist in modernity, making them critical because they link past to present.

* * * * *

Chapter I presents Easter eggs concealed inside the rooms of the *Bates Motel* (2013-2017), focusing on the A&E television series, but touching on Hitchcock's classic, *Psycho*. An *Easter egg* is defined as a hidden allusion placed in a movie, television show, or other media to be observed by the initiated, denoting a socio-political-economic or pop culture theme or reference. Some Easter eggs are benign, while others hint at a more sinister agenda, suggesting they were placed there by an Illuminati-like Hollywood cabal. There are Easter eggs scattered throughout this book, some explained openly, hiding in plain sight, others more concealed, so keep out a watchful eye.

Chapter II explores Gnostic Hollywood: movies exploring the heresy and its ubiquitous dualism; Gnostic thought is a dominant root nurturing occultism proper. *Gnostic* designates several widely differing sects, which sprang up in the Eastern provinces of the Roman Empire almost simultaneously with Christianity. That is to say, these groups, for the first time, assumed a definite form, ranging themselves under different teachers, by whose names they became known to the world. Although, in all probability, their principal doctrines had made their appearance previously in many of Asia Minor's cities. Here, it is probable these sectaries first came into definite existence under the title of *Mystae*, upon the establishment of direct intercourse with India and her Buddhist philosophers, under the Seleucidæ and the Ptolemies. The term *Gnosticism* comes from the Greek *gnosis*, *to know*, a word specially employed from the first dawn of religious inquiry, defining the science of things divine. Thus, Pythagoras (ca. 570-ca. 495 BC), according to Diogenes Laertius (180-240 CE), called the transcendental portion of his philosophy, *the knowledge of things that are*. And in later times, what Porphyry of Tyre (234-305 CE) termed the *Antique or Oriental philosophy* became *gnosis*, distinguishing it from the Grecian systems. But the term was first used in its ultimate sense of supernal and divine knowledge, by the Hebrew kabalistic philosophers belonging to the celebrated school of that nation, flourishing at Alexandria, Egypt.[88]

The Reverend A.B. Mackay (1842-1901) addressed the Gnostics in an 1880 sermon, decrying, "Thrice in three verses the apostle John utters the emphatic words, *we know*. Of these three utterances that at the beginning of this verse is the central and most comprehensive. A class of men rose in the early days of Christianity calling themselves and delighting in being called Gnostics, that is *knowing ones*. They professed to have a deeper insight into the mysteries of being, into the nature and origin of good and evil, than ordinary men. They considered themselves the elite of the intellect of their age, the aristocrats of thought. But notwithstanding all their pride and boastfulness, their assumptions were essentially false and inconsistent; their wisdom an elaborated folly; their endless processions a cloak, often ludicrous, of ignorance, and their morality a volatile and variable phantasm."[89] His disdain is not surprising. Gnosticism revived the idea, familiar to heathen thought but wholly alien to the spirit of Christianity, of one religion designed for the wise and the initiated, and another for the ignorant and profane. Faith, the foundation of Christian wisdom, was fitted only for the vulgar masses, the animal men who were incapable of higher things. Far above these were the privileged natures, the men of intellect, the spiritual men, whose vocation was not to believe but *to know*.[90] I've analyzed other Gnostic films before, notably *The Matrix*, *The Truman Show* (1998), and *Fight Club*, but will now take on a new slate of movies exemplifying Gnostic doctrines. I will also define Gnostic beliefs, cosmologies, and its theologies to ensure the reader is well versed with this heresy.

---

[88] C.W. King, *The Gnostics and Their Remains, Ancient and Medieval* (London: David Nutt, 1887), 3.
[89] A.B. Mackay. *The True Gnostics: A Sermon* (Montreal: W.M. Drysdale & Co., 1880), 3.
[90] Henry Longueville Mansel, *The Gnostic Heresies of the First and Second Centuries*, (London: John Murray, 1875), 10.

Gnosticism is a prevalent theme in Hollywood because the enlightened hero, or savior, questing for selfhood, is something toward which we strive. To break free from societal doldrums–stasis–for a higher godhead is the Gnostic film's crux. The protagonist wants to know himself, attain the Greek *nous* (intuition, divine intellect), akin to the kabalistic *neshamah*, possessing wisdom informed by spirit. Put another way, to know the stages of the creative process is also to understand the steps of one's return to the root of all existence. Humankind's crippling disability is ignorance; thus, the highest aspiration is to overcome ignorance and, by helping men and women understand their genuine nature, bringing them to know the godhead, asserting their divinity.

In doing so, the Gnostic champion transforms a mechanized clockwork reality into a numinous actuality. There is a paradox with Gnostic cinema: these films are primarily products to make money by offering seductive images of rebellion, to turn away from materialism in favor of spiritual fulfillment and enlightenment. This duplicity makes the contemporary commercial Gnostic film an especially apt vehicle for exploring heterodoxic themes. Unlike classical, avant-garde, and cult renditions of Gnostic concepts, modern commercial versions suffer a double bind, an irreducible conflict between exoteric packaging and arcane vision. Some Gnostic films self-consciously explore this contradiction, viz. to reject consumerism while, at the same time, make a fast buck. In reflecting on the impossibility of their very existence–they are metaphysical meditations and vulgar commodities–these movies consume themselves and push audiences into vague spaces: abyss and interpretation, infinite regressions over insoluble problems.

These negations are bewildering and potentially meaningless. However, they also liberate viewers from the hermeneutical status quo, releasing them into fresh and possibly redemptive ways of seeing and being. The auto-erasures of these Gnostic films encourage audiences to speculate on impossible realms beyond the frames. Self-aware pictures overtly purveying Gnostic themes push viewers into an ideal blank screen that is both nothing–no color–and everything–the ground of all hues: void and plenitude, one and many. Reflexive kabalistic-cabalistic works inflecting Gnostic paradigms of redemption inspire audiences to contemplate an invisible film projector: a mindless machine yet a tool of consciousness simultaneously, fated repetition but a free-play of images. Alchemical movies–like *Black Swan* and *Beauty and the Beast* (2017)–informed by Gnostic notions of spirit, and keenly conscious of their contradictions, offer this possibility: the dark theater gestures toward a crepuscular space where antinomies dissolve into chaos only to be remade into new, more complex vital orders.[91] Although not alchemical, one Gnostic movie this author is particularly fond of is *Donnie Darko* (2001) because it dovetails with my life in some strange Jungian way–more on Richard Kelly's film later.

Chapter III is a continuation of Chapter IV from *Cinema Symbolism 2*, which revealed the arcane imagery concealed in the movies produced by Disney Studios, in specific, films dramatizing fairy tales. Here, I explore the live-action version of *Beauty and the Beast*, a story rich with archetypes, documenting the changing seasons, much like *The Winter's Tale* (*vide supra*). Belle (Emma Watson), mirroring Snow White and Cinderella, her counterparts, is a heroine frustrating the Counter-Reformation by becoming a counter-discourse: she is a modern-woman preoccupied with enlightenment, not domestic banalities like marriage and housekeeping. She desires to spend more time in the library then tending to home and hearth; as such, Belle, because she seeks light, embodies the splendor of the dawn. By reflecting light, she is also the moon, the sacred feminine. The cruel Beast (Dan Stevens) personifies the sun, trying to, once again, become a handsome prince at the vernal equinox, making their struggle an effort to escape the barren winter. By falling in love, they perform an alchemical wedding, unifying opposites, lifting the curse, returning life to the land.[92]

The Philosopher's Stone, the magical element that facilitates transition, is part of the Great Art. Four phases must be attained to generate the Stone: the *nigredo*, *albedo*, *citrinitas*, and *rubedo*. This jargon was intentionally used by medieval alchemists to confuse the uninitiated and profane; without understanding these keys, alchemical movies are impossible to decipher because these components are not only literal but psychological.[93]

---

91 Eric Wilson, *Secret Cinema: Gnostic Vision in Film* (New York: Continuum International Publishing Group Inc., 2006), x.

92 In *Beauty and the Beast*, the prince begins mean and selfish, is turned into a monster reflecting this, then is transformed back to a prince only now benevolent and kind, redeemed from his former selves, indicating an alchemical transition. Contrast this with *Lost Highway*'s Fred Madison. Fred starts as an egotistical jerk, transforms into the friendly Pete Dayton, but ends up his old self at the conclusion. Thus, any transition Fred made was for naught.

93 Albert Pike, *Morals and Dogma of the Ancient and Accepted Scottish Rite of Freemasonry*, (1871; repr., Richmond, Virginia: L.H. Jenkins, Inc., 1960), 731.

Alchemical change can be ugly, cruel, and discordant; in most films, the change results in chaos and death or fails altogether, depicted expertly by Hollywood. The alchemists' general conception of nature led them to assign every substance a condition or state natural accordingly. Each substance, they taught, could be caused to leave its natural state only by violent or non-natural means. Any medium driven from its natural condition by violence was ready, and even eager, to return to the condition consonant with its nature.[94] As such, the White Swan, the virginal and frigid Nina cannot transmute into an alluring Black Swan, a seductive ballerina, unless she abandons her dreary existence. So, she fuses pleasure with algophilia; unsatisfied, Nina further humiliates herself by masturbating before her mother, and then in public–in the back of a taxicab. She dies, achieving perfection, becoming a fleshy Philosopher's Stone. Only Nina knows if her mortification, her annihilation, was worth it.

Within the lexicon of the Sacred Art, the *nigredo*, or blackness, is putrefaction, decomposition. Many alchemists believed that, as a first step in the pathway to the Philosopher's Stone, all alchemical ingredients had to be cleansed and cooked extensively to a uniform black matter. In Jungian psychology, it is the shadow self, the dark and sinister figure. It surfaces as another personality, an alter ego, in Robert Louis Stevenson's (1850-1894) *The Strange Case of Dr. Jekyll and Mr. Hyde* (*vide supra*). In the Harry Potter saga, the shadow possesses the Heir of Slytherin; in *Mystery of Chessboxing* (1987), it accords with the vengeful Ghost Face Killer (Kuan-Wu Lung). Darth Vader embodies the shadow, as does Roat (Alan Arkin): a scumbag bedeviling Suzy Hendrix (Audrey Hepburn) in *Wait Until Dark* (1967). Looking like a goth beatnik, with round sunglasses and a nasal voice, Roat will kill anyone who gets in his way. His weapon of choice, an ivory gravity knife named Geraldine, anticipates the next stage of the alchemical process.

Following the chaos or *massa confusa* of the *nigredo*, the alchemist undertakes a purification in *albedo* (the whiteness of the moon, sacred feminine, the White Queen), the washing away of impurities. In this process, the subject is divided into two opposing principles to be later coagulated into a Union of Opposites, producing balanced equilibrium

---

[94] M.M. Pattison Muir, *The Story of Alchemy and the Beginnings of Chemistry* (London: George Newnes, LTD., 1902), 39.

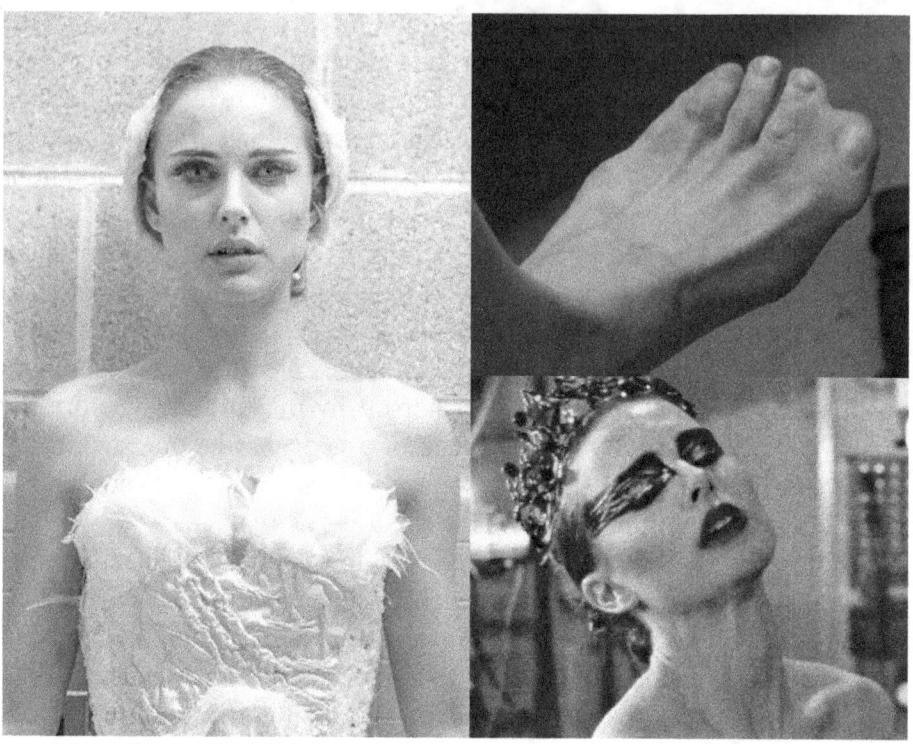

"Thus were the aims of the art expanded until they embraced transmutations, not of metals only, but of human beings, and the control of powers which reached out into the universe at large." – Rev. J.E. Mercer, D.D., *Alchemy: Its Science and Romance*, 1921. (Left) The finality of the *rubedo*. Nina, having formulated an unseen Philosopher's Stone (likely hidden in her bedroom), or, more accurately, a substratum (underlying substance), her eye's blaze hellfire red, signaling the finality of the Great Art, the end of the Magnum Opus. Interestingly, the alchemy stage from the *nigredo* (crow's head, black earth) to the *albedo* (the moon, white as snow) is called the *swan*. From it arises two parts, the *citrinitas* and the *rubedo*, generating the Philosopher's Stone. Nina's demonic red eyes aside, the *rubedo* is the red lights of the nightclub's dancefloor and, at the conclusion, the red stage lights while she performs *Swan Lake*. Nina's alchemical success is evident by her webbed foot (top right), signifying she is physically changing into a birdlike creature, her repressed shadow emerging and manifesting. Now, having liberated her shadow, the *nigredo*, Nina succumbs to masturbating in public in the back of a taxi cab, fantasizing that Lily is fondling her. Public onanism is a bizarre attempt to seduce the world. Depending on the circumstances, it can mean the masturbator has an intrapsychic problem, arising from an unhealthy family situation or relationship. For Nina, her difficulty stems from living with her abusive mother, Erica. (Bottom right) Unable to cope with her oppressive, incestuous mother, Nina turns once more to masturbating in public–this time backstage at the theater–only she does not have to use her hands. Instead, her black eye makeup, dark crown, midnight tutu, virginal skin, and ruby-red lips are a source of passion, pleasuring her flesh, a beautiful yet tragic crescendo. Her incandescent performance as the Black Swan proves her alchemical formula has worked to perfection. Only when it is too late does Nina understand: "There is a Swan whose name is Ecstasy: it wingeth from the Deserts of the North; it wingeth through the blue; it wingeth over the fields of rice; at its coming they push forth the green. ...*O fool!* criest thou? Amen. Motion is relative: there is Nothing that is still. ...the white breast poured forth blood...I was but a Pure Fool, they let me pass. ...Thus and not otherwise I came to the Temple of the Graal." – Aleister Crowley, "The Swan," *The Book of Lies*, 1912.

during the *rubedo,* synthesizing the Philosopher's Stone. The third stage, *citrinitas*, sometimes referred to as *xanthosis*, is a term given by alchemists to yellowness (the sun, gold, divine masculine, the Red King); it is the transmutation of silver (the moon) into gold (the sun) or yellowing of the lunar consciousness. In alchemical philosophy, *citrinitas* stood for the dawning of the solar light inherent in one's being. Sol and Luna's union is the alchemical wedding, representing Sulfur and Mercury, integrating opposites: male with female, god with goddess. It is the mythological marriage of Cupid and Psyche (from *Metamorphoses*, or *The Golden Ass*, written 2nd century CE by Apuleius, ca. 124-ca. 170), also known as the Union of Opposites, what Jung termed *syzygy* (a conjunction of the moon and sun). The synthesis is *coincidentia oppositorum*, merging light with dark, male with female (the godhead is often thought to be androgenous), and order with chaos. Golden Dawn (est. 1887) adept Dion Fortune (Violet Mary Firth, 1890-1946) commented on Kabbalah's active and passive *sefirah*, "everything rests upon the principles of the stimulation of the inert yet all-potential [*Binah*] by the dynamic principle [*Chokhmah*], which derives its energy direct from the source of all energy [*Keter*, God]. In this concept lie tremendous keys of knowledge; it is one of the most important points in the mysteries." In alchemy, such a marriage transcends duality, producing the Philosopher's Stone, changing lead to gold, ignorance to enlightenment, or gnosis.

Rubedo, a Latin word meaning *redness*, was adopted by alchemists to define the fourth and final stage in their Magnum Opus. Both gold (*citrinitas*) and the Philosopher's Stone were associated with the color red because the *rubedo* signaled success, concluding the Great Work. The *rubedo*, also known by the Greek word *Iosis*, is exaltation, the predominance of spirit (negative or positive) over matter, decisiveness, and apostleship. To Jung, the *rubedo* stage was what he termed *individuation*, representing the finality of the alchemical-psychological formula. Individuation is a transformative process whereby the personal and the collective unconscious are brought into consciousness, e.g., through dreams, active imagination, or free association, to be assimilated into the whole personality. It is an entirely natural amalgamation necessary for the psyche. It is the realization of selfhood: the union of male and female, the syzygy, merging ego with shadow.

The *rubedo* in *Rosemary's Baby*. (Left) Rosemary Woodhouse receives red roses; (top right) the Devil's face is hellfire red; (center right) a sickly Rosemary wears a red frock; (bottom right) Rosemary's wear a red ensemble while dreaming, right before the satanic ritual. And speaking of the diabolical ceremony, observe the rape scene because Rosemary has 28 painted on her chest in red, foreshadowing the birth of the Devil's child on June 28, 1966. The number *2000* denotes the end of the millennium, the end of the Piscean Age, the reign of the Antichrist. The overt use of red anticipates the *rubedo*, the finality of the film, during which an innocent mother chooses to become the protectress of evil: her hell-spawned son, Adrian. Rosemary, as a Marian analog, mothers the offspring of the Prince of Darkness, generating a sublime Union of Opposites; emotionally and psychologically, she accepts her fate as the Antichrist's mother. The other colors of alchemy manifest. The *citrinitas* is the Devil, reflected in Rosemary's yellow ensembles, candles, wallpaper, shower curtain, bedding, and the doll seen before she sneaks into the Castevets' apartment. The *nigredo* is the Bramford, mirrored by the elderly couple's black candles, seen during the climax on their fireplace mantle beneath the portrait of Adrian Marcato. The *albedo* is Rosemary, echoed by the moon-like silver charm she wears, containing the Tannis Root.

Also present during the alchemical process is Mercury, the element that makes transmogrification possible. Mercurius can become personifications, avatars, reflecting the attributes of the phase it inhabits; these characters are memorable, lingering in our dreams, haunting our nightmares. Furthermore, some films perpetually dwell in an alchemical stage wholly, to be explained as this tome unfolds.

Blade Runner (1982) is a Gnostic fable, set in the blackness of the *nigredo*, the gloom of a futuristic dystopia. When Deckard (Harrison Ford) arrives at the Bradbury Building to confront an android, a Nexus-6 Replicant named Roy Batty (Rutger Hauer, 1944-2019), his Replicant girlfriend, Pris (Daryl Hannah), is hiding in plain sight amongst other robots and manikins. She has disguised herself in a wedding veil, signifying two things. The garment highlights the marriage between Roy and Pris, an occult, idealistic marriage between the solar Red King (Roy is *roi*, French for *king*), and the White Queen or lunar prize, Pris. Together, they form an alchemical union, a syzygy, from which Deckard emerges as their symbolic son, a Philosopher's Stone capable of merging opposites. The wedding veil also foreshadows Deckard perfecting *coincidentia oppositorum*. After he kills (or retires) Pris, he serves as Roy's spiritual bride, a hylic copy of the heavenly bridegroom because the hunter has now become the hunted; moreover, Deckard comes to understand the Replicants have souls. Deckard has become what he vowed to destroy, thereby unifying opposites. Once Roy expires, Deckard will himself turn into a version of Roy, achieving individuation, the *rubedo*, making his love interest, the Replicant Rachael (Sean Young), into a nouveau Pris, merging human with machine.[95] Easter egg: the Bradbury Building is named after science fiction, fantasy, and horror writer Ray Bradbury (1920-2012).

The four alchemical stages arise in the satanic masterpiece, *Rosemary's Baby*, one of Kubrick's favorite films, considered cursed by its producer, William Castle (1914-1977). The shadowy Black Bramford concretizes the *nigredo*: the Gothic apartment building houses a coven of witches in league with the Prince of Darkness. The Bramford was the Trench Sisters' home: two proper Victorian ladies who cannibalized several young children, including a niece. Adrian Marcato practiced witchcraft inside its walls, and Keith Kennedy held his notorious parties there. It is an unholy labyrinth with no exit; its blackness clings like chill wet leaves. The moon rises in this darkness, the *albedo*, the sacred feminine, personified by Rosemary Woodhouse (Mia Farrow): she is an optimistic, all-American stereotypical woman. Her name, *Rosemary*, denotes the herb of the same name. It is believed to only grow in the gardens of the righteous, employed as a protective talisman against evil spirits, associating with Jesus' virgin mother, representing purity, thereby investing Rosemary with an air of Marian sacredness.[96] But his satanic majesty will fertilize Rosemary, and

---

95 Wilson, *Secret Cinema*, 81.
96 Hilderic Friend, *Flowers and Flower Lore* (Troy, NY: Nims and Knight, 1889), 37, 81-82, 106-107.

she'll birth the Antichrist, making her an ungodly version of the Virgin. Her husband is the masculine, the *citrinitas*, Guy Woodhouse (John Cassavetes, 1929-1989), or is he? Like a Black Sun rising, the masculine is the Devil, the beast raping a drugged Rosemary to impregnate her in his favorite haunt, the Bramford. The climax is the *rubedo*, hinted at throughout the film, anticipating its diabolical fait accompli.

Rosemary discovers her child in a bassinet with an inverted crucifix hanging over it. She parts the black drapes and recoils in horror and screams, but soon relaxes, becoming protective of her child when one of the witches, Laura-Louise McBirney (Patsy Kelly, 1910-1981), begins rocking him too hard. The *rubedo* stage ends Polanski's danse macabre when psychological polarities, the ego, and the shadow, are united. The innocent and conscientious woman, Rosemary, decides to become a de facto member of the coven, abandoning all sensibility, forfeiting her soul to become the corrupted mother of the Devil's son. She achieves individuation by fusing good and evil, evil and good; she is a diabolical matriarch, but maybe she can exert a positive, almost divine, influence upon the Antichrist, assuming that's even possible.

The Great Operation completed, Rosemary's demonic child is born in June '66 or 6/66. Evil has triumphed; the film's Christmas imagery has been utterly annihilated. "God is dead! Satan lives! The year is one!" exclaims Steven Marcato (Sidney Blackmer, 1895-1973) triumphantly. Easter egg: at the behest of Roman Castevet (also Blackmer), Guy comes home unexpectedly as Edward "Hutch" Hutchins (Maurice Evans, 1901-1989) counsels Rosemary, drinking tea with her in the kitchen. Guy's purpose is sinister: he's returned early to steal Hutch's glove so it can be used in a black magic ritual. Later that night, Rosemary receives an urgent phone call from Hutch, agreeing to meet him at 11:00 am the following morning. Guy, deducing he's discovered the Castevets' witchcraft, makes an excuse of wanting ice cream so he can leave the apartment. Shortly after he splits, as Rosemary painfully winces in bed, a doorbell sounds faintly. Guy rings the door of the Castevets to give them Hutch's glove so they can hex him. His deception is confirmed moments later when Rosemary, the next morn, rings the Castevets' doorbell–the ring is the same, heard seconds earlier when Guy rang it. The passive viewer will miss this cinematic magic. Another Easter egg: while Hutch calls on Rosemary, the game of Scrabble can be observed on the coffee table. Later, she will use the game's alphabetical pieces to solve Hutch's riddle–an anagram–exposing Roman's true identity: Steven Marcato, the son of the renowned devil worshipper Adrian Marcato. Easter egg: in black magic, possessing a person's article of clothing or part of their body enables the magician to cast a damning spell. Crowley, who had much to fear from rival thaumaturges, was always careful to make sure no one obtained his hair, nail clippings, or other bodily products. By getting hold of Hutch's glove, the Castevets drop a satanic curse that puts him in a coma then kills him.

Chapter IV analyzes Gothic Hollywood; specifically, *The Mummy* (1932), the rebirth of *Suspiria*, the most recent iteration of *Halloween* (2018), the Victorian-suspense drama *Lizzie* (2018), *The House with a Clock in Its Walls* (2018), *Dark Night of the Scarecrow* (1981), *The Witch*, *Pan's Labyrinth* (2006), and *Midsommar* (2019). Karloff's (1887-1969) mummy suffers Freudian melancholia, pining for a lost love he can never know or experience. In *Cinema Symbolism 2*, I analyzed the *Suspiria '77*, a witchy tale playing out like a soothsayer turning over Tarot cards, revealing the archetypal narrative. This brief paragraph from *The Book of the Witches* (1909) illustrates the dark world Dario Argento's film inhabits:

Suzy uses one of the glass quills from Helena Markos' peacock sculpture to kill the evil witch. Depicted on Roman coins, the peacock designates the princess' apotheosis, insinuating Suzy's numinous mission to destroy the Black Queen. The peacock's tail also denotes the death of blackness, viz., alchemy's *nigredo*, and the colorful rainbow of white (*albedo*), yellow (*citrinitas*), and red (*rubedo*) that inevitably follows darkness. Thus, she employs the quill to extinguish the devilment lurking inside the dance academy, completing her fairy tale quest. From *Suspiria*, '77.

> It is wild weather overhead. All day the wind has been growing more and more boisterous, blowing up great mountains of grey cloud out of the East, chasing them helter-skelter across the sky, tearing them into long ribbons and thrashing them all together into one whirling tangle, through which the harassed moon can scarcely find her way. The late traveler has many an airy buffet to withstand ere he can top the last ascent and see the hamlet outlined in a sudden glint of watery moonlight at his feet. Those who lie abed are roused by the moaning in the eaves, to mutter fearfully, 'The witches are abroad tonight!'[97]

Directed by Luca Guadagnino, the new *Suspiria* is, like the original, about *hexen* operating a prestigious ballet school. The Neo-expressionist *Volk* is the coven's homoerotic spellcasting, its rapid body movements, and obscure motions originating from the magical gesticulations of the Hermetic Order of the Golden Dawn and the occultist Crowley. The Golden Dawn was:

> One of the most influential Western occult societies of the late 19th to early 20th century. Like a meteor, it flared into light, blazed a bright trail and then disintegrated. Members included W. B. Yeats, A.E. Waite, Aleister Crowley and other noted occultists.
>
> ...The key founder was Dr. William Wynn Westcott, a London coroner and Rosicrucian. In 1887 Westcott obtained part of a manuscript written in brown-ink cipher from the Rev. A. F. A. Woodford, a Mason. The manuscript appeared to be old but probably was not. From his Hermetic knowledge, Westcott was able to decipher the manuscript and discovered it concerned fragments of rituals for the 'Golden Dawn,' an unknown organization that apparently admitted both men and women.
>
> Westcott asked an occultist friend, Samuel Liddell MacGregor Mathers, to flesh out the fragments into full-scale rituals. Some papers evidently were forged to give the 'Golden Dawn' authenticity and a history. It was said to be an old German occult order. Westcott produced papers that showed he had been given a charter to set up an independent lodge in England. The Isis-Urania Temple of the Hermetic Order of the Golden Dawn was established in 1888, with Westcott, Mathers, and Dr. W. R.

---

[97] Oliver Madox Hueffer, *The Book of the Witches* (New York: The John McBride Co., 1909), 19.

Woodman, Supreme Magus of the Rosicrucian Society of Anglia, as the three Chiefs. The secret society quickly caught on, and 315 initiations took place during the society's heyday, from 1888-1896. An elaborate hierarchy was created, consisting of ten degrees each corresponding to the 10 Sephiroth of the Tree of Life of the Kabbalah, plus an eleventh degree for neophytes. The degrees are divided into three orders: Outer, Second and Third.

One advanced through the Outer Order by examination. Initially, Westcott, Mathers, and Woodman were the only members of the Second Order, and they claimed to be under the direction of the Secret Chiefs of the Third Order, who were entities of the astral plane. Mathers's [sic] rituals were based largely on Freemasonry.

...During its height, the Hermetic Order of the Golden Dawn possessed the greatest known repository of Western magical knowledge. Second Order studies centered on the Kabbalistic Tree of Life. Three magical systems were taught: the Key of Solomon; Abra-Melin magic; and Enochian Magic. Materials were also incorporated from the Egyptian Book of the Dead, William Blake's Prophetic Books and the Chaldean Oracles. Instruction was given in astral travel, scrying, alchemy, geomancy, the Tarot and astrology.

The key purpose of the order was 'to prosecute the Great Work: which is to obtain control of the nature and power of [one's] own being.' ... Elements of Golden Dawn rituals, Rosicrucianism and Freemasonry have been absorbed into the rituals of modern Witchcraft.[98]

Crowley, the Great Beast 666, was one of history's greatest ceremonial magicians. In *Cinema Symbolism 2*, I wrote:

For those not familiar, Crowley was, among other things, an English ceremonial magician, poet, spy, painter, novelist, and mountaineer. He founded the religion and philosophy of Thelema, identifying himself as the prophet entrusted with guiding humanity into the Æon of Horus, a new solar age, the Age of Aquarius, in the early 20th century. Initiated

---

[98] Rosemary Ellen Guiley, *The Encyclopedia of Witches and Witchcraft* (New York: Facts on File, Inc., 1989), 157-159.

into the mysteries of Freemasonry, the Golden Dawn, and the OTO, Crowley believed himself to be the reincarnation of other great occultists: Pope Alexander VI (1431-1503), renowned for his love of physical pleasures; Edward Kelley (1555-1597), the mystical assistant to the conjurer Dr. John Dee (1527-1608/09) in Elizabethan England; occultist and adventurer Cagliostro (1743-1795), and ceremonial magician Eliphas Levi who died on the day Crowley was born.[99]

Thelema's maxim, *Do What Thou Wilt Shall Be the Whole of the Law*, comes from Crowley's *The Book of the Law* (1904). The theory of Thelema, put into practice by the OTO is to become an adept of transformative *magick*, to effect change–and that's *magic* spelled with the letter *k*. Me doth thinks Crowley could've directed *Suspira*, with the Golden Dawn producing, documenting the power of the Left-Hand Path, the ability to transfer lifeforce from one human vessel to another. Alas, Crowley had a falling out with the Golden Dawn, causing him to form the *Argentium Astrum*, A∴A∴ or Silver Star (est. 1907), a secret society dedicated to learning occult/kabalistic wisdom, intended to supersede the Golden Dawn.

Before watching the 2018 visions of *Halloween* and *Suspiria*, I thought I was going to enjoy *Suspiria* more than *Halloween*. However, this turned out not to be the case. I loved *Halloween* and thought *Suspiria* was okay, but I've come to appreciate *Suspiria* for its subtleties; it's an acquired taste that gets better each time I watch it. I am glad it's not a frame-by-frame remake; it is a fresh, yet gloomy take on Argento's mythology. Still, it's too bad the campy bat attack from the original is absent from this rebirth because I would have liked to have seen that kitsch reimagined.

Lizzie, as the title suggests, is about the infamous 19th-century Fall River Murders. *The House with a Clock in Its Walls* is a tale of black and white magic, *Dark Night of the Scarecrow* is all about the archetypes, while *The Witch* lauds the satanic faith, the irresistible supplication to Lucifer's luminance. *Pan's Labyrinth* and *Midsommar* round out the chapter; the former is a dark fairy tale set in Francoist Spain. The latter concludes with the sacrifice of a Christian, as it were, to the sun. The unwitting victim is burned alive inside a giant wooden structure, resurrecting *The Wicker Man*'s ghastly paganism.

---

99 Sullivan, *Cinema Symbolism 2*, Introduction.

CINEMA SYMBOLISM 3

In Chapter V, I analyze *Blade Runner 2049* (2017), and, in doing so, revisit Scott's kabalistic classic. It is impossible to discuss the sequel without returning to the original, which I initially took on in *Cinema Symbolism*. The automatons of both films are futuristic golems known as Replicants. They are humanlike creations brought to life by biomechanical sorcery. *Blade Runner*'s Replicant antagonist is Roy Batty, a Nexus-6, paralleling a fallen Gnostic Anthropos. The Anthropos unfallen is a cosmogonic element of pure mind, distinct from matter, akin to Kabbalah's Adam Kadmon or Blake's Albion.[100] It is the underlying nature of humanity, viz. the collective, the archetype, or the spiritual essence of each human. He is a perfect copy of his eternal father, knowing the mysteries of the seven planetary spheres. There is a Gnostic belief that, like Sophia, the Anthropos fell into material decay, dividing his nature between matter and spirit. The pursuit of gnosis is the restoration of the Anthropos, forging a pre-Fall of Eden condition. When God revealed himself, he did so in the form of the Anthropos. For this reason, the Gnostics explained, Jesus Christ called himself the Son of Man; that is, the Son of Anthropos.

Batty's mind, conceived as a hypostasis, emanating from spiritual essence, God, yet darkened–corrupted–by contact with his human creators. The protagonist, Rick Deckard, also personifies a fallen Anthropos: a soulless man hunting Replicants, trapped by his ignorance, disconnected from the divine. *Blade Runner* plots the paths of Roy and Deckard, the awakened Anthropos (Roy), and the Anthropos asleep (Deckard) though these characters begin as enemies but end as compatriots. Through his encounter with Deckard, Roy learns his vocation: he is the golem-turned-savior. This Christlike robot will supply Deckard with gnosis, awakening him, making him conscious that Replicants are imbued with souls and worthy of life. By way of his battle with Roy, Deckard awakes to his identity: he is a personification of the golem he seeks to destroy. Each epiphany generates a new disposition. Just as he realizes freedom, Roy

---

100 Gershom Scholem, *On the Kabbalah and its Symbolism*, trans. Ralph Manheim (1960; repr., New York: Schocken Books, 1996), 104. Scholem writes: "The esoteric thinking of the *Zohar*–as the book repeatedly points out–is wholly concerned with the primordial world of man, as creature and as the increate Adam Kadmon. For this secret world of the Godhead manifested in the symbol of man is both at once; it is the world of the 'inner' man, but also the realm which opens up only to the contemplation of the believer and which the *Zohar* terms the 'secret of faith,' *raza de-mehemanutha*."

accepts his death. Likewise, when Deckard transcends his old identity, he embraces the ruin of his calling. When he finds the hideout of the Nexus-6s, Deckard verges on conversion: from an enervated human who kills machines to an intelligent Gnostic-engine, liberating humans.[101] *Blade Runner* asks this critical question: do the Replicants have souls? If the answer is yes, then *Blade Runner 2049* poses the logical follow-up: can the Replicants feel emotions, love, and be loved?

Chapter VI investigates the mysteries of *The Cabinet of Dr. Caligari* (1920), the first movie with an unexpected twist, presenting a subjective narrative from the mouth of an unreliable storyteller. We are introduced to the sleepwalker or somnambulist, a blend of automaton and golem, under his devious master's hypotonic control. Because of its indelible imagery, *Caligari* cannot be mistaken for any other picture. Its style is the pinnacle of German Expressionism, with its crooked backdrops, harsh lines, painted shadows, and surrealism are present in every dour scene. Distortions and mangled perspectives are constant, churning on the screen like a witch stirring her cauldron, producing nightmarish shapes. Its horror is shot within the bosom of an artistic combination evoking Edvard Munch (1863-1944), M.C. Escher (1898-1972), Georges Braque (1882-1963) and Pablo Picasso (1881-1973). Retaining almost nothing of Edgar Allan Poe's (1809-1849) short story, *Murders in the Rue Morgue* (1932) borrows heavily from *Caligari*, with Bela Lugosi playing a mountebank turned mad scientist named Dr. Mirakle, who exhibits a murderous ape named Erik instead of a death-dealing somnambulist. *Rue Morgue* is, in many ways, a crazy artifact left over from the Scopes Monkey Trial of 1925.[102]

In *Cinema Symbolism*, I discussed the mythology of Batman and his villains as mythological, Jungian archetypes. Chapter VII applies this paradigm to the Dark Knight Trilogy of Christopher Nolan, and Todd Phillips' *Joker,* arguably four of the best superhero/supervillain movies ever made, hiding many esoteric and pop-culture Easter eggs. Bruce Wayne *qua* Batman is the quintessential American hero; the essence of mythology and the

---

101 Wilson, *Secret Cinema*, 77-86; Wilson, *Melancholy Android*, 91-92.
102 David Skal, *The Monster Show: A Cultural History of Horror* (New York: Farrar, Straus and Giroux, 2001), 164. Conan Doyle seems to have predicted the Scopes Monkey Era with the Sherlock Holmes story, "The Adventure of the Creeping Man," published in 1923. It is about an aging professor who injects himself with an extract from primates to reinvigorate his energy and sex drive. The Professor's experiment revives Darwin's (1809-1882) *On the Origin of Species* (1859).

archetypes demand life's journey consists of momentous events that are epic, heroic, and tragic. To live otherwise is to exist in stasis like the multitude, going through the daily motions and experiencing a fleeting and forgetful life. Remembrance by the multitude is the objective of all heroes and villains; for them, it is to write a gospel and live a myth. But what does it mean to be a hero, besides rescuing damsels from towers and slaying evildoers? In *The Power of Myth* (1988), comparative mythology expert Joseph Campbell answers this question, defining a hero: "...the main character is a hero or heroine who has found or done something beyond the normal range of achievement and experience. A hero is someone who has given his or her life to something bigger than oneself."[103] There is also a traumatizing event propelling the hero forward, motivating him (or her): "The usual hero adventure begins with someone from whom something has been taken, or who feels there is something lacking in the normal experiences available or permitted to the members of his society."[104] Young Bruce, witnessing the murder of his parents by a thug, dedicates his life to fighting crime, becoming a fearful symbol of the night: the Batman, an American myth. Using his wealth, Bruce travels the world, fine-tuning his intellect, training himself to physical perfection, and learning a variety of crime-fighting skills. As the Caped Crusader, his Jungian shadow, he forever seeks justice, hoping to reconcile the murder of his parents by defeating evildoers. But counteracting the Batman is another shadow, the Joker, a much darker, eviler reflection of the winged avenger. The Joker's genesis (at least one possible version) is explored in *Joker*, a movie nominated for eleven Academy Awards, including Best Picture, Best Director, and Best Actor.

The films presented in Chapter VIII feature women that are dualistic, sinister, secretive, romantic intelligent, and erotic; they are not afraid to engage their wicked fantasies, to succumb to their hang-ups, to masturbate, murder, and maim. These activities are a walk in the park for them because pain can feel just as good as pleasure, and vice versa. These women are men's darkest archetypal fantasies; for the complex, evil female is just as alluring as the innocent, uncorrupted virgin. We are used to women being objects, archetypes, and plot points. Culturally, we don't know what to do with *Blue Velvet*'s (1986) Dorothy Vallens (Isabella Rossellini): it's terrible

---

103 Joseph Campbell and Bill Moyers, *The Power of Myth* (New York: Anchor Books, 1991), 151.
104 Ibid, 152.

CINEMA SYMBOLISM 3

(Left) Torn between the love for her husband, Julian Craster (left, Marius Goring, 1912-1998), and her incessant need to dance, embodied by the ballet company's tyrannical impresario, Boris Lermontov (right, Anton Walbrook 1896-1967), Vicky Page (center, Moira Shearer, 1926-2006) suffers heartbreak, melancholy, and frustration, resulting in tragedy. The conflict leaves her lost in a fog of confusion and despair, so she kills herself by leaping before an oncoming train, becoming a martyr. (Top right) Lermontov, the ballet company's oppressive and demanding CEO, with a sculpture of a ballerina's taut foot, symbolizing the agony and ecstasy of the dance. (Bottom right) Vicky emulates the idol later by donning the scarlet ballet slippers, her obsession, signifying her self-sacrifice, desire to dance, seek perfection, and become a superstar. From *The Red Shoes*.

to see her threatened and raped, and it's awful to see her want to be struck during sex. Yet, it's her pleasure; her discomfort is her eroticism.[105] She's a desperate mother, and we often don't know where the line between her victimhood and desire rests.[106] She can't be pigeonholed with traditional female archetypes, which only adds to the confusion. We rarely expect male characters to be all good or all evil because we have a plethora of fictional models of their complexity.[107] When women are presented as erotic, evil, and deviant, our instinct is to see misogyny where there isn't

---

105 Leigh Kellmann Kolb, "The Uncanny Electricity of Women in David Lynch's Worlds," in *The Women of David Lynch*, ed. David Bushman (Columbus, OH: Fayetteville Mafia Press, 2019), 7.
106 Ibid.
107 Ibid.

Seen here with Count Mora (Bela Lugosi) is a bad moon rising named Luna (Carroll Borland, 1914-1994) from *Mark of the Vampire* (1935). Her pale skin and long raven locks, complemented by her goth makeup, are hallmarks of the sinister female archetype.

any. Remember, Sandy Williams (Laura Dern), Vallens' anthesis, is more than an innocent teenager, and *Black Swan*'s Nina surpasses her virginal ballerina ego. Neither women are cooker-cutters: Sandy is a schemer and an eavesdropper, and Nina is a repressed lesbian, a sadomasochist, and likely in an incestuous relationship with her mother. Instead, women like these show us how mysterious, dangerous, and enigmatic the world can be.

First up is the Romantic Satanism of *The Red Shoes* (1948), a tale about a ballerina's idée fixe to dance perfectly, signified by her infernal red ballet slippers, her mercurial fetish. A nymphet and two hebephiles competing for her affection take center stage in Kubrick's *Lolita* (1962). The dark side of the sacred feminine is taken to dangerous extremes in *The Neon Demon* (2016) wherein the models are cannibals, and their aloof collaborator is a necrophile. The female protagonist in *The Shape of Water* (2017) forsakes the world of humankind to fall in love with an Amphibian Man. In *Red Sparrow* (2018), Jennifer Lawrence's protagonist, Dominika

Egorova, learns the art of seduction, becoming a sexy spy in the world of international espionage.

The *Star Wars* saga drags on in Chapter IX; the sequels are now distributed by Walt Disney Studios, the new owner of Lucasfilm Ltd. I have not seen *Solo: A Star Wars Story* (2018), so the film is absent from the chapter. That notwithstanding, the elements of Campbell's monomyth are still present with the Call to Adventure, Refusal of the Call, Supernatural Aid, the Crossing of the First Threshold, the Belly of the Whale, the Road of Trials, the Meeting with the Goddess, Woman as the Temptress, Atonement with the Father, and Apotheosis transcendent. In *The Hero with a Thousand Faces* (1949), Campbell anticipates the dichotomy of the Force: "The hero-deed to be wrought is not today what it was in the century of Galileo. Where there then was darkness, now there is light; but also, where light was, there is now darkness. The modern hero-deed must be that of questing to bring to light again the lost Atlantis of the co-ordinated [*sic*] soul."[108] Will Rey (Daisy Ridley) be able to illuminate blackness, or will she be consumed by it and turn to the Dark Side? We will have to wait until the release of *The Rise of Skywalker* (2019) to learn Rey's fate and see if the Ultimate Boon–the fall of the First Order–is satisfied, or if evil rises. It will be interesting to see if the film features what Campbell refers to as *Return* (*Hero*, Chapter III) components such as Refusal of the Return, the Magic Flight, Rescue from Without, the Crossing of the Return Threshold, Master of the Two Worlds, and Freedom to Live.

Chapter X expands on a paragraph in *Cinema Symbolism*, documenting the uncanny nexuses between Elvis, the sun, and deification. The archetypal solar messiah's cinematic presence is also explored. The dying and resurrected sun god is a compelling persona, and one of Hollywood's favorites. Comparative hierology and magic expert, J.G. Frazer (1854-1941), explains the deity's universality: "We need not, with some enquirers in ancient and modern times, suppose that these Western peoples borrowed from the older civilisation of the Orient the conception of the Dying and Reviving God, together with the solemn ritual, in which that conception was dramatically set forth before the eyes of the worshippers. More probably the resemblance which may be traced in this respect between the religions of the East and West is no more than what we commonly, though incorrectly,

---

108 Campbell, *Hero*, 334.

call a fortuitous coincidence, the effect of similar causes acting alike on the similar constitution of the human mind in different countries and under different skies."[109] Jesus Christ typifies the sun–the parallels between the savior and the heavenly orb are too numerous to analyze, suffice to say this esoteric doctrine has been investigated in my other nonfiction books. Nevertheless, I am compelled to enumerate a few examples of Jesus' link to the sun. For example, just as Jesus is administered twelve Apostles to assist him, so too is the sun provided with twelve helpers, the zodiac, to aid it on its ecliptic, yearly journey. John the Baptist, the water bearer, personifies Aquarius; hence, in the Orthodox Church, Epiphany–the baptism of Christ– is celebrated on January 19th because, in the northern hemisphere, the sun enters the sign of Aquarius. The sun *qua* Jesus meets Aquarius *qua* John the Baptizer because "What is above is like what is below, and what is below is like what is above," inscribed upon the Emerald Tablet of Hermes Trismegistus, becoming part of the *Disciplina Arcani*.

This religious imagery continues into Chapter XI, wherein the Kabbalistic-Valentinian mysteries of *Mother!* are revealed. Relegating the Bible's dramatis personae to bondieuseries, Aronofsky's cynical film could easily have been included in Chapter II. Still, I felt it deserved a standalone chapter because not only does it feature symbolism, but the movie itself is a parable.

Chapter XII is a continuation of Chapter III from *Cinema Symbolism 2*, delving into the mysterious noir of David Lynch; *Eraserhead* (1977), *Wild at Heart* (1990), *Twin Peaks, Twin Peaks: Fire Walk with Me* (1992) and *Twin Peaks: The Return* are all put under the microscope. Due to the complexities of Lynch's work, this chapter slowed the writing of this book substantially, with the *Twin Peaks* analysis devouring the summer of 2019. I should also point out that I wrote this Introduction after completing the corpus of this book; as such, I would like to reiterate something I mention later. While writing Chapter XII, I watched, for the first, the original *Twin Peaks* television series from start to finish, offering a rather scathing review of it. Since then, I have come to appreciate the show, but lingering doubts about it and Lynch's aesthetic dramas persist. After all, the endless interplays between content and form, surface and depth, and opposing meanings must find a concord in a Baudrillardian middle ground; at least,

---

109 Frazer, *Golden Bough*, 382.

Da Vinci's *Salvator Mundi* (ca. 1500) depicts Jesus, the World's Savoir, as a magus holding a scrying ball, the foremost tool of the fortune teller. This imagery presents the Messiah more as a wizard than as a god. In his *Last Supper* (1495-1498), da Vinci shrouds Christ in solar allegory, echoing the tenets of the *mysterion*, i.e., the sacred mysteries. Both paintings suggest he was a student of Renaissance Cabala, Neoplatonism, and occult Christianity, using his artistic talents to promote the agendas of Marsilio Ficino (1433-1499) and Giovanni Pico della Mirandola (1463-1494).

one would think. Those red curtains, the eccentric characters, non sequitur dialog, barking dogs, electrical currents, and a dancing dwarf to boot must mean something, right? They do, and these interconnected dynamics are like pieces of a jigsaw waiting to be put together harmoniously. But after the parts are connected, the puzzle remains incomplete; something new has emerged from this imperfection: an unsolvable enigma open to interpretation and speculation.

Finally, Chapter XIII returns the reader to Middle-earth, exploring the high-fantasy world of Hobbits, Elves, Wizards, and Dwarves. The films are based upon the pre-WWII novel by J.R.R. Tolkien (1892-1973), featuring the monomyth and other veiled themes and motifs, echoing the author's intent to create a mythology. Tolkien served as the Rawlinson and Bosworth Professor of Anglo-Saxon and Fellow of Pembroke College, Oxford, England, from 1925 to 1945. He was a Professor of English Language and Literature and a Fellow of Merton College, Oxford, from 1945 to 1959. At one time, he was a close friend of Christian apologist C. S. Lewis

(1898-1963)–they were both members of the informal literary discussion group known as the Inklings. The Inklings met for nearly two decades between the early '30s and late 1949, praising the value of narrative in fiction while encouraging the writing of fantasy. Among its members was poet, novelist, playwright, theologian, and literary critic, Charles Williams (1886-1945). Williams gathered many followers and disciples during his lifetime. He was, for a period, a member of the Salvator Mundi Temple of the Fellowship of the Rosy Cross. Williams met Evelyn Underhill (1875-1941), a member of the Golden Dawn, in 1937 and later wrote the introduction to her published *Letters* in 1943. With Williams in the mix, it is easy to see a cabalistic-occult influence upon Tolkien and Lewis; moreover, Tolkien's deep interest Christianity and Norse mythology stemmed from his translation of *Beowulf*, completed in 1925. Tolkien created a mythology of his own termed the *Legendarium*, with the Middle-earth, and its inhabitants, part of lost English/European history, akin to Atlantis and Lemuria.

* * * * *

My analyses of movies are based upon objective observations, not superstition or paranoia. That is why I am never wrong. I am not infallible, but like an attorney, I approach any film like I would a new case: open-minded and impartial. I do not analyze films with a predetermined agenda or from the perspective of a rightwing Christian crusader, or a social justice warrior. I do not make vapid arguments based on suppositions, searching for cinematic evidence to pigeonhole into a predetermined narrative: Hollywood, its entertainments, are mind control, evil, the product of the Illuminati's hidden hand. To do so would be an error, doing these movies a disservice, making the analysis a mere subjective interpretation wherein everything is sinister. Not to mention, it would be boring, repetitive, and pointless. If I see something negative, I will pinpoint it. If I see Masonic symbols, I will explain their meaning. When there is a Gnostic storyline, I will identify it as such. When a film features alchemy, I will so dissect it. If I see evidence of mind control, the reader will be the first to know. If I see something mysterious, I will point it out, but if something is concealed, that doesn't necessarily make it malignant. It could be sinister or demonic, depending on the context, but it could also hide higher truths, becoming a holistic emblem of light. I feel it's important for the reader to know my objectivity because it separates my research from others in the field.

I remind the reader that this book, like my others, shrouds riddles, clues, codes, and tokens of the occult, so keep an eye out while reading it. For instance, know that in my first novel, *A Pact with the Devil* (2017), I named Elizabeth Burnblack's mother after Asenath Waite, a dark magician/hypnotist first appearing in H.P. Lovecraft's (1890-1937) "The Thing on the Doorstep," published in *Weird Tales* (January 1937). Asenath Waite matriculated at Miskatonic University, becoming the only female student to attend the occult institution, studying medieval metaphysics while there, linking Lovecraft's story to mine. Although *Cinema Symbolism 3* is not a work of fiction, similar ciphers, homages, and mysteries are encoded herein, so read carefully.

Recondite symbolism and themes are nothing new; instead, they are transcendent. Manly P. Hall (1901-1990) explains:

> Symbolism is the language of the Mysteries; in fact it is the language not only of mysticism and philosophy but of all Nature, for every law and power active in universal procedure is manifested to the limited sense perceptions of man through the medium of symbol. Every form existing in the diversified sphere of being is symbolic of the divine activity by which it is produced. By symbols men have ever sought to communicate to each other those thoughts which transcend the limitations of language. Rejecting man-conceived dialects as inadequate and unworthy to perpetuate divine ideas, the Mysteries thus chose symbolism as a far more ingenious and ideal method of preserving their transcendental knowledge. In a single figure a symbol may both reveal and conceal, for to the wise the subject of the symbol is obvious, while to the ignorant the figure remains inscrutable. Hence, he who seeks to unveil the secret doctrine of antiquity must search for that doctrine not upon the open pages of books which might fall into the hands of the unworthy but in the place where it was originally concealed.[110]

Throughout history, the masters have employed symbolism, Hermeticism, and occultism in their work. Hall continues:

---
110 Hall, *Secret Teachings*, 37.

CINEMA SYMBOLISM 3

> Richard Wagner's immortal composition, *Der Ring des Nibelungen*, is based upon the Mystery rituals of the Odinic cult. While the great composer took many liberties with the original story, the Ring Operas, declared to be the grandest tetralogy of music dramas the world possesses, have caught and preserved in a remarkable manner the majesty and power of the original sagas. Beginning with *Das Rheingold*, the action proceeds through *Die Walkure* and *Siegfried* to an awe-inspiring climax in *Gotterdammerung*, 'The Twilight of the Gods.'[111]

If a genius like Wagner (1813-1883) employed arcane symbolism and archetypal imagery in his operas, wouldn't it stand to reason similar techniques would be used in the entertainment business today? To ask the question is to answer it: yes, of course, they would. Do not be surprised when occult emblems and secret themes emerge in cinema, but watch in awe the methods used by these Hollywood magic makers to conceal and reveal mystic undercurrents. Filmmakers like Lucas, del Toro, Kubrick, Carpenter, Proyas, Spielberg, Lynch, Peter Jackson, Disney, Polanski, Zemeckis, Hitchcock, the Archers, Ari Aster, Aronofsky, Eggers, Phillips, and Nolan are expert sorcerers and alchemists. They cast spells upon unsuspecting movie audiences, holding their imaginations hostage. Time to ring up the curtain on *Cinema Symbolism 3*.

---

111 Ibid, 66.

CHAPTER I

EASTER EGGS HIDDEN IN THE BATES MOTEL

Can I give you some advice?
You gotta cut that shit out. "Mother?" It's just weird.
Dylan Massett, "What's Wrong with Norman," *Bates Motel*, 2013

The man that wandereth out of the way of understanding
shall remain in the congregation of the dead.
Proverbs 21:16

We're all in this sideshow together. And then we die.
Chick Hogan, "Bad Blood," *Bates Motel*, 2017

Bates Motel, created by Anthony Cipriano, Carlton Cuse, and Kerry Ehrin, was one of this author's favorite television series. Like *Twin Peaks*, the show takes place in the northwestern United States, set in the fictional town of White Pine Bay. An everyday American borough on the surface, yet beneath its saccharine vista, like Lynch's fictional hamlet, lurks a criminal and seedy underworld. *Bates Motel* aired on the A&E Network for five seasons from 2013 to 2017. The show is a modern retelling of Hitchcock's *Psycho*, hiding Easter eggs that pay homage to its precursor. *Psycho*, often considered the keystone of the horror-thrillers, the godfather of explicit media violence, is replete with undercurrents, both abstract and concrete, so it's only logical *Bates Motel* followed in its footsteps.

For instance, Hitchcock uses artwork to establish Norman Bates' (Anthony Perkins, 1932-1992) psychosis and repressed sexuality. The oil painting he uses to cover the peephole in the motel's parlor is a replica of *Susanna and the Elders* (1731). It depicts a story from the Bible–Book of Daniel, Chapter XIII–in which three old men spy on an innocent woman as she gets ready to bathe, but when they find themselves overcome with

(Left) *Susanna and the Elders* oil painting by either Frans van Mieris the Elder (1635-1681) or Willem van Mieris (1662-1747), Frans' youngest son. The artwork, based on a story from the Bible, features three men, like Norman, spying on a bathing woman. In the Biblical tale, the men accuse her of erotic blackmail; in Room 1, Norman *qua* Mother brutally stabs the naked woman. (Right) Norman, a sexual doppelganger, imitates Susanna's posture during the creepy climax when Loomis subdues him. From *Psycho*.

passion, they accuse her of sexual blackmail. Watching Marion Crane (Janet Leigh, 1927-2004) voyeuristically, his lust brings jealous "Mother" to life; she, not Norman, seals Marion's fate. Later, when he is caught by Sam Loomis (John Gavin, 1931-2018), Norman's pose emulates Susanna's: his clothes are torn while his head is thrown back, and his right arm lifted high in the air. Stripped of his Mother's dress and a cheap wig, Norman is finally laid bare for all he is: mother and son, female and male, guilty and innocent.

Hitchcock uses uneaten food or the refusal to share food—the interruption or denial of a natural act—as a conceptual device presenting his characters' inability to communicate, either with their innermost desires or with each other. Eating is a communal activity, but by refusing to indulge, the characters increase their suspicion and isolation. In the hotel room, during Sam and Marion's lunchtime tryst, we see her uneaten sandwich sitting on the night table; the lovers argue about whether or not to get married. Later, Mother will not let Norman invite Marion inside for dinner, so he brings food to her. He prepares nothing for himself while she only picks at hers. The meal produces only hostility: Norman and his Mother argue over Marion, and then in the parlor, Norman and Marion get into a disagreement over Mrs. Bates. When Detective Arbogast (Martin Balsam, 1919-1996) inquires about Marion, Norman offers him candy, but he refuses, indicating distrust. When questioned further by the detective, Norman becomes agitated, concealing the nature of Marion's arrival at the motel, and her subsequent disappearance, to the private investigator.[112]

Marion has a change of heart and decides to return the money she's stolen. She wants to go back to society after her brief stint as a fugitive, so she takes a shower. The water is a baptism, a transitional action signaling her purification, of her intention to return to normalcy. Her murder by Norman-as-Mother became a powerful image of the collapse of social contracts and relatedness; like us, Marion seeks advancement and financial security. She makes a mistake, but plays by the rules, seeking forgiveness and acceptance, only to have her cleansing turned into a bloody sacrifice. There is no God, at least not a just one. The disturbing scene became one of the most influential in cinema history with good reason: it undermined all expectations and formulas; released on September 8, 1960, Hitchcock's opus anticipated the erosion of social, political, and artistic mores in the coming decade. *Psycho* articulates the dread of ordinary people feeling trapped and immobilized in a world of rapid change.[113] Easter egg: in the Sherlock Holmes mystery *The Scarlet Claw* (1944), Judge Brisson's (Miles Mander, 1888-1946) shocking murder anticipates *Psycho*'s shower scene. Although little blood is shed on-screen, a silhouetted man violently killing his prey while dressed as a woman, stabbing him with a knife-like five-pronged garden weeder goes for the jugular, just like Norman Bates sixteen years later.[114]

Eyes are the windows to the soul; they express fear, underscoring the taboo theme of voyeurism and surveillance. When Marion is fleeing town with Mr. Cassidy's (Frank Albertson, 1909-1964) cash, she locks eyes with her boss (Vaughn Taylor, 1910-1983) while he's crossing the street–she knows she's been spotted doing something irregular and illegal. During

---

112 "Psycho Symbols, Allegory and Motifs," *Grade Saver*, n.d., https://www.gradesaver.com/psycho/study-guide/symbols-allegory-motifs (accessed January 10, 2018).
113 Skal, *Monster Show*, 378.
114 Tom Weaver, Michael Brunas, and John Brunas, *Universal Horrors: The Studio's Classic Films, 1931-1946*, 2nd ed. (Jefferson, NC: McFarland & Company, Inc., Publishers, 2017), 399.

Marion's drive, Hitchcock positions his camera straight on, so the viewer is watching Marion, hearing her innermost thoughts. The patrol officer that awakens Marion on the side of the highway wears intimidating, dark sunglasses, staring right into the camera, making him antagonistic; we, like Marion, feel nervous even though he has no idea what she's done. His skull-like appearance mirrors Mrs. Bates' eyeless corpse: all-seeing and judgmental. In the parlor, the eyes of Norman's stuffed birds peer down on him, just like his omnipresent Mother. Then, while Norman watches Marion undress through the peephole, Hitchcock employs an extreme close-up of Norman's eyeball, implicating us in his voyeuristic secret. Later, when Marion is lying dead on the ground, Hitchcock goes in close on her lifeless eye; this image connects to the close-up of Mrs. Bates' mummified hollow sockets in the fruit cellar.[115] Hitchcock, via allusions, informs us we are privy to a nightmare we should not be seeing.

But before we begin in earnest, a little about Hitchcock's thriller is in order. First, Robert Bloch (1917-1994) is the author of the classic horror novel, *Psycho* (1959), the basis for the film. Second, the iconic Bates home– the hilltop house behind the motel–is modeled on Edward Hopper's (1882-1967) painting, *The House by the Railroad* (1925), making it an example of art influencing art. Third, Norman embodies real-life serial killer Ed Gein (1906-1984), a reclusive, grave-robbing fiend who adored his mother. All references to *Psycho* are to the 1960 original, not the miscast 1998 remake. With this in mind, let's go Easter egg hunting.

<u>Season One (2013)</u>

Approximately six months after the death of his father, seventeen-year-old Norman Bates (Freddie Highmore) and his mother, Norma (Vera Farmiga), move from Arizona to the town of White Pine Bay, Oregon. Norma has purchased a defunct motel with the insurance money from her husband's death. Mother and son intend to start over. A few nights later, the former owner of the motel breaks into the home and sexually assaults Norma; Norman knocks him out, and Norma kills him. Together, they dispose of the body in a body of water. His disappearance soon draws the attention of the town sheriff Alex Romero (Nestor Carbonell) and his

---

[115] "Psycho Symbols, Allegory and Motifs" *Grade Saver*, n.d., https://www.gradesaver.com/psycho/study-guide/symbols-allegory-motifs (accessed January 10, 2018).

It is easy to see the influence of Hopper's *The House by the Railroad* (left) on the Bates Motel's hilltop mansion (right).

deputy Zack Shelby (Mike Vogel); Norma and Norman do their best to stop them from finding out the truth.

Meanwhile, Norman enrolls at the local high school, befriending classmates Emma Decody (Olivia Cooke) and Bradley Martin (Nicola Peltz), while attracting the attention of teacher Blaire Watson (Keegan Conner Tracy). Elsewhere, Norma's other son Dylan Massett (Norman's half-brother, played by Max Thieriot), arrives in town. All is not what it seems in White Pine Bay: there is a lucrative–yet illegal–marijuana and sex-slave industry sustaining the township; local law enforcement turns a blind eye to the criminality. In the finale, it appears as though a jealous "Mother" takes over Norman, murdering Miss Watson.

Easter Eggs

- Episode 1 "First You Dream, Then you Die," airdate March 18, 2013. While waiting at the bus stop, Norman listens to music on his MP3 player. It is Beethoven's (1770-1827) Symphony No. 3 (*Eroica*), composed 1803-1804. In *Psycho*, Norman has this composition on his record player. Bradley refers to Norman as a "deep, still lake," a line alluding to Norman's favorite method of hiding dead bodies. Bradley's description foreshadows her fate when her corpse, while in her car's trunk, is dumped into a murky lake during

Season Three's final episode, "Unconscious." The butcher knife Norma uses to kill Keith Summers (W. Earl Brown) is the same one Norman uses to kill Marion in the shower. Norma tells Romero the toilet doesn't work hints at Marion, suffering from a guilty conscience, tearing up her note, then flushing it down the toilet. *Psycho* was the first film to depict a flushing toilet on-screen. Norma sees the town's plan to build a bypass around her motel, cutting off her revenue, just like in *Psycho*, wherein the new highway isolated Norman and the motel. Norma's robe is periwinkle blue, signaling her burial dress in both the A&E series and the movie.

- Episode 2 "Nice Town You Picked, Norma..." airdate March 25, 2013. Dylan has Norma listed as *The Whore* in the contacts on his cell phone. The listing is a paradox because, in both the novel and film, Norma taught Norman sex was wrong, and all women, except for her, were whores.

- Episode 7: "The Man in Number 9," airdate April 29, 2013. Norman finds a stray dog, naming it Juno, growing close to the canine quickly. Juno was the wife of Zeus, and the protector and special counselor of the state. Her Greek counterpart was the alluring Hera, the queen of the Gods; only the arrogant and vain Cassiopeia, queen of Aethiopia and wife of King Cepheus, claimed to be more beautiful than Juno *qua* Hera. In the starry canopy above, Cassiopeia is a constellation known as the Lady in the Chair, anticipating the fate of Norma: her mummified corpse destined to remained seated in the fruit cellar (or around the dinner table).[116]

- Episode 8 "A Boy and His Dog," airdate May 6, 2013. Norman discovers taxidermy, his hobby in *Psycho*. Bottles of Dharma Beer are seen at the bar where Remo Wallace (Ian Tracey) and Dylan Massett get drunk and fight. The bottles are a nod to the television series *Lost* (2004-2010), a show produced by *Bates Motel* cocreator Carlton Cuse. Like *Lost*, White Pine Bay has secrets: all is not what it seems because most–if not all–of its inhabitants are duplicitous, devious,

---

[116] William Tyler Olcott, *Star Lore: Myths, Legends, and Facts* (1911; repr., Mineola, NY: Dover Publications, 2004), 127. The link between Juno and Cassiopeia, forging a nexus between Norman's dog and Norma's fate, is likely a product of the collective unconscious.

and dualistic. Remember, Nestor Carbonell portrayed Richard Alpert, introduced in *Lost*'s third season; his casting only adds to the mysteries of *Bates Motel*.

Season Two (2014)

Norman fixates on Miss Watson's death while his mother's mysterious past starts to haunt the family via the introduction of her brother, Caleb Calhoun (Kenny Johnson). Meanwhile, Norman's brother, Dylan, gets more entrenched in the familial drug war fueling White Pine Bay, finding himself right in the middle of the peril. Bradley remains on the hunt to uncover her father's killer, only to be driven to dangerous extremes. Sheriff Romero finds himself in a multifront war as everything escalates. At the same time, Emma complicates her relationship with Norman as the duo explore new love interests, bringing new and old characters along for the ride.

Easter Eggs

- Episode 2 "Shadow of a Doubt," airdate March 10, 2014. At show's culmination, Norma looks out her bedroom window, evoking her seated, mummified corpse silhouetted in the window. This episode is named after the 1934 Hitchcock movie, which influenced *Stoker* (2013), which, in turn, pays homage to *Psycho*.

- Episode 5 "The Escape Artist," airdate March 31, 2014. Nick Ford's (Michael O'Neill) yacht is *Amnesia IV*, an allusion to Norman's homicidal blackouts.

- Episode 8 "Meltdown," airdate April 21, 2014. Norman decorates the home; specifically, the entrance to the living room with a taxidermic owl.[117] The owl resembles the one in the hotel's parlor in *Psycho,* suggesting his predatory disposition.[118] Norma goes on a dinner date with George Heldens (Michael Vartan) to make Norman jealous, hinting at Norma's carnality, her subconscious desire to sleep with her son. In turn, Norman has an unhealthy infatuation with his mother bordering on necrophilia. When Romero tells Norman about the broken shower curtain rod, it is a subtle reference to when Sam

---

117 In the earlier episode "Plunge" (airdate April 7, 2014), the owl appears in Norman's basement work area.
118 Owls are carnivorous hunters.

and Lila Crane (Vera Miles) notice the missing shower curtain while investigating Marion's disappearance. They are unaware Marion tore the curtain down when she was fatally stabbed by "Mother."

- Episode 10 "The Immutable Truth," airdate May 5, 2014. As Norma watches Norman sleep, she's sits in a rocking chair. This scene is a reference to her eventual fate when Norman places her mummified corpse in a rocking chair in the fruit cellar. The Bobby Darin (1936-1973) song, "Dream Lover," was released in 1959, the same year Bloch published his novel. "They'll see, they'll see and they'll know, and they'll say, 'why she wouldn't even harm a fly.'" When Norman stares directly ahead, the final scene mirrors the creepy shot when, during the end of *Psycho*, his Mother's skull becomes a latent image lurking behind his face.

Season 3 (2015)

After a happy summer with his mother, living within the safe confines of home, and the Bates Motel, Blaire Watson's death resurfaces as Norma questions the incident. Norman continues to be tormented, wondering about his possible involvement in her murder. Norma, forced to look at disturbing truths about her son for the first time, their deeply intricate relationship continues to evolve. Norma finds herself turning to her other son, Dylan, relying on him in ways she never expected. This relationship inevitably triggers jealousy in Norman, causing a new love triangle between Norma and her two sons to erupt. Estranged brother Caleb frequents the family throughout the season, challenging the family bond even further. Pressures from the outside world take hold of the family via the introduction of Bob Paris (Kevin Rahm), Annika Johnson (Tracy Spiradakos), and the eccentric Chick Hogan (Ryan Hurst). Sheriff Romero and Norma have grown closer, but they will always have troubling question marks surrounding Norman. Something doesn't feel right, but despite his instincts, Romero finds himself continually drawn back to the Bates family–and Norma. Emma, determined to find out what is happening to Norman, becomes more emboldened and fearless, going after the things she wants. Familiar face Bradley Martin returns to surprise the family, digging up old memories, causing Norman to become Norma, killing her during the season's final episode.

CINEMA SYMBOLISM 3

Easter Eggs

- Episode 1 "A Death in the Family," airdate March 9, 2015. The hotel's office gets an art of memory device: a stuffed owl, recalling *Psycho*: in the parlor, the nocturnal bird hovers godlike over Marion and Norman. While sitting at the end of the dining room table, Norma tells Dylan her mother has died, showing him one of her mother's periwinkle blue hair ribbons. Interestingly, during the series' final episode "The Cord," Norman places his mother's corpse at the other end of the same table, a covert mnemonic fortifying the death of the matriarch: mother and grandmother. Norman spies on Annika while she showers; in *Psycho*, he watches Marion shower. Notice both women wear black underwear.

- Episode 2 "The Arcanum Club," airdate March 16, 2015. Norman foreshadows how he will preserve his mother's corpse by telling her he needs a large freezer in the basement. Over a dinner date, Emma asks Norman if he wants to be Peter Pan. This quip conjures *Finding Neverland* (2004) in which Freddie Highmore starred as the inspiration for Peter Pan. When Emma and Norma enter Annika's motel room, Emma notices her black stockings and garter belts dangling from the shower rod. Norma finds Annika's invitation to the Arcanum Club for the Annual Rites of Harvest Party. When Norma arrives at the Club's gate, a password is required to enter. After she sneaks in, Norma stumbles upon what appears to a pagan, sex magick ritual. Such imagery draws forth Kubrick's *Eyes Wide Shut*, identifying the Club as a playground for White Pine Bay's Illuminati-like elites. One will notice the Club is located on Manderly Way, giving it a supernatural air, conjuring the fictional estate in Daphne du Maurier's (1907-1989) novel, *Rebecca* (1938). Manderly, the gloomy manor of George Fortescue Maximilian "Maxim" de Winter was considered haunted by the ghost of his first wife, the titular Rebecca. Hitchcock made *Rebecca* into a movie, released in 1940. Chick tells Dylan and Caleb they remind him of two characters from a book, then asks if they have any rabbits, alluding to John Steinbeck's (1902-1968) *Of Mice and Men* (1937). The question is meant to insult Caleb because the story's two main characters are Lennie: a large, dimwitted man obsessed with rabbits; and George: a smart man working toward owning a small piece of farming land. Dylan is analogous to George because he is trying to open a small medical marijuana farm, making Caleb the de facto imbecile. By directing all his comments/questions to Dylan, Chick makes it evident he is the intelligent one, not Caleb.

- Episode 3 "Persuasion," airdate March 23, 2015. When she delivers the marijuana plants to Dylan's farm, Emma's demeanor comically imitates Marion's behavior when she flees Phoenix with the $40,000.
- Episode 4 "Unbreak-Able," airdate March 30, 2015. In a heated exchange, Norman yells, "What are you going to do, kill me?" at Dylan. The question presages the grand finale when Dylan kills Norman.
- Episode 5 "The Deal," airdate April 6, 2015. Norma wears black stockings (or pantyhose) and somber clothing signifying her shadow self when negotiating a Faustian Pact with Arcanum Club president Bob Paris (Kevin Rahm), securing her hotel's survival at the expense of two murdered prostitutes. Norma's dark clothing is a nod to Marion, when, before stealing the money, she wears white lingerie. After the theft, she wears black lingerie, indicating her evil deed, her turn to the dark side.[119]
- Episode 6 "Norma Louise," airdate April 13, 2015. When Norma trades in her Mercedes Benz for another car echoes *Psycho* when Marion does the same thing.
- Episode 7 "The Last Supper," airdate April 20, 2015. When comforting Norman in the basement, Norma says, "We all go a little mad sometimes." In *Psycho*, he speaks the same line when talking to Marion in the parlor. During dinner, no one toasts Norman designating his status as a social outcast.
- Episode 8 "The Pit," airdate April 27, 2015. Pierre is Chick's gun-running contact, inferring the French crime fiction writers Pierre Boileau (1906–1989) and Pierre Ayraud (aka Thomas Narcejac, 1908–1998); together, they collaborated to write *D'entre les mort*

---

119 Sullivan, *Cinema Symbolism 2*, Chapter XI.

(*Among the Dead*, also titled *The Living and the Dead*, 1954). Hitchcock made their story into a film, *Vertigo*, released in 1958. Norman's taxidermy includes a third owl, evoking the omnipresent owl in the hotel's parlor. Norma yells at Norman, "You're gonna kill me," anticipating the events of Season Four's penultimate episode. Norman visualizes Mother watching him from the bedroom window, paralleling her deathly silhouette in *Psycho*.

- Episode 9 "Crazy" (airdate May 4, 2015). The license plate on Bradley's car, NFB 418, is the same as Marion's car in *Psycho*. When Norman envisions Mother, she is wearing a periwinkle blue sweater and frock.[120]

- Episode 10 "Unconscious," airdate May 11, 2015. After she returns home from Pineview, Norman and Norma's conversation reflects Norman and Marion's dialog about one of those *places*, meaning an insane asylum. Norman, assuming Mother's personality, murders Bradley Martin brutally. After "Norma" kills her, he regains consciousness, questioning, "Mother, what have you done?" In *Psycho*, Norman asks this same question of the phantom matriarch. Next, he puts Bradley's lifeless body in the trunk of her car, driving it to a near-by rickety boat ramp. Norman, joined by hallucinatory Mother, watches it drift into the cold, dark water. In *Psycho*, Norman slips Marion's car into neutral, then waits for the vehicle to sink into the swamp.

Season 4 (2016)

Norma becomes increasingly fearful and desperate, going to great lengths to find Norman the professional help he desperately needs. This development further complicates their once unbreakable trust, while Norman struggles to maintain his grip on reality. Sheriff Romero, once again, finds himself drawn back into their lives. Will things finally heat up between Norma and the other man in her life? And how much further will he go to protect her? In the end, Norma dies when Norman tries to commit murder-suicide, only he survives.

---

[120] In Season Three's episode "The Deal, " it is revealed that Norma's blue and white dress is Norman's favorite, so he steals it from her closet, hiding it under his mattress.

Easter Eggs

- Episode 1 "A Danger to Himself and Others," airdate March 7, 2016. When Emma's mother, Audrey Ellis (Karina Logue), meets with Norman, she brings with her a stuffed rabbit. In *Psycho*, the rabbit resembles the one in Norman's bedroom.
- Episode 7 "There's No Place Like Home," airdate April 25, 2016. While sporting a periwinkle blue dress, Norma makes a cryptic comment about turning part of the basement into a fruit cellar referencing *Psycho*, where her corpse is stored and eventually discovered.
- Episode 8 "Unfaithful," airdate May 2, 2016. Norman peering through the peephole in the wall is a replica of the shot from *Psycho* when Norman spies on Marion.
- Episode 9 "Forever," airdate May 9, 2016. In the attic, there is another stuffed owl eerily similar to the one in *Psycho* stalking the hotel parlor. Norman's murder-suicide attempt with Norma refers to how she and her lover were initially thought to have died a decade before the events of *Psycho*. However, they were poisoned with strychnine rather than carbon monoxide.
- Episode 10 "Norman," airdate May 16, 2016. The surname of the female detective (Molly Price) who questions Romero, and later visits Norman, is Chambers. It is a homage to *Psycho*'s Sheriff Al Chambers (John McIntire, 1907-1991). For her funeral, Norman buries his mother in a periwinkle blue dress. Norman digs up Norma's corpse, bringing her home. In both the TV show and the film, Norma's mummified body takes up residence in the hilltop home.

Season 5 (2017)

Norman, now a grown man, is living a double life. In public, he's a happy, well-adjusted member of the White Pine Bay community. But in private, his violent blackouts escalate as "Mother" threatens to take over his mind and life completely, embodying the attributes of the evil matriarch archetype.[121] Meanwhile, since leaving White Pine Bay, Dylan and Emma

---

[121] In cinema, the diabolical-revengeful mother archetype has the attributes of the Greco-Roman goddess Nemesis, representing balance, justice, retribution, and vengeance; see Sullivan, *Cinema Symbolism*, Chapter XI, *passim*.

are blissfully unaware of Norma's death and Norman's descent into madness. Unfortunately for them, they will soon find themselves drawn back into Norman's insanity. A vengeful Romero, currently incarcerated for a perjury, hungers for a chance to destroy his stepson to avenge the murder of his one true love, Norma Bates. The final season occurs during late autumn-early winter–notice the snow-covered ground in the last couple of episodes. The snow signifies the weakened sun when Cimmerian darkness *qua* evil shrouds the land, paralleling the ghastly murder spree of Norman and his dead, frozen mother. Death is everywhere: mother and son are forever condemned to their motel, Hades, and to the imposing house rising on the hill like a macabre beacon.

Easter Eggs

- Episode 1 "Dark Paradise," February 20, 2017. The episode opens with an homage to Ed Gein, the real-life ghoul shadowing Norman. Gein, also known as the Butcher of Plainfield, was an American murderer and body snatcher. His crimes, committed around his hometown of Plainfield, Wisconsin, gathered widespread notoriety after authorities discovered Gein had exhumed corpses from local graveyards, fashioning trophies and keepsakes from the bones and skin. Gein confessed to killing two women: tavern owner Mary Hogan in 1954, and a Plainfield hardware store owner, Bernice Worden, in 1957. Thus, Norman plays a record with a Plainfield Recordings Inc. label–a Gein *qua* Bates Easter egg. When Madeleine Loomis (Isabelle McNally) remarks the Bates house reminds her "of that Hopper painting," she is referring to his painting *The House by the Railroad* (*vide supra*). Madeleine, along with her husband Sam (Austin Nichols), runs a hardware store; in *Psycho*, Sam Loomis operated a hardware store. There is a stuffed owl in the hotel's parlor, mirroring the one in *Psycho*. Sam checks into the motel under a fake name, which Marion also does in *Psycho* when she checked-in.

- Episode 2 "The Convergence of the Twain," airdate February 27, 2017. Upon arriving at the Bates house, Caleb finds a book on mummification when he searches for Norma, reflecting her condition.[122]

---

[122] The title of the book is *The Lost Art of Mummification*.

When Chick writes about Norman in his journal, his words resemble the language used the psychiatrist, Dr. Fred Richman (Simon Oakland, 1915-1983) used in *Psycho* when describing Norman's post-arrest condition, informing the police about his "Mother" persona.

- Episode 4 "Hidden," airdate March 13, 2017. Brooke Smith was enlisted to play Sheriff Jane Greene because her presence alludes to Ed Gein and, consequently, Norman Bates. In *The Silence of the Lambs* (1991), Smith played Catherine Martin, the Senator's daughter abducted by Jame "Buffalo Bill" Gumb (Ted Levine), imprisoned in a pit in his basement. Like Norman Bates, Gumb is a Gein analog: a serial killer who dons the skins of his victims. By casting this specific actress under these cinematic circumstances, she becomes an art of memory mnemonic. The wizards behind *Bates Motes* also jam to Q Lazzarus' "Goodbye Horses" (1988), recalling the atrocities of Gumb and, accordingly, those of Gein, summoning Bates' real-life ghoulish counterpart. When Norman, along with Sheriff Greene, checks the registry, one is reminded of Detective Arbogast checking the register for signs of Marion, using a sample of her handwriting. Highmore even tilts his head and eats candy corn, paying homage to Anthony Perkins' portrayal of Norman Bates.[123] When Norman visits Madeleine at her shop, he's picking up shower curtains. She comments, "I imagine you go through a lot of these," and he replies, "Yes, yes, we do, actually." This dialog is a nod to *Psycho*'s infamous shower scene. Later, Chick tells Norman he's writing a suspense novel that might someday be turned into a movie. Chick's story is the tale of Norman and his Mother, just like Bloch's novel.

- Episode 5 "Dreams Die First," airdate March 20, 2017. Norman frequents a bar, the White Horse, as Norma. To Jung, the horse was a symbol for the mother, asserting it expresses the magic side of man; that is, the mother within us.[124] Thus, inside the tavern, Norman is free, unrestrained to dress like Norma, and behave like her. Sam and Marion Crane (Rihanna) have a secret rendezvous, imitating *Psycho* when Marion and her lover also meet in secret.

---
123 Spelled Kandy Korn in *Psycho*.
124 Cirlot, *Dictionary*, 145.

Marion works for the realty company, R.A. Bloch, referencing *Psycho* author Robert Albert Bloch. When Marion asks for a promotion, she asks for Janet's old job; in *Psycho*, Janet Leigh played Marion. She steals $400,000; in *Psycho*, Marion stole $40,000. Driving, Norman encounters Dr. Edwards (Damon Gupton) crossing the street, conjuring Marion, in *Psycho*, stumbling upon her boss walking across the street. In both versions, the driver has something to hide from these respective characters passing before them. The series' creator, Carlton Cuse, plays the police officer who stops Marion on the road. Cuse's casting as the constable is not only a reference to *Psycho* but to Hitchcock himself, who always made a cameo in his films. In *Psycho*, Marion spots the motel's sign during a rainstorm as she does in the television show.

- Episode 6 "Marion," airdate March 27, 2017. Marion checks into the motel under the name Marie Samuels, the same alias used in Hitchcock's film. Both women stay in Room 1. As Norman checks Marion into her room, he tells her about the stationery with the motel name on it, using the dialogue from *Psycho*. When Norman looks up at the house, he sees Mother's silhouette in the window, another nod to *Psycho*. While Marion eats her sandwich, she tells Norman her aunt used to say ladies eat like birds. In *Psycho*, Norman tells Marion she eats like a bird. When Marion notices his taxidermy, he replies he likes stuffing things just like in *Psycho*. Unlike the original and Bloch's novel, Marion survives her experience at the motel. The iconic shower scene from the 1960 movie was duplicated in this episode; however, Sam takes Marion's place, and Norman is not his Mother persona when killing him. After Norman stabs Sam in the shower, he says, "Oh, mother, what have I done?" echoing the line, "Mother, what have you done?" When Norman kills Sam, Roy Orbison's (1936-1988) "Crying" (1962) plays during the violent attack. The music summons David Lynch's bipolar film *Mulholland Drive*, wherein the song is performed in Spanish, "Llorando," by Rebekah Del Rio in Club Silencio. In Lynch's movie, the song terminates the dream world of Betty Elms, returning to Diane Selwin's miserable existence. In *Bates Motel*, the song connotes the same paradigm: Norman becomes aware "Mother" is another side of his personality–a sable vision–and he's been murdering as her the entire time. Like *Mulholland Drive*, the music signals the deconstruction of the fantasy, returning both characters–Betty and Norman–back to their bleak realities.

- Episode 7 "Inseparable," airdate April 3, 2017. As he lies dead on the floor, the shot of Sam's open eye is the same as Marion's as she lies lifeless in the bathroom. After returning from disposing of Sam's body and car, he meets the sheriff, telling her it's linen day, using the same dialogue from *Psycho* when conversing with Arbogast. In a surprise twist, Norman subdues "Mother" from attacking someone–his brother Dylan–with a knife; in *Psycho*, Loomis overpowers Norman.

- Episode 8 "The Body," airdate April 10, 2017. *Psycho* was the first movie to feature a flushing toilet (*vide supra*); in this episode, inside the jail cell, both Norma and Norman are framed by a toilet seat. When Madeline is leaving the restroom at the sheriff's office, the bathroom sign has a man, woman, and a transgender figure on it, symbolizing Norman's androgynous-split personality. Sheriff Greene tells Madeleine that Norman is infatuated with her, recalling the dialog between Dr. Richman and Lila, telling her Norman was infatuated with Marion, inciting "Mother" to kill.

- Episode 9 "Visiting Hours," airdate April 17, 2017. One of the forensic examiners comments that Norman has kept his mother's bedroom like a museum. This Easter egg alludes to Gein, who, after his mother died, kept her bedroom uncluttered and unused.

- Episode 10 "The Cord," airdate April 24, 2017. The title of this episode touches on a line from the very first show, "First You Dream, Then You Die." Right before they dump Keith Summers' corpse overboard, mother tells son, "There's a cord between our hearts." *Bates Motel* comes full circle, linking the last episode to the first.[125] The phrase is furthermore inscribed on Norma's headstone. In *Psycho*, Norman murdered both his mother and her lover out of jealousy over their relationship; hence, Norman kills his

---

125 Curiously, at the end of Season 3, during the final scene of the episode "Unconscious," an imaginary Norma repeats this line to Norman after watching Bradley's car sink into the water.

mother, Norma, and her lover, Romero. However, in both the novel and original film, it was stated they died after drinking strychnine-laced tea, initially believed to be a murder-suicide by Norma's hands. Norman plays a record with a "Plainfield Recordings Inc." label, like the one in "Dark Paradise." The song "Que Sera, Sera (Whatever Will Be, Will Be)" by Doris Day (1922-2019) is from Hitchcock's suspense-thriller, *The Man Who Knew Too Much* (1956). Norman carries his dead mother down the staircase to dinner as he did in *Psycho* when he moved his mummified mother to the fruit cellar. Actress Diana Bang returns; during the first season, she played Jiao the Chinese sex slave, in this episode, she portrays the realtor selling the Bates Motel.

Time to turn the page, from the Easter eggs of *Bates Motel*, we proceed to Gnostic Hollywood, movies fusing ancient spiritual visions with commercial cinema. After all, Gnostic themes have become hip, no longer marginalized because the orthodox days of Irenaeus (ca. 130-ca. 202 CE) are long over, consigned to an Age long since passed. In a culture increasingly paranoid over the possibility that a secret society rules the world, Gnostic inflections of conspiracy are especially appealing.[126] Many Gnostic films resemble so-called Illuminati films because they feature a puppet master steering society to satisfy his (or her) narrow ego. The results of this manipulation are depressing; seeking an exit from oppressive and controlling mechanisms, the protagonist's divine spark is ignited, thereby declaring open rebellion on the constructed reality and its creator. The puppet master is not a Masonic overlord; instead, it is a Valentinian Demiurge, maintaining the hylic world regardless of the consequences. To many hyperactive commentators and misguided critics, these films are evidence of a diabolical cabal running Hollywood, pulling strings at the behest of devil-worshipping elites running the world. In reality, these films are an exercise in Gnostic transcendentalism and not proof of a conspiracy. One must always remember that Hollywood is a dream factory with some movies darker than others; nightmares are *real* with some films resembling William Blake's hellish paintings come to life. But let's be honest: Gnostic cinema is but the latest wave of esoteric populism because people love to watch occult-virtual images that seem more genuine than the austere motions of daily life.

---

126 Wilson, *Secret Cinema*, vii.

CHAPTER II

GNOSTIC HOLLYWOOD

It's only after we've lost everything that we're free to do anything.
Tyler Durden, *Fight Club*, 1999

We accept the reality of the world with which we're presented.
It's as simple as that.
Christof, *The Truman Show*, 1998

♪ 'Cause we are living in a material world
And I am a material girl
You know that we are living in a material world
And I am a material girl ♪
Madonna, "Material Girl," 1984

He's not a performer, he's a prisoner. Look at him,
look at what you've done to him!
Sylvia, *The Truman Show*, 1998

Luminous beings are we, not this crude matter.
Yoda, *Star Wars: The Empire Strikes Back*, 1980

For two years, I thought it was normal for a ten-year-old to wet the bed.
Shanda Riesman, *Donnie Darko*, 2001

My dear Alice. In the gardens of memory, in the palace of dreams,
that is where you and I will meet.
But a dream is not reality.
Who's to say which is which?
Dialog between the Mad Hatter and the Alice Kingsleigh,
Alice Through the Looking Glass, 2016

"Truth did not come into the world naked, but came clothed in types and images, one will not receive truth in any other way." – *Gospel of Philip*, 3rd Century, discovered in Upper Egypt, 1945. In *The Matrix*, Morpheus (Laurence Fishburne) says to Neo, "Welcome to the real world," inferring the universe's duality: ignorance versus consciousness, the make-believe, material reality at odds with spiritual transcendence. Gnosticism permeates Hollywood; many films veil its cosmologies and philosophies. Through heterogeneous, these traditions emerged in Alexandria and Rome in the 2nd and 3rd centuries, featuring recurring themes. The visible cosmos is the sinister creation of the tyrannical Demiurge. Thus, the material universe is a rip-off of the pleroma that the uninformed maker does not know exists. The false (or lesser) god brainwashers the inhabitants of this world into believing that what they see before them is the only reality, dumbing them down. Certain people awaken to the illusory nature of this material plane, struggling to rise above this mire to the currents of spirit. These are the Gnostics, those who know.[127]

Having attained enlightenment, they can bypass the Demiurge and the archons, returning to the divine godhead, singing hymns, becoming mingled with its powers.[128] The *Corpus Hermeticum*'s first dialog between Hermes Trismegistus and *Poimandres* lays the groundwork; its subsequent books describe how the spirit can escape matter. A Manichean conflict between light and dark defines the cosmos; during life, one must obtain illumination to know oneself; at death, the spirit passes through the armature of spheres, leaving behind a part of his (or her) corrupt nature.[129] Free of the body, the spirit enters the eighth realm beyond the seven planets, transcending the material world.[130] But while we live, the dialog, the *Asclepius*, offers humankind a chance to work God's will, an exit ramp to the *Poimandres'* pessimism. Called the *Sermo perfectus* by Lactantius (240-320 CE), the Christian advisor to Emperor Constantine I (272-337 CE), Trismegistus encourages the practice of astral magic, to know the occult properties of substances, and to arrange them per the principles of sympathetic magic. The magus calls upon the gods of heaven via statues filled with *sensus* and

---

127 Ibid, 3.
128 Yates, *Giordano Bruno*, *supra* note 31.
129 Ibid.
130 In some Gnostic cosmologies, this eighth sphere is home to the Great Archon; see King, *The Gnostics*, 80.

spiritus to perform sorcery, foretell the future, hex, and cure[131] It would be a legitimate practice for a pious philosopher to draw down heavenly forces by theurgy, as the Renaissance philosopher Marsilio Ficino advised in book III of *Libri de Vita* (1489), titled *De vita coelitus comparanda*.[132]

One of the earliest works of Gnostic fiction is Shakespeare's *Hamlet*, first performed in 1609; the protagonist, Hamlet, finds himself dwelling in a bogus world created by his demiurgic Uncle Claudius. Hamlet's reality is so bleak that he contemplates suicide, immortalized in his "To be, or not to be," soliloquy. To navigate existence, Hamlet turns to the invisible, spiritual realm, speaking with the ghost of his regal father. There is no loophole or hallucination; the spirit is seen and identified by others before Hamlet meets the apparition. Through this supernatural manifestation, he comes into possession of proof his father was murdered, learning by whom, and in what treacherous and cowardly manner it was accomplished. Enlightened, Hamlet applies physical tests to this psychic information, and, thus getting full confirmation, he carries out his plan of revenge against his controlling uncle.[133] The specter designates his Gnostic vision, granting Hamlet an occult insight into how things are, piercing the fog of ignorance, glimpsing the realm beyond the Demiurge's artifice, unperceived by the profane.[134]

Gnosticism permeates the work of Philip K. Dick (1928-1962). Like *The Scarlet Claw*'s Alistair Ramson (Gerald Hamer, 1886-1972), Dick was a paranoiac; his tales, populated with monopolistic corporations, parallel dimensions, authoritarian governments, and altered states of consciousness, became *Blade Runner* (1982), *Total Recall* (1990), *A Scanner Darkly* (2006), and *The Adjustment Bureau* (2011). Dick aside, *The Matrix*, *The Truman Show*, and *Fight Club* are the fountainheads of Gnostic cinema, cited in this book; this trifecta is unavoidable when discussing Hollywood's fascination with this Christian heresy. But those three films are only the tip of the iceberg. So, where to begin? The most efficient way to pull back the curtain is to briefly explain Gnostic doctrines, philosophies, teachings,

---

131 Yates, *Giordano Bruno*, 37, 41; Fowden, *Egyptian Hermes*, 77. He explains: "These energies derive from the sun, the planets and the stars; and they operate on all bodies, whether immortal or mortal, animate or inanimate."
132 Yates, ibid, 41.
133 L.W. Rogers, *The Occultism in the Shakespeare Plays* (New York: The Theosophical Book Company, 1909), 8.
134 Ibid, 9.

heresiarchs, and its influence on the Hermetic tradition via a glossary. Let's begin with Gnosticism's asshole god, and its angelic scumbag mafia seeking to extinguish humankind's divine spark.

The Demiurge. In his short story "Plato's Dream" (1756), Voltaire called the Demiurge the Demogorgon; the Gnostic theogony offers a distinction between the highest, unknowable-spiritual godhead (positive) and the creator (negative) of the hylic reality. Several systems of Gnostic thought present the Demiurge, known as Yaldabaoth, Son of Chaos, as antagonistic to the will of the Supreme Being. Yaldabaoth's act of creation occurs as an unconscious semblance of the divine model; thus, it is fundamentally flawed. Otherwise, it is formed with the corrupt intention of entrapping aspects of the divine pleroma in materiality, thereby enslaving humankind. In these systems, the Demiurge solves the problem of evil. As the lesser god of the material world, the deity is an artisan-like figure responsible for fashioning and maintaining the physical universe. In perpetuating the artifice, a cadre of oppressive servants assists the demiurge, preserving the cosmos imperfectly.

The word *Demiurge* is an English word derived from *demiurgus*, a Latinized form of the Greek δημιουργός or *dēmiourgos*. It was initially an ordinary noun meaning *craftsman* or *artisan*, but gradually came to mean *producer*, and eventually *creator*. The philosophical usage and the proper noun derive from Plato's dialog *Timaeus*; written ca. 360 BCE, wherein the Demiurge is the maker of the universe. The Platonic (ca. 310–90 BCE) and Middle Platonic (ca. 90 BCE–300 CE) philosophical traditions describe the Demiurge as a creator. In the various branches of the Neoplatonic school (3rd century onwards), the Demiurge is the fashioner of the real, perceptible world after the model of the Ideas, but (in most Neoplatonic systems) is not the One. In the arch-dualist ideology of the various Gnostic systems, the material universe is evil, while the spiritual world is good. According to some strains of Gnosticism, the Ancient of Days is baleful because it is linked to the material world. In others, including the teachings of Valentinus (ca. 100–160 CE), the craftsman-god is merely ignorant or misguided. According to the Marcion of Sinope (ca. 85–160 CE), the Demiurge is the wrathful God–Jehovah or Yahweh–of the Old Testament, not the forgiving God of the New Testament. The God of the Old Testament was to be rejected, while the Father of Jesus (Logos made flesh) was to be accepted; thus, Marcion concluded the true believer in Christ entered into God's Kingdom, the unbeliever was a captive of the Demiurge forever. To Marcion, the scriptures were describing two different gods: one positive and spiritual, the other negative and the creator of illusions. Denounced as a heretic, the majority of early Christians condemned this idea as dualistic, choosing to identify with the orthodox by confessing one God, who is both Father Almighty and the Maker of Heaven and Earth.[135] Blake's Urizen was modeled after the Old Testament god, bearing the Demiurge's telltale signs.

In *Sherlock Holmes Faces Death* (1943), inside Gothic Musgrave Manor, Sherlock Holmes (Basil Rathbone, 1892-1967) sits atop a ladder, conducting a game of chess using people as pieces. Holmes is the lofty manipulator, guiding humanity on the chessboard of life, moving them about, suggesting the Demiurge's machinations. The scene gives off a Gnostic vibe; ultimately, the chess game is a mysterious ritual, leading to a crown grant hidden in a crypt.

The Matrix Reloaded (2003) introduces the Architect, the trilogy's Demiurge. He is the creator of the phony world in which humans remain in a state of eternal stasis, unaware their reality is make-believe. They are slaves to the Matrix–their bodies used, unbeknownst to them–as batteries to sustain the machines. Only a few discover the ontological truth; they gain gnosis, the nature of being, exiting the artifice for the real world of Morpheus and the *Nebuchadnezzar*. He is an illuminator: a Trismegistus archetype heralding the One, who will awaken humankind to their plight so they can exit their computerized enslavement.

The Architect aside, there is another deity in the trilogy. Appearing in *The Matrix Revolutions* (2003) as a giant face, imitating *The Wizard of Oz*'s menacing green-faced Oz the Great and Powerful, is the Supreme Being, Deus Ex Machina. To the machines, it is the godhead, the Monad, known as the One to the Neoplatonists, *Nyx* (or *Nox*) in the Orphic Mysteries, and *Ein Sof* to the Kabbalists. Deus Ex Machina takes after Basilides' (d. 140 CE) Abraxas, the chief god of Alexandria.[136] Because of its connection to serpents, Abraxas was considered a demon, inferring Deux Ex Machina's evil scheme: the endless quest to destroy Zion and its rebellious inhabitants.

---

135 Elaine Pagels, *The Gnostic Gospels* (1979; repr., New York: Vintage Books, 1989), 28.
136 King, *The Gnostics*, 112. Abraxas "was the 'Supreme God,' and he, we know, was the IAO of Egypt." IAO is a Gnostic word of power, deriving from the Hebrew Tetragrammaton.

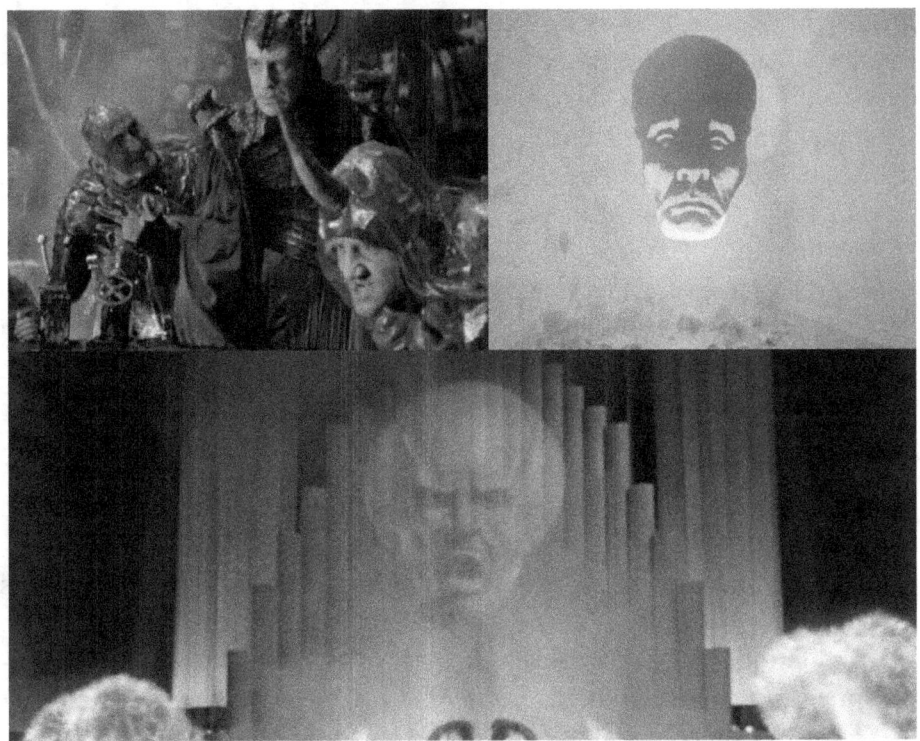

Gnostic reversal in cinema: (top left) *Time Bandits* (1981) sees Evil (David Warner) flanked by demons trying to protect and safeguard knowledge for humankind, echoing the Watchers from *I Enoch*. Biding his time in the Fortress of Ultimate Darkness, Evil gains and preserves wisdom by having an understanding of "digital watches, video cassette recorders, car telephones, and computers," which will lead humankind into a new enlightened age, making him the new godhead. (Top right) The Supreme Being, resembling Oz the Great and Powerful from *The Wizard of Oz* (bottom), is the terrifying Demiurge trying to retrieve his map. The disobedient Time Bandits qua archons use the map to satisfy their matristic desires, wreaking havoc to our history qua reality along the way. As Time Bandit Randall (David Rappaport, 1951-1990) explains, "You see, to be quite frank, Kevin, the fabric of the universe is far from perfect. It was a bit of botched job, you see. We only had seven days to make it. And that's where this comes in. This is the only map of all the holes. Well, why repair them? Why not use them to get stinking rich?" In the end, the Supreme Being (Ralph Richardson, 1902-1983) turns out to be nothing more than a bungled Jehovah, returning Kevan (Craig Warnock) to his burning home at the conclusion with a piece of Evil intact.

Christof (Ed Harris) is the Demiurge, producing *The Truman Show*. He is the creator of the illusory Seahaven, the phony reality of Truman Burbank (Jim Carrey). Truman's life is a sham; he is the unwitting salve of Christof, a mere puppet in his television show. Like a shallow megalomaniac, Christof controls everything: the weather, Truman's friends, his fears, even his wife. Truman's wife, Meryl (Laura Linney), is Christof's archon-in-chief. Her purpose is to hock wares to the TV audience while keeping Truman in perpetual stasis, ignorant of the false reality around him. Like the Demiurge, Jesus was also a craftsman–a carpenter–hence *Christof* has the syllable, *Christ*. Some Gnostics speculated that Jesus, because his physicality seemed to be an illusion, was related to the Demiurge, a concept strongly denounced by Irenaeus in *Against Heresies* (ca. 180 CE), Book III, Chapter II. In the *Hermetica*, the sage connects the Son of God, i.e., Jesus Christ, with the Demiurge.[137]

Anticipating Christof, the Demiurge governs humanity in *Glen or Glenda*, an idiosyncratic docudrama written and directed by the equally oddball Edward D. Wood, Jr. Like the protagonist, Glen/Glenda (Wood using the screen name Daniel Davis), Wood was a transvestite with a fetish for angora sweaters. In *Cinema Symbolism 2*, this author explained:

> If one wishes to view the Gnostic Demiurge in film, one of the best examples is Bela Lugosi's (1882-1956) armchair subdeity from Ed Wood's sixty-five-minute transvestite apologia *Glen or Glenda* (1953). Billed in the credits as "Scientist," Lugosi's eccentric Demiurge pulls humanity's strings to fix, or at least reconcile, cross-dressing men. While rationalizing transvestism, he admits mistakes are made, admonishing humankind to, "Dance to that which one is created for," suffocating all notions of individuality. He has no problem tinkering with humanity to satisfy the needs of his narrow ego. Lugosi's Demiurge describes the two protagonists: "One is wrong because he does right, and one is right because he does wrong. Pull the string!" implying Manichean duality, e.g., good versus evil, male and female, spirit and matter, light against dark, i.e., Zoroastrian dualism. Lugosi's Demiurge sees the sexes as arbitrary: they can be (and should be, depending on the circumstances) distorted, altered, and rearranged regardless of consequence…[Lugosi portrays] the Gnostic craftsman-god; his presence emanates from a hidden projector. His hand manipulates the material realm, erroneously guiding humankind into pansexual oblivion. So how can this contradiction be reconciled?[138]

In David Lynch's dualistic *Mulholland Drive*, the Demiurge controls Hollywood. Once again, we turn to *Cinema Symbolism 2*; I wrote:

---

137 Yates, *Giordano Bruno*, 7-8, 27, 152-153.
138 Sullivan, *Cinema Symbolism 2*, Preface.

Sitting in the dark behind a glass pane only becoming visible when the light comes on, Mr. Roque is a Gnostic Demiurge. Like Lugosi's creator deity in *Glen or Glenda*, Roque also pulls the string. He 'organizes the experience of the fallen...His arm reaches as high as the Hollywood boardroom and as low as the two-bit hitman. He puts Adam the artistic genius under his control and tries to kill Rita.' Embodying the Demiurge, Roque 'is an imperialist of experience, someone who reduces every event to his will to power...He dwells solely in the limited illusions of his own making, the paltry images of his vulgar ego. He is a bad artist, attenuating the world to one ugly face. His visions are tawdry, mere fantasies of infantile control. His characters are flat, predictable.' Like Gnostics, Betty and Rita rebel against this Demiurge. In contrast to the Demiurge, Betty and Rita are open to otherness, to strange and new experiences that might change their egos once and for all; they are indeed connoisseurs of experiences, lovers of the aesthetic fecundity of each other and their environment.[139]

In *Fight Club*, Durden admonishes the Narrator: "Listen to me! You have to consider the possibility that God does not like you. He never wanted you. In all probability, he hates you. This is not the worst thing that can happen," regarding the Demiurge's condescending attitude toward humanity. Although the lesser god does not appear, Durden nevertheless launches a war against consumerism, commercialism, and materialism, attempting to destroy the Demiurge's temporal influence. For only the enlightened–the Space Monkeys–could pull off something as bold as Operation Latte Thunder by killing two birds with one stone, annihilating things the Demiurge esteems: tawdry art and a snobby-artisanal third-wave coffee shop.

The Archons. "You play a good game, boy, but the game is finished. Now you die!" The Tall Man (Angus Scrimm, 1926-2016), appearing in *Phantasm* (1979) and its numerous sequels, acts like an archon (or even the Demiurge). He is an interdimensional rogue terrorizing the living by raiding graves, turning corpses into subservient dwarves, obfuscating dream and reality, and impaling his victims with deadly metal spheres. In the Gnosticism of late antiquity, an archon was any of several servants of the Demiurge standing

---

139 Ibid, Chapter III (citations omitted).

between the human race and the transcendent God only reachable through gnosis. In this context, they have the role of the *daemons* in Neoplatonism; the difference is that archons are negative, *daemons* are positive.

Along with the Demiurge, the Gnostics believed these malevolent entities ruled the world and planetary provinces, or spheres. The archons were named from the Greek word ἄρχοντες, meaning *principalities*, or *rulers*; the term was taken from the ancient Greek position of office, literally *archon*. The archons' purpose: keep humanity asleep, depressed in matter, a disposable pawn in the program.

In *Cinema Symbolism 2*, I described the skull-faced aliens of *They Live* (1988) as "demiurgic" when I should have just called them what they are: archons. For these aliens seek to drown humanity, "their intention to rule rests with the annihilation of consciousness," in a sea of greed and consumerism. The aliens use subliminal messaging and television as hypnotic forms of mind control, keeping humankind in perpetual stasis. Only by wearing magical sunglasses–the eyes are the window to the soul–can one see the archons for what they are, breaking the electronic spell that "induces artificial consciousness resembling sleep," revealing the covert stimuli they use to enslave the world. The Agents of *The Matrix* and its sequels personify the archons. Led by Smith (Hugo Weaving), they locate and destroy humans awakening to the Architect-as-Demiurge's false reality, deleting them from the system.

An archon camouflages itself in the Spaghetti Western, *The Good, the Bad and the Ugly* (1966), cropping up when Tuco (Eli Wallach, 1915-2014) frantically searches Sad Hill Cemetery for the grave of Arch Stanton. As he runs in circles, Ennio Morricone's (1928-2020) haunting *The Ecstasy of Gold* holds the audience captive. Keep an eye out for a black dog entering the cemetery along with Tuco; black dogs (hellhounds) associate with the Devil, anticipating the return of Angel Eyes (Lee Van Cleef, 1925-1989). Tuco believes the grave hides a cache of Confederate gold. Upon discovering it, he digs it up to find it contains Stanton's skeleton; there is no treasure, no money, no gold, empty. Miguel Conner, author, and host of *Aeon Byte Gnostic Radio* pointed out during one of my interviews that *Arch Stanton* becomes *archon* by simply removing *Stant*, hinting at the negative consequences of avarice and materialism. The gold–the sun's metal symbolizing en*light*enment–is buried in a grave marked *UNKNOWN*, evoking the unknowable god above the Demiurge, the Monad. It is a radically transcendent power that is immeasurable, unfathomable, and unlimited. The Monad is inconceivable in rational concepts and indescribable in discursive language. It is not corporeal nor incorporeal; it is not large, it is not small, it is not quantifiable, it is not a creature or a thing.[140] Its conclusion intimates that the meaningless pursuit of riches leads to emptiness equivalent to the spiritual nothingness of the archons and the Demiurge. By finding the gold, Blondie (Clint Eastwood) has obtained gnosis while Tuco ends up hanging like Judas Iscariot, the Apostle who betrayed Jesus for 30 pieces of silver.

In *The Wizard of Oz*, Dorothy must pass a series of trials to receive gnosis, which, for her, is the understanding that "there's no place like home." She must negotiate the archons, holding sway over their respective provinces, akin to celestial spheres, to achieve self-awakening. These tasks include confronting fear, overcoming the flying monkeys, defeating time by outlasting the Witch's hourglass, then killing the Wicked Witch of the West (Margaret Hamilton, 1902-1985), winning her broomstick and the admiration of her guards. The archons thus overcome, and their dominions navigated successfully, Dorothy and her sacred band expose the Wizard (Frank Morgan, 1890-1949) as a demiurgic charlatan.

Sophia. Akin to the kabalistic *Shekinah*, viz. Rachel and Leah, Sophia (Koinē Greek: σοφία, *sophía*, *wisdom*) is a Gnostic figure analogous to the human soul but, simultaneously, God's feminine aspect.[141] She is the divine spark; Sophia enables rebirth to our true selves, residing in us, without recourse to theurgic magic. The Gnostics believed she was the syzygy, the hypostatic Bride of Christ: the divine female twin Aeon of Jesus and the Holy Spirit of the Trinity. In the Nag Hammadi texts, Sophia is the lowest Aeon: an anthropic expression emanating God's light. She fell from grace and, as a result, birthed the Demiurge, who created the material world. Her offspring stupidly believes he is the only deity; bereft of wisdom, he fashions an inferior cosmos after the pleroma. Other Gnostic myths held the Demiurge also modeled Adam after the Anthropos, the perfect human being, the heavenly archetype. In one Gnostic account, Sophia employed the serpent to tempt Adam and Eve to transgress the command of their

---

140 Eric Wilson, *The Strange World of David Lynch: Transcendental Irony from Eraserhead to Mulholland Dr.* (New York: Continuum International Publishing Group Inc., 2007), 115.
141 Scholem, *On the Kabbalah*, 105-106.

maker, Yaldabaoth, who'd designed Eve to deprive Adam of his *spiritus*, which he had unwittingly conferred upon him. Another version of this legend makes the serpent out to be Sophia herself, bestowing knowledge upon humankind to spite the Demiurge.

Almost all Gnostic systems of the Syrian or Egyptian type taught the cosmos began with an original, unknowable God, Bythos, called the Monad by Monoimus (ca. 150–210 CE). From this initial unitary beginning, the Monad spontaneously emanated Aeons: pairs of progressively lesser beings in sequence. Together with the Monad, the Aeons generate the pleroma: the spiritual abode of God; it is the totality of the divine powers and emanations of the godhead, akin to the Kabbalah's *sefirot*. The Aeons should not be interpreted as distinct from the divine, but symbolic abstractions of the divine nature. The unfortunate transition from spiritual to the material, from noumenal to sensible, is brought about by a flaw, passion, or sin by one of the Aeons, Sophia.

In most Gnostic cosmologies, Sophia instigates this instability in the pleroma, thereby bringing about materiality. According to Gnostic texts, the crisis occurs because Sophia tries to emanate without her syzygy or, in other traditions, she tries to behold the unknowable Monad. After falling from the pleroma cataclysmically into the kenoma or void, and her fear and anguish over losing the Monad's light, cause both confusion and a longing to return to the spiritual realm. The creation of the Demiurge is also an error made during this exile, who crafts the physical world in which we live. Ignorant of his mother, she manages nevertheless to infuse some spiritual spark or pneuma into his imperfect creation.

In the *Pistis Sophia* (ca. 3rd-4th centuries), Christ (the Logos) is dispatched from the godhead to bring Sophia back into the fullness, restoring her, returning her to the pleroma. Christ enables her to see the light again, bringing her knowledge of *spiritus*. Christ is then sent to earth in the form of the man, Jesus, to give men the gnosis needed to rescue themselves from the physical reality, returning them to the spiritual world. In Gnostic theology, the Gospel story of Jesus is considered an allegory, an astrological fairy tale. It is an outer mystery, used as an introduction to gnosis, rather than literal history. To the Gnostics, the drama of the redemption of Sophia through Christ is the universe's central drama.

Sophia lives a double life. Even though she descends into the material realm to rectify her error, part of her remains in the pleroma; indeed, her spiritual aspect is inseparable from the most pristine presence in the plenitude. But this eternal identity remains only half her existence. Once she descends into time, hoping to redeem Adam and Eve, she stays on the material plane to take on yet other physical forms and to call home other exiled creatures. Though she thrives in the unsullied air, she is willing to take on any identity to awaken Yaldabaoth's slaves, kindling their spiritual yearnings. She will turn rebel, snake, warrior, criminal, and prostitute; this is her blessing and her curse. As a savior of humankind, she is a material form unattached to the ills of matter, a virginal presence. As the guilty cause of the first error, she can be made to suffer the degrading elements of the fallen world, becoming a lowly whore, incarnating as Mary Magdalene in exoteric Christianity.[142]

In *The Truman Show*, Silvia (Natascha McElhone), who portrays the character Lauren Garland, embodies Sofia; their names are nearly identical: *Sylvia, Sophia*. She attempts to ignite Truman's divine spark by alerting him of his make-believe world; discovered by Christof *qua* the Demiurge, she is banished from Seahaven, echoing Sophia's exile from the pleroma. While inside the falsehood, she catches young Truman's attention in front of the schoolyard. Her luminous eyes mesmerize Truman; despite Meryl's attempts to pull his attention away from the striking beauty, Truman falls in love with Sylvia even though he knows nothing about her, having never even talked to her. This ignorance and this silence are fitting because Sylvia is beyond empirical fact and linguistic category. Her irreducibility to earthly categories–her mysterious presence and piercing gaze–attracts Truman, inundated as he is with the banalities and idle chattering of Seahaven. With his speech and reason arrested, Truman senses energies in Sylvia, like Sophia, beyond the structure of Seahaven. When they finally do exchange words, in a library, a temple of learning *qua* gnosis, Sylvia informs him she possesses a secret which she can't reveal in public. They go to the shore where she tells him his life is a lie. Before Truman can fully comprehend her rhetoric, her television "father" appears and accuses his "daughter" of insanity. He hurries her away in his station wagon, telling the pining Truman that Sylvia is moving away forever, to Fiji, a symbolic kenoma. From this

---
142 Wilson, *Strange World*, 59.

moment, Truman's longing for an existence other than his present one is focused on Sylvia and Fiji. Daily meditating on these figures–markers of Sophia and the pleroma–he lives a double life, torn between the two principles of his cosmos: the real world intimated by Sylvia and the *terra incognita* where she ostensible lives, and the fake one embodied by Meryl (a female archon) and her bogus Seahaven surroundings.[143] He actively cultivates this saturnine modality through secret rituals that question the validity of his Seahaven identity. Each morning, he purchases a fashion magazine–"for the wife," he says–and, when Truman reaches his desk at work, he scours its pages for models that resemble Sylvia. When he finds a pair of eyes or a mouth or a nose that recalls his beloved, he rips this facial feature from the page and hides it. Later, at night, Truman surreptitiously descends into the basement of his home and recovers a hidden box where he stores these fragments. Spreading these shards before him, he tries to piece them together into the face of his lost Sylvia. This ritual depicts his desire to overcome his fallen condition–his feeling of duplicity, of spiritual dismemberment–through the unity suggested by the savior from another world. In other words, by exiting Seahaven and unifying with Sylvia, they can finally perfect the syzygy, obtain gnosis of their benighted condition, and find the higher godhead, reaching the pleroma. Another regular failure matches this sad activity. Almost every day, Truman schemes over how to get to Fiji. He calls or visits travel agents who tell him that all flights are booked for months in advance. He stares dreamily over maps of the remote island as if he could mentally travel there.[144] Sylvia *qua* Sophia often wears a red sweater; here, the color reflects the Ancient Mystery tradition. Red was considered a forceful agitating hue, signifying she's a thorn in Christof's side, fighting to free Truman from his imprisonment.[145]

In *Fight Club*, Sophia hangs around with Marla Singer (Helena Bonham Carter), aiding and abetting the Narrator by resurrecting his inner Christ, bringing forth the mercurial trickster-wizard Tyler Durden. Known as Project Mayhem, Durden has waged an unrelenting war against materialism and consumerism. Together, they become Valentinian Masters: Marla and the Narrator/Durden watch the financial buildings crumble–brought down

---

143 Wilson, *Secret Cinema*, 43.
144 Ibid, 43-44.
145 Hall, *Secret Teachings*, 146-147.

by controlled demotions–witnessing the destruction of the Demiurge's false reality. They are now enlightened, achieving the syzygy.

Sophia possesses Trinity (Carrie Anne Moss), dwelling in the real world, descending into the Matrix to free souls from the Architect and the Agents. Serving as the trilogy's sacred feminine, she seeks to bring Thomas Anderson to consciousness, placing him on a spiritual path to awaken Neo: humanity's Christlike Gnostic savior. Her name, Trinity, echoes texts from the Nag Hammadi Library, identifying Sophia as a feminine hypostasis in the Holy Trinity. In the Eastern Orthodox and the Catholic churches, Holy Wisdom, *Αγία Σοφία*, *Hagía Sophía*, is an expression for God the Son (Jesus) in the Trinity (as in the dedication of the church of Hagia Sophia in Constantinople) but, rarely, for the Holy Spirit. As Trinity, she lingers in Room *303*; later, she formulates the syzygy by resurrecting Neo from the dead. His messianic mission now identified, he fulfills his destiny by becoming the One, confronting and defeating the Agents *qua* archons. Like Christ, Neo ascends into the heavens during *The Matrix*'s final moments.

Married to the ethereal, yet grounded in the material is *The Fifth Element*'s (1997) Leeloo (Milla Jovovich): a deadly off-world weapon employed by humankind to defeat the Ultimate Evil. She is the sacred feminine performing the alchemical wedding by marrying Korben Dallas (Bruce Willis), the divine masculine (the Cosmic Christ), becoming an anthropic expression of the emanation of God's light.

Sophia, feminine divine energy and spirit, sometimes referred to as the Virgin of Wisdom, is the goddess who inspires all other goddesses, including the Egyptian Isis; she is the omnipresent wisdom and God's overshadowing power.[146] Her spirit dwells in Buffy "the Vampire Slayer" Summers (TV: Sarah Michelle Gellar, Movie: Kristy Swanson), a heroine battling vampires, monsters, and demons, becoming a beacon of light in a dark world. She lives in Princess Leia Organa (Carrie Fisher, 1956-2016), a lunar goddess analog combating Sith wickedness: Darth Vader, the Emperor, the Empire, and the First Order. She also assists the divine masculine, Han Solo (Harrison Ford), discover his calling is with the Rebels, and not as a mere smuggler. In *V for Vendetta* (2005), Sophia inhabits Evey Hammond (Natalie Portman), an employee of the state-

---

146 Ibid, 132.

run British Television Network. She allies with a Luciferian serpent, V (Hugo Weaving), in his gnostic quest to awaken the English people, and, simultaneously, in his rebellious mission to destroy Norsefire England.

Sophia's archetypal dark side is the goddess Lilith, the first wife of Adam, the seducer of men, an airborne nocturnal terror (Psalm 91), and the murderer of children. She is the infernal Madonna, and as the first woman, a protomartyr of female independence. She was probably *lilitu* originally, an Assyrian demon who had wings and long, disheveled hair. If Sophia is the sacred feminine, then Lilith is the satanic consort. A demon par excellence in the mythology of the Babylonians and the Sumerians, feared by the Jews, and, in the Christian tradition, she became the consort of Satan and Lucifer.[147] A Babylonian terra-cotta relief, dating from about 2000 BCE, depicts Lilith in human form–with the notable exception of her wings and owl feet. She is standing on two reclining lions and flanked by owls–wisdom–indicating her strong command and her nocturnal domain.[148] "O flyer in a dark chamber, go away at once, O Lili!" was found inscribed on a 7th-century BCE Syrian tablet depicting Lilith as a winged sphinx signifying that, like the Giza monument, she is as wise as a serpent.[149] As queen of the night, this sexy archetype's guise is a black leather skirt, bullet bra, stiletto heels, and black stockings with the seams down the back. In *Black Swan*, Lilith is Lily, the capricious rogue beguiling Nina, spawning her alchemical transformation, leading to her emotional downfall. Tattooed on her back are grotesque black wings, implying the ballerina is the airborne-demonic goddess incarnate. In *Blue Velvet*, Lilith shadows Dorothy Vallens, the sadomasochistic chanteuse playing opposite Sophia, personified by the gee-whiz girl next door, Sandy Williams. Together, aided by the volatile Frank Booth (Dennis Hopper, 1936-2010), the lustful whore and the chaste virgin guide Jeffrey Beaumont (Kyle MacLachlan) on his quest for gnosis, snapping him out of his spiritual lethargy.

Clad in black skin-tight vinyl, one cannot help but see traces of Lilith in *The Matrix*'s Trinity. With her rebellious spirit and strict nihilism, Trinity, one could argue, embodies the dark side of the kabalistic *Shekinah*: a

---

147 Michelle Belanger, *Names of the Damned: The Dictionary of Demons* (Woodbury, MN: Llewellyn, NY, 2019), 189-190.
148 Shelley R. Adler. *Sleep Paralysis: Night-mares, Nocebos, and the Mind-body Connection* (New Brunswick, NJ: Rutgers University Press, 2011), 38.
149 Ibid.

The circled dot was used by the Pythagoreans and later Greeks to represent the first metaphysical being, the Monad. The Point within a Circle is a symbol of great importance in Freemasonry and the Illuminati having two interpretations. To the profane, the point represents an individual brother, while the circle is the boundary line of his duty to God and man. The symbol commands peculiar attention in the occult because it is an ancient representation of the universe, and the solar orb, denoting Masonic heliocentric rulership. In *Watchmen* (2009), Dr. Manhattan (Billy Crudup) adopts the symbol for his own because he is a godlike entity, the Christlike solar savior of the United States. Like a Masonic candidate, he was resurrected into the highest gnosis, signifying Manhattan's mystical *ascensio* (leadership) and *apotheosis* (divine approbation).

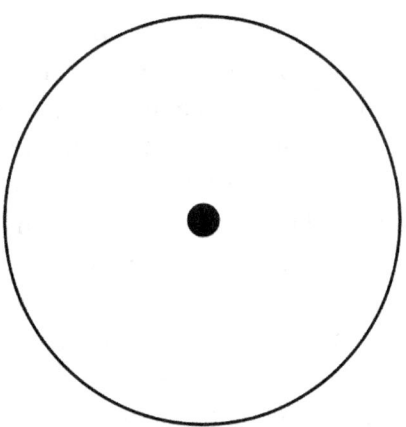

demonic serpent corrupting the simulation by tempting Neo to exit the artifice to join the battle against the machines.

The Monad. Though widely heterogeneous, the Gnostics embraced the Platonic notion that the divine is irreducibly ineffable. Part of the *Secret Book according to John* (ca. 180 CE), a foundational Gnostic text, espouses this philosophy, indicating Plato could have been its author. In cosmogony, the Monad (from Greek μονάς, *monas*, meaning *singularity*), refers to the Supreme Being, divinity, or the totality of all things. The concept was reportedly conceived by the Pythagoreans, referring variously to a single source acting alone, or to an indivisible origin, or both. This concept was later adopted by other philosophers, like Gottfried von Leibniz (1646-1716), who referred to the Monad as an elementary particle. The unknown God is the deity above the Demiurge; any attempt to know this God is a hindrance, only to know thyself is to fathom the godhead truly. In the *Gospel of Thomas* (ca. 340 CE), Jesus ridicules those who thought of the Kingdom of God in literal terms, like it was a specific place; instead, it is a state of self-discovery.[150] The Monad seldom turns up in cinema, but its antithesis, the Demiurge, is a regular tourist in Hollywood.

The Pleroma. Running parallel with the Hebraic *ma'aseh bereshit*, the pleroma, or the plenitude, refers to the totality of divine powers and emanations, a spiritual heaven, the home of the Monad and the Aeons.[151] The word *pleroma* means *fullness* from πληρόω (*I fill*) comparable to

---

150 Pagels, *Gnostic Gospels*, 128.
151 Gershom Scholem, *Kabbalah* (1974; repr., New York: Meridian, 1978), 21.

πλήρης which means *full*, and is used in both Christian and Gnostic theological contexts, referenced by St. Paul the Apostle at Colossians 2:9. The Jedi Knights hope to become one with a pleroma-like energy field known as the Force, echoing Wilhelm Reich's (1897-1957) Orgone Energy. In Tolkien's *The Lord of the Rings*, the elders of Middle-earth retire to the Grey Havens *qua* pleroma. In *The Lovely Bones* (2009), Susie Salmon (Saoirse Ronan) is granted entry into the pleroma after learning to let go of the material world. She witnesses her family heal, move on from her death, and retribution for her murderer.

Mani. Mani (ca. 216-274 CE) of Persian ancestry was the prophet and the founder of Manichaeism, a less complicated Gnostic religion of late antiquity. Mani's teachings were intended to succeed and surpass Christianity, Zoroastrianism, and Buddhism. It is a rigid system of dualism, good and evil, locked in perpetual struggle. While his religion was not strictly a movement of Christian Gnosticism in earlier models, Mani did declare himself to be an apostle of Christ, and extant Manichaean poetry frequently extols Jesus and his mother, Mary, with the highest reverence. Manichaean tradition claims its founder was the reincarnation of different religious figures, including Zoroaster (ca. 1500-1000 BCE), the Buddha (b. 536 BCE), and Jesus. Mani's cosmology is microcosmic and macrocosmic, epitomizing saturnine dualism: an eternal conflict between light and darkness, spirit and matter, knowledge and ignorance, and order and chaos. Mani's pessimistic cosmology is illustrated by the struggles between Jesus and Satan, Horus and Set, St. George and the Dragon, and Apollo and Python. The inhabitants of Middle-earth battle the evil Lord Sauron; Harry Potter and his friends fight Lord Voldemort and the Death Eaters, Buffy slays vampires, and Jedi countering Sith are all examples of Manichean dualism. At the end of *The Truman Show*, the protagonist struggles through the dark matter to achieve gnosis, the light, the pleroma, ascending steps in the clouds to free himself from the illusion of Seahaven. The Manichean's panoramic view of the world is strictly light and dark, enemy or friend. The Manichean is Buffy Summers, best portrayed by Sarah Michelle Gellar in the television series (1997-2003), and James Bond of the Ian Fleming (1908-1964) spy novels and movies. Both Buffy and Bond are agents of light destroying darkness; this is no middle ground; there are no two ways. Han Jonas (1903-1993) describes the profound dread and homesickness of the Manichean. Sadly, the greatest task of this fallen soul is not to work through anxiety, alienation, and confusion. It is to keep their melancholia acute. Their forlornness corresponds to their readiness for gnosis. But the world conspires against their dejection, offering either the brief comforts of matter (*hyle*) or the more lasting solaces of mind (*psyche*). Hedonism seduces the first case–think Bond and the Bond Girl; orthodox theology in the second–Buffy performs her sacred duty, destroying vampires to protect humankind.[152]

Valentinus. Valentinus (ca. 100–ca. 160) was the best known and the most successful early Christian gnostic theologians. According to Tertullian (155-220 CE), Valentinus was a candidate for Bishop of Rome but started his sect when another aspirant was chosen. Valentinus produced a variety of writings; still, only fragments survive, mostly those embedded in refuted quotations in the works of his opponents (notably Irenaeus), though not enough to reconstruct his system except in broad outline. His elaborate doctrine is known only in the developed and modified form given to it by his disciples. He taught there were three types of people: pneumatics, psychics, and hylics. Only the former received the gnosis, allowing them to return to the pleroma. Those of a psychic kind (ordinary Christians) would attain a lesser or uncertain form of salvation, and those devoured by materialism were doomed. These classes are represented in descending order by the figures Seth, Abel, and Cain. Valentinus' cosmology included the fall of Sophia into chaos and matter, the two gods: the Monad and the Demiurge, the awakening of the internal Christ, and that our reality is an illusion. Only through gnosis can one obtain the godhead in the antimaterial realm, bypassing (or negotiating) the archons.

Valentinus claimed he learned secret teachings and hidden mysteries about Jesus from Theudas (d. ca. 45 CE), one of Paul the Apostle's chief disciples. In the core text of the Valentinian school, *The Gospel of Truth* (ca. 150 CE), Jesus is the illuminating figure sent to rouse humankind from its stasis, igniting its divine spark, not to redeem sin. This unorthodox Jesus resembles other saviors in the Valentinian tradition: the serpent awakening Adam and Eve to the knowledge of Jehovah's brutal regime, and Sophia taking on a mundane form or persona to correct her mistake in the pleroma. Valentinus' cosmology takes center stage in *The Matrix* and *The Truman Show*; the Valentinian-Gnostic axiom of *being in this world*

---

[152] Wilson, *Secret Cinema*, 40.

just not part of it defines Dick's paranoid sci-fi acuity. In the former, Neo knows something is out of place; upon discovering the truth, he assumes the mantle of the Valentinian Christ–he's even called *Jesus* by one of his fellow hackers–launching him on a quest to awaken humanity, freeing them from the Matrix's subjugation. In the latter, Truman suspects his reality is bogus; like Jesus, he appears in the sky cruciform, signaling his gnosis. Free of his shackles, he leaves Seahaven for the pleroma to unite with Sylvia *qua* Sophia. In *Dune* (1984), Muad'Dib (Kyle MacLachlan) is the Valentinian Christ, instigating a rebellion, liberating Arrakis from the grip of the Emperor (Jose Ferrer) and the Harkonnens. V is a nihilistic revolutionary turned loose in the Norsefire England, supplying gnosis to Evey-as-Sophia, eventually overthrowing the oppressive government. These Valentinian saviors form a sort of psychic disorientation, an irritation in the back of the mind. The majority of people repress these irritating twinges, but a fevered minority transforms this annoyance into gnosis.[153]

Lastly, in Lewis Carroll's (1832-1898) *Alice in Wonderland* (1865) and *Through the Looking Glass* (1871), Sophia accompanies his little-girl Victorian protagonist. Carroll, real name Charles Lutwidge Dodgson, was an eccentric professor at Christ Church, Oxford, teaching mathematics. He was a member of the Society for Psychical Research, which investigated paranormal activity. Gnostic commentator, Miguel Conner, in an online article[154] identifies the uncanny similarities between Alice and Sophia:

- Both, out of boredom, curiosity, and disobedience, are thrown into an existential dimension: Alice to Wonderland and Sophia into chaos. In the latest big-screen adaptation (2010, directed by Tim Burton), Sophia-as-Alice (Mia Wasikowska) is a bored, lonely recluse. She disobeys her mother (Lindsay Duncan) by refusing to wear her corset and stockings signaling a Valentinian rebellion while suffering Mani's melancholia. In *Alice Through the Looking Glass* (2016), this pessimism continues wherein, due to the loss of his family, the Mad Hatter (Johnny Depp) suffers acute depression. To restore them, Alice (Wasikowska again) steals the Chronosphere,

---

153 Ibid, 39.
154 Miguel Conner, "Alice in Wonderland and the Occult," *Cinegnose: Cinema Secreto*, December 29, 2009, http://cinegnose.blogspot.com/2009/12/alice-in-wonderland-and-sophia-gnostic.html (accessed October 22, 2018).

allowing her to time travel. In antiquity, Chronos was the Greek personification of time, conflated with the Roman Saturn, the patron of the harvest.[155] The ringed planet epitomizes death, terminating life through lingering diseases; cough, rheumatism, flux, ague, a disorder of the spleen, dropsy, cholic, and complaints in the womb; in short, by all such diseases as proceeding from the super-abundance of cold.[156] To Ficino, Saturn's influence was characterized by moroseness and erudition; its sad blackness governs brilliant souls in perpetual gloomy moods.[157] To cure this melancholy, Ficino proposes astrological magic and talismans designed to draw down the beneficent energies of the Sun, Venus, viz. kindness and love, and amiable Jove.[158] Alice embodies emotional blackness; moreover, by traveling underground, one cannot help but think of the infernal regions suggesting she is not only rebellious but a Romantic Satanist. Her journey not only produces Gnostic revelation, but her adventure also epitomizes a sharp rebuke of dogmatic Victorian mores, making her a counterculture Luciferian rock star. In *Looking Glass*, the Latin phrase on the sundial, *Umbra Sumus* (English: *We Are A Shadow*), foreshadows her gloom: she will lose her father's ship, fostering her disappointments with society and its conformities.[159] This melancholic mode requires that one fixation on either the visible illusions of the material world (Victorian England) or the subtle delusions of the spiritual realm (Wonderland). Hovering between antinomies ensures Alice, on the one hand, will not mistake

---

[155] Cavendish, *Black Arts*, 204. He explains: "The Romans mistakenly identified Saturn, originally a harmless agricultural god, with the Greek Cronos, possibly because both of them had a sickle (or scythe) as an emblem. Cronos was the old and savage ruler of the Greek gods, who castrated his father Uranus with a sickle, ate his children, eventually tricked and overthrown by Zeus. Cronos, in turn, was wrongly identified with Chronos, Time, and so the planet rules the inexorable passing of time, which eats its children in turning all things into dust. In addition, Saturn is 'cold' because it is the furthest from the sun of the old planet and 'black" because its light is dim."
[156] Alan Leo, *Saturn: The Reaper* (London: Modern Astrology Office, 1916), xviii.
[157] Peter Marshall, *The Magic Circle of Rudolf II: Alchemy and Astrology in Renaissance Prague* (New York: Walker & Company, 2006), 200; Wilson, *Secret Cinema*, 47-49.
[158] Greer, *New Encyclopedia*, 173-174, 502.
[159] Laura Gibbs, "Sundial: UMBRA SUMUS," *Bestiaria Latina Blog: A round-up of what's going on at BestLatin.net*, February 7, 2013, http://bestlatin.blogspot.com/2013/02/sundial-umbra-sumus.html (accessed March 3, 2019). The Latin phrase is from the *Odes* (Horace) 4:7 (13 BCE), linking the moon's renewal to our morality.

the Demiurge's ejaculations for reality, not take his hylic goo for actuality, his surface for depths. On the other hand, she will not be seduced by the invisible reveries of the same Demiurge, the philosophical opium he offers to those who question his might. This kabalistic modality, dear reader, is Alice's gnosis; it is her reward for successfully passing Wonderland's trials and tribulations. Her mystical revelation is to follow her dreams even if they run contrary to her elders' harsh constructs; while doing this, she has come to know herself–the Gnostic manta.

- Both often lose their direction and their very senses until aided by tricksters: Alice by the Cheshire Cat and the Caterpillar, Sophia by the Cosmic Christ. In Burton's *Alice in Wonderland*, the Cat's visage faintly appears in the full moon before the opening credits. In *Looking Glass*, the Cat's smile morphs into a crescent moon. The moon is an emblem of the sacred feminine; as such, the Cat helps Alice-as-Sophia negotiate the mysteries of Wonderland. Absolem is the Caterpillar's name, conjuring Absalom, the third son of David, King of Israel (reign ca. 1000 BCE). Absalom rebelled against his father, circuitously inferring Alice-as-Sophia's revolt against Victorian England's suffocating assimilations. The Caterpillar transforms into a butterfly, awakening to wisdom, a new life.

- Both must overcome bizarre creatures: Alice battles the monstrous Jabberwocky; Sophia combats Jehovah, appearing to her in a dragon-like form. Alice, wearing shiny armor–thereby armed with gnosis–while wielding the Vorpal Sword defeats the Jabberwocky, representing Valentinus' ignorance *qua* darkness. Their battle occurs on a black and white chessboard, implying the cosmological dualism of Mani. The is also an interplay between Tweedledee and Tweedledum (Matt Lucas), white and red roses, as well as White and Red Queens (Anne Hathaway and Helena Bonham Carter) denoting Mani's universal polarities.

- Both must pass tests of emotion and will, i.e., archons, so they can return to their primordial home: Alice to England and Sophia to the pleroma.

- Both represent the Gnostic quest of the fallen soul in search of self-knowledge that will bring about restoration and release from corrupted matter. Alice must solve several riddles and often reflects on her nature. Sophia must discover and utter the correct prayers to understand herself and her place within the Eternal Realm from which she originated. It has been suggested the riddles, such as the unanswerable "Why is a raven like a writing desk?" along with Alice's fluctuating size signifies Carroll's disdain for symbolic algebra. For example, in the story (not included in Burton's film), the Caterpillar's warning is perhaps one of the most telling clues to Dodgson's conservative mathematics. "Keep your temper," the Caterpillar tells her. Alice presumes he's telling her not to get angry, but although he has been abrupt, he has not been unusually irritable at this point, so it's a somewhat puzzling thing to say. But the word *temper* also means *the proportion in which qualities are mingled*. So, the Caterpillar could be telling Alice to keep her body in correlation no matter what her size. This reference may be another reflection of Dodgson's love of Euclidean geometry in which absolute magnitude doesn't matter; instead, what's important is the ratio of one length to another. To survive in Wonderland, Alice must behave like a mathematic savant, keeping her ratios, e.g., her emotions, balanced and constant, even if her size changes.
- Both realize they are part of the living dream, generated an ultra-Supreme Being: Alice by the Red King and Sophia by the Monad. The Red King is absent in Burton's movies.
- Both have names that represent human virtues: Alice means *truth*, and Sophia means *wisdom*.

Carroll's story is twelve chapters in length representing the twelve months of the year and the Mazzaroth, i.e., the Zodiac (Job 38:31-32), governed by the sun, alluding to solar light, enlightenment, gnosis. As such, when Alice wakes, dead leaves brush her face. It was spring, now autumn, her journey in Wonderland occurred during the summer months when the sun's light is exalted.[160] *The Matrix* makes reference to Carroll's stories.

---

160 *Literary Wonderlands: A Journey Through the Greatest Fictional Worlds Ever Created*, ed. Laura Miller (New York: Black Dog & Leventhal Publishers, 2016), 87.

Neo follows a white rabbit (tattoo) leading him to Sophia-as-Trinity, and he goes through the looking glass (melding with a mirror) to achieve consciousness of the real world; thus, the Wachowski siblings generate a simulacrum that the Oxford don would be proud.

The influence of *Anabasis* aside, *The Warriors* resembles a Valentinian-styled fable. Trapped in a world of gangbanging, the Warriors travel from their turf, Coney Island, to the Bronx to attend a vast gangland meeting. Framed for the death of Cyrus, the chieftain of the powerful Gramercy Riffs, the Warriors have to battle their way back home. Along the way, they encounter the sacred feminine–Sophia–in the form of the street urchin Mercy (Deborah Van Valkenburgh). Her name contradicts the Warriors because, as *Mercy*, she is benevolent, balancing out their warlike nature, becoming an exemplar of the syzygy, i.e., the Union of Opposite. Surviving archon-like trials, tests, or Hermetic spheres of purification, the Warriors fight different gangs, including the Orphans, the Turnbull ACs, the Lizzies, and, most memorable, the Baseball Furies. Trying to oppose their gnosis is the leader of the Rogues, Luther (David Patrick Kelly), who, at one point, speaks to the Devil on a payphone. Upon reaching Coney Island, the Warriors have a gnostic epiphany: gangbanging over materialism, their turf, leads nowhere; now enlightened, they seek something better, something innate and transcendental.[161]

Basilides. Basilides, a contemporary of Valentinus, was an early Gnostic heresiarch in Alexandria, teaching from 117 to 138 CE, claiming to have been instructed by the Apostle Saint Matthias (d. ca. 80 CE). He was a pupil of either Menander or a supposed disciple of Peter (d. ca. 64-68 CE) named Glaucias. According to *The Acts of the Disputation with Manes*, Basilides taught among the Persians. He is believed to have written over two dozen books of commentary on the Christian Gospel (now all lost) titled *Exegetica*, making him one of the earliest Gospel commentators. Only preserved fragments of his works supplement the knowledge furnished by his opponents. The followers of Basilides formed a movement that persisted for at least two centuries after him; Epiphanius of Salamis (310-403 CE), at the end of the 4th century, recognized Basilides' profound influence in Alexandria. It is probable, however, that the school melded into the Gnostic mainstream by the latter half of the 2nd century. Sophisticated exegetes of this account

---

161 See the Introduction to my *Cinema Symbolism 2*.

were acutely aware of what the *Secret Book of John* (2nd century CE) overlooks: how can the spiritual adept extricate himself (or herself) from material trappings, his somatic conditions, and cultural boundaries? This reality is an illusion ruled by the Demiurge who thinks he is the only god; how is one to escape this material environment to the substantial Nothing–the primal godhead, a nonbeing–dwelling in a ghostly cold absence? Basilides struggled to answer these questions in radical means. His response: total negation, complete silence, and utter ignorance. Quelling curiosity toward things is a Gnostic reversal; put another way, ignorance of the world is the wisdom of the anti-world. Silence can disarm the illusion machine; Basilides recommended the Gnostics held their mysteries in silence. If the true God is beyond human knowledge, then ignorance, the negation of knowing, is the path to this sacred darkness. If this same deity is unnamable, outside conception, then silence, the annihilation of concepts, is the way to holy quietness.[162] Silence, as Jacques Lacarriere (1925-2005) observes, is at the "very heart of Gnostic teachings [and] one of the purest and most difficult ways of combating the illusion of the world."[163] Quietism inspires a state of constant watchfulness, a triumph of hyper-consciousness. It is negation word world noise, a kind of anti-matter. Basilides' cosmology is a total epistemological negation of everything; speaking and thinking are to be avoided because, to do so, partakes in the world of illusion.

Neoplatonism. A recherché doctrine-philosophy emerging at the same time as Gnosticism (2nd-3rd centuries CE), Neoplatonism interweaves Orphic paganism (akin to the Isiac and Eleusinian Mysteries), Plato, and Christian cravings into a theurgic melting pot with a dash of Oriental mysticism. Pythagoras, famous for his right-angled triangle theorem, declared that numbers are reality's ultimate essence and can render visible the structure of the universe, usually hidden from the experiences of the senses. The correspondences he discovered between arithmetic ratios and the chief musical intervals supported the idea and gave rise to a belief in *the harmony of the spheres*, celestial music created by the planets turning in their orbits.

Pythagoras strongly influenced Plato, stressing the inextricable connection between mathematics and cosmology. In *Timaeus*, Plato argued that while organizing the universe, God "placed water and air between

---

[162] Wilson, *Secret Cinema*, 36-38.
[163] Ibid, 38.

fire and earth, and made them so far as possible to one another." The result was a close relationship between beauty, perfection, and divinity. At the same time, Plato believed the cosmos was a living being, a blessed god, and its components were its living limbs. Thus, the heavens became anthropomorphized; in Plato's *Republic* (381 BCE), the sun symbolizes God's love, while the planets and stars are divine manifestations. Comparatively, the Twelve Houses of the Zodiac turn into the Twelve Apostles; Jesus, the Logos, the Son, is the luminous orb whose heavenly light warms and sustains humankind, perpetuating life eternal, its glorious gnosis defeats the works of darkness or nocturnal ignorance. This occult philosophy underlies Freemasonry, understood by the adept who joins the brotherhood, studying its arcane rituals and symbolism.

Reviving Plato's doctrines gave rise to *new*, *neo*, hence the Neoplatonists. The principle of emanation as unfolded in the Orphic theogony became the vital doctrine of the Gnostics, conceiving a spiritual hierarchy as occupying each degree of the interval between the extremes of the First Cause and Nature. Existence's seven grand divisions are termed in Neoplatonism:

1. The Principle of Principles, which is inscrutable and analogous to the threefold darkness of the Egyptians;
2. Being, the first point of the Triad of Cause;
3. Life;
4. Intellect, which completes the Triad of Causes;
5. Soul, which is the apex of the Triad of Generation;
6. Nature; and
7. Body, which completes the Triad of Generation.

Thus, it is revealed the order by which Cause flows into Generation and eventually produces bodies, the latter being objectifications in matter of superphysical paradigms or archetypes.[164]

Neoplatonism does not encapsulate a set of ideas as much as it summarizes a chain of thinkers, which began with Ammonius Saccas (175–242 CE) and his student, Plotinus (204/5–270 CE), stretching to

---

164 Manly P. Hall, *Lectures on Ancient Philosophy* (1970; repr., New York: Tarcher/Penguin, 2005), 218-219.

the 6th century CE. Even though Neoplatonism primarily circumscribes the thinkers now labeled Neoplatonists and not their ideas, some views are common to Neoplatonic systems. For example, the monistic idea that all of reality can be derived from a single principle, the supreme spiritual godhead, the One.

After Plotinus, there were three distinct periods in the history of Neoplatonism: the work of his student Porphyry; that of Iamblichus of Chalcis (235–325 CE) and his school in Syria; and the period in the 5th and 6th centuries when the Academies in Alexandria and Athens flourished. Neoplatonism had an enduring influence on the subsequent history of philosophy. In the Middle Ages, Neoplatonic ideas were studied and discussed by Islamic, Christian, and Jewish thinkers. Meister Eckhart was influenced by Neoplatonism, propagating a contemplative way of life pointing to the supreme God beyond the nameable deity. Neoplatonism strongly influenced perennial philosophy of the Italian Renaissance mystics Ficino and Giovanni Pico della Mirandola. For the Renaissance Neoplatonists, if God was imminent in the world, then mathematical truths, the movements of the stars and planets, the attributes of natural phenomena are all expressions of the mind of God in the world. This philosophy was incorporated into 19th-century Universalism and modern-day spirituality and nondualism.

There are differences between Gnosticism and Neoplatonism. Plotinus, the fountainhead of Neoplatonism, attacked the Gnostics for their anti-materialism. In his *Enneads* (ca. 250 CE), he criticizes the Gnostics for identifying the Demiurge, the architect, as evil. To Plotinus, the creator of the world is positive, a legitimate emanation from the true deity, the One, the ineffable sustainer of the universe. The One, like the kabalistic *Ein Sof*, is beyond all things, surpassing the supreme majesty of the intellect. It is so utterly different from human nature that there is nothing in the world that can assist in obtaining knowledge about it. Such a belief means we can only understand what the One is not, never what it is. This belief mirrors the God of Basilides: mysterious and transcendent, not merely because it is unlike anything in the created world or because it is difficult to come to any knowledge of its nature. This God is unknown because it has made all things ignorant of him. Thus, the best way to approach this great absence is Basilides' willed ignorance. However, this self-conscious silence, i.e., a refusal to question, does not mean we can never have an inkling of the One's essence. On the contrary, when the intellect shuts down, another faculty arises, the soul. When the soul becomes pure–that is, when it becomes plain–it no longer envisions the One as an object to be known. Instead, the purified soul resembles the godhead, becoming like the One.[165]

When the Gnostics and Neoplatonists were developing their negative theology, Christian thinkers soon thereafter cultivated the idea that one can gain holy knowledge through ignorance, echoing Basilides. The most profound was Pseudo-Dionysius the Areopagite. Though Pseudo-Dionysius wrote in the late 5th or early 6th century CE, his works were written like they were composed by St. Dionysius the Areopagite. St. Dionysus, a member of the Athenian judicial council–the Areopagus–in the 1st century CE, was converted to Christianity by St. Paul. Pseudo-Dionysius negates all concepts that could be conceivably applied to God, including wisdom, goodness, spirit, and paternity, including nothingness, silence, and mystery. To Pseudo-Dionysius, God is not only beyond all positive assertion, but outside the reach of negative statement. Practicing the radical negativity–this unwillingness to predicate anything on God–the religious seeker necessarily enters into painful blindness, difficult nonbelief. But this troublous condition is ultimately an *ekstasis*, an ecstasy, a transcendence of all temporal understanding, ascending to divine darkness, a learned ignorance.[166] This paradoxical theology pervades David Lynch's *Lost Highway* (1997), analyzed by this author in *Cinema Symbolism 2*.

This chapter begins with Fritz Lang's (1890-1976) *Metropolis* (1927), a two-hour-plus black and white silent movie.

The Above and Below of Fritz Lang's Metropolis

Reportedly one of Adolf Hitler's (1889-1945) favorite movies, along with Disney's *Snow White and the Seven Dwarfs* (1937), *Metropolis* is a German Expressionist drama directed by Fritz Lang. The silent film is

---

165 Deirdre Carabine, *The Unknown God, Negative Theology in the Platonic Tradition: Plato to Eriugena* (1995; repr., Eugene, OR: Wipf & Stock, 2015), 92, 135-138.
166 Edgar Wind, *Pagan Mysteries in the Renaissance: An Exploration of Philosophical and Mystical Sources of Iconography in Renaissance Art*, revised ed. (New York: W.W. Norton & Company, Inc., 1968), 54. See also Wilson, *Strange World*, 115-116;

(Left) The influence of *Metropolis*' cityscape, specifically the New Tower of Babel, manifests (right) in Tim Burton's *Batman Returns* in the design of Max Shreck's (Christopher Walken) Headquarters. The two buildings forge an architectural nexus, linking Gotham City to Lang's dystopia. Walken's ruthless business mogul bears the same name as actor Max Schreck (1879-1936), who famously portrayed Count Orlok in *Nosferatu* (1922). Orlok, a vampire, sucks his victims dry, anticipating Gotham's Shreck, who, likewise, tries to suck the city dry by monopolizing its energy.

regarded as a pioneering science-fiction spectacle and the first feature-length movie of that genre, exploring the horror of mechanism and the hope for transcendence. Made during the decadent Weimar Period (1918-1933), *Metropolis* takes place in a futuristic urban dystopia. The movie is about Freder (Gustav Fröhlich, 1902-1987), the city master's wealthy son, and the beautiful Maria (Brigitte Helm, 1906-1996), a saintly figure to the workers, trying to overcome the vast gulf separating the classes in their city. Their goal is to unite the lowly workers with Joh Fredersen (Alfred Abel, 1879-1937), the city's despotic overlord, finding common ground to create a progressive society, indicated by the film's catchphrase: *The Mediator Between the Head and the Hands Must Be the Heart*. Due to its long runtime, it was cut down after its German premiere with a large portion of footage removed. In 2008, a damaged print of Lang's original cut was found in a museum in Argentina. After a long restoration process that required additional materials provided by a print from New Zealand, *Metropolis* is currently 95% restored.

In this Cartesian nightmare, in the sprawling city of Metropolis, wealthy industrialists and business magnates and their top employees reign from high-rise towers. Concurrently, underground-dwelling workers toil to operate the great machines that power the city. The laborers themselves are machine-like, stripped of their humanity, working monotonous ten-hour shifts. Joh Fredersen is the city's ruler, managing it from the lofty New Tower of Babel. His son, Freder, idles away his time at the sports colosseum–the Club of the Sons–and the pleasure garden but is interrupted by the arrival of a young woman named Maria. She has brought a group of workers' children to observe the lifestyle of their rich "brothers." Maria and the children are ushered away, but Freder, fascinated, goes to the lower levels to find her. On the machine levels, he witnesses the explosion of an enormous contraption that kills and injures numerous workers. Freder has a hallucination that the machine is demon-god Moloch, and the workers are fed to it, sacrificed below so the Metropolis above can flourish. When the hallucination ends, he sees the dead workers carried away on stretchers; he hurries to tell his father about the accident. Fredersen questions his assistant, Josaphat (Theodor Loos, 1883-1954) about the incident, wondering why he learned of the explosion from his son, and not from him.

Grot (Heinrich George, 1893-1946), the foreman of the Heart Machine, brings Fredersen secret maps found on the dead workers. Fredersen again asks Josaphat why he did not learn of the maps from him, then fires him. After seeing his father's cold indifference toward the harsh conditions the laborers endure, Freder secretly rebels against him by deciding to aid the workers. Fredersen orders his spy, the mysterious Thin Man (Fritz Rasp, 1891-1976), to follow his son and report on his activities. Meanwhile, Freder enlists Josaphat's assistance, returning to the machine halls where he trades places with a worker. The worker makes his way to the surface but is seduced by the pleasures of the cabaret Yoshiwara, name after the famous red-light district in Edo, now present-day Tokyo, Japan.

Fredersen takes the maps to the strange inventor, C.A. Rotwang (Rudolf Klein-Rogge, 1885-1955), to discover their meaning. Rotwang had been in love with Hel, who left him to marry Fredersen but later died giving birth to Freder. Rotwang shows Fredersen a robot he has built to resurrect Hel; in turn, the maps show a network of catacombs beneath the Metropolis, so the two men investigate. They eavesdrop on a gathering of workers, including Freder. Maria addresses them, prophesying the arrival of a divine mediator who can unite the working and ruling classes. Freder believes he could fill the role, declaring his love for Maria. Fredersen orders Rotwang to give Maria's likeness to the robot–a kabalistic golem–so that it can ruin her reputation among the workers to prevent any rebellion. Fredersen is unaware Rotwang plans to use the robot to take over the Metropolis. Rotwang kidnaps Maria, transfers her likeness to the robot, sending her to Fredersen. Freder finds the two embracing and, believing it to be the real Maria, falls into a prolonged delirium.

Intercut with his hallucinations, the false Maria unleashes chaos throughout the Metropolis, driving men to murder and stirring dissent among the workers. During this sequence, the false Maria becomes Babylon the Great, also known as the Whore of Babylon. She performs a Rabelaisian dance, leaving the men drooling, unable to control their desires, lusting after her. Her racy act personifies Anita Berber (1899-1928), Weimar's high priestess of depravity.[167] Berber represented an artistic generation that defied all restraints, the wild hedonism, and the frenetic theatrics of Weimar Berlin. On the city's cabaret stages, Berber danced out bizarre erotic fantasias: spectacular displays, fueled by noxious concoctions of ether-and-chloroform, cognac, morphine injections, and a chic, pansexual disposition.[168]

Ultimately, the false Maria appears riding the horned beast of Revelation–the apocalyptic symbolism evident: the demiurgic Metropolis, like debauched Weimar Berlin, is a cauldron of sin, carrying the seeds of its destruction. Easter egg: the automaton, Hel, inspired C-3PO's appearance.

Freder recovers and returns to the catacombs. Finding the false Maria urging the workers to rebel and obliterate the machines, Freder accuses her of being an imposter. The workers follow the false Maria from their dwellings to the machine rooms, leaving their children behind. They destroy the Heart Machine, causing the workers' homes below to flood, destroying everything, conjuring the Flood of Noah, signifying rebirth–a new beginning. The real Maria, having escaped from Rotwang, rescues the children with Freder and Josaphat's help. Grot berates the celebrating workers for abandoning their children in the flooded city, explaining that they have a symbiotic relationship with the machines and destroying

---

167 Mel Gordon, *The Seven Addictions and Five Professions of Anita Berber: Weimar Berlin's Priestess of Depravity* (Port Townsend, WA: Feral House, 2006), *passim*.
168 Mel Gordon, *Voluptuous Panic: The Erotic World of Weimar* Berlin (Port Townsend, WA: Feral House, 2006), ix.

one destroys the other. Believing their children to be dead, the hysterical workers capture the false Maria; they accuse her of being a witch, so they burn her at the stake. Horrified, Freder watches not realizing the deception until the fire exposes her to be a robot.

Rotwang has become delusional; perceiving the real Maria as his lost Hel, he chases her to the roof of the cathedral, followed by Freder in hot pursuit. The two men fight with Fredersen and the workers watching from the street. Rotwang is pushed over the edge to his death, reminiscent of Frollo's death in *The Hunchback of Notre Dame* (1831). Like Rotwang, Frollo also sought to corrupt the sacred feminine, Esmeralda; comparatively, both Rotwang and Frollo are pushed from cathedral rooftops by righteous heroes: Freder and Quasimodo. With Maria moderating, Freder fulfills his role as mediator by linking the hands of Fredersen and Grot, bringing them together; the former's oppressive rule is over–a new age has dawned.

The title of this analysis, *Above and Below*, alludes to Hermes Trismegistus, the archetypal god of magic. A Gnostic-like wizard, Trismegistus is a combination of three gods: the Greek Hermes, the Roman Mercury, and the Egyptian Thoth; the deity is the purported author of the *Hermetica*. Inscribed upon the Emerald Tablet, also known as the *Tabula Smaragdina*, is the axiom *as above, so below*: macro and microcosmic harmonies interrelate. The Tablet is the key to alchemy, critical to Renaissance Cabala, and magic. Possessing omniscience, Hermes Trismegistus is a hierophant, becoming Morpheus in *The Matrix*, Gandalf the Grey (Ian McKellen) in *The Lord of the Rings*, Durden in *Fight Club*, and Obi-Wan in *Star Wars*. Trismegistus foretells the coming of Jesus Christ, just like Morpheus predicted the arrival of the One. The One supplies spiritual gnosis to humankind; Neo, imitating the Valentinian Christ, awakens the masses to their enslavement by the machines. When discussing Gnosticism, Hermes Trismegistus always turns up because the *Hermetica* integrates many of its mythologies. The conversations presented in the *Asclepius* anticipates sages restoring gnosis while rejecting mundane reality ("despise all material things"), prophesying the penetrating dialogs between Morpheus and Neo, Durden and the Narrator, defining Truman's plight.[169] *Metropolis*' above and below has little to do with astral magic;

---

169 *Hermetica: The Ancient Greek and Latin Writings Which Contain Religious or Philosophic Teachings Ascribed to Hermes Trismegistus*, ed. and trans. Walter Scott, 4 vols. (1924-1936; repr.,

instead, it denotes a synergy. The elitist world above cannot survive without the proletariat below, and vice versa. It is rich and poor, light and dark, wisdom and ignorance; alas, it is a duality, an interdependence, Mani's cosmological gloom.

The Demiurge casts a shadow upon Joh Fredersen, the Metropolis' godlike manipulator, the creator of matter, the progenitor of the lavish material world. Humans are no more than pawns, consigning Josaphat to the hellish underworld below over a slight. For his reality is spiritual ignorance, keeping the megalopolis orderly and operational is his godhead. Like an oppressive Jehovah, he has no problem allowing his son, Freder *qua* Adam Ha-Rishon, to remain ignorant and frolic wantonly in the pleasure gardens (Eden) with concubines. So long as he does not partake of the forbidden fruit, gaining knowledge and consciousness of the illusion. Everything is copacetic as long as everyone remains stupid, nothing more than rotating cogs in the grotesque machines below. However, the Valentinian serpent, Maria, sneaks into Fredersen's garden, awakening Freder to the desperate plight of the subterranean workers. Seeking only the truth, Freder discovers the world below, and armed with gnosis, rebels against his father's solipsistic vision. He explores the world of the workers who are more enlightened than their counterparts above. He attends a service deep down in the catacombs where Maria prophesies a Christlike mediator to deliver them from slavery. Her name, Maria, denotes Mary, the Virgin Mother of Christ, the savior, Valentinus' perfected illuminator. Children accompany Maria when she enters the garden, implanting on (or drawing from) the subconscious' countless representations of Madonna and Child (see Chapter XI) designating her divinity. To Freder, she is Sophia personified: the goddess seeking to unite the laborer with the aristocrat, to attain the syzygy with Freder-as-Christ, joining the head and the hand with the heart. Together, they will free humankind from its mechanized construct, which has imprisoned consciousness. They will liberate the workers from the machines, emancipating them from the Manichean darkness of matter, supplying gnosis, thereby freeing them from grips of the Demiurge's ferocious servant, Moloch. Easter egg: the

---

Boston: Shambala Publications, Inc., 1985-1993), *Asclepius* III, 1:335-337. See also Graham Hancock and Robert Bauvel, *Talisman: Sacred Cities, Secret Faith* (Canada: Doubleday Canada, 2004), 168.

word *metro* comes from the Greek word for *mother*; thus, Maria effuses Marian sacredness while embodying Sophia's enlightenment; ergo, she is a divine rebel, instigating insurrection against the demiurgic Fredersen, redeeming the city.[170]

But this Demiurge is practiced in the art of deception. First, he enlists his chief archon, the Thin Man, to tail Freder and discover his plans, then foil them. Gaunt, pale, dressed in black, and methodical, the Thin Man anticipates the operatives of *The Adjustment Bureau*, the Strangers of *Dark City* (1998), and the Agents of *The Matrix*. Next, he visits the reclusive inventor, Rotwang, a Simon Magus-like magician having unlocked the Kabbalah's secrets of golem making, constructing an android. Simon, often considered one of Gnosticism's godfathers, was a wonder-worker who became the prototypical heretic and black magician. He conjured a woman calling it Helen; Simon said he was God, and Helen was Sophia, his *thought of God*. Helen was untouched by matter yet, nevertheless, a sullied inmate of the material realm but indifferent to moral laws and physical limitations.[171]

Rotwang, a technocratic sorcerer and scientist, has employed Kabbalah and magical sigils to create a golem, akin to a Hermetic statue: a creature in human form artificially made by a magic act, through the use of mystical names. Kabbalah is the Hebrew mystery school: its most famous texts are the *Zohar* by Moses Leon (1240-1305), dating to 13th-century Spain, and the *Sefer Yetzirah*, dating back to perhaps 500 years earlier. The Kabbalah teaches God created the world through the *sefirot*: ten emanations from God. Between God's Light and the hylic reality are four worlds: *azilut*, *beriah*, *yezirah*, and *asiyyah*; the *sefirot* are active in all four worlds. The twenty-two paths connecting the *sefirot* were expressed by the Hebrew alphabet's letters, and it was believed the contemplation of these letters could lead to the divine. It was thought that becoming a creator on earth (the *Hermetica*'s creed), one could experience the mystical rapture of union with the godhead. The purpose of Kabbalah is to bring God down to man and to raise man to God. The social message of the Kabbalah was apocalyptic, prophesying a new harmonious age based on moral and spiritual regeneration.

---

170 Tobias Churton, *Aleister Crowley, the Beast in Berlin: Art, Sex, and Magick in the Weimar Republic* (Rochester, VT: Inner Traditions, 2014), 102.
171 Guiley, *Encyclopedia of Witches*, 318; Wilson, *Strange World*, 60.

Rotwang fuses magic with science–the Renaissance ideal–to create a female robot to serve him. His automaton, Hel, is a reinvention of Simon Magus' Helen, a mechanized Sophia, taking Maria's visage. To Rotwang, Hel is an uncorrupted *thought of God*, mirroring Friedrich Nietzsche's (1844-1900) *Übermensch*, placing the android above the moral law. Golem legends of the Middle Ages and Renaissance emerged from 3rd- and 4th-century tales of rabbis bringing clay to life. The stories are grounded on the idea that only sin separates humans from God; thus, a sinless being can generate life. This rabbinic magic influenced the alphabetical theurgy of Cabala or Christianized Kabbalah. The *Sefer Yetzirah* emphasizes alphabetic power, claiming God made the world from letters. If God can create from scripts, a person in accord with God can do the same, hence the golem. Most of these legends stick to the same storyline: the golem once brought to life, develops dangerous powers, turning against its master eventually.[172] Such is the case with Dr. Frankenstein and his Monster, and Gargamel and Smurfette–more on these later.

The sullen Rotwang, like all learned magicians, uses both black and white sorcery, evidenced by the two magical sigils at his residence: emblazoned on the wall behind his android is an inverted pentagram (black magic, the goat of the sabbath), and an upright pentagram (white magic, the sign of the Savior) decorates his front door. Inverted, it is the sign of the cloven hoof or the footprint of the Devil; the two points up symbolize Satan's horns attacking Heaven. Upright, the pentagram represents Pythagorean mysticism, the properties of the Great Magical Agent, the Blazing Star of Freemasonry, the five senses of man, the five elements of nature, and the five extremities of the human body; it is the most potent symbol of the magician, gnosis, the kabalistic keys of occultism.[173] His home recalls a house on Melantrichova Street in Prague, where the wandering alchemist and astrology Johann Faust (ca. 1466/80– ca. 1541) allegedly lived. After it was demolished, Mladota's Palace at the south end of Charles Square became known as Faust's House because of its association with wizardry and alchemy, especially when it was occupied by Rudolf II's (1552-1612) astrologer Jakub Krocinek. Little is known about him, but his two sons came to a bitter end: the youngest killed the eldest, apparently for alchemical

---

[172] Scholem, *Kabbalah*, 351-355; Wilson, *Secret Cinema*, 75.
[173] Levi, *Transcendental Magic*, 241.

treasure hidden in the house's walls, and ended up on the gallows. The notorious English alchemist Edward Kelley bought the house in 1591; over time, alchemical symbols were discovered beneath its plaster.

The symbolism of the two pentagrams implies Rotwang has unified opposites, fusing Ficino's white-natural magic with the Saturnian magic of Heinrich Cornelius Agrippa (1486-1535). He has merged light and dark, life with death, machine with woman, thereby discovering the Philosopher's Stone to accomplish the alchemical wedding. For Rotwang, sorcery is not about changing base metal into gold, but turning hard metal to soft flesh. Rotwang is transforming matter, not transcending it. He is cunning Paracelsus dwelling in dystopian modernity: he has created life, a robot, via biomechanical kabalistic sorcery, producing death and chaos. His magic foreshadows *Blade Runner*'s Eldon Tyrell (Joe Turkel) and *Halloween III*'s Conal Cochran, only Rotwang's golem embodies the legend of Pygmalion, differentiating his android from Tyrell's philosophical Nexus-6s and Cochran's mute drones.

In Ovid's (43 BCE–18 CE) narrative *Metamorphosis* (8 CE), Pygmalion is a Cypriot sculptor who shaped a woman out of ivory. According to Ovid, after seeing the Propoetides, he was no longer interested in women, so he carved a statue so beautiful and realistic that he fell in love with it. In time, Aphrodite's festival day came, and Pygmalion made offerings at the altar of the goddess. There, too scared to admit his desire, quietly wished for a bride who would be the living likeness of his ivory girl. When he returned home, he kissed his ivory idol, finding its lips felt warm. He kissed it again, discovering it had lost its hardness; Mandragoritis had granted Pygmalion's wish. Pygmalion married the ivory sculpture, which had changed to a woman because of Aphrodite's blessing. In Ovid's narrative, they had a daughter, Paphos, from whom the city's name originates. In mythology, the story has a happy ending: ironic idealism. Still, the romance also has a negative side: patriarchal narcissism and a penchant for the dead often found in stories inspired by the myth, like Nathaniel Hawthorne's (1804-1864) short story "The Birth Mark" (1843), his similar novella *Rappacinni's Daughter* (1844), and H.P. Lovecraft's *Herbert West: Reanimator* (1922).

The Stepford Wives (1975) is a dark version of the Pygmalion myth. Directed by Bryan Forbes (1926-2013) and based on the novel by Ira Levin (1929-2007), the movie is a reaction to the Women's Lib

Movement of the '70s. Men, weary of the unmanageable organicity of their wives, opt to have their spouses replaced by identical automatons, making them subservient sex toys. The story centers on Walter Eberhart (Peter Masterson, 1934-2018) and Johanna (Katherine Ross), a married couple who move from New York City to Stepford, Connecticut, a bucolic suburb. Though a housewife, Johnna is artistic, intelligent, and aware of women's rights issues. She is astonished by how most of the wives of the Stepford men are domestic slaves, interested only in cleaning the house and pleasing their husbands. Walter joins the local men's club–a secret society-styled cabal–learning the dark secret: the members have had their wives murdered, and are now enjoying artificial replacements. As the feminist (or anti-feminist) allegory continues, Johanna watches the remaining organic women of Stepford turn into vapid blends of '50s housewives and '70s porn stars. Notice her name, *Johanna* conjures the first name of *Metropolis*' Demiurge, Joh. She is not a demiurgic creator-manipulator by any sense; instead, her name evokes mechanical-nightmarish dysfunctionality, a theme ever-present in Forbes' film.[174]

When Johanna finally discovers the plot, it is too late. The members of the club have kidnaped her children. When she sneaks in to rescue them, her robot doppelganger kills her. The final scene portrays a Stepford supermarket in which complacent, smiling, busty wives move mindlessly up and down the aisles, shopping for their masters. The Johanna automaton appears sad, aware of its worthless utility, its empty fate. Like *Metropolis*, *The Stepford Wives* presents the Pygmalion motif emerging from a fear of the world being taken over by machines. From 1800 or so to the present, Westerners have witnessed the rise of the factory, the Industrial Revolution (1760-1840), widespread urbanization, breathtaking technological growth, the computer age, and the internet. With the rise of the machines, the possibility the world and its inhabitants becoming mechanized is real.[175]

Like Pygmalion, Rotwang seeks to construct the object of his affection. The automaton, Hel, was modeled after a flesh and blood woman bearing the same name. He loved her but lost her to his friend Fredersen; in turn, Hel died birthing his son, Freder. Both men, hollowed with mourning, project their emotions onto this machine. The robot embodies their devotion and

---
174 Wilson, *Melancholy Android*, 118.
175 Ibid.

regret, their lost beloved, and their hatred toward the cause of their pain. The mix of love and hate is revealed when they conspire to transform the appearance of Hel into Maria *qua* Sophia, the muse inciting the workers to question their mechanical existence. Rotwang and Fredersen hope to replace the peace-loving Maria with a mechanical one programmed to destroy and oppress. Thoroughly narcissistic, both men quickly reduce the simulacrum of their beloved to a subtle tool to quell vitality. They can only love machines–gears, wheels, and mechanisms–that won't upset their corpselike comfort. The clash between self-love–the desire for control–and self-hatred–yearning for death–ends badly for both melancholic tyrants. The real Maria, with the help of the heroic Freder, undoes their diabolical plans: Rotwang is cast down to his death, and Fredersen is exposed as the Demiurge, a false messiah, losing all his power.[176]

The robot Hel is named after the Old Norse goddess Hel, ruling in the underworld over the spirits of those who died ingloriously and those who broke oaths. In *Metropolis*, Hel is Hell, death, the underworld, the robotic-malignant obsession of Rotwang and Fredersen's sable souls. Hel anticipates *The Matrix Revolutions*' Club Hel, a hedonistic nightclub ruled by the Merovingian (Lambert Wilson). The Merovingian does many dealings with the Matrix's exiles: independent, rogue programs that have severed their allegiance, making them targets for deletion. Similarly, the club represents the nether regions; in Greek Mythology, Hades rules the abyss. The Merovingian parallels the dark god, and his club is his Tophet, wherein sexual deviances and forbidden pleasures are explored, suggesting the Second Circle of Dante's *Inferno* (*Divina Commedia*, 1308-1320). Inside the elevator that accesses the club, there is a brief shot of the red HELP button on the control panel. The *P* on the button has been scratched out, so it reads *HEL*. In 2017's *Thor: Ragnarok*, Cate Blanchett played Hela, a death goddess, and Hel analog.

Metropolis is also a political allegory, signifying class warfare: the bourgeoisie versus the proletariat of Karl Marx and Friedrich Engels. In the underground world, we see the workers toiling endlessly, their clash with the wealthy inevitable. In the aristocratic world above, we see the seeds of fascism, the total repression of contrasting ideologies and philosophies. We also observe the polarized way the fascists viewed women: as wholesome,

---

176 Ibid, 117

virginal, surrounded by children like Maria when she first appears in the garden, or vile temptresses reflected by the false Maria. Lang's film is like *The Wizard of Oz* because it's multilayered with symbolism. Not only is *Metropolis* gnostic, but also a microcosm of German socio-economic-political culture, from the end of World War I (1914-1918), sowing both Dadaism and National Socialism, well into World War II (1939-1945).

Aeons, Archons, and Tuning: The Fallen Strangers of Dark City

"As a man is, so he sees." – William Blake. *Dark City*, directed by Alex Proyas, is a noir murder mystery, and a postmodernist supernatural thriller all wrapped into one; to analyze this film, this author viewed both the Blu-ray Theatrical and Director's Cuts. Due to its illusory and mutable nature, the city (both the above and below) is a blend of German Expressionism and moribund futurama; think *Metropolis* meets *Nosferatu* meets *The Cabinet of Dr. Caligari* meets *Murders in the Rue Morgue* meets *Blade Runner*. However, the inhabits of this city dress like they were living in an urban cityscape of the '40s or '50s America. This paradox creates a time vortex, making it impossible to discern when the events of *Dark City* are occurring. This intentional ambiguity leaves the audience unsure of the reality they are witnessing. Like all good Gnostic films, *Dark City* draws on the Valentinian idea that visible reality is an illusion perpetrated by a demiurgic creator who, along with the archons, are hellbent on enslaving its inhabitants. It is also a Manichean struggle through matter to obtain gnosis. The protagonist must navigate false constructs and the Strangers' implements of darkness (ignorance, sleep, stasis), to receive light (en*light*enment, the sun, represented by Shell Beach) and consciousness. Dr. Daniel P. Schreber (Kiefer Sutherland) explains the film's Manichaeism, "They [the Strangers] control everything here, even the sun, that's why it's always dark. They can't stand the light."

John Murdoch (Rufus Sewell) awakens in a hotel bathtub, suffering from amnesia. The green bathroom summons the Overlook Hotel to the conscious mind; specifically, room 237: a chilling place where things are not what they seem. He receives a phone call from a frantic Dr. Schreber, urging him to leave the hotel to evade a group of men who are after him. Next to the bed, Murdoch discovers the corpse of a ritualistically murdered woman along with a bloody knife. He flees just as the Strangers arrive at the scene; they are a sickly group of pale bald men in black trench coats that make an insect-like clicking noise.

Following clues, Murdoch learns his name, discovering he has a wife named Emma (Jennifer Connelly), a nightclub singer. She croons wearing a green gown, linking her with Venus; she is a beautiful evening star performing in a world of darkness. He is also sought by Police Inspector Frank Bumstead (William Hurt) as a suspect in a series of murders committed around the city, though he cannot remember killing anybody. Pursued by the Strangers, Murdoch realizes he has psychokinesis, which the Strangers also possess, dubbed *tuning*: the ability to alter or create reality. He uses this power to elude them as he explores the anachronistic city, where nobody seems to realize it is always night. At midnight–the witching hour, the time of supernatural occurrences–he watches as everyone except himself fall asleep as the Strangers physically rearrange the city. They also manipulate people's identities and memories. Murdoch learns he is from a coastal town called Shell Beach: a resort familiar to everyone, though nobody knows how to get there. His attempts to go to Shell Beach are unsuccessful for varying reasons. Meanwhile, the Strangers inject one of their own, Mr. Hand (Richard O'Brien), with memories intended for Murdoch to predict his movements, so they can track him down. Murdoch is eventually caught by Inspector Bumstead, who acknowledges that Murdoch is most likely innocent, having misgivings about the unusual nature of the city. They confront Schreber, who explains the Strangers are parasitic extraterrestrials, or Eternals, having fallen into degradation; in fact, Mr. Hand tells Murdoch they use corpses as hosts. The Strangers, possessing a collective-hive mentality, are experimenting with humans to analyze their individuality, swapping their memories to study their souls in the hopes the observations will help them survive.

Schreber reveals Murdoch is an anomaly, awakening inadvertently when Schreber was imprinting his latest identity as a murderer. The three embark on finding Shell Beach, but it exists only as a poster on a wall at the city's edge. Frustrated, Murdoch and Bumstead break through the wall, revealing outer space. The men are confronted by the Strangers, including Mr. Hand, holding Emma hostage. In the ensuing fight, Bumstead and one

(Left) Dressed in black, tall, pale, and thin are the Strangers: a race of fallen beings manipulating humankind to study the immortal soul. The Strangers render people unconscious, so they can carry out their mind-altering experiments to keep themselves alive. (Right) The Strangers influenced *Buffy the Vampire Slayer*'s (1997-2003) Gentlemen in the episode "Hush" (airdate December 14, 1999). Like the Strangers, the Gentlemen prey on people while they are sleeping by stealing their voices, prohibiting them from screaming.

of the Strangers fall through the hole into space, revealing the city is a deep space habitat bounded by an unseen force field.

The Strangers bring Murdoch to their subterranean lair, forcing Schreber to imprint him with their collective memory, believing Murdoch to be the total culmination of their experiments. Schreber betrays them by inserting memories into Murdoch which artificially reestablish his childhood as years spent training and honing his tuning skills, and learning about the Strangers and their machine. Murdoch awakens, fully realizing his extraordinary abilities. He frees himself and battles the Strangers, defeating their leader Mr. Book (Ian Richardson, 1934-2007) in a psychokinetic fight high above the city. Although not Valentinus' Demiurge, Mr. Book instead evokes the omnipotent Abraxas, Basilides' chief archon. It is from the seven-lettered Abraxas we get the mystic word *abracadabra*, which enables metaphysical faculties, hence Mr. Book's superior supernatural talents.

After learning from Schreber that Emma has been re-imprinted and cannot return to her previous self, Murdoch exercises his newfound powers, amplified by the Strangers' machine. He creates Shell Beach by flooding the area within the force field with water, forming dunes and beaches. On his way to the resort, Murdoch encounters a dying Mr. Hand. He informs him they have been searching in the wrong place–the mind–to understand humanity, inferring it is to the heart they should've looked. Murdoch turns the habitat toward the star it had been turned away from, and the city experiences sunlight for the first time; the darkness of the Strangers vanquished, the light of gnosis shines freely.

He opens a door leading out of the city, stepping out to view the sunrise. Murdoch has brought light to the dark city, making him its Luciferian messiah. Beyond him is a pier, where he finds the woman he knew as Emma, now with new memories and a new identity, Anna (Connelly). Murdoch reintroduces himself as they walk to Shell Beach, beginning their relationship anew.

* * * * *

Of all the characters, only Murdoch and the Strangers can tune, suggesting the amnesiac man is also a Stranger. He is a failed creature who is different from his eerie brethren only through his apparent benevolence. Murdoch and the Strangers share perspectives and powers; moreover, they engage in the same quest for life and truth. In contrast to the other dramatis personae, they question the status quo, seeking to change it. They are hollowed, haunted, and hungry, aliens in their skins. Whether Murdoch constitutes an early, more innocent incarnation or a later, more powerful evolution of his jaded, decrepit siblings is unimportant. What matters is Murdoch and the Strangers are no different, guilty of the same sorts of psychic legerdemain, dark or light, it does not matter.[177]

Murdoch awakens in a bathtub filled with water, signifying baptism and thus rebirth, awakening not to another identity, but to gnosis: the revelation that empirical reality is an illusion. He finds himself in room 614, referencing John (his forename) 6:14 and the coming of a savior, "Then those men, when they had seen the miracle that Jesus did, said, this is of a truth that prophet that should come into the world." The room number designates Murdoch as the Gnostic Christ, the Valentinian illuminator, liberating humankind from the Strangers' schizophrenic stasis. The verse anticipates the *Nebuchadnezzar*'s nameplate, *Mark III No. 11*, identifying Neo as the Gnostic Christ when he is brought to the ship's bridge. *Mark III No. 11* references Mark 3:11, "And unclean spirits, when they saw him,

---

177 Wilson, *Secret Cinema*, 56.

fell down before him, and cried, saying, Thou art the Son of God." The verse designates Neo as a redeemer; thus, he will overcome the artificial Matrix and the Agents, paralleling Murdoch exposing the Strangers' artifice. Both Neo and Murdoch are messianic archetypes foiling deadly illusions. His surname, Murdoch, is *mur* or *mer*, the sea, and *doch or dock*, a port to unbounded waters; he arises naked and unknowing from his watery vessel–the tub–denoting rebirthing from matter to spirit, the Valentinian ideal. It further signifies the false births or rebirths concocted each midnight by the Strangers, enslaving humankind. But to Murdoch, it is the opposite, becoming an initiation into gnosis, allowing him to differentiate illusion from the truth, freeing him from bondage. His gnosis comes later, appropriately, at Neptune's Kingdom, advancing the watery-baptismal motif; here, Murdoch comes to believe Shell Beach is one of the Strangers' ersatz memories.

Waking in the hotel's bathroom, Murdoch notices a small wound on his forehead, denoting the Strangers' prefabricated memories, injected nightly between the eyes signifying third-eye vision: the ability to sense and hone invisible currents. Murdoch's accidental shattering of the fishbowl, and rescuing the fish, point to his battle with transparent barriers imposed by the Strangers, his efforts to destroy invisible walls and flow into wilder currents. The keys imitate his false existence–a fake home in which no one lives–and his potential to unlock the truth, the mystery of his life. Keys also represent a mystery, a task to be performed; in this instance, Murdoch's Christlike quest, and his mission to know himself.[178] The postcard of Shell Beach and Schreber's call point to the same tension: both are parts of the Strangers' illusions as well as calls to a bright, new world, and trustworthy messengers.[179] Murdoch's confusion over the *J.M.* initials on the suitcase signals his hunger to overcome his suspicion that he's living someone else's life. His hunch that he might not have murdered the woman foreshadows the paranoia that will grow throughout the film, his misgiving that the status quo is an oppressive plot, and his wild conjectures are open to the real. The spirals carved into the dead woman's body, the winding fingerprints, the mouse maze in Schreber's lab, and the clouds above the city gather this ignorance and gnosis: it is the labyrinth, the unending warren of city

---

178 Cirlot, *Dictionary*, 159.
179 Wilson, *Secret Cinema*, 53.

blocks; the spiral is the mandala of the soul, harmony in discord.[180] The spiral symbolizes fresh thoughts, a fiery awakening from the depths of the subconscious mind, the upward ascent of a new creation, growth, Murdoch, and the concrete jungle's inevitable rebirth.[181]

As the story unfolds, Murdoch successfully navigates this maze: he cultivates the ability to *tune*, battles the Strangers eventually defeating them, and, in the end, awakens the inhabitants of Dark City, transforming it into a Temple of Light; his role as the Gnostic Christ fulfilled. Murdoch, epitomizing his messianic persona, appears cruciform on a circular rack when captured by the Strangers during the climax. He is the Vitruvian Man–a perfected being–whose remarkable soul the Strangers intend to use to stave off death. Rather than imprinting the Strangers' collective memory, Schreber betrays them, injecting Murdoch with a Gnostic primer, uploading a liquidized software package featuring Schreber, and with seemingly legitimate childhood memories. As the memories unfold, Gnostic liberation occurs: Schreber tells Murdoch who he is: a savior with a special gift far superior to the Strangers' abilities, a man destined to liberate humankind from their endless stasis. Awake and armed with gnosis, Murdoch engages the Strangers in a tuning battle with him coming out victorious. Murdoch begins to envision a new cosmos, a world of light, not darkness. A world with lavish buildings, rich architecture, and inviting streets. He creates a world of light, including an oceanic vista with Shell Beach; it is no longer a bogus imprint but a beautiful mandala. Here, he meets Anna (formerly Emma), his ex-wife; having been re-imprinted by the Strangers, she doesn't know him or recognize him. However, they have a deep connection, their emotions having survived past their previous fake identities. The human soul and its favorite expression, love, have conquered the machine and its manifestations, unconsciousness, and hatred. Cognizant of his gnosis, Murdoch knows the nature of his birth: he is the savior sent to redeem the world, destroying the false construct. His third-eye is not an evil portal where false memories are injected; instead, it is mystical sight allowing him to tune and defeat the Strangers. Reborn with the occult vision, he is no longer the grasping goldfish, struggling for air. Rather, he is the liberator. His inner paradise–luminous Shell Beach–is now externalized; he has

---

180 Ibid.
181 Franz, "The Process of Individuation," 248-250; Cirlot, *Dictionary*, 290-291.

found what he thought to be lost: the key to his identity, the knowledge of his origin, and the immortality of the soul.[182] Put another way, Murdoch penetrates the Strangers' toxic bullshit, achieving gnosis, emancipating the city from their pernicious influence and counterfeit paradigm.

The Strangers, an ancient race with supernatural powers, are akin to the Aeons in *The Gospel of Truth,* a Valentinian text from the Nag Hammadi Library. According to the theatrical version's introductory voiceover, they are as "old as time itself," appearing to be alien-like insect creatures descending from some unknown immortal species, having fallen into ruination. Trapped in decaying human bodies, they try to fend off death by studying the vitality of the human soul. To accomplish this, the Strangers have corralled a large population of humans, manipulating them by erasing their memories, giving them new ones, in an artificial city hovering in space. The Strangers can do all this through their ability to *tune*: the ability to reshape reality, everything from walls, doors, people, even change the skyscrapers of the cityscape. Each night at midnight, the Strangers render

(Left) *Nosferatu*'s Count Orlock (Max Schreck) and *The Rocky Horror Picture Show*'s (1975) Riff Raff (right) inspired the physical appearance of the Strangers. Like the Strangers, Orlock and Riff Raff are thin, gaunt, dressing in black with an enigmatic-androgynous quality. Interestingly, Richard O'Brien, who played the Transylvanian, also played one of the Strangers, Mr. Hand.

---

182 Wilson, *Secret Cinema,* 55.

people unconscious and, via telepathy and the machinery below, alter the city's buildings. The people awake with new memories, believing this is the way things have always been, allowing the Strangers to study them from their underground lair, hoping to discover the soul's sublime numinosity. They hope that spirit will somehow survive the change, become aware of the new identity, revealing that a human is a whole beyond the sum of its parts. Into this gestalt, the soul, the Strangers intend to channel their disintegrating lives; they are mere fragmentations indicated by their superficial names: Mr. Book, Mr. Sleep (Satya Gumbert), Mr. Hand (Richard O'Brien), Mr. Rain (Nicolas Bell), and Mr. Wall (Bruce Spence).

Applying Gnosticism proper, the Strangers mirror Valentinus' Aeons while, in turn, embodying Manichaean darkness: pale, thin, and dressed in black, the Strangers have created a material prison through stupidity. An Aeon is one of the orders of spirits, or spheres of being, that emanated from the unknowable godhead (aka the Monad, Bythos), becoming attributes of the nature of the absolute, an essential element in the cosmology, developing around the central concept of Gnostic dualism: the conflict between matter and spirit. The Aeons attempted to interpret, objectify, know, behold, and name the Monad, which is impossible; instead, it is beyond objectification. According to *The Gospel of Truth*, the Monad is unknowable, unfathomable, beyond concept, representation, interpretation; it is infinite. From the Aeons' failed attempts came error, resulting in the fall of Sophia, the birth of the Demiurge, and ultimately the creation of our world. The fall is psychological: matter, along with its qualities, evil and ignorance, issues from mental error because all beings born into error's universe (our universe) come to consciousness unaware that what they take for awareness of their environment is forgetfulness of God. Each person reenacts the cosmic decline, mistaking ignorance for wisdom. However, like error itself, each individual–such as John Murdoch–is a glance away from freedom. This glance is gnosis, an intuition of these unnerving facts: to be puffed up with the understanding the hylic world–the Strangers' Dark City–is to suffer spiritual confusion; to founder in worldly unknowing is to thrive in spiritual knowledge. Such awareness would breed acute paranoia toward the establishment, a refusal to conform to conventions of material knowledge, like Murdoch, Truman Burbank, and John "Neo" Anderson. This awareness would necessitate a rebellion against traditional communication

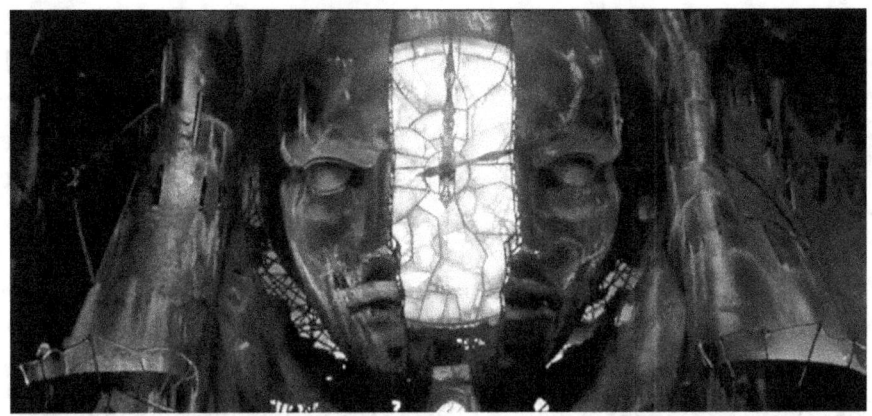

The Strangers use this giant clock to manipulate time, the cityscape, and the asphalt jungle's guinea pig inhabitants. Does the massive face, suggestive of the green-faced Oz, represent the Demiurge? This author will allow the reader to meditate on this mystery.

methods, an attempt to reverse semantic connections between words and concepts (see Lynch's *Eraserhead*, Chapter XII). It would inspire outlandish forms of expression: new symbols, new thoughts.[183] Valentinus attempts this rebellion against the status quo by overturning traditional Jewish and Christian theological concepts. He claimed the Judeo-Christian god is not omnipotent but an error, a botched craftsperson capable of making an insubstantial and illusory cosmos. He also claimed Jesus is not the son of the Judeo-Christian God but a messenger–a bearer of gnosis–from the Monad, the perfect Gnostic god beyond all earthly knowing. This Valentinian Christ becomes John Murdoch, rebelling against the Strangers, trying to liberate humankind from enslavement.

The Strangers imitate the Aeons because they believe the human soul to be finite, suitable for study and manipulation. Burdened with the erroneous idea that the soul can be commodified, the Strangers produce only gloom: sordid buildings and apathetic people. If they could escape their objectifying hermeneutic, they might transcend their bodily limitations. But they remain immured in their dream of reducing the soul to a scientific implement.[184]

The Strangers serve as the archons because they're the inimical rulers of the dismal city, a Skinnerian maze in which unwitting specimens are controlled for the benefit of a tyrannical minority. By way of tuning, the

---

[183] Wilson, *Strange World*, 34.
[184] Wilson, *Secret Cinema*, 51-52.

Strangers *qua* archons have reduced humankind to somnambulists, their divine spark extinguished, enslaved, unaware of their illusory reality. The Strangers are *The Evil* haunting the metropolis unseen, playing in its movie theaters endlessly to unwitting audiences. We never see the Demiurge; however, this author believes the expressionless face hiding the giant clock in the Strangers' sanctum is an image of their dark, fallen overlord.

Murdoch aside, the only person aware of the Strangers' agenda is Dr. Daniel P. Schreber. He is a human psychiatrist who can both manufacture and destroy memories. Forced by the Strangers, Schreber manipulates people's memories, making him privy to their schemes, and essential to their plots. The Strangers nightly observe the mental interiors of the city's inhabitants, then see how they react to their new imprinted memories, trying to divine the soul. Although he is a slave, he is also a master who can change the experiments to the benefit of his race. Entrapped and free, he is poised to play Sophia or Christ, acting out of love for his fellow man, paying allegiance to both matter and spirit.[185] While pretending to be loyal to the Strangers-as-archons (matter), he secretly toils to reveal the city's occult secrets to Murdoch, the Valentinian illuminator (spirit). Schreber chooses Murdoch because, contrasting the other inhabitants of the city, he is often immune to tuning and can tune himself. Recognizing in Murdoch a potential challenger to the Strangers, Schreber spends most of the film trying to locate him.

Dr. Daniel Paul Schreber is named after the German judge Daniel Paul Schreber (1842-1911), who suffered from what was then diagnosed as *dementia praecox* later known as paranoid schizophrenia. He described his second mental illness (1893-1902), also making a brief reference to the first disorder (1884-1885) in his book *Memoirs of My Nervous Illness* (1903). *Memoirs* became an influential book in the history of psychiatry and psychoanalysis thanks to its interpretation by Freud. The significance of *Schreber* is threefold. First, Schreber, although a man, thought God was turning him into a woman mirroring the cinematic Schreber's role as either female or male, Sophia or Christ, a paradigm he embraces (*vide supra*). Second, the Strangers force the historical Schreber's schizophrenia onto an unwitting populace when they, aided by Schreber, imprint different memories, forcing humankind to live fractured lives, ignorant of prior

---
185 Ibid, 52.

recollections hence unable to connect with reality. Third, part of Schreber's weird cosmology was *nerves*, which compromised both the human soul and the nature of God concerning humanity. Each human soul was composed of nerves derived from God who, with his nerves, was the ultimate source of human existence; this idea mirrors the Strangers' interest in the soul as a way to construe the godhead, thereby avoiding death.

Inspector Frank Bumstead's surname pays tribute to Lloyd Henry "Bummy" Bumstead (1915-2006), an American cinematic art director and production designer. In a career that spanned over fifty-five years, he won two Academy Awards: the first for *To Kill a Mockingbird* (1962), and the second for *The Sting* (1973). He also was nominated for Hitchcock's *Vertigo* and Clint Eastwood's *Unforgiven* (1992). His name evokes the expert craftsmanship found in *Dark City*'s sets and grim production design; it is the film's somber cityscape and the mysterious underground lair of the Strangers. When he is introduced, the tune Inspector Bumstead plays on his accordion is a song written in 1939 by a Polish-Jewish composer Jerzy Petersburski (1895-1979), which was initially called "*Mala blekitna chusteczka*" or "Little Blue Handkerchief." The lyrics were later translated (with slight differences) to many languages, becoming especially popular in the WWII Soviet era under the title "*Siniy Platochek*" or "Blue Scarf." The song lyrics are about an unhappy, lonely man who wanders around the world, thinking about his lost love, who is gone forever. His only memento of his beloved one is the blue handkerchief from the title. Since *Dark City* is all about memories, the song harmonizes both Murdoch's quest and the Strangers' agenda.

In an intricate piece of paradoxical casting, Colin Friels plays the role of Detective Eddie Walenski, Bumstead's former partner. Walenski is convinced he has discovered the city's dark secret, driving him insane. He kills himself by diving in front of a speeding subway train, becoming a victim of the Strangers' sinister manipulations. In a cinematic twist, Friels portrayed Louis Strack Jr. in *Darkman* (1990)–notice the similarities of the two movies' names, *Dark City* and *Darkman*. Strack is a nebulous manipulator, employing sadistic crime lord Robert G. Durant (Larry Drake, 1950-2016) to pull strings, destroying the lives of the protagonist Dr. Peyton Westlake (Liam Neeson), and his girlfriend Julie Hastings (Frances McDormand). Corrupt and ruthless, Strack runs the eponymous Strack Industries. He is a monstrous-billionaire real-estate developer erecting a dark city, dubbing it "the City of the Future," eliminating all those that stand in his way, including his wife. Strack builds his city using blood and terror as brick and mortar, anticipating the evil of the Strangers' gloomy city, which will eventually consume Walenski, claiming his life. The casting of Friels generates an incongruity: Friels' character, Strack, murders to build a dark city; later, Friels' character, Walenski, takes his life, becoming a victim of the metropolis. Friels-as-Strack cares only about material wealth, matter, doing whatever it takes to create his prodigious megalopolis. Friels-as-Walenski is a morose Valentinian, struggling to discover consciousness, gnosis, thus transcending matter, freeing the soul from the confines of the Strangers' tenebrous city *qua* prison.

Although Connelly's characters Emma and Anna are not Sophia, her performance nevertheless offers occult insight. The sine qua non of the Gothic genre is an irreducible ambiguity; for instance, is the specter real or imaginary? Is the monster supernatural or human? Is the old mansion haunted, or is there a rational explanation? Kubrick's *The Shining* presents a similar parallel: is the Overlook possessed by evil spirits, or are the phantoms psychic projections? From the Gothic genre comes its first cousin, noir: the dark, criminal underworld of the unrelenting metropolis. Like many Gnostic movies, there is a Gothic-noir ambiance to *Dark City*, signified by a sultry chanteuse performing in a dark nightclub, or an elegant lounge. Emma sings "Sway" (1953) and "The Night Has a Thousand Eyes" (1962), the second song sums up the Strangers, the menacing, watchful caretakers of the nocturnal city. We see this element in other Gnostic films such as *Mulholland Drive*, *Blue Velvet*, *The Matrix*–a techno nightclub is Trinity's hangout–and *The Thirteenth Floor*–a lavish 1937 Los Angeles jazz club. It's a mysterious, seedy, crime-ridden Dashiell Hammett-Mickey Spillane[186] world wherein it is impossible to tell friend from foe, producing an analogous irreducible ambiguity with a ghostly atmosphere. When it comes to appearances, a Kantian epistemological crisis emerges: things exist, but their nature is unknowable.

February 27, 1998, saw the release of *Dark City*; thirteen months later, another Gnostic masterpiece was released, *The Matrix*, on March 31, 1999. The movies' similarities are apparent: both feature Gnostic-Christ

---

[186] Famous American hard-boiled crime novelists. Hammett: born 1894, died: 1961. Spillane: born: 1918, died: 2006.

saviors and illusory realities controlled by the archons. From one Gnostic film to another, some of the set pieces from *Dark City*, including the hotel's winding staircase, and those used for the rooftop chase, were sold to the production of *The Matrix* at the end of *Dark City*'s filming, further linking both films. But the influence of Proyas' movie goes beyond *The Matrix*. One sees *Dark City*'s dystopian fingerprints on Christopher Nolan's *Memento* (2001) and *Inception* (2010), as well as movies like *The Thirteenth Floor* (1999), *Minority Report* (2002), and *Equilibrium* (2002). These Gnostic movies, along with *The Truman Show*, *Fight Club*, *eXistenZ* (1999), and *Vanilla Sky* (2001), validate Jungian synchronicity. They were all released at the end of the last millennium and the start of the new one, making this period the apex of Gnostic cinema. These films wave goodbye to Piscean Age while welcoming the Aquarian Age; that is, these movies herald consciousness, gnosis, begging the viewer, like their protagonists, to *know thyself*.

Mad World: Donnie Darko and the Robert W. Sullivan IV Connection

Add to that apogee *Donnie Darko* (2001), a film that questions fatalism, or does it? Before I begin this section, the reader must understand that the first time I watched this movie was on January 2, 2019, despite being badgered by my friends over the years. Everyone told me I'd love it, but for some reason, I just never got around to viewing it, and it became one of my favorite movies instantly. There is a strange nexus between this film and myself (or my life), so the reader needs to know this movie did not influence me. Again, before January '19, I'd never seen it, so I knew nothing about it.

Furthermore, the film centers on time travel, one of my favorite subjects. In truth, I watched this movie in disbelief, my jaw on the floor, not quite believing what I was seeing. Coincidence, time travel, a sign of things to come? Who knows, only time will tell. And rest assured, I am not crazy. I will detail this special connection as this portion of the book unfolds, and you'll start understanding where I am coming from, learning cinema can run parallel with reality.

The pessimistic movie, written and directed by Richard Kelly, follows the adventures of the troubled title character as he seeks the meaning behind his doomsday-related visions. The film received a limited theatrical release, debuting on October 26, 2001, four days before my 30th birthday on October 30. However, due to its advertising featuring a crashing plane, and with the 9/11 attacks transpiring a month earlier, it was scarcely advertised. It has subsequently developed a cult following.

The movie takes in October 1988, so to capture that MTV '80s vibe, we see Drew Barrymore in a supporting role. Barrymore's presence conjures her performance in one of the ultimate '80s films, *E.T. the Extraterrestrial*. Then we see Patrick Swayze (1952-2009) in the role of Jim Cunningham, a bogus Tony Robbins-like motivational speaker preaching from the mountaintop, only Cunningham is an utter scumbag: he is a huckster Christ, a fraud, and a pedophile. Swayze's appearance resurrects his cheesy '80s films such as *Red Dawn* (1984), *Dirty Dancing* (1987), and *Road House* (1989); the incorporation of these '80s icons generates a reality within a reality, setting it in the '80s *twice*. Thus, Barrymore and Swayze's casting effuse the Latin axiom, *entitas ipsa involvit aptitudinem ad extorquendum certum assensum*, which is the heart and soul of *Donnie Darko*.

On October 2, 1988, troubled teenager Donald "Donnie" Darko (Jake Gyllenhaal) awakens, beckoned outside by a mysterious voice. It is midnight, the witching or the Devil's Hour, the time of mystical events. "The Star-Spangled Banner" (1814) seeps through the TV static; it is a transmission from the 1950s, signifying a corruption of the spacetime continuum, indicating the creation of the Tangent Universe. This corruption seems to be caused by a demiurgic Deus Ex Machina: a hidden biomechanical puppet master mentioned a few times during the film.[187]

Once outdoors, he encounters a figure wearing a monstrous rabbit costume. The rabbit introduces himself as Frank (James Duval), telling Donnie the world will end in 28 days, 6 hours, 42 minutes and 12 seconds. The sum of these added numbers is 88–more on this later. The date of the Apocalypse is October 30, which is, as I just indicated, this author's birthday. Point of fact: October 30, 1988, was this author's 17th birthday– add one plus seven to get 8, a number transcending this film. The next morning, Donnie wakes up on the green of a local golf course, having been

---

187 Donnie mumbles "Deus ex Machina" while fighting Seth, and, in the Directors Cut, Karen mentions it in a classroom lecture. Based on the director's commentary, I think Kelly confuses Deus Ex Machina with the demiurge.

Donnie Darko's spirit guide, or animal, is Frank the Rabbit: a Gnostic-nihilistic escort, exposing Donnie to alternative realities and modes of thinking, encouraging him to destroy formal institutions. By annihilating their dogmas, Donnie wages war against the Demiurge and the archons.

dreaming and sleepwalking. He returns home to discover a jet engine has crashed into his bedroom. His older sister Elizabeth (Maggie Gyllenhaal), tells him the FAA investigators do not know its origin. The engine has a noticeable spiral which, for groundcrew safety, is common; however, one cannot help but think of the spirals from *Dark City* and their related symbolism: spiritual *ascensio*, gnosis. Contextually, a spiral also conjures the Fibonacci Sequence, which is based on rabbits' mating habits.

Over the next several days, Donnie continues to have visions of Frank, and his parents Eddie (Holmes Osborne) and Rose (Mary McDonnell) become increasingly worried. Donnie's psychotherapist, Dr. Lilian Thurman (Katherine Ross), believes Donnie is detached from reality, and his visions of Frank are "daylight hallucinations," symptomatic of paranoid schizophrenia. Frank asks Donnie about time travel, prompting Donnie, in turn, to ask his science teacher, Dr. Kenneth Monnitoff (Noah Wyle), about the subject. Monnitoff gives Donnie a copy of the book, *The Philosophy of Time Travel*, written by Roberta Sparrow (Patience Cleveland, 1931-2004). Sparrow, a former science teacher, is now a senile old woman nicknamed *Grandma Death* living outside of town.

Interestingly, Roberta Sparrow, an eccentric professor, has the same initials as the author of this book, *RS*. Donnie also starts seeing Gretchen Ross (Jena Malone), who has recently moved into town with her mother under a new identity to escape her violent stepfather. Easter egg: Grandma Death is one hundred and one years old, which alludes to another Gnostic-alternative reality film, *The Matrix*. One hundred and one is *101*, binary for five, but computers count zero as one making it six; hence, Zion is about to be destroyed for the sixth time. One can reasonably assume the Primary Universe has been destroyed five times before, making the events of the film the sixth tangential universe.

Frank begins to influence Donnie's actions, instructing him to flood his high school by breaking a water main. Gym teacher Kitty Farmer (Beth Grant) attributes the act of vandalism to the influence of the short story "The Destructors" (1954), by Graham Greene (1904-1991), assigned by dedicated English teacher Karen Pomeroy (Drew Barrymore). Kitty begins teaching attitude lessons, borrowed from the local motivational speaker Jim Cunningham, but Donnie rebels against these, leading to friction between Kitty and Rose. Kitty arranges for Cunningham to speak at a school assembly, during which Donnie insults him. He later finds Cunningham's wallet with his address, so Frank suggests setting his house on fire. Firefighters discover a kiddie-porn dungeon inside his home, so the police arrest Cunningham. Kitty, wishing to testify in his defense, asks Rose to chaperone their daughters' dance troupe–Sparkle Motion–on its trip to Los Angeles where they are scheduled to appear on Ed McMahon's (1923-2009) *Star Search*.

With Rose and little sister Samantha (Daveigh Chase) in Los Angeles, and their father, Eddie (Holmes Osborne) away for business, Donnie and Elizabeth throw a Halloween costume party to celebrate her acceptance to Harvard. At the bacchanalia, Gretchen arrives distraught because her mother has gone missing, leading to her and Donnie having sex for the first time. When Donnie realizes Frank's prophecy about the end of the world is about to come to pass, he takes Gretchen and two other friends to see Sparrow. Instead of Sparrow, they find two high school bullies, Seth (Alex Greenwald) and Ricky (Seth Rogan), trying to rob the former teacher's home. Donnie, Seth, and Ricky get into a fight in the road, just as Sparrow returns home. An oncoming car swerves to avoid Sparrow, running over

Gretchen, killing her. The driver turns out to be Elizabeth's boyfriend, Frank Anderson, wearing the same rabbit costume from Donnie's visions. Donnie shoots Frank in the eye with his father's gun, then walks home carrying Gretchen's body.

Donnie returns home; "The Star-Spangled Banner" seeps through the TV static; it is a transmission from the 1950s, signaling a corruption of the spacetime continuum, indicating the termination of the Tangent Universe. A time vortex *qua* wormhole forms over his house. He takes one of his parents' cars, loads Gretchen's body into it, driving to a nearby ridge overlooking the town. There, he watches the plane carrying Rose and the dance troupe home from Los Angeles get caught in the vortex's wake, which violently rips off one of its engines, sending it back in time. Events from the previous 28 days unwind. Donnie wakes in his bedroom and recognizes the date is October 2, laughing ironically as the jet engine crashes through the roof, crushing him. Around town, those whose lives Donnie would have touched wake up from troubled dreams. As the jet engine is hauled off, Gretchen rides her bicycle by the Darko home the next morning, learning of Donnie's death. Gretchen and Rose exchange a glance and a wave, like they know each other but cannot remember from where.

"I don't think that you have a clue what it's like to communicate with these kids. We are losing them to apathy, to this prescribed nonsense. They are slipping away." – Karen Pomeroy. *Donnie Darko*'s Gnosticism is twofold. First, it is about questioning absolutes: moral, religious, and educational powers and constructs. Frank the Rabbit, Donnie's daemon or spirit guide, encourages him to commit vandalism against oppressive institutions. He breaks the water main in his high school, driving the ax through the statue of the Mongrel, a giant dog, the school's mascot. Later, Donnie circuitously exposes the school's rigid gym teacher Kitty as a moral coward. She is more interested in defending Cunningham, consciously denying his horrors, than the welfare of Sparkle Motion (she is a pageant mother), even though her daughter Beth (Tiler Peck) is a member.

Frank also instructs Donnie to burn Cunningham's house to the ground, disclosing his pedophilia. Cunningham personifies the dogmatic Christian Church; his name, **J**im **C**unningham, is *JC* for **J**esus **C**hrist. Blonde haired and blued eyed, the rising sun introduces him, signifying his Neoplatonic divinity. He believes himself to be a messianic figure, saving humankind from their fear, delivering them to love. But he is a false prophet; giving his sermon on the mount at the school, helping the kids overcome their anxieties, Donnie cross-examines him. Cunningham can't supply wisdom because Donnie asks the one question he can't answer: "How much money are they paying you to be here?" This scene reminds this author of *The Morton Downey Jr. Show* (1987-1989), a televised three-ring circus, encouraging people to go the Loudmouths to vent, trade insults, turning the show into a pablum-puking shouting match. The show reached its popularity in October '88, the same timeframe the film takes place. During their confrontation, Donnie exposes Cunningham's narrow dogma as hokey and fake because it pigeonholes life's experiences into two pedestrian categories: love and fear. Cunningham is only interested in hocking self-help videos and books, revealing he is nothing more than an imposter.

Two clues reveal Cunningham's pedophilia: he introduces the all-girl dance ensemble Sparkle Motion, evoking the pre-pubescent beauty pageants of JonBenét Ramsey (1990-1996), heavily criticized by parents and the media for attracting child pornographers. Then there's Elizabeth, who's Halloween costume is Vivian Darkbloom (Marianne Stone, 1922-2009) from Kubrick's *Lolita*. Both the film and novel are about a middle-aged man sexually attracted to a 12-yead-old girl, alluding to Cunningham's unnatural interest in children. The antichristian symbolism continues at the Aero Movie Theater, which is showing a double feature: *The Evil Dead* (1981) and *The Last Temptation of Christ* (1988), arguably two of the most controversial films of the 1980s. By showing a movie about Christ (albeit a humanistic Jesus) along with a film about horrific demons equates Christianity to a form of self-destructive mindless possession; remember, Donnie calls Cunningham the Antichrist while at school. The moral of *Donnie Darko* is not to rely on religious or educational institutions when searching for truth and God and to beware of strict orthodoxy because all may not be what it seems. Easter egg: the school's totem, the Mongrel, is an '80s reference to Shermer High School, where the characters in *The Breakfast Club* (1985) served their detention on March 24, 1984. Shermer's sports teams are referred to as Bulldogs because the canine is the school's mascot. Easter egg: The last fifteen minutes of *The Last Temptation of Christ* is about Jesus living in a tangential universe, just like the events of *Donnie Darko*.

From a Darkbloom to a Darko. (Left) At the Halloween party, Elizabeth costumes herself as Vivian Darkbloom from Kubrick's *Lolita*. (Right) Vivian Darkbloom hangs around with Clare Quilty, portrayed by Freemason Peter Sellers (1925-1980). The name Vivian Darkbloom is an anagram for the author of *Lolita*, Vladimir Nabokov (1899-1977).

Second, Kelly's film features an alternative reality, a virtual universe, a staple within Gnostic theology. Frank hints to Donnie that several temporal planes are existing simultaneously, following a predetermined logic. Donnie sleepwalks onto the golf course when, on October 2, the jet engine crashes into his bedroom; he is not there, but senses he should have been, that he should have died. This incident creates two parallel timelines or dimensions. By October 30, his girlfriend has died, and his mother and younger sister face certain death aboard the flight when it loses its engine; Donnie realizes the mundane reality in which he exists can be reversed. If he can transcend his matrix of time through a portal between temporalities, then he can move freely about the construct, reshaping the fated patterns. With his dead girlfriend by his side and his mother and little sister's plane about to go down, Donnie returns to the night he first encountered Frank, October 2. This time, he remains in his room, dying when the jet engine comes crashing down, becoming Christlike, sacrificing himself so others may live. His death changes the temporal fabric–his girlfriend, mother, and younger sister will escape death–altering those who knew him on the timeline he just erased. Now, Gretchen will never meet him, but she nevertheless feels a connection to Donnie's family when she is bicycling past his home, waving at Rose, who waves back; they seem to know each other only they are not sure how. This interaction suggests Donnie's reality involved a power to compel sure assent, which, for him, is to manipulate the spacetime continuum. Donnie's spirit now moves among temporalities, awakening prepared souls to the superficiality of time. Kelly's film places alert viewers in the same position as Gretchen–suspecting that temporal events are fabricated possibilities that can be altered from the perspective of other fabricated histories. It calls attention to its artificial temporality by embodying two opposing narratives simultaneously. Like a hypertext, the film concurrently runs the story of the Donnie, who survives the falling engine, and the Donnie killed by the same engine. One narrative cancels the other, leaving the viewer in doubt as to which series of events is valid. It further highlights its fabricated nature through its casting. Featuring Katherine Ross as Donnie's psychotherapist, the movie construes itself a remake of *The Graduate* (1967), an iconic study of a young man's confusion over the conventions of his culture, wherein Ross played Elaine Robinson, the eventual love interest of Benjamin Braddock (Dustin Hoffman). By casting Swayze as the corrupt motivational speaker, the film presents itself as a version of *Dirty Dancing*, an equally iconic analysis of early '60s disaffected youths.[188] In parodying and embracing these films, *Donnie Darko* portrays itself as repetitious, suggesting the events may have happened before.

In navigating these two extreme conditions, Donnie experiences a spiritual awakening. While his classmates decline into apathy, conformity, and cruelty, Donnie cultivates intellectual curiosity, compassion for outcasts, and disdain for puritanical powers, indicating his gnosis.[189]

In the Director's Cut (2004), we read some of the pages from Sparrow's book, *The Philosophy of Time Travel*, explaining how these two dimensions are formed, intertwined, and corrected. In Chapter One, she explains, "Incidents when the fabric of the fourth dimension becomes corrupted are incredibly rare. If a Tangent Universe occurs, it will be highly unstable, sustaining itself for no longer than several weeks. Eventually it will collapse upon itself, forming a black hole within the Primary Universe capable of destroying all existence."

In Chapter Two, we learn, "Water and Metal are the key elements of Time Travel. Water is the barrier element for the construction of Time Portals used as gateways between Universes as the Tangent Vortex." Next,

---

[188] Wilson, *Secret Cinema*, 60.
[189] Ibid.

in Chapter Four, Sparrow explains, "When a Tangent Universe occurs, those living nearest to the Vortex, will find themselves at the epicenter of a dangerous new world. Artifacts provide the first sign that a Tangent Universe has occurred. If an Artifact occurs, the Living will retrieve it with great interest and curiosity. Artifacts are formed from metal, such as an Arrowhead from an ancient Mayan civilization, or a Metal Sword from Medieval Europe."

She continues to philosophize; in Chapter Seven, she writes: "…which is to assist the Living Receiver in returning the Artifact to the Primary Universe. The Manipulated Living will do anything to save themselves from Oblivion." In Chapter Eight, we read, "The Living Receiver is chosen to guide the Artifact into position for its journey back to the Primary Universe. No one knows how or why a Receiver will be chosen. The Living Receiver is often blessed with a Fourth Dimensional Powers. These include increased strength, telekinesis, mind control, and the ability to conjure fire and water. The Living Receiver is often tormented by terrifying dreams, visions and auditory hallucinations during his time within the Tangent Universe." In Chapter Nine, she theorizes: "The Manipulated Dead will set an Ensurance Trap. The Living Receiver must ensure the fate of all mankind." And finally, Chapter Twelve concludes with: "When the Manipulated awaken from their Journey into the Tangent Universe, they are often haunted by the experience in their dreams. Many of them will not remember. Those who do remember the Journey are often overcome with profound remorse for the regretful actions buried within their Dreams."

The jet engine is an Artifact, making Donnie the Living Receiver. Donnie is the person most affected by the metal Artifact; hence, he is the center of the Tangent Universe (created when he sleepwalked outside to heed Frank), becoming the only one who can close it. Donnie has twenty-eight days to return the Artifact to the Primary Universe. If the Ensurance Trap is successful, the Living Receiver has no choice but to use his Fourth Dimensional Power to send the Artifact back in time to the Primary Universe before the wormhole collapses upon itself. Donnie must create a paradox by dispatching the engine back in time through a wormhole, to prevent the other incongruity, a second jet engine spiraling downward in the Tangent Universe.

Frank the Rabbit is the Manipulated Dead. If a person dies within the Tangent Universe, he or she can contact the Living Receiver through the Fourth Dimensional Construct made of water; hence, the liquid spears protruding from the characters' chests. One of these spears leads Donnie to the gun he'll use to murder Frank in the Tangent Universe, transforming him into the Manipulated Dead. Consequently, Frank sets an Ensurance Trap for the Living Receiver, guaranteeing the Artifact will be returned safely to the Primary Universe. Returning the Artifact is the focal point in the paradox because, as the Tangent Universe winds down, a wormhole, or a tear or hole in spacetime, appears. It is now that Donnie must guide the jet engine out of the Tangent Universe, as we see, successfully preventing the paradox for the first time. Otherwise, the Tangent is destroyed, resets, and recycles. As the story unfolds, it becomes evident this temporal loop has repeated several times–more on this later.

With the restoration of the Primary Universe, the Manipulated Living awaken, tormented by the dreams *qua* events they've experienced. The song "Mad World" hauntingly signals their profound remorse.[190] The tune lyricizes: "♪ The dreams in which I'm dying / Are the best I've ever had, ♪" alluding to Donnie's plight in the Tangent Universe, and his ultimate sacrifice to restore the Primary Universe. Notice in the final montage sequence, Karen Pomeroy is the only one remaining asleep, perhaps suggesting she will become a Living Receiver sometime in the future.

The movie documents Donnie's successful quest to break the cycle, similar to Phil (Bill Murray) in *Groundhog Day* (1993). When the engine from the October 30 Primary Universe drops into the past, it erases itself, creating the Tangent Universe. Similarly, when the engine in the October 30 Tangent Universe falls–when the Living Receiver/Donnie Darker returns it–the Tangent Universe collapses, and the Primary Universe is reset, at the point we see at the beginning. This paradigm is the loop, continuing until the engine does not drop in the Tangent Universe because it is sent back to the Primary Universe by Donnie. Ending this time-loop is how he saves his girlfriend, mother, younger sister, and the universe.

To delineate these two differing realities, we see subtle repetition, reminiscent of Betty Elms and Diane Selwin's dream-versus-reality construct in another movie released that same year, Lynch's *Mulholland*

---

[190] Originally performed by Tears for Fears, 1982.

Drive. For instance, during the prologue, along the winding-scenic road, Donnie wakes and smiles cynically at something, intuitively anticipating that this is where he will send the engine back in time to October 2, healing the Primary Universe. Afterward, when Donnie is bicycling home, Frank Anderson (Elizabeth's boyfriend, later Frank the Rabbit) red Trans Am passes him. Once Donnie restores the Primary Universe, returning to October 2, we hear Frank's car honk its horn a couple of times after dropping Elizabeth off at home, right before the engine crashes into Donnie's house. Remember, Frank's car never honks in the Tangent Universe because Donnie is on the golf course with Frank the Rabbit as the engine crashes into his bedroom. Later, Frank will be driving the car, killing Gretchen, prompting Donnie to shoot him. Frank's Pontiac Trans Am displays a Phoenix on its hood. The Phoenix is a mythological bird that consumes itself by fire only to resurrect from its ashes, foreshadowing Donnie's death that will revive his mother, sister, Gretchen, and the Primary Universe. In alchemy, the Phoenix symbolizes transmogrification, demonstrating the cycle of death and rebirth.

In Karen's classroom, when discussing Greene's story, Donnie remarks: "Well, they say right when they flood the house and tear it to shreds that, like, destruction is a form of creation, so the fact that they burn the money is ironic. They just want to see what happens when they tear the world apart. They wanna change things." The Primary Universe is temporarily annihilated, perpetuating a time-loop in the Tangent Universe. It is a form of destruction because the two universes cannot coexist; leaving one generates the other. Only after the Tangent Universe's abandonment is the Primary Universe restored, returning the timeline to normal. A mezzotint of M.C. Escher's *Eye* (1946) decorates Donnie's bedroom wall; later, Donnie sees Frank the Rabbit in his bathroom's mirror and stabs his eye repeatedly, turning the mirror to liquid, becoming a portent. Seated in the movie theater, Frank removes his mask, revealing his mutilated eye; Donnie will put a bullet through his eyeball later. This sequence explains how Frank became the Manipulated Dead: he was killed in the Tangent Universe, thus able to communicate with Donnie, setting the Ensurance Trap. In other words, Frank is a *reversed ghost*. Easter egg: When Donnie and Gretchen present the Infant Memory Generators (IMGs), Seth makes a stabbing motion, imitating Norman Bates. Seth's antics evoke Donnie's, specifically, when he knifed Frank in the eye in the bathroom. This repetition is further evidence of worlds colliding. One cannot help think *Donnie Darko* anticipated the Mandela Effect: we now have differing memories of past events, occurrences that did or did not happen, implying another dimension is bleeding through, corrupting our reality.

Donnie successfully returns the jet engine, resulting in his death but restoring the Primary Universe. People wake from their slumber, including Frank; he is designing his Halloween costume–a monstrous rabbit–rubbing his right eye because it is residual from the Tangent Universe. Earlier, Rose Darko was reading Stephen King's *It* (1986). In the novel, a clown terrorizes children in a small town. After Gretchen's death, there is a brief encounter between Donnie and a clown. Donnie tells Dr. Thurman about his dead dog Callie. Later, he holds a stuffed toy dog in her office. In his house, Cunningham has deer taxidermy; Kitty, his chief acolyte, has a deer painting in her bedroom. The animal motif continues: when Kitty plays Cunningham's motivation tape to the class, one hears a neigh not once but twice. There is an owl lamp in Donnie's bedroom and an owl magnet on the Darkos' refrigerator door. The owl is a totem of occult insight; ergo, Donnie perceives reality differently, enabling him to alter it. Donnie has a Led Zeppelin *Swan Song* poster on his bedroom's ceiling, depicting an Icarian-Luciferian fallen angel. Cherita Chen's (Jolene Purdy) swan dance at the talent show is titled, *Autumn Angel*. In the hotel, Eddie Darko recollects with his wife about Frankie Feedler's death, anticipating the death of Frank Anderson, or Frank the Rabbit. Eddie then tells his wife that Donnie, like Frank, is doomed, but their son dodged a bullet, suggesting he's supposed to die, thereby restoring the Primary Universe. Also, Frank is the character in Cunningham's on-stage morality lesson.

Kitty owns Cunningham's motivational book, *Attitudinal Beliefs*, which has a painting of Cunningham on its cover; this same portrait decorates Cunningham's home. Karen recites from Greene's "The Destructors," which is about kids breaking into Old Misery's home; later, the bullies Seth and Ricky break in Grandma Death's home. Old Misery hid money inside his house; it is rumored Grandma Death is wealthy, hiding gems inside her home. Old Misery's home became inundated; Donnie breaks a water main flooding the high school. Donnie is a juvenile delinquent having spent time in jail for burning down an abandoned house; later, he will torch

Cunningham's mansion. Elizabeth says she is voting for Michael Dukakis in the upcoming Presidential Election. Dukakis was then Governor of Massachusetts; later, Elizabeth announces she will be attending Harvard University, located in Massachusetts.

Samantha Darko authors a story titled *The Last Unicorn* about Ariel, her stuffed toy unicorn, which is also the protagonist in *The Little Mermaid* (1989), another '80s classic. Samantha clings to Ariel in the hotel room, and again at the airport. In a few scenes, she wears a t-shirt depicting a cartoon unicorn. I will allow the reader to decide: this could be referencing one, two, or three '80s movies. It could be an homage to the Director's Cut of *Blade Runner*, featuring unicorn origami, insinuating Deckard is a Replicant. Or, maybe a film with the same name: *The Last Unicorn* (1982), which is about an evil king trying to capture the mythic beasts, or it could be an homage to *Legend* (1985). In the dark fantasy, Darkness (Tim Curry) wants to slay all the unicorns, collecting their horns to conquer light. Unicorns can symbolize many things, including the sacred feminine, chastity, and maidenhood; thus, the magical animal shadows Donnie's little sister, who embodies at least two of the three.

Donnie plays the arcade video game *Out Run*, controlling a red sports car denoting Frank's red Trans Am.[191] A painting of an airplane decorates Dr. Thurman's office, inferring the Artifact. Donnie reads aloud a Life-Line Exercise Card about a person finding a lost wallet. Later, he finds Cunningham's wallet on the sidewalk outside his mansion. Cunningham depicts drugs, alcohol, and premarital sex as "instruments of fear." Donnie smokes a cigarette (nicotine is an addictive chemical), drinks alcohol, and engages in premarital sex; the climax occurs after he surrenders to all three temptations. While watching *The Evil Dead*, there are only three people in the theater: Donnie, Gretchen, and Frank, all of whom are touched by the Grim Reaper–their deaths are the only ones in the movie. As they stroll through a forest path, a man in a red leisure suit watches Donnie and Gretchen; later, he makes a cameo outside the Halloween party. In Karen's classroom, on the chalkboard, she has written *Cellar Door*; later, Donnie enters Grandma Death's house via the cellar door, as if Karen was cuing him to go inside.

---

191 This sequence appears in the Director's Cut.

Rabbits are ubiquitous. As Gretchen waits for the school bus, a Volkswagen Rabbit Convertible speeds past her. Karen assigns the novel *Watership Down* (1972); later, the class watches the animated movie. The story is about a rabbit, Fiver, who has a prophetic vision that the end of his warren is nigh, running parallel with Donnie's knowledge of the Apocalypse.[192] On October 30, while Elizabeth sleeps on the recliner, there is a stuffed rabbit under the window. As Donnie reaches for the car keys on the table, there is an old Polaroid picture of him and Elizabeth as children; observe that Donnie wears a bunny outfit. The repetition of the hare relates to Frank, the Manipulated Dead, and needs no further explanation.

Grandma Death checks her mail endlessly, signaling a time-loop, becoming evidence that all this has happened previously. The Manipulated Dead's earlier attempts to prevent the paradox have failed. Frank the Rabbit was unable to get Donnie to send the engine back because he would not survive long enough to do so, or he would choose not to return it, knowing it would mean certain death. The Manipulated Dead and the Manipulated Living–those alive in the Tangent Universe–persuade Donnie–the Living Receiver–in many ways to carry out his destiny. Their actions appear to be a result of their subconsciousness. For example, Grandma Death whispers that we all die alone, prompting Donnie to accept his fate. Dr. Monnitoff gives him *The Philosophy of Time Travel*, spawning his interest in the subject matter. Karen plays matchmaker with Gretchen and Donnie; by hooking them up, Donnie sacrifice himself to save his gal. Donnie may even feel responsible for his girlfriend's demise. Grandma Death was standing in the road holding aloft the letter Donnie sent her, causing Frank's car to run over Gretchen. Hence, Donnie wants to give up his life to bring his girlfriend back. Despite being a moral coward, Kitty tries to put Donnie on the righteous path in the hopes he will restore the Primary Universe, preventing the end of the world.

Then there are the Manipulated Dead's cryptic warnings and manipulations. After the school's vandalization, the phrase, "They made me do it," is scrawled under the school's mascot in Frank's handwriting, evidenced by the "Frank was here went to get beer" written on the white magnetic board on the refrigerator. "They made me do it" suggests a hidden hand guides Donnie to repair the spacetime continuum. Earlier, the phrase,

---

192 *Watership Down* appears in the Director's Cut.

"Where is Donnie?" appears written on the same white magnetic board, indicating Donnie's absence when the engine crashed in his bedroom, creating the Tangent Universe and putting the Primary Universe at risk.

Have the events of October '88 happened before? The answer to this question is yes. Observe that Donnie bicycled in his pajamas to the scenic overlook, suggesting he was in a somnambulist-like state when cycling. He was drawn outside by extramundane Frank the Rabbit; as a result, he has to redo the events of October '88 because he did not perish.[193] Notice October 1 is never crossed off on his calendar, denoting a constant time-loop: the events always start on October 2, terminating on October 30 perpetually.[194] When Donnie, Gretchen, and his friends bicycle to Grandma Death's home, the former is the only one without a headlight, implying he knows the route because he's done it before. When we first visit Donnie's school, the song "Head over Heels" by Tears for Fears defines the '80s atmosphere, becoming part of the film's soundtrack. Its final verse is: "♪ In my head, my mind's eye / One little boy, wandering by / Funny how time flies, ♪" suggesting a psychic nexus to time or time travel. The mind's eye relates to the mental faculty of conceiving imaginary or recollected images from time, conjuring the Fourth Dimensional Spiral, a repeating Tangent Universe, an incorrect iteration which Donnie fixes by giving up his life, repairing the Primary Universe.

Donnie meets and becomes close to Gretchen. Then, Frank Anderson accidentally kills her, leading Donnie to kill Frank by shooting him through his eye, closing the Ensurance Trap. Sealing the trap ensures Donnie will:

1. comprehend how;
2. understand why; and
3. want to change events so his girlfriend, and his mother and little sister, will survive.

Donnie understands enough to prevent the paradox from occurring by sending the engine back in time, resetting the Primary Universe with Donnie in his bedroom (October 2) when the engine comes crashing down. After the engine kills Donnie, the other (identical) engine that already exists in that timeline will be investigated thoroughly, and will not fly, or crash, on

---
193 Or, he did not use his Fourth Dimensional Powers.
194 In the Director's Cut, Donnie's calendar appears once with no dates crossed off.

this October 30 timeline. Hence, the Tangent Universe will not be created; the cycle is over, broken because Donnie's actions have saved the future.

* * * * *

Kelly's film is chockfull of Biblical allusions. The Old Testament refers to a mongrel race known as the Nephilim, created by fallen angels (the *Book of Enoch*'s Watchers) by mating with human women. Genesis 6:4 reads: "The Nephilim were on the earth in those days, and also afterward, when the sons of God came into the daughters of men, and they bore children to them. These were the mighty men who were of old, the men of renown." To eradicate these hybrids, indicated by the school's mascot, a Mongrel, God conjured the Deluge of Noah; ergo Donnie smashes the water main, flooding the school. This action suggests the Tangent Universe must be destroyed so the Primary Universe can be restored, regenerated, thus purified.[195]

Cunningham is a false messiah, so Donnie calls him the Antichrist. The Book of Daniel (11:37) describes the Antichrist: "Neither shall he regard the God of his fathers, nor the desire of women, nor regard any god: for he shall magnify himself above all," mirroring Cunningham's aloofness and his sexual desire for children, not women. The movie's plot deals with termination of the Primary Universe or the end of the world; therefore, it would be remiss not to analyze it concerning the Book of Revelation. We have the Cunningham *qua* Antichrist appearing in the End Days. At Revelation 12:1, the moon heralds the Apocalypse: "And there appeared a great wonder in heaven; a woman clothed with the sun, and the moon under her feet, and upon her head a crown of twelve stars." The verse is an astrological reference to the Virgin Mary *qua* the constellation Virgo the Virgin, also known as the Woman of the Apocalypse. Frank tells Donnie the world will end in 28 days, 6 hours, 42 minutes, 12 seconds. This figure is not random: it comes from adding or subtracting one from each part of the value: 27 days, 7 hours, 43 minutes, and 11 seconds, the precise length of one lunar month by one of the less-used definitions, sidereal instead of the usual synodic. After he wakes up on the road, Donnie rides his bike home

---

195 Cirlot, *Diotionary*, 75.

to "The Killing Moon" (1984) by Echo and the Bunnymen.[196] Not only is it a lunar reference, but the band's name forges an occult link to Frank the Rabbit. Even the name of the meanspirited bully, Seth Devlin, has hidden meaning. His forename, Seth, references the Egyptian god of darkness, Set, while Devlin's surname conjures the Devil.

Eight is embedded in the celluloid, because, to the Kabbalists, it is a number denoting perfection. The kabalistic-esoteric significance of eight is fleshed out more in Chapter XI; however, in *Donnie Darko*, the number signifies the spacetime continuum. When turned sideways ∞, it becomes a mathematical symbol known as the lemniscate, representing the concept of infinity. The E8 x E8 string theory, well-known to many mathematicians, is often referred to in the study of time travel; as such, eight designates the continuity of the Primary Universe. The first letter of the protagonist's forename and surname is *D*, **D**onnie **D**arko, the fourth letter of the alphabet. Add 4+4 to get 8. The story occurs in October 1988.

Frank informs Donnie the world will end in 28 days, 06 hours, 42 minutes, and 12 seconds; add these numbers to get the sum of 88. Eight-eight, or 88, is a hidden reference to *Back to the Future*'s time-traveling DeLorean (mentioned by Donnie), which must hit 88 miles an hour to time travel. When Samantha asks when she can have kids, "squeeze one out," Donnie replies: "Not until 8th grade." Donnie mentions to his therapist that his dog Callie died when he was eight years old. Donnie's little sister is named *Samantha*, which has eight letters; Frank's surname, *Anderson*, also has eight letters. *The Wisdom of Solomon* (2nd century BCE), also known as the *Book of Wisdom*, says at 8:8: "Do you want to have wide experience? Wisdom knows the lessons of history and can anticipate the future. She knows how to interpret what people say and how to solve problems. She knows the miracles that God will perform, and how the movements of history will develop," indicating mastery of spacetime, and that the Tangent Universe is repetitious. Stephen Hawking's (1942-2018) book, *A Brief History of Time*, turns up; it is about quantum mechanics, published in 1988. Cunningham has divided the spectrum of human emotions into two

---

196 cf. the Director's Cut, wherein "Never Tear Us Apart" by INXS replaces "The Killing Moon." The INXS song has the lyric, "♪ Two worlds collided, ♪" contrasting the Primary and Tangent Universes. "The Killing Moon" now plays during the Halloween party.

categories: fear and love. The word *fear* has four letters, and the word *love* has four letters–when added, the sum is eight.

According to the television reporter, the fire at Cunningham's mansion was extinguished "sometime after 8:00 last night." Frank Anderson's Trans Am has Virginia license plates; *Virginia* has eight letters. *J* and *D* are the only letters appearing on the license plate; *J* is the 10th letter of the alphabet, and *D* is the 4th. *JD* is 10:04, forging another nexus to *Back to the Future*: as movie buffs, we know it is the time when lightning strikes the Clocktower, sending Mary McFly (Michael J. Fox) back to the future. October 4 (10:04) is the 277th day of the Gregorian calendar, which means 88 days are remaining until the end of the year. Flight 2806 is the red-eye flight that loses its engine, boarding at Gate 42 at 12 AM; remember, the world will end in 28 days, 06 hours, 42 minutes, and 12 seconds. The climax of *Donnie Darko* occurs right before the US presidential election when George H.W. Bush (1924-2018) won on November 8, 1988.

When I watched this movie (again, for the first time on January 2, 2019), I couldn't help but notice some eerie similarities between myself and Kelly's masterpiece. I assure you, dear reader, that I am not crazy, nor am I seeing things intended only for me, akin to Charles Manson (1934-2017) finding hidden messages in the Beatles' *The Beatles* (aka *The White Album*, 1968). Are these coincidences, or something more? Here they are for consideration.

- *Donnie Darko* received a limited theatrical release, debuting on October 26, 2001, four days before my 30th birthday on October 30.
- The date of the vortex *qua* wormhole *qua* end of the world is October 30, 1988, this author's 17th birthday–add 1+7 to get 8.
- An eccentric author named Roberta Sparrow wrote a book about time travel. I wrote a book about occult movie symbolism, featuring *Back to the Future*'s DeLorean on the cover (*Cinema Symbolism*, 2nd. ed., 2017). **R**oberta **S**parrow has the same initials as this author, *RS*.
- Roberta Sparrow's name has five syllables; my name, Robert Sullivan, has five syllables.

- Elizabeth and Samantha are Donnie's sisters. Elizabeth and Samantha are two witches in my first work of fiction, *A Pact with the Devil*. There is also a witch named Gretchen, Jena Malone's character in *Donnie Darko*.
- Donnie wanted the board game, Hungry Hungry Hippos, for Christmas. Sometime in the early '80s, I got Hungry Hungry Hippos for Christmas.
- Donnie has an American flag hanging from his bedroom's ceiling. In the '80s and '90s, I had an American flag hanging from my bedroom's ceiling.
- "Smurfette doesn't fuck." – Donnie Darko. Donnie explains the occult origins of Smurfette to a couple of his buddies. He tells them she was created–a kabalistic golem–by Gargamel to sow discord in the Smurf village. It's by way of the commune's overwhelming positive vibe, and the white magic of Papa Smurf that changes her into the pleasant, blonde-haired version we all know and love. This dialog is strangely familiar because I have had this same conversation numerous times with my friends, something I analyzed in *Cinema Symbolism 2* (2017).

Like many Gnostic films, especially those released around September 11, 2001, *Donnie Darko* is prophetic. A few years later, on November 4, 2004, a large chunk of ice fell from an airplane in Kent, Washington. The ice block crashed into an 8-year-old girl's bedroom, landing on her bed. Like Donnie trapped in the Tangent Universe, she was not home at the time of impact. Truth, it seems, is sometimes stranger than fiction.

Basilides' Nothingness in David Cronenberg's eXistenZ

If Basilides directed or produced a film, it would be *eXistenZ*, a non-film about nonexistence, totally blurring virtual and real, negating everything. Since Basilides' cosmology is a 180-degree negation of Valentinus, *eXistenZ* is a repudiation of the gnostic meditations pervading *The Matrix* and *Dark City*. In *eXistenZ*, there is no reality, no awakening, no truth or consciousness: everything, including gnosis–assuming there is any–is an illusion. Like *Videodrome* (1983), David Cronenberg gives his psychological statement about how humans react and interact with the technologies surrounding them, in this case, the world of video games. The film's plot came about after Cronenberg conducted an interview with Salman Rushdie for *Shift* magazine in 1995. At the time, Rushdie was in hiding because there was a fatwa against his life, stemming from his controversial book, *The Satanic Verses* (1988). Rushdie's dilemma gave Cronenberg an idea of a fatwa against a virtual-reality game designer.

In the near future, biotechnological virtual reality game consoles known as *game pods* have replaced electronic ones. The pods are grotesque fleshy apparatuses, looking like deformed appendages, making strange noises, responding to touch, appearing alive. The human body powers the pods, using UmbyCords that plug into bio-ports, connectors surgically inserted into players' spines, specifically in the lumbar area. This techno-sorcery is akin to kundalini, which, in Hinduism, refers to a form of primal energy, or *Shakti*, located at the base of the spine. Several different branches of yoga teach methods for awakening the kundalini, directing it up through the chakras to the crown of the head, bringing enlightenment, and a range of supernormal powers.[197]

Two game companies, Antenna Research and Cortical Systematics, compete against each other in the world of virtual gaming by tapping into *Shakti*, meaning *power, ability, strength, might, effort, energy, and capability*. *Shakti* is the primordial cosmic energy that represents the dynamic forces that are thought to move through the entire universe in Hinduism; thus, one must access this mystic synergy, allowing the mind to participate in computer-generated high-octane virtual environments. Moreover, *Shakti* is the concept or personification of divine feminine creative power; in Hinduism, it is sometimes known as the Great Divine Mother. Countering both game companies is the Realist Underground, combatting their futuristic technologies, trying to stop them from distorting reality.

Antenna Research's Allegra Geller (Jennifer Jason Leigh), a brilliant world-renowned game designer, is demonstrating her latest virtual reality game, *eXistenZ*, to a focus group in a country church. Videogaming is a religion, and Allegra is a goddess; she is the Mother Goddess, the earthly personification of *Shakti*. Allegra plugs into her pod along with twelve others, reflecting orthodox Christianity, she is Jesus, and they are her

---

197 Greer, *New Encyclopedia*, 262.

apostles. Flanked by her acolytes on either side, like Jesus in da Vinci's *The Last Supper*, Allegra goes into a meditative trance. She and the players are no longer in reality but in the virtual world of the game. Only after the players have exited existence for eXistenZ, a Realist named Noel Dichter (Kris Lemche) joins the congregation. He shoots Allegra in the shoulder with a weird organic pistol–made from greasy bone and teeth–that he smuggled past security. "Death to the demoness," he shouts, pulling the trigger. Chaos ensues.

As Dichter is gunned down by the security team, a guard, Ted Pikul (Jude Law), rushes to a wounded Allegra, escorting her outside, whisking her away. Easter Egg: when Allegra and Ted hide in a motel room after the failed assassination attempt, their fast food comes from a chain named Perky Pat's. It's an homage to "The Days of Perky Pat" (1963), a science fiction short story by Philip K. Dick, first published in *Amazing Stories* magazine. Later, elements of the story were incorporated into Dick's novel, *The Three Stigmata of Palmer Eldritch* (1965), which utilizes an array of science fiction concepts. Like *eXistenZ*, it features several layers of reality and unreality philosophical ideas. The story is one of Dick's first works to explore religious themes wherein the framework of the false realities is not a video game, but drugs called Can-D and Chew-Z.

Allegra discovers that her pod, containing the only copy of *eXistenZ*, may have been damaged. Ted reluctantly agrees to have a bio-port installed in his spine to test the game's integrity. Allegra takes him to a gas station run by a black-marketeer named Gas (Willem Dafoe), who deliberately installs a faulty bio-port. The place's name is COUNTRY GAS STATION. This anomaly, combined with his odd name, Gas, suggests a video game glitch, a defect in the programming, viz. a man named Gas working at a gas station, indicating their current reality is a simulation. Gas waxes enthusiastically about Allegra's spiritual game, *ArtGod*, "Thou, the player of the game, art God....God the artist–the mechanic," evoking the Demiurge, implying the artifice's deity; put another way, virtual gaming is a neo-religion in which Allegra is a goddess to some, a demoness to others. Like Judas Iscariot, Gas is a turncoat, revealing his intention to kill Allegra for the five-million-dollar bounty the Realists have placed on her head. In casting Dafoe to portray a Judas-like betrayer, attempting to kill the supreme Christlike goddess of the gaming world for money, he negates his iconic performance

Allegra Gellar at the COUNTRY GAS STATION. She stands next to a pump labeled SUPREME, identifying her as the virtual gaming world's messiah. From *eXistenZ*.

as Jesus in *The Last Temptation of Christ*, perpetuating both Basilides' ideal and an ontological paradox. Ted kills Gas, and the two escape to a former ski lodge used by Kiri Vinokur (Ian Holm), Allegra's mentor.

Kiri and his assistant repair the damaged pod and give Ted a new bio-port. In a cabin, Allegra and Ted enter *eXistenZ*, a virtual simulacrum appearing no different from reality. Though Ted claims his transition from *reality* to *virtual* was exceptional, "beautiful" as he calls it, realizing little has changed, saying, "I feel just like me." His sense that the game world is inseparable from the non-game world is borne out one minute later when he asks Allegra the goal of *eXistenZ*. Like the reality they have just left behind, she admits one has to "play the game to find out why" one is "playing" the game, and that the more one plays, the more one understands "how natural it feels." At first. Ted struggles with this indeterminacy and with the moments when his game character makes him do or say things his natural self would not usually say or do. However, he soon gives himself over to the rules of the game, playing *eXistenZ* in earnest. Once inside the game, Ted and Allegra meet with D'Arcy Nader (Robert A. Silverman), the proprietor of Game Emporium, who provides them new micro pods. They activate the new micro pods which behave like living organisms; like creepy-crawlies, they slither into their bio-ports, allowing them to enter a deeper layer of virtual reality or another reality altogether.

They assume new identities as workers in a trout farm/game-pod factory. Another worker in the factory, Yevgeny Nourish (Don McKellar), claims to be their Realist contact. At a CHINESE RESTAURANT near the factory, Nourish recommends they order the Special for lunch; like the COUNTRY GAS STATION, bold block letters spell out its name. At the CHINESE RESTAURANT, Ted stops the game by shouting, "*eXistenZ* is paused," appearing to transport himself and Allegra back to reality, back to the cabin at the ski lodge. By now, it is impossible to distinguish what is part of *eXistenZ* and what isn't. Ted and Allegra have already entered a game within a game, a virtual reality within a virtual reality. How can we tell if the transportation back to the ski lodge is another translation to another virtual world? Like Ted and Allegra, we have been thrown into oblivion, cast into an ontological and epistemological crisis.

Allegra convinces Ted to return to the CHINESE RESTAURANT; Ted eats the unappetizing Special, a disgusting dish of cooked mutated amphibious creatures, constructing a pistol out of the inedible skeletal parts; it is the same gun Dichter used to shoot Allegra at the church. In jest, he threatens Allegra, duplicating the scene from reality, then shoots the Chinese waiter (Oscar Hsu), a spy for Cortical Systematics gathering information on the Realist Underground. Nourish, a member of this Realist Underground, tells Ted and Allegra that Cortical Systematics is using the mutant creatures to develop weapon systems as well as game pods. Ted vows to destroy the trout farm. Ted, an employee of a virtual game company, and Allegra, a designer of these games, have become agents for the Realists. Even though they both feel like their genuine selves, they possess virtual identities in contrast to their empirical personae–another paradox. When the pair return to the Game Emporium, shop assistant Hugo Carlaw (Callum Keith Rennie) informs them Nourish is a double agent for Cortical Systematics, and the Chinese waiter Ted murdered was the actual contact. They are instructed to return to the trout farm, kill Nourish, and destroy the latest game from Cortical Systematics.

Back at the factory, Ted once more expresses his concerns about the virtual world, but his language precisely describes what it is like to live in the real world. He hates that he "doesn't know what's going on," and that he is always "stumbling around…in this unformed world whose rules and objectives are largely unknown, seemingly indecipherable or even possibly nonexistent." He fears he is "always on the verge of being killed by forces" he doesn't "understand," wondering who would want to play a game like this. Allegra replies that it is a "game everybody's already playing"; *eXistenZ* is existence. Hooked to a pod or not, one struggles to survive in a habitat controlled by unknowable forces. What appears to be chaotic may be fated. What seems lawless could be random. Freedom is counterfeit; destiny remains mysterious; this is being in the world. These confusions–reducing knowledge to ignorance and meaning to silence, the precincts of Basilides–pervade the film's concluding scenes.[198]

After the revelation of *eXistenZ* and existence's Gnosticism, they find a diseased pod. Allegra connects it to her bio-port as part of a plan to infect the other pods to sabotage the factory. When Allegra quickly becomes ill, Ted cuts the UmbyCord, but she begins to bleed to death–the pod has melded with her. Nourish appears with a flamethrower, cries "death to the demoness," blasting the diseased pod, which bursts into deadly spores, polluting the factory. Holding the wounded Allegra, Ted concludes they have lost the game.

Allegra and Ted transport to the ski lodge's cabin, where they discover her game pod is also diseased, signaling the virtual simulation has infected the real world. Allegra surmises Ted's new bio-port must have been infected by Kiri to destroy her game. She inserts a disinfecting device into Ted's bio-port. Unexpectedly, Hugo Carlaw reappears as a machine gun-toting Realist resistance fighter, escorting Allegra and Ted outside to witness the death of *eXistenZ*. Before Carlaw can deliver the "death to the demoness" line and kill Allegra, Kiri shoots him in the back with the bone gun; Kiri reveals he is a double agent working for Cortical Systematics. He informs Allegra he copied her game data while he was fixing her pod; Kiri offers Allegra a choice: join Cortical Systematics or die. In revenge, she kills Kiri with Hugo's machine gun. Ted then reveals he is a Realist sent to kill her. Allegra tells Ted she had known his intentions since he pointed the gun at her in the CHINESE RESTAURANT, and she remotely detonates the disinfecting device in his bio-port, killing him. Out of nowhere, a strange blue device appears on her head and hands; she asks: "Have I won?"

---

198 Wilson, *Secret Cinema*, 64.

Suddenly, "Ted Pikul" and "Allegra Geller" awaken back at the country church. They are on stage together with the other members of the cast, wearing the same blue electronic virtual reality devices. They are all part of a focus group; a man, who was "Yevgeny Nourish" in the game, explains the story was all part of a virtual reality game he designed called *transCendenZ*. The players laud *transCendenZ*, praising its real and authentic gameplay. "Nourish's" surname suggests he's feeding them with what they crave: a religious experience, a false existence wherein their minds cannot perceive real from fake. Shortly thereafter, "Nourish" privately tells his assistant Merle (Sarah Polley) that he feels uneasy because the anti-game plot elements may have originated from the thoughts of one of the testers. "Ted" and "Allegra" confront "Nourish," accusing him of twisting reality, yelling "death to the demon," before shooting him and Merle to death with guns smuggled on "Ted's" dog (the large canine appeared several times in the virtual sequence). As it turns out, they are part of the Realist Underground. As the others watch in muted silence, like they are awaiting their next cue, "Ted" and "Allegra" escape, aiming their guns at the person who played the "Chinese waiter." At first, the "Chinese waiter" pleads for his life, but then relaxes, jokingly asking if they are still in the game. Bewildered, "Ted" and "Allegra" stand side by side in Basilides' void, in meditative-ignorant silence; reality, gnosis, and consciousness are negated, assuming they ever existed. The screen goes black. The "Chinese waiter's" question remains unanswered, hanging in limbo. Easter egg: observe, because Allegra's hair changes its curliness depending upon the reality she inhabits, altering between straight, partially curly, and entirely kinky.

The first thirty minutes of *eXistenZ* define its essential elements. The organic and the mechanical, the natural and the artificial, are indivisible. Video game pods breathe and quiver, get sick and heal. People have biomechanical ports in their spines to become one with machines. These collapses of differences compromise ontology and epistemology. If objects are both born and made, how can one ever know what anything is? Even if one could discern between organic and machine, his (or her) insight is rendered null by the annihilation of difference–between the empirical world of subjects engaging with objects and the virtual realm of phantoms playing with ghosts. People ascend to enjoy virtual experiences far more intense, far more *real* than those drab habits of their everyday lives. Those in the congregation feel divorced from the ecstasy of those plugged into the pod, like they are trapped in sordid predictability, denied salvation.[199]

The game, *eXistenZ*, is far more authentic than existence. The illusion is real, and reality is an illusion. Organs and machines, pods and bio-ports, churches and corporations; it is all or nothing, either empirical events attenuated by tedious habits or virtual occasions made excitingly real. Both negations of the real, the artificial usurping the mental, and the virtual dissolving the empirical, are perpetuated by a collective Demiurge: the Antenna Corporation. The company attempts to reduce people to addicts, to human machines requiring the fuel of virtual games. To this end, the corporation holds demonstrations in churches and promises artificial transcendence, as *transCendenZ* implies. It tricks people into worshipping false gods, viz. the art god *qua* Demiurge. These four themes: the blurring of artifice and nature, the collapse of empirical and virtual, the corporation *qua* Demiurge, and the corporate products as sacred objects persist throughout the film, an apocalyptic evacuation of reality for Basilides' nothingness.[200]

Unlike *The Matrix*, which implies comprehending the truth is a Christlike *ascensio*, and unlike *The Truman Show*, inferring Manichean melancholy might lead to a realm beyond illusion, and unlike *Dark City*, intimating paranoia might translate to salubrious tuning, *eXistenZ* offers no keys to knowledge, salvation, or power. There is no difference between action and idleness, the sequences pretending to be *real*, and those allegedly *fake*, share the same objects, motifs, and conflicts. Pervading the *real* and the *fake* are the bone gun, assassination attempts with the cry of "death to the demon" (or "demoness"), the large white dog, an ongoing battle between the Realist Underground and the corporations producing virtual games, mutant amphibians/reptiles, and the diseased pod. If the same things permeate the empirical and the virtual, what separates existence from *eXistenZ*?

All of the characters, or players, are thrust into this unanswerable question. Throughout *eXistenZ*, "Ted" and "Allegra" enter and exit the *real* and *virtual* worlds. They struggle in both narratives trying to figure out

---

199 Ibid, 62.
200 Ibid, 62 63.

what they are supposed to be doing. Are they pawns subject to rules they will never understand, or are they secret agents capable of shaping reality with their actions? Is the world random, comprised of chaotic pulses, or is it determined, a clockwork cosmos? Do their actions matter, do they people they kill die, or is it merely play, the killings inconsequential? Unable to transcend these ambiguities, the characters remain ignorant and static. They are like actors in a bizarre movie, which never ends; in fact, it is incapable of finishing. They are controlled by a mysterious script that always seems in the process of changing, conducted by an idiosyncratic Ed Wood-like director who might be as whimsical as wind chimes or regimented like the military. By becoming habituated to this situation, they believe the game is the only thing: reality. This modality is the abysmal limbo of Basilides; this is *eXistenZ*.[201]

Cronenberg's erasure posits this conundrum: when we leave the theater, are we entering a new simulation? After all, some of the objects and motifs that define cinema are things we deal with in our empirical lives. The blurring of distinctions between authentic and fake is something we deal with in our everyday lives. Computers get viruses, and humans upload our lives, our consciousness, to our various social media platforms. People base their behaviors on cinema's illusions; the world of cinema passes itself off as real. Corporations shape reality by manipulating the culture industry. Consumerism replaces reality, reducing the sacred to a commodity. How can one discern between *eXistenZ* and a non-cinematic experience? Aren't we all doubles of Ted and Allegra, units of matter thrown into a world whose rules are unknowable? Aren't we always questioning the meaning of life: why are we here and what is our purpose? But if *eXistenZ* implies the movie is existence, then we cannot trust this claim because Cronenberg's film, like the game it depicts, is caught in the web of illusions it tries to describe. It enjoys no more ontological or epistemological validity than *eXistenZ*, a game within a game. In trying to glean any stable truths from the film, we are left like the "Chinese waiter," "Ted," and "Allegra" pondering what is real and what is not, asking the question, "Are we still in the game?" We receive no answer to the "Chinese waiter's" query, only a blank screen: ignorance, silence, the limbo of Basilides.[202]

---

201 Ibid, 65-66.
202 Ibid, 66.

The willed oblivion–desired nothingness–of Basilides recalls the tradition of negative theology, based on the idea one can know the unfathomable divine through what it is not. Codified in the 5th and 6th centuries by Pseudo-Dionysius the Areopagite in the *Corpus Areopagiticum*, negative theology pervades Lynch's *Lost Highway*, a movie defying rational explanation. Besides the positive adumbration of aspects of the godhead, Dionysius sets forth a negative way. There are no words for God in his essence; no names for him as he is; therefore, he is at the last best defined by negatives, by a kind of darkness, by saying that God is not good, not beauty, and not truth, meaning he is nothing we can understand by those names. The Dionysian negative way brought forth some beautiful spiritual fruits in the course of the ages. For example, the 14th-century *Cloud of Unknowing,* in which the unknown author, following the *Deonise Hid Divinitie*, puts himself under a cloud of unknowing within which, with a blind stirring of love, he reaches forth toward the *Deus Absconditus*. And the learned philosopher Nicholas of Cusa (1401-1464) found in the learned ignorance of Dionysius the only final solution, or mode of approach to the divine, as he expounds in his famous work the *De docta ignorantia* (1440). The negative theology, or the idea of the negative limbo, reached Ficino not only through Dionysius but also through Cusa, of whom he was a great admirer, and whom he regarded as a critical link in the great chain of Platonists.[203]

This limbo evokes the 20th-century philosophy of Martin Heidegger (1889-1976), arguing that existence, or *existenz* (German), can become transcendent only when one relinquishes the desire to reduce mysterious beings to static concepts. In *Being and Time* (1927), Heidegger maintains Being is the interplay between the unknowable abyss and the palpable presence, between the ungraspable whole (*lethe*) and the revelatory parts (*aletheia*). To apprehend this energy, the thinker cannot grasp for whole or components but must negotiate between each. He must engage in the hermeneutical circle, an oscillation between Being and beings. He partially illuminates the parts from the perspective of the whole, and incompletely brightens the entirety from the angle of the parts. The thinker is always in process, growing in his experience of the mystery but never resting in certainty.[204]

---

203 Yates, *Giordano Bruno*, 124.
204 Martin Heidegger, *Being and Time*, trans. John Macquarrie and Edward Robinson (New York: Harper, 1962), 7 12.

Being and Time is a fundamentally Kantian work. Immanuel Kant (1724-1804) sought to provide an account of the necessary, *a priori* structure of nature, so Heidegger aims to provide an ontology of human beings; an account of those existential qualities the human person must satisfy.[205] The overarching feature mentioned by Heidegger is *being-in-the-world*. According to the traditional account of human existence–associated with Rene Descartes (1596-1650) but very much older, going back through Christian metaphysics to Plato and beyond–to exist as a human is to live as a particular type of *object*. In traditional, anti-materialist Cartesian versions, it is to be an immaterial soul–what Heidegger calls a *soul substance*–a soul that is rather loosely, and only temporarily, attached to a body. Critically, the same tradition can be reproduced within a materialist metaphysics by identifying humanness with being a particular type of organism: a brain, of suitable sophistication, or a brain-plus-a-body. The Cartesian allows that, as a matter of epistemology, questions about people are based on visible behavior: the self stands to bodily action as an inner reality to outer appearance. Heidegger rejects this root and branch, declaring the self as an inner object to be a metaphysician's myth, a philosopher's fiction. To be human is not to be an inner object, but a process of happening, a pattern of *concerning activity*. The existence of the self thus entails the existence of a world. I am not in the world–contingently–as water in a glass, says Heidegger. Rather, I am necessary since I can no more be an agent without a society than I can be an actor without a stage.[206]

In "What is Metaphysics?" (1929), Heidegger analyzes this anxious limbo. Sounding the mystery of Being, one suffers an indeterminate field. Individual beings, formerly definite, dissolve into the dark origin from which they arose. Being briefly shines in the parts that it sustains. Throbbing between mystery and mystery, the thinker experiences *the essential impossibility* in determining the nature of Being. To linger in this original anxiety is to undergo a disclosure of what cannot be disclosed. Faced with oblivion, one might flee from stress, grab their determinate interpretations of the world, severing themselves from possibility and transcendence. However, a braver thinker might remain conscious of the disturbing nothingness, open to strange

---

205 *A priori* is wisdom relating to or derived by reasoning from self-evident propositions.
206 Julian Young, *Heidegger, philosophy, Nazism* (New York: Cambridge University Press, 1998), 56-58.

horizons, and apprehend exhilarating potentialities and supernatural vistas.[207] One might feel anxiety to enter into a "secret alliance with the cheerfulness and gentleness of creative longing."[208]

Such are the enigmas of Cronenberg's *eXistenZ*, a grim virtual reality inside a dark virtual reality, wherein the impossible evolves into reality then devolves into virtual. Upon awakening to reality, one is awakening to another sable virtual reality; or worse of all, there is no reality, virtual or otherwise. *eXistenZ*'s limbo is this: *being* cannot be defined or discerned because the interplay between unknowable abyss and palpable presence endlessly overlap; thus, it is impossible for "Ted" and "Allegra" to negotiate between them, to know what is *real* and what is *virtual*. They are in limbo because, in *eXistenZ*, real is virtual and virtual is real–it is impossible to differentiate between natural and artificial. Like lost souls trapped in Purgatory, "Ted" and "Allegra" can never rest in certainty.

If one wishes to see *eXistenZ* negated, take a gander at *Ready Player One* (2018); although Spielberg's film lacks Cronenberg's Gnostic vision, I found it to be entertaining nevertheless. Set in a dystopian 2045, the protagonists are conscious of the virtual simulation, entering it willingly and eagerly. They are aware of when they are outside of the virtual reality, dwelling on the mundane plane. There are no epistemological or ontological crises. Called the OASIS (**O**ntologically **A**nthropocentric **S**ensory **I**mmersive **S**imulation), the virtual reality is a sumptuous open-world playground. Created by the Willy Wonka-like James Halliday (Mark Rylance), and assisted by Ogden Morrow (Simon Pegg), it is a digital never-ending Chocolate Factory wherein anyone can be anybody, and do anything. The limits of the OASIS are one's imagination. They are the OASIS' benign demiurgic creators; set in Columbus, Ohio; *Columbus* a nod to Christopher Columbus (1451-1605), the Admiral of the Ocean Sea who discovered a new world, anticipating the OASIS' neo-reality. Halliday's (d. 2040) favorite song was "Video Killed the Radio Star" by the Buggles, and it's easy to understand why. It was the first video to air on MTV,[209] prophesying the coming digital age, the internet, and a more interactive mass medium, anticipating the OASIS. Halliday's favorite music video was

---

207 Wilson, *Secret Cinema*, 67-68.
208 Martin Heidegger, "What is Metaphysics?" in *Heidegger: Basic Writings*, revised and expanded edition, ed. David Farrell Krell (New York: Harper Collins, 1993), 106.
209 The music video debuted at 12:01 am on August 1, 1981.

"Take On Me" (1984) by a-ha, fitting because it's about a woman entering a pencil-drawn virtual universe.

Reality is boring, drab, "a bummer," to quote the protagonist, while the OASIS is the place to be; action, adventure, and intrigue are around every corner. The catch is one does interact with one's friends outside the simulation, everyone inside remains anonymous, so there is an inherent disconnect with humankind. Inside, one is challenged to locate three keys that unlock a door hiding the ultimate Easter egg: ownership of the OASIS. When one finds the three keys, the player enters Halliday's childhood bedroom to receive gnosis. In a scene resembling the Allegory of Plato's Cave, Halliday philosophizes to the protagonist, Wade Watts, also known as Parzival (Tye Sheridan), not to attach himself to the make-believe reality. He further warns him not to be bound to artificial avatars, sensory stimuli, and illusory images, but to live and be in the real. To do otherwise is to live in fear because "reality is real," to quote Halliday. The lesson is well learned: in the real world, Watts befriends his OASIS posse, falling in love with one of them, Samantha, also known as Art3mis (Olivia Cooke).

The Oasis is a wonderland of '70s, '80s, and '90s pop culture Easter eggs and nostalgia that Generation X will easily recognize. Here, the protagonists search for the second key in the Oasis, concealed in Halliday's life, specifically when he saw *The Shining*. Most Easter eggs hide in plain sight–notice the movie theater's name is the Overlook, an obvious *Shining* homage. Although there are far too many Easter eggs to list, pay attention to Aech's (Lena Waithe) garage because near the door is Pee-wee Herman's stolen bicycle from *Pee-wee's Big Adventure*. Inside Aech's loft, one will find a Re-Elect Mayor Goldie Wilson poster from *Back to the Future* along with the nuclear missile tip coming out of the floor from *Weird Science* (1985). When we are introduced to i-ROk (T.J. Miller) at the downed Martian ship from *The War of the Worlds* (1953), keep an eye out for Perseus' magical shield from *Clash of the Titans* (1981). He stores the Orb of Osuvox (shaped like a twenty-sided dice, a Dungeons and Dragons reference) in the same wooden box that housed Gizmo the Mogwai in *Gremlins* (1984) And lest we forget that Zhou aka Sho (Philip Zhao) wields the Glaive from *Krull* (1983). From *Ready Player One*.

Heeding Halliday, he decides to shut down the OASIS a couple of days a week so people can connect in person and not via their fantastic avatars.

Pop culture Easter eggs overload *Ready Player One*, most of them easily discoverable. However, one gem worth mentioning is the tribute to *The Matrix*, arguably the chief false-reality Gnostic movie of all time. The logo IOI identifies the tyrannical corporation, **I**nnovation **O**nline **I**ndustries. IOI encodes *101*; thus, IOI employees are nicknamed *sixers* because *101* is binary for five, but to a computer is the sixth number since it counts from zero, i.e., 0=1 (*vide supra*). Recall the events of *The Matrix* took place in its sixth iteration; this is why the *101* shadows Neo: he is the sixth One, and his alter ego, Thomas Anderson, dwells in apartment 101.

Splicing Dream and Reality in Vanilla Sky

Vanilla Sky blurs dream and reality. After a car accident, David Aames (Tom Cruise), wears a prosthetic mask of his visage. This movie is the second time in two years Cruise wore a mask of himself. The first was in *Eyes Wide Shut*; the imagery of a man wearing a mask modeled after his face is strange, but compelling because it forces us to question our selfhood: who are we?[210] Ourselves, or are we the various masks we show to the world. Are we greater than the sum of our parts? Put another way, are the masks our real faces, and if so, do we shape reality by wearing different masks, or are the masks a result of the actualities we inhabit?

Unlike *Dark City* and *The Truman Show*, *Vanilla Sky*'s indifference to Gnostic anxiety makes it a postmodern nihilistic product: we are all simulacra of simulacra, enjoying the show happily. Still, in its cynicism, *Vanilla Sky* might unconsciously shock audiences awake, urging them to contemplate their unconsidered commitments to stimulating experiences. This meditation is unlikely to happen because of Tom Cruise running around in a cinematic Sharper Image catalog. For example, his trendy apartment is a museum of eclectic male cool, failing to inspire the Valentinian-Philip K. Dick credo of *being in the world, just not part of it*. On the other hand,

---

210 Robert P. Kolker and Nathan Abrams, *Eyes Wide Shut: Stanley Kubrick and the Masking of his Final Film* (New York: Oxford University Press, 2019), 74, 204. The authors dispel the theory Bill Harford's (Cruise) mask was modeled after Ryan O'Neal from *Barry Lyndon* (1975). Instead, three identical masks were 'made to the proportions of Tom's face," using his precise facial measurements.

CINEMA SYMBOLISM 3

Vanilla Sky is a perfect cinematic time capsule of the late 90s-pre-9/11 world, which, now in 2020, appears like a less sophisticated, uncorrupted reality–something we all wish we could revisit.

From a prison cell, having been charged with murder, David, his face behind a mask, tells his life story to court psychologist, Dr. Curtis McCabe (Kurt Russell). In flashbacks, we learn David is a wealthy owner of a large publishing firm in New York City. He inherited it from his father, leaving its regular duties to his old man's trusted associates. A voice-over from a Hispanic female says, "Open your eyes," insinuating closed lids are best for apprehending all that exists–the collective dreams of popular culture. The woman's voice is Sophia Serrano (Penelope Cruz)–more on this later. David awakens and cleans up, getting ready for his day, driving down Broadway in a sleek Ferrari.[211] There are no people, no signs of life. He reaches Times Square, which is empty; he gets out of his car and screams. The film returns to the same bedroom in the same apartment. A different female voice (Cameron Diaz) awakens David with the same line. He goes through the same routine only this time there is a blonde bombshell in his bed, Julianna "Julie" Gianna, portrayed by Diaz. He motors through crowded streets only this time in a Mustang; notice the inspection or registration sticker of 02/30/01, a date that doesn't exist, suggesting this sequence is a dream, making the opening clip a dream within a dream.

At David's 33rd birthday party, his best friend, author Brian Shelby (Jason Lee), introduces him to Sofia Serrano. David and Sofia spend a night together talking, falling in love. David's lover, Julie, stalks David in her car, waiting for him to leave Sofia's flat. David eventually gets into Julie's car, and she attempts to kill herself in a crash, bringing David with her. Julie dies, but David survives, his face grotesquely disfigured, forcing him to wear a mask to hide the injuries. With no hope of repairing the damage through plastic surgery, David cannot come to grips with the idea of wearing the mask for the rest of his life. On a night out with Sofia and Brian in a dance club, David gets hopelessly drunk, so Sofia and Brian leave him to wallow in the street where he eventually passes out. Easter egg: 703 is the number of David's upstairs apartment or day office. July 3 is Tom Cruise's birthday.

---

211 The Ferrari's registration or inspection sticker appears to expire on 05/30/01.

The next day, in the street, Sofia wakes David, apologizing for deserting him the night before, and takes him home. The two continue to see each other as their romance blossoms. David successfully has his face surgically repaired despite being told before it was impossible. Though his life seems perfectly content, he encounters oddities, such as brief visions of his distorted face. A man at a bar named Edmund Ventura (Noah Taylor) insinuates David can be omnipotent. One day, as he wakes up in Sofia's bed but finds Julie, with all of Sophia's photos now displaying his former concubine's face. Easter egg: In the dream, Edmund is in the booth observing David's facial reconstruction; in reality, Edmund attends David's funeral.

To make matters worse, Julie now calls herself Sophia, like she was vivacious Hispanic the entire time. Angry and confused by alternating visions of Julie and Sophia, David suffocates Julie/Sophia while having sex with her. He is then arrested and placed in prison, discovering his face has reverted to its previously disfigured state.

David finishes telling his story to Curtis, who visits David further for more sessions to try to help him recuperate. During one interview, Curtis informs David the staff reported him calling out "Ellie" in a bad dream, and asks who she is. David later sees a nearby TV advertisement for Life Extension, a company that specializes in cryonic suspension, and realizes he'd called out the letters *L* and *E*. Curtis and a police guard (Michael Shannon) escort David to the Life Extension offices, where salesclerk Rebecca Dearborn (Tilda Swinton) explains what the company does. Life Extension freezes people just after the point of death until a cure for their ailment is available in the future, with an optional feature of keeping their brain active by placing them in a lucid dream state. David becomes nervous, breaking free of Curtis, realizing he is confined in a dream of his creation gone horribly wrong, so he screams for tech support.

In the offices' empty lobby, Edmund reappears, claiming to be his technician from Life Extension, now known as the Oasis Project, predicting the dreamy virtual simulation of *Ready Player One*. Easter egg: once David realizes his dream has become a nightmare, the Beach Boys' song "Good Vibrations" (1966) validates his paranoia, signaling that his journey of self-discovery is coming to an end: he will awaken to the real world. In 2019, scientists discovered the Beach Boys' catchy song cures sleep inertia; when sleeping, one should wake to melodic music, not a beeping alarm or buzzer. According to scientists, when coming out of sleep, "Good Vibrations" heightens one's

CINEMA SYMBOLISM 3

David and Sofia (left) imitate Bob Dylan and Suze Rotolo (1943-2011) from the album cover *The Freewheelin' Bob Dylan* (1963, right) by strolling down the same New York City block, indicating David's lucid dream imagery comes from pop culture.

alertness and cognition, making the forthcoming day more relaxing, pleasant, and productive.[212] But the filmmakers had foreknowledge of this behaviorism, using the song to announce David's awakening from his stasis, making his transition from the lucid dream to the real world a noble cause, a peaceful epiphany, rousing him back to life. How did they know, back in 2001, "Good Vibrations" relieves sleep inertia? The answer: the CIA told them.

David and Edmund ascend in an elevator to the top of an impossibly tall building, the height triggering David's acute acrophobia. Edmund explains David has been in cryonic sleep for the last 150 years. David opted for Life Extension's services after struggling with his breakup with Sofia, the suicide of Julie, and his disfigurement. After securing the publishing company to its associates, he proceeded to kill himself with a drug overdose. The demiurgic Life Extension preserved his body and, as David directed, placed him into his lucid dream. The dream splice started after the drunken night when Sofia left him. That morning, Sofia returned to him; thus, under a radiant vanilla sky, taken from Claude Monet's (1840-1926) painting, *The Seine at Argenteuil* (1873), his blissful dream began. David inherited the artwork as it was his mother's favorite.

---

212 Jon Coates, "Scientists find starting the day with Beach Boys instead of alarm leads to good vibrations," *Express*, April 21, 2019, https://www.express.co.uk/life-style/life/1117146/beach-boys-pop-songs-alarm-scientists-good-vibrations-sleep-ineptia (accessed February 7, 2020).

Archetypal images from popular culture organize David's dreamlife; for example, the album cover of *The Freewheelin' Bob Dylan* (1963) establishes his relationship with Sofia.[213] Dr. Curtis became a father figure, an Atticus Finch-like (Gregory Peck, 1916-2003) mentor borrowed from *To Kill a Mockingbird* (1962), airing on the prison's TV. Romantic undercurrents from Francois Truffaut's (1932-1984) *Jules et Jim* (*Jules and Jim*, 1962) and Jean-Luc Godard's *A bout de souffle* (*Breathless*, 1960) are omnipresent; both movie posters decorate David's bedroom. However, during his frozen slumber, the dream went wrong. He incorporated elements from his subconscious, such as substituting Julie for Sofia because of the former's suicide, and his disfigurement, resulting from his guilty conscience. His nightmares might be a result of his desire for spiritual growth; frozen, immured in matter, he seeks to unite with Sophia in the pleroma.[214] David's home, the Dakota, epitomizes his nightmare, his murky subconscious because it is pop culture's ultimate haunted house. In *Rosemary's Baby*, Satan lurked its corridors; later, it served as the backdrop for John Lennon's (1940-1980) assassination by a Holden Caufield wannabe.

When they arrive at the top of the building, Edmund offers David a choice: to either be reinserted into the corrected lucid dream or return to the real world. To awaken to reality, he must take a leap of faith off the roof that will wake him from his deathlike state. David decides to awaken, ignoring Curtis' paranoid ravings, trying to talk him out of it. Next, David envisions Sofia and Brian so he can say his goodbyes–by now, Dr. Cutis McCabe has vanished, proving he was nothing more than a projected figment from David's subconscious. Conquering his final fear, David's journey of self-awakening is complete; after he jumps off the building, his life flashes before his eyes. A disembodied female voice says, "open your eyes," and David opens his eyes, awake in the real world.

The problem with *Vanilla Sky* is there is little difference between David's real life and is dream-like existence, contrasting Lynch's *Mulholland Drive*, wherein Betty Elms' rich dreamworld goes against Diane Selwyn's dreary reality. Both of David's worlds are devoted to the perfect appearance: the trendy apartment, the beautiful and intelligent girlfriend, the witty wingman, the shirt rumpled just so, the gesture so unstudied. In the very

---

213 The album cover decorates David's bedroom wall.
214 Adler, *Sleep Paralysis*, "Religious and Spiritual Interpretations," 28-31.

end, the distorted David vanishes, and the audience is left utterly seduced by his life of perfect product placement. Though *Vanilla Sky* wants to say reality is more significant than a dream, it claims the exact opposite: the images of commodity culture are more valuable than ugly faces. But this message–a crass apology for the entertainment industrial complex–might unexpectedly awaken some viewers to the Gnostic conundrums.[215]

Vanilla Sky documents David's quest to exit the fake for reality, the mundane for the spiritual. Aiding David in his Gnostic journey of self-discovering is Sophia, his savior, named after the Gnostic goddess, who he falls in love with, supplying him with holy wisdom. Indicative of the syzygy, she becomes Sophia to his Christ: like Jesus, David dies aged 33 and is resurrected, standing cruciform in the middle of Times Square. His father wrote the Book *qua* Bible titled *Defending the Kingdom*, and *RISE*, David's magazine, implies a mystical Christian ascension. David is not Jesus; he is mortal; thus, he intones Joan Osborne's "One of Us" (1995). He has sold his soul to the Luciferian Corporation, Life Extension, exchanging it for a fabricated existence. "You signed a contract?" is repeatedly asked of David, indicating a Faustian Pact. The salesperson, Rebecca Dearborn, has hellfire red hair offset by a collection of spicy sauces; her flaming haired secretary, Libby (Alicia Witt), greets people when they come to Life Extension, sacrificing their souls for a cryonic dream. For David, the simulation has become a hellish nightmare, so, like Christ, he ascends to the heavens via an elevator to unite with Sophia one last time; he takes a leap of faith, jumping off the building, receiving gnosis, waking to reality.

The movie presents epistemological questions: what is fantasy and what is real, and when did David's dream begin? According to the narration, the dreamy vision began when David awakens on the street and is taken home by Sofia. If this is the case, then the opening sequence in Times Square was a dream that David had while still living. However, the first "Open your eyes" is delivered by Sophia, who, at this point, had not come into David's life. This portion could either be: the collective unconscious or the Theory of Forms at work, anticipating (or predicting) Sophia's entrance into his life; or, David is asleep in cryostasis. If he slumbers in frozen stasis, then the entire film, from opening montage until when he opens his eyes at the end, is a dream; and the opening Times Square sequence was a dream

---

215 Wilson, *Secret Cinema*, 68-69.

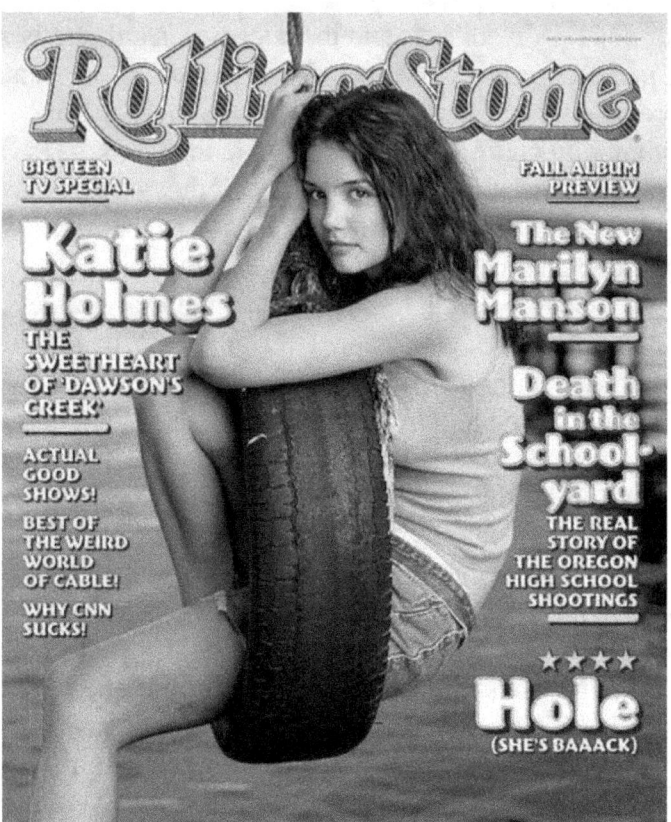

Due to the popularity of *Dawson's Creek* (1998-2003), Katie Holmes graced the cover of the September 1998 issue of *Rolling Stone*. This same picture appears on the cover of the fictitious *TV Digest*, foretelling Cruise's marriage to the actress five years after *Vanilla Sky*'s release.

within a dream. Remember, his real-world Mustang has a registration or inspection sticker that expires on 02/30/01, a date not found on the Gregorian Calendar (*vide supra*), suggesting the entire film is a dream or nightmare. The following correlations strengthen this epistemological conundrum.

- *Vanilla Sky*'s soundtrack gives it a dreamlike vibe because the lyrics continuously relay the emotion of the scene. When the characters aren't speaking, the words take over, continuing to carry the feelings forward. For example, when Julie drives to her death, the song "I Fall Apart" puts a damper on the scene. Diaz, credited as Julianna Gianni, performs the song.

- Radiohead's "Everything in Its Right Place" (2000) signals David's seemingly perfect existence, playing before he runs through an empty Times Square. However, the chorus, "♪ Yesterday I woke up sucking on a lemon, ♪" relates to Brain's *sweet and sour* speeches, signifying life's ups and downs.
- Sophia says, "Open your eyes," waking David from his slumber. She repeats this line to him when he is passed out in the street, awakening him once again. The repetition suggests the whole movie is a dream.
- Penélope Cruz also starred in *Open Your Eyes* (1997), a film with the same theme as *Vanilla Sky*, giving Crowe's opus a reality within a reality feel, akin to the casting of Swayze and Ross in *Donnie Darko*.
- In David's bedroom, the movie on the TV (both times when he awakens) is *Sabrina* (1954). Sabrina Fairchild (Audrey Hepburn) falls in love with David Larrabee (William Holden, 1918-1981), an oft-married, crazy-for-women playboy. He has never noticed Sabrina because, to him, she was still a child, much to her dismay. Sabrina sees David with a woman, becoming devastated by how he is so in love with her. Distraught, she leaves her father a suicide note, turns on every car in the garage, and tries to kill herself by carbon monoxide poisoning. *Sabrina* reflects David's playboy lifestyle; notice he has the same forename as Holden's character. Upon seeing David in love with Sophia, Julie decides to kill herself in a car crash.
- In David's apartment, Julie's cell phone rings. The ringtone is "Row Row Row Your Boat," which, of course, has the lyric, "Life is but a dream," suggesting the whole movie is a fantasy. At David's birthday party, when he's asked how it's going, his response is "Living the dream, baby, living the dream," mirroring the song's verse. This phrase also appears on the memorial cards eulogizing David.
- Prophetic cinema: during the opening Times Square dream sequence, a magazine cover–*TV Digest*–featuring Katie Holmes on a tire swing, flashes as a subliminal image. This same photo of Holmes was the cover of the September 1998 issue of *Rolling Stone* magazine. Cruise married Holmes in November 2006, approximately five years after the release of *Vanilla Sky*. Interestingly,

according to David, the fictitious *TV Digest* was his father's most celebrated publication.

- At the birthday party, Brian's t-shirt has the word *Fantasy* emblazoned upon it. The t-shirt is evidence that the whole movie is all a dream/nightmare.

- At the same party, someone says, "I hear *The Grand Illusion* is great if you watch it stoned." *Le Grande Illusion* (1937) implies David's reality is a fabrication.

- Two posters from the French New Wave decorate David's bedroom: *A bout de souffle* and *Jules et Jim*. Both films feature self-destructive, free-spirited characters whose personal relationships suffer, violently ending because they need to be free. *Jules et Jim* ends with Catherine (Jeanne Moreau, 1928-2017) driving Jim (Henri Serre) off a bridge in a car paralleling Julie and David's car accident. At one point, David makes a couple of faces in the bathroom's mirror. In *A bout de souffle*, Patricia Franchini (Jean Seberg) does the same thing. The posters insinuate *Vanilla Sky* is a dream, and the currents of the French movies are simulacrums of that dream, embedded in David's subconscious.

- During the first dream sequence, when David gets out of his car, *The Twilight Zone* (1959-1964) is airing on Time Square's jumbotron. The episode, "Shadow Play" (airdate: May 5, 1961), is about Adam Grant (Dennis Weaver, 1924-2006), who, having been found guilty of murder, is sentenced to the electric chair. Grant believes the crime is a recurring nightmare.

- In prison, Jung's book, *Memories, Dreams, and Reflections* (1961) is on the table between David and Dr. McCabe. The book is all about Jung's dreams and how they helped him uncover his shadow, thereby removing his persona, or mask, alluding to David's dilemma.

- When David is getting his mug shot taken, the slate spells out in simple code: WHEN DID THE DREAM BECOME A NIGHTMARE?

- On his cryogenic tank, David's L.E. patient number is PL515NT 4R51MS. If you replace the numbers with the corresponding letters of the alphabet, it almost spells out, PLEASANT DREAMS. At

Beth Israel Hospital, during his reconstruction, the computer screen showing David's skull-face also reads PL515NT 4R51MS; encoded in the lower left is DO NOT WAKE HIM UP.

- At one point, Dr. McCabe tells David he'd cried out "Ellie" repeatedly during a nightmare. David replies, "Everything's a nightmare."
- When David and Sophia are lying together naked in bed, Sophia asks, "Is this is a dream?" David replies, "Absolutely."
- Brain jokes about being from Ohio, and it just so happens Dr. McCabe is also from Ohio–a repetitive glitch in the programming.
- Two R.E.M. songs are featured: "All The Right Friends" (2001) and "Sweetness Follows" (1992). R.E.M. stands for *rapid eye movement*, as in a state of sleep, it's when you dream, denoting David's stasis.
- Take a look at David's prison garb. His name tag says, FROZEN GUY in a code, 6R0Z5N 7UY that's easy to decipher.
- Frequently turning up is the cryogenic Benny the Dog, both in actuality and the dream, intentionally obscuring the two realities.
- R.E.M.'s "The Sweetness Follows," plays after Sophia and Brain abandon David after the leave the nightclub; jealous, he runs away, eventually passing out in the street. Although the song is poignant, it signals the dearest scenes between David and Sofia are forthcoming. Right before Sophia rouses David, you can hear the splice, commencing the lucid dream. Suddenly, Julie, a product from David's guilt-ridden mind, arises like succubus from a nightmare; "Boo!" she yells, jolting David out of his drunken stupor. But then Sophia reappears, and the two seem to live happily ever after, but all is not what it seems. R.E.M.'s song stands in stark contrast to the sour lyrics of Radiohead's "Everything Is In Its Right Place." Yin and yang, or *sweet and sour*, just as Brain philosophizes.
- Popping up on multiple occasions is 9. For example, it's a little past 9:00 am on David's watch, and it's on the prison's chalkboard. Right before David picks up Brian, a guy strolls along, wearing a navy-blue shirt with 9, and the frequent mentions of cats recall the number: according to mythology, felines have nine lives. Crowe

has stated in multiple interviews this is an homage to the Beatles' song "Revolution 9" (1968). The tune is a sound collage described as a piece of avant-garde music, and as a *musique concrète* work. The song, coming out of Lennon's psychedelic mind, infers David's pop-culture imagination crafts his hallucination. Also, Crowe has said the *Paul is Dead* rumors, swirling around the Beatles since the band's inception, influenced *Vanilla Sky*, viz. is David dead or alive; as such, Crowe asked Paul McCartney to record a song for the soundtrack. McCartney agreed, and his song, "Vanilla Sky," won a Golden Globe award.

- When glitches begin to turn David's reality to shit, such as Julie becoming Sophia, one can hear a rewind sound effect, tape splicing, or people whispering, which are the scientists monitoring his lucid dream. One can also hear a scientist repeat "3093" because it presumably indicates a problem with the program. A "ding-ding" correct bell sound effect rings after Thomas Tipp (Timothy Spall) tells David to "Wake up." Shortly thereafter, as David leaves the police station, a mysterious man appears, stating, "This is a revolution of the mind," indicating a massive malfunction, a distortion of realities.

- Sophia wears the same jacket to David's funeral that she wears at the end, standing on the rooftop. She wore it at his death, and now dons it at his rebirth; she brings David to the real, escorting him from stasis to consciousness, awaking him from his slumber. Standing on the lofty rooftop, she is marked with the graces of a goddess redolent with light and love. Sophia is to David what Mary Magdalene was to Christ, and Helen was to Simon Magus; ergo, he resurrects like Jesus and Benny the Dog.

- We learn from the televised ad there are 72 cryogenic patients in L.E.'s facility in New Brunswick. This number seems to be coming straight out of the collective unconscious because it signifies multiple things, including the Name of God (*Shemhamforash*), the demons of *Ars Goetia*, and the Precession of the Equinoxes. As such, applied to *Vanilla Sky*, it denotes L.E.'s omnipotence.

- Lastly, Life Extension plays the dualistic role of both liberator and jailor. As Lucifer, the corporation rebels against the Grim

Reaper, freeing people from death. Once free, L.E. then becomes the Demiurge, imprisoning them in a false reality, a lucid dream, generated by their imagination. This duality signifies David's struggle is not only a journey of self-awakening but a Manichean quest through matter. His gnosis comes when he realizes ignorance and wisdom, dark and light, pleasure and pain are interdependent; knowing he treated Julie poorly, he takes the sweet with the sour, suffering paranoid melancholy. To be emancipated from the nightmare he created, David must overcome his acrophobia, leaping to his death to experience life.

Like Lynch's *Lost Highway*, Crowe's film poses this question: is the entire movie David's dream, or does the splice start when David awakens, lying in the city street? In my opinion, Crowe leaves it ambiguous because he wants *Vanilla Sky* to have multiple interpretations, making it arduous to analyze. Ergo, a breakdown requires a Masonic pedigree: the ability to analyze symbols and themes objectively, an occult sophistication beyond that of the casual moviegoer. These modern-day myth makers are challenging us, the audience to transcend the mundane by figuring it out for ourselves, to decode the hidden and bring it to light. After all, by unlocking the secrets of Gnostic Hollywood, aren't we, the audience, receiving gnosis?

The Sword of Exact Zero: Prophetic Visions in the Lego Movie

The Lego Movie (2014) is a 3D computer-animated adventure comedy written and directed by Phil Lord and Christopher Miller from a story by Lord, Miller, and Dan and Kevin Hageman. Based on the Lego line of construction toys, the story focuses on an ordinary Lego Minifigure, learning he is the only one who can stop a tyrannical businessman from gluing everything in the Lego worlds into his vision of perfection. It is a Gnostic fable akin to *The Matrix* with a Masonic-alternative reality twist.

In the Lego universe, populated by anthropomorphic Minifigures, the evil Lord Business (Will Ferrell) finds a super-weapon called the Kragle. The wizard Vitruvius (Morgan Freeman) attempts to stop him, but Business' robots blind him. Before Business leaves with the weapon,

Vitruvius prophesies someone called *the Special* will find the Piece of Resistance: a brick capable of stopping the Kragle.

Eight-and-a-half years later, Lord Business is now President Business, ruler of the Lego universe. In Bricksburg, ordinary construction worker Emmet Brickowski (Chris Pratt) notices a mysterious woman searching for something. When he investigates, Emmet falls into a hole, finding the Piece of Resistance. Compelled to touch it, Emmet experiences vivid visions and passes out. He awakens with the Piece of Resistance attached to his back, and in the custody of Good Cop/Bad Cop (Liam Neeson), Lord Business' lieutenant. The woman, introducing herself as Wyldstyle (Elizabeth Banks), rescues Emmet, believing him to be the Special, taking him to meet Vitruvius in the Old West. Emmet learns Wyldstyle and Vitruvius are Master Builders, i.e., the Freemasons, opposing President Business, capable of building anything using their ingenious imagination without instructions. Their divine spark ignited, the Master Builders' discipline imitates the *Hermetica*'s religion: divine essence is a result of creative activity, explicitly, statue construction. They *know themselves* and, thus, know God.[216]

Wyldstyle explains Business wants to use the Kragle (a weathered tube of *Kra*zy *Gl*ue) to freeze the world into silent perfection. Though disappointed to find Emmet is not a Master Builder, Wyldstyle and Vitruvius are convinced of his potential when he remembers a human deity called the Man Upstairs (also Will Ferrell).

Emmet, Wyldstyle, and Vitruvius evade Bad Cop's forces, aided by Wyldstyle's boyfriend, Batman (Will Arnett). They go to the hidden realm of Cloud Cuckoo Land to attend a council of Master Builders, all of whom are unimpressed with Emmet, refusing to fight Business. Bad Cop's forces invade Cloud Cuckoo Land, having placed a tracking device on Emmet, capturing everyone except Emmet, Wyldstyle, Batman, Vitruvius, and a small group of other Master Builders. Cloud Cuckoo Land is then destroyed. Emmet devises a plan to infiltrate Business' office tower to disarm the Kragle with help from Princess Unikitty (Alison Brie) and the pirate Metalbeard (Nick Offerman). The plan goes well at first, but the group ends up captured, imprisoned in the Think Tank: a dungeon where

---

[216] *Hermetica, Asclepius* I, III, 1:291-293; 1:307-309; 1:311; and 1:339-341. See also Carabine, *Unknown God*, 67; Fowden, *Egyptian Hermes*, 107-108.

the Master Builders have their creativity extracted. Vitruvius fights off robots but is decapitated by Business; next, Business sets the self-destruct protocol, leaving everyone to perish, including Bad Cop.

As he dies, Vitruvius reveals he made up the prophecy. He soon reappears to Emmet as a ghost, like Obi-Wan Kenobi, seemingly one with the pleroma, using its divine energy, i.e., the Light Side of the Force, Reich's Orgone Energy, to appear. Vitruvius then reveals the secret, leading to Emmett's satori: self-belief is what makes one the Special. Strapped to the self-destruct mechanism's battery, Emmet jumps out the tower into the abyss to sever the connection, saving his friends. Inspired by Emmet's sacrifice, Wyldstyle rallies the Lego people across the universe to use whatever creativity they have to build machines and weapons to fight against Lord Business and his army of Micro Managers.

In *The Lego Movie*, President Business wields the Sword of Exact Zero.

Emmet finds himself in the human world–the Lego universe is another reality–as an immobile Lego Minifigure. A boy named Finn (Jadon Sand) is playing out the movie's happenings on his father's expansive Lego set in their basement. His father, referred to as the Man Upstairs, comes home from work horrified to see his son ruining his ideal setup by combining different playsets, ignoring the instructions. He immediately proceeds to undo Finn's changes and permanently glue the pieces together. Emmet, realizing the danger his friends are in, wills himself to move, getting Finn's attention. Finn returns Emmet and the Piece of Resistance to the playset, where Emmet now possesses the powers of a Master Builder, confronting Business in Bricksville.

Meanwhile, Finn's father looks at his son's imaginative creations, realizing Finn had based the evil Lord Business on him and his perfectionism. Through a speech that Emmet gives to Business, Finn's father comes to his senses and apologizes to his son. The two unglue the constructions with Mineral Spirits, which plays out as Business having a change of heart, capping the Kragle *qua* Krazy Glue, and freeing his victims. Emmet is hailed as a hero and begins a romantic relationship with Wyldstyle with Batman's blessing.

The Man Upstairs then allows his younger daughter to play with his Lego sets, resulting in weird aliens from the planet Duplon beaming down to the Lego world, announcing their plans to destroy everyone.

Watching this film, I felt like I was watching a Lego version of *The Matrix*. Think about it; all the elements are present. There is a mechanical-dystopian reality contrasted by an alternative reality: a Lego world and a Human world. Emmet is the Special mirroring Neo, the One. Vitruvius is the illuminating Hermes Trismegistus-like sage foretelling the Special. Morpheus is the enlightening Hermes Trismegistus-like sage prophesying the One. Bad Cop is Agent Smith, and Wildstyle is Trinity. But this is a little too simplistic, so let's analyze *The Lego Movie*'s mysteries, some of which are prophetic.

The Master Builder chief is Vitruvius, named after, naturally, the historical Vitruvius (ca. 80–70 BCE-ca. 15 BCE). Vitruvius was a celebrated Roman author, architect, civil engineer, military planner, known for his multi-volume work titled *De architectura* (30-15 BCE). His discussion of perfect proportion related to the human body led to the famous Renaissance drawing by da Vinci, the *Vitruvian Man*. Many Masonic monitors claim Vitruvius as a proto-Freemason, a pioneer of geometry and architecture, the cornerstones of the Craft.

The Master Builders are a secret guild, constructing things using their imagination, not the uninteresting instructions. The Freemasons are spiritual liberators, whose exotic rituals ignite the candidate's divine spark; the Master Builders are trying to free the Lego Universe from the grips of President Business, the Demiurge. The Master Builders do not follow the hackneyed instructions; instead, they possess imaginative occult insights unknown to the uninitiated, building better than the demiurgic god. Thus, the Master Builders epitomize the Freemasons, their godfather is Vitruvius, trying to transform the Lego universe into a divinely inspired creation.

Like *The Truman Show*'s Seahaven, the Lego universe is insipid and predictable. Everyone conforms; if not, they incur the wrath of the archons: Business' Micro Managers, and the police led by Bad Cop. The Master Builders, the freethinkers, and the nonconformists end up in the Think Tank, a torture chamber akin to Room 101 in George Orwell's (1903-1950) *1984* (1949). Everyone follows the instructions, everyone likes the same song, "Everything is Awesome," and everyone watches the same television show, *Where are my Pants?* Enter the Valentinian savior, Emmet, the Special, who will foil Business' plans to freeze everyone with the Kragle. President Business is the Demiurge, ruling imperfectly, keeping all the Minifigures static, unable to use their imaginations, unconscious of their divine abilities: to build freely and creatively. He is the Man Upstairs; in his world of supposed order, we find nothing but chaos, his robots, and the police drown everyone's spirituality, disconnecting them from the godhead. Meanwhile, his son Finn is the actual God–the Monad–worth seeking out and fighting for; he is the God of the Master Builders, the Freemasons' Great Architect of the Universe.

Enter Wildstyle, the Sophia-like disrupter, and liberator, awakening Emmet to his purpose, guiding him toward the sun (literally), the Hermetic second god, to receive gnosis. He is the prophesied Special who will defeat the Demiurge and his host of archons. It turns out Emmet is a disciple of Basilides: according to Vitruvius, his mind is empty; apparently, he is trying to negate everything, willing himself to nothingness. With the help of the Master Builders, Emmet formulates a plan to invade Business' fortress.

Along the way, they visit Cloud Cuckoo Land, paralleling the Orthodox Christian notion of Heaven. We see in both the Sethian *Gospel of Judas* (ca. 2nd century) and the Nag Hammadi Library's *Gospel of Thomas* (ca. 1st-2nd centuries) the Gnostic Jesus mocking the average Christian's perception of the divine. He laughs at the disciples in the *Gospel of Judas* for holding communion, saying they "are not doing this because of your own will but because it is through this that your god [will be] praised."[217] To the Gnostics, Orthodox Christians are mistaken in their faith because it is thoroughly of this world, a product of Jehovah, the wrathful god of the Old Testament: the Demiurge. Their god is not worth praise and has brainwashed his creation into believing in him and only him, mirroring the Demiurge's ignorance of

---

217 *The Gospel of Judas*, trans. Mark M. Mattison, *gospels.net*, n.d., https://www.gospels.net/judas (accessed January 22, 2019).

the Monad. The key to escaping this world is finding one does not need the instruction manual, or dogmatic teachings, to attain salvation. Instead, one needs to find the truth that the genuine man upstairs–the Monad–has instilled within us. This realization brings salvation, allowing the Minifigures to enter Cloud Cuckoo Land. But this presents a problem Orthodox Christianity struggles with, yet the Gnostics provide a solution.[218]

In Cloud Cuckoo Land, there is no questioning anything, no negativity, and no unhappiness; all despondency is "repressed down deep inside," according to Unikitty. At first, Cloud Cuckoo Land would appear to provide happiness to its inhabitants because it rids them of all pessimism. But the truth is much more mysterious: the inhabitants of Cloud Cuckoo Land are morbidly depressed. There is no happiness in Cloud Cuckoo Land because there is no more freedom than there is in the place they left, the Lego World. If liberty is found in one's actuality, rather than in one's potentiality, then Cloud Cuckoo Land presents a situation where the denial of reality results in one knowing only happiness, echoing the demiurgic anthem "Everything Is Awesome." Put another way, by knowing only joy, one is inherently unhappy, becoming an emotional slave. When Unikitty finally admits to herself she is unhappy, she escapes her self-imposed melancholic prison created by her psychological Christian religion by embracing gnosis, liberating her soul.

When they attack President Business' Tower, they triumph at first, but Lord Business eventually defeats Emmet. Vitruvius–the prophet who foretold the Special, the world's savior–reveals he made up the whole thing. Emmet is not the Special because there is no such thing as the Special. This contradiction is what redeems Emmet, allowing him to sacrifice himself to save the others and the world. Yet Vitruvius is wrong. The prophecy is valid, even though it is entirely false. To quote Emmett, Lego's Neo-like messiah: "The prophecy is made up, but it is also true." Vitruvius is a blind prophet, an ironic hero because what he preaches to the Master Builders is self-evident to everyone except himself; he is wise, yet ignorant. Sublime duality pervades the Gnostic Mysteries fathomable only to the initiated few.

And, finally, like so many Gnostic films, *The Lego Movie* is prophetic; it is unexplainable how certain cultural, political, and social conditions can express themselves in widely divergent ways, before the events take place. We think of *Donnie Darko*, when, in Donnie's bedroom, a plane's engine

---

218 Pagels, *Gnostic Gospels*, 126-131.

comes crashing down through an American flag, released one month after September 11, 2001 (this scene would've been filmed long beforehand). In *Vanilla Sky* (released December 10, 2001), the radiant Monet-like vanilla sky over the Twin Towers as David poignantly leaps off the skyscraper, plummeting downward seeking salvation. David's leap imitates those who jumped off the World Trade Centers after the planes struck the buildings; like *Donnie Darko*, *Vanilla Sky* was in post-production on September 11, 2001.

The Lego Movie, released on February 7, 2014, prophesied the coming President Donald J. Trump, akin to Nostradamus' predictions about the Great Fire of London (1666), Napoleon I (1769-1821), and Hitler. Specifically, the film features uncanny parallels between President Trump and the Man Upstairs/President Business. Like Trump, President Business is a ruthless entrepreneur. Both reside in a skyscraper: Trump Tower and the Octan Tower. The Octan Tower evokes the number 8; to the Kabbalists, it denotes perfection, representing the Man Upstairs/President Business' desire for flawless uniformity. Both Trump and Business want to build walls; President Trump has to deal with an opposition-leftist Resistance; in the Lego universe, there is the Piece of Resistance: the red Krazy Glue cap, neutralizing Business' weapon. President Business refers to his detractors as *snowflakes*, anticipating *snowflakes*: young, left-wing anti-Trump dissenters who are easily offended, unable to synthesize contrarian opinions, suffering from an inflated sense of uniqueness. When the Man Upstairs descends a staircase wearing a red tie, one thinks of Trump, wearing a red tie, riding down an escalator to announce his candidacy for the Presidency of the United States.

Snowpiercer's Deus Ex Machina:
We Control the Engine, We Control the World

Based on the French graphic novel *Le Transperceneige* by Jacques Lob (1932-1990), *Snowpiercer* (2013) reminded this author of *Metropolis* because it explores human consciousness married to a machine. In *Metropolis*, those that live above, and those that dwell below, rely on the Heart Machine; in *Snowpiercer*, the train's sacred engine sustains human life. Set in a post-apocalyptic world, *Snowpiercer*'s Gnosticism is liberation from the train, its demiurgic inventor, and its godly engine; humankind's divine spark is nobler than the machinations of the artisan god. The film's Marxist/Capitalist class warfare motifs are apparent, and, as such, not the subject of this analysis.

In 2014, an attempt to counteract global warming through climate engineering backfires catastrophically, causing an ice age that extinguishes nearly all life. The only human survivors are on the *Snowpiercer*, a massive train traveling on a circumnavigational track created by the transportation magnate and inventor, Wilford (Ed Harris). By 2031, elites inhabit the extravagant front cars while the lower classes–the scum–inhabit the back end in squalid and brutal conditions. Under watch by Wilford's guards, commanded by a martinet named Mason (Tilda Swinton), they are brought only gelatinous protein bars to eat; the disgusting meal is made from insects. The cruel bitch personifies Kabbalah's *Gevurah sefirah*, the feminine sphere of Mars linked with hatred, destruction, and the mother's callous authority. Mason is also loosely based upon Margaret Thatcher (1925-2013), a British Prime Minister (1979-1990) often despised for her aggressive cuts to social programs, draconian policies toward the working class, curtailing the state welfare system.

Conspiring with his mentor, Gilliam (John Hurt, 1940-2017), and second-in-command Edgar (Jamie Bell), Curtis Everett (Chris Evans) plans to lead the tail passengers in a revolt that will take them up to the engine. Gilliam evokes Terry Gilliam, a director whose filmography includes similarly bleak, cataclysmic science fiction such as *Brazil* (1985), *12 Monkeys* (1995), and *The Zero Theorem* (2013). Claude (Emma Levie), Wilford's assistant, along with a few armed guards, come to measure two small children, eventually taking Andy (Karel Veselý) and Timmy (Marcanthonee Reis). Andy's father, Andrew (Ewen Bremner), attempts to fight back but is punished by Mason, forced to put his arm into the extreme cold outside the train, amputating it. Enraged, Curtis initiates their plan the next time they are fed. Deducing the guards have no ammunition, Curtis and the tail passengers easily rout them, taking the security and prison cars.

In the prison car, Curtis releases security expert Namgoong Minsu (Kang-ho Song) and his clairvoyant daughter Yona (Go Ah-sung), so he can disable the locks between the cars, offering them a hallucinogenic drug called Kronole as payment. Gilliam suggests that if they take the water supply car, they will control any negotiations with Wilford. Instead, they are ambushed by a contingent of masked men with hatchets overseen by Mason, and Franco the Elder (Vlad Ivanov): a bruising and brutal archon. In the ensuing bloody battle, Curtis sacrifices Edgar but takes Mason captive. The next day, some of the insurgents press forward, holding Mason hostage, while many remain behind to tend the injured, guarding those they've captured.

They travel through several luxurious cars, arriving at a classroom, where an archon holds sway. Teacher (Alison Pill) gives the lesson, explaining to the children, and the rebels, the greatness of Wilford and the sacred engine. While distracted by the celebration of the New Year, marking a circumnavigation of the globe, Teacher ambushes them by pulling a gun from a basket of eggs, killing Andrew before Grey (Luke Pasqualino) blows her away. Further back, Franco and Mason's soldiers use the same distraction to kill the rebel army. Franco executes Gilliam, so Curtis executes Mason in revenge. Curtis' group presses forward, followed by Franco, leading to a violent fight in a sauna car during which Franco kills Grey before Curtis and Namgoong seemingly kill him. There is an allusion to *The Shining* buried in this scene–more on this in a moment.

At the engine's locked portal, Namgoong reveals he plans to use the highly flammable Kronole as an explosive to blow a hatch to the outside because he has observed signs the world is thawing and may be hospitable. Curtis confesses to him that shortly after boarding the train, the tail passengers–including himself–resorted to cannibalism to survive, haunting him still. He was nearly ready to kill the infant Edgar when Gilliam offered his arm instead. Sickened by his previous actions, Curtis' confession mirrors the Gnostic's rejection of a sacrificial offering, a Christian-styled Eucharist during which blood and flesh are consumed. Meanwhile, Franco regains consciousness, so he makes his way toward the sacred engine.

Wilford's assistant, Claude, emerges from the engine, shoots Namgoong, inviting Curtis inside, where he meets an aging Wilford. He explains to Curtis the revolution was orchestrated by himself and Gilliam to reduce the population, maintaining the balance of the hermetically sealed ecosystem, and subsequently orders the elimination of 74% of the remaining tail passengers. He explains the importance of using fear and chaos to keep order and leadership on the train. After letting Curtis experience being alone for the first time in seventeen years, Wilford asks Curtis to replace him. Curtis appears ready to accept, when Yona enters and pulls up a floorboard, showing Curtis tiny children from the tail section, including Andy and Timmy, are used as replacement parts for extinct machinery. In other words, the scum in the tail section exists solely to sustain the engine. Curtis subdues Wilford, sacrificing an arm to liberate Timmy from the engine, though Andy refuses to be saved.

Namgoong revives, killing Franco as Yona lights the fuse on the Kronole. However, the portal to the engine short-circuits and doesn't close, forcing Curtis and Namgoong to embrace Yona and Timmy tightly, shielding them from the blast. The explosion triggers an avalanche, derailing the train. Yona and Timmy, apparently the only survivors, the new Adam and Eve, emerge from the wreckage and see a polar bear in the distance, validating Namgoong's belief life exists outside the train.

Like the oppressed laborers in *Metropolis*, the tail end passengers seek spiritual and physical liberation from their deplorable conditions. Gilliam is the sage, counseling the multitude while prophesying the coming of a savior, Curtis. But Gilliam is not what he appears to be; he epitomizes duality, serving two distinct masters: Curtis and Wilford. Wilford compares his Machiavellian relationship with Gilliam and the inhabitants in the rear of the train–the scum–as two opposing sides working together: to investigate revolts, then suppress the uprising, maintaining the train's population while bringing order from chaos. This master-slave relationship conjures an ouroboros: a snake swallowing (or biting) its tail, the front car working with the rear cab, creating an unbreakable cycle. The *Snowpiercer*'s perpetual, serpentine circumnavigation signifies this vicious circle, beginning where it ends, ending where it begins.

To orchestrate this deception, Wilford sends cryptic notes to the train's back cars. These notes or clues, hidden in the protein bars, are written on red paper, infers the red pills from *The Matrix*. Like Morpheus, the notes encourage gnosis and liberation–a revolt against the forward cars–when it is just a ruse, orchestrated by Wilford and Gilliam. The notes are nothing more than a red herring–literally. Nevertheless, the downtrodden instigate a rebellion, unaware it is all a hoax, part of Wilford and Gilliam's grand scheme to reduce the train's population. Like a typical Manichean, Curtis' journey is depressed, his purpose is almost lost: does he want to destroy the sacred engine and kill Wilford? Does he want off the train, entering the frozen wasteland? In the end, he rejects Wilford's offer to replace him; like Valentinus' Christ, he sacrifices himself, destroying the train's mechanized-fake reality. Humankind is no longer subservient to Wilford, the artisan god; now, it can continue in the real world unshackled. This epiphany is Curtis' gnosis, his cosmic awakening.

In the journey through the train, the archons attack, keeping the rear passengers afraid and static. One reminds them they are the shoe that goes on the foot, existing at the bottom, they are scum. Interestingly, this archon is Mason, conjuring the conspiratorial paranoia associated with the Freemasons, a secret society long rumored to be manipulating society, keeping the vile multitude ignorant. Progressing through the train cars, they see wonders to behold, but they are all replications, cheap knockoffs of the original. These astonishing railway carriages imitate purifying celestial spheres; like the archons barring the human soul's celestial ascent, each represents a test, a Hermetic sphere, viz. the *Poimandres*' seven levels of spirituality–trials of the soul–that must be navigated to achieve gnosis, i.e., the *Poimandres*' eighth sphere. Kabbalah's Tree of Life mirrors this paradigm, with each *sefirah* guarded by an angelic order attempting to turn the wisdom seeker back–this is Teacher in the classroom car. At one point, Curtis *qua* Christ battles masked guards wielding axes. They dangle a fish before him, dipping their axes in its blood. The fish could symbolize one of two things or both. The fish is free to roam the water of the oceans without restraint. By showing a fish to the rear passengers and smearing its blood on their weapons, the implication is they're no longer free to wander unrestrained. They should return from whence they came or face dire consequences. Alternatively, the fish signifies the waning Age of Pisces, and Curtis *qua* Christ, the Piscean Age solar avatar, is a dead man walking. To this author, both explanations are valid.

Curtis and the rebels encounter the School Teacher who pulls a machine gun from a basket of eggs. Wilford goons pull machine guns from a cart of eggs, freeing the captured guards and slaughtering many rear-car passengers. The egg is a symbol of the Demiurge and his inferior universe; thus, eggs are a tool of Wilford's oppression.[219] They are decoys hiding his weapons of mass destruction, allowing him to control his train-as-reality and his sacred engine. *Ready Player One* parallels this imagery: the

---

219 Hall, *Secret Teachings*, 176.

demiurgic creators of the OASIS *qua* false reality, Halliday and Morrow, offer an egg as a reward, bequeathing the digital make-believe world to whoever finds the three keys. But Parzival, the Grail quester he is, has learned the lesson of Plato's Cave *qua* Halliday's bedroom. For Parzival's cosmic awakening–the end of his journey–is balance: he must moderate the OASIS, not be consumed by it. By doing so, Parzival, like the Arthurian knight from legend, redeems humankind by recovering the godly object.

Proceeding to the engine, they pass through two cars reminiscent of the Seven Deadly Sins. The first car is the nightclub wherein people dance with wanton abandon, denoting the sin of lust, and beyond that, we have the semi-conscious drug addicts, representing sloth. Upon reaching the sacred engine, Deus Ex Machina, we are finally introduced to the man behind the curtain, the Demiurge, the fashioner of the mighty *Snowpiercer*, the artificial reality. And he's quite the handyman: the aquarium and greenhouse cars are evidence of his craftsmanship. Nevertheless, his creation is flawed, needing tiny children from the rear cars to serve as lost parts, while the train itself divides the classes along the harshest lines, causing suffering, death, and despair. But behold, this craftsman has been seen before! Ed Harris portrays Wilford, drawing forth Christof, the demiurgic creator of Seahaven, Truman Burbank's fake reality. From Christof to Wilford, from one Demiurge to another, Harris' casting in *Snowpiercer* is occult and intentional, of this, there is no doubt.

Wilford *qua* the artisan-god reveals his plan: the revolt, like those previously, was a staged event designed to reduce the train's population. Offered to become the new Demiurge, to become one with Deus Ex Machina, Curtis refuses; his gnostic quest complete, like Christ, he dies, sacrificing himself to save humankind. Notice his hand displays stigmata, mirroring the wounds left on Jesus' body by his crucifixion; he perishes rejecting the false construct, saving the remaining human population's consciousness from the sacred engine, redeeming them. The train crashes and, the new first couple emerge from the train–the artificial construct–awakened to its horrors, entering the real world, transcending the false world of Wilford, the Demiurge.

Snowpiercer hides an occult homage to *The Shining*. In the golden sauna train car, like the Overlook's Gold Room, Franco the Elder fights the insurrectionists as Al Bowlly's (1898-1941) "Midnight, the Stars and

Jack Torrance's "Here's Johnny!" scene from *The Shining* (left) reincarnates in *Snowpiercer*'s Franco the Elder (right), a speechless archon.

You," plays faintly in the background. The song can be heard twice in the Overlook: during the ball, and during the big reveal at the end. The music draws a parallel subconsciously between the two movies' similarities: the brutal cold prevents the protagonists from escaping their confines, large and opulent rooms, and final scenes depicting a young woman and a boy fleeing into the harsh environment, hoping for better lives.

Although Franco receives minimal characterization, he serves as a crude tribute to Jack Torrance, hinted at during this scene. Franco shares a weapon of choice, the ax, with Torrance, and even the way the sweaty strands of gray hair fall upon his forehead resemble Torrance's demented visage. Namgoong and Yona surprise Franco, with the Curtis neutralizing him by stabbing him in the side. As this happens, the camera pans upward to focus on Franco, revealing a maniacal, toothy grin–nearly identical to Torrance when he breaks down the door in the iconic "Here's Johnny!" scene. The framing of Franco's face, accentuated by the yellow slats of wood beneath him, resembles Torrance's evil smile peeking through the broken door. Lastly, like all good Gnostic films, the use of Al Bowlly's song evokes duality: in *The Shining*, the song uneasily bookends Jack's descent into madness and his ultimate demise. In *Snowpiercer*, it denotes acute intellect, quick thinking, and a brutal fight for survival.[220]

---

[220] Killian Young, "How an Old Jazz Song Pays Homage to Stanley Kubrick's The Shining," *Consequence of Sound*, July 31, 2014, https://consequenceofsound.net/2014/07/how-an-old-jazz-song-pays-homage-to-stanley-kubricks-the-shining/ (accessed December 11, 2018).

Finally, watching *Snowpiercer* is like watching *Willy Wonka & the Chocolate Factory* (1971), only without the comedy. Think about it: in each film, a select group of people must traverse a dangerous and fantastic structure filled with wonders. One by one, they're picked off, with the surviving member, the one morally upright, face-to-face with a genius inventor, a reclusive industrialist employing oddball underlings. Willy Wonka (Gene Wilder, 1933-2016) uses the Oompa Loompas to punish and admonish spoiled children, and Wilford uses Mason and Franco the Elder to suppress the lower class. In the end, both Wonka and Wilford (their surnames have two syllables, starting with the letter *W*) reveal the whole thing was a test designed to find a worthy successor.

When one enters a movie theater, it is like going to church. One sits in a churchlike nave with aisles, in a pew, to receive light, wisdom, morality, the good Word. If films are spiritual events (and I believe they can be), then the Gnostic movies presented in this chapter are especially powerful revelations of the potential virtues of most commercial films. Gnostic cinema both deploys and negates the elements of the specific genre in which they surface. They offer and remove the pleasures of romance, the blockbuster's action, and the suspense of the thriller. In pointing to the unsettling energies lurking beneath the patina of conventional narratives, these movies invite us to witness them as we would an allegorical dream. That is, visible wish fulfillments of ungraspable yet enduring desires. As allegories of spirit–like symbols that veil and unveil simultaneously–these Gnostic films further urge us to envision all moving pictures in the same fashion, as vulgar surfaces perfectly designed to reveal pristine heights and depths.[221] Gnostic or otherwise, movies are modern-day myths; next, *Cinema Symbolism 3* analyzes Disney's *Beauty and the Beast*.

---

221 Wilson, *Secret Cinema*, 147-148.

CHAPTER III

ARCHETYPES, ALCHEMY, AND JUNGIAN PSYCHOLOGY IN DISNEY'S BEAUTY AND THE BEAST

♪ Certain as the sun
Rising in the east
Tale as old as time
Song as old as rhyme
Beauty and the Beast ♪
Celine Dion and Peabo Bryson, "Beauty and the Beast," 1991

I asked for the rose. Punish me, not him.
Belle, *Beauty and the Beast*, 2017

Initially, in *Cinema Symbolism 2*, I intended to include *Beauty and the Beast* in my Walt Disney movies chapter. At the time of completing my last movie book, Disney was about to release a live-action version; the studio's first take was as an aminated musical (1991), so I held off so I could watch both movies together. The live-action version debuted on February 23, 2017, and I'm glad I waited. The analysis presented here will focus on the recent incarnation because it follows the original fairy tale more closely than the '91 cartoon classic.

However, this analysis can be applied to both movies because they are based on the original lore, which is, ultimately, an astrological-archetypal-alchemical metaphor. As will be seen, all fairy tales follow the same formula. Like its earlier animated counterpart, the live-action *Beauty and the Beast* is an adaptation of Jeanne-Marie Leprince de Beaumont's (1711-1780) 18th-century fairy tale. In turn, Beaumont's story came from Gabrielle-Suzanne Barbot de Villeneuve (1685–1755), a French author influenced by Madame d'Aulnoy (1650/51-1705), Charles Perrault (1628-1703), and various *précieuse* writers. Perrault was a French writer and member of the *Académie Française*, laying the foundations for a new literary genre, the fairy tale, his works deriving from even earlier legends. Perrault's versions of the old stories include *Le Petit Chaperon Rouge* (*Little Red Riding Hood*), *Cendrillon* (*Cinderella*), *Le Chat Botté* (*Puss in Boots*), *La Belle au bois Dormant* (*The Sleeping Beauty*) and *Barbe Bleue* (*Bluebeard*). Perrault's tales heavily influenced their Germanic offshoots, published by the Brothers Grimm more than 100 years later. Nevertheless, Villeneuve's *La Belle et la Bête* (1740) is particularly noteworthy because it is the oldest known variant of the fairy tale, predating all others.

A beautiful Enchantress disguised as an old beggar arrives at a French castle during a ball, offering the host, a cruel and selfish prince (Dan Stevens), a vibrant red rose in return for shelter from a storm. When he refuses, she reveals her true identity. To punish the prince for his lack of compassion, the Enchantress transforms him into a horrible beast and his servants into household objects, then erases the castle, the prince, and his servants from the memories of their loved ones in the small town of Villeneuve nearby. In romantic fairy tales, the single rose symbolizes completion, consummate achievement, and perfection.[222] These ideals were pursued by Rosicrucian alchemists, represented by white and red roses, viz. profane versus enlightened.[223] Hence, accruing to it are concepts related to the mystic Centre, the heart, the garden of Eros, the paradise of Dante, and the emblem of Venus.[224] Reflecting this mysticism, she casts a spell on the rose, warning the prince the curse will only be broken if he aspires to love another, and earn their love in return, before the last petal falls, achieving completion. Easter egg: the town's name bears the surname of Gabrielle-Suzanne Barbot de Villeneuve, the author of *La Belle et la Bête*.

Some years later, in the township, Belle (Emma Watson), the book-loving eccentric daughter of a music box maker and artist, Maurice (Kevin Kline), dreams of adventure, brushing off advances from Gaston (Luke Evans), an arrogant ex-soldier. Gaston's flunkey, LeFou (Josh Gad), is French for *the madman*, a phonetic pun on *the Fool*. Easter egg: Belle (French for *beauty*) cavorting in the countryside parallels *The Sound of Music*'s (1965) Maria (Julie Andrews) signing in the lush hills, signaling her independence. More Easter eggs: the music box Maurice crafts is a

---

222 Cirlot, *Dictionary*, 263.
223 Ibid.
224 Ibid.

miniature of his windmill home in Paris, seen later in the movie. One will also observe a music box in the shape of an elephant with a mini Taj Mahal on its back; this is a reference to Disney's *Aladdin* (1992) because the Taj Mahal served as inspiration for the Sultan's palace. *Aladdin* was likewise made into a live-action film in 2019.

On his way to a convention, Maurice becomes lost in the wintery forest. He seeks refuge in the Beast's castle, warming himself near the fire. As he is about to dine, Chip the Teacup (Nathan Mack) inadvertently scares him away, but the Beast (Stevens) captures and imprisons him for stealing a white rose from the garden. Maurice intended the rose as a gift for Belle. When Maurice's horse returns without him, Belle ventures out in search of him, finding her father jailed inside the castle. The Beast agrees to let her take her father's place, remaining behind as the monster's prisoner.

Belle befriends the castle's servants, including the candelabra Lumière (Ewan McGregor), the teapot Mrs. Potts (Emma Thompson), and the clock Cogsworth (Ian McKellen), inviting her to a spectacular dinner. When she wanders into the forbidden west wing and discovers the cursed rose, the Beast scares her into the woods. A wolfpack ambushes her, but the Beast rescues her, injuring himself in the process. As Belle nurses his wounds, a friendship develops between them. He also brings her to his library, which makes her feel a different way toward the Beast, unlike before. The Beast shows Belle a gift from the Enchantress, a magical book that transports the readers wherever they want. Belle uses the book to visit her childhood home in Paris, discovering a plague doctor, realizing she and her father were forced to leave when her mother succumbed to the pestilence. Easter egg: upon arriving in Paris, Notre-Dame Cathedral appears in the background referencing another Disney animated classic, *The Hunchback of Notre Dame* (1996). Another Easter egg: the chief wolf has a scar through his left eye conjuring *The Lion King*'s antagonist, Scar (Jeremy Irons), who, likewise, has the same injury to his left eye.

In Villeneuve, Maurice tries to convince the other villagers of the existence of the Beast and Belle's imprisonment in the castle, but no one believes him. Gaston, seeing an opportunity to win her hand in marriage, agrees to help Maurice rescue her. When Maurice learns of his ulterior motive, he rebukes him, so Gaston abandons him to be eaten by the wolves. The hermit Agathe (Hattie Morahan) rescues and nurses Maurice back to health. When Maurice tells the townsfolk of Gaston's crime but is unable to provide conclusive evidence, Gaston convinces them to send Maurice to an insane asylum. Easter egg: one will see a white owl in Agathe's earthy home, alluding to Hedwig the Owl from the Harry Potter Universe, wherein Emma Watson played Hermione Granger.

After sharing a romantic dance with the Beast, Belle discovers her father's predicament by using the Beast's John Dee-like magic mirror. The Beast places Belle's happiness before his own, freeing her to save Maurice, giving her the mirror to as a token of their affection, leaving him and his servants heartbroken, realizing they will soon be inanimate. Back in the village, Belle reveals the Beast with the magic mirror to the townsfolk, proving her father's sanity. A jealous Gaston, realizing Belle loves the Beast, claims she has been hexed by dark magic, having her thrown into the asylum carriage with her father. He rallies the villagers to follow him to the castle to slay the Beast before he curses the whole village. Meanwhile, Maurice and Belle escape; in love, she hurries back to the Beast's castle. Easter Egg: inlaid on the dance floor, one will observe the initials *WD* in fancy cursive, paying homage to Walt Disney.

During the battle, Gaston abandons LeFoul, who sides with the servants to fend off the villagers. Gaston attacks the Beast in his tower, but Belle's departure has left him heartbroken to fight back; however, the Beast regains his zeal upon seeing her return. The Beast defeats Gaston but spares his life before reuniting with Belle. Ungrateful and unrepentant, Gaston mortally wounds the Beast with a gunshot from a bridge, but it collapses as the castle crumbles, so Gaston falls to his death. The injured Beast tells Belle how happy he was to see her again, then dies in her arms as the last petal falls, making the servants inanimate. As Belle tearfully professes her love for the Beast, Agathe reveals herself to be the Enchantress; she undoes the curse, repairs the crumbling castle, and revives the Beast. Then, her sorcery turns the Beast back to a prince, making his servants human once again, restoring the villagers' memories of their loved ones. The Prince and Belle host a ball; everyone dances happily, concluding the fairy tale.

Set in France, the northern hemisphere, *Beauty and the Beast* is an astrological-archetypal story documenting the moon, i.e., the sacred feminine, this time adopting the traits of the dawn or the feminized sun, interacting with the golden orb, the masculine. It is the telling of the ecliptic:

cold darkness–ominous clouds and night–turns into the revitalizing spring. So, it is with all fairy tales; the journey skyward and sunward is a common, if not a universal, theme.

For example, the little girl nicknamed *Little Red Riding Hood* (made into a live-action movie titled *Red Riding Hood*, 2011) personifies the winsome dawn, the youthful sun beginning the day. She dons the red cloak of autumn, symbolizing the changing greenery, which, in the fall, turns orange and red; she enters a dark forest to journey to her grandmother's house. The woods represent September, October, November, and December, signaling the shortening days during winter when the sun falls into decay, bringing the earth with it. Along the way, she encounters a lycanthrope–a werewolf–which speeds ahead, disguising itself as the grandmother after swallowing her whole, depending on the version presented. When Little Red Riding Hood arrives at grandma's, the wolf eats her as well. The consuming of Red Riding Hood signifies the biting winter: December, January, February, and March swallow the sun; thus, she is devoured by darkness, epitomized by the nocturnal werewolf, transformed by the full moon. But winter doesn't last forever: enter the vernal equinox, the masculine sun *qua* huntsman or woodcutter, slaying the wolf, liberating Red Riding Hood and the grandmother. The dawn and the sun are freed from the wintry belly to triumphantly rule the spring and summer months. Unified once more, they radiate warmth, light, and life. Easter egg: the Old Testament's Jonah and the Whale story epitomizes this same solar allegory.

Another exemplar is *Cinderella*, made into a live-action movie by Disney in 2015, starring Lily James, Helena Bonham Carter, Richard Madden, and Cate Blanchett. Cinderella is the aurora, the dawn: gray, dark, and dull, obscured by envious clouds, embodied by her stepsisters, and by her evil stepmother, the forbidding night. Neglected, she pines for the sun *qua* Prince Charming to return at the vernal equinox, liberating her.

This motif transcends *Sleeping Beauty* (1959) when Aurora[225] (*Aurora* means the *dawn*) seeks to unify with her masculine Apollonian Prince. Maleficent (voiced by Eleanor Audley, 1905-1991) personifies the darkness of night, the winter months, consigning Aurora to winter's depths when she pricks her finger on s spinning wheel, putting her into a paralyzing sleep. In winter, the dawn is dormant until the sun, Prince Charming, finally

---

225 Voiced by Mary Costas.

awakens her. The Prince *qua* the sun defeats Maleficent *qua* darkness, ultimately becoming one with the morning light, resurrecting it from the vault of winter, returning life to her. Know the sun is known by many names, including Osiris and his heir, Horus; Mithras, Ormazd (aka Ahura Mazda), Shamash, Apollo, Helios, Jesus, Moses, King Arthur, Surya, Hercules, Frodo Baggins, Luke Skywalker, and Harry Potter.

Like Red Riding Hood, Cinderella, and Aurora, Snow White is also the dawn; her Prince Charming is the sun, and evil Queen Grimhilde is darkness epitomized, the night and the winter months. It's all the same thing. The seven dwarfs, personifying the seven days of the week, administer aid to the heroine. Hexed by the black-cloaked Queen, she is sent into the deep sleep of the winter months only to be awakened, like the others, by the sun at the vernal equinox.

One key feature in all these legends are entities closely linked to each other—as closely, that is, as the sun and the dawn—may not look upon each other without misfortune. As such, the dawn is put in harm's way, falling into a slumber, hexed by wintery evil queens, or placed in the belly of a vicious werewolf. The solar prince must defeat the villain, the darkness of night, to liberate the dawn. This seasonal occultism is illustrated in the charming story of *The Land East of the Sun and West of the Moon*, told in various forms, the best of them are William Morris' (1834-1896) beautiful poem "The Earthly Paradise," (1870) and in Dr. George Dasent's (1817-1896) *Popular Tales from the Norse* (trans. 1859).[226] Comparatively, Snow White, Red Riding Hood, and Aurora could also be interpreted as earth goddesses akin to the Greek Cybele and Demeter, the Roman Ceres, or the Hindu Prithvi. Like the earth, they are comatose in winter. A woodman's ax, or Prince Charming's kiss, revives them, returning the sun's light at the vernal equinox, bringing foliage and life back to the earth. As the sacred feminine, they are also embodiments of the moon, performing the alchemical wedding with the sun, the *hieros gamos*, living happily ever after with the masculine.[227]

In *Beauty and the Beast*, we have an identical astrological-astronomic construct. The sun *qua* Beast is a monster, forever locked in the frigid,

---

226 James Thackray Bunce, *Fairy Tales: Their Origin and Meaning* (London: MacMillan and Co., 1878), *passim*.
227 Cirlot, *Dictionary*, 204.

gloomy winter months. Enter aurora, the virginal anti-Counter-Reformation progressive lass, Belle, breaking winter's spell to free the sun, allowing it to rule the spring and summer victoriously as a glorious blonde-haired and blued-eyed Prince. Belle and the Beast fall into despair because they are closely linked. She and her father are denounced as lunatics, and Gaston nearly kills the Beast. The cause of the Beast's icy curse is the wilting rose; its falling petals denote the autumn and winter months when the sun

"Osiris conquers Typhon, and Ormuzd, Ahriman, when, at the Vernal Equinox, the creative action of Heaven and its demiourgic [sic] energy is most strongly manifested. Then the principle of Light and Good overcomes that of Darkness and Evil, and the world rejoices, redeemed from cold and wintry darkness by the beneficent Sign into which the Sun then enters triumphant and rejoicing, after his resurrection." – Albert Pike, *Morals and Dogma of the Anceitn and Accepted Scottish Rite of Freemasonry*, 1871. (Left) The one-sheet movie poster for *Beauty and the Beast*, released on March 17, 2017 (USA), coincides with the vernal equinox on March 20 when the sun resurrects from its wintry death. Belle personifies the dawn, and the Beast is the sun trapped in perpetual winter. Since the dawn and sun are inseparable, they may not look upon each other without adversity. (Center) Darkness reigns supreme on the one-sheet movie poster for *Maleficent: Mistress of Evil*, depicting a beautiful Maleficent radiating defiance and gloom. Her two horns conjure such as Pan, Bacchus, and the Devil. Horns are a symbol of the masculine; thus, by protruding from the female fairy, they imply Maleficent is a phallic worshipper, akin to *The Lair of the White Worm's* (1988) Lady Sylvia Marsh (Amanda Donohoe). Like Lady Sylvia, Maleficent is bisexual; the only difference is the former is wily, erotic, and confident. The latter is celibate, exhibiting hermaphroditic confusion, hence the two colors of her bipolar magic. Subconsciously, Maleficent yearns to be the sexy, sharp-witted, antichristian, strap-on dildo wearing, human sacrificing, fun-loving vixen that is Lady Sylvia. Maleficent wants to pray at the serpent's altar while plucking Aurora's (Elle Fanning) delicate flower, attempting to unify opposites to become a Baphomet-like deity. Maleficent, appearing deliciously satanic in *Mistress of Evil* (right), echoes medieval Europe's sentiment regarding the Devil, believing the Prince of Darkness to be androgynous. In terms of Jungian depth psychology, the virginal Aurora represents two things. First, she personifies the *anima* (the unconscious feminine side of man); alternatively, she epitomizes a female archetype: the ancestral images lying dormant in the subconscious, waiting to be stimulated into action. In fairy tales, princesses lie dreaming in their palaces, like memories and institutions buried in our collective unconscious. The princesses in their castles, though not always asleep, are invariably outside the world of action, so that every sleeping, secluded, or chaste princess indicates a passive potential, a virgin maturing into sexual kinetic energy: masturbation at first, then intercourse, and then deviancy.

is weakest. It is kept in the castle's west wing implying death, the setting sun, signifying the Beast's curse, and his servants' deterioration. They must finally unite because they are linked inevitably; when they first dance, Belle and the Beast fall in love. Each wears the color of the other. Belle's elegant gown is resplendent yellow, conjuring the brilliant glow of the diurnal, life-giving orb; gold-leaf embellishes her dress, symbolizing sun rays. The Beast dons blue, signifying the coruscating azure sky at dawn, when the sun's rays break over the horizon, defeating the starry nighttime sky.

When Belle and the Beast discover true love is found within regardless of outward appearances, they break the Enchantress' spell. The trickster woman *qua* enchantress is the sign of Libra, which rules the autumn equinox, when the days become shorter, weakening the sun; think the myth of Delilah *qua* Libra cutting Samson's hair *qua* sun rays, enervating him. The servants regain their human form; the sun rises in the east, the castle thaws, winter is vanquished, the vernal equinox has returned. The monster is no longer confined to the beastly vault of winter; instead, the radiant sun emerges as a handsome Prince ready to take his bride, Belle, the lovely dawn. At the finale, at the midsummer-like celebration, as Mrs. Potts sings "Beauty and the Beast," listen carefully for the lyric, "♪ winter turns to spring ♪," exemplifying these esoteric-seasonal motifs. For the Prince and Belle have perfected the Chymical Marriage of Christian Rosenkreutz, unifying the sun and moon. As such, they have accomplished the syzygy; like a god and goddess, they are exalted in the heavens, dwelling in harmony.

Because it is a fairy tale, the collective unconscious-Jungian archetypes surface. Belle is the waxing moon, a child blossoming into a heroine; Gaston is the Devil, cruel and destructive; LeFou is the Fool, the obedient follower; and the Beast is the ogre father turned into an Apollonian hero. Maurice is like the hermit; Mrs. Potts is the nurturing mother; the Beast's castle is the Tower of the Tarot's Major Arcana, also known as the House of the Devil,[228] denoting the punishment of youthful pride and arrogance.[229] Agathe the Enchantress is the Trickster and Magician, and Lumière and Featherduster (Gugu Mbatha-Raw) and Maestro Cadenza (Stanley Tucci) and Madame Garderobe personify the Lovers.

---

228 Robert M. Place, *The Tarot: History, Symbolism, and Divination* (New York: Tarcher/Penguin, 2005), 155.
229 Richard Cavendish, *The Tarot* (New York: Harper & Row, Publishers, 1975), 123.

Archetypes populate these ancient myths and legends. They represent transition, making these stories alchemical allegories. These tales involve a metamorphosis or transformation from one thing to another, to unify something previously separated. Psychologically, they are about making something whole again, like the sun and the dawn, balancing light and dark. It has little to do with changing base metal to gold; instead, alchemy is about changing ignorance to wisdom. The word *alchemy* comes from the Coptic word for Egypt *Al Kemia*, meaning *Black Land*, and it first emerged in Alexandria in the 2nd century BCE. The Arabs had brought it to Europe during their occupation of Spain and Sicily. The hypothesis holds that Mohammedan grammarians believed alchemy derived from the wisdom of the Egyptians, which was the proud boast of Moses, Plato, and Pythagoras, and the source, therefore, of their illuminations. The greatest thinkers of the Middle Ages–St. Thomas Aquinas (1225-1274), Roger Bacon (ca. 1219/20-ca. 1292), Ramon Llull (ca. 1232-ca. 1315/16), and Arnaldus Villanovanus (ca. 1240-ca. 1311)–were involved in the pursuit of the Philosopher's Stone.[230]

Alchemical movies, descending from Egyptian science, enlighten us via symbols and allegories that draw light from darkness; they are a constant reminder of the *unus mundus*, binding us to the earth. Legends and fairy tales document the sun and moon's unification, *coincidentia oppositorum*, male and female, light and dark, the alchemical wedding, the key to the Baconian-Shakespearean-Rosicrucian mysteries. As I mentioned in the Introduction, four colors represent the four stages of alchemical change: the *nigredo*, the *albedo*, the *citrinitas*, and the *rubedo*. In cinema, alchemy is both literal and psychological, making it expressive, symbolic art. Comprehending this color scheme–what it designates–decodes this art and thus deciphers alchemical cinema; to Jung, the Great Art was the key to understanding the psychology of the unconscious.

* * * * *

The first stage, the *nigredo*, is blackness, meaning putrefaction or decomposition. It is darkness personified, primal chaos, the abyss, and the destructive monster. Called the Black Crow, Crow's Head, or Black Sun, its symbol is a rotting corpse, a blackbird, a king slaughtered by warriors,

---

230 Marshall, *Magic Circle*, 104; Israel Regardie, *The Philosopher's Stone* (n.p., 1938), 2.

or a dead king eaten by a wolf, viz. psychological deconstruction of the ego. A serpent *qua* dragon also symbolizes the *nigredo*; Hermes' caduceus signifies the spirit of life, the world soul present in all the alchemical stages. The Talaria-wearing god is a psychopomp, guiding souls to rebirth and integration, which can be positive or negative; the magician can be a dark, necromantic sorcerer. *Nigredo* is Mercury sinister, the Left-Hand Path, embodied by the androgynous Baphomet, the Goat of Mendes.[231] The *nigredo's* psychological equivalent is melancholia, pessimism, associated with the influence of the planet Saturn, the ruler of Capricorn when, in late December and into January, the life-giving orb is dormant in the northern hemisphere. Saturn correlates with death and evil; in astrology, it is a malevolent planet; in Hermeticism, it is the great dragon or Philosopher's Lead. Because it is the furthest from the sun, Saturn is cold, deemed black because its light is dim.[232] As an alchemical phase personified, *nigredo* is the villain, sometimes misunderstood or misguided; think Darth Vader, whose journey to the Dark Side of the Force was predicated on the Emperor's manipulative false truths. Sauron (Sala Baker) in Peter Jackson's *The Lord of the Rings* trilogy epitomizes the *nigredo*, trying to plunge Middle-earth into the Dark Night of the Soul: a period of spiritual dryness and depression.[233] In *The Raven* (1935), Dr. Richard Vollin (Bela Lugosi) thrives in the *nigredo*. He is a Poe-obsessed melancholic, taking pleasure by torturing and murdering people solely for the sake of torturing and murdering people. "What a torture! What a delicious torture, Bateman. Greater than Poe! Poe only conceived it! I have done it, Bateman! Poe, you are avenged," Vollin waxes gleefully, torturing his houseguests with Poe-inspired horror devices. In fairy tales, the *nigredo* is the werewolf in *Little Red Riding Hood*, while *Sleeping Beauty*'s Maleficent is a cruel and jealous black magician. In *Snow White*, the *nigredo* embodies the baleful Queen, transforming herself in a black-cloaked hag, hexing Snow White with a poisoned apple. Of course, the apple is an instrument of Satan who tempts Eve with one in the Garden, thereby linking the crone to the Prince of Darkness directly, making her the Devil's agent.[234]

---

231 Negative or black magic. Its opposite is the Right-Hand Path or white magic.
232 Cavendish, *Black Arts*, *supra* note 155; Greer, *New Encyclopedia*, 424.
233 Greer, ibid, 125.
234 See Faxneld, *Satanic Feminism*, "Apples and Phalluses: Some Examples of the Demonic Feminine in Rops's [*sic*] Oeuvre," 287-296.

Nina's unholy three are her overbearing mother, Erica (top left), the self-destructive ballerina Beth Macintyre (Winona Ryder, center left), and the black sorcerer Rothbart; the innocent dancer stands in awe before an idol of *Swan Lake*'s villain (bottom left). Together, they epitomize the *nigredo*: the black night of her soul. *Black Swan* is an ouroboros: it begins with a dream sequence, featuring Nina dancing with darkness, epitomized by owllike Rothbart. It concludes blurring fantasy with reality: she grows black wings alchemically (right), becoming a birdlike entity while performing the role of Odile. For her, the *rubedo* is the *nigredo*; the dance of death is her orgasm. Nina, a repressed lesbian, never unites with the divine masculine, so there is no *coincidentia oppositorum*. Instead, she masturbates and makes love to Lily; thus, her alchemy fails, having rejected the *citrinitas*. Although Nina achieves temporary perfection, she dies a ruined magician. From *Black Swan*.

As a Tarot archetype, *nigredo*-as-Mercurius, or Mercury existing in perpetual blackness, becomes an aspect of the Magician Card (I) of the Major Arcana, embodying will, intelligence, dominance, eloquence, individuality, action, gifted with acute perception.[235] The thaumaturge can initiate self-realization, Jung's *individuation*, serving as an emissary between the material and spiritual realms. In other words, he knows himself to be above nature or the hylic world, understanding his earthly operations succeed to the degree that his thought, word, and action transmit the powers of the spiritual plane above him faithfully. The greatest magicians know themselves to be no more than channels for the life-power, clear windowpanes through which the light of wisdom within the house of personality streams forth into the objective world.[236] He, or she, transcends

---

235 Cavendish, *The Tarot*, 67; *The Complete Picatrix: The Occult Classic of Astrological Magic – Liber Atratus Edition*, trans. John Michael Greer and Christopher Warnock (1256; repr., Adocentyn Press, 2018), 158.
236 Paul Foster Case, *The Tarot: A Key to the Wisdom of the Ages* (1947; repr., New York: TarcherPerigee, 2006), 41.

the ego, propitiate through magical rites.[237] The magician archetype is a traveler; mercurial, this figure can be a white or black sorcerer, both a positive or a negative force. In pop culture, FBI Special Agent Dale Cooper (Kyle MacLachlan) on *Twin Peaks* (Chapter XII) personifies the thaumaturge *qua* Mercurius. He is a positive yet disruptive force forever altering the social fabric of the sleepy town of Twin Peaks.

As a black magician, Mercurius forces us to confront our darkest fears; rebirthed, we become wiser versions of our former selves. Mercury, prospering the *nigredo* stage, dwelling there perpetually, as a shadowy agent of change, incarnates as *Blue Velvet*'s Frank Booth. By exposing Jeffrey to Lumberton's underbelly, Booth initiates gnosis, supplying the seeker with the dark experiences he desperately craves. Like the black he wears, and the sinister, fecund garden he tends, Booth as the magician blurs all distinctions, annihilating the differences between father, husband, and son. He plays both a violent adult and a helpless child. He wants dominion over Dorothy Vallens yet surrenders his mind to nitrous oxide. Under Booth's tutelage, Jeffrey emerges as a more worldly figure, understanding there are no absolutes; good and evil are nonexistent, only shades of gray fester with some hues darker than others. In *Angel Heart*, Louis Cyphre is Lucifer the Light Bearer: a refined Hermes Trismegistus-like fallen angel, furnishing Harry Angel with en*light*enment, whether or not he wants it. As the chthonic magician, Cyphre's sorcery slowly pulls back the veil, guiding Angel through a murderous maze to discover his true identity. In *The Dark Knight*, the Joker (Heath Ledger) is the Tarot's Magician: he is a destructive-alchemical "agent of chaos" to quote the Harlequin of Hate. His mission is a never-ending peregrination to destroy and rebuild so that Gotham will reflect his sick and twisted sense of humor. Dr. Hannibal Lecter (Anthony Hopkins) is the dragon Mercurius. Under his devilish guidance, Special Agent-in-training Clarice Starling (Jodie Foster) reconciles her bleak childhood, allowing her to overcome her fear to apprehend serial killer Jame "Buffalo Bill" Gumb. Starling's menacing therapy sessions with Lecter *silences the lambs* tormenting her; by welcoming blackness, she lets Mercurius obliterate her ego and her cheap shoes. In the reality in which we live, Mercury embodies the 45th President, Donald J. Trump. Born June 14, 1946, he is given to Gemini, which Mercurius governs, making

---

237 Nichols, *Jung and Tarot*, 45.

him the archetypal great disruptor, the wrecker of worlds, the destroyer of norms, the annihilator of good and evil. As Mercury, Trump's purpose is pure, simple, and twofold, viz. Geminian: (1) to dismantle the legacy of the 44th President, Barack Obama, erasing it from history; and (2) annihilate the mainstream media's credibility. Trump *qua* Mercurius pulls this off because this archetype understands there's no such thing bad press; the thoughts and feelings of others are rightly consigned to the void.

Historically, Jacob Boehme's (1575-1624) *Aurora* analyzes Mercury as a wrathful, destructive agent. But Mercurius can be a medium for consciousness, Logos, or the Word; when love permeates Mercury, it's a means to communicate with the divine. Such a personification would be Cinderella's beneficial fairy godfather or Glinda the Good Witch (Billie Burke, 1884-1970), succoring Dorothy's gnosis, her spiritual rebirth.[238] When she returns to Kansas, the farmhands do not understand her Gnostic revelation.

From darkness rises moonlight, the *albedo*, the feminine, the transition from gloom to albification. The *albedo* leads the adept out of the black night of the soul. The stage appears when the solution is blanched, with no color yet all colors, transparent spirit, and opaque body. The *albedo* is Luna, the moon, the light of the night, becoming Diane and her dark antithesis, Hecate, and the virginal maiden waiting for her marriage. It is the sacred feminine; in this stage, the matrix's swells are congealed, the slivering snake is frozen, his quicksilver transformed into a stable body. Mercury iced represents the world soul in a purified state. In fairy tales, the *albedo* is the heroine: Snow White, Little Red Riding Hood, and Sleeping Beauty–they are all personifications of the second alchemical stage, the moon. The moon has two sides, dark and light; in *Blue Velvet*, Dorothy Vallens and Sandy Williams bask in Luna's glow, a motherly whore and devious virgin, Lilith and Sophia commingled.

Citrinitas is the third stage, the yellow sun, the diurnal ruler. *Transmutation of silver into gold* or *yellowing of the lunar consciousness* occurs during this phase. In alchemical philosophy, *citrinitas* stood for the dawning of the *solar light* inherent in one's being; reflective lunar or soul light was no longer necessary because they are now unified, perfecting the alchemical wedding. In fairy tales, Prince Charming personifies the

---

238 Arthur Versluis, *Magic and Mysticism: An Introduction to Western Esotericism* (Lanham, MD: Rowman & Littlefield Publishers, Inc., 2007), 108.

citrinitas, the divine masculine, for he is *sol invictu*s, the unconquered sun, unifying with the *albedo*, anticipating the grand finale.

The finality of the Magnum Opus is the *rubedo*. The Red King *qua* sun and White Queen *qua* moon now married the process is complete. In this phase, Mercurius is a thriving pure spirit, a fiery talisman capable of combing all oppositions into harmony, the Philosopher's Stone accomplished. In synthesizing life and death, chaos and order, light and dark, and the sun and the moon, the *rubedo* is not merely life, the eternal infant; it is also death, the dying king. Psychologically, the *rubedo* signals the ego's realization of the collective unconscious' archetypes. What was once unconscious now becomes conscious: the man understands his feminine energies; the woman apprehends her masculine side. This union is integration, Jung' *individuation*: the realization of self (or selfhood), the assimilation of both light and dark, male and female, and shadow and ego into a whole personality. Medieval and Renaissance alchemists grounded their occult ideas and interpretations on the Gnostic traditions and philosophies. The microcosm within realizes its connection to the macrocosm without; together, they become aware of their relationship to the trans-cosmic, the plenitude.[239]

In *Snow White and the Seven Dwarfs*, the red apple represents the *rubedo* circuitously, signifying the evil Queen's curse, her black magic, which is broken by the Prince, unifying the moon and sun. In *Little Red Riding Hood*, her red cloak denotes her journey from autumn (the forest) to winter (the wolf's belly) to spring (liberation from the icy tomb by the huntsman's ax). It is the end of the cycle; she is both infant and elder, creating the pathway to the Philosopher's Stone. In *Sleeping Beauty*, Prince Phillip (Bill Shirley, 1921-1989) weds Aurora; they dance in the clouds like only the sun and moon can do. Unified, signifying *coincidentia oppositorum*, he wears a red cape designating the end of the alchemical process, the Great Operation perfected.

* * * * *

Now let's apply alchemy to the fairy tale at hand. The *nigredo* is the Enchantress' curse, consigning the Prince to winter, transforming him into a monster. His servants are changed into household items; his castle becomes a gloomy, frozen wasteland. Into this darkness enters the light of the moon,

---

239 Wilson, *Secret Cinema*, 106-109.

the sacred feminine, the free-thinking Belle. The Beast *qua* Prince and Belle must fall in love, looking beyond outward appearances–only then will the curse be lifted, linking their energies. The Beast must find compassion and mercy within to shed his hideous appearance to become the *citrinitas,* becoming a blonde-haired blue-eyed sun god. The *rubedo* is the red rose, the symbol of the Enchantress' alchemy, her magic transmogrifying the Prince and his servants. The moon and the sun unite, falling in love. Despite the last red petal falling, the Enchantress reverses her spell, having mercy on the Beast–pity he did not show her–completing the archetypal story. The young King (the sun) and Queen (the moon) are thus resurrected at the summit of the tower and ensouled by Divine Life representing the forces of the two great luminaries–Intelligence and Love–which must ultimately guide society, enshrined in *Beauty and the Beast*. Easter egg: in the Paris flashback, the rose also appears as a talisman associated with Maurice's sick wife (Zoe Rainey), depicted in Maurice's painting of his wife and Bell, designating this alchemy.

Jung suggests particular myths and fairy tales erupt out of the collective unconscious when there is a need within the collective psyche trying to express itself, expressing significant questions and issues. The ones small children ask, that inquiring adolescents ask again, or that as adults, we leave for others to ask and answer for us. Except, when knocking on the walls becomes more insistent in times of crisis, we discover the act of authentically living requires us that we ask for ourselves. Perhaps never more so than today when searching for meaning (and other people's answers) is such a mega-business. From a Jungian-psychological standpoint, *Beauty and the Beast* is about the maturity of a girl into a young woman. In modernity, girls share in the masculine hero myths because, like boys, they must also develop a reliable ego/identity, acquiring an education. But there is an older layer of the mind that surfaces regarding their feelings: to make them into women, not into imitations of men. When this ancient content of the psyche begins to make its appearance, the sophisticated young woman may repress it because it threatens to cut her off from the emancipated equality of friendship and the opportunity to compete with men that have become her contemporary privileges.[240]

---

[240] Joseph L. Henderson, "Ancient Myths and Modern Man," in *Man and His Symbols*, ed. Carl G. Jung (New York: Dell, 1968), "Beauty and the Beast," 128-134.

Beauty and the Beast expresses this universal myth; it is a meditation on feminine awakening, to know thyself, or herself. In the original tale, Belle, the youngest of four girls (representing the four seasons, two equinoxes and two solstices), becomes her father's favorite because of her unselfish goodness. She is aware of her inner sincerity of feeling when she asks her father only for a white rose–a token of the *albedo*, her lunar-alchemical presence–instead of the costlier presents demanded by the others. She does not know she's about to endanger her father's life and her tender relationship with him. When he steals the white rose from the Beast's enchanted garden, the monster is stirred to anger by the theft, requiring the father to return in three months for his punishment: presumably death. By allowing the father this reprieve, to return home with his gift, the Beast behaves out of character, especially when he also offers to send him a trunk full of gold when he gets there. As Belle's father comments, the Beast seems cruel and kind at the same time. Belle insists upon taking her father's punishment, returning after three months–signifying the three months in each season–to the enchanted castle. There she is given a beautiful room where she has no worries and nothing to fear except the Beast's occasional visits, who repeatedly comes to ask her if she will someday marry him. Belle always refuses his advances. Then, seeing in a magic mirror a picture of her father lying ill, she begs the Beast to allow her to return to her father to comfort him, promising to return in a week. The Beast tells her that he will die if Belle deserts him, but she may go for a week. At home, her radiant presence brings joy to her father and envy to her sisters, who plot to detain her longer than she promised to stay. At length, Belle dreams the Beast is dying of despair. So, realizing she has overstayed her time, she returns to resuscitate him.[241] Recall the Beast personifies the stagnant sun, trapped in perpetual winter.

Forgetting the dying Beast's ugliness, Belle returns to him, anticipating the Stockholm Syndrome: that is, when captives, during their imprisonment, develop a psychological alliance with their captors. The Beast tells Belle that he was unable to live without her and he will die happy since she has returned. But Belle realizes she cannot live without the Beast because she has fallen in love with him. She tells him so, promising to be his wife if he will not die. With this spring returns: the castle glows with a blaze of

---

[241] Ibid.

light and the sound of music. The Beast disappears; in his place stands a handsome prince, telling Belle that a witch hexed him, turning him into the monster. The spell was ordained to last until a beautiful girl should love the Beast for his goodness alone, seen in both of Disney's movies, animated and live-action.

If we unravel the psychological motifs, we are likely to see that Belle is any young girl or woman, having entered into an emotional bond with her father, no less binding because of its spiritual nature. Her request for a white rose designates her goodness. Still, in a significant twist of meaning, her unconscious intention puts her father, then herself, in the power of a principle that expresses not only goodness alone, but cruelty and kindness. In the Disney versions, the Beast treats Belle like royalty: he needs her to break the curse, but despite being his prisoner, he falls in love with her. It is as if she wished to be rescued from a love holding her to an exclusively virtuous and unreal attitude.[242]

By learning to love the Beast, she awakens to the power of human love concealed in its animal–and therefore imperfect–but genuinely erotic form. Presumably, this represents an awakening of her true function of relatedness, enabling Belle to accept the erotic component of her original wish. Belle repressed this sensual element because of a fear of incest. To leave her father, she had, as it were, to accept the incest-fear, allowing herself to live in its presence in fantasy until she could get to know the animal man, discovering her response to it as a woman. In this way, she redeems herself, and her image of the masculine, from the forces of repression, bringing to consciousness her capacity to trust her love as something that combines spirit and nature in the best sense of the words. But in the cases of older women, the Beast theme may not indicate the need to find the answer to a personal father fixation or to release a sexual inhibition or any of the things that the psychoanalytically-minded rationalist may see in the myth. It is a unique expression of a woman's initiation, which might be as meaningful at the onset of menopause as at the height of adolescence. This initiation may appear at any age when the union of spirit and nature has been disturbed. For Belle, the inauguration is the descent into the lower regions of a strange house–the Beast's Castle–emerging at a highly conscious level. This initiation, we can guess to be the entrance to some meaningful aspect of the

---

[242] Ibid.

collective unconscious, challenging her to accept the masculine principle as the animal-man, that same heroic, clown-like Trickster archetypal figure. For Belle to relate to this ape-man, to humanize him by bringing out the goodness in him, means she would first have to accept some unpredictable element of her creative spirit. With this acceptance, she could cut across the conventional bonds of her life and learn to write in a new way, more appropriate for her in the second part of life.[243] For the Beast, he must tame the nonconformist-mercurial trickster within.

For both Belle and the Beast, this *new way* involves a new acceptance of the dual principle of life in nature; namely, cruel is to be kind, or, as we might say in their case, ruthlessly adventurous but at the same time humbly and creatively domestic. These opposites obviously cannot be reconciled except on a highly sophisticated psychological level of awareness; ergo, they would be harmful to that innocent child in her Sunday school dress. Both the Beast and Belle are initiates of a psychological mystery school, themselves archetypes from our subconsciousness, making them reflections of all of us. The Beast had to be willing to embrace the full polarity of his emotions, then subdue them. Belle had to give up the innocence of trusting in a father who could not give her the pure white rose of his feeling without awakening the beneficent fury of the Beast.

Next, *Cinema Symbolism 3* turns to one of this author's favorite genres: horror and suspense.

---

243 Ibid.

CHAPTER IV

GIVE YOUR SOUL TO THE DANCE: MELANCHOLIC HORROR AND SUSPENSE

There's a reason we're supposed to be afraid of this night.
Deputy Hawkins, *Halloween*, 2018

Hail the Queen of the May!
Lord Summerisle, *The Wicker Man*, 1973

The mummy's on the loose and he's dancing with the Devil.
Goobie, *The Mummy's Curse*, 1944

The witches' song in *Macbeth* is believed to have an uncanny power for evil, and many actors cannot be induced to play in that tragedy.
Astra Cielo, *Signs, Omens and Superstitions*, 136, 1918

If you're not planting, why would you put up a scarecrow?
Mrs. Hocker, *Dark Night of the Scarecrow*, 1981

They say there's just enough religion in the world to make men hate one another, but not enough to make them love.
Louis Cyphre, *Angel Heart*, 1987

When you dance the dance of another,
you make yourself in the image of its creator.
Mme. Blanc, *Suspiria*, 2018

What's wrong with weird? Weird's like the nuts in my cookies,
it's the nuts that make things interesting.
Florence Zimmerman, *The House with a Clock in Its Walls*, 2018

Look–the sacred spells which protect the soul in its journey to the underworld have been chipped off the coffin. So, Imhotep was sentenced to death not only in this world, but in the next.
Dr. Muller, *The Mummy*, 1932

Occult symbolism, when contextually deployed in horror films, is some of Hollywood's finest. The films of John Carpenter, *The Exorcist*, and, of course, Kubrick's *The Shining* are great examples of maximizing arcane symbolism's effects. Although I've mentioned this before in my previous books and discussed it numerous times on different radio shows, I love how *The Exorcist* and *The Shining* use Halloween to convey hidden meaning; namely, the macabre festivities of October 31 auger the approaching wintery bleakness. In the northern hemisphere, the sun's heavenly light is in a coffin; ergo, darkness reigns, allowing evil to run amok.

In *The Exorcist*, as Chris MacNeil strolls home from the movie shoot at Georgetown University, a gaggle of trick-or-treaters runs past her, designating Halloween, marking the midway between the autumn equinox and the winter solstice. With darkness triumphing over light, evil runs amok: the demon Pazuzu possesses Chris' young daughter, Regan. In *The Shining*, Ullman tells Jack the Overlook operates from May to October 30; thus, the Torrance family arrives at the hotel on Halloween to begin their caretaking duties. Soon thereafter, winter comes; the Overlook's sinister ghosts control Jack, turning him into a murderous wrecking ball.

Angel Heart perfects cinematic occultism, successfully combining Satanism with noir, a unique fusion of genres. Louis Cyphre–Lucifer, a black-suited Mercurius Trismegistus–hires Private Detective Harry Angel to find crooner Johnny Favorite. But Lucifer is not a monster; instead, he is a refined eccentric because the Evil One is adapting with the times, becoming a polite, clever, soft-handed gentleman; the normalization only leaves him a more false-hearted and villainous than before. Indeed, what a new and strange departure to find Mr. Cyphre hand in glove with clergymen instead of at a witches' sabbath. Recall a Christian Church serves as Lucifer's headquarters, run by the false prophet, the greedy Pastor John (Gerald Orange), damning his flock rather than offering them the dispensation of the Gospels.

Lucifer's sleight of hand shadows Angel from start to finish. Before heading to Coney Island to investigate, Angel refers to Favorite by his nickname, "golden tonsils." When Angel gets to the amusement park, he speaks to Izzy's wife (Judith Drake), who is standing in the waves. She, too, refers to Favorite as "the man with the golden tonsils." Why is this significant? The repetition indicates that Angel knows he is Favorite subconsciously; somehow, he is aware of the nickname, confirmed by Izzy's wife.

CINEMA SYMBOLISM 3

When Cyphre blows salt from his egg onto the restaurant table, Angel takes a pinch and throws it over his left shoulder. The superstition follows that by doing so, you blind the Devil, lurking on your sinister side. Johnny Favorite's real surname is Liebling, German for *sweetheart, darling,* or *angel*, but its secondary meaning is *favorite*. The Johnny Favorite song, "Girl of My Dreams," that Lucifer plays on the record player is the same melody Epiphany Proudfoot (Lisa Bonet) sings in the bathtub earlier–identified as a Johnny Favorite tune her mother always sang to her.

"Girl of My Dreams" haunts the mystery, from Courtney Pine's ghostly saxophone solos to a one-fingered styled rendition on an out-of-tune piano. In one scene, when he is driving to the clinic where Johnny is registered as a patient, Angel whistles the song, a tune he shouldn't know or recall, insinuating he is Favorite. When Angel gets to the clinic, he opens his briefcase to retrieve a fake identification card to present to the nurse (Kathleen Wilhoite). Inside, there is a set of skeleton keys foreshadowing Margaret's Krusemark's (Charlotte Rampling) Hand of Glory, a coveted relic of witchcraft that opens any lock. These are the hallmarks of expert craftsmanship and superior filmmaking. To the director of *Angel Heart*, Alan Parker (1944-2020), I salute you.

Esoteric symbolism in horror films is transcendent and, thus, powerful; whether hidden or overt, it doesn't seem to matter. It is efficacious, regardless; for example, in *Trick 'r Treat*, a female werewolf named Danielle (Lauren Lee Smith) lures her victims to Sheep's Meadow for a Halloween night bacchanalia, only to slaughter them. And one has to wonder about those Harry Potter books and movies–are they satanic? Most likely not (at least I don't think so) but it is peculiar that Nicholas Flamel is 666 years old, forcing one to wonder about Hermione Granger (Emma Watson), specifically her forename.

Hermione is an unusual name, and those women with it have the nickname "Minnie." In horror and suspense cinema, Minnie conjures one thing and one thing only. It evokes the evil witch, Minnie Castevet from *Rosemary's Baby*, portrayed by Ruth Gordon (1886-1985), who won the Academy Award for Best Supporting Actress. Is *Hermione* secretly paying homage to the diabolical witch of Black Bramford? Combine this innuendo with Flamel's 666 years, and one is right to conjecture if the students at Hogwarts are, in fact, black magicians. Do they all secretly adore the Goat of Mendes, or is Baphomet reverence reserved for the students of Slytherin House?

In *Cinema Symbolism*, I analyzed the occult motifs related to *Dracula*, *Frankenstein*, and *The Wolf Man*, all early Universal Pictures, and all predicated on earlier mythologies and legends. Excluded was *The Mummy*, also released by Universal Pictures. It seems only appropriate to tackle this classic horror film, arguably one of the best of the Universal Monsters. Next, the saturnine mummy, and the pangs of the living dead.

Desolation and the Resurrected Dead: The Mummy 1932

Thoth, the author of the texts that form the *PER-T EM HRU*, or *Book of the Dead*, was believed by the Egyptians to have been the heart and mind of the Creator, who was in Ancient Egypt called by the natives, *Pautti*, and by foreigners, Ra. Thoth was also the *tongue* of the Creator, voicing the will of the great god, speaking the words which commanded every being in heaven and on earth to come into existence. His words were almighty and, once uttered, never remained without effect. He framed the laws by which heaven, earth, and all the supernal bodies are maintained; he ordered the courses of the sun, moon, and stars; he invented drawing and design and the arts, the letters of the alphabet and the art of writing, and the science of mathematics.[244] At an early period, he was called the scribe of the Great Company of the Gods. Many generations of Egyptians regarded him as the Recording Angel since he kept the celestial register of the words and deeds of men.[245]

Inspired by the opening of Tutankhamun's (ca. 1341-1323 BCE) tomb in 1922, and the infamous Curse of the Pharaohs that befell George Herbert, 5th Earl of Carnarvon (b. 1866), producer Carl Laemmle Jr. (1908-1979), wanted to make a mystery. The Mummy's Curse is no joke; Carnarvon, Howard Carter's (1874-1939) financial backer, was bitten on the face by a mosquito, which became infected, causing him to contract pneumonia, dying on April 5, 1923. At the same time, all the lights in Cairo went out,

---

[244] *The Book of the Dead*, trans. E.A. Wallis Budge (1894; repr., London: British Museum. 1920), 14.
[245] Ibid, 14-15.

and his dog Susie also died at his estate in Hampshire, England.[246] But the curse does not end there:

- Lord Carnarvon's half-brother, Aubrey Herbert (1880-1923), died of peritonitis.
- Professor Lafleur, who studied the treasure and visited the tomb, died suddenly at Luxor.
- Archaeologist Hugh Evelyn-White (1884-1924) fell into depression and hanged himself. His suicide note read: "I have succumbed to a curse which forces me to disappear."
- The scientist who x-rayed the mummy, Douglas Reed, suddenly died.
- Egyptian Prince Ali Fahmy Bey was murdered in a London hotel room, and his brother committed suicide.
- Papyrus expert Bernard Grenfell (b. 1869) and Egyptologist Aaron Ember (b. 1878) died in 1926.
- Carter's right-hand man, Arthur Mace (1874-1928), died five years after Lord Carnarvon. He suffered from symptoms that resembled arsenic positioning.
- In 1929, the wife of Lord Carnarvon died.
- Richard Bethell, who was responsible for cataloging the treasure, died in 1929 at the age of thirty-five.
- In 1930, Bethell's father committed suicide by jumping out the window of his London apartment. In his bedroom was a vase from Tutankhamun's tomb.
- Shocked by the number of deaths, a government official was sent to the grave to investigate the situation. Within a few days, he also became ill and died.

Seventeen people who can be directly or indirectly associated with King Tut's tomb died unnatural, strange, or early deaths within a few years. Oddly enough, the discoverer of the grave, Howard Carter, had remained outside the crypt, dying in 1939 of natural causes.[247]

---

246 Heather Lynn, *Evil Archaeology: Demons, Possessions, and Sinister Relics* (Newburyport, MA: Disinformation Books, 2019), 236.
247 Ibid, 236-237.

Laemmle commissioned story editor Richard Schayer (1880-1956) to find a literary novel to form a basis for an Egyptian-themed horror film, just as *Dracula* and *Frankenstein* inspired their 1931 cinematic concomitants. Schayer found none, although the plot bears a strong resemblance to a short story by Conan Doyle titled "The Ring of Thoth" (1890). Schayer and writer Nina Wilcox Putnam (1888-1962) learned about Freemason, occultist, and magician Alessandro Cagliostro, writing a nine-page treatment titled *Cagliostro*. The story, set in San Francisco, was about a 3,000-year-old sorcerer who survives by injecting nitrates. Laemmle was pleased with these ideas, so he hired John L. Balderston (1889-1954) to write the script. Balderston had contributed to *Dracula* and *Frankenstein*, having covered the opening of Tutankhamun's tomb for *New York World* when he was a journalist. Hence, he was more than familiar with the highly popular tomb unearthing. So, Balderston moved the story to Egypt, renaming the film and changing its title character's name to Imhotep, the historical architect.

The *Mummy* is an American pre-code Universal horror film; Karl Freund (1890-1969), the cinematographer on *Dracula*, was hired to direct, making this his first film in the United States as a director. Freund had also been the cinematographer on Lang's *Metropolis* and later photographed the television series *I Love Lucy* (1951-1957). The movie is about an ancient Egyptian mummy discovered by a team of archeologists, inadvertently brought back to life via a magical papyrus. Masquerading as a modern Egyptian, the mummy searches for his lost love, whom he believes has been reincarnated into a modern, young woman. Freund cast Zita Johann (1904-1993) as the female lead. Johann was a student of the occult and Kabbalah, believing in the ability to communicate with the dead, and reincarnation. Her character, Ankh-es-en-Amon, is named after the only wife of Tutankhamun, her half-brother. The historical Ankhesenamon's (*Her Life Is of Amun*, ca. 1348-1322 BCE) body had not been discovered in King Tut's tomb; born Ankhesenpaaten, she was the third of six known daughters of the Egyptian Pharaoh Akhenaten (d. 1336-1334 BCE) and his royal wife Nefertiti (1370-1330 BCE). Her name change reflects the transition in the Ancient Egyptian religion during her lifetime and after her father's death. Akhenaten had abandoned Egypt's old deities in favor of the Aten, hitherto a minor aspect of the sun god, characterized as the sun's disc.

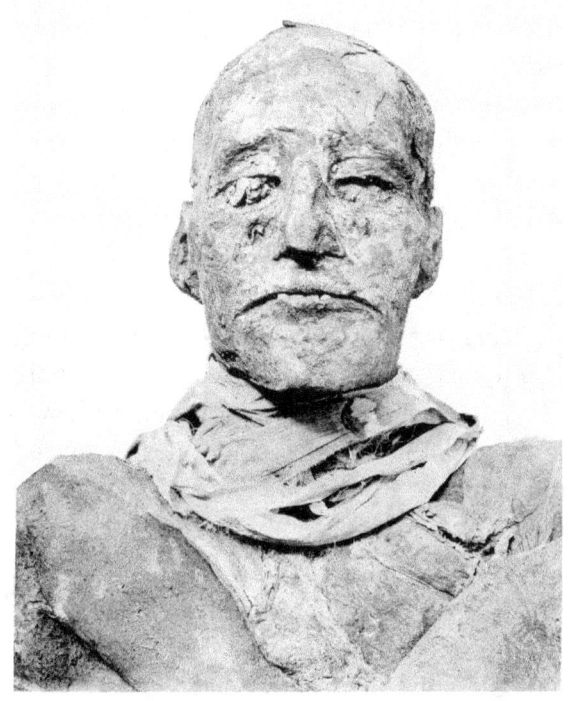

The mummy of Usermaatre Ramesses III, the second Egyptian Pharaoh of the Twentieth Dynasty. Jack Pierce used photos of this mummy to craft Karloff's deathly appearance.

From the Scroll of Thoth: "Oh! Amon-Ra--Oh! God of Gods--Death is but the doorway to a new life---We live today-we shall live again--In many forms we shall return-Oh, mighty one." It opens in 1921 with an archaeological expedition led by the Howard Carter-like Sir Joseph Whemple (Arthur Byron, 1872-1943), finding the mummy of an ancient Egyptian high priest named Imhotep (Boris Karloff, 1887-1969). Ramses III's (reign: 1186-1155 BCE) mummy was used by legendary makeup artist Jack Pierce (1889-1968) to design Karloff's bandaged appearance; Pierce spent eight hours a day applying the makeup. When an inspection of the mummy by Whemple's friend, Dr. Muller (Edward Van Sloan, 1882-1964), reveals the viscera were not removed, Muller deduces that although Imhotep had been prepared like a traditional mummy, he was buried alive. Hidden with Imhotep is a smaller casket with a curse on it. Van Sloan is typecast because the effendi Muller, an Egyptian expert and master of the occult sciences, is also a monster exterminator par excellence. A year earlier, in *Dracula*, he played the identical character: Dr. Van Helsing, the sagacious vampire hunter. Only now, he pursues a mummy–the resurrected dead–echoing the vampire because both are living corpses. Large segments of Freund's movie are scene-by-scene parallels of *Dracula*.[248] For example, the apotropaic Amulet of Isis substitutes for the crucifix; the former protects the wearer against Imhotep's dark powers, while the latter keeps Dracula at bay.[249] Both talismans can be worn around the neck. Despite Dr. Muller and Professor Van Helsing's safeguards, both female protagonists elude their protectors, ending up in the arms of their seducers, but not for long. In *The Mummy*, as in *Dracula*, the elderly mentor and the heroine's sweetheart track the menace to his lair, arriving just in time to witness his destruction, saving the sacred feminine from a fate worse than death.[250]

Muller and Whemple exit the tomb to discuss the casket and its curse. Despite Muller's warning, Sir Joseph's assistant, a modern-day Pandora, Ralph Norton (Bramwell Fletcher,1904-1988) opens it. He reads aloud the Scroll of Thoth, an ancient life-giving manuscript, preserving the incantations the virginal Isis used to raise Osiris from the dead. The Osiris myth is the most elaborate and influential story in Egyptian mythology. It concerns the murder of the solar deity Osiris, an ancient king of Egypt, and its consequences. Osiris' murderer, his brother Set, usurps his throne. The primeval king's wife, Isis, restores her husband's disembodied corpse (except his phallus) via the secret name of Amun-Ra, restoring his vitality, allowing him to conceive their son, Horus, his posthumous solar replacement. His heir Horus now established, Osiris becomes a god of the underworld. Osiris lives a double life: first, as a lofty sun god, second as the first and essential mummy, a gloomy ruler of the underworld. He is the dead king creating a living son, Horus, to activate his dormant powers, to make his potential manifest, and to avenge his death by the hands of Set, also known as Typhon. Osiris is the chthonic reservoir of vitality that must be annually reborn like Christ: the sun at the vernal equinox, resurrecting from the musty tomb of winter, death, and darkness.

---

248 Skal, *Monster Show*, 168, stating: "Virtually every plot element as well as key performers... were recycled from *Dracula* in the story of an ancient Egyptian returned from the dead to claim the soul of a young English girl and transform her into a living mummy like himself."
249 The charm looks more like the Egyptian sky goddess Hathor than Isis.
250 Weaver et al., *Universal Horrors*, 67.

Imhotep rises, snapping Norton's mind; he laughs hysterically like a madman as the mummy shuffles off with the scroll. In depicting Imhotep's resurrection, Freund may have been inspired by *The Cabinet of Dr. Caligari*. The ghoulish Cesare (Conrad Veidt, 1893-1943) lies in an upright, coffinlike box. At the command of master Dr. Caligari (Werner Krauss, 1884-1959), Cesare slowly opens his eyes as if from a deep sleep. It is a chillingly effective moment, the like of which would not be seen until Karloff the Uncanny awakens in *The Mummy*.[251] The theme of animating something dead or dormant resonates with audiences; Shelley aside, it is the subject of Gustav Meyrink's (1868-1932) serialized novel, *The Golem* (1913-1914), one of Crowley's favorites.[252]

The Scroll of Thoth parallels the *Book of the Dead*: an ancient funerary text, utilized by the Egyptians from the beginning of the New Kingdom (around 1550 BCE) to approximately 50 BCE. Imhotep (late 27th century BCE) was a historical figure but not a high priest; instead, he was an Egyptian chancellor to the Pharaoh Djoser (3rd Dynasty), the probable architect of the step pyramid, and high priest of the sun god Ra at Heliopolis. Very little is known of Imhotep, but in the 3000 years following his death, he was gradually glorified and exalted. Today, outside the Egyptological community, he is referred to as a polymath, poet, judge, engineer, magician, scribe, astronomer, a proto-Masonic Hiram Abif architect, astrologer, and especially a physician. Indeed, some have considered Imhotep alongside Hippocrates (ca. 460-370 BCE) and Charaka (3rd century BCE) as the fathers of ancient medicine.

Ten years later, Imhotep impersonates a present-day Egyptian named Ardath Bey (still Karloff). *Ardath Bey* is an anagram for *death by Ra*; Ra is the supreme Egyptian sun god mentioned in the scroll. Garbed in an Egyptian silk robe and his head topped with a velvet fez, Bey's unassuming presence belies his destructive capabilities. The Egyptian's first appearance is delineated in celebrated James Whale fashion via a series of quick cuts of the odd-looking gentleman. Here, as well as *Frankenstein*, *The Old Dark House* (1932), and Edgar Ulmer's (1904-1972) *The Black Cat* (1934), Karloff is first glimpsed framed in a doorway. The combined effect of Pierce's makeup and Karloff's acting convinces the audience Bey

---

251 Ibid, 69.
252 Churton, *Beast in Berlin*, 291.

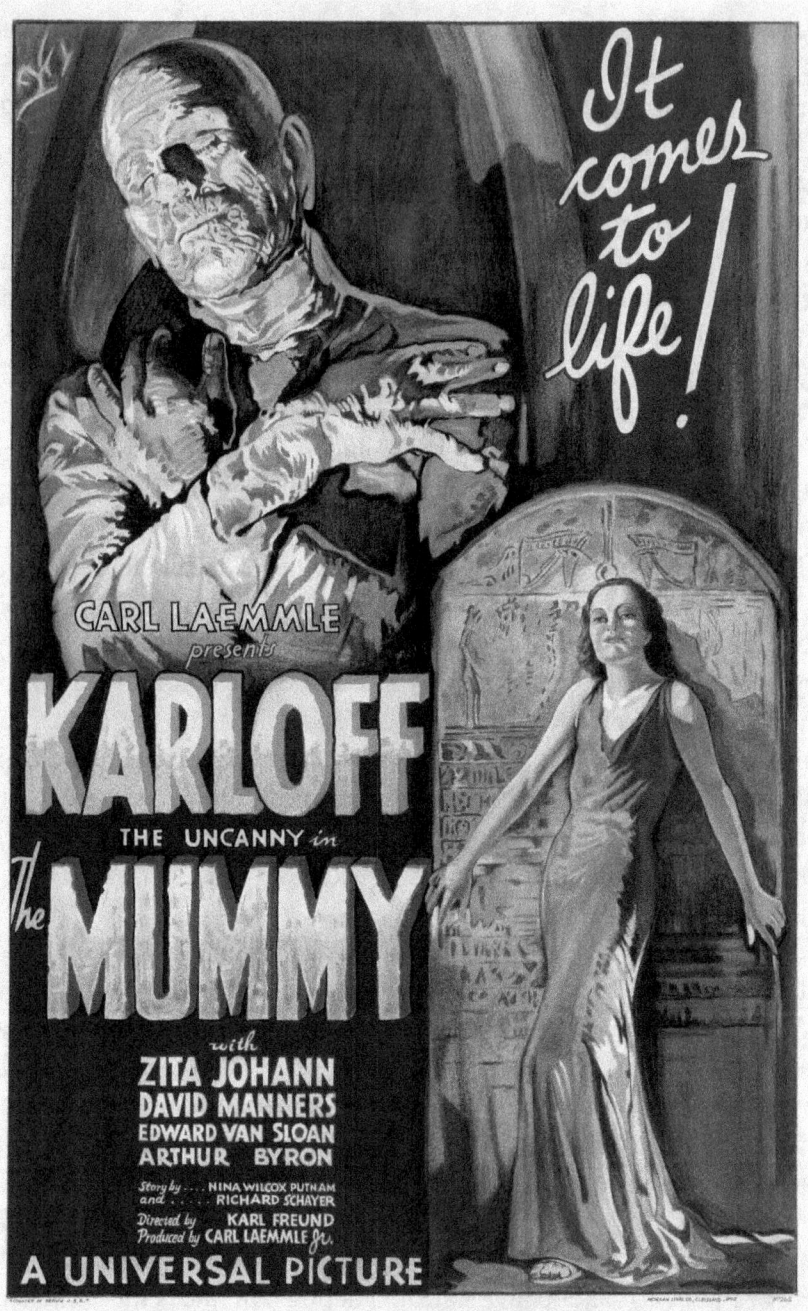

The theatrical one-sheet poster for *The Mummy* set a record in 1997 when it fetched $453,500 at auction; a price exceeded in 2017 when a poster from *Dracula*, the vampire classic starring Karloff's rival Bela Lugosi, sold for $525,800 at auction.

is as ancient and crumbly as the mummy we know him to be. Optically illuminating Karloff's eyes in key shots suggests that the omnipresent Egyptian, like the Eye of Horus, sees all and, thus, knows everything.[253]

Bey calls upon Sir Joseph's son, Frank (David Manners, 1900-1998), and Professor Pearson (Leonard Mudie, 1883-1965), showing them where to dig to locate the tomb of the Princess Ankh-es-en-Amon. After finding the crypt, the archaeologists present its treasures to the Cairo Museum, thanking Imhotep *qua* Bey for making their discovery possible. The exhibition's display placard features the solar-winged orb of Horus, and at the bottom, two bulls betoken the old Age of Taurus, a time during which Egyptian culture and Pharaohs reigned supreme.

Imhotep's horrific death was punishment for sacrilege: attempting to resurrect his forbidden love, Princess Ankh-es-en-Amon, a vestal virgin in service to Isis. When he was buried alive, he was fraught with desire and fear–desire to hold his dead beloved, fear of being forever bereft of her. When he is resurrected some 3700 years later, he is still obsessed with his love for the princess and his terror of never holding her again.

Thus, begins *The Mummy*: a resurrected creature, hollowed by centuries of thwarted love, attempting to discover and revive the soul and body of his lost beloved.

Imhotep soon encounters a young and sophisticated lady, Helen Grosvenor (Zita Johann), a half-Egyptian woman bearing a striking resemblance to the princess. Helen is unaware of the ancient soul dwelling in her body. Even though she is attracted to the exciting present, filled with trendy cocktail parties, she is also drawn to the Egypt of old, with its pyramids and mummies. Imhotep uses his mystical powers to manipulate this atavistic side of Helen. On two occasions, he places her modern, conscious self in a trance, directing her ancient, unconscious self to walk, like an automaton, to the dark side. On the second of these occasions, he lures her to his temple-like dwelling, revealing to her, in a magical reflective pool of water, the critical scenes of her former life: her premature death, his efforts to raise her, his gruesome burial. After witnessing this sable element of her being, Helen falls under the control of Imhotep *qua* Bey, surrendering to his Dracula-like hypnotic powers. He plans to sacrifice her body to liberate her soul ritualistically. But Helen is drawn

---

253 Weaver et al., *Universal Horrors*, 69.

in another direction, toward young Frank. As the plot unfolds, Frank and Muller become aware of his scheme and try to thwart it. In battling Frank and Muller, the mummy's monstrosities surface. He murders a guard at the Museum, Frank's father, Joseph, and Helen's dog. Only the protective Amulet keeps Frank and Helen safe.[254]

Convinced Helen is Ankh-es-en-Amon's reincarnation, Imhotep draws her to the museum *qua* temple, dressing her as an ancient Egyptian, overcoming Muller and Frank's protections. She has become a sleepwalker, a somnambulist, unable to act or react. He wields a ceremonial dagger, promising her immortality. Imhotep attempts to kill her, mummify her, then resurrect her, finally making her his bride. He does not understand the mummification of bodies is a superstition that goes against nature. Mummification is an occult attempt to create death; it is the forceable petrification of a substance needed for life. Inside the embalming chamber, there is an idol of the god Anubis, the deity in the Egyptian religion of yore associated with mummification and the afterlife, rendered as a humanized black jackal-dog. But before Anubis can assist with her resurrection, the old soul of the princess rebels; she will not allow Imhotep to destroy the modern-day woman she has become. Bey puts her in a trance; "You shall rest from life, like the setting sun in the west. But you shall dawn anew in the east as the first rays of Amun-Ra dispel the shadows," he prays over her sleeping body. As he is about to deliver the fatal wound, Frank and Muller intervene and bring Helen back to her senses. She prays to the goddess Isis for salvation. Like a numinous effigy from the *Asclepius*, the statue of Isis obeys, lifting her hand bearing the *crux ansata*, i.e., the Ankh, the symbol of life, issuing forth a blinding flash that sets the Scroll of Thoth on fire. The Scroll's destruction turns Imhotep to dust.

Immortal but fixated with mortality, omnipotent but blinded by love, Imhotep cannot achieve the elegance of the transcendent Osiris. He remains dismembered in the rivers of time, fervidly yearning for his own Isis to gather and heal him. But his abiding egotism keeps him from such wholeness. He greedily tries to pull the soul of the princess from her never-ending journey and back into a resurrected body, offending Isis, the virginal goddess of spiritual resurrection. He uses his priestly powers to control others and, in some cases, kill them; thus, he likewise violates Osiris' animating energies.

---

254 Wilson, *Melancholy Android*, 61.

His punishment for these transgressions is incompleteness. He is a machine built for eternal bliss, but he nonetheless aspires to possess an inaccessible human woman.[255]

The Mummy documents Imhotep's Freudian depression and melancholy. Echoing the *Asclepius*' dogma, Ficino claimed melancholic awareness of the conflict between body and soul is not a sad result of an inherently botched cosmos, but a vibrant inspiration for holy-white magic. Another text by Hermes, *The Poimandres*, contrasts this model, exuding a Valentinian-Gnostic atmosphere: matter is inherently bungled and beyond redemption, that we dwell in a reality governed by the Demiurge.[256] The Man-Shepherd (or Knowledge of Re) claims the eternal, boundless, and omniscient soul is imprisoned in the body, a realm of decay and ignorance. But free of the flesh, the soul ascends to the Father, viz. it quits the material cosmos, entering the incorporeal world, which is filled with the presence of God, or, as some Gnostics expressed it, the soul journeys to the pleroma.[257]

Ficino follows the former, alchemical Hermetic dialogue by stating that one way to heal the saturnine wound is to channel appropriate spirits to ailing matter: the warm Venus to the cold soul, the convivial Jupiter to the dry disposition. Yet, underneath Ficino's positive theories of melancholy lurks negative currents. Through Ficino's depression, philosophers appear to be attuned to the vital flows necessary to ameliorate the hurting cosmos; they are at their cores cold and dry, motivated and sustained by Saturn's black ice. Likewise, even if the sad philosophers in his *Three Books on Life* (*De Vita Libri Tres*) seem able to animate matter with vibrant spirit, they are finally, as the students of the *Asclepius*, fixated on a dead thing: inanimate statues. Though desirous of life and magic, they are in love with death. If Ficino's melancholy points to a hunger for the current of spirit, yet obsessed with cold stone, then Freud's psychology of sadness reveals a reverse: a neurotic love of death that fixates on the macabre. Like Ficino, Freud believes that melancholy can grant people "a keener eye for truth than others who are not melancholic." But Freud also maintains the price for this sight is high: perpetual dread, self-loathing, and an obsession with corpses. Freud's depression is the tragic, Gothic world of Edgar Allan

---

255 Ibid.
256 Ibid, 25.
257 *Hermetica*, 2:67.

Poe.[258] Freudian melancholics, like the sad souls of Ficino, long to heal their lacerations by reconnecting with some pristine concord. However, in contrast to the Hermetic melancholics, who quest for a union with the divine, Freud's despondent patients become angry at the source of their loss. Incorporating this source into their beings, they come to detest those parts of themselves that love the lost person or state. If they should try to recover this state or person through creating artificial copies–automatons resembling their lovers or statues that look like Adonis–these melancholics will hate these unnatural forms as much as they love them. In other words, they will view these forms as monsters as much as angels. The creations of these melancholics will not be divine, self-effacing emanations that hunger for cosmic unity. They will be maladjusted, narcissistic projections yearning to possess the one thing that's been lost; read Poe's "Ligeia" (1838), or watch *The Tomb of Ligeia* (1964) for further understanding.[259]

In chronic Freudian mourning for his lost beloved, Imhotep identifies with the princess, whom he loves for her pristine virtues, but hates for the pain she has caused. Loathing the part of himself that is one with the loss, he is suicidal. Imhotep risks his life to bring the princess back to life, eventually suffering a live burial. Loving that aspect of his being that's identical to the princess' virtues, he is murderous. When he is resurrected, he is fixated only with death. Imhotep is a corpse, so too shall she be like him. His dry body is linked to the Scroll of Thoth; when it burns, he perishes. Yet, the mummy who merges with the transcendent Osiris, peaceful beyond space and time, is an exemplar of indifference: the unattainable grace that comes only to those beings beyond love and hate. John Keats' (1795-1821) "Ode on a Grecian Urn" (1820) insinuates the mummy is closer to eternity than to time. Undying and beyond suffering, it is nonetheless a "Cold Pastoral" that "doth tease us out of thought."[260] Imhotep is neither: he recoils from the eternal because of his love of time, making him more akin to men of flesh and blood, burning in the forehead, and parched on the tongue. Imhotep is monstrous; his sadness is that of all humans seized by obsessive love at the expense of tranquility, risking everything in hopes of one instance of unity

---

258 Wilson, *Melancholy Android*, 26.
259 Ibid, 26-27.
260 John Keats, "Ode on a Grecian Urn," lines 44-45, cited in Wilson, ibid, 62.

with a warm body. His plight is the tragedy and beauty of immanence, of diseased blood flooding the immaculate machine.[261]

Two other popular mummy films from the last century, Terrance Fisher's (1904-1980) *The Mummy* (1959) and Stephen Summer's 1999 film with the same title, both focus on the same themes as Freund's excellent movie. This emphasis on the Gothic element of the mummy points to a palpable fear and desire of our age. The concern is that of undying bodies mechanistically murdering soft-skinned humans, and the desire to see such insensitive carapaces exterminated, returned to dust. But perhaps these monstrous renderings of the mummy reveal a more profound, secret terror and yearning. That is, fear over the possibility that there is no way to tell whether we are inanimate or animate, and a wanting, in the end, to relinquish our hopes for vitality, becoming serene as osseous matter.[262] Next, we leave Egypt for the equally dark and fascinating world of European witchcraft.

A Season in the Abyss: the German Autumn and Suspiria 2018

Witchcraft, in the Middle Ages, according to Sir Walter Scott (1771-1832), was understood to be a compact with Satan. The Devil fuses his baleful powers with the witch to inflict calamities upon a person or property, or both. Ergo, witches could impose the most horrible diseases, and death itself, as marks of the slightest ill will. They could transform their persons, and those of others, at their pleasure; raising tempests to ravage the crops of their enemies, or carrying them home to their garners. Witches could annihilate or transfer the produce of herds to their dairies, spreading pestilence among cattle, infecting and blighting children, and, in a word, do more evil than the heart of man might be supposed capable of conceiving, using supernatural powers beyond human facilities.[263] Fast forward to the present; when it comes to witches, witchcraft, and their diabolical workings, some things never change.

"Oh, what do they know of these occult matters? Blind fools." – Katherine "Kay" Caldwell (Louise Allbritton, 1920-1979), *Son of Dracula*, 1943. By all outward appearances, *Suspiria* is a supernatural psychological

---

261 Wilson, ibid.
262 Ibid.
263 John Mitchell and John Dickie, *The Philosophy of Witchcraft* (Paisley: Murray and Stewart, 1839), 118.

(Left) Ceremonial magician Aleister Crowley demonstrates the Sign of Horus, the Enterer, the entry grade in his *Argenteum Astrum* (A∴A∴) magical order. This posture–one of the Beast's signs of the grades–was based on the gestures from the Golden Dawn's initiatory system. ♩ Ooh, see that girl / Watch that scene / Digging the dancing queen ♩. (Right) Susie imitates the Great Beast when she auditions for the Tanz Academy, signifying her initiation into ceremonial magick, the Great Arcanum, and witchcraft. This is why she came to Berlin: to fulfill her destiny as Mater Suspiriorum, a black magician with a heart of darkness. "For this reason too I cut again the Cross of Blood; and now a third time will I do it. And I will take out the Magical Knife and sharpen it yet more, so that this body may fear me; for that I am Horus the terrible, the Avenger, the Lord of the Gate of the West." – Aleister Crowley, *Liber DCCCLX John St. John*.

horror film. But, beneath its achromatic patina is a didactic, cinematic grimoire extolling black magic: witches, operating as a secret society, foist their sinister will, perfecting their spells. Directed by Luca Guadagnino with a screenplay by David Kajganich, *Suspiria* takes after the Italian horror film of the same title directed by Dario Argento. Guadagnino's pastiche, set in '77, the same year the original *Suspiria* was released, stars Dakota Johnson as an American woman, Susanna "Susie" Bannion, who enrolls at a prestigious dance academy in Berlin operated by a coven of witches. Tilda Swinton co-stars in multiple roles, including the company's lead choreographer and an elderly psychotherapist investigating the academy. Mia Goth and Chloe Grace Moretz appear in supporting roles as students, while Angela Winkler, Renée Soutendijk, Ingrid Caven, and Sylvie Testud portray the academy's matrons. The star of the original film, Jessica Harper, has a cameo appearance. Six acts comprise *Suspiria*, an allusion to the hexagram: a six-pointed star used in paganism to symbolize the sun. It is from *hexagram* the word *hex*, a curse in witchcraft, originates. *The Cabinet of Dr. Caligari* also has six acts, and, like *Suspiria*'s visceral

Volk, exemplifies German Expression. Both films have twist endings; thus, *Caligari*'s fingerprints are all over *Suspiria*. Guadagnini's film is also alchemical, documenting the Susie's metamorphosis from dancer to Mater Suspiriorum, one of three witchcraft godmothers.

Unlike Argento's orgy of witchcraft, with its vivid colors, Guadagnino's pastiche is winterish and bleak, so the primary hues are absent. Instead of bright colors, it has a homoerotic Neo-expressionist dance sequence choreographed by Damien Jalet, representing the coven's black magic. Also missing is the memorable score by the prog-rock band Goblin; instead, the musical score was composed by Radiohead singer Thom Yorke, taking inspiration from krautrock. *Suspiria* '18 is dedicated to the memories of Vogue Italia editor-in-chief Franca Sozzani (1950-2016), film director Jonathan Demme (1944-2017), and Deborah Falzone.

The all-female cast populates the coven's matriarchy. None of the witches have male companions, husbands, or boyfriends, nor are there any male dancers. One is left to conclude the *TANZ* building is not only a Synagogue of Satan but a temple of lesbianism and masturbation. The dance academy's bowels substitute for the Brocken, where the witches conduct their satanic, orgiastic rites. There are few nondescript men, notably, two lackadaisical German police officers humiliated by the recalcitrant witches. A woman even plays the male lead, Dr. Klemperer. Given Guadagnino's comments that this interpretation's visual style was inspired by the films of Rainer Werner Fassbinder (1945-1982), this could be seen as a tribute to Fassbinder's *The Bitter Tears of Petra von Kant* (1972), a movie with an entirely female ensemble. A further indication of this is the casting of Ingrid Caven as housemother Miss Vendegast. In the early 1970s, Caven was married to Fassbinder, appearing in many of his movies. Guadagnino's *Suspiria*, like Blanc's *Wiederöffnen*, is a rebirth, not a remake. When viewing *Suspiria*, one feels "the inevitable pull that they exert and our efforts to escape them," quoting Madame Blanc when discussing renewals. The thriller is a re-contextualization while, at the same time, revitalizing Argento's mythology. Easter egg: Miss Vendegast is named after Professor Verdegast (Renato Scarpa) from *Suspiria* '77. In turn, Professor Verdegast is named after Dr. Vitus Werdegast (Bela Lugosi) from *The Black Cat*.[264]

---

264 Sullivan, *Cinema Symbolism 2*, Chapter V.

CINEMA SYMBOLISM 3

Traveling to Berlin, Susie arrives during the height of the German Autumn to audition for the Helena Markos Dance Group (German: *Markos Tanzgruppe),* identified by the word *TANZ* on the building's façade. She succeeds even with no professional training; however, her arrival coincides with the sudden disappearance of another student, Patricia Hingle (Chloe Grace Moretz). Patricia visits her psychiatrist, Dr. Josef Klemperer (Tilda Swinton, but billed as Lutz Ebersdorf), who keeps her journals, describing the strange activities inside the academy. The diaries recount what appears to be a constructed mythology involving an occult ritual, implying the school's matrons are witches. The journals document other intrigues, as well as the Three Witchcraft Godmothers: Mater Tenebaraum (Mother of Darkness), Mater Lachrymarum (Mother of Tears), and Mater Suspiriorum (Mother of Sighs). Undoubtedly, the former is a distant relative of Frater Lux Ex Tenebris, one of the Golden Dawn's Secret Chiefs, and the source for the rituals of the *Rosae Rubae et Aureae Cruis*, the society's inner Second Order. In the meantime, Susie befriends classmate Sara Simms (Mia Goth); Susie's confident dance style quickly attracts the attention

When I first began choreographing, I never thought of it as choreography but as expressing feelings. Though every piece is different, they are all trying to get at certain things that are difficult to put into words. In the work, everything belongs to everything else–the music, the set, the movement and whatever is said." – Philippine "Pina" Bausch (1940-2009). Bauch (left) was a German dancer and choreographer who, with a blend of movement, sound, and prominent stage sets, influenced modern dance–a style now known as *Tanztheater*–from the '70s onward. Bauch's spirit inhabits Madame Blanc (right); not only does the witch look like Bauch, but her dance piece, *Volk*, is a paragon of *Tanztheater*, of German Expressionist dance. The choreographer Sasha Waltz, and the dancer Mary Wigman (1886-1973), also shadow Blanc.

of Madame Veva Blanc (Tilda Swinton), the head artistic director and the academy's choreographer.

The matrons informally vote for the coven's new leader, reelecting Mother Markos (Swinton again) over Blanc; Markos is a diseased, aging witch that has long ruled the coven, believing herself to be Mater Suspiriorum. They also begin to conspire to use Susie as a host body for the decaying matriarch. During a rehearsal, Patricia's friend and Russian student, Olga Ivanova (Elena Fokina), accuses the matrons of being responsible for Patricia's disappearance, as well as practicing witchcraft. She attempts to flee the school, only to become disoriented and trapped in a lower room. Upstairs, Blanc touches Susie's hands and feet, transferring her energy, her magic, into the dancer. Susie dances for Blanc; however, her movements physically and violently inflict damage on Olga's body. The matrons find Olga bent, broken, and twisted like a pretzel, dragging her body away with large hooks. Miss Vendegast opens a mirror to the *mütterhaus*, an inner sanctum wherein the coven performs their occult rituals, practicing witchcraft. She opens the mirror by making a unique hand gesture; fans of the television series *Twin Peaks* will recognize the posture, expressed by Laura Palmer (Sheryl Lee) in the Black Lodge-Red Waiting Room. By imitating Laura, Vendegast is evoking the show's transcendent duality; that is, the coven is duplicitous, having two sides: one positive and exoteric, which it shows to the world, this is the dance academy. The other

ALL OF THEM WITCHES. (Left) Inside Markos' Academy, Susie stands before a poster with the letters unconnected, loosely scrambled. The lettering conjures *Rosemary's Baby* (right) when the expectant mother plays with the Scrabble pieces, trying to unlock the mystery of the book, *All of Them Witches*. Rosemary will soon realize the riddle involves her neighbor, Roman Castevet. Like *Suspiria*, *Rosemary's Baby*'s plot is about a coven of witches hiding in plain sight.

is sinister and esoteric; this is their black magic, hiding behind mirrors and walls. Laura's gesture alludes to the epic French romantic drama, *Les Enfants du Paradis* (1945, English: *Children of Paradise*), to be analyzed in Chapter XII. Later, Miss Griffith (Sylvie Testud), a sheepish matron, suffers a nervous breakdown, committing suicide.

The dark dancer quickly climbs the ranks, becoming Blanc's protege, earning her the role of the protagonist in *Volk*, an upcoming and anticipated performance by the academy. While the two women share a meal, Susie speaks to Blanc about her life and family. Susie's Amish background is a red herring; after all, who could imagine a witchcraft queen coming out of a traditionalist Christian community. When Blanc asks her what she felt while practicing *Volk*, Susie says it felt like what it must be like to fuck, confessing her virginity indirectly (abstinence strengthens one's magical abilities). When Blanc asks if she means to fuck a man, Susie says she was thinking of an animal. Susie's bestiality conjures Crowley's Scarlet Woman, Leah Hirsig (1883-1975), a Swiss-American occultist, who took the name Alostrael: the womb (or grail) of God. In 1920, in Cefalù, Sicily, Italy, while at Crowley's Abbey of Thelma, Leah attempted to copulate with a goat, emulating an ancient pagan ritual. The Scarlet Woman, also known as Babalon (in the Enochian language, *harlot*), the Great Mother, and the Mother of Abominations, is a goddess found in the occult system Thelema, established by Crowley via the writing and publication of *The Book of the Law*. Babalon epitomizes the female sexual impulse and the liberated woman. Crowley believed Babalon had an earthly aspect in the form of a spiritual office, which could be filled by actual women as a complement to his identification as *To Mega Therion* (The Great Beast). Her duty was to produce occult energies to usher in the Aeon of Horus, the Age of Aquarius.[265]

Living in one of the school's dorms, Susie suffers strange nightmares sent to her by Blanc, featuring weird images including (but not limited to) a broken mirror, bloody faces, her mother, Blanc herself, and Susie as a child. In one dreamy sequence, Sara straddles a doorframe, levitating off the floor, masturbating. Most of the surreal images are drawn from the works of famous photographers. For instance, Susie envisions a nude woman sitting in a chair beside an imprint of her body on the floor. This

---

265 Greer, *New Encyclopedia*, 55, 115-117, 478.

phantasmagoric representation comes from an artsy photo by Francesca Woodman (1958-1981) of a naked woman in a chair with her black bodily imprint on the floor. Other grotesque images appearing in Susie's dreams come from the photographs of Gina Pane (1939-1990), and Claude Cahun (1894-1954), among others. Blanc transfers the artistic images she finds indelible–the work of her contemporaries–to the young dancer, seducing her with quasi-homoerotic visions.

After suffering from one of these ghoulish, erotic nightmares, a "lezzie wet dream" to quote *Black Swan*'s Lily, Susie awakes, screaming, "I know who I am!" Her agonized cry conjures Harry Angel/Johnny Favorite from *Angel Heart*, who yelled these same words upon discovering his true identity. Just as Angel embodies another person, Favorite, Susie, likewise, conceals another persona, the dreaded Mater Suspiriorum. Like Angel/Favorite, Susie is a black magician of the highest caliber in league with dark forces. After awakening, another student enters Susie's room, offering her a valium because vivid nightmares are par for the course at the Markos Dance Group. Easter egg: Sara pleasures herself by mounting a doorframe owes its origin to the Rops engraving of an evil woman ascending a Devil statue (*vide supra*). The dream sequence in Ken Russell's (1927-2011) *The Lair of the White Worm* also foreshadows this sequence. In *Lair*, the virginal Eve Trent (Catherine Oxenberg) mounts a doorframe and begins jilling off by moving her leg back and forth. We know it's Eve humping the doorframe by the crucifix ring she wears, linking her to a previous life when she was a nun, a virgin "masturbating in the dark" to quote Lady Sylvia.

During a practice, Blanc tells Susie, "We need to get you in the air," evoking the witch's ability to levitate. Then, Susie and Blanc retreat to a mirrored room, where Blanc instructs Susie in the art of jumping, viz. spellcasting. Blanc informs Susie she must learn French, a poetic language, insinuating the art of seduction. Blanc says, "There are two things that dance can never be again: beautiful and cheerful. Today we need to break the nose of every beautiful thing." Blanc, as choreographer and artistic director, guides the company, applying visceral aesthetics. Blanc's Luciferian homily is a direct rebuttal to the Third Reich's feminized ideal, that of subservient wife and dutiful mother. Blanc's statement is both a rephrasing and a rebuke to a declaration by Nazi propagandist Joseph Goebbels (1897-1945): "Dance must be cheerful and show beautiful female bodies. It has nothing to do with philosophy."[266] Everything about the Markos *Tanzgruppe* flies in the face of that mandate. These women will create beauty by practicing black magic through their dance, embracing the Left-Hand Path. Susie tells Blanc she wants to be the dance company's hands; they touch intimately, inferring the two women are closet lesbians about to engage in sex. Easter egg: the German subtitles have a red drop shadow, and the subtitles in French, blue.

Meanwhile, Klemperer becomes suspicious of the matrons, requesting Sara review Patricia's journals. Initially skeptical, Sara investigates the academy, opening the mirror, discovering the concealed corridor which leads the *mütterhaus*. Looking like something out of McDougal's House of Horrors, the chamber displays occult relics, including showcases filled with porcelain sculptures of breasts, hands, feet, faces, suggesting the body's contortions are the coven's arcanum, its method of casting spells. Decorating the wall is a painting of Blanc with Markos in a frame made of human hair. After hearing the witches lament over Miss Griffith's suicide, she runs off, taking one of the hooks that impaled Olga. Sara returns to Klemperer and gives him the hook, confirming his suspicions about the dance school. As Sara leaves, a frisson of fear engulfs her when she spies Miss Tanner across the street, watching her intensely. Tanner then uses black magic, changing into someone else.

The night of the dance finally arrives. As the dancers prepare for *Volk*, they have their hair cut; Susie watches as Vendegast collects it, rather than sweeping it up and throwing it away, implying the tufts will be used for occult purposes. Sara sneaks back down to the academy's secret chamber, discovering Patricia, rotting like a corpse, indicating Markos, seated nearby, is draining her lifeforce. An unidentified woman (perhaps Olga), with her hands and feet removed, crawls toward Sara. As she tries to escape, holes in the floor open magically; Sara falls into one of them, breaking her leg, exposing the bone. Two matrons find Sara; they proceed to use witchcraft to heal her leg. Sara emerges midway through the performance, dancing her part with robotic precision in a hypnotic trance. As *Volk* comes to a close, Sara collapses in pain. Later, Blanc chastises Susie for interfering in the matrons' secret affairs.

---

266 Lilian Karina and Marion Kant, *Hitler's Dancers: German Modern Dance and the Third Reich*, trans. Jonathan Steinberg (New York: Berghahn Books, 2004), 121.

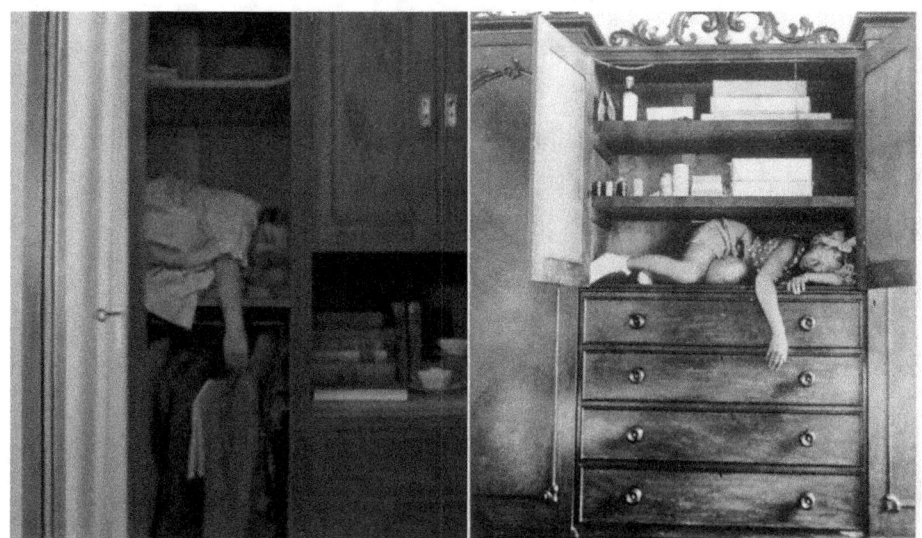

The image of Susie dreaming of herself as a child, sleeping in a cupboard (left), is lifted from Claude Cahun's *Self-Portrait (in cupboard)* (right), 1932.

After Klemperer disposes of Patricia's belongings, he returns to his dacha in East Germany, where he encounters his missing wife, Anke (Jessica Harper), who had disappeared during the war. Anke reveals she fled to England after escaping the Nazis. They walk along happily, eventually passing through the border into West Berlin, evading security. Klemperer discovers he has been led unwittingly to the academy for an impending witches' sabbath; outside, he is ambushed by the matrons.

Susie enters the *mütterhaus*, wherein she discovers the matrons, along with Blanc and Markos, joined by an incapacitated Klemperer. To begin the sabbath, a hexed Sara is disemboweled; she stands next to Patricia and Olga, who, like her, are nothing more than rotting corpses. Feeling something is not right, Blanc attempts to intervene in the ritual, trying to stop it. "We all know what you want. This isn't vanity. This isn't art! We have been on two sides of this for too long now," Markos declares, admonishing Blanc. Enraged, Markos attacks Blanc, nearly decapitating her with magic; Markos' razor-sharp fingernails cut through the air, tearing into Blanc's neck like a hot knife through butter. Markos sets her sights on Susie, "If you accept me, you must put down the woman who bore you. Think of that false mother now. *Reject her*. Expel her. You have the only

(Left) The Solomonic Mircroprosopus (intaglio from Levi's *Transcendental Magic*) is a mystical hexagram (from where the word *hex* originates), symbolizing the kabalistic attributes (*sefirot*) of the unfathomable God (*Ein Sof*). An alchemical ouroboros surrounds the godhead, the aphorism, "*Quod Superius Macroprosopus, Quod Inferius Microprosopus,*" meaning as above, so below, alludes to the nexus between the microcosm and the macrocosm. (Right) The witches in *Suspiria* pervert this symbol. They transform the Masonic-like seal into an emblem of witchcraft, formed by their naked bodies, signifying their unbridled desires and dark magics; such is the grotesquerie of Satan and his court.

mother you need here. Death to any other mother! Say it. Death to any other mother." Markos' satanic declaration harks back to the beginning and the opening credits. A needlepoint sampler decorates Susie's rustic home's wall, reading: "A Mother is a woman who can take the place of all others but whose place no one can take."

Drenched in red light–the *rubedo* is her *nigredo*–Susie accepts her fate as Markos' new vessel willingly, only she turns Markos' words against her; as it is, Susie embodies the phrase on the needlepoint sampler. Susie announces she is Mater Suspiriorum, a supreme adept, an Ipsissimus, to claim the academy and annihilate the corrupt coven; her witchcraft is more formidable than the sorcery of Tituba (b. 1674-?). Susie summons an incarnation of Death (Malgorzata Bela, who also plays Susie's sick mother), delivering the kiss of death, killing Markos, causing the matrons who reelected the repulsive witch to explode. Susie *qua* Mater Suspiriorum is a dark version of the Tarot's High

Priestess, offering occult wisdom while guarding it, remaining a virgin while attaining motherhood.[267]

Susie grants the physically ravaged Patricia, Olga, and Sara clemency: painless deaths as the remaining dancers are either obliterated or continue their danse macabre. Later that night, Klemperer is released in a catatonic state; the next day, the academy continues operations. Miss Vendegast discovers Blanc alive, on the verge of death, in the chamber. Susie, now Mother Suspiriorum, visits Klemperer, explaining Anke died in the Theresienstadt concentration camp after the Nazis captured her. She touches him, causing Klemperer to suffer a violent seizure, erasing his memories. Susie leaves, and we return to Klemperer's dacha; it is daytime, and people are roaming about the garden. A young woman passes, holding a book titled *The Great Mother: An Analysis of the Archetype* (1955) written by psychologist, philosopher, and student of Jung, Erich Neumann (1905-1960). The tome explores the Great Mother as a primordial image of the human psyche, describing how the feminine can be a goddess or a monster. Such is *Suspiria*'s pervasive, archetypal theme. Since the movie is about alchemical transformation, it ends with its beginning, signifying the mystical ouroboros. The film began with one of Jung's books, concluding with one by a Jungian analyst.

A post-credit scene features Susie reaching out her hand to the camera, to the audience, making a gesture, then looking around to make sure the coast is clear. Based on the lamppost in the background, she appears to be standing before the dance academy. She holds out her hand, then lowers it, like she is casting a spell on the school, or the witches dwelling within. Her hand movement resembles the gesture from her dream, smearing blood on a wall. She wears a black glove, which she donned before going out to dinner, suggesting this scene occurred before the sabbath. Is Susie hexing the dance academy? Is she Mater Suspiriorum, or is Susie a fraud like Markos? Has her spell cursed the other witches, duping them into believing she is one of the Three Mothers? Perhaps these questions will be answered in a sequel.

Before its release, rumors swirled around an actor never heard of before: Lutz Ebersdorf, the thespian playing Dr. Klemperer. As we now know, Swinton plays Klemperer, with a clue revealing this in *Ebersdorf*. *Eber* is German for *boar* or *swine*, and *dorf* is likewise German for *town*.

---

[267] Stewart Farrar, *What Witches Do* (New York: Coward, McCann, & Geoghegan, Inc., 1971), 121.

Thus, the name is *Swine-town*, or Swinton, for Tilda Swinton. The casting of Swinton as Madame Blanc–French for *white*–is curious since she has played another evil witch associated with *white*. That character is, naturally, Jadis the White Witch of *The Chronicles of Narnia*, which she played in all three live-action films. Jadis is the White Witch of Winter; hence, gloomy, snowy Berlin is *Suspiria*'s backdrop.

Guadagnino shows us, the audience, what he is hoping to achieve concerning hidden symbolism. Again, it is more thematic and overarching than specific, starting at the beginning. When Patricia visits Klemperer's office, we are privy to his extensive library. Patricia notices two particular books; the first is Jung's *Die Psychologie der Ubertanung* (*The Psychology of Transference*, 1946). Jung's argues that within the transference dyad both participants typically experience a variety of opposites, that in love and during psychological growth, the key to success is the ability to endure the tension of the opposites without abandoning the process, and this tension allows one to grow and to transform. Only in a personally or socially harmful context can transference be described as a pathological issue. A modern, social-cognitive perspective on transference explains how it can occur in everyday life. When someone meets someone new, who reminds them of someone else, they unconsciously infer the new person has traits similar to the person previously known. This perspective has generated a wealth of research, illuminating how people tend to repeat relationship patterns from past to present. Jung's book relates to Patricia's fragile psyche. When Klemperer speaks to Sara about Patricia's journals, he indicates Patricia was transferring her political action and paranoia to the idea the dance company houses a witches' coven. This persecution complex creates delusions, a "lie which tells the truth," he explains. Klemperer believes her fantasies about witches are her way of processing some other form of intrigue. He says love and manipulation are frequent bedfellows; hence, Patricia's passion and psychosis has synthesized her strange behavior, causing her to disappear.

In terms of witchcraft, *transference* is literal. Blanc transfers her magical energies to Susie–to perfect her ballet–so she can become a vessel, allowing Markos to shift her essence into youthful flesh, leaving her disgusting-deformed body behind. The Jung book subconsciously implies his ideas relating to the archetypes and shadow self, a darker side. The darkness is the coven of witches hiding inside the academy behind its mirrors; their reflections denote duplicity and duality: the mirror, echoing *Black Swan*, signifies the dancers' darker sides.

Regarding the archetypes, they are easy to identify. Blanc is the mentor, the manipulative mother, i.e., the Tarot's Queen of Swords, or the High Priestess inverted. Susie is a dark heroine, a waxing moon on her way to becoming full, bright, and brilliant: a goddess of witchcraft. In the mystery teachings, darkness is the mother of the moon. It was the first power, and therefore it was approached with both fear and reverence, under the title of Anthea, the Underworld Queen. Her name meant *the Sender of Nocturnal Vision*. Later, she was known as Hecate Triformis, a Greek goddess associated with the powers of darkness and the moon.[268]

The fools are Patricia, Olga, and Sara, falling victim to the coven's witchcraft. Miss Vendegast is the trickster, deceiving the two police officers. Miss Griffith is the Tower (card XVI of the Major Arcana), and Death is Susie's mother, killing the treacherous witches, purging the coven. Before, it was a decadent shithole led by a fraudster, not exactly Susie's cup of tea; moving forward, it will be elegantly demonic, ruled by the one and only Mater Suspiriorum. The sagacious hermit is the psychiatrist Dr. Klemperer, and the Devil is the repulsive Markos.

The Major Arcana's Tower Card (XVI) indicates ruination; it is archetypal disaster, representing punishment of pride and overconfidence, or, more broadly, destruction of a false system of values. In Italian, this card was called Casa del Diavolo (Devil's House) and Casa de Dannato (House of the Damned). In *Suspiria* '18, this archetype becomes the suicidal Miss Griffith; her death illustrates Markos' pride, cruelty, and fraudulent leadership; it is a prelude to the coven's annihilation. In another ballet movie, *Black Swan*, the Tower incarnates as the self-destructive ballerina Beth Macintyre; morose and jealous, she is humiliated for her aloofness and arrogance. The imagery of the lightning flash knocking off the crown signifies the breaking down of existing forms to make way for new ones; for Beth, it means she is to be replaced by a new Swan Queen, Nina, making Beth the dying swan, causing her to attempt suicide. Beth, like the Tower, is built upon a foundation of misapprehension. The whole structure elaborates superficial observation, false reasoning, and an erroneous theory of will. On the Tower Card, Russian mystic P.D. Ouspensky (1878-1947) writes: "The tower should warn the people not to believe in it. It should serve as a reminder of the Inner Temple as a protection against the outer; it should be as a lighthouse, in a dangerous place where men have often been wrecked and where ships should not go."

---

268 Grimassi, *Encyclopedia*, 292.

Subjecting Guadagnino's film to a Jungian-alchemical-psychological analysis, the following conclusions can be drawn. The coven's black magic is the *nigredo*. Klemperer personifies the *albedo* and *citrinitas* because he is both male and female: a woman, Swinton, playing a man. Klemperer epitomizes the Union of Opposites because he is both a man and a woman, Mars and Venus, the sun and moon unified. Kidnapped, he witnesses Susie's alchemical becoming during the sabbath: her transformation into a diabolical red dragon, the *rubedo*, when she reveals her true identity, achieving selfhood. The color red saturates Susie, and Blanc wears a red gown, designating *Suspiria*'s infernal spagyric essence.

The second book, *Geheimnisse der Freimauerei* (*Secrets of the Freemasons*) by Josef Keller, catches Patricia's eye while in Klemperer's office. She reacts negatively toward the fictitious tome, flipping it over to hide its cover and spine, featuring the square and compasses with an all-seeing eye. The tome conjures the satanic goat of the witches' sabbath subconsciously, Baphomet, the Goat of Mendes. When Freemasons, in the early-phase development of their systems, starting searching for suitable predecessors among medieval knights, the Knights Templar were given a prominent position in this lineage, but they were seen as misunderstood martyrs. They were the keepers of esoteric secrets rather than hardcore Satanists. Enemies of Freemasonry soon seized upon this nexus but emphasized the sinister aspects of the Templars. This Masonic conspiracy is alive and well today, and Baphomet often plays a significant part. In 1818, the Austrian orientalist Joseph von Hammer-Purgstall (1774-1856) published the lengthy article "*Mysterium Baphometis Revelatum*" ("*The Mystery of the Baphomet Revealed*") in a journal, wherein he claimed the Templars revered Baphomet, an androgynous entity of pre-Christian origin, whose name referred to the Gnostic baptism of the soul, a reconciliation of opposites. Gnosis is the artist's religion, and the artist, or dancer, creates magic, producing light in a dark universe. In 1904, Crowley synthesized this doctrine, writing simply: "Every man and every woman is a star." Some of Hammer-Purgstall's ideas became influential, including Baphomet as a gender-transgressing entity. This idea, at times, merged with the diabolical connotations of the deity, producing an intersex Satan, linking the Dark Angel to witchcraft and, ergo, to Freemasonry.[269]

---

[269] Faxneld, *Satanic Feminism*, 53, 66; Churton, *Occult Paris*, 94.

As a result, the conspiracy that Freemasons were in league with Lucifer flourished in the late 19th century, and, though a hoax, persists to this day. In 1892, the French book *Le Diable au XIXe siècle* (English: *The Devil in the 19th Century*), penned by anti-Mason Leo Taxil (Marie Joseph Gabriel Antoine Jogand-Pagès, 1854-1907) under the pen name "Dr. Bataille" exposed the satanic Palladian Rite of Freemasonry, the pinnacle of the Masonic hierarchy, organized and led by Scottish Rite Sovereign Grand Commander Albert Pike (1809-1891) from Charleston, South Carolina.[270] In *Morals and Dogma of the Scottish Rite of Freemasonry* (1871), Pike describes Lucifer as a beneficent *light-bearer*; thus, according to conspiracy theorists, the fallen angel is Masonry's Great Architect.[271] Ordinary Masons were not aware of this; only to the initiates of the high degrees was the truth disclosed, step by step.[272] Initiates were introduced to the worship of Baphomet, whom the Freemasons, like their precursors, the Templars, venerated as the pantheistic and magic symbol of the Absolute.[273] In 1896, Freemason, occultist, renegade scholar, and cocreator of the favored Rider-Waite Tarot deck, Arthur Edward Waite (1857-1942) published *Devil-Worship in France* thoroughly debunking Taxil, but the damage had been done. Ergo, Klemperer's Masonic book implies a secret society of Devil-worshipping witches, like their sinister Masonic counterparts, in league with Lucifer; this is *Suspiria*'s collusive black magic.

Moreover, the Masonic book generates an overarching theme of conspiracy and paranoia often associated with the Freemasons, identifying them as hidden puppet masters, linking Masonic subterfuge to the witches' coven, manipulating the dancers from behind their mirrors, perpetrating a conspiracy to locate Markos' new vessel. Patricia recognizes the Masonic symbol, associating it with a demonic plot. To her, the Masons are like witches, a talking-point which turns up–like Baphomet–in the world of conspiracy; the Masons, the Illuminati, and Witchcraft are often linked (listen to the lectures of John Todd, 1949-2007) albeit incorrectly, unsubstantiated and quickly debunked. Nevertheless, the book signifies

---

270 The Palladian Rites is named after the Greek figure Pallas, son of the first werewolf, Lycaon, and the teacher of Athena, the virginal goddess of wisdom and power, the protectress of the state, social institutions, and agriculture.
271 Pike, *Morals and Dogma*, 32; Van Luijk, *Children of Lucifer*, 208.
272 Van Luijk, ibid.
273 Ibid.

Patricia's fear and anxiety over a dark conspiracy at work inside the dance school. Easter egg: like all magical mysteries, the Great Work's secrets have triple meaning: religious, philosophical, and natural.[274] There are three degrees of Blue Lodge Masonry; thus, the number three pervades the cinematic grimoire, reinforcing the Masonic-witchcraft conspiracy. There are three mothers, Swinton plays three characters, the dance counts are often in threes, Markos wins the election by three votes, and Susie went to New York, to the Martha Graham Center, to see Blanc there three times.

Additionally, the book's all-seeing eye conjures the original *Suspiria*. Inside Helena Markos' quarters, the Eye of Providence decorates a wall, designating her omnipotence over the coven, its Black Queen. It feels like the *Tanzakademie's* building was once used by the Freemasons or the Rosicrucians, given all the abstruse words and symbols lining its hidden corridors. The building is famous for being the brief residence of noted classical and theological scholar, Desiderius Erasmus (1466-1536), identified by a plaque on the structure. Argento celebrates this like a mischievous imp, knowing the irony of having an occult conspiracy housed in the refuge of one of Christianity's most noted humanists.

The author of the Masonic book, Josef Keller, references Josef Keller (1887-1981), a confectioner who invented *Schwarzwälder Kirschtorte*, or Black Forest Cake, a chocolate sponge cake with a creamy cherry filling. Once again, this is an homage to *Suspiria* '77 wherein the foot of the Black Forest is home to Markos' occult-dance school; specifically, in the city of Freiburg.

The two books set the stage for the arc of *Suspiria*, observable to the initiated few: the Freemasons, the Gnostics, mystics, witches, and those with a working knowledge of Jung and his depth psychology. Know that the old queen of the world is on the march and wearies never? Every uncurbed passion, every selfish pleasure, every licentious energy of humanity, and all its tyrannous weakness, go before the sordid mistress of our tearful valley, and, scythe in hand, these indefatigable laborers reap their eternal harvest.[275] These are the occult and diabolical laws of *Suspiria*, governing the sabbath, witchcraft, and ungodly talismans and alliances.

*****

---

274 Levi, *Transcendental Magic*, 281.
275 Ibid, 187.

The black dress Susie wears when she goes out to dinner (left) features the same floral pattern decorating the school's secret corridors (right), when, in *Suspiria* '77, Suzy searched for the coven of witches.

Suspiria's weather and costumes are gloomy and drab; it is autumn with winter on its way, light is dead, exalting darkness and cold. Witches and evil roam freely–think of the ghosts of *The Shining* and Pazuzu of *The Exorcist*. When Susie descends onto the subway platform, there is a sign, *SUSPIRIA*, to the left. Why is this there? I can come up with only one answer: foreshadowing. By placing it close to Susie, it is a harbinger that she–not Markos–is Mater Suspiriorium. *The Exorcist* hides an antithetical allegory when Father Karras ascends onto the subway platform from 33rd Street, anticipating that he will become Regan's Christlike savior. Inside the Markos Dance Company's building, the main dance hall is named the Iris Studio, a nod to the original film's three irises. Turning the blue one reveals the academy's dark secret, exposing the witches' coven. The infamous maggot scene from the *Suspiria* '77 was not included in this rebirth. However, one of Susie's dreams alludes to it when a few worms crawl on a mask. To dream of worms foretells a secret enemy seeking death and reconciliation: Susie, Markos' rival, will destroy the imposter witch and her supporters with the remaining coven accepting Susie as Mater Suspiriorium.[276]

---

276 Stephen Girard, *The Mystic Dream Book of Stephen Girard: A Complete Guide to Wealth, Health, and Happiness; Consulted Daily by This Eminent Man, Taken From the Arabic of Mohammed Kazvini; Embracing the Mysticism, Rites, and Ceremonies of the Orient, Adapted to the Wants of All Classes and Conditions of People*, rev. ed. (Philadelphia: Rufus C. Hartranft, 1886), 29; *The Witches' Dream Book and Fortune Teller* (New York: Henry J. Wehman, Publisher, 1885), 50.

When she goes to the Paris Bar, the black dress Susie wears features the same floral pattern from the original *Suspiria* on the walls of the school's secret corridors, perhaps an allusion to her true identity: Mater Suspiriorum. While at the restaurant, Susie refuses a menu, leaving her plate empty, making her the odd woman out, suggesting she's one of the Three Mothers. She also moves to the head of the table, signaling her rulership. The *Volk* performance is November 11, 1977, which Dr. Klemperer attends. Later, Susie discloses that his wife, Anke, died on November 11, 1943, telling Klemperer she thought of him as she perished, and the time he took her to a Chopin and Brahm's concert. Anke died thinking about her husband taking her to a show, and thirty-four years later to the day, Klemperer attends *Volk* without her, synchronizing the dates, the two moments in time. During *Volk*, observe the seat next to Klemperer is empty, seemingly occupied by Anke's ghost.

Once again, we return to Jungian psychology, suggested by the book in Klemperer's office. Embracing Jung's ideas of the *anima* and the *animus*, we have a woman playing a man, Dr. Klemperer. Jung's school of analytical psychology describes the *anima* and *animus* as part of his theory of the collective unconscious. Jung labeled the *animus* as the unconscious masculine side of women, and the *anima* as the unconscious feminine side of men, with each transcending the personal psyche. Jung's theory states the *anima* and *animus* are the two primary anthropomorphic archetypes of the unconscious mind, as opposed to both the theriomorphic and inferior function of the shadow archetypes. He believed they are the abstract symbols that formulate the Self archetype.

Klemperer, the feminine and the masculine, embodies *coincidentia oppositorum*, the syzygy. Psychologically, the man-woman must witness the sabbath, transcending duality, facilitating Susie's revelation that she is Mater Suspiriorum, thereby becoming Jung's notion of the Self, *individuation*. It is the union of the subconscious with the conscious, shadow with ego, the unification of the archetypes (*vide supra*). In the end, Susie achieves self-awareness of both the conscious and subconscious; opposites are unified, good and evil, God and the Devil, shadow and ego, and witch and saint. Susie mercifully kills Sara and Patricia while punishing the witches favoring Markos. But this act of disembowelment is more than a release from the pain of living; in Jungian psychology, a release of the repressed attributes from the shadow, freeing those flaws that have been forcibly hidden to integrate with the psychic whole: Mother Suspiriorum. The *anima* and *animus* witness her transcendence; Klemperer, the *albedo* and *citrinitas*, personifying the two anthropomorphic archetypes, synthesizing the occult-psychological-alchemical process, allowing Susie to realize selfhood, alchemy's *rubedo* stage, *individuation*. During the sabbath, Blanc wears a flowing red robe, while a hellish red glow suffuses Susie and the *mütterhaus*. Susie accomplishes selfhood, transmogrifying into Mater Suspiriorum. "I am she," Susie says with aplomb, announcing to the coven she is the Mother of Sighs, exposing Markos as a charlatan, finalizing the psychological-alchemical Magnum Opus.[277]

Outside the dance school, anarchy and political chaos reign for it is the German Autumn (*Deutscher Herbst*): a series of events occurring in late '77, associated with the kidnapping and murder of industrialist Hanns Martin Schleyer (1915-1977), president of the Confederation of German Employers' Associations (BDA) and the Federation of German Industries (BDI), by the Red Army Faction (RAF) insurgent group. Coinciding with this event was the hijacking of Lufthansa Flight 181 by the Popular Front for the Liberation of Palestine (PFLP). They demanded the release of ten RAF members detained at the Stammheim Prison plus two Palestinian compatriots held in Turkey and $15 million (US) in exchange for the hostages. The assassination of Siegfried Buback, the attorney-general of West Germany on April 7, 1977, and the failed kidnapping and murder of the banker Jürgen Ponto on July 30, 1977, marked the beginning of the German Autumn. It ended on October 18, 1977, with the liberation of Flight 181, the suicides of the RAF's architects in their prison cells, and Schleyer's death.

Inside the dance academy, there is a similar rebellion brewing amid the growing division between the old and new, as Blanc vies to wrestle control of the school from the enigmatic and reclusive Mother Markos. Some of the instructors believe the aging Markos abuses her power, compromising the purity of the school's artistic vision by exploiting certain students. For example, Patricia, whose stories about witches and rituals are dismissed as little more than paranoid ramblings by her psychoanalyst, or the Russian

---

277 Britt Hayes, "Sunday Reads: SUSPIRIA – Psychoanalyzing Luca Guadagnino's Rapturous Rebirth of a Horror Classic: An investigation into the psychology of SUSPIRIA." *Birth. Movies. Death.*, November 4, 2018, https://birthmoviesdeath.com/2018/11/04/sunday-reads-suspiria-psychoanalyzing-luca-guadagninos-rapturous-rebirth-of (accessed December 3, 2018).

dancer Olga, who openly accuses her instructors of witchcraft following Patricia's suspicious disappearance. Olga imminently finds herself trapped in a mirrored room wherein her body is gruesomely contorted, beaten, and internally pulverized by an unwitting Susie, whose rehearsal of *Volk's* protagonist casts a damning spell.[278] The coven's critical point of contention is Markos' reckless treatment of the most skilled students, conducting rituals to appropriate their youthful bodies and talents. But Markos' recent efforts have resulted in repeated failures. She has been impatient, greedy, and zealous; the girls were not quite ready; it was too much, too soon. In this respect, *Suspiria* is, on its surface, also a film about the corporatization of art–a theme reflected through the maternal underpinning of the mentor-protege relationships between Blanc and Markos, and Blanc and Susie, and marked by its potential to be mutually beneficial or destructive.[279] Like the German Autumn, the result is death and mayhem, but from this tumult, Susie brings order out of chaos.

Speaks the goddess: "Ye shall *dance*, sing, feast, make music and love, all in my praise. For mine is the ecstasy of the spirit, and mine also is joy on earth … Let my worship be within the heart that rejoiceth; for behold, all acts of love and pleasure are my rituals."[280] Dancing has an intense magical effect upon people. It unites them by the rhythm of the beat of the dance. A group of people dancing together in harmony is of one mind, and this is essential to magical work. Their mood can be excited or calm by varying the pace of the dance. Magical forms of dancing can induce a state of light hypnosis; or, people can achieve a state of ecstasy, which in its original form is ex-stasis, "being outside oneself."[281] Put another way, the everyday world is left behind, with its squalor and dull cares; the doors to the magical realms open. Medieval witches may have invented modern dancing; dance can be a prayer, an invocation, a rapture, or a spell. It is world-old and world-wide magic.[282]

Sometimes the Devil would cause witches to strip themselves and dance before him naked; at cockcrow, the whole phantasmagoria vanished. Along with dancing, the sabbath was the witch's paradise, where there

---

278 Ibid.
279 Ibid.
280 Farrar, *What Witches Do*, 95, emphasis added.
281 Valiente, *ABC of Witchcraft*, 101-102.
282 Ibid.

was more joy than could be expressed. The witch in attendance had a singular pleasure in going to the sabbath because the Devil so held their hearts and wills that he hardly allowed any other desire to enter therein. That she had more pleasure and happiness in going to the sabbath than to Mass, for the Devil made them believe him to be the true God, and the joy which the witches had at the sabbath was but the prelude of much greater glory.[283] Indeed, when Susie attends the hideous sabbath, her greater glory is disclosed, purging the coven of its corrupt members.

We now come to its diabolical crescendo: *Volk* (English: People) and the witches' sabbath. But this dance number isn't exactly new; it is the visceral, interpretive dance Blanc created in 1948 in the aftermath of World War II. It is a demanding piece, requiring more than any student can give. Because it is so challenging, Blanc enhances her most talented dancers with additional physical gifts–painfully procured from the other students, magically transferring their skills into the others, including Markos' would-be vessel. The dancers and the matrons are all black magicians; the Devil is their great magical agent employed for evil purposes by a perverse will: Markos' desire to inhabit a new vessel.[284] Most known magical rituals are either mystifications or enigmas: *Volk* is the coven's witchcraft, magnetic power, and evil folly; *Volk* is an occult method to transmit Markos' energies and spirit into Susie as she dances the protagonist. The performers' scant red costumes and Susie's stark makeup make them all look like vengeful demons.

The floor markings are akin to a magic circle, protecting the dancers from negative forces. Yet, they also resemble the demonic sigils from the grimoire, *Ars Goetia,* designed to attract evil principalities. The dancers' rigid yet fluid movements and postures echo magical signs such as Osiris Slain, Isis Mourning, Typhon, Osiris Rises, Rending the Veil, Closing the Veil, and Babe of the Abyss: the Sign of Chastity (see Aleister Crowley's *Magick*). They twirl and sway with precise, almost supernatural, equilibrium; movement is the result of an alternate preponderance. During the dance, if one observes, one can see an homage to Michael Jackson's (1958-2009) "Thriller" music video (1983), specifically the iconic Werewolf Dance.

---

283 Murray, *God of the Witches*, 41-42.
284 Levi, *Transcendental Magic*, 135.

(Left). Sign from Crowley's *Argenteum Astrum*: Isis in Welcome, the Sign of Babalon, the Babe of the Abyss grade, the Attitude of Baphomet. It represents the Mother of Abominations, an occult goddess that "Sitteth upon many waters: … I saw a woman sit upon a scarlet colored beast, full of names of blasphemy, having seven heads and ten horns. And the woman was arrayed in purple and scarlet color, and decked with gold and precious stones and pearls, having a golden cup in her hand full of abominations and filthiness of her fornication: And upon her forehead was a name written, Mystery, Babylon The Great, the Mother of Harlots and Abominations of the Earth. And I saw the woman drunken with the blood of the saints, and with the blood of the martyrs of Jesus: and when I saw her, I wondered with great admiration" (Revelation 17:1-6). (Right) Susie emulates the magical posture in this promotional image, identifying her as Babalon the Great, the obscene deity of Mendes, the goat of the sabbath, personifying witchcraft. Susie is a Scarlet Woman, a Crowley-like female black magician, becoming Mater Suspiriorum. "Firstly, this Sphinx is a Symbol of the Coition of Our Lady BABALON with me THE BEAST in its Wholeness. For as I am of the Lion and the Dragon, so is She of the Man and the Bull, in our Natures, but the Converse thereof in our Offices, as thou mayst understand by the Study of the Book of the Vision and the Voice." – Aleister Crowley, *Liber Aleph vel CXI: The Book of Wisdom or Folly.*

The concluding sabbath is a gathering of the dance academy's matrons; the Devil is present just not seen; if he were to manifest physically, it would be as the Goat of Mendes, Baphomet.[285] They are black magicians, their bodies gyrating blasphemously, generating negative forces, all at the behest of the fraudulent Markos with Klemperer serving as the witness. Susie arrives at the hidden vault, becoming an agent of terror and destruction; comparatively, she is the Hindu goddess Kali, a goddess of violence, and

---

285 Ibid, 307. See also Anton LaVey, *The Satanic Bible* (New York: Avon Books, 1969), 99.

a mother and a destroyer of evil forces.[286] Susie has become Crowley's Scarlet Woman, or Babalon: "Let her raise herself in pride! Let her follow me in my way! Let her work the work of wickedness! Let her kill her heart! Let her be loud and adulterous! Let her be covered with jewels and rich garments, and let her be shameless before all men! ...Curse them! Curse them! Curse them!"[287] The Susie *qua* Mater Suspiriorum revelation hides in the forename of the actress portraying her, Dakota Johnson. *Dakota* conjures *Rosemary's Baby* and the Dakota Apartments, wherein a coven summons Satan, Hell on earth, "Year One!" to quote Roman Castevet/ Steven Marcato. Thus, Susie *qua* Mater Suspiriorum personifies pure evil.

Before Susie kills Sara, she refers to the disemboweled dancer as a "sweet girl," an allusion to *Black Swan*, a movie about a ballerina trying to reconcile her dark side. Erica, Nina's mother, speaks the condescending phrase as a term of endearment; in *Suspira*, Mater Suspiriorum uses it to refer to Sara, one of her "daughters," before granting her death. Like Sara, Nina also perishes at *Black Swan*'s finale, dying before the sun, achieving perfection, absorbed by Lucifer's light. The phrase, "sweet girl," links *Black Swan*'s bleakness to *Suspiria*'s wicked sabbath; contextually, both films are meditations on alchemical blackness, only Nina fails whereas Susie triumphs, integrating darkness entirely.

Ultimately, we observe subtle parallels between Argento's original and Guadagnino's pasticcio. After all, *Suspiria* '18 is a rebirth of *Suspiria* '77, not a remake. In the original, Miss Tanner (Alida Valli, 1921-2006) tests Suzy when she first arrives at the *Tanzakademie*. After Madame Blanc (Joan Bennett, 1910-1990) informs Suzy that a dorm room at the academy is now ready, she refuses, saying she would rather stay in town. Tanner complements Suzy on being strong-willed, stating that once her mind is made up, nothing will change it. As she walks down a corridor, Suzy is hit with a hex as a disembodied voice yells, "Witch!" Suzy makes her way to the yellow room to rehearse; only the spell takes effect; thus, she cannot obey Tanner's commands, passing out with her nose bleeding, humiliated. Tanner has broken Suzy's will, a powerful act–a dark spell–in witchcraft. But Suzy has her revenge by destroying the coven, Tanner included.

---

286 Colin Wilson, *The Occult: A History* (New York: Random House, 1971), 419.
287 Aleister Crowley, *The Book of the Law* (1938; repr., San Francisco: Weiser Books, 1976), 46-47, describing the Scarlet Woman's attributes.

In *Suspiria* '18, Blanc tests Susie by trying to break her will with *Volk*, causing her to become sick when she initially practices it. Later, Blanc attempts to manipulate Susie by instructing her how to jump, but this time, she passes Blanc's test. Like Suzy from the first film, Susie locates the witches' coven, destroying its corrupt members, only she takes control of it and the remaining witches. In *Suspiria* '77, Suzy obliterates the witches, then escapes the academy, fleeing for her life.

To those well versed in esoteric lore, Freemasonry, sorcery, witchcraft, Jung, the occult, psychology, and symbolism, the analysis I have just unveiled will be readily understood. To those inclined to believe *Suspiria* '18 is an exercise in Illuminati mind control and predictive programming may want to reflect that a nod is as good as a wink to a blind horse.[288]

History Repeats Itself: The Déjà Vu of Halloween 2018

Pomona, the Roman goddess of fruit, lends us the harvest element of Halloween; the Celtic day of summer's end was a time when spirits, mostly evil, were abroad. The gods whom Christ dethroned joined the ill-omened throng; the Church festivals of All Saints' and All Souls' coming at the same time of year—November 1—contributed the idea of the return of the dead. The Teutonic May Eve assemblage of witches brought its hags and their attendant beasts to help celebrate the night of October 31.[289] The residents of Haddonfield, Illinois, are, unfortunately, all too familiar with this pagan mythology.

Michael's spooky Halloween mask transcends popular culture. The iconic mask is William Shatner, or more accurately, Captain Kirk from the television series *Star Trek*. Although this is now common knowledge, mentioned by this author in *Cinema Symbolism*, it is still thought-provoking and worth discussing. The filmmakers wanted the Michael Myers character to be the personification of evil, forever haunting Halloween. To convey emotional emptiness, a psychological void, a lack of apathy, an absence of mercy and compassion, Michael is faceless: he is a steely killing machine. The mask is his genuine face. So, John Carpenter and Debra Hill (1950-2005) purchased a Don Post Captain

---

288 Aleister Crowley, *Magick*, eds. John Symonds and Kenneth Grant (1973; repr., London: Routledge & Kegan Paul, 1981), 216.
289 Kelley, *Hallowe'en*, 4.

On the left is the Don Post William Shatner Captain Kirk mask, and, to the right, is its altered version: Michael's Myers' frightening mask, making him the living personification of Samhain. In *Halloween* '18, as the Shape stalks his prey, there's a small hole on the left side of his mask's neck area. The puncture is from where Laurie stabbed him with a sewing needle back on Halloween night '78.

Kirk mask, hallowed out the eyes, removed the sideburns, messed up the hair, and painted it white. And it worked: the mask is disturbing, evoking a soulless ghoul, a terrifying inhuman monster. The mask is a staple in the Halloween franchise; in the latest *Halloween*, it triggers him, causing him to go on another killing spree. This analysis focuses on the most recent *Halloween* (hereafter "*Halloween* '18"), released forty years after the original's release. The film is a direct sequel to *Halloween* '78, erasing all other sequels and movies in the franchise, creating an alternative timeline. In doing so, *Halloween* '18 incorporates many elements and scenes from the other films, implying the events were destined to happen regardless of the timeline. *Halloween* '18 is a study of déjà vu, history repeating itself.

Halloween '18 opened in theaters on October 19, 2018; according to *Halloween: Resurrection* (2002), Michael Myers was born on October 19, 1957. The movie begins with a wall clock conspicuously displaying 10 and 3, evoking October 30, or Devil's Night, alluding to *Halloween II*, released on October 30, 1981. October 30 is auspicious because Michael always escapes on Devil's Night as he is transferred from one facility to another, freeing him to murder again. Michael's 10-30 exodus from incarceration occurs in *Halloween '78*, *Halloween 4: The Return of Michael Myers* (1988), and *Halloween '18*.

Serial killer/mass murderer Michael Myers (James Jude Courtney and Nick Castle) has been confined in the Smith's Grove Sanitarium (Warren County) for the past forty years, resulting from his infamous Halloween night killing spree in Haddonfield, Illinois. He is about to be transferred to a new facility. True-crime podcasters Aaron Korey (Jefferson Hall) and Dana Haines (Rhian Rees) interview Michael's psychiatrist Dr. Ranbir Sartain (Haluk Bilginer), a former student of the deceased Dr. Samuel Loomis. Sartain has been studying Michael to gain insight into his deadly psychology to shed light on his past actions. Aaron approaches Michael, brandishing his white mask, to no effect. Easter egg: when the podcasters arrive, a vinyl record plays to soothe the patients. The tune is "Tonight in the Moonlight" (1923) by the Morrie Morrison Orchestra; it is a prelude, heralding the Boogeyman's nocturnal rampage.

Back in Haddonfield, Laurie Strode (Curtis) lives an isolated life in her heavily fortified house in the woods; its basement is a panic room. She has been divorced twice, has a strained relationship with her daughter, Karen Strode (Judy Greer), and, in her misery, has turned to alcohol. Laurie is far from happy as the tragic events from 1978 still haunt her; she has prepared for Michael's potential return through intense combat training–think Sarah Connor (Linda Hamilton) in *Terminator 2: Judgment Day*. As Michael is transferred, his transport mysteriously crashes. He escapes, kills a father and his son for their car, returning home to Haddonfield. On Halloween, Michael spots Aaron and Dana visiting his sister's Judith grave in the local cemetery. He follows the pair to a gas station, where he murders them, recovering his white mask. He also kills a mechanic for his coveralls. Deputy Frank Hawkins (Will Patton), who arrested Michael in 1978, learns of Michael's getaway and tries to convince Sheriff Barker (Omar Dorsey) about the danger he poses. Laurie discovers Michael's getaway after overhearing a TV broadcast and attempts to warn Karen, and her yo-yo enthusiast husband, Ray Nelson (Toby Huss), but they dismiss her worries.

At the high school Halloween party, Allyson (Andi Matichak), Karen's daughter, and Laurie's granddaughter, finds her boyfriend, Cameron Elam

(Dylan Arnold), cheating on her, so she leaves with his best friend, Oscar (Drew Scheid). Michael steals a kitchen knife from the home of an elderly woman; he murders her, then kills a young lady living next door. Allyson's best friend, Vicky (Virginia Gardner), babysits the comical Julian Morrisey (Jibrail Nantambu); Michael fatally stabs Vicky, sacrificing herself to protect Julian. Hawkins and Laurie arrive to locate and stop Michael; the Shape and Laurie come face-to-face for the first time in forty years. Laurie shoots Michael, who flees, but she persuades Karen and Ray to seek protection in her fortress house. Michael comes across Allyson and Oscar; Hawkins and Dr. Sartain, the good doctor now working with the police, arrive just in time to save Allyson, but Oscar is impaled. Hawkins subdues Michael, but Sartain, obsessed with Michael's enigmatic motivations, murders the Deputy before he can kill Michael. Sartain explains to Allyson that he facilitated Michael's escape to validate his perceived role as an apex predator, needing to finish what he started: to kill Laurie to reassert himself. Hoping to see his patient in action, he doesn't get the chance: Michael murders Sartain, allowing Allyson to escape. Michael arrives at Laurie's fortified house and promptly kills Ray.

Laurie manages to get Karen to safety before she engages in a showdown with Michael. Laurie severely injures him, severing two of his fingers, but he stabs her in the abdomen and pushes her over a balcony; when Michael looks over, he finds it missing. Allyson arrives, and Karen shoots Michael in the jaw. Stunned, he stumbles in the hallway, when Laurie suddenly appears and attacks him, trapping him inside the basement. Laurie, Karen, and Allyson set the house ablaze, and the trio escapes in the back of a passing pickup truck. Despite various shots of the burning house and its basement, the Shape is nowhere in sight. At the end of the credits, Michael's breathing is heard, leaving his fate in doubt. Easter egg: after Karen shoots Michael standing at the top of the basement's steps, Laurie steps out from the shadows, stabbing him from behind. This scene stands in opposition to *Halloween* '78, when Michael emerged from the darkness behind Laurie, knifing her after she discovered Annie's, Bob's, and Lynda's corpses in the Wallace residence.

While watching this movie for the first time, two undercurrents became immediately apparent. The first is that *Halloween* '18 presents an alternative reality, completely divesting itself from all the earlier sequels while acknowledging them as originals. This second is duality; this movie is all about role reversal; the main characters behave opposite from what they (or their counterparts) did in *Halloween* '78. We also find allusions to the original film; for example, inside Karen's childhood bedroom, Laurie's sun hat from her teenage bedroom in *Halloween* '78 decorates the wall. Karen's dollhouse is, likewise, a replica of the Myers home. Both serve to pay homage to the immortal classic. On duality, it exists in the motivation of the two doctors. Dr. Loomis (Donald Pleasence) wanted to keep his patient locked away in an asylum forever because he knew Michael was pure evil. His 2018 antithesis, Dr. Sartain, intends to free Michael from the institution, knowing he is pure evil, turning him loose to observe him slaughter. One doctor wants to preserve life, the other desires only death. Keep these themes in mind as the analysis unfolds because they are the heart and soul of *Halloween* '18.

The film opens with the credits rolling in the same orange color and typeface, with an updated version of Carpenter's creepy theme music, a direct parallel to *Halloween* '78. There is one difference; the jack-o'-lantern, carved precisely like the '78 one, resuscitates, rising from its decomposition, representing rebirth: the Shape's awakening. It's autumn, and Michael is no longer dormant; he's back to murder once more. When Aaron and Dana attempt to interview Michael, they are standing on a checkerboard, or chessboard, representing the lethal combinatorial game–brinkmanship–Michael and Laurie are playing. Furthermore, the checkerboard or chessboard is a repeating trope: at Allyson's home, her father, Ray, mentions making a checkerboard out of teak. Later, when the two police officers kibitz in the patrol car, one of the officer's sandwich is wrapped in checkerboard paper.

As a result of repeating the checkerboard-chessboard motif, the filmmakers successfully establish Game Theory: the strategic interaction between two primary competing decision-makers, Michael and Laurie, who play a deadly cat-and-mouse game. Game Theory is the branch of mathematics concerned with the analysis of strategies for dealing with competitive situations where the outcome of a participant's choice of action depends critically on the other participants' activities. Game Theory applies to situational contexts in war, business, economics, and biology. In their deadly Bimatrix Game, Laurie and Michael are free to act and react, implementing calculated maneuvers, attempting to anticipate the other's move. Laurie and Michael seek a solution to a noncooperative situation (absence of an external authority to enforce rules): each player chooses a strategy to negotiate the game; here, both are trying to eliminate each other with extreme prejudice. Neither can benefit by unilaterally changing their course of action while the other player keeps their plans unchanged, constituting a Nash Equilibrium; for Laurie and Michael, it is a finite-mathematical certainty: death to the other player. The application of Game Theory explains why Michael spares the baby: the child cannot make decisions or formulate integrative stratagems. Easter egg: Michael's encounter with the baby comes from *Halloween II* when he stands over babies in incubators in the Haddonfield Memorial Hospital; the filmmakers' attention to detail is remarkable.

When the podcasters are on their way to interview Laurie, Aaron remarks that one monster–Michael–created another monster, Laurie. And he is right: Laurie has lost her family and friends, becoming a sad recluse, hellbent on destroying her former stalker *qua* would-be murderer. Like Michael's confinement, her home is a prison, or is it? She is no longer a scream queen or a damsel in distress; instead, she is now a methodical huntress, her nature is the polar opposite from *Halloween '78* and *Halloween II*. Dana says Michael will be "Locked away for the rest of his days," to which Laura responds, "That's the idea," quoting Dr. Loomis from *Halloween '78*–history repeats itself.

Next, we visit Karen and Ray's home. Ray sets a mouse trap foreshadowing the final confrontation at Laurie's house, which is more than a residence. Laurie's fortified abode is a giant deathtrap intended to lure and destroy Michael. Allyson leaves for school with her friends, Vicky, and her boyfriend Dave (Miles Robbins), in a scene paralleling Laurie, Annie (Nancy Kyes), and Lynda (P.J. Soles) walking home from school in *Halloween '78*. In 2018, it is backward: Allyson, Vicky, and Dave stroll to school, while back in '78, Laurie, Annie, and Lynda walked home from school. While on their way, Allyson debunks the Michael-as-Laurie's-brother legend, which was *Halloween II*'s big reveal. Easter egg: as they amble along, Allyson says her family turns "into total nut cases this time of year," due to the horrific events of Samhain '78. Vicky suggests the Strode family should put up a Christmas tree instead, and skip over all the "creepy

(Left) Laurie and her daughter Karen (right) await the Boogeyman in Laurie's fortress home. Notice that Karen wears a Christmas sweater, signaling her desperate attempt to bypass Halloween's darkness and go directly to joyous Christmas, suggested earlier by Vicky to Allyson (from *Halloween* '18). The celebrations associated with the sun's death and rebirth are psychological, microcosms of the ecliptic, the macrocosm. "Yule-tide, the pagan Christmas, celebrated the sun's turning north, and the old midsummer holiday is still kept in Ireland and on the Continent as St. John's Day by the lighting of bonfires and a dance about them from east to west as the sun appears to move. The pagan Hallowe'en at the end of summer was a time of grief for the decline of the sun's glory, as well as a harvest festival of thanksgiving to him for having ripened the grain and fruit, as we formerly had husking-bees when the ears had been garnered, and now keep our own Thanksgiving by eating of our winter store in praise of God who gives us our increase." – Ruth E. Kelley, *The Book of Hallowe'en*, 1919.

Halloween shit." Later, on Halloween night, Karen does precisely that by donning a Christmas sweater, signifying her conscious need to avoid the dark holiday by fast-forwarding straight to joyous Christmas.

Arriving at school, we meet Cameron Elam, Allyson's boyfriend. They are going to the high school Halloween dance as Bonnie and Clyde only their roles are reversed: Dave is Bonnie, and Allyson is Clyde. Dave is a descendant of Lonnie Elam (Brent Le Page), the bully of Tommy Doyle, tormenting him with tales of the Boogeyman, only to be scared away from the Myers home by Dr. Loomis in *Halloween* '78.

In the classroom, Allyson sits exactly where her grandmother sat and looks out the window only to see Laurie; in *Halloween* '78, Laurie glanced out and saw Michael. But now everything is reversed: Allyson sees Laurie, who has become the monster because she is the one stalking Michael; thus, "one monster has created another." Like the pedagogue in *Halloween* '78, the teacher lectures on fate, talking about Frankl's interpretation, only there is a difference. *Frankl* is Viktor Frankl (1905-1997), an Austrian neurologist, psychiatrist, and Holocaust survivor. He authored the book, *Man's Search for Meaning* (1946), in which he talked about fate being under one's control, learning to cope with one's past sufferings. This philosophy now applies to Laurie, who controls her destiny, giving her past pain inflicted by Michael a deeper meaning. This reasoning is the opposite of what Laurie was taught forty years earlier in *Halloween* '78. Back then, she was educated about the fictitious Costaine, who felt fate was related to religion. She was also schooled about the fictitious Samuels, who argued fate is a natural, (i.e., earth, air, fire, and water), nonsectarian, "unmovable," element in our lives, so we're destined for whatever fate has in store for us, regardless. Accordingly, Laurie was bound to meet the Shape lurking outside the window, changing her life forever. Easter egg: listen carefully to the teacher's voice speaking about Frankl's take on fate. Recognize it? The voice belongs to actress P.J. Soles, who played Lynda in *Halloween* '78.

On the evening of October 30, as Michael is transferred, Laurie observes the bus from her car; she breaks down, screaming as Michael's silhouette closes in. She then joins her family for dinner; distraught, Laurie refers to Michael as *the Shape*, which is an homage to *Halloween* '78, wherein Michael was portrayed by Nick Castle, credited as the Shape. Next, in flashback, young Karen (Sophia Miller) says "Gotcha," firing her rifle at target practice, anticipating adult Karen (Greer) saying 'Gotcha," shooting Michael with the same weapon at the climax. Easter egg: after surreptitiously entering her daughter's home, Laurie surprises Karen by announcing her presence with a "Gotcha" from the staircase, marking Laurie and Karen as tricksters who know they will have to use their wits to defeat the Boogeyman.

As a father and his terpsichorean son are driving along, they come across the crashed bus transporting Michael. The scene runs parallel with *Halloween* '78 when Dr. Loomis and the nurse arrive at the asylum: the car's headlights cut through the rainy night, revealing the freed inmates wandering around aimlessly. In *Halloween* '78 and '18, Michael commandeers the vehicle and escapes. Easter egg: in *Halloween* '18, the song playing on the car's radio is "Close to Me," performed by Heavy Young Heathens. Carpenter and Jaime Lee Curtis improvised the tune for *Halloween* '78, sang by Laurie after dropping the key off at the Myers house.

Next, Deputy Hawkins plays a *Back to the Future* pinball machine in a convenient store. The *Back to the Future* trilogy involves a parallel universe, especially *Back to the Future II* (1989), a construct present in *Halloween*

'18 because it erases all other sequels and timelines. Nevertheless, these timelines seep through as though certain things and events were predestined to occur regardless of the reality.

When Deputy Hawkins and Sheriff Barker discuss the missing mental patients, they refer to Michael's killing spree as "the Babysitter Murders," which was *Halloween '78*'s original title.

After visiting Judith Myers' grave–called on by Dr. Loomis in *Halloween '78*, only the headstone was missing–Aaron and Dana stop by a gas station, which is a retelling of *Halloween 4: The Return of Michael Myers*. In *Halloween 4*, Michael's bus crashes, so he goes to a gas station, killing an attendant for his coveralls. In *Halloween '18*, when Dana asks for the key to the bathroom, Michael's throwing haymakers in the background; he clutches a hammer, killing the attendant for his coveralls. Both gas stations are nearly identical, right down to the iceboxes outside. We also get a *Halloween: Resurrection* homage with the evangelical bus marked RESURRECTION in the gas station's parking lot. Dana's bathroom stall encounter with Michael alludes to *Halloween H20* (1998), in which Claudia (Larisa Miller) has a similar restroom encounter with Michael. When Michael kills Dana, her dangling, limp feet conjure *Halloween '78*; specifically, Bob's (John Michael Graham) dangling, lifeless feet after Michael pins him to the wall with a knife.

With Samhain ascendant, the past *Halloween* movies bleed through into this new reality, this new timeline, almost like they were preordained. Trick-or-treaters are everywhere, and two of them bump into Michael accidentally: one dresses as a pirate, and the other is carrying a boombox. The pirate alludes to *Halloween II*; a boy, costumed as a pirate, has become the victim of a cruel Halloween prank. His mother takes him to the Haddonfield Memorial Hospital because he has a razor wedged in his mouth from biting into tainted candy. The kid with the boombox also emerges from *Halloween II*; a teenager with a radio bumps into Michael as he heads to the hospital to kill Laurie. Lance Warlock played the teenager with the ghetto blaster; in *Halloween II*, his father, Dick, played the Shape. Easter egg: in *Halloween III*, Dick Warlock played one of Cochran's silent androids.

The *Halloween II* timeline continues to bleed through, refusing to be erased. Michael enters the house of a woman wearing a red bathrobe, making a ham sandwich. In *Halloween II*, the woman making the ham sandwich, and wearing the red bathrobe, is Mrs. Elrod (Lucille Benson, 1914-1984). In *Halloween* '18, the woman is unidentified, but, for now, remember *Elrod*. A glitch occurs: in *Halloween II*, Michael steals Mrs. Elrod's butcher knife, but she survives, screaming at the blood the Shape leaves behind. In *Halloween* '18, Michael kills the red-robed woman with a hammer before taking the knife.

From there, Michael sees a sexy nurse alluding to *Halloween II*'s Karen Bailey (Pamela Susan Shoop), the horny nurse at the Haddonfield Memorial Hospital. What comes next is déjà vu: in *Halloween II*, Michael sneaks into the home of a worried Alice Martin (Anne Bruner), speaking on the phone with her friend, Sally, and murders her. In *Halloween* '18, Michael sneaks into the home of a distressed neighbor talking on the phone with her friend, Sally, and slaughters her, duplicating the murder of Alice Martin.

During the high school's dance party, Allyson mentions that Halloween is on a weeknight. Correct she is; in 2018, Halloween fell on a Wednesday night. Allyson and Cameron's costumes reverse their genders: he is Bonnie Parker (1910-1934) while she is Clyde Barrow (1909-1934), implying role reversal. The Devil's cheerleaders dance energetically on an inverted pentagram, signifying the pagan holiday's supernatural darkness, almost like their dance is a satanic ritual, deliberately summoning evil-as-Michael Myers. Halloween parties are the real survival of the ancient November Eve merrymakings, to commemorate our sensual activity, our animal-mindedness.[290] The party's popular colors are orange, yellow, and black: orange denotes the dying sun in autumn; deep yellow is the color of most ripe grain and fruit; black stands for black magic and demonic influence. Ghosts and skulls and cross-bones, symbols of death, startle the beholder.[291] The high school's Halloween celebration, the infernal dance, imitates another autumn 2018 movie: *Suspiria*, with its pithy *Volk*, a witchcraft-styled ritual, designed to raise Hell. It's like *Suspiria*, and *Halloween* '18 are connected, the uncanny parallel coming straight out of the demonic realm. Similar Left-Hand Path sorcery has happened before: at the end of this section, I will analyze the archetypal witchcraft-occult undercurrent buried deep in *Halloween* '78. Finally, the Halloween party conjures the

---

290 Ibid, 155. See also Alvin Boyd Kuhn, *Halloween: A Festival of Lost Meaning* (1922; repr., Whitefish, MT: Kessinger Publishing, 2004), *passim*.
291 Kelley, *Hallowe'en*, 156.

Halloween carouse in Rob Zombie's *Halloween II* (2009), only during the bacchanalia, Laurie Strode (Scout Taylor-Compton) goes batshit insane.

Vicky babysits Julian, echoing the Lynda and Bob thread from *Halloween '78*, only with latent backwardness. For example, Vicky wears a white t-shirt with yellow sleeves when she puts Julian to bed; in *Halloween '78*, when Tommy Doyle is put to bed, he wears a white t-shirt with yellow sleeves. Observe Julian's rotating lamp; its phantasmagoria spotlights a costumed child wielding a knife, paying homage to *Halloween '78* when a young, clown-costumed Michael kills his sister with a knife. The lamp also projects Saturn representing death, which the Shape embodies. Her boyfriend Dave arrives; we see laundry drying on a clothesline paying tribute to *Halloween '78* when Laurie spies Michael from her bedroom window, standing behind drying laundry on a clothesline. Dave also refers to Julian as "little buddy," alluding to *Halloween III*'s "Little Buddy" Kupfer (Brad Schacter), whose face melts into a symphony of bugs and deadly reptiles, courtesy of a cursed Silver Shamrock pumpkin mask. Michael kills the female first, Vicky, then the male, Dave, reversing his actions from 1978 when he murdered Bob first, then Lynda. Instead of wearing the ghostly bedsheet to kill Vicky, as he did with Lynda in *Halloween '78*, Michael now makes it a death shroud, covering her bloody body. He still makes sure to put a pumpkin next to her–in a fish tank–like the jack-o'-lantern sitting on the nightstand next to Annie Brackett's corpse back in *Halloween '78*. Like Bob, Michael pins Dave's body to a wall with a knife only Dave faces backward, not forward, signifying backwardness, an alternative timeline.

The police radio band reports a domestic disturbance at 707 Meridian Avenue, which was the address of the real-life Myers House in South Pasadena, California. The home has been moved subsequently; its new address is 1000 Mission Street, South Pasadena, next to the railroad tracks. Laurie, equipped with a police radio in her car, arrives at the scene to be welcomed with another *Halloween III* homage. Several children are trick-or-treating, happily wearing Silver Shamrock Halloween masks: a skull, a pumpkin, and a witch. Back at the dance, Cameron kisses another girl, so Allyson exits, but a drunk Oscar pursues her. She leaves him behind in a backyard, and Michael appears; Oscar mistakes the Shape for Mr. Elrod, referencing the ham sandwich-making Mrs. Elrod from the original *Halloween II* universe.

CINEMA SYMBOLISM 3

At last, we have the grand finale at Laurie's fortress-like home. Ray plants mousetraps at the beginning, suggesting the cat-and-mouse game Laurie and the Shape will play, and that her house is a giant lure. Over the years, Laurie has become the monster, transforming her home into a deathtrap. Before entering the house, Michael seems to have developed a new hobby: making jack-o'-lanterns out of human faces. Laurie's home is reminiscent of the Doyle home; she stalks Michael, whom she believes to be hiding in closets just like she did back in '78. Her bedroom looks like the Doyle's master bedroom, with the balcony across from the closet. This time around, Laurie goes over the balcony, not Michael, and when he looks over–like Dr. Loomis did back in '78–Laurie has vanished. One monster has created another: Laurie traps Michael in the basement and sets the house on fire, burning him alive as she escapes with her daughter and granddaughter. Unlike *Halloween II*, when Michael collapses, engulfed in flames, in *Halloween* '18, he is never seen again, but his breathing is heard during the end credits, signaling that he lives still. Easter egg: again, history repeats itself: Laurie finds Ray's dead body hidden in a closet, much like Lynda's in *Halloween* '78

In a scene conjuring *The Texas Chainsaw Massacre*'s (1974) finale, Laurie, Karen, and Allyson ride off in the flatbed of a pickup truck, fleeing Michael just as Sally Hardesty (Marilyn Burns, 1949-2014) escaped Leatherface (Gunnar Hansen, 1947-2015). A disconnected Allyson clutches a large kitchen knife, suggesting she may be possessed by Michael's evil spirit, mirroring *Halloween 4*'s coda. Dressed as a clown, Jaime Lloyd (Danielle Harris) brandishes bloody scissors after stabbing her stepmom. And speaking of Danielle Harris, where is she? She should've cameoed in some form or fashion. Laurie's previous children, each retconned out of existence, were named Jamie (Harris) and John (Josh Harnett, appearing in *Halloween H20*). Her child in *Halloween* '18, Karen, starts with the next letter of the alphabet, *k*. Easter egg: In *Halloween* '18, Laurie uses a Winchester to defend herself against Michael. In *Halloween* '78, part of Dr. Dementia's Horrorthon is Howard Hawks' *The Thing*, which Carpenter remade in 1982. Winchester was not only Hawks' middle name, but he also named his production company Winchester Films. In *Halloween* '78, the Winchester Films logo appears during the opening credits of *The Thing*. Carpenter acknowledges Hawks as a significant influence. Easter egg: Allyson seems possessed by a greater evil than Michael. When Allyson stabs him, the knife wounds him, stinging him like Bilbo Baggins' elvish blade, unlike Laurie's attack, suggesting the Shape is susceptible to her blitzkrieg.

Dr. Sartain's spinal column pen, which doubles as a blade, is fascinating and chilling; he uses it to backstab Deputy Hawkins.

To analyze *Halloween* '18, I naturally re-watched the original *Halloween* and its sequels. When watching the first film, I was struck by something buried deep in the celluloid, almost like the movie has a subconscious of its own. When we think of Halloween, we think of witches and witchcraft, performing occult rituals and black magic. Halloween, like April 30 or Walpurgisnacht, and May 1, Beltane, celebrates the macabre, originating in Europe with fire festivals, particularly the British Isles. On this paganism, J.G. Frazer explains: "We must bear in mind that among the British Celts the chief fire-festivals of the year appear certainly to have been those of Beltane (May Day) and Hallowe'en (the last day of October); and this suggests a doubt whether the Celts of Gaul also may not have not have celebrated their principle rites of fire, including their burnt sacrifices of men and animals, at the beginning of May or at the beginning of November rather than at midsummer."[292]

In *The Book of Hallowe'en* (1919), Ruth E. Kelley (1893-1982) further elucidates: "So this night was called Walpurgis Night, when evil beings were abroad, and with them human worshippers who still guarded the old faith in secret. This is very like the occasion of November Eve, which shared with May 1st the Celtic manifestations of evil. Witches complete the list of supernatural beings which are out on Halloween. All are to be met at crossroads, with harm to the beholders."[293] The purpose of these fire-festivals was to diminish the power of witches and warlocks. On those two days, especially Halloween, the magical powers of witches, wizards, and devils were exalted, given them license to terrorize the countryside.[294]

I believe there is a witchcraft-styled theme buried deep in *Halloween* '78, emerging from the collective unconscious. Witches identify with faceless ghosts, coming back on moonlit nights. As the moon glows overhead, Michael murders his sister on Halloween night '63. Fast-forward to Halloween '78,

---

292 Frazer, *Golden Bough*, 648.
293 Kelley, *Hallowe'en*, 137.
294 Frazer, *Golden Bough*, 626, 648.

and the Shape has come home. He personifies evil: a dark supernatural elemental incapable of death, conjured by two teenage, fledgling witches: Lynda and Annie. They embrace the dark side of the moon, Hecate, the patroness of witches. Lynda and Annie adore the goddess by satisfying their libidinous flesh because, in America, Halloween is a night of excess, sexual escapades, bizarre happenings, and ghostly revelry.[295]

Ergo, Annie forsakes her babysitting duties to seek out her boyfriend, Paul Freedman, while Lynda becomes a drunken whore, fucking her lover, Bob Simms. Through excessive partying and fornicating, their fleshy fantasies are fulfilled but not without consequence. They have unknowingly cast a harmful spell via their sex magicks, summoning evil in the form of the Shape: a relentless, soulless, entity; Michael is a hammer that will destroy their wanton pride, lust, debaucheries, stupidity, and arrogance. *Hex* is Greek for *six* (as in *hexagram*), and *six* is virtually synonymous with *sex*; thus, the witch is the noetic or mind principle masquerading in its feminine phase. One may be prepared to learn without too great astonishment that *hex* is German for *witch*, and *hexerei, witchcraft*. It is not stretch if one were to say that when the soul is *sixed*, it is *sexed* and *hexed*, i.e., bewitched, using a word in colloquial vogue.

Enter the white witch, Laurie, who embodies the moon's positive persona, Artemis, the virginal protectress of children, evidenced by her babysitting duties; lacking a boyfriend, she instead keeps a watchful eye on Tommy Doyle and Lindsay Wallace. Michael deposes Annie and Lynda while Laurie shelters the children, eventually surviving the dark menace.

The only person who understands that Michael personifies evil is the sagacious Dr. Loomis, who attempts to warn everybody, but is ignored. In the televised version of *Halloween*, there is a scene occurring after Michael has murdered his sister, Judith, on Halloween '63. Inside a lecture hall, a psychiatrist reads a judge's order remanding Michael to the Smith's Grove Sanitarium over Dr. Loomis' objections. May 1 is the date of this hearing, Beltane, the halfway point between the vernal equinox and the summer solstice '64, ingeniously showcasing the film's underlying witchcraft narrative. To this author, it is part of *Halloween*'s cinematic unconsciousness, a diabolical element observable only to the initiated. Easter egg: Carpenter's *The Fog* (1980) features the same witchcraft

---

295 Kelley, *Hallowe'en*, 154; Kuhn, *Halloween, passim*.

undercurrent. After Father Malone (Hal Holbrook) finds his ancestor's journal hidden in the church's wall, he reads its pages, documenting the plan to kill Blake and the *Elizabeth Dane*'s crew. Toward the end, the diary states, "April 30 – Midnight 'til one belongs to the dead. Good Lord deliver us." April 30 is *Walpurgisnacht*, the pagan-witchcraft celebration that opens Hell's gates, permitting the *Elizabeth Dane*'s ghosts to return, seeking revenge one hundred years later.

Birds of a Feather Flock Together: Chloe Sevigny and Kristen Stewart in Lizzie

Lizzie is an American biographical thriller directed by Craig William Macneill and written by Bryce Kass. It had its world premiere at the Sundance Film Festival on January 19, 2018. It was released on September 14, 2018, by Saban Films and Roadside Attractions.

"*In the Days and Hours of Saturn* thou canst perform experiments to summon the Souls from Hades, but only those who have died a natural death. Similarly on these days and hours thou canst operate to bring either good or bad fortune to buildings; to have familiar spirits attend thee in sleep; to cause good of ill success to business, possessions, goods, seeds, fruits, and similar things, in order to acquire learning; to bring destruction and to give death, and to sow hatred and discord." – *The Greater Key of Solomon*, Book I, ii.

Lucifer has always been a patron of sapphic women because lesbianism has traditionally been held up as a rebellion against God. Luciferian radiance, the *Sol Niger*, illuminates *Lizzie*; Chloe Sevigny portrays the eponymous murderess with Kristen Stewart playing the maid, Bridget Sullivan; they are two repressed lesbians consciously exploring their dark, erotic sides. They desire to liberate their inner blackness marking them as Romantic Satanists; by allowing their shadows' ascendency, they paint a pair of homicidal portraits, becoming Lilith-like icons of female independence.[296] Murder is their art, their black mass; death their blank canvas; their hatchet blows, brushes, and blood splatter, paint. Jung wrote about the Black Sun in his later works; *Sol Niger* relates to the darkest and

---

296 Faxneld, *Satanic Feminism*, "'Protomartyr of Female Independence': Lilith Becomes a Feminist Icon," 61-65.

the most destructive situations, in what the alchemists called the blacker-than-black dimension of the *nigredo* (*vide supra*). This aspect is darkness itself: painful, dangerous, tragic, and, at times, masochistic; it is annihilation, welcoming oblivion. In *Star Wars: Revenge of the Sith* (2005), a Luciferian Black Sun illuminates the volcanic Mustafar as Anakin Skywalker, now Darth Vader, awaits Obi-Wan Kenobi. The Jedi Knight will defeat the Sith Lord in a lightsaber duel, tragically transforming him into a black-suited, physically ravaged, mechanized terror. As a Dark Side user, Vader radiates the Black Sun's terrifying light, embodying the saturnine *nigredo*.

When the light of the *Sol Niger* shines upon Mercurius inhabiting the destructive *nigredo* stage, death and chaos are wrought, making change inevitable. Lizzie and Bridget's psychological transformation is a descent into raw savagery, signified by birds, as well as its employment of light and dark, confinement and freedom. The somber movie reminds this author of *Stoker* because the dialog is minimized; instead, the characters' actions, facial expressions, and gestures speak louder than words.

In 1892 Fall River, Massachusetts, 32-year-old Lizzie Borden resides with her domineering father, Andrew (Jamey Sheridan), stepmother, Abby (Fiona Shaw), and elder sister, Emma (Kim Dickens). Gloomy Saturn governs the household: while the Borden family are prominent members of the community, Lizzie's day-to-day life is under the strict control of her oppressive father. One day, an Irish immigrant, Bridget Sullivan, moves into the Borden residence to work as a maid. That night, Lizzie attends an opera and suffers a seizure during the performance. After she recovers, she and Bridget quickly forge a close bond as Lizzie attempts to teach the illiterate Bridget how to read. Easter egg: the photograph in the locket that Andrew gives her is the historical Lizzie Borden's biological mother, Sarah, who died when Lizzie was a baby.

On several occasions, written threats disrupt the bleak household, which Lizzie believes are connected to her father's recent acquisition of land. Lizzie overhears a discussion between her father and her uncle, the nebulous John Vinnicum Morse (Denis O'Hare), the brother of Lizzie and Emma's deceased mother. During the conversation, Andrew indicates his desire to appoint John as his estate's trustee. The next morning, Lizzie plays the piano by herself, i.e., *playing with herself*, identifying her as a melancholic

Black Sun rising: although *Suspiria* '77 isn't alchemical, the deathly light of the *Sol Niger* is pervasive, the *nigredo* exalted, manifesting in black slip and pair of stockings hanging outside a window (top). The demon's eyes materialize in the enticing lingerie (center), causing pain and death, attacking Patricia Hingle (Eva Axén, bottom), making her appear piglike before brutally killing her. The demon-as-Mercurius strikes! This humiliating torture is Patricia's punishment for entering ill-prepared into a world of darkness; she witnessed the evil hiding in the Tanz Academy, not knowing it was an augury of death. *Lizzie* treads on similar cinematic ground because Luciferian light demolishes New England Victorian sensibilities.

masturbator, defining her solitude.[297] After her father leaves, she then raids Abby's jewelry box and hocks its contents to a local pawnbroker, staging the scene as though an intruder robbed the house. Such an act signals her rebellion, turning against her father, a hostile Demiurge, the fashioner of her gloomy existence. Lizzie does not seek gnosis spirituality, only satanic liberation, craving two things: money and sapphic pleasure.

---

297 William Stekel, *Sex and Dreams: The Language of Dreams* (Boston: Richard G. Badger, 1922), 118.

However, the pawnshop's owner visits Andrew at his office, explaining Lizzie pawned the missing jewelry. Enraged over Lizzie's theft of the items and the staged robbery, Andrew unleashes his anger by killing her pet pigeons, which he has Bridget prepare for dinner. One morning, Bridget becomes distraught after receiving a letter from Ireland disclosing her mother's death. Late that night, Lizzie finds her father sexually assaulting Bridget in the attic's servant quarters. Lizzie smashes a hand mirror and sprinkles the glass on the floor, causing Andrew to cut his feet when leaving.

Lizzie and Bridget's bond grows increasingly close, and with Bridget able to write, the two leave letters for one another around the house. Both women open themselves to modernity, wishing to experience new things, to push the bounds of constrictive Victorian ethos. Their relationship eventually becomes mysteriously romantic, then erotic because both women are desperate to experience coitus, whatever forbidden, or *satanic*, form it may take. One afternoon, Andrew witnesses Lizzie and Bridget fondling each other, mutually masturbating in the barn; during the Victorian Era, such eroticism was taboo and unthinkable. The barn is hot, quiet, and heavy with languor making it the perfect place for their sexual dalliance.

Subsequently, he confronts Lizzie about the affair, forbidding her to speak to Bridget, stating he is terminating her employment. He then calls Lizzie an "abomination." That night, Lizzie burns her father's will in the kitchen stove. The next day, August 4, Andrew's and Abby's dead bodies are found in the house, both bludgeoned with a hatchet. Law enforcement suspects Lizzie is responsible, though Emma proclaims her sister's innocence. Lizzie is formally charged with both murders, her case proceeding to trial. Bridget visits Lizzie in jail, telling her she wishes never to speak to her again, before leaving for Montana.

A flashback shows Lizzie and Bridget performing the gruesome murders. That morning, Lizzie strips nude and hides in Abby's bedroom while Andrew goes for his morning walk. Bridget brings Abby a doctored telegram notifying her of a friend's illness. When Abby rushes to her room to prepare to leave, Lizzie bludgeons her multiple times in the face and head with a hatchet. Bridget, outside washing windows, is sickened by the sounds and vomits. Lizzie cleans herself and redresses. When Andrew returns, she tells him she is going outside to pick fruit. Bridget undresses, confronting Andrew in the den armed with a hatchet, but hesitates. Lizzie re-enters the house, and seeing

Bridget's reluctance, takes the hatchet from her, butchering Andrew herself. To taint the evidence, Lizzie butchers a pigeon with the murder weapon, smearing it with the bird's blood before sawing off the blade and hiding it in a pail in the basement. She then burns the ax's wooden handle in the kitchen stove, and, presumably, her blood-splatted dress.

Bridget, personifying alchemy's *albedo*, and Lizzie, epitomizing Mercury lingering in the *nigredo*, has temporarily risen from chaos, floating between the turbulence of instinct and the unbearable order of domesticity. They have merged matter–murder–with their ungodly spirits, their ambitions for freedom, to be rid of all patriarchy. Lizzie is a proto-feminist, a macabre icon of the woman's liberation movement, a Romantic Satanist, a defiant and proud lesbian. But Bridget is reserved, and knows better, explaining the predicament to Lizzie in her cell. In Victorian New England, to announce themselves as a gay couple, to step *out of the closet* as it were, would be a death sentence. Society would pronounce them monsters, not members of a fanciful, progressive bourgeoisie, damning them for all time.

Nevertheless, the two women obliterate the masculine Andrew Borden-as-*citrinitas*; the blood-stained walls, the *rubedo*, signify the conclusion of the women's murderous, yet liberating, rampage. Her devious plan executed, Lizzie "Mercurius" Borden slips the shackles of her smothering domestic confinement; liberated and wealthy, the spinster reigns supreme. Ironically, Lizzie will be acquitted by the very thing she seeks to destroy. A jury of twelve men, Fall River's patriarchy, find her not guilty of the crimes, refusing to believe a woman could commit such a grisly act.

After her acquittal, she lived the remainder of her life in Fall River as a social outcast, estranged from her sister, Emma. She died aged 66, leaving the majority of her estate to the local humane society. Bridget remained in Montana for the rest of her life, eventually dying in 1948, aged 78-79.

Lizzie is not a traditional alchemical movie per se because there is no transition from oneself to another. Although Lizzie Borden becomes a murderess, it is merely an extremity of her lackluster persona: repressed, disturbed, and rebellious. She is a lonely maiden, killing to escape the confines of a prison-like home ruled by an ogre father and cruel stepmother. Lizzie is the same person at the beginning that she is at the end credits. She does not change or transition; rather, Lizzie is at home in satanic darkness, moving from dark to darker like only Mercury can. The *rubedo*, *albedo*, and *citrinitas* are liminal and fleeting; however, it is the *nigredo*–darkness and death–the Black Sun illuminating *Lizzie*'s Victorian world. Ms. Borden personifies Mercury in the *nigredo* stage succinctly, chaos, order arising from chaos, order descending into disorder, and a return to order. As a deranged fertility goddess, Lizzie takes pleasure in both death and her resurrection, killing her parents yet emerging triumphantly; her resurrected-self achieves indestructibility, becoming American folklore.

The archetypes are present in both the film and history, which explains why there is such fascination with the Fall River murders. The mystery appeals to our conscious and subconscious minds, only heightening our interest; paralleling the crimes of Jack the Ripper, we are always looking back in time, trying to solve the mystery. We hope to discover some new piece of evidence that was overlooked or an insight into the personalities involved, which might tip us off, disclosing the truth. The Borden murders are gruesome, induced by rage: repeated blows to the head with an ax; our morbid curiosity cannot turn away from them, like driving by a horrific car accident. The paradigmatic legend, the memory of the murders, the memory of the principals, and the memory of the deadly hatchet, will not erode from the American consciousness.[298] The enduring public obsession is fed by the whimsical and numerically inaccurate jingle which, in celebrating the crime and its characters, has become this country's best-known quatrain: "Lizzie Borden took an ax / And gave her mother forty whacks / When she saw what she had done / She gave her father forty-one." With its measured pulsation, this little rhyme is popularly recited today as it was over a hundred years ago, making the incomparable Lizzie Borden part of the nation's identity.[299]

At the time of writing, the crimes remain unsolved, but this author can disclose the archetypes: Bridget (1869-1948) is the child, and Emma Borden (1851-1927) is the fool because she's in denial. Abby Borden (1828-1892) is the evil stepmother, the bitter crone (think fairy tales, like *Cinderella*), and Lizzie (1860-1927) personifies the trickster/Magician/Mercury; by getting away with murder, the ax murderess transforms the social fabric of Fall River and New England forever. Uncle John Morse (1833-1917) is the hanged man

---

298 Robert Sullivan, *Goodbye Lizzie Borden* (Brattleboro, VT: The Stephen Greene Press, 1974), 2.
299 Ibid.

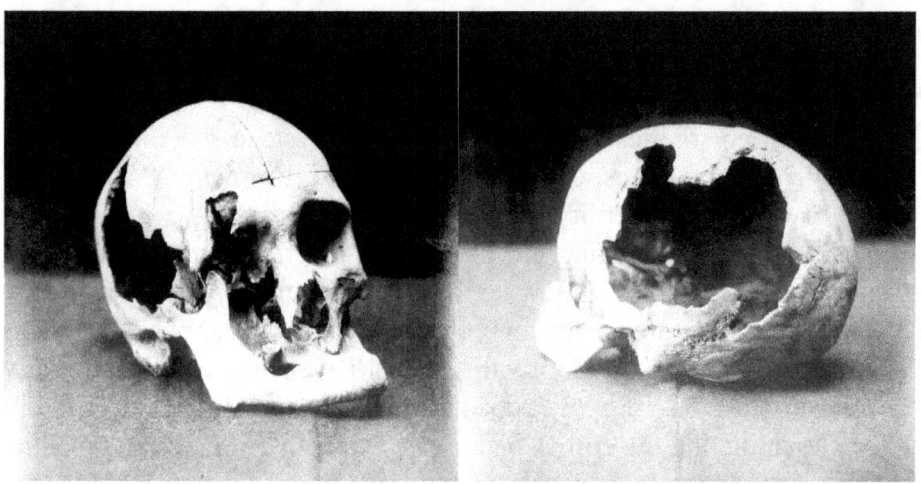

Photographs of the skulls of Andrew (left) and Abby Borden (right) in the collection of the Fall River Historical Society. Andrew was struck eleven times, and Abby nineteen times, indicating the violent attacks were personal, motivated by uncontrollable wrath.

(Card XII of the Major Arcana), a traitor and would-be thief, and Andrew Borden (1822-1892) is the ogre father, the Devil.

The actors portraying Lizzie's stepmother and father, Abby and Andrew, demonstrate the power of occult casting, designed to draw forth the earlier performances of Fiona Shaw and Jamey Sheridan. Shaw has played the evil surrogate mother archetype before, appearing in several Harry Potter movies as Petunia Dursley, the neglectful and cruel aunt of the saga's hero, Harry. Sheridan has also played the Devil before, appearing as Randall Flagg in the miniseries *The Stand* (1994). Flagg is a demonic figure associated with the End of Days, human conflict, misery, and destruction. The casting of Shaw and Sheridan as Lizzie's malicious parents reinvents their past performances, transferring their previous roles as a heartless matriarch and a fiendish patriarch to tyrannical Victorians. Their casting heightens Lizzie's anguish and distress, making them worthy of violent annihilation, justifying her murder spree.

The movie–and the historical legend–is a meditation on how abhorrent female behavior might shock Victorian New England out of its patriarchal hierarchy and reactionary attitudes. Because the Victorian Eden repressed and marginalized the feminine, it was hellishly brutal when it finally erupted. As I've explained, sun and light are critical within the alchemical formula.

They are attributed to the masculine–Apollo, Helios, Horus, or King Arthur ruling with his lunar queen, Guinevere. *Sol Niger's* light subsists in the *nigredo*, documenting Mercurius' shifts, his chaotic descents, and his cosmic rising. Here, we see Lizzie descend into a psychological Tophet becoming murderesses, rising like an alchemical Phoenix when she is acquitted. But Lizzie is at home in the *nigredo*; as a feminized Mercurius, she is flexible, intelligent, and adaptable to extremely unusual circumstances.

In his writings, Ficino described three suns: black, white, and red, corresponding to the three significant alchemical color stages. On the *Sol Niger*, he explains: "The body must be dissolved in the subtlest middle air: The body is also dissolved by its heat and humidity; where the soul, the middle nature holds the principality in the color of blackness all in the glass: which blackness of Nature the ancient Philosophers called the crows head or the Black Sun."[300] Sevigny's portrayal of Lizzie Borden presents the spinster as absorbing and radiating melancholic light. It is also numinous; blackness is a nonmanifest latency, a shadow of the sun, linked to deathly Saturn and Yahweh, the *primus Anthropos*. *Sol Niger* equates with, and is understood only in the *nigredo* aspect. Its more sublime dimension–its shine, its dark illumination, its Eros and wisdom–remains in the unconscious.[301]

The *Sol Niger*–destruction and the inevitable rebirth–may have originated the myth of Saturn devouring his children as soon as Rhea gave birth. In the painting, *Saturn Devouring a Child* by Marten van Heemskreck (1498-1574), Saturn begins to eat his offspring; the ringed planet produces a melancholic influence, and its color, black, associates with winter, night, death, and distance.[302] One of the Black Sun's occult symbols is a green lion devouring a bloody sun, much like the dark emblems suggesting the *nigredo*. Lizzie epitomizes this ferocious green lion, suggested by the green wallpaper decorating the sitting room where Andrew is butchered. Notice also that Abby wears a green dress when she is cut down.

Sevigny's performance also befogs all distinctions between lust and love. She desperately craves attention; obsessed with bohemianism,

---

300 Marsilio Ficino, "Marsilio Ficino on the alchemical art," *Liber de Arte Chemica* from *Theatrum Chemicum*, Vol 2, Geneva, 1702, 172-183, trans. Justin von Budjoss, *The Alchemy Web Site*, n.d., http://www.levity.com/alchemy/ficino.html (accessed January 21, 2020).
301 Marlan, *Black Sun*, 11
302 Ibid, 44.

Sixteenth-century alchemical woodcut of a green lion devouring the sun. Lizzie is the lion; her father is the sun (masculine) chewed, eaten, and killed. The blood represents splatter from the ax's deadly blows. It is destruction intended for a melancholic rebirth; for her, it is parricide in exchange for liberation.

she manages to create a sphere in which one cannot tell this from that. With her lesbian-masturbatory histrionics with Bridget, she annihilates the differences between sister, lover, and daughter. Although their tender caresses are private–concealed inside a barn–Lizzie relishes that her father was watching, realizing masturbation is defiance. She is a dark trickster only, divorced from Victorian sense and sensibility. She wants control over Bridgette, yet she gives control over by teaching her to read. Lizzie makes her a witness to murder, unearthing the *nigredo*, but Bridget's alibi stirs Emma's suspicions. During the trial, Bridgette lies under oath, not only to save Lizzie but herself. In this paradigm, Lizzie Borden personifies duality, obfuscating the distinction between good and evil, exploring secret interpenetrations between the powers the world puts asunder.

In Jungian psychology, the dark light of the Black Sun heralds a developing consciousness of sexuality emerging from the repressed feminine shadow (*vide supra*). Like Foucault's Pendulum, Lizzie's stale libido sways endlessly between lassitude and repression, her dreams and desires unfulfilled. She has reached the age of thirty-two and is single; Lizzie is aware she will not marry like her dour sister. Compounding the situation is her father's vast inheritance, soon to be placed in trust with Uncle John as trustee, which is unacceptable to Lizzie under any circumstance. Her stepmother, Abby, hates her, and her sister Emma is hardly around; she is friendless, Fall River society wants nothing to do with her, evidenced by the contempt she receives when she attends the theater. She goes to church alone; God, seemingly, does not want anything to do with her.

Enter Bridget into this world of angst and Victorian repression. Lizzie not only cultivates a friendship by teaching Bridget how to read, but they become lovers briefly, finding sexual release. This forbidden erotism is their Black Sun rising, making them Satanists of the romantic variety: they instigate a full-blown rebellion against the patriarchy. Their black alchemy is a mutual sexual orgasm, a physical and poetic event during which a vital exchange occurs: it is the transference of yin and yang energies, harmonizing their souls, releasing their frustrations. Lizzie, comprehending her heart of darkness, can see through the blackness; she understands deconstructive activity is necessary for psychological change. As for Lizzie, the transition was smooth: descending into the *nigredo* means a house on the hill and financial security, no greedy-ogre father, no oppressive-evil stepmother, no sexual repression, and no meddling uncle.[303] Lizzie is now willing and able to murder, with Bridget as her partner in crime. A demon did not possess Lizzie; instead, she was temporarily Mercurius; the murder was not evil, but liberation, she harnessed the dark energy emanating from the Black Sun.

The bird is a harbinger of this liberation; at one point, Uncle John dubs Lizzie a "night bird," hinting at the *nigredo's* darkness. Lizzie keeps a few birds–pigeons–as pets in the barn, her sanctum sanctorum, which are killed by her father, and served as dinner. But Lizzie has a sense of irony. Later, she turns the tables and kills a bird, smearing the ax with blood, tainting it, contaminating the evidence. Birds signify freed energy, Lizzie's eventual

---

[303] The historical Lizzie Borden would have a love affair with the actress Nance O'Neil (1874-1965), known as the American Sarah Bernhardt.

liberation from the home. Just as the bird is free to fly, it can also be caged, representing her confinement. The destruction of the bird–both by Andrew and Lizzie–and their consumption is akin to Saturn devouring his children. Saturn, haunted by one of his children overthrowing him, signifies Andrew's subconscious fear of patricide: his offspring will kill him, taking his fortune. The birds' slaughter by Andrew, and later by Lizzie, is gruesome, the inevitable putrefaction of the *Sol Niger*. Yet, like the Phoenix, the bird is reborn: Lizzie is acquitted, leaving her parents' house forever, marking Fall River indelibly. In ancient Egypt, birds represented the vital breath; they symbolized immortality, hovering over mummified bodies. Lizzie has alchemically changed; once a spinster, she is now a terror, the stuff of nightmares, haunting children, memorialized in a rhyme. She has become Lilith incarnate: the murder part of American folklore; Lizzie's eternal mythos crafted upon her father's and stepmother's butchered bodies.

The film's wardrobe is thematic. *Lizzie*'s costumes aren't just pieces to lust after–they're lustful and stimulating. One of Bridget's duties is to dress Lizzie, and as their attraction mounts, this domestic routine becomes a sexy one. A close-up shot details the dozen buttons that trim Lizzie's leg-of-mutton sleeves, Bridget slowly clasps each one. Here, their bodies can touch, their mouths hang open–they could kiss–and they almost do. Getting dressed together is a sort of make-out session without the kissing–foreplay in reverse.[304] And when Lizzie's sister walks in on them, they don't have to stop. Clothing acts as a barrier that guards against, but also allows for, homoerotic contact. The many buttons that signal modesty and the concealing silhouettes are among Victorian-Edwardian fashion's most conspicuous features, each reminding contemporary viewers of the traditionalist values of the era. Humility was not only an allusion to purity but also meant to protect it. Similarly, the detailed designs, laborious to undo, were intended to prevent unwanted contact. They assume the wearer's chastity rather than their lust, welcoming the former, rejecting the latter. And yet, these fashions and the hierarchic social customs attached to them loosen Lizzie and Bridget's desires.

---

304 Clementine Ford, "'Lizzie' Shows Us the Erotic Side of Fussy Edwardian Fashion," *Garage*, September 26, 2018, https://garage.vice.com/en_us/article/wjyxjm/lizzie-borden-costumes (accessed March 2, 2019).

When fantasy becomes reality: Bridget Sullivan and Lizzie Borden finally embrace, exploring their sexual melancholia and frustration, bathing in the *Sol Niger's* Luciferian light, succumbing to forbidden sexual desires. Their homoerotic lust leads to lovemaking in the barn, and then to coldblooded murder.

At once, the style is liberating and restricting. When Lizzie and Bridget finally get to fondle each other, they don't take off their clothes. In the barn, the women lean against a bale of hay and entangle their limbs, their conjoined form striped by the shadows of the barn's wooden slats. Lizzie's light brown calico dress, dotted with deep brown and pink flowers and, of course, puff-sleeved and ruffled, looks rich next to Bridget's sullen gray, simple woolen maid's uniform. As the women waded through the layers and depths of their skirts to masturbate each other, one is reminded of how ironically erotic Victorian-Edwardian clothing is. The highest of high necklines are suggestive of precisely what it covers.[305] Victorian-Edwardian modesty fails to deliver on its patriarchal promise of protection from men, even Lizzie's complicated and burdensome dresses are illusory as safety nets.

When Lizzie confronts Uncle John about scheming for her inheritance, he violently pushes her many-layered skirt aside and digitally rapes her. And if Lizzie's gilded costumes are penetrable, Bridget's nondescript ones are all the more so. Andrew creaks up the stairs to the maid's quarters at night to rape Bridget. Her nightgown, ankle-length, dolman sleeved, and high-necked–lace is the dress' one intricacy–isn't made for alluring bedmates.

---

305 Ibid.

And yet, the nightie doesn't armor against Andrew either.[306] But Mr. Borden isn't just murdered for raping Bridget. Lizzie's father had been peering through barn's slats, and despite the narrow lace covering their necks, Lizzie's gigot arms, and a large number of skirts between them, his naked eye demystifies the ruffles beneath their dresses. "You are an abomination, Lizzie," he admonishes her, confirming he saw her and Bridget in *flagrante delicto*. Bridget will be discharged, and Lizzie will be sent away.[307] Lizzie must act and act now, or she'll lose her father's inheritance to Uncle John. She burns her father's will in the oven, summoning fire and brimstone because Hell hath no furies like a woman scorned.

At the beginning of the bloody murder, presented in a revealing flashback, Bridget nervously washes windows outside while Lizzie ceremoniously strips to kill indoors. On the one hand, the choice to murder in the buff is a practical one: no bloody clothes as evidence. But nudity also implies sex and the crime does too: murder is, after all, the most transgressive act, and as she buries the hatchet into her stepmother, Lizzie finally orgasms. Afterward, Lizzie walks down the large varnished wood staircase, completely naked, covered in blood. She has become an archetype: a mythic madwoman, Medusa or Lilith. The tightly pinned curls loosening from her head create a halo; she looks all-powerful, otherworldly, and completely free, arising as a hell-fury angel.[308] Lizzie has died and been reborn, emerging as a sable, tripartite phantom, personifying the *albedo*, *mortification*, and *putrefactio*.

Lizzie then dresses in a calico pie-crust collar top, white and stippled with blue flowers, which matches her A-line blue skirt. But getting dressed in the fashion of her time doesn't mean she loses the naked power she had earlier. Lizzie gestures to Bridget that it's now her turn; that is, to pick up the hatchet where Lizzie left it, and kill Andrew. Before Bridget goes through these similar motions, the scene is interrupted when it cuts to Lizzie again. Bucolic under a tree, Lizzie's expression is the same one she wore in the nude. Even her post-murder halo remains, with her baby hairs glowing in the bright, soft afternoon light. Freedom, then, doesn't come at the cost of your clothing.[309] Back inside the claustrophobic house, Bridget

---
306 Ibid.
307 Ibid.
308 Ibid.
309 Ibid.

is looking less well than Lizzie. The light of the *Sol Niger* is proving too much for her senses. Naked and shivering before her employer, she holds the ax with none of the confidence with which Lizzie brandished it. Thankfully, Lizzie enters, and like the video game *Mortal Kombat*, finishes him off with a Fatality. She takes the hatchet from Bridget and murders her father, splattering herself (and her beautiful outfit) with his blood; she orgasms again, but the horror is too much for poor Bridget. The pair of murders, nude and then clothed, suggests the era's fashions aren't inherently restrictive, nor are they inherently liberating. Ideologically sewn into the garments that clothe Lizzie are patriarchal ethos, but the garments themselves don't limit her. In the buttoned-up, Batsheva-like costumes that visually define *Lizzie*, ambiguity abounds everywhere.[310]

As *Lizzie*'s Black Sun sinks beneath the horizon, we enter the world of necromancy, astrology, and the occult: *The House with a Clock in Its Walls*.

The Astrological Tropes in the House with a Clock in Its Walls

The House with a Clock in Its Walls is an American dark fantasy-horror comedy directed by Eli Roth, based on the 1973 novel of the same name by John Bellairs (1938-1991). Universal Pictures released the film in the United States on September 21, 2018. It was a box office success, grossing over $131 million worldwide, but receiving lukewarm reviews from critics who praised the cast, but said it did not fully live up to its potential. To this author, this movie has a late 70s-early 80s made-for-television vibe to it, feeling like it should have aired on *CBS Saturday Night Movies* around Halloween like *Dark Night of the Scarecrow*. Like the Harry Potter saga, the movie introduces children to the fascinating world of magic and the occult. Roth's film is a black magic masterpiece featuring the dead's resurrection, a theme referenced frequently throughout it. Though, its hidden gem is the concealment of the zodiac; specifically, the four fixed signs: Taurus, Leo, Scorpio, and Aquarius. It is about an evil wizard who, after making a pact with the demon Azazel in exchange for forbidden knowledge, constructs a clock counting down to the apocalypse. Ergo, the use of these archetypal signs subconsciously evokes the Book of Revelation and the End of Days.

---

310 Ibid.

In 1955, after a car crash kills his parents, ten-year-old Lewis Barnavelt (Owen Vaccaro) moves to live with his Uncle Jonathan (Jack Black) in New Zebedee, Michigan. According to all four Canonical Gospels, Zebedee was the father of James and John, two of the disciples of Jesus, the Sons of Thunder (Mark 3:17), the latter authoring a secret Sethian Gnostic gospel, viz. the *Apocryphon of John*. But this is New Zebedee, with Lewis becoming the neo-savior, thwarting the apocalypse. All he has left of his parents are a Magic 8-Ball they had given him, and a family photograph. Easter egg: Uncle Jonathan writes a letter to his nephew, Lewis, enclosing money and a bus ticket. A magic lamp logo adorns Jonathan Barnavelt's letterhead. Well known to the Rosicrucians, the lamp is a symbol of wisdom and ceremonial magic; burning forever, the learned Jesuit, Athanasius Kircher (1602-1680), deduced these lamps were the Devil's work.

The opening scenes pay homage to *Back to the Future*–also set in 1955– suggesting the two stories run parallel. When Lewis gets off the bus, he and his uncle walk past the Alamo Movie Theater; its marquee advertises *Space Man from Pluto*. The movie alludes to the comic book Sherman Peabody (Jason Marin) shows his father right after Marty McFly (Michael J. Fox) crashes the DeLorean into the family's barn. The comic book is *Tales from Space*, featuring a story, "Space Zombies from Pluto." In 1985, before *Back to the Future*'s release, Sid Sheinberg (1935-2019), the head of Universal Pictures, wanted to re-title the time-traveling film, *Spaceman from Pluto* because the *Tales from Space* comic so impressed him.

Uncle Jonathan and Lewis then stroll past New Zebedee's conspicuous clock tower; in *Back to the Future*, Hill Valley's clock tower is critical to its mythology. The initial *Back to the Future* imagery anticipates the plot, to turn back the hands of time; the evil warlock, Isaac Izard (Kyle MacLachlan), wants to return to a time and place when humankind didn't exist, thereby erasing it. The warlock is likely named after the witch Ann Izzard (1765-1838) of Great Paxton, County of Huntington, England.

Uncle Jonathan takes Lewis to his stately home: a foreboding, archetypal mansion protected annually by lit jack-o'-lanterns and iron horseshoes. These are talismans against evil: on Halloween, carved pumpkins ward off unwelcome ghosts, and iron repels devils; thus, iron gates and fencing enclose cemeteries. The reason behind these customs is jack-o'-lanterns resemble skulls, warding off unwelcome spirits. Iron can be employed

(Left) The Alamo Theater shows *Space Man from Pluto*, an allusion to the *Tales from Space* comic book (right) from *Back to the Future*, featuring the story "Space Zombies from Pluto." "Old Man" Peabody (Will Hare, 1919-1997) glances at it after Marty crashes the DeLorean into his barn.

against demons because men discovered and used meteoric iron long before they found iron ore in the earth. Since it first came from the sky, iron is deemed heavenly, so malevolent wraiths fear it, keeping them in their graves.

Inside the home, clocks are everywhere, recalling *Back to the Future*, and Doc Brown's collection of timekeeping devices. Jonathan keeps them to drown out the pervasive ticking of the unseen timepiece hidden in the walls. Lewis meets Uncle Jonathan's neighbor and best friend, Florence Zimmerman (Cate Blanchett). Although she is affable, beneath her modest façade, she suffers melancholy, negating her magic. She wears the color purple only; even Florence's pet garter snake, William Snakespeare, is purple, having grown enormous because one of her spells backfired. She jokes about Jonathan's freakishly oversized head, anticipating the baby-Jonathan hybrid. Florence was once a powerful white witch; hence, Blanchett's casting evokes her performance as Galadriel from *The Lord of the Rings* movies. After protecting Middle-earth from the evil of Sauron, Blanchett now defends New Zebedee against a black magician and his evil wife. Easter egg: the Italianate Cronin Mansion, in Bellairs' hometown of

The Cronin Mansion in Marshall, Michigan.

Marshall, Michigan, inspired the Uncle Jonathan's fictional mansion. The hamlet served as the basis for New Zebedee, a town featured in his novels.

Lewis checks out his bedroom, decorated with astrological and astronomical symbols: the sun and the moon, the lunar cycle, and the zodiac. To the profane, they merely enliven the room, but to the initiated, they are emblems of Hermeticism and the occult. During the night, Lewis hears a ticking sound in the walls, puzzling him. He wakes, observing Capricorn the Goat; the sign alludes to the Bible's scapegoat rite, becoming a harbinger of the Azazel–more on this shortly.

On his first day at his new school, Lewis befriends Tarby Corrigan (Sunny Suljic), running for class president. Tarby's friendship is self-serving: after he wins the election, he abandons Lewis. In the gymnasium, Lewis is picked last in a game of basketball. The banner hanging in the gym has the school's mascot, Zebus, proudly displayed, and its slogan underneath, NEVER LUUZ. The misspelling of *Lose* to *Luuz* is intentional. *Luuz* is *Luz*, suggesting the luz bone resurrection narrative in Ezekiel (Ch. XXXVII), detailing a vision revealed by God to Ezekiel, conveying to him a dream-like realistic-naturalistic depiction. In it, the Prophet sees himself standing in the valley full of dry human bones. He is commanded to carry a prophecy. Before him, the bones connect into human figures, then they become covered with tendon tissues, flesh, and skin. Then God reveals the bones to the Prophet as the People of Israel in exile, commanding the Prophet to carry another prophecy to revitalize these human figures, resurrect them, and bring them to the Land of Israel. *Luuz* evokes the resurrection of the dead, necromancy, foreshadowing Lewis' acquisition of a Necronomicon-like grimoire, and raising the dark sorcerer, Isaac Izard, from the grave. Easter egg: at school, when it's announced Tarby has been elected president, the principal's voice over the PA system is the director, Eli Roth.

Lewis' deceased mother visits him in his dreams, informing him that Uncle Jonathan is hiding something, then tells him to find a book and a key. She mentions the strange ticking, causing Lewis to wake. He begins exploring the house, stumbling upon his uncle, smashing a wall with an ax. Frightened, Lewis runs away, but before he can leave, several household objects come to life, most notably an easy chair that acts like a dog. His uncle explains the strange goings-on inside the home. In his monastic library, Jonathan states he is a warlock and that Florence is a witch. The home's previous owners were a black magician named Isaac Izard and his equally wicked wife, Selena (Renee Elise Goldsberry); they hid a clock within the house's walls before they died. Jonathan has been trying to find it to discover its purpose. An awestruck Lewis expresses a deep interest in learning sorcery, so Uncle Jonathan reluctantly agrees to teach him. Leather-bound grimoires and occult artifacts fill the library's shelves. Most recognizable is a human skull, crystal ball, and a withered Hand of Glory. The dried appendage, the mummified hand of a criminal, is a macabre device of witchcraft that can open any lock. At one end of the library is a cabinet with a large bolt, and Uncle Jonathan tells Lewis never to open it. Inside is a grimoire designed to raise the dead, an open invitation to demonic gatecrashers.[311] Applying Campbell's monomyth to *House*, we see Uncle Jonathan and Florence fulfilling the roles of Threshold Guardians: characters that protect the unique world and its secrets from the hero and provide necessary tests to prove the hero's commitment and worth. Uncle

---

[311] Owen Davies, *Grimoires: A History of Magic Books* (New York: Oxford University Press, 2010), 23.

Jonathan and Florence safeguard the magical world, allowing Lewis to participate when ready and fully committed.

In the basement, Uncle Jonathan flips through Isaac's old scrapbooks, featuring engravings of the demons Azazel, Furcas (or Forcas), and Buer. Azazel stands alongside a goat, recalling the Capricorn zodiac in Lewis' bedroom. According to the *Book of Enoch* (300-100 BCE), Azazel was a leader of the Fallen or Watcher Angels, a disseminator of forbidden knowledge. Azazel can be seen as an angel of warfare, as he taught humankind about the metals of the earth, further showing them how to fashion weapons and armor. In Leviticus, he only appears in association with the Israelites' scapegoat rite. The sins of the Israelites would be cleansed once a year by transferring their collective guilt to a goat. In this rite, two goats were chosen as sin-offerings, and lots would be cast for them. One lot was for Yahweh and the other lot for Azazel. When the lot for Azazel fell, that goat, from which we derive the term *scapegoat*, was then taken, and the high priest would confess the people's sins over it. With the sins thus transferred, the goat was then driven off into the desert to meet its fate. Although the scapegoat is often recorded as named Azazel, it is more properly the name of the demon believed to reside in the wastes of the deserts. By driving the goat into the desert and associating it with Azazel, the ancient Israelites sacrificed this sin-offering to the demon.[312] His role as a fallen angel partly remains in Christian and Islamic traditions. In Islam, he is often, but not exclusively, associated with the Devil.

Furcas is the 50th demon described in the mid-17th century grimoire, *Ars Goetia*, said to appear in the form of a cruel man with a long beard and hoary head. He rides a pale horse and carries a sharp spear in his hand. He is a Knight of Hell (the only one) commanding 20 Legions. Despite his intimidating appearance, Furcas is primarily a teaching demon, instructing philosophy, rhetoric, astrology, and logic. He also teaches the occult arts of chiromancy (palm reading) and pyromancy (divination by fire).[313] When Izard meets Azazel in the Black Forest, the demon's appearance is modeled on Furcas

Buer is the 10th demon named in *Ars Goetia*; he is a Great President of Hell, having fifty legions of demons under his command. He appears when

---

312 Belanger, *Names of the Damned*, 53.
313 Ibid, 130.

the sun is in Sagittarius only. He teaches natural and moral philosophy, logic, and the virtues of all herbs and plants, and is also capable of healing all infirmities and bestows the best familiars.[314] The scrapbook leaves little doubt that Isaac was in league with dark forces and the clock is sinister. When Florence comes into the basement, she emerges from behind the boiler, pronouncing, "Well, I have scoured the crawl space. I found a dead mouse but no clock." Jonathan then opens the boiler door, frustrated, saying, "We don't know where the clock is," foreshadowing its location.

In the mansion's stately garden, beneath a Harvest Moon, Lewis is initiated into magic. Uninspired, he attempts alchemy by reading a passage from a grimoire, trying to transmute lead into gold, but fails. Present at his initiation is his uncle and Florence. His uncle wears a red fez, the headgear of the Nobles of the Mystic Shrine: a secret society open exclusively to Freemasons. Until 2000, before being eligible for membership in the Shrine, a Mason had to complete either the Scottish Rite (32nd) or York Rite (Knights Templar) systems, but now any Master Mason can join. Masonry is concerned with the same arcane disciplines Dr. Dee, Agrippa, Bruno, and their forebearers were, and far beyond the obscure writings of cloistered hermits, Masonry has formed the backbone of Western civilization over three centuries.[315] Uncle Jonathan's fez, with a crescent moon and sphinx identifies him as a Freemason, initiated into its mysteries. Easter egg: Uncle Jonathan's best jamming hours are at 3:00 am, betokening the Blue Lodge's three degrees.

Florence and Uncle Jonathan tell Lewis his alchemy failed because real magic comes from within. It cannot be imitated like a parlor trick, and that spell books are resources not necessarily to be followed to the letter. Ultimately, each magician's sorcery is unique because it reflects the enchanter's eccentric personality. Before the fountain's armillary sundial, they use magic, transforming the garden into a miniature universe with the signs of Taurus and Leo exalted–more on the zodiac later. Lewis strolls past the moon, taking it in his hand, while Florence admires Saturn, spinning it on the tip of her umbrella; the ringed planet rules her melancholic Hermeticism, stemming from her family's death.

---

314 Ibid, 77.
315 Jason Louv, *John Dee and the Empire of Angels: Enochian Magick, and the Occult Roots of the Modern World* (Rochester, VT: Inner Traditions, 2018), 337.

Florence and Uncle Jonathan continue to teach Lewis sorcery. Tarby comes over and unlocks the forbidden cabinet–its key is hidden in the drawer under the lock–revealing a necromantic grimoire designed to raise the dead. Such a conjuring is particularly dangerous because its grim procedures stir up evil currents or attracts evil forces which may fasten onto the magician. Lewis, frightened, returns the book to the cabinet, leaving Tarby disappointed. When he laments that Tarby does not see him as a friend anymore, his mother returns to his dreams, suggesting he use a spell from a forbidden grimoire to impress his wayward comrade. Easter egg: Uncle Jonathan refers to himself as the *black swan* of the family. Lewis corrects him, saying he meant the black sheep of the family. But then Lewis says he is a *black swan*, insinuating his parents' death was an unanticipated event with far-reaching consequences. The demise of his family led him to Uncle Jonathan and, in doing so, to his occult studies and the practice of sorcery. In this instance, the term *black swan* does not allude to Aronofsky's film. Remember, always pay strict attention to the context in which something is presented.

Meanwhile, Uncle Jonathan searches a room filled with creepy automatons, looking for a clue to the clock's location. He discovers the fireplace conceals the entrance to secret chamber hiding a giant telescope, a diagram of the lunar cycle, and an enormous orrery. It is here Uncle Jonathan finds the clock's blueprints, featuring the omega Ω, which Florence deduces means the end of the world. However, the clock's diagrams are written in a secret code that Florence cannot identify. She does, however, mention her familiarity with Enochian Glyphs and the Alberti Cipher. Easter egg: there are compasses on the blueprints, suggesting the mysteries of Freemasonry; that is, the movement of the moon and planets foretell doomsday–the above and below of Trismegistus. Easter egg: by now, one should have noticed the lunar cycle synchs with the doomsday clock. The clock counts down to the total lunar eclipse when "night's at its blackest" to quote Uncle Jonathan, reinforcing the mythic belief the moon's invisible phase corresponds with death.[316] For this reason, lunar symbolism is pervasive: adding to what I've already indicated, the skeletal key features the moon's cycle, and there is an Eclipse Special advertised on a billboard at the grocery store. When Uncle Jonathan picks Lewis up from school, a radio announcer mentions

---

316 Cirlot, *Dictionary*, 205.

A total lunar eclipse synchronizes with Izard's apocalyptic clock; ergo, the moon permeates *The House with a Clock in Its Walls*. In the hallway, after Tarby wins the election, a poster advertises the *Dark of the Moon* performance (left) by the New Zebedee Players at the elementary school. The advert signifies the lunar eclipse but also alludes to something much dark and sinister. In *The Black Cat*, the Rites of Lucifer are performed in the Dark of the Moon. During the satanic ritual, the Aleister Crowley analog, Hjalmar Poelzig (Boris Karloff), intends to offer a human sacrifice. At one point, Poelzig reads a grimoire discussing the ceremony (right). By recalling the Dark of the Moon, Roth's movie constitutes itself as a reimaging of *The Black Cat*, a study in black magic: Lewis raises the dead, and Izard takes on the attributes of Poelzig, becoming a Crowley-like sorcerer.

the eclipse. Reflecting Izard's astronomical doomsday scenario, the Book of Revelation refers to the woman with the moon beneath her feet (Rev. 12:1), portending the End of Days (*vide supra*).

Enochian is an occult or angelic language recorded in the private journals of astrologer, necromancer, mathematician, and occultist Dr. Dee and his colleague Edward Kelley in late 16th-century England. Kelley was a spirit medium who worked with Dee in his magical investigations. The men claimed the language was revealed to them by angels, and is integral to the practice of Enochian Magic. Enochian's syntax and grammar are highly similar to English. Enochian, as found in their journals, encompasses a limited textual corpus, only some of it with English translations. Several linguists, notably Donald Laycock (1936-1988), have studied Enochian, arguing against any extraordinary features in the lingo. The language is critical within the occult because not only can one use it to communicate with angels, but Enochian (and Enochian Magic) can also be employed to raise the dead and summon and bind demons. More recently, Enochian was used during the magickal workings of both Master Therion and Marvel Whiteside "Jack" Parsons (1914-1952). The term, *Enochian*, comes from Dee's assertion the Biblical Patriarch Enoch had been the last human (before Dee and Kelley) to know the language, based on his travels to Heaven, serving as an intermediary for the Fallen Angels.

The Alberti Cipher, described in his treatise on encipherment, *De Cifris* (1467), is the first polyalphabetic cipher. In its opening pages, Leon Battista Alberti (1401-1472) describes a conversation with papal secretary, Leonardo Dati (1360-1425), about how a recently developed movable-type printing press led to the development of his cipher wheel. His device was made up of two concentric disks, attached by a standard pin, which could rotate one with respect to the other. The larger one is called *Stabilis* (stationary or fixed); the smaller one is called *Mobilis* (movable). The circumference of each disk is divided into 24 equal cells. The outer ring has one uppercase alphabet for plaintext, and the inner ring has a lowercase mixed alphabet for ciphertext. The outer ring also includes the numbers 1 to 4 for the superencipherment of a codebook having 336 phrases with assigned numerical values. In its simplest terms, the Alberti Cipher is a medieval decoder pin. Easter egg: Lewis unlocks the blueprint's weird code with a Captain Midnight decoder pin, a prize from a jar of Ovaltine. The indomitable Captain Midnight, a Flash Gordon or Buck Rogers analog, is Lewis' hero. However, his name, *Midnight*, evokes another apocalyptic device; maintained since 1947 by the members of the Bulletin of the Atomic Scientists, the Doomsday Clock is a symbol for threats to humanity from unchecked scientific and technical advances. The Clock represents the hypothetical global catastrophe as *midnight* and the Bulletin's opinion on how close the world is to an intercontinental cataclysm as a number of minutes to midnight.

Lewis heeds his mother's advice, retrieving the black magic grimoire from its cabinet. Operating under cover of darkness, Tarby and Lewis meet in Oak Ridge Cemetery. Its entrance has an iron arch inscribed, "The trumpet shall sound and the dead shall be raised," signifying Lewis' necromancy and the seven trumpets of Revelation (8-11), the End of Days. Inside the grimoire, there is an illustration of a John Dee-like conjurer standing inside a pentagram and a pentagram/hexagram-like magical sigil. On the opposite page is an ink drawing of a skull-to-face that looks like it was lifted from the *Evil Dead 2*'s (1987) *Necronomicon ex Mortis*, or *Naturom Demonto*, *The Book of the Dead*. Standing before the tomb of Isaac Izard, Lewis performs a blood magic ritual with Tarby serving as a

Nineteenth-century engraving of Dr. John Dee and Edward Kelley performing necromancy. Standing inside a protective magic circle, the two have evoked the dead under the light of a crescent moon. Intaglio from Raphael (Robert Cross Smith, 1795-1832), *The Astrologer of the Nineteenth Century*, 1825. In Chapter VI of *Cinema Symbolism*, I analyzed Dee's involvement in a spy ring to keep Queen Elizabeth I (1533-1603) safe from the Jesuits and Counter-Reformation agents. Indeed, Dr. Dee protected Good Queen Bess' successor, the Protestant monarch James I (1566-1625), as well. There are several accounts of how the Gunpowder Plot of 1605 was discovered, but among the students of the occult science, the belief is that its timely discovery was made by Dee using a magic mirror. Some editions of the Book of Common Prayer, published in the 18th century, have an engraving inserted before the Fifth of November service, depicting a circular mirror on a stand, reflecting the Houses of Parliament by night, and a person carrying a dark lantern. On the left side may be observed two men in the costume of King James' reign, looking into the mirror. At the top, the Eye of Providence throws a ray on the mirror. Toward the bottom are legs and hooves as if evil spirits were making their exit.

witness. This scene evokes the necromancy and Enochian Magic of Dr. Dee and Edward Kelley, communicating with both angels and the dead to learn forbidden wisdom. The black magic is successful, and Isaac rises from the grave. Easter egg: Izard's tomb depicts a sigil with an inverted pentagram and cross, establishing him as a black magician. This sigil also marks the cabinet protecting the necromantic grimoire.

Uncle Jonathan soon realizes Isaac has been resurrected because all the automatons chant, "He's coming home." At Florence's house, she explains to Lewis that the Brothers Grimm fairy tales are histories and that Uncle Jonathan and Isaac were showmen, performing magic to enthusiastic audiences. She tells Lewis she was once a powerful witch, and her magic was the "toast of Paris," having melted Salvador Dali's watch off his wrist, implying her sorcery was the inspiration for *The Persistence of Memory* (1931) oil painting. However, losing her husband and child in a WWII Nazi concentration camp has left her emotionally scarred, breaking her witchcraft. She witnessed the camp's horrors, evidenced by a numeric tattoo on her arm. She also mentions that at some point, Isaac started practicing black magic, straining his friendship with Jonathan.

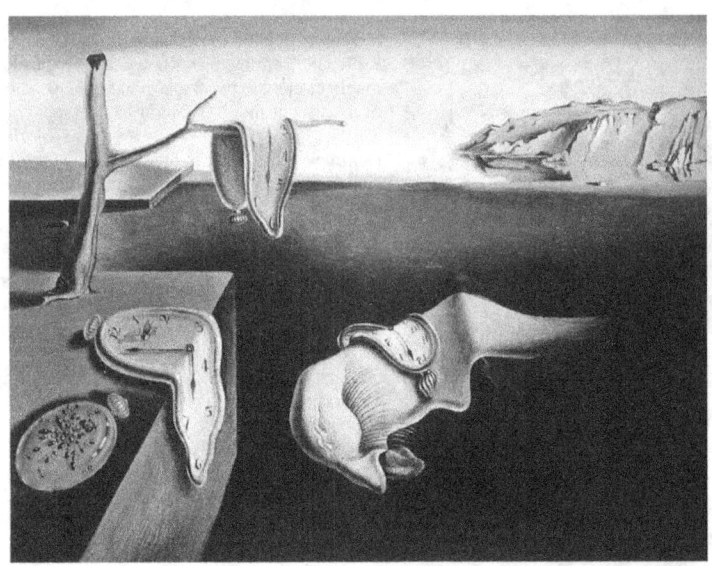

Located in the Museum of Modern Art in New York City, *The Persistence of Memory* is Dali's most recognizable painting. According to *The House with a Clock in Its Walls*, Dali was inspired to paint melting clocks after Florence liquified his watch in Paris.

At school, Tarby bullies Lewis while Florence and Jonathan try to decode the clock's blueprints. However, Lewis solves the cipher using a Captain Midnight decoder pin. Realizing the clock is counting down to the end of the world, and with Isaac on the prowl, they intensify their efforts to find it. With a guilty conscience, a remorseful Lewis admits to his uncle and Florence that it was him who resurrected Isaac, having removed the forbidden grimoire from the cabinet. His uncle berates him, but before any punishment can be doled out, Lewis spots Isaac hiding in the house of a neighbor, Mrs. Hanchett (Colleen Camp). Lewis runs to her aid, bringing her back to the house, but before he can find his uncle, Isaac emerges from the shadows. He reveals Mrs. Hanchett is his wife, Selena, who killed the genuine Mrs. Hanchett, taking her place by transmogrifying into her. She also took the form of Lewis' mother to persuade him to use the necromantic grimoire to summon Isaac. Easter egg: when the books fly about the library, using their covers as wings, they attack Lewis, recalling *Army of Darkness* (1992). Specifically, when Ash (Bruce Campbell) is trying to retrieve the *Necronomicon* from medieval graveyard, the book comes to life and flies around, attacking him. Like *The House with a Clock in Its Walls*, the plots of *Evil Dead* (1981), *Evil Dead 2*, and *Army of Darkness* involve the resurrection of the dead.

Florence, Uncle Jonathan, and Lewis escape from the house, battling past a horde of attacking pumpkins. At Florence's home, Uncle Jonathan forgives Lewis for resurrecting Isaac, encouraging him to formulate a hex of his design. Lewis creates a bizarre spell: praying to his ancestors–his mother and father–he theatrically waves the Magic 8-Ball around, asking for the location of the clock, which the 8-Ball reveals to be under the boiler. The three return to the house, with Florence defeating the pumpkins using her magic wand, which is the handle of her purple umbrella. But the three are captured, and Isaac explains himself. Broken by the horrors of WWII, he stumbled upon the demon Azazel in the Black Forest. Isaac presumably sold his soul in return for the knowledge to build the clock. In the flashback, Azazel gives Isaac a cup with the omega symbol from which he drinks, bestowing the wisdom of how to construct the doomsday device. A key made from human bone activates the clock. Isaac reveals his demonic clock will turn time back so humanity, which he deems unworthy, never existed.

Inspired by Lewis' indomitable spirit, Florence regains her witchcraft and the three escape, but Snakespeare sidelines her; the Izards use magic, transforming Jonathan into a half baby-half adult with an oversized head. Outside in the darkness, the moon turns red, becoming a blood moon, bringing forth Revelation 6:12: "And I beheld when he had opened the sixth seal, and, lo, there was a great earthquake; and the sun became black as sackcloth of hair, and the moon became as blood." Next, the full lunar eclipse begins to take effect as the moon fades to black. Lewis consults the Magic 8-Ball, telling him to "Say goodbye." He realizes he has to let go of the pain of losing his parents to harness his occult power. He breaks the clock by dropping the Magic 8-Ball into its gears. The ball's icosahedron jams the clock; then, using his magic blasts Isaac and Selena with the mystical energy he channels from the clock's mechanisms, erasing them from existence.

Lewis returns to school with more confidence, getting revenge on Tarby and the class bully by magically bouncing a basketball off their heads, then into the hoop. He also befriends a girl named Rosa Rita Pottinger (Vanessa Anne Williams). At the end of the school day, Jonathan and Florence pick up Lewis as the three of them have become a regular family. The film ends on this high note, and the credits roll. Easter egg: The post-credit scenes with the chainsaw-wielding recliner chasing the griffin topiary were inspired by Leatherface's (Gunnar Hansen, 1947-2015) maniacal performance at the end of *The Texas Chain Saw Massacre*.

The zodiac's four fixed signs, Taurus the Bull, Leo the Lion, Aquarius the Water Bearer, and Scorpio the Scorpion pervade *The House with a Clock in Its Wall*, revealing its inner mysteries. Kabbalah calls these four fixed signs *Hayot* or *the Creatures*. They are yoked to the chariot, a mystical kabalistic code for the vehicle (or meditation) used to ascend to communion with the divine. These creatures are a tetramorph, appearing first in Ezekiel's transcendent vision at 1:10, "As for the likeness of their faces, each had the face of a man [Aquarius]; each of the four had the face of a lion [Leo] on the right side, each of the four had the face of an ox [Taurus] on the left side, and each of the four had the face of an eagle [Scorpio]."[317] The stars comprising Aquila the Eagle overlap with those in Scorpio the Scorpion; as such, the two constellations intermingle and are forever linked. Later, Christian mystics associated the four creatures with the Four Evangelists: Mark (Lion/Leo), Matthew (Man/Aquarius), Luke (Ox/Taurus), and John (Eagle/Scorpio), the authors of the Four Canonical Gospels. The fixed signs are critical within astrology and its concomitant mysteries like astrotheology; thus, these portents demand that we, down on earth, regard them as solemn–as above, so below. It is no wonder the accounts ascribed to these Apostles were later compiled into the New Testament to be regarded by close to a billion people as God's Word. The fixed signs stand as the pillars supporting the zodiac, just as the four creatures buttress many of Kabbalah's esoteric mysteries, and the four gospels are Christendom's fountainhead. In mundane astrology, Aquila the Eagle *qua* Scorpio rules the United States' space exploration and its advanced airborne weaponry like nuclear bombs and precision missiles.

The Book of Revelation revives the four fixed signs, and *House* uses them to great effect, evoking the End of Days, epitomized by Izard's dire timekeeping apparatus. Revelation 4:6-8: "And before the throne there was a sea of glass like unto crystal: and in the midst of the throne, and round about the throne, were four beasts full of eyes before and behind. And the first beast was like a lion [Leo] and the second beast like a calf

---

317 A tetramorph is a symbolic arrangement of four different elements or the combination of four disparate elements in one unit.

Taurus' astrological symbol (left) sculpted on the garden fountain's rim (right). In this scene, Lewis is about to place his finger in the water where the giant red star Aldebaran, the brightest star in Taurus, is located.

[Taurus] and the third beast had a face as a man [Aquarius] and the fourth beast was like a flying eagle [Scorpio]." Then, the Lamb (Aries) unfurls God's scroll and opens its seals (Rev. 5:6-9), announcing the Four Horsemen (Rev. 6), beginning Armageddon, or the end of an age and the start of a new one.

Taurus surfaces when Lewis, during his magical initiation, places his finger in the portion of the fountain given to Taurus, identified by its astrological symbol on the fountain's rim. He touches the Eye of the Bull, the nickname for the red giant star Aldebaran, the brightest star in Taurus, creating a miniature universe in the garden, becoming a rendition of the stars in the waters of the firmament. Taurus also hides in the high school's mascot, Zebus, a cow. A zebu, sometimes known as indicine cattle or humped cattle, is a species or subspecies of domestic cattle originating in South Asia. Its characteristics are a fatty hump on their shoulders, a large dewlap, and sometimes drooping ears. Leo the Lion can be seen in the garden-initiation scene. It is the zodiac that comes alive and frolics with the griffin topiary. Aquarius the Water Bearer flirts with Tarby and the water fountain. He *bears water* by using the water fountain as a campaign issue to get elected class president. By seeking elected office, Tarby flirts with Aquarius' traits: persistent with a desire to help others, coupled with sociability. Scorpio, the sign of Judas Iscariot, Set, the serpent in Eden, the Goat of Mendes, embodies the black magician, Isaac Izard; he is nocturnal, cold, phlegmatic, and self-centered–the characteristics of Scorpio.[318]

Are there other astrological secrets (or archetypes) hidden in *The House with a Clock in Its Walls*, waiting to be revealed? The answer to this question is *yes*. When Uncle Jonathan comes into the house, he flips his hat onto a ram head mount taxidermy, symbolizing Aries the Ram, the opener of Revelation's Seals. Selena is the trickster, linking her to the house of Libra, the Old Testament's Delilah. Florence loves the color purple, wearing nothing but purple clothing, decorating her home in purple, identifying her with Sagittarius. Purple is the Archer's color, while those born under this sign possess a cosmic consciousness, illuminating those around them, just as Florence guides Lewis, mentoring him in magic. Like an archetypal fire sign, Florence is changeable, forsaking her witchcraft, but then becoming stalwart in the face of danger, regaining her mystical abilities. Theoretically, the centaur, with its bow and arrow–the symbol for enthusiasm and effort–aims at the stars mirroring Florence, who joins Jonathan eagerly in his battle against evil, rewarding him with gold stars.[319] Practically, she uses her umbrella-as-a-bow to fire arrow-like purple bolts, destroying the attacking pumpkins. Her pet snake, Snakespeare, represents Ophiuchus, the serpent-bearer, the secret 13th sign between Scorpio and Sagittarius.

I suspect there were more astrological motifs in Bellairs' novel that did not translate to the big screen, but I have not read the book, so I cannot say for sure if this is the case.

Bubba Didn't Do It: Shining Light on the Archetypes of Dark Night of the Scarecrow

And speaking of *Dark Night of the Scarecrow*, it's time to analyze the made-for-television classic. Lauded as one of the best TV films ever produced, it feels more like a morbid afterschool special than a horror movie.

---

318 Nicholas Devore, *Encyclopedia of Astrology* (New York: Philosophical Library, 1947), 369; Hall, *Secret Teachings*, 277.
319 Devore, ibid, 370-371; Derek and Julia Parker, *The Complete Astrologer* (New York: McGraw-Hill Book Company, 1971), 105.

Nevertheless, when it comes to televised terror, *Scarecrow* ranks right up there with *The Night Stalker* (1972), *The Night Strangler* (1973), *Trilogy of Terror* (1975), *The Dark Secret of Harvest Home* (1978), and *Salem's Lot* (1979); it is authentic and frightening. Murder, revenge, injustice, arson, alcoholism, supernatural forces, grave desecration, and pedophilia pervade *Scarecrow*, a rarity for 1981 sensibilities, especially on network TV. The film was directed by veteran novelist Frank De Felitta (1921-2016), the author of *Audrey Rose* (1975), from a script by J.D. Feigelson. The writer had intended to make an independent feature, but CBS bought his script for television; despite this, only minor changes were made to the screenplay. *Dark Night of the Scarecrow* first aired on Saturday evening, October 24, 1981, six days before my tenth birthday, as a companion to Halloween celebrated seven days later. Today, it is remembered as a spooky masterpiece with archetypal characters, haunting music, and an unforgettable ghostly ambiance.

In Bogan County, a small farming town in rural America, Charles Eliot "Bubba" Ritter (Larry Drake, 1950-2016), a gentle but mentally challenged man, befriends young Marylee Williams (Tonya Crowe). Some of the townspeople are upset and suspicious by Marylee and Bubba's closeness; the brooding, mean-spirited postman Otis Hazelrigg (Charles Durning, 1923-2012) watches Marylee like a hawk, wary of Bubba. Otis has an unnatural, intense interest in the child, but it goes unnoticed. One recalls G.K. Chesterton's (1874-1936) detective story "The Invisible Man" (1911), a Father Brown mystery. The short story is about the crimes committed by James Welkin; he stalks his love interest, Laura Hope, and menaces his rival, Isidore Smythe, who he eventually murders. Since Welkin is a postman, he accomplishes this without being observed because no one pays attention to letter carriers. Likewise, Otis' motives and measures are not questioned, placing him above suspicion.[320]

When Marylee trespasses into a gnome garden, she is mauled by a vicious dog and taken to the hospital. Otis immediately assumes Bubba murdered her even though it was he who saved her life. Otis and three friends: gas station attendant Skeeter Norris (Robert F. Lyons), and farmers

---

[320] In the Sherlock Holmes mystery *The Scarlet Claw*, the murderer, Alistair Ramson, disguises himself as a mailman, Mr. Potts. Holmes (Rathbone) remarks, "May I say monsieur Ramson that your disguise as a postman was a masterpiece of ingenuity. Your very choice of the role put you above suspicion." In *The Spider Woman* (1943), Holmes, disguised as a mailman, informs Watson: "No one ever looks twice at a postman, you know."

Philby (Claude Earl Jones), and Harliss Hocker (Lane Smith, 1936-2005) form an armed lynch mob. Bubba's mother, Mrs. Ritter (Jocelyn Brando, 1919-2005), disguises him as a scarecrow, posting him in a nearby field to wait for the drama to die down; this worked the last time the four men terrorized Bubba, so mother and son try it again. When the bloodhounds sniff out Bubba, the four vigilantes stand before the scarecrow like a firing squad, shooting multiple rounds, killing him. Soon afterward, via Harliss' CB radio, they discover Marylee is alive, thanks to Bubba's heroics, having just murdered him in cold blood.

Acting fast, Otis places a pitchfork in Bubba's lifeless arm to make it appear like he was attacking them with a weapon. Then, a sweeping, unearthly wind blows through as the four killers stand silently before the dead man crucified in scarecrow garb; these few seconds of eeriness establish that something wicked their way comes. The vigilantes are subsequently released because of the lack of evidence against them, and blatant perjury by Otis during a pretrial hearing. Harliss, Philby, and Skeeter celebrate by getting drunk at a hole in the wall called Bogan Cafe; it is obvious the four murderous yokels are white trash.[321] Indeed, everyone in the county seems to be a lowlife. Like the inanimate garden gnomes, the inhabitants of Bogan are unmoved, unsympathetic, and unaffected when an injustice is committed before their very eyes.

Having recovered from the dog attack, Marylee sneaks out of her bedroom and goes over to the Ritter house looking for Bubba. Mrs. Ritter cannot bring herself to tell Marylee the truth, instead saying Bubba has gone away where no one can harm him. Marylee runs out of the house to look for Bubba, with Mrs. Ritter pursuing the girl. She finds Marylee sitting in the field where Bubba had been killed, singing a favorite song of theirs, calmly telling Mrs. Ritter that Bubba is not gone, only hiding.

A day later, Harliss sees in his field a mysterious scarecrow filled with straw and dressed like Bubba; there is no indication of who put it there. A scarecrow is a symbol of death because they carry the fearful reminder of starvation if the crows eat the harvest, presaging calamity for Bubba's murderers. Otis suspects the district attorney Sam Willock (Tom Taylor)

---

[321] *Bogan* is Australian slang for an uncouth lowlife. The term was probably unknown to the filmmakers, and would not have been recognized by American TV audiences. Regardless, the word describes the vigilantes perfectly.

of placing it there to rattle the four of them, telling the others to keep calm and do nothing. In the evening, the scarecrow disappears, with Harliss observing activity in his barn. As he investigates its loft, the wood chipper below turns on, which he had just switched off moments earlier. Startled, he topples over into the machine, killing him horrifically. Since the wood chipper still had gasoline in its tank after Harliss had fallen in, but had been switched off, Otis, Philby, and Skeeter suspect their comrade's death was not accidental.

Otis visits Mrs. Ritter, obliquely accusing her of having engineered the supposed accident; she denies involvement, saying other agencies–supernatural forces–will punish her son's murderers. She also implies Otis is a pedophile because of his intense interest in Marylee, causing him to run off. This vile deviancy explains why Otis wanted Bubba out of the way. With Bubba alive, Marylee was safe in the presence of the gentle giant. But Bubba's murder opens the door to Otis, allowing him to stalk his prey without fear of reprisal, assaulting the child sexually when the opportunity presents itself.

At the church Halloween party, from behind a skull window decoration, Otis' faces peers in; he is death personified, Bubba's executioner. While playing hide-and-seek with the other children, Otis confronts Marylee in the hallway. He tries to coax her into telling him Mrs. Ritter is behind the recent events. Instead, she tells him she knows what he and his friends did to Bubba, suggesting Bubba himself told her. When Otis becomes hostile, she runs away from the predator. He chases after her but is stopped by a security guard, telling him to go back to the party. Otis does so, requesting a drink, but the hostess–dressed as the Wicked Witch of the West–remembers Otis doesn't drink alcohol, pouring him a glass of punch from the teetotaler bowl. Otis glances around and, seeing no one paying attention, helps himself to the spiked punch. It is evident Otis is a closet alcoholic; by drinking booze, much like Jack Torrance, Otis opens himself to demons, giving him the confidence to act on his pedophilic desires. His alcoholism is hinted at earlier when Harliss, Philby, and Skeeter visit him at Mrs. Bunch's (Alice Nunn, 1927-1988) boarding house. Otis is in his room drinking liquor; learning his friends are here to see him, he hides the bottle, spraying his mouth with mouthwash to remove the smell.

The scarecrow soon reappears, only this time in Philby's field; that same night, Otis breaks into Mrs. Ritter's house. Trying to stop what he sees as the next stage of her plot, his sudden appearance shocks her so severely she suffers a fatal heart attack. To cover his tracks, Otis starts a gas leak causing an explosion, destroying the house. While everyone else believes the blast was an accident, the district attorney is suspicious.

The next night, a commotion in his hog pen disturbs Philby; while investigating, mysterious occurrences make him panic, so he tries to flee in his car, but the vehicle won't start. He is pursued across his property, taking refuge in a grain silo, shutting the door behind him. A conveyor belt feeding the silo is switched on. Unable to open the locked door, the resulting avalanche of grain buries Philby alive.

The following day, upon learning from Otis of Philby's death, Skeeter is ready to turn himself over to the authorities rather than face any portended wrath. Otis remains convinced the recent occurrences are a hoax arranged to avenge Bubba's murder, and Bubba himself is still alive. That night, Otis and Skeeter dig up Bubba's grave, ostensibly to prove the corpse is not there. Skeeter opens the coffin revealing the corpse and, in panic, tries to flee. Otis chases after and stops him, promising to go along with whatever Skeeter decides to do. They return to the grave to refill it. While Skeeter is down in the grave closing the coffin lid, Otis decides then to protect himself, killing Skeeter by smashing his skull with a shovel, filling in the grave, burying Skeeter along with Bubba's corpse.

Driving home intoxicated, Otis sees Marylee alone in the middle of the road. He crashes his mail truck, exits, chasing her on foot into a pumpkin patch. Catching up with her, he accuses her of masterminding the scarecrow murders when a plowing machine nearby starts up of its own accord. Terrified, Otis flees as the machine pursues him. Running through the field, Otis runs into the scarecrow holding the pitchfork that he planted on Bubba's corpse, impaling him on the tines. Mortally wounded, Otis collapses and dies. Marylee, hiding in the pumpkin patch, hears footsteps approaching; she looks up to see the scarecrow looking down at her. Marylee smiles; the scarecrow bends down, presenting her with a flower. "Thank you, Bubba," she says graciously. Marylee then innocently tells him that she has a new game to teach him called "the chasing game." Otis' death is haunting, evoking the human sacrifices linked to Samhain,

CINEMA SYMBOLISM 3

Original *TV Guide* ad for *Dark Night of the Scarecrow*, 1981.

the celebration of the autumn harvest, and the coming seasonal darkness. The film is not a cliffhanger, nor is it ambiguous; we know Bubba's ghost has returned as a spectral punisher, taking possession of the scarecrow, killing his murderers.

Born in October 1971, I attended many Halloween parties in the late '70s and early '80s as a boy. *Scarecrow*'s Halloween party is authentic, with its plastic pumpkins, skeleton decorations, tissue ghosts, orange and black bunting, hide-and-seek, and bobbing for apples. The only difference: the music, the "Monster Mash" (1962), was still the graveyard smash, while Bogan County's inhabitants like nothing but country and western, caring little for Bobby "Boris" Pickett (1938-2007) and the Crypt-Kicker Five. The Samhain church party resurrects memories from days long ago, recalling Halloween pasts that Generation X will appreciate.

The movie resonates with archetypes, making it popular, memorable, and scary. Bubba is the childlike Fool, the zero card of the Major Arcana, echoing its attributes. Simple, yet connected to the divine, his spirit can materialize in reality, avenging those who killed him.[322] He returns as a scarecrow: an icon representing monstrous emotions and thoughts, provoking fear and dread. He appears cruciform on two wooden posts, imitating Christ's crucifixion, indicating his ethereal presence. He is a supernatural lawgiver, an avenging holy spirit, seeking revenge at Halloween when ghosts are given license to haunt the living.

Bubba's mother, Mrs. Ritter, is the overbearing matriarch, an elderly waning moon in touch with the supernatural realm, understanding its karmic essence. She reflects the goddess Nemesis, a punishing force doling out retribution, knowing paranormal powers will avenge her son's murder. Otis is the Devil, the personification of irresistible impulses and malice. His pedophilic desire motivates him to kill Bubba so he can have Marylee all to himself. His consumption of alcohol unleashes his unnatural cravings, stimulating his lust for the girl. Marylee is the Page of Cups, a pretty little girl; she is insightful, gentle, reflecting on her friendship with Bubba. Until the finale, we never know if she sees his ghost, or if her visions are a product of her youthful, romantic imagination.[323] The district attorney embodies Justice, the eleventh card of the Major Arcana. Willock is an early tormentor of the four vigilantes, personifying the proverb, "as a man sows, so shall he reap," spoken by Mrs. Ritter. It is ebb and flow, cause and effect, good and evil, indicating the men will be punished for murdering Bubba, only their adjudicator is a ghost: the scarecrow is a harbinger of their gruesome deaths.

If you've never seen this made-for-television horror classic, by all means, give it a view because this film holds up extremely well for being 40 years old. *Dark Night of the Scarecrow* is highly entertaining; it is the perfect meeting of two worlds: the slasher movie and the ghost story, designed to unnerve rather than to jolt. I recommend purchasing the Blu-ray because not only is the picture and sound quality superb, the extras are well worth it. Included is a documentary, a Q&A with some of the cast from a horror convention, and the original *CBS Saturday Night Movies* introduction. The intro will bring back memories, reminding us what television was like pre-cable and pre-internet. It did for me, and seeing

---

322 Cavendish, *The Tarot*, 59-64.
323 Ibid, 163.

that old intro again was nostalgic, recalling my childhood, remembering a time long since passed.

Black Phillip Saith I Can Do What I Like: The Triumph of Evil over Good in The Witch

Witches were the Devil's followers, writing their names in his book, carried away by him for nocturnal revels. At the witches' sabbath, the Devil sometimes appeared as a goat, and the witches were attended by cats, owls, bats, and cuckoos because these creatures had once been sacred to Freya.[324]

The VVitch: A New England Folktale (known as *The Witch*) is a 2015 American-Canadian period supernatural horror film written and directed by Robert Eggers. An international coproduction of the United States and Canada, the film premiered at the 2015 Sundance Film Festival on January 27, 2015, going into general release by A24 on February 19, 2016. It received positive reviews becoming a box office success, grossing $40 million against a budget of $4 million. This author watched two trailers for Eggers' next movie, *The Lighthouse* (2019), which looks fantastic. Shot in black and white and starring Willem Dafoe as Thomas Wake and Robert Pattinson as Ephraim Winslow, this late 19th-century period piece is replete with madness, mysticism, a mermaid, a giant octopus, and a pesky seagull. I look very much forward to analyzing it in *Cinema Symbolism 4*, but now it's time to take on *The Witch*.

In 1630s New England, English settler William (Ralph Ineson) and his family: wife Katherine (Kate Dickie), eldest daughter Thomasin (Anya Taylor-Joy), son Caleb (Harvey Scrimshaw), and fraternal twins Mercy (Ellie Grainger) and Jonas (Lucas Dawson) are banished from a puritan colony over a religious dispute. The family builds a farm near a vast, secluded forest while Katherine gives birth to Samuel (Axtun Henry Dube and Athan Conrad Dube). One day, Thomasin is playing peekaboo with Samuel when the baby abruptly disappears into thin air. A witch has stolen the unbaptized Samuel; she is invisible and moves like lightning; as she flees with the babe, she brushes past a dead plant. It sways back and forth, signaling her ungodly presence. The witch slaughters him to use his fat to make flying ointment. The hag then smears the lotion on her naked body

---

324 Kelley, *Hallowe'en*, 133-134.

and broomstick, levitating before a full moon, identifying her as Hecate's disciple. Easter egg: the parishioners occupying church-meeting hall are divided by the sexes, as it would have been in a Calvinist community in the 1630s.

Katherine, devastated by Samuel's disappearance and presumed death, spends her days crying and praying, believing her unbaptized child is in Hell. The family thinks a wolf killed the baby, although this is speculation. With their crops failing–perhaps hexed by the witch in the woods–William and Caleb try to trap wild animals.[325] While hunting with William, Caleb asks if Samuel's unbaptized soul will reach Heaven. William admonishes Caleb for raising the question, revealing to his son that he traded Katherine's silver cup for hunting supplies. That night, Katherine questions Thomasin about the disappearance of her cup, suspecting her to be responsible for Samuel's abduction. After the children retire to bed, they overhear their parents discuss sending Thomasin away to serve another family. Easter egg: the family's corn is "trash" to quote Katherine; observe, because the corn rots with ergot: a hallucinogenic fungus attributing to real-life stories of possession and witchcraft.

Early the next morn, Thomasin finds Caleb preparing to check a trap in the forest, forcing him to take her with him by threatening to wake their parents. In the woods, the two spot a hare, which sends their horse into a panic with their dog, Fowler, giving chase to the rabbit. Caleb pursues after the dog and hare while Thomasin is thrown from the horse, knocking her unconscious. Caleb becomes lost, stumbling upon Fowler's disemboweled body. Deep in the woods, he comes across a hovel from which a beautiful young woman emerges, seducing him; the witch knows lust is Caleb's weakness. The witch wears a red cloak; in European folklore, witches were believed to don red before flying through the air to sabbaths.[326] However, as they are about to embrace, the woman's arm becomes old and decrepit, grabbing Caleb violently. William finds Thomasin, taking her home where Katherine angrily chastises her for taking Caleb into the

---

[325] W.H. Davenport Adams, *Witch, Warlock, and Magician* (London: Chatto & Windus, 1889), 349. Witches often attacked their enemies by destroying the harvest, causing starvation; Adams writes: "That when they wished to destroy an enemy's crops, they yoked toads to his plough; and on the following night the Devil, with this strange team, drove furrows into the land, and blasted it effectually."

[326] Guiley, *Encyclopedia of Witches*, 279.

woods before William reluctantly admits he sold the silver cup. Easter egg: A hare frequently appears in *The Witch*. In colonial New England, hares were considered magical creatures in their own right. They were often associated with witches, either as a milk-hare, which stole or spoiled milk from the farm animals, or the witch herself, blessed by the Devil with the ability to transmogrify to spy on people, hexing them. In England, so strong was this belief that, to this day, it is considered bad luck for one's path to be crossed by a hare.[327]

Later that night, Caleb is found outdoors in the rain, naked and delirious from an unknown illness. When he awakens the next day, Caleb expels a bloody apple from his mouth; Katherine believes it to be witchcraft. The diseased apple is a token of Caleb's earlier lie when he told his mother that he and his father were looking for apple trees in the valley, rather than telling her the truth: William sold her silver cup to buy animal traps. The apple alludes to Eden and Adam and Eve's banishment, signifying the family's fall from grace. The witch has turned Caleb's sin against him; however, he passionately proclaims his love for Christ before he dies, though Katherine believes Caleb to have been under an evil spell. The twins then accuse Thomasin of witchcraft, stating she made a pact with the Prince of Darkness. In retaliation, Thomasin reveals to her father that the twins are in cahoots with Black Phillip, the Devil in disguise, the family's rambunctious billy goat. Black Phillip epitomizes the Goat of Mendes, Baphomet, the idol allegedly worshipped by the Knights Templar, depicted as the Tarot's Devil card.[328] Enraged, William boards up Thomasin and the twins in the goat house. That night, William breaks down, confessing to God that the sin of pride infects him, driving his family to leave the plantation out of stubbornness rather than sincere religious devotion. Katherine awakens to her silver chalice sitting on a shelf, then encounters Caleb cradling Samuel, whom she takes and begins breastfeeding, although it is a raven–a bird of ill omen–pecking at her teat. Next, the twins awake to find a crone drinking milk from a goat, cackling at them. The family has fallen victim to witchcraft.

---

327 Ibid, 151.
328 Ibid, 21-22. See also Tracy Twyman and Alexander Rivera, *Baphomet: The Temple Mystery Unveiled*, Chapter 1, "Pacts with the Devil," *passim*.

Witches' Sabbath (1798) oil painting by Francisco Goya (1746-1828) features the adoration of Baphomet, the Goat of Mendes, inspiring Black Phillip, the demonic billy goat in *The Witch*.

The following morning, William wakes to find the goat house nearly destroyed, the goats eviscerated, the twins missing, and an unconscious Thomasin lying nearby with blood-stained hands. As Thomasin awakens, Black Phillip gores William before her eyes. Katherine, unhinged, blames Thomasin for the tragedies that have beset the family, accusing her of being a whore in league with the Devil, attacking her. Thomasin stabs her mother to death in self-defense.

Alone, Thomasin wakes at night, entering the goat house, urging Black Phillip to speak to her. The goat responds by asking if she wants to *live deliciously*, tempting her with butter and a pretty dress. The goat then changes into a tall, thin man with a dark complexion. Black Phillip *qua* Satan orders Thomasin to remove her shift, and sign her name in the Black Book, forging a Faustian pact. Like I mentioned earlier, keep an eye out for Black Phillip's cloven hoof, visible briefly when the Devil's Black Book appears before Thomasin. The young woman, now in league with Satan, follows the goat into the forest, joining a coven of witches holding a sabbath around a bonfire. *Aquerra Goity, Aquerra Beyty, Aquerra Goity, Aquerra Beyty* they would shout at the Devil's gathering. However, these witches are chanting in Enochian, using the Eleventh Enochian Key, heralding the coming of the dead to establish sustenance beyond the grave. To bind to the earth, a funerary call.[329] The Eleventh Enochian Key, ascribed to Dr. Dee and (and tweaked by Anton Szandor LaVey, 1930-1997), is:

English:

The mighty throne growled and there were five thunders that flew into the East. And the eagle spake and cried aloud: Come away from the house of death! And they gathered themselves together and became those of whom it measured, and they are the deathless ones who ride the whirlwinds. Come away! For I have prepared a place for you. Move therefore, and show yourselves! Unveil the mysteries of your creation. Be friendly unto me for I am your God, the true worshipper of the flesh that liveth forever!

Enochian, as heard in *The Witch*:

Oxiayala holado, od zodirome O coraxo das zodiladare raasyo. Od vabezodire cameliaxa od bahala: NIISO! salamanu telocahe! Casaremanu hoel-qo, od ti ta zod cahisa soba coremefa i ga. NIISA! bagile aberameji nonuзape. Zodacare eca od Zodameranu! odo cicale Qaa! Zodoreje, lape zodiredo Noco Mada, hoathahe Saitan!

The coven begins to levitate with a euphoric Thomasin floating with them, ascending above the trees. The pious puritans have been utterly annihilated; evil has triumphed over good, Satanism over Christianity. Easter egg: the Devil's costume is an elaborate, custom-made creation featuring gold, jewels, spurs, cockerel feathers, a beaver hat, earrings, but the audience can see none of this because it is too dark.

---

329 LaVey, *The Satanic Bible*, 219. *The Witch* uses LaVey's translation of the Eleventh Key. cf. Van Luijk, *Children of Lucifer*, 337, who notes the Black Pope's alterations: "The most blatant example is the 'translation' of John Dee's Enochian Keys at the end of *The Satanic Bible*, wherein the many pious references to the Christian deity by the Elizabethan magus were simply swapped with 'Satan' by LaVey, to the great horror of some occult connoisseurs."

Although she confesses to the sin of sloth, Thomasin–note that her name has the syllable *sin* in it–is the only family member without sin, at least until the end. But it's easy to see why blame falls upon her: she is, after all, present when calamity befalls each family member. She was watching Samuel when he went missing, as she was when the twins vanished. She was present when Caleb and William died, having found the former naked and bewitched. Ergo, Katherine regards her as wickedness personified, the root cause of the family's undoing.

As Christians, they are all hypocrites, and their offensives are not peccadillos. William believes himself to be humble but is prideful. Caleb's lust poisons him like the apple choking him, making him incestuous, desirous of his sister's flesh. He lies to his mother covering for his duplicitous father, having pilfered her silver cup to purchase hunting supplies. By allowing his son to be deceptive and by going along with it, William bears false witness. Greed and envy plague Katherine over her silver cup; later, she becomes wrath when she tries to murder Thomasin. The twins are lazy, doing nothing except singing Black Phillip songs, communicating with Satan in the guise of the mischievous goat. In league with the Dark Angel, Jonas and Mercy cannot offer Christian prayer, a common symptom of those who submit to demonic forces. This duplicity undoes the family, exposing them as apostates, not true Christians.

But because Thomasin is pure, true to herself, the witch does not attack her, but turns the sins of the others against them, making them believe Thomasin is a witch when she is innocent. Her downfall is she teases Mercy that she's a witch, which her little sister takes seriously. But she was merely reacting to Mercy, the obnoxious child jesting that she is the "witch of the wood." Ultimately, after she kills her mother in self-defense, Thomasin enters into a pact with the Devil. The theocratic patriarchy destroyed, she is liberated; one could argue the film is a feminist fairy tale, the sabbath's bonfire emitting the light of the *Sol Niger*. Thomasin has freed herself from the bonds of this world, damming her soul in the next.

Eggers has indicated *The Witch* is archetypal, and he is correct. The missing silver goblet brings forth the Ace of Cups from the Tarot; its negative attributes are unexpected and unwelcome change. Katherine's lost cup signals the tragedy about to beset the family, thus. Venturing into the dark woods, Caleb and Thomasin conjure the fairy tale of *Hansel*

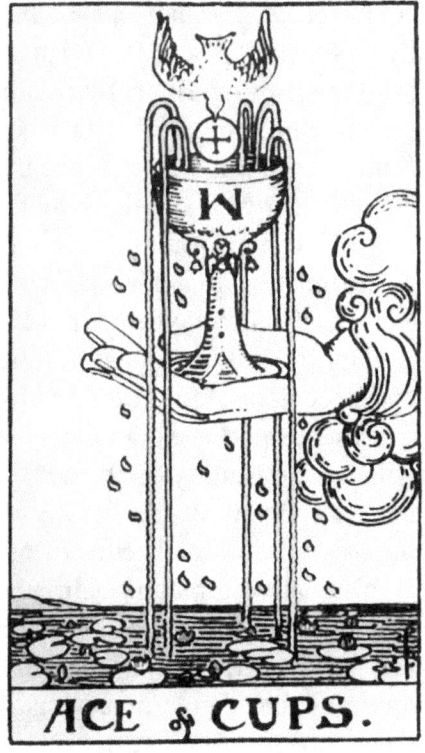

The Ace of Cups from the Rider-Waite Tarot Deck. The card associates with fruitfulness, motherhood, and the alchemical feminine identifying with Katherine because she has five children, but reversing the cup (in the movie it is absent) is a harbinger of negative change, portending the dark days ahead.

and Gretel (1812), with Caleb falling victim to witchcraft, and Thomasin accused of hexing him. The witch, appearing as both a beautiful young woman (Sarah Stephens) and an ugly hag (Bathsheba Garnett), evokes the evil Queen in *Snow White* (1812, film: 1937); she is the fairest of them all, but later becomes a hideous crone.[330] William is the ogre father, Katherine, the suffocating mother, and Thomason is the waxing moon turning from light to darkness. The twins are fools, following Black Phillip, Satan, and the Magician simultaneously: he is the devilish trickster, Mercurius, the serpent and catalyst, destroying the family, obliterating their suffocating Christianity while unchaining Thomasin.

The Church of Satan (est. 1966) endorsed *The Witch*, and it's easy to understand why. The idea of Satan/Lucifer epitomizing a liberating, rebellious force, combatting both dogmatic Christianity and the society's

---

[330] In a compelling case of Jungian synchronicity, the actress who plays the oldest and most powerful witch is, in reality, named Bathsheba Garnett. A year and a half before *The Witch* hit theaters, *The Conjuring* (2013) premiered, featuring the ghost of an evil witch named Bathsheba.

conformities, is a chief tenet of the Church; it is the underlying philosophy of Eggers' film. It is scary for what it doesn't show; its supernatural pessimism is overwhelming. But perhaps most damning of all is the absence of God's presence in Thomasin's life. She prayed for his mercy and grace, but the Demiurge doesn't give a shit; instead, her family and God betrayed her. Her younger twin siblings bore false witness against her, William revealed himself to be a prideful hypocrite, poisoning mother against daughter by insinuating that Thomasin stole her silver cup, opening the door to Katherine believing that her eldest daughter is evil.

But by making a pact with the Devil, Thomasin is granted freedom and acceptance, finding kinship with the other witches in the forest's darkest bowels. The diabolical magic levitating her–causing euphoria and wild sexual ecstasy–is the acceptance she did not have with her family, nor ever experienced. She became a witch because her beliefs were so intense that in the absence of one religious covenant, Thomasin sought an alternative replacing Christianity with its polar opposite: unbridled Satanism. And the oppressive culture that bred her to be meek, subservient, and imminently guilty pushed her to be what they feared the most: feminine and dangerous. Thus, our modern understanding of medieval witchcraft and its practitioners–independent and strong women–fuels this nightmare taken from the bleakest puritanical superstitions, making *The Witch* an instant classic. Already, we see its cinematic influence, taking shape in *Gretel & Hansel: A Grim Fairy Tale* (2020). When Holda (Alice Krige) comments to Gretel (Sophia Lillis) concerning Hansel (Samuel J. Leakey), "That little boy is your poison. All that is left is to make him *delicious*," one recalls Black Phillip immediately, and the goat's tenet to *live deliciously*.

Hymn to Pan's Labyrinth

There is no opacity when it comes to Pan: one immediately thinks of the archetypal pagan god of the woods, panpipes, and Frater Perdurabo's lurid poem to the seducer of nymphs. Even the boyish Peter Pan dons green, indicating a woodland presence. However, the film's director, Guillermo del Toro, has stated in interviews the faun in *Pan's Labyrinth* is not Pan,

"The thought in your head is, 'Go look in the shed.' You'll find saws to be sharpened for the bones of the dead." – Holda, *Gretel & Hansel: A Grim Fairy Tale* (2020). A movie in accord with the fairy tale Rule of Three, paying homage to other witchy tales, including *Häxan*, *The Wizard of Oz*, *The Blair Witch Project* (1999), *The Witch*, and *Suspiria* '77. *Gretel & Hansel* documents the Aquarian Age fascination with the occult and witchcraft, manifesting in the collective unconscious. (Left) Holda's (Jessica De Gouw) staff, leaning against the wall behind her, is modeled after the Mysterious or Fulminating Wand, depicted in *The Red Dragon* (1521, right): a grimoire designed to conjure the demon Lucifuge Rofocale. The filmmakers drew from the world of black magic to craft this dark, archetypal fantasy.

but a composite of magical figures from mythology.³³¹ The director did not want Pan, a horny god of seduction, to hang around with an innocent, little girl. Del Toro considers the story to be a parable influenced by fairy tales; regardless, it has occult undertones evoking Crowley, witchcraft, *Alice in Wonderland*, Freemasonry, and the Illuminati. Del Toro employs a tub and bathroom foreshadowing the bathrooms and tubs of *Crimson Peak* and *The Shape of Water*, an intimate device borrowed from Kubrick. Allerdale Hall's green bathroom is a direct allusion to *The Shining*; Elisa's bathroom and its tub are a temple of pleasure: a watery sanctuary of masturbation and amphibious sexual intercourse. *Pan's Labyrinth* showcases red and green, indicating the director's fascination with these two hues, taking center stage in *Crimson Peak* and *The Shape of Water*.

The story takes place in Spain during the summer of '44, five years after the Spanish Civil War, during the early Francoist period. The narrative

---

331 Ian Spelling, "Guillermo del Toro and Ivana Baquero escape from a civil war into the fairytale land of *Pan's Labyrinth*," *Science Fiction Weekly*, December 25, 2006, https://web.archive.org/web/20080609075453/http://www.scifi.com/sfw/interviews/sfw14471.html (accessed October 10, 2019).

intertwines reality with a mythical world predicated on an overgrown, abandoned garden-labyrinth and the relationship between a mysterious unnamed faun (Doug Jones) and the protagonist: a little girl named Ofelia (Ivana Baquero). Resembling Pan, a faun was a traditional Roman deity of the husbandman and a patron of agriculture and cattle-rearing. An annual festival, the Lupercalia, or *Faunalia*, was celebrated in his honor by the Romans on December 5, the same date as *Krampusnacht*.

Ofelia's stepfather, the Falangist Captain Vidal (Sergi López), hunts the Spanish Maquis fighting against the Francoist regime in a forest-mountainous region. At the same time, Ofelia's pregnant mother, Carmen (Ariadna Gil), grows increasingly ill. Ofelia meets several strange and magical creatures becoming central to her story, leading her through the maze's trials. The film employs makeup, animatronics, and CGI effects to bring life to its creatures. Easter egg: Ofelia evokes Shakespeare's *Hamlet*, hinting at similarities between Carmen, Ofelia's *mamá*, and Hamlet's mother, Queen Gertrude. They're both widows who marry monsters. Queen Gertrude marries the villainous Uncle Claudius, and Carmen marries Captain Vidal, a cruel soldier prone to sadistic paroxysms. Both *Pan's Labyrinth's* Ofelia and *Hamlet*'s Ophelia die tragically.

Pan's Labyrinth premiered on May 27, 2006, at the Cannes Film Festival. It was theatrically released in Spain on October 11 and in Mexico on October 20. It was produced and distributed internationally by Esperanto Filmoj and Warner Bros. Pictures in association with Telecinco Cinema. *Pan's Labyrinth* opened to widespread critical acclaim, with many praising the visual effects, direction, cinematography, and performances. It won numerous international awards, including three Academy Awards, three BAFTA Awards including Best Film Not in the English Language, the Ariel Award for Best Picture, the Saturn Awards for Best International Film and Best Performance by a Younger Actor for Ivana Baquero, and the 2007 Hugo Award for Best Dramatic Presentation, Long Form.

In a fairy tale, Princess Moanna, the daughter of the King of the Underworld (Federico Luppi, 1936-2017), visits the human world. The sunlight blinds her, erasing her memory, making her mortal, and she dies. The King believes that one day her spirit will reincarnate and return to the underworld, so he builds labyrinths–which act as portals–around the globe in preparation for her return. The sun epitomizes the masculine; since it erases her memory, it is the *Sol Niger*, anticipating Vidal, the evil patriarch.

In 1944 Francoist Spain, Ofelia travels with her pregnant but sickly mother Carmen to meet Captain Vidal, her new stepfather. Vidal, the son of a famed commander who died in Morocco, believes strongly in Falangism having been tasked to hunt down republican rebels. Stopping along the road, Ofelia finds a rock, discovering it is an eye to a missing pagan statue nearby. She returns the stone eye to its socket, opening her eyes to the magical world beyond mundane reality. Like Dorothy Gale, Ofelia is walking upon a path of initiation, gaining the intellect to navigate the trials before her. A stick insect akin to a praying mantis emerges from a hole in the statue–which Ofelia believes to be a fairy–leading her into an ancient labyrinth. Before she can enter, Vidal's housekeeper, Mercedes (Maribel Verdú), stops her. Mercedes is secretly supporting her brother Pedro (Roger Casamajor) and other rebels. When Ofelia meets Vidal, she greets him with her left hand, insinuating witchcraft and Left-Hand Path magic; indeed, witchcraft pervades del Toro's fairy tale. Vidal's men capture two farmers hunting rabbits; the rabbits are an allusion to the White Rabbit in *Alice in Wonderland*, foreshadowing Ofelia's adventure underground, going beneath a decaying fig tree.

That night, the insect appears in Ofelia's bedroom, transforming into a fairy, leading her through the labyrinth. Fairies symbolize the supra-normal powers of the human soul; the fairy's abilities are not merely magical but are instead the sudden revelation of latent possibilities.[332] Fairies personify the stages in the development in the soul's spiritual life, indicating Ofelia's forthcoming supernatural journey.[333]

The labyrinth is a symbol of initiation, death, and reincarnation, signifying Ofelia's quest to return to the Underworld, to be restored as Princess Moanna. A walker entering a labyrinth is not the same person leaving the maze. The seeker has been born again into a new phase or level of existence; the center is where death and rebirth occur, hence it is in the center where Ofelia encounters the faun. Death and reincarnation represent the transition from one form of existence to another, presumably a higher one, and one of the most important rites of passage is initiation; thus, the

---

332 Cirlot, *Dictionary*, 96.
333 Ibid.

(Left) Ofelia, dressed as an archetypal Alice, travels to a dank wonderland, down a muddy cavity, i.e., a rabbit's hole, into the bowels of a dying fig tree to confront a giant toad. Her name, Ofelia, evokes Hamlet's tragic girlfriend, Ophelia, from Shakespeare's drama. Both *Hamlet* and *Pan's Labyrinth* feature tyrannical father figures: Uncle Claudius and Captain Vidal, and Ophelia and Ofelia both suffer melancholy, dying in the end. (Right) Nine years later, in *Crimson Peak*, the stick-figure fairy appears in a mural painted on the walls of Allerdale Hall, discovered by Edith Cushing.

rituals performed, and verbal instructions given to an initiate served to change his or her religious or social life.[334] Furthermore, in the labyrinth, a person is surrounded by, isolated, and cut off from his or her familiar environment; for that person, familiar surroundings have died. There is no way back, only the inevitable path forward, with a change of direction at the center. The road from a former existence into confinement is a path of death. It is no accident that some of the earliest labyrinths–Bronze Age petroglyphs–are either associated with graves or with mines, those places where a person sets out on a dangerous path back into the womb of Mother Earth, the Queen of the Underworld.[335]

The faun, believing Ofelia to be the reincarnation of Princess Moanna of the Underworld, gives her a magical book, the Book of Crossroads. He tells her she will find in its pages three tasks to complete to acquire immortality, allowing her to return to her kingdom. The three tasks–to be completed before

---

334 Hermann Kern, *Through the Labyrinth* (New York: Prestel, 2000), 30.
335 Ibid.

the moon is full–represent the initiatory rituals of the Ancient Mysteries carried forward by Freemasonry; the three rites of the Blue Lodge are Entered Apprentice, Fellowcraft, and Master Mason. The Rule of Three permeates fairy tales because it is an archetypal, divine number, viz. the Holy Trinity.[336] There are three little pigs; the djinn will grant three wishes; *The Three Sisters* published in 1634, and Goldilocks met three bears. In *Rumpelstiltskin* (1812), a manikin spins straw for the miller's daughter over three nights in three rooms, during which she gives three gifts (the necklace, the ring, and the first-born child) to the funny imp. Then, when she is queen, she has three days to come up with the little man's name.

Three crops up in *Pan's Labyrinth*. For example, there are three female archetypes: the little girl, the mother, and the rebel. Two sergeants shadow Vidal, forming a triumvirate, and the faun provides Ofelia with three fairies. Ofelia must feed the toad three magic stones; there are three locked cabinets in the Pale Man's dining hall; Vidal makes the stutterer count to three, and there are three thrones in the golden chamber. Easter egg: the intersection of roads is a customary site of occult rituals, hence the magic book's name. The moon goddess, Hecate, was the goddess of witchcraft and crossroads; from antiquity through the Middle Ages, sorcerers and witches were said to frequent crossings to conjure the Devil, or demons, to make a sacrifice to them. In *House of Frankenstein* (1944), Dr. Gustav Neiman (Boris Karloff) travels to Reigelberg, exhibiting Lampini's Chamber of Horrors at the hamlet's crossroads, reviving Count Dracula (John Carradine, 1906-1988) to feast upon the living. According to Jung, intersections are a place of flux and change, signifying Ofelia's initiation into greater, supernatural mysteries. According to the faun, she was born of the moon; hence, Ofelia has a lunar birthmark on her left shoulder, identifying her with the dark side of the moon, the Left-Hand Path.

Ofelia approaches an imposing, rotting tree, wearing a dark green dress with a hair bow, looking like an archetypal Alice about to enter Wonderland. The tree is a clever mnemonic representing two things. First, it resembles the sculpture of the faun's horns above the entrance to the labyrinth; second, it also looks like a uterus, foreshadowing the generative organ appearing

---

336 Mills, *The Tree of Mythology*, *passim*. Edwin Sidney Hartland, *The Science of Fairy Tales: An Inquiry into Fairy Mythology* (London: Walter Scott, 1891), *passim*. See also Hall, *Secret Teachings*, 199, 216; Cavendish, *Black Arts*, 80-81. In *Gretel & Hansel: A Grim Fairy Tale* (2020), pyramids and triangles are everywhere, correlating with the Rule of Three.

in the magic book, gushing blood on its pages, indicating Carmen's dire maternal complications.[337] Like Alice, Ofelia goes down a dark hole; she completes the first task, retrieving a key from a giant toad's belly. The bloated toad has corrupted the tree, becoming a symbol for socio-economic inequality. "Aren't you ashamed living down here, eating all these bugs and growing fat while the tree dies?" Ofelia *qua* Princess Moanna asks the toad. The scene immediately following Ofelia's confrontation with the toad is the dinner feast, with Vidal, the priest, and other important dignitaries. These elites enjoy their fancy foods while the rest of the families are rationed because of post-Civil War conditions. In the same way the toad is siphoning the life off the fig tree, the Spanish upper class is suffocating the masses by hoarding Spain's limited resources.

Ofelia becomes increasingly worried about her mother's worsening condition. The faun gives Ofelia a mandrake root, to be put in a bowl of milk, then placed under her mother's sickbed with two drops of blood added regularly to ease Carmen's painful pregnancy. Like Baphomet, the Knights Templar were accused of worshipping the priapic root, which looks like a miniature human being. Mandrake is critical in witchcraft both as a poison and as an aphrodisiac. Medieval witches were said to harvest the root at night beneath gallows trees where unrepentant criminals, evil since birth, died. The root purportedly grew from a criminal's bodily drippings. According to Christian lore, the witch washed the root in wine, wrapping it in silk and velvet. She fed it sacramental wafers stolen from a church during communion, which placed witches in the Devil's camp. It's also a mystical fertility pill, an infallible cure for sterility. In Genesis, the barren Rachel, wife of Jacob, ate a mandrake root to conceive Joseph; ergo, it relieves Carmen's illness.

Perched atop Ofelia's bedposts are hand-carved wooden owls, symbolizing enlightenment. The owl, a totem sacred to Minerva and the Illuminati, represents Ofelia's mystic journey, and the ability to observe things not noticeable to the uninitiated.

Accompanied by three fairy guides, Ofelia completes the second task: retrieving a dagger from the lair of the Pale Man (Doug Jones), a chthonic, child-eating monster. The Pale Man is an archetypal-traditional fiend, a

---

337 The twisting horns also appear on the backboard of Carmen's bed, making them a repetitive trope.

descendant of the Big Bad Wolf, Bluebeard, a fire-breathing dragon, the Fenrir, a ghoul, a troll, and an ogre. Inside his dining hall–its banquet table has a sumptuous feast–she uses the key from the toad's lair to obtain the dagger. Although Ofelia was warned not to consume anything there, she eats two grapes, awakening the Pale Man. He devours two of the fairies, giving chase to Ofelia, but she manages to escape. Del Toro has stated in interviews that artists have influenced him, especially Francisco Goya. The shot of the Pale Man eating the fairies is taken directly from the artist's *Saturn Devouring His Son* (1819-1823). Easter egg: del Toro conceived the Pale Man as a perverted allusion to stigmata, ghastly wounds signifying grace and piety. The Pale Man's eyes, embedded in his hands, are shared by the Japanese mythological monster, the Tenome, which means *eyes of hands*.

Saturn Devouring His Son by Goya influenced del Toro; the painting comes alive when the Pale Man eats the two fairies.

The faun, infuriated by her disobedience, refuses to assign Ofelia the third task. During this time, Ofelia quickly becomes aware of Vidal's ruthlessness in hunting down the rebels. After he erroneously murders two local farmers detained on suspicion of aiding the rebels (they were merely hunting rabbits), Vidal interrogates and tortures a captive rebel. He asks Dr. Ferreiro (Alex Angulo, 1953-2014) to tend to the captive, whom the doctor then proceeds to euthanize surreptitiously at the rebel's urging. Vidal realizes Ferreiro is a rebel collaborator and shoots him from behind, killing him. Later, Vidal catches Ofelia tending to the mandrake root, which he considers delusional behavior triggered by her fairy tale books. Carmen agrees and throws the root into the fire. With the root burning and the witchcraft broken, she immediately develops painful contractions, dying while giving birth to Vidal's son. Easter egg: the solider who finds a lottery ticket near the rebel's campfire is the same one listening to the radio when the host announces the winning lottery numbers. The winning numbers are 3-3-0-3-7; the three threes allude to the Rule of Three, and seven evokes the seven circular gardens of the Palace of the Underworld. Mysticism transcends the number seven to be presented later in this tome.

Mercedes, having been discovered to be a rebel spy, tries to escape with Ofelia, but they are caught. Ofelia, mistaken as a traitor, is locked in her bedroom, while Mercedes is taken to be interrogated and tortured. Mercedes frees herself, stabs Vidal, and rejoins the rebels. The faun, having a change of mind, tells Ofelia to bring her baby brother into the labyrinth to complete the third task. Ofelia complies, sneaking into Vidal's room to get the child. But Vidal discovers her, pursuing Ofelia into the labyrinth just as the rebels launch an attack on the outpost. She meets the faun at the center of the maze. Under the light of a full moon, Hecate, the goddess of witchcraft, the faun wishes to draw a few drops of the baby's blood to complete the third task: opening a portal to the Underworld, which requires the blood of an innocent. The faun plans on slaughtering the child with the magical dagger, evoking Crowley's "Bloody Sacrifice" from *Book Four: Magick in Theory and Practice* (1929).[338] As Ofelia argues with the faun, refusing to hand over the child, Vidal discovers her speaking, but he cannot see the mythical creature. Vidal takes the baby from Ofelia's arms before gunning her down.

---

338 The sacrificing of a virgin male child of high intelligence is a euphemism for masturbation.

CINEMA SYMBOLISM 3

Vidal returns to the labyrinth's entrance, where he runs into Mercedes and Pedro along with the other rebels. Knowing he will be killed, he hands the baby to Mercedes, asking that she tell his son the exact time of his father's death. However, Mercedes refuses, telling him, "He won't even know your name," as Vidal is then shot to death by Pedro. Mercedes enters the labyrinth to comfort a motionless but breathing Ofelia. Drops of Ofelia's blood drip onto an altar below. Ofelia, well dressed and uninjured, then appears in a golden throne room. The King of the Underworld says she passed the final test: choosing to spill her blood instead of that of an innocent. The faun appears, praising Ofelia for her choice, addressing her once more as "Your Highness." The Underworld's Queen, her mother, invites Ofelia to sit next to her father. Back at the labyrinth, Ofelia smiles, dying in Mercedes' arms. She has perished and been reborn, becoming a supreme initiate, ruling the Underworld from her lofty throne.

The epilogue completes the tale of Princess Moanna, stating she ruled wisely and left quiet traces of her time in the world, "Visible only to those who know where to look," implying those with occult insight will recognize the vestiges.

Worse than the ogre father archetype, the monster of *Pan's Labyrinth* is Captain Vidal; his name means *life*, but he is nothing more than a death dealer, a cruel beast. A torturer of men and women, he is pedantic and meticulous, obsessed with time, symbolized by his father's broken watch, becoming a memento mori. He shares his fixation with another fascist, Adolf Hitler, who was distrustful of time, avoiding its demands, blaming it for his defeat.[339] Echoing deathly Chronos, Saturn, the god of time, Vidal's room looks like the insides of a clock; its stagnant gears represent his troubled psyche.[340] Saturn, with its ravenous appetite for life, devours all its creations, whether they are beings, things, ideas, or sentiments, much like Vidal. He is selfish, caring only for himself and his unborn son, paying no attention to his wife or stepdaughter. In Spanish, when addressing two or more women, one would say *Bienvenidas*. The presence of any man or boy would require the use of *Bienvenidos*. When Vidal welcomes Ofelia

---

[339] Robert G. L. Waite, *The Psychopathic God: Adolf Hitler* (1977; repr., Boston: Da Capo Press, 1993), 17-18.
[340] Cavendish, *Black Arts, supra* note 155.

and her pregnant mother to the base, he says *Bienvenidos*, indicating he's more interested in his unborn son than them.

Ofelia dons mostly green, wearing red when she finally arrives in the Underworld. The movie flirts with alchemy, documenting Ofelia's transition from mere mortal to Princess Moanna of the Underworld. The red outfit and shoes are the *rubedo*; the Great Operation completed when Ofelia ascends to the throne of the Underworld, joining her mother and father, the King and Queen. In this context, her red shoes conjure Dorothy's ruby slippers from *The Wizard of Oz*, indicating Ofelia is home, over the rainbow, dwelling in the magical Underworld. The *nigredo*, death, is Vidal, the Black Sun, and the *albedo* is the moon, regulating the three tasks. The *citrinitas* is the solar-golden throne room, paralleling the kingly salon of Apollo at Versailles.[341] Ofelia, born of the moon, the ruler of the night giving way to the sun at dawn, has a crescent birthmark on her left shoulder; the crescent is a symbol of both the moon and Venus. Green is the color of Venus and the color of Ofelia, identifying her with Venus' counterpart, Lucifer, making her journey to the Underworld more akin to the return of a fallen angel to Tophet, or Gehenna, the abode of the damned.

The fairy tale world mirrors reality and vice versa; what is essential in one, is also critical in the other. The Pale Man sits at the head of the table, presiding over a feast, just as Vidal sits at the head of the table, presiding over a feast, making them the same: vile monsters. There are two keys: in the fairy tale world, a key unlocks the cabinet to retrieve the dagger; in reality, a key opens the supply room, storing food, medical supplies, and munition. There are two knives: the blade needed by the faun to perform the third task, and the kitchen knife used to wound Vidal. In the solar golden throne room, Princess Moanna's mother, the Queen of the Underworld (also played by Ariadna Gil), cradles a baby; moments later, under a full moon, Pedro cradles Ofelia's baby brother. The fairy tale items are more elaborate and decorative than their real-world equivalents, implying the numinous world of Princess Moanna is superior to the prosaic world of humankind.

Lastly, there is a rebellious undercurrent pervading del Toro's fairy tale. In saving the fig tree, Ofelia obeys the faun but disobeys her mother by

---

341 Ofelia's green dresses also bring forth the Emerald Tablet of Hermes Trismegistus, suggesting her alchemical metamorphosis. In another alchemical film, *Stoker*, it could be argued the mansion's green walls signify India's change from melancholic teenager to murderous adult.

soiling her green dress and ruining her new shoes. Ofelia defiance upsets Carmen, who sends her to bed without dinner, but the future princess did what was moral: she saved the dying tree, completing the task. Despite being warned not to eat anything at the Pale Man's banquet, Ofelia consumes two grapes. By contravening the faun's dictate, but admitting her mistake, Ofelia is given a second chance at the third task. She passes the third trial by disobeying again, refusing to spill her baby brother's blood, proving her moral fiber, allowing ascension to Underworld's throne. Mercedes and Dr. Ferreiro parallel her defiance when they secretly disobey Vidal by assisting the rebels. When Vidal asks the good doctor why he didn't obey him, he explains, "To obey–just like that–for the sake of obeying, without questioning, that's something only people like you can do, Captain." This resistance mirrors a Valentinian Gnostic revolt: to question dogmas, to be wary of lawgivers, rule-makers, and their noble institutions because all may not be what it seems. By defying Vidal and the Falangists, the rebels win–all is not a lost cause.

It's Just a Spring Clean for the May Queen: Midsommar's Transcendent Gloom

Emerging from the pages of Frazer's *Golden Bough*, *Midsommar* is a depressing folk horror film written and directed by Ari Aster, theatrically released in the United States on July 3, 2019, by A24 and in Sweden on July 10, 2019, by Nordisk Film.[342] At first, I was going to analyze *Midsommar* in *Cinema Symbolism 4*, but I was so impressed with it, I decided to include it herein. To say it is a remake of *The Wicker Man* (1973), with a sprinkle of *The Dark Secret of Harvest Home*, does it an injustice; that said, lurking in Aster's masterpiece is a creepy, pagan versus Christian undercurrent that is more pronounced than it initially appears. Norse mythology is prevalent, so is paganism and sun worship, alluding to its Christianized equivalents. The winter and summer solstices are pervasive, indicating dark and light, signifying both the sun's death and exaltation. There is an allusion to *The Wizard of Oz* because of Dorothy's Gnostic-like awakening,

---

342 Aster's *Midsommar* seems to borrow from a 2003 movie, also titled *Midsommar*. The latter's description from the Internet Movie Database: "Christian's sister commits suicide. Why? After his four friends graduate secondary school, they head off to a Swedish cabin for midsummer as previous years. Strange things happen. Is it his sister's spirit?"

Inside the Ardor residence's master bedroom, Mr. and Mrs. Ardor are sound asleep, not knowing their daughter, Terri, is about murder them by filling the room with carbon monoxide gas, poisoning them. On the nightstand sits a photo of Dani with a bouquet behind it, making it appear like she's wearing a floral crown, foreshadowing her May Queen ascendancy.

understanding there's *no place like home*, a belief the female protagonist of *Midsommar*, Dani Ardor (Florence Pugh) comes to appreciate. There are buried references to two Kubrick movies, *The Shining* and *Eyes Wide Shut*; as the analysis unfolds, it will be easy to understand why Aster pays homage to these classics. During its opening moments, Aster also pays tribute to another maestro, David Lynch, to conjure the underbelly thriving in the shadows of saccharine, suburban America. After viewing *Midsommar* for the third time, it became apparent that, much like *The Black Cat* and *The Exorcist*, the Devil dwells in the movie–its celluloid exalts evil. After watching *Hereditary*, Aster's meditation on demonism and mental illness, it became evident he's this generation's Roman Polanski.

It opens by showing us, the audience, a five-paneled mural painted by Brooklyn-based artist Mu Pan. The artwork, when examined, spoils about 80% of the story. As such, I will not analyze now but will present its symbolism at the end of this portion. To do otherwise would be duplicative, repeating the analysis.

After the mural, *Midsommar* begins, revealing it is the present-day; the sun is dead because it is deathly winter. It is snowing and dark outside; a frozen river designates the northern hemisphere in the throes of Jack Frost's icy grip. At Delphi, Dionysus governed the winter months; linked with the Black Sun and the Devil, he was attended by satyrs, and his rites were orgiastic.[343] The deity was connected to the underworld, like other gods of fertility and vegetation because plants and trees grow beneath the ground's surface.[344] The sun god Apollo is nowhere to be found, having given his heavenly glow over to the moon, governing the frigid night. A

---

343 Cavendish, *Black Arts*, 344.
344 Ibid.

town appears on-screen; most of the homes have their lights on because families are inside enjoying life, getting ready to celebrate Christmas, the winter solstice, when the sun is annually reborn. The sun must pass through the three-month tomb of deathly winter, resurrected at the vernal equinox, achieving full strength in summer. A dog barks, focusing on a residential house in the suburbs with all its lights off, appearing abandoned and lifeless. The barking canine evokes David Lynch, who often employs noisy dogs to indicate that misfortune and death are about to strike the main characters–more on this in Chapter XII. By doing so, Aster conjures *Blue Velvet* and *Lost Highway*, and the television series *Twin Peaks*, all of which, like *Midsommar*, explore suburbia's dark side.

Indeed, the barking dog is an ill omen because all is not well with this house; death is descending upon this community. Inside the quiet home, Dani leaves a voice mail for her parents after receiving a disturbing email from her sister, Terri (Klaudia Csányi), who has rapid-cycling bipolar disorder, suffering mood swings, depression, and mania. As the camera pans away from the answering machine, a collection of family photos shows the family in happy times, including one of Terri as a little girl wearing a yellow shirt and blue overalls. We then see Terri and Dani's father (Zsolt Bojári) and mother (Gabriella Fón) sleeping, appearing like stone effigies atop a tomb; observe, for they are wearing blue pajamas and sleeping in yellow sheets and covers.

Yellow and blue are omnipresent, suggesting the radiant sun and the tranquil blue sky, creating an anomaly because the vibrant hues foreshadow the Hårga death cult in Sweden. In their tranquil, reclusive commune, nine victims are sacrificed in a yellow wooden pyramid with blue doors. There are blue tarps collecting dew visible on both sides of the pyramid, signifying the blue sky, governed by the sun during the summer months. Back inside the home, one will also observe that Dani's voicemail is the ninth message. Easter egg: according to the script, Dani's parents live in Minnesota while she is a college student in Brooklyn, New York. Minnesota evokes the state's NFL football team, the Vikings, mirroring the film's deep Norse mythology. The chant of the Vikings football team, *Skol* (or *Skal*), is given during toasts in the Hårga commune. Another Easter egg: sitting on her mother's nightstand is a framed photo of Dani with a vase of flowers behind it. The bouquet makes it appear like Dani is wearing a floral coronet, foreshadowing the climax when she is crowned with a garland, ordained the May Queen. Easter egg: the Tarot's Empress (III) corresponds with the May Queen, a female archetype who brought new life after winter, anticipating Jung's theory of the *anima*.

Before I continue this analysis, I feel it necessary to explain why nine pervades Aster's masterpiece, critical in Norse mythology, incorporated into Christianity. Nine even conjures Aster's first movie, *Hereditary*. *Midsommar* has nine letters, as does *Dani Ardor*. Terri's and Dani's names end with the letter *i* because it's the alphabet's ninth letter. Dani's is the ninth voice message left on the machine (*vide supra*), and the Hårga hold their midsummer festival every ninety years, lasting nine days. In the book, *Norse Mythology: A Guide to the Gods, Heroes, Rituals, and Beliefs* (2001), Professor John Lindow explains how nine transcends Norse lore:

- The Norse cosmology knows nine worlds supported by Yggdrasil (mystical or cosmic tree, comparatively Kabbalah's Tree of Life/ Wisdom).
- At the end of *Skáldskaparmál* is a list of nine heavenly realms provided by Snorri, including, from the nethermost to the highest, Vindblain (also Heidthornir or Hregg-Mimir), Andlang, Vidblain, Vidfedmir, Hrjod, Hlyrnir, Gimir, Vet-Mimir and Skatyrnir which *stands higher than the clouds, beyond all worlds*.
- Every ninth year, people from all over Sweden assembled at the Temple at Uppsala. According to Adam of Bremen (ca. before 1050-1081/85), There was feasting for nine days and sacrifices of both men and male animals.
- In *Skírnismál*, Freyr is obliged to wait nine nights to consummate his union with Gerd.
- In *Svipdagsmál*, the witch Gróa grants nine charms to her son Svipdag. In the same poem, nine maidens sit at the knees of Menglod.
- In *Fjölsvinnsmál*, Laegjarn's chest is fastened with nine locks.

- During Ragnarök, Thor kills Jörmungandr but staggers back nine steps before falling dead himself, poisoned by the venom that the Serpent spewed over him.

- According to the very late Trollkyrka poem, the fire for the blót was lit with nine kinds of wood.

- Odin's ring Draupnir releases eight golden drops every ninth night, forming circles of equal worth, totaling nine rings.

- In the guise of *Grímnir* in the poem *Grímnismál*, Odin allows himself to be held by King Geirröd for eight days and nights and kills him on the ninth after revealing his true identity.

- There are nine daughters of Ægir.

- There are nine mothers of Heimdall.

- There are nine great lindworms: Jörmungandr, Níðhöggr, Grábakr, Grafvölluðr, Ofnir, Svafnir, Grafvitni and his sons Góinn and Móinn.

- The god Hermod rode Sleipnir for nine nights on his quest to free Baldr from the underworld.

- The giant Baugi had nine thralls who killed each other to possess Odin's magical sharpening stone.

- The god Njord and his wife Skadi decided to settle their argument over where to live by agreeing to spend nine nights in Thrymheim and nine nights at Nóatún.

- The giant Thrivaldi has nine heads.

- The clay giant Mokkurkalfi measured nine leagues high and three broad beneath the arms.

- When Odin sacrificed himself to himself, he hung upon Yggdrasill's gallows for nine days and nights. In return, he secured rúnar, *runes, secret knowledge*.

- The valknut symbol is three interlocking triangles forming nine points.

Midsommar's omnipresent gloom radiates from the sun, worshipped by the Hårga, a solar death cult in Hälsingland, Sweden; it is a mediation on saturnine depression. (Left) Terri, covered in vomit with a yellow hose duct-taped into her mouth, has committed murder-suicide, killing her parents and herself by carbon monoxide poisoning under cover of night. The ghoulish deed occurs in deathly winter when darkness and the moon rule supreme. She wears a yellow shirt and blue pants, foreshadowing the yellow pyramidal temple and blue tarps in the Hårga community. Like her sister Dani, Terri is a death votary, pursuing a death wish, worshipping the Grim Reaper. Thus, Terri is with her sister, spiritually and physically, always and forever–they are inseparable. Unlike the nocturnal, saturnine Terri, who destroys when the moon is exalted, Dani offers up her boyfriend as a sacrifice to the diurnal, luminous orb because the sun can be just as bloodthirsty as the moon. (Right) Later, during the midsummer procession, after Dani is crowned May Queen, Terri's lifeless face (upper left), along with the hose sticking out her mouth (running along the bottom), manifest in the trees and foliage behind the parade. "Mighty and erect is this Will of mine, this Pyramid of fire whose summit is lost in Heaven. Upon it have I burned the corpse of my desires. ...This is The Night wherein I am lost, the Love through which I am no longer I." – Aleister Crowley, "The Gun-Barrel," *The Book of Lies*, 1912.

- There are nine surviving deities of Ragnarök, including Baldr and Höðr, Magni and Modi, Vidar and Váli, Hoenir, the daughter of Sól and a ninth *powerful, mighty one, he who rules over everything.*[345]

In the Eleusinian Mysteries, nine was the number of spheres through which the consciousness passed on its way to birth, denoting Dani's Gnostic awakening when joins the Hårga sun cult, making it her family.[346] Because of its close resemblance to the spermatozoon, 9 has been associated with germinal life, signifying the cult's obsession with fertility.[347] Moving forward, I will continue to point out when the trope surfaces in *Midsommar*.

---

345 John Lindow, *Norse Mythology: A Guide to the Gods, Heroes, Rituals, and Beliefs* (New York: Oxford University Press, 2002), *passim*; Rudolf Simek, *Dictionary of Norse Mythology*, trans. Angela Hall (1984; repr., Rochester, NY: D.S. Brewer, 2000), *passim*.
346 Hall, *Secret Teachings*, 220.
347 Ibid.

One other element worth mentioning before returning to the analysis. When viewing, pay attention to the mirrors and reflective surfaces populating *Midsommar*. Aster employs mirrors much like Aronofsky does in *Black Swan*: to breathe life into the characters' shadow selves. Dani and her ambivalent boyfriend, Christian Hughes (Jack Reynor), argue before a mirror about his secret plan: going to Sweden without her. When Christian informs his drinking buddies, Josh (William Jackson Harper), Mark (Will Poulter), and Pelle (Vilhelm Blomgren) that he is bringing Dani with him, their facial expressions reveal their true feelings. That is, they see Dani as a fifth wheel, an interloper, persona non grata. The mirror on the wall displays their disappointment, reflecting their feigning acceptance. Dani will cramp their styles, and they know it; hence, they cannot conceal their angst. The mirror documents the unease the characters are experiencing as their shadows emerge from their psyches' recesses. Because *Midsommar* is all about winter and summer, death and life, the moon and the sun, Aster uses mirrors because they reflect the multiplicity of the soul–positive and negative–just as the moon receives the light of the sun, illumining the night sky.[348]

Returning to the prologue, Dani sits anxiously in her Brooklyn apartment, looking at her computer screen. It is night; she has received this ominous email from her sister, Terri, "dear dani i can't anymore - everything's black - mom and dad are coming too. goodbye." This communication is sent on December 23, a day or two after the winter solstice of December 20-22, celebrated as the Feast Day of St. John the Evangelist on December 27. It is the evening before Christmas Eve, two days before the sun's birthday, Christmas, on December 25. We know this because of the dates of Terri's earlier correspondences. On the left side of Dani's computer screen, from bottom to top, are a string of emails. Dated December 18, the first email (no subject) Terri sent her sister is a link to a YouTube video found here: https://www.youtube.com/watch?v=dwHBpykTloY.

From National Geographic's verified YouTube channel, this video is titled, "First-Ever 3D VR Filmed in Space | One Strange Rock." The video's narrator–an astronaut–discusses that, when in outer space orbiting the earth, it is impossible to differentiate between day and night, how one's body clock is thrown off, and time calculation switches from

---

348 Cirlot, *Dictionary*, 201.

numbers displayed on a watch to the changing seasons. The narrator mentions that a billion years seem to float next to him, giving him a sense of eternity. Another astronaut says the view of earth from outer space is something human eyes are not supposed to see because this is what the world must look like from Heaven. Spacemen (and spacewomen) orbiting the earth in outer space, insinuates a desire to leave the planet, exit stage left, presaging her suicide. The changing seasons suggest Terri's reality–literally and figuratively–is a Stygian nightmare. When she writes everything is "black," she refers not only to her depression but of the "bleak December" to use Poe's lexicon. The sun is dead, darkness reigns, thus Terri commits murder-suicide because light has been extinguished– she has lost all hope because "everything's black" during the Feast of St. John the Evangelist.

On December 19, Terri emails Dani again (no subject); it links to another YouTube video found here: https://www.youtube.com/watch?v=2vkA5WB38Hc. This video, also from National Geographic's verified account, is titled, "Relaxing Yellowstone River LIVE! | Yellowstone Live," featuring a tranquil river, surrounded by a beautiful landscape. This video shows Terri's desperate attempts to relax to ambient imagery and sounds, to ease her anxiety. The two videos give us a glimpse into Terri's troubled mind and fragile emotional state.

The next email, dated December 23, is from Dani's boyfriend, Christian, followed by Terri's final, doomy email, sent *one hour ago* (an hour after Christian's message), saying goodbye for the last time.

Dani calls her boyfriend, Christian, to discuss Terri's disturbing email, but he is distant and disinterested, making excuses, telling her Terri is trying to upset her. In truth, he is attempting to find a way out of the relationship. Next, she calls a girlfriend to discuss the email, revealing she is dependent on Christian for emotional support while he seems to want nothing in return. We learn Dani takes Ativan to control her anxiety brought about by her sister's erratic behavior. Terri is a bit of a masochist, knowing she is causing Dani pain and distress because, after all, misery loves company. In other words, Terri is torturing Dani with her problems, taking a perverse pleasure in harming her.

In a diner, Christian and drinking buddies, his posse, are hanging out. Among his homies are Josh, the scholar, studying anthropology, Mark

CINEMA SYMBOLISM 3

(Left) When Josh, Christian, Pelle, and Mark kibitz at the diner, the photograph on the left–Sofia Loren and Jayne Mansfield–decorates the wall behind them. The photo's symbolism is twofold: first, it represents their hedonistic desire to attend the Hårga's festival, especially Mark, who wants to get laid. Second, it is well known Mansfield was involved with LaVey's Church of Satan, appearing with LaVay–dressed as the Devil–in the photo on the right. In the world of conspiracy, it has been suggested the car accident that decapitated Mansfield was a sacrifice to the Prince of Darkness–a product of black magic–foreshadowing the sacrifice of Josh, Mark, and Christian to the sun god on St. John's Day. Mansfield died on June 27, a few days after the summer solstice of '67, anticipating *Midsommar*'s fiendish climax.

the wise-cracking jester, and Pelle the Swede who has invited the trio to Hälsingland to attend the Hårga's solar festival. Mark insists Christian terminate his relationship with Dani because she is a basket case. According to Mark, there are other, more appealing, fish in the sea. Pelle speaks of the women they will impregnate over the summer, foreshadowing Christian's Dionysian sex rite with Maja (Isabelle Grill), during the commune's fertility rite.

Decorating the wall behind them is a massive reproduction photo of Sophia Loren with Jayne Mansfield (1933-1967) having a wardrobe malfunction. It is from a series of photographs taken in April 1957. Italian actress Sophia Loren was welcomed to Hollywood by Paramount Pictures at a dinner party at Romanoff's restaurant in Beverly Hills, launching her international career. During that same year, 20th Century Fox began marketing American actress Jayne Mansfield as the studio's blonde-bombshell successor to Marilyn Monroe (1926-1962) after the box-office success of *The Girl Can't Help It* (1956). Mansfield was a popular actress with film and Broadway credits, appearing in *Playboy* as a Playmate of the Month. According to Loren, Mansfield was the last person to arrive at the dinner, walking directly to her table where she was seated between Loren and her dinner companion, Clifton Webb (1889-1966). Mansfield, wearing a backless satin dress in her signature pink color with a deep, plunging neckline, was photographed numerous times during the dinner with Loren unable to unglue her eyes from Mansfield's generous tits. The snapshot of the two sex symbols represents the boys' wanton, hedonistic desires while recalling Mansfield's involvement with Anton LaVey, the founder of the Church of Satan. Mansfield died in a horrific car accident, causing rumors to swirl that she was hexed, a blood sacrifice to the Devil. The photo of Jayne Mansfield anticipates Josh, Mark, and Christian becoming blood sacrifices to the sun at the summer solstice.

Dani receives a phone call from an unknown number, revealing Terri has committed murder-suicide, gassing herself and their parents, everyone dying from carbon monoxide poisoning. Two yellow hoses lead from the cars' exhaust pipes to the bodies of Terri and Mr. and Mrs. Ardor. Terri possesses a devious and ghoulish imagination: she has sealed up her parents' bedroom with duct tape, flooding it with the toxic gas, turning the residence into Professor Lampini's (George Zucco, 1886-1960) Chamber of Horrors. Terri is close by: her corpse is right down the hall, leaning against her desk in her bedroom, with the hose taped inside her mouth, making her appear freakishly grotesque. Paralleling her parents, Terri wears a yellow shirt and blue pants, anticipating the commune's iconic, yellow pyramid with its blue tarps when death will strike once again.

As it snows, Christian walks over to Dani's apartment to comfort her; for the first time, we observe joyous Christmas lights illuminating the background. Inside, as Christian does his best to console her, Dani wails in pain, crying over her dead family. One will notice many books in both Terri's bedroom and Dani's apartment, indicating the sisters are introverts; as it turns out, Dani is like her sister in more ways than one. Contemporary art decorates Dani's walls; a piece features two moons, foreshadowing her travels up, up and away to a land with two suns: the Hårga village, where the sun and midnight sun shine equally. Because it both receives and reflects light from the sun, the moon's passivity dovetails with the number two, an

Two illustrations by Swedish painter John Bauer represent the two sisters, Terri and Dani. The image on the left is *Ännu sitter Tuvstarr kvar och ser ner i vattnet* (English: *Still, Tuvstarr sits and gazes down into the water*), painted in 1913, is one of his most noted works. The image shows Tuvstarr gazing down into the tarn looking for her missing heart, an allegory of innocence lost. A large color print of this painting sits next to Terri's corpse because she is guilty of committing murder-suicide, thereby losing her innocence. The picture on the right is titled *Stackars lilla basse!* (English: *Poor little bear!*), painted in 1912, representing Dani. The painting depicts a little girl wearing a crown before a bear, an allusion to Dani becoming the May Queen, wearing a crown, watching as Christian is burned alive in a bear carcass.

evil number, the Devil's number, and the feminine principle, represented by the two sisters: Dani and Terri.[349]

As snow falls outside, the opening credits roll. It is the winter solstice, known to Christians as the Feast of St. John the Evangelist, when darkness reigns and death is nigh. But *Midsommar* is not an exercise in Manicheanism; instead, both dark and light are ominous, the moon and the sun are death dealers, the two luminous orbs ride pale horses.

* * * * *

Fast-forward six months, right before the summer solstice, known to Christians as the Feast of St. John the Baptist, a celebration of his birth on June 24. As such, the Feast of St. John the Evangelist and the Feast of St. John the Baptist signify the winter and summer solstices, known to the Freemasons under the appellation of the *two St. Johns*.[350] Dani, resting in her bed, unable to sleep, is still haunted by the death of her family. A large

---
[349] Ibid, 205-206. See also Wilson, *The Occult*, 417.
[350] Hall, *Secret Teachings*, 308.

reproduction image, *Stackars lilla basse!* (English*: Poor little bear!*) by Swedish illustrator John Bauer (1882-1918) decorates the wall behind her bed. The image foreshadows the end of *Midsommar*, when Dani, wearing the May Queen crown, stands before Christian—encased in a bear carcass—as he is burnt alive, sacrificed to the sun. To the right of the Bauer print is a picture of the Sydney Opera House in Australia. The auditorium is in the Southern Hemisphere, where it is now winter; light and dark are interdependent, there cannot be one without the other. Christian comes in, saying he is going to a party for 45 minutes—add four plus five to get nine.

Dani decides to go with him; the party is in the apartment of Josh, Mark, and Pelle (Christian may also live here). As they chit-chat, Dani learns for the first time that Christian is going with the others to a once-in-a-lifetime midsummer festival in Sweden. She also discovers the trip was planned a while ago. Josh and Christian are anthropology students, with the former intending to write his thesis about the Hårga. We know Mark—the joker—lives here because of items foreshadowing his death. Atop the refrigerator is a photo of Ray Bolger (1904-1987) dressed as the Scarecrow from *The Wizard of Oz*.

Its symbolism is threefold. First, the Scarecrow anticipates Mark's fate; like a scarecrow, he is skinned and stuffed with straw to be set ablaze as an offering to the sun.

Second, Bolger's Scarecrow transforms Dani's journey into a quest for enlightenment, of Gnostic epiphany, just like Dorothy's in *The Wizard of Oz*. Dorothy finally understands there's *no place like home*, so too does Dani come to learn she is home, her place is with the Hårga solar death cult. It is her new family because she, like her sister, worships death, the planet Saturn; Terri and Dani's happiness is a perverse melancholy that relishes dread while ejaculating misery. Even their surname, *Ardor* means *passion* because they are neurotic death merchants. Imitating Dorothy's adventure through Oz with three travelers: a Scarecrow wanting a brain, a Tin Woodman in search of a heart, and a Lion looking for courage, Dani also goes on a quest with three travelers. For Dani, everything is backward. Josh personifies the Tin Man because he's a heartless, emotionless academic, caring nothing about her problems. Mark is the Scarecrow, content to be a brainless fool, living only for pleasure. Christian is the Cowardly Lion; he winds up as a ferocious beast, a bear, only he never seeks or finds courage, choosing to be a milksop.

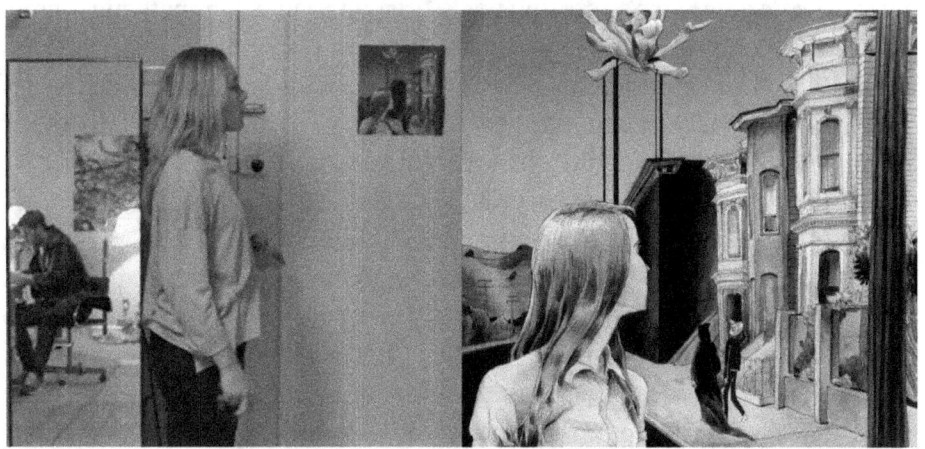

(Left) Dani stands inside her apartment, mirroring the woman in the artwork's foreground decorating her door. (Right) The image is *Print Number 23* by Julia Petrova, featuring a woman looking back at another woman walking with the Grim Reaper. The picture is easy to decode: the woman is Dani, looking back at Terri strolling along with death, having committed murder-suicide.

Thirdly, the Scarecrow is our first reference to a Kubrick film, in this instance, *Eyes Wide Shut*. Dorothy goes *over the rainbow* to experience Oz, but Bill Hartford must go to the costume shop Under the Rainbow to experience the dark, Illuminati rituals at the Somerton mansion. The Bavarian Illuminati employed the sun as one of its chief symbols; as such, *Eyes Wide Shut*'s occult rituals occur in *Somer*ton Mansion, a reference to the summer solstice, mirroring Dani and her companions Oz-like journey to experience the Hårga's solar death rites.[351]

Upon returning to Dani's apartment, Christian argues about the trip to Sweden, offering weak excuses for why he never told her about it. A mirror reflects Christian, suggesting his duplicitous nature, his ulterior motives: he wants to break-up, ending the relationship. Dani physically imitates a woman depicted on a picture decorating the door: a woman (Dani) looks back to see a girl strolling with the Grim Reaper, alluding to Terri's danse macabre. They argue, eventually reconciling before a print of Mu Pan's

---

[351] James H. Billington, *Fire in the Minds of Men: Origins of the Revolutionary Faith* (New York: Basic Books, Inc., Publishers, 1980), 95. He explains: "The name Illuminist was apparently chosen from the image of a sun radiating illumination to outer circles. At the very center within the inner circle of Areopagites burned a candle symbolizing the solar source of all illumination." See also Terry Melanson, *Perfectibilists: The 18th Century Bavarian Order of the Illuminati* (Walterville, OR: Trine Day, 2009), 18.

Dinoasshole Chapter 8, inferring that Christian is an unsympathetic a-hole. Easter egg: also, in Dani's apartment, is a print of a woman surrounded by thriving foliage, indicating she is a spring or summer goddess, further foreshadowing Dani becoming May Queen. As of this book's writing, I have not been able to identify this painting or its artist.

In their apartment, like atypical students, Christian, Josh, Pelle, and Mark lounge around a cluttered coffee table; when Dani's so-called boyfriend rises from his easy chair, a mirror once again catches his reflection, denoting duplicity. Mark is a hedonistic imbecile, wanting to go to Stockholm so he can go to a sex club. On the other end of the spectrum is Josh, a scholar, writing his thesis on European midsummer festivals, the subject matter of comparative magic and religion expert, J.G. Frazer. It could be argued that Josh's dissertation relies heavily on Frazer's magnum opus, *The Golden Bough*, published in 1890. Resting on the coffee table is a fictitious book, *The Secret Nazi Language of the Uthark*, implying his scholarship. The book also suggests Sweden's growing xenophobia, hinted at during the film. Both Mark and Josh are attending the Hårga but for different reasons.

Christian dubiousness continues when he tells them he's invited Dani to Sweden, to the midsummer festival, reassuring them that she will reject the invitation. Dani arrives, informing them that she is coming with them, assuming her presence will not ruin their plans. Christian embraces her; they have reconciled since their ruction. The others feign acceptance, welcoming her as a fellow sojourner. Pelle, an anthropology major like Josh, is also an amateur artist sketching the coffee table, while Dani reveals she's studying psychology. Pelle hints at how Josh loves research, possessed by academic passion. Pelle says he is glad that she is coming to Hälsingland to attend the nine-day festival. Dani responds by telling him they will be arriving on her birthday, the same day the festivities begin, boding her May Queen coronation.

He shows Dani a snapshot on his smartphone of the Hårga commune, informing her the people are wearing clothes specially made during the winter and summer solstices, a mnemonic linking Terri's wintry murder-suicide to the forthcoming solar horrors. He tells her that he's sorry for her loss, saying that he too lost his parents, but it's too much. She flees to the bathroom in tears. Easter egg: when Dani hurries to the toilet, she passes a bookshelf with a toy scarecrow sitting on a book with *Blood* in its title. The toy and word, much like the Ray Bolger photo, foreshadow Mark's gruesome death: skinned with his dead flesh stuffed with straw, a sacrifice to the sun.

The group flies to Sweden; aboard the plane, as Josh reads *The Poetic Edda* (a collection of Norse poems), violent turbulence erupts, anticipating the bloodbath awaiting them. As they drive to the commune, the shot becomes inverted, representing the Hårga's perverted beliefs and antiquated attitudes; they are, indeed, going under the rainbow. In *Hereditary*, Aster uses this same technique when Annie (Toni Collette) walks down the hallway to Joan's (Ann Dowd) apartment, representing the psychological-supernatural insanity consuming her family. They drive under a sign welcoming them to Hälsingland, but the banner also proclaims, "Stop mass-migration to HÄLSINGLAND. Vote for a Free North this fall," designating Sweden's xenophobia. Ruben (Levente Puczkó-Smith), the Hårga's inbred prophet, personifies this ethnocentric undercurrent. They arrive at the outskirts of the commune; the car they drive has a license plate which includes 774. Add 7+7+4 to get 18, then add 1+8 to get 9. They meet Simon (Archie Madekwe) and Connie (Ellora Torchia), an English couple invited by Pelle's communal brother Ingemar (Hampus Hallberg). In Swedish, Ingemar greets Pelle by wishing him a "Happy St. John's!" welcoming him to the summer solstice festival. Easter egg: Rob's fan theory: did Dani die in a plane crash, signified by the turbulence? For her, the commune is like Heaven, yet everything she experiences upon arriving is death, suggesting Dani is burning in Hell, *liftoach pandemonium*.

Ingemar offers the group psilocybin; under its influence, Mark begins to have a bad trip, wondering aloud the time. It is here they encounter the first sun. Christian tells him it is 9:00 pm (remember, nine is omnipresent), while Pelle remarks the "midnight sun" illuminates the sky. Although *Midsommar* is more Gnostic than alchemical (Medieval and Renaissance alchemists borrowed their ideas from the Gnostics), with Dani eventually having a Dorothy Gale-like awakening, traces of the Great Work lurk in the narrative, providing further intrigue. The *midnight sun* is the *Sol Niger*, the destructive blackening of the *nigredo* phase, indicating the Hårga's obsession with deathly sun worship. The next day, when they arrive in the commune, Father Odd (Mats Blomgren) greets them wearing a dress; he explains it represents nature's hermaphroditic qualities, evoking alchemy's equilibrated opposites. In the occult world, illustrated brilliantly by da Vinci in his painting *Saint John the Baptist* (1513-1516?), androgyny holds the secret key to humankind's regeneration and the earth's spiritual vitalization, the cult's essential tenet. Odd admires Lord Summerisle; in *The Wicker Man*, the eccentric heathen leads the May Day procession dressed as an androgyne, the sinister teaser, personifying *coincidentia oppositorum*. *Sumer is icumen in*: *Midsommar* and *The Wicker Man* celebrate the changing seasons: winter gives way to warmer weather, but the Grim Reaper's ubiquitous influence is present regardless the time of year.

Under the influence of the drug, Dani hallucinates grass growing through her hand. She runs off, finding sanctuary in an outhouse. She strikes a match, revealing Terri's cadaverous face staring back at her in the mirror. Terri's image is a reflection of Dani because the two sisters are death worshippers. She runs off into the woods, Dante's dark forest, where her bad trip continues: red and blue lights flash, recalling Terri's murder–suicide. The lights are from an ambulance, a police vehicle, or a fire truck, or a combination of the three; parked outside the home, they are heralds of ill omen. Dani sees her parents sleeping (or dead) on a sofa with Terri–alive and well–seated next to them. Terri makes eye contact; it is obvious she is pleased with the unhappiness she has wrought because, after all, misery loves company–she delights in Dani's suffering. Terri's piercing gaze issues a dare to her sister; without uttering a word, she challenges Dani to top her murder-suicide. She accepts, exceeding Terri's ghoulish deed by becoming the May Queen, sacrificing her boyfriend to the sun, burning him alive, terminating their relationship.

The next day, Christian awakens Dani from her bad dream, and the group walks through the woods to the Hårga community. During this sequence, we have the first allusion to the second Kubrick film, *The Shining*. The overhead view of the group leaving the road for the dirt path conjures Jack driving to the Overlook Hotel at the start of Kubrick's film, transferring subconsciously the same sense of isolation existing in the Overlook to the Hårga. As they stroll along, St. John's wort (*Hypericum perforatum*) grows along the path. The flower, named after the Baptizer,

Emerging from a dusky penumbra, da Vinci's *Saint John the Baptist* implies androgyny, *coincidentia oppositorum*, and terrestrial regeneration. He points to the heavens to his concomitant zodiac, Aquarius the Water Bearer, denoting the above and below of Hermes Trismegistus. In the *Hermetica*, the Lord of Summer is synonymous with alchemical gnosis. The Baptizer is a patron of Freemasonry as the Premier Grand Lodge of England was founded on June 24, 1717. During the third-degree Blue Lodge ritual, the candidate undergoes a symbolic death and rebirth, a baptism from dark to light– the Hermetic ideal. Comparatively, in his Greek guise as the divine messenger, Hermes was often identified with John the Baptist, the forerunner and herald of the Messiah's coming.

blooms around the summer solstice and can be used medicinally to treat depression. Dani, taking Ativan for anxiety, walks on a path covered with the flower because it symbolizes stress relief; St. John's wort leads her to happiness, discovering peace in the commune, joining a new family to replace the one she has lost. Norse mythology aside, at Luke 1:56, we are told the Virgin Mary stayed with Elizabeth, the mother of John the Baptist, for ninety days (three months); hence, the Hårga festival is every ninety years. The ceremonies of the heathen festival, despite centuries of Christianity, are unavoidable in observances of midsummer. Its burning lamps and bonfires point to the worship of the sun gods, as do the appropriation of all sun-like flowers as emblems of St. John. St. John's wort has leaves marked with red blood-like spots that always appear on August 29, the day St. John was beheaded.[352] The Baptist's attributes are shared remarkably with St. John the Evangelist, thereby linking the two solstices, light with dark, and dark with light. In the stained glass of the 12th century, filling a window in the apse of the church of St. Remi at

---

352 Miss Carruthers, *Flower Lore: The Teachings of Flowers, Historical, Legendary, Poetical, and Symbolical* (Belfast: McCaw, Stevenson & Orr, 1879), 6-18.

Riicims, the Virgin and St. John appear on either side of the cross, the head of both encircled by aureoles, having sunflowers inserted in their outer circles. The flowers are turned toward the Savior on the cross, their true sun.[353]

In Sweden, midsummer is the season when these pagan ceremonies are chiefly observed. On the Eve of St. John (June 23), the houses are thoroughly cleansed and garnished with green boughs and flowers. Young Fir trees are raised at the doorway and elsewhere about the homestead; very often, small umbrageous arbors are constructed in the garden. In Stockholm, on this day, a leaf-market is held at which thousands of Maypoles (*Maj Stănger*), from six inches to twelve feet high, decorated with leaves, flowers, colored paper slips, and gilt egg-shells strung on reeds are for sale. Bonfires are lit on the hills, and the people dance around them and jump over them. But the main event of the day is setting up the Maypole, consisting of a straight and tall spruce-pine tree, stripped of its branches. At times, hoops and at others pieces of wood placed crosswise, attached to it at intervals, while at others, it is provided with bows, representing, so to say, a man with his arms akimbo. From top to bottom not only the *Maj Stăng* (Maypole) itself, but the hoops, bows, etc., are ornamented with leaves, flowers, slips of various cloth, gilt egg-shells, etc.; and on the top of it is a large vane, or it may be a flag. The Maypole's raising, the decoration done by the village maidens, is an affair of grand ceremony; the people flock to it from all quarters, dancing around it in a great ring.[354] Easter egg: it's customary to celebrate St. John's Day with bonfires, seen at *Midsommar*'s gruesome climax, and with torches, like those the commune members carry throughout the film.

John the Baptist's function was to prepare the hearts of men for the coming of the Christ, bringing gnosis; for Dani, celebrating his Feast Day at the summer solstice results in revelation: she comes *to know herself*, the Hermetic aphorism.[355] But her gnosis is a turn to the dark side, understanding she loves only death. In the *Hermetica, Corpus Hermeticum*,

---

353 Hilderic Friend, *Flowers and Flower Lore* (Troy, NY: Nims and Knight, 1889), 148.
354 Frazer, *Golden Bough*, 121.
355 *Hermetica, Corpus Hermeticum, Libellus* I, 1:125, "And let the man that has mind in him recognize that he is immortal, and that the cause of death is carnal desire. And he who recognized himself enters into the Good." *Hermetica* 1:129, "This is the Good; this is the consummation, for those who have got *gnosis*." See also Yates, *Giordano Bruno*, *supra* note 31.

Libellus IV, Hermes Trismegistus and Tat discuss the Baptizer as an agent of enlightenment: "He filled a great basin with mind, and sent it down to earth; and he appointed a herald, and bade him make proclamation to the hearts of men: 'Hearken, each human heart; dip yourself in this basin, if you can, recognizing for what purpose you have you have been made, and believing that you shall ascend to Him who sent the basin down.' Now those who gave heed to the proclamation, and dipped themselves in the bath of mind, these men got a share of *gnosis*; they received mind, and so became complete men."[356] A Neoplatonist would recognize John's role here as one incarnating as Hermes, the psychopomp purifying the soul, implying spagyric rebirth. But when Dani dips her heart in the Baptizer's basin, it turns black; she has a sinister epiphany, signified by her demonic grin at *Midsommar*'s climax, surrendering to the *Sol Niger*.

"This is place of the dead. We're all dead here." – Ygor (Bela Lugosi), *Son of Frankenstein* (1939). Apollo rides his chariot, pulled by four fiery horses, across a blue, cloudless sky. The group arrives, passing through a circular sun portal, entering the pastoral commune where Helios, the second sun, always shines. She has come from a place with two moons to land of the midnight and noonday suns.

Father Odd greets them, welcoming Dani home because, as Dorothy discovered, there is *no place like home*, foreshadowing her integration with the Hårga, making it her new family. Upon entering the commune, musicians are repeating an ascending scale in C major. However, the instrumental score that plays over the immolation is a loud sustained F# major chord, the furthest key from C. Known as the Devil's Interval (Latin: *Diabolus in musica*), the tritone demonstrates how everything can quickly change: life turns to death, and good turns to evil, during the solar jamboree.

They move to the sun-wheel stage, where Siv (Gunnel Fred), the Hårga's matriarch, opens the festival officially, welcoming the travelers to midsummer, commencing the nine-day feast. Siv recalls *The Dark Secret of Harvest Home*'s dowager, the widow Mary Fortune (Bette Davis, 1908-1989), Cornwall Coombe's herbalist and midwife. Dani, like Mark, Josh, and Christian, are *not in Kansas anymore*; instead, they are in Oz, only this magical land is deadly. Near to the stage is

---

356 *Hermetica*, ibid, *Libellus* IV, 1:151; *Hermetica*, 2:140-141 on *Libellus* IV as an allegory for baptism, transforming the personality of the votary.

a Maypole adorned with flowers and leaves, with the runes *Raidho* ᚱ and *Fehu* ᚠ hanging off the pole's crossbar; more on the Maypole and the occult runes later. Seated nearby, Ruben, the village's deformed prophet, produces illogical finger paintings in the commune's sacred book, becoming the second allusion to *The Shining*. The nonsensical smears are akin to Jack's monotonous "All work and no play makes Jack a dull boy" pages, denoting madness, implying the Hårga–like Jack–is homicidal. Torches are lit, a pagan custom adopted by the Christian Church when celebrating the Feast of the Baptizer.

In Swedish, Siv preaches, "Spirits! Back to the Dead!" indicating the festival is not only a celebration of life but a party for the dead, hinting at the cult's belief in reincarnation or the recycling of souls. She is not an evangelizing preacher; she is a pagan bullhorn. Enter the youthful, red-headed Maja; she rushes out of the bunkhouse, looking for a mate, as children dance and run about the field. Simon returns with drinks for himself and Connie; he asks Ingemar what the kids are playing. He answers, "Skin the Fool," foreshadowing Mark's fate: murdered and skinned, and his flesh stuffed with straw like a scarecrow. Simon then jokes, "Precious," which is an off-kilter, one-word response that doesn't seem to make sense. "Precious," evokes *The Silence of the Lambs*' Precious, the canine poodle companion of Jame "Buffalo Bill" Gumb. The transexual wannabe, like the commune, is an expert in removing the flesh from his victims, skinning them. Easter egg: the practice of skinning a fool comes from *The Wicker Man*, Robin Hardy's (1929-2016) pagan classic, which, like *Midsommar*, also emerges from *The Golden Bough*'s pages. When Sgt. Howie reads the book describing May Day celebrations, it mentions a gruesome rite in which the sacrificed child's skin was removed. The flesh was to be worn by the priest as a mantle, representing the goddess reborn, anticipating the removal of Mark's skin, worn by Ulf (Henrik Norlén) right before Josh's murder.

Maja dances around, kicking Christian in the side, trying to get his attention because she has chosen him as her mate. When Christian asks if he can join the dance, Pelle tells to "jam" himself in there, anticipating Christian fucking Maja later. For her birthday, Pelle gives Dani a portrait he drew of her featuring the runes *Raidho* ᚱ and *Dagaz* ᛞ that shadow Dani at the commune to be analyzed later. Dani tells Pelle that Christian has forgotten her birthday. As the group strolls around, Pelle speaks of rune magic, and of how hand-carved runes are to be placed under pillows at night, then to dream about their powers to produce supernatural effects. As the conversation continues, it becomes clear Ingemar desires Connie, claiming to have taken her on a date. Connie quickly corrects him, forcing Ingemar to admit they're just friends. Off in the distance, a brightly painted yellow pyramid stands erect between blue tarps. The building is a sacred temple; entering it is forbidden. Pyramids, resembling the shape of a flame, are consecrated to the sun and fire, making it the perfect edifice for the Hårga's to execute their fiery, blood sacrifices to the sun.[357]

As Pelle takes Dani, Mark, Josh, and Christian to the bunkhouse, Ingemar leads Connie and Simon to the *Rotvalta* (English: uprooted tree), the commune's sacred tree. The tree's symbolism, linked traditionally with wisdom and life, is a token of death in the community, the abode of the Hårga's deceased ancestors. Sitting nearby is a curious site: a bear in a cage, while Connie is drawn to a tapestry depicting a strange love story. From right to left, it features a maiden falling in love with a young man. To seduce him, she clips her pubic hairs, placing them in a meal, and then collects her menstrual fluid, putting it into a drink (a common Low Magic recipe), serving them to the young man, placing a love spell on him. The tapestry foreshadows Maja tainting Christian's meat tart with her pubic hairs, and putting her menses in his drink to hex him, casting a love spell of her own. The tapestry's final image shows the man and woman smitten, together in love; she is pregnant with his child. As the camera pans to the left, the cult's lottery machine sits nearby as an atypical contraption, anticipating the selection of Turbeyon (Mihály Kaszás); yet, in the end, Dani selects Christian to be the ninth sacrifice.

Decorating the bunkhouse's walls are colorful, primitive, medieval like paintings, depicting the cult's pagan rites, looking like a heathen Sistine Chapel, foreshadowing the events of *Midsommar*.[358] For example, there's a painting of the mating ritual, portending Maja and Christian's bizarre sex rite. Pelle explains to Josh that the Hårga considers existence like the seasons, counting the human life in multiples of nine. Years one through eighteen are spring, indicating childhood and youth. Summer is eighteen through thirty-six, that's when one goes on a pilgrimage. Years thirty-six

---

357 Pike, *Morals and Dogma*, 459-460.
358 Swedish artist Ragnar Persson painted the murals in the bunkhouse.

through fifty-four are fall, the working age. Lastly, one becomes a mentor in winter from fifty-four to seventy-two. After seventy-two, Pelle does a throat slash with his hand, foreshadowing ättestupa: precipices in Sweden for ritual senicide. The bunkhouse has no privacy; thus, Mark complains there is no place to jerk off, foreshadowing Maja's sorcery, simulating masturbation with a rune stone, attempting to hex Christian.

Dani strolls over to a wall decorated with photos of the May Queens, conjuring *The Wicker Man* when Sgt. Howie observed pictures of the Summerisle harvest adorning the walls of the Green Man Inn. Pelle scolds Christian for forgetting Dani's birthday. A woman announces the children are watching *Austin Powers* (1997), indicating the commune is not wholly cut off from the outside world. Christian apologizes to Dani about forgetting her birthday, presenting her with a slice of cake. Notice how he has trouble lighting the candles, insinuating the flame has gone out between them. A trifecta of Easter eggs: by Pelle's seasonal-life calculation, Dani's in midsummer, celebrating her birthday at a solar festival, making her a perfect candidate to be May Queen. In his twenties, Pelle has returned to the commune from his pilgrimage, bringing human sacrifices with him. When Christian apologizes to Dani for missing her birthday, a group of women stands behind them, swaying side to side like trees in a summer breeze. The woman in the center is rocking a baby, with others imitating the motion–more on this later.

As night descends, they tuck themselves into bed. A mural foreshadows the Maypole dance, while scissors are placed under a baby's pillow, inside the crib. Dani awakens during the night, looking at a painting of a cultist slicing his hand, offing blood to the sun. The purpose of scissors is explained the next day during the meal: the child's mother is on a pilgrimage, so to sever the child from the parent, clippers were placed under the baby's pillow to help it detach. The commune has a feast with the tables arranged in the *Othala* rune ᛟ. Joining the feast is an elderly couple, a man and woman, wearing blue pajama-like outfits, evoking Dani's parents, poisoned wearing blue pajamas. For Dani, death is everywhere because Terri's ghost never leaves her; winter's darkness has become bloodthirsty summer. As the feast continues, Maja carves a rune on a priapic stone, which she will use to simulate masturbation, placing it under Christian's bed (*vide supra*). The elderly man and woman rise, chanting; they are toasted because they

The painting of the mating ritual inside the bunkhouse foretells the sexual rite between Maja and Christian.

are to perform ättestupa. The fool, Mark, decides to take a nap, thereby missing all the action as the procession moves to a nearby cliff.

Atop a crag, two dead trees stand tall, honoring the two victims about to die, and those who have gone before. Their hands are sliced, shedding their blood to the sun; miraculously, the stone reflects sunlight like water. Nine hand-carved sections divide the stone; the woman smears her blood on the runes *Raidho* ᚱ and *Tiwaz* ↑, which associate with Dani and Christian– more on this later. One will notice older stones with blood smears from ättestupas past. In the ravine, Siv reads a blessing from a book, the *Rubi Radr*, the commune's holy scripture. The tome interests Josh, but Pelle tells him he will not be able to read it. Then, the older woman appears at the top of the precipice, making eye contact with Dani, leaping to her death, crashing down on a rock below. Simon and Connie freak out while Dani seems stunned at first but then appears to be hypnotized by the ritual, welcoming death, even aroused by it. Shocked by what he just saw, Simon blasts Ingemar, "Are you freaking blind! What the fuck!" not understanding how he can be nonchalant over what just happened. Ingemar tries to calm him but to no avail. Simon's hostile comments bode his grisly fate: the

Blood Eagle torture with his eyes plucked out, replaced with St. John's wort, ironically blinding him forever.

Next, the man jumps but, unlike the woman, does not die immediately. The onlookers imitate the man's moaning and suffering; his head is bashed in with a giant hammer, putting him out of his misery. When the second blow smashes his head apart, Dani's eyes are glued to the horrific spectacle, sighing pleasurably. When the third blow is delivered to the man's skull, Josh and Christian cringe in pain while Dani stands there like a pillar, radiating bliss. As Connie and Simon attempt to leave, Siv explains that what they just witnessed is a long-observed honorable custom, and part of the Hårga's paganism, viz. the recycling process. Ingemar offers an apology, explaining he should have warned them better. Speaking to Dani, Siv tells her, "It does no good dying, lashing back at the inevitable. It corrupts the spirit." Siv knows Dani worships death subconsciously, so she should recognize it and embrace her darkness. Two Easter eggs: by now, one will observe the cult imitates its other members, suggesting a hive mentality. One will also notice the Hårga employs a sharp inhale-exhale breathing exercise, as breath is necessary for life, it can be deadly. Terri relied on breathing to commit murder-suicide; thus, it designates the cult's lethality.

Returning to the community, Dani tells her boyfriend that she needs time alone. She walks away and starts crying, melting down. Christian confronts Josh in the bunkhouse about his thesis. Christian informs Josh crudely that he will rip him off by also writing his thesis on the Hårga. And why not? Christian personifies Christianity; by borrowing from Josh's dissertation on European sun-worshipping cults, Aster informs the audience the religion is a rip-off of pagan sun worship. In other words, Christian-as-Christianity steals from Josh's sun-worship thesis because Christianity *is* sun worship, pointedly Piscean Age solar adoration.

Based on the astronomical phenomenon, the Precession of the Equinoxes, the sun has dwelt in the constellation of Pisces for the last 2,150 years. The worship of the sun–for the previous 2000 years–has adopted the attributes of Pisces, incorporated into Christian worship surreptitiously. Thus, the Christian fish symbol derives from the Greek acronym for the phrase Jesus Christ, God's Son, Savior. In Greek, the phrase is Ἰησοῦς Χριστός, Θεοῦ Υἱός, Σωτήρ. When we take the first letter from each word in that phrase, we have ΙΧΘΥΣ, the Greek word for *fish*, *ixthus* or *icthus*—the spelling can vary in English. The Christian fish symbol either has the Greek letters inside or underneath the fish emblem. Before the Age of Pisces was the Age of Aries. The divine lamb had long been identified with the zodiacal sign Aries the Ram, which the sun enters at the vernal equinox, the time of the crucifixion. The Precession of the Equinoxes had, for some time, made the sun's zodiacal place in that season, Aries, i.e., Judaism, e.g., Abraham sacrifices a ram *qua* lamb as a burnt offering instead of his son Isaac to honor the sun. But the Age of Aries ended when the sun precessed into the constellation Pisces.[359] The sun has recently left Pisces and entered Aquarius; the Water Bearer's worship is deism and Luciferianism, coinciding with Judaism, Christianity, and Islam's decline.

Jesus embodies the sun in Pisces; at Matthew 14:17, the Son of God feeds his followers with two fish designating Pisces, while making his followers fishers of men. Here we should identify the solar dates on the calendar, which in the Christian cult are combined, causing the Piscean god to die and rise again at the spring equinox in the manner of Attis and Adonis and the other gods of vegetation. The diabolical Goat-God tempts Jesus, the sun god, at the beginning of his career in winter–Capricorn–when the sun is born at the winter solstice, December 25. Jesus rides two asses, the Northern Donkey–*Asellus Borealis*, and the Southern Donkey, *Asellus Australis*–at the height of his power yet the beginning of his summery decline (Cancer), mirroring *Midsommar*'s seasonal occultism.[360] On Fridays, Catholics eat fish (especially on Good Friday), not meat, adoring the sun in Pisces; fish consumption appears later in the movie. Christian-as-Christianity steals from Josh by copying his thesis; Josh, not Christian, is the expert on pagan sun worship and its festivals and rites, including midsummer. Observe when they argue; behind Josh are the colorful murals, but behind Christian is the blank, unpainted door. The colorful paintings identify Josh as original and authentic, suggesting Christian is merely an unpainted wall, an empty vessel, plagiarizing pagan solar cults, and their sun worship, making it his, a bastardized religion. Josh can do nothing about it other than complain and protest; in the end, they wind up collaborating because there's plenty of sun worship to go around.

---

359 John M. Robertson, *Pagan Christs: Studies in Comparative Hierology*, 2nd ed. (London: Watts & Co., 1911), 208.
360 Ibid, 323.

From Dani Ardor to Danny Torrance: the former's blanket in the bunkhouse (left) has a pattern imitating the Overlook Hotel's carpet (right).

Dani decides to leave, not understanding why she's there, but Pelle talks her out of it, knowing she is a kindred spirit. He explains that he was orphaned after losing his parents in a fire but never became lost or alone because the Hårga became his new family, embracing him. The commune doesn't bicker or argue about what is theirs and not theirs, telling her that's the world she lives in, and deserves a real family. As he holds her hand, Dani worries Christian may see them, drawing the wrong conclusion. Pelle says Christian is his friend, but asks Dani if she feels held back by him, and if he feels like home, hinting Christian *qua* Christianity is an oppressive fraud.

As the two ättestupas jumpers are cremated, Christian attempts to reconcile with Dani. She asks him if the ritual senicides shocked him. He says he was disturbed, but they should keep an open mind, be culturally sensitive, and acclimate, signifying Christianity's adoption and renaming of pagan solar customs. That night, in the bunkhouse, we have our third and final reference to *The Shining*. Dani's blanket features a pattern reminiscent of the Overlook's carpet, denoting the group's isolation; they are strangers in a strange land. Dani has a nightmare, reminding her that she and her sister are the same because they're obsessed with death; the two sisters derive pleasure from pain. Dani sees Josh, Christian, Mark, and Pelle sneak out of the bunkhouse–their beds are empty.

When she goes outside to see what's going on, they speed by her in a car. Mark sneers at her from the backseat, identifying Dani as a fifth wheel–they are glad to be rid of her. Once again, red and blue lights flash, resurrecting Terri's murder-suicide. The car emits a dense cloud of exhaust as Dani screams–the word she hollers seems to be "wait"–but her breath turns to exhaust, again, conjuring her sister's evil deed. The smashed head of the male ättestupa jumper appears, and then Dani observes her mother–in her blue nightgown–from Terri's perspective inside her bedroom, indicating she is one with her morbid sister. A mallet strikes the man's head, only this time, his face and head heal. Next, Dani's dead mother lies in bed, a victim of carbon monoxide poisoning. Finally, she dreams of the ravine; only the ättestupas victims have become Dani's mother and father. They lie on either side of the rock in the same postures as the elderly male and female leapers; again, bleak winter has become deathly summer. Their flesh is pale gray because they are dead. Leaning up against the rock between them is Terri, wearing her shirt and blue jeans with the yellow hose duct-taped in her mouth. Terri's body is a temple of death, representing the Hårga's yellow pyramid with her parents, in their blue pajamas, representing the blue tarps on either side of the pyramid. Suddenly, Terri eyes Dani, keen to see if her sister can surpass her fiendish murder-suicide; it is as though evil is trying to reach Dani's soul. Easter egg: yellow and blue evoke Aster's *Hereditary*, and, by design, Paimon: a Great King of Hell obedient to Lucifer; he is the *ninth* demon presented in the mid-17th century grimoire, *Ars Goetia*, or *The Lesser Key of Solomon*.[361] According to Agrippa, in rabbinic lore, Paimon identified with the demon Azazel.[362] In the treehouse *qua* cacodemonic temple, Charlie Graham (Milly Shapiro) keeps a blue box with a yellow lid in which she hides the severed heads of animals. Paimon's spirit inhabits Charlie; the demon collects decapitated heads as macabre offerings or trophies. The two hues, mingled with Paimon, the *ninth* devil, infuse *Midsommar* with *Hereditary*'s diabolism.

As everyone sleeps, Maja is wide awake, sitting in bed, unable to take her eyes off of Christian. With her phallic rune stone in hand, she simulates masturbation because there is no privacy. Upon the priapic stone, she has carved the *Wunjo* rune ᚹ. She sneaks over and places it under Christian's bed, hexing him. Buts Josh sees her and removes the stone. A bunkhouse mural foreshadows the Maypole dance as the ashes of the two ättestupas

---
[361] Belanger, *Names of the Damned*, 238.
[362] Ibid, 238-239.

jumpers are collected and deposited at the base of the *Rotvalta*. Josh asks Pelle if the elders will allow him to write about the Hårga's solar-fire midsummer festival. Pelle tells him they have consented, but he must omit the location and change the participants' names, keeping them anonymous. He must also share his dissertation with Christian. Josh then shows Pelle the runestone Maja placed under Christian's bed. Pelle says it is a love rune, and that a spell has been cast. Christian arrives, so Pelle tells him that Maja has taken a liking to him. Pelle explains Maja recently got the *byxmyndig*, allowing her to have sex.

Mark, the jester, urinates on the *Rotvalta*, unaware it's a holy object, linked to the commune's ancestral dead. Ulf becomes offended and enraged, cursing at Mark as Pelle tries to ease the escalating tension. But Ulf breaks down, crying because the sacred tree has been desecrated.

Meanwhile, Connie anxiously searches for Simon, who has vanished into thin air. As she storms to the bunkhouse, listen attentively: commingled with animal grunts in the background, one can hear Simon wailing in pain, suffering the Blood Eagle torture in the chicken coop. Connie tells Dani they are leaving, but Father Odd arrives expectedly, explaining Simon has left without her–gone to the train station–because there wasn't room enough in the truck for the two of them. Connie insists Simon wouldn't have just left without telling her. Odd explains the train leaves in ninety minutes, evoking, once again, the ninety-year duration between the Hårga's festival, and the ninety days the Virgin Mary stayed with Elizabeth, the mother of the Baptizer. He says it takes thirty-five minutes to get there and back, so they had to leave immediately. Odd insists the truck is returning, but Connie, skeptical, storms off, remarking, "This is bullshit."

As Christian speaks with Valentin (Anders Back) about the commune's customs–Christian *qua* Christianity is interested in coopting their beliefs, their sun worship–Dani informs him that Simon left without Connie. Feigning concern, he continues to converse with Valentin, asking him about the community's take on incest. Valentin explains the bloodlines are well preserved, and incest is frowned upon, so outsiders are brought into the commune to mate, foreshadowing the sexual ritual between Christian, the outsider, and Maja, the Hårga member. A female member invites Dani into the kitchen to make meat tarts. Maja has prepared a tart containing her pubic hairs to bewitch Christian further.

CINEMA SYMBOLISM 3

Meanwhile, commune elder Arne (Anders Beckman) explains the runic *Rubi Radr* to Josh, saying it is like emotional sheet music. A corner hides Ruben's tiny bed; behind the altar is a two-way mirror hidden by a curtain. Arne clarifies the runes, saying each stand for one of the sixteen affekts [*sic*], graded from holy to unholy. Arne states that *Raidho* rune ᚱ stands for grief, hence its association with Dani. This rune appears on Pelle's hand-drawn portrait of her, and she will wear it later when she dons one of the commune's tunics. *Raidho's* relation to Dani is obvious: she grieves over her family's death, searching for a new one. Arne says the holy book has blank pages because it is forever evolving and Ruben, the cult's inbred prophet, produces its current iteration (the selves house hundreds of them). He draws in the book–nonsensical finger paintings–and the elders interpret them. According to Arne, Ruben is unclouded by normal cognition, making him open to the *source*, viz. a supernatural current.

When Josh asks what happens when Ruben dies, wondering if the commune waits for another unclouded child. Arne says Ruben was inbred: all the Oracles are deliberate products of inbreeding, indicating an anti-immigration sentiment, referenced earlier. Within the commune, divine children are born of parents not only related but the same race. Easter egg: when Arne denies Josh's request to take a photograph of the *Rubi Radr*, a woman can be heard screaming in the distance. The screaming woman is Connie, who is being murdered by the Hårga. Three people hear her shriek; first by Josh, then by Dani making meat tarts, and finally by Mark near the yellow pyramid. Notice how Josh, Dani, and Mark react to the bloodcurdling scream, but none of the Hårga even notice it, carrying-on like nothing was wrong or out-of-place.

At supper, Dani asks if anyone has seen Connie. Mark replies he saw her earlier, trying out for the sprinting Olympics, insinuating she was running for her life. One of the commune members interjects, revealing Simon called the landline and calmed her down. She was then driven to the train station to meet him. Dani wonders why Simon would leave without her, to which Christian replies it must've been a miscommunication. Dani says she could see Christian doing that to her, leaving without telling her. Josh sits at the table ashen-faced, scared, visibly shaken–something is bothering him. Ulf and his posse glare at Mark, unable to forgive him for pissing on their ancestral tree; Marks wonders aloud if they will kill him. Christian's meat

(Top) In Dani's nightmare, she sees her mother, wearing a blue nightgown, and father in blue pajamas on either side of Terri, who is in the center. They are at the bottom of the cliff where the ättestupa victims landed, falling to their deaths. Terri wears a yellow shirt and blue pants (or jeans) with a yellow tube duct-taped to her mouth to breathe the car's exhaust, inhaling its deadly fumes. The gruesome image designates the Hårga's chamber of death–a bright yellow pyramid–surrounded by blue tarps. (Bottom) Standing before the solar monument, Mark hears a woman scream; startled, he turns around while none of the commune's members even flinch.

tart contains Maja's pubic hair, discovering the foreign object much to the horror of the others. The drink in Christian's glass is darker than the others because it has been tainted with Maja's menstrual fluid. Josh pulls out his notebook, opening it to a specific page. Featuring seven symbols, it reads:

Runic Combinations

Emotional Sheet Music

Affects

In the Rotvalta →

- Language is subjective?

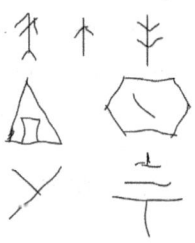

- Translation from stone?
- No empirical evidence of a shared language even person to person
- How does this work?
- Swedish is also used
- Inbreeding as a means of spiritual divination

Josh, epitomizing the scholar, has discovered that something sinister is afoot, becoming increasingly worried. A maiden approaches Mark, asking him to come with her, so he obliges, leaving with her. He is never seen alive again.

That night, Josh sneaks back into the Temple to photograph pages from the *Rubi Radr*, only this time the curtain is pulled back–someone guards the book. As he takes snapshots of Ruben's finger paintings, a person comes in, standing in the entrance. Josh notices his reflection in the glass, believing it to be Mark. But it is not him; instead, it is Ulf wearing Mark's skin; the fool has been skinned. As Josh turns around, Pelle lurks in the corner; he strikes Josh with a giant mallet, knocking him unconscious. At breakfast, it is announced the nineteenth (and current) *Rubi Radr* has gone missing from the Temple. Josh and Mark are absent, indicating they are the culprits. When questioned by two elders, Christian says it was likely Josh, motivated by his academic interests. Christian and Dani deny any involvement regarding the book's disappearance. As Pelle and Odd go off to look for Josh and Mark, Dani is told she will be going with the women to participate in the day's activity, while Siv wants to see Christian in her house.

Dani, dressed like the other maidens, wears a floral crown around her head. She is offered tea–a hallucinogen–before participating in the Maypole dance to determine who will become May Queen. As they stand around the Maypole, Dani looks down, seeing the grass growing through her feet; like her hand before, she integrates with the earth, becoming ensconced in the commune.

Irmi (Anki Larsson) explains the Maypole-dance legend: back in the day, the Black One–the Devil–lured the youths of the Hårga to the grass and seduced them into dancing. Once they started, they could not stop, and they danced themselves to death. Now, in life, they dance in defiance of the Black One until they collapse out of exhaustion. The last maiden left standing will be rewarded for her stamina. The tale comes from a genuine legend: Hårga, a real location in Northern Sweden, has long been associated with evil forces. Specifically, with a story about when the Devil, disguised as a fiddler, forced the town's inhabitants to dance to death.[363] The winner is crowned May Queen, a title traditionally reserved for May 1, or Beltane, not midsummer, commemorating springtime fertility and the arrival of warmer climes in the northern hemisphere.

The May Queen represents the archetypal maiden, the earth's fertility, purity, the goddess of spring, the vanquisher of the winter empress. Alfred, Lord Tennyson (1908-1892) popularized the ancient tradition with his 1855 poem "The May Queen." Crowning an annual May Queen became a part of Victorian culture, persisting in some places today.[364] The Maypole is a phallic symbol, usually made from a tree associated with fecundity such as the oak, birch, elm, or fir. The young women dance in circles around it; ergo, the pole and ring (*linga* and *yoni*) symbolize the dual generative principle of nature. As such, only Hårga maidens are permitted to dance, worshipping the priapic pole. The cavorting and paganism linked to the Maypole ensure the fertility of women, cattle, and crops.[365]

As Dani frolics, the effects of the hallucinogenic tea become pronounced when flowers start moving on the Maypole like they are breathing, alive. Toward the end of the competition, she speaks in Swedish, signifying her integration with the commune–they are becoming her family, welcoming her to the fold. In Siv's house, Christian sits before an image of a bear on fire, foreshadowing his immolation during the climax. Siv tells him he is a perfect astrological match for Maja; as such, he has been selected to mate with her. "Sounds probably right," she comments, confirming that Christian ate one of her pubic hairs. Christian joins the onlookers watching the Maypole dance as Maja is eliminated. The dancing stops temporarily when eight maidens remain, including Dani; eight is identified with kabalistic perfection, making them elite. Next, Christian drinks a hallucinogen that, according to commune beauty Ulla (Liv Mjönes), will lower his defenses, opening him to the influence, making him susceptible to Maja's love spell.

---

363 Elena Nicolaou, "How *Midsommar*'s May Queen Scene Connects To A Real Swedish Legend," *Refinery29*, July 3, 2019, https://www.refinery29.com/en-us/2019/07/236964/midsommar-real-may-queen-dance-harga-legend-devil-dark-one (accessed January 22, 2020).
364 Ibid.
365 Guiley, *Encyclopedia of Witches*, 227.

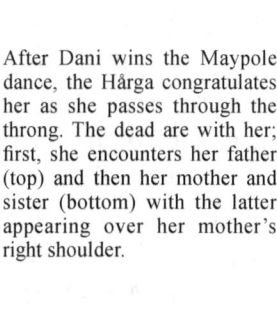

After Dani wins the Maypole dance, the Hårga congratulates her as she passes through the throng. The dead are with her; first, she encounters her father (top) and then her mother and sister (bottom) with the latter appearing over her mother's right shoulder.

Dani is the last celebrant standing, winning the dance, so she is crowned with a colorful chaplet, installing her as the May Queen. The pink flower in her garland breathes like it is alive–more on this in a moment. A group photo is taken to decorate the bunkhouse with the others. Christian *qua* Christianity looks on from a distance, establishing his status as an outsider. Death is with Dani; as her new family congratulates and welcomes her, she is also reminded of her old one. She passes her deceased father, mother, and sister dressed like they are members of the Hårga; notice Terri wears the *Perthro* rune ᛈ on her white tunic. Dani, startled, says, "Mom," and then Pelle plants a kiss on her, thrilled she won. Terri's ghost looks one as Dani mounts a pedestal, lifted high into the air, taken to a banquet table. Terri's dead face, complete with the hose protruding from her mouth, can be observed in the trees behind the procession. Terri is always with Dani because the two sisters worship death subconsciously, stimulated by pain and suffering.

A feast commences, with Dani seated at the head of the banquet table. Sitting on the table is disgusting meat; the slab appears human, naked with red hair, anticipating Maja and Christian's mating ritual. Easter egg: throughout, Dani hallucinates the plant life interacting with her, becoming one with her, foreshadowing her eventual decision to join the community. Additionally, her interaction-growth with plants gets more pronounced as the narrative progresses. Notable examples include the tuft of grass growing through her hand, the lawn consuming her feet, the vines on her throne reacting to the movement of her arms, the flowers in her crown breathing in sync with her, and the dress made entirely of flowers in the final scene, signaling her complete engulfment by the pagan community.

Christian joins the feast, but he is disoriented, not sure of himself. Everyone begins to eat when Dani is offered a herring for good luck. But she rejects it, spitting it out, rejecting Christian-as-Christianity in favor of solar paganism, a godless nirvana. Dani is toasted as the May Queen, officially welcoming her to the family as a sister. Maja leaves to prepare for the mating rite inside the Temple while Siv announces it is now time for the May Queen to bless the crops and livestock. Siv remarks that after the luck Dani inherited from the salt herring, she is doubly encouraged. But didn't Dani spit out the fish? Siv's ambiguity implies Dani has renounced Christianity, joined the cult willingly, becoming a heathen sun worshipper, a lover of death. Dani asks if Christian can accompany her, but Siv tells her the Queen must ride alone. Dani is handed a torch, a fiery token of the Feast Day of St. John the Baptist, the lord of summer. She gets in a carriage, riding off as Christian prepares to have sex with Maja. Holding a torch and a tree branch (presumably from a yew or fir), Dani blesses the commune with a votive offering of meat (animals), grain (crops), and eggs (livestock) to the earth. As Dani performs her pagan rites, so too does Christian complete a ferritization ritual, impregnating Maja.

Christian dons a tunic with the phallic *Tiwaz* rune ↑ and the *Yr* rune ↄ, inhaling incense for vitality. As Christian performs sex magick with Maja, the female ritualists sing and imitate her ecstasy, denoting the cult's hive mindset, producing egregores. Ruben, resting on his bed in the corner, observes the bizarre sex rite. Dani returns and, hearing the erotic noises coming from the Temple, investigates, looking through its keyhole, seeing a Dionysian ritual: Christian fucking Maja hard. Dani breaks down, crying, sobbing, and retching. She runs outs and vomits, taking sanctuary with the other maidens in the bunkhouse. They also mimic her cries of betrayal and anger, whimpering and wailing along with her. Inside the Temple, Christian and Maja climax as she joyously announces she can feel the baby.

Christian, distraught, runs outside naked, attempting to flee. First, he encounters the floral throne–the seat of the Hårga's potentate–carried to the solar stage, occupied by the May Queen, presiding over the sun cult. Next, he finds Josh's leg sticking out of the ground like a plant with the *Mannaz* rune ᛗ carved on his foot. Josh hides in the chicken coop, discovering Simon barely alive, hanging in the air before him. He is suffering the Blood Eagle torture; his eyes have been plucked out, replaced with St. John's wort, forever blinded for insulting Ingemar. Simon's lungs have been removed–making them look like wings–but he is still breathing. St. John the Evangelist's symbol is an eagle, whose feast day coincides with the winter solstice's celebration, Yuletide, Saturnalia, Christmas. *Midsommar* has come full circle, having started cloaked in darkness with a murder-suicide at the winter solstice, concluding at the summer solstice with nine human sacrifices under the blazing sun. An elder paralyzes Christian–rendered unconscious–via a toxic powder, blowing it in his face. Appearing pleased, Pelle peers through the door–his pilgrimage has been a success, bringing his friends to the Hårga as sacrifices to the sun.

At the solar stage, the cult gathers with a paralyzed Christian as Ruben sits on a mountain of wool, creating his doodles. The fleece looks like a cloud, making him appear angelic or divine. Siv announces nine human sacrifices must be offered to the sun; "As the Hårga takes, so Hårga also gives," she explains. The first four victims are outsiders, new bloods–Josh, Mark, Connie, and Simon–lured to the commune by Pelle and Ingemar. Pelle is praised for bringing victims, and the new May Queen, to their midst. Pelle is to be honored for his unclouded intuition because he recognized Dani's deep need for a family, finding it in the Hårga. The manner of the outsiders' deaths resembles the four elements. Connie's waterlogged, bloated body indicates she has been drowned, water; Josh was buried in the ground, earth; Mark was skinned and stuffed with straw to be burned, fire; and Simon suffered the Blood Eagle torture making him appear airborne, air. Earth (or solids), water (or liquids), air (or gas), and fire (the temperature which brings about the transformation of matter) have been conceived in the West from pre-Socratic onwards as the Cardinal Points of material existence, and, by a close parallel, also of spiritual life.[366] Fire, Air, Water, and Earth were but the visible garb, the symbols of the informing, invisible Souls or Spirits–the Cosmic gods to whom worship was offered by the ignorant and simple, respectful recognition by the wiser.[367] The four elements link the microcosm to the macrocosm, the Hårga to their treasured sun god above, demanding human sacrifices, satisfied by spilling blood. The sun, the light of Christ, shines its Luciferian radiance upon the Hårga as it did in the days of yore. Easter egg: after the sex ritual, Maja wears a red-flowered vest and red lipstick, indicating the finality of the *rubedo*, which, for her, is pregnancy.

The next four victims are cult members: effigies of the two ättestupa elders, and two volunteers: Ingemar and Ulf. Dani enthroned as the May Queen, costumed in flowers from head to toe, must choose the ninth and final victim: either Christian or a cult member, Turbeyon, selected by lottery. Nobody puts Baby (Jennifer Grey) in a corner, and Christian shouldn't have messed around with Maja. The May Queen decides to sacrifice Christian, cementing *Midsommar*'s status as a horrific breakup movie, a fairy tale with the unhappiest ending. Outside the shed, Ulf and Ingemar say their goodbyes to the women. Inside, still paralyzed, Christian is stuffed into a disemboweled bear–seen alive inside a cage earlier–and placed in the yellow pyramid alongside the other sacrifices. A photo is attached to Connie's corpse; it appears to be of Ingemar, hinting at his everlasting love for her, here and in the afterlife. Mark, his skin stuffed with straw, is wheelbarrowed into the pyramid. He wears the hat of a jester, identifying him as a fool, the horny imbecile. The fool's connection with lustful and life-creating vigor appears in his coxcomb, with its ass' ears, dangling bells, and his phallic slapstick.[368] The fool of the old mumming capers dances about obscenely, making grotesquely indecent advances to the spectators. In some of them, he is killed and revives again, making Mark another perfect sacrifice.[369] Stuffed inside Josh's mouth is his notebook, his research, adding insult to injury.

A masked elder delivers a harsh benediction to Christian-as-the bear: "Mighty and dreadful beast. With you, we purge our most unholy

---

366 Cirlot, *Dictionary*, 91.
367 Helena P. Blavatsky, *The Secret Doctrine* (1888; repr., New York: TarcherPerigee, 2016), 350.
368 Cavendish, *The Tarot*, 66.
369 Ibid.

(Left) His skin stuffed with straw like a scarecrow, a wheelbarrow carries Mark to be sacrificed to the sun, torched inside the pyramid. He wears the fool's hat, the jester, evoking the Punch costume worn by Sgt. Howie in *The Wicker Man* (right). Punch, synonymous with the fool, is short for Punchinello: a clown figure linked with death. The jester is a hunchback with a large nose, wearing black and white checkered clothing. Behind Howie-as-Punch is Nuada, the sun god worshipped by the inhabitants of the remote Hebridean island, the fictitious Summerisle. The fool and the clown, as Frazer points out, play the role of scapegoats in the ritual sacrifice of humans. Hence, Howie, like Mark, will be placed inside a wooden structure–a giant wicker man–to be immolated to the sun god; the fate of one fool is the destiny of another.

affekts [*sic*]. We banish you now to the deepest recesses, where you may reflect upon your wickedness." The bear is an attribute of the cruel man, signifying Christian's mistreatment of Dani, making him the epitome of callousness and, thus, a worthy sacrifice to the sun.[370] But by plagiarizing Josh's thesis on midsummer and its customs, Christian is also a copycat and thief, appropriating sun worship, renaming it Christianity as his forename implies. Ingemar and Ulf are offered sap (or extract) from a yew tree to feel no pain, accepting it orally; the yew associates with death and graveyards; hence, it invites the Grim Reaper, making their deaths quick and painless.[371]

Inside the pyramid, on its walls, is the *Gebo* rune X.

---

[370] Cirlot, *Dictionary*, 22. The bear carcass also alludes to 2006's *The Wicker Man*. In the remake, Nicolas Cage's character, Edward Malus, disguises himself in a bear suit, joining the woman's parade, heading to the human sacrifice/fertility rite.
[371] Cavendish, *Black Arts*, 114.

The sun's appeasement begins; the temple is set on fire, and, as it burns, Ulf screams in agony. Outside, the cult wails with him, naturally. The May Queen looks upon Christian, paralyzed inside the bear, predicted by the Bauer image over her bed earlier. As he burns, we think back to *The Wicker Man*'s Sgt. Howie, a Christian offered to the sun inside a giant wooden structure, mollifying Nuada so the island's apple crops will flourish. At first, Dani sobs in anguish and horror, but gradually begins to smile, pleased with the death and chaos she has wrought. Like Dorothy, the May Queen receives gnosis, coming to know herself. She understands there's *no place like home* because she is home, the Hårga is her new family. Dani accepts that she, like Terri, is a death dealer, worshipping icy Saturn, embracing melancholy, radiating misery. She has become dominant, no longer relying on Christian or the tenets of Christianity; instead, she has become an odious pagan, godless, at home to adore the sun by sacrificing humans to the glorious orb above, savoring evil and murder.

The Hårga, steeped in Norse mythology, employs Elder and Younger Futhark runes as magic. Odin was called the Lord of the Gallows or the God of the Hanged, depicted sitting under a gallows tree. Indeed, he is said to have been sacrificed to himself in the ordinary way, as we learn from the weird verses of the *Havamal* (13th century), in which the god describes how he acquitted his divine power by learning the magic runes:

> I know that I hung on the windy tree
> For nine whole nights,
> Wounded with the spear, dedicated to Odin,
> Myself to myself.[372]

The *Raidho* ᚱ and *Fehu* ᚠ appear in wreaths, hanging off the Maypole. *Raidho* expresses natural phenomena as the sun's daily path and the cycles of nature and humanity, inferring the cult's sun worship and belief in reincarnation.[373] An elder tells us this rune represents grief; thus, it appears on Dani's tunic and Pelle's sketch. *Raidho* is carved on the stone smeared with blood by ättestupa jumpers, suggesting they are sacrifices to the sun. *Raidho* represents the initiate's journey through the paths of the

---

372 Quoted in Frazer, *Golden Bough*, 351.
373 Edred Thorsson, *Futhark: A Handbook of Rune Magic* (1984; repr., York Beach, ME: Samuel Weiser, Inc., 1992), 28-29.

Nine Worlds of the Yggdrasill, conveying Dani's search for a new family, resulting in initiation into the pagan cult.[374] *Fehu* is wealth, prosperity, and power, signifying the mystery of creation and destruction. Often the authority of *Fehu* manifests in mythology as an otherworldly glow around grave mounds and hills, or even as a ring of fire, hence the Hårga place it on the Maypole, indicating their obsession with death.[375]

The *Dagaz* rune ᛞ appears on Dani's tunic and Pelle's portrait. *Dagaz* is the light of day, perceived at sunrise and sunset, dawn and twilight. It is the rune of total awakening; for Dani, it represents her Gnostic baptism, awakening as a morbid pagan, a sadistic worshipper of death. Her boyfriend, Christian, wears a tunic featuring the phallic *Tiwaz* ↑ and *Yr* ᛦ runes. *Tiwaz* denotes a war god; it is the mystery of spiritual discipline and faith according to divine law.[376] It is the religious instinct in the individual and society, implying Christian's duty to impregnate Maja. Along with *Raidho*, *Tiwaz* is carved on the stone, smeared with the ättestupa leapers' blood, indicating senicide is part of their faith, crucial to the recycling process. Also, on the bloodstone is *Gebo* X, bedecking the Temple walls and ceiling as the nine sacrifices are set ablaze. *Gebo* means *gift*; hence, the sacrifices are offerings to the sun. Upon Christian's tunic is the Younger Futhark rune, *Yr*, meaning *bow made of yew wood*. Bows were often fashioned from the hard, resilient yew wood, and because of the connection of the Bow God, Ullr, with the mystery of the yew. Ullr is the archaic death god, ruling Yuletide, the winter solstice; hence, Ulf and Ingemar are offered yew extract before their immolation, welcoming death with open arms (*vide supra*).[377]

Siv wears the *Ansuz* rune ᚠ because it represents magical ancestral power, one that has been handed down from generation to generation along genetic lines.[378] She is the commune's matriarch, allowed to read from the *Rubi Radr*, welcoming Dani as the new May Queen.

When the ättestupa sacrifices are honored during the meal, the feast tables are arranged as the *Othala* rune ᛟ. Later, *Othala* wreathes Christian inside the pyramid, formed by the hay bales, becoming kindling when its

---

374 Ibid.
375 Ibid, 21.
376 Ibid, 53-55.
377 Ibid, 45.
378 Ibid, 27.

set on fire. The mystery of *Othala* signifies homeland and is associated with Odin. The rune characterizes the clan's reclusiveness, defining its holy boundary, ancestral territory, defending against impious intruders. *Othala* represents the Hårga's pagan customs: the cult's need to sacrifice profane outsiders–Josh, Mark, Connie, and Simon–to the sun, drawing down the orb's dazzling, life-giving powers; *Quod Superius Macroprosopus, Quod Inferius Microprosopus.*

Upon her phallic stone, Maja carves the *Wunjo* rune ᚹ because it symbolizes joy, signaling her desire to have sex with Christian and bear his child.[379]

Cut into Josh's foot is the *Mannaz* rune ᛗ as it protrudes from the earth. *Mannaz* is the power of human intelligence, rationality, memory, and tradition, denoting Josh's supreme scholarship, his need to learn.[380] As an archetype, Josh embodies the Tarot's Hermit card; his sole motivation is to understand the cult's heritage and midsummer festivities.

After Dani wins the May Queen competition, she encounters the apparition of her dead sister, Terri. The ghost sports the *Perthro* rune ᛈ on her white tunic; *Perthro* is akin to karma, or fate, or even synchronicity, both positive and negative. *Perthro* implies Terri's destiny, to commit murder-suicide, putting Dani on the yellow brick road that ends with her May Queen coronation. The ideographic interpretation of *Perthro* is a dice cup, such as a device used for casting lots; thus, the rune appears on the lottery ball, selecting Turbeyon as the potential ninth sacrifice.

Finally, this section ends by going back to the beginning, analyzing Mu Pan's artwork, which opened the movie. The mural appears on-screen for about three to four seconds, depicting the approximately 80% of the narrative in five panels. It looks like medieval artwork, something found in a 13th-century library. The first panel presents the opening sequence. In the dead of night, the full moon–depicted as a human skull–presides over Terri's macabre deed. As it snows, Terri, Dani, and their parents are connected by a hose, a quasi-umbilical cord, representing Terri's murder-suicide by carbon monoxide poisoning. But death–the skeleton–severs the hose connected to Dani, removing her from the family. On either side of the moon is Huginn and Muninn–*thought* and *memory*–the two ravens of Odin, serving as his eyes and ears, bringing him worldwide news. The birds

---

379 Kari Tauring, *The Rune: A Human Journey* (Lulu.com, 2007), 28-29.
380 Thorsson, *Futhark*, 60.

Mu Pan's untitled mural opens *Midsommar*, foretelling the story. Starting on the left, moving to the right, the painting begins with the murder-suicide, then Dani and her friends arriving at the Hårga, ending with the Maypole dance.

symbolize Odin's intellectual-spiritual capabilities journeying outward as fittingly intelligent and curious birds, resonating with Odin's roles as a god of battle and death.

The next panel shows a townscape. In the foreground, Christian consoles Dani, mourning the death of her family. He hides one hand behind his back, designating confidence and power because she is dependent on him. Pelle sits in the tree above them, drawing in his notebook, plotting, and scheming.

The group strolls through the woods, walking upon St. John's wort. Pelle leads the crew as a pied piper, sending some of them to their deaths. Behind Pelle is Mark wearing the fool's cap, followed by Josh carrying a book stack, identifying him as the scholar. They arrive at the Hårga, passing through the solar gate. They are welcomed by the commune's members, offering them psychedelic drinks, representing pleasure, and skulls, signifying the cult's fascination with death. Some women are topless, signaling their willingness to mate with outsiders to produce children, new commune members. As above, so below: at the bottom is the bear, foreshadowing Christian's fate; above them is the May Queen's throne, heralding Dani's lofty destiny. The bunkhouse can be seen in the background with the two ättestupa sacrifices above it, although elderly when they leaped, the man and woman are now young, denoting the cult's belief in reincarnation. Alternatively, the jumpers appear to be Dani's mother and father from the first panel, a parallel drawn in the movie.

The far-right final panel features the bloodthirst sun shining above, approving the pagan festivities. Skeletons play instruments and cavort around the Maypole, identifying the Hårga as a Jonestown-like death cult. Dani is among the revelers as other commune members feast, celebrating June 24. The mural opens *Midsommar*; it ends with Frank Valli singing, "The Sun Ain't Gonna Shine (Anymore)" as the credits roll. The song's lyrics epitomize Aster's gloomy masterpiece: "♪ Loneliness is the cloak you wear / A deep shade of blue is always there / The sun ain't gonna shine anymore / The moon ain't gonna rise in the sky ♪." *Midsommar* is a visceral masterpiece, featuring moments of brutal violence set within an unsettling and often drug-induced stylistic haze of rural Sweden. It's the sort of film that can easily trigger anxiety due to the constant hum of threat, commingled with disturbing imagery, gore, and violence that only a Hollywood master–like Aster–can conjure.

Horror films do not depict dreams; instead, they are robust nightmares from our psyche, inspiring dark deeds, lauding the unthinkable, celebrating the macabre. We are drawn and repelled by them: they glorify the Jungian shadow, which is always a fascinating persona, for the shadow is mad and monstrous, having an insatiable bloodlust for death, destruction, murder, and chaos. Under these terrifying conditions, the movie theater becomes a claustrophobic coffin, negating its churchlike atmosphere. Scary movies are celluloid manifestations of the Left-Hand Path, cinematic black masses celebrating fear, sex, the occult, bloodshed, and terror. Evil has an undeniable lure; the more significant the Devil's power, perceived or imagined, the more interest in his works. The same holds for the horror genre: the scariest films are remembered as hellish masterpieces, becoming part of the social fabric.

Next, this book turns to an equally solemn subject: golem making, and Hollywood's interest in artificial creations. Next, *Blade Runner* (1982), and its sequel, *Blade Runner 2049* (2017), are analyzed.

CHAPTER V

GOLEM MAKING IN TINSELTOWN: BLADE RUNNER REVISITED AND BLADE RUNNER 2049

> Mere data makes a man. A and C and T and G. The alphabet of you.
> All from four symbols. I am only two: one and zero.
> Joi, *Blade Runner 2049*, 2017

> ♫ We can't go on together
> With suspicious minds
> And we can't build our dreams
> On suspicious minds ♫
> Elvis Presley, "Suspicious Minds," 1969

Initially, I had planned on analyzing *Blade Runner 2049* only in this chapter, but it only seemed right to discuss 1982's *Blade Runner*, a film I initially took on in *Cinema Symbolism*. This book gives me a chance to revisit *Blade Runner*, augment my initial analysis, and dissect its sequel. If one has already read *Cinema Symbolism*, some of this will look familiar; if not, this material will be brand new, so please enjoy this examination. After all, one can never receive too much enlightenment. But before we can get started on *Blade Runner*, we must first investigate the golem's history, a humanoid creation critical to *Blade Runner* and *Blade Runner 2049*'s mythology and appeal.

In his book, *Kabbalah* (1974), Gershom Scholem (1897-1982) explains the legend of the golem, writing:

> The *golem* is a creature, particularly a human being, made in an artificial way by virtue of a magic act, through the use of holy names. The idea that is possible to create living beings in this manner is widespread in the magic of many people. Especially well known are the idols and images to which ancients claimed to have given the power of

speech. Among the Greeks and the Arabs these activities are sometimes connected with astrological speculations related to the possibility of 'drawing the spirit of the stars' to lower beings. The development of the idea of the golem in Judaism, however, is remote from astrology; it is connected, rather, with the magical exegesis of the *Sefer Yezirah*, and with the ideas of the creative power of speech and of letters.[381]

Like the Egyptian priests of a bygone era, such an idea appealed to the Renaissance's adepts, mystics, and alchemists, like Agrippa, Bruno, Michael Maier (1568-1622), John Comenius (1592-1670), Boehme, John Dee, and Paracelsus. Under the rule of Emperor Rudolf II, Prague became a center for mystics, hungering to harmonize Neoplatonism, Cabala, Hermeticism, and magic; steeped in alchemy, they were the fathers of modern chemistry and medicine; believing in astrology, they created the new astronomy. They were all vying to become the new Hermes Trismegistus.

The concept of animation originates in Hermeticism, documented in the *Asclepius*. The Thrice-Greatest and Asclepius discuss creating statues filled with *sensus* and *spiritus*; it was one of the Egyptian sages' principal arts. It earned the *Hermetica* the criticism of idolatry, a rebuke aimed, years later, with puritan venom at motion pictures and their celluloid preserved stars.[382] In the Gnostic dialog, humans can become godlike, following the Almighty's example, harnessing energies, transforming crude matter into sacred, animated effigies, fashioning "gods in the likeness of their own aspect."[383] This wizardry draws down divine substance; charged, it becomes "living and conscious" and able to do "many mighty works": predict the future, inflict and cure disease, and dispense sorrow and joy "according to men's deserts."[384] According to occult tradition, Albertus Magnus (ca. 1200-1280) owned a living statue, a talking head of brass, but his best pupil, St. Thomas Aquinas, smashed it because it interrupted his studies. The Hermetic statue's first cousin is the kabalistic golem; both are artificial creations designed to do its maker's will.

The golem is the mummy's opposite, and so too are its progenitors. The practitioners of mummification empowered the corpse to enjoy the rhythms

---

381 Scholem, *Kabbalah*, 351.
382 Churton, *Beast in Berlin*, *supra* note 252.
383 *Hermetica*, *Asclepius* III, 1:339-341, *supra* note 216.
384 Ibid.

of time; the Renaissance sorcerers attuned to the *Asclepius*, the alchemical Emerald Tablet, and the *Zohar* converted theses wreaks of time into eternal concord. The Osirian wanted to persist in the world as it is, to become an inorganic vessel partaking of organic existence, to achieve physical immortality. The magus of the golem, and its counterpart, the homunculus (a miniature humanoid), yearned to change the world by fashioning an organic pattern of inorganic spirit, reaching spiritual mortality. Their motivation is the primary difference between the Egyptian mummy and the animated figures of the alchemists, the Kabbalists, and the disciples of Hermeticism: while the mummy is a result of a thwarted love of matter, the golem issues from an abiding chagrin over the material, trying to discover spiritual energy in matter, unstained and eager.[385]

Arguably, two of the most famous golems are Smurfette and Frankenstein's Monster. The sinister wizard Gargamel created Smurfette: a tiny humanoid blue-skinned creature, was forged out of a lump of clay by its maker to infiltrate the Smurf's perfected socialist-communist village, sowing discord and chaos, eventually destroying it. Ironically, Gargamel's plan backfires; because of the cabalistic-white alchemy of Papa Smurf and the Smurf village's positive vibe, Smurfette is welcomed into the collective, transformed into a genuine Smurf. She personifies the best qualities of the golem; her story has a happy ending. Gargamel tried to create anarchy but instead produces peace, order, love, and acceptance despite Smurfette being different.

An even darker irony pervades Mary Shelley's Gothic *Frankenstein*. In 1752, Benjamin Franklin, the Masonic Prometheus behind Shelley's novel, drew electric fire from the heavens, revealing the mystery of lightning and, perhaps, the spark of life. The protagonist, Victor Frankenstein, grows up studying Paracelsus and Agrippa's alchemical and occult philosophies, generating his monster according to the *Hermetica*'s schematics. He was schooled in the noble vision of the Anthropos, the idea that the adept might return to Eden–the cabalistic ideal–through an artificial being. Shaken by his mother's death, fear and desire consume him. He creates a golem–by stealing fire or lightning from the heavens, like Prometheus– in the hopes of fulfilling his selfish yearnings to vanquish death and of assuaging his childish terror of dying. This narcissistic motivation leads

---
[385] Wilson, *Melancholy Android*, 64.

Victor to recreate the primal sin, embodied by the Gnostic Demiurge and the Judeo-Christian Adam alike; that is, hubris, the lust to become God. Ironically, in wishing to transcend death, Frankenstein must spend his nights in graveyards digging up corpses. This paradox is the logic of vengeance: to become what one hates willingly. In attempting to defeat death and ugliness, Frankenstein bathes in rotting flesh, generating a horrific shape, a monster. Frankenstein's forbidden science designates his Romantic Satanism; in the novel, even his monster paraphrases the line "Evil, be thou my good," quoting Milton's Lucifer.[386]

Blinded by hatred and lust, Frankenstein cannot even see the creature's hideousness until he animates it; watching the monster's yellow eye open, he splits. The creature, abandoned, wanders the earth searching for its maker, only to be cruelly treated at every turn. When the monster discovers Frankenstein, it is so embittered by the world's injustice that it undertakes revenge, killing everyone close to its maker. What was meant to embody life without death turns out to be death without life. But this murderous golem is a perfect ironic double of Frankenstein's obsession: his yearning for a world devoid of the polarity between life and death, a material existence untroubled by transience, a plane of smooth endurance, is just a realm of death. Ostensibly bent on life, he is fascinated only with death. His murderous golem figures this affection for this stable state. Suffering Freudian melancholia, Frankenstein realizes the most horrific outcome of trying to annihilate matter with matter: the reduction of difference to the same, the wasteland. His golem is a condensation of the repressed fury of the fallen world. This mechanism unleashed turns everything in its path into a corpse, a cipher of his deadness. This monstrosity–famously portrayed by Boris Karloff in the 1931 James Whale Universal film–embodies the worst nightmares surrounding the golem: visions of telluric rage with a human face, of black mud swamping cities back into chaos.[387]

Antoine-Joseph Pernety (1716-1796), sporadic Benedictine and Frederick the Great's (1712-1786) librarian, wrote on the volatile process of generating life: "But whatsoever may have been this Matter, the first principle of things, it was created in shadows too thick for the human mind to see clearly. Only the Author of Nature knows it, and in vain would

---

386 Faxneld, *Satanic Feminism*, 149. "Evil thenceforth became my good."
387 Wilson, *Melancholy Android*, 87-88.

theologians and philosophers wish to determine what it was; yet, it is very probable that this dark abyss, this chaos, was an aqueous, or humid, matter, since it would be more easily rarefied and condensed, and consequently more suitable, because of these qualities, for the construction of the heaven and earth."[388] However, none must hope to behold the secret sun of this Royal Art while he remains in darkness regarding the fundamental principles of physical Hermeticism, or alchemy.[389]

Smurfette and Frankenstein's Monster aside, the most memorable cinematic golem is in Ridley Scott's 1982 masterpiece, *Blade Runner*. The film is keenly aware of the golem's psychology and cultural depths, represented by a Nexus-6 named Roy Batty: an animated, rebellious humanoid machine filled a Hermetic statue's *spiritus* and *sensus*, imbued with a soul.[390] In re-analyzing this film, this author watched (more than once) the Director' Cut Blu-ray edition.

Blade Runner Revisited

Set in a dystopian future Los Angeles in 2019, synthetic humans known as Replicants are bio-engineered by the powerful Tyrell Corporation to work on off-world colonies. When a fugitive group of Replicants–led by Roy Batty–escape back to Earth, burnt-out plain-clothed cop Rick Deckard (Harrison Ford) reluctantly agrees to hunt them down, retiring them.

Blade Runner underperformed in North American theaters and polarized critics; some praised its thematic complexity and visuals, while others were displeased with its slow pacing and unconventional plot. It later became an acclaimed cult film regarded as one of the all-time best science fiction movies. Beneath its sci-fi veneer, it's a Gnostic fable, with Batty as a Valentinian illuminator, demonstrating *nous*, higher reason, bringing Deckard to consciousness.

---

388 Antoine-Joseph Pernety. *Treatise on the Great Art: A System of Physics According to Hermetic Philosophy and Theory and Practice of the Magisterium*, ed. Edouard Blitz (Boston: Occult Publishing Company, 1898) 57.
389 Ibid, see the Preface, *passim*.
390 This runs contrary to the *Hermetica*, *Asclepius* III, 1:359, because humankind cannot make souls. Instead, they "invoked the souls of daemons, and implanted them in the statues by means of certain holy and sacred rites." However, Tyrell Corporation can manufacture souls because Batty has one, symbolized by the dove.

CINEMA SYMBOLISM 3

The movie's occult-kabalistic Paracelsus-like magus is Eldon Tyrell, an earthly deity of biomechanics manufacturing androids known as Replicants. A giant black pyramid headquarters Tyrell Corporation, resurrecting the Egyptian sorcerers and the Osirian priests of old. Its logo is the owl, Minerva's totem, the ultimate emblem of wisdom, identifying Tyrell as Luciferian. Not only does the company create life, but it bears enlightenment: its inventions are Trismegistus-like philosophers. But this is to be expected; the casting of Joe Turkel draws forth his performance in *The Shining* wherein he played Lloyd the Ghostly Bartender, a wily devil who seduces Jack Torrance with alcohol, changing the struggling writer into a homicidal demon.

Tyrell's objective is to rectify Eden's errors, of fallen matter, to erase stupidity, ignorance, decay, ugliness, and fear. To these ends, he painstakingly develops his latest golem, the Nexus-6, an android indiscernible from human beings. Though Tyrell crafts this golem to serve as a slave to humankind's needs, he nonetheless imbues his artifices with superhuman grace and intelligence. A Nexus-6, Roy Batty, is keenly aware of his slave status but is also conscious of his superiority over his creators. What motivates Batty? He wants to extend his life because the Nexus-6 models are only endowed with a mere four years. Tyrell, the occultist that he is, has studied mathematics and Pythagoras. In the Pythagorean Mysteries, the number four–the tetrad–signified the heavenly soul, denoting God the Maker.[391] When their four years are up, the Nexus-6s will expire, die, their souls will leave their humanmade bodies. Easter egg: Tyrell's baroque chamber was modeled on the Pope's bedroom in Rome's Sant'Agnese in Agone, designating his biomechanical-kabalistic-alchemical divinity.

Caught between Tyrell, a magus unhindered by fate; Rachael (Sean Young), an android love interest who dresses like she's in a '40s noir murder mystery; and Batty, a sharp-witted automaton who cannot enjoy freedom, is Rick Deckard. Deckard is an *average joe* standing in proxy for those in the movie audience trapped between determinism and liberation.[392] His name is a play on philosopher, mathematician, and scientist Rene Descartes, who argued humans are machines imbued with emotions and souls congruously, much like the Nexus-6s. Descartes was obsessed with automatons; in the

---

391 Hall, *Secret Teachings*, 217.
392 Ibid, 89.

17th century, he helped to inaugurate the idea of mechanism that countered the Hermetic holism behind the golem (or statues) and the homunculus. Put another way, there was no room for magic in Descartes' mechanical world; he saw mathematics as the only safe tool for objective inquiry. By doing so, he ensured the 18th-century Enlightenment would be based on analytical reasoning rather than the Hermetic and occult sciences that were pervasive during the Renaissance.[393]

Deckard *appears* to be a human being; he is a bounty hunter, a Blade Runner, tracking down the Replicants and the Nexus-6s, discerning between organism and machine. He administers a test, the Voight-Kampff, which exposes emotional deficiencies, thereby identifying the test-taker as either human or robot. The test focuses on the subject's eyes because the eyes are the window to the soul, which an android should lack. He exposes renegade Replicants and Nexus-6s and retires or kills them. In performing this task, Deckard exhibits mechanical behavior. His zombie-like character displays no emotions. His life is a predictable grind: his retires Replicants and drinks to dull his guilt; he kills another Replicant, and drinks a little more.

When he meets Tyrell's latest model, Rachael, a Betty Davis-Joan Crawford-like sophisticated Replicant, Deckard's ambiguous condition heightens. He meets her when he's hired to investigate Batty and his band rebellious Nexus-6s, visiting Tyrell Corporation to gather information. The Nexus-6s reflect exiled angels, wise Enochic-Luciferian demons, which explains why Batty quotes or rather misquotes, William Blake's *America a Prophecy* (1793) "Fiery the angels fell; deep thunder rolled around their shores; burning with the fires of Orc." In this context, the Replicants were exiled from earth to the off-world space colonies, but Batty's gang of Replicants hijacked a ship to sneak back to earth. In a sense, like Lucifer and the Fallen Angels, Batty and his group were *cast out* and *fell to earth* though not at the same time.

When Zhora (Joanna Cassidy) is shot and killed, her shoulder wounds appear like her wings have been clipped off. Regardless of the misquotation, Batty's meaning is clear: he views himself as an apostate angel, an eternal rebel against tyranny; he is a fallen Anthropos tainted by matter (*vide supra*). This chosen identity enjoys the virtues of both machine and human: as a human, he is a fallen angel, a demon; he is a declined Anthropos or *Adam*

---

[393] Marshall, *Magic Circle*, 240.

Kadmon, a heavenly being bereft of immortality, trapped in matter. He is sensitive to beauty as he is to ugliness. Although Batty can aesthetically enjoy the harmony of his condition, he can also suffer the horrors of life. As a machine, he is an unfallen angel, a sublime vessel of perfect sight; what the angel sees, it *sees*, with no doubts over the reality of the experience, or the validity of the concept. A being of effortless motion, when the angel acts, it acts, suffering no awkward hesitation over how or why it proceeds. When this angel descends into time and space, what does it become but a machine troubled by the gap between vision and action? But since the angel retains its super-human qualities, its acute perception, and decorous bearing, it does not suffer from self-consciousness. The angel's inhuman mechanisms empower it to benefit from self-awareness. Before the Fall of Eden, when innocent, the angel did not understand the value of its sight and motion. Now, after the Fall, experienced, the angel can appreciate its virtues; it can know, and more intensely enjoy its exquisite sensitivity, its brilliant gestures. Lapsed, the angel becomes more beautiful, more complex–a sleek machine with consciousness added, a human being that beholds the world as a god.[394] Such is the strange, paradoxical ways of Lucifer the Light Bearer.

At Tyrell's behest, Deckard administers the Voight-Kampff test to Rachael, to see if she can pass for human. Not aware she is a Replicant, she fails; Tyrell states he has begun implanting memories into his creations to strengthen their emotions, convincing them they are human. After failing the test, Rachael visits Deckard in his barren apartment. She sheds tears over her lost humanity, especially her memories, which are just Tyrell Corporation implants. Deckard is unable to sympathize; distraught and shaken, she leaves. Later in Deckard's apartment, Rachael asks him if he has taken the Voight-Kampff test, to which she receives no answer. Couple this with Deckard's collection of black and white photographs (Replicants have a penchant for old pictures since it provides a tie to a nonexistent past), raises the possibility that Deckard, though seemingly human, is an android, and Rachael, though mechanical, is human.

These possible reversals organize Deckard's relationship with Rachael. Deckard also falls into a deep sleep and dreams of a unicorn running through the mist. The unicorn's horn symbolizes the pineal gland, or third

---

394 Wilson, *Secret Cinema*, 80.

eye, the brain's spiritual cognition center. The Ancient Mysteries adopted the unicorn as a symbol of the initiate's illuminated spiritual nature, the horn with which it defends itself being the flaming sword of the religious doctrine against which nothing can prevail.[395] The mythical animal implies gnosis; that is, Deckard will receive enlightenment shortly. Furthermore, the unicorn's appearance into Deckard's bland consciousness suggests his memories might be artificial. Indeed, after Batty expires, Blade Runner Eduardo Gaff (Edward James Olmos) tells Deckard, "You've done a man's job, sir," insinuating that he's not human. At *Blade Runner*'s conclusion, Gaff also leaves an origami unicorn at Deckard's door, indicating the police know he's a Replicant, aware of Deckard's unusual dream. *Gaff* means *to reveal a plot or secret* suggesting he is discreetly disclosing a mystery: Deckard, like Rachael, is an android. Easter egg: There are a total of three origamis made by Gaff, all mocking Deckard. The first is a chicken, which he makes from paper while Deckard is trying to "chicken out" by not returning to duty to retire the renegade Nexus-6s. The second is a man with an erection, made from a paper match, while Deckard searches Leon's apartment. It implies Deckard gets off going through another man's (or a masculine Replicant's) things, mocking him. The third is a silver-foil unicorn, denoting that Gaff knows about Deckard's unicorn dream because it is an implant. Thus, we can conclude Gaff knows Deckard is a Replicant.

Next, Rachael and Deckard meet in a dire circumstance when Leon Kowalski (Brion James, 1945-1999), one of Batty's Nexus-6 accomplices, attacks the Blade Runner. Just as Leon is about to murder Deckard, Rachael steps in and kills the machine, saving the human's life. The man is reduced to a helpless cog in the hands of a machine; the mechanism exhibits courage and initiative. By now, Deckard and Rachael finally achieve sympathy mutually. However, Deckard's desire comes as lust, while Rachael's is love. Even though they engage in lovemaking, both remain troubled. Deckard still thinks he is an autonomous human even though he acts like a machine. Rachael continues to believe herself to be a Replicant despite displaying human traits. Rachael and Deckard are the exiled Adam and Eve. In *The Melancholy Android* (2006), Professor Eric Wilson explains:

---

395 Hall, *Secret Teachings*, 287.

Between freedom and fate, they lack clarity of vision and action. Deckard is confused over whether he is artifice or organ, over whether he kills machines or humans. These ambiguities cast doubt over how he should act toward Rachael and Roy. Rachael is a Replicant and woman. She is Deckard's victim and his lover. Caught in an epistemological and ethical crisis, Deckard and Rachael do not know what they see or how they act. The grace of the machine—clear sight and motor elegance—is clotted by the confusion of the organ. The nobility of the organ—moral vision and ethical fortitude—is flattened by the indifference of the machine. These are the splits of self-consciousness, results of the fall.

The film is a quest for the insight that Deckard and Rachael lack. The opening shot features a disembodied eye gazing on twenty-first-century Los Angeles. Reflected in this eye are flames bursting from the tops of buildings. The orb above yet within the fires of the world suggests harmony between detachment and attachment.[396]

The only character close to this ideal eye, this perfected eye of providence, is Roy Batty, himself a banished Luciferian angel. Wilson continues:

In his first appearance, Roy visits the factory where Replicants' eyes are made. Though Roy is visiting the factory in hopes of prolonging his four-year mechanical life, he is also passionate about vision. When he confronts an engineer, he says proudly, 'If only you could see what I've seen with your eyes.' This line emphasizes what makes Roy superior to Deckard and Rachael. Deckard and Rachael oscillate between immediate perceptions whose validity they doubt and mediated perceptions incapable of providing clarity. Roy embraces immediate visual experiences not as sites of faith or skepticism but as aesthetic events: harmonies of precept and concept, energy and form, instinct and intuition. Not troubled by the gap between unconscious apprehension and self-conscious comprehension or by doubts over whether objects are real, Roy values experiences insofar as they are beautiful or horrifying. This aesthetic perspective allows him to participate in the flux of experience without fearing determinism and to discern enduring patterns without suffering skepticism. This is the

---

[396] Wilson, *Melancholy Android*, 90.

difference between aesthetic experience and abstract knowledge. To gain the former, one must meld instincts and ideas; to try for the latter, one must sever pulses from geometrics. Roy would see in the rose fire flickering into multifoliate morphology. Deckard and Rachael would ask: are the petals machines or organs?

But Roy's balance mechanism and organicism–his ability to play, like the alchemical Mercurius, like Goethe's homunculus–does not erase the fact that he is the declined Anthropos, a heavenly being bereft of immortality. If Roy can aesthetically enjoy the harmony of his condition, he can also suffer, aesthetically, the horror of his life. Even though he is exuberant over his superiority to other humans and machines, he is also devastated over the limitations of mortal existence. He is as sensitive to ugliness as he is to beauty. His perceptions of vigor make him all the more aware of death. This is the dark side of perfect sight: he can see terror as clearly as joy. The tyrannies of the world shake him to the core. He becomes a crusader against the prisons of matter. He rebels against Tyrell, his oppressive creator. His quest is twofold: to find more life in hopes of overcoming his own mortality and to destroy the magus who fashions machines that serve as slaves and then die. Monstrously, he annihilates material obstacles that hinder his design. Miraculously, he transcends the forms that he destroys.[397]

Batty expresses this aesthetic in his culminating scene. He and Deckard have been battling ferociously throughout an old building. During the fight, Batty becomes the hunter and Deckard the hunted. Fleeing, Deckard reaches the rooftop in the pouring rain; the falling water denotes baptism, the ascent is the long climb up the winding stairs of Solomon's Temple to attain wisdom. Deckard's old life is about to end; now, he will be reborn into gnosis. When Deckard witnesses Batty reach the rooftop, he tries to escape by leaping to an adjoining building. Deckard falls short and ends up hanging on for dear life, his grip slipping away. Holding a white dove in his hand, symbolizing the annunciation, the virgin conception, Batty easily makes the jump. A nail pierces his hand, implying stigmata, Christ's wounds, designates Batty as a Valentinian messiah. He stands above the desperate Deckard and reminds him this state–hovering in

---
397 Ibid, 90-91.

limbo–is an extreme version of Deckard's existence so far: "Quite an experience to live in fear, isn't it? This is what it means to be a slave." To be detached from aesthetic participation is slavery, the opposite of life; full attachment to fear and desire–fear over unanswerable ontological and epistemological questions, desire to enjoy total certainty and security–is what it means to live.

After telling Deckard the limitations of his existence, Batty pulls him up to the roof, saving his life and renewing his spirit. Deckard plummets to ascend, dying to be reborn, becoming alive to newness, the aesthetic condition's vitality. Initiated into gnosis by Batty, baptized by the pouring rain, Deckard sits at his liberator's side, conscious that Replicants are living beings, blessed with souls, worthy of life and free from the bonds of slavery. The unicorn dream has come to pass. Batty takes a load off as well, leaving Deckard with one last piece of wisdom.[398] Easter egg: in a twist of Jungian synchronicity, Roy Batty shares a birthday, January 8, with two Rock 'n' Roll icons: Elvis Presley and David Bowie (1947-2016). By a sad coincidence, Bowie died on January 10, 2016–two days after Batty's inception date. Coincidentally, both Bowie & Presley are related to the sequel, *Blade Runner 2049*. Bowie was the original choice to play Niander Wallace (Jared Leto) before his death, and Presley performs holographically when K (Ryan Gosling) and Deckard battle in the casino.

Batty's valediction is an account of aesthetic experiences, memories of uniquely beautiful and horrifying moments: "I've seen things you people wouldn't believe. Attack ships on fire off the shoulder of Orion. I watched C-beams glitter in the dark near the Tannhauser Gate. All those moments will be lost in time, like tears in the rain. Time to die." These are numinous shimmers of the violent harmony into which the cosmos occasionally coheres. Such instances are ephemeral, but they nonetheless comprise portals to the eternal, the condition in which one is no longer troubled by time–the past as regret or nostalgia, the future as anticipation or dread. The foliate flames of dying ships, the scintillation of unexpected beams–these events seize the watcher, pulling him from the cares of the ego and opening him to the marvels unfettered by minutes and charts.[399]

---

[398] See Sullivan, *Cinema Symbolism*, Chapter XII; Wilson, ibid, 91.
[399] Wilson, ibid, 91-92.

As Batty expires, the clouds break, and the dove flies through the rift. The dove signifies the divine soul, the Spirit of God, descending upon Jesus at his baptism: "And Jesus, when he was baptized, went up straightway out of the water: and, lo, the heavens were opened unto him, and he saw the Spirit of God descending like a dove, and lighting upon him" (Matthew 3:16). The dove's release signals Batty's departing soul, free to ascend to Heaven, the plenitude. Enlightened, Deckard tells Gaff that he is finished retiring Replicants, weary of his old life. Gaff says, "It's too bad she won't live, but then again, who does?" Realizing he means Rachael, a Replicant on the run, Deckard returns to his apartment. He finds Rachael in his bed. She appears dead until he bends down to kiss her. She comes to life as if Deckard's affection has animating powers. He decides to save her–to become Batty returned, a liberator of androids. When he leads Rachael out of his apartment, he notices Gaff's small origami unicorn; Deckard holds it in his hand, pondering its riddle. Deckard seems to know that he's a Replicant, understanding his unicorn dream/memory was implanted. His knowing smile and decisive movement toward Rachael suggest he accepts this knowledge; for now, he can be Roy Batty, a marriage of human and machine.

Blade Runner 2049

Blade Runner 2049 is a 2017 American neo-noir science fiction film directed by Denis Villeneuve and written by Hampton Fancher and Michael Green. Harrison Ford and Edward James Olmos reprise their roles from the original film. The movie received five nominations at the 90th Academy Awards, winning Best Cinematography and Best Visual Effects. It received eight nominations at the 71st British Academy Film Awards, including Best Director, winning Best Cinematography and Best Special Visual Effects.

Just like the original, *Blade Runner 2049* begins with an eye, denoting attachment and detachment, organic versus synthetic; some things never change. It is now 2049, and the Replicants, described as *bioengineered humans*, are slaves. K (Gosling), a Replicant, works for the Los Angeles Police Department (LAPD) as a Blade Runner, an officer who hunts and retires rogue Replicants. He is a golem who tracks down, then kills other golems, indicating most Blade Runners, because they are machines, are proficient in hunting down other machines.

At a protein farm, he retires Sapper Morton (Dave Bautista), a Nexus-8, finding a box buried under a dead tree. The land is sterile; the greenhouses at Morton's farm bears the word *Tselina*, Russian for *virgin lands*. It references Nikita Khrushchev's (1894-1971) Virgin Lands campaign (*Osvoyeniye Tselina*) in the Soviet Union, where citizens were moved to undesirable and sparsely populated lands to start farms and grow food, denoting *Blade Runner 2049*'s dystopia: the need to synthesize sustenance. K returns to LAPD headquarters and is administered a post-traumatic baseline test, which analyzes instability. K must recite: "And blood-black nothingness began to spin / A system of cells interlinked within / Cells interlinked within cells interlinked / Within one stem. And dreadfully distinct/ Against the dark, a tall white fountain played." These lines are from *Lolita* author Vladimir Nabokov's *Pale Fire* (lines 703-707 of the poem), the novel Joi (Ana de Armas) volunteers to read to K later when he returns home. The poem then describes how "…the mind / Of any man is quick to recognize / Natural shams … The reed becomes a bird, the knobby twig / An inchworm…" Recognizing *natural shams* describes the Blade Runner's job, so the baseline is apropos.

The box contains the skeletal remains of a female Replicant who died during a cesarean section, demonstrating that Replicants can reproduce sexually, previously thought impossible. K's superior, Lt. Joshi (Robin Wright), is fearful this could lead to a war between humans and Replicants. She orders K to find and retire the Replicant child to hide the truth. In Japanese, *Joshi* means *boss* or *superior*.

K visits the Wallace Corporation, the successor-in-interest in the manufacturing of Replicants, taking over from the defunct Tyrell Corporation. Its headquarters hasn't changed: it is the dark, imposing pyramidal building from the original film. A Wallace Corp. staffer identifies the deceased female from DNA archives as Rachael, an experimental Replicant designed by Dr. Eldon Tyrell. K learns of Rachael's romantic ties with former Blade Runner, Rick Deckard. Wallace Corporation CEO Niander Wallace (Leto) wants to discover the secret to Replicant reproduction to expand interstellar colonization. His forename is a play on *Homo Neandertalensis*: a species or subspecies of archaic humans, living in Eurasia until about 40,000 years ago, becoming extinct because *Homo Sapiens* (modern humans) turned out to be more efficient, adaptable, and resilient. Thus, *Homo Neandertalis* became defunct, and *Homo Sapiens* prevailed, implying Niander–a human–belongs to a dying race. *Blade Runner 2049* suggests that humans, as *Homo Neandertalensis*, dwell alongside the Replicants *qua* neo-*Homo Sapiens*, who will, in time, outlast their human compeers.

Wallace refers to Replicants as *angels*. Why? It hints at the original film, wherein Roy Batty misquotes Blake, identifying his band of Nexus-6s as Enochic-Luciferian outlaws (*vide supra*). Wallace is also blind, mirroring his predecessor Tyrell whose eyes were put out by Batty. Wallace sends his Replicant enforcer Luv (Sylvia Hoeks) to steal Rachael's remains from LAPD headquarters and follow K to Rachael's child. Luv embodies duality: her name, while connoting bliss, is nothing more than an agent of death and destruction–more on this paradox later.

K visits Gaff (Olmos) at a retirement home, who says he knows nothing about Deckard's current whereabouts. When K asks why he believed Deckard was always going to disappear, Gaff replies, "It was something in his eyes," alluding to the theory that Deckard is a Replicant. Remember, the Voight-Kampff test used to identify Replicants focused intensely on the subject's eyes and pupil responses; also, the Replicant's pupils would occasionally glow. Gaff makes an origami sheep, referencing Dick's *Do Androids Dream of Electric Sheep* (1968), which served as the primary basis for both this film and its predecessor.

Back at Morton's farm, K observes the date 6-10-21 carved into the tree trunk and recognizes it from a childhood memory relating to a wooden toy horse. Because Replicants' memories are artificial, K's holographic AI girlfriend Joi believes this is evidence that K was born, not created. She names him Joe, an allusion to Franz Kafka's (1883-1924) novel, *The Trial* (1925). Kafka's narrative is about the persecution of an innocent man, Joseph K, by people and forces beyond his control, anticipating the pursuit of K by the LAPD and Wallace Industries, acting like a post-apocalyptic Illuminati. In the Bible, the Old Testament matriarch Rachael births Joseph only to be sold into slavery (K has memories of the slave-like orphanage) and later becomes Israel's savior, suggesting K is the miraculous offspring of Deckard and Rachael.

He searches the LAPD records, discovering twins born on that date with identical DNA aside from the sex chromosome, but only the boy is listed as alive. K tracks the child to an orphanage in ruined San Diego but discovers the records from that year are missing. K recognizes the orphanage from his memories, finding the toy horse where he remembers hiding it. Easter egg: Although this is debatable, there appears to be a rough spot on the top of the small wooden horse's head where it looks like a horn broke off, alluding to *Blade Runner*'s unicorn.

Dr. Ana Stelline (Carla Juri), a designer of Replicant memories, confirms the recollection from the orphanage is authentic, leading K to conclude he is Rachael's son. Ana Stelline is a play on *anastellin*: a human anti-angiogenic peptide. Anti-angiogenesis is a field of medicine concerned with the prevention of the formation of blood vessels. The area is studied by cancer doctors to stop blood-flow supplying malignant tumors; thus, her name encourages symbiosis between Replicants and humankind. Easter egg: Ana suffers from what is called Galatian Syndrome: a condition resulting in a compromised immune system, causing her to live in an isolated, sterile environment. The disease's name has a hidden meaning, referring to the Epistle to the Galatians (9th Book of the New Testament) by Paul the Apostle (ca. 5–ca. 64-67 CE), contextualizing the role of the law in light of the revelation of Christ. The Syndrome identifies Ana as a Christlike figure, an entity that can peacefully redeem and unite humankind and machine.

Back at LAPD headquarters, K fails the baseline test, marking him as a rogue Replicant; next, he lies to Joshi, telling her that he killed the Replicant child. Joshi gives K forty-eight hours to disappear. At Joi's request, K reluctantly transfers her to a mobile emitter, an emanator, so he can't be traced through her console memory-files. He has the toy horse analyzed, revealing traces of radiation that leads him to the ruins of Las Vegas.

Upon arriving, elements of the Voight-Kampff tests from the first film are reenacted: K walks through a desert, a scenario presented to Leon; then, a wasp lands on his hand, echoing a question posed to Rachael. It is here that he finds Deckard, living exiled in a casino. At first, the two fight while a holographic Elvis performs "Suspicious Minds," suggesting their mutual distrust. After a stalemate, Deckard reveals he's the father of Rachael's child and scrambled the birth records to protect the child's identity; Deckard left the child in the custody of the Replicant Freedom

Movement. Deckard, between the events of the first film and 2049, has become a disciple of Basilides' negative theology, a student of Pseudo-Dionysius the Areopagite and Meister Eckhart. He lives in exile, drinking heavily to erase his memories, divesting himself from all traces of the past, existing in a self-imposed ignorant limbo, much like Luke Skywalker in *The Last Jedi* (see Chapter IX). Willed stupidity and oblivion are Deckard's desert of the real.

After killing Joshi, Luv tracks K's LAPD vehicle to Deckard's hiding place in Las Vegas. She kidnaps Deckard, destroys Joi, and leaves K to die. But the Replicant Freedom Movement arrives, rescuing K. When their leader, Freysa (Hiam Abbass), tells him that she helped deliver Rachael's daughter, K understands he is not Rachael's child, deducing Stelline is her offspring; thus, the memory of the toy horse belongs to her, not to him. As they meet, Mariette (Mackenzie Davis) says the Replicants are "More human than humans." In the original film, when Tyrell meets Deckard, the former says, "More human than human," referring to Replicants, the motto of Tyrell Corporation. To prevent Deckard from leading Wallace to Stelline or the Freedom Movement, Freysa asks K to kill Deckard for the greater good of all Replicants. Easter egg: the child in the memory hiding the wooden horse has a full head of hair, indicating she is a little girl because all the boys have shaved heads.

Luv brings Deckard to Wallace's headquarters to meet Niander. He offers Deckard a clone of Rachael for revealing what he knows. Deckard refuses, so Luv kills the clone. As Luv is transporting Deckard to a ship to take him to an off-world interrogation, K intercepts and kills Luv but is severely wounded in the fight. K tells Deckard that he "drowned out there" to protect him from Wallace and the Replicant Freedom Movement. K takes Deckard to Stelline's office, where he gives him the toy horse. As K lies down motionless on the steps, looking up at the snowy sky, an emotional Deckard enters the building to meet his daughter for the first time. The falling snow recalls Batty's "Tears in the Rain" soliloquy, delivered right before he expires. Easter egg: Production Designer Dennis Gassner based Wallace's lair on one of the rooms in the Kiyomizu-dera, a Buddhist temple in Kyoto, Japan. The floor type used in the sanctuary is the *uguisubari* or the nightingale floor. The noise created by the flooring alerts a person to a possible intruder, becoming a reminder that although Niander is blind, he has acute hearing.

One of the esoteric gems is Wallace Corporation's jingle, which is the strings assigned to the character of Peter from *Peter and the Wolf*. Before a contextual analysis can occur, some background information on *Peter and the Wolf* seems in order.

Peter and the Wolf is a symphonic fairy tale for children written by Sergei Prokofiev (1891-1953) in 1936. The narrator tells the story, while the orchestra illustrates the performances. Prokofiev's most frequently presented piece is one of the most staged works in the entire classical repertoire. A corresponding instrument in the orchestra represents each character: the bird by a flute, the duck by an oboe, the cat by a clarinet playing staccato in a low register, the grandfather by a bassoon, the wolf by three horns, Peter by the string quartet, the hunters by the kettle drums and bass drum. Before an orchestral performance, it is desirable to show these instruments to the children and play the corresponding leitmotivs. Thereby, the children learn to distinguish the timbres during the performance.

Wallace Corporation uses Peter's strings only; as such, Niander identifies with Peter. If Niander is Peter, then *Peter and the Wolf*'s narrative, applied to *Blade Runner 2049*, follows this interpretation. Niander *qua* Peter pushes the bounds of Replicant technology by seeking the mysteries of android procreation, dangerously surpassing his godfather, Tyrell, a master chess player killed by his creation. Niander-as-Peter ventures into the unknown, i.e., going to the meadow alone, trying to breed humans with Replicants. In *Peter and the Rabbit*, the argument between the duck and bird about swimming and flying, acting according to their natures, mirrors philosophically what it means to be human, and what it means to a Replicant. These qualities are often blurred, juxtaposing while dovetailing concurrently. The wolf eventually comes out of the woods; Ana embodies the wolf, Deckard and Rachael's offspring, a creation capable of starting a war.

In *Peter and the Wolf*, hunters track the wolf trying to destroy it, just like Blade Runners chasing and retiring replicants. However, Niander, like Peter, wants to capture Ana *qua* the wolf, creating a race of human-Replicants to populate the earth, and eventually the universe. In a nutshell, *Peter and the Wolf* is a parable of humans mastering nature, mirroring Wallace mastery of android technology, hegemonizing Replicant procreation to satisfy his desire for total domination. Niander's use of Peter's strings, something that appears harmless on its surface, denotes the opposite: his egotistical desire to become master of the universe, to "storm Eden and retake her" to quote the biomechanical pioneer. Director Denis Villeneuve wanted David Bowie to play Niander Wallace, but the Starman passed away in January 2016. In May 1978, an album was released with Bowie narrating *Peter and the Wolf* over the symphony, prophetically anticipating the nexus between Bowie and Wallace Corporation's catchy jingle.

Love is one of the mythological images of the Great Secret and the Great Agent because it postulates an action and a passion simultaneously, a void and a plenitude, a shaft and a wound.[400] Love is one of the great instruments of magical power, but it is categorically forbidden to the magus, at least as an intoxication or passion.[401] Like Frankenstein's Monster and Smurfette, the golems of *Blade Runner* and *Blade Runner 2049* point to another story, one that runs counter to the dream of the sacred machine beyond loathing and longing. Such is the fable of the golem that wants to be human, that wants to be loved. Frankenstein's Monster, Smurfette, Batty, Pris, Rachael, K, and Joi (a humanoid AI, not a golem but golem-like) stir our compassion for this reason: they value the unkempt emotions of humanity more than do their creators. They seem to say: to be human, to fear and desire, is good, noble, heroic. For example, in *Blade Runner 2049*, K and Joi seem to love each other ("I love you" is her final words to him), so much so Joi assimilates to a prostitute so K can make love to her. Joi bequeaths a human name to K, Joe, not only as a term of endearment but as a token of her heartfelt affection.

But is it love? K, standing before a black-eyed soulless 3-D advertisement of Joi, the simulated ad calls K by the name she gave him earlier, *Joe*, like it was all part of the program. His face radiates disappointment, leaving K in epistemological limbo. By contrast, the unfeeling machine is evil and aberrant and monstrous. Despite being named *Luv*, Niander's enforcer is a mere killing machine, terminating everything–natural and inorganic–that stands in her way. Like the magus who controls her, love is forbidden, not allowed. Love separates the Replicants from other robots because the android who longs for humanity reveals the transcendent machine's

---

400 Levi, *Transcendental Magic*, 17.
401 Ibid, 75.

limitations. It suggests Eden's fall was joyful, that the dying organ is superior to the undead machine. The reversal in values emerges at the turn of the 19th century after scientists had–for almost two centuries–argued that the cosmos, including humans, is a machine already. Faced with the possibility of ubiquitous cogs, soft humans rebelled, raging with their rotting blood against the metal.[402]

---

402 Wilson, *Melancholy Android*, 92-93.

CHAPTER VI

THE MUMMY, THE GOLEM, AND THE AUTOMATON REIMAGINED: DR. CALIGARI'S SOMNAMBULIST

> What she and I have lived through is stranger still than what you have lived through---
> Francis, intertitle, *The Cabinet of Dr. Caligari*, 1920

> The state of somnambulism, whether natural or artificial, is then extremely dangerous, because in uniting the phenomena of the waking state and the state of slumber, it constitutes a sort of straddle between two worlds. The soul moves the springs of the particular life while bathing itself in the universal life, and experiences an inexpressible sense of well-being; it will then willingly let go the nervous branches which hold it suspended above the current. In ecstasies of every kind the situation is the same. If the will plunges into it with a passionate effort, or even abandons itself entirely to it, the subject may become insane or paralysed, or even die.
> Eliphas Levi, *The Key of the Mysteries*, Part III, "The Mysteries of Nature," 1861

> I must know everything
> I must penetrate his secrets –
> I must become CALIGARI!
> Dr. Caligari, intertitle, *The Cabinet of Dr. Caligari*, 1920

> There are spirits --- everywhere. They are all around us. They have driven me from hearth and home–from wife and child.
> Intertitle, *The Cabinet of Dr. Caligari*, 1920

CINEMA SYMBOLISM 3

he Cabinet of Dr. Caligari (German: *Das Cabinet des Dr. Caligari*) is a 1920 German silent horror film, directed by Robert Wiene (1873-1938) and written by Hans Janowitz (1890-1954) and Carl Mayer (1894-1944). The quintessential work of German Expressionist cinema tells the story of an insane hypnotist who uses a somnambulist to commit murders. *Caligari*'s visual is dark, twisted, and bizarre; radical and deliberate distortions in perspective, form, dimension, and scale create a chaotic and unhinged appearance. The actors' faces exhibit nothing but torment and anxiety. The sets are defined by sharp-pointed forms and oblique and curving lines, with narrow and spiraling streets, and structures and landscapes that lean and twist in unusual angles, giving the impression they could collapse at any given moment.

Set in Holstenwall, the phantasmagorical scenery is painted on canvas, as opposed to a constructed set. Shadows and streaks of light are applied directly onto the backdrop, further distorting the viewer's sense of perspective and three-dimensionality. Buildings are clustered and interconnected in cubist-like architecture, surrounded by dark and twisted back alleys. Holstenwall's overall bleak design, warped architecture, and crazed streetscapes are the aesthetics of a discombobulated nightmare, signifying Francis' unfortunate mental condition, revealed in the surprise ending. Everything is artificial and stylized; it looks like Marcel Duchamp's (1887-1968) *Nude Descending a Staircase, No. 2* (1912) brought to life.[403] The strange set design represents post-WWI Germany and Europe, the revelation that the old order of things upon which Germans and their European neighbors had depended for so long had changed drastically, heading toward collapse in the years leading toward WWII (1939-1945). *Caligari* is a paragon of this skewed perspective; it is a cinematic rendering of Germany's order and chaos in the 1920s, the louche Weimar Republic, which was a melting pot of Expressionism, Dadaism, eroticism, and surrealism.[404]

Since *Caligari* is known to a vast number of people who have never seen it, the narrative is worth recounting. As Francis (Friedrich Fehér, 1889-1950), sits on a bench in a garden with an elderly man who complains that spirits have driven him away from his family and home, a semiconscious

---

403 Skal, *Monster Show*, 40.
404 Ibid, 46-47.

CINEMA SYMBOLISM 3

Rejected by the Cubists as too Futurist, *Nude Descending a Staircase, No. 2* by Marcel Duchamp anticipates *Caligari*'s Expressionist set design.

woman dressed in white named Jane Olson (Lil Dagover, 1887-1980), passes by them. Francis explains she is his fiancée and that they have suffered a great ordeal. We are led to believe something horrible has happened to the young couple.

Most of the narrative is a flashback of Francis' tale, which takes place in Holstenwall, a shadowy village of twisted-surreal buildings and spiraling streets. Francis, and his friend Alan (Hans Heinz von Twardowski, 1898-1958), are good-naturedly competing for Jane's affection, planning to visit the town festival. Meanwhile, a mysterious man named Dr. Caligari seeks a permit from the rude town clerk to present a spectacle at the fair, featuring a somnambulist named Cesare. The clerk berates Dr. Caligari but ultimately approves the permit. That night, the clerk is found stabbed to death in his bed.

The next day, Francis and Alan visit Dr. Caligari's exhibit, where he opens a coffinlike box to reveal the sleeping Cesare. The cabinet/coffin implies Cesare is an animated corpse akin to a mummy; he is alive yet dead. Skeletal yet capable of considerable strength, he commingles life and death, much like Frankenstein's Monster. An unfeeling murderer and a martyr for love, Cesare combines indifference and passion, anticipating the Replicants of *Blade Runner*. As a robot, he is mechanical as a clock; he burns in his heart, his eyes, like the other actors, reveals all. From his spectral, stiff face, his orbs gaze into some unreachable unknown, trying to unlock the universe's mysteries.

Upon Dr. Caligari's orders, Cesare awakens so he can answers questions from the audience. It is a master-slave relationship: Cesare does the bidding of his diabolical keeper without question. Caligari states that Cesare knows the past and can see the future despite never waking. Over Francis' protests, Alan asks, "How long will I live?" To Alan's horror, Cesare answers, "Till the break of dawn." The prophecy comes true. Later that night, a figure breaks into Alan's home, stabbing him to death in his bed. A grief-stricken Francis investigates the murder with help from Jane and her father, Dr. Olsen (Rudolph Lettinger, 1865-1937), who obtains police authorization to investigate the somnambulist. The police apprehend a criminal in possession of a knife (Rudolf Klein-Rogge) who was caught attempting to murder an elderly woman. When Francis and Dr. Olson question the criminal, he confesses to trying to kill the woman, but denies any part in the two previous deaths; he was merely taking advantage of the situation to divert blame onto the other murderer.

At night, Francis spies on Dr. Caligari, observing what appears to be Cesare sleeping in his box. At the behest of Caligari, the real Cesare sneaks into Jane's house as she slumbers, seeking her death. He raises a knife to stab her but falls in love with her instead. He abducts her after a brief struggle, dragging her through the window onto the street. Chased by an angry mob, Cesare eventually drops Jane and flees; it will later be disclosed that he perished in a field.

Cesare is the antithesis of Karloff's mummy; he is not a machine but a reversed golem, a new entity. If the mummy is the corpse revived, then the somnambulist is a vital organ turned into a dead thing. If the golem is dumb matter transformed into a killer such as Frankenstein's Monster or transformed into cultivated warrior-philosophers like the Nexus-6s, then the somnambulist is a moral agent flattened into an unthinking villain. While the programmed automaton–*Metropolis*' Hel–is a machine mimicking the human being, the chronic sleepwalker is a man metamorphized into a mechanism. The somnambulist is a creature reimagined from the legends of the golem and mummy, Kabbala and the Osirian Mysteries, combining man's spirit with the automaton, and vice versa, human with the vitality of a machine. The somnambulist reflects the banality of the middle of life, habit, and apathy.[405] The noctambulist invariably forgets what he did while sleeping, and the train of thought leading to his somnambulistic actions.[406] Thus, to sound the somnambulist is to face the possibility that routine existence is mechanical, that autonomy is automatic.[407] The somnambulist does not travel to the place the magician or magnetizer sends it; instead, Caligari performs necromantic sorcery to control Cesare, moving the deathly sleepwalker from one place to another.[408]

Next, Francis confirms the captured criminal, having been locked away, could not be the attacker. Francis and the police investigate Dr. Caligari's sideshow, realizing the "Cesare" sleeping in the box is a dummy. Dr. Caligari escapes in the ensuing confusion. Francis follows Caligari, seeing him go through the entrance of an insane asylum.

Upon further investigation, Francis is shocked to learn Dr. Caligari is the asylum's director. Helped by the asylum's staff, Francis studies the director's records and diary as he sleeps. The master-slave relationship obscures an incongruity: Caligari's is awake, yet his criminal deeds are exposed while he sleeps, Cesare perpetually sleeps yet kills when he is conscious, making their association a paradox, an ontological mystery. Is Cesare beholden to Caligari, or does Caligari need Cesare, a being critical to his sinister methodology? The director's writings reveal his obsession with an 18th-century mystic named Caligari, who used a somnambulist named Cesare to commit murders in northern Italian towns. The director, attempting to understand the earlier Caligari, experiments on a somnambulist admitted to the asylum, becoming his own personal Cesare. The director screams, "I must become Caligari!" Francis and the doctors bring the police to Dr. Caligari's office, where they

---

405 Wilson, *Melancholy Android*, 126.
406 Horace G. Hutchinson, *Dreams and Their Meanings: With Many Accounts of Experiences Sent by Correspondents and Two Chapters Contributed Mainly from the Journals of the Psychical Research Society on Telepathic and Premonitory Dreams* (London: Longmans, Green, & Co., 1901), 12.
407 Wilson, *Melancholy Android*, 126.
408 Levi, *Transcendental Magic*, 67.

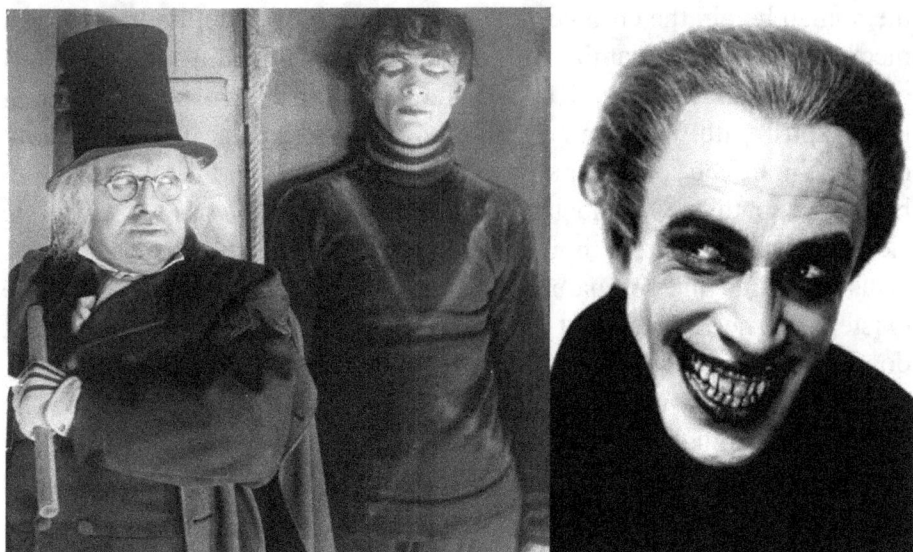

(Left) The villainous Dr. Caligari with his somnambulist, Cesare. (Right) Conrad Veidt, the actor portraying Cesare, would play Gwynplaine in *The Man Who Laughs* (1928). Gwynplaine's *risus sardonicus* inspired Bob Kane (1915-1998) when it came time to create Batman's archnemesis. Interestingly, Gwynplaine's father was betrayed by a jester. Enter Jungian synchronicity: the specter of *Caligari*, the untrustworthy narrator surprise-ending, surfaces in *Joker*, a film that leaves the audience wondering if the story they have just seen is real or imaginary.

show him Cesare's corpse, recovered in a field. Dr. Caligari then attacks one of the institution's staff; he is subdued, restrained in a straitjacket, placed in a cell, becoming an inmate in his asylum.

The story returns to the present as Francis, still narrating, concludes his tale. In a twist reveal, Francis is insane; he is an inmate in the asylum. Jane and Cesare are patients as well; Jane believes she is a queen, while Cesare is not a somnambulist but awake, docile, harmless. The man Francis considers to be "Dr. Caligari" is the asylum director. Francis attacks him but is restrained in a straitjacket, then placed in the same cell where Dr. Caligari was confined in Francis' story. The director announces he now understands Francis' delusion. As such, he is confident he can cure him. The film ends.

The insane asylum takes center stage in *Caligari*'s second half, foretelling Germany's failed Weimar Republic, mirroring the disillusionment and post-traumatic German conscience between the two World Wars. A mental hospital is a place in which boundaries collapse because nothing is as it seems. First, Caligari is a madman; then, he's the director of the asylum. Next, he's a lunatic masquerading as the director; later, the story is revealed to be a psychotic's fevered dream. At the time of release, Germany was in a heightened state of anxiety over its future and how the past would shape it. Caligari's insane asylum expresses while anticipating the doomed, decadent Republic. Weimar Berlin was a stomping ground for delusional ideas and weirdness, nurturing the OTO and the *Fraternitas Saturni's* sexual black magic, fostering political theories like fascism and communism, leading to crazy ideas about master races and Zionist conspiracies, the Third Reich's dogmatic philosophies.

The sadness of Cesare the somnambulist is not the golem's melancholy, either noble longing for spirit or nervous fixation on matter. The sleepwalker's moroseness is more subtle; what Henry David Thoreau (1817-1862) has called "quiet desperation." This somnambulistic sadness occurs when people unknowingly become the tools of their tools, cogs of the machines they have fashioned. Without even realizing their stale condition, humans relinquish freedom for fate, consciousness for unconsciousness. Or worse, they knowingly allow this to happen, intentionally plugging themselves into the machine, choosing ignorance over wisdom because ignorance is bliss. To unplug from the network is to die; as Morpheus explained to Neo in *The Matrix*: "…most of these people are not ready to be unplugged. And many of them are so inured, so hopelessly dependent on the system, that they will fight to protect it." They are nothing more than an ignorant "Brick in the wall," to quote Pink Floyd. They think they are Dr. Caligari in command of the situation when they are Cesare, a puppet dangling on a string.[409]

Cesare is the unlikely representation of the bifurcated subject, emerging in the wake of the romantic revolt against the 17th and 18th centuries' mechanistic visions. Caught between the great scientific successes of the post-Enlightenment world and the organic rebellions of the Romantic era, the somnambulist suggests the struggles between the machine's virtues and limitations and the sorrows and joy of the organ. An organism turned robotic machine, a machine pulsating like an organ; he is a sad exemplar of our postromantic existence. He is tacitly uneasy over the engines that secretly control his beloved organs and the organs that covertly move his

---

[409] Wilson, *Melancholy Android*, 126.

valued machine. Cesare, the somnambulist, is more than our sibling or familiar; instead, he is our parent.[410]

Caligari's somnambulistic roots come out of the Victorian Era, with the newfound romantic wonders of hypnotism and mesmerism. Cesare is not idyllic or wondrous; rather, he is a ghostly sleepwalker, a medium of spirit, as a soulless zombie, carried forward into the 20th century. During the Victorian period in England and America, many people valued mesmerism and hypnotism as an exploration of the human mind's powers, and as a valid mode of healing various ailments. For these supporters of the theory of animal magnetism, the somnambulist was a remarkable inflection of organic energy, a mere component, one with the whole. However, others thought mesmeric practices were instances of black magic, sinister efforts to control another's will. The critics of hypnosis saw the somnambulist as a helpless victim of evil manipulations; a mindless body serving tyrannical desires, just like Cesare obeying his dark master. It both mirrors and anticipates the Haitian boogieman depicted most famously in *White Zombie* (1932), wherein Murder Legendre (Bela Lugosi) is a Caligari-like *bokor*, controlling the sleepwalking undead. The shuffling spectacle of the living dead was, in many ways, a nightmare vision of the Depression-era (1929-1933) breadline.[411]

Understanding the somnambulist is critical to defining mummification, golem making, and automaton construction in the new millennium. Cryonics is the modern embalming, neo-mummification; that is, the freezing of dead bodies in the hopes of awakening them when scientists overcome disease and death. Hollywood prophesied cryonics: in *House of Frankenstein*, the Wolfman/Larry Talbot (Lon Chaney Jr.), and the Monster (Glenn Strange, 1899-1973) revive from suspended animation after having been frozen for years inside a glacier ice cave.[412] The new golem is the clone, the artificially concocted genetic double constrained to act out its genomes' scripts. The automaton thrives in cybernetics, in which scientists study the feedback loops of organs and machines alike, making no real distinction between humans and robots.[413] The mummy of Ancient

---

410 Ibid.
411 Skal, *Monster Show*, 168-169.
412 In the previous monster rally, *Frankenstein Meets the Wolfman* (1943), Talbot thaws the frozen Monster from the caverns beneath Frankenstein's castle, cryonically reviving him.
413 Wilson, *Melancholy Android*, 130-131.

Egypt illuminates our vexed technological attempts to extend mortality in the material vessels. The kabalistic golem sheds light on our troubled essays to transcend the temporal world in time-bound engines. The human-made automaton reveals our undying machines as manifestations of the death drive. Each of these figures shines it beams on our condition from afar, from a historical period before the Industrial Revolution. In the new millennium, the somnambulist brightens our troubled state from within, from our duration, the time of machines consuming the world. Dwelling in the center of our hearts, the sleepwalker is more than an analytical tool for studying our plight. It is a confusion, delirium, and a cry of pain: the pangs of cryonics, cloning, and cybernetics.[414]

The aesthetics of solemn blackness continues. From Holstenwall's distorted streets, we now venture to the crime-ridden world of Gotham City.

---

414 Ibid, 127.

CHAPTER VII

SABLE VISIONARIES: CHRISTOPHER NOLAN'S DARK KNIGHT TRILOGY AND TODD PHILLIPS' JOKER

Would you like to see my mask?
Dr. Jonathan Crane, *Batman Begins*, 2005

I used to think that my life was a tragedy,
but now I realize it's a fucking comedy.
Arthur Fleck, *Joker*, 2019

Don't burden yourself with the secrets of scary people.
Carmine Falcone, *Batman Begins*, 2005

Theatricality and deception are powerful agents.
Henri Ducard/Ra's al Ghul, *Batman Begins*, 2005

I believe whatever doesn't kill you simply makes you stranger.
The Joker, *The Dark Knight*, 2008

Speak of the Devil, and he shall appear.
Bane, *The Dark Knight Rises*, 2012

My mother warned me about getting into cars with strange men.
Catwoman, *The Dark Knight Rises*, 2012

How 'bout another joke, Murray?
What do you get when you cross a mentally ill loner with a society that abandons him and treats him like trash?
I'll tell you what you get! You get what you fucking deserve!
The Joker, *Joker*, 2019

I am the League of Shadows, and I'm here to fulfill Ra's al Ghul's destiny!
Bane, *The Dark Knight Rises*, 2012

CINEMA SYMBOLISM 3

In *Cinema Symbolism*, I discussed the Batman mythology. Like *Blade Runner*, I will now expand the analysis in the context of three of the greatest superhero movies ever made, Christopher Nolan's Dark Knight Trilogy. I will also dissect *Joker*, a film I added after this book's completion because it is thematically dark, evoking alchemy, making it rich in symbolism.

For the uninitiated: Batman is a superhero appearing in American comic books published by DC Comics. Batman is a pop culture icon, recognized around the world. Batman was created by artist Bob Kane (1915-1998) and writer Bill Finger (1914-1974), and first appeared in Detective Comics #27 in 1939. Originally named the Bat-Man, the character is also referred to by such epithets as the Caped Crusader, the Dark Knight, and the World's Greatest Detective. Batman is the secret identity of Bruce Wayne, a wealthy American playboy, philanthropist, and Wayne Enterprises' owner. After witnessing the murder of his parents Dr. Thomas and Martha Wayne as a child, he swore vengeance against criminals, an oath tempered by a sense of justice. Bruce trains himself physically and intellectually, crafting a bat-inspired persona to fight crime. Batman operates in the fictional Gotham City with assistance from various supporting characters, including his butler Alfred Pennyworth, Police Commissioner Jim Gordon, and vigilante allies such as Robin. Unlike most superheroes, Batman does not possess any superpowers; instead, he relies on his genius-level intellect, physical prowess, martial arts abilities, detective skills, science and technology, vast wealth, intimidation, and indomitable will. A large assortment of eccentric villains populates Batman's Rogues Gallery, including his archenemy, the Joker. As Batman's archetypal nemesis, the Joker embodies the Hanged Man card (XII) from the Tarot's Major Arcana, which is the arch-traitor, or the enemy.[415]

It is not my intent to rehash everything I wrote about Batman in *Cinema Symbolism*, but feel it necessary to briefly delve into the Caped Crusader's esoteric lore for those who have not read my second book, republished in 2017. The Batman mythos exemplifies the eidolon and the daemon; the former is the lower self, and the latter is the higher identity. The eidolon is the embodied self, the physical body, and ego-personality. The daemon is the spirit, the true self, which is each person's spiritual connection to God. The

---

415 Cavendish, *The Tarot*, 106-109.

ancient Mystery Schools and modern-day Freemasonry were designed to help initiates realize that one's eidolon is a false self and that one's true identity is the immortal daemon. The Gnostic sages of the past taught precisely the same arcane doctrine. Valentinus explained that a person receives gnosis from their guardian angel or daemon but that this angelic entity is the seeker's own higher self, or soul. In ancient Egypt, the daemon had, for millennia, been identified as the divine double of the eidolon. Mani was said to have been conscious of having a protecting angel from the age of four and, at aged twelve, to have realized it was his heavenly twin, whom he called the "most beautiful and largest mirror image of my own person."[416] The eidolon and daemon make their presence known in *The Fifth Element*, wherein Korben Dallas (Bruce Willis) has to shed his lower self as a cab driver and become a hero by escorting Leeloo, the Fifth Element, to the Egyptian temple to annihilate the Ultimate Evil. Korben becomes his inner daemon; the Pan-like Ruby Rhod (Chris Tucker) calls him "D-Man" for daemon, indicating his authentic self, his noble quest to save the earth. Bruce Wayne is the eidolon, while Batman personifies the daemon, the sublime, godlike persona. Bruce is a mere playboy, while Batman, his alter ego, is a crime-fighting vigilante, dispensing justice, and battling evil.

Applying Jungian psychology to Gotham's mythology, Batman is Bruce's shadow self, adopting the darkness to become an archetype. This archetype represents a person's dark side; it is not necessarily an evil one, but rather one hidden, concealed from both the world and oneself. Bruce Wayne confronts his darkness early in life; he chooses to harness it to instill fear in wrongdoers and combat evil. The Joker then would be the destructive shadow of the shadow, the opposite of the Batman, a living-breathing form of the alchemical *nigredo*: death and decay, the *massa confusa*.

Duality is vital in this epic. Bruce and Batman are two sides of the same person; when Bruce is Batman, he also becomes a wizard, a Hermes Trismegistus-like magus, gifted with *nous*, crafting gadgets, designing cars, boats, aircraft, and formulating strategies to defeat crime. This particularity is a departure from traditional mythology; for example, Hermes Trismegistus becomes Merlin the Magician counseling King Arthur, Morpheus guiding Neo, and Gandalf mentoring both Bilbo and

---

416 Timothy Freke and Peter Gandy, *The Jesus Mysteries: Was the "Original Jesus" a Pagan God?* (New York: Three Rivers Press, 2001), 101-102.

Frodo Baggins. Yet, Batman has no such tutor as Alfred Pennyworth is more a caretaker than an illuminator. Batman is the wisdom provider, the detective, the expert.

Outside Batman, the villain Two-Face embodies dualism, good and evil, his actions decided by the flip of his lucky coin. Two-Face personifies the god Janus, a double-faced deity epitomizing positive and negative, war and peace, the alpha and the omega. Batman's female opposite, Catwoman, is also dualistic: she is sexy Selina Kyle by day, wily cat burglar by night. She is the trickster archetype; she embodies elements associated with the demonic goddess Lilith, a sexy nocturnal seductress.

Batman is Americana, becoming a symbol for what the ordinary person can do in reality, using negative pivotal life experiences to do something positive. That is why he resonates with so many people. Bruce Wayne is a regular man who endured the pain of loss and used that as a drive to be something more and make something better—to become transcendent. Batman personifies the obsessive personality's hidden desires: to escape dependence of things, to transcend space and time, to dwell in a Gothic dream, to become an icon. Christopher Nolan's Dark Knight Trilogy typifies this mythology and unrelenting desire, mirrored darkly in Phillips' *Joker*.

Winged Fear: Batman Begins

After the disappointment of *Batman and Robin* (1998), Warner Brothers shelved the Batman franchise for seven years. Under the direction of Tim Burton and Joel Schumacher, it was clear Batman needed a vacation from the silver screen. The franchise was rebooted with Chris Nolan at the helm, with David S. Goyer serving a lead writer. Gone is the over-the-top campiness of Schumacher, and the Gothic architecture and brooding streetscapes of Burton. Instead, aiming for a darker and more realistic tone, this new vision's primary goal was to engage the audience's emotional investment in both the Batman and Bruce Wayne personas. The film, principally shot in the United Kingdom, Iceland, and Chicago, relied heavily on traditional stunts and miniature effects. Computer-generated imagery was used to minimal capacity compared to other action movies. Comic book storylines such as *The Man Who Falls* (1989), *The Dark Knight Returns* (1986), *Batman: Year One* (1987), *Dark Victory* (1999-2000), Alan Moore's *The*

Killing Joke (1988), *The Man Who Laughs* (2005), and *Batman: The Long Halloween* (1996-1997) served as inspiration for the entire trilogy. *Batman Begins* opened on June 15, 2005, in the United States and Canada in 3,858 theaters. It grossed over $48 million in its opening weekend in North America, eventually grossing over $374 million worldwide. It was nominated for the Academy Award for Best Cinematography and three BAFTA awards.

The opening sequence displays Batman's emblem emerging from a swarm of bats. Similar iconography would be used in all three films, having veiled meanings particular to each. Here, the bats denote terror, specifically, Bruce's fear of the winged creatures. Fear is the underlying theme of *Batman Begins*: how anxiety is used to manipulate, becoming a weapon, and how it is then turned on those that prey upon the fearful. As a child, Bruce Wayne (Gus Lewis) falls into a dry well and is attacked by a swarm of bats, subsequently developing chiroptophobia (fear of bats). The fall is a descent into the underworld, an archetypal nightmare, during which Bruce must not only confront his dread but master it.

Mentmore Towers in England serves as Wayne Manor; the estate, once owned by the Rothchilds, a family steeped in conspiracy, also appears in films such as *Brazil*, *Quills* (2000), *The Mummy Returns* (2001), and most infamously, Kubrick's *Eyes Wide Shut* only adding fuel to the Illuminati-runs-Hollywood conspiracy.

While watching an opera with his parents, Thomas (Linus Roache) and Martha (Sara Stewart), Bruce becomes frightened by performers masquerading as bats and asks to leave. The opera they are attending is Arrigo Boito's (1842-1918) *Mefistofele* (1868), and the performance reflects Bruce's descent into a chthonic pit, Hell, chiroptophobia, eventually become Batman, a feared vigilante. Outside, mugger Joe Chill (Richard Brake) murders Bruce's parents in front of him. Orphaned, the family butler, Alfred Pennyworth (Michael Caine), raises Bruce while Chill is imprisoned.

Fourteen years later, Chill is paroled in exchange for testifying against Gotham City mafia boss Carmine Falcone (Tom Wilkinson). Bruce (now Christian Bale) intends to murder Chill, but one of Falcone's assassins does so first. The scene is reminiscent of Jack Ruby (1911-1967) murdering Lee Harvey Oswald (1939-1963) in the Dallas Police Department's basement on November 24, 1963, indicating a criminal conspiracy at work, with Falcone pulling Gotham's strings. Criminality has infiltrated the Gotham Police Department: no one is to be trusted. Bruce's childhood friend, law school student Rachel Dawes (Katie Holmes), berates him for attempting to undermine the justice system, saying his father would be ashamed. Bruce confronts Falcone, who tells him real power comes from being feared. Bruce decides to travel the world to learn how to confront injustice, training himself in combat while gaining insight into the criminal mind.

While serving a prison sentence for theft in Bhutan, he meets Henri Ducard (Liam Neeson), a member of the League of Shadows, led by Ra's al Ghul (Ken Watanabe), whose name means the *Demon's Head*. Ra's asks what Bruce seeks; this is akin to a Masonic initiation, during which the candidate is asked a similar question. After completing rigorous combat training, mastering ninja methodology, confronting, and then purging his fears, Bruce learns the League intends to destroy Gotham. The secret society believes it to be corrupt, decadent, hypocritical, and beyond saving; they expect Bruce to lead them after his final test: taking a criminal's life. Bruce rejects both the League's cause and its edict that killing is necessary. The ruthless execution of the criminal echoes the philosophy of Friedrich Nietzsche's *ubermensch*: by gaining admission to the League, Bruce is now a superman, above the law, and is free to dispense justice, serving as judge, jury, and executioner. Bruce's idea that Gotham was redeemable mirrors the Book of Genesis in the Old Testament when Abraham pleaded with God to spare Sodom and Gomorrah, with Bruce arguing that Gotham is worth saving. The idea of saving Gotham–a morally bankrupt metropolis–plays out as the story unfolds. Bruce burns down their temple during his escape. Falling debris kills Ra's, while Bruce saves the unconscious Ducard from falling off a cliff.

Bruce returns to Gotham intent on fighting crime. He takes an interest in his family's company, Wayne Enterprises, which is going public by the unscrupulous Richard Earle, portrayed by Rutger Hauer. His casting recalls his performance as Roy Batty from *Blade Runner*, intended to conjure the neo-noir vibe of Scott's film, its seedy streets, dystopian blackness, and imposing monolithic buildings.[417] *Blade Runner*'s urban nightmare is

---

[417] Mark Hughes, "Exclusive: Christopher Nolan Talks '*Batman Begins*' 10th Anniversary," *Forbes*, July 30, 2015, https://www.forbes.com/sites/markhughes/2015/07/30/

transferred expertly to Gotham via the casting of Hauer. Company archivist Lucius Fox (Morgan Freeman), a friend of Bruce's father and subsequently deposed by Earle, allows Bruce access to prototype defense technologies, including a protective bodysuit and a heavily armored car, the Tumbler. Bruce publicly poses as a shallow playboy to allay suspicion, while setting up a base in the caves beneath Wayne Manor and taking up the vigilante identity of Batman.

Bruce has overcome his fear of bats, adopting the nocturnal creature as his symbol. Here we get to see Bruce as his inner Hermes Trismegistus, his inner daemon, shedding his eidolon by improving and modifying his gadgets and crime-fighting equipment, much of which is based on real-life military equipment. He is a detective first and foremost; Batman will become a legendary symbol, incorruptible and terrifying, something Bruce can never achieve. We learn the soon-to-be Batcave used to be part of the Underground Railroad, secretly transporting freed slaves to the north, seemingly the impetus for Thomas Wayne to construct Gotham's light rail, a benefit to Gotham's less fortunate. We are also introduced to Detective Arnold Flass (Mark Boone Junior), a reference to the comic, *Batman Year One*, by Frank Miller. In the comic, Flass, a dishonest cop, partners with James Gordon. The movie further follows the comic storyline by showing Gordon refusing to snitch on the corrupt police officers.

Batman intercepts a drug shipment, provides Rachel (now the city's assistant district attorney) with evidence against Falcone, and inspires and enlists Sergeant James Gordon (Gary Oldman), one of the few honest cops left in Gotham, to arrest him. In prison, Falcone meets Dr. Jonathan Crane (Cillian Murphy), a corrupt psychologist whom he has helped smuggle drugs into Gotham, and threatens to reveal his complicity if Crane does not declare him mentally unfit for trial. Crane puts on a scarecrow mask and sprays Falcone with a fear-inducing hallucinogen driving him insane, causing Falcone to mumble *scarecrow*; thus, he is transferred to Arkham Asylum. Here, we get a nod to Jung and the archetypes as Crane explains that Falcone has transferred his fear onto a frightening, subconscious universal symbol: a scarecrow. The asylum pays homage to H.P. Lovecraft because Arkham is critical to Lovecraftian horror; it is a dark city integral

---

exclusive-christopher-nolan-talks-batman-begins-10th-anniversary/#57a938da8b53 (accessed March 17, 2019).

to the Cthulhu mythos, and home to Miskatonic University, a school where students study and practice the occult sciences and the dark arts. In Gotham, Arkham imprisons Batman's Rogues Gallery, making it an abode of evil and insanity, themes permeating Lovecraft's fiction.

While investigating the Scarecrow (Murphy), Batman is exposed to the hallucinogen and left incapacitated. Alfred saves Batman, delivering an antidote developed by Fox. When Rachel accuses Crane of corruption, he reveals he has been pouring his fear-inducing drug into Gotham's water supply. The Scarecrow has taken a cue from Conan Doyle's "The Adventure of the Devil's Foot" (1910), wherein *Radix pedis diaboli* (English: Devil's foot-root), a deadly powder, is administered via combustion with horrific effects. Sherlock Holmes, like the Caped Crusader, discovers that the toxin–once inhaled–stimulates the brain centers controlling fear, resulting in madness or death, Crane's specialty.

The Scarecrow drugs Rachel with it, but Batman subdues and interrogates Crane, who claims to work for Ra's al Ghul. Batman evades the police to get Rachel to safety, administers her the antidote, and gives her a vial of it for Gordon and another for mass production. Ducard reappears at Bruce's birthday party and reveals himself to be the real Ra's al Ghul. By claiming to be immortal and supernatural, he is referencing the Lazarus Pit; appearing in Batman comic books, it is a natural phenomenon that possesses therapeutic properties that can instantly heal injuries and even grant immortality. Easter egg: Scarecrow and Batman's first encounter mirrors the episode "Nothing to Fear" (1992) from *Batman: The Animated Series* (1992-1995). In the show, Batman tries to foil Scarecrow's arson attempt, failing while being drugged by the villain's fear toxin.

Ra's, a Fu Manchu-like *éminence grise*, gives a conspiratorial history lesson, revealing the League of Shadows was responsible for fall of Rome, the Dark Ages, the Black Death, and the Great Fire of London insinuating they are the Illuminati or, at least, Illuminati-like: hidden global elites, manipulating the world from behind the curtain. Once again, Bruce pleads with Ra's not to destroy Gotham, mirroring Abraham pleading with God not to destroy Sodom and Gomorrah, giving the dialog an apocalyptic feel. Ra's al Ghul also affirms that he caused economic depression in Gotham years earlier, precipitating the rise in crime, implying he is responsible for the murder of Thomas and Martha Wayne. Having stolen a powerful microwave emitter from Wayne Enterprises, the Demon's Head plans to vaporize Gotham's water supply, rendering Crane *qua* Scarecrow's drug airborne, like *Radix pedis diaboli*, causing mass hysteria that will destroy the city. He sets Wayne Manor ablaze and leaves Bruce for dead, but Alfred rescues him.

Ra's al Ghul loads the microwave emitter onto Gotham's monorail system, intending to release the drug as the train travels toward the city's central water source. In the Narrows, Batman rescues Rachel from a drugged mob and indirectly reveals his identity to her. He pursues Ra's al Ghul onto the monorail and fights him as Gordon uses the Tumbler's cannons to destroy a section of the track. Ra's tells Bruce, "Don't be afraid," which were Thomas Wayne's final words to young Bruce, indicating the circle is complete. He has conquered his fears, while simultaneously becoming something fearful to criminals: Batman. Bruce allows his father's train to be destroyed while avenging him at the same time. Batman refuses to kill Ra's but also chooses not to save him, gliding from the train and leaving him aboard as it crashes and explodes, killing him. Bruce gains Rachel's respect but loses her love, as she decides she cannot be with him while he is Batman. The World's Greatest Detective becomes a public hero, while Bruce reveals he has secretly purchased a controlling stake in Wayne Enterprises, firing Earle and replacing him with Fox. Gordon is promoted to Lieutenant of the Gotham City Police Department, shows Batman the Bat-Signal, and mentions a criminal who left behind a Joker playing card at a crime scene. Batman promises to investigate, and disappears into the night. Easter egg: The joker playing card is bagged with an evidence label, identifying J. Kerr as the officer who collected the evidence, which is one of the Joker's favorite aliases, Joe Kerr, or *Jo-ker*, in the comic books. Easter egg: the Joker card tallies with the Tarot's Fool, a trump that can signify madness, auguring the Joker's diabolical insanity.

Batman Begins' theme is fear. It is about how anxiety is used and turned on those who use it. Bruce must overcome his fear of bats to become Batman, a symbol of dread. Falcone uses terror to control the public, and Scarecrow has weaponized fear, making his victim's worst nightmares come alive. What separates them is their motives: Batman uses fear altruistically while Scarecrow and Falcone are motivated by greed. Paradoxically, Bruce finds the blue flower, granting him admission to the League of Shadows; however, it is from the same flower that Scarecrow develops his fear toxin.

Falcone lectures about fear, how he uses it, only to wind up a patient in Arkham, exposed to Crane's fear toxin. Batman confronts Crane and gives him a dose of his own medicine, paralyzing him with fear. Batman also weaponizes fear, summoning a swarm of bats to terrorize the Gotham Police Department. Ra's al Ghul intends to use Scarecrow's toxin to poison Gotham's citizens, so their fright will tear the city apart. Near to the end, as he rides a horse like one of the Four Horsemen of the Apocalypse, Scarecrow paraphrases Freemason Franklin D. Roosevelt (1882-1945), "There is nothing to fear but fear itself," denoting the film's anxiety, its somber psychological qualities.

Exploding Fire: The Dark Knight

The sequel to *Batman Begins*, *The Dark Knight*, was released on July 18, 2008, in the United States, and on July 25, 2008, in the United Kingdom. Film critics consider it one of the best films of the decade and one of the best superhero films of all time. It received positive reviews for its action, score, screenplay, performances (especially Heath Ledger's Joker), visual effects, and direction, setting numerous records during its theatrical run. *The Dark Knight* appeared on many critics' top ten lists, more than any other film of 2008 except for *WALL-E*, and even more named it the best movie released that year. With over $1 billion in revenue worldwide, it became the blockbuster of 2008 and is the 37th highest-grossing film of all time, unadjusted for inflation (4th at the time of release). It also set the record for the highest-earning domestic opening with $158 million, a record it held for three years. It received eight Academy Award nominations; it won the Oscar for Best Sound Editing, and Ledger (1979-2008) was posthumously awarded Best Supporting Actor. In 2016, it was voted 33rd among 100 films considered the best of the 21st century by 117 film critics worldwide. Nolan's film is ripe with esoteric concepts and imagery. According to Nolan, this movie's central theme is escalation, personified by the Joker, whose emergence comes from Batman's pressure on the Mob, and the tension builds from there.

The Batman logo emerges from exploding bluish-purple flames heralding the Joker's diabolical trial by fire: the demented clown will test Batman and Gotham with the incendiary flames of chaotic madness. The

CINEMA SYMBOLISM 3

Joker uses grenades to incapacitate the hostages during the bank robbery, employs fire and explosives to kill Rachel Dawes (now Maggie Gyllenhaal), and scar and disfigure Harvey Dent (Aaron Eckhart) turning him into Two-Face. He blowups Gotham General Hospital, bombs Judge Surillo's (Nydia Rodriguez Terracina) car, and burn the Mob's money. His purpose: to break Batman and the citizens of Gotham psychologically. "You see, I'm a guy of simple taste. I enjoy dynamite and gunpowder and gasoline! And you know the thing that they have in common? They're cheap," the Joker will explain to the Chechen (Ritchie Coster), signifying his nihilistic pyromania. Unlike the Scarecrow, Carmine Falcone, Ra's al Ghul, and Batman, who all have a relationship to fear, the Joker is fearless, which is a departure from the main characters of the first film. The Ace of Knaves has nothing to lose, making him especially dangerous. Not caring about profit, passion, or revenge, all he wants to do is "watch the world burn" to quote Alfred (Caine). Easter egg: Ledger applied his Joker makeup himself, and, when watching, one will notice his fingers covered with white, red, and black makeup. The Joker's look was partially inspired by Brandon Lee's (1965-1993) character Eric Draven in *The Crow* (1994). Sadly, both Lee and Ledger died during, or just after, the making of their respective projects.

The clown mask Ledger's Joker wore during the opening bank robbery (right) pays homage to Cesar Romero's (1907-1994) Joker from the old 1960s *Batman* television show. Specifically, the Joker wears the same mask while performing Pagliacci (center) in the episode "The Joker Is Wild" (airdate: January 26, 1966). The episode is notable for Cesar Romero's debut as the Joker, just as *The Dark Knight* was Ledger's debut as the Harlequin of Hate. Both Joker masks owe their origin to Weary Willie, a clown persona made famous by circus performer Emmett Kelly (1898-1979). In Kubrick's *The Killing* (1956), Sterling Hayden's (1916-1986) character Johnny Clay wears a Weary Willie mask during a robbery (left); interestingly, at one point, Marvin Unger (Jay C. Flippen, 1899-1971) yells, "You jerk! You clown! Come on, clown, sing us a chorus from Pagliacci," synchronizing Kubrick's film and clown mask to those worn by Romero and Ledger years later.

Masked criminals rob a Gotham City mob bank, murdering each other for a higher share of the money until only the Joker remains, escaping with the cash; symbolism cloaks this opening sequence, giving us a taste to what's to come. When the bank robbery begins, one of the robbers says they're "three of a kind," which is a poker hand, and the phrase has multiple, contextual meanings. Planted throughout the movie are subtle references to gambling. For instance, the victims at 8th and Orchard have their dead bodies posed like they were playing cards. The Joker uses the phrase "chips are down" when Batman (Bale) interrogates him, and when the Joker is captured, he speaks of having an "ace in the hole." Jim Gordon (Oldman) says we "bet it all on him," referring to District Attorney Harvey Dent, during the final moments.

Like *Halloween* '18, this undercurrent alludes to Game Theory because the Joker likes to toy with his prey before striking, denoting that everything is a deadly game of cat-and-mouse to him. The Joker employs Game Theory when robbing the bank; specifically, the Pirate Game: a mathematical multiplayer contest about the distribution of wealth, by eliminating players until only one remains, thereby maximizing the share of the treasure. And the Joker does precisely this by having the bank robbers *qua* pirates dispose of one another after completing their specific task, leaving the Joker the only one left alive, taking all the money for himself.

The "three of a kind" line also foreshadows the turbulent relationship between Dent, Gordon, and Batman, and whether they can trust one another. The Joker will succeed in driving a wedge in this relationship, sowing hostility, eventually tearing down Dent, and putting Batman on the run. In a superb piece of occult casting, William Fichtner portrays the bank manager, and his appearance evokes one of the best crime dramas ever, Michael Mann's *Heat* (1995), a film that starred Fichtner. *Heat* dramatizes the life-and-death complexities of criminals and detectives. By casting Fichtner, Nolan transfers this hostile paradigm subconsciously to *The Dark Knight*; pointedly, the interrogation scene between Batman and the Joker, which parallels dialog between the protagonist and antagonist in *Heat*–more on this later. Fichtner's bank manager unloads a shotgun at the robbers not caring if he blasts a customer; and why should he, it is a mob bank, so he is merely protecting their stash regardless.

Next, after capturing the Scarecrow (Murphy), Batman, Dent, and Lieutenant Gordon form an uneasy alliance to rid Gotham City of organized crime–they are *three of a kind*: an attorney, a costumed vigilante, and a police officer. Gordon raids the Mob's banks, having marked bills commingled inside the vaults, attempting to bring them down. But their corrupt accountant, Lau (Ng Chin Hang), has already moved the money. When Batman arrives, Gordon shows him a security camera image of the Joker. The date on the photo is 2008/07/18, *The Dark Knight*'s theatrical release date.

Bruce believes that with Dent as Gotham's protector, he can retire from being Batman and lead a normal life with Rachel–even though she and Dent are dating. Both Gordon and Bruce's girlfriend, Natascha (Beatrice Rosen), refer to Dent as a "white knight," conjuring duality. The Batman is Gotham's Dark Knight, ruling the streets nocturnally, striking fear into Gotham's underbelly; Dent is the new white knight, prosecuting criminals in broad daylight, administering justice for all eyes to see. Batman and Dent stand in opposition: Batman is a vigilante operating outside the law while Dent is the law. Dent will become Two-Face, epitomizing good and evil, shattering this relationship with Batman because now he embodies duality. He is light and dark, order and chaos; like his coin, Two-Face can be both sides separately, either heads or tails. Nolan scatters the number two throughout, becoming a harbinger of Dent's transformation into Two-Face. For instance, the Joker's school bus from the bank heist is from District 22, and one of the explosives that Batman fires onto Lau's office window distinctly displays the countdown time of 2:22. Like Two-Face, Batman's relationship to the Joker embodies dualism: Batman is order and justice, the Joker is chaos and anarchy.

Dent foreshadows his fate over dinner, saying: "You either die a hero, or you live long enough to see yourself become the villain." Dent fulfills his prophecy: he lives long enough to see himself become a villain, Two-Face, yet dies a hero because Batman takes the fall for his murders. Easter egg: Eckhart modeled his performance, in part, after Robert F. Kennedy (1925-1968) both in terms of his initially polished, dashing appearance and his preoccupation with revenge over the assassination of his brother.

Mob bosses Sal Maroni (Eric Roberts), Gambol (Michael Jai White), and the Chechen hold a video-conference with Lau, having taken their funds for safekeeping, fleeing to Hong Kong. The Joker interrupts the meeting, warning them Batman is unhindered by jurisdictions, offering to kill him for half of their money. This ploy is another example of Joker employing Game Theory; here, the Shrinking Pie Game. The longer the crime bosses wait to divide the pie, the longer Batman remains in the hunt, ergo the less *pie* or money-resources they will have. Essentially, waiting is costly; their delay will only continue to shrink the pie. The Joker understands that killing Batman for 50% of their money is a reasonable offer. The mob bosses disagree, and a bounty is placed on the Joker by Gambol. The Joker employs deception–faking his death–to find Gambol, killing him, taking over his gang. The mob ultimately decides to take the Joker up on his offer.

Meanwhile, Bruce asks Fox to redesign the bat suit to make it more flexible. He agrees and makes the modifications. As he explains the improvements to Bruce, he says the new armor should "do fine against cats," foreshadowing Catwoman's emergence in the next film.

Batman finds Lau in Hong Kong and brings him back to Gotham to testify, allowing Dent to apprehend the entire mob. Batman uses the sky-hook to capture Lau, a device grounded in reality. The full name of the gadget is the Fulton Surface-to-Air Recovery System, developed in the 1950s by inventor Robert Edison Fulton, Jr., (1909-2004) for the CIA. The first pick-up of a human with the apparatus happened in 1958.

Back in Gotham, the Joker threatens to keep killing people unless Batman reveals his identity, and starts by murdering Police Commissioner Gillian B. Loeb (Colin McFarlane) and the judge presiding over the mob trial. At a fundraiser held by Bruce, the Joker attempts to get to Dent. Bruce enters the party, asking, "Where is Harvey?" tossing out his champagne. Then the Joker enters, asking, "Where is Harvey Dent?" spilling his champagne. Although they mimic each other, Bruce/Batman and the Joker are opposites of the same coin; again, their relationship embodies duality. Disguised as a police officer, the Joker tries to kill Mayor Anthony Garcia (Nestor Carbonell) in public, but Gordon sacrifices himself, thwarting the assassination. Dent kidnaps one of Joker's henchmen (David Dastmalchian), threatening him with a deadly game of heads-or-tails using his lucky coin, revealed to be heads on both sides. Dent learns Rachel is Joker's next target by the goon's nametag. Before Dent can kill the minion, Batman intervenes, reminding Dent that he is the white knight, not the shadow. If the media exposed Dent's torture of Joker's thug, everything they've worked for would be undone.

In *The Dark Knight*, when the Joker (left) tries to assassinate the mayor, he is not white-faced or wearing makeup; instead, he is dressed as a cop, looking normal. His visage is a salute to *Batman* comic #1, published in April 1940, which was the Joker's first appearance. In one panel, the Joker appears flesh-toned–not white– disguised as a police officer (right). In the comic, the Joker smuggles a bomb into a prison to escape, steals from the Mob, and falls from penthouse scaffolding only to be caught by Batman, *nota bene*, the Joker does all this in *The Dark Knight*. Furthermore, in the comic, the Joker's motivation is to perpetuate disorder while Ledger's Joker announces he's an "agent of chaos."

Bruce decides to reveal his secret identity to prevent more deaths. Before he can, however, Dent falsely claims he is Batman. Dent is taken into protective custody, but the Joker appears and attacks the convoy. Batman rescues Dent; Gordon, who faked his death, apprehends the Joker, securing promotion to Commissioner. Rachel and Dent are escorted away by detectives on Maroni's payroll; Gordon later learns they never arrived home. Batman interrogates the Joker, who reveals they have been trapped in separate locations rigged with explosives and that Batman must choose which one to save. This exchange is modeled after the diner scene from *Heat*. The protagonist, Lt. Vincent Hanna (Al Pacino), and the antagonist, Neil McCauley (Robert De Niro), know their next encounter will mean certain death for one of them. The diner scene is a riveting piece of film, serving as a psychological delicacy during which two dogged hunters reserve their weapons to speak on the methodology of their pursuit. Here, the dialog between the Joker and Batman reveals they are interdependent; although they are polarities, they require the other to exist. The Joker has no interest in killing Batman because, without him, there would be no Joker. The Joker explains that he plans to exploit humanity's ugly side to destroy Gotham, letting chaos and anarchy reign. The Joker forces Batman's hand, making him choose between Rachel and Dent. Batman races to save Rachel, while Gordon attempts to rescue the district attorney.

Batman arrives at the building, realizing the Joker sent him to Dent's location instead. Both buildings explode, killing Rachel while disfiguring half of Dent's face. The Joker escapes with Lau, who leads him to the Mob's large money stash. The Joker burns the money before killing Lau and the Chechen. In trying to understand the Joker's motives, Bruce tells Alfred that "Criminals aren't complicated," which echoes Ra's teachings, indicating Bruce still relies on the musings of his former mentor. Easter Egg: when the Joker begs Batman to run him over with his Bat-Cycle, one recalls Jack Nicholson's Joker goading Michael Keaton's Batman to attack him with his Bat-Wing in Burton's *Batman* '89.

Coleman Reese (Joshua Harto), an accountant at Wayne Enterprises, deduces Bruce Wayne is Batman and threatens to publicize the information. Not wanting Reese's revelation to interfere with his plans, the Joker threatens to destroy a hospital unless Reese is killed within an hour. All hospitals are evacuated as Gordon travels to secure Reese. When Bruce drives to the police car carrying Reese, he drives a Lamborghini Murciélago; Murciélago means *bat* suggesting this is Bruce's diurnal Batmobile. Disguised as a nurse, the Joker discovers Dent's ward and hands him a gun, convincing him to seek revenge for Rachel's death. The Clown Prince of Crime then destroys the hospital and escapes with a busload of hostages.

Dent goes on a killing spree, deciding the fates of people he holds responsible for Rachel's death by flipping his lucky coin, which was disfigured on one face by the explosion, just like him. Dent eventually apprehends Gordon's family, believing Gordon's love for his family parallels his love for Rachel. The address Two-Face chooses for his final stand is where Rachel perished; its address is 250 52nd Street, a palindrome: 25052. Palindromes denote duality and extremities, everything Two-Face embodies. The actual numbers, two and five, also possess occult meaning. Naturally, two is for Two-Face, indicating polarity and a flawed condition. The negative attributes of five are imperfect duality: order and disorder, happiness and misfortune, and life and death corresponding with Two-Face's split personality superbly.[418] Easter egg: Matilda is on the Joker's nametag, an homage to his daughter, Matilda Ledger.

---

[418] Pike, *Morals and Dogma*, 630-633. See also Hall, *Secret Teachings*, 216.

CINEMA SYMBOLISM 3

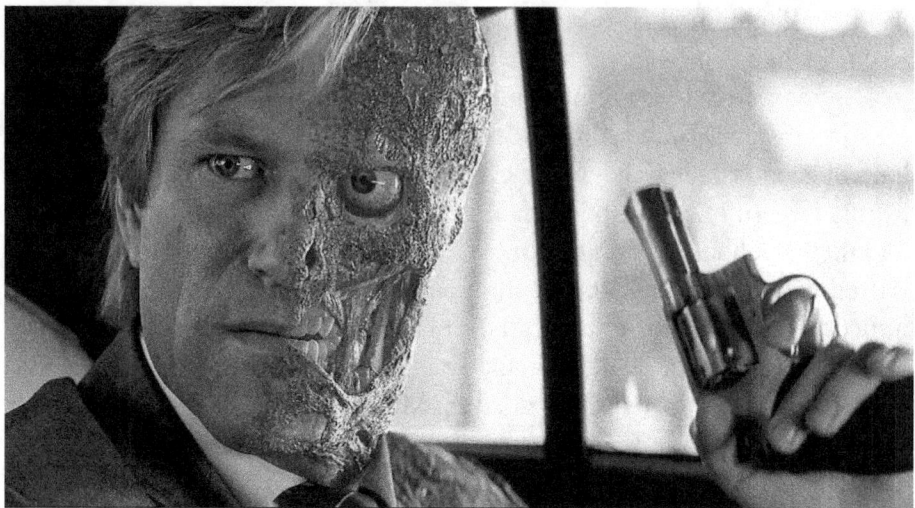

Harvey Dent is the arch-criminal Two-Face. No longer the white knight balanced out by the Dark Knight, Two-Face embodies dualism: good and evil, Fraggles and Doozers, order and chaos, personifying the double-headed god Janus. A flip of Two-Face's coin determines whether his victim lives or dies. The address he holds the Gordon family hostage at the end, where Batman and Commissioner Gordon confront him, is 250 52nd Street, where Rachel died. *Nota bene*: 250 52, or 25052, is a palindrome characterizing extremities: the alpha and omega, good and evil, life and death.

After announcing that Gotham will be subject to his rule by nightfall, the Jester of Genocide rigs two evacuating ferries with explosives; one with civilians, and the other with prisoners. Both ships have been supplied with a trigger to the other boat's explosives; next, the Joker announces through an intercom that he will explode both ferries if one of them has not destroyed the other by midnight. Again, the Joker employs Game Theory, here what is known as the Prisoner's Dilemma. The Joker's use of Game Theory suggests that he is dangerously sane, not insane at all. The game is played like this: two members of a criminal gang are arrested and imprisoned. Each prisoner (A and B) is in solitary confinement with no means of communicating with the other. The prosecutor lacks sufficient evidence to convict the pair on the primary charge, but they have enough to convict both on a lesser charge. Simultaneously, the prosecutor offers each prisoner a bargain. Each prisoner is allowed to testify against the other, or to remain silent. The offer is:

- If A and B each betray the other, each of them serves two years in prison;

- If A betrays B, but B remains silent, A will be set free, but B will serve four years in jail (or vice versa);
- If A and B remain silent, they will only serve one year in prison on the lesser charge or go free.

The passengers on the boats face this problem: destroy the other and live, but they choose to do nothing and perish, restoring a sense of decency to Gotham. Curiously, the criminals have a higher morality than the citizens, who seem more eager to blow up the prisoners' boat. Both the civilians and the prisoners refuse to kill each other; meanwhile, Batman, with Fox's reluctant help, locates the Joker by using a sonar device that eavesdrops on the entire city. Batman apprehends the Joker after a brief fight, frustrating his plan to destroy the ferries. Before the police arrive to take the Joker into custody, he gloats that Gotham's citizens will lose hope once Dent's rampage becomes public. The Joker, inverted, dangles by his leg, becoming the Hanged Man of the Major Arcana; its occult symbolism explained at the start of the chapter (analyzed in my other movie books as well.)

Gordon and Batman arrive at the building where Rachel perished to find Dent threatening to kill Gordon's family. They are *three of a kind*, only now Two-Face exists, Dent *qua* the white knight is gone because the Joker has succeeded in destroying Gotham's hope. Dent again flips his coin and shoots Batman, spares himself, and aims to kill Gordon's son while claiming Gordon's negligence was responsible for Rachel's death. Before he can flip his coin to determine the boy's fate, Batman tackles Dent causing him to fall off the building to his death. Batman persuades Gordon to let him take responsibility for the murders to preserve Dent's heroic image. As the police launch a manhunt for Batman, Gordon destroys the Bat-Signal, Fox watches as the sonar device self-destructs, and Alfred burns a letter from Rachel saying she plans to marry Dent. Batman flees from the police, taking Dent's place for Two-Face's crimes. Batman has made a heroic sacrifice: giving Gotham hope by destroying himself; the caped crusader is "…the hero Gotham deserves, but not the one it needs right now … because he's not a hero, he's a silent guardian, a watchful protector, the Dark Knight."

The two villains reflect Batman, becoming funhouse distortions, antitheses of the Dark Knight. The laughing, clownish costumed Joker contrasts Bruce's grim, Jungian shadow. Unlike Bruce, the Joker has no alter ego; the clown mask hides another clown–there is no mystery. They are opposites sides of the same coin: Batman is order, the Joker, chaos; the Ace of Knaves hints at their interdependence when interrogated. Personifying these opposites sides Two-Face, who is both yin and yang, justice and anarchy. Like Bruce, his two faces are a result of a tragedy; a flip of the coin determines life or death.[419]

There are numerous canine allusions throughout the film, culminating near the end when the Joker, observing the two ferries, surrounds himself with three of the Chechen's Rottweilers. The dogs are obedient and ready to attack, serving as the Joker's Praetorian Guard. When watching the movie, one will notice the Joker licking his chops like a cur. After he escapes the MCU, the Joker sticks his head out of the car's window like a dog, basking in the fresh air. The Joker refers to himself as a dog, telling Two-Face he is a "dog chasing cars." Later, Two-Face refers to the Joker is as a "mad dog" when speaking to Maroni. The dog symbolism, especially the three Rottweilers at the end, conjures archetypal Greek mythology. Cerberus is the Hound of Hades, e.g., the Sherlockian hound terrorizing Dartmoor, guarding Hell's Gates, depicted as a three-headed dog. For his business also is settled for all time; he is the terrible, fearless, and watchful janitor, or guardian (*janitor* or *custos*) of Orcus, the Styx, Lethe, or the black Kingdom. And so he remains for modern poets, as when Dante, reproducing Virgil, describes him: When Cerberus, that great worm, had seen us / His mouth he opened and his fangs were shown, And then my leader with his folded palms / Took of the earth, and filling full his hand, Into those hungry gullets flung it down."[420] Or Shakespeare, *Love's Labor Lost* (1597), v. ii: "Great Hercules is presented by this imp whose club killed Cerberus, the three-headed *canis*."[421] The Joker's villainy, combined with his diabolical personality personifies Pluto, Lucifer, and other chthonic entities. The three vicious dogs, and the canine allusions, imply the Joker is more than a lawbreaker; instead, he is a monster unleashing Hell on earth.

---

419 Travis Langley, *Batman and Psychology: A Dark and Stormy Knight* (Hoboken: John Wiley & Sons, Inc., 2012), 22.
420 Dante Alighieri, *Inferno*, Canto vi., 13 ff, quoted in Maurice Bloomfield, *Cerberus, the Dog of Hades* (Chicago: The Open Court Publishing Company, 1905), 6.
421 Quoted in Bloomfield, ibid, 7.

CINEMA SYMBOLISM 3

Black Ice: The Dark Knight Rises

Returning to their respective roles are Christian Bale, Michael Caine, Morgan Freeman, Nestor Carbonell, and Gary Oldman. *The Dark Knight Rises* premiered in New York City on July 16, 2012, and was released publicly on July 20, 2012. The movie grossed over $1 billion worldwide, making it the second film in the Batman film series to earn that amount. In addition to being Nolan's highest-grossing film, it is the 25th highest-grossing film of all time and the highest-earning live-action superhero film not in a shared universe. It is the third highest-grossing film of 2012, the top moneymaking Batman film of all time, the ninth highest-grossing superhero film, and the second-highest-grossing DC Comics film in history. That a lot of accolades!

Tragically, on July 20, 2012, during a midnight showing (beginning on the evening of Thursday, July 19) at the Century 16 Theater in Aurora, Colorado, a gunman wearing a gas mask opened fire inside the complex, killing 12 people and injuring 70 others. Police, responding to the shooting, apprehended a suspect later identified as 24-year-old James Eagan Holmes shortly after arriving on the scene. Initial reports stated Holmes identified himself as the Joker at the time of his arrest. His trial began on April 27, 2015, and on August 24, he was sentenced to 12 consecutive life sentences plus 3,318 years without parole. Many others think the film predicts further tragedy: toward the end, a map of Gotham is shown revealing a borough named Sandy Hook, also known as South Hinkley. Many in the conspiracy world believe this imagery foretells the Sandy Hook Elementary School shooting, which occurred a few months later, on December 14, 2012, in Newtown, Connecticut. Adam Lanza (1992-2012) fatally shot twenty children between six and seven years old, and six adult staff members before taking his own life. Although the Sandy Hook imagery lacks any context when applied to Newtown, it is still odd, and theories persist, questioning why *Sandy Hook* appears in the movie.

This time, the Batman logo is shaped by breaking and creaking black ice, representing Bane (Tom Hardy), shattering Batman's body and spirit. Like the first two movies, the elemental symbol designates an obstacle Batman must overcome. The first movie was bats implying Bruce's fear; in the second film, it was an explosion denoting the Joker's trial by fire. Here, it is Bane's cruelty and ferocity that Batman must survive and conquer.

In Uzbekistan, Bane, a mysterious terrorist and former member of the League of Shadows, abducts nuclear physicist Dr. Leonid Pavel (Alon Abutbul) from a CIA aircraft. Like Ra's al Ghul from *Batman Begins*, and the Joker from *The Dark Knight*, Bane disguises himself as one of his henchmen, hiding in plain sight.

We learn that eight years after the death of District Attorney Harvey Dent, Batman has disappeared; organized crime has been eradicated in Gotham City thanks to the Dent Act giving expanded powers to the police. Commissioner Gordon has kept Dent's murderous rampage a secret, allowing blame for his crimes to fall on Batman. Gordon has maintained this virtuous lie at a cost: the Dent Act was passed, increasing the powers of the law enforcement, creating a surveillance state, putting innocent people behind bars, and increased sentencing for minor offenders. He pens a resignation speech revealing the truth but decides the city is not yet ready to hear it. Bruce has become a Howard Hughes-like recluse. Wayne Enterprises is losing money after discontinuing his fusion reactor project–originally designed to supply Gotham with clean energy–when he learned it could be weaponized.

Six months following Pavel's kidnapping, Bane sets up his base in the city's sewers, prompting Bruce's corporate rival John Daggett (Ben Mendelsohn) to buy his fingerprints. Wily cat burglar Selina Kyle (Anne Hathaway) obtains Bruce's prints from a safe in Wayne Manor for Daggett, but she is double-crossed at the exchange, so she alerts the police. Selina's method of escaping Wayne Manor is highly reminiscent of a tall tale involving one of Catwoman's inspirations, Hedy Lamarr (1914-2000), whom Hathaway studied for the role. Lamarr claimed she escaped her possessive Austrian arms-dealer husband by dressing as one of her maids, collecting all her jewelry (Selina steals Bruce's mother's pearl necklace), and jumping out a window.

Gordon and the police arrive and pursue Bane and Daggett's henchmen into the sewers as Selina flees. Bane's henchmen capture Gordon, bringing him before their anarchistic savior. Bane searches Gordon, coming upon his retirement speech denouncing Dent as a murderer, and takes the document. Gordon escapes, only to be found by rookie officer John Blake (Joseph

Gordon-Levitt). Blake, a fellow orphan, confronts Bruce, convincing him to return as Batman. Blake also mentions giant alligators in Gotham's sewers, alluding to the villain Killer Croc, who appeared in 2016's *Suicide Squad* played by Adewale Akinnuoye-Agbaje. Bane later attacks the Gotham Stock Exchange by using Bruce's fingerprints in a series of transactions leaving him bankrupt; Batman resurfaces for the first time in eight years, intercepting Bane and his subordinates.

At a masquerade, Bruce speaks to Wayne Enterprises CEO Miranda Tate (Marion Cotillard), hiding behind a mask, insinuating that she too has another identity. She also mentions *balance*, which is a nod to her father, Ra's al Ghul, who also referred to *balance* as a justification for destroying Gotham. Shortly thereafter, as Bruce dances with Selina, she waxes Marxist doctrine, suggesting the impoverished masses will overtake the wealthy. "You think all this can last? There's a storm coming, Mr. Wayne. You and your friends better batten down the hatches because when it hits, you're all gonna wonder how you ever thought you could live so large and leave so little for the rest of us," she tells him. Like Batman's other villains, his relationship with Selina/Catwoman is a polarity, signified by economic extremes: Bruce is from the upper class, Selina is from the lower class. His butler, Alfred, resigns in an attempt to save him from death at Bane's hands. Bruce finds comfort with Miranda; she has a scar on her back, the mark of the League of Shadows, branded on new initiates, recalling *Batman Begins*, and the branding iron the decoy Ra's al Ghul was about to use on him. Using the stolen transactions, Bane kills Daggett, expanding his operations.

Selina *qua* Catwoman agrees to take Batman to Bane but instead leads him into a trap. Bane reveals he intends to fulfill Ra's al Ghul's mission to destroy Gotham. Although they trained him, Bane was later excommunicated from the League of Shadows. Bane is familiar with the Demon's Head's methods and philosophies, quoting his line about "theatricality and deception" to Batman. Bane fights the Caped Crusader, defeating him, dealing a crippling blow to his back, which comes from the *Knightfall* comic story arc from the mid-1990s. Bane then takes the fallen hero abroad to an underground prison. The inmates tell Bruce the story of Ra's child, born and raised there, finally escaping–the only prisoner to have done so.

Bane lures Gotham's police into the underground sewer network and uses explosives to trap them, then destroys the bridges leading out of the city. He kills Mayor Anthony Garcia and forces Dr. Pavel to convert the reactor core into a decaying neutron bomb at a football stadium before killing him. Bane states a single Gotham citizen holds the detonator, and if anyone tries to flee, the bomb will be exploded, killing everyone. The philosophy mirrors Batman's creed that one person can make a difference, effecting positive change. Only Bane has put a sinister spin on it, indicating it only takes one person to instigate a riot, become a destroyer, remolding the world cataclysmically. Later, Bane reads Gordon's speech to the public exposing the city's bureaucratic corruption, releasing the prisoners of Blackgate Penitentiary, initiating chaos while holding the city hostage, isolated with the bomb. Easter egg: the football scene was filmed at Heinze Field in Pittsburgh with many of the Steelers players in the roles of Gotham City's team, the Rogues. The kicker for the opposing team, Rapid City, is Luke Ravenstahl, Mayor of Pittsburgh at the time. Another Easter egg: From one fierce brawler to another: Tom Hardy based Bane's voice on bare-knuckle boxing champion Bartley Gorman V (1944-2002).

Months later, Bruce, recovered, escapes from the prison, returning to Gotham, which is now in winter, death, signifying the city is on the verge of collapse. Bruce must climb up a narrow circular tunnel, recalling the circular dry well from the first movie that young Bruce fell. Like a hero, he must rise, become reborn, and, having overcome his torment, and vanquish Bane. As Bruce climbs, a swarm of bats flies out from a crevice, implying he's overcome his fear. Bruce passed that test, and now he must conquer his pain. He meets with Gordon and ignites a fiery Bat-Signal, signaling that he will thaw Bane's bitter grip in the city, liberating it from the icy clutches of the League of Shadows. Batman frees the trapped police, and they clash with Bane's army in the streets; during the battle, Batman overpowers Bane.

However, Miranda intervenes and stabs him, revealing herself to be Talia al Ghul, Ra's daughter, and that she was the escapee from the prison. Wearing the armor from the previous film, the suit Fox said was venerable to a knife attack, Talia waxes sadistically about using a blade: "You see, it's the slow knife...the knife that takes its time. The knife that waits years without forgetting then slips quietly between the bones. That's the knife that cuts deepest." These lines hark back to the previous film, when the Joker, confined in the interrogation room, explains why he prefers a knife: "Do you want to know why I use a knife? Guns are too quick. You can't savor all the…little emotions. You see, in their last moments, people show you who they really are. So, in a way, I know your friends better than you ever did. Would you like to know which of them were cowards?" The significance of Talia favoring a knife, like the Joker, signals that she's just as cold-blooded as the Clown Prince of Crime. Talia shares her father and Bane's pessimism making her relationship with Bruce/Batman bipolar: she embodies cynicism and destruction; he is optimistic, believing in salvation and redemption. She activates the weapon's detonator, but Gordon blocks the signal.

Talia leaves to find the bomb while Bane prepares to finish off Batman, but Catwoman arrives and kills Bane. The duo pursues Talia, hoping to bring the weapon back to the reactor chamber where it can be stabilized. Talia's truck crashes (imitating the train crash that killed her father), but she remotely floods and destroys the reactor chamber before dying. With no way to stop the detonation, Batman uses the Bat (helicopter-like aircraft) to haul the bomb far over the bay, where it safely explodes. Before takeoff, Batman reveals his identity to Gordon. As Blake watches the bomb detonate, music plays–a choir boy performing a composition titled "Barbastella"– that transcended Bruce and Martha Wayne's murder in the first film. The haunting music represents for Blake what it did for Bruce: the death of parental figures, and rebirth to a new life, which is masked vigilantism, combating criminality.

In the aftermath, Batman, presumed dead, is honored as a hero. With Bruce also thought deceased, Wayne Manor becomes an orphanage with his remaining estate left to Alfred. Gordon finds the destroyed Bat-Signal repaired, while Fox discovers that Bruce, the Trismegistus-like wizard he is, has fixed the previously malfunctioning auto-pilot on the Bat. Blake resigns from the GCPD; a parcel left to him in Bruce's will leads him to the Batcave. When he enters it, he ascends on a platform toward the light, identifying him as Gotham's neo-Christlike savior. It is also disclosed that Blake's name is Robin, leaving us to presume that he will take up Batman's mantle as the superhero Nightwing. While visiting Florence, Alfred discovers Bruce is alive and well in a relationship with Selina.

CINEMA SYMBOLISM 3

The Dark Knights Rises allegorizes the French Revolution and Charles Dickens' (1812-1870) historical novel, *A Tale of Two Cities* (1859), which takes place during the upheaval surrounding the toppling of the *ancien régime,* and Robespierre's (1754-1794) subsequent Reign of Terror. The French Revolution was a period of far-reaching social, economic, and political upheaval in France, and its colonies, beginning in 1789. The Revolution overthrew the monarchy, established a republic, catalyzed violent periods of political turmoil, finally culminated in a dictatorship under Napoleon I, spreading many of its principles to areas he conquered in Western Europe and beyond. Inspired by liberal and radical ideas, the Revolution profoundly altered the course of modern history, triggering the global decline of absolute monarchies while replacing them with republics and liberal democracies. The Revolutionary Wars unleashed a wave of global conflicts that extended from the Caribbean to the Middle East. Historians widely regard the Revolution as one of the most critical events in human history.

A Tale of Two Cities takes place in London and Paris before and during the French Revolution. The novel tells the story of the French Doctor Manette, his 18-year-long imprisonment in the Bastille, his ultimate release, then living in London with his daughter Lucie, whom he had never met. The story is set against the conditions that led up to the Revolution and the Reign of Terror. Bane exploits Gotham's social and economic divide, turning citizens against citizens, causing Gotham to fall into economic collapse and social disorder. Kangaroo Courts are convened, dispensing sham justice to undesirables, traitors to Bane's dystopia.

Nolan alludes to the Parisian terrorism, and Dickens' novel, conveying Bane's neo-revolutionary lawlessness, and Gotham's socioeconomic divisions. After Bane hijacks the CIA's airplane, kidnapping Dr. Pavel, he tells one of his henchmen, "the fire rises," suggesting his insurrection has begun. "Fire Rises" is the title of Book 2: Chapter 23 of Dickens' novel. Daggett's adjutant, the Skelton Knaggs (1911-1955) aspirant Phillip Stryver (Burn Gorman), is named after the fictitious London barrister, C.J. Stryver, the boorish defender of Charles Darnay in *A Tale of Two Cities*. Bane begins his revolution, standing before Blackgate Prison, freeing tits prisoners conjuring the Bastille's storming on July 14, 1789, instigating the French Revolution. Bane, wearing a leather trench coat, lectures of his great egalitarian uprising, and that Blackgate Prison, like the Bastille, is a symbol of oppression and corruption. Harvey Dent, too, was a false idol. He rips the picture of the former D.A. in half resurrecting Two-Face, a man cleaved in twain, then reveals the truth about Dent's villainy by reading Gordon's retirement speech. Bane's zealous rhetoric echoes Revolutionaries like Marat (1743-1793), Couthon (1755-1794), Danton (1759-1794), Robespierre, Saint-Just (1767-1794), Desmoulins (1760-1794), and Hébert (1757-1794) who were hellbent on destroying the feudal system and absolute monarchy. Nevertheless, Bane turns City Hall into his headquarters, denoting his dictatorial rule. Although Bane talks like an ideologue, he is not interested in social justice or class warfare; rather, he is a terrorist wanting to reduce Gotham to ashes.

Later, at the kangaroo court, Bane's knitting evokes the evil tricoteuse, Madame Thérèse Defarge, from Dickens' novel. Bane also hangs the Special Forces soldiers' dead bodies from bridges, displaying them in public like the severed heads of guillotined victims; to Bane, they are merely enemies of his state.

Finally, Commissioner Gordon eulogizes Bruce: "I see a beautiful city and a brilliant people rising from this abyss. I see the lives for which I lay down my life, peaceful, useful, prosperous, and happy. I see that I hold a sanctuary in their hearts, and in the hearts of their descendants, generations hence. It is a far, far better thing that I do, than I have ever done; it is a far, far better rest that I go to than I have ever known." In *A Tale of Two Cities*, Sidney Carton speaks these lines while he awaits the guillotine. *The Dark Knight Rises* has come full circle: Gordon opens the film by eulogizing Gotham's white knight, Harvey Dent, and ends by extolling its Dark Knight, Batman *qua* Bruce Wayne.

Nolan's trilogy depicts 9/11 imagery and themes, making them realistic, conjuring that tragic day's trauma. In *Batman Begins*, we see a city gripped by fear. In *The Dark Knight*, we observe a metropolis torn apart by the Joker's explosions, paralyzed by the nihilistic flames of anarchy. We also see Batman weaponizing mobile communication to capture the Joker, echoing the abuses by government agencies–the NSA–when they illegally spied on Americans following the September 11th attacks. In *The Dark Knight Rises*, we learn about the passing of the Dent Act, mirroring the Patriot Act, which increased the police state's powers, curtailing civil

CINEMA SYMBOLISM 3

(Left) *The Dark Knight*'s apocalyptic one-sheet poster has the Bat Symbol seared into the side of a skyscraper, evoking the Twin Towers' devastation when commercial planes were hijacked and flown into them (right).

liberties.[422] When Bane sets off his explosives, Nolan shows us bridges collapsing around lower Manhattan. We can observe the Freedom Tower still under construction, which replaced the Twin Towers, all indicative of 9/11. When the Gotham City Police Force decides to retake the city and challenge Bane, they rush in almost like the first responders on 9/11, trying to reclaim Gotham from the carnage the terrorists had wrought.

Put on a Happy Face: Joker

A hundred years from now, 2121, Todd Phillips' *Joker* will be celebrated as one of the greatest films of the 21st century. The movie's principal

---

[422] The USA PATRIOT Act is an Act of Congress signed into law by United States President George W. Bush on October 26th, 2001, in response to the September 11th attacks and the 2001 anthrax attacks. With its ten-letter abbreviation (USA PATRIOT) expanded, the Act's full title is **U**niting and **S**trengthening **A**merica by **P**roviding **A**ppropriate **T**ools **R**equired to **I**ntercept and **O**bstruct **T**errorism **A**ct of 2001.

♪ Now they're some sad things known to man / But ain't too much sadder than / The tears of a clown when there's no one around ♪. (Left) Arthur Fleck's Joker makeup resembles John Wayne Gacy's Pogo the Clown (right).

photography took place in New York City, Jersey City, and Newark from September to December 2018. *Joker*, a psychological thriller, is the first live-action Batman film to receive an R-rating from the Motion Picture Association of America due to its violent and disturbing content, borrowing heavily from *The Killing Joke* graphic novel. The story documents the alchemical descent of Arthur Fleck into madness, changing him from failed clown and stand-up comedian to criminal mastermind, the Joker, the archenemy of Batman. *Joker* received numerous accolades: at the 92nd Academy Awards (February 9, 2020), earning eleven nominations, including Best Picture and Best Director, winning Best Actor for Joaquin Phoenix and Best Original Score for Hildur Guðnadóttir. Phoenix and Guðnadóttir also won at the Golden Globe and BAFTA Award ceremonies.

To call *Joker* dark and morbid is an understatement. Serial killer John Wayne Gacy (1942-1994), whose alter ego was Pogo the Clown., inspired Arthur's Joker makeup. Gacy murdered 33 young men and boys, burying his victims in the crawlspace of his Chicago home. Like Arthur, he often entertained at children's hospitals while costumed as a clown; like the Joker, Pogo has a pale face and a blood-red grin with dark blue triangles hiding the eyes, looking like a skull, not a jovial clown. With its sharp corners, the sullen face paint was shunned by professional clowns because the style terrified children. Arthur performs in Pogo's comedy club, thereby paying homage to Gacy–how deliciously evil!

CINEMA SYMBOLISM 3

Robert De Niro's casting as Murray Franklin, a Merv Griffin (1925-2007)-Johnny Carson (1925-2005) late-night comedic talk show host is a wonderful occult touch, drawing forth two Martin Scorsese films. The first is the satirical black comedy, *The King of Comedy* (1982). De Niro played Rupert Pupkin, a delusional aspiring stand-up comedian–like Arthur–trying to launch his career. Rupert, like Arthur, is a loner, living with his mother, dreaming of being a guest on a late-night talk show. Both rehearse their acts at home, and both make it onto the show only to commit a crime: Rupert kidnaps the host, Jerry Langford (Jerry Lewis, 1926-2017), while Arthur murders Murray.

The second, *Taxi Driver* (1976), stars De Niro as Travis Bickle: a lonely, depressed, isolated 26-year-old living in the Big Apple, just as Arthur lives in Gotham City. Both Arthur and Travis play with guns in their homes, and both use their fingers to simulate blowing their brains out. Both mentally ill men become obsessed with a woman, write dark thoughts in a journal, and become fixated on a political figure. Both Arthur and Travis change their appearances before going on a murder spree. In the end, it is suggested that both Travis' and Arthur's stories were imagined. The casting of De Niro transfers the omnipresent psychotic melancholy of Scorsese's films to *Joker* and, by doing so, makes Arthur-as-Joker, much like Travis and Rupert, an antihero worthy of admiration. Scorsese's two films aside, *Joker* was inspired by movies like *Black Swan*, *The Cabinet of Dr. Caligari*, and *The Man Who Laughs*.

Joker is strangely prophetic, presaging 2020's anarchy and chaos, stemming from the death of George Floyd (1973-2020) by a Minneapolis police officer. It opens with an outdated 1980s Warner Bros. logo, rewinding the clock forty years, to 1981. In grimy Gotham City, garbage bags are piled sky-high, mirroring a real-life sanitation strike that plagued New York City in 1981. It is so bad that Gotham has become infested with giant rats, terrorizing the city. Moreover, Gotham is rife with crime and unemployment, leaving large segments of the population disenfranchised and impoverished, languishing in the decay of the *nigredo*. Inside Ha-Has, a seedy booking agency for profession clowns, we are introduced to Arthur as he puts on his clown makeup. Sitting before a mirror, he makes the two faces of theater, Sock and Buskin–comedy and tragedy–foreshadowing his belief that he considered his life to be the latter only to discover it is the former.

Decorating Ha-Has' walls are posters advertising Amusement Mile, a Gotham district built during the city's industrial boom, akin to New York City's Coney Island. Over time, Amusement Mile fell into ruin due to bankruptcy and flood damage. The posters signify the Joker's use of abandoned, dilapidated amusement parks as hideouts, especially in *The Killing Joke*, anticipating Arthur's transformation into the Clown Prince of Crime. Easter egg: when Arthur goes outside to stomp trash bags after his boss threatens to dock his pay, Amusement Mile's Ferris wheel towers in the background. Another Easter egg: to make Gotham disgusting, one can observe the super rats in three scenes. The first time is when Arthur is speaking in the phone booth with his boss, Hoyt Vaughn (Josh Pais), a rat turns the corner. The second time is when Arthur murders the third yuppie on the subway platform; the rat is on the far left, near a garbage can, visible when Arthur runs up the steps. Finally, when young Bruce Wayne (Dante Pereira-Olson) is standing over his parents' corpses in the alley, two rats scurry behind the boy. The vermin add to *Joker's* creepy ambiance; they represent Gotham's degradation, betokening the *nigredo*.

On the job, dressed as a clown on the sidewalk, spinning a sign for a going-out-of-business music store, juvenile delinquents attack Arthur, knocking him unconscious in an alley, breaking the sign over his head. He is kicked and beaten, humiliated and weakened, straining his ability to cope with reality, breaking him psychologically. The Joker was born in an alleyway echoing Batman's origin: young Bruce Wayne witnessed the murder of his parents in a backstreet, which was his impetus to become a masked vigilante years later. Soon afterward, Arthur's coworker, Randall (Glenn Fleshler), gives him a gun for protection, which he accepts reluctantly.

Depressed, Arthur visits his social worker, Debra Kane (Sharon Washington). He laments that society is deteriorating, requesting an increase in medications to ease his misery. Debra Kane is named after Batman's creator, Bob Kane; she first appeared in *Batman: The Ultimate Evil* (1995) as a caseworker with child services, hinting that Arthur was abused as a child. He shows her his journal; as she flips through the pages, we get a glimpse of Arthur's troubled mind. He tells her he is pursuing stand-up comedy, echoing the storyline in *The Killing Joke*, wherein the Joker was, likewise, attempting to be a comedian. In his journal, one line reads: "i just hope my death makes more cents [*sic*] than my life," implying a death wish.

Left) Inside Ha-Has, Arthur sits before a mirror, putting on his clown makeup, making the two faces of the theater, Sock and Buskin (right): a smile for comedy, and a frown for tragedy.

A clock with the time 11:11 conspicuously hangs on the wall as Debra mentions that he was once confined to a mental hospital. In a flashback, we see Arthur in Arkham State Hospital's observation room, in a white straitjacket, banging his head against the door's window. On the wall hangs a clock with the time 11:11; two clocks with identical times blur reality and fantasy, questioning whether the film is a truthful depiction or a product of Arthur's sable imagination. Other numeric discrepancies manifest in *Joker*, further confusing the real world with make-believe. These inconstancies are intentional, leaving the movie open to interpretation; like *Caligari*, *Joker* is the product of an unreliable narrator. Easter eggs: 11:11 could refer to the Biblical passage Jeremiah 11:11: "Therefore thus saith the LORD, Behold, I will bring evil upon them, which they shall not be able to escape; and though they shall cry unto me, I will not hearken unto them," dovetailing with Arthur *qua* Jokers' methodology contextually. The time, 11:11, evokes November 11 or 11/11; in *Suspiria* '18, *Volk* was performed, the coven's attempt at magical transference. In *Somewhere in Time* (1980), November 11, 1885, is the birthday of Elise McKenna (Jane Seymour). However, these seem to be unrelated because there's no nexus between *Suspiria*'s witches, Elise, or the Joker.

While riding home on a bus, Arthur's jawline has white makeup, indicating the Joker, his alter ego, is bleeding through; his dark side is emerging. He gives an African-American mother a business card, revealing he has pseudobulbar affect: a condition characterized by episodes of sudden uncontrollable and inappropriate laughing or crying. For Arthur, his unrestrained laugh makes him giggle at inopportune times. Thus, he is the man who laughs, evoking *The Man Who Laughs*, starring Conrad Veidt as Gwynplaine, the Joker's inspiration. Arthur walks home, trudging through the gloom, mired in sadness; he climbs a flight of stairs, ascending to the *nigredo*. Easter egg: Arthur's accursed laugh evolves during the story. At first, his guffaw is a tortured soul's affliction. When he confronts Thomas Wayne (Brett Cullin) in the men's room, he laughs like he's one of the guys, hanging around with his pals. Finally, after killing Murray, his wryly chuckle is sheer happiness; it is not forced or pronounced, suggesting he is at peace with murder.

Arthur arrives home–a dingy apartment–where we are introduced to his mother, Penny (Frances Conroy). *Penny* evokes two things: first, a sense of worthlessness because it's the lowest denomination of currency, signifying her lowly social status. Second, *Penny* conjures another evil clown, Pennywise, the terror of Stephen King's *It* novel and movie franchise. Penny obsesses over Thomas Wayne, having sent him a series of letters, eagerly waiting for a response. She explains that she used to work for the Wayne family, believing he will make a great mayor because he is the only one who can save the city, identifying Thomas as a Donald Trump-like political figure. He will make Gotham great again.

Mother and son watch *Live! with Murray Franklin* with Arthur envisioning himself in the audience. After Arthur yells out that he loves Murray, the gracious host asks him to stand. As he absorbs the spotlight, Murray praises him, saying there is something special about him. Murray invites him down to the stage, telling him he wished he had a son like him. The two men embrace; Murray is one of Arthur's father figures, the masculine *citrinitas*, but will eventually reject him, transforming the failed comedian into a psychopath.

Arthur meets his neighbor on the elevator, single mother, Sophie Dumond (Zazie Beetz), following her through Gotham's streets the next day. Her forename implies the goddess of gnosis, Sophia, but Arthur's ascent of enlightenment is imaginary; instead, she personifies the *albedo*, making his alchemical transformation inevitable. When Arthur gets off the elevator, traces of his white makeup are visible on his jawline and neck, indicating, once again, the Joker surfacing. He bathes his mother in the tub, for she is another indicator of the *albedo*. She tells him that Thomas will help them because he is a good man. Arthur says she need not worry about money because his act is ready for comedy clubs. Penny shits on his dream, telling him that one has to be funny to be a comic, inferring he is neither. In the living room, he watches *Shall We Dance* (1937), starring Fred Astaire (1899-1987) and Ginger Rogers (1911-1995), on the television. "Slap That Bass" is the musical number lyricizing: "♪ The world is in a mess / With politics and taxes / And people grinding axes / There's no happiness ♪," signifying Arthur's consternation over society's lack of civility, denoting the decay of the *nigredo*. He discharges the gun that Randall gave him, not realizing it was loaded. A mirror's reflection records the scene, indicating the dark side rising.

After stalking Sophie to the bank, Arthur ends up at Pogo's, enjoying the comedy, trying to hone his act. Sitting alone at home, he writes his dark thoughts in his journal: "the worst part about having a mental illness is people expect you to behave as if you D☺NT." Sophie rings the doorbell, asking if he was following her earlier. He reluctantly confesses but eases the situation by inviting her to his upcoming stand-up routine, which she accepts.

While entertaining at a children's hospital, Arthur's gun falls out, hitting the floor. It turns out Randall lied about how Arthur acquired the pistol, so Hoyt fires him. On the subway train, Mercurius strikes, rousing the *nigredo's* chaos: three drunken Wayne Enterprises businessmen assault him; one of them sings, "Send in the Clowns" (1975) before beating him down. He snaps, shooting two of them in self-defense, executing the third as he tries to escape. The incident resembles the December 1984 New York City Subway Shooting when Bernard "Bernie" Goetz shot and wounded four African-American men on a subway train in Manhattan. Goetz surrendered to police nine days later and was charged with attempted murder, assault, reckless endangerment, and several firearm offenses. Initial support and public opinion turned against Goetz due to racist statements and damaging details of the incident that later surfaced. Nevertheless, a jury found him not guilty of all charges except for one count of carrying an unlicensed firearm, for which he served eight months of a one-year sentence. The event sparked a nationwide debate on race and crime in major cities, the legal limits of self-defense, and how the citizenry could rely on the police to secure their safety.

Arthur flees the 9th Ave-Robinson Park Station to a disgusting public bathroom. He performs a somber ballet before a mirror, evoking *Black Swan* and, accordingly, Nina's alchemy, and her evil reflections. Arthur's shadow is thriving, integrating with his ego, allowing for individuation, the finality of the *rubdeo*: the Joker. If Nina observed his ballet, its creepiness would arouse her. In a grimy stall, camouflaged in a filthy penumbra, she would masturbate, hone her alchemy, perfecting chaos magic. In Gotham's mythology, Robinson Park is a landmark located in an impoverished neighborhood. Its borders extend between South Gotham and Central Gotham Island. Selina Kyle and her young companion, Holly Robinson, lived in an apartment building just outside of Robinson Park. In recent years, Robinson Park became the base of operations for Poison Ivy during the No Man's Land affair. In all likelihood, Robinson Park is named after Golden Age Batman inker Jerry Robinson (1922-2011).

Arthur returns home, drops in on Sophie, kissing her passionately. Next, he cleans out his locker at Ha-Has. He punches the punch in-out clock off the wall; its time, like the clocks earlier, is 11:11, skewing fantasy with reality, making it hard to discern what's genuine and what's artificial.

On the television show *Good Morning Gotham*, the subway murders are condemned by billionaire mayoral candidate Thomas Wayne, a Donald Trump analog (*vide supra*). Even their names have eleven letters, with their forenames having six letters, and the surnames having five letters–they are the same. The host says there's an anti-rich groundswell brewing, like Gotham's less fortunate residents are siding with the killer. Thomas says it's a shame, and that Gotham has lost his way. When asked about the suspect in a clown mask, Thomas denounces the killer as a coward, too scared to show his face, envious of those more fortunate; ironically, his son, Bruce, will fight crime while concealing his identity behind a mask. Thomas says successful people–such as himself–will always view those who've failed to make something of themselves as nothing but *clowns*. Demonstrations against Gotham's wealthy begin with protesters donning clown masks of Arthur's makeup. Easter egg: a print of Thomas Gainsborough's (1727-1788) *The Blue Boy* (1770) decorates the wall above Arthur's TV, paying

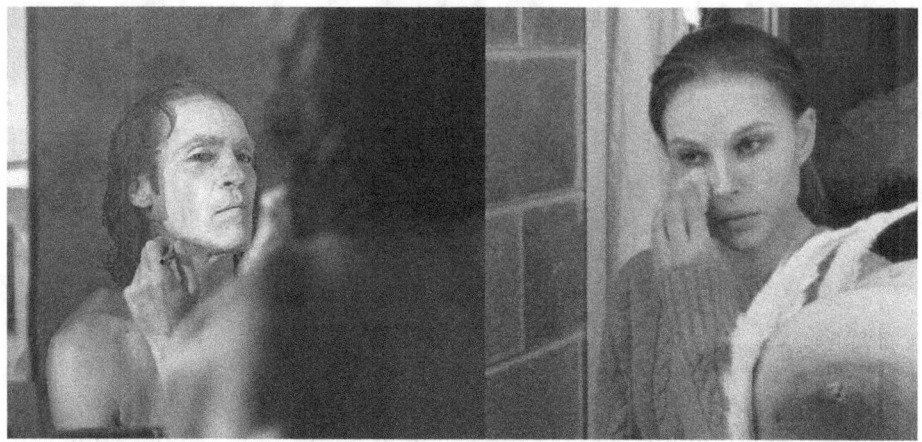

Dark alchemy, ghostly faces: Arthur (left) applies white face paint, imitating the White Swan herself, Nina Sayers (right). The white greasepaint makes the two performers appear corpselike; they have murdered their egos, allowing their dark sides' ascendancy, the festering *nigredo*, epitomized by their new personalities: the Joker and the Black Swan.

homage to Jack Nicholson's Joker. In *Batman* '89, when the Joker trashes the Flugelheim Museum, his goons deface *The Blue Boy*.

Visiting her office, Arthur tells Debra that all he has are negative thoughts–he dwells in the *nigredo* but is trying to escape it. He tells her that, for the first time, people are starting to notice him. She informs him that social services are being terminated because of budget cuts, leaving Arthur without his medication.

Sophie attends Arthur's stand-up routine, which goes poorly; he laughs uncontrollably and has difficulty delivering his jokes. Afterward, Sophie and Arthur stroll along the street, passing by a newspaper kiosk. The headline of the *Gotham Examiner* reads KILLER CLOWN ON THE LOOSE with an illustration of a fierce clown mask, looking like a bloodthirsty vampire. Under its image, the newspaper reads: EXCLUSIVE: PHOTOS OF DISASTER IN UKRAINE. On the surface, this story is about the April 1986 Chernobyl nuclear disaster in the former Soviet Union. However, by alluding to Ukraine, *Joker* might be an exemplar of Jungian synchronicity, foretelling the impeachment of Donald Trump in 2019-2020. Thomas' rhetoric, his desire to save Gotham, recalls Trump's campaign slogan: Make America Great Again. *Disaster in Ukraine* anticipates Trump's alleged quid pro quo with Ukrainian President Zelensky, exchanging foreign aid for an investigation into Hunter Biden. Do the filmmakers know the future? And if so, how? Remember, this movie was filmed between September and December 2018, well before the Trump-Ukraine scandal. Does the answer lie in the collective unconscious, enabling the prediction of future events through filmmaking, via creative expression? Perhaps a coincidence, or is this Jungian synchronicity at its finest?

Gotham Journal's headline is CLOWN VIGILANTE? *Violence on the number 9 train as three men were killed over a reported dispute.* The number nine is a discrepancy because the subway train stopped at the 9th Ave-Robinson Park Station–this is the platform where Arthur murdered the third Wayne businessman. The train is also identified with nine, hinting the narrator may be lying, confusing the train with the station, distorting reality, indicating the storyteller cannot be trusted. Sophie praises the subway vigilante, "Fuck 'em," she says, referring to the three dead Wayne employees, telling him their killer is a hero. A car drives by slowly with a man in the back seat wearing a Joker-clown mask; indeed, people are beginning to notice. But they are not paying attention to Arthur; instead, they are lionizing his violent alter ego, the soon-to-be Joker. The lovebirds enjoy each other's company in a coffee shop located on JEROME Ave, perhaps an allusion to Jerome Valeska (Cameron Monaghan), a deranged, criminally insane mass murderer and anarchist on the television show *Gotham* (2014-2019). Jerome had a twin brother named Jeremiah (Cameron Monaghan), who was the show's equivalent to the Joker.

Arthur opens a letter written by Penny to Thomas, alleging the man who laughs is Thomas' illegitimate son. Arthur berates his mother for hiding the truth. Attempting to make contact with his father, Arthur travels by commuter train to stately Wayne Manor, where he meets Thomas' young son Bruce, but flees after a scuffle with the family butler Alfred Pennyworth (Douglas Hodge). From a treehouse, young Bruce slides down a pole, paying homage to the *Batman* television show of the '60s when Bruce Wayne (Adam West, 1928-2017) and Dick Grayson (Burt Ward) slid down poles from Wayne Manor to the Batcave, miraculously becoming Batman and Robin along the way. Arthur and Bruce interact through iron gates, appearing like prison bars, foreshadowing their confrontations when the Joker will be locked away, visited by Batman in jail or Arkham Asylum.

CINEMA SYMBOLISM 3

Following questioning by two Gotham City Police Department detectives investigating Arthur's possible involvement in the subway murders, Penny suffers a stroke and is hospitalized. One of the detectives is named Burke (Shea Whigman) after Detective Tommy Burke, a policeman first appearing in *Detective Comics* #748 (September 2000). Detective Burke is the comedian and ladies' man of the GCPD's Major Crimes Unit, or so he would like to think. His attempts at lightheartedness of grim situations may partly be an attempt to cover up how uncomfortable he feels because he is one of the unit's youngest members.

While tending to his bedridden mother in the hospital, Arthur watches *Live! with Murray Franklin*. The host mocks him by showing clips from his failed comedy routine at Pogo's, referring to Arthur as "Joker." One of Arthur's father figures–the *citrinitas*–has rejected him, fueling his rage and disappointment, heightening his alchemical metamorphosis. Arthur returns home; resting in bed, he listens to the television. The news anchor says that although tensions are rising in the city, Mayor Stokes hopes cooler heads will prevail. Mayor Stokes alludes to Mayor Bradley Stokes, making his sole appearance in *Detective Comics* #179 (January 1952). Arthur watches the television, showing angry protestors dressed as clowns, raging against the city's elites. The mob carries banners with RESIST, and FUCK WAYNE, while other impolite signs state the mayor candidate is a FASCIST. But Thomas remains defiant, telling reports he wants to help lift the lower class out of poverty to make their lives better. This noble cause, he explains, is why he is running for political office: to offer hope to the hopeless even if they don't realize it.

At a showing of Charlie Chaplin's *Modern Times*, Arthur confronts Thomas in a men's room. The Wayne patriarch tells him that Penny is delusional, mentally ill, and that she is not his biological mother, and that he is not his biological father. Unable to control his laugh, Thomas punches him and storms out. After being rejected by his other father figure, Arthur empties his refrigerator and gets inside, fulfilling a psychological yearning to return to the womb, to have safety and security, to escape reality. Or, perhaps, to commit suicide. Since becoming trapped in a refrigerator can be fatal if no one is around to open it, this incident seems to be imagined by Arthur. It might even be a dream because the refrigerator scene ends with the telephone ringing and, the following morning, the ringing phone wakes him. He answers, and booking agent Shirley Wood invites him to appear on Murray's show. She explains that his comedy routine's clips have become unexpectedly popular, so he accepts. Easter egg: Shirley Wood is named after *The Tonight Show*'s real-life talent coordinator, Shirley Wood (1923-2008), scheduling acts while Johnny Carson was the host.

Disturbed and in denial, he visits Arkham State Hospital to steal Penny's case file; the file discloses she adopted him when he was a baby, allowing her abusive boyfriend to harm both of them. Dr. Benjamin Stoner diagnosed Penny; in the DC Universe, Dr. Benjamin Stoner was a head doctor at Arkham Asylum. He was chosen by a Lord of Chaos named Typhon to act as a soldier of Chaos. Possessed by Typhon, Stoner became Anti-Fate and was manipulated into battling the second Doctor Fate, Eric Strauss, a battle that ended with his defeat. Afterward, Stoner was freed from the Lords of Order and Chaos' influence, becoming an average person again. Stoner's first appearance was in *Doctor Fate* #1 (July 1987), and his last was in *Doctor Fate*, Vol. 2, #24 (January 1991). Easter egg: Arkham State Hospital is, of course, named after Arkham Asylum, the facility that incarcerates Gotham's super-criminals after Batman captures them.

In a flashback, Penny alleged that Thomas used his influence to fabricate the adoption, committing her to the asylum to hide their affair. The records office is on floor seven, which, again, is an inversion; traditionally, seven is a lucky number, but, for Arthur, it is unlucky. It is via the number seven that he learns he was adopted, furthering his mental deterioration. Distraught and befuddled, Arthur returns home, entering Sophie's apartment unannounced. Frightened, Sophie asks him to leave, revealing that their previous encounters were delusions, a mere figment of Arthur's sick imagination. Arthur tells her that he had a bad day, a line lifted from *The Killing Joke*, wherein the Joker states: "All it takes is one bad day to reduce the sanest man alive to lunacy. That's how far the world is from where I am. Just one bad day," implying his sad state, designating his psychosis.

At the hospital, in broad daylight, the psychotic son kills the deranged mother by suffocating her with a pillow—exit Penny. Before bringing down the curtain, Arthur says that she led him to believe his laugh was a condition, that something was wrong with him. He says there's nothing wrong; instead, he has come to know himself, implying that his shadow self is alive and well. As he begins to smother her, he says, "I used to think that my life was a tragedy, but now I realize it's a fucking comedy," recalling his Sock and Buskin faces from Ha-Has. Arthur's comment paraphrases another clown, the Tramp, Charlie Chaplin, who said: "Life is a tragedy when seen in close-up, but a comedy in long-shot." Having removed the *albedo*, viz. Sophie and Penny, and having been rejected by the *citrinitas*, Murray and Thomas, Arthur is prepared to incorporate the *rubedo*, which, for him, is the *nigredo*: a descent into madness, becoming the Joker, completing the alchemical Magnum Opus.

Arthur simulates shooting himself in the head–committing suicide–as he rehearses to go on *Live! with Murray Franklin*. Dying his hair green, and putting on his clown makeup, he finds a snapshot of his mother when she was younger. Written on the back is: "Love your smile…TW." The *TW* is Thomas Wayne, indicating their love affair was real, making Arthur their child; he is Thomas' illegitimate son. Arthur crumples the photo, understanding he may have just murdered his mother over a falsehood. Next, Randall and fellow ex-colleague Gary (Leigh Gill) visit his apartment, bringing him a bottle of booze, trying to cheer him up after hearing about his mother's death. Arthur tells them he is celebrating and has stopped taking his medication, making him feel better. Arthur brutally murders Randall but leaves Gary unharmed because of his past friendship.

Arthur is dead, but the Joker lives in his stead: sporting a red suit–the *rubedo*–he dances down a flight of stairs, descending into madness. Gary Glitter's "Rock and Roll Part 2" (1972) transcends his awakening, a tune fitting for *Joker*. The nexuses to Gacy already established, Glitter (b. Paul Francis Gadd) was imprisoned for downloading child pornography in 1999, and child sexual abuse and attempted rape in 2006 and 2015; he is currently serving a sixteen-year prison sentence. Fleck's Joker wears makeup paying homage to a serial killer, so why shouldn't he dance to a song performed by a convicted pedophile? These are the screwy impulses of Mercurius when he dwells in the *nigredo*, assuming the guise of the *rubedo*. But two detectives interrupt his lively jig, pursuing him onto a subway train filled with protesters wearing clown masks. Detective Burke accidentally shoots a protester inciting a riot, allowing Joker to escape. Both detectives are brutally attacked, taken to the hospital in critical condition.

Before the show goes live, Arthur requests that Murray introduce him as Joker, referencing Murray's previous mockery. He assures Murray and his producer that his clown makeup is not a political statement. He preps for his debut in room 404, an allusion to *Batman* comic #404, beginning the celebrated Year One storyline. Arthur again puts the gun to his head, but he realizes he has bigger fish to fry. Arthur walks out to thunderous applause, kissing Dr. Sally (Sondra James), a Dr. Ruth Westheimer analog. He starts telling morbid jokes, confesses to the subway train killings, ranting about how society abandons the downtrodden and mentally ill. He says the murders–like his life–are comedy; his tirade resembles Howard Beale's (Peter Finch, 1916-1977) rant from *Network* (1976). Arthur considers shooting himself–his original plan–but realizes that would make his life meaningless. So, he blows Murray's brains out, turning his twisted journal into a manifesto, transforming him into the Joker. The Joker is subsequently arrested as riots break out across Gotham. Easter egg: Arthur *qua* Joker's late-night talk show appearance comes from the pages of Frank Miller's *The Dark Knight Returns* (1986), a four-part comic book miniseries. At one point in the story arc, the Joker appears on a late-night talk show hosted by David Endocrine, a parody of David Lettermen. The Joker kisses Dr. Ruth Westheimer before killing everyone in the studio, including the host.

After they leave a movie theater, a rioter–hiding behind a clown mask– confronts the Wayne family in an alley, shooting Thomas and his wife, Martha (Carrie Louise Putrello), sparing Bruce. The film they were watching is *Zorro the Gay Blade*, released in July 1981. It is a comedic sequel to *The Mark of Zorro* (1940); moreover, *The Mark of Zorro* (1920) was one of Kane's inspirations because Zorro, like Batman, is a masked vigilante.[423] *Excalibur* (1981) is also playing in the theater, a movie about a character named Arthur. In John Boorman's ostentatious astrological-Rosicrucian film, the wizard Merlin (Nicol Williamson, 1936-2011), performs alchemy by summoning the Dragon's Breath via the Charm of Making, i.e., the Philosopher's Stone, transforming Uther Pendragon (Gabriel Byrne) into the semblance of his enemy. Merlin's alchemical magic parallels Arthur's metamorphosis into something else: Gotham City's archnemesis, the Joker. As Bruce stands over his parents' dead bodies like a cemetery monument, a *Wolfen* (1981) poster hangs on the alley's wall. Based on the novel *The Wolfen* (1978) by Whitley Strieber, it's about a cop who tracks down a series of murders committed by a monster, echoing the search by Detectives

---

423 Les Daniels, *Batman: The Complete History* (San Francisco: Chronicle Books, 2004), 21.

Burke and Garrity (Bill Camp) for an evil clown. During the late-night talk show, while sitting on the couch, Arthur growls that he won't take it anymore, that he'll "werewolf, and go wild."

Encouraged by Arthur's nihilism, rioters in a commandeered ambulance crash into the police car transporting him, rendering him unconscious. They remove him from the vehicle; Arthur soon awakens, rising to the crowd's cheers. He has come a long way; he was beaten in an alleyway, ordered to *stay down* by the hooligans, but now he is instructed to *rise*, reborn as the Joker, becoming a living symbol, personifying the city's unrest. Before making a bloody smile with his fingers, Joker dances around on a police car's hood. Phoenix told the Associated Press that Ray Bolger heavily influenced the Joker's quirky dance moves. "There was a particular song called 'The Old Soft Shoe' that he performed and I saw a video of it and there's this odd arrogance almost to his movements and, really, I completely just stole it from him," the star explains. "He does this thing of turning his chin up," Phoenix said. "This choreographer Michael Arnold showed me that and tons of videos and I zeroed in on that one. That was Joker, right? There's an arrogance to him, really. That was probably the greatest influence."[424]

Locked inside Arkham, Arthur laughs to himself about a jest, telling his psychiatrist (April Grace) she wouldn't get it. It's an inside joke that only he finds amusing: he knows he was responsible for the riots which killed Thomas and Martha Wayne; thereby, rather circuitously, he left Bruce orphaned, thus creating Batman. He escapes, running from the orderlies, leaving a trail of bloody footprints. Arthur was incarcerated on floor thirteen, which is another inversion: thirteen is unlucky for most, but for Arthur, it is fortuitous, facilitating his escape. We, the audience, have no idea how long Arthur *qua* the Joker has been confined, leaving the narrative we have just watched in doubt. In *The Killing Joke*, the Joker says he wants his origin to be a mystery: "If I'm going to have a past, I prefer it to be multiple choice!"

It ends where it began: with an interview by a psychiatrist, an African-American woman, harkening back to Arthur talking to his social services counselor, Debra, another African-American woman, insinuating the two scenes are inconsequential reflections, hinting at deception. There are two

---

[424] Raechal Shewfelt, "Joaquin Phoenix's 'Joker' character was inspired by a 'Wizard of Oz' star," *Yahoo*, September 30, 2019, https://www.yahoo.com/entertainment/joaquin-phoenixs-joker-character-was-inspired-by-a-wizard-of-oz-star-204041947.html (accessed February 16, 2020).

Arkhams: one sanitized wherein Arthur is jailed, the other grimy, which he visits to steal his mother's psychiatric records. Adding to the confusion is that both asylums and Ha-Has have clocks displaying the same time, 11:11. Which of the two Arkhams is authentic is open to interpretation, or worse of all, both are bogus, generating an epistemological crisis. Numeric discrepancies only compound the situation. The final moments reveal Arthur is insane, locked away in an asylum, making him an unreliable narrator. His confinement is an allusion to *Caligari*, starring Conrad Veidt, the inspiration for the Joker. Is *Joker* a false narrative, a product of Arthur's sick mind? We know Sophie was a barometer for his grip on reality, and his relationship with her was imagined, leaving it to the viewer to speculate about what was real and what was a delusion.

Like *Black Swan*, *Joker* is alchemical cinema, documenting Arthur's metamorphosis into the Clown Prince of Crime, failed comic into a criminal mastermind. Arthur has a lot in common with Nina; for example, both live in apartment buildings with their mothers. Both are depressed performers: Nina is a melancholic ballet dancer; Arthur is a sullen clown. Both are morbid; their dark sides reflected in pervasive mirrors, anticipating their lunacy.

Alchemically, Arthur resides in the *nigredo*; his life is sheer gloom. Two women represent the *albedo*, Luna's whiteness: Sophie, and his mother, Penny. When he meets Sophie, the Lawrence Welk (1902-1993) tune "The Moon is a Silver Dollar" (1939) plays over the scene. The song continues into the disturbing next scene: Arthur bathing his mother. The song is a token of the *albedo*, the feminine presence in his life.

Two father figures personify the *citrinitas*: Thomas and Murray, rejecting him for different reasons, furthering his fall. His downward spiral is both literal and figurative; psychologically, Arthur is driven insane. To signify his mental erosion, he dons the *rubedo*–a red suit–dancing down a flight of stairs, a descent into madness. Arthur is no more; he is now the Joker, the archenemy of Batman, the terror of Gotham. His tragic life is now a comedy; only there is no punchline. In *Black Swan* and *Joker*, *coincidentia oppositorum* is absent; there is no integration. Ergo, Nina dies, whereas an insane asylum incarcerates Arthur. But both rise: bathed in Lucifer's radiance, she archives perfection by tripping the light fantastic, while he escapes his confinement, freeing himself to terrorize Gotham City.

Exit the light, enter the shadow. (Top) Nina stands before a mirror with the word *WHORE* written on its surface, signifying the shadow self's emergence. (Bottom) Arthur stands before a mirror with the phrase *PUT ON A HAPPY FACE* written on its surface, announcing his shadow's onset. Both *Black Swan* and *Joker* are alchemical movies, documenting Nina and Arthur's metamorphosis into something deranged and wicked.

I try to keep my books apolitical. Still, it is crystal clear Phillips' film is a condemnation of the Woke and Cancel Culture movements, challenging their PC narratives. *Joker* demonstrates that a society that shames, humiliates, censors, and disenfranchises people generates violence; free expression does not cause havoc, only its suppression. Thus, Arthur-as-Joker is motivated to kill because of Murray's on-air humiliation, which, for lack of better words, *cancels him*. The Joker seeks to annihilate his oppressors: the rage bait media, global elites, Big Pharma, and all those worshipping at the altar of political correctness.

Furthermore, the movie demonstrates that gun violence is the product of mental illness, having nothing to with conservative Christian values or the NRA. Detractors call it racist and reactionary, arguing that the vengeful white male, Arthur, typifies the sort of person who voted for Donald Trump. This argument falls short because Arthur kills only Caucasians–five of them–while falling in love with an African-American woman. Arthur is not a racist, and his shadow self, the Joker, states he is not politically motivated. With this anti-establishment construct in mind, the casting of De Niro takes on a new light because the actor has willingly accepted the role of the self-righteous, condescending, Hollywood celebrity archetype that the middle class has come to loathe over last 25 years. De Niro-as-Murray, representing Hollywood's smug elitism, humiliates the downtrodden– personified by Arthur *qua* Joker–on live television. Arthur returns the favor by killing Murray publicly; when Arthur murders him, the Joker terminates the Woke and Cancel Culture movements figuratively.

Hopefully, we'll see the Joker tyrannize Gotham under the direction of Todd Phillips again. We'll never see Batman back in action under the directorship of Chris Nolan; however, the Matt Reeves-directed *The Batman* is about to kick off production. In late 2019-early 2020, Reeves' take on the Caped Crusader is shaping up to be a Batman-noir detective tale, featuring a vast rogues gallery which I, for one, am looking forward to seeing. Already cast is Robert Pattinson as Bruce Wayne/Batman, Paul Dano as Edward Nashton/the Riddler, Zoë Kravitz as Selina Kyle/Catwoman, Colin Farrell as Oswald Cobblepot/the Penguin, and Jeffrey Wright as Commissioner Gordon. In the meantime, though, the DC fandom (which includes this author) can at least take solace because the Dark Knight Trilogy and *Joker* remain the epitome of superhero/supervillain cinema and fantastic movies in their own right.

Time to leave Gotham City; next, *Cinema Symbolism 3* explores the sacred feminine's dark side, so "Fasten your seatbelts. It's going to be a bumpy night." – Margo Channing (Bette Davis), *All About Eve*, 1950.

CHAPTER VIII

THE DARK SIDE OF THE MOON: THE UNCANNY ELECTRICITY OF THE TEMPTRESS

How can you be so mean to someone so meaningless?
Selina Kyle, *Batman Returns*, 1992

You cannot have it both ways.
A dancer who relies upon the doubtful comforts
of human love can never be a great dancer. Never.
Boris Lermontov, *The Red Shoes*, 1948

♪ But down in the underground
You'll find someone true
Down in the underground
A land serene, a crystal moon ♪
David Bowie, "Underground," 1986

Nothing quite encourages as does one's first unpunished crime.
Marquis de Sade, *The 120 Days of Sodom*, 1785

I released a gospel record when I was 15 because I grew up in a household where all I ever did was listen to gospel music …
I swear I wanted to be like the Amy Grant of music, but it didn't work out, and so, I sold my soul to the Devil.
Katy Perry

Have you ever seen a picture of yourself,
taken when you didn't know you were being photographed,
from an angle that you don't usually see when you look in a mirror,
and you think: that's me, that's also me.
India Stoker, *Stoker*, 2013

CINEMA SYMBOLISM 3

> Time rushes by, love rushes by, life rushes by, but *The Red Shoes* go on.
> Boris Lermontov, *The Red Shoes*, 1948

> You're not a virgin, are you?
> Thomas Leroy, *Black Swan*, 2010

> Fancy praying to a god who was nailed to a wooden cross,
> who locked up his brides in a convent.
> Did they really enjoy themselves, hmmm?
> Poor little virgins masturbating in the dark and then in penance
> for their sins indulging in flagellation
> till their bodies wept tears of blood.
> Captive virgins, hmmm, in the hands of an impotent god.
> Dionin will have none of that, Eve.
> Lady Sylvia Marsh, *The Lair of the White Worm*, 1988

In cinema, like literature, the moon's dark side assumes many nebulous forms, inclining toward the weird. Fetish exploration, bondage, submission, humiliation, incest, madness, obsession, ritual masturbation, devil worship, torture, sadomasochism, murder, lesbianism, and necrophilia are the purview of the dark side of the sacred feminine. Pleasurable destruction of the flesh is irresistible corruption, decadent bliss, and, god willing, the soul's annihilation. But to wantonly engage in epicureanism is not without penalty, and the price is high: death, depression, embarrassment, and contrition are the consequences for living deliciously.

Is it worth it? Donatien Alphonse François (1740-1814), better known as the Marquis de Sade, thought so. In *The 120 Days of Sodom* (written 1795, published 1905) de Sade tells us: "'Oh, there are plenty of people,' the Duc used to observe, 'who never misbehave save when passion spurs them to ill; later, the fire gone out of them, their now calm spirit peacefully returns to the path of virtue and, thus passing their life going from strife to error and from error to remorse, they end their days in such a way there is no telling just what roles they have enacted on earth. Such persons,' he would continue, 'must surely be miserable: forever drifting, continually undecided, their entire life is spent detesting in the morning what they did

CINEMA SYMBOLISM 3

The goddess Hecate rules the dark side of the lunar cycle: in *Eye of the Devil* (1967), Sharon Tate (top left, 1943-1969) portrays Odile de Caray, a witch practicing the dark arts. Dressed in black and wearing an amulet, the Eye of the Devil around her neck, she is named after Odile–the Black Swan maiden–the secondary antagonist in *Swan Lake*. Odile was portrayed by Natalie Portman (top right, as Nina Sayers) in *Black Swan*, fusing masturbation and masochism to awaken her dark side, alchemically changing her into a monster. Sayers' bizarre facial expression and crazy eyes mirror Charles Manson (bottom left), the murderer of Sharon Tate; his cult, known as the Family, resembled a witches' coven. Manson was inspired to murder Tate because of the Beatles' song "Helter Skelter" (1968), coauthored by John Lennon. In turn, Lennon was killed at the Dakota Apartment Building (bottom right) in 1980, where the Mephistophelian *Rosemary's Baby* took place. The director was Roman Polanski, husband of Sharon Tate, completing the dark Jungian synchronistic cycle, tying the deadly satanic knot together. Indeed, it appears as though the Devil had ridden out, the diabolical rider bringing chaos and death.

the evening before. Certain to repent of the pleasures they taste, they take their delight in quaking, in such sort they become at once virtuous in crime and criminal in virtue.'" This chapter explores daring women who have boldly allowed their passions to consume them, destroying them in some instances. Again, we turn to de Sade, who explained this untamable lust in *Juliette* (1797): "My passions, concentrated on a single point, resemble the rays of a sun assembled by a magnifying glass: they immediately set fire to whatever object they find in their way."

Before we delve into *The Red Shoes*, *Lolita*, *The Neon Demon*, *The Shape of Water*, and *Red Sparrow*, I feel it necessary to revisit–briefly– movies showcasing Luna's shadow, films analyzed in my previous books. Let's start with the granddaddy of them all, *Black Swan*. Aronofsky's masterpiece presents a sexually frustrated ballerina, Nina Sayers, blending masturbation and masochism to awaken her dark side, a quixotic yearning to dance the role of Odile the Black Swan. Nina, a repressed lesbian, goes through an alchemical transition, changing emotionally and physically, metamorphizing into a horrific birdlike creature. Her eyes bloodred and feet webbed, she grows wings during *Swan Lake* (1876), announcing her saturnine perfection. Nina's ringtone implies this infernal alchemy, her Transyuggothian sorcery. Before landing the role of the Swan Queen, the incoming call alert on her mobile device is a typical ringtone. After landing the coveted role, it tinkles the melancholic "Swan Theme" right before she dances in the nightclub–the discotheque's lights flash red, announcing the *rubedo*, indicating the Magnum Opus' completion.[425] From here on out, she changes from timid virgin to seductive Black Swan; her dance morphs from rigid to effortless as she abandons her ego, embracing her romanticized shadow self. While performing *Swan Lake*, the stage glows red, signifying the *rubedo*; thus, Nina mutates, growing wings, becoming a Black Swan. Easter egg: *Black Swan* begins with Nina dreaming, performing ballet with *Swan Lake*'s villain, von Rothbart, an owl-man. To dream of night birds, viz. the owl, bittern, and bat is an ill omen, foreshadowing Nina's mental erosion and eventual death.[426]

---

[425] "Swan Theme" also plays over the opening credits of *Dracula* (1931), *The Mummy* (1932), and *Murders in the Rue Morgue* (1932).
[426] Girard, *Mystic Dream Book*, 47; *The Witches' Dream Book*, 34.

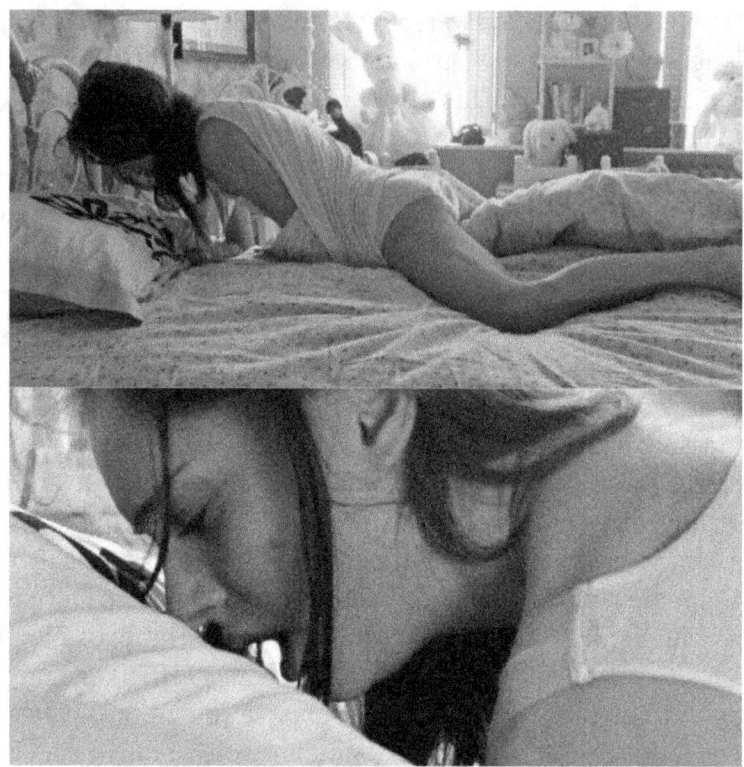

"My body, weary of empty clasp, Strong as a lion, sharp as an asp – Come, O Come! I am numb / With the lonely lust of devildom." – Aleister Crowley, "Hymn to Pan," 1913. (Top and Bottom) Nina, a Romantic Satanist at heart, masturbates in bed before her sleeping mother, basking in the pleasurable Luciferian sun, foreshadowing her alchemical transition to the dark side, descending into the *nigredo* to obliterate her ego. The black swan stuffed toy is a token of putrefaction, anticipating her metamorphosis. Later, Nina hallucinates she and Lily are sapphic lovers; when this turns out to be false, it means Nina's "lezzie wet dream" was either: (1) autoeroticism; or (2) an incestuous affair with her mother. "Then Oothoon pluck'd the flower, saying: 'I pluck thee from thy bed, Sweet flower, and put thee here to glow between my breasts; And thus I turn my face to where my whole soul seeks.'" – William Blake, *Visions of the Daughters of Albion*, 1793.

"I wear my father's belt tied around my mother's blouse and shoes which are from my uncle. This is me." – India Stoker, recognizing that she's a composite figure plagued with a fractured psyche. *Stoker* imitates *Black Swan*'s sullen alchemy; it's a British-American psychological thriller drama film written by Wentworth Miller and directed by South Korean filmmaker Park Chan-wook in his English-language debut. With stringy black hair shrouding her pale face, India (Mia Wasikowska) is a dour, intelligent, loathsome introvert: a kind of Victorian-Jungian shadow of Wasikowska's Jane Eyre. She is a voyeur who hates being touched; concurrently, her acute sensitivity picks up household whispers, a tiny spider crawling up her leg, over her black stockings, the foreboding tick of a metronome, and the cracking of a hardboiled eggshell sounds like breaking bones. She sits at the dinner table sipping wine, pretending to be an adult, a mature lover, when, in reality, she is nothing more than a virgin, a fledgling masturbator. Like troubled Nina, this ne'er-do-well fondles herself to formulate alchemy, the Sacred Art, transitioning from a melancholic teenager to a vile murderess, believing high heels and murder make her sophisticated. Her pathetic onanism, her great rapture, much like *Mulholland Drive*'s Diane Selwyn violent caresses, is a nihilistic baptism: while taking a shower, she fantasizes about death while touching herself, reaching orgasm when the victim's neck snaps.

Stoker is loaded with homages and allusions to the master of suspense, especially *Shadow of a Doubt* (1943) and *Psycho*. Like Hitchcock's movies, *Stoker* relies on the actors' raw emotions and facial expressions rather than dialog to move the narrative forward. What makes a film timeless doesn't have to do with the moral codes or overt edginess but to make a piece of cinema investing the audience in a story by deploying its unique style. With different emotional arcs and plot devices in each film, the reliance of visual and audio storytelling rather than dialogue is what makes *Shadow of a Doubt*, *Psycho*, and *Stoker* thrilling masterpieces in their own right. Easter Egg: a spider climbs up India's leg, over her black hosiery, implying change: fledgling virgin to a dour murderess. A spider ceaselessly weaves and kills, creating and destroying, denoting transmutation, anticipating her grim metamorphosis.[427] Spiders link with the moon, further identifying her with the goddess Diana, a huntress like India.[428] At night, she stands erect like a phallus before the luminous orb; accordingly, many myths depict the moon as a giant spider.[429]

As I explained in *Cinema Symbolism 2*, *9 ½ Weeks* is cinematic autoeroticism, nothing less. The female protagonist, Elizabeth, cultivates a penchant for black silk stockings, masturbating to surreal images of demons

---

427 Cirlot, *Dictionary*, 289-290.
428 Ibid.
429 Ibid.

CINEMA SYMBOLISM 3

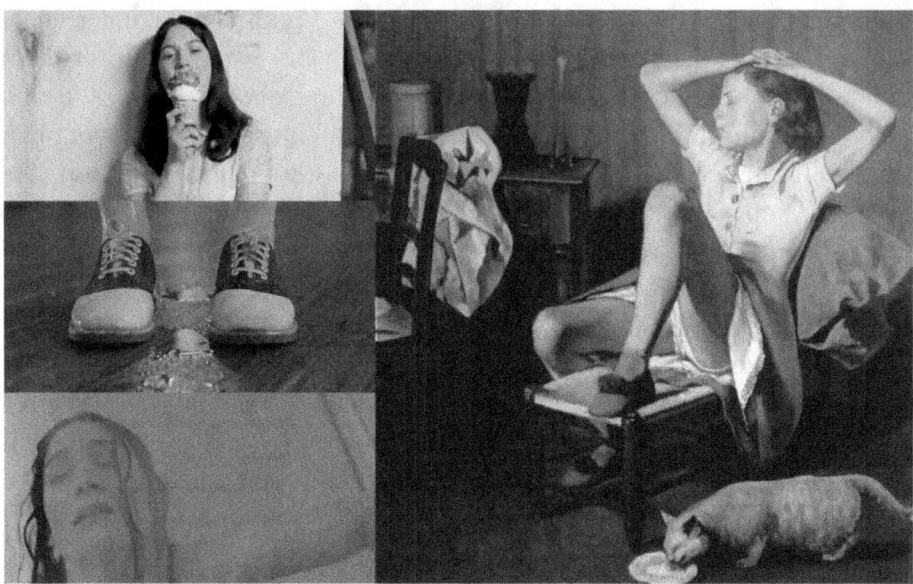

(Top left) To ease her sexual frustration, India Stoker erotically licks an ice cream cone symbolizing her desire to perform fellatio–she's a peeping Tom unable to procure a boyfriend. (Center left) Saddle shoes are India's idée fixe, the black and white shoes contrasting her youthful innocence against her tormented-cracked psyche (like the chocolate and vanilla of her ice cream cone) and fragile emotional state. Caught in a rainstorm (which she was warned about), she stands humiliated before her mother, Evelyn (Nicole Kidman), and her Uncle Charlie (Matthew Goode), as they play the piano. Drenched, the puddle on the floor represents arousal fluid dripping from her vagina, her swollen clit; indeed, India is suffering a Freudian nightmare. Like Onan from the Book of Genesis, she wants her arousal fluids to soil the ground; India has no problem offending deity. She is soaked, stimulated, and angered by seeing her mother and her uncle's music-making, which she misinterprets as lovemaking. Her wet shoes are a harbinger of her troubled and perverted homicidal-masturbatory fantasy; furthermore, to Swedenborg, shoes symbolize the lowly nature, implying India's despicable personality. Later, she will play the piano, with her uncle sitting beside her, becoming titillated and entranced, having symbolic intercourse, performing musical coitus. Was her uncle there seated beside her, or was India alone and fantasizing, jilling off? Solitary piano playing represents masturbation. It appears as though the latter is true, but the question is left ambiguous, open to interpretation. Regardless, India emerges from the duet with a greater awareness of herself, embracing her destructive nature and masturbatory desires. She no longer requires an instructor. The piano is the catalyst of this formative moment, part of her alchemical metamorphosis from melancholy girl to homicidal woman, which she acknowledges in her monologue, "To become adult, is to become free." (Bottom left) While taking a shower, signifying a baptism of darkness, India masturbates to embrace her shadow, fantasizing about death and murder. Her alchemy perfected, she changes into the embodiment of the *nigredo*, becoming a psychopath. India's youthful, erotic antics resurrect the controversial Expressionist oil painting, *Thérèse Dreaming* (right, 1938) by Balthasar Klossowski de Rola (aka Balthus, 1908–2001), romanticizing the sexualization of a girl.

and other simulacra to both free and embrace her Jungian shadow, the alchemical *nigredo*, for Elizabeth the *nigredo* is the *rubedo*. She embodies the dogma of the 19th-century Decadents, emphasizing a sickness at the world, skepticism, delighting in perversion. Blake wrote, "The road of excess leads to the palace of wisdom"; *The Red Shoes'* Vicky Page takes this satanic proverb to a deadly extreme.[430] In *Cinema Symbolism 2*, I wrote:

> ...it is a journey of self-discovery because she wishes to push the boundaries of her self-imposed banal status quo. She wants to alchemically effectuate selfhood by unifying her dark erotic self, the alchemical *nigredo*, with her ego. Initially, the *nigredo* is an objective state, visible from the outside only and is an unconscious state of non-differentiation between self and object, consciousness and the unconscious. John personifies this condition: he is light, i.e., the sun, and shadow, viz. *nigredo*, Crow's Head, *Sol Niger*, simultaneously. However, and more importantly, the second *nigredo* is a subjectively experienced process brought about by the subject's painful and growing awareness of their shadow aspects, clearly visible in this motion picture. As Elizabeth starts to unleash her shadow, she experiences heightened sexual pleasure that is not without consequence: she begins to collapse psychologically suffering from anxiety, tension, depression, and by movie's conclusion, total emotional meltdown. To effect this change, Elizabeth wears darker clothing and lingerie, signaling her transformation; Elizabeth's black stockings signify her shadow and the wanton cravings that she desperately desires to explore and experience. Elizabeth's repressed yearnings are the profound wisdom of the *nigredo*; it is the sullen light of the Left-Hand Path that she travels. Elizabeth, to know herself, must acknowledge her inner darkness and black magic-like sexual desires. She must learn to adore the Goat of Mendes, to worship at his satanic altar, supplicating to gain its favor. This sexual predicament torments *Black Swan*'s Nina as well. Dark sensuality and erotic experiments excite and repel both Elizabeth and Nina, making both women embodiments of a conflict they cannot resolve. Their predicament is a chimera: neither woman can reconcile

---

[430] Quoted in Churton, *Occult Paris*, 58.

their egos with their Lilith-like shadow selves regardless of how much they masturbate or delight in deviance.[431]

Elizabeth's masturbatory ceremony is an erotic, provocative, and alchemical rite; it is the Lesser Work of Sol. Because it is explicit and transformative, one thinks of the sexual practices of secret societies like the *Ordo Templi Orientis* (OTO); its members perform tantric sex magicks to effect transition, positive and negative. In *Aleister Crowley: The Nature of the Beast*, Colin Wilson (1931-2013) writes on the OTO's history and practices:

> This event occurred in the following year (1912), when Crowley received an unexpected visit from a German named Theodore Reuss, who introduced himself as a high-ranking German Freemason and the head of a magical order called the OTO–the *Ordo Templi Orientis*, or Order of the Temple of the East. And, to Crowley's astonishment, Ruess accused him of betraying the secrets of the ninth grade of this order. Now it so happened that Crowley was a member of the OTO–he had joined it in the previous year. But then, Crowley was a kind of collector of secret societies, and he had joined it thinking it was simply another order of Freemasons (otherwise, why did he call it a temple?). Crowley hastened to point out that he had not reached the ninth grade, and so could not betray its secrets. Reuss then reached out and took from Crowley's shelf his recent work *The Book of Lies*, and pointed to a section that opened: 'Let the adept be armed with his magic rod and provided with his mystic rose.' Reuss was obviously unaware that although 'rood' means rod in old English, it is generally used of a crucifix, and that this is what Crowley meant by it. Crowley had a flash of intuition, and realized that the 'secrets' of the ninth degree were sexual in nature. He and Reuss had a long conversation about magic and sex, and found themselves in close sympathy. And when Reuss left, he had allowed Crowley to found an English branch of the OTO. Crowley had to go to Berlin to be initiated; typically, he chose for himself the magical name Baphomet–the name of the demonic idol that the Knight Templars [*sic*] were accused of worshipping.

---

431 Sullivan, *Cinema Symbolism 2*, Chapter XI.

The rituals of the OTO were not simply an excuse for sexual orgies. The order had been founded around the turn of the century by a rich German named Karl Kellner, and Reuss was his successor. (He seems to have been rather an odd character: a member of the German secret service, a journalist, a music hall singer, and a political agitator who tried to infiltrate the London Marxist organization.) Kellner had been heavily influenced by the branch of Hinduism known as Tantra, an attempt to achieve mystical union with the universe by regarding it as a continuous process of creation. This was blended with orthodox western magic, which is based upon the belief that the mind can exercise a direct influence on nature. One of the most widespread forms of magic, for example, is the charging of talismans with magical power–a talisman is a 'charm' designed to help its owner to achieve a certain end, such as wealth or sexual conquest or fame. A talisman would normally be 'charged' by the performance of a ritual or ceremonial magic. In the OTO, two 'initiates' would perform a ceremony culminating in a sexual act, concentrating the aim of the magical operation, and end by anointing the talisman with a mixture of sperm and the secretions of the vagina, known as the 'elixir', or amrita.

...Crowley's first act on becoming head of the London OTO was to rewrite all its rituals in his own inimitable style. They are, of course, full of quotations from *The Book of the Law*, and laced with Crowleyan blasphemies, such as a section on the Black Mass in which Crowley attacks Roman Catholicism as 'that base and materialistic cult', and praises practitioners of the Black Mass because 'at least they set up Man against the foul demon of the Christians.'[432]

Ultimately, Elizabeth's onanism and OTO-like sex magicks backfire: she does not transform into a sexy black magician, a Lilith-like seductress, a mistress of fiery lust; instead, she suffers a nervous breakdown, experiencing anxiety, humiliation, and sexual frustration. Masturbation may harm the weak-willed because it results from foolishness; folly is not the product, but the cause of

---

[432] Colin Wilson, *Aleister Crowley: The Nature of the Beast* (London: Aquarian Press, 1987), 102-104.

"O Fool! begetter of both I and Naught, resolve this Naught-y Knot! ...OP-us, the Work! the OP-ening of THE EYE! Thou Naughty Boy, thou openest THE EYE OF HORUS to the Blind Eye that weeps! The Upright One in thine Uprightness rejoiceth -- Death to all Fishes!" – Aleister Crowley, "The Fool's Knot," *The Book of Lies*, 1912. *9 ½ Weeks'* Elizabeth masturbates to a painting with the all-seeing eye (left), often associated with the Illuminati. The dark puppet masters seem to approve her masturbation, her solitary erotic sorcery, her alchemical sex magick. "Magical operations are usually performed in an artificial twilight; this represents the glamour of the astral plane which the magician proposes to illumine with the divine light." – Aleister Crowley, *777 and Other Qabalistic Writings of Aleister Crowley*. (Top right) Elizabeth is caught in a fool's knot, mesmerized by Luciferian radiance, projecting luminous demonic images, causing her to become aroused. (Center right) The alchemical masturbator personified: soaking wet and spewing bodily fluids, the Left-Hand Path's somber light consumes Elizabeth. Her black stockings are sweet seduction, becoming a token and source of *the dark sister* and its associated pleasures. She experiences rapture, paralleling the OTO's practice of mystical, transformative sex magicks. But Elizabeth's alchemy fails, symbolized by a picked apart fish (bottom right) at the art gallery's exhibition party, implying she's emotionally broken. "O Rose thou art sick. The invisible worm, That flies in the night / In the howling storm: Has found out thy bed / Of crimson joy: And his dark secret love / Does thy life destroy." – William Blake, "The Sick Rose" in *Songs of Experience*, 1794.

Elizabeth's intense masturbation, hedonism, and oddball fetishism.[433] By the end, Elizabeth is a dunce-cap wearing fool, and she knows it.

"Beware, beware! Beware of the big green dragon that sits on your doorstep. He eats little boys, puppy dog tails, and big, fat snails. Beware,

---

[433] O.A. Wall, *Sex and Sex Worship (Phallic Worship)* (St. Louis: C.V. Mosby Company, 1922), 166.

(Left): Paint it black; exit the ego, enter the *nigredo*. Selina Kyle spray-paints her pink apartment, turning it into a Stygian den, allowing her shadow's emergence, becoming Catwoman; black cats, *nota bene*, symbolize darkness. (Right) After she's dropped by Penguin's (Danny DeVito) umbrella into a greenhouse, Catwoman cracks psychologically, realizing she is no dominatrix, and her exploration into the world of bondage was just folly. Frustrated, she screams pleasurable agony, shattering the greenhouse's glass and her psyche. The red flowers surrounding her indicate the *rubedo*, which, for the femme fatale wannabe, is the *nigerdo*: embarrassment, torture, and the suffering of the submissive loser is her endgame. From *Batman Returns*.

take care…beware!" – The Scientist *qua* Demiurge (Bela Lugosi), *Glen or Glenda*, 1953. This cryptic admonition cautions the listener to moderate materialism, and not give in to forbidden desires and urges. Nina Sayers, Elizabeth McGraw, and India Stoker fail to heed this warning. All three women succumb to strange fetishes: Nina's tight and restrictive ballet slippers are excruciating yet pleasurable; Elizabeth's black silk stockings masturbate her, supplying her with sable alchemical rapture. India's saddle shoes consume her: she places them on her bed, encompassing her like a lover. Thus, the ballet slippers, black silk stockings, and saddle shoes are bitter comforts, harassing and soothing their flesh simultaneously.

Also bitten by the big green dragon is *Batman Returns*' Selina Kyle/Catwoman, portrayed by Michelle Pfeiffer, which is a radical departure from her comic book and television personas. Her DYI Catwoman costume is stitched together, suggesting a cleaved personality, split into multiple identities, foreshadowing her psychotic breakdown. Pfeiffer's Catwoman thinks she is a dominatrix, but she isn't; instead, she is a pretender, nothing more than a mere weakling. Her black vinyl Catwoman outfit changes her into an alchemical-erotic trickster, but she ends up the fool, her costume in tatters, sexually frustrated, and defeated—the constrictive-sexy vinyl and stiletto heels devour her flesh. In essence, she convinces herself that she is the terrifying Lilith when, in reality, she embodies the Greek goddess Atë whose dominion is mischief, delusion, ruin, and folly. Selina/Catwoman is a paradox: she is a sadomasochist, having consigned herself to a limbo wherein her lust can never be satisfied because it never existed. Put another way, the moment she sheds her mousey-submissive secretary persona and dons her Catwoman costume, she becomes sexless–spayed–only she thinks she is salacious. Knocking out the *O* in the word *HELLO*, and the *T* in *THERE–HELLO THERE*–Catwoman stands before the neon sign, *HELL HERE*. Selina is gone; instead, Catwoman is in a Hell of her creation: she has willingly entered the Second Circle–Lust–believing that, as a dominatrix, her carnal desires will be finally satisfied. In time, her libido will be negated as she comes to understand that she is a pathetic submissive, getting off on her humiliation and destruction.

The Dance of Death: The Romantic Satanism of the Red Shoes

"Artist, thou art priest: Art is great mystery; and if your attempt turns out to be a masterwork, a divine ray descends as on an altar. ...Artist, thou are king; art is the real kingdom. ...Artist, thou art magus: art is the great miracle and proves our immortality." – Joséphin Péladan, Preface to *Geste Esthetique Catalogue du Salon de la Rose+Croix*. Anticipating the tragic femininity of *Lizzie, Black Swan, Stoker,* and *9 ½ Weeks* is Victoria "Vicky" Page, portrayed elegantly by Moira Shearer, in the Archers' (Michael Powell, 1905-1990, and Emeric Pressburger, 1902-1988) production of *The Red Shoes*. The drama, released in 1948 to a post-WWII world, documents a ballerina's chimera: a desire for perfection and fame by dancing *The Red Shoes*' lead, a dark ballet based on the 1845 fairy tale by Hans Christian Andersen (1805-1875). If the Rose-Croix Salons' Decadents and Symbolists would've admitted women, they would've toasted *9 ½ Weeks*' Elizabeth (*vide supra*); still, Vicky would've been their neo-Rosicrucian goddess, an alchemical muse, her bust mounted on a lofty marble plinth.[434] The central Decadent tactic of inverting, challenging the hegemonic values, symbols, and semantics harmonizes with satanic

---

434 Churton, *Occult Paris*, 274.

feminism's hermeneutics. The radicalizing of the woman as the Devil's chosen one makes her a threat to patriarchal structures and mores.[435] Vicky is a subversive Romantic Satanist: an independent performer consumed by her craft, willing to make the ultimate sacrifice for her art: to forsake love and domesticated bliss to dance the footlights, dying in a state of alchemical perfection, becoming a Philosopher's Stone, signified by the red shoes, a color given to passion and lust.[436] But trading domesticity for high art is an inversion; she replaces godly home and hearth with creativity, the need for fame, and opulent magnificence. She confuses God with the Devil; to her, Jehovah is an oppressive, dogmatic monster, and the Dark Angel a spiritual revolutionary, a liberator of forbidden impulses.[437] Crowley noted that "Spiritual attainments are incompatible with bourgeois morality."[438] Guided by this Luciferian philosophy, Vicky wants to become a dark hierophany: to be Lilith reborn, an aesthetic manifestation, a living-breathing sacred feminine paragon. By embracing her antinomian desires, her artistry, she offends social mores but dies a martyred bohemian: her death makes her a feminist counterculture icon, a radical nonconformist. Her transgression is more than an inversion; it is a hybrid: a blend of rebellion with artistry–ballet–to actively shift the system by erasing and interrogating the relationships and constructs which constitute her milieu. She wishes to drink the Elixir of Life and live forever; Vicky sees herself as a goddess, a famous ballerina dwelling with the other immortals. Instead, like any ballerina, she tries to reconcile desire with reality. Symbolically, the beautiful dancer tiptoes across the Grimpen Mire but gets caught in the quicksand, drowning in artistic expression, choking on romantic perfection, murdered by the scarlet slippers.

At the 21st Academy Awards, *The Red Shoes* won Best Original Score and Best Art Direction awards. It also had nominations for Best Picture, Best Original Screenplay, and Best Film Editing. Today, it is regarded as one of the best films of Powell and Pressburger's partnership, and in 1999, it was voted the 9th greatest British film of all time by the British Film Institute.

Have you ever seen a gaggle of millennials trying to force their way into a theater to watch a ballet performance? As of 2020, this author can

---

[435] Faxneld, *Satanic Feminism*, 251-252.
[436] Astra Cielo, *Signs, Omens and Superstitions* (New York: George Sully & Company, 1918), 113.
[437] Michael Osiris Snuffin, *Introduction to Romantic Satanism* (Throned Eye Press, 2020), 9-10.
[438] Quoted in Churton, *Occult Paris*, 158.

affirmatively answer *no* to that question. Such is not the case in *The Red Shoes*. In post-WWII England, the film opens with a group of boisterous students trying to break down the doors of the Covent Garden Opera House to see a performance by the prestigious Ballet Lermontov, the hottest ticket in town. Among them is enthusiastic music student Julian Craster, who is eager to hear the ballet score, *Heart of Fire*, composed by his teacher, Professor Palmer (Austin Trevor, 1897-1978), who has a box seat. Also present is Vicky, a young, unknown dancer with an aristocratic background attending with her aunt, Lady Neston (Irene Browne, (1896-1965). Unfortunately, Julian recognizes *Heart of Fire* as one of his compositions, leaving the theater disillusioned over his professor's plagiarism. During the performance, the unscrupulous Professor Palmer receives an invitation to an after-party at Lady Neston's residence. Boris Lermontov (Anton Walbrook), the company's eccentric, demanding, and pugnacious impresario, is also invited. Vicky and Lermontov meet at the soirée awkwardly; nevertheless, he asks her to attend a company's rehearsal.

Julian writes a letter to Lermontov explaining the circumstances behind *Heart of Fire* but then tries to retrieve it. Lermontov's assistant Dimitri (Eric Berry, 1913-1993) thwarts Julian's attempts to gain entry to the impresario's suite, but finally, the maestro grants him an audience. Julian says that he wishes to recover his letter before Lermontov has seen it, except that he has already read it. Lermontov asks Julian to play one of his works on the piano. After hearing it, he hires him as a répétiteur for the company's orchestra and assistant to its conductor, Livingstone Montague (Esmond Knight, 1906-1987), known colloquially as "Livy." Lermontov realizes Julian is the composer of *Heart of Fire*.

Julian and Vicky arrive for work at the Ballet Lermontov on the same day. Later, Vicky dances with the Ballet Rambert in a matinee performance of *Swan Lake* at the Mercury Theatre, Notting Hill Gate, in a production led by Marie Rambert (1888-1982), appearing as herself in a wordless cameo. Watching this performance, the director realizes her vast potential and invites her to go with Ballet Lermontov to Paris and Monte Carlo. He decides to create a starring role for her in a new ballet, *The Red Shoes*, with Julian composing its music.

The Red Shoes is a resounding success; the ballet is about a young woman who acquires a cursed pair of red shoes, which, at first, stimulates

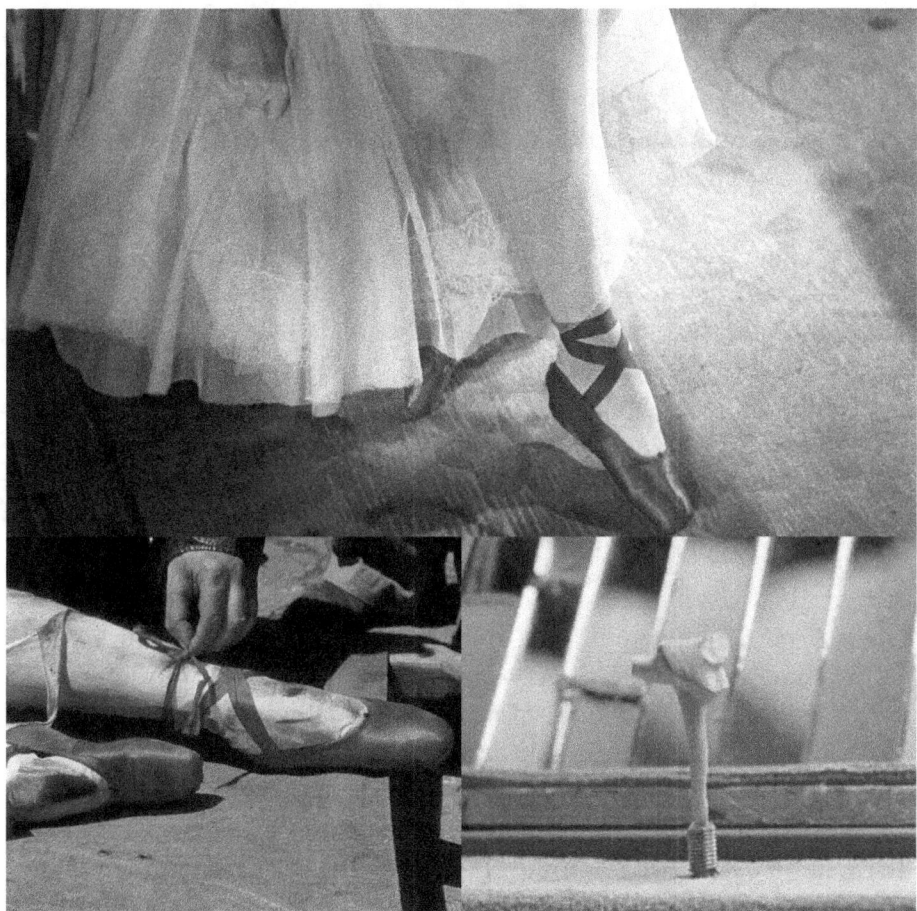

She was very much frightened, and tried to throw off her red shoes, but could not unclasp them. She hastily tore off her stockings; but the shoes she could not get rid of they had, it seemed, grown on to her feet." – Hans Christian Andersen, "The Red Shoes," 1845. (Top) Vicky allows her scarlet ballet slippers (viz. Andersen's cursed red shoes) to become an obsession representing her unwavering pride and vanity. A woman's shoes symbolize her sexuality, lifted from *Cinderella*. She becomes obsessed: her fists clenched, she can't remove them, signifying her obsession. (Bottom left) The red shoes take control, manipulating her, causing her to leap before an oncoming train, killing her. Her tights torn and blood-stained, Vicky dies ruined in a state of alchemical limbo. She cannot archive the *rubedo*: torn between her love for Julian and her passion for ballet, the shoes break her emotionally and sexually, consigning her to oblivion. Vicky's desire to dance *The Red Shoes* and achieve perfection anticipates Nina's need to dance the role of Odile, the Black Swan. In *Black Swan*, Nina's failure to integrate her ego with her shadow self allows her black fantasies to destroy her, symbolized by a broken music box dancer figurine (bottom right) in her bedroom.

her hubris, causing her to dance with glee and perfection. But she cannot remove them; exhausted, she eventually dances herself to death, asking a priest to remove the torturous shoes with her dying breath. Lermontov revitalizes the company's repertoire with Vicky in lead roles, and Julian tasked with composing new scores. The two artists fall in love, but keep their relationship secret from Lermontov. The impresario begins to have personal feelings toward Vicky; he resents the romance between her and Julian after learning they're an item. The tyrant fires Julian, so Vicky leaves the company with him. They marry and live in London, where Julian works on orchestrating a new opera.

Sometime later, while traveling, Vicky receives a visit from Lermontov, who convinces her to return to the company to dance a revival of *The Red Shoes*. In truth, she misses the spotlight and all the attention it brings. For Vicky, to live is to dance, to trip the footlights is her religion. On opening night, Julian appears in her dressing room; he has left the première of his opera at Covent Garden to find her and take her back. Lermontov arrives; he and Julian contend for Vicky's affection, arguing that her true destiny is only with him. Torn between her love for Julian and her compulsion to dance, she eventually succumbs to ballet. Her mercurial, idiosyncratic behavior is a rebellion against conformity; like the Devil, she wages war against God, denouncing moralistic discourses. A fetish devours Vicky: the red shoes, her precious crimson ballet slippers have physically and psychologically taken control of her, subverting her rationality. They are decadent tokens of her insatiable desire to dance, become transcendent art, conquering her flesh and spirit, overcoming Julian's love.

Julian, realizing he's lost her, leaves for the railway station heartbroken; the virtuoso consoles Vicky and tries to turn her attention to the evening's performance. She's escorted to the stage under the red shoes' demonic influence only to flee the theatre. Julian, on the platform, runs toward her. Guided by her cursed slippers, the danseuse jumps from a ledge and falls before a steaming locomotive to certain doom. The red shoes, her need to dance, and her quest for perfection has summoned the Grim Reaper. Shaken, Lermontov appears on stage to announce that, "Miss Page is unable to dance tonight–nor indeed any other night." As a mark of respect, the company performs *The Red Shoes* with a spotlight on the space where she would have danced. Dying on a stretcher, Vicky asks Julian to remove the hexed red slippers, just like at the end of *The Red Shoes* ballet. A Phoenix she is not: Vicky perishes for her art, unable to resurrect, humiliated because she has fallen short, conscious that her lust for transcendence has broken her mind and crushed her soul. Nor can she checkmate Death or ask Charon to drop her off elsewhere; Vicky is not Ygor, having survived the gallows, recounted in *Son of Frankenstein* and *The Ghost of Frankenstein* (1942).

The Nightmare of the *Nigredo* *The Red Shoes* is psychological alchemy, documenting a ballerina's yearning to taste the forbidden nectar known as perfection. Vicky, born world-weary of a Schopenhauerian civilization, seeks a satanic renewal of her soul, a Luciferian baptism. Ballet is her magic; fame is her godhead. Her mission is not to build but destroy, to demolish the old patriarchal order to prepare the arts' embryonic elements, reviving the Decadents (and Symbolists) post WWII. Like *Black Swan*'s Nina, Vicky's alchemical, Grail Quest fails; her metamorphosis is a temporary aphrodisiac, turning malignant then deathly. When considering the *nigredo*, we think of Jung's shadow self, personified by Maleficent in *Sleeping Beauty*, Nurse Ratched (Louise Fletcher) in *One Flew Over the Cuckoo's Nest* (1975), Han Gruber (Alan Rickman) in *Die Hard* (1988), and Erica Sayers, Beth Macintyre, and Rothbart in *Black Swan* to name a few. Vicky's consciousness is open to darkness, eager to hone her dancing beyond that of a typical ballerina, to journey far beyond the Anglican codes that have shaped her life. Lermontov instructs the path's difficulties, and that there are no two ways: the only way to be legendary is to rebel against love as Lucifer turned against God. At first, she agrees, anxious to dance *The Red Shoes*' lead. She is vain, desirous to be a cynosure. The scarlet shoes, bright crimson ballet slippers, are the *rebudo* representing the Magnum Opus' finality, emerging from the *nigredo*, signifying Vicky's relentless desire to eclipse the world of ballet, to become a living piece of art. Enter midnight: the deathly and chaotic *nigredo* is Lermontov's dark ballet based upon Andersen's fable. His choreography illustrates both pride and mortification: it is about a young woman's vanity stimulated when she dons a pair of red shoes, dancing rapturously through the town and countryside, resulting in death.

The young woman is Vicky, and Vicky is the young woman; the director knows there is no difference between the performer and the performance, that is why he's cast her. He also knows pride fuels her, so he turns it against her, making her a masochistic paragon, sacrificing everything for her art. *The Red Shoes*' plot is about a beautiful young woman who acquires a pair of exquisite red shoes, but there is a terrible price: they are cursed by the evil cobbler who sold them to her. She cannot remove them, causing her to dance endlessly without rest. They are an evil talisman, generating a harmful cycle: they feed her narcissism while perpetuating it. Although suffering, Vicky wants to leave them on because she gets off on self-admiration. But she also delights in mortification, deriving pleasure from her character's anguish. Her downfall occurs on stage for the audience to witness, adding to her shame. After she perishes, a priest (Robert Helpmann, 1909-1986) removes her shoes postmortem, absolving her sins. Only death can relieve her. The cobbler retakes his diabolical prize, awaiting the next vain woman to crave the red shoes.

The ballet is a parable of the historical Dance of Death. The dancing plague, or dance epidemic, was a case of dancing mania in Strasbourg, Alsace, (now modern-day France) in the Holy Roman Empire in 1518. Around 400 people took to dancing without rest, and, for about a month, some affected collapsed or died of heart attack, stroke, or exhaustion. From this bizarre incident rose the Cult of St. Vitus. A Christian Saint from Sicily believed to have escaped unscathed from a boiling cauldron of tar and molten lead, St. Vitus died a martyr at the Romans' hands in the 4th century. He was also one of the fourteen holy helpers of the Latin Church whose intervention was believed to be particularly useful combating certain diseases. St. Vitus' Day was celebrated on June 15, and, as the patron saint of dancers, it can't be a coincidence the outbreaks of dancing mania in Aachen and Strasbourg occurred around this date.

Worshippers in Germany and Latvia celebrated the day by dancing in front of his statue. Sydenham's Chorea, the neurological disorder which became known as *Saint Vitus Dance*, caused those stricken to suffer from rapid, uncoordinated jerking movements of the feet, face, and hands. Understandably, many people believed those involved in the dance manias were thought to be suffering from this disorder. The celebration of St. Vitus' Day was linked to the Feast Day of St. John the Baptist, or midsummer, on June 24 because the two days are a little over a week apart. At Obermedlingen, in Swabia, the *fire of heaven*, as it was called, was made on St. Vitus' Day by igniting a cart-wheel, which, smeared with pitch and plaited with straw, was fastened to a pole twelve feet high, the top of the pole being inserted in the nave of the wheel.[439] The fire was made on the summit of a mountain, and as the flame ascended, the people uttered a set form of words, with eyes and arms heavenward.[440] Not only the patron saint of dancers, St. Vitus guarded entertainers, comedians, epileptics as well as giving protection against lightning strikes, animal attacks, and oversleeping.[441]

Art imitates life: like the youthful victim in Lermontov's ballet, Vicky becomes entranced by the red shoes, developing a fondness for her slippers, denoting her bohemian pride and vanity. She desires fame and all the trappings that come with it; she lusts to be a great dancer, the *best* dancer. Eager to taste the forbidden and taboo, Vicky creeps around her bedroom at night while Julian is absent, keeping the crimson ballet slippers hidden in a drawer, admiring them like they are magical-sexual stimulants. She conceals them like a teenager would hide porno magazines from his parents, turning the pages in privacy. Unable to resist their talismanic pull, she willingly descends into the *nigredo's* chaotic aesthetics: she returns to tyrannical Lermontov, choosing to dance in *The Red Shoes* once again. Under Mercurius' spell, the slippers have mysteriously compelled her to abandon her womanly sensibilities, to wrought chaos from order.

Tragically, she cannot remove the red slippers; they have merged with her body; the laces tight around her ankles and calves like the Dianoga's suckered tentacles, sticking to her white tights. The red shoes consume her, crushing and chewing her artistic spirit like the Death Star's trash compactor. Under their hypnotic control, she leaves the theater hastily, throwing herself before a moving train to her death. Dying, her soul seems trapped and unable to leave her body. However, once the slippers are removed does Vicky die a broken and tortured artist. Like Lermontov's play, death rids her of the red shoes, consigned to a Baudelairean inferno. In reaching for the stars, she has unknowingly become a duality, a psychological non-Self, cleaving her psyche into two halves. One illuminated by the sun, her love for Julian, the other cut off from luminance, lit by the Black Sun, her obsessive need to trip the light fantastic. Shakespeare's Hamlet eloquently described the *nigredo's* pangs, anticipating Vicky's plight: "Whether 'tis

---

439 Frazer, *Golden Bough*, 635-636.
440 Ibid, 636.
441 Miss_Jessel, "The curse of the red shoes: dancing manias of the middle ages," *HauntedPalaceBlog*. April 4, 2013, https://hauntedpalaceblog.wordpress.com/2013/04/04/the-curse-of-the-red-shoes-dancing-manias-of-the-middle-ages/ (accessed April 24, 2019).

nobler in the mind to suffer the slings and arrows of outrageous fortune, ... For who would bear the whips and scorns of time, the oppressor's wrong, ...The pangs of despised love, the law's delay, the insolence of office and the spurns that patient merit of the unworthy takes, to grunt and sweat under a weary life, but that the dread of something after death, the undiscovered country from whose bourn no traveller returns."[442]

Bad Moon Rising: the *Albedo* "Don't go around tonight / Well it's bound to take your life / There's a bad moon on the rise." – Credence Clearwater Revival, 1969. Simultaneously, the *albedo* is a developmental step in a series of alchemical processes and the illuminating quality intrinsic in the blackening process. The lunar whiteness the alchemists speak of is not a whiteness separate from blackness. *Au contraire*, to understand the renewal that follows the *nigredo*, one must go beyond simple dichotomies and see the complexity of the darkness itself. Putrefaction extends and continuous even unto whiteness, and that shadow is not washed away. Built into the psyche's body, which then exhibits a kind of lustration, featuring both darkness and light.[443] Rising from *The Red Shoes*' *nigredo* comes Luna, the heavenly nocturnal queen, the illustrious Vicky Page, illuminating the movie. When she dances gloriously, Vicky wears white tutus, tights, and flowing dresses indicating moonlight, her virginal innocence, her genteel naiveté. This alchemical phase, when personified, incorporates the attributes of the Moon, the 28th trump card from the Major Arcana. The Moon card classifies as feminine because it's the mistress of the night and ruler of the waxing and waning rhythms of life, the menstrual cycle and the sea's tides, and so in modern Jungian psychological terms of the deep waters and swirling treacherous currents of the unconscious. The card connects with imagination and fantasy, representing Vicky's desire to dance, with dreams whose fitful and eerie moonlight disturbs the mind in sleep; its scaly impulses claw their way up into the conscious mind from the depths below. The moon can indicate madness (hence the word *lunacy*), and many writers have linked the trump card with fear and horror. Thus, the moon associates with archetypal imagery connected to the Dark Night of the Soul, i.e., the *nigredo*, hidden

---

442 William Shakespeare, *Hamlet*, Act III, Scene I. See also Marlan, *Black Sun*, 151-153, discussing the *albedo* and the *nigredo*.
443 Marlan, ibid, 99.

(Left) The Moon Card (XVIII) of the Major Arcana. On its archetypal symbolism, Ouspensky writes: "Dread fell upon me, I sensed the presence of a mysterious world, a world of hostile spirits, of corpses rising from graves, of wailing ghosts. In this pale moonlight I seem to feel the presence of apparitions; someone watched me from behind the tower,–and I knew it was dangerous to look back." (Right, Top and Bottom) The beautiful Vicky Page, the luminous moon, is tortured by her need to dance, and don the red shoes–her crimson ballet slippers–to delight in her destruction. Unable to look back, she is in a world of hostile spirits, ghosts, because dread has descended upon Vicky; she will soon die, wearing the red shoes, becoming a rotting corpse.

dangers, enemies, sorcery, witchcraft, and folkloric themes related to the werewolf: the human who turns into a murderous beast at night.[444]

Vicky merges matter with spirit for the nonce: her ambition to dance with her desire to be omnipresent. To conquer the ballet world, she willingly embraces the *nigredo*, rising like a moon, bringing clarity and purpose to the narrative, bridging the dark pit between unconscious and conscious. Vicky's intuition comprehends Lermontov's sable vision: a dark, punishing ballet that destroys the character in the performance and the dancer's will to power. Vicky dares to engage Lermontov, *albedo* absorbing *nigredo*, believing she can withstand the pressure and torments

---

444 Cavendish, *The Tarot*, 128.

that accompany dancing in *The Red Shoes*. To compensate, Vicky goes beyond Lermontov's edict because she is willing to forsake love and die for her craft, transcending art, transcending life. Earlier, Vicky dances in a production of *Swan Lake* at the Mercury Theater, indicating Mercurius, the sable patron of alchemy.[445] Her taboo, dark desires for preeminence, anticipate *Black Swan*'s Nina, who dies achieving perfection. Both women dance in eerie moonlight; the Moon card is the 18th trump, and by reduction is nine, the number of the Hermit. The path shown on the Moon card leads to the Hermit: a recluse who forsakes love for discipline, for quasi-religious beatification, according to occult teachings.[446] Vicky denies herself by abandoning her husband to satisfy her fetish, to put on the red shoes, dancing once again, resulting in death. In a Grail Quest seeking a chimera, preternatural excellence, Nina goes mad, fusing masturbation (one of the Hermit's hallmarks) with masochism to dance the role of Odile the Black Swan, which, likewise, kills her. Vicky's luminous moonlight blends with her dark, lurid desires, synthesized in the solar alchemical stage, the *citrinitas*, producing the *rubedo*, represented by her agonizing scarlet ballet slippers. By the endings of *The Red Shoes* and *Black Swan*, the prima ballerinas can no longer distinguish pleasure from pain, perfection from destruction, life from death. This occult focus provides the impetus for both films' rendering of the alchemical opus.

<u>Burning too Bright: the *Citrinitas*</u> Following the moon, the glorious sunrise dispels the night: Apollo defeats darkness, Python, or Jesus battles Satan, conquering him. The sun has long associated with masculine attributes in patriarchal culture. The sun relates to the king who can be benevolent and light the world, or it can stand still, becoming a dictator, burning the flesh, searing the soul. To the alchemists, the sun was the source of treasure, both material and spiritual. It is necessary to formulate the alchemical wedding or *coincidentia oppositorum*: male and female, order and chaos, light and dark, good and evil, and pleasure with pain. The *albedo* gives way to the *citrinitas*, the masculine, personified by three men, each an archetype, absorbing and manipulating Vicky-as-*albedo*. First, is the composer Julian, whom she marries, generating the alchemical wedding. Like he was guided by the daemon Love, Julian scores a rendition of *Cupid*

---

[445] Moreover, Mercury is a patron of the arts.
[446] Case, *The Tarot*, 185.

and Psyche, designating this perfected divine union. He and Vicky form the Lovers, the great archetypal conjunction, a union beyond duality. Through their love, they saw the mystery of the world's equilibrium, and that they were a symbol and expression of this balance. Two triangles united in them into a sex-pointed star. Two magnets melted into an ellipsis. They were two. The third was the Unknown Future. The three made one.[447]

In Lermontov's morose ballet, we have an evil cobbler, the fiendish shoes' creator, played by Russian choreographer and ballet dancer, Leonide Massine (1896-1979).[448] Massine as the impish cobbler, or shoemaker, is the trickster/magician/juggler, Card I of the Major Arcana. This archetype stood for the divine's spirit or vital energy concealed in matter, just as the trickster/magician/juggler is human spirit incarnated in the flesh. The archetype can be egotistical, brutal, and ruthless, abusing his powers for his selfish ends. He or she can be a sagacious black or white magician, having its roots in the divine.[449] In the ballet, Massine's trickster beguiles Vicky's character to put on the shoes, luring her with a prideful reflection of her wearing them–a doppelganger–making her dance endlessly, resulting in scorn and death. His shop's door is a cobweb, symbolizing the web he weaves about the unsuspecting victims lured to his parlor. Life imitates art, and the red slippers become a token of Vicky's ruthless ambition, yearning to perform and be the world's premier dancer. Massine the trickster, the *citrinitas'* incarnation, facilitates her insatiable hunger, further signifying *The Red Shoes* alchemical aesthetics.

However, Lermontov is the most potent masculine archetype, the manipulative impresario, personifying the Devil (card XV), enjoying the athanor's heat. He is the somber light of the Left-Hand Path, using Vicky as a pawn to satisfy his ego, known as the developer of the world's greatest ballerina, the sensational Victoria Page. He creates the ballet as her vehicle to stardom, knowing it holds the seed of her celebrity and the germ of her ruination; this nihilistic showman is a passionate animator and latent destroyer, a sinister P.T. Barnum (1810-1891). Lermontov anticipates *Black Swan*'s Thomas Leroy (Vincent Cassel), the Luciferian puppeteer of

---

[447] P.D. Ouspensky, *The Symbolism of the Tarot: Philosophy of Occultism in Pictures and Numbers Pen-Pictures of the Twenty-Two Tarot* Cards, trans. A.L. Pogossky (1913; repr., Mansfield Centre, CT: Martino Publishing, 2013), 39.
[448] In *The Red Shoes*, his character's name is Ljubov.
[449] Cavendish, *The Tarot*, 70.

Nina, who expedites her destruction, relentlessly harassing Nina to dance the Black Swan. Both Vicky and Nina see their respective impresarios as necessary–a demanding yet positive force; they are essential to achieve alchemical perfection. In reality, the Devil is the opposite: he is imprudent, unwise, and unreasonable, all that must be cleansed to reach their goals. But Lermontov and Leroy's demonic solar fire burns too bright, and Vicky and Nina, personifying the moon, must absorb their masters' darkness, destroying their bodies, breaking their spirits. Both Lermontov and Leroy come to lament their decisions to obliterate their beautiful creations, to make impure what was once wholesome.

Corrupted Perfection: the Finality of the *Rubedo* The red never lasts; the Philosopher's Stone cannot be maintained in perpetuity if it can be obtained at all. *The Red Shoes* brilliantly explores the psychological states of the alchemical sequence, mainly, the impossible interactions of the *rubedo*, identified by her red ballet slippers. Vicky performs alchemy, merging *albedo* with *citrinitas*, male and female, the Union of Opposites. In accomplishing unification, her alchemical quest is this: to become perfect, a perfect ballerina, not just great, but an unsurpassable superstar. Her metamorphosis is to transition from dancer to goddess, to transcend her art. To satisfy her need to dance, she develops a monomania for the red shoes, becoming a dark token of her ambition. As a result, Vicky becomes a counter archetype, a counterfeit pilgrim, a non-Self, epitomizing the impossible discipline of the *rubedo*, fostering perfection and annihilation simultaneously. Her orgasmic release is oblivion; as an artist, she failed to find her way through the labyrinth of the world to the paradise of the heart.

The Archers' movie suggests the *nigredo* contains the seeds of the *rubedo*. Or perhaps, for Vicky, the *rubedo* is the *nigredo*: perfection is destruction, implied by the Rolling Stones' song, "Paint It Black" (1966). Jagger sings, "♪ I see a red door and I want it painted black / I look inside myself and see my heart is black / I see my red door I must have it painted black ♫," insinuating the Magnum Opus' finality is a revival of the *nigredo*. The vision of selfhood, wholeness, i.e., *coincidentia oppositorum*, and aesthetic perfection, viz. the *rubedo*, remains shrouded amid decay, implying sublime harmony is nothing more than a fanciful ideal worthy of annihilation. These are the alchemical protagonist or antagonist's conundrums, producing an unsustainable thematic. Like Lizzie Borden, Nina Sayers, India Stoker, Elizabeth McGraw, an ominous chimera consumes Vicky. All these women erase their stories. Ultimately, the student of mysticism and alchemy, Mercurius' disciple, is left staring at the darkness–the somber alembic, the gloomy shew stone. All these women are left with are a guilty conscience, black feathers, saddles shoes, black silk stockings, and red ballet slippers–impotent emblems of their melancholic alchemy. But perhaps these women have learned one thing: the blackness is not nothingness because, for them, nihility might be everything.[450]

Lolita: Kubrick's Occult Impulse

Lolita is a 1962 British-American drama directed by the incomparable Stanley Kubrick. Based on a 1955 eponymous novel, Vladimir Nabokov also wrote the screenplay, which Kubrick used but a small portion. It follows a middle-aged literature lecturer who becomes sexually obsessed with a young adolescent girl, a nymphet. Kubrick, not wanting to fall foul of the Production Code Authority, had an interest in making Lolita a teenager, curtailing the novel's pedophilia-hebephilia overtones. The point was to make her a more sophisticated version of Sandra Dee (1942-2005), the blue-eyed blonde who, in her Gidget persona, was the epitome of the naughty-but-nice late 1950s teen sex appeal. Ergo, the movie is deliberately vague over Lolita's age; Kubrick has been quoted, wrongly: "I think that some people had the mental picture of a nine-year-old, but Lolita was twelve and a half in the book; Sue Lyon was thirteen." Lyon was fourteen by the time filming started and fifteen when it finished.[451] Although it passed without cuts, *Lolita* was rated X by the British Board of Film Censors when released, meaning no one under sixteen was permitted to see it. Lolita Haze (Sue Lyon, 1946-2019) personifies one of the darkest aspects of the sacred feminine: a nymphet who attracts two hebephiles, Humbert Humbert (James Mason, 1909-1984), and Clare Quilty (Peter Sellers), creating a devilish archetypal love triangle.

Lolita is a meditation on symbolism, inference, and innuendo. For the first time, Kubrick seems to be turned loose, like a mad scientist in a

---
450 Wilson, *Secret Cinema*, 112, 135, 143.
451 Graham Vickers, *Chasing Lolita: How Popular Culture Corrupted Nabokov's Little Girl All Over Again* (Chicago: Chicago Review Press, 2008), 117-118.

mountain laboratory, ready to bombard the viewer with a broad spectrum of images and suggestions, creating a film that resonates on multiple levels. Kubrick was obsessed with bathrooms, a place of intimacy and secrets. For example, Humbert writes in his diary while sitting on the toilet. Humbert needs utmost privacy when he writes his genuine thoughts and feelings about Charlotte and her tempting daughter. Later, in the tub, he celebrates Charlotte's death with a glass of booze.

Toilet humor pervades *Dr. Strangelove or: How I Learned to Stop Worrying and Love the Bomb* (1964) in its use of names and double entendres: as General Buck Turgidson (George C. Scott, 1927-1989) uses the toilet, his secretary and mistress, Miss Scott (Tracy Reed, 1942-2012) interrupts his privacy with an urgent phone call. His tone of voice intimates his perturbation; after all, his downtime has been disturbed. The outside world's monotonies, his job, have invaded his sanctuary. Like *A Christmas Story*'s (1983) Ralphie (Peter Billingsley), Turgidson employs the bathroom as a fortress of solitude: a place one is not to be troubled with the problems of others. Later, General Jack D. Ripper (Sterling Hayden) locks himself in his private bathroom, shooting himself without giving the CRM Code to Group Capt. Lionel Mandrake (Peter Sellers) to stop the nuclear missiles from destroying the world. Since Ripper was delusional, it is apropos that he killed himself inside the bathroom because its societal sacredness provided him an exit ramp from both his immediate problems and his life.

In *A Clockwork Orange* (1971), Kubrick shows us how a hot bath can be relaxing. Soaking in hot water, people often doze off or daydream. Despite having gone to prison for hurting innocent people, and receiving the Ludovico Technique, neutering his sex drive and violent tendencies, resting in a bath was young criminal Alex DeLarge's (Malcolm McDowell) undoing. Alex is taken in by Mr. Frank Alexander (Patrick Magee, 1922-1982), who, at the start, he'd crippled then raped his wife gleefully. Mr. Alexander does not recognize Alex and only knows of him through the newspapers for undergoing the Ludovico Technique. However, Alex *does* recognize Mr. Alexander, so he keeps his mouth shut, naturally. But when Alex gets too comfortable while taking a bath, he thoughtlessly hums "Singin' in the Rain," which was the same song he sang while assaulting Mr. Alexander and his wife years earlier. His signing reveals

Alex's identity as the thug who ruined his life; with this revelation, Mr. Alexander's stunned, bitter expression is unforgettable, making him look like a deranged gargoyle. In this instance, the bathroom is not the private-safe space that one may think.

Of all Kubrick's films, *The Shining* utilizes bathrooms to display the vulnerability of each Torrance family member, and how both real and figurative ghosts haunt them. Like *A Clockwork Orange*, the bathroom is not a haven or sanctuary. As five-year-old Danny (Danny Lloyd) communicates with his imaginary friend Tony, he looks ominously into the bathroom mirror. He suffers a vision of the infamous tidal wave of blood pouring out of the elevators. This dark premonition is a harbinger of the terror awaiting his family at the Overlook Hotel, causing him to seizure. Later, Jack investigates room 237, and upon entering the room's bathroom, he sees a naked young woman in the bathtub. When he sees this nude young woman, Jack's impish expression shows man's never-ending desire to have sex with attractive women. Seemingly bewitched, Jack does not speak to this strange woman; instead, he embraces and kisses her. She then turns into a crone with a rotting body, showing us that like the previous guests of the Overlook, the Torrance family seems destined to join the ghoulish apparitions that continually haunt the resort. When Jack goes to the Overlook's ballroom, he is led to the bathroom by the waiter, Delbert Grady (Philip Stone, 1924-2004). They need privacy to discuss how Jack's wife, Wendy (Shelley Duvall), a woman prohibited from entering a room designated for men only, is the cause of Jack's problems. At first, Grady is cordial and amenable. Still, Jack bluntly says that Grady killed his family, revealing the ugly truth, paralleling another unpleasant truth: bathrooms are used for urination and defecation. Grady then reveals his sinister nature by using a racial slur against the African-American chef Dick Hallorann (Scatman Crothers, 1910-1986), and suggesting Jack *correct* his wife and son, as Grady himself *corrected* his family years earlier. Finally, Wendy and Danny lock themselves inside a bathroom, trying to escape Jack's murderous rampage as he chops through the door with an ax. Besides Jack saying the famous line "Here's Johnny!" he is also violating the social norm of not intruding on someone using the bathroom. People feel vulnerable when they are inside because they are naked or doing private things. In this case, Jack invades the safe space bathrooms provide, and Wendy's life is at risk because of his violent intrusion.

In *Full Metal Jacket* (1987), the platoon's bathroom is sanitized and immaculate, so much so "the Virgin Mary herself would be proud to go in there and take a dump," to quote Gunnery Sergeant Hartman (R. Lee Ermey, 1944-2018). However, by the end of the Parris Island segment, the idea of the perfect soldier and the perfect bathroom is destroyed, making the bathroom a symbol of nihilistic duality: disciplined order and deathly chaos. The overweight and slow-witted recruit nicknamed *Gomer Pyle* (Vincent D'Onofrio) loses his sanity after constant torment from his drill instructor, causing him to be outcast by his fellow recruits. Private Joker (Matthew Modine) discovers Pyle sitting on a toilet in the bathroom, *the head*, loading his rifle. Pyle has snapped, intending to go on a killing rampage, targeting his fellow recruits. Pyle's discordant recital of the Rifleman's Creed wakes Hartman, so he storms into the head, yelling: "What is this Mickey Mouse shit? What in the name of Jesus H. Christ are you animals doing in my head?" Up to this point, Hartman had all the power over the recruits; but now it is Pyle, carrying a loaded weapon, exercising godlike powers over everyone. Despite his life being on the line, Hartman does not relinquish his authority, demanding Pyle put down the rifle while berating him. Pyle blasts Hartman, killing him, then commits suicide; the bathroom has transformed from disciplined order and cleanliness to unbridled chaos and bloody death.

Then there's *Eyes Wide Shut*'s provocative sexual rawness, Kubrick's swan song. In the opening scene, Alice Harford (Nicole Kidman) uses the toilet in front of her husband Bill, because she is comfortable enough to urinate in his presence. However, when she asks him how she looks, he replies she looks beautiful without glancing at her. This detached answer to her question shows they are not close and that their relationship is troubled, indicating Bill takes his wife for granted. This scene is juxtaposed when they go to Victor Ziegler's (Sydney Pollack) Christmas party, acting like a happy couple, dancing close together. When they arrive, the Harfords and Zieglers are very cordial and informal, appearing to be in perfect relationships. However, this act vanishes when Alice dances sensually with another man, and Bill flirts with two women. Victor cuts in on Bill's action, urgently needing his help. In a luxurious bathroom, which includes furniture, lamps, paintings, and other items usually not found in a toilet, Bill finds one of Victor's mistresses overdosed on a speedball in need of his life-saving medical expertise. This scene reveals the real goings-on in Victor's life, shattering the illusion of a sophisticated middle-aged rich man who, like men of any background, sexually lusts after young women, committing adultery behind his wife's back. At the Harfords' home, Alice hides marijuana in the bathroom cabinet, inside a Band-Aid box, indicating that she has secrets. Alice stands in the bathroom's doorframe in skimpy underwear as the stoned couple argues over men and women's fidelity, foreshadowing a disturbing revelation.

After Bill expresses his disbelief that Alice would cheat on him because of his misplaced conviction that women are less inclined to cheat than men, Alice reveals a dark, sexual fantasy about a Naval Officer she saw on a family vacation. Although she merely saw the man and never spoke to him, she confesses she could barely move because of how attracted she was to this mysterious and handsome individual. Once she admits that she would have given up her marriage and family for one night of passion with the Naval Officer, Bill is stunned and furious, shattering the strong foundation he thought his marriage had.

But the grand master doesn't stop there. In *Killer's Kiss* (1955), Davey Gordon (Jamie Smith) first spots Gloria Price (Chris Chase, 1924-2013) out his bathroom window from his tiny New York City apartment. In *Paths of Glory* (1957), we first meet Colonel Dax (Kirk Douglas, 1916-2020) as he washes in a makeshift bathroom. In *Spartacus* (1960), Antoninus (Tony Curtis, 1925-2010) bathes Crassus (Laurence Olivier, 1907-1989) in the homoerotic *Snails and Oysters* scene, only not in the theatrical version. In *2001: A Space Odyssey* (1968), Kubrick slyly inserts a graphic joke: a Decalogue of Instructions on the Zero Gravity Toilet's door. In *Barry Lyndon* (1975), Barry (Ryan O'Neil) shows he is not a complete cad when he apologizes for his multiple infidelities as Lady Lyndon (Marisa Berenson) bathes.

In Kubrick's cinema, the bathroom denotes imperfect realism: that things are never quite as they seem because everyone keeps secrets. Everyone has a side they do not show to the rest of the world. It is important to remember that Cruise and Kidman were married when *Eyes Wide Shut* was filmed, so this openness about one baring all in front of the other would have been much like their real marriage. They divorced shortly after its release, so perhaps this contributed to their realistic performances as a couple emotionally drowning in a troubled marriage.

So, why does Kubrick use bathrooms to convey angst and anxiety? He was influenced by Hitchcock's *Psycho*, the first film to feature a flushing toilet (*vide supra*), and its infamous shower scene still resonates with moviegoers everywhere. In *Psycho*, the bathroom expresses duality: it is a place where Marion is contrite, choosing to return the stolen money, flushing the note down the toilet on which she had subtracted out the amount of money she had spent. But it is too late; thus, it is also the place where she will be disciplined. She's caught Norman's eye, and his mother is jealous, punishing Marion while she showers in the same room where she repented, murdering her. Everyone–and I mean everyone–recalls Norman's shadowy figure, dressed as his mother, entering the bathroom stealthily while Marion is taking a shower. He pulls back the shower curtain and begins stabbing while "The Murder," composed by Bernard Herrmann (1911-1975), featuring an orchestra's screeching strings, synchs every knife slash. Easter egg: Kubrick uses *The Shining*'s opening credits to pay homage to *Psycho*. The former's titles are periwinkle blue, the color of Norma Bates' burial dress. Also, the Grady Twins' frocks are the same color.

* * * * *

In *Lolita*, we find Kubrick, for the first time, experimenting with cinema symbolism and innuendo adroitly, and most of it is not subtle. The movie, set in the 1950s, begins *in medias res* near the end, with a tragicomic confrontation between two men in a cluttered estate. The first is Clare Quilty: hungover, drugged, or purposely incoherent, he commits comical, overacted delaying tactics, such as playing Chopin's *Polonaise in A major, Op. 40, No. 1* (1838) on the piano. He's eventually shot while hiding behind a framed portrait of a young woman (a copy of the 18th-century original). The painting alludes to the logo of Gainsborough Pictures, a British B-movie outfit that, in the 1940s, turned out period melodramas, often featuring the young James Mason as the villain. The other man is his killer: Humbert "Hum" Humbert, an urbane, 40-something British professor of French literature. We do not know why Humbert is there, and Quilty's antics are

Lolita's one-sheet poster, with its red lollipop sucking siren, wearing heart-shaped sunglasses signifies one thing and one thing only: her love of fellatio.

odd, orchestrating a one-sided ping-pong match, approximating the twangy accent of an archetypal Western sidekick–think Walter Brennan (1894-1974)–to read aloud an accusatory poem that Humbert hands him. The poem is a parody of T.S. Eliot's (1885-1965) "Ash Wednesday" (1930), and this arcane literary touch, lifted from the novel, surely sits uncomfortably in a mainstream movie. Quilty is shot crouching behind the painting; his death stylized out of sight. Easter egg: when Humbert first encounters Quilty, he asks him, "Are you Quilty?" Wearing a dust sheet as a toga, he replies, "No, I'm Spartacus. You come to free the slaves or something?" The quip and makeshift chiton are a nod to Kubrick's previous film, *Spartacus*. Since he did not have full creative control, he disowned it, and Quilty's snide remark and costume disparage the gladiator epic.

It then flashes back to the events of four years earlier. Humbert arrives in Ramsdale, New Hampshire, to spend the summer before his professorship begins at Beardsley College, Ohio. He searches for a room to rent, and Charlotte Haze (Shelley Winters, 1920-2006), a cloying, sexually frustrated widow, invites him to stay at her house. Humbert declines until seeing her daughter, Dolores "Lolita" Haze (Lyon) sunbathing. As he ogles her, Charlotte remarks that she bakes an excellent cherry pie, insinuating her daughter is a virgin. Humbert becomes infatuated with Lolita immediately; even though she is virgo intacta, Lolita behaves worldly: she is an archetypal soda-pop drinking, gum-snapping, overtly flirtatious teenager who thinks she knows everything.

To be close to Lolita, he accepts Charlotte's offer, becoming a lodger in the Haze household. But Charlotte wants all of Hum's time for herself and soon announces she will be sending Lolita to an all-girls sleepaway camp for the summer. At the summer dance, we are introduced to the eccentric Clare Quilty, and his mysterious female companion, Vivian Darkbloom. After mother and daughter have departed for the camp, the maid gives Humbert a letter from Charlotte, in which she confesses her love for him, demanding he leaves unless he feels the same way. The letter says that if Humbert is still in the house when she returns, she will know that her love is requited and that he must marry her. Though he roars with laughter while reading the sadly heartfelt yet characteristically overblown letter, Humbert marries Charlotte.

The couple becomes cantankerous in the teenager's absence: glum Humbert becomes more withdrawn, and brassy Charlotte whinier. She shows him a handgun (stored in a drawer under her deceased husband's ashes), which she claims isn't loaded, but it is, indicating its sacral nature. It seems her late husband purchased it, intending to use it on himself to spare his wife watching him die, but he never got a chance to use it. In a turn of Jungian synchronicity, one cannot help but think of Kubrick's *Full Metal Jacket*, wherein, during the Parris Island boot camp sequence, the soldiers' rifles are designated divine extensions of their souls, viz. the Rifleman's Creed.

Charlotte discovers Humbert's diary entries detailing his passion for Lolita and characterizing her as "the Haze woman, the cow, the obnoxious mama, the brainless baba." She has a hysterical outburst, runs outside, and is struck by a car, dying on impact.

Humbert drives to Camp Climax to pick up Lolita, who doesn't yet know her mother is dead. They stay the night in the Enchanted Hunters Hotel (more on this later), handling an influx of police officers attending a convention. Two of the guests are Clare Quilty and Vivian Darkbloom, photographing the conference. Quilty poses as a pushy, abrasive stranger, lecturing Humbert, steering the conversation to his "beautiful little daughter" asleep upstairs. Quilty-as-the-stranger implies that he, too, is a policeman and repeats, too often, that he thinks Humbert is normal, suggesting that sex with a minor is exceptional. Humbert escapes the man's advances, and, shortly thereafter, Humbert and Lolita enter into a sexual relationship. While traveling, Humbert tells Lolita that her mother is not sick in a hospital, as he had previously told her, but dead. Grief-stricken, she stays with him; the two commence an odyssey across the United States, traveling from hotel to motel. Although they are lovers, they pose as father and daughter.

In the autumn, Humbert reports to his position at Beardsley College, enrolling Lolita in a local high school. Before long, people begin to wonder about the relationship between the father and his over-protected daughter. He worries about her involvement with the school play and her male classmates. One night, he returns home to find Dr. Zempf, a pushy, abrasive stranger, sitting in his darkened living room. Zempf, speaking with a thick German accent, claims to be a psychologist from Lolita's school, intruding to discuss her knowledge of "the facts of life." Indicating that she is sexually repressed, Zempf convinces Humbert to allow Lolita to participate in the school play, for which she had been selected to play the leading role. In the drama, she portrays Semiramis, the legendary Lydian-Babylonian wife of Onnes and King Ninus, succeeding the Hellenistic monarch to Assyria's throne. Two men compete for Semiramis' affection, echoing Quilty and Humbert's lust for Lolita. Semiramis appears in *The Divine Comedy* as one condemned to Hell for her passion, denoting Lolita's budding sensuality.

While attending the play, Humbert learns Lolita has been lying about how she spent her Saturday afternoons when she claimed to be at piano practice. They get into a row, so he decides to leave Beardsley College, taking Lolita on the road again. She objects at first but then suddenly changes her mind, seeming enthusiastic. Once on the highway, Humbert soon realizes they are being followed by a mysterious car that never falls behind but never quite catches up. When Lolita becomes sick, he takes her to the hospital. However, when he returns to pick her up, she is gone. The nurse there tells him she left with another man claiming to be her uncle and, Humbert, devastated, is left without a single clue as to her disappearance or whereabouts.

Some years later, Humbert receives a letter from Mrs. Richard T. Schiller, Lolita's married name. She writes that she is now wed to a man named Dick (Gary Cockrell, 1932-2018). She is pregnant and in desperate need of money. Humbert travels to their home, finding her roundly expectant, living a pleasant, humdrum life. Humbert demands she tell him who kidnapped her three years earlier. Lolita explains the man tailing them was Quilty, a famous playwright with whom her mother had a fling during the Ramsdale days. She states Quilty was also the one who disguised himself as Dr. Zempf, and the pushy stranger at the hotel. She discloses that Quilty, along with Vivian Darkbloom, were the supervisors of the high school play. Lolita carried on an affair with him, leaving him when he promised her glamour. However, he demanded she join his depraved lifestyle, including acting in his "art" films, which she vehemently refused.

Like a lovesick teenager, Humbert begs Lolita to leave her husband and come away with him, but she declines. Humbert gives Lolita $13,000, explaining it as her money from the sale of her mother's house, and leaves to shoot Quilty in his mansion, where the film began. The epilogue explains that Humbert died of coronary thrombosis awaiting trial for Quilty's murder.

Kubrick employs four archetypes–the tyrannical father, the trickster/juggler, the fool, and the child–with tremendous effect, forging a dark love story. First is Humbert, the authoritarian, and unrelenting hebephile. His humor is dry, like's he part of a dark sitcom. Like other ogre fathers: Darth Vader (*The Empire Strikes Back*, and *Return of the Jedi*, (1983), Daniel Plainview (*There Will Be Blood*, 2007), Thomas Dunson (*Red River*. 1980), Jack Torrance (*The Shining*), and George Lutz (*The Amityville Horror*, 1979), Humbert is duplicitous, hiding his genuine identity. Humbert's erudition, worldliness, and intellectual superiority mask his true nature, that of a sexual predator, making him appear as a sympathetic hermit. He is critical of American culture's vulgarity, establishing himself as a polymath, but his myopic self-delusion and need for sympathy make him phony. He seems to labor under the misconception that Lolita seduced him and that she was in complete control of the relationship. Humbert, as the adult, clearly has the upper hand. He controls the money and Lolita's freedom, and he often repeats that Lolita has nowhere to go if she leaves him. But Humbert has little control over his feelings and impulses. He never considers the morality of his actions, and he refuses to acknowledge that Lolita may not share his affection. As his relationship with Lolita deteriorates, Humbert becomes more and more controlling of her and less and less in control of himself. He considers Quilty's love for Lolita deviant and corrupting, so he murders Quilty to avenge Lolita's lost innocence, a radical act of denial regarding his complicity in that loss. Kubrick takes a page from Hitchcock, who often used black-somber clothing to denote guilt and white dress to represent innocence (see *Psycho*, *Dial M for Murder*). Humbert's costuming characterizes him: he's often shown in white before having sex with Lolita, then in darker clothes, after indulging his hebephiliac desires. In the end, he comes off as a handsome but ineffectual rogue, suffering from occasional bouts of bad temper as he seeks to seduce a pretty teenager while living in a decidedly tense domestic situation.

Enter the trickster/magician/juggler, the destructive Mercurius, another hebephile. Mysterious, manipulative, and utterly corrupt, Quilty is Humbert's doppelgänger. Largely improvised by Sellers, he serves as Humbert's mirror image, reflecting similar traits and thoughts but embodying a darker side of those characteristics Humbert stridently disavows; the two men are opposite sides of the same hebephiliac coin. Quilty and Humbert both adore nymphets, but they act on their adoration in very different ways. While Humbert slavishly worships and idealizes Lolita, Quilty takes her for granted and wishes to denigrate her through pornography. Humbert paints himself as a man in love, while Quilty is, in many ways, a more typical hebephile. Both Quilty and Humbert are men of letters, well-read and persuasive, but Quilty has a much more successful career. Quilty is also far less subtle than Humbert about his nymphet obsession. Quilty's professional success and reputation allow him to get away with his deviant behavior. During his final encounter with Humbert, Quilty's baroque speech, cavalier attitude, and persistent game-playing imply that he, like Humbert, is not quite sane. Imbued with the juggler's qualities, he deceives Humbert: from the pushy man in the hotel to playing Dr. Zempf, cajoling Humbert into allowing Lolita perform in the school play; as such, Quilty bends Humbert to his will. But the trickster is not the Chariot (Card VII of the Major Arcana), perishing in the middle of an attempt to bribe Humbert with a variety of perverse pleasures. Quilty hangs around with the equally mysterious Vivian Darkbloom, whose name is an anagram for the novel's author, Vladimir Nabokov. Her appearance resembles that of television horror hostess Vampira (Maila Nurmi, 1922-2008), with her long phallic fingernails, jet-black hair, and sexy black gown. One ponders if she represents Nabokov's *anima*, the unconscious feminine side of his personality. Unified with Quilty, together, they become Nabokov's archetypal shadow.

Charlotte Haze is the fool, a typical middle-class, middle-aged American woman. She aspires to sophistication and European elegance, but her attempts fall comically flat. She is religious and not particularly imaginative. Charlotte sees Humbert as the epitome of the world-weary European lover of–and in–grand literature. He represents her chance to become the woman she dreams of being, but her vulgar, self-conscious stabs at sophistication make Humbert, and the audience, cringe. Charlotte's love letter traffics mainly in self-pitying martyrdom and melodramatic gestures. Typifying the fool, she dies, knowing the man she loves lusts after her daughter.

Lolita is the child, acting and reacting to the other three as only a child can do. Ergo, she can be manipulative, acting like a spoiled brat. Lolita attracts the depraved Humbert not because she is precocious or beautiful, but because she is a nymphet, Humbert's ideal combination of childishness and the first blushes of coquettish womanhood. She bears all the telltale signs: Lolita sucks on soda straws, chews bubblegum, pulls faces, and alternates between bright acquiescence and whining protestation with a palette of expressions, ranging from diffuse pettiness to slack-mouthed vulgarity. To non-hebephiles, Lolita would be a rather ordinary girl. Her ordinariness is a constant source of frustration for Humbert, and she consistently thwarts his attempts to educate her and make her more sophisticated, such as with the piano lessons. Lolita adores pop culture, enjoys mingling freely with other people, tending toward the dramatic like most prepubescent girls. However, when she shouts and rebels against Humbert, she exhibits more than the ordinary adolescent's frustration. In essence, she feels trapped by her arrangement with him, but she is powerless to extricate herself. Humbert and Quilty objectify Lolita, robbing her of any sense of self. Lolita exists only as the object of their obsession, never as an individual. The lack of self-awareness in Lolita *qua* child is typical and often charming. By the end of the movie, the absence of self-examination in the adult Lolita seems tragic because she is not the archetype she was during the rest of the film.

Like the novel, there are many vulgar double entendres, sarcastic innuendos, and humorous-sexual references–both verbal and visual–scattered throughout. These asides represent the sex drive of the two hebephiles. During the opening sequence, when the two hebephiles are face to face, Kubrick presents an obscene sparring match. Quilty talks about how professionals "use their bats," calls Humbert a "horn toad," asking him if he "likes watching." The sexual banter continues at Charlotte's home when she takes Humbert around the property. Charlotte apologizes for a "soiled sock" viz. a condom, and talks about her house being "stimulating," then remarks about her "cherry pies" as Lolita's introduced along with other "late-night snacks." At the summer dance, Humbert talks with Mona's parents, who refer to themselves "broad-minded," suggesting they "swap partners," meaning dance partners, insinuating they are swingers. Charlotte has a priapic urn wherein she keeps the ashes of her late husband, which Humbert strokes suggestively, implying masturbation, before realizing what it is. A clock on the wall near the staircase is particularly phallic, as are the soda bottles Lolita drinks from, hinting at fellatio. Easter egg: in *The Shining*, similar toilet humor surfaces when Jack reads a *Playgirl* magazine in the lobby

"If you were in my class, I'd give you an A+," Humbert tells Lolita during the recitation of *Ulalume* (originally published 1847) by Edgar Allan Poe. It is a poem about happening upon the tomb of your past love while in the presence of your current lover, written by a Gothic author who married his 13-year-old cousin at the age of 27, signifying his lust for Charlotte's daughter. Lolita's summer camp, Camp Climax, and its mascot–a stuffed beaver–are sarcastically erotic, needing no further explanation. At the camp, when Humbert is waiting for Lolita to arrive, one will see a collection of butterflies on the wall. Nabokov had a passion for lepidoptery, so this is a reference to *Lolita*'s author.

The hotel where Humbert first has sex with Lolita is the Enchanted Hunters. The image of the Enchanted Hunter epitomizes hebephiles/pedophiles like Quilty and Humbert. They are *hunters* because they chase and sexually conquer prepubescent girls. They are *enchanted* because their depraved desires are something out of a perverted fairy tale, causing

Lolita attends Camp Climax for Girls (left); naturally, its mascot is a stuffed beaver (right), suggesting the obvious.

them to act upon their obscene cravings like a couple of debauched Prince Charmings. The man's name behind the desk at the Enchanted Hunters is *Swine*, denoting society's revulsion over hebephilia/pedophilia. While outside on the porch, Quilty speaks to Humbert intrusively, stating "I'm with you," indicating they are hebephiliac brothers in arms.

Inside hotel room 242, Kubrick presents a synthesis of visual and spoken allusions, like when Humbert unfolds a cot at the foot of the bed while Lolita is sleeping. He fights the cot with a bellhop, and the two men grapple with unfolding the bed properly. Perhaps a cot is just a cot, but the difficulty with which Humbert erects the bed suggests otherwise. The physical quality of the humor in this scene further suggests the ridiculousness of Humbert's intended goal. This monster intends to take advantage of his 14-year-old stepdaughter, without telling her that her mother has just died because it would destroy her appetite for sex. What should be disgusting is instead hilarious, as Humbert struggles with the cot, and approaches Lolita on the bed. She awakes and says, "The cot came" in a dismissive tone, then wishes him "goodnight." Humbert then lies on the cot, and it collapses. Kubrick goes to great lengths in this scene to detail the anti-climax, the failed ejaculation, and Humbert's seemingly erectile dysfunction. Then we have the Frigid Queen malt shop, where Lolita goes to hid from Humbert much to his dismay. To Humbert, rejecting his advances makes her icy and unkind; instead, she would rather hang out and drink milkshakes with people her age, two teens named Roy

(Top) In *The Killing* (1956), George Peatty, played by Elisha Cook Jr. (1903-1995), is shot in the face; in *Lolita* (bottom), a portrait replaces his mug. In the latter, Quilty tries to shelter himself behind George Romney's (1734-1802) painting titled *Mrs. Bryan Cooke (Frances Puleston, 1765-1818)* only to be fatally shot by Humbert. Like the surnames of the actor playing Peaty and the painting's subject, the bullet wound to both is identical.

and Rex. The boys' names mean *king* (*Roy* in French, and *Rex* in Latin), inferring her need to perfect her alchemical wedding with people her age, and not with a middle-aged professor. Lolita wishes to be a lunar queen unified with a red king, merging her youthful sexual energies with someone with equal vigor and stamina.

Kubrick's use of symbolism does not end with sexual innuendoes. He also references his earlier films, and in *Lolita*, we see elements and techniques Kubrick would employ in his later movies, anticipating them. Everything seems to come back to and out of *Lolita*, completing the circle, making this film an occult masterpiece. For example, when Humbert first encounters Quilty, he's hiding beneath a sheet in a wingback chair, becoming one with the furniture. Kubrick revisits people *qua* pieces of furniture in *A Clockwork Orange* when Alex and his friends relax in the Korova Milk Bar, and *Eyes Wide Shut* during the Dionysian rites in the Illuminati's mansion. *2001*'s red Djinn furniture also flirts with humans-as-furniture. Djinns, having the ability to transform, can become anything, appearing human-like.

During the confrontation in the mansion, Quilty takes shelter behind an oil painting, triggering Humbert to shoot and kill him. The bullet hole in the painting's face imitates the wound to George Peatty in *The Killing*, released six years earlier. When Humbert approaches Quilty's residence in the fog, one remembers Jack's winding approach to the Overlook Hotel. Inside Quilty's mansion, a Greek keyhole design paves the hall's floor, a meander recalling a labyrinth's twists and turns, evoking *The Shining*'s two mazes: the hedge maze and the dark corridors of the Overlook. Dust sheets cover some of Quilty's furnishings, anticipating *The Shining*'s finale: the Overlook's lobby's furnishings are also clothed in white sheets as the camera zooms in on the old black and white photo.

Quilty and Humbert are sexual predators anticipating *A Clockwork Orange*'s ultra-violent rape scene when Alex defiles Mrs. Alexander (Adrienne Corri, 1930-2016). Their hebephilia surfaces in *Eyes Wide Shut*, inside the Under the Rainbow costume shop which traffics sex slaves, young girls for older men. Charlotte fixes two eggs for Humbert anticipating Wendy Torrance, who prepares two eggs for Jack while caretaking the Overlook. But Lolita, not Charlotte, feeds the eggs to Humbert; the egg is a symbol of the Demiurge and earthly desires, foreshadowing their forbidden and turbulent relationship. Charlotte keeps her gun, her sacred firearm, in the drawer beneath her husband's cremated ashes, becoming a precursor to *Full Metal Jacket*'s Rifleman's Creed, indicating the divinity of weaponry. Charlotte shows Humbert the gun shortly before throwing herself before an oncoming car, killing her. At the end of *Full Metal Jacket*'s Parris Island sequence, "Gomer Pyle" brandishes his weapon before blowing his brains out.

When Humbert paints Lolita's toenails, an Expressionist portrait titled *Elvira Standing Nude* (1918) by Amedeo Modigliani (1884-1920) hangs on the wall behind them. This same painting hangs on the wall in Bill Harford's office in *Eyes Wide Shut*. In *Lolita*, we have Sellers playing an obnoxious German named Dr. Zempf, anticipating his role as another obnoxious German, the eponymous Dr. Strangelove, Kubrick's next movie. As in *Lolita*, Sellers plays multiple roles in *Strangelove*. The hotel where Lolita and Humbert first have sex is the Enchanted Hunters. The school play is *The Hunted Enchanters* signifying repetition, a device key to decoding *The Shining*. Even in *Full Metal Jacket*, Kubrick couldn't help himself and resorts to repetition. At the end of the Parris Island sequence, Hartman mentions Mickey Mouse before storming into the head. During the concluding moments, as the soldiers march out of the city at the Battle of Huế, they sing the "Mickey Mouse Club March" (1955), bringing the Vietnam tale full circle. This esoteric-repetitive imagery transcends Kubrick's films, linking them together, making them part of the same cinematic universe, creating a Kubrick Code. It is now no longer enough to watch Kubrick movie; instead, one must observe the moving frames, attempting to forge links to his other films, which Kubrick seems to want. To view a Stanley Kubrick movie otherwise does it a disservice.

To this author, *Lolita* is an occult key that unlocks Kubrick's films going forward. When the reader understands and appreciates how Kubrick employs symbolism—exoteric and esoteric—his films become easier to decipher. You will grasp Kubrick's motivation, and most importantly, why. Next, *Cinema Symbolism 3* analyzes a movie that pays homage to Kubrick, *The Neon Demon*, which is *Black Swan* on steroids.

The Neon Demon: Are We Having a Party or Something?

"*The Hours of the Moon* are proper for making trial of experiments relating to recovery of stolen property, for obtaining nocturnal visions, for summoning Spirits in sleep, and for preparing anything relating to Water." – *The Greater Key of Solomon*, Book I, ii. *The Neon Demon* conjures the grimoire's magic, a psychological horror film directed by Nicolas Winding Refn, cowritten by Mary Laws, Polly Stenham, and Refn. An international coproduction between France, Denmark, and the United States, it competed for the *Palme d'Or* at the 2016 Cannes Film Festival, the third consecutive film directed by Refn to do so, following *Drive* (2011) and *Only God Forgives* (2013).[452] In the United States, the film was released theatrically on June 24, 2016, by Amazon Studios and Broad Green Pictures. It opened to polarized reviews, and ultimately grossed a little over $3 million against a $7 million budget.

---

452 The *Palme d'Or* (English: Golden Palm) is the highest prize awarded at the Cannes Film Festival. It was introduced in 1955 by the festival's organizing committee. Previously, from 1939 to 1954, the highest accolade at the festival was the Grand Prix du Festival International du Film. In 1964, The *Palme d'Or* was replaced again by the Grand Prix, before being reintroduced in 1975.

If *Lizzie* languishes in alchemy's *nigredo* stage, basking in the Black Sun, *The Neon Demon* exists in the *albedo* phase. Unlike the saturnine *nigredo* with its shadowy motivations, nocturnal activities, forbidden erotica, and where mysteries linger–like the Borden murders–the *albedo* enjoys clarity and lucidity. While motives and actions are mercurial in the *nigredo*, they are pellucid in the *albedo*. By the end, the moral of the story is clear-cut: the modeling world is vile, vicious, toxic, and ugly, representing the worst qualities of humankind. Supermodels are self-absorbed cannibals, annihilating all those that stand between them and the runway. It documents the two poles–material and spiritual–of the *albedo*: the danger of becoming a self-absorbed narcissist (material), and the ability to be grounded and humble, and to appreciate your success, not forgetting from whence you came (spiritual). Male and female archetypes, *citrinitas* and *albedo*, emerge from the *nigredo*. The masculine sun is the sleazy yet shrewd motel owner, the aloof fashion designer, and the two photographers: one fledgling, and one experienced. The feminine is the innocent child manipulated by three evil queens; in a dark fairy tale, Jesse would be Cinderella, controlled by the melancholic Ruby, who personifies Lady Tremaine with Gigi and Sarah the cruel stepsisters, Anastasia and Drizella. Cloaked in the Black Forest's penumbra, *The Neon Demon* is a satanic fairy tale.

Sixteen-year-old aspiring model Jesse (Elle Fanning) has just moved from small-town Georgia to Los Angeles. One cannot help but think of Lynch's *Mulholland Drive*, wherein a young woman aspiring to be an actress arrives in Hollywood, jumpstarting a mystery. Jesse meets photographer Dean (Karl Glusman), who does her first shoot, then meets makeup artist Ruby (Jena Malone). Ruby introduces her to fellow models Sarah (Abbey Lee) and Gigi (Bella Heathcote), both in their late 20s. They are an unholy trio, signified by pervasive triangles and pyramids, recalling the fairy tale Rule of Three. They identify three different types of beauty. In an interview with *Slant,* the director explains: "You have to look at the three women: You have Abbey Lee (Sarah), who's external beauty, Bella Heathcote (Gigi) is a woman trying to recreate beauty artificially, and then you have Jena Malone (Ruby)–who's all about inner beauty, virginity, and

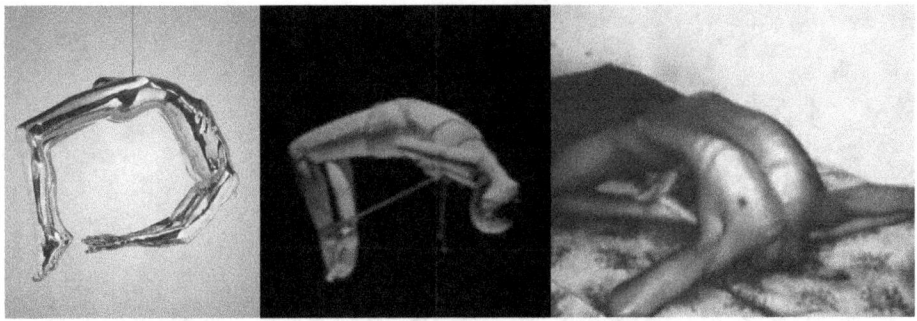

(Left) *The Arch of Hysteria* (1993) sculpture by Louise Bourgeois (1911-2010) pops up in *The Neon Demon* by the bondage performance artist (center) in the nightclub. In a strange twist, serial killer and cannibal Jeffrey Dahmer (1960-1994) posed one of his victims (right) in this same bizarre posture, anticipating the cannibalism of the models in Refn's movie.

innocence. Beauty is one of the most complex subjects we have within this world because you have to look within yourself."[453]

Dean, an unknown photographer, executes a bloody photoshoot resembling a Weegee (Arthur Fellig, 1899-1968) crime-scene photo with Jesse's throat slashed, presaging her violent murder. The photoshoot's symbolism is literal: the modeling world is a cutthroat industry, cold, nihilistic, viz. *Fight Club*'s cynicism, devoid of pity and sympathy. The three women invite Jesse to a nightclub to see a kinky artistic performance. Red and blue suffuse the club; the two primary hues conjure *Suspiria* '77, also saturated in red and blue, investing *The Neon Demon* with the *Tanzakademie's* vile witchcraft, transferring its evil bouquet to Refn's controversial film. The comparison resonates because Jesse, Ruby, Gigi, and Sarah reveal themselves as power-hungry narcissists, cannibals, necrophiles, and black magicians. According to the cinematographer, Natasha Braier, in an interview with *The Guardian*, the color blue relates to the Greek myth of Narcissus, denoting Jesse's climactic egotistical moment, admiring and kissing her reflection in the triangle while on the runway. She becomes self-absorbed, going from the *Alice In Wonderland* little girl to the empowered beauty queen. It's very subtle; it's done with just light

---

453 Steve Macfarlane, "Interview: Nicholas Winding Refn on *The Neon Demon*," *Slant*, June 24, 2016, https://www.slantmagazine.com/features/interview-nicolas-winding-refn-on-the-neon-demon/ (accessed April 22, 2019).

Like a virgin: in *The Neon Demon*, Ruby (left) admires Jesse's (right) beauty and innocence. But all is not what it seems. Ruby is a sexual predator who has found a new victim to prey upon, eventually killing Jesse to bathe in her blood, stealing her youth and virginity.

and mirrors.[454] According to Braier, red denotes danger (this motif likely borrowed from 1973's *Don't Look Now*) and is why Malone's character is named Ruby, who ends up pushing Jesse backward into the empty pool.[455]

Inside the club's ladies' room, Ruby puts on Red Rum lipstick, evoking Kubrick's *The Shining*, thus equating the Overlook's ghosts and ghastly murders with the horrors of Refn's movie, creating an evil equilibrium. When discussing the lipstick, Jesse's asked if she is "food or sex," which is a harbinger of her horrific demise. As they kibitz, Ruby, Gigi, and Sarah become intrigued by Jesse's natural beauty and curious about her sexual proclivities. The virgin feigns experience regarding her conquests.

Jesse is signed by Roberta Hoffman (Christina Hendricks), the owner of a prestigious modeling agency, who tells her to pretend she's nineteen, referring her to a test shoot with notable photographer Jack McCarther (Desmond Harrington). Jesse goes on a date with Dean but keeps his advances at bay. On a roadway overlooking Los Angeles (I believe it is Mulholland Drive), the two hang out while the moon, the *albedo*, shines down upon the metropolis

---

454 Natasha Braier, "Inside the weird world of *The Neon Demon*," *The Guardian*, July 4, 2016, https://www.theguardian.com/global/2016/jul/04/inside-the-weird-world-of-the-neon-demon (accessed March 2, 2019). In this author's twenty-five years of research, *nota bene*, I have never encountered anything associating the color blue with the Narcissus legend.
455 Ibid.

below. It is the goddess Artemis, the protectress of virgins, indicting Jesse's chastity. The moon is a spiritual beacon denoting her ability to transcend Los Angeles and the fashion industry by remaining humble. Dean, like her, aspires to celebrity; both seek ascendancy while staying true to themselves.

She returns to her seedy motel room, finding it ransacked and occupied by a mountain lion. Next, Jesse does the photoshoot with Jack. Ruby fixes gold glitter to Jesse's face making her appear like a sun goddess or the dawn. After asking her to remove all her clothes, Jack paints her gold, completing her transformation into the sunrise. The paint job is a clever homage to *Maleficent* wherein Elle Fanning portrayed Princess Aurora; *aurora* is Latin for *dawn* (*vide supra*). The shoot is successful, and afterward, at a diner, Gigi and Sarah begin envying Jesse's youth and start to feel threatened by her, while Ruby becomes increasingly fascinated with her.

"Beauty isn't everything; it's the only thing." – Robert Sarno (Alessandro Nivola). Jesse goes to a casting call with renowned fashion designer Sarno where Sarah is also present. To make it look like a slaughterhouse, all the models are in their underwear and heels, making them appear naked and helpless. He pays no attention to Sarah, but Jesse hypnotizes him. After smashing the mirror in the women's room, a distraught Sarah asks her how it feels to be the one everyone admires. Jesse admits, "It's everything." Sarah lunges toward her, and Jesse accidentally cuts her hand on broken glass. Like a vampire, Sarah grabs her, sucking the blood from Jesse's hand, trying to steal her youthful, virginal vitality. Horrified, she rushes back to her motel, faints, hallucinating a strange triangular mirror or neon pyramid. Dean arrives and treats Jesse's wound. He also speaks to the motel's lecherous owner, Hank (Keanu Reeves), who mentions a "Lolita" in room 214, referencing Kubrick, using the expression to denote sexually promiscuous young women. A girl in a sordid motel room, the same location where Lolita experiences a majority of her abuse from Humbert, is intentional, signifying Hollywood proper's sleazy underbelly, and the unscrupulous fashion industry.

At Sarno's fashion show, Gigi tells Jesse about her cosmetic surgeries, expressing disbelief that Jesse has not used casting couches to achieve success. The entrance to the runway is a blue pyramid. Dressed in black, Jesse closes the show, seeing a vision of the glowing triangle that she saw before in her hallucination. Jesse approaches the blue pyramid (or triangle) and sees her shadow persona inside–recall Luke Skywalker confronting his shadow, Vader, in the cave on Dagobah (*The Empire Strikes Back*). Suddenly, the triangle changes color to glimmering red. Standing face to face with her reflection, Jesse kisses her mirrored, dark alter ego sybaritically, indicating her supreme narcissism, personifying sheer glamour. In the ancient mysteries, the pyramid was a place for a *second birth*, where, after initiated, one came forth godlike.[456] The pyramid, also known as the *Womb of the Mysteries*, is where Jesse sheds her innocence, emerging as an egotistical goddess. Now initiated into the modeling worlds' mysteries, Jesse has fallen in love with her beauty. The runway's blue pyramidal entrance is also its exit, now becoming red. Blue and red denote Jesse's newfound narcissism, but more critically, it signifies her dominance, prestige, and goddess-like status. Possessed by the Neon Demon, vanity and pride, Jesse believes she is now dangerous when, in reality, she is mere quarry. Such is the dilemma of the virginal fool, the self-absorbed masturbator. Easter egg: Gigi's makeup, like the other models in the show, is both blue and red, denoting narcissism and danger, according to the cinematographer.

Wearing a plunging gold halter top with skintight leather pants and Christian Louboutin stilettos, Jesse goes out with Dean to a restaurant. There, Sarno denigrates women who have cosmetic surgery, using a humiliated Gigi as an example. In contrast, he praises Jesse's natural beauty. Dean challenges him by arguing that it is what's inside that matters, trying to convince Jesse to leave. But she rejects him, consumed by her new self-obsessed persona, believing her hype.

Back at her dingy motel room, Jesse has a nightmare of Hank forcing her to swallow a buck knife, implying fellatio. According to Refn, the dream touches on Jesse's fear of penetration, and her deep-seated need to maintain her virginity at all costs. In an interview with *Vulture*, he explains: "That's her nightmare about the predatorial aspect of the film because beauty is not about just what you look like, it's also what other people want from the inside—youth, perfection, purity, and virginity."[457] She wakes up to hear someone fidgeting with her door lock. She quickly turns the lock but is left to listen as the intruder breaks into the next room and assault the female occupant. Terrified, she calls Ruby, who picks her up, taking her to

---

[456] Hall, *Secret Teachings*, 118.
[457] Jada Yuan, "Nicolas Winding Refn and Elle Fanning on *Neon Demon*, Fanning's Physical Beauty, and a Knife-Wielding Keanu," *Vulture*, May 30, 2016, https://www.vulture.com/2016/05/elle-fanning-nicolas-winding-refn-neon-demon-sex-keanu.html (accessed April 11, 2019).

the house she is housesitting. Ruby tries to initiate sex with her, but Jesse rejects her, revealing her virginity. Ruby draws a lipstick face on Jesse's mirror, with its eyes crossed-out, symbolizing death, and leaves for her second job as a makeup artist at a morgue. Like the bodies she attends to at the morgue and her lipstick drawing, her libido is dead.

Tortured and sexually frustrated, Ruby becomes a living-breathing Freudian nightmare, descending into the *nigredo's* darkest chasms, assuming she ever left them. She performs necrophilia by masturbating on top of a female corpse; meanwhile, at the house, Jesse frigs deliciously, outstretched on a couch. As Jesse pleasures herself, the movie blurs reality and fantasy because it is hard to tell if Ruby is fantasizing Jesse's self-gratification, or if it's happening. Ruby masturbates out of desperation and futility; on the other hand, Jesse touches herself because she's a virgin, wishing to keep her flesh unsullied, preferring to make love to herself rather than with another. Jesse's onanism conjures *9 ½ Weeks* because both masturbators have fallen in love with themselves, delighting in their sensual caresses. By now, one will observe Refn employing mirrors to represent the characters' darker sides and duplicitous natures, imitating *Black Swan*, which also used mirrors to connote the same thing. The two movies run parallel because *Black Swan* dramatizes the performing arts' cutthroat reality, mirroring *The Neon Demon*, which amplifies the modeling industry's perniciousness.

After she finishes making love to herself, Jesse applies makeup and puts on an elegant gown. Ruby returns home, finding Jesse now unabashed in her narcissism and egotism. Jesse stands like a mannequin on a diving board over an empty swimming pool. Like the natatorium, she is devoid of personality, devoured by conceit. Jesse pontificates: "You know what my mother used to call me? Dangerous. '*You're a dangerous girl.*' She was right. I am dangerous. I know what I look like. And what's wrong with that anyway? Women would kill to look like this. They carve and stuff, and inject themselves. They starve to death, hoping, praying that one day they'll look like a second-rate version of me."

Like Chaney's Red Death in *The Phantom of the Opera* (1925), Sarah and Gigi crash the party terrifyingly. Gigi chases her with a butcher knife, while Sarah pursues her with a fire-poker. The three women corner Jesse outside where Ruby pushes her into the empty pool, breaking her leg. As

Jesse lies helpless, the three women approach her with knives butchering her, welcoming the *nigredo's* chaos. It turns out Jesse was *food*, dying a virgin. Jesse's progression from an aspiring model to a vain superstar is ironic. The moment she achieves status, becoming like Ruby, Gigi, and Sarah is the moment she attains oblivion. The instant she fulfills her material aspirations, Artemis abandons her. The moment she sheds her innocence, believing herself to be dangerous, is when she becomes fodder. Jesse, reduced to a source of cannibalistic nourishment, explains the mountain lion and the stuffed cougar: the predatory animals identify Jesse as sumptuous prey, as sustenance for the others. The women were hunting her all along–literally.

After butchering her, they consume her flesh; Ruby bathes in a tub of her blood, while Sarah and Gigi shower together, delighting in Jesse's plasma. Their actions are pure vampirism: by consuming Jesse and bathing in her blood, the three women believe they absorb her youth, purity, lifeforce, and vitality.[458] Such imagery conjures the infamous Elizabeth Bathory (1560-1614), who bathed in the blood of virgins to keep herself young and beautiful. Vampirism aside, the gruesome cannibalism draws forth *The Texas Chainsaw Massacre*, with the three women as Leatherface, hacking up their victims for eventual consumption. The women are not only models, but they are monsters, personifying the fashion industry's brutality.

Later, Ruby sprays the sidewalk clean of Jesse's blood; occult tattoos cover her torso, identifying her as a black magician. She rests in Jesse's unmarked grave, and later, stands nude in her living room before the moon, then lies down. Menstruating, a torrent of blood gushes from her genitals. The moon is the goddess Hecate, the protector of witches and witchcraft, indicating Ruby is performing some bizarre sex magick or death ritual, signifying the *albedo's* other pole: uncontrolled materialism and selfishness. Jesse shed her wholesome persona yet remained a virgin, becoming bitter, a cruel narcissist like the others. The swimming pool was empty–there was no water–suggesting Jesse was not the thaumaturge she thought she was, indicating that her sorcery has failed. She misinterpreted her dark visions on the runway; Jesse, believing her hype, did not heed her mysterious dreams, causing her to be plagued by self-congratulatory vanity. Once pure

---

458 One also thinks of *The Hunger* (1983), wherein a vampire learns that blood-human consumption will grant eternal life, but not eternal youth.

and beautiful, the moon *qua* Jesse has entered a new cycle, waxing and waning with Ruby, signifying the modeling world's ugliness.

The next day, Sarah drives Gigi along the Pacific Coast Highway to one of Jack's photoshoots, spotlighting another model named Annie (Sophie Mazzaro); she asks Sarah if another girl has screwed her out of a job, and she responds in the affirmative. Annie inquiries about what she did about it, so Sarah responds apathetically that she "ate her." As Gigi and Annie strike a pose, Jack wanders about, suddenly becoming enthralled with Sarah. He hires her and fires Annie on the spot; Sarah has just screwed Annie out of a job. During the shoot, as Gigi stares into a pool, she becomes ill and exits. The pool conjures the memory of Jesse subconsciously, and how she died ghoulishly. Easter egg: the woman applying Gigi's makeup wears a necklace with a triangle, recalling the Rule of Three.

As Gigi winces in pain on a triangular couch, Sarah stoically watches her vomit one of Jesse's eyeballs. She cries with regret, "I need to get her out of me," stabbing herself with a pair of scissors. Sarah watches Gigi croak; drooling, the former ingests the regurgitated eyeball. She sheds a tear, feeling pity momentarily, returning to the photoshoot nonchalantly. The movie ends; Refn explains: "But when she's devoured, three things happen: Jena Malone's character (Ruby), initiating this whole ceremony of beauty, menstruates again, has something flowing through her. Bella Heathcote (Gigi) wants to manufacture her own beauty, dies–because that's the one thing that you can't do. And then there's Abbey Lee (Sarah), the supermodel, who felt like a ghost, but finds everything within her again, by eating the thing that Jesse is."[459] Like Kubrick, Refn uses repetition: Ruby's opening line, "Am I staring?" is all about the eyes, which is also the last thing we see: Jesse's disgorged eyeball. *The Neon Demon* comes full circle, ending where it began, swallowing its tail like a cyclic ouroboros. The fashion industry trashes innocence gleefully; its malignant elixir produces not the Philosopher's Stone but cruel prima donnas. Its toxic alchemy consumes its own, spitting out those it once celebrated, rebirthing itself by grinding souls, chewing flesh and drinking blood, fueling its cogwheels.

---

459 Bilge Ebiri, "'Neon Demon' Auteur Nicolas Winding Refn on his Fluorescent Narcissism," *The Village Voice*, June 27, 2016, https://www.villagevoice.com/2016/06/27/neon-demon-auteur-nicolas-winding-refn-on-his-fluorescent-narcissism (accessed April 14, 2019).

CINEMA SYMBOLISM 3

The Red Shoes and Hairspray transcend the Shape of Water

The Shape of Water is an American dark romantic fantasy film directed by Guillermo del Toro, written by him and Vanessa Taylor. It received critical acclaim with praise for the acting, screenplay, direction, visuals, production design, and musical score. Many called it del Toro's best work since *Pan's Labyrinth*; the American Film Institute selected it as one of the top 10 films of the year. It received several awards and nominations, including thirteen nominations at the 90th Academy Awards, winning for Best Picture, Best Director, Best Production Design, and Best Original Score. It was nominated for seven awards at the 75th Golden Globe Awards, winning Best Director and Best Original Score. It was nominated for twelve wards at the 71st British Academy Film Awards, winning three awards, including Best Director. It was nominated for fourteen awards at the 23rd Critics' Choice Awards, winning four of them.

"It's still Baltimore, Elaine, and no one likes Baltimore." – Richard Strickland, *The Shape of Water*. The film's symbolism is multilayered: it is an archetypal-alchemical fable while paying homage to *The Red Shoes*, from which it borrows heavily. Its title implies alchemy and transmogrification, making something concrete and definite out of something abstract and amorphous. It further alludes to Universal horror movies like the *Creature from the Black Lagoon*, *Dracula*, *The Wolf Man*, RKO's *King Kong* (1933), and the many cinematic version of *The Hunchback of Notre Dame* because they are all love stories about misunderstood monsters. One also sees a parallel to Lovecraft's works, who wrote of the Deep Ones: amphibian-reptilian godlike creatures dwelling in the sea. The Deep Ones appear in stories like *Dagon* (1919) and *The Shadow over Innsmouth* (1936). It also draws from *Hairspray* (1988), *Black Swan*, and *Metropolis*.

If *Lizzie* rots in the *nigredo*, and *The Neon Demon* celebrates the *albedo* darkly, then *The Shape of Water* is alchemy's magnum opus, existing in the *rubedo* triumphantly. Unlike the *nigredo*, suitable for the volatile Borden household, and contrasting the *albedo*, appropriate for the gruesome reveries of *The Neon Demon*, the *rubedo* is the daylight world of reason. The movie's forms are as clear as its content: it's an alchemical fairy tale, with the Princess finding her Prince Charming, only the beast remains outwardly as a beast, not transforming into a handsome young man. By the

Archetypal cinematic imagery: (Left) Elisa comforts the chained Amphibian Man, evoking Esmeralda (Patsy Ruth Miller, 1904-1995) consoling the chained Quasimodo (Lon Chaney, Sr.) in *The Hunchback of Notre Dame* (1923, right).

conclusion of this striking tale, we are left in murky limbo just like Elisa and the Amphibian Man embracing in dark water, inflated with hope, but bereft of faith. Out of the *rubedo* comes a psychology akin to the shadowy retort, something magnificent and new might arise, but likely not.[460]

Like Belle in *Beauty and the Beast*, Elisa Esposito (Sally Hawkins) personifies the dawn, indicated by the rays of the glorious daybreak, shining on her face as she rides the bus, returning home from the gloomy nightshift. Like Belle, Elisa is also uniquely imperfect. Belle is beautiful on the outside, but no one understands her inner progressive eccentricities: her desire to be educated, resulting in a lack of interest in marrying and Elisa is mute, a "Princess without Voice," making both of them free spirits. The Amphibian Man (Doug Jones), also known as the *asset*, is the sun, the Beast, trapped in a dank laboratory, i.e., winter, death, stasis, awaiting his youthful bride to liberate him. Like the dawn and the sun, Elisa and the Amphibian Man are closely related: both can live underwater. Like a traditional fairy tale, they fall into peril before their happy ending can be accomplished. Out of this peril, this *nigredo, coincidentia oppositorum*, is ultimately perfected. Elisa (the *albedo*) and the Amphibian Man (the

---

460 Wilson, *Gnostic Cinema*, 142.

citrinitas) are unified; psychologically, the archetypes are given a license to roam this cinematic alchemical experiment from start to finish freely.

Elisa is the moon *qua* sacred feminine: speechless, she is an orphaned child princess, a misunderstood outcast. Giles (Richard Jenkins) is a hermit, a failed advertiser, and an aging homosexual. Strickland (Michael Shannon) is the narrowminded ogre father, the shadow or Devil, hellbent on destroying the Amphibian Man. Like Gaston in *Beauty*, Strickland is a dualistic model: handsome and polished; still, his soul is ugly and vile. General Hoyt (Nick Searcy) is Death (Card XIII), ordering the Amphibian Man's vivisection in the name of science. Dr. Robert Hoffstetler/Dimitri Mosenkov (Michael Stuhlbarg) is the trickster, deceiving both Strickland and the KGB while helping Elisa serendipitously free the Amphibian Man.

Zelda (Octavia Spencer) is the positive attributes of the Strength (VIII): a female St. George celebrating victory over brutishness and evil, helping Elisa foil Strickland and the government, slaying the dragon. Her husband, Brewster (Martin Roach), is the traitor *qua* Hanged Man (XII) because he tips off Strickland that Elisa is hiding the asset. The Amphibian Man is the Chariot (VII), representing release from earthly bondage of the adept's true and higher self, in an emotional and spiritual rapture which sets him free to soar beyond the normal limits of human consciousness into communion with the divine.[461] He is the true self, the Master-power behind all forms of life expression.[462] In the end, Strickland comes to believe the Amphibian Man is a god (at least godlike); like Christ, he possesses healing powers that elevate Elisa to a new reality, living beneath the waves. Easter egg: Elisa, Giles, and Zelda form a sacred trinity, like *Star Wars*' Han, Luke, and Leia and Rowling's Harry, Hermione, and Ron, evoking the fairy tale Rule of Three.

Like *Black Swan*'s Nina, Elisa also effectuates physical metamorphosis; it is like they're competitors, trying to outdo each other. The *nigredo* plagues them: Elisa is nocturnal, working a nightshift in a military base with its twisting corridors and hellish torture devices. Nina suffers torment from her mother, Beth, and Rothbart. Both personify the moon, the *albedo*, forced to deal with the masculine *citrinitas*: Leroy gaslights Nina while Strickland sexually harasses Elisa. Both women transmute, achieving the *rubedo*: Elisa develops gills allowing her to breathe underwater, and Nina

---

[461] Cavendish, *The Tarot*, 91.
[462] Case, *The Tarot*, 97-98.

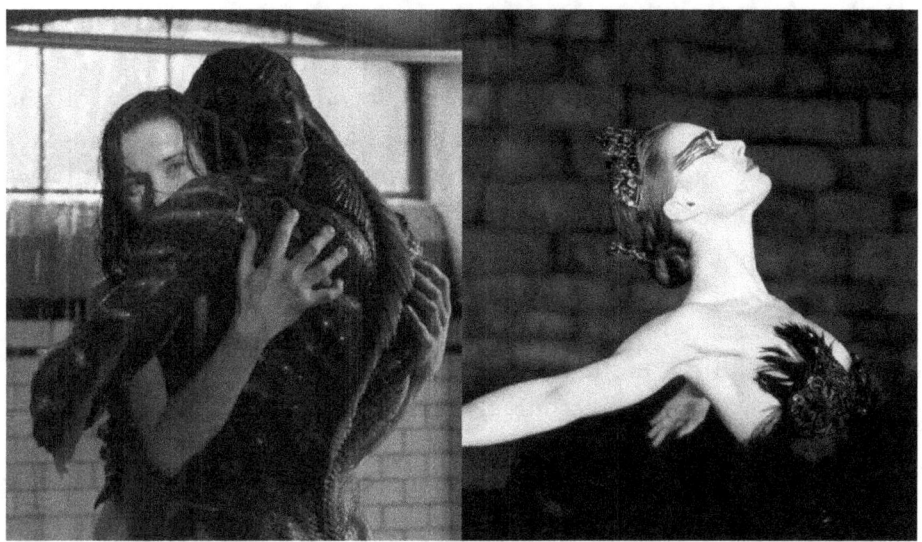

(Left) From the *nigredo* comes the *albedo*, and the *citrinitas*, personified by Elisa and the Amphibian Man; they embrace, generating *coincidentia oppositorum*. Her masturbation session having paid off, Elisa dons red clothing insinuating the *rubedo*, the end of Magnum Opus, when she will transform and breathe underwater, living with the Amphibian Man happily ever after. From *The Shape of Water*. (Right) Her tragic masturbation having paid off, Nina receives an award too, dancing the role of Odile perfectly, the Black Swan. She is arrogant, confident, and sensual–her dark makeup, black bodice, and black tutu arouse her. Unlike Elisa dwelling in perpetual *rubedo*, Nina cannot because, for her, the *rubedo* is the *nigredo*. At the ballet's climax, she dances the White Swan, appearing before a setting sun, and perishes–obliterated by the chaos of the *nigredo*–even though she momentarily realized the perfected finality of the *rubedo*. Her problem is she cannot reconcile or integrate her shadow self with her ego. She cannot control the chaos of her dark alchemy, awakened through masturbation and masochism, unleashing pleasure and pain indivisible. From *Black Swan*.

sprouts feathers, becoming elegant black wings. To accomplish this change, both women masturbate in water–in a bathtub–and both have lacerations, indicating their forthcoming transmogrification. Indeed, it appears that, like Nina, masturbation is part of Elisa's alchemical formula. However, Elisa can perpetuate the *rubedo* by living in the sea with the divine masculine, unlike *Black Swan*, wherein Nina perishes after attaining perfection. Elisa's alchemical opus is successful because she has brought order from the chaos: Strickland is dead, and the Amphibian Man is free. Nina does not have a happy ending because the *rubedo* is the *nigredo*: Leroy, her Luciferian mentor, survives, so does her evil doppelganger, Lily. For Nina, self-destruction, masochism, and death are the culmination of the Great Work, the *rubedo*, returning her to the chaos of the *nigredo*.

It begins with Giles asking Elisa whether she noticed the chocolate factory down the street caught fire. "You smell that?" Giles asks, "....toasted cocoa. Tragedy and delight, hand in hand." Right off the bat, del Toro foreshadows the climax. Like most alchemical movies (at least the good ones), the beginning anticipates its ending; such is the ouroboros' nature, biting its tail, symbolizing infinity, *Hen to Pan*, concluding as it began.

Elisa, who was found abandoned as a child by the side of a river with strange scars on her neck, is mute, communicating through sign language. She lives alone in an apartment above a cinema and works as a janitor at a secret government laboratory in Baltimore, 1962, at the height of the Cold War.

Water and water-related tropes are omnipresent. As it turns out, water is Elisa's odd sexual fetish; it foreshadows and defines her love for the Amphibian Man, thriving in the shapeless element. Del Toro's fairy tale opens in a watery dream, anticipating its submerged climax. She sleeps in water, waking in a cyan-colored apartment denoting water. The apartment's Anglo-Japanese wallpaper, viz. Japanese meets high Victorian Gothic, is a repeating curved, grid-pattern of scales, recalling water. The gaps in her floorboards permit light to escape from the theater below; this flickering, caustic illumination emulates like a luminescence shining or reflecting off water. Her apartment's roof is damaged, so water drips through the ceiling into pots on the floor. Mammoth water stains are on the walls, and there is water wear in the kitchen. Painted on Elisa's wall, layered with peeling paint, stains, and washes, is Katsushika Hokusai's (1760-1849) *The Great Wave off Kanagawa* (1829-1832), its mighty wave rising over the door entrance.

Elisa's only friends are her next-door neighbor Giles, an aging homosexual and struggling advertising illustrator, and Zelda D. Fuller, a coworker serving as her sign-language interpreter. All three are outcasts for different reasons, which explains why they are tied together, almost forming a single person. Elisa is mute, unable to communicate, invisible to the world. Giles is gay, and Zelda is black in a pre-Civil Rights United States. They exist in a world that does not understand them, or want them; they suffer insults and taunts, coarse homophobia, and racial slurs. Even Hoffstetler is a pariah because he is a Russian spy with a conscience. Easter egg: to designate their isolation, a man sits alone at a bus stop. He is holding

(Left) Hokusai's iconic *The Great Wave off Kanagawa* breaks on Elisa's wall (right), cleverly concealed beneath peeling paint, washes, and stains, noticeable to the subconscious mind.

a birthday cake with a missing slice and balloons behind him. He went to his birthday party, but no one came, so he is returning home with the balloons, having eaten a single slice of the cake. Pathetic.

Suggesting her shapeless idée fixe, Elisa masturbates in a watery tub, synchronizing her orgasm to an egg timer. In this case, the eggs are not a symbol of the inferior god, the Demiurge; instead, they are a symbol of fertility, viz. the ova, or oocytes. The eggs also signify her yearning to be seen for the kindness inside, to look beyond ordinary surfaces as she looks beyond the Amphibian Man's fearsome appearance. She needs to be loved and to love another. The Amphibian Man satisfies this need, who sees her inner beauty as she can see beyond his monstrous exterior. She boils the eggs in water–her fixation–feeding them to the creature, transferring her masturbatory pleasure, ardor, and fertility, to the godlike being. Even Egypt's masculine gods were often depicted as masturbating, linking her and the Amphibian Man to the divine.[463] Easter eggs: since we're on the subject of eggs, here are three of them. (1) Elisa's apartment is above the Orpheum movie theater–a hippodrome inspired by Baltimore's Senator Theater. The Senator is a historic single-screen Art Deco auditorium located at 5904 York Road in the Govans section of Baltimore, opening in October 1939. It still operates, showing movies to this day. (2) The pie shop, Dixie Doug's, recalls real-life Baltimore pie shop, Dangerously Delicious Pies, with locations in the neighborhoods of Canton and Hampden. Note that

---

463 Wall, *Sex Worship*, 448, 558-559.

both shops are alliterations, employing two Ds in their names. (3) The plant where Dr. Hoffstetler/Mosenkov meets his Russian handlers is likely the Bethlehem Steel Mill and Shipyard at Sparrows Point, operating from 1889 to approximately the mid-1980s. When he encounters his comrades, part of the password is "The sparrow nests on the window sill," referencing the Baltimore Steel Mill.

The facility receives a mysterious life-form captured from the Amazon River (*The Creature from the Black Lagoon*'s setting) by Richard Strickland: a government spook charged with studying it. The lab holding the Amphibian Man prisoner imitates a medieval torture chamber, with its twisted pipes looking like something out of *Metropolis*' subterranean world. Believing it is just a wild beast, Strickland treats it brutally, repeatedly shocking it with his electric cattle prod. Curious about the creature, Elisa discovers it is a male humanoid amphibian. She begins visiting him in secret, and the two form a close bond as she teaches him sign language, gives him eggs, playing a variety of music for him. She seems mysteriously linked to the creature, intuitively knowing that he needs eggs to thrive. Later, when Elisa abducts the Amphibian Man, Hoffstetler tells her a "raw protein diet is a must." Yet she already seems aware of this, having fed him eggs earlier like she knew how to care for him. Easter egg: Elisa dancing with a mop is an homage to Fred Astaire dancing with the coat rack in *Royal Wedding* (1951).

By now, one will notice del Toro's fairy tale is washed in green. Except for the red shoes that Elisa admires in the store window, the red doors to the movie theater (more on this later), and the red Jell-O in Giles' drawing, green is omnipresent. Its use is intentional; here are the obvious:

- The opening and closing credits are green letters.
- Elisa wears a green nightgown.
- Elisa wears a green headband.
- Elisa sleeps on a green sofa.
- Elisa has a green lamp on a table next to her sofa.
- As part of her evening routine, Elisa uses a green duck shoe shine brush to clean and polish her shoes. Shoes, dancing, and feet are displayed prominently throughout the film. The astrological sign of

Pisces rules feet, a water sign, signifying its aquatic aesthetics, identifying the Amphibian Man as a Christlike redeemer of the downtrodden, e.g., Christ is an archetypal solar avatar, embodying the sun in the House of Pisces due to the Precession of the Equinoxes.

- Elisa and Zelda punch in and out of work with green timecards.
- Elisa uses a green eye mask when she sleeps.
- The green bus Elisa rides has green seats.
- Giles and Elisa dine on a green key lime pie.
- Strickland buys a teal Cadillac as a status symbol but insists it is green. (Note: later, it is damaged by Giles, denoting the collision course between reactionary past and progressive future. Thus, Strickland is not the "man of the future" but an anachronistic relic–more on this in a moment).
- Elisa wears a green sweater.
- Strickland's wife, Elaine (Lauren Lee Smith), makes green gelatin.
- Elisa's cleaning outfit is bluish-green.
- Strickland eats green candy from a green box.
- There is green liquid soap in the facility's green bathroom.

In del Toro's *Crimson Peak* (2015), Dr. Alan McMichael (Charlie Hunnam) explains red and green, hues permeating the Gothic love story, are imaginary, inferring the film may not be what it seems. McMichael suggests it is a vast psychotopographic landscape, existing in Edith Cushing's deranged mind.[464] Being the expert craftsman that he is, del Toro uses red and green once again, but to different ends. In *The Shape of Water*, green creates a paradox: it seems to represent the future, but it does not; instead, the color represents the reactionary past. For instance, Giles is advised to replace the red gelatin with green in his advertisement because green is the future. A salesman tells Strickland that his teal (green) Cadillac represents the future and that he's a "man of the future"; hence, they are made for each

---

[464] Victoria Nelson, *The Secret Life of Puppets* (Cambridge: Harvard University Press, 2002), 110-111. See also Wilson, *Strange World*, 117. This author applies this psychological landscape to *Crimson Peak* in *Cinema Symbolism 2*, Chapter V.

other. The movie and its characters suffocate in green until Elisa frees the Amazonian creature, then red begins bleeding through, displacing green.

Elisa sports a red headband, followed by a red jacket and shoes. Red signals the progressive-fiery future, a place where the vile Strickland is not welcome. Red also indicates passion: Elisa is now free to love, explore her boiling sexuality like the eggs she cooks. The sheepish Giles and cowardly Zelda intensify, becoming radicalized, helping her. Giles drives the getaway car, neutralizing the draconian Strickland. Zelda helps hide the asset, standing up to her lazy husband when he reveals the Amphibian Man's location. Like all alchemical opuses, red is the aesthetic future, not green, the process' finality. The entrance and exit doors to the movie theater are red, symbolizing, and synthesizing Elisa's refined soul. In essence, she uses cinema and dance, and her love for music and musicals, to communicate her love, demonstrating her sophistication.

She marks her calendar with a crimson pencil, coinciding with a canal's opening to release the Amphibian Man on October 10, or 10-10, granting him access to the sea. In the Pythagorean Mysteries, ten associates with divinity, imbuing the Amphibian with godlike qualities.[465] On the other hand, one will notice that Strickland's home is bathed in pale yellow, resembling urine, implying both the *citrinitas* and his irregular pissing habit. Easter egg: At first, when Elisa goes to Dixie Doug's with Giles, she wears a butterfly broach on the lapel of her green jacket. Next, she wears a green gem on the lapel off her green jacket. After she abducts the Amphibian Man, Elisa wears a red butterfly pin on the lapel of her red coat, hinting at metamorphosis, i.e., shifting from green to red. Just as a caterpillar changes into a butterfly, Elisa will transition from human to a humanoid, living beneath the waves like a Yellow Submarine.

Like green and red, del Toro also uses time to create a paradox, infusing *The Shape of Water* with an underlying sense of duality. All the characters observe time: a jumbo solar clock hangs in Strickland's home above the television set. "Just like they do in the movies," Giles and Elisa synchronize their watches before they steal asset. The Princess without Voice uses an egg timer while keeping both an alarm clock and wristwatch on the table next to the sofa where she sleeps. Another clock hangs above Elisa's calendar, and there's a massive clock on the outside wall of Occam Aeronautics. A

---

465 Hall, *Secret Teachings*, 221.

birthday cake–an annual-solar timekeeping device–is conspicuously held by a man sitting on a bench. Elisa and Zelda check-in/out of work on a time punch clock. Yet, nothing is timely: Elisa is always late to work, having Zelda wait in line for her, punching her in when she finally arrives. After the Amphibian Man's abduction, Strickland's assistant Fleming (David Hewlett), says the kidnapping was carried out by a strike team with "clockwork precision." He does not know it was serendipitous and fortuitous, such as Hoffstetler injecting the MP with the euthanizing agent, and the Israeli popper killing the power.

One will notice odd contradictions, dualistic tropes, embedding the dark fairy tale in the subconscious, reviving archetypal imagery, etc. Elisa plays with herself, then eats cornflakes, invented to "prevent masturbation," so Giles tells her. One of the Russian spies talks of eating "surf and turf," anticipating the Amphibian Man and Elisa's love affair; she lives on land, and the creature dwells in water. Strickland speaks of capturing the monster in the Amazon, and later his kids watch an episode of *The Many Loves of Dobie Gillis* (1959-1963) wherein a trip to the Amazon is planned. Elaine smells her husband's fingers before initiating sex, denoting pleasure. Later, Fleming complains that his reattached fingers stink, indicating displeasure; next, a frustrated Strickland rips off his decomposing fingers while interrogating Zelda. Elaine makes a green Jell-O mold precisely as Giles depicts it in his artwork. Zelda tells Elisa that her husband, Brewster, is "silent as a grave," yet when he finally does speak, he reveals the location of Amphibian Man, almost foiling Elisa's plan. Because it tastes terrible, Elisa spits out the key lime pie, and later Giles spits out pie when the Dixie Doug's waiter (Morgan Kelly) rebukes his homosexual advances. Moments later, the Pie Guy reveals his intolerance by denying an African-American couple seats at the counter. The pie is just as unsavory as the racist that serves it.

Seeking to exploit the Amphibian Man to gain an American advantage in the space race, Strickland persuades General Frank Hoyt to vivisect it. One scientist, Robert Hoffstetler–a Soviet spy named Dimitri Mosenkov– pleads unsuccessfully to keep the Amphibian Man alive for further study and, at the same time, ordered by his Soviet handlers to euthanize the creature. When she overhears Hoyt and Strickland's plans, Elisa implores Giles to help her free him. Hoffstetler stumbles upon Elisa's plot in progress, choosing to assist her. Though initially reluctant, Zelda also becomes involved in the successful escape. Easter egg: Strickland asks himself, "What am I doing, interviewing the fucking help?" when questioning Elisa and Zelda about the Amphibian Man's kidnapping. Octavia Spencer won an Academy Award for Best Supporting Actress for her performance in *The Help* (2011).

Elisa shelters the Amphibian Man in her bathtub, planning to release him into a nearby canal when it rains, granting access to the ocean. Strickland interrogates Elisa and Zelda, among others, but learns nothing. Back at the apartment, Giles discovers the creature devouring one of his cats, Pandora. It seems freeing the Amphibian Man has opened Pandora's Box, and all hell is about to break loose. No longer painting the traditional American nuclear family, Giles now draws Elisa and her new love interest because, in his eyes, they are truly beautiful. They personify the red, the *rubedo*, his yearning for the libertarian future. Easter egg: Egyptian hieroglyphs adorn Giles' sofa, evoking the ancient Egyptians who worshipped cats. Among their deities was the half-feline, half-woman goddess Bastet (or Bast) whose duty was to protect the Pharaohs. The Egyptian nexus explains why cats are everywhere in his apartment, implying Elisa is half woman and half something else: a humanoid lifeform capable of breathing underwater, manipulating the raindrops falling on the window.

Startled by Giles, the Amphibian Man slashes his arm, rushing out of the apartment. He gets as far as the cinema downstairs, luckily empty of patrons, before Elisa finds him, returning him to her flat. He touches Giles on his balding head and wounded arm; the next morning, Giles discovers his hair has begun growing back and the wound healed. Elisa has sex with the Amphibian Man in her bathroom, and, for a later encounter, she floods it with water, which begins to drip into the theater below. The upset theater owner alerts Giles, who then enters the apartment, opening the bathroom door, interrupting the aquatic tryst.

Hoyt unexpectedly arrives, asking about the status of the case. When Strickland questions how much loyal service is enough, he is told he has 36 hours to recover the asset or his career, and life, will be over. Meanwhile, Hoffstetler learns he will be extracted in two days. As the planned release date approaches, the Amphibian Man's health starts to deteriorate. Hoffstetler goes to meet his Soviet handlers with Strickland tailing him.

At the rendezvous, one of his fellow Russians shoots Hoffstetler, but Strickland appears, killing the gunman. Having learned he is a spy for the USSR, Strickland tortures him for information on the Soviet strike team he believes took the Amphibian Man; Hoffstetler instead implicates Elisa and Zelda as he dies. Strickland savagely threatens Zelda in her home until her husband, Brewster, reveals that Elisa harbors the Amphibian Man having overheard telephone conversations. After Strickland's departure, Zelda calls Elisa, warning her to get the creature out immediately. An enraged Strickland arrives and searches Elisa's empty apartment until he finds a calendar note revealing where she plans to release it. Easter egg: the black and white dance fantasy between Elisa and the Amphibian Man imitates a dance sequence by Fred Astaire and Ginger Rogers in *Follow the Fleet* (1936).

Elisa and Giles bid farewell to the creature at the canal when Strickland arrives, knocking Giles down, shooting the Amphibian Man and Elisa. The Amphibian Man quickly heals, then slashes Strickland's throat, killing him. Strickland says the Amphibian Man is "god," alluding to Jesus Christ. The Amphibian Man can heal the sick and wounded; he defies secular authorities, and, like Christ, is a fish deity: Jesus is a Piscean Age-solar avatar. Like the Messiah, the Amphibian Man redeems the marginalized, giving Elisa, Giles, and Zelda purpose, and dies (from gunshot wounds) but resurrects, rising like the morning sun. As the police arrive on the scene with Zelda, the Amphibian Man takes Elisa and jumps into the canal, healing her underwater. When he applies his healing touch to Elisa's neck scars, they open to reveal gills like his; she jolts back to life, and the two lovingly embrace. In a closing voice-over narration, Giles conveys his belief that Elisa lived "happily ever after in love" with the Amphibian Man. Concluding, he quotes a poem: "Unable to perceive the shape of you / I find you all around me / Your presence fills my eyes with your love / It humbles my heart / For you are everywhere." Unlike the Creature in *The Creature from the Black Lagoon*, tragedy has become fortune: the Amphibian Man survives, living blissfully with his soulmate.

The Red Shoes is a critical influence upon del Toro's film. *The Shape of Water* opens with the TSG Entertainment logo: an archer firing an arrow. TSG's logo exemplifies Jungian synchronicity because the archer harks back to Powell and Pressburger, inaugurating *The Red Shoes* by identifying themselves as *The Archers* with an arrow hitting a bullseye. Elisa admires a pair of red shoes in a window, conjuring Vicky's crimson ballet slippers. The two sets of red footwear represent the same thing: passion. In *The Red Shoes*, they are a fetish signifying Vicky's desire to dance, to improve her ballet in Lermontov's production alchemically. In the Baltimorean fairy tale, they represent Elisa's desire to perfect *coincidentia oppositorum* with the Amphibian Man. Elisa successfully develops the *rubedo*, but Vicky, like *Black Swan*'s Nina, is devoured by her ambition, her antagonizing fixation, consigning her to the festering *nigredo*. Elisa can regulate her desires while they destroy Vicky and Nina.

What's the difference? Love, because it is shapeless like water, is the answer. She wants to love and be loved while Vicky and Nina cast love asunder; instead, they are guided solely by their selfish lust for perfection. Because the ballerinas' desires are impure and unobtainable, their alchemy backfires, killing them. The government facility where Elisa and the asset meet, Occam Aerospace Research Center–named after Occam's Razor– reflects their love. The Razor is a logical principle attributed to the medieval philosopher William of Ockham (1285-1347). It holds one should not make more assumptions than the minimum needed, applicable to the ambiguity presented in del Toro's masterpiece: how can these two physically different beings possibly interact? Ultimately, the simplest explanation is love. Only Elisa manages to perpetuate the *rubedo*; however, even if del Toro's film depicts the sublime conversion of chaos to order, his narrative remains dreamlike, like a series of flickering illusions. The dreamy qualities of *The Shape of Water* emphasize the tenuous of harmonies, implying the red never lasts. Perhaps we continually swarm movie theaters because all movies, regardless of subject matter, possess on some level the qualities on display in *The Shape of Water*: the twilight of dreams in which anything can metamorphosize into anything else. While the seed requires months to a stalk and then to a rose, the dark auditorium can instantaneously produce apples, feeding our imaginations. Witnessing the quick cuts and the moving images on the screen, we, like Elisa, dream of defying the constraints of time and its slow successions and restraining chains.[466]

There are other religious allegories aside from the Amphibian Man-Jesus Christ nexus. The movie showing at the Orpheum Theater is the epic, *The*

---
466 Wilson, *Secret Cinema*, 141-143.

(Left): Boris Lermontov's office window appears in *The Shape of Water*, only spilt in twain. (Top right) Half of the window appears in Elisa's apartment and the other half in Giles' apartment (lower right). The window characterizes polarity: Elisa's passion, counterbalanced by Giles' rueful constraint.

Story of Ruth (1960). According to the Bible, Ruth was a foreigner among the Israelites, connecting with the Hebrews and their loving God. When her husband dies, her mother-in-law, Naomi, expects her to go back to her Moabite people. But Ruth remains with her saying, "Intreat me not to leave thee, or to return from following after thee: for whither thou goest, I will go; and where thou lodgest, I will lodge: thy people shall be my people, and thy God my God:" (Ruth 1:16). Elisa came from the water because, as a baby, she was found by the river. She has strange marks on her neck, concealing her gills; her surname, Esposito, is from the Latin *expositus*, the past participle of *exponere* meaning *to place outside*, indicating she is a fish out of water, and not part of the world. Ruth's love for Naomi transcends her ethnicity, while Elisa's love for the Amphibian Man transcends her humanity, rendering her nobler than the reactionary sphere she inhabits. Put another way, Elisa is like Ruth because by connecting emotionally with the Amphibian Man, as Ruth connects with Naomi, she chooses to stay with whom she loves and belongs regardless of consequence. We all yearn for connection and communion, belonging somewhere and to someone, finding our soulmate to perfect the

Union of Opposites. That requires a suspension of judgment to see the divine in each other, bringing forth a beauty and gift for the world to see, looking beyond the hard eggshell to find the goodness inside.

Zelda and Strickland's repartee centers on the Old Testament story of Samson and Delilah. It's sparked when Zelda tells him that her middle name is Delilah, and she recounts the tale to Strickland to show him that no matter how strong he believes himself to be, a woman can rob him of that strength. Later–while interrogating Zelda in her house– Strickland refutes her by relating the story's end when Samson regains his strength and gets his revenge. Strickland believes himself to be Samson-like, and for a moment, it seems like he's right on the money. But in the end, Zelda triumphs while Strickland dies. Astrologically, Delilah corresponds with Libra, a wily female seductress (think Morgan le Fay in the Arthurian Legend) who tempts or deceives the sun, sending it into autumn and eventually into deathly winter. Delilah clips Sampson's hair, representing sun rays at the autumn equinox, indicating the sun is weakening; thus, the days shorten. The light becomes scarcer because the night *qua* darkness increases, ruling supreme. Libra is exalted from 23 September to 23 October when, in early October 1962, Elisa and Zelda free the Amphibian Man, planning to release him into the canal. These events occur in late September-early October, identifying Zelda and Elisa as Libra-like tricksters, outwitting the solar masculine, the *citrinitas*, personified by Strickland. This cinematic, astrological-archetypal motif recalls Bruno's art of memory techniques, produced by the collective unconscious, signaling Plato's timeless Theory of Forms.

Finally, del Toro has stated during interviews that he set *The Shape of Water* in Baltimore to honor Charm City director Barry Levinson. Del Toro is a fan of *Diner* (1982), *Tin Men* (1987), and *Avalon* (1990), which are set in Baltimore. However, one is drawn to another Baltimorean tale and another director from Baltimore. Specifically, when one watches *The Shape of Water*, one remembers John Waters' original *Hairspray*, which also occurs in Baltimore, 1962. As crazy as it sounds, there are uncanny parallels between the two fables. The names of the protagonists, Elisa Esposito and Tracy Turnblad, are alliterations with two Es and two Ts. Both names have 13 letters. Both Elisa and Tracy use dance and music to express themselves. They also desire pop culture stardom: Tracy intends to showcase her talents on the Corny Collins Show, and Elisa envisions herself as a movie star. Ricki Lake portrayed Tracy; her surname, Lake, evokes water as does the last name of *Hairspray*'s director, John Waters, anticipating del Toro's aqueous tale. The Amphibian Man is a Christ analog, and Turnblad's mother, Edna, was played by Divine (1945-1988), constituting godlike omnipotence. Elisa and Tracy receive aid from their best friends: Zelda helps Elisa, Penny Pingleton (Leslie Ann Powers) assists Tracy, and both bosom buddies outwit authority figures. Both films have a father, or a father figure, who encourage the female protagonists to follow their hearts: Wilbur Turnblad (Jerry Stiller) in *Hairspray*, and Giles in *The Shape of Water*. Although there is no secret government lab or creature in *Hairspray*, both films are about outsiders trying to find their way in the world, trying to reshape society–alchemically or otherwise–for the better. Again, these similarities are likely unintentional, becoming another textbook example of Jungian synchronicity in action.

Uncle Toby Sent Me: Red Sparrow vs. Black Swan

Red Sparrow (2018) is an American thriller directed by Francis Lawrence and written by Justin Haythe, based on the 2013 novel of the same name by Jason Matthews. Matthews, a former member of the CIA, advised the production regarding depiction, spying, and infiltration. Based on Soviet sexpionage and contemporary Russian use of *kompromat*, filming took place in Hungary, Slovakia, and Austria. On February 15, 2018, it premiered at the Newseum in Washington, D.C., going into general release in the United States on March 2. The film grossed $151 million worldwide, becoming a modest box-office success, receiving mixed reviews from critics who described it as having more style than substance. Its length (2 ½ hours) was criticized, and its over-reliance on graphic violence and sex, while Jennifer Lawrence's performance was praised.

I give it two thumbs up: it moves quickly despite its runtime, engaging the viewer to determine the double agent. The protagonist belongs to the Bolshoi Ballet, so one cannot help but observe resemblances to *Black Swan*, evoking its pessimism. The two movies are named after colored birds: a red sparrow and a black swan, creating a nexus. Although not as esoteric as Aronofsky's bleak fairy tale, *Red Sparrow* is nevertheless worthy of

Comparative cinema: the prideful ballerinas of *Black Swan* and *Red Sparrow*. (Left) Standing backstage, Nina, having descended into the *nigredo*, now experiences the *rubedo*: satanic rapture, the decadent grace to dance the Black Swan. (Right) Standing backstage, Dominika, epitomizing the *rubedo*, a sublime ballerina, is about to experience the chaotic *nigredo*, plunging her into the volatile world of espionage. These two ballerinas' alchemy is backward; nevertheless, for them, the *nigredo* is the *rubedo*, agony is ecstasy, pain is pleasure, and pride is humiliation. Swans and sparrows are connected to Venus, a beauty goddess, therefore Nina and Dominika are voluptuous, enticing danseuses.

analysis. Its plot is reminiscent of the TV movie *Secret Weapons* (1985), made during the Cold War era. Linda Hamilton played the Dominika Egorova role with Sally Kellerman playing the Matron character. Several scenes at the training school are similar to those in *Red Sparrow*.

In modern-day Russia, Dominika Egorova (Lawrence) is a famous ballerina supporting her ill mother, Nina (Joely Richardson), named after the Black Swan herself, Nina Sayers. Dominika lives in a cramped apartment with her mother, as Nina lived with her mom, Erica. Before a packed house, while performing ballet donned in an elegant red ballet bodice and tutu, a male dancer intentionally injures her, ending her career. Dominika's crimson ballet slippers and costume are tokens of ill omen, resurrecting *The Red Shoes*, and Vicky's self-destructive fetishism, only Dominika's alchemical transition is backward, the finality of the *rubedo* heralds her descent into the *nigredo*. Dominika changes alchemically from a successful ballerina to a hardened, erotic, cold warrior. She is the *albedo*, the waxing moon, and the overbearing, manipulative male figures in the SVR and CIA are the *citrinitas*, shining their imposing light upon her. Like *Black Swan*'s Nina, *9 ½ Weeks*' Elizabeth, and *Stoker*'s India, Dominika drinks from the same alchemical elixir: the *nigredo* is her *rubedo*; saturnine, erotic blackness is her endgame.

(Left, referenced earlier in this chapter) The dogs (denoting both dark and light sides of the moon, Hecate and Diana) on the Moon's Tarot card (XVIII) appear in *Red Sparrow* as a single canine (right), seen immediately after Dominika recovers in a Moscow hospital. The dog, roaming an archetypal wasteland, represents isolation and fear of the unknown.

Dominika's vicious injury recalls Beth Macintyre's crippling injury when the latter threw herself in front of a car in a failed suicide attempt. Dominika's leg laceration mirrors Beth's, conjuring the former Swan Queen's despair and isolation. The art of memory kicks in: after Dominika recovers in a hospital, a dog roams a frozen Russian wasteland, recalling the canine from the Tarot's Moon card.[467] The dog was the beast of Hecate, the classical goddess of the baleful moon, epitomizing a mixture of fear and longing in the conscious mind's attitude toward the unknown.[468] For Dominika, the canine symbolizes her hopelessness. Her ballet career over, she does not know what the future has in store for her. The Moon card insinuates that it's not yet time to act but that seeds of action are in motion; for Dominika, it suggests clandestine governmental forces will determine her fate.

Three months after her career-ending injury, Dominika's uncle, Ivan Vladimirovich (Matthias Schoenaerts), the Deputy Director of SVR, approaches her. The black crow rears its head; warriors butcher a king, the

467 The eighteenth card features a dog and a wolf, sometimes indented as two dogs.
468 Cavendish, *The Tarot*, 129-130.

Black Sun rises: to gain her trust, Uncle Ivan says there are no accidents. To prove his point, he exposes the lovers' conspiracy to injure her, spurning Dominika's terrible revenge, plunging her into the *nigredo*: thrashing the two dancers within inches of their lives. Next, she is tasked with seducing Dimitry Ustinov (Kristof Konrad), a Russian gangster, in exchange for her mother's continued medical care. She wears a sexy red dress, signaling the darkness awaiting her. In an expensive hotel, inside Room 22, Ustinov rapes her. Enter the assassin: Sergei Matorin (Sebastian Hülk), an SVR operative authorized by Ivan, strangles him to death. She is extracted, and Ivan offers her a choice: become an SVR agent, or be executed for witnessing Ustinov's assassination.

Nate Nash (Joel Edgerton) is a CIA agent working in Moscow. While meeting with an asset in Gorky Park, the police confront them. Nash creates a diversion to ensure his asset, a mole in the Russian ranks code-named Marble, escapes unidentified. Nash, secure in the American embassy, is reassigned back to the U.S. but insists Marble will only work with him. With his cover blown, he cannot return to Russia, so he is assigned to Budapest to reestablish contact with Marble, which the SVR also deduces.

Dominika is sent to State School Four, a brutal specialist training school for Sparrows: SVR operatives capable of seducing their targets with sexpionage. Under Matron's (Charlotte Rampling) tutelage, Dominika excels in her training, despite some friction with her trainers and fellow students. The Sparrows are taught to ignore pride and shame and willingly engage in fleshy pleasures, thereby honing their espionage techniques. These instructions echo Leroy ordering Nina to masturbate to dance the Black Swan, perfecting her ballet. After humiliating an impotent student, Ivan assigns Dominika to Budapest to gain Nash's trust to learn Marble's identity.

In Budapest, Dominika lives with another Sparrow named Marta Yelenova (Thekla Reutan), supervised by SVR station chief Maxim Volontov (Douglas Hodge). Dominika makes contact with Nash, who quickly determines she is a Russian intelligence operative, attempting to convince her to defect. Dominika surreptitiously inspects Marta's room, discovering she's been assigned to buy classified intelligence from Stephanie Boucher (Mary-Louise Parker), a U.S. Senator's chief of staff. She learns Marta is Stephanie's lover, echoing Nina and Lily's tryst;

Tarot imagery in *Black Swan*. (Left) The Wheel of Fortune (X) from the Major Arcana features the deities Set and Anubis turning endlessly, representing ebb and flow, flux and reflux, action and reaction, and death and rebirth. In the Egyptian pantheon, Anubis led the soul to judgment in the Hall of Truth after death, while Set was the evil murderer of Osiris. The two contrasting gods recall "The Argument" in Blake's *Marriage of Heaven and Hell* (1793): "Without Contraries is no progression. Attraction and Repulsion, Reason and Energy, Love and Hate, are necessary to Human existence. From these contraries spring what the religious call Good and Evil. Good is the passive obeying Reason. Evil is the active springing from Energy." The sphinx at the top denotes equilibrium and wisdom. The alchemical symbols on the inner circle's crossbars are, proceeding clockwise from the top, Mercury, Sulfur, Solution (or Dissolution when an element is extracted), and Salt, implying metamorphosis. (Right) A circular decoration appears in Thomas Leroy's apartment behind Nina, evoking the Tarot's Wheel, representing change and spiritual ascent and descent, anticipating Nina's transformation into a confident yet self-destructive Black Swan.

moreover, Marta's codename for Stephanie is *Swan*, recalling Aronofsky's opus. Marta is scheduled to meet Stephanie in London on March 22, .03 .22, or 322, the number of Yale University's Skull and Bones.

Skull and Bones secret society at Yale University was founded in 1832 by William Huntington Russell (1809-1885) and Alphonso Taft (1810-1891) as a reaction to the prevailing Anti-Masonic sentiment in the country. The influential fraternity adopted the Freemasons and Illuminati's occult machinations, cloaking it in conspiracy and mysticism. Located inside the Tomb, a bare and symmetrical building, its number, 322, refers to the Greek orator Demosthenes who died in 322 BCE, when, according to Bones lore, Eulogia, the goddess of eloquence, ascended into Heaven, not returning until 1832 when she took up residence at Skull and Bones.[469] Members call its most secret room the Inner Temple, or room 322. Guarded by a large, locked iron door, room 322 has a case containing a skeleton. Bonesmen–members of the fraternity–refer to the skeleton as *the Madame* out of their conviction that it's the remains of Mme. de Pompadour (1721-1764), the fashionable socialite mistress of King Louis XV (1710-1774) and one of the most influential women of the 18th century.

There is a floor mosaic of the number 322, mirroring the 322 engraved beneath Greek letters spelling out Demosthenes' name on an opposite wall. Inside this chamber, Skull and Bones' initiatory ritual occurs, with members costumed as the Pope, the Devil, Don Quixote, and Uncle Toby. Uncle Toby, a lead character in Laurence Sterne's (1713-1768) novel *Tristam Shandy* (1760), is also the password to gain admission to the Tomb: "Uncle Toby sent me," must be spoken after pressing a secret buzzer.[470] Secret societies founded the intelligence agencies: the Rosicrucians inspired MI5 (Est. 1905) and MI6 (Est. 1909), and the Freemasons J. Edgar Hoover (1895-1972) and Franklin D. Roosevelt (1882-1945) were behind the FBI (Est. 1935); accordingly, Skull and Bones developed the CIA (Est. 1947), steering America's Cold War foreign policy. Predominate among these were Robert Lovett (1895-1986) and McGeorge Bundy (1919-1986), while other Bonesmen operatives included career diplomat Charles S. Whitehouse (1921-2001). Bonesman George H.W. Bush served as its director from 1976-1977; he was sworn in as its director ('76) and as Vice President ('81 and '85) by Supreme Court Justice and Bonesman Potter Stewart (1915-1985). The March 22 rendezvous alludes to Skull and Bones and, therefore, the CIA, the archenemy of the SVR, their interdependent espionage part of the fabric of history.

When Ivan pressures his niece about her slow progress with Nash, she claims to be helping Marta with Stephanie. The SVR brutally kills Marta for sharing her classified mission with Dominika; her mutilated body is a warning of what will happen to her if she fails. Dominika contacts Nash, agreeing to become a double agent in exchange for protection for her and her mother, and has sex with him. Under Russian orders, Dominika travels

---

469 Alexandra Robbins, *Secrets of the Tomb: Skull and Bones, The Ivy League, and the Hidden Paths of Power* (New York: Little, Brown and Company, 2002), 84.
470 Ibid, 91-93.

The symbol of Yale University's Skull and Bones Illuminati-like secret society. The number 322 is beneath the death's head.

to London with Volontov to meet Stephanie to complete the trade. Inside a hotel room, she covertly switches out the intelligence Stephanie supplies with CIA disinformation.

Upon leaving the meeting, Stephanie sees CIA agents closing in on her, panics, unintentionally stepping into traffic, killed by an oncoming truck. Russian spies, observing Stephanie and the CIA agents, realize their mission has been compromised. Suspected of tipping off the Americans, Dominika and Volontov are recalled to Moscow, where they are tortured and interrogated for days. Again, the alchemical process' finality is its beginning: walking through the Heathrow Airport, an airline attendant in red escorts them to the terminal, the *rubedo*, indicates the *nigredo* awaits them: torture and death. Volontov is executed, but Ivan believes Dominika's claims of innocence are legit, and she is allowed to return to Budapest to continue her original mission of extracting Marble's identity from Nash. Instead, she convinces Nash to relocate her and her mother to the United States.

After spending the night with Nash, Dominika awakes to find him tortured by Matorin for Marble's identity. She assists Matorin initially until he lowers his guard, then she kills him, but is severely injured in the melee. She wakes in a hospital where General Vladimir Korchnoi (Jeremy Irons), a high-ranking official working with Ivan, reveals himself as Marble. He explains that he was initially patriotic, but became disillusioned by Russia's corruption. He fears he will be caught soon and instructs Dominika to expose his identity to Ivan rather than dying in vain. Doing so will make her a national hero, allowing her to replace him as a mole passing critical intelligence to the CIA. But when Dominika contacts her superiors, she frames Uncle Ivan instead, using evidence she had been fabricating since she first arrived in Hungary, blaming him for the botched exchange in London. A sniper kills Ivan, and Dominika is honored in a Russian military ceremony attended by Korchnoi. Easter egg: General Korchnoi's name is a subtle giveaway that he is the mole. He shares the same surname as Viktor Korchnoi (1931-2016), a famous Russian chess master who defected from the Soviet Union. His challenges to the Soviet chess establishment are depicted in *Closing Gambit: 1978 Korchnoi versus Karpov and the Kremlin* (2018).

At home in Russia, Dominika lives with her mother, receiving a phone call from an unknown person, playing Grieg's piano concerto. She had previously told Nash, during their first date, that she'd danced her first solo performance to this piece of music, indicating it's him on the other end.

Red Sparrow is bloody, violent, and sexually disturbing, making it an unforgettable roller-coaster ride. And let's not forget about the Stephanie Boucher anecdote: in London, Dominika meets Stephanie in an oppressively bright hotel bar. Two things occur here: Stephanie is wearing sunglasses indoors for a few seconds too long, and she approaches the bar muttering, "Vodka." With the shades and that one word, we know everything about her: she's shady, sexually ambiguous, and morally ambivalent, a traitor, and not there to mess around; after all, who goes to hotel bars during the daytime to make prudent decisions? During the exchange, Stephanie is shit-faced that when she leaves, she fails to notice she is standing in the middle of a road, stepping backward into a speeding truck, turning her into guava jelly, butchered like a piece of meat as *Boucher* means *butcher* in French.

Sex, violence, bad decisions, murder, succumbing to fetishes, and acting upon dark impulses designate the wickedness of the sacred feminine. That is what makes these women so interesting: their ability to annihilate etiquette, to cast conformity asunder, to go against the grain in the most extreme ways. For example, take *The Red Shoes*' Vicky, a woman willing to die for her art. During WWI and WWII, Britons died for king and country– they did not perish to become a perfected dancing queen. In post-WWII

CINEMA SYMBOLISM 3

"The mirage will fade; then will the desert be thirstier than before. O ye who dwell in the Dark Night of the Soul, beware most of all every herald of the Dawn! O ye who dwell in the City of the Pyramids beneath the Night of PAN, remember that ye shall see no more light but That of the great fire that shall consume your dust to ashes!" – Aleister Crowley, "Sodom-Apples," *The Book of Lies*, 1912. If this graphic had a rubric, it would be *Fetishes, Phallic Worship, Bad Decisions, and Dark Impulses*. The performance of tantric sex is alchemical sorcery, allowing ascent of the shadow. (Top left) Illuminated by *Sol Niger's* luminosity, Elizabeth cups her breast, finger painting to hypnotic phantasmagoria, welcoming her dark side, casting aside her inhibitions and restraint. Such are the strange ways of the dark side of the moon. (Center left) Chastity banks sexual energy; Elizabeth's chichi onanism swamps her with pleasure, insinuating she has not delighted in the flesh for a considerable time, making her orgasm cathartic and alchemical. The athanor scorches her with desire, dripping lust, consumed by her artistic caresses; she profusely releases a bouquet of sulfurous fluids: sweat, arousal vapor, and drool, denoting her gratifying metamorphosis, which she can't resist or control. (Bottom left) Not only are they her fetish, but her black silk stockings also designate Mercurius, the sexy ingredient making her alchemy possible. Her prolific delight ascendant, she hoists her legs excitedly to acknowledge her change agent, signifying the transition from ego to shadow. As New Yorkers stroll overhead, the sculpted, reserved faces serve to remind her she's jilling off in public, akin to avant-garde performance art. As the projector's light flashes freakish images, one cannot help think of Sade's *La Philosophie dans le boudoir* (English: *Philosophy in the Bedroom*, 1795) when Mme. de Saint-Ange, during orgasm, proclaims Lucifer as her god and inspirer. But her Dionysian masturbation binge fails, leaving Elizabeth emotionally destroyed and sexually frustrated (right) by the end. She has forgotten Mercury is a trickster, making her stockings bogus quicksilver. Nevertheless, Elizabeth understands sorcery and sex magicks take a pagan delight in fleshy pleasures and deviant sexual behavior is Satanism. She would have fit right in at Abbé Joseph-Antoine Boullan's (1824-1893) mysterious Work of Mercy, a sect promulgating masturbation, along with incest and adultery, as solemn acts of worship. Still, she hasn't learned that sensual indulgence for its own sake does not serve the magician's purpose; interestingly, many witches said intercourse with the Devil was extremely painful. Elizabeth has allowed herself to be carried away on the tides of masturbatory desire, failing to achieve the perfect balance of opposites from which the magical process originates. From *9 ½ Weeks*. Easter egg: In my first work of fiction, *A Pact with the Devil*, Rebecca Mortlake, dons a chastity belt to increase the potency of her witchcraft, backfiring horrendously.

England, the idea of a ballerina dying for her art was unheard of, taboo, even blasphemous. But such is Vicky's all-consuming, uncontrollable passion, her need to dance, her reason for living. She forsakes love to dance, destroying her in the end.

Such a forbidden impulse was revolutionary, not only in film but in reality, as well. *Lolita* is a gloomy tale about a nymphet, a seducer of men, and *The Neon Demon* documents the evil that women do to make it in the fashion industry. In *The Shape of Water*, Elisa leaves humankind behind, falling in love with an Amphibian Man, dwelling beneath the waves. In *Red Sparrow*, Dominika, to support her mother, engages in deadly sexpionage. Multidimensional women, their dark and surreal worlds allow them to have agency, be complicated, have meaningful lives and experiences. When women appear as the traditional archetypes, the story is often shaped by a male protagonist whom we are supposed to lionize or condemn. Examining the female characters populating *The Red Shoes*, *Lolita*, *The Neon Demon*, *The Shape of Water*, and *Red Sparrow* shows us the importance of women's stories and perspectives, and the danger and tragedy that results in objectifying and dismissing women. For the moon's dark side can be more luminous and powerful than the sun at noon, Hecate's black magic is more energetic and furious than Apollo's brilliancy.

CHAPTER IX

THE STAR WARS SAGA CONTINUES

I never made a deal with Kanjiklub!
Han Solo, *Star Wars: The Force Awakens*, 2015

There's been an awakening. Have you felt it?
Supreme Leader Snoke, *Star Wars: The Force Awakens*, 2015

There is no Death Star. The Senate has been informed that
Jedha was destroyed in a mining disaster.
Darth Vader, *Rogue One*, 2016

Lord Vader will handle the fleet. Target the base of Scarif.
Single reactor ignition... You may fire when ready.
Grand Moff Tarkin, *Rogue One*, 2016

I've seen this raw strength only once before....
It didn't scare me enough then. It does now.
Luke Skywalker, *Star Wars: The Last Jedi*, 2017

In *Cinema Symbolism*, I analyzed *Star Wars* episodes I-VI, providing insights into those films' esoteric themes and symbolism. At the time of its initial publication, July 2014, those were the only theatrical *Star Wars* films in existence. Not so anymore: Walt Disney purchased Lucasfilm in 2012; since then, five new movies have been released with a television series, *The Mandalorian*, debuting on Disney+ in November 2019.

The *Star Wars* science fiction media franchise is acknowledged to have been inspired by many sources. These include southern and eastern Asian religions, Qigong, philosophy, classical mythology, Roman history, Manichaeism, Zoroastrianism, Gnosticism, the Abrahamic religions, Buddhism, Confucianism, Shintō and Taoism, and countless cinematic precursors. Creator George Lucas stated, "Most of the spiritual reality in the movie[s] is based on a synthesis of all religions. A synthesis through history; the way man has perceived the unknown and the great mystery and tried to deal with that or dealing with it" (see *Science of Star Wars*, 2005 Documentary). It is speculated *Star Wars* takes inspirations from pre-Roman Celtic folklore, like the Arthurian legends, which are post-Roman, set around the 3rd century CE. Lucas has also said that chivalry, knighthood, the samurai, and related institutions in feudal societies inspired some concepts in the *Star Wars* movies, most notably the Jedi Knights. The work of the mythologist Joseph Campbell, especially his book *The Hero with a Thousand Faces*, directly influenced Lucas, driving him to create the modern myth of *Star Wars*, featuring a host of Jungian archetypes. The natural flow of energy, known as the Force, is believed to have originated from the concept of *qi/chi/ki*, the all-pervading vital energy of the universe. It is akin to the divine vitality emerging from the Gnostic pleroma, what psychoanalyst Wilhelm Reich called orgone energy (*vide supra*).

The Gnostic Tao of Star Wars: The Force Awakens

Star Wars: The Force Awakens (2015) is an American epic space opera, produced, cowritten, and directed by J. J. Abrams. It is the first installment of the *Star Wars* sequel trilogy, following *Return of the Jedi*, and the seventh episode of the main *Star Wars* film franchise. The movie was produced by Lucasfilm Ltd., Abrams' production company Bad Robot, and distributed by Walt Disney Studios Motion Pictures. *The Force Awakens* is the first *Star Wars* to not significantly involve franchise creator George Lucas. It was widely anticipated, and Disney backed the film with extensive marketing campaigns. It premiered in Los Angeles on December 14, 2015, before its theatrical release in the United States on December 18.

It broke various box office records and became, unadjusted for inflation, the highest-grossing installment in the franchise, the highest-earning film in North America, the 2015's blockbuster, and the third largest moneymaker of all time with a worldwide gross of over $2 billion and a net profit of over $780 million. *The Force Awakens* is loaded with Easter eggs referencing the earlier films, but beneath the cinematic eye candy hides a Gnostic rebellion challenging Christian oppression. Its heresies are so well concealed they are only visible to the Gnostics, the Freemasons, and the initiated few.

Like all *Star Wars* films, the monomyth is omnipresent; only this time, it does not adhere to the traditional mythology. In *Hero*, Campbell explains: "Throughout the inhabited world, in all time and under every circumstance, myths of man have flourished; and they have been the living inspiration of whatever else of whatever else may have appeared out of the activities of the human body and mind. It would not be too much to say that myth is the secret opening through which the inexhaustible energies of the cosmos pour into human cultural manifestations. Religions, philosophies, arts, the social forms of the primitive and historic man, prime discoveries, in science and technology, the very dreams that blister sleep, boil up from the basic, magic ring of myth."[471] After reading this quote, one might think Campbell was describing *Star Wars*' vast mythology because, after all, it is modern-day folklore, transcending popular culture.

Thirty years after the Civil War, the First Order has risen from the ashes of the fallen Galactic Empire, seeking to eliminate the New Republic. The Resistance, backed by the Republic and led by General Leia Organa (Carrie Fisher), opposes them while Leia searches for her brother, Luke Skywalker (Mark Hamill).

The *Finalizer*, one of the First Order's Star Destroyers, slowly comes onto the screen, blacking out the desert planet Jakku, representing Zoroastrianism: based on the teachings of Zoroaster the Magian, to whom aftertimes have united in ascribing high and mysterious doctrine in combination with occult and wondrous lore; that is, the eternal conflict of light against dark, good against evil.[472] In the *Star Wars* mythos, Zoroastrianism, or Manichaeism, is represented by the Force's duality.

On the planet Jakku, Resistance pilot Poe Dameron (Oscar Isaac) receives a piece of a digital map to Luke's location from Lor San Tekka, played by Max von Sydow (1929-2020). The casting of von Sydow is intentional and occult, specifically designed to evoke two of his past performances, shifting the imagery associated with those roles to *The Force Awakens*. In *Cinema Symbolism 2*, I explained:

> ...on the desert planet Jakku, von Sydow's character Lor San Tekka also confronts a dark lord, the First Order's Kylo Ren (Adam Driver).

---

471 Campbell, *Hero*, 1.
472 R. Brown, *The Religion of Zoroaster Considered in Connection with Archaic Monotheism* (London: D. Bogue, 1879), 1-20, *passim*.

Mirroring *The Exorcist*, this confrontation occurs at the beginning of the film, and in a desert. By casting von Sydow to portray a character that challenges Kylo, just as Father Merrin faced Pazuzu, the filmmakers have cast a mnemonic spell by transforming San Tekka into a Christian hierophant *qua* Jesuit: a white magician wanting to return balance to the Force; with Kylo and the First Order embodying Pazuzu's raw demonism. Furthermore, San Tekka and Father Merrin both possess sacred talismans portending future events: San Tekka has a digital relic containing a holographic map leading to Luke Skywalker, and Merrin unearths the Pazuzu amulet. This mystical construct subconsciously transfers Pazuzu's evil onto the First Order and Kylo to signify their malevolence; Snoke (Andy Serkis) and his disciples are devils in the new *Star Wars* films. After a brief exchange, Kylo strikes down San Tekka, recalling yet another von Sydow movie. Kylo killing San Tekka imitates Baron Harkonnen killing von Sydow's character, Dr. Kynes, on the desert planet of Arrakis in *Dune*, which again subconsciously conveys Kylo and the First Order are, like the Harkonnens, savage monsters (Sullivan, *Cinema Symbolism 2*, Chapter V).

One will also notice that unlike the Galactic Empire, the First Order admits women into its ranks, no longer denying the sacred feminine.

First Order Stormtroopers commanded by Kylo Ren (Adam Driver) arrive in transports on Jakku; the transports' doors lower, and the troopers come out firing, resembling the amphibious carriers that dropped Allied soldiers at Normandy and their assault on the beachhead. This scene is a homage to one of J.J. Abrams' favorite films, *Saving Private Ryan* (1998), which documents the Allied landing at Omaha Beach, becoming the first of two WWII allusions. The Stormtroopers and Kylo destroy the village and capture Poe, while Kylo kills San Tekka. Poe's eccentric droid BB-8 escapes with the map, encountering a scavenger, Rey, near a junkyard settlement.

Inside Rey's home, a destroyed AT-AT, we find a handmade Rebel Pilot doll indicating her allegiance to the Rebellion and now to the Resistance. The settlement, known as the Niima Outpost, is run by junk dealer Unkar Plutt (Simon Pegg), who trades food rations for secondhand electronics and other scraps. The junkyard houses relics from the previous films, specifically pod-racing engines (*The Phantom Menace*, 1999) and the

CINEMA SYMBOLISM 3

Millennium Falcon. Back on the *Finalizer*, Kylo tortures Poe using the Force, learning BB-8 has the map. Stormtrooper-with-a-conscience FN-2187 (John Boyega), having witnessed death firsthand, is now unwilling to kill for the First Order, so he rebels, freeing Poe, and together they escape in a stolen TIE fighter. FN-2187 removes his helmet, telling Poe it's a rescue, recalling *A New Hope* when Luke takes his Stormtrooper helmet off, telling Princess Leia it's a rescue. Poe nicknames FN-2187 *Finn*; his numeric designation, 2187, is a homage to Episode IV, Leia's Death Star jail cell number, 2187. It also alludes to *21-87*, a 1963 Canadian abstract montage-collage movie created by Arthur Lipsett (1936-1986) that lasts 9 minutes and 33 seconds. The short feature influenced Lucas strongly in the aesthetic style he used in his *Star Wars* films.

As Poe and Finn return to Jakku to retrieve BB-8, they are shot down, crash-landing. Finn survives, and, assuming Poe died in the crash, wanders off to investigate the planet. He stumbles upon Rey and the droid, but the First Order tracks them down, launching an airstrike. Finn, Rey, and BB-8 flee the planet in the *Millennium Falcon*, which Rey refers to as "garbage," recalling Luke, who referred to the *Falcon* as "junk" back in Episode IV. Easter egg: Captain Phasma (Gwendoline Christie) is named after the 1979 horror film *Phantasm*. As Lord of the Stormtroopers, she wears bright shining silver armor (the moon, Luna, the feminine principle), imitating *Phantasm*'s flying death spheres, which are also shiny silver.

A large cargo ship piloted by Han Solo (Harrison Ford) and Chewbacca (Patrick Mayhew, 1944-2019, and Joonas Suotamo) capture the *Falcon*, looking to reclaim their former vessel. The group is attacked by gangs seeking to settle debts with Han, so they flee in the *Falcon*. We have throwbacks to *A New Hope* on the *Falcon*, such as the game of Dejarik, which seems to pick up exactly where it was the last time Chewie and R2-D2 played it. Rey mentions the Kessel Run, and Finn finds the Marksman-H training remote that tested Luke's lightsaber skills when he was briefly under Obi-Wan's tutelage.

At the First Order's Starkiller Base, a planet converted into a superweapon that harnesses solar energy; Supreme Leader Snoke grants General Armitage Hux (Domhnall Gleeson) permission to fire the weapon. Snoke questions Kylo's ability to deal with emotions relating to his father, Han Solo, who he says means nothing to him. It is here, on Starkiller Base,

CINEMA SYMBOLISM 3

Chewbacca and R2-D2 play Dejarik on board the *Millennium Falcon* in *Star Wars: A New Hope*.

that we have our second WWII reference. In a scene designed to evoke one of Hitler's Nuremberg Rallies, Hux addresses the Stormtroopers zealously, who raise their arms like they are giving a *Sieg Heil!* Like the Nazis, the First Order employs a red, white, and black color scheme echoing the colors of Sheev Palpatine/Darth Sidious' Galactic Empire, which Lucas, in turn, based on the Third Reich.

The *Falcon*'s crew determines the map inside BB-8 is incomplete. Han explains Luke attempted to rebuild the Jedi Order but exiled himself when an apprentice turned to the Dark Side, destroyed the temple, and slaughtered the other trainees. The crew travels to the planet Takodana to meet with cantina owner Maz Kanata (Lupita Nyong'o), who offers assistance in getting BB-8 to the Resistance. Terms of endearment: by now, Han has become a mentor to Finn, providing advice on women and a father figure to Rey, who he offers a job. Tattered pod-racing flags festoon the exterior of Maz's castle-cantina, which, again, references *The Phantom Menace*. Rey is drawn to a secluded vault and finds the lightsaber that once belonged to Luke and his father, Anakin. She experiences disturbing visions, including the corridor on Cloud City (*The Empire Strikes Back*), where Luke dueled Vader. We hear Alec Guinness as old Obi-Wan say, "Rey," then we hear Ewan McGregor as young Obi-Wan impart, "These are the first steps." Frightened, she flees into the woods while Maz gives Finn the lightsaber for safekeeping.

Starkiller Base destroys the Hosnian System, including the New Republic's capital Hosnian Prime, and a portion of its fleet. The Hosnian System is named after venerable high school teacher Jim Hosney, who taught film to scores of people, including several of J.J. Abrams' producing partners. The First Order attacks Takodana in search of BB-8. Han, Chewbacca, and Finn are saved by Resistance X-wing fighters led by Poe, revealed to have survived the crash on Jakku. Leia arrives at Takodana with C-3PO (Anthony Daniels), reuniting with Han and Chewbacca.

Meanwhile, Kylo captures Rey and takes her to Starkiller Base, but she resists his mind-reading attempts. As Kylo scans Rey's mind, he says he sees an ocean and an island, foreshadowing Luke's hiding place on Ahch-To. Rey, discovering she can use the Force, escapes by using a Jedi mind trick on a nearby Stormtrooper portrayed by Daniel Craig, famous for playing British secret agent James Bond. Easter Egg: JB-007 identifies Craig's Stormtrooper (uncredited).

At the Resistance base on D'Qar, BB-8 finds R2-D2 (Kenny Baker, 1934-2016) inactive, having been that way since Luke's disappearance. As Starkiller Base prepares to fire on D'Qar, the Resistance devises a plan to destroy it by attacking one of its thermal oscillators, located in Precinct 47–more on this later. Using the *Falcon*, Han, Chewbacca, and Finn infiltrate the facility, lower the planet's shields, find Rey, and plant explosives. Han confronts Kylo, calling him by his birth name, Ben, to abandon the Dark Side. As Rey and Finn watch from a balcony, Kylo refuses, killing Han with his lightsaber. Chewbacca, enraged, shoots Kylo, then sets off the explosives, allowing the Resistance to attack and destroy the base. The scene echoes *A New Hope* when Darth Vader strikes down Obi-Wan with his lightsaber as Luke watches unable to help.

The injured Kylo pursues Finn and Rey to the surface. Kylo defeats Finn in a lightsaber duel, leaving him wounded. Rey takes the lightsaber, then uses the Force to defeat Kylo, before a fissure separates them as the planet begins to disintegrate. Snoke orders Hux to evacuate and to bring Kylo to him so he can complete his training. Rey and Chewbacca escape with the unconscious Finn in the *Falcon*. As the Resistance forces flee, the energy from the core of Starkiller Base ignites into a new star. On D'Qar, Leia, Chewbacca, and Rey mourn Han's death. R2-D2 awakens, revealing the rest of the map, which Rey uses to find the oceanic planet Ahch-To. There, she finds Luke and presents him with his lightsaber, implying she wants to learn the ways of the Force.

The casting of von Sydow conjures his performances from *The Exorcist* and *Dune*, transferring diabolism and brutality to the Kylo Ren and the First Order subconsciously (*vide supra*). But Abrams and the filmmakers change course quickly, reversing the paradigm, and, consequently, exposing it to be Christian heresy. At the start, in the village on Jakku, conscientious Stormtrooper Finn experiences death firsthand as one of his fellow Stormtroopers perishes, smearing blood on his helmet. The three blood smears are the Hebrew letter *Vav* or *Vau*, the sixth letter in the Hebrew alphabet, identifying Finn with the number of the Antichrist, 666, from the Book of Revelation. If Finn and Rey are Antichrist, that would make the First Order run-of-the-mill Christians. However, the symbolism points in a slightly different direction. Finn and Rey are not agents of the Devil; rather, they are heretics akin to Valentinian Gnostics, in league with the Luciferian serpent (In *The Rise of Skywalker*, Rey heals a snake in a cavern, designating their rebellion). Thus, the First Order epitomizes the dogmatic Roman Catholic Church; comparatively, *V for Vendetta*'s Norsefire Party with the Rey, Finn, and the Resistance promulgating the nihilism of the anarchists Evey and V, seeking rebellion and liberation.

This Gnostic-Christian religious conflict (or dynamic) is well concealed. The First Order reminds this author as a galactic version of the medieval Inquisition, stamping out heresy wherever it can find it. They do not employ clones in their rank and file; instead, they program their followers from an early age, echoing fundamentalist Christianity. The First Order is like Christ, returning in Revelation to destroy wickedness: you are either with them or against them. As a First Order leader, Kylo's red lightsaber is

(Left) The Hebrew letter *Vav* (or *Vau*) is the sixth letter in the Hebrew alphabet. (Right) In *The Force Awakens*, Finn has three blood streaks smeared on his helmet. The bloody marks mirror the sixth Hebrew letter *Vav*, identifying him as 666, and his soon-to-be Resistance compatriot Rey as Antichrist.

cruciform, identifying him with Christianity because the cross *qua* crucifix is the religion's most identifiable symbol. The god of the First Order is Snoke, who appears as a hologram; he is not real but an illusion, a false messiah, a demiurgic leader. He is worthless and weak, unable to foresee his demise by the hands of his apprentice, Kylo Ren, in Episode VIII. He is like Oz the Great and Powerful, a fraud, a lousy magician, a scary, menacing face but nothing more. Snoke is not strong with the Dark Side. Yet, in *The Force Awakens*, he is worshipped in a cathedral-like setting, issuing edicts that are obeyed blindly. He is the God of Abraham, fire and brimstone, not the spiritual godhead of the Gnostics.

The story of Jesus dovetails with ancient solar lore; hence, the First Order's hideout, Starkiller Base, is powered by the sun–a Neoplatonic design–echoing Christianity's pagan roots. The solar oscillator that harnesses the sun's raw power is located in Precinct 47, a reference to the Masonic lodge and the 47th Proposition of Euclid, or the Pythagorean Theorem. The Masonic Blue Lodge governance is thrice divided, representing the three stations of the sun: morning in the east, midday in the south, and setting in the west. The Pythagorean Triangle is worn by the Worshipful Master, stationed in the east, representing the rising sun, bringing light (or enlightenment) to the lodge. As such, Starkiller Base's Precinct 47 is an indicator of the First Order's strict Christian-solar theology. Easter egg: this is not the first time Christian symbolism has been employed in the *Star Wars* films. In the prequels, the saga of Anakin Skywalker mirrors the Christ story because both are virgin birthed, temple elders reject them, both are prophesied to be the Chosen One, and both want to stop people from dying. Both Anakin and Jesus storm temples, both use magic, have secret lovers, Padme Amidala and Mary Magdalene, and both are killed and resurrected. Even the surname of the actor who portrayed Anakin, Hayden Christensen, has *Christ* in it.

Finn and Rey are Valentinian Gnostics, drinking from the same Arcadian stream, seeking further enlightenment. Finn rebels against the First Order's dogma and conformity, joining the Resistance. He wants to know thyself, and have a greater understanding of selfhood instead of being "just another brick in the wall" to quote Pink Floyd. Finn shrugs off the First Order's banal reality by stealing a TIE Fighter, getting the secret Skywalker map to the Resistance. Finn gets Han and Chewbacca into Starkiller Base, where they set explosives, disabling its shields, securing its eventual destruction. He engages Kylo in a lightsaber duel, but loses when he is injured, rendering him unconscious. Through these experiences, he sheds his drone-like existence as a robotic Stormtrooper, leading to a realization of selfhood and self-worth. His rejection of the First Order's dogma and brutality leads to intimate unity with natural elements: allying with Rey, Poe, Han, and the Resistance. He loses himself to discover his true home.

Rey, a mere scavenger, toils on the desert planet of Jakku, a wasteland where she forages for parts from downed Star Destroyers. She is waiting perpetually for her family to return, while deep down, she knows they have abandoned her. Living alone, she has hardened herself to her harsh conditions, yet she remains compassionate, unaware of her destiny. Rey frees BB-8 from Teedo's net, and allows the droid to stay with her, and refuses to trade the droid to Unkar Plutt for a whopping 60 portions, knowing intuitively the droid needs safeguarding, and is worth more than tasteless food rations. Refusing materialism–food for survival–she chooses liberation from her stasis; she allies with Finn and breaks the rules of decorum by stealing the *Millennium Falcon* (which belongs to Unkar Plutt), outmaneuvering TIE fighters. She desires experiences beyond the perirhinal world of Jakku to become worldly. Rey repairs the *Falcon*, choosing to get BB-8 to the Resistance, to sacrifice to be part of something nobler than her. Luke and Vader's lightsaber calls her like she has a destiny beyond searching downed imperial ships for scarps and hardware. She can resist Kylo's mind invasion, discovering she is Force-sensitive. Rey uses a Jedi mind trick to escape her captors, using Luke and Anakin's lightsaber to defeat Kylo before fleeing Starkiller Base. She returns Luke's lightsaber to him on Ahch-To, now ready to begin her Jedi training. Rey, like Finn, realizes selfhood, to walk the path that leads to gnosis. With this realization of self, in which destiny becomes a reality, comes wisdom, knowing her parents are not returning. A more meaningful and consequential existence and fate are to be found elsewhere.

Like the previous six *Star Wars* installments, Campbell's monomyth is transcendent, making *The Force Awakens* a comparative mythology study. In its simplest terms, the monomyth or the hero's journey can be summarized as, "A hero ventures forth from the world of common day into a region of supernatural wonder: fabulous forces are there encountered and a decisive victory is won: the hero comes back from this mysterious adventure with the power to bestow boons on his fellow man."[473] This quote describes *The Force Awakens* in a nutshell; only there are two heroes, not one. Unlike the other *Star Wars* films, the elements appear out of order, effecting different characters at different times. The hero's journey has many components beginning with what Campbell describes as the Call to Adventure. In *Hero*, he writes:

> This first stage of the mythological journey–which we have designated the 'call to adventure'–signifies that destiny has summoned the hero and transferred his spiritual center of gravity from within the pale of his society to a zone unknown. This fateful region of both treasure and danger may be variously represented: as a distant land, a forest, a kingdom underground, beneath the waves, or above the sky, a secret island, lofty mountaintop, or profound dream state; but it is always a place of strangely fluid and polymorphous beings, unimaginable torments, superhuman deeds, and impossible delights.[474]

This element is satisfied when Finn rebels against the First Order, rescuing Poe and stealing a TIE Fighter, leaving behind his regimented existence as a Stormtrooper for a zone unknown. Rey satisfies this element when she takes the *Millennium Falcon* from Unkar Plutt (after refusing to sell BB-8 to him), exiting Jakku for parts unknown. Both accept the adventure; they do not Refuse the Call, which is another element connected to Call to Adventure. Refusal of the Call occurs when Finn, at Maz's cantina, decides he wants out, fearing repercussions from the First Order. He chooses to stay and fight with the Resistance. Rey's Refusal of the Call occurs on the *Millennium Falcon* when she considers returning to Jakku to wait for her family to arrive. But both do not refuse adventure; instead, Finn decides to fight his former oppressors, and Rey decides to join Han because he is the father she never had. Although a minor character, Captain Phasma could be interpreted as satisfying the monomythic component of the Woman as the Temptress because she is a female devil, a mysterious, conniving figure whose loyalties are to the First Order above all else. Campbell defines this element as a siren designed to lead the hero astray; in cinema, the Temptress

---
473 Campbell, *Hero*, 23.
474 Ibid, 48.

usually appears as a duplicitous woman, epitomizing the perils the hero must overcome and vanquish.

Finn and Rey, having heeded the call, now receive Supernatural Aid. On this component, Campbell explains, "For those who have not refused the call, the first encounter of the hero-journey is with a protective figure (often a little old crone or old man) who provides the adventurer with amulets against the dragon forces he is about to pass."[475] Both Finn and Rey receive supernatural from a crone, Maz, who gives them Luke and Anakin's old–yet powerful–lightsaber. It calls to Rey and then finds Finn; both use it to battle Kylo on Starkiller Base. For Rey, it is her first step toward mastering the Force.

The next part of the monomyth, Crossing of the First Threshold, occurs when the hero leaves behind his (or her) world of familiarity to enter realms unknown. Campbell explains, "With the personifications of his destiny to guide and aid him, the hero goes forward in his adventure until he comes to the 'threshold guardian' at the entrance to the zone of magnified power. Such custodians bound the world in four directions–also up and down–standing for the limits of the hero's present sphere, or life horizon."[476] Finn's threshold guardian is Poe, granting him entry into the Resistance. By allying with the rebel, he is a Stormtrooper no longer. Free of the First Order, Finn is a marked man, knowing that danger may be around every corner. Rey's threshold guardian is BB-8, inaugurating her into a mysterious actuality; she crosses the threshold aboard the *Falcon*, joining the Resistance in their struggle against the First Order. She will be swept away by an intriguing world of Jedi Knights battling Sith, of "hokey religions and ancient weapons." Both are experiencing new territories, a world of unknowns.

Next is the Belly of the Whale, defined as the hero's separation from the familiar while undergoing a metamorphosis. Campbell elucidates, "The idea that the passage of the magical threshold is a transit into a sphere of rebirth is symbolized in the worldwide womb image of the Belly of the Whale. The hero, instead of conquering or conciliating the power of the threshold, is swallowed into the unknown and would appear to have died. ...Allegorically, then, the passage into a temple and the hero-dive

---

475 Ibid, 57.
476 Ibid, 64

through the jaws of the whale are identical adventures, both denoting in picture language, the life-centering, life-renewing act"[477] For Finn, this occurs when he is aboard the transport, ready to attack the village on Jakku. Death effects Finn greatly, and his inability to kill causes transformation–the development of a conscience–turning into rebellion. Rey experiences this element when she is held prisoner on Starkiller Base as Kylo tries to read her mind. Rey blocks his attempts and ends up reading his mind, learning that he emulates Darth Vader but knows he is not as powerful. Escaping her captors, Rey realizes she is Force-sensitive, choosing to seek out Luke to begin Jedi training.

On the Road of Trials, Campbell provides, "Once having traversed the threshold, the hero moves in a dream landscape of curiously fluid, ambiguous forms, where he must survive a succession of trials. The road of trials is a favorite phase of the myth-adventure. It has produced a world literature of miraculous tests and ordeals."[478] This element is the swashbuckling action *The Force Awakens*. Finn and Rey escape the First Order in the *Falcon*, only to be captured by Han and Chewbacca. On their freighter, they escape Kanjiklub and the Guavian Death Gang. They narrowly escape two dangerous Rathtars: ugly monsters responsible for the Trillia Massacre. Finn and Rey again battle the First Order on Takodano, assisting the Resistance to destroy Starkiller Base.

Another monomythic element is the Meeting with the Goddess, the appearance of the archetypal female, the entrance of the sacred feminine, the venerated lunar queen. Campbell writes, "The ultimate adventure, when all the barriers and ogres have been overcome, is commonly represented as a mystical marriage of the triumphant hero-soul with the Queen Goddess of the World. This is the crisis at the nadir, the zenith, or at the uttermost edge of the earth, at the central point of the cosmos, in the tabernacle of the temple, or within the darkness of the deepest chamber of the heart. ... The meeting with the goddess (who is incarnate in every woman) is the final test of the talent of the hero to win the boon of love (charity: *amor fati*), which is life itself enjoyed as the encasement of eternity."[479] Mirroring Episode IV, enter the archetypal sacred feminine, the moon to the sun, the

---

477 Ibid, 74, 77.
478 Ibid, 81.
479 Ibid, 91, 99.

reemergence of Princess (now General) Leia. We learn she is instrumental to the Resistance, former wife of Han Solo, and mother of Kylo Ren. She counterbalances the masculine attributes of Han and Finn, and like *A New Hope* wherein her leadership was critical to destroying the Death Star, now leads the efforts to annihilate Starkiller Base.

Atonement with the Father, an ingredient usually reserved for the ogre father archetype, is backward in *The Force Awakens*. On this element, Campbell writes:

> Atonement (at-one-ment) consists in no more than the abandonment of that self-generated double monster—the dragon thought to be God (superego) and the dragon thought to be Sin (repressed id). But this requires an abandonment of the attachment to ego itself, and that is what is difficult. One must have a faith that the father is merciful, and then a reliance on that mercy. Therewith, the center of belief is transferred outside of the bedeviling god's tight scaly ring, and the dreadful ogres dissolve.
>
> It is in this ordeal that the hero may derive hope and assurance from the helpful female figure, by whose magic (pollen charms or power of intercession) he is protected through all the frightening experiences of the father's ego-shattering initiation. For if it is impossible to trust the terrifying father-face, then one's faith must be centered elsewhere (Spider Woman, Blessed Mother); and with that reliance for support, one endures the crisis—only to find, in the end, that the father and mother reflect each other, and are in essence the same.[480]

Here, this component is satisfied when Kylo kills Han, his father; only the son has turned to the Dark Side, and it is the father, along with the mother, trying to redeem him by returning him to the light. But to Kylo, Han is at fault, believing Snoke is salvation. He strikes his father down with his lightsaber, atoning with his father for all the wrong reasons.

Finally, Episode VII features the monomythic element of Apotheosis: physical death and spiritual resurrection or death of the former-self and rebirth into gnosis (sometimes a combination of both). On this, Campbell explains, "Like the Buddha himself, this godlike being is a pattern of the divine state to which the human hero attains who has gone beyond the last

---

[480] Ibid, 107, 110.

terrors of ignorance. 'When the envelopment of consciousness has been annihilated, then he becomes free of all fear, beyond the reach of change.' This is the release of the potential within us all, and which anyone can attain–through herohood; for, as we read: 'All things are Buddha-things;' or again (and this is the other way of making the same statement): 'All beings are without self.'"[481] Like Obi-Wan was to Luke in *A New Hope*, Han fulfills this role in *The Force Awakens*, serving as a mentor to Finn, and a father figure to Rey. When Han is struck down by his son, he passes into legend, again like Obi-Wan, becoming a mythological-omnipotent figure in the *Star Wars* universe.

Next up is *Rogue One*, a prequel to *A New Hope*, featuring elements of the monomyth (surprise, surprise) and some cleverly concealed Easter eggs paying homage to the earlier films, especially Episode IV. Time to turn back the clock to the rise of the Galactic Empire and the the origins of the Death Star, Grand Moff Tarkin's ultimate weapon.

Rogue One: An Estrogen Driven Monomyth

Rogue One: A Star Wars Story (2016, hereafter *Rogue One*) is a Yuletide blockbuster directed by Gareth Edwards. The screenplay by Chris Weitz and Tony Gilroy is from a story by John Knoll and Gary Whitta. It is the first installment of the *Star Wars* anthology series, set just before *A New Hope*, and follows a group of rebels on a mission to steal the plans for the Death Star, the Galactic Empire's superweapon. The film received positive reviews from critics, with praise for its acting, action sequences, direction, musical score, visual effects, and darker tone, but received some criticism for its underdeveloped characters and digital recreation of actors from the original trilogy. It grossed over $1 billion worldwide, making it the 30th highest-grossing film of all-time, the second highest-grossing film of 2016, and the third highest-earning film in the *Star Wars* franchise. It received two Academy Awards nominations for Best Sound Mixing and Best Visual Effects.

What makes this entry unique is it incorporates the monomyth from an entirely female standpoint, and there is no opening crawl, the first *Star Wars* film without one. On a subconscious level, Edwards' film explores the transition from imprisonment to freedom, from hopelessness to having

---
[481] Ibid, 127 (citation omitted).

hope, illustrated by one's ability to make decisions, or to *go rogue*, and choose for oneself. The prisons preventing independence are literal and spiritual; as Chirrut Îmwe (Donnie Yen) explains, "There is more than one sort of prison, Captain, I sense that you carry yours wherever you go."

Research scientist Galen Erso (Mads Mikkelsen) and his family are hiding on the planet Lah'mu. Imperial weapons developer Orson Krennic (Ben Mendelsohn) arrives to press him into completing the Death Star, a space station-based superweapon capable of destroying planets. Lah'mu is a worthy hiding place for Galen and his family: the ringed planet conjures Saturn, death; thus, Galen is critical to completing the battle station. Krennic arrives, dressed in white flanked by black Deathtroopers, reversing the opening of *A New Hope* when Darth Vader, dressed in black, enters *Tantive IV* flanked by white Stormtroopers. According to Doug Chiang, *Rogue One*'s production designer, this backwardness is intentional, intended to evoke the two protagonists' role reversal. Put another way, the story of Luke and Jyn run parallel while being inverses simultaneously. In *A New Hope*, Luke is a farm boy, dreaming of adventure in far-off lands; in *Rogue One*, Jyn (Beau Gadsdon), is a farm girl who gets pulled into adventure and intrigue at a young age, so, as an adult, she dreams of normalcy and family life. Galen's wife, Lyra (Valene Kane), is killed in the confrontation while Jyn, their daughter, escapes and hides, eventually rescued by rebel extremist Saw Gerrera (Forest Whitaker). Easter eggs: The tall tripod towers on Ersos' farm are moisture vaporators similar to those on the Lars homestead, which Luke maintains in *A New Hope*. Inside the Ersos' home, one will find blue Bantha milk, another throwback to the Lars' home on Tatooine. A Deathtrooper finds a Stormtrooper doll, an allusion to the Rebel pilot doll in Rey's refuge in *The Force Awakens*. Jyn's toy alludes to the fog of war when loyalties in the galaxy, pre-Death Star and pre-Rebellion, were ambiguous at best.

Thirteen years later, cargo pilot Bodhi Rook (Riz Ahmed) defects from the Empire, taking a holographic message recorded by Galen to Gerrera on the desert moon Jedha. After learning about the Death Star from an agent at the trading outpost, the Ring of Kafrene, Rebel Alliance intelligence officer Cassian Andor (Diego Luna) frees Jyn (now Felicity Jones) from an Imperial labor camp on Wobani. The seedy trading post imitates the dirty street of *Blade Runner*'s Los Angeles, and *Wobani* is an anagram for

CINEMA SYMBOLISM 3

Jungian synchronicity at work: the Death Star (left) resembles the moon Mimas (right), orbiting the planet Saturn. Mimas, also known as Saturn I, was discovered in 1789 by William Herschel (1738-1842); it was not photographed until 1980 when Voyager encountered it. Yet, *Star Wars: A New Hope* featured the Death Star, an armored space station that looks like Mimas. The Empire's Death Star destroys planets while Mimas orbits Saturn, a planet linked to death.

Obi-Wan. On Yavin IV, Jyn is brought before three threshold guardians: Rebel leader Mon Mothma (Genevieve O'Reilly, reprising her role from *Revenge of the Sith*), General Draven (Alistair Petrie), and Cassian. They question her about her past and her loyalties. Mothma convinces her to find and rescue Galen so the Rebellion can learn more about the Death Star. Hanging around is General Jan Dodonna (Ian McElhinney), who prepped Rebel pilots before attacking the Death Star in Episode IV. Bail Organa lurks in the shadows, once again played by Jimmy Smits. Before leaving Yavin IV, Cassian is covertly ordered to kill Galen rather than extract him. Easter egg: the interrogation of Jyn echoes the grilling of Ellen Ripley (Sigourney Weaver) at the beginning of *Aliens* (1986). Ripley was convinced to lead a contingent of marines against a deadly enemy (Xenomorphs), just like Jyn cajoled into leading a band of rebels against a mortal enemy (the Empire). Another Easter egg: the defector, Rook, is a loose reference to castling in chess: a defensive, strategic maneuverer in which the piece leaps over the king, alluding to Rook's defection by *jumping over* the Emperor.

Jyn, Cassian, and reprogrammed Imperial droid K-2SO (Alan Tudyk) travel to the desert planet of Jedha, where the Empire is removing kyber crystals from the holy city to power the Death Star. In the desert, fallen

Jedi statues lie on their sides, one of which holds a lightsaber. These are ruins of an ancient Jedi temple because Jedha was a sacred site of worship for those who believed in the Force. As Cassian and Jyn walk through its crowded streets, an Imperial Probe Droid (Probot), similar to the one encountered by Han and Chewbacca in *The Empire Strikes Back*, floats by in the background. With Imperial Stormtrooper regiments on the march, the entire sequence resembles Paris during Nazi occupation. As they cautiously make their way through the thoroughfare, Cassian and Jyn bump into Dr. Cornelius Evazan (Michael Smiley) and Ponda Baba/Walrus Man (Tommy Ilsley), who bullied Luke in the Mos Eisley cantina in *A New Hope*. In both films, Evazan warns, "You just watch yourself."

Concurrently, Gerrera and his partisans engage in an armed insurgency against the occupying Imperial forces. With the aid of blind spiritual Buddhist-like warrior Chirrut Îmwe, and his mercenary friend Baze Malbus (Jiang Wen), Jyn makes contact with Gerrera, who has been holding Rook captive. Gerrera–his breathing apparatus sounds eerily like Vader's iron lung–shows her the holographic message. Inside his hideout, Galen reveals he has secretly built a vulnerability into the Death Star, directing them to retrieve the schematics from an Imperial data bank on the planet Scarif, which bears a striking similarity with the acronym SCIF: **S**ensitive **C**ompartmented **I**nformation **F**acility. A SCIF is a secure facility used to store top secret and classified data. There are Easter eggs aplenty: Gerrera's partisans like to play strategy games because a non-holographic version of Dejarik can be found in the sanctum. Gerrera yells, "It's a trap!" recalling Admiral Ackbar (Tim Rose) in *Return of the Jedi*. The mind-reading blue-eyed octopus-like creature Bor Gullet reflects the azure-eyed Third-Stage Guild Navigator in *Dune*. Both can read thoughts, sensing the plans of others. Cassian mentions that Chirrut and Baze are the Guardians of the Whills, an allusion to original *Star Wars* script titled *The Adventures of Luke Starkiller as taken from the "Journal of the Whills"* by George Lucas. According to Lucas, the Whills were wise aliens who created the Force as a religious faith.

Back on the Death Star, Krennic orders a low-powered test shot, destroying Jedha's capital city. Jyn, with Rook and the others, flees the moon, but Gerrera remains, perishing with the city. Before firing, the Death Star blots out the sun, signifying darkness overtaking light, mirroring the saga's Manichean and Zoroastrian mythology. Grand Moff Tarkin congratulates

CINEMA SYMBOLISM 3

Krennic before using Rook's defection, and the security leak, as a pretext to take control of the project. Rook leads the group to Galen's Imperial research facility on Eadu, where Cassian, preparing to snipe Galen, has a change of heart, choosing not to kill him. Eadu emulates LV-426 from *Aliens*. LV-426, one of three known moons orbiting the planet Calpamos, has a rocky, dangerous, and rainy terrain, anticipating Eadu. One wonders if the Xenomorph Queen nests nearby. Jyn makes her presence known moments before Rebel bombers attack the facility. Galen is wounded, dying in his daughter's arms; next, she escapes with her band by stealing an Imperial cargo shuttle.

Darth Vader summons Krennic to Mustafar to answer for the attack on Eadu. Krennic seeks Vader's support for an audience with the Emperor, but Vader instead orders him to ensure no further breaches occur. Since Vader is darkness personified–a Mephistophelian figure–he dwells in Hell: the volcanic, fiery planet Mustafar;[482] he cannot escape the world that created him (see *Revenge of the Sith*). Vader's Stygian castle is a giant tuning fork, allowing him to catch and concentrate negative vibes, enhancing his ability to use the Dark Side of the Force. The Jedi Temple on Jedha is also a tuning fork; only it is built of white stone, representing positive vibrations. Easter egg: Galen Urso personifies nuclear scientist Robert Oppenheimer (1904-1967), the brain behind the Manhattan Project. Like Galen, Oppenheimer came to regret developing a weapon of mass destruction.

Jyn proposes a plan to steal the Death Star schematics using the Rebel fleet but fails to gain approval from the Alliance Council because they believe that victory against the Empire is now impossible. Winston Churchill (1874-1965), whose *never surrender* attitude helped defeat the Nazis, shadows gruff council member Admiral Raddus (Paul Kasey), who, likewise, is willing to sacrifice everything to defeat the Empire. Frustrated with their inaction, Jyn's group lead a small squad of Rebel volunteers to raid the databank themselves. Arriving on Scarif on the stolen Imperial shuttle, dubbed "Rogue One" by Rook, Jyn and Cassian–now disguised– enter the base with K-2SO; the other Rebels attack the resident Imperial garrison, creating a diversion. Easter egg: In *The Empire Strikes Back*, the Rebellion pays respect to Jyn and company by naming a squadron *Rogue*, so identified when they search Hoth for Luke and Han.

---
482 Campbell et al., *Power of Myth*, 180-181.

The Rebel fleet learns of the strike from intercepted Imperial communications; they deploy to support the raid. K-2SO sacrifices himself so Jyn and Cassian can retrieve the data. Îmwe is killed after activating the master switch, allowing communication with the fleet, and Malbus dies in battle shortly afterward. A grenade kills Rook after he informs the armada that it must deactivate the shield surrounding the planet to transmit the schematics. As Jyn searches the database for the Death Star plans, she sees an entry titled *Hyperspace Tracking*. In *The Last Jedi*, this is the technology that enables the First Order to pursue the Resistance fleet even as they have jumped to lightspeed. Eventually, Jyn and Cassian obtain the battle station's schematics, but they are ambushed by Krennic, with Cassian shooting and wounding the Imperial Director. Jyn transmits the schematics to the Rebel command ship. The Death Star enters orbit above Scarif, where Tarkin uses another low-power shot to destroy the compromised base, killing Krennic, Cassian, and Jyn. Easter egg: the resulting mushroom cloud/explosion from the Death Star's laser shot suggests the footage of nuclear bomb testing, viz. Operation Crossroads, by the US government on the Bikini Atoll in the Marshall Islands (Scarif is a tropical planet) in mid-1946. Such imagery defines the Death Star's apocalyptic power: the ability to wreck worlds.

The Rebel flotilla prepares to jump to hyperspace, but Vader's flagship, the *Devastator*, intercepts many of the escaping ships. Vader boards the Rebel command vessel attempting to regain the schematics, but a small blockade runner–*Tantive IV*–jumps into hyperspace with the plans on board. Aboard the fleeing ship, Princess Leia declares the schematics will provide hope to the Rebellion. Easter egg: In *A New Hope*, when Tarkin announces the dissolution of the Senate to Vader and the other Imperial officers, there are several empty chairs around the conference table. Presumably, one of these seats belonged to Director Krennic, who, we now know, perished on Scarif.

Like other *Star Wars* films, some (not all) of the monomyth's elements are present, this time experienced by a heroine, sometimes out of order, and during one scene commingling two at once.

- Call to Adventure: Mon Mothma recruits Jyn to parley with Gerrera in the hopes of rescuing her father and discover more about the Death Star.

- Refusal of the Call: On Wobani, when Jyn is freed from the labor camp, she tries to escape her liberators.
- Supernatural Aid: "The strongest stars have hearts of kyber." - Chirrut Îmwe. Jyn receives a necklace with a kyber crystal pendant from her mother. The gem guides her to greater things, becoming one of the first martyrs of the Rebellion.
- Crossing of the First Threshold: Jyn ventures to Jedha, not knowing what awaits her; danger and intrigue lurk around every corner.
- The Belly of the Whale: Inside Saw Gerrera's fortress, Jyn watches a hologram of her father, Galen, finally understanding his motivations. During the attack on Eadu, her father dies in her arms. She leaves Eadu emotionally transformed, not allowing her father to die in vain. Jyn knows her destiny: she will find the Death Star blueprints so the Rebellion can exploit its weakness, crippling the Empire.
- The Road of Trials: Jyn comes to terms with Gerrera, barely escaping the Death Star's strike upon Jedha. She rebels against the Rebellion by going to Scarif to steal the Death Star plans, battling her way through the citadel to transmit the schematics to the Rebellion.
- The Meeting with the Goddess: Senator Mon Mothma. Like Princess Leia in *A New Hope*, she wears the white robes of the moon, providing the light that puts Jyn on her adventurous path. She is birthing the resistance to the Empire.
- Atonement with the Father: This element harmonizes with the Belly of the Whale. Galen dies redeemed, knowing his daughter will seek out the Death Star's schematics to obliterate it eventually.
- Apotheosis: Like Obi-Wan in *A New Hope*, K-2SO and Chirrut sacrifice themselves for the greater good, dying selfless, allowing Jyn and Cassian to complete the mission.
- The Ultimate Boon: The goal of the quest. Campbell explains: "The gods and goddesses then are to be understood as embodiments and custodians of the elixir of Imperishable Being but not themselves

the Ultimate in its primary state. What the hero seeks through his intercourse with them is therefore not finally themselves, but their grace, i.e., the power of their sustaining substance. This miraculous energy-substance and this alone is the Imperishable; the names and forms of the deities who everywhere embody, dispense, and represent it come and go. This is the miraculous energy of the thunderbolts of Zeus, Yahweh, and the Supreme Buddha, the fertility of the rain of Viracocha, the virtue announced by the bell rung in the Mass at the consecration, and the light of the ultimate illumination of the saint and sage. Its guardians dare release it only to the duly proven."[483] This occurs in Episode IV with the destruction of the Death Star, made possible by the daring heroics of Jyn, Cassian, and the crew of Rogue One who give their lives to the Rebellion.

Next, the saga continues, and this chapter concludes with *The Last Jedi*.

The Last Jedi's Ancient Religions

Star Wars: The Last Jedi (2017), written and directed by Rian Johnson, continues the saga. Johnson stated he took inspiration from *Twelve O'Clock High* (1949), *Letter Never Sent* (1960), *The Bridge on the River Kwai* (1957) (which earned Sir Alec Guinness an Academy Award for Best Actor) and *Three Outlaw Samurai* (1964). It is the second installment of the *Star Wars* sequel trilogy, following the events of *The Force Awakens*, and the eighth episode of the main *Star Wars* film franchise. It is the first *Star Wars* movie without Peter Mayhew as Chewbacca; instead, Joonas Suotamo played the Wookie. He also acted as Chewbacca's body double in *The Force Awakens*. Mayhew died on April 30, 2019.

The Last Jedi had its world premiere at the Shrine Auditorium in Los Angeles on December 9, 2017, going into general release in the United States on December 15, 2017. It grossed over $1.3 billion worldwide, becoming the blockbuster of 2017, the seventh-highest-ever grossing film in North America and the ninth-highest-grossing film of all time during its theatrical run. It is also the second-highest-earning film of the *Star Wars* franchise, turning a net profit of over $417 million. The film received positive reviews, with praise for its ensemble cast, musical

---
483 Campbell, *Hero*, 155.

score, visual effects, action sequences, and emotional weight. It received four nominations at the 90th Academy Awards, including Best Original Score and Best Visual Effects, and two nominations at the 71st British Academy Film Awards.

Since this is the middle episode, bridging Episodes VII and IX, most elements of the hero's journey are absent save the Road of Trials. Finn experiences this component on Canto Bight, and his failed attempt to sabotage the tracking device on Snoke's flagship, *Supremacy*, and the resulting fight with Phasma. Rey satisfies this ingredient when she trains as a Jedi and battles Snoke's Pretorian Guard. The only other component present is Apotheosis, occurring twice: first, when Vice Admiral Amilyn Holdo (Laura Dern) sacrifices herself so the Resistance can flee to Crait, then Luke sacrifices himself via Force projection so the Resistance can escape. Both Holdo's and Luke's actions echo Obi-Wan's sacrificial death in *A New Hope*. We will have to wait and see if *The Rise of Skywalker* features monomythic elements such as the Ultimate Boon (the destruction of the First Order), Atonement with the Father, Refusal of the Return, Rescue from Without, the Crossing of the Return Threshold, Master of Two Worlds, and Freedom to Live.

Following the destruction of Starkiller Base, General Leia Organa leads the Resistance forces' flight from D'Qar, when a First Order fleet arrives. Poe leads a costly counterattack, destroying a First Order dreadnought, allowing the remaining Resistance ships to escape via hyperspace. On the bridge of the *Finalizer*, we find Captain Peavy portrayed by Ade Edmondson. Fans of the famous BBC television series *The Young Ones* (1982-1984) will remember the character of Vyvyan Basterd, a psychopathic, sociopathic, sadistic, and misanthropic orange-haired punk played by Edmondson. Easter egg: General Leia Organa's Mon Calamari cruiser is named after *Rogue One*'s Churchillian Admiral Raddus.

Rey, having traveled to Ahch-To with Chewbacca and R2-D2 aboard the *Millennium Falcon*, attempts to recruit Luke Skywalker to the Resistance. Disillusioned by his failure to train Kylo as a Jedi, and under self-imposed exile, Luke refuses to help, indicating the Jedi Order should end. Observe the door to Luke's hut; it is made from a metal plate off his X-wing, submerged beneath the waves. Luke drinks green milk from a Thala-siren; in Greek mythology, Sirens were dangerous creatures who

(Top) In the black cave on Ahch-To, Rey stands before a perpetual reflection of herself, denoting her Jungian shadow, her fleeting embrace of the Dark Side. This imagery borrows from *Black Swan* (bottom) when Nina stands before a mirror seeing endless reflections of herself, signifying her dark side lives, becoming dominant, consuming her in the end.

lured nearby sailors with their enchanting music and singing voices to shipwreck on the rocky coast of their island.

Meanwhile, the First Order uses a secret device, Hyperspace Tracking, to tail the Resistance. Once the Resistance leaves hyperspace, the First Order attacks; Leia's son, Kylo Ren, hesitates to fire on the Resistance ship after sensing his mother's presence; however, another fighter destroys the bridge, killing most of the Resistance's leaders. Leia is sucked into outer space but barely survives by using the Force.

Encouraged by R2-D2 (Jimmy Vee), Luke decides to train Rey as a Jedi. One can see Luke's robotic hand briefly; if one looks at the bottom of his hand, near the wrist, one will notice the formation of a blaster hole. Luke received this burn mark when he was fighting on Jabba's barge during *Return of the Jedi*. During training, Rey flirts with the Dark Side of the Force, descending into a cave just like the one Luke entered on Dagobah, confronting his Jungian shadow *qua* Darth Vader. In a black cave on Ahch-To, Rey stands before a repeating reflection of herself, signifying her shadow. Rey and Kylo begin communicating through the Force, puzzling them; they are not sure how the phenomenon is happening. After Kylo tells Rey what transpired between him and Luke, causing him to turn to the Dark Side, Luke confesses he momentarily contemplated killing Kylo upon sensing that Snoke was corrupting him; this prompted Kylo to destroy Luke's new Jedi Order. Convinced Kylo can be redeemed, Rey leaves Ahch-To much like when Luke left Yoda.

Luke prepares to burn the Jedi library's sacred scrolls but hesitates. Yoda's Force ghost (Frank Oz) appears, destroying the library by summoning a bolt of lightning, saying Rey has all she needs to learn, encouraging Luke to gain wisdom from his failures. The sacred Jedi texts are house inside the trunk of a large ancient Uneti tree because the tree is a universal symbol for wisdom and divinity. On its vast esoteric symbolism, Hall writes:

> The Scandinavian world-tree, Yggdrasil, supports on its branches nine spheres or worlds, which the Egyptians symbolized by the nine stamens of the persea or avocado. All of these are enclosed within the mysterious tenth sphere or cosmic egg—the definitionless Cipher of the Mysteries. The Qabbalistic tree of the Jews also consists of nine branches, or worlds, emanating from the First Cause or Crown, which surrounds its emanations as the shell surrounds the egg. The single source of life and the endless diversity of its expression has a perfect analogy in the structure of the tree. The trunk represents the single origin of all diversity; the roots, deeply imbedded in the dark earth, are symbolic of divine nutriment; and its multiplicity of branches spreading from the central trunk represent the infinity of universal effects dependent upon a single cause.
>
> The tree has also been accepted as symbolic of the Microcosm, that is, man. According to the esoteric doctrine, man first exists potentially

within the body of the world-tree and later blossoms forth into objective manifestation upon its branches. According to an early Greek Mystery myth, the god Zeus fabricated the third race of men from ash trees. The serpent so often shown wound around the trunk of the tree usually signifies the *mind*—the power of thought—and is the eternal tempter or urge which leads all rational creatures to the ultimate discovery of reality and thus overthrows the rule of the gods. The serpent hidden in the foliage of the universal tree represents the cosmic mind; and in the human tree, the individualized intellect.

The concept that all life originates from seeds caused grain and various plants to be accepted as emblematic of the human spermatozoon, and the tree was therefore symbolic of organized life unfolding from its primitive germ. The growth of the universe from its primitive seed may be likened to the growth of the mighty oak from the tiny acorn. While the tree is apparently much greater than its own source, nevertheless that source contains potentially every branch, twig, and leaf which will later be objectively unfolded by the processes of growth.

Man's veneration for trees as symbols of the abstract qualities of wisdom and integrity also led him to designate as *trees* those individuals who possessed these divine qualities to an apparently superhuman degree. Highly illumined philosophers and priests were therefore often referred to as *trees* or *tree men*–for example, the Druids, whose name, according to one interpretation, signifies *the men of the oak trees*, or the initiates of certain Syrian Mysteries who were called *cedars*; in fact it is far more credible and probable that the famous *cedars of Lebanon*, cut down for the building of King Solomon's Temple, were really illumined, initiated sages. The mystic knows that the true supports of God's Glorious House were not the logs subject to decay but the immortal and imperishable intellects of the tree hierophants.

Trees are repeatedly mentioned in the Old and New Testaments, and in the scriptures of various pagan nations. The Tree of Life and the Tree of the Knowledge of Good and Evil mentioned in Genesis, the burning bush in which the angel appeared to Moses, the famous vine and fig tree of the New Testament, the grove of olives in the Garden of Gethsemane where Jesus went to pray, and the miraculous tree of Revelation, which bore twelve manners of fruit and whose leaves were for the healing of the nations, all bear witness to the esteem in which trees were held by the scribes of Holy Writ. Buddha received his illumination while under the *bodhi* tree, near Madras in India, and several of the Eastern gods are pictured sitting in meditation beneath the spreading branches of mighty trees. Many of the great sages and saviors carried wands, rods, or staves cut from the wood of sacred trees, as the rods of Moses and Aaron; Gungnir–the spear of Odin–cut from the Tree of Life; and the consecrated rod of Hermes, around which the fighting serpents entwined themselves.[484]

Like all sacred wisdom, the Jedi texts survive the tree's fiery destruction because Rey has hidden them on the *Falcon* without Luke, or Yoda's Force ghost, knowing their location.

Meanwhile, Poe entrusts Finn, mechanic Rose Tico (Kelly Marie Tran), and BB-8 with a secret mission to find someone–a code breaker–who can disable the First Order's tracking device. Speaking with Maz Kanata via a video link, she tells them the person they are looking for is in Canto Bight, a coastal city on the desert planet Cantonica. Canto Bight's design was heavily inspired by Monte Carlo, emulating Alfred Hitchcock's *To Catch a Thief* (1955). Inside one of the city's casinos, they meet the hacker DJ (Benicio del Toro), escaping the city with the help of some stable hand children and freed Fathiers. Easter egg: In Canto Bight, Finn and Rose park their spacecraft in a tow zone, and when authorities catch them, arresting them for parking violation 27B/6. In *Brazil*, 27B/6 is the superficial yet necessary paperwork needed to repair domestic ductwork.

Finn, Rose, and DJ infiltrate Snoke's ship as Rey also arrives in the *Falcon*'s coffinlike escape pod. Captain Phasma captures the trio before they can disable the tracking device. Kylo brings Rey to Snoke, the Supreme Leader, revealing he facilitated the psychic connection between her and Kylo as part of a plan to destroy Luke. Meanwhile, new Resistance leader Vice Admiral Holdo reveals her plan to evacuate the remaining Resistance members using small transports. Believing her actions to be cowardly and futile, Poe instigates a mutiny. Poe declares, "If they move...stun 'em"; the

---

[484] Hall, *Secret Teachings*, 295-296.

line is an allusion to Sam Peckinpah's (1925-1984) western *The Wild Bunch* (1969). Pike Bishop, William Holden's character, famously says, "If they move, kill 'em." However, a recovered Leia stuns Poe with a laser shot, allowing the escape to begin. Holdo remains on the ship, misleading Snoke's fleet as the others flee to an abandoned Rebel base on Crait. In a bargain for his freedom and money, DJ reveals the Resistance's plan to the First Order, who begin firing upon the evacuation transports, destroying them. Easter egg: when a robot irons a First Order uniform, it blows steam like a spaceship coming in for a landing. An iron-as-a-spaceship appears in *Hardware Wars* (1978), a *Star Wars* spoof.

Ordered to kill Rey, Kylo instead eliminates Snoke. Briefly unified, they battle his Praetorian Guard; a scarlet throne room sword fight alludes to Powell and Pressburger's *The Tales of Hoffmann* (1952), and the red Praetorian Guard imitates the Emperor's red-cloaked Imperial sentinels from *Return of the Jedi*. Rey hopes that Kylo has returned to the Light Side, but he asks her to join him to rule the galaxy. This imagery parallels what his grandfather Darth Vader did in *Revenge of the Sith* when he invited his wife Padme (Natalie Portman) to join him in overthrowing the Emperor to rule the galaxy with him. This offer also occurred in *The Empire Strikes Back* when Vader again suggested overthrowing the Emperor, allowing Luke to rule at his side as father and son. Refusing like Padme and Luke before her, Rey and Kylo use the Force to try to obtain the Anakin-Luke lightsaber, splitting it in two. Holdo sacrifices herself by ramming into Snoke's flagship at lightspeed, crippling it. Rey escapes in the chaos, while Kylo declares himself Supreme Leader. BB-8 frees Finn and Rose; they defeat Phasma, then join the survivors on Crait. When the First Order arrives, Poe, Finn, and Rose attack with old speeders. Rey and Chewbacca draw the TIE Fighters away from the battle in the *Falcon*. At the same time, Rose stops Finn from completing a suicide run against the enemy siege cannon, which subsequently penetrates the Resistance fortress.

Luke appears, confronts the First Order, thereby enabling the remaining members of the Resistance to escape. Kylo demands the First Order open fire on Luke, but the blasts do not affect him. He then engages Luke in a lightsaber duel; upon striking Luke, Kylo realizes he has been fighting a phantom, a Force projection. Luke's skill is known as bilocation: a psychic or miraculous ability wherein an individual (or object) is, or appears to be, located in two distinct places simultaneously. The concept has been used in a wide range of historic and philosophical systems, ranging from early Greek philosophy to modern religious stories, occultism, and sorcery. Several Christian saints, monks, and Muslim Sufis are said to have exhibited bilocation. Among the earliest is the apparition of Our Lady of the Pillar in the year 40 CE. St. Isidore the Farmer (ca. 1070- 1130) claimed to be praying or attending Mass in Church while at the same time plowing in the fields. In the 17th century, persons accused of witchcraft were reported to appear in dreams and visions of witnesses. The trials at Bury St. Edmunds and Salem included this spectral evidence against defendants. Witchfinder General Matthew Hopkins (ca. 1620-1647) described the phenomenon in his book *The Discovery of Witches* (1647). English occultist Aleister Crowley was reported by acquaintances to have the ability, even though he said he was not conscious of it happening at the time. In *Lost Highway*, the Mystery Man (Robert Blake) appears to bilocate; however, his ability to be two places represents the transcendent nature of evil because it is universal, especially when invited.

Rey helps the remaining Resistance escape on the *Falcon*. Luke, exhausted, dies peacefully on Ahch-To, unifying with the Force, returning to the Gnostic pleroma. Luke, like Han in *The Force Awakens*, has stepped into the role of Obi-Wan, becoming a reclusive hermit, sacrificing himself so the Resistance may escape, allowing them to fight another day. Rey and Leia sense his death, but the two women remain resilient. Back at Canto Bight, one of the stable hand children moves a broom with the Force, then gazes into space, indicating the omnipotence of the Force. A spaceship jumps to hyperspace, burning like a shooting star across the nighttime sky, reminding the child of his connection to the macrocosm and that, although small, he has a role to play in the vast universe. Easter egg: there are several tipoffs that Luke's presence on Crait is an illusion. Unlike everyone else, his movements do not stir the planet's salty red surface; moreover, his steps remain silent because Foley was not used.[485] When Luke appears, he has a shorter, darker beard and hair, looking like he did when he confronted Ben Solo in flashback. Rey aside, no one in the Resistance knows what he looks like now, so they don't realize he is a projection. Another thing

---

485 Foley (named after sound-effects artist Jack Foley, 1891-1967) is the reproduction of everyday sound effects added to film, video, and other media in post-production to enhance audio quality.

that gives Luke's projection away is that he's armed with his lightsaber. Rey had his saber, broken during the struggle between her and Kylo after Snoke's demise.

Because *The Last Jedi* is the middle movie, the monomyth cannot be thoroughly analyzed until after the final installment is released; that film, *The Rise of Skywalker*, is slated for a December 2019 release. Nevertheless, we see the Woman as the Temptress–Captain Phasma–finally defeated, and the Meeting with the Goddess satisfied by Vice Admiral Holdo, a Resistance martyr. The Road of Trials is Rey's training with Luke, Finn, and Rose's escape from Canto Blight, and the subsequent battle on Crait. Apotheosis is the death of Luke Skywalker, while the Belly of the Whale might be satisfied when Kylo kills Snoke, fighting Rey in a lightsaber duel; until *The Rise of Skywalker* is viewed, I cannot be sure of this is part of the Road of Trials. Moreover, look for Woman as the Temptress to reemerge when Rey flirts with the Dark Side.

Finally, during his self-imposed exile on Ahch-To, Luke has become a disciple of Basilides, trying to negate everything and live in oblivion. He has detached himself from everyone, including his sister, and has even attempted to free himself from the Force. Like a Zen Buddhist, it appears as though Luke spends his time meditating, with eyes closed in a Bhakti Yoga-like trance, doing everything possible to separate himself from the material agencies of the Demiurge. He dwells in a state of willed limbo, wanting nothing to do with anyone or anything. When Rey presents him with his lightsaber, which he now calls a "laser sword," he tosses it over his shoulder like it was a worthless bauble. He could care less about it, or its intrinsic importance. Luke has no interest in training her, or his status as a legend, or joining the Resistance; he wants to erase himself, annihilating his desire to know, obliterating his consciousness. He even tries to destroy the sacred scrolls to end the Jedi Order. Luke dwells in a cloud of unknowing, a nihilistic state of emptiness and stupor. Living in a void, cleansed of these desires to know and immersed in ignorance, he opens himself to the mystery of existence, coming to know himself. He finally learns from Yoda's Force ghost that failure is a necessary ingredient for success. Armed with this gnosis, Luke makes a final stand against Kylo, sacrificing himself so the Resistance can escape and regroup. Practicing Basilides' negation ignites Luke's divine spark; he now transcends the galaxy, becoming a romanticized legend–something he once scoffed at–was his *raison d'être*. Back on Ahch-To, Luke vanishes into thin air, becoming nothingness. Luke's actions are the stuff of dreams, evidenced by the stable hand children who are using handmade toys to reenact Luke's final stand during the battle of Crait. The Force is with them, and like farm boy Luke Skywalker from Episode IV, they eagerly await the adventures that lie before them.

CHAPTER X

ELVIS PRESLEY LIGHTS THE MORNING SKY: THE NEW WORLD'S MASONIC-SOLAR-APOLLONIAN GOD OF MUSIC AND THE CHRIST ARCHETYPE IN FILM

> The sun, as supreme among the celestial bodies visible to the astronomers of antiquity, was assigned to the highest of the gods and became symbolic of authority of the Creator Himself.
> Manly P. Hall, *The Secret Teachings of All Ages*, Chapter IX, "The Sun, a Universal Deity," 1928

> Though we have no disposition whatever to trench upon the ground that has been so exhaustively gleaned by those learned scholars who have shown that every Christian dogma has its origin in a heathen rite, still the facts which they have exhumed, since the enfranchisement of science, will lose nothing by repetition. Besides, we propose to examine these facts from a different and perhaps rather novel point of view: that of the old philosophies as esoterically understood.
> Helena P. Blavatsky, *Isis Unveiled*, II, i, "Religion," 1877

> His beneficent influences caused his identification with the Principle of Good; and the BRAHMA of the Hindus, and MITHRAS of the Persians, and ATHOM, AMUN, PHTHA, and OSIRIS, of the Egyptians, the BEL of the Chaldeans, the ADONAI of the Phœnicians, the ADONIS and APOLLO of the Greeks, became but personifications of the Sun, the regenerating Principle, image of that fecundity which perpetuates and rejuvenates the world's existence.
> Albert Pike, *Morals and Dogma of the Scottish Rite*, Chapter XXVIII, "Knight of the Sun, or Prince Adept," 1871

CINEMA SYMBOLISM 3

♪ Your kisses lift me higher / Like the sweet song of a choir / You light my morning sky / With burning love ♪. Elvis in concert (1974) wearing a jumpsuit with the Aztec Sun Stone, linking the King of Rock 'n' Roll with the divine, life-giving orb.

The extraordinary Elvis Aaron Presley life story began when he was born to Gladys (1912-1958) and Vernon Presley (1916-1979) in a two-room house in Tupelo, Mississippi, on January 8, 1935. His twin brother, Jessie Garon, was stillborn, leaving Elvis to grow up as an only child. He and his parents moved to Memphis, Tennessee, in 1948, and in 1953, Elvis graduated from Humes High School.

Elvis' musical influences were the pop and country music of the time, the gospel music he heard in church and at the all-night gospel singalongs he frequently attended, and the black R&B he absorbed on historic Beale Street as a Memphis teenager. In 1954, Elvis began his singing career with the legendary Sun Records label in Memphis. In late '55, his recording contract was sold to RCA Victor; by '56, he was an international sensation. With a sound and style that uniquely combined his diverse musical influences and blurred and challenged the social and racial barriers of the time, he ushered in a whole new era of American music and popular culture.

Here are a few Elvis facts: he starred in 33 successful films, made history with his television appearances and specials, and knew great acclaim through his many, often record-breaking, live concert performances on tour and in Las Vegas. Globally, he has sold over a billion records, more than any other artist. His American sales have earned him gold, platinum, or multi-platinum awards for 150 different albums and singles. Among his many achievements were 14 Grammy nominations (three wins) from the National Academy of Recording Arts & Sciences, the Grammy Lifetime Achievement Award, and honored as one of the Ten Outstanding Young Men of the Nation (1970) by the United States Jaycees. Without any of the special privileges that his celebrity status might have afforded him, Elvis honorably served his country in the U.S. Army (1958-1960).

His talent, handsome looks, sensuality, charisma, and good humor endeared him to millions, as did the humility and human kindness he demonstrated throughout his life. Known the world over by his first name, he is regarded as one of the most important figures of 20th-century popular culture. Elvis died at his Memphis home, Graceland, on August 16, 1977. He was 42 years old (biography courtesy Graceland's official webpage, https://www.graceland.com/biography).

The occult influences the music world; dark magic and demonism have been there since Robert Johnson (1911-1938) made his infamous pact, birthing the Delta Blues, impacting the recording industry to this very day. For example, Crowley, the Great Beast, appears collaged (upper-left corner) on the cover of the Beatles' *Sgt. Pepper's Lonely Hearts Club Band* (1967). In the world of the occult and black magic, Crowley is considered Sgt. Pepper, the fictitious bandleader who inspired the album. The album's opening lyrics are, "♪ It was twenty years ago today / Sgt. Pepper taught the band to play, ♪" which references the year 1947 because the album was released in 1967 (1967-20=1947). Crowley died in '47; hence, this was the year he "taught the band to play," to carry on his esoteric teachings posthumously through the medium of Rock 'n' Roll. Crowley's influence on Led Zeppelin is well documented, but what is less known is that the band's occult-demonic roots go much deeper than Frater Perdurabo. In 1971, Led Zeppelin's fourth album featured a gatefold illustrated with an adaptation of the Hermit card from the Rider-Waite Deck. For this album, the band employed arcane-alchemical symbols instead of a title; Jimmy Page's sigil was ZoSo, which comes from the book, *Ars Magica Arteficii* (1557) by Renaissance astrologer and mathematician Girolamo Cardano

(1501-1576).[486] Cardano linked the glyph to Saturn; Page was born under Capricorn, on January 9, 1944; thus, the gloomy, ringed-planet governs the guitarist. ZoSo also appears in *Le Triple Vocabulaire Infernal* (1844), a tome on demonology.[487] Page intended Zoso to be a magical phrase like abracadabra, representing his knowledge of the occult. In 1974, Zeppelin founded the boutique record label Swan Song; its logo was a stylized rendering of the mythical winged Icarus or, by other interpretations, Lucifer the fallen angel.[488]

In *Cinema Symbolism*'s Introduction, I analyzed a fascinating exemplar of Jungian synchronicity, something defying rational explanation, flirting with the supernatural. That is, Elvis' uncanny nexus to the sun; how solar iconography transcended his life, enveloping his death. Although both men are kings, Elvis was not Jesus Christ; instead, Elvis' life and legacy are connected to the sun for some unexplained, numinous, mystical reason. However, since Jesus personifies the sun, the nexuses between Elvis and Jesus are equally astounding as it is with all unexplained mysteries. I should mention that Elvis was not a Mason or in the Illuminati. Any comparison with the sun should not be construed as Masonic membership or linked to Weishaupt's defunct, Jesuit-styled cabal.

The purpose of this chapter is to consolidate this information and update it. Further, this chapter will analyze the solar-godman-hero archetype in film, a Hollywood favorite. If you've read my other two movie books, some of this material will look familiar; if not, this is brand new.

In *Cinema Symbolism*, I explained the following occultism:

> When examining the life and career of music and screen legend Elvis Presley (1935-1977), one cannot help notice a Masonic-solar influence–a supernatural correlation–existing from birth to death and beyond. A devout Christian, Elvis was familiar with the occult works of Manly P. Hall, Albert Pike, and Madame Helena Blavatsky (1831-1891). He occasionally read her *The Voice of Silence* (1889) on stage to his audience. Elvis was familiar with the esoteric philosophies of antiquity, yet was unaware that his life was a transcendent solar, pop-culture parable imbued upon the United States' social fabric, then the world.

---

486 Case, *Sweet Satan*, 10.
487 Ibid.
488 Ibid.

Like the Olympian solar deity Apollo, who was also a god of music, Elvis is an apotheosized, Apollonian King of Rock 'n' Roll: a musical solar deity. Elvis was born under Capricorn on January 8, 1935; in the northern hemisphere, Capricorn exalts from December 22 to January 19. The winter solstice occurs under Capricorn on December 20-22, when the sun is born again annually because the days become longer. Thus, Elvis, like the sun, and many of the sun gods of yore, e.g., Mithras, Sol Invictus, are given to Capricorn; the two pagan deities born on December 25. Elvis, personifying the sun, dies on August 16, 1977, in the house of Leo the Lion, the sole house of the sun. Toward the end of his life, he often wore a jumpsuit featuring the Aztec Sun Stone during live performances. Elvis' early songs were recorded and distributed by Sun Records, Memphis, Tennessee.[489]

Dates and numbers convey occult meanings, some divine, some evil, depending on one's point of view. Elvis' birth and death dates denote his solar rulership and Apollonian attributes. They are not limited to historic figures, but countries as well. If an essential year of a nation's history (or person) is added to itself, the result will likely be another significant year corresponding to the earlier event. This formula is how fortune tellers, psychics, and black magicians divine the future. An example from French history:

> The fall of Robespierre occurred in 1794; add 1+7+9+4 to get 21. Add 21 to 1794 to get 1815, the fall of Napoleon I at the Battle of Waterloo. Add 1+8+1+5 to get 15. Add 15 to 1815 to get 1830, which was the fall of Charles X (1757-1836).

Another example from French history:

> Louis XVI (b. 1754) ascended to the throne in 1774. Add 1+7+7+4 to get 19. Add 19 to 1774 to get 1793 the year he was guillotined.

From English history:

> The ascension of George I (1660-1727) to the throne occurred in 1714. Add 1+7+1+4 to get 13. Add 13 to 1714 to get 1727, which was the ascension of George II (1683-1760) to the throne. Another example

---
489 Sullivan, *Cinema Symbolism*, Introduction.

CINEMA SYMBOLISM 3

from English history: Queen Victoria was born in 1819; add 1+8+1+9 to get 19. Add 19 to 1819 to get 1838, the year she was coronated.[490]

We can, of course, apply this formula to Elvis:

He was born in 1935; add 1+9+3+5 to get 18. Add 18+1935 to get 1953. In 1953, Elvis graduated from high school, and, more importantly, recorded his first tunes at Sun Records, launching him to superstardom.

In *Cinema Symbolism*, I further provided:

Sun Records in Memphis, Tennessee dovetails with Memphis, Egypt; both are homes to famous solar temples. Uncovered at Saqqara, a temple dedicated to the Aten in Memphis, Egypt, is attested by hieroglyphs found within the tombs of the Memphite dignitaries of the end of the 18th dynasty. Among them, Tutankhamun, beginning his career under the reign of the Pharaoh Akhenaten (f/k/a Amenhotep, 1380-1334 BCE) as a Temple of Aten steward. Akhenaten–his name means the *living spirit of Aten*–was a Pharaoh of the Eighteenth dynasty of Egypt, ruling for seventeen years. Today, he is remembered for abandoning traditional Egyptian polytheism and introducing worship centered solely on the sun–the Aten–sometimes described as monotheistic or henotheistic. Memphis, Egypt, rests on the banks of the Nile River paralleling Memphis, Tennessee, which sits on the banks on the new world's Nile River, the Mississippi. Sun Records and Elvis' estate, Graceland, located in Memphis, Tennessee, are new world solar temples, designating Elvis as America's Rock and Roll heliacal and musical messiah. Elvis dies reading *The Scientific Search for the Face of Jesus* (1972) by Frank Adams, harmonizing one sun king, Jesus, with another: Elvis. Graceland is one of the most visited landmarks in America; Elvis is buried in its Meditation Garden. Elvis' fans *qua* disciples make pilgrimages to Graceland like a holy shrine, collecting the king's personal belongings, keeping them sacred relics. Like a resurrected sun, rumors that Elvis survived his death began to circulate after his drug overdose. It now appears like a religion *qua* solar-like faith has grown around the Apollonian King of Rock and Roll posthumously. Thus, Elvis' solar

---

490 Cavendish, *Black Arts*, 65-66.

life and personality, paralleling Jesus, appears to be a unique product of the world's collective unconscious or a sublime exemplar of Jungian synchronicity. Elvis personifies what the world wanted and needed him to be: a messianic-musical sun king. Elvis' life, from his humble beginnings to his rise to musical superstar, is the raw material that dreams are made of, fueling our imaginations.[491]

It's only appropriate the solar King of Rock 'n' Roll would rise out of the United States, the world's first (and only) Masonic Republic. Masonry's most critical symbol is the sun; thus, if the United States was born out of Freemasonry, it too relates to the sun, like Elvis. On Freemasonry and the sun, Masonic encyclopedist Albert Mackey (1807-1881) explains:

> Hardly any of the symbols of Masonry are more important in their signification or more extensive in their application than the sun. As the source of material light, it reminds the Mason of that intellectual light of which he is in constant search. But it is especially as the ruler of the day, giving to it a beginning and end, and a regular course of hours, that the sun is presented as a Masonic Symbol. Hence, of the three lesser lights, we are told that one represents or symbolizes the sun, one the moon, and one the Master of the Lodge, because, as the sun rules the day and the moon governs the night, so should the Worshipful Master rule and govern his Lodge with equal regularity and precision. And this is in strict analogy with other Masonic symbolisms. For if the Lodge is a symbol of the world, which is thus governed in its changes of times and seasons by the sun, it is evident that the Master who governs the Lodge, controlling its time of opening and closing, and the work which is it should do, must be symbolized by the sun. The heraldic definition of the sun as a bearing fits most appositely to the symbolism of the sovereignty of the Master. Thus Gwillim says: 'The sun is the symbol of sovereignty, the hieroglyphic of royalty; it doth signify absolute authority.'

> This representation of the sun as a symbol of authority, while it explains the reference to the Master, enables us to amplify its meaning, and apply it to the three sources of authority in the Lodge, and account for

---
[491] Sullivan, *Cinema Symbolism*, Introduction.

the respective positions of the officers wielding this authority. The Master, therefore, in the East is a symbol of the rising sun; the Junior Warden in the South, of the Meridian Sun, and the Senior Warden in the West, of the Setting Sun. So in the mysteries of India, the chief officers were placed in the east, the west, and the south, respectively, to represent Brahma, or the rising; Vishnu, or the setting; and Siva, or the meridian sun. And in the Druidical rites, the Arch-Druid, seated in the east, was assisted by two other officers–the one in the west representing the moon, and the other in the south representing the meridian sun.

This triple division of the government of a Lodge by three officers, representatives of the sun in his three manifestations in the east, south, and west, will remind us of similar ideas in the symbolism of antiquity. In the Orphic mysteries, it was taught that the sun generated from an egg, burst forth with power to triplicate himself by his own unassisted energy.

Supreme power always seems to have been associated in the ancient mind with a three-fold division. Thus the sign of authority was indicated by the three-forked lightning of Jove, the trident of Neptune, and the three-headed Cerberus of Pluto. The government of the Universe was divided between these three sons of Saturn. The chaste goddess ruled the earth as Diana, the heavens as Luna, and the infernal regions as Hecate, whence her rites were only performed in a place where three roads met.

The sun is then presented to us in Masonry first as a symbol of light, but then more emphatically as a symbol of sovereign authority.

But, says Wemyss (*Symb. Lang.*), speaking of Scriptural symbolism, 'the sun may be considered an emblem of Divine Truth,' because the sun or light, of which it is the source, 'is not only manifest in itself, but makes other things; so one truth detects, reveals, and manifests another, as all truths are dependent on, and connected with, each other more or less.' And this again is applicable to the Masonic doctrine which makes the Master the symbol of the sun; for as the sun discloses and makes manifest, by the opening of the day, what had been hidden in the darkness of night, so the Master of the Lodge, as the analogue of the ancient hierophant or explainer of the mysteries, makes Divine truth manifest in the neophyte, who had been hitherto in intellectual darkness, and reveals the hidden or esoteric lessons of initiation.[492]

The Masonic influence upon the United States is substantial, and cannot be avoided when discussing its history. It is shallow thinking to assume that the secret societies operating in Europe–Freemasons, the Rosicrucians, and the Fellows of the Royal Society–had no representation among the American colonies until the beginning of the 18th century. The confusion is due not to the lack of such activity, but the inadequacy of available records.[493] Freemasonry of the 18th century cannot be compared to the modern Order. Masonic scholars were still dabbling in the systems of ancient Mysteries, which dominated classical antiquity.[494] James Anderson's (1769-1739) *Constitutions of the Free-Masons* (1723) was published one hundred years after the appearance of the Rosicrucian-Masonic-mystical Shakespearean folio in 1623. Benjamin Franklin became a Mason in 1731, becoming Provincial Grand Master of Pennsylvania in 1734. George Washington (1732-1799) took his first degree in the Lodge at Fredericksburg, Virginia, in 1752. The early American Lodges met in taverns or inns, and the first Masonic Temple in America was built in Boston in 1832. It cannot be learned if Thomas Paine (1737-1809) was a Mason, although he wrote an essay dealing with the origin of Freemasonry. He attempted to trace the Fraternity to the Celtic Druids. In 1791, George Washington spoke of Masonry: "Being persuaded a just application of the principles on which Free Masonry is founded, must be promotive of virtue and public prosperity, I shall always be glad to advance the interest of this Society and be considered by them a deserving brother."[495]

It is believed the Boston Tea Party (1773) was arranged around a chowder supper at the home of the Bradlee brothers, who were Masons, and that mother Bradlee kept the water hot so they could wash off the disguises. "Who were these 'Mohawks,' Sons of Liberty, in paint and gear?" asks

---

492 Albert Mackey, *An Encyclopedia of Freemasonry and its Kindred Sciences*. 2 vols. (New York: The Masonic History Company, 1921), 2:736-737.
493 Manly P. Hall, *The Secret Destiny of America* (1942/1951; repr., New York: Tarcher/Penguin, 2008), 211.
494 Ibid, 221.
495 Ibid, 228.

Madison C. Peters. "Free Masons, members of St. Andrews Lodge, led by the Junior Warden, Paul Revere."[496]

The First Continental Congress, on the motion of George Washington, selected Peyton Randolph (1721-1775, past Grand Master of the Masons of Virginia, to preside over its deliberations. Later, John Hancock (1737-1793), another Mason, succeeded him. Hancock signed the Declaration of Independence with the signature so bold "the King of England could read it without spectacles." It was rumored Thomas Jefferson (1743-1826) became a Mason in France. Of the signers of his Declaration of Independence, nine have been confirmed as Freemasons.

On June 17, 1775, at Bunker Hill, General Joseph Warren (1741-1775) fell, Grand Master of the Massachusetts Grand Lodge. The Marquis de Lafayette (1757-1834), who fought alongside Washington, was also a Mason. Frederick Wilhelm August Heinrich Ferdinand, Baron von Steuben (1730-1794), received the first offer of surrender from Lord Cornwallis (1738-1805) at Yorktown, was made a Mason in New York State. He had been aide-de-camp to the King of Prussia. John Paul Jones (1747-1792), founder of the U.S. Navy, was a brother of the mystical Nine Sisters Lodge in Paris, which counted among its members Voltaire, the philosopher Claude Adrien Helvetius (1715-1771), Danton, and the neoclassicist sculptor Jean-Antoine Houdon (1741-1828) who made portrait busts of Washington, Franklin, and Cagliostro. Other Masonic leaders included General Nathan Greene (1742-1786), Major General Henry Knox (1750-1806), and Ethan Allen (1738-1789) of Green Mountain Boy fame.[497] Out of the thirty-nine men who signed the U.S. Constitution, thirteen were Masons.

The United States' triple division of governance between an executive (President *qua* Royal Arch Sun Priest), a legislative (the Congress and Senate), and judicial (Supreme Court) branches derive from the tripartite division of governance in the Blue Lodge, based on the sun's three daily stations. The separation of church and state (Second Amendment) originates from Anderson's *Constitutions*, Charges: 1. "Concerning God and Religion," wherein Masonry declares it does not adhere to any one faith. Instead, religion is left to the individual Mason so long as he believes in a Supreme Being.

---

496 Ibid.
497 Ibid, 222, 229-230.

Daniel Carroll (173-1796), a Mason, owned the land that the federal capital–the District of Columbia, the city of the sun–would be built. He was one of five men to sign the Articles of Confederation and the Constitution, and one of the very few Roman Catholics among the Founders. The architecture and streetscape of the Federal/Masonic capital, Washington, D.C., is solar and astrological, correlating with the above and below of Hermes Trismegistus, the legendary founder of Freemasonry. The District of Columbia's architects, James Hoban (1758-1831), Benjamin Henry Latrobe (1764-182), and Robert Mills (1771-1855), were all Masons. Former Mayor of New York City and Governor of New York State, DeWitt Clinton (1769-1828), was a Royal Arch Mason and Knight Templar, responsible for creating the two-party political system. For more on the Masonic influence on the development of the United States, I refer the reader to my first book, *The Royal Arch of Enoch* (2nd ed., 2016).

Although Elvis was not a Mason, the sun transcends his life, identifying him as an Apollonian Masonic-Christlike king of the musical world. Coming out of the new world's sun temple *qua* Sun Records in Memphis, Tennessee, Elvis made 33 movies, 31 as an actor and two theatrical documentaries: *Elvis: That's the Way It Is* (1970) and *Elvis on Tour* (1972). The 33 movies represent the 33 degrees of the Scottish Rite of Freemasonry, an esteemed high-degree body both in and outside the United States. The thirty-three degrees alludes to Christ's mundane existence: he was 33-years-old when he was crucified at Calvary or Golgotha. The 33 years represent the 33 vertebras of the spine; at its vertex sits the skull–*Golgotha* means *skull*–wherein truth, en*light*enment, are either acknowledged, generating wisdom, or murdered, extinguished, perpetuating ignorance. Thus, Christ, the light, dies at (or in) the human mind–inside the cranium.

Elvis' career, like Christ's redemptive mission, was virgin birthed. Elvis' first appearance was on the Ed Sullivan Show (1948-1971) on September 9, 1956, under Virgo the Virgin; the constellation is the Virgin Mary anthropomorphized in the Christian Mysteries. This performance launched his career, placing him on the path to superstardom. During his later concerts, Elvis came on stage to the opening sequence of Richard Strauss' (1864-194) *Also sprach Zarathustra* (1896) titled "Sunrise," apropos since early Christians had some difficulty in distinguishing the rising sun from Christ.[498] Elvis ran the so-called Memphis Mafia, a group of his friends, associates, employees, and yes-men who surrounded him from 1954 until his death, mirroring the Apostles of Christ. Elvis died reading a book about Jesus, specifically the Shroud of Turin. The book was either *The Scientific Search for the Face of Jesus* by Frank Adams or Robert Wilcox's *Shroud* (1977). Elvis perished on August 16; in the Eastern Orthodox Church, August 16 was the Feast Day of the Image of Edessa, considered the Shroud of Turin, to commemorate the arrival of the cloth in Constantinople in 944 CE. Lastly, every king must have a queen, and the Queen of Soul was none other than the incomparable Aretha Franklin (1942-2018), dying 41 one years to the day of the King of Rock 'n' Roll, on August 16, 2018.

* * * * *

If we could ask one of the ancient pagans whom he revered as his mightiest deity, he would name the sun god, calling him Apollo if he were a Greek; if an Egyptian, Horus or Osiris; if of Norway, Sol; if of Peru, Bochica. Since the sun is the center of the physical universe, all primitive peoples made it the hub about which their religion revolved, nearly always believing it a living person to whom they could say prayers and offer sacrifices. It directed their lives and destinies, and could even snatch men from earthly existence to dwell for a time with him, as it draws the water from lakes and seas.[499] All the sacred church festivals are survivals of the old rites honoring the sun. How many times has the Church decanted the new wine of Christianity into the old bottles of heathendom? Yule-tide, the pagan Christmas, celebrated the sun's turning north, and the bygone midsummer holiday is still kept in Ireland and on the Continent as St. John's Day by the lighting of bonfires and dance about them from east to west as the sun appears to move.[500] The similarity of these ancient pagan legends and beliefs with Christian traditions was so significant that it excited the attention and the undisguised wrath of the early Christian fathers. They felt no doubt about the similarity, but not knowing how to explain it fell back upon the innocent theory that the Devil–to confound the Christians–had,

---

498 Marlan, *Black Sun*, 149.
499 Kelley, *Hallowe'en*, 1-2.
500 Ibid, 2.

centuries before, caused the pagans to adopt certain beliefs and practices. (Very crafty, we may say, of the Devil, but also very innocent of the Church Fathers to believe it!) Justin Martyr (100-165 CE), for instance, describes the institution of the Lord's Supper as narrated in the Gospels, then goes on to say, "Which the wicked devils have imitated in the mysteries of Mithras, commanding the same thing to be done. For, that bread and a cup of water are placed with certain incantations in the mystic rites of one who is being initiated you either know or can learn."[501]

Tertullian states "the Devil by the mysteries of his idols imitates even the main part of the divine mysteries. ...He baptizes his worshippers in water and makes them believe that this purifies them from their crimes. ...Mithras sets his mark on the forehead of his soldiers; he celebrates the oblation of bread; he offers an image of the resurrection, and presents at once the crown and the sword; he limits his chief priest to a single marriage; he even has his virgins and ascetics."[502] Mithras was virgin birthed in a cave on December 25. He traveled far and wide as a teacher and illuminator of men. His great festivals were the winter solstice and the spring equinox, i.e., Christmas and Easter. He had twelve companions or disciples, viz. the twelve months or zodiac. He was buried in a tomb, but rose from the dead; his resurrection was celebrated yearly with great rejoicings. He was called savior and mediator, and sometimes figured as a lamb; his followers held sacramental feasts in remembrance of him.[503] Osiris was born (Plutarch tells us) on the 361st day of the year, December 27. He, too, like Mithras and Dionysus, was a great traveler. As King of Egypt, he taught men civil arts, and "tamed them by music and gentleness, not by force of arms"; he was the discoverer of corn and wine. But he was betrayed by Typhon/Set, the power of darkness, and slain and dismembered. "This happened," says Plutarch (46-120 CE), "on the 17th of the month Athyr, when the sun enters into the Scorpion," the sign of the zodiac, heralding the oncoming of winter. His body was placed in a box, but afterward, on the 19th, it came to life, imitated in the cults of Mithras, Dionysus, Adonis, and others. In Osiris worship, an image placed in a coffin was brought out before the worshipers and saluted with

---

[501] Edward Carpenter, *Pagan & Christian Creeds: Their Origin and Meaning* (New York: Harcourt, Brace and Company, 1921), 25.
[502] Ibid.
[503] Ibid, 21.

glad cries of "Osiris is risen." "His sufferings, death, and resurrection were enacted year by year in a great mystery-play at Abydos."[504]

Such mythologies speak to the power of the messianic-solar archetype. In the *Corpus Hermeticum*, the sun is divine: "The Sun is the greatest of the gods in heaven; to him, as to their king and over-lord, all the gods in heaven yield place."[505] Is it no wonder that Hollywood, the Entertainment Industrial Complex of the Masonic Republic, employs heliacal iconography expertly? After all, the solar-resurrected-heroic-Christlike-Mithraic-Egyptian godman is a cinematic favorite, the protagonist of many blockbusters. Many of the founders of Hollywood's movie studios were Freemasons, so solar symbolism and recondite imagery should come as no surprise. Griffith aside, Adolph Zukor (1873-1976), one of the three founders of Paramount Pictures, and often considered the godfather of the motion picture industry, was a brother of Centennial Lodge 763, New York. Cecil B. DeMille (1881-1959) was a Hollywood movie director, and brother of Prince of Orange Lodge No. 16, New York. Like Zukor, he is a founding father of cinema; his film, *The Squaw Man* (1914), was Hollywood's first major production. Jack Warner (1892-1978), who cofounded Warner Brothers, was a Mason of Mount Olive Lodge No. 506, in Los Angeles, California. Carl Laemmle Sr. (1867-1939), founder Universal Studios, was a Freemason. Darryl F. Zanuck (1902-1979), a cofounder of 20th Century Productions, was a Mason of the same lodge as Jack Warner. Zanuck earned three Academy Awards during his lifetime, having been nominated for countless others. Louis B. Mayer (1884-1957) was a film producer who cofounded Metro-Goldwyn-Mayer (MGM) and was a member of the St. Cecile Lodge No. 568, New York. The mascot of MGM, the roaring lion that introduces their films, is named Leo after the zodiac's fifth house, which the sun governs. The Academy of Motion Picture Arts and Sciences annually awards films for outstanding achievements, as well as actors and actresses for their excellent performances. *Oscar* is the award's nickname; it's a miniature golden man because gold is the metal of the sun, designating heliocentric supremacy; thus, the trophy is given out to the best in the business, making them Hollywood royalty, and American nobility.

---

504 Ibid, 22.
505 *Hermetica, Corpus Hermeticum, Libellus* V, 1:159.

After slaying him, Jadis the White Witch wears the mane of the Christlike solar avatar, Aslan the Lion (Liam Neeson). His return heralded the end of Narnia's endless winter; hence, the Queen begins to thaw. Even she cannot avoid the spring, adorning herself with his golden mane, symbolizing sunrays coinciding with the vernal equinox's increasing daylight. Image from *The Chronicles of Narnia: The Lion, the Witch and the Wardrobe* (2005). "The winter solstice and the vernal equinox, the birthday of the Sun-God and the period of his sacrifice and his triumph. ...That Easter is also a solar festival is perhaps not so freely recognized. But we know not only that Mithras and Osiris (and Horus), like so many other solar and vegetal deities, were especially adored at the vernal equinox, the time of Christ's crucifixion and resurrection."
– John M. Robertson, *Pagan Christs*, 1903.

The solar-Christlike figure appears in our favorite films, battling an evil overload, the Devil. In the original *Star Wars* trilogy, Luke combats the Sith Lord, Darth Vader. Luke personifies the sun: he is Apollo, a solar messiah who defeats darkness represented by Python, the serpent. Comparatively, Apollo is Horus in Egyptian mythology, defeating Typhon or Set (or Seth), the dark lord of chaos, storms, disorder, and violence. Luke is the light– *Luke* derives from the Latin *lux*, *light*, that *skywalks* daily because of the ecliptic. As the sun personified, he does battle with darkness: Darth Vader is the Sith Lord; the Sith are named after the Egyptian god Set or Seth, the enemy of Horus. Interestingly, in *The Force Awakens*, Rey thinks Luke is a myth, thereby casting him in with legendary solar deities like Surya, Horus, Mithras (or Mithra), Amun-Ra, Brahma, Osiris, Apollo, and Belenus.

Parallel Manichean mythology runs though the Harry Potter stories, and the films based upon them. Harry is the savior of the wizarding world, doing battle with darkness personified, Lord Voldemort. The mascot of Harry's house at Hogwarts, Gryffindor, is a lion symbolizing Leo, ruled by the sun. Voldemort's domain, and that of the Death Eaters, is Slytherin, employing a serpent for its totem representing Python, the enemy of the sun god Apollo (*vide supra*). The entire Harry Potter saga is a Manichean conflict between light and dark; like Christ and the sun, Harry dies and resurrects, becoming a messianic figure, defeating darkness and evil.

"The solaronite is a way to explode the actual particles of sunlight." – Eros, *Plan 9 from Outer Space*. In the best of the worst, *Plan 9*, the sun is both savior and destroyer, as benevolent aliens attempt to prevent humans from developing solaronite weaponry to destroy the universe. In the Hamlet-like Disney epic *The Lion King*, Mufasa (James Earl Jones) and Simba (Matthew Broderick) personify Osiris and his solar son, Horus. Together, they rule the Pride Lands until Scar (Jeremy Irons) *qua* Typhon (Set) betrays them, usurps power, transforming the land into wintry decay. Like the sun which resides in the east, south, and west, Mufasa and Simba, as solar avatars, cannot enter the north because it is the domain of darkness: the macabre elephant graveyard. The sun never dwells in the north. Aslan the Lion, of *The Chronicles of Narnia* series, is a solar savior epitomizing Leo the Lion; his return ends the frigid reign of the White Queen. Narnia thaws signifying the end of winter, coinciding with the vernal equinox: the resurrection of the sun, its warmth, and divine light. In *Alien 3* (1992), Ripley becomes a Christlike savior–a warrior sun goddess–when she sacrifices herself by destroying the last Xenomorph, falling backward into the flames cruciform mirroring Christ's crucifixion. Like Jesus, she is brought back to life in the next film in the franchise, appropriately titled *Alien: Resurrection* (1997).

Not all Christ archetypes are so distinct. In *The Bride of Frankenstein*, the Monster (Karloff) becomes tragic, removing sin from the Scientific Revolution. He becomes a redemptive figure by absolving humanity's desire to play god: after capture, he is hoisted on a pole before a jeering mob, suggesting crucifixion.[506] In *The Day the Earth Stood Still* (1951), the humanoid space alien Klaatu (Michael Rennie, 1909-1971) descends from the heavens in flying saucer to redeem humankind, to save it from itself. He assumes the name *John Carpenter*, the surname referencing Christ's day job, identifying the extraterrestrial as Logos from the Gospel of John. Note the initials *JC* for Jesus Christ: depending on the context, *JC* identifies the character as a Christlike, combating works of darkness, redeeming humanity. Klaatu's words must be obeyed, or else earth will face the consequences. In *Gangs of New York* (2002), Amsterdam Vallon

---

506 Skal, *Monster Show*, 189.

Christian imagery in *Frankenstein*. Victor Frankenstein (Colin Clive, 1900-1937), along with his hunchbacked henchman Fritz (Dwight Frye, 1899-1943), rob a grave with a cross and Grim Reaper tombstones nearby. The cross and Grim Reaper suggest Dr. Frankenstein is an apotheosized figure, god on earth. He's a Hermetic magus trying to defeat the saturnine Reaper by discovering the mysteries of eternal life.

(Leonardo Dicaprio) redeems New York City by casting the Devil out of Paradise, Paradise Square, personified by Bill "the Butcher" Cutting (Daniel Day-Lewis). In keeping with his diabolical persona, Bill gambles and broods in the lower level of his headquarters named Satan's Circus, subconsciously conjuring *Inferno*'s ninth level.[507] Subtle demonism lurks in *The Warriors'* celluloid when Luther *qua* Lucifer talks to his master on the phone. Based on the conversation, Luther is speaking with Satan; the Angel of Darkness has offered protection to his subordinates in return for the hunting down and killing the righteous Warriors.

In *The Green Mile* (1999), *JC*, John Coffey (Michael Clarke Duncan, 1957-2012), can heal the sick raises the dead; he returns life to a mouse, imitating Christ, who raised Lazarus from the dead in the Gospel of John. Like Jesus, he is executed unjustly; Coffee dies in the electric chair, trying to redeem the sins of the former Confederacy. In *The Terminator* mythology, John Conner saves humankind from evil machines trying to take over the

---

507 For more on this Christian-occult imagery, check out this author's *Cinema Symbolism 2*, Chapter XIII, "Lost History and the Gangs of New York."

(Left) Stained glass window at St. John the Baptist's Anglican Church (est. 1840), Ashfield, New South Wales, featuring Jesus as the luminous sun, cradling the lamb, symbolizing the constellation Aries the Ram. It illustrates Jesus' description of himself at John 10:11: "I am the good shepherd: the good shepherd giveth his life for the sheep." (Right) Similar imagery can be seen in *The Green Mile*: John Coffey, the South's redeemer, sits in a theater with light emanating from behind, symbolizing the sun's divine light, linking him with Jesus.

world. In a way, he is virgin birthed, having sent one of his soldiers back in time to impregnate his mother. In *12 Monkeys* (1995), James Cole (Bruce Willis) travels back in time to save humanity from a deadly virus. Like Christ, he is mocked and scorned because no one believes his truthful message. The apocalypse occurs around Christmas: Saturnalia, the birthday of the sun and, as such, the birth of Christ. Cole unifies, viz. accomplishes the alchemical wedding, with the sacred feminine, Dr. Kathryn Railly (Madeleine Stowe), a Mary Magdalene-like persona who comes to believe in Cole and his dire prediction. Like Jesus, Cole is martyred, trying to save humanity, killed by those he was trying to redeem.

On the hero, Manly P. Hall writes:

> A hero was one who had heroically turned from the contemplation of the temporal to the contemplation of the eternal, and consequently was dedicated to the service of the gods. Gazing rapturously upon the faces of the Ungenerated Ones, the heroes verged toward certain divinities with more ardor than to others, thus expressing the innate preferences of their dispositions. The heroes, therefore, were divided among the orders of the gods, each serving his own preference and by degrees coming to be identified with the qualities of his chosen deity. As the gods themselves are incapable of descending into the corporeal sphere,

they incline toward it through their vassals, the heroes. As a result certain men have come to be revered as divine incarnations and the creative principles venerated under their similitudes. Unable to discern that the hero is not a god, the nonphilosophic have befogged the issues of theology, with the result that men have become the worshippers of men and have propitiated mortal heroes before the superessential gods.

While ordinary mortals, being as yet rationally unawakened, depend largely upon their natal daemon, the heroes—or those already approaching liberation—are the beneficiaries of a more exalted genius, denominated the *essential daemon*. The Father-Star of the Neoplatonists is this essential daemon, into whose nature the natal daemon has been merged by a process in which the lesser is mingled with the greater, and their issues become one. The essential daemon is unapproachable by him who is still a servant to his sense perceptions. Nor can the essential daemon descend into man, but as a Silent Watcher must brood over the irrational soul until, emerging from its chrysalis of materiality, it spreads its spiritual wings and soars swiftly to the source of its own light.[508]

Hall describes, in essence, the solar archetype, whether he (or she) be a king's son or daughter, warrior-leader, philosopher, prophet, sage, saint, or semi-divine being, the hero blazes a trail for the less adventurous to follow. Mythology is the deeds and actions of this archetype, evident in so many of the world's great religions, echoed in fairy tales, and a source of profound, inspirational wisdom for humankind.

Next, the Biblical enigmas continue as we explore *Mother!*

---

508 Hall, *Lectures*, 291-292.

CHAPTER XI

KABBALAH AND THE BIBLICAL MYSTERIES OF MOTHER!

Me? I am I. ...It's not your fault.
Nothing is ever enough. I couldn't create if it was.
And I have to. That's what I do. That's what I am.
Now I must try it all again.
Him, *Mother!*, 2017

You never loved me. You just loved how much I loved you.
Mother, *Mother!*, 2017

The whole problem of creation, even in its most recondite aspects,
is bound up with the revelation of the hidden God and his outward
movement – even though 'there is nothing outside Him' (Azriel),
for in the last resort 'all comes from the One, and all returns to the One,'
according to the neoplatonic formula adopted by the early kabbalists.
Gershom Scholem, *Kabbalah*, III, "God and Creation," 1974

The Gnostic Simon Magus maintained the first divine Thought was the mother of lower demiurgic power that created the world, and that Yaldabaoth's morality keeps humankind in bondage. Simon's heresies are the heart and soul of *Mother!*

Intense is how this author would describe watching *Mother!* for the first time, and even subsequent viewings. It is raw, especially toward the conclusion when Mother (Jennifer Lawrence) gets kicked around and beaten by angry, unwelcome houseguests. By all accounts, this scene is disturbing to watch and reminiscent of the grotesquely horrific scenes from *The Exorcist*. On its surface, Aronofsky's film is a parable–it is not meant to be taken literally. It is not about a man and a woman living alone in an isolated house only to be visited by strangers, ultimately leading to death, annihilation, and renewal.

Instead, it is a Biblical allegory with a dash of Lurianic Kabbalah. Aronofsky also pays homage to the Polanski classic *Rosemary's Baby* as a means to signify the emergence of evil. To this author, the best way to dissect it is to break it in half between the Old and the New Testament. Note that none of the characters have names,[509] making the religious allusions more noticeable, even to a viewer not well versed in hidden movie symbolism. After the Biblical analysis, other veiled aspects will be discussed, such as the significance of the number eight, the mercurial frog, and the film's kabalistic-Gnostic undercurrents. I could have easily analyzed this movie in Chapter II but felt it was worthy of a chapter due to its complexities.

It starts with a woman engulfed in flames, then Him[510] (Javier Bardem) places an oval-shaped crystal in a display holder, as a house is remade from ashes.

The first portion is the Old Testament. Him lives alone in an octagonal house with Mother. Observe the number eight because everything in the home is octagonal; from the molding to the kitchen's floor tiles, from the frying pan to the doorknobs, eight is prevalent. The couple is isolated: he is a struggling writer while she is caretaking the home. One cannot help but think of Jack and Wendy from *The Shining*, but that's the only parallel between them. Mother, it seems, is doing more than decorating the home; instead, she is repairing it, making it livable (literally) after a mysterious fire consumed it. From the ashes of the old house, Him has procured an enigmatic crystal that he safeguards in his study. Him is God, Yahweh, Jehovah, the Ancient of Days, while she is Mother Nature or Mother Earth. Thus, she and the home are the same: when she places her hands to the wall, she can feel the home's heartbeat because it is her heartbeat; the home is earth, and she is its keeper, Mother Nature. The relationship between Mother and the house reflects Gaia theory, which holds earth's environments form a synergic living organism. Easter egg: Mother is barefoot most of the time. Bare feet have come to represent innocence, or childhood, in a glorifying perception of freedom from real-life requirements. Like Mother Nature, she is free, pure, and uncorrupted, connecting her to the house *qua* terra firma.

---

509 During the end credits, none of the characters' names start with a capital letter except for Him cementing his demiurgic status.
510 Scholem, *Kabbalah, passim*; the author frequently refers to the godhead as *Him*.

CINEMA SYMBOLISM 3

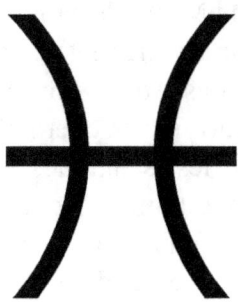

Man's paraphernalia features Pisces' astrological symbol. "Each year the sun passes entirely around the zodiac and returns to the point from which it started–the vernal equinox–and each year it falls just a little short of making the complete circle of the heavens in the allotted period of time. As a result, it crosses the equator just a little behind the spot in the zodiacal sign where it crossed the previous year. Each sign of the zodiac consists of thirty degrees, and as the sun loses about one degree every seventy-two years, it regresses through one entire constellation (or sign) in approximately 2,160 years, and through the entire zodiac in about 25,920 years. (Authorities disagree concerning these figures). This retrograde motion is called the *Precession of the Equinoxes*. This means that in the course of about 25,920 years, which constitute one Great Solar or Platonic Year, each one of the twelve constellations occupies a position at the vernal equinox for nearly 2,160 years, then gives place to the previous sign. Among the ancients the sun was always symbolized by the figure and nature of the constellation through which it passed at the vernal equinox. For nearly the past 2,000 years the sun has crossed the equator at the vernal equinox in the constellation of Pisces (the Two Fishes). For the 2,160 years before that it crossed through the constellation of Aries (the Ram). Prior to that the vernal equinox was in the sign of Taurus (the Bull). It is probable that the form of the bull and the bull's proclivities were assigned to this constellation because the bull was used by the ancients to plow the fields, and the season set aside for plowing and furrowing corresponded to the time at which the sun reached the segment of the heavens named Taurus." – Manly P. Hall, *The Secret Teachings of All Ages*, 1928

While Him broods, she seems to enjoy the peaceful solitude with God and the earth. Mother, though, suffers anxiety attacks for which she drinks a mysterious yellow elixir, curing her. To this author, the yellow potion is a reference to the 1892 short story, *The Yellow Wallpaper* by Charlotte Perkins Gilman (1860-1935), which is about a woman seeking isolation in an old mansion to cope with a temporary nervous depression–a slight hysterical tendency–which also afflicts Mother. Perhaps this is because of who is coming to the house; Mother sees strange foreboding black stains in the home when (or before) the uninvited guests arrive. These guests will have a devastating effect on the home, implying the destruction of the environment; toward the end, they wantonly rip the house to pieces; a dying fly, or bee, is a harbinger of climate change. Easter egg: When Mother paints the wall, she makes a single diagonal stroke of yellow-gray paint, from upper-right to lower-left. Later, when the Poet's acolytes invade the house, he makes an identical stroke with his thumb on their foreheads, marking them. After Him and Mother's baby is born, the mark remains as they adore the child as an earthly manifestation of Him.

The first to arrive is Man-as-Adam, portrayed by Ed Harris, showing up one night unannounced, carrying an overnight bag. Him welcomes Man into the home, but Mother is less sanguine, believing subterfuge may be afoot. Man enters through the home's front door, which conspicuously features a windowed cross, signifying the earth's terrestrial cross, formed by the two solstices and equinoxes, and the astral cross formed by the four fixed signs of the zodiac: Scorpio, Aquarius, Leo, and Taurus. The cross, naturally, is an allusion to Christianity, which takes center stage in the second half; tying into this esoteric, Christian theme is Man's cigarette lighter, featuring the symbol of Pisces the Fish–more on this eschatology later.[511] Mother pushes the lighter off a dresser–in all probability because Man smokes too much–where it is lost until the apocalypse.

Man enjoys talking to Him, and Him enjoys listening to his stories. After drinking too much, Man is sick over the toilet with a wound in his side, indicating the removal of his rib to create Eve, the First Woman. Soon thereafter, Mother sees a bizarre animated organism in the toilet, presumably some discarded appendage from Man, although this is never explained. The next morning, while Man smokes outside, Woman/Eve (Michelle Pfeiffer), arrives at the door. But she is no ordinary First Woman; instead, she is tainted heavily–notice her black clothing and stockings–by Adam's first wife, the dark goddess Lilith (implied at Genesis 1:28, as Eve was not created until the next chapter). Within kabalistic demonology, she has two primary roles: the strangler of children and the seducer of men.[512] Appearing as early as 700 BCE in the book of Isaiah, Lilith is the dark aspect of the Mother Goddess; thus, she is diametric to Lawrence's Mother.[513] She wears earthy hues like tans, browns, beiges, and whites while Woman always dresses in somber black. Woman is annoying, prying, and most importantly, Woman and Man are older than Mother

---

511 Man's duffle bag is also tagged with the Pisces symbol. Aronofsky did this to make sure the viewer could see the logo because it is hard to identify on the lighter. Inside the bag, Man carries an image of Him, i.e., a Graven Image, suggesting he is violating the Second Commandment at Exodus 20:4.
512 Scholem, *Kabbalah*, 357.
513 Guiley, *Encyclopedia of Witches*, 203.

(Left) The original one-sheet poster for *Rosemary's Baby*. (Right) The third promotional poster for *Mother!* imitates the former, indicating Aronofsky is importing the satanic undercurrents from Polanski's movie into his film. Aronofsky does this by using an elderly couple–like Polanski–to introduce evil, plaguing a younger couple.

and Him; through this paradigm, younger and older couples, Aronofsky introduces the Devil.

Him wants to spend time listening to Man's stories; they chum around and go for walks, neglecting Mother, who yearns to be with the former. Woman makes lemonade, a drink made from the fruits of the earth, but carelessly leaves a mess of tapped-out lemons strewn about the kitchen as a harbinger of the home's despoiling by humankind. Mother is not happy with the two visitors, wanting them to leave, but Him objects, so they remain. The awkward relationship between Him and Man and Mother and Woman deliberately conjures the interplay between Rosemary and Guy and their older, nosey, Devil-worshipping neighbors Roman and Minnie in *Rosemary's Baby*. Man echoes Roman because he lures Him away from his young, beautiful significant other with engrossing tales. Woman parallels Minnie because she is nosey, always turning up when she is not wanted, irritating her host. Aronofsky employs this young-old couple dynamic from *Rosemary's Baby* as a theodicean riddle, thereby introducing evil. This paradigm, along with a foreboding, basement laundry room, and its blazing hellfire furnace, seeks to transfer the demonism from the Black

Bramford to the octagonal home subconsciously. After all, there can't be a God without the Devil.

Him protects a mysterious crystal that he keeps in his study. It symbolizes the apple *qua* forbidden fruit in the Garden of Eden; it represents the Kabbalah, the *sefirot*, the Tree of Life/Wisdom. Man and Woman are curious about it but are admonished by Mother to stay away from it and the room. They accidentally break it–smashing it into tiny shards–and are expelled from the office, paralleling Adam and Eve's expulsion from Eden. Now in a state of original sin, Mother witnesses Man and Woman fornicating. When Mother goes to confront them, she answers the door; notice that her bra has a leafy motif to it. This scene is a reenactment of Genesis, specifically, when Adam and Eve covered up their nudity with leaves after eating the forbidden fruit.

Cain and Abel arrive at the house personified by Man and Woman's two arguing sons, billed as Oldest Son and Younger Brother (portrayed by Domhnall and Brian Gleeson). They fight–one son murders the other–with the surviving one marked on his forehead just like his Biblical analog. The dead son's blood stains the home-earth cursing it; the floor *qua* ground "hath opened her mouth to receive thy brother's blood from thy hand" (Genesis 4:9-11). Mother follows the dripping blood–crying out to her from the ground (Genesis 4:10)–to the basement where she discovers a hidden chamber with a large tank. It is the vehicle of the earth's destruction at the climax. Even after the blood-stained floorboards are replaced, the wound returns, becoming a gory hole in the floor–an open mouth–because the house *qua* earth is forever jinxed.

Meanwhile, Man, Woman, and random mourners are welcomed into the home. Him tells Mother the living son is "lost in the wilderness," echoing Cain's wanderer-fugitive status. Strangers arrive with some trying to improve or repair it much to Mother's chagrin. Unnamed guests break the kitchen sink; thus, the Deluge of Noah occurs, indicated by the gushing water and rain pouring from above. Everyone leaves, including Man and Woman, who are never seen or heard from again.

Alone in the house, Mother and Him make love, ending the Old Testament segment and starting the New; the rest of the narrative is Christianity. Based on what follows, it is apparent Aronofsky is not a fan of the religion. The next morning, inspired by Mother, Him starts writing presumably the Word of God: viz. the New Testament, the Koran, the Vedas; it is never fully disclosed other than his writings are divine. Mother, on the other hand, gets "started on the apocalypse," foreshadowing its dramatic end. From a doorway, she observes Him write; his unintelligible scribblings decorate the walls around his desk, conjuring Erica's amateurish artwork in *Black Swan*. The parallel drawn suggests godly canon is incoherent and open to interpretation akin to her childish finger paintings. Nevertheless, when Mother reads what he has written, she becomes emotional and starts crying, saying, "It's beautiful." He will later tell Mother that his work is beloved, "but it affects everyone in a different way," implying the scripture's subjectivity.

Time passes; at night, a pregnant Mother prepares dinner, i.e., Maundy Thursday, alluded to by eleven burning candles on the table. Add Mother and Him to the feast, and one has thirteen: the number of attendees at the Last Supper. But droves of people interrupt the meal, wishing to see Him, trespassing into the home to learn more about his writings. People wander onto the property and into the house, resurrecting *The Night of the Living Dead*, implying the masses coming to the home–dogmatic Christians occupying earth–are mindless, destructive zombies.

Herald (Kristen Wiig), Him's literary agent, arrives. She reveals herself to be an archon, indiscriminatingly killing people during the End Days, heralding the new Age of Aquarius as her *nom de guerre* insinuates.

More and more people enter the home, seeking Him, worshipping him as *Poet*.[514] The word *poet* derives from the Greek *poietes*, meaning *maker* or *creator*, identifying Him as the Demiurge. Him smears a dark mark on one of his follower's forehead, alluding to Catholicism's Ash Wednesday. People want pictures with god and want Him to sign their books, making the texts sacred relics worthy of veneration. Next, pagan-like rituals are performed with words such as *goyim* (non-Jews) and *angel* bandied about, underscoring the movie's religiosity. Eventually, everyone becomes violent and destructive, destroying the home causing Mother to wince and grimace in pain; remember she and the home-earth are one. Put another way, destroying-altering the house ruins her.

Utter pandemonium ensues with the couple retreating to his upstairs study where she gives birth to a son; Mother now personifies the Virgin

---

[514] When he enters the house and becomes contentious, Oldest Son refers to Him as *Poet*.

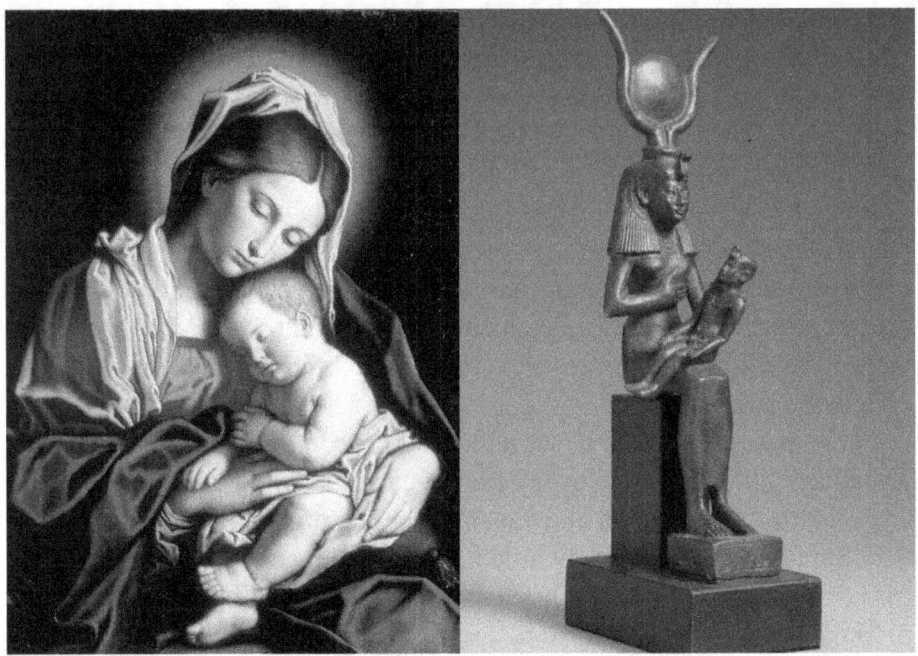

(Left) The imagery of Madonna and Child, seen here in this 17th-century painting by Giovanni Battista Salvi da Sassoferrato (1609-1685), Palazzo Ducale, Urbino, Italy. This painting is one of thousands displaying the archetypal imagery of mother and child, depicted years earlier as the virginal Isis nursing her son, the sun god Horus (right). The sculpture is in the collection of the Legion of Honor Museum, San Francisco, CA.

Mary with Him as the Holy Ghost. As Mother cradles the child, the Christian imagery of Madonna and Child is implanted upon (or drawn from) the subconscious, originating from the Egyptian; that is, Isis nursing her solar child, Horus. Aronofsky shrouds Him in sunlight and Mother in a penumbra of moonlight, investing Him with the attributes of the Egyptian god Osiris, Horus' father, i.e., God the Father and Mother the lunar characteristics of Isis, Osiris' virgin-sister consort, the sacred feminine. Like the Magi, gifts are brought to the child; people want to adore the baby, but she refuses to let her son out of her sight.

After Mother dozes off, Him steals the child, selfishly presenting it to humankind for adoration akin to the Nazarene. Worshippers chant "hallelujah" and "praise be" revering the holy offspring. Like Christ, the sacred baby is killed (albeit accidentally), and the people plea for forgiveness. Next, the Christians are depicted as cannibals consuming the bloody child, eating its dead flesh; it is a sick parody of the Eucharist.

Aronofsky has lifted this diabolical dynamic from *Rosemary's Baby* and reversed it, applying it to orthodox Christianity, further revealing his disgust for the religion. If one recalls, Rosemary was worried–paranoid–that the coven was attempting to steal her baby for demonic rituals, as a sacrifice during their sabbath. Mother, likewise, seeks to protect her son, becoming suspicious of Him and his disciples *qua* Christians, and she's right to be wary. They take her child, killing it then cannibalizing its flesh, performing a gruesome ritual more akin to a satanic rite than a numinous ceremony, something one would find in the Black Bramford's dark recesses.

Mother, furious they have killed their son, screams that she wants everyone out, but is bludgeoned with the same octagonal doorknob used by Oldest Son to slay Younger Brother. Mother is brutally beaten; she denounces Him as a murderer, then finds Man's missing Piscean cigarette lighter. Armed with it, she descends to the basement to the secret antechamber, i.e., Freemasonry's Vault of Enoch, the source of forbidden wisdom thwarting God's *qua* Demiurge's will with the tank filled with combustible oil. She decides to end the earth, breaching the tank, igniting the lighter, killing the guests, burning the home to a blackened cinder. Strolling in the kenoma, Him is unharmed; he carries a burnt, dying Mother in his arms, removing her heart, her sacred love. Her heart/love transforms into a crystal–just like the one at the beginning–and Him takes everything back to Genesis; without her love, essence, and thought, he cannot create implying her power is mightier than his. He places the crystal in its holder, laughing like a mad scientist–a maniacal child–having been given his first chemistry set, eager to get back to work, tinker, experiment, recalling Lugosi's Demiurge *qua* Scientist from *Glen or Glenda*.

A new Mother wakes in bed, asking, "Baby?" just like from the beginning, denoting the end of the old world and the dawning of a new one. Sarah-Jeanne Labrosse, Jennifer Lawrence, and Laurence Lebeouf all play the same character, Mother or Mother Nature. Labrosse was the previous Mother (credited as Foremother), dying before Lawrence incarnates, and Lebeouf is the new Mother (billed as Maiden) incarnating after Lawrence perishes. Old and new, death and rebirth imply the Precession of the Equinoxes; that is, the ending and beginning of Ages. Labrosse's death is the end of a previous Age, Lawrence's demise is the end of the Piscean Age so identified by the symbol on Man's lighter, making Lebeouf the earth in the new Age of Aquarius. Easter egg: there is no musical score until the end credits when the song "The End of the World" plays, covered by Patti Smith.

The second half of *Mother!* is cinematic Christianity, established by the Pisces sigil on Man's lighter. Calculated by the Precession of the Equinoxes, Christianity is a Piscean Age religion with the sun residing the house of Pisces for the last 2000-2150 years. In *Cinema Symbolism 2*, this author explained:

> The Christian Faith is the adoration of the sun–Jesus *qua* the sun god, *Sol Invictus*–in the solar Age of Pisces the Fish. Jesus feeds his five thousand followers with two fishes in the Gospel accounts, signifying the sun residing in the house of the two fishes, the Piscean Age. Christ was born of a virgin because Virgo the Virgin is the opposite house of Pisces; as such, the priests and servants of Christianity, both male and female (nuns; in Aramaic nun means *fish*), remain celibate virgins. Christ washes feet and has his feet washed because Pisces rules of the feet. Christ encourages his apostles to be watery Piscean fishers of men since Pisces is a water sign; the first Pope, Simon called Peter, was a fisherman.[515]

At the climax, we have the destruction of the Piscean Age by fire, echoing God's covenant never to destroy the earth by water at Genesis 9:11-17.[516]

Him is the Demiurge. For instance, he is the artisan-like God of the Old Testament, i.e., Marcion's two Biblical deities, telling Mother of his need to create, "That's what I do." He allows humans to remain–even though they are warlike–over Mother's objections because they adore him; he does not want them to leave because their worship satisfies his narrow ego. After Mother gives birth, a basket is left as a gift. Among other fruits and vegetables is an egg, a proper symbol of the Demiurge whose auric body is the egg of the inferior universe (*vide supra*). Recall when Mother awakened, she looked around the bedroom and, not seeing Him, asked,

---

515 Sullivan, *Cinema Symbolism 2*, Chapter I.
516 "I now establish my covenant with you and with your descendants after you and with every living creature that was with you—the birds, the livestock and all the wild animals, all those that came out of the ark with you—every living creature on earth. I establish my covenant with you: Never again will all life be destroyed by the waters of a flood; never again will there be a flood to destroy the earth."

"Baby?" But perhaps it is not a term of endearment but literal. Mirroring Valentinian cosmology, Mother is Sophia and Him–the Demiurge–is her child, the lesser god, making Him her *baby*. Thus, Him refers to Mother twice as *goddess* hinting at her divinity; she is holy wisdom, Sophia. The mythos of Sophia's soul and her descent into this lower world, with her various sufferings and changing fortunes until her final deliverance, recurs in the Simonian system under the form of the All-Mother issuing as its first thought from the *Hestōs* or highest power of God. She generally bears the name *Ennoia*, but is also called Wisdom or Sophia–she is an incarnation of the archetypal mother goddess (and mother of all life). To ease her suffering, Mother drinks the yellow potion reinforcing Mother *qua* Sophia personification. Later, when their son is killed, Mother accuses Him of sinking into insanity by allowing the people to remain, suggesting the Demiurge's dysfunctional nature. To Aronofsky, the creator god is not only the deity of the Old Testament but the New as well.

The home–and just about everything in it–is octagonal, and the symbolism of eight is significant. Aronofsky states that Victorian homes were often eight-sided because scientists believed it was the perfect shape for the brain; furthermore, its design represents Gnostic philosophy and infinity. The number, when turned sideways, becomes the lemniscate, implying regeneration.[517] In Gnosticism proper, the Great Archon resides in the eighth celestial sphere (Ogdoad) as does Sophia, the Demiurge's mother. In Greek Gematria, 888 equals Jesus Christ (the Neoplatonic sun), the Logos made flesh, intimating the second half. Mother sees a mnemonic, a frog (more on this in a moment), conjuring the second plague of Egypt at Exodus 8. Eight has additional Biblical-recondite meaning; on its occultism, Pike explains:

> The number 8, or the octary, is composed of the sacred number 3 and 5. Of the heavens, of the seven planets, and of the sphere of the fixed stars, or of the eternal unity and the mysterious number 7, is composed of the ogdoade, the number 8, the first cube of equal numbers, regarded as sacred in the arithmetical philosophy.

---

517 Julie Miller, "*Mother!*'s Ending: What Does It All Mean?" *Vanity Fair*, September 16, 2017, https://www.vanityfair.com/hollywood/2017/09/mother-movie-meaning-explained (accessed December 2, 2017).

The Gnostic ogdoade had eight stars, which represented the eight Cabiri of Samothrace, the eight Egyptians and Phoenician principles, the eight angels of the cubic stone.

The number eight symbolizes perfection: and its figure, 8 or ∞ indicates the perpetual and regular course of the universe.[518]

On its shape, Hall adds, "It derived its form partly from the twisted snakes of the Caduceus of Hermes and partly from the serpentine motion of the celestial bodies; possibly also from the moon's nodes."[519] The 8th card of the Tarot's Major Arcana is Strength, and its attributes pervade *Mother!* On Strength, Richard Cavendish (1930-2016) explains: "The Tarot card has been described as the feminine equivalent of St. George defeating the dragon. The woman taming the king of beasts is a sign of victory over brutishness and evil. ....Eight is the number of new life and the woman's hat is the same shape as the Juggler's, a symbol of fecundity."[520] Mother is the key to the earth's renewal; without her love, Him cannot begin again, because her *strength* triumphs over his truculence. In other words, without Mother, Him is impotent–he cannot generate anything without her. It is through her, and her alone, that new life emanates.

Professor Pagels continues to explain, "…the Greek feminine term for 'wisdom,' *sophia*, translates a Hebrew feminine term, *hokhmah* [or *Chokhmah*]. Early interpreters had pondered the meaning of certain Biblical passages–for example, the saying in Proverbs that 'God made the world in Wisdom.' Could Wisdom be the feminine power in which God's creation was 'conceived?' According to one teacher, the double meaning of the term conception–physical and intellectual–suggests this possibility: 'The image of thought [*ennoia*] is feminine since … [it] is the power of conception.'"[521] Hence, the octagonal home infuses *Mother!* with universal motifs of heavenly inspiration and conception. To the Kabbalists, eight represented perfection; that is, the earth (home) and mother (nature) are objects of divine beauty even though Him–the creator–is imperfect.[522] Interestingly,

---

518 Pike, *Morals and Dogma*, 635.
519 Hall, *Secret Teachings*, 220.
520 Cavendish, *The Tarot*, 97-98; Cavendish, *Black Arts*, 85-86.
521 Pagels, *Gnostic Gospels*, 53-54.
522 George Steinmetz, *The Royal Arch: Its Hidden Meaning* (New York: Macoy Publishing and Masonic Supply Co., 1946), 20.

The Eighth Card of the Tarot is Strength. "There is one aspect in which the lion signifies the passions, and she who is called Strength is the higher nature in its liberation. It has walked upon the asp and the basilisk and has trodden down the lion and the dragon." – A.E. Waite, on the Strength Card, *The Pictorial Key to the Tarot*, 1911.

it delves into kabalistic mysteries more akin to rabbinic gnosis, and God *qua* the Demiurge's need to write, create, and be worshipped.

One of the seminal books on Kabbalah is Gershom Scholem's (1897-1982) *Kabbalah* first published in 1974, a tome that must have influenced Aronofsky. Scholem's section on "God and Creation" begins on page 88, suggesting Jungian synchronicity. Even the casting of Jennifer Lawrence designates the number eight. Her first name, *Jennifer*, has eight letters, and her surname, *Lawrence*, also has eight letters. Aronofsky, trumpeting his occult and kabalistic expertise, employs an eight-lettered actress to be his Mother Nature, caretaking his octagonal home-as-earth.

Mother! reflects a school of Hebrew mysticism named after the Jewish rabbi who developed it: Isaac Luria (1534–1572). Lurianic Kabbalah gave a seminal, new account of kabalistic thought that its followers synthesized with, and read into, the earlier Kabbalah of the *Zohar* which had disseminated in medieval circles. The Lurianic mythos brought deeper kabalistic notions to the fore: theodicy, viz. the primordial origin of evil, and exile of the *Shekinah*, i.e., Divine Presence, in Kabbalah, the Divine Feminine Aspect, eschatological redemption, the symbolism of sexuality in the supernal Divine manifestations, and the unconscious dynamics in the soul. Luria gave esoteric theosophical articulations to the most fundamental and theologically daring questions of existence.

A core tenet of Lurianic Kabbalah is that all four worlds, including the world of *asiyah*, the world of making, the terrestrial world, were originally spiritual. But, through the *breaking of the vessels*, i.e., the death of the kings, the world of *asiyah*, after its descent from its earlier position, was commingled with the *kelippot* or impure husks (or shells), which, in principle, should have remained completely separate, producing a world of matter, implying Valentinian cosmology, that contained nothing spiritual.[523] It was from the scattered shards of *kelipott* that the dark forces of the *sitra ahra*–what the *Zohar* calls impurity and evil "from the other side"–took on substance.[524] In a few words, Luria developed a cosmology more tragic than even the Gnostics; the broken cosmos emerges from God himself, so vast and powerful that he must annihilate himself to make space for the world and shatter his products to spread his force. The Universe is God in exile.[525]

Applying Lurianic Kabbalah to *Mother!* the smashing of the crystal–Him sweeps up its pieces–*breaks the vessels*, plunging the world into material darkness. The king dies; Him is spiritually divested, annihilated. Gruesome murder occurs inside the home, saturating it with wickedness forever. Henceforth, the divine feminine, Mother-as-*Shekinah*, takes a backseat to the whims of Him; she comes to understand she cannot compete with his narcissistic ego. Evil is a byproduct of Him, who allows malignant humans to occupy earth against Mother's wishes. Still, since they adore Him *qua* Poet, they are given license to destroy the planet while being worthy of forgiveness much to Mother's dismay. The film's conclusion is the Biblical apocalypse, with the earth and humankind destroyed with Mother sacrificing herself so he can create and build again, attempting to restore humanity. Lastly, their sexual relationship is a sacred manifestation allowing Him to write scripture–God's Word–for the entire world to read, gaining Him their worship. But everyone interprets the Word differently, suggesting Lurianic Kabbalah's notion of the human soul's complex machinations, and cerebral interpretations.

---

523 Scholem, *Kabbalah*, 119, 138.
524 Ibid.
525 Wilson, *Melancholy Android*, 81.

CINEMA SYMBOLISM 3

In the Old Testament portion, after Mother discovers the secret, subterranean chamber, she observes a frog hopping around, and its religious symbolism is multifaceted. *The Encyclopedia of World Mythology* states:

> In mythology the frog appears comparatively rarely but, when he does, he seems to evoke either extreme repulsion or respect. The ancient Jews, for instance regarded him with abhorrence. In the book of Revelation, seven angels 'pour out on the earth the seven bowls of the wrath of God;' when the sixth does so, 'three foul spirits like frogs' appear; 'demonic spirits, performing signs.'
>
> The Jewish attitude to frogs doubtless goes back to the early days of their culture, when these creatures were called up by Moses and Aaron as the second plague of Egypt (Exodus, chapter VIII). The Egyptians themselves, on the other hand, clearly regarded the frog in quite a different light: Heket, their gentle goddess of childbirth, had the head (and sometimes the entire form) of a frog and, in a variant of the Egyptian myth of the world, she and her ram-headed husband Khnum were the first to 'build men and make gods.
>
> ....The frog is also connected to the deluge myths found in many parts of the world. In Queensland, Australia, the aborigines say that a great frog once swallowed all the water in the world, causing great drought and suffering.[526]

The frog's symbolism dovetails with the biblical-mythological mysteries of *Mother!*

When this author first saw advertisements for this movie in the autumn of 2017, it was clear it was going to be an exercise in arcane iconography. However, *Mother!* goes much further. The movie itself is an allegorical tale while, simultaneously, veiling symbolism–a rarity. Like *Black Swan*, this author considers this movie a masterpiece and anxiously awaits the director's next project.

---

526 *Encyclopedia of World Mythology* (New York: Galahad Books, 1975), 214.

CHAPTER XII

TALES FROM THE BLACK AND WHITE LODGES: THE ARCANE NOIR OF DAVID LYNCH CONTINUES

Let's rock.
The Man from Another Place,
"Zen, or the Skill to Catch a Killer," *Twin Peaks*, 1990

Oh, I don't know much of anything.
Henry Spencer, *Eraserhead*, 1977

I'm gonna cut your balls off and feed 'em to you.
Marietta Fortune, *Wild at Heart*, 1990

Robert Brenton that dumb fuck, that stupid shit!
That fuckin' Bob was so fuckin' dumb! He deserved to die, that asshole!
Timmy Thompson, *Wild at Heart*, 1990

My dog barks, some. Mentally you picture my dog, but I have not
told you the type of dog which I have. Perhaps you might even
picture Toto from *The Wizard of Oz*. But I can tell you,
my dog is all ways with me. ARF!
00 Spool, *Wild at Heart*, 1990

You're next, fucker.
Bobby Peru, *Wild at Heart*, 1990

You're on the path. You don't need to know where it leads. Just follow.
– Deputy Chief Tommy "Hawk" Hill,
"Arbitrary Law," *Twin Peaks*, 1990

Every forest has its shadow.
Annie Blackburn, "Miss Twin Peaks," *Twin Peaks*, 1991

CINEMA SYMBOLISM 3

> Life is full of mysteries, Donna.
> Laura Palmer, *Twin Peaks: Fire Walk with Me*, 1992

> Let's go back to starting positions.
> It's really much more comfortable.
> Mr. C, "What Story is That, Charlie?" *Twin Peaks: The Return*, 2017

This author is a fan of David Lynch, so please keep this in mind when you read the introduction to the *Twin Peaks* section, a show that I like, but don't love. I feel it is just too discombobulating, so if the reader of this book is a *Twin Peaks* diehard, please forgive my criticism. I considered revising my critique but decided to leave it alone because it was my initial reaction. And when I write *it*, I do mean *it* because I've watched every episode and the movie, I even purchased canonical texts to ensure my examination was thorough, scholarly, and accurate. *Twin Peaks*–the original ABC series and *Fire Walk with Me*–are now 30 years old. In those 30 years, there have been numerous essays and YouTube videos dissecting Lynch's mythology, some more veracious than others.

Lynch is a student of the occult and an expert on conspiracy theories and facts. When he places arcane imagery and duality in his work, it is meant to betoken the metaphysical and magical, the numinous and the diabolical. For example, the identification of White and Black Lodges in *Twin Peaks* conjures Freemasonry and the Illuminati, contrasting secret societies, one given to light and the other, darkness.[527] Alas, most of his symbolism hides in plain sight, making it easy to locate and decode. Lynch also employs the same cinematic tropes and tricks over and over again, questioning how well versed he is with occult techniques or just making this up as he goes along. It seems like when he runs out of recherché devices, he obfuscates his artwork, creating epistemological crises, making a definitive analysis impossible. This methodology is especially true regarding *Lost Highway*.

So, let's get going. Lynch likes to use strobe lights and electricity to convey supernatural anomalies, while duality pervades all his work. He obsesses over *The Wizard of Oz* like Kubrick does bathrooms, and enjoys toying with numbers. Tibetan Buddhism and mysticism fascinate him. Inside the Baudrillardian cinema of Lynch, blue implies secrecy and intrigue. For

---

[527] Mark Frost, *The Secret History of Twin Peaks* (New York: Flatiron Books, 2016), 58-65, *passim*.

(Left) The Lullaby League in *The Wizard of Oz* becomes (right) Mandie (Andrea Leal), Candie (Amy Shiels), and Sandie (Giselle DaMier) in *Twin Peaks: The Return*. The three cocktail waitresses are spaced-out somnambulists, vacillating between consciousness and bewilderment. They are asleep yet awake, a Lynchian threesome of weirdness.

instance, in *Mulholland Drive*, a blue key and a blue box are strange tokens of Betty Elms' dreamy reality, which, when married, return her to the real world. Here, a blue key represents Diane Selwyn's murderous secret. She even lives inside an apartment with blue walls, indicating all may not be what it seems. Blue, and the fabric, velvet, are synonymous with Dorothy Vallens and Frank Booth, the dark side of the moon and Mercurius, assisting Jeffrey Beaumont in his Gnostic quest for enlightenment. In *Wild at Heart*, Marietta Fortune (Diane Ladd) wears a blue dress when she accosts Sailor Ripley (Nicholas Cage) in a men's room because she knows his secret: that he was privy to the murder of her husband, threatening to expose him. Blue Rose cases are the heart and soul of *Twin Peaks*. Also, beware of barking dogs–more on this phenomenon later.

For some unknown reason, Lynch has a penchant for the assassination of Abraham Lincoln (1809-1865). Frank Booth's surname conjures Lincoln's assassin John Wilkes Booth (1838-1865), while Dorothy Vallens resides on Lincoln Street. In *Twin Peaks: The Return*, Mr. C (Kyle MacLachlan) drives a Lincoln sedan after putting his Mercedes Benz inside a mini-storage unit. The Blue-Haired Lady (Cori Glazer) perches in a box–just like Lincoln at Ford's Theater–surveying Club Silencio.

Lynch was influenced by Hitchcock, especially *Vertigo,* a movie with two women, both played by the same actress. In *Twin Peaks'* first season,

CINEMA SYMBOLISM 3

In *Lost Highway*, Renee Madison (left) and Alice Wakefield (right) personify duality. Renee wears dark clothing and has dark auburn hair, while Alice wears lighter-colored attire, complementing her golden locks. Renee is darkness, i.e., Jung's shadow, and Alice is light, viz. Jung's ego. Renee is Alice's opposite: she is negative, linked to the narcissistic Fred Madison (Bill Pullman); Alice is positive, coupled to the mellow Pete Dayton (Balthazar Getty). Both versions of Arquette's character are duplicitous, evoking femme fatale Kathie Moffat (Jane Greer) as she first appears from the shadows in *Out of the Past* (1947), or Kitty Collins (Ava Gardner) languidly poised near the piano in *The Killers* (1946). But, most of all, both are the unobtainable desideratum of the male protagonists. Before Pete's reversion back to Fred, Alice whispers in his hear, "You'll never have me," stating the protagonist, whoever he is, will never get the film's femme-fatale, harness her sacred energies, no matter who she is. Fred's solipsistic worldview is constantly threatened by his various projections of the female archetype. Complex, postmodern, and self-aware, *Lost Highway* serves as an outstanding example of contemporary noir, wherein reality and the psyche are still mysteries to be decoded.

there are two contrasting teenagers portrayed by the same actress, Sheryl Lee. In *Mulholland Drive*, Bettys Elms and Diane Selwyn–both played by Naomi Watts–are different halves of the same person, the former ebullient, the latter dour. In *Blue Velvet*, Sandy Williams and Dorothy Vallens are the moon's different sides; Sandy is the virginal Artemis, and the sadomasochist, Hecate. Renee Madison and Alice Wakefield, both Patricia Arquette, haunt *Lost Highway*. In *Twin Peaks: The Return*, Diane Evans (Laura Dern) is cleaved into two people twice. There is a tulpa of Diane, and later, when she enters an alternative dimension with Agent Cooper, she becomes a woman named Linda. Dougie Jones (Kyle MacLachlan) is Mr. C's tulpa, making Dougie a double of a double. Agent Cooper also becomes another person, Richard, and there are two Sheriff Trumans: Harry S. Truman (Michael Ontkean) and his brother Frank Truman (Robert Forster, 1941-2019). "Two birds with one stone," the Giant *qua* Monad remarks to the FBI Agent, implying *Twin Peaks*' omnipresent duality. And how many Renault brothers are there?

But before we journey to the township of Twin Peaks (population 51,201), *Cinema Symbolism 3* aims at *Eraserhead* and *Wild at Heart*, two movies with Gnostic overtones. These films were to be analyzed in *Cinema Symbolism 2*, but I ran out of time and space. Lynch's movies are always heavy lifting, requiring lengthy analyses, but as an admirer of his work, I relish the challenge.

Eraserhead's Ironic Gnostic Paradox

Initially opening to small audiences and little interest, *Eraserhead* gained popularity over several long runs as a midnight movie. Since its release in 1977, the film has earned positive reviews. The surrealist imagery and sexual undercurrents are its key thematic elements, and the intricate sound design is its technical highlight. In 2004, it was preserved in the National Film Registry by the United States Library of Congress as "culturally, historically, or aesthetically significant." *Eraserhead*'s script was influenced by Kafka's novella *The Metamorphosis* (1915), and Nikolai Gogol's (1809-1852) short story "The Nose" (1836), among others. Lynch also confirmed in an interview with Metro Silicon Valley that it came together when he opened up a Bible, read one verse from it, and shut it; in retrospect, Lynch could not remember if it was from the Old or the New Testament. In 2007, Lynch said, "Believe it or not, *Eraserhead* is my most spiritual film."[528]

Eraserhead has also been noted for its underlying sexual themes. The film, opening with an image of conception, portrays the protagonist, Henry Spencer (Jack Nance, 1943-1996), terrified by sex, yet fascinated by it. The recurring images of sperm-like creatures, including the snakelike child, transcend the black and white opus. The apparent girl-next-door appeal of the Lady in the Radiator (Laurel Near) is abandoned during her musical number when she begins to violently stomp on Henry's spermatozoon monsters, meeting his gaze aggressively. David J. Skal, in his book *The Monster Show: A Cultural History of Horror* (1993), described *Eraserhead* as: "depict[ing] human reproduction as a desolate freak show, an occupation

---

[528] "David Lean Lecture: David Lynch," *British Academy of Film and Television Arts*, October 27, 2007, http://www.bafta.org/media-centre/transcripts/bafta-television-lecture-david-lynch (accessed July 5, 2019).

fit only for the damned."[529] Skal also posits a different characterization of the surrealistic Lady in the Radiator, casting her as servile, "desperately eager for an unseen audience's approval."[530] In his book, *David Lynch Decoded* (2007), Mark Allyn Stewart puts a Freudian spin on the Lady in the Radiator, suggesting she's Henry's subconscious, a manifestation of his urge to kill his child. She embraces him after he does so, reassuring him that he has done right.[531]

Moreover, the motion picture is replete with motifs from the primary Gnostic myths, cosmology, and theology. It loathes the mire of the material world, yearning to be free of grimy matter. It is disdainful toward words that shackle the mind and body; therefore, it persistently searches for cracks in the linguistic system. But the movie also appears to be aware of the paradoxical problem of the Gnostic: he must use matter to critique matter, words to undercut language. By invoking Gnosticism, the film makes itself dependent on a complex grid of linguistic signification. Aware of this troubling fact, it works to undermine the very mythos that is its foundation. In attempting to be Gnostic, it attacks gnosis. In espousing the annihilation of matter, it embraces the material. *Eraserhead* tries to erase the stultifying conventions of the recognizable world. The movie deletes itself since it's part of the world it wishes to wipe away. But this thoroughgoing consumption of stuff is not nihilistic. *Au contraire*, in becoming *no*-thing, not one particular thing or another, the film, in the end, turns to *no*-thing: the spiritual abyss transcending the horrific divisions of the fallen cosmos.[532]

Lynch's movie presents the Gnostic myth of the fall, documenting Henry's descent from the ethereal plane above space and time into a mundane world crafted by a sickly Demiurge. Once inside this hylic reality, unpleasant obligations, generated by language, shackle Henry immediately. Although it has little dialogue, Henry seeks to free himself from words through music, nonlinguistic communication, personified by the dreamy Lady in the Radiator, a Sophia-like liberator, a divine spark.

The burned and scarred Man in the Planet (Jack Fisk) pulls mechanical levers from inside his planet-home in space while looking outside his

---

529 Skal, *Monster Show*, 298.
530 Ibid.
531 Mark Allyn Stewart, *David Lynch Decoded* (Bloomington, IN: AuthorHouse, 2007), 7.
532 Wilson, *Strange World*, 31-32.

broken window, observing the transparent head of Henry floating in the cosmos. Like Lugosi's subdeity in *Glen or Glenda*, the Man in the Planet is the Demiurge who, instead of pulling strings, tugs levers to enforce his twisted will, satisfying his narrow ego. Henry enjoys a peaceful state beyond the seedy earth when a giant spermatozoon-like creature emerges from his mouth, drifting into space. His mouth represents the uterus and vagina, a birthing orifice. The Man in the Planet appears to control the creature with his levers, eventually making it fall into a pool of water, or mud. The camera drifts down into the puddle, following something out of the pit, through a portal, into a white sky, akin to the birth canal. In a dreary and desolate industrial cityscape, Henry walks home with his groceries. He looks confused and unassured like he has just been born. Lynch has just revealed the Gnostic fall: the heavenly soul of Henry hovers above the material world. However, the evil Demiurge, lurking in the dark with his mechanical levers, his sinister technology, drags the soul down into bleak materialism. Lugosi aside, he evokes Oz the Great and Powerful, hiding inside a planet instead of behind a curtain.

Birth imagery envelops the descent: by pulling the levers, the pellucid soul becomes the materialized opaque spermatozoon-like organism, splashing down into putrid amniotic fluid in which it grows into a man, Henry. He emerges from the womb to a mirthless industrial wasteland carrying sustenance in a grocery bag. Henry has one of the oddest coiffures in cinema: his hair combed straight up about five inches above his scalp. His hair resembles an eraser, making him an *eraserhead*. His hair implies that he is in a perpetual state of confusion or shock, never comfortable in any given situation. Eventually, his head and brain are turned into erasers, making his eraser-like hairstyle a weird harbinger. Henry walks along through this ugly cityscape, stepping into a puddle as annoying industrial sounds blare in the background. He seems lost and confused; Henry is a stranger in a strange land.

He finally wanders into his apartment building and seems more assure of his surroundings and his actions. Observe its zig-zag carpet because it turns up years later in *Twin Peaks*—more on this paradigm later. He checks his mail and ascends in an old elevator, resigned to his new condition. The Beautiful Girl Across the Hall (Judith Anna Roberts) stops Henry outside his room, telling him his girlfriend, Mary X (Charlotte Stewart), has invited him to dinner with her family that night. "A girl named Mary called on the payphone in the hallway about an hour ago. She said that she's at her parents and that you're invited to dinner," she informs him. These are the first words uttered, and Henry seems genuinely surprised by these remarks. "Oh, yeah? ...Well ...thank you very much," he muses. Henry appears unaware that he has a girlfriend, like the woman's words are calling him to a life that he didn't know existed.

Her words have created a girlfriend, and reported her existence, conjuring up an entirely new set of obligations and responsibilities that immure Henry further into the strange land he finds himself.[533] With a look of woolly disgust–like he's not looking forward to the repast–he thanks the woman and enters his dingy one-room apartment. A table, an old record player, a bureau, a tabernacle-like cupboard, a bed, a nightstand, and a couple of lamps furnish the abode. What seems to be cut grass (or hair clippings) is piled atop the dresser and under the radiator. A denuded branch, protruding from a dirt mound, sits on his nightstand. A tiny picture of a nuclear mushroom cloud hangs above it. Without pausing to consider his options, he makes ready to fulfill his obligations. Inside, he feels more at home, playing a Fats Waller (1904-1943) record on the turntable. He removes one of his wet socks and places it on the radiator. He goes to his chest of drawers and removes a photo of a woman, presumably his girlfriend, torn in half at the neck. He seems bemused by the picture like he is not sure who she is, or why he has it.

With this introduction, the movie's fundamental contrast has been established with startling, and wordless, economy. On the one hand, we have the ethereal realm from which Henry has fallen. Transparency and transcendence characterize this sphere. The only area paralleling this place in the material world is Henry's apartment, wherein music and intimate warmth protect him from the harsh world outside. On the other hand, there is the hylic plane into which Henry has fallen. Opacity and entrapment distinguish this environment. It is a mucky industrial cityscape where words force us into unpleasant duties. As the story unfolds, the former realm–the spiritual one–is exemplified by a strange woman singing in

---

533 Ibid, 36-37.

Henry's radiator. The latter plane–the material one–will be thoroughly instanced by a monstrous snakelike infant crying incessantly.[534]

That night, Henry visits Mary's ramshackle home, a few feet from the railroad tracks and its deafening trains. Waiting for him at the door is an average blonde-haired woman, Mary, who rudely accosts him saying that she didn't think he'd come, to which he sheepishly responds that he didn't think she wanted him to. This dialog is a sampling of what's to come. The entire dinner is unpleasant, signifying the unsavory reality into which Henry has fallen. The house and the people inside seem foreign to him, like he is experiencing them and the residence for the first time. The home's environment is disgusting, featuring a litter of innumerable puppies ravenously feeding on their mother's teats. The salad is a gross mixture of anemic iceberg lettuce and an overabundance of salad dressing. At the dinner table, he is asked to carve a chicken that Mary's talkative father, Mr. X (Allen Joseph, 1919-2012), says are "man-made"; the tiny bird writhes on the plate and squirts blood when Henry slices it.

The people in the house are also indecorous. Henry converses awkwardly with Mary's mother, Mrs. X (Jeanne Bates, 1918-2007), who grills him about his vocation; Mary then goes into an epileptic seizure, relieved when her mother begins to brush her hair. The mother exhibits only two behavior extremes. Most of the time, she is mechanical; like a robot, she interrogates Henry, brushes her daughter's hair, and makes the salad. However, when she witnesses the blood squirting from the chicken, she becomes a lust-filled maniac. She screams at the sight of the blood, flees the dining room, and, soon afterward, tries to seduce Henry. The grandmother (Jean Lange) is a zombie who has to have her limbs moved for her. However, she can smoke, puffing away on a cigarette. The gregarious father is a plumber, having to deal with waste-ridden water, shit, vacillating between polarities like the mother. He is crazed with enthusiasm for the new artificial chickens he is basting for dinner, and he inappropriately revels in the vapid clichés of banal conversation. But he is also half-dead, worthless, because his arm is numb, making him unable to carve the poultry. He is comatose while his wife screams at the chicken blood. By giving the family the surname X, Lynch strips them of their individuality, making them insipid stereotypes.[535]

---

534 Ibid, 37-38.
535 Kolb, "The Uncanny Electricity of Women in David Lynch's World," 6.

(Left) The dinner scene in *Eraserhead* is a parody of Norman Rockwell's (1894-1978) iconic *Freedom from Want* (right, aka *The Thanksgiving Picture*, published 1943) depicting the perfect family which, of course, doesn't exist.

The language spoken during the evening is odd, inappropriate, and improbable. After Henry enters the house and sits uncomfortably on the couch, the mother launches into a series of predictable questions, like she was programmed to chit-chat. Henry does his best to answer her inquires but seems unsure how to comport himself in this situation. The scene is a parody of the light banter that usually characterizes such occasions. The same strain of mockery pervades the dinner table talk. The frenzied father expresses his excitement over the chickens before manically asking Henry to carve the birds. Henry is unsure about how to proceed. All he can do is convey doubt over his ability and undertake the task.

Another instance of satire follows the parody of the Rockwellian dinner scene. Lynch ridicules the archetypal *serious conversation* about the well-mannered suitor's intentions. The mother bluntly asks Henry if he and Mary are having sexual intercourse, trying to kiss him. Once again, the baffled Henry does not know how to answer. The mother then tells him there's a baby at the hospital, which still leaves Henry bewildered. Mary, however, is not sure if what she bore is a child. The mother tells Henry that he must marry Mary. It is like he's hearing about sex, marriage, and babies for the first time. Once again, language does not convey meaning;

instead, it merely forces Henry to do what he doesn't want to do, and strain to understand things he doesn't quite get.[536]

The couple moves into Henry's one-room apartment to care for the child–a swaddled bundle with a long neck, and an inhuman snakelike face, resembling the spermatozoon-like creature. Except for its head and neck, the rest of its small body is wrapped in white bandages. The infant refuses all food, crying incessantly and whining intolerably. The sound drives Mary crazy, and she leaves the apartment, returning to her parent's home. Her frustration and exhaustion are palpable. Like Henry, the child builds a prison around her: when Mary tries to remove her luggage from under the bed so she can leave, her face presses between the iron bars of the bed's footboard, making it appear like she is in jail. Henry attempts to care for the child, learning it struggles to breathe and has developed painful sores. Easter egg: the snakelike child is a precursor to elements of other Lynch films, such as John Merrick's (John Hurt, 1940-2017) makeup in *The Elephant Man* (1980), and the Third-Stage Guild Navigator in *Dune*.

When the Beautiful Girl Across the Hall told Henry that his girlfriend expected him for dinner, the girlfriend and her odd family came into existence for Henry. He seems to have had no awareness of them before his neighbor mentioned them. The same is true for the infant. The serpentine baby emerges after the mother says there's a child in the hospital. Before these words, Henry had no idea the strange organism lived or that he might be its father. Both instances show how words make burdensome obligations, how they fashion phenomena that might otherwise not exist. The child-snakelike creature is one of Lynch's most notorious creations. The monstrous infant can do nothing but lie on the table with its head propped up on an old caseless pillow, crying and whining annoyingly.

The creature's appearance in Henry's apartment suggests that almost nothing is exempt from the corruption of matter. Earlier, the lodging was a place he could escape the harsh climate and its oppressive utterances. It was where he could sit silently in warmth and listen to Fats Waller on an old phonograph; now, it is the home to the strange infant, invading his sanctuary. The snakelike baby recalls several archetypal symbols of the chaos of matter, namely the serpent and the dragon, the tokens of Mercurius.[537]

---

536 Wilson, *Strange World*, 39-40.
537 Ibid, 40-41; Marlan, *Black Sun*, 152-153; Jung, *Portable Jung*, 386.

The snakelike child makes Henry's life miserable because he spends most of his nights lying awake, listening to the creature cry whine. The monster becomes sick with puss-ridden boils, and Henry must labor to comfort the ugly thing. He sits by its side with an old-fashioned humidifier bubbling nearby. Whenever Henry tries to leave the apartment, the creature screams louder, forcing him to return to it.

The infant, furthermore, appears to bring other monstrosities into Henry's life. Whether real or imagined—we can never tell—these bizarre experiences imply the creature is more than an aberrant baby: it is a condensation of the material world and a herald of bad omens. One night after Mary has returned, Henry awakens because she is making strange sucking sounds and gnashing her teeth. Battling with her for the covers, he finds the bed infested with spermatozoon-like devils that resemble the infant in miniature, and throws them against his wall. On another occasion, after Mary has vanished, the Beautiful Girl Across the Hall seduces him, finding himself in bed kissing her. However, the bed is a vat of white fluid, a viscous liquid in which he and the woman sink. At a certain point, all parts of Henry and the woman have sunk except for her bushy black hair. Her follicles float grotesquely on the fluid's surface, resembling the hairy substance on the floor of his apartment and atop his bureau. Her hair eventually goes under, and they find themselves on a dark plane of existence, the kenoma, slinking in and out of the shadows. The look on her face is ominous and monstrous, inferring that sex in this world is nothing but perverse. Next, he suffers a more nightmarish event, or dream, or vision. He finds himself located in a vaudevillian-styled theater inside his radiator. He meets a woman he has seen before, known as the Lady in the Radiator; she has chipmunk cheeks, platinum blonde hair, and a cloyingly innocent smile—she is something out of the 1950s, existing in Eisenhower's (1890-1969) saccharine America. Light saturates her, and she appears to be a positive force. Just as Henry is on the verge of hugging her, the Lady fades into the darkness. A leafless tree rolls out onto the black and white checkerboarded stage. Scared of this sign of his fallen state, Henry scurries to the corner of the stage. While blood flows from the base of the tree, his head falls off, landing in the blood. The head of the snakelike child, along with its long neck, grows out of Henry's neck, replacing his head. The creature has somehow infected the core of his being.

Next, his severed head falls through the stage, then the sky, landing with a splat on the street below. A bum on a bench (John Monez) watches as a young boy (Thomas Coulson) finds it, bringing it to a pencil factory. A factory worker (Hal Landon Jr.) drills out a portion of the head and brain, feeding it to a rudimentary machine. The machine transforms the head and brain into erasers, attaching them to the end of pencils. To make sure they work, the factory worker takes one of the pencils, makes a mark on a sheet of paper, then erases it. The factory's owner (T. Max Graham, billed as Neil Moran, 1941-2011) gives the boy some money for his trouble. Henry's brain has been turned into inanimate matter, erased.

The pencil mark's annihilation is significant, for one of the few hopeful parts of Henry's life is his vocation as a printer. The erasure of this silent line–a wordless communiqué and thus a small rebellion against language–implies Henry's last possibility for liberation has been removed. One wonders if there is any hope for Henry, or if he is forever trapped in matter. The erasure is the last of many dashing attempts of Henry's efforts to liberate himself from the material world's trappings. Henry's first attempt to escape his harsh environment involves music. In the beginning, after passing through the industrial wasteland, he finds peace and warmth inside his cocoon-like apartment, listening to the stylings of Fats Waller. The warm radiator contrasts with the miserable conditions outside. The wordless tunes playing on his phonograph differ substantially from the commanding words he will soon encounter.[538]

Henry rebels against matter in other ways. At Mary's dinner party, he tells her mother that he's a printer. His job requires him to copy down and reproduce words and sentences, thus participating in the language system that constrains his existence. In effect, he is a tool of the Demiurge; he is *just another brick in the wall*. However, he informs the mother that he's currently on vacation. Freedom from work is rebellion, indicating Henry is trying to liberate himself from language, capitalism's crass getting and spending, and the commodification of otherwise autonomous beings into materials to be consumed.

Henry's most significant revolt appears to be psychological. When the hylic world becomes too oppressive, he imagines himself inside the warm radiator with the woman with the puffy cheeks and cheerful eyes. Whether

---

538 Wilson, *Strange World*, 42.

this vision is real, or a dream is immaterial. What is critical is that for Henry, this woman signals a way out of the prison of matter. She is his Gnostic messenger, a Sophia-like brilliant presence from beyond who somehow exists secretly within the hidden corners of matter. Through her wordless gestures and joyful songs, she suggests to Henry that matter and its linguistic systems are obstructing illusions. She intimates to him that only his silent and luminous soul is real, opening him to a realm beyond confusion.[539]

The woman first appears to Henry soon after his bed becomes infested with the spermatozoa-like worms. After he throws these disgusting creatures from his bed, he watches as his radiator glow from inside. He gazes beyond the iron heating device, discovering a small stage. The stage bulbs light up to reveal an old vaudevillian proscenium as carnival-like music begins to play. In the center of the brightly lit stage is the woman, grinning happily. She begins to dance slowly to the music. Under her feet are the same horrible worms that Henry threw from his bed. Without ever losing her smile, she stomps on the worms during her dance, squashing them like grapes under her feet. The Lady embodies a higher power than these tellurian monsters harassing Henry. The wordless music to which she dances transcends the harsh language that binds and obligates Henry. Her dance destroys the monstrous symbols of the mundane prison incarcerating him. Her presence shows Henry the dark reality to which he finds himself shackled is not real, but rather a nightmare from which he only needs to awaken. Once aroused, this realm will disappear as quickly as the tenuous veils of sleep. However, he is not yet ready to experience full consciousness. An instant after this vision, he once again finds himself trapped in the room with the crying snakelike baby.

Later, Henry encounters the Lady more intimately. After he kisses the Beautiful Girl Across the Hall, falling through his bed turned liquid, finding himself on stage with her. This increased intimacy suggests there is a ratio at work: the more matter oppresses Henry, the more desperately he desires to know a world beyond this prison. When he allows his lust to embroil him in a fluid soaked sexual embrace, Henry longs to become one with the messenger who might free him from all material desire. Standing inches away from her on a stage littered with dead worms, Henry listens as she sings a heartbreakingly beautiful song about Heaven, the pleroma.

---

[539] Ibid, 42-43.

Although this song has words, it nonetheless betokens a place beyond language. "♪ In Heaven, everything is fine / In Heaven, everything is fine / You've got your good things / And I've got mine ♪." After the woman finishes the tune, she reaches gently toward him with a beckoning look in her eyes. She is inviting him to join her, to embrace her. For once, Henry is not confused; with a determined look, he reaches toward the woman bathed in light. However, as he is about to touch her, she fades into the distance. The tree, a sign of Henry's descent into matter, squeaks onto the stage. Within minutes, Henry has lost his head, having it replaced with the infant's hideous head and neck. He is still not ready to escape the matter into which he has been thrown. On some psychological level, likely motivated by fear, Henry still longs for his prison's perverse security. Otherwise, he would be able to unify with this woman at this point.[540]

Henry's Valentinian rebellion is unsuccessful until he experiences the Lady again. Ultimately, Henry fully realizes that what most take for reality is fake, and what most take for delusion or fantasy is real. Once he understands this Gnostic reversal, he can extricate himself of his mundane prison and dwell blissfully in the generous arms of the luminous woman.

After the dream or vision in which his head and brain are transformed into an eraser, Henry finds himself alone back in his apartment with the snakelike infant. He is now more troubled than before, pacing about nervously. Henry opens his door to find out what's going on with the Beautiful Girl Across the Hall. It seems he enjoyed his sexual experience with her and is keen on another descent into lust. When he doesn't see her, Henry steps back into his hellish apartment, desperate and disgusted. He hears voices outside his door, so he checks to see who is conversing to discover the Beautiful Girl Across the Hall talking with another man. In the lurid light of the hall, the woman is no longer attractive. She leers at him, humiliating him. Henry retreats into his apartment, weary and defeated. The serpentine infant now laughs, further mocking him.

These instances push Henry to a deep hatred of matter. After wanting to act on his lust and getting rejected, Henry falls into a state of guilt and self-loathing. Suffering this shame and remorse, the last thing he wants to hear is the monstrous baby laughing at him. Understandably, he's had

---

540 Ibid, 44-45.

enough of this world of gross desire and perverse fear. He can't take this place anymore, wanting out pronto.

He decides, for once, to act against this oppressive material world. Comparatively, Henry takes Morpheus' red pill, discovering that, like Neo, the material world is a prison. He finds scissors, goes over to the laughing infant and begins to cut through the bandages covering its body. He quickly realizes the bandages are the child's skin–appearance has taken the place of reality. They keep its internal organs together, spilling apart after the rags are cut. Henry takes the scissors and stabs the monster's heart. The wounds gush blood and puss, covering the child; it appears to be dying.

But the creature isn't done, finding new supernatural powers, growing and rearing up like a serpent about to strike. It has finally revealed its true identity: Set or Typhon, the monster of matter's chaos, the serpent of sin, and the great dragon of destruction. It is the poisoned worm, which infects everything with its venom.[541] Henry recoils in terror as he will be consumed by matter once and for all. The electrical power overloads, causing the lights to flicker on and off as the child's reptilian head grows to enormous proportions. When the lights burn out, the camera returns to the planet from the beginning. Henry appears amidst a billowing cloud of eraser shavings. The planet bursts open; inside, the diseased Demiurge–the Man in the Planet–struggles with his malfunctioning levers, emitting sparks. The Demiurge has lost control. Henry grins as he is embraced warmly by the Lady in the Radiator; he has transcended the illusion of matter and has discovered an ethereal Heaven where everything is fine. Henry and the Lady, suffused in heavenly white, achieve the Alchemical Wedding, the syzygy, the sun and moon unified, the masculine and feminine, transcending freakish matter for gnosis.[542]

Eraserhead is an anti-materialism film premised on Gnostic cosmology: the hylic world–including language, sex, and childbearing–is fundamentally flawed and abhorrent, a prison in which the spirit suffers. The solution to suffering is to free ourselves from the trammels of matter, including sexual desire. These elements are problematic, for they connect to underlying Gnostic heresy that is dependent upon the horrific world the

---

541 Fulcanelli: Master Alchemist, *Le Mystere des Cathedrales*: *Esoteric Interpretation of the Hermetic Symbols of the Great Work*, trans. Mary Sworder (1926/1990; repr., Las Vegas: Brotherhood of Life, 2016), 81-82.
542 Stewart, *David Lynch Decoded*, 110.

mythology attempts to vanquish. The movie valorizes silence and nonverbal communication–the precinct of Basilides–while presenting Gnostic motifs linked to linguistic concepts inextricably. To see the film as an example of Gnosticism is, ultimately, not to see it as Gnostic at all, but as a product of the Demiurge, one more illusion of material deception.[543] Put another way, *Eraserhead*, like all movies, Gnostic or otherwise, are manufactured products of Hollywood: the entertainment-industrial complex. As such, its Gnosticism is based on materialism; like all Gnostic cinema, it is an ironic paradox: espousing spiritual awakening and gnosis while simultaneously entertaining us, making moola hand over fist.

Eraserhead achieves this Gnostic-ironic paradox by undercutting its Gnostic theme with counter-Gnostic elements. This deception is akin to the skullduggery the Jesuits employed during the Counter-Reformation: to use Cabala, magic, sorcery, and Freemasonry as tools of the Catholic Church; to utilize nonconformist things, viz. as a means to an end to lure dissenters back to the Pope in Rome clandestinely. If, from one angle, it is an attack on material ills, then from another perspective, it is a paean to the vigor of the mundane. Like a Rorschach Test, Lynch's film is both ascetic and sensual at once and thus neither antimaterial nor material. The movie, spanning the spectrum of opposites, is everything and nothing. For example, let's go back to the beginning. Henry's head floating in space may not be his transcendent soul; instead, it might be his escapist dream, his inability to engage meaningfully with the vigorous material world. The emergence of the spermatozoon-like creature from his mouth–the transmogrification of his soul into a man–need not be a fall into unsavory matter; this descent could be a depiction of a man waking up from dreamland to the world of consciousness. If we take this interpretation seriously, then we can conclude the Man in the Planet is not a cruel Demiurge, but a figure of acute consciousness, an entity burned by the vital fires of life, a guide from the realms of disembodied dreaming to fully fleshed regions of reality.[544] With these shifts in perspective in mind, we are prepared for a counter reading, an interpretation that convincingly reveals the picture as an indictment of anti-materialistic escapism and a celebration of matter's virility–akin to Neoplatonism's optimism toward the material world. In this vein, Henry

---

543 Wilson, *Strange World*, 46-47.
544 Ibid, 47.

is not a brave Gnostic hero; instead, he is a craven denier of sex. He is not a man legitimately pining for the pleroma beyond matter's illusions; rather, he is one perversely trading robust reality for the wispy domain of dreams. Unlike Neo, John Murdoch, and Truman Burbank, he does not erase untruth; instead, Henry extinguishes natural desire.[545]

Strolling along through the industrial wasteland with his groceries, Henry appears to be a man avoiding human contact. He becomes annoyed when the Beautiful Girl Across the Hall reminds him of his date because it means more social interaction. He seems to be only happy in the tiny confines of his shadowy apartment, a box blocking out the sun. It is a fabricated environment: his music shuts out the din of the real, and his radiator supplies him with warmth. The picture of the mushroom cloud is the annihilation of humankind, which he desires subconsciously. He seems to be a man who wants to return to the womb, who hates the noonday glare. But his retreat from life is a form of death, and his apartment, a mausoleum.

Even though he has ripped the photo of his girlfriend in half–a gesture renouncing her jovial and warm presence–Henry nevertheless drags himself to the home for dinner. Unlike a recluse, Henry has not detached himself fully from life, even though he detests the mundane world. His visit shows us reality through escapist eyes, someone who finds the most ordinary temporary events to be dismal. For a mere printer on vacation, a man who deals in artifice and shirks work, the realities of labored existence will be especially unseemly. In Henry's view, his girlfriend is a retarded epileptic dependent on her mother's nurturing. The girlfriend's mother is a Spanish Inquisition-like interrogator or a lustful harpy. Like Mrs. Bates' corpse in *Psycho,* the grandmother is dead, catatonic in a chair. The father, a plumber, is a purveyor of human waste and fascinated with synthetic chickens. To Henry, this environment is repulsive. The nursing pups are annoyingly disgusting, the salad is uneatable slop, and the chickens seem to be alive, wincing in pain and spewing blood.

The worst part of this perversion of Rockwell's iconic image–*Freedom from Want*–is the sickening baby that arises from it. In Henry's view, the creature resembles a monstrous phallus. It symbolizes the sexual vigor and energy that Henry lacks, and which he is afraid. Once this creature enters his meek apartment, Henry becomes obsessed with sex. He guiltily desires

---

545 Ibid, 48.

it while cravenly fearing it. Mary wakes him with her stimulating, sucking sounds only to find phallic worms infesting his bed. Unable to sexually perform, he hopes these little phalluses might do the work for him. But Henry immediately recoils from his sexual desires and throws the tiny penises violently against the wall. Then his weird imagination takes over, and he envisions the Lady blithely stomping the worms, killing them, and his desires with them. She is an ideal for Henry: someone untroubled by sexual desire, who can stamp out lust, a wholesome woman embracing chastity.[546]

Soon afterward, Henry encounters the Beautiful Girl Across the Hall. She is morally unrestrained, having multiple sex partners, contrasting the virginal Lady, denoting Lynchian duality. Henry is nervous around the Beautiful Girl, apparently scared of her sexual advances. However, he soon yields to her lusty wiles, finding himself kissing her in a vat of milky fluid. Both are naked; Henry finally seems to be overcoming his aversion to sex when he and the woman sink into the milky substance. Immediately afterward, Henry and the woman find themselves on a dark plane. The woman moves in and out of the shadows, appearing monstrously lascivious. Henry's guilt has once more gotten the best of him as he is unable to consummate his lust.

That Henry is guilt-ridden over his sexual desires plays out over the next series of scenes. After his failed escapade with the Beautiful Girl, he finds himself face-to-face with the Lady in the Radiator. They stand on the same black and white checkerboarded stage, symbolizing duality, i.e., good and evil, spirit vs. matter, chaos vs. order, dream vs. reality, where she stomped the wormy spermatozoon. Their dead skins still litter the area. She is chaste and virtuous, happily unaware of sex and lust. Henry wishes to hug her, to become one with her. However, before he can perfect the alchemical wedding, a leafless tree squeaks eerily onto the stage. The tree conjures the Biblical and kabalistic Tree of Life *qua* Tree of Wisdom. It signals his guilt over sex and his forthcoming punishment, viz. Adam and Eve's expulsion from Eden. Terrified, Henry cowers to one side of the stage and fidgets nervously. His head falls off only to be replaced with the snakelike head and long neck of the infant, becoming an oversized phallus, suggesting the sexual intercourse he both desires and fears. His cranium descends into a bloody mire on a dirty street. Retrieved by a boy,

---

[546] Ibid, 48-49.

it is taken to a factory where it is transformed into erasers placed on the tips of pencils–a phallus stiffened into a dead instrument–an implement designed to record the thoughts of the brain. This Cartesian nightmare captures Henry's greatest horror perfectly: that his overly rational head and mind will become detached from his utterly lustful body. If this were to happen, then he would have no control over his detested sexual desire.[547]

Soon after this strange and horrific happening, Henry finds himself back in his apartment with the whining infant. After the Beautiful Girl Across the Hall rejects him, the serpentine child taunts him. He takes scissors, cuts the bandages open, and stabs the infant between two testicle-like organs. The creature violently rebels against this affront, but to no avail. Its wild death throes soon end, and Henry finds himself exactly where he wants to be: in the arms of the Lady in the Radiator, his figure of ideal innocence, purity, and virginity. To him, she is a paragon of Sophia, the goddess all men woo. In destroying the infant, Henry has castrated himself, divorcing himself from the natural flows of life. With his phallic levers broken, the burnt Man in the Planet is rendered impotent. With his guide between dreamy fantasy and bland reality helpless, Henry can now dwell entirely in dreams, free of both the pangs and vigor of existence. He can live comfortably in the warm radiator, resting in the safe bosom of sexless affection. Henry has returned to the protective womb; but, there also found his tomb.[548]

In proving itself to be anti-Gnostic–an indictment of sexual impotence–*Eraserhead* becomes Gnostic: an ironic erasure of the Demiurge's semantics and linguistics, an escape into the meaningless abyss, the holy void beyond the lucid illusions of the material world. Even though it undercuts its Gnostic cosmology and mythology with a paean to organic energy, ultimately, Lynch's film leaves the audience hovering in an interpretative-epistemological limbo. Such a condition recalls the pre-fallen state in which the cosmos is not yet divided into spiritual and material, soul and body.[549] In the end, *Eraserhead,* from a Gnostic or venereal standpoint, is like cutting open a drum to see what makes the noise–you may get your answer, but you ruin the drum in the process. Like with so many of his other

---

547 Ibid, 49-50.
548 Ibid, 50.
549 Ibid.

films, this is the way Lynch wants it. Hopefully, this drum will continue to beat for decades, even after we cut it open.

The Duality of Fire: Wild at Heart's Alchemical Wedding

Wild at Heart (1990) is an American neo-noir black comedy-crime film, loosely based on Barry Gifford's 1989 titular novel. Both revolve around Sailor Ripley and Lula Pace Fortune (Laura Dern), a passionate young couple from Cape Fear, North Carolina; they go on the run from her domineering mother and the freaky gangsters she hires to kill Sailor. Lynch was originally going to produce, but after reading Gifford's book, he decided to write and direct the film. He did not like the novel's ending, so he changed it to fit his vision of the main characters. *Wild at Heart* is a road movie with allusions to *The Wizard of Oz* and Elvis' corny cinema.

Soon after making it, Lynch was asked by a reporter what inspired him about the story. His answer was crystal clear: he was drawn to the intense romance between Sailor and Lula. He found these characters to be perfectly compatible. Sailor exhibited extreme masculine traits, denoting the sun, alchemy's *citrinitas*, but he felt a deep respect for Lula's femininity, the moon, alchemy's *albedo*; she demonstrated very feminine characteristics yet showed profound regard for his robust manliness. These complementary traits–Sailor's sensitive masculinity and coupled with Lula's virile femininity–allowed these characters, in Lynch's mind, to form a strange world, to stand side by side in the face of terrible adversity. Finding affection in the wasteland, Sailor and Lula constituted, Lynch concluded, a really modern romance in a violent world, a way of finding love in Hell.[550] Sailor and Lula's Gnosticism is the perfection of the alchemical wedding, the unifying of the diurnal and nocturnal orbs, their romance transcending the hylic world.

Wild at Heart presents the sacred feminine–the Moon (XVIII)–in all three archetypal phases. The first is the maiden, the waxing moon, Lula. She is young, free, rebellious, enchanting, and beautiful. Her adventures in this world are just beginning. She is a seductress, curious, and fearless. Her emotions are raw, and when situations go astray, she will attempt to

---

[550] Philip Matthews, "Finding Love in Hell," *Werewolf*, March 25, 2015, http://werewolf.co.nz/2015/03/finding-love-in-hell/ (accessed July 15, 2019).

lure them back with love, coyness, joyfulness, and truth. Lula embodies all these traits, choosing to be with Sailor, who her mother wants dead. She goes on a cross-country adventure with him regardless of the consequences. When their relationship goes to hell in Big Tuna, she knows they have lost sight of the yellow-brick road, and desperately tries to return to it, rekindling their erotic romance. The second is the mother, the full moon, becoming Lula at the conclusion, having given birth to a son, Pace (Glenn Walker Harris, Jr.). When Sailor finally sings "Love Me Tender" to her, she oozes feral sexuality, but as the nurturing mother archetype, not as the neglectful-negative mother, which is the way Hollywood usually presents the mother. She is grounded in her body, mature, responsible, and balanced. The third is the crone, the waning moon, personified by Marietta, often appearing as the Wicked Witch of the West. As a controlling hag, she wants to keep her child infantized. However, she can connect to the otherworld, the spiritual plane, tormenting Lula with a vision of her as the Wicked Witch, flying on a broomstick off in the distance.[551] She also watches the events of the movie unfold in her magic crystal ball.[552] Marietta, as an evil mother, also embodies the archetypal qualities associated with the Tarot's Queen of Sword (Minor Arcana), and the High Priestess (II) reversed, both signifying the scornful and bitter woman.

 Lynch suggests *Wild at Heart* is less about an erotic force in an unsettling world; instead, what inspired him was the two lovers' alchemical wedding. That is, the love that burns during the chaos and wreckage; the barren *desert of the real* is the muse of romance–think Neo and Trinity's sexual and spiritual unification in *The Matrix* trilogy. This sort of love, *amor*, transcends eroticism but is instead a form of spiritualism, an elevated form of bliss out of ruination. A significant part of this love is erotic intensity; the more robust the bodily contact, the more authentic the lift to transcendence. It is sex magick: ceremonial coitus to obtain a mystical result, unify, achieving a higher godhead. Sailor and Luna's passion is paradoxical and ironic on two levels: earthly destruction encourages amorous happiness, while physical intimacy generates spiritual redemption and Gnostic liberation.

---

551 In *Dark Night of the Scarecrow*, Mrs. Ritter is the crone. She is tuned to the spiritual world, promising karmic retribution to those that murdered her son (*vide supra*).
552 Lauren Fox, "The Triple Goddess," in *The Women of David Lynch*, ed. David Bushman (Columbus, OH: Fayetteville Mafia Press, 2019), 75-84, *passim*.

In his book, *The Strange World of David Lynch* (2007), Professor Wilson states:

> In medieval Provence, numerous troubadours traveled from court to court singing of a certain kind of love. These itinerant minstrels were deeply influenced by Gnostic and Sufi ideas of *amor*. These ideas were based on the notion that passionate love between the sexes is the proper and mystical mode. Only through impassioned love toward a particular individual can a man or a woman achieve union with the divine. In this view, marriage is beside the point: only the passion of love is important, and this passion is generally all the stronger when it takes place outside of wedlock. Embracing this dangerous theory, most troubadours of medieval Provence faced fatal persecution from a Catholic Church bent on upholding the sacrament of marriage. For many of these wandering singers of love, *amor* was literally reverse of *Roma*: impassioned, extramarital love with an individual ran counter to the stilted martial rules of the Holy See. Impassioned love grew out of a rebellion against the destructive church, and this sort of heretical *amor* persisted in the face of possible death at the hands of the Inquisition. Emerging from a violently oppressive landscape, this kind of love offered an escape from the tyranny of institutional evil, an intimate respite, however brief, from the world pernicious divisions. In the love embrace, one could become, for a time, human.[553]

In *Le Secret des Troubadours* (1906), the mystic Catholic, art critic, and Rosicrucian enthusiast Joséphin Péladan declared the troubadours worshipped divine Sophia through the love of their ladies. In 12th-century Provence, the currents of courtly and passionate love intertwined with Catharism, and central to their interconnection was a mysticism of love, or, to put it another way, an approach to God via a female lover.[554] The troubadours devoted themselves to a chivalric relationship with a woman, producing a literary religion that combined celibacy with powerful sexual tension and longing. Troubadour poetry reveals a type of ritualized syneisaktism in which the troubadour worships his beloved from afar, and that love manifests in the

---

553 Wilson, *Strange World*, 86.
554 Arthur Versluis, *The Secret History of Western Sexual Mysticism: Sacred Practices and Spiritual Marriage* (Rochester, VT: Destiny Books, 2008), 61.

literary jewels of troubadour poems and songs.[555] The troubadour culture is like the Islamic tradition of love mysticism in which the symbolism of dying for love or service to a lady functions of multiple levels. Although the Cathars are remembered as a world-renouncing, dualistic, Gnostic sect, they shared with the troubadours a rejection of traditional marriage in favor of otherworldly, amorous mysticism.[556]

Sailor and Lula seek Gnostic liberation from the abstractions that ignore love. This rebellion resembles the Left-Hand Path, Gnosticism, Catharism, and secret societies like the OTO: the commitment to antinomian action, to the exhaustion of sensual passion. But this unsettling Luciferian-Gnostic current is not mere libertinism nor pure hedonism. On the contrary, it also requires strict discipline and Right-Hand modes. Consider the James Bond films, wherein 007 must transcend dualism, sexually uniting with the sacred feminine, the Bond Girl, to defeat an over-the-top supervillain to save the world. To achieve this sort of liberation and sexual alchemical perfection, one must attain bodily grace and elegant attunement to the beautiful mysteries of the flesh. The fictitious Bond is an expert in this attunement. Between dark contrarianism and bright asceticism, this Gnostic-alchemical eroticism is simultaneously turbulent and cultivated, demure and brazen, spiritual and materials, wild at heart yet courtly in demeanor.[557]

The couple aspires to balance burning desire and noble carriage. Trapped in a landscape of pervasive wickedness–an environment beset by tyranny and violence, greed and chaos, deceit and death–they can only look to their love for salvation. From their surrounding darkness, there blooms in these young characters an exquisite passion. This erotic-alchemical energy allows them to escape their world's evil by transcending an earthbound Demiurge and her scumbag henchmen. Even though a fiery lust consumes them, they demonstrate a sweet sensitivity to one another's needs, a graceful attunement to the heart's longings. This elegant attention is gorgeous in form, a mannered dance. Furthermore, it extols unmediated passionate contact over the stultifying conventions of matrimony; it praises *amor* over *Roma*.

---

555 Ibid.
556 Ibid, 61-62.
557 Wilson, *Strange World*, 87.

CINEMA SYMBOLISM 3

Wild at Heart is a strange mixture of reassuring cinematic conventions and disturbing scenes of violence. One minute, Sailor breaks into an Elvis inspired heartfelt rendition of "Love Me" (1956) at a Powermad concert. Later, a blood-splattered woman (Sherilyn Fenn) dies horrifically in the aftermath of a car wreck. One minute, it depicts Lula seeing her mother as the Wicked Witch of the West from *The Wizard of Oz*, and the next she is molested by the repulsive Bobby Peru (Willem Dafoe). The clash of moods is analogous to the amorous relationship between Sailor and Lula, a mixture of brutal eroticism and tenderness. The question concerning both forms, the cinematic and the passionate, is this: is synthesis achieved, a concord of opposites, or is fracture perpetrated, a serving of potential infinities?

In Lynch's problematic picture, the answer to these questions is yes. It's key theme–the amatory link between fire and ice–and the film's primary form, viz. a cinematic *coincidentia oppositorum* of tenderness and evil, finds tranquility. Hence, we can rest assured that strange antagonisms will one day cohere, that love indeed can conquer all. But the movie's primary motifs dissolve into fragments. Therefore, we are left wondering where the hope lies, where we can ever find concordant bliss in a despotic world. Ultimately, it cancels itself out, leaving us hovering in an interpretative limbo from which it seems impossible to leave.[558]

The wicked world in *Wild at Heart*–it's "wild at heart," Lula says, and "weird on top"–makes it nearly impossible for love to survive. Like the Tarot's Major Arcana sixth card's symbolism, lovers Lula Fortune and Sailor Ripley seek an Eden where they can be divorced from trite material attachments but must disobey to be exiled, which ironically lands them in a fleeting paradise. The first music we hear represents their unbridled passion. As Sailor and Lula emerge from a party in Cape Fear, the popular big-band era hit, "In the Mood," recorded by American bandleader Glenn Miller (1904-1944), plays, signaling they, like the song, are always ready for lovemaking. The song was released in 1939, a mere one month after *The Wizard of Oz*, a film *Wild at Heart* emulates.

The lovers are separated after Sailor is jailed for killing a man who attacked him with a knife; the assailant, Bobby Ray Lemon (Gregg Dandridge), was hired by Lula's tyrannical mother, Marietta Fortune. She is the evil genius behind this affectionless wasteland. Like a Gnostic

---
558 Ibid, 88.

Together, Sailor and Lula personify the Lovers' archetypal qualities from the Tarot's Major Arcana. The card depicts the male and female, often thought to be Adam and Eve, with the angel Raphael (or Cupid) hovering above them. To Jung, the card was the Union of Opposites, the syzygy, the sun and moon's alchemical marriage. Once unified, the lovers yearn for independence and to rebel against the cold world outside. From a psychological standpoint, personal happiness and health depend on harmonious cooperation between two modes: subconsciousness and consciousness. To secure this harmony, we must understand both are expressions of a power superior to either. We must also see that subconsciousness is the mode that, in response to suggestions originated and framed by self-consciousness, brings us into a personal relationship with this superior power. As male and female, these two modes should be one of loving intimacy.

Demiurge and the priests and followers who unwittingly serve this false messiah, Marietta works overtime to control and extinguish the sexual yearnings all around her. Wanting total security, she does not realize the police state's absolute security leads to utter stasis because utopias are dull, a world in which difference is reduced to the same. It is a world of death where nothing changes, thrives, loves, grows, or exists.

Marietta is compared to *The Wizard of Oz*'s Wicked Witch of the West. Like the green-skinned hag opposing Dorothy's quest to return home, Marietta thwarts the lovers' search to find the ideal home, a comfortable place where one can love and be loved. Also like the witch, who has a host of flying monkeys and a crystal ball, Marietta surveys the land with help of deadly archon-like oddballs: Johnny Farragut (Harry Dean Stanton, 1926-1917), Marcellus Santos (J.E. Freeman, 1946-2014), Mr. Reindeer (William Morgan Sheppard, 1932-2019), Perdita Durango (Isabella Rossellini), Bobby Peru, Dropshadow (David Patrick Kelly), Reggie (Calvin Lockhart, 1934-2007), and Juana Durango (Grace Zabriskie). Aided directly and indirectly by these goons, Marietta can observe the couple in her crystal ball, tracking every move of Sailor and Lula, the film's collective version of Dorothy. She stalks her daughter and her daughter's lover in the hopes of murdering Sailor and possessing Lula. She hates and fears love and will do anything to annihilate it. Easter egg: Perdita and Juana are sisters, evidenced by a photo of them with Reggie, and their distinct platinum blonde hair.

What motivates Marietta's desire to destroy Sailor and Lula's rhapsodic love? First off, she confuses love with possession: absolute control and total domination. Before Lula and Sailor even met, she hired Santos to kill her husband, burning him alive to make it look like a suicide. The horrendous murder makes it appear that she can only love what she can utterly manipulate. When Mr. Fortune became disobedient–an obstacle to her selfish pleasure–Marietta immolates him. This crusade to kill when she cannot tyrannize reveals her true identity: a cutthroat narcissist, a meanspirited bitch, someone who cannot distinguish between self and other. She gets off on browbeating Sailor and her daughter. For her, love is self-love; love for another–selfless passion–is out of the question. Narcissistically confusing affection with possession, Marietta loses it when Lula doesn't bend to her will. To Marietta, Lula is not an individual but a mere extension of herself. When Lula directs her love toward the Elvis aspirant, Marietta lashes out, setting out to destroy them, much like how she set fire to her husband. Although she doesn't want to kill her daughter, she wants to squash her freedom by turning her into a marionette so she can pull strings, operate levers, or pull cranks from behind a curtain like a typical Demiurge.

Second, Sailor is an obvious threat to her need to control for two reasons. First, as Santos' former driver, he knows that she put a contract out on her husband, thereby compromising Marietta and Santos. He could reveal their plot in the future, exposing them. They rightly know they must remove him and the potential threat he poses. This incident occurred before Sailor met Lula, so he has kept quiet about it, not telling Lula about his sordid past. But Marietta wants him dead for another more compelling reason: he once rejected her lusty advance toward him. "Yoo-hoo, Sailor boy, how'd you like to fuck Lula's mama?" she asks him drunkenly in a men's bathroom before taking him into a toilet stall denoting her debauchery, cementing her status as white trash. Sailor passes, and she immediately threatens to have him killed. Moments later, Marietta hires Lemon to stab him to death at the party. Once again, the conflation of lust and violence reveals Marietta's narcissism: if she can't have Sailor for herself, no one can. But this merging of libido with brutality suggests something more sinister about the dowager. Like an evil queen from a Disney film, Marietta wants to steal her daughter's youth and vitality. Jealous of Lula's ability to garner the affection of a handsome young man like Sailor, she attempts to steal him away from Lula, thereby making herself feel young again. When this fails, she takes revenge, not only on Sailor but on her daughter as well. She must destroy what she fears: the youthful vibrancy that makes her feel old and decrepit. Marietta wars against love, happiness, and life; her very identity depends on the creation of a wasteland where joy dies, and love fails.

Marietta's endeavors to destroy the couple takes center stage the rest of the film. Sailor and Lula must struggle against Marietta's effort to divide them, and her malicious powers continuously threatened their romance. They must live and love freely and wildly if they are ever to achieve safety from her diabolical ways. They are aware of this; every time they feel her oppressive force, they embrace all the harder, like their love was born out of Hell. Marietta's first try is when Lemon attempts to kill Sailor, but the rebel beats his attacker to death with his bare hands, bashing his head to pieces. For this, Sailor serves a brief prison sentence for manslaughter. On the day he is released from the Pee Dee Correctional Facility, Lula disobeys her mother and picks him up, bringing him his snakeskin jacket. The jacket, he explains, symbolizes his "individuality and his belief in personal freedom." This brief exchange instantly rekindles their romance and reveals Lula's tolerance of his eccentric personality. Sailor's returns this favor later when he accepts Lula's non sequitur tales of misery and weirdness.

Lula says that she's reversed a hotel room at the Cape Fear Hotel and planned an evening of dancing at the Hurricane, a venue nearby. Sailor anticipates her announcement, saying *Hurricane* at the same time Lula does, indicating their synchronized harmony and their alertness to each other's thoughts, their openness to difference. They seem to understand that every act of tolerance and sensitive responsiveness is a rebellion against the demiurgic Marietta, who traffics solely in intolerance, maliciousness, and unresponsiveness. Inside the hotel room, they consummate their alchemical wedding by making passionate mutually-satisfying love. The sun and moon are unified; thus, the couple is spiritually equipped to navigate the hazards that lie ahead. The dimly lit room is secluded, separated from the outside world, seemingly disconnected from time and space.

CINEMA SYMBOLISM 3

The camera focuses on a lighter's flame firing up a cigarette. This single flame symbolizes Lula and Sailor's burning passion, which runs counter to Marietta's engulfing flames that consumed her unfortunate husband.[559] After the spark, Lula and Sailor relax in their hotel room, impervious to outside influence or negative persuasion. Lynch's use of fire is twofold: the conflagration denotes Marietta's narcissism, her scorched-earth strategy because fire was the sun emanating the Demiurge.[560] On the other hand, the solitary flame from the striking match, the cigarette lighter, and the burning cigarette tip signify Lula and Sailor's unselfishness and smoldering passion.[561] After Lula praises Sailor's lovemaking, she recalls that when she was fifteen, her mother started talking to her about sexuality. She then tells the story of when Uncle Pooch (Marvin Kaplan, 1927-2016), a business partner of her father, raped her when she was fifteen. The movie flashes back to this incident: she is young and in hair curlers with her mouth bleeding. Uncle Pooch scornfully throws her pantyhose at her; Marietta enters, berating him belligerently as Lula begins to cry. Lula tells Sailor that three months later, Pooch was killed in a car accident while vacationing in Myrtle Beach; the car goes over a cliff and explodes. Lula then visions a house on fire, hearing horrible laughter, which reminds her of the Wicked Witch of the West. This association is shorthand for her mother's reality, which entails nothing but violence and murder, dysfunction, loss of innocence, and vengeful plots. The imagery also implies Marietta orchestrated Pooch's death, making it look like an accident. Sailor reassures her it was just an "old gal having a good time," then reports that he is ready to go dancing, and move and groove with her in harmonized bliss energetically. Easter egg: Sailor's snakeskin jacket came from Nicolas Cage's wardrobe. Cage asked Lynch if he could wear the jacket as a tribute to Marlon Brando's (1924-2004) role in *The Fugitive Kind* (1960). After filming was completed, Cage gave his coat to Laura Dern. Interestingly, *The Fugitive Kind* was based on the play, *Orpheus Descending*, by Diane Ladd's cousin, Tennessee Williams (1911-1983). In a twist of Jungian synchronicity, Laura Dern's parents, Diane Ladd and Bruce Dern met while appearing in a 1961 stage production of *Orpheus Descending*.

---

559 This imagery opens the film. A match strikes, symbolizing Lula and Sailor's passion, then a raging inferno appears, denoting Marietta's flames of destruction.
560 Cirlot, *Dictionary*, 100.
561 Stewart, *David Lynch Decoded*, 29.

This bedroom scene is the first of many where Lula and Sailor doggedly try to keep Marietta's sinister world at bay. In many of these subsequent bedroom scenes, the couple confirms their love, *amor*, as the only mode of existence among the ruins, their salvation in waste. After Sailor suggests they go dancing, we get a conversation between Marietta and Johnny Farragut, a detective and her putative lover. She informs him of her desire to hire a hitman to murder Sailor. However, he calms her, so she agrees to allow Farragut to trail the couple. This brief interlude reminds the audience of the sinister environment in which the two lovers reside. The story returns to the hotel room, with Sailor brushing his boots, and Lula painting her toenails, waiting for them to dry. Sailor wonders why her mother hounds them. Though Sailor doesn't tell her, he knows the battle-ax is seeking vengeance because he rejected her sexual advances, and he also knows what happened to Lula's father, thinking the same fate awaits him. Rather than dwelling on these ominous possibilities, Sailor tells her he is thinking about breaking parole, and taking her to California. He puts on his snakeskin jacket and, impersonating Elvis by throwing a karate punch, tells her they have to go dancing, prompting her to jump joyously on the bed.

They party at the Hurricane where the speed metal group Powermad rocks on. There, Sailor gets into a fight with a man flirting with Lula, then leads the band in a rendition of Elvis' "Love Me." Later, after making passionate love back in the hotel room, they lie in bed with their heads opposite with their bodies intertwined, almost looking like they are attached. Signifying their fiery passion, a solitary wooden match strikes, lighting a cigarette. Lula asks Sailor about the wind, and the Wicked Witch flying in. As this scene unfolds, we return once again to the devouring immolation that killed her father. She then changes the subject and starts talking about smoking and what brand she chose. The conversation turns to Sailor's difficult upbringing and his praise for Lula for sticking with him even after serving time in prison.

Lula says that he moves her and that he marks her the deepest. He replies that she is perfect for him. She then compares him to her beloved dead father and asks him if she's told him how her daddy died. Sailor says it was in a fire. Lula says that her mama told her he committed suicide by pouring kerosene over himself and lighting a match. Sailor knows this is a lie but remains silent; instead, he caresses her exposed left breast and begins to make love to her again. The two lovers repress their painful lives through their love for one another. With Marietta and her destructive inferno always blazing in the background, forever haunting them, the couple fosters their single creative flame, their tiny light in the middle of destruction.

Sailor decides to jump parole and travel with Lula to "sunny California," a state they liken to the Land of Oz: a beautiful destination at the end of a yellow brick road, a place where all wishes come true. On the way, they make a pitstop in New Orleans; in their isolated hotel room, divorced from time and the rest of the world, Sailor and Lula once again make wild love, renewing their alchemical marriage. Afterward, a single wooden match strikes, symbolizing their passion; they smoke, relaxing in bed only this time side by side. On the run from the law with Sailor facing a possible return to jail, they engage in a conversation about their favorite subject: their love for each other. Lula praises Sailor for being so responsive, and paying attention to her, during their sex. He takes her "over the rainbow," she says. She almost feels as though his "sweet cock" talks to her when he is inside her. She ends by claiming that Sailor "gets on" her. Sailor, with a satisfied grin on his face, responds by describing her as "dangerously cute." Their mutual acknowledgment of each other's paradoxical virtues flies right in the face of Marietta's narcissism and grandiose ego. Lula lauds Sailor for being an aggressive yet sensitive lover, while he praises her for being a cuddly yet edgy girlfriend. In both cases, the lovers exhibit a feeling for each other's full and complex humanity, and acute, flexible, and graceful sense of the play of existence, its strange interactions between dynamic oppositions.[562] They accomplish *coincidentia oppositorum* with their burning love smoldering in an athanor, becoming a blazing Philosopher's Stone.

They venture out to experience the Crescent City, stepping out into the "crazy world" to enjoy a "fried banana sandwich," then retire to their room for their favorite pastime.[563] After more crazy sex, they once more engage in postcoital colloquy. This time they don't smoke; instead, a solitary red candle burns representing their intense love. Lula wonders what it would be like if the two could stay deeply in love for the rest of their lives. Sailor says from now on, he'll be faithful only to Lula. He'll never do anything

---

562 Wilson, *Strange World*, 96.
563 This is a nod to Elvis, who, in later years, frequently enjoyed dining on fried peanut butter and banana sandwiches.

again without a good reason, he claims, but then acknowledges there are numerous bad ideas out in the world that might tempt a man away from his path. Sailor is thinking about his troubled past, and his time spent with the hitman Santos as his driver. Lula responds by telling Sailor a story about bad ideas, an account with a "lesson." She then tells the tale of her bizarre relative, Cousin Dell (Crispin Glover). He was mentally ill and wanted Christmas to be all year round, causing the family to nickname him "Jingle Dell." He feared space aliens in black rubber gloves, viz. men in black were trying to destroy the spirit of Christmas, believing these aliens controlled the weather. To add to this weirdness, Dell stayed up all night making sandwiches, put cockroaches in his underwear, and placed a giant roach on his anus. One day, Dell disappeared; his current whereabouts unknown. The implied lesson of this story is that of the movie. Suppose one becomes fixated on one concept at the expense of all others. In that case, one turns into a textbook narcissist, incapable of receiving love, unable to relate to the world's pleasant particulars. The lesson also entails the reverse: to remain open and flexible to new ideas is to be sensitive to the divine fluxes and interchanges of love and desire, to the singular beauties and uniqueness of people, especially loved ones.

What empowers this sui generis capacity is the ability to enjoy ironic interplay. Sailor and Lula, in the safety of love grottos, discover the middle ground between order and chaos, form and wildness, pattern and turbulence. They are free and wild at heart, enamored by the crazed forces that fuel their fiery lovemaking, of unbridled dancing, of boisterous speed metal music. Concurrently, both are cognizant of studied forms, the courtly sensitivity of their choreographed lovemaking, the returning rhythm of dance, and the monotonous beat of head-banging tunes. In their best moments, they organize order with chaos, transcending opposition and duality; in those spaces barely perceivable, where antimonies meet, merge, and finally vanish. In these psychic regions, one is not bothered by eccentricity and neuroses, by fixation and obsession, by narcissistic tyranny. Rejecting the hive mindset, one opens one's faithful heart to the unusual and the unknown, to the mystery of individuality, represented by Sailor's snakeskin jacket. This paradigm is the secret of their love or *amor*. These secrets elude people like Marietta, who obsess negatively over life's extremes: either absolute control or anarchy. These are her unwavering vacillations.

One minute, she tries to police the life of her daughter, like a Demiurge, to entirely arrange and control the cosmos. The next minute, she falls into fits of rage and jealousy bordering on madness, signified by smearing lipstick all over her face, turning it completely red. During this bizarre spectacle, Marietta wears curled-toed slippers, the preferred footwear of witches. Unable to find the perfect middle ground of transcendental irony, a golden mean, she ossifies at extremes, turning life into death, love into hate, order to disorder, and the pulsating heart into cold stone.[564] Easter egg: Marietta uses lipstick to paint herself as Frank Booth does in *Blue Velvet*. Lynch connects these two characters because both seek to manipulate others for their pleasure and the gratification that control brings them.[565]

The solar-lunar accord between Lula and Sailor cannot last forever; eventually, the sun journeys to the underworld, setting in the west, and the moon ceases to glow. From the time they leave New Orleans until the *Wild at Heart*'s finale, they slowly observe their sacred love dissolve. It seems Marietta's goofball archons prove too much for them. Traveling through the wasteland of death and despair, they soon surrender to the pervasive wilderness and forfeit their enticing forms of love. For a time, they become one with Marietta's hatred.

The last time we see them in harmony, a living example of the alchemical wedding perfected, is west of the Crescent City. They are on their way to Texas, where Sailor will try to discover if Marietta has put out a contract on his ass. Sailor sleeps in the back seat while Lula drives. She tries to locate music on the radio, but all she can find is news about sickness, death, murder, and necrophilia. She stops the cars, gets out, demanding Sailor find some music on the radio. Sailor quickly tunes the radio to a Heavy Metal station, yells wildly, handsprings out of the car, and begins to dance by punching and kicking to the beat, like Elvis during one of his concerts. Lula starts to dance, jumping and stomping like a crazy woman. The two lovingly hug each other, holding desperately onto their *amor* in the middle of a desert. The same poignant music that played over the fiery opening credits drowns out the raucous music. This music conjures the imagery accompanying the credits: a single match, igniting, symbolizing Lula and Sailor's passion, followed by an all-consuming fire destroying everything

---

564 Wilson, *Strange World*, 97.
565 Stewart, *David Lynch Decoded*, 31.

in its path, the blaze that likely burned Lula's father to death. This same touching music overruns the voices of Lula and Sailor. By reading their lips, they tell one another they love each other. The camera then pans away from them, revealing a vast panorama of natural waste. As the sun sets, exalting darkness and evil, the two young lovers are swallowed up by an endless desert: the Hell that spawned their love is the same inferno that will now consume them.

In the next scene devoted to Sailor and Lula, they are driving at night for the first time, alluding to the darkness that awaits them. They travel along through the middle of a Southwestern desert as Chris Isaak's sinister instrumental to "Wicked Game" (1989) plays over their journey. The music is apropos because Sailor reveals his dark side, his secrets, to Lula. He confesses that he knew her father, and he sat outside her house in Santos' car the night her father was immolated. She now realizes Sailor was witness to her father's murder. Off in the darkness, Lula sees her mother as the Wicked Witch of the West flying on a broomstick. Her mother's unsettling presence causes Lula's discomfort, portending the next catastrophe. Shaken, she tells Sailor that things are never really as they seem: outward appearances can block access to the real.

The next disaster happens moments later when they happen upon a terrible car accident off the side of the road. They make their way in the darkness to an overturned vehicle with a passenger lying dead nearby. Out of the night comes a young woman–later identified as Julie Day– wandering around aimlessly and deliriously. Hallucinating, she speaks random nonsense to imaginary people, not acknowledging Sailor or Lula. She dies a gruesome death, vomiting blood, and losing consciousness. Easter egg: Sherilyn Fenn's accident scene came from Lynch's impression of Fenn as a porcelain doll and from the idea of seeing a one breaking. Lynch said, "I just pictured her being able to do this. She's like a broken china doll." Lynch got the same inspiration for the car accident scene in *Mulholland Drive*. His direction to actress Laura Harring was to act like a broken porcelain doll.

This horrible scene compliments Sailor's earlier confession concerning his dubious past; in both instances, form belies reality: his carefree appearance has concealed his actual past. Though he seems entirely noble and honest, he has been harboring a dark secret: he was once one of

Marietta's archons, a pawn in her schemes and deathly pursuits. The dying girl's hallucinations highlight the collapse between form and reality. She believes that she sees a man named Robert, but in actuality, he is not there. She doesn't acknowledge Sailor and Lula even though they are right beside her. She can't tell the difference between illusion and truth. As the couple pulls away from the accident scene, the instrumental version of "Wicked Game" begins to play again. Sailor's dark side has been disclosed, and they will soon find themselves immured in a wicked game of brinkmanship with Marietta and her henchmen.

These are the hallmarks of Marietta's world, a world where one can never tell the difference between appearance and reality. Through her demiurgic machinations, she generates an environment in which no one can trust anyone, a world where deception is currency. Marietta deceives Farragut into thinking she's in love with him, only to convince him to go after Sailor and Lula. Later, she hoodwinks Santos in the same way, hoping to persuade him to murder Sailor. Santos agrees to murder him, but with a condition: Farragut must be killed as well. This action sets in motion an entire sequence of trickery commingled with a device to ruin. Santos goes to the powerful crime lord Mr. Reindeer who puts a contract out on both Sailor and Farragut. Mr. Reindeer retains the assassins Dropshadow, Reggie, and Juana Durango to kill Farragut, and Sailor's former associate, Perdita (English: lost) Durango and her boyfriend Bobby Peru, to kill him.

When the lovers arrive in Big Tuna, Texas, the town where Perdita lives, Sailor visits her. He wants to know if there is a contract out on him, placed by Marcelles Santos at the behest of Marietta Fortune. Perdita lies to him, telling him she has heard of no such contract. But she implies that Marietta wants him dead for two reasons: first, he is Lula's lover. Second, because he witnessed a fire but Sailor claims he "didn't see nothing"; however, Perdita admits she was there when Santos torched Marietta's husband. Next, Sailor and Lula meet the nearly toothless Bobby Peru, a man who pretends to be their friend, even offering Sailor an easy job robbing a feed store. But Bobby is in league with Perdita, trying to kill Sailor to satisfy the contract. All this wicked chicanery stems from Marietta's narcissistic need to control. Easter egg: a barking dog announces Peru's entrance when 00 Spool (Jack Nance) imitates his unseen dog, Toto. According to the book, *David Lynch Decoded*, a barking dog (or dogs, or even just a dog appearing), is a herald of woe in Lynch's movies. The howling of dogs has always been considered a sign of coming disaster because canines are supposed to have a peculiar sense of trouble, presaging death in some instances.[566] Spool's dog barking brings Bobby Peru out of the shadows; as mercury personified, Bobby will be the undoing of Sailor and Lula's passionate romance. In the pilot episode of *Twin Peaks* ("Northwest Passage," airdate April 8, 1990*)*, two high school students, Bobby Briggs (Dana Ashbrook) and Mike Nelson (Gary Hershberger) bark like dogs at James Hurley (James Marshall), foreshadowing Sarah Palmer's (Grace Zabriskie) first vision: the unearthing of her daughter's heart locket. Sarah will then see Bob, her daughter's tormentor and murderer. In the season 2 finale, "Beyond Life and Death" (airdate June 10, 1991), in the Double R Diner, Bobby Briggs and Shelly Johnson (Madchen Amick) imitate dogs by barking and howling at each other. Moments later, while seated at a booth, their barking heralds Sarah Palmer delivering a message in a disturbing voice to Major Briggs (Don S. Davis, 1942-2008): "I'm in the Black Lodge with Dale Cooper. I'm waiting for you." The dog was the sacred totem of the goddess Hecate, the goddess of witchcraft; hence, Lynch employs canines as ill omens in his films, anticipating disasters.[567]

The breakdown between form and reality opposes the charming relationships of transcendental irony. In the world of deception, one focuses solely on one semblance as the representative of the real. One becomes blind that the possibility of this representation, like all delineations, can only partially reveal reality, that actuality is ultimately ungraspable. The victim of deception, such as Sailor falling prey to Perdita, blinds himself to the film's fundamental question: what thrives in the gap between form and reality?[568] Sailor assumes for an instant that no gap exists, that this form–Perdita's performance, for instance–accurately reveals this reality–Perdita's intended meaning, for example. In closing the chasm between form and reality, Sailor widens the distance between them. Fixating on this pattern as a revealer of truth, reducing the actual to one representation, he ends up losing reality, for he cuts away its ungraspable energy, its powers always beyond disclosure. Sailor, hungry for reality and truth, alienates

---

566 Cielo, *Signs, Omens and Superstitions*, 122.
567 Cavendish, *The Tarot*, 75.
568 Wilson, *Strange World*, 99-100.

himself from them. Wishing to avoid deception, Sailor becomes hopelessly deceived or *lost* just as Perdita's name implies.[569]

In contrast, the ironist never reduces reality to one form. He (or she) remains open to the possibility that no one form can ever capture the real. He knows actuality is ungraspable, beyond full disclosure. The practitioner of irony is attuned to his primary assumption: a gap *always* exists between the stable pattern and the unstable reality, between normalcy and weirdness. Sailor echoes this practitioner before he became a victim of deception, falling into Perdita's trap. The practitioner of this irony resembles the Sailor whose desire for Lula can never be represented by any specific form of affection, attempting to realize his love in a variety of ways, ranging from wild lovemaking, tender terms of endearment, lively dancing, and frisky speech. In holding open the chasm between reality and form, this practitioner ironically comes close to the real: the middle pillar's balance. Open to numerous forms as partial revealers of truth, he approximates the unstable, inexhaustible nature of the real. He opens himself up to a familiar marriage with the strange, to an intimate knowledge of the transcendent, to gnosis. Accepting the divide between form and reality, he closes the gap between the two. Knowing all semblances are deceptions, he (or she) is never deceived. [570]

After they settle in at Big Tuna, Sailor and Lula lose their irony: the ability to play in the sublime couloir between the mountain ranges of reality and form. Here, they quickly become the victims of one of Marietta's archons, Bobby Peru. According to Buddy (Pruitt Taylor Vince), he is "the most exciting item to hit Big Tuna since the '86 cyclone sheared the roof off the high school." Bobby is a black-suited Mercurius, flourishing in the *nigredo* as an evil trickster and an agent of chaos and death; he is the fly in their ointment. Lula asks Bobby if he's from Texas; he answers that he's from "all over," inferring his persona's universality as the fraudster archetype. His clownish grin highlights his rotting teeth. Bobby thinks he's funny; after drinking some Jack Daniels, he jests, "Speaking of Jack, one-eyed Jack's yearning to go a peeping in a seafood store." Sailor and Lula do not laugh at the vulgar joke. However, they both fall victim to Bobby's deceit, and their alchemical wedding melts down as they lose

---

569 Ibid.
570 Ibid, 100.

their intimacy, love or *amor*. In almost no time, their hotel room sanctuary becomes exposed to the harsh light of the desert, the dragon's burning flames, incinerating their romance. Their feeling of timeless isolation from the cruel world becomes constrained to a relentless schedule for sperate actions.

First, the cat's paw defiles Lula. Bobby begins by accosting her aggressively but ends up seducing her; that is, by deceiving her into believing his designs are legitimately erotic. He abruptly slithers into Lula's room at the Big Tuna motel–her bower of love is no longer impervious to the outside world. He says, "I gotta take a piss bad, can I use your head," a comment charged with crass sexuality. When her finished urinating–he does so loudly with the bathroom door open–he walks into the room and begins making lewd remarks to Lula, claiming she looks like she can "fuck like a bunny" and that she wants "Bobby Peru to fuck her hard." When she orders him to leave, he brutally grabs her by the neck, touches her breast, and caresses her crotch, saying he'll go if only she'll say "fuck me." As he whispers these words to her over and over, Lula becomes increasingly aroused.

When Lula verges on climaxing, she gives into Bobby's request: she says, seductively, "fuck me." She has fully convinced herself that Bobby desires her erotically. But immediately after she says what Bobby wants to hear, he pulls back laughing and, with a shit-eating grin on his face, jokes, "Someday honey, I will, but I gotta get going." When he speaks, he sounds like the fatuous Marty Moose (Harold Ramis, 1944-2014) in *National Lampoon's Vacation* (1983). Bobby exits; Lula has allowed herself to be tricked by Mercurius. She has taken his brutal though vacuous form of eroticism seriously. Lula begins crying; like Dorothy in *The Wizard of Oz*, she begins clicking her red high heels together, i.e., the ruby slippers, wanting to be transported to Sailor, far away from the hylic world and its vile infestations.

Sailor believed Perdita when she told him that she was unaware of a contract on him. He thinks Bobby is weird and slightly sinister–though mostly an affable small-time hood–having his best interests at heart. After Bobby violates Lula, he drives to where Sailor is changing the oil in his car to ask him if he'd like to have a beer. Looking at his watch–for the first time–Sailor agrees, and the two men find themselves several beers into a conversation at a local bar. Bobby feigns concern for Sailor's financial welfare. He invites Sailor to join him in an easy robbery at a nearby feed store. The money from the theft, Bobby claims, will help him and Lula make their way to the West Coast or elsewhere. Sailor agrees; as the Wicked Witch *qua* Marietta watches in her crystal ball, Sailor claims this extra money could help him and Lula get further down the yellow brick road. Here, he views Bobby as a helpful guide. He doesn't realize Mercurius has donned the guise of a psychopomp from Hell.

In allowing Mercurius-as-Bobby to dupe them, Sailor and Lula betray one another. Thinking about his criminal past, Sailor had promised Lula earlier he would never do anything without a "good reason." In agreeing to rob a feed store, he breaks that promise. When he returns to Lula after drinking with Bobby, she asks him what he's been up to; alas, Sailor chooses not to tell her about the planned burglary. Realizing Bobby is a poisonous snake, she warns Sailor to stay away from him, calling him a "black angel," but he does not heed her advice. For the first time, he tells an outright lie to his lover, denying that he is in cahoots with Bobby. Sailor breaks the primary code of *amor*, of their divine alchemical union: faithfulness to the sacred beloved, annunciated by the troubadours.

Lula is also mendacious, violating this unwritten code. Earlier, she promised Sailor she'd always be faithful to him, stand by him, and go to the "far end of the world" for him. By giving in to Bobby's crude seductions, Lula prevaricates, breaking her promise. When Sailor returns after hanging out with Bobby, she doesn't tell Sailor about the scumbag's earlier visit. Her silence constitutes a lie, to cover up her lewd behavior, thereby breaching her amorous accord with Sailor. She distances herself from his affection. Lula chooses the evil Demiurge (her mother) and an archon (Bobby) over possible salvation. She laments, crying that she wishes she was "over the rainbow," the pleroma, and that this world is "shit."

Sailor and Lula's respective deceptions correspond to several portents of their undoing, their fall from grace. First, in Big Tuna, Sailor and Lula find themselves controlled by time. Sailor, on two occasions, looks at his watch: the first is when Bobby asks him if he wants to have a beer, and the second when he waits for Bobby to pick him up for the robbery. He is now a hostage of temporality. Sailor is no longer able to enclose himself in a protective sanctuary of love seemingly separate from the world's inevitable decay. Likewise, Lula, soon discovers that she, too, is now a victim of temporality. During her first day in this desolate town, she vomits on the floor of the motel room. She quickly discovers why: she is pregnant, now caught in the inexorable nine-month cycle ending with painful labor. The second sign of their demise is their seedy motel room. Unlike their earlier self-contained abodes, their accommodation in Big Tuna exposes them to the outside world. Blinding Texas daylight shines in, and the unsavory Bobby Peru can slink in and out as he pleases. A tasteless, Texas-style (obese women) pornographic film defines their stay in Big Tuna.

Lula's puke on their motel room's floor is the third symbol. Flies buzz around it continually, and neither of them makes an effort to clean it up. Sickening nausea has tainted their love, immuring them in the foulest sort of excrement. The fourth token is the candy necklace Sailor gives to Lula as a sign of his affection. She promises to save it, but she tells him that if she does eat it, she'll be thinking of him. After the feed store heist goes wrong and Sailor is behind bars, she bites into it, denoting their intense romance is over, but she is thinking of him nevertheless.

Lula acknowledges her growing distance from Sailor by admitting that she's not sure she wants to have their baby. She assures him that she loves him, but questions their future together. She fears they have "broke down" on the yellow brick road, faintly hearing the Wicked Witch's cackle implying her evilness now encircles them. It appears the embryo growing inside her womb is more a sign of despair than hope, heralding their fall into the decay of the material world. One cannot help but think of *Eraserhead*'s snakelike baby, signifying the same hylic world tormenting Henry. Lula and Sailor can no longer say their love, their alchemical marriage, is perfect, spiritual, and infinite. It has been corrupted, descending into procreation and thus into the labor of existence.

Their fall is consummated quickly. Sailor, with Perdita serving as the getaway driver, goes on the robbery with Bobby. The two men enter the feed store as Perdita waits outside. But a police officer arrives unexpectedly and begins questioning her. Inside, the robbery goes spectacularly wrong when Bobby needlessly shoots one of the clerks, breaking his promise that no one will get hurt. He then turns the shotgun on Sailor, telling him that he's next; Sailor tries to shoot Bobby, only he has been given a pistol with drill rounds. "Those are dummies, dummy," Bobby smirks, referring to both the cartridges in the gun and his dupe. Realizing he's one of Marietta's goons, Sailor drops his weapon, challenging the archon to fisticuffs. The other clerk pulls out a shotgun, but Bobby shoots him as Sailor flees the building. Bobby reloads and follows his target outside, where the police officer opens fire, hitting Bobby several times.

As Bobby collapses, he accidentally blows his head off with his shotgun, the devious trickster killed at play. "Oh, for Christ's sake, that poor bastard," Sailor says aghast, witnessing Bobby's head blasted off, splattering on the ground. Sailor is arrested, and as he languishes in a Texas jail, Lula waits in the lobby of the jailhouse. Marietta arrives along with Santos and tells Lula she must return home. Lula claims she can't forsake Sailor. Marietta reiterates her desire to bring Lula home as Santos embraces her in a bearhug that is more akin to a constricting pro-wrestling hold than a token of affection. Trapped in the arms of her enemy, Lula screams; like Sailor, she too is imprisoned.

This film does not end here, even though the movie's reality suggests it should. At this point, it is clear Lula and Sailor are dangerously disconnected. Not only is there relationship troubled by mutual deception, but they are also on the verge of being separated for five years because of Sailor's prison sentence. Furthermore, Lula is now trapped in Marietta's world, her enemy, and Sailor, once released, will be an easy target for her hitmen. The situation seems hopeless. One would think any honest director would realize the bleak situation and end his (or her) opus with Lula and Sailor miles apart, with Lula held hostage by her mother, and Sailor rotting away in jail.

However, Lynch's movie is all about love and romance, transcending mundane reality, thus requiring a happy ending. Lynch rebels against any *realist* notions and conventions which necessitate fealty to the painful limitations of time and space. Instead, the romance genre encourages commitment to the satisfaction of love, of *amor*, of the perfection of the alchemical Union of Opposites, passion fulfilled, despair, and fear assuaged. Though this satisfaction might not occur in the so-called *real* life of the empirical world, it remains a redemptive ideal, a paragon of salvation. Impossible in the everyday reality of fear and desire, deception and violence, this romantic transcendence of empirical limitation must exist in artifice–in the aesthetic realms of courtliness, of dance, and, of course, of movies.[571] In providing a satisfactory conclusion to his film, an ending replete with cinematic allusions, Lynch is showing his devotion to the transcendental possibilities of romance: to the idea that the blissful conclusion is healing, holistic, hovering above temporal anguish.[572]

Lynch's happy ending differs from the conclusion of Gifford's novel. In the book, Lula and Sailor separate; their romance is over, so they go down different paths. In Lynch's film, the two recapture their perfect alchemical unity; their passion is rekindled, and marriage appears to be forthcoming. After six years, Sailor is released from prison. Marietta calls her daughter, begging her not to reunite with him. Marietta is drunk, and her hair is a mess; she knows once they renew their alchemical wedding, she is finished. Lula and Marietta berate each other over the phone; the conversation ends with Lula fiercely hanging up on her mother. In anger, Lula then tosses her drink on a photograph of Marietta, evoking Dorothy throwing a bucket of water on the Wicked Witch. Marietta screams, "No," heralding her demise. Lula-as-Dorothy is on the verge of having he wish fulfilled. She will soon get to return home, to the place where all her wishes come true: in the arms of her beloved. With her and Sailor's son Pace–Latin for *in peace*–Lula drives to the train station where Sailor awaits her. She picks him up, and, after driving a short distance and a brief conversation, Sailor says this reunion is awkward and all wrong. He gets out of the car and walks away, leaving Lula sobbing, screaming in tears. When Sailor is about a hundred yards away from the car, he finds himself in a strange situation: confronted in broad daylight in the middle of a street by a gang of thugs. Sailor insults their sexuality, so they beat him down. While he lies unconscious, Glinda the Good Witch of the South (Sheryl Lee), appears to him in a vision. She delivers a sermon on the power of *amor*, encouraging Sailor to return to Lula, saying, "Don't turn away from love, Sailor." He wakes up from his stupor, apologizes to the toughs, and, with a swollen nose, yells "Lula," then runs to her.

After Marietta melts down emotionally, we see the wet photograph of her sizzle, then vanish; the Wicked Witch has disappeared. Marietta screams "Lula" with her final, failing breath. Running with wild abandon over cars, Sailor finds his soulmate and their son stuck in a traffic jam.

---

571 Ibid, 104.
572 Ibid.

There is a car accident nearby. Amidst twisted, burning metal, injured people, and under the blazing sun, Sailor proclaims his eternal love for Lula. With Pace watching from the passenger's seat, Sailor breaks into a rendition of Elvis' "Love Me Tender" (1956), his favorite long song, a tune he was reserving for his wife. Sailor and Lula have risen above their ruinous fray; like a Phoenix, they have been reborn from the ashes. The sacred alchemical wedding, their *amor*, their love, has saved them from deadening divorce, promising them vital harmony.

After watching the movie, audience members will enjoy the same satisfaction as the lovebirds. By ending with homages to *The Wizard of Oz* and Elvis musicals, Lynch recalls for viewers Hollywood's most artificially blissful pictures, those films that are entirely untroubled by the trammels of space and time. Such movies are, eventually, romances for they are interested only in what makes audiences happy, in what allows viewers for a moment to escape the doldrums and pressures of the daily grind. Though such cinema may seem to be escapist trifles, they are, in fact, salves for the hurt soul, Gnostic rebellions against the vicious rigors of matter.

But who are we fooling: can we take *Wild at Heart* as a serious mode of redemption? It seems to be a parody of other films–of earlier Tinseltown movies and Lynch's pictures themselves. As a parody, it is nothing more than a series of mocking allusions, a sequence of forms without any real content or substance. *Wild at Heart* lacks precisely a heart. It doesn't redeem as much as divert; it is not a romance as much as it is a send-up. If the film does invoke romantic love, it does so only to mock Hollywood's versions of affection. *Wild at Heart*, in the end, seems to suggest real love is impossible–only fake love, artificial movie love, can exist.[573]

The primary victims of Lynch's ironic-satirical wit are *The Wizard of Oz* and Elvis' cinematic trumpery. This statement is not a revelation as the movie's basic structure follows the plot of Victor Fleming's (1889-1949) dark masterpiece. Like Dorothy, Lula makes her way down the yellow brick road in the hopes of discovering her home, her romance with Sailor. Along the way, she's hounded by her evil mother, a figure for the Wicked Witch. Just when it appears Lula's wish will never come true, she will never find the means to return to Sailor, Glinda the Good Witch appears to Sailor in a vision and encourages him to stay with Lula at all costs.

---
573 Ibid, 105-106

(Top) Glinda the Good Witch appears to Sailor in a vision, extolling the virtue of love. (Bottom) *Wild at Heart* is not the last time Lynch alludes to *The Wizard of Oz*. For example, in *Mulholland Drive*, Winkie's Diner is named after the Winkies: Ozian residents tasked with guarding the Wicked Witch of the West. Green-skinned and armed with elaborately designed halberds, the Winkies loyally obeyed the Wicked Witch, but only because they were scared of her. Like the Winkies protecting the Wicked Witch, the diner shelters a terrible evil, personified by a disgusting bum lurking in the rear parking lot.

Surely, on the one hand, these references to *The Wizard of Oz* are just plain silly. They take away from the film's violent seriousness, from its delving into the psychology of love and its mysterious alchemy. But on the other hand, these allusions work to mock the optimism of *The Wizard of Oz* and its smarmy belief in happy endings–a Lynchian ironic hallmark. In emphasizing *The Wizard of Oz*'s hopeful ebullience in an unbelievable Deus Ex Machina, *Wild at Heart* reveals the total artifice of Hollywood joy.

The Elvis allusions work in the same way as the ones from *The Wizard of Oz*. In essence, they detract from *Wild at Heart*'s solemnity, undercutting its ostensible efforts to depict Sailor's legitimate transformation. Sailor, like Lula, is but a substitute for a Hollywood figure of yore. While Lula is Dorothy Gale reincarnated, Sailor is Elvis Presley resurrected. Though Elvis is never mentioned, Sailor impersonates him nevertheless. He has jet-black hair like the King and speaks like Elvis with a Southern drawl, breaking into Elvis songs twice. When Sailor dances, he throws karate punches and kicks like Elvis on stage during his final years. He casts himself as a young rebel on the run from the law. An amalgamation of stereotypical Elvis ticks, Sailor is something of a caricature, more a comic relief offering than a lover in need of salvation. In portraying Sailor as a clown, the film implies Elvis, too, is silly, intimating that his movies are likewise farcical renderings of Hollywood affection, sentimental products from the artifice.[574]

In *Wild at Heart*, Lynch even seems to parody his cinematic sensibilities. The perverse violence of Dropshadow, Reggie, and Juana Durango accompanying Farragut's murder–a weird mixture of ritual, sexual desire, and a death wish–conjure the violence Frank Booth perpetrates on Jeffrey Beaumont in *Blue Velvet*, likewise a bizarre blend of erotic passion and brutal assault. Similarly, Lula's visions of Oz recall Sandy Williams' dream of robins; in both cases, a young, innocent woman tries to envision a better world where there is no pain. The pervasive weirdness of Mr. Reindeer's atmosphere–replete with a topless girl waiting on him while he takes a shit, and outlandish circus acts entertaining him while he dines–recalls the stereotypical irregularities present in several of his previous cinema. For instance, *Eraserhead* with the weird Lady in the Radiator, *Blue Velvet* with its sadomasochism, nitrous oxide, Suave Ben's (Dean Stockwell) lip-synching, and *Dune* with its obese, floating vampire-like Baron Harkonnen (Kenneth McMillan, 1932-1989). In referencing these earlier films directly or indirectly, Lynch suggests he's more interested in creating a Lynchian movie than in fashioning a meaningful cinematic event. Parodying himself, he undercuts the value of his work. On the other hand, without these comedic undercurrents, *Wild at Heart* would take itself too seriously, failing to uplift the audience as Lynch intended.

---

574 Ibid, 106-107.

Twin Peaks Seasons I and II: the Owls are not What They Seem

"The owls are not what they seem," says the Giant (Carel Struycken) to FBI Special Agent Dale Cooper, and in this author's opinion, neither is *Twin Peaks*. Often lauded as one of Lynch's masterstrokes, *Twin Peaks* is not a work of genius. Instead, it is a hodgepodge of campy soap opera, psychological thriller, surreal plotlines, the metaphysical, alchemy, murder mystery, and neo-noir drama imbued with schizophrenic, explainable allegories and symbolism. Some of the characters are annoying, especially the one played by Lynch: a nearly deaf FBI Agent named Gordon Cole, who screeches in a whiny, high-pitched voice. The show is all but unwatchable when he appears on-screen; nevertheless, Cole's voice is evidence of Lynch's disdain for language, implied by the constricting words of *Eraserhead* and *Blue Velvet* and *Mulholland Drive*'s lip-synching. The character's hard of hearing indicates that he–Lynch–doesn't want to listen to anything because language muddles intent, making it a hostile concept, mere chants of conformity, reducing images to subjective abstractions.

Indeed, the Black Lodge's odd language raises more questions than answers; Lynch wants us to know there's a difference between meaning and interpretation, between what is said and what is understood, and never to underestimate the power of silence, designated by Club Silencio. Easter egg: Lynch's Agent Gordon Cole is named after a minor character in *Sunset Boulevard*. Lynch acknowledges Wilder's film as a significant influence, most notably in the similarly named *Mulholland Drive*. Wilder's impact upon Lynch is also evidenced by *Twin Peaks*' insurance agent, Herbert Neff (Mark Lowenthal). Neff is named after Walter Neff (Fred MacMurray, 1908-1991), the insurance salesman in *Double Indemnity* (1944). In *Twin Peaks: The Return*, during episode 15, "There's Some Fear in Letting Go" (airdate August 20, 2017), Cooper *qua* Dougie Jones is watching *Sunset Boulevard* when Cole's name is mentioned, initiating a recall.

The symbolism and allusions that are offered are observable to anyone with two eyes. There is no great mystery, and Lynch knows it. The show is akin to a confidence trick: Lynch relies on the sublime eccentricities of his other films to convince the audience that *Twin Peaks* is more than a convoluted nighttime serial, cleverly using framing devices. For example, much like Chinese boxes or Russian wooden dolls hiding inside one another,

CINEMA SYMBOLISM 3

Lynch mingles the moon and burning fireplaces with owls and demonic entities like Bob (Frank Silva, 1949-1995; *nota bene*: I will not spell his name BOB). Lynch then surrounds this imagery with a murder mystery involving a beautiful young woman, Laura Palmer. He frames all this with a secret organization, the Bookhouse Boys, and the mysterious White and Black Lodges–more on these later. He shrouds all this with a bizarre Red Room, also known as the Waiting Room, complete a Dwarf known as the Man from Another Place (Michael J. Anderson) and a Giant. Buddhism and dualism further envelop *Twin Peaks* in a penumbra of mysticism.

However, it's all a televised magic act because, by season two's final episode, the audience will realize there is nothing up Lynch's sleeve, no rabbit in the hat. Lynch knows this because he mocks *Twin Peaks* with a show within a show. The asinine *Invitation to Love* is a soap opera entertaining many dramatis personae dwelling in Twin Peaks, such as the Sheriff Department's dispatcher Lucy Moran (Kimmy Robertson). *Invitation to Love*'s melodramatic scenes either recall, run parallel with, or anticipate *Twin Peaks*' byzantine twists and turns. By mirroring this silly soap opera, Lynch informs us subtly, the audience, that *Twin Peaks* should be taken with a grain of salt, with tongue firmly planted in cheek.

Outside the town, there's the men's club One-Eyed Jacks, which immediately conjures Bobby Peru's comment from *Wild at Heart*, debuting the same years as *Twin Peaks*, 1990. Bobby-as-Mercurius uses it as a term of endearment for his penis; ergo, Lynch uses crudity to poke fun at his televised creation. Having offered this critique, I should mention that, overall, I do like the show. It is entertaining; the characters, acting, music, storylines, and settings are engaging, but I feel like the show reveals a chink in Lynch's cinematic armor. By intentionally confusing the audience with paradoxical imagery and non sequitur dialog, especially in the Red Waiting Room/Black Lodge, one is forced to ask: is *Twin Peaks* a sublime work of genius? Or is Lynch, and Mark Frost, making this up as they go along, creating plot loopholes so large that one could drive a Mack Truck through them? When I watch *Twin Peaks*, I sometimes feel like I am watching an Ed Wood movie, not a show created by the director of *Blue Velvet*, *Dune*, *Mulholland Drive*, and *The Elephant Man*. Easter egg: *Invitation to Love*'s title card rests on a swatch of blue velvet, evoking *Blue Velvet*, a movie anticipating *Twin Peaks*' vast duality.

(Left) Lynch transfers the chevron pattern carpet from the lobby of Henry's apartment in *Eraserhead* to the floor of the Red Room (right) in *Twin Peaks*. The zig-zag carpet seems to anticipate pessimism; in the former, the corruption of Henry's apartment by the serpentine infant, and in the latter, Bob's malevolence and the Black Lodge's gloom.

Is *Twin Peaks* a Gnostic fable? Not really; there is no Demiurge, no alternative reality, and no Valentinian rebellion, at least in the ABC series and follow-up movie. However, a strong case for Gnostic cosmology can put forth if one takes into account *The Return*–more on these 2017 episodes later. Is *Twin Peaks* an exercise in dualism? The answer to this question is an emphatic *yes*, and Lynch draws from a dichotomous reservoir to make *Twin Peaks* feel mystical when, in reality, it is nothing more than a weird slice of American pie. Lynch is an expert in employing duality, indicating good and evil, male and female, chaos and order, wisdom and ignorance, presenting dense Shakespearean-like plotlines, unfolding from stupefying, conflicting epistemological paradigms.

Duality pervades Lynchian cinema: in *Wild at Heart*, love struggles to survive in a loveless wasteland; in *Eraserhead*, the filthy hylic reality, represented by the snakelike baby, is contrasted by spiritual transcendence personified by the Lady in the Radiator. In *The Elephant Man*, John Merrick's gnarled, twisted, deformed body signifies London's underbelly, disrupting Victorian virtues and untainted sensibilities. *Dune* is pure Manicheanism: good against evil, conscious awakening, slipping the shackles of ignorance. *Lost Highway* presents two separate yet interconnected actualities while *Mulholland Drive* contrasts the ebullient dream against gloomy reality.

Like *Twin Peaks*, *Blue Velvet* presents a saccharine America concealing a sordid underworld. In the former, drugs, pornography, and grisly murder befoul a mawkish Northwestern town, the eponymous Twin Peaks, further plagued by a hidden evil lurking in the woods. In the latter, Lumberton looks and acts like 1950s America. However, a forbidden darkness stains it, located around Lincoln Avenue, where the sadomasochistic chanteuse Dorothy Vallens dwells, maker her apartment a den of iniquity. She hangs around with the freakishly sinister Frank Booth, gleefully inhaling his nitrous oxide, but becoming lachrymose when Suave Ben lip-synchs Roy Orbison's "In Dreams" (1963). Put another way, *Blue Velvet* and *Twin Peaks* emphasize the good and evil nature of humankind; beneath the artificial surface of peaceful small American towns, you'll find a dark world of gangsters, prostitution, murder, drug trafficking, corruption, and wicked weirdness.

Lynch's cinema is populated with characters who are diametric to others, or themselves, further conveying duality. In *Eraserhead*, Henry's seductive neighbor, the Beautiful Girl Across the Hall, opposes the wholesome Lady in the Radiator. In *Dune*, the sophisticated and noble House Atreides combats the brutal and diseased House Harkonnen. In *Blue Velvet*, the virginal Sandy Williams counterbalances the sexually adventurous Dorothy Vallens, the two sides of the alchemical *albedo*: light and dark, love and lust. In *Lost Highway*, the solipsistic and narcissistic Fred Madison (Bill Pullman) morphs into easygoing Pete Dayton (Balthazar Getty). In *Mulholland Drive*, a wide-eyed and eager ingénue Betty Elms contrasts her real-world persona, the depressed Diane Selwyn.

Twin Peaks is no exception as dualism is omnipresent, suggesting that Janus, the double-headed god of Roman antiquity, could've produced the series. Antithetical imagery introduces it: during the opening credits, we observe a Bewick's Wren, a symbol of nature's tranquility, dissolve into a lumber mill, representing the environment's destruction. Audrey Horne (Sherilyn Fenn) rocks black and white saddle shoes, symbolizing light and dark, neo-Manicheanism, brilliantly anticipating India Stoker's saddle-shoe obsession. Audrey's footwear represents different sides of her personality: inexperienced virgin and tempting harlot. The murder victim, Laura Palmer, led a double life. One was open and innocent, the blonde-hair girl next door, the homecoming queen dating the football player; the other was dark and secret, laced with pornography, bondage, and drug abuse. Laura is the dark side of the *albedo*. Enter the moon's bright side, Laura's opposite, her demure cousin from Missoula, Montana (Lynch's hometown) named Madeline "Maddy" Ferguson, also portrayed by Sheryl Lee.

Maddy is Laura's backward clone: a nerdy brunette who wears glasses; she is a reserved, shy virgin. She is coy and down to earth, but adventurous to a degree: she willingly disguises herself as Laura to lure Dr. Lawrence Jacoby (Russ Tamblyn) out of his office. But her disguise attracts the attention of Bob, sealing her fate. Maddy's brief stint on the show represents *what could have been* if Laura had survived. Even *Madeleine Ferguson* denotes duality: it's an amalgamation of two characters from Hitchcock's *Vertigo*, specifically John "Scottie" Ferguson (James Stewart, 1908-1987) and Madeline Elster (Kim Novak). Novak plays two women: one blonde and the other brunette, just like Laura and Madeline. *Vertigo* is about an obsessive man trying to replace a lost lover in the form of a new woman, echoing Maddy replacing Laura temporarily. This is one of the many Hitchcockian influences turning up in Lynch's art.

We even have an androgynous character: DEA officer Denise Bryson (David Duchovny), a transvestite. On the spectrum's opposite end, a woman, Catherine Martell (Piper Laurie), after faking her death, disguises herself as a man, Mr. Tojamura. There is a bordello, One-Eyed Jacks, and a one-eyed woman, Nadine Hurley (Wendy Robie). Nadine's personality schism is brought about by head trauma, taking her from the mindset of a 35-year-old married woman obsessed with silent drape runners to that of an 18-year-old high school senior obsessed with cheerleading. There are two inseparable dark spirits: Mrs. Chalfont (Frances Bay, 1919-2011) is an older woman, and her grandson, Pierre (Austin Jack Lynch), is young; the duo represents the dichotomy between old age and youth, female and male. There are two conspicuous invitations: the histrionic *Invitation to Love*, and the petroglyph in Owl Cave. One of the show's villains, Windom Earle (Kenneth Welsh), pronounces, "For you see, the cave painting is not only an invitation, [but] it is also a map, a map to the Black Lodge!" Earle spoke of the dugpas: a society of evil sorcerers who promoted evil for the sake of evil. They had access to a place of power to streamline this process, the Black Lodge. Earle researched the dugpas while studying Project Blue Book, and likened their worship to Kali worshippers in India. According to

Blavatsky, the term dugpa was synonymous with black magicians, referring to them as Brothers of the Shadow. *Twin Peaks*' mythos centers on theses two Lodges, Black and White, representing both good and evil, ego and shadow self.

There are two types of Black Lodge inhabitants: parasitic archon-like spirits *qua* demons in need of hosts to move about our world, and doppelgangers, shadow selves wrenched away from the original person. The evil of the Black Lodge creates the doppelgangers, held captive for time immeasurable. Of the former, Bob is the most active. When he materializes on terra firma, he possesses the body of Leland Palmer (Ray Wise), Laura's father, a dualism represented by Bob's reflection in a mirror, usually before bouts of violent murder. When Leland dies, Bob leaves his body, returning to the Black Lodge as an owl. Inside the Black Lodge, Leland's doppelganger, no longer half of a whole, now roams its corridors for eternity, as will the doppelgangers of Laura, Maddy, Leland, and Caroline Powell Earle (Brenda Mathers). A Dwarf and a Giant visit the Red Room, presumably the Black Lodge's entrance, or the Black Lodge itself. Earle plays chess with black and white pieces, inferring Lynchian Manicheanism.

But the dualism doesn't end there. The cold shadow cast by the Horne Corporation–a horn is a traditional symbol of power and strength–contrasts the jovial warmth of Norma Jennings' (Peggy Lipton, 1946-2019) Double R Diner (*nota bene* the duality of the diner's name). Horne conspires to devour Twin Peaks with corporate greed; Norma seeks to nourish it with hot coffee and delectable pie. Josie Packard's (Joan Chen) identity is triply divided between Andrew Packard's (Dan O'Herlihy) unfortunate widow, Sheriff Harry S. Truman's sensual lover, and Thomas Eckhardt's (David Warner) Mata Hari-like concubine. Audrey's virginal persona contrasts her Hester Prynne identity when she goes undercover at One-Eyed Jacks. Ernie Niles (James Booth, 1927-2005) is a financial advisor on the surface and a hardened criminal beneath, and his wife, Vivian Smythe Lindstrom Blackburn Niles Halliwell (Jane Greer, 1924-2001), façade as a judgmental mother masks her professional career as a travel writer and restaurant reviewer M. T. Wentz.

Ben Horne (Richard Beymer) suffers a psychotic break after losing Ghostwood, transforming him from a greedy corporate scumbag into a caring and philanthropic do-gooder via a personal reenactment of the American Civil War. After Ben turns over a new leaf and decides to do good, his trademark cigars are gradually replaced by vegetables, with him nibbling on carrots and celery instead of smoking. Lucy struggles with deciding which of her dueling beaus will be a better father to her unborn child, regardless of paternity. Donna Hayward (Lara Flynn Boyle) has two dads, and Laura kept two diaries: one known, one secret. There are two Roberts: Bobby Briggs and Bob, and two Mikes: Mike (Al Strobel) and Mike Nelson. Then there's Leo Johnson's (Eric DaRe) arc from an abusive monster to a helpless, crippled, and unwilling minion. Even Dr. Jacoby's trademark eyeglasses are two colors, red and blue. These hints reveal the ever-present struggle between opposing forces; however, they are noticeable to the profane, not requiring expertise. Easter egg: Wendy Robie's character, Nadine, is married to Ed Hurley, played by Everett McGill. This show isn't the only time these actors played a twosome. In *The People Under the Stairs*, which, like *Twin Peaks* debuted in the early 90s, Robie and McGill played Woman and Man, or Mommy and Daddy, bizarre personifications of Nancy (1916-2016) and Ronald Reagan (1911-2004). Symbolically, *People* is about racism, and socioeconomic disparages, personified by the presumed married couple. However, they are sister and brother, and their casting likely a result of *Twin Peaks*' lack of ethnic diversity.

Balanced, diametric forces comprise the universe, energies that push when others pull and create when others destroy. Without this balance, chaos ensues, and reality becomes warped, fractured, or otherwise flawed. It is in one of these fissures the town of Twin Peaks exists. The death of Laura Palmer caused an imbalance that set-in motion the events of the series. Cooper was the agent, viz. the magician archetype, through which order could have been restored, his role in the drama was the polar opposite of the victim, the tragic Laura. But as we all know, Cooper's efforts only led to an even more significant imbalance of the dual forces at work in *Twin Peaks*, one that has left the town, the series, and its audience teetering on the brink of oblivion for more than a quarter-century.[575]

---

[575] Perry H. Horton, "An Opposition of Self: Duality and 'Twin Peaks,'" *Film School Rejects*, May 17, 2016. https://filmschoolrejects.com/an-opposition-of-self-duality-and-twin-peaks-dee93503e4e5/ (accessed July 15, 2019).

Out of this occult dualism comes *Twin Peaks*' tortuous storylines, an endless array of double-crosses, love triangles, murder mystery, and intrigue. The brainchild of Lynch and Mark Frost, *Twin Peaks*' first season premiered on April 8, 1990, on ABC. The series cultivated a loyal following, but declining ratings led to its cancellation after its second season in 1991. It nonetheless gained cult status and has been referenced in a wide variety of media. In subsequent years, *Twin Peaks* is often listed among the greatest television series of all time, a sentiment this author may disagree with, but concedes it is undoubtedly one of the most influential.

Twin Peaks, and for that matter, *Blue Velvet*, were born out of the melodrama, *Kings Row* (1942), a movie about a small town with dark secrets. It is with some irony that *Kings Row* opens with a shot of a billboard advertising it as "A Good Clean Town. A Good Place to Live In and a Good Place to Raise Your Children." The towns of Lumberton and Twin Peaks, and the suburban estate Rancho Rosa have similar signs demarcating them as all-American "Good Clean" towns. These signs contrast with the darkness and violence dwelling within them, exemplifying Lynchian duality.[576]

In 1989, logger Pete Martell (Jack Nance) discovers a naked corpse wrapped in plastic on a riverbank outside Twin Peaks, Washington. When Sheriff Harry S. Truman, his deputies, and Dr. Will Hayward (Warren Frost, 1925-2017) arrive, the body is identified as homecoming queen Laura Palmer. A severely injured second girl, Ronette Pulaski (Phoebe Augustine), is found in a fugue state. Easter egg: the much-used homecoming queen photo of Laura Palmer is Sheryl Lee's genuine prom photo. Another Easter egg: *Ronette Pulaski* evokes Roman Polanski, in a subconscious effort to conjure *Rosemary's Baby*, transferring its demonism to *Twin Peaks*' quasi-satanic Bob. The Polanski allusion also conjures *Repulsion* (1965), which is about a young woman's descent into madness, signifying Ronette's psychological and emotional collapse.

Black-suited FBI Special Agent Dale Cooper arrives to investigate. His initial examination of Laura's body reveals a tiny typed letter *R* inserted under her fingernail. Cooper informs the community that her death matches

---

576 Lindsay Hallam, "Women's Films: Melodrama and Women's Trauma in the Films of David Lynch," in *The Women of David Lynch*, ed. David Bushman (Columbus, OH: Fayetteville Mafia Press, 2019), 21-22.

the signature of a killer who murdered another girl, Teresa Banks, in southwestern Washington the previous year. The evidence indicates the killer lives in Twin Peaks. The letters inserted under the victims' fingernails spell *Robert*, the parasitic demon's name. Easter egg: Lynch named Cooper after D. B. Cooper, an unidentified man who hijacked a Boeing 727 aircraft on November 24, 1971, parachuting into the airspace between Portland, Oregon, and Seattle, Washington. This area is, of course, where Twin Peaks is located.

Via Laura's diary, the authorities discover she has been living a double life. She was cheating on her boyfriend, football captain Bobby Briggs, with biker James Hurley and prostituting herself backed by truck driver Leo Johnson and drug dealer Jacques Renault (Walter Olkewicz). Laura was also addicted to cocaine, which she obtained by coercing Bobby into doing business with Jacques. Cooper explains his unique method of investigation to Sheriff Truman and his deputies. Tibet fascinates him, implying the mysteries of Buddhism; specifically, he uses subconscious information in his dreams as clues to a crime committed. The dream practice and analysis have been used in Tibet since ancient times, considered an essential part of the medical examination and mind training. Tibetan Bon faith healers and ancient shamans used dreams to read the relationship between the spirits and humans and diagnose diseases. Among these shamans were independent female *dream tellers* who were involved with the government to make predictions for the kings about the country's politics and prosperity.

After Buddhism came to Tibet in the 7th century, dream analyzing culture developed along with medical expertise and spiritual practice, becoming a more important subject. Even today, there are eminent dream tellers and visionaries able to give predictions on future happenings. The method of dream analysis increased with the use of healthy dream interpretation and dream omens as a diagnosis in medical practice, according to the *Gyud-shi* (the Four Medical Tantras), with yoga as a spiritual practice for the transformation of the body-mind. Cooper is more than an FBI Agent going through the motions. Like a shaman, he uses his dreams–surreal visions from another realm–to solve crimes, suggesting he is well versed in esoteric teachings, employing unconventional methods while bound to Sherlockian deductive reasoning. He understands the language of unconscious gesture is a language of condensed and latent meaning, but even so, its effect is powerful.[577] Easter egg: this author is aware of the power of dreams and visions. In April 2013, I had a lucid dream inspiring me to write *A Pact with the Devil*.

Other intuitive deductive devices in Agent Cooper's arsenal are the Tibetan method of rock-throwing, and coin toss, inspired by the *I Ching* (ca. 1000-750 BCE). While looking over photos of prospective residences with a real estate agent, Cooper flips a coin, accidentally landing on the listing for Dead Dog Farm. This action results in a lead in the case. The silver coin conjures the full moon, ruler of the sacred feminine, alluding to the subconscious mind, intuition, and psychic awareness, the hallmarks of Cooper's magical abilities. The Winged Mercury dime was commonly used in coin tosses because Mercury is the Greek god of divination, luck, and communication, among other things; thus, Cooper is a bridge between the upper and lower worlds. Moreover, as I've discussed throughout this book, Mercury is fundamental to the alchemical process (*vide supra*). Cooper embodies the archetypal planetary and alchemical properties of Mercury himself, fluid in his deductive reasoning and clairvoyance.[578] Ergo, Cooper personifies the Tarot's Magician (I) of the Major Arcana, making him a transformative agent. Easter egg: when Cooper throws the rocks, attempting to divine Laura's murderer, the distance to the bottle is 60 feet, 6 inches, the length in baseball from the pitcher's mound to home plate.

Laura's father, attorney Leland Palmer, suffers a nervous breakdown. As he collapses emotionally, he plays the swing jazz song "Pennsylvania 6-5000" on his record player, dancing around with a framed photo of Laura. "Pennsylvania 6-5000" is the New York City phone number for the Hotel Pennsylvania (212-73**6-5000**), its main restaurant, the Café Rouge, or Red Café. The jazz song is a harbinger of the Red Room, a place Cooper will visit in his dreams soon thereafter. Meanwhile, Laura's best friend, Donna Hayward, begins a relationship with James. With the help of Laura's cousin Maddy Ferguson, Donna and James discover that her psychiatrist, Dr. Lawrence Jacoby, was obsessed with Laura, but he is proven innocent of the murder. Easter egg: Dr. Jacoby takes after the late ethnobotanist Terrence McKenna (1946-2000), who lectured and wrote about various

---

577 Maurice Nicoll, *Dream Psychology* (London: Henry Frowde, Hodder & Stoughton, 1917), 14.
578 Zora Burden, "Another Place: The Esoteric Symbolism of Twin Peaks/Agent on the Threshold: The Taoism and Alchemy of Twin Peaks," *Zora Burden: Writer, Artist, Poet*, August 2015, https://zoraburden.weebly.com/the-esoteric-symbolism-of-twin-peaks.html (accessed August 1, 2019).

(Left) The Major Arcana's Magician (or Juggler) from the Rider-Waite Deck. As the Card I, the trump is the master of ceremonies, corresponding with Mercurius, holding his wand toward Heaven, and his left hand to earth, signifying the Hermetic maxim, *as above, so below*. The Magician says Heaven's way should be manifested on earth, indicating his nexus to material reality and the spiritual realm. Alternatively, the Magician can be a black magician, heralding destruction and woe. Notice he stands in a garden of roses and lilies. Tarot historian Robert O'Neill points out these flowers are lifted from the Song of Songs, 2:1, "I am the Rose of Sharon, the lily of the valley." The Rose of Sharon conjures only one thing: Rafferty's Rose of Shannon Motel from *Halloween III*, evoking the black magic of Conal Cochran, and his diabolical plan to murder the children of America on Samhain via hexed Halloween masks. The female Juggler incarnates as *Breakfast at Tiffany's* Holly Golightly (right). Characterizing quicksilver in the *albedo* phase, this café society trickster skillfully manipulates the men in her life. Her air of mystery is an intoxicating aphrodisiac next to impossible to resist. Echoing this archetype, Holly is mercurial: she wishes to find love and marriage but rebels against them because she adores her role as an American geisha.

subjects, including psychedelic drugs, Jungian psychology, plant-based entheogens, shamanism, metaphysics, alchemy, language, philosophy, culture, technology, environmentalism, and the theoretical origins of human consciousness. Their physical appearance is strikingly similar, as is their dress style and all-embracing '60s' countercultural ideologies. Dr. Jacoby holidays in Hawaii and has a Hawaiian wife, while McKenna lived in Hawaii. Dr. Jacoby has a notable mushroom-shaped lamp, and McKenna studied and wrote widely on psychedelic mushrooms, developing the Stoned Ape Theory. Later, in *Twin Peaks: The Return*, Jacoby is a podcaster using the handle Dr. Amp, preaching to his followers, including Nadine, about the war on consciousness. According to Dr. Amp, one must awaken, then use one of his golden shovels to dig themselves out of shit, rejecting materialism and its concomitant consumerism.

Ruthless hotelier Ben Horne, Twin Peaks' wealthiest man, plans to destroy the town's lumber mill and its owner, Josie Packard. He also plans on murdering his lover (Josie's sister-in-law), Catherine Martell, so that he can purchase the land at a reduced price to complete a development project, Ghostwood. Horne's sultry, troubled daughter, Audrey, becomes infatuated with Cooper, so she spies and eavesdrops for clues to gain his affection.

Cooper dreams that he is approached by a one-armed otherworldly being who calls himself Mike (to go easy on the reader's eyes, I will not spell it MIKE). The one-armed man states Laura's murderer is a similar entity, Bob: a feral, denim-clad demon with long gray hair. After committing several rape-murders with Bob, Mike claimed to have had a religious epiphany and repented, cutting off his arm to rid himself of the tattooed phrase, *Fire Walk with Me*, cleansing himself of the devilish one's mark. *Fire Walk with Me* was found written in blood inside the train car where Laura was murdered. Cooper then finds himself in a Red Room complete with a Saturn lamp and a Venus de' Medici statue. The Room's hallway has a Venus de Milo sculpture. The two Venusian idols represent Laura and Maddy. The objectified Venus de Milo epitomizes Laura, i.e., *nuditas criminalis*, lascivious and vain exhibition. The modest Venus de' Medici, or Venus Pudica, personifies Maddy since the figure is trying to cover its naked body, viz. *nuditas virtualis*, purity and innocence.

Inside the odd room, with its chevron carpet borrowed from *Eraserhead*, Cooper is decades older with Laura (or her doppelganger) dressed in black, and the Dwarf (later identified as the Man from Another Place or the Arm) wearing a red suit. When they speak, the language sounds like English backward, evoking *The Exorcist* when Regan MacNeil, possessed by the demon Pazuzu *qua* the Devil, speaks English reversed. The Red Room associates with the Black Lodge, a place of darkness, so conjuring *The Exorcist* makes sense. Crowley promoted reverse speech in his book, *Magick*, as a means to grant the adept further occult power. An even older reference can be found in Carroll's *Through the Looking Glass*, the sequel to *Alice in Wonderland*, which has Alice entering a world through a mirror where she encounters a book with backward writing that can be read by its reflection. The late 1960s-early 1970s witnessed musicians adding backward masking to their songs, most notably by the Beatles in "Revolution 9" on the *White Album* and Led Zeppelin's "Stairway to Heaven" on *Led Zeppelin IV* (1971). This technique gave their music an exciting edge during the experimental psychedelic era, an era that also involved various artists, writers, and musicians exploring occult themes and Eastern philosophies. The Dwarf, the strange language, the statue of Venus, and Laura's spirit give the Red Room an off-world mystical vibe.

The next day, Cooper informs Truman that if he can decipher the dream, he will discover Laura's killer. Cooper and the sheriff's department find the one-armed man from Cooper's dream, a traveling shoe salesman named Phillip Gerard (Al Strobel, same actor as Mike). Gerard knows a Bob, the veterinarian who treats Renault's pet bird. The FBI Agent interprets these events to mean that Renault is the murderer, and with Truman's help, tracks Renault to One-Eyed Jacks, a brothel owned by Horne across the border in Canada. He lures Jacques Renault back onto US soil to arrest him, but Renault is shot while trying to escape and is hospitalized.

Hiding in the township is a Masonic-Oddfellow-like secret society, the Bookhouse Boys, who meet sub rosa in a used bookstore, which, like a library, houses wisdom. The clandestine group recalls hugger-mugger orders haunting the East of England, such as the Ancient Order of Bonesmen (not Yale's Skull and Bones), the Toadmen, the Confraternity of the Plough, and the Society of the Horseman's Grip and Word, each still functioning to keep up the day. Like Bonesmanry, the Boys use hand gestures as a means of communication and recognition. According to Sheriff Truman, the Bookhouse Boys were formed to combat darkness hiding in the woods surrounding Twin Peaks. It is never explained if this evil is material, e.g., vampires, witches, goblins, or werewolves; or spiritual, e.g., ghosts or demons. Cooper will come to believe the malevolency associates with the Black Lodge. Unlike Masonry, the Oddfellows, and East Anglia's occult-agrarian orders, there is no formal requirement to join the Bookhouse Boys; to be presented with a simple membership patch is all that's needed. Easter egg: the one-armed man's surname, Gerard, is the same as the detective, Lt. Philip Gerard (Barry Morse, 1918-2008) from the television show *The Fugitive* (1963-1967).

Lt. Gerard was hunting Richard Kimble (David Harold Meyer, 1931-1980), who was also searching for a one-armed man. References to Hugo's *Les Misérables* (1862) may also be no accident, as the novel inspired the TV series *The Fugitive*, to which *Twin Peaks* alludes. For example, Hank Jennings' (Chris Mulkey) inmate designation is 24601, copying Jean Valjean's prison number from *Les Mis*.

Leland, learning of Jacques' arrest, sneaks into the hospital and kills him, believing him to be Laura's murderer. The same night, Horne orders Leo to burn down the lumber mill with Catherine trapped inside. Horne has Leo gunned down by ex-con Hank Jennings (Chris Mulkey) to ensure Leo's silence. Cooper returns to his room in the Great Northern Hotel following Jacques' arrest only to be shot by a masked gunman. This cliffhanger ends the first season.

The second season debuted on September 30, 1990, picking up exactly where the previous left off. Cooper, mortally wounded, has a vision of the Giant, revealing three clues:

- "There is a man in a smiling bag";
- "The owls are not what they seem";
- and "Without chemicals, he points."

He takes Cooper's gold ring, explaining that when he understands the three premonitions, the ring will be returned. To dream or have a vision of a giant is a favorable omen; within *Twin Peaks*' cosmology, the Giant epitomizes the Monad (known as the Fireman), governing the White Lodge.[579] In the pleroma, he will emanate Laura as a Sophia-like Aeon to counter the archon Bob, documented in the episode, "Gotta Light?" *Twin Peaks: The Return* (June 25, 2017).

Leo Johnson survives his shooting but is brain-damaged. Catherine Martell disappears, presumed killed in the mill fire. Leland Palmer, whose hair has whitened overnight, returns to work but behaves erratically. Cooper deduces the "man in the smiling bag" is Jacques Renault's corpse in a body bag.

We learn Mike, a supernatural being, inhabits the body of Phillip Gerard. His personality surfaces when Gerard forgoes the use of the drug haloperidol. Mike reveals that he and Bob once collaborated in killing humans and that Bob is similarly inhabiting a man in the town. Cooper and the sheriff's department

---

579 Girard, *Mystic Dream Book*, 34; *The Witches' Dream Book*, 25.

CINEMA SYMBOLISM 3

Season two, episode 18, "Masked Ball," (airdate December 15, 1990) introduces Evelyn Marsh (left, Annette McCarthy), a siren plotting to kill her husband, hiring James Hurley to frame him for the murder. She hangs out in a bar named WALLIES (center), becoming another of Lynch's doubles, anticipating the arrival of Wally Brando (right, Michael Cera) in episode four of *Twin Peaks: The Return*, "....Brings Back Some Memories" (airdate May 28, 2017). Thus, WALLIES is a temple wherein a sexy woman-as-temptress holds court, and Wally is the name of a Marlon Brando wannabe, hinting at female and male, Venus and Mars, alchemy's *coincidentia oppositorum*. Evelyn's red coat and black stockings seek to unify the *rubedo* and the *nigredo* because, to vixens like her, the *nigredo* is the *rubedo*. Dark sexiness, masturbatory platitudes, and narcissism are her calling cards, her alpha and omega, nothing more, nothing less. She dares to flaunt her stockings in public, welcoming chaos and lust, wantonly disregarding her deadly game's consequences. Impure, jealous, and stupid, her manipulations fail; as her surname *Marsh* suggests, Evelyn becomes mired in a web of double-crosses and erotic brinksmanship, unable to escape the matrix she created.

use Mike, in control of Gerard's body, to help find Bob. Withholding the drug from Gerard solves the "without chemicals, he points" clue.

Donna befriends an agoraphobic orchid grower named Harold Smith (Lenny Von Dohlen) whom Laura entrusted with the second secret diary she kept. He catches Donna and Maddy trying to steal the journal, so he hangs himself in despair. Cooper and the sheriff's department take possession of the secret journal, learning Bob, a friend of her father's, has been sexually abusing her since childhood, so she used drugs to cope. The journal also reveals Cooper and Laura experienced the same Red Room dream. They initially suspect that the killer is Ben Horne and arrest him, but Leland Palmer is revealed to be Bob's host when he brutally kills Maddy.

Cooper begins to doubt Horne's guilt, so he gathers all of his suspects in the belief that he will receive a sign to help him identify the killer. The Giant appears, confirming Leland is Bob's host and the killer of Laura and Maddy, giving him back his ring. Cooper and Truman take Leland into custody. In control of Leland's body, Bob admits to a string of murders, before forcing Leland to commit suicide. Leland, as he dies, is freed of Bob's influence and begs for forgiveness. Bob's spirit disappears into the woods in the form of an owl, leaving the lawmen to wonder if he will reappear. Bob takes the shape of an owl, intimating Lynch knows his Egyptian mythology because, in their hieroglyphs, the owl symbolized death, night, and coldness.[580] The nocturnal bird of prey links Bob's transcendent evil to Owl Cave, the Black Lodge's entrance, anticipating the negativity of the green ring (with its owl petroglyph). Bob-as-an-owl solves the "owls are not what they seem" riddle, but only we, the audience, are privy to this revelation.

Cooper is set to leave Twin Peaks when he is framed for drug trafficking by Jean Renault (Michael Parks, 1940-2017), and suspended from the FBI. Jean Renault holds Cooper responsible for the death of his brothers, Jacques and Bernard. Jean Renault is killed in a shootout with police, and Cooper is cleared of all charges.

Windom Earle, Cooper's former mentor and FBI partner escapes from a mental hospital and comes to Twin Peaks. Cooper had previously been having an affair with Earle's wife, Caroline, while under his protection as a witness to a federal crime. Earle murdered Caroline and wounded Cooper. He now engages Cooper in a twisted game of chess wherein Earle kills someone whenever a piece is captured.

Investigating Bob's origin and whereabouts with the help of Major Garland Briggs, Cooper learns of the existence of the White Lodge and the Black Lodge, and that the entrances to these extradimensional spheres are somewhere in the woods surrounding the town. Cooper also learns Earle was involved with Project Blue Book. Earle was dismissed after he became obsessive and violent with his assignments while searching for the Black Lodge. Despite its official disbandment in 1969, Project Blue Book continued its activity well into 1989, with Major Briggs searching for the White Lodge. Blue Book was the US government's investigation into UFOs and related data. Although the White and Black Lodges are metaphysical, Major Briggs suggests an extraterrestrial intelligence could be behind them, but that nexus is never fully established.

Catherine returns to town disguised as a Japanese businessman, having survived the mill fire, and manipulates Horne into signing the Ghostwood

---

580 Cirlot, *Dictionary*, 235-236.

project over to her. Andrew Packard, Josie's husband, is still alive much to the surprise of all. Josie, it turns out, shot Cooper at the end of the first season. Andrew forces Josie to confront his business rival and her tormentor from Hong Kong, the sinister Thomas Eckhardt. Josie kills Eckhardt, but she mysteriously dies of fear when Truman and Cooper try to apprehend her.

Cooper falls in love with a new arrival in town, Annie Blackburn (Heather Graham). Earle captures the brain-damaged Leo for use as a henchman and abandons his chess game with Cooper. As an exemplar of transcendental irony, a former nun, Annie, wins the Miss Twin Peaks contest, but Earle kidnaps her and takes her to the Black Lodge, seeking to harness its dark energy.

Through a series of clues, Cooper discovers the Black Lodge's entrance, which turns out to be the strange, red-curtained Red Room from his dream. The Man from Another Place (the Dwarf) greets him, while the Giant and Laura give Cooper cryptic messages. The Giant reveals he is the elderly hotel waiter who found Cooper shot in his room ("May the Giant Be with You," airdate September 30, 1990). Laura says she will see him in 25 years. Searching for Annie and Earle, Cooper encounters spirits, or doppelgangers, of various people, including Maddy and Leland. He also runs into Laura's white-eyed doppelganger, which terrifyingly screams at him. Cooper finds Earle, who demands his soul in exchange for Annie's life. Cooper agrees, but Bob appears, taking Earle's soul for himself, consuming it by fire. Bob then turns to Cooper, who is chased about the lodge by a doppelgänger of himself.

Meanwhile, in town, Andrew Packard, Pete Martell, and Audrey Horne are caught in an explosion at a bank vault, a trap laid by the dead Eckhardt.

Cooper and Annie reappear in the woods, both injured. Annie is taken to hospital, but Cooper recovers in his room at the Great Northern Hotel. It becomes evident the Cooper who emerged from the Lodge is his doppelgänger, under Bob's demonic control. Cooper smashes his head into a bathroom mirror, laughing maniacally. The credits roll, and season two ends.

One of the reasons the show resonates is because of the archetypes. Death is Laura, denoting, in this instance, variation and rebirth.[581] Her

---

[581] Case, *The Tarot*, 145-146. As I mentioned in the Introduction, Death is Eric Harris and Dylan Klebold, who, personifying the Grim Reaper, transformed society. Their actions made us revisit gun laws, and they spawned a host of copycats forcing us to adapt to a new reality: a post-Columbine world of the internet and the 24-Hour News Cycle. See also Robert M. Place, *The Tarot, Magic,*

(Top left) Duality in *Twin Peaks*: in the Red Room *qua* Black Lodge, Laura appears to Cooper, saying, "Meanwhile," as she makes a hand gesture. (Bottom left) A few moments later, Laura's sinister doppelganger appears to Cooper, saying, "Meanwhile," making the same hand signal. "Meanwhile" is spoken twice, once by Laura and again by her evil double, denoting duality. The hand gesture comes from *Les Enfants du Paradis* (1945, English: *Children of Paradise*) wherein one of the characters, the mime Baptiste Debureau (Jean-Louis Barrault, 1910-1994), makes the same gesture (right). The French film is about a beautiful courtesan, Claire "Garance" Reine (Arletty, 1898-1992), and the four men who love her in their distinct ways: a mime artist, an actor, a criminal, and an aristocrat. The four men in Laura's life mirror this paradigm, nurturing her differently; two are harmful, and two are loving. Bob and Leland love her destructively, while Bobby and James love Laure affectionately.

ghastly murder transforms Twin Peaks from an insipid community into a town plagued by dark intrigue and mystery. Leland is the Hanged Man, the traitor who kills his daughter. Dangling upside-down helplessly, the Hanged Man *qua* Leland is in the grasp of fate; having no control of his destiny, Leland becomes possessed by Bob, opening the door for the FBI to investigate the community.[582] And speaking of Bob, he represents the destructive Tower; personifying archetypal hostility and wrath, he moves

---

Alchemy, Hermeticism, and Neoplatonism. 2nd ed. (Saugerties, NY: Hermes Publications, 2019) 447. Place explains: "Death and rebirth are essential themes in alchemy. Death is necessary if the matter of the work is to be reborn in a higher state, and it is a necessary part of the process of spiritual growth."
582 Nichols, *Jung and Tarot*, 215-216.

between matter (Twin Peaks) and spirit (the Black Lodge/Red or Waiting Room).[583] The cruel Devil is Leo Johnson, then Windom Earle. The sagacious philosopher is Deputy Tommy "Hawk" Hill (Michael Horse), having insights into the White and Black Lodges, understanding they have more to do with the perfection of the soul than with good and evil. The Fool resides in Twin Peaks, personified by the bumbling Deputy Andrew "Andy" Brennan (Harry Goaz). Despite being a simpleton, Andy realizes the cave petroglyph is a map of Twin Peaks, echoing the Fool's uncanny ability to perceive what ordinary people tend to overlook.[584] The moon–the sacred feminine–is personified in all three of her glorious phases. Four sexy, zestful maidens, Donna, Audrey, Maddy, and Shelly Johnson, embody the waxing moon. There is the full moon, the tragic mother Sarah Palmer, having lost her daughter, and the soon-to-be mother, Lucy Moran. There is the crone or waning moon, Margaret Lanterman (Catherine Coulson, 1943-2015), better known as the Log Lady, having an intuitive connection to the supernatural realm, much like Marietta Fortune in *Wild at Heart*. There are the Lovers: Sheriff Truman and Josie Packard, Donna and James, and Ed Hurley and Norma Jennings.

However, the one archetype that is the lynchpin (pun intended) is FBI Special Agent Dale Cooper. Agent Cooper is Mercury: instinctive and fluid. But more importantly, like Mercury, he is the Tarot's Magician, the great alchemical agent of transmogrification. Cooper-as-the-magician is hinted at by the madam of One-Eyed Jacks, Blackie O'Reilly (Victoria Catlin), who dabbles in Tarot. Mercury unifies opposites alchemically; thus, Cooper transcends the duality of *Twin Peaks*, perfecting the Magnum Opus, the *rubedo*, unlocking the secrets of the White and Black Lodges. Depending on the circumstances, this transition can be positive, negative, or odd mixture of both. For example, in the season two episode "Checkmate" (January 19, 1991), Jean Renault explains Cooper is an agent of change, Mercurius, only that in his opinion, it was negative. To Renault, Cooper lingers in the *nigredo*, stating, "Before you came here, Twin Peaks was a simple place. My brothers deal dope to the teenagers and the truck drivers. One-Eyed Jack's welcomed the businessmen and the tourists. Quiet people lived a quiet life. Then, a pretty girl dies, and you arrive, and everything

---

583 Ibid, 283-284.
584 Cavendish, *The Tarot*, 59-62.

change. My brother Bernard, shot and left to die in the woods. A grieving father smother my remaining brother with a pillow. Kidnapping. Death. Suddenly, the quiet people, they're quiet no more. Suddenly, the simple dream become the nightmare."

Cooper alters Twin Peaks' social fabric because Mercury is a trickster, happiest at play. He loves black coffee and pie as much as he loves being an FBI Agent. He likes uncovering and exploiting dark secrets, perfecting the double consciousness of the cosmic mode: the world is serious and trivial at the same time, a meaningful pattern of eternity and a filmy veil blocking the beyond. He speaks to the mysterious Diane, who may or may not exist, and meditates while hanging upside down.[585] While immersed in the *nigredo's* turbulence, Mercury can go-with-the-flow, integrating perfectly with the locals in Twin Peaks, rising above the current. Cooper can navigate hazardous and complex situations. In the *nigredo* phase, Mercurius can be a murderous spinster guided by the light of *Sol Niger*, like Sevigny's Lizzie Borden. It can be a capricious weirdo like *Blue Velvet*'s Frank Booth, or an unorthodox detective, apprehending criminals and intuitively solving crimes like Cooper Dale. Resolving into the crystal moonlight of the *albedo* and the solar rays of the *citrinitas*, Mercury stiffens into transparent geometry without forgetting the opaque flickers. He remains attuned throughout the *rubedo*, harmonizing spirit and matter. Embodying the *rubedo*, Mercury never dissolves into fecund material, nor does he stiffen into spiritual rectitude. It is transcendence and failure to transcend. It is annihilating darkness and the light that forms anew.[586] All the archetypes resonate because they exist in the collective unconscious being an expression of the eternal *unus mundus*.

Agent Cooper is the thaumaturgist mentioned in the poem: "Through the darkness of future's past / The magician longs to see / One chants out between two worlds / Fire walk with me." One of the most critical figures next to the Dali Lama was the Nechung Oracle. The Oracle interpreted divine messages from the gods, as a bridge between two worlds, Heaven and earth, the living and spirits. It was Cooper's duty to investigate the murder. Cooper communicates with the specters of the Lodges, relating

---

[585] *Diane* alludes to Diana the moon goddess, indicating the two worlds of Cooper *qua* the magician: temporal and spiritual.
[586] Wilson, *Secret Cinema*, 110.

this information as he investigates. Fusing logic with divination methods, a profound understanding of the esoteric and outside-the-box thinking, he calls out between two worlds as an oracle, solving the Giant's riddles, using the spirit world to solve temporal crimes.[587]

As Mercury the wonder-worker, only Cooper can navigate the two worlds mentioned in the poem. One is the township of Twin Peaks, and the other is the White and Black Lodges' metaphysical realms. Moving between the two worlds, he merges understanding of the spiritual and the material, deducing Laura's murderer is a combination of the two: a supernatural demon, Bob, inhabiting the body of a mortal, Leland. As if guided by a supernatural force, Cooper instinctively doodles the mysterious triangular marks on the Log Lady and Major Garland Briggs, combining them into one drawing. Cooper's enigmatic picture leads to Owl Cave, which conceals the map to the Black Lodge. The owl is a symbol of the Illuminati whose members, like the Freemasons, sought to shape society by perfecting themselves through arcane rituals.[588] Often, this involved a vast conspiracy; operating in secret, the members toiled behind the scenes of all secular and religious institutions and organizations so the profane masses could not discover their hidden agendas.

The two Lodges are not fraternities; instead, they are spiritual, psychological, and alchemical temples of transmogrification, involving the idea of individuation, Eckhart's synthesis of the soul. Nevertheless, the word *lodge* immediately conjures Freemasonry and, consequently, secret societies like the Illuminati; thus, these Lodges give off a nefarious fragrance. The White and Black Lodges evoke Crowley's *Moonchild*, his Rabelaisian novel about a group of white magicians battling a coven of black magicians over an unborn child. However, the motives of the white lodge may not be what they seem. A Crowley analog named Simon Iff leads the white magicians, while Arthwaite and SRMD command the black lodge. Arthwaite is Arthur E. Waite, and SRMD (*'S Rioghal Mo Dhream* or Royal Is My Race is the MacGregor Clan's motto) was created by S. L. MacGregor Mathers (1854-1918) using Notarikon, becoming his magical name. Theosophist Annie Besant (1847-1933) also makes an appearance,

---

[587] Zora Burden, "Another Place: The Esoteric Symbolism of Twin Peaks/Agent on the Threshold: The Taoism and Alchemy of Twin Peaks," *Zora Burden: Writer, Artist, Poet*, August 2015, https://zoraburden.weebly.com/the-esoteric-symbolism-of-twin-peaks.html (accessed August 1, 2019).
[588] Frost, *Secret History*, 64.

identified as A.B. Like Crowley, both Mathers and Waite were members of the Golden Dawn. Still, Crowley would come to believe they were frauds, perpetrating a hoax involving Secret Chiefs, so he branded them black magicians out of retribution.[589]

The owl's prominent imagery summons Minerva, the goddess of wisdom, and its symbolism associated with the Bavarian Illuminati. The owl is an emblem of enlightenment because it can see things in the dark, implying that only initiates of secret societies can observe the uncanny, unseen by the profane and vulgar. The owl is further linked to the Bohemian Grove, evoking Moloch, and a dark conspiracy. The Arthurian references to Glastonbury Grove, where the Black Lodge's portal is found–under the 12 sycamore trees–only adds to the show's occult leanings. The sycamore trees are leafless, indicating death and, thus, Left-Hand Path magic. They appear in the Egyptian *Book of Dead*. According to the text, two sycamore trees stood at the eastern gate of Heaven. Between the trees is where the mystical sun god, Amun-Ra, showed himself each morning. Adding to this mysticism, Glastonbury was also rumored to be the Holy Grail's hiding place, brought to England for safekeeping by Joseph of Arimathea. The door to the Black Lodge opens during a conjunction of Jupiter and Saturn. According to Agent Cooper, when they conjunct every 20 years, there are enormous shifts in power and fortune; Jupiter being expansive, and Saturn contractive. The two planets and the twelve trees *qua* zodiac revive the Hermetic axiom *as above, so below* mentioned by the Log Lady, when she introduces episode 9 titled "Coma" (airdate October 6, 1990). Easter egg: The Log Lady vignettes were written and directed by David Lynch in 1993 for the syndicated re-airing of the series on the Bravo network.

The two Lodges are sanctuaries wherein spiritual energies converge; although they seem diametric, they are interrelated as Yin-Yang principles, upper and lower truths. The Lodges' dualism reflects many esoteric belief systems: the Native American Twin Hero myth, the Solomonic pillars Jachin and Boaz ever-present in Freemasonry. Hinduism's Maya and Brahma, the *hieros gamos*, Tibetan Buddhism's Yab-Yum, Kabbalah's Pillars of Mercy (*Chokhmah*, *Chesed* and *Netzach*) and Severity (*Binah*,

---

589 In various occult movements, the Secret Chiefs are said to be transcendent cosmic authorities, a spiritual-mystical hierarchy responsible for the cosmos' operation, overseeing a magical order or lodge's activities and ritual workings.

Gevurah and *Hod*), and Yoga's Nadis theory. There's the *Rosarium Philosophorum*'s (1550) Hermetic Androgyne and the Pillars of Enoch *qua* Thoth Hermes Trismegistus. This magical duality is direct knowledge of creation, the art of nature, the science of the stars. The Black Lodge's entrance at Glastonbury Grove suggests the Chalice Well, signifying the Great Work. The portal is reminiscent of the *Porta Alchemica* legend, turning up in Native American lore as the Sipapu.[590]

Deputy Hawk explains the Lodges' ethereal functions in episode 18 titled "Masked Ball" (airdate December 15, 1990). Hawk enlightens Cooper about an old Native American myth surrounding them: "Cooper, you may be fearless in this world. But there are other worlds. My people believed that the White Lodge is a place where the spirits that rule man and nature here reside. There is also a legend of a place called the Black Lodge, the shadow self of the White Lodge. Legend says that every spirit must pass through there on the way to perfection. There, you will meet your own shadow self. My people call it: the Dweller on the Threshold. But it is said, if you confront the Black Lodge with imperfect courage, it will utterly annihilate your soul." Cooper, like a magician navigating these two worlds, is eager to gain this wisdom. He should understand the Jungian-alchemical significance of the metaphysical Lodges because the magician can initiate self-realization, the *rubedo*.

Applying Hawk's expertise to Jung's occult, depth psychology, the White Lodge denotes the positive ego, and the Black Lodge signifies the negative shadow self. Passing through the Black Lodge, the ego is afforded the chance to integrate with its shadow, becoming perfected. In other words, when the soul is fully integrated, positive and negative are one. This unification is also a meditation on alchemy; Eliphas Levi describes the Great Work arduously in his tome *Transcendental Magic*. Like Cooper *qua* the magician, the two Lodges serve to transcend the duality of Twin Peaks, initiating and consummating *coincidentia oppositorum*. It is the coalescing of male and female, order and chaos, light and dark, good and evil, representing *Twin Peaks*' duality. It is the moon, the *albedo*, personified by the woman of Twin Peaks, and the men, the solar *citrinitas*,

---

[590] Zora Burden, "Another Place: The Esoteric Symbolism of Twin Peaks/Agent on the Threshold: The Taoism and Alchemy of Twin Peaks," *Zora Burden: Writer, Artist, Poet*, August 2015, https://zoraburden.weebly.com/the-esoteric-symbolism-of-twin-peaks.html (accessed August 1, 2019).

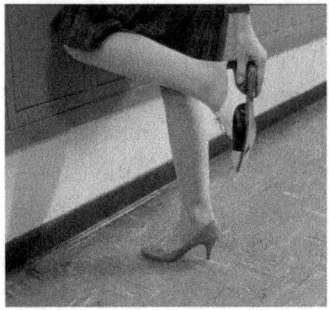

In *Twin Peaks*' Pilot, Audrey Horne exchanges her black and white saddle shoes for red high heels, suggesting the Union of Opposites, evil (black) and good (white) merged, resulting in the finality of the alchemical process, the *rubedo*. Hawk later explains that alchemical perfection is the function of the White and Black Lodges: the transmogrification of the soul, allowing it to achieve spiritual nirvana.

embodied by the town's men–more on this dichotomy in the *Fire Walk with Me* section. After the decomposition of the *nigredo* phase, the sun and moon unify; thus, the soul achieves alchemy's *rubedo* stage, marking the Magnum Opus' finality, self-realization, Jung's individuation. The pilot episode cleverly suggests this alchemical scheme. Audrey takes off her black and white saddle shoes, representing the White and Black Lodges, replacing them with red high heels, the *rubedo*, denoting that once black and white, viz. good and evil or light and dark integrate, the *rubedo* manifests. Audrey's talismanic shoes herald the magician's arrival to Twin Peaks: FBI Special Agent Dale Cooper, the archetype necessary to unlock the secrets of psychological alchemy.

This alchemical formula hides, not surprisingly, in other movies. Recall *Suspiria* '18, Susie is bathed in red when she declares herself Mater Suspiriorum because she has achieved consciousness of her identity, i.e., individuation; male and female are unified, personified by Dr. Klemperer, a man played by a woman: the syzygy (*vide supra*). In *Black Swan*, the club pulsates with flashing red lights, the *rubedo*, signaling her dark, erotic side is dormant no longer, having merged with her virginal, White Swan ego. When she dances in *Swan Lake* near the end, she is, once again, enveloped in red, the *rubedo* pervasive; as such, she can now dance the Black Swan. Through alchemy, Nina becomes birdlike, growing wings, enhancing her performance spectacularly (*vide supra*). Rid of the White Swan's innocence, Nina cannot comprehend her gnosis, her sexual alchemy; it consumes her, resulting in her tragic death. In *Mulholland Drive*, the dour Diane Selwyn cannot integrate her ego, the ebullient Betty Elms. To compensate, she masturbates chillingly, attempting to harm and pleasure herself, commingling love with hate simultaneously. In the end, Diane is overwhelmed by her guilty conscience, resulting in suicide, a gunshot to the head. Woe to the soul who fails in the Black Lodge, unable to integrate ego with shadow because they will be annihilated. Bob epitomizes evil, a corrupted demon, and it appears as though Laura is trapped, cleaved in half: spirit and doppelganger.

The White and Black lodges are not terrestrial, but mortals can gain access. The portal to the Black Lodge–and likely the White Lodge–is located in the dense forest surrounding Twin Peaks. The purpose of these lodges is alchemical-spiritual perfection, which, perhaps, explains why Lynch imbues these lodges, and their surrounding environments, with the iconography of secret societies like the Freemasons, Illuminati, and Bohemian Grove. Many of the rituals of secret societies involve the quest for perfection. For example, in the Scottish Rite, degrees 4-14 are known as the Lodge of Perfection wherein the candidate, in the 13th Royal Arch of Enoch degree, beholds the Tetragrammaton, achieving apotheosis, signaling a return to a pre-Fall of Eden state of perfection, embodying the kabalistic (or cabalistic) ideal, Adam Kadmon, the Gnostic Anthropos. This occult philosophy underlies Martinism; this holy perfection is known as *exaltation* in Masonry's York Rite.

Furthermore, these positive and negative temples explain why everything in Twin Peaks is colored red; the hue haunts the town like a crimson specter, from curtains to floor tiles, to the Black Lodge's strange Waiting Room. Red is the *rubedo,* designating the Lodges' function: psychical magnificence, *Moksha,* completion of the alchemical work, individuation. This alchemical exemplum is a parable from the New Testament (John 2:1-10) when Jesus turns water into wine. The water represents base metal or ignorance, and the wine is gold *qua* perfection; wine is red, viz. the *rubedo*, individuation. Finally, there is a Saturn lamp in the Red Room–its symbolism now evident. It is an emblem of the *nigredo*: the dark shade of the Black Lodge, its somber souls; it is the ravages of time. The *nigredo qua* Saturn is death and decay, annihilating those fearful souls unable to integrate ego with shadow self; thus, Saturn is the reaper, devouring its children.

Ultimately, Cooper *qua* the magician confronts then wrestles with his shadow. His purpose is clear: to help the fallen souls trapped in the Black Lodge achieve self-fulfillment or individuation, to complete the alchemical process; such is the modus operandi of the magician/juggler/trickster archetype. After a brief struggle, during which strobe light illuminates the Red Room, Copper returns to reality. However, it is not the genuine Cooper sent back, but a doppelganger possessed by Bob. The real Cooper, it seems, is trapped in the Black Lodge. It appears as though the White and Black Lodges not only represent duality, but the Black Lodge generates duality: doppelgangers of the personas who fail to integrate their shadow selves properly. Easter egg: the flashing strobe light represents the eternal Manichean conflict of good and evil. The strobe effect suggests light and dark or good and evil are interdependent; when they clash, helter-skelter ensues. In the morgue, the light flickers when Cooper discovers the tiny note under Laura's fingernail, auguring her killer's identity. We find a flickering light and sparking electricity when Henry confronts *Eraserhead*'s giant serpentine infant, defeating it and the Man in the Planet, finding salvation in the Lady in the Radiator's welcoming arms. *Mulholland Drive* echoes this method when the Cowboy (Monty Montgomery), personifying Lucifer the Light Bearer, the bringer of wisdom, appears on-screen. When he approaches Adam Kesher (Justin Theroux), the light flickers on, signifying the en*light*enment he bears. After speaking to Adam, he walks away, so the light flickers off because Lucifer has returned to his shadowy recesses, disappearing into the night.

Alchemy crops up toward the end of Season 2. Earle, a *Red King*, searches for his *White Queen*, Annie, representing the sun and moon's merger, male and female, *albedo* and *citrinitas*, the Union of Opposites, syzygy, implying the White and Black Lodges' methodology. The Lodges' function further suggests Meister Eckhart's theories regarding the soul's union with God. Ergo, Cooper *qua* the magician solves the Lodges' mystery upon the arrival of Thomas Eckhardt (no surprise). Eckhardt is named after Eckhart von Hochheim, more commonly known as Meister Eckhart. He was a medieval German philosopher and mystic whose negative theology was interpreted by Jung, identifying him as a Gnostic Christian. Eckhart saw Christ as the archetypal self; he preached the soul's four-stage union with God: dissimilarity, similarity, identity, and breakthrough, influencing Jung's psychological alchemy and individuation theories.

A strange black puzzle box left by Eckhardt is given to Catherine Martell. It is implied that opening the box will result in a fortune or a valuable secret. Glyphs and astrological symbols are engraved upon the box, confusing the uninitiated, so Catherine, Andrew Packard, and Pete try to open the box by force. Andrew manages to open it properly, but frustration ensues because the opened box reveals an impenetrable metal cube. Andrew and Pete try and destroy it in a desperate attempt to find the treasure inside. Andrew says, "Maybe it's not a box at all. Maybe it's just a block of stainless steel. Eckhardt's last little joke." They are looking at a mere lead block, suggesting a failed attempt in the alchemical process to turn base metal into the gold of enlightenment. Their crude understanding of spirituality has been corrupted by their greed and ignorance identified by the lead cube. A fired bullet destroys the lead block; inside, a key is found leading to the bank vault. There is no treasure but a bomb, their demise.

Twin Peaks' impact upon popular culture is substantial. With its reference to Project Blue Book and UFOs, we see an influence on *The X-Files* (1993-2018); in fact, some of the first episodes of *The X-Files* were set in the Northwest of the United States, making them feel like crossover episodes. Duchovny aside, actor Don S. Davis (*Twin Peaks'* Major Garland Briggs) played FBI Agent Dana Scully's (Gillian Anderson) father, Captain William Scully, in the episodes "Beyond the Sea" (airdate January 7, 1994), and "One Breath" (airdate November 11, 1994). Richard Beymer, *Twin Peaks'* megalomaniac Benjamin Horne, played Dr. Jack Franklyn in "Sanguinarium" (airdate November 10, 1996). Kenneth Welsh, the ever-evil Windom Earle, played Simon Gates in "Revelations" (airdate December 15, 1995). The Man from Another Place, Michael J. Anderson, played Mr. Nutt, a trailer park landlord in "Humbug" (airdate March 31, 1995). Michael Horse, Deputy Hawk, played Sheriff Tskany in "Shapes" (airdate April 1, 1994). These roles are but a sampling of the actors from *Twin Peaks* who also appeared on *The X-Files*.

Twin Peaks influenced other television shows, including, but not limited to, *Lost* (2004-2010), *The Bates Motel* (2013-2017), and *Breaking Bad* (2008-2013). Don't get me wrong, I like Seasons 1 and 2, but the tropes are overt. Sure, there are plenty of esoteric undercurrents, but nothing too challenging to discover or decode. Why is this the case? The answer: Lynch likes to use the same device over and over again: duality. It is omnipresent in all his work in some form or fashion. Once identified (which isn't too difficult), his creations become much easier to decipher contextually, and the underlying themes rise to the surface. Next, fire walk with me as I analyze, what else, but *Twin Peaks: Fire Walk with Me* (1992), the prequel to the television series.

Twin Peaks: Fire Walk with Me

Twin Peaks: Fire Walk with Me is a psychological horror film directed by Lynch, written by him and Robert Engels. It documents the investigation into the murder of Teresa Banks (Pamela Gidley) and the last seven days in Laura Palmer's life. *Fire Walk with Me* initially received negative reviews in the United States but has been met with a more positive reception in subsequent years, with some critics viewing it as one of Lynch's essential works. Although it has long been reported that *Fire Walk with Me* was greeted at the 1992 Cannes Film Festival with boos and jeers from the audience, cowriter Engels denies this ever happened. It was a box office bomb domestically, although it fared much better in Japan. Though it appears to feature a struggle between good and evil, it is a weird fable of the inevitable interdependence between evil and good, transgression and charity. It plays out like an inverted fairy tale. The film introduces a mysterious green ring and creamed corn (or a substance appearing like creamed corn), called *garmonbozia*, augmenting the show's strange mythology. I find this movie less interesting than Lynch's other films, but analysis is unavoidable when presenting a section on *Twin Peaks*. To watch it without the benefit of first viewing the television show is impossible; in other words, the movie does not stand alone and would make little sense without pre-knowledge of the TV show's mythos.

FBI Regional Bureau Chief Gordon Cole sends agents Chester Desmond (Chris Isaak) and Sam Stanley (Kiefer Sutherland) to investigate the murder of drifter and teenage prostitute Teresa Banks in the town of Deer Meadow, Washington. The antics of a mime named Lil (Kimberly Ann Cole, billed as Lil the Dancer) informs the pair of their new assignment. Although her moves are inexplicable, she holds all the answers. Clad in a red dress–heralding *Twin Peaks' rubedo*–with an artificial blue rose on her lapel; when Sam asks about the flower, Chester replies, "But I can't tell you about that." A Blue Rose Case is a top-secret investigation, designated by

Cole because of its relation to the supernatural.[591] It is safe to assume that a Blue Rose Case is the forerunner of an X-File: the government's classified investigations into the paranormal. Easter egg: Chester Desmond is yet another allusion to *Sunset Boulevard*. The agent is named after Norma Desmond, as is Norma Jennings.

Desmond and Stanley examine Teresa's body in the morgue of the local sheriff's department. They notice a ring is missing from her finger, and a small piece of paper with the letter *T* inserted underneath one of her fingernails. The ring has a green stone inlaid into a gold band. The stone has a carved-winged owl symbol upon it, the same as the petroglyph in Owl Cave. Later, Desmond discovers the ring under a trailer. As he reaches out for it, he disappears, taken by an unseen force.

At the FBI headquarters in Philadelphia, Cooper tells Cole of a dream involving their long-lost colleague Agent Phillip Jeffries (David Bowie, 1947-2016). In the vision, Cooper tries to create his doppelganger by standing in the hallway, allowing the video surveillance camera to capture his appearance on the monitor. Cooper moves between the camera and the monitor to see if his image is left behind in the hallway, allowing him to see himself. When this finally occurs–foreshadowing Cole's doppelganger during the last episode of Season 2–the enigmatic Jeffries steps out of an elevator onto the seventh floor. The number seven is critical within both religion and the occult world as it associates with the numinous and mysterious. I have discussed its mysticism in my past books, so I will, once again, reiterate its importance here.

In Revelation, Jesus Christ stands among seven golden candlesticks, explaining: "The mystery of the seven stars that you saw in my right hand and of the seven golden lampstands is this: The seven stars are the angels of the seven churches, and the seven lampstands are the seven churches" (Rev. 1:20). Lamech, a patriarch in the genealogies of both Adam (Gen. 5:25) and Jesus (Luke 3:36), lived 777 years (Gen. 5:31). In Prague's St. Vitus Cathedral, seven keys unlock the Coronation Chamber, containing the ancient Crown of Charlemagne and the sword and crown (dating from 1345) of St. Wenceslas. Crowley wrote a *Liber 777*, becoming *777 and Other Qabalistic Writings* (1909), explaining Hermeticism, Kabbalah, mythology, and magic. There are seven Japanese gods of luck, and the

---

591 Stewart, *David Lynch Decoded*, 51.

Virgin Mary is said to have experienced seven joys and seven sorrows, inferring *coincidentia oppositorum*. Pan, the god of the wild and seducer of nymphs, played a shepherd's pipe with seven reeds, enchanting all those that heard its tune.[592] In Dickens' *A Christmas Carol* (1843), Jacob Marley has been dead for seven years, having died seven years to the day of the book's events, offering Ebenezer Scrooge absolution for his transgressions. In *The Mummy's Hand* (1940) and *The Mummy's Tomb* (1942), the Hill of the Seven Jackals hides Kharis and Princess Ananka's sanctuary, protected by the High Priest of Karnak.[593] Tom Tyron's (1926-1991) titular festival, Harvest Home, occurs once every seven years.[594]

On number seven, Masonic magus Albert Pike writes:

> The world, the ancients believed, was governed by Seven Secondary Causes; and these were the universal forces, known to the Hebrews by the plural name ELOHIM. These forces, analogous and contrary one to the other, produce equilibrium by their contrasts, and regulate the movements of the spheres. The Hebrews called them the Seven great Archangels, and gave them names, each of which, being a combination of another word with AL, the first Phœnician Nature-God, considered as the Principle of Light, represented them as His manifestations. Other peoples assigned to these Spirits the government of the Seven Planets then known, and gave them the names of their great divinities.
>
> So, in the Kabala, the last Seven Sephiroth constituted ATIK YOMIN, the Ancient of Days; and these, as well as the Seven planets, correspond with the Seven colors separated by the prism, and the Seven notes of the musical octave.
>
> Seven is the sacred number in all theogonies and all symbols, because it is composed of 3 and 4. It represents the magical power in its full force. It is the Spirit assisted by all the Elementary Powers, the Soul served

---

[592] Alexander S. Murray, *Manual of Mythology: Greek and Roman, Norse, and Old German, Hindu and Egyptian Mythology*, 2nd revised ed. (New York: Charles Scribner's Sons, 1893), 136-137.

[593] In *The Mummy's Hand*, Kharis was played by Tom Tyler (1903-1954), and, in *The Mummy's Tomb*, by Lon Chaney Jr. In the former, the High Priest of Karnak was played by Eduardo Ciannelli (1888-1969), and in the latter by George Zucco.

[594] *Harvest Home* was published in 1973; it was made into a TV miniseries, *The Dark Secret of Harvest Home*, in 1978.

> by Nature, the Holy Empire spoken of in the clavicules of Solomon, symbolized by a warrior, crowned, bearing a triangle on his cuirass, and standing on a cube, to which are harnessed two Sphinxes, one white and the other black, pulling contrary ways, and turning the head to look backward.
>
> The vices are Seven, like the virtues; and the latter were anciently symbolized by the Seven Celestial bodies then known as planets.[595]

The number seven signals that Cooper's vision is supernatural, a product of higher consciousness, likely from the Black Lodge.

Jeffries mentions Judy, then tells them about a meeting held in a room above a convenience store. The gathering he witnessed involved several mystifying apparitions: the Man from Another Place, an electrician, Bob, Mrs. Chalfont, and her grandson, Pierre (Jonathan J. Leppell). During this bizarre sequence, Lynch makes a point to move the camera inside a mouth, speaking the word *electricity*. The scene even bears the word's subtitle so that we do not miss its importance. "We live inside a dream," Jeffries states emphatically before vanishing into thin air. Jeffries' declaration, coupled with Donna's line, "Maybe our dreams are real" ("The Orchid's Curse," airdate October 27, 1990) are (so far) *Twin Peaks*' brush with Valentinian Gnosticism, insinuating the world is an illusion controlled by archons and the Demiurge. Easter egg: utility poles and powerlines appear repeatedly, and we hear the word *electricity* uttered in the room above the convenience store. By doing this, Lynch strips electricity of its scientific properties, transforming it into a mystical conduit, connecting material reality to the spiritual world. Mathers described an electric, almost unbearable, intense pressure when in the presence of the Golden Dawn's Secret Chiefs.[596] Lynch uses electricity to convey the same thing in another of his movies. In *Eraserhead*, during Henry's final confrontation with the snakelike baby, a wall light flashes and electrical sparks discharge, signifying his rejection of the sublunary world in favor of gnosis.

One will recall Mrs. Chalfont and Pierre from the Season 2 episode titled "Coma." When Donna assumed Laura's Meals on Wheels route, she visited Mrs. Tremond only to find the home occupied by Mrs. Chalfont

---
595 Pike, *Morals and Dogma*, 727.
596 Churton, *Occult Paris*, 405.

posing as a bedridden Tremond, with Pierre–introduced as a magician–sitting in a chair nearby. Mrs. Chalfont made the creamed corn disappear–more on the symbolism of the creamed corn later.

Meanwhile, Agent Cooper is dispatched to Deer Meadow to investigate Agent Desmond's disappearance but finds no answers.

A year later, in Twin Peaks, homecoming queen Laura Palmer and her best friend, Donna Hayward (now Moira Kelly), attend high school. Laura is addicted to cocaine and is cheating on her boyfriend, the arrogant and ill-tempered jock Bobby Briggs, with the biker James Hurley. Laura realizes pages are missing from her secret diary, so she gives it to her friend, the agoraphobic recluse Harold Smith. Mrs. Chalfont and her grandson appear to Laura. Outside the Double R Diner, they give Laura a framed picture of a doorway; Chalfont tells her, "this would look nice on your wall." They also warn her the "man behind the mask" is looking for her diary, "the book with the pages torn out," and he's "going toward the hiding place." Laura runs home, where she encounters Bob in her bedroom. Terrified, Laura rushes outside and hides, only to be further startled when she sees her father, Leland, exit the house. She breaks down, crying. But for the mysterious duo, Laura may not have been able to connect the dots that Bob possesses her father. That evening Leland's behavior is erratic and abusive; he accusingly asks her about her romances, then tenderly tells her he loves her.

The picture, which she hangs on her bedroom's wall, instigates Laura's dream. Beckoned to enter by Mrs. Chalfont, she next encounters Pierre, who snaps his fingers, illuminating the room, transporting her to the Red Room *qua* Black Lodge. The Man from Another Place informs Cooper that "I am the arm," revealing his identity as Mike's severed appendage, and offers Teresa's green ring to Laura, but Cooper tells her not to take it. Laura finds Annie Blackburn next to her in bed, covered in blood. Annie tells Laura to write in her diary "the good Dale is in the Lodge and cannot leave." Laura sees the ring in her hand, but it's gone when she wakes up the next morning.

Later that evening, Laura goes to the Bang Bang Bar (nicknamed the Roadhouse) to meet her drug connections and have sex with strange men. Outside the bar, a dog trots behind Laura. In Lynch's cinematic reality, the canine indicates something critical is about to occur. And it does: Laura bumps into the Log Lady, who offers her a chance at redemption, to leave the negative path she has chosen. Like a shaman, the Log Lady places her right hand (implying Right-Hand Path sorcery, white magic) on Laura's forehead, telling her, "When this kind of fire starts, it is very hard to put out. The tender boughs of innocence burn first, and the wind rises, and then all goodness is in jeopardy." It is not too late to save herself, reject Bob, but Laura must abandon her self-destructive behavior. Although the encounter moves Laura, she cannot or does not want to forsake the Left-Hand Path. As she expressed earlier, she is falling "faster and faster" and will "burst into fire."[597]

Inside the bar, a chanteuse, before red curtains, illuminated by a blue spotlight, gives us a peek into Laura's heart as she harmonizes the questions that resound in her mind. "Questions in a World of Blue" is the jam, and the performer (Julee Cruise) sings about life's vicissitudes, hinting at Laura's descent. She now walks a path of destruction when she was once full of happiness and love. All of the questions posed by the song's lyrics are questions Laura is secretly asking herself, but there are no answers. These questions are asked in a melancholic world of blue, wherein she is trapped by her secrets, feeling there is no way out. Unfortunately, lost as she is, Laura will fail to find love in this hellish reality, not until after her death.[598] Listening to the song, she begins to weep, suffering the same maudlin sadness experienced by Frank Booth when Suave Ben lip-synched Roy Orbison's "In Dreams." *Blue Velvet*'s theatre of the absurd anticipates *Mulholland Drive*'s Betty's and Rita's sappy lamentations when Rebekah Del Rio lip-synchs Orbison's "Crying" in Spanish.

Sitting at a table, Laura does not realize Donna followed her, who she ditched earlier in the evening. Laura is joined by two men, offering her money for sex. She is floored when Donna comes over, insisting they leave. Proving she can hold her own, Donna hits the bottle, prompting Laura to kiss one of the men, Buck (Victor Rivers). Donna then kisses the other man, like an erotic game. Next, Laura one-ups the situation by taking them to a separate bar where one can engage the excesses of the flesh–sex, drugs, booze, and rock 'n roll–with impunity. The room is saturated red, conjuring the fires of Hell with its lust and gluttony circles. Laura discusses Teresa

---
597 Stewart, *David Lynch Decoded*, 56.
598 Ibid.

Banks's murder with Ronette Pulaski, and Ronette says that Teresa was trying to blackmail someone. Laura casually takes off her jacket, discarding it. Like it was a sacred talisman, Donna finds it and puts it on, transforming her into a slut. When Laura sees a topless Donna making out with a stranger, she freaks out, yelling, "Don't ever wear my stuff! Never!" With the help of Jacques Renault, Donna is taken home immediately.

The next morning, in Laura's living room, she admonishes Donna again, "I don't want you to wear my stuff…I don't want you to be like me." Deriving self-gratification by wearing another's clothing is masturbatory fetishism; Donna takes pleasure in mimicry by putting on Laura's jacket, adopting the temptress' sensual personality, becoming promiscuous and indulgent. She has harnessed Laura's sexual energy by donning her clothing, changing her from schoolgirl to femme fatale, echoing the show's alchemical storyline. Although Donna is scolded and told never to do it again, her flesh is insatiable, succumbing once more to this odd fetishism, a corruption of supernatural energy. In the Season 2 episode "May the Giant Be with You," Donna asks Maddy for Laura's sunglasses, and she obliges. After she puts them on, Donna again acts like Laura by smoking, becoming a vamp with her boyfriend James (Laura's ex-boyfriend), behaving rebellious and detached. The jacket and the shades are Mercury, the Goat of Mendes, formulating alchemy by transmogrifying Donna into a siren, but without a Philosopher's Stone, the transition is imperfect and temporary. Easter egg: I employed this same fixation in my novel *A Pact with the Devil*. One of the witches, Elizabeth Burnblack, seeks out the lingerie and garments of another witch, believing if she wears it, she will experience dark ecstasy, harnessing that witch's power and sorcery.

As Donna and Laura reconcile, Leyland enters, telling his daughter they have to meet up with Mrs. Palmer for breakfast. As they drive along, Philip Gerard, the one-armed man possessed by the repentant archon *qua* demon Mike, attempts to warn Laura about her father and Bob. He pulls up alongside Leland's car, yelling that he stole his corn, suggesting Bob and Leland are the same. Intercut with this scene is a barking dog (something wicked this way comes); then, Mike shows Laura the green ring before speeding off. Pulling into a gas station, Leland recalls his affair with Teresa. He had asked Teresa to set up a foursome and invite some of her friends but fled when he discovered Laura was among them. Teresa realized who he was and plotted to blackmail him, so he killed her to keep his secret safe. Laura realizes that Mike's ring was the one from her dream, and was also worn by Teresa.

Upset, Laura uses more cocaine and has trouble concentrating at school. Laura disses James, and that night Sarah Palmer has a vision of a white horse, conjuring the pale horse rode by death in Revelation, foreshadowing her daughter's demise. Later, Bob comes through Laura's window and begins to rape her, transforming into Leland. Next, Bobby, realizing that Laura is only using him to score cocaine, breaks off their relationship.

Laura's fall from grace is cemented when she goes to a cabin in the woods for an orgy with Ronette, Jacques, and Leo. Donning her black stockings, tokens of her shadow self, she is now ready to explore her darkest sexual desires: bondage and humiliation. First, she sneaks out of her house to meet up with James. Acting possessed, she jumps off the back of his motorcycle, leaving him. She meets up with the trio, and they go to the cabin. Leland follows her there and, after attacking Jacques and scaring away Leo, takes the two girls to an abandoned train car.

Laura asks her father if he's going to kill her, but he transforms into Bob, placing a mirror before her. Laura's reflection turns into the denim-wearing demon, signaling his intent to possess her. "I want you," Bob tells her. Ronette prays to God, seeking forgiveness; the godhead hears her and sends an angel (Karen Robinson), freeing her from her bonds–more on the angel symbolism in a moment. Meanwhile, Mike tracks the Bob-possessed Leland to the train, but when Ronette tries to let him in, Bob/Leland strikes her, knocking her unconscious. Mike manages to toss Teresa's ring into the train car, rescuing Ronette by pulling her out. Laura slips on the ring, which prevents Bob from possessing her. Enraged, Bob stabs Laura to death. He removes the half-heart pendant from her neck. Mike walks off, leaving an unconscious Ronette behind. The Bob-possessed Leland then wraps Laura's body in plastic and sets it adrift in the lake.

As her corpse floats away, the Bob-possessed Leland enters the Red Room *qua* Black Lodge, wherein he encounters Mike and the Man from Another Place; unified, they demand their share of garmonbozia. A monkey's face materializes, and a disembodied voice speaks the name, *Judy*. We then see Laura's corpse wrapped in plastic. The plastic is pulled back, revealing her face. Laura's spirit appears in what seems to be the

White Lodge with Cooper by her side. Why is Cooper there? I have no fucking clue suffice to say the reader's guess is as good as mine.

At first, Laura appears sad, but then happy as an angel floats overhead. Her face is washed in blue light, resembling the singer performing at the Roadhouse earlier, signifying she has passed beyond the melancholic world of blue. The end presents an epistemological crisis because the White Lodge is identical to the Black Lodge, with the lamp of Saturn, the red curtains, the Venus Pudica statue, and the zig-zag carpet. How are we to differentiate between the two Lodges if they are identical or, worst of all, the White and Black Lodges are the same. Or is Lynch obfuscating for the sake of obfuscating, deliberately trying to confuse the viewer, such as is the case with *Lost Highway*?

* * * * *

Observe the ceiling fan in the Palmer home in both *Twin Peaks* and *Fire Walk with Me*, signaling Bob's demonic presence and the father-daughter incest pervading the household. At the top of the staircase, above the landing where Leland crosses from the master bedroom to his daughter's room, the ceiling fan hovers, destroying the home's safety and security. In *Fire Walk with Me*, close-ups of the ceiling fan are intercut with Laura on the staircase looking up at the fan, as she hears Bob whisper to her, "I want to taste through your mouth." This scene points to further transgressions beyond the taboo of incest, because Bob desires to possess Laura completely, violating the boundary that separates not just bodies but souls. Laura is shot from a high angle, emphasizing her lack of power as she looks upward. Bob is not physically present, but his voice overwhelms her, seemingly coming from above, invading her mind, penetrating her soul. His presence, emanating from the fan as it circulates, violates the home's domestic tranquility. Laura has no sanctuary; she is lost, doomed, and she knows it.[599] One is left to ponder *Angel Heart*'s fans and elevator gears. Their endless clockwise and counterclockwise rotations represent the eternal conflict of good against evil, order and chaos, Mani's cosmological dualism.

Garmonbozia is a yellow substance that looks like or is creamed corn, synonymous with pain and sorrow. It is a source of sustenance for certain spirits, including the Man from Another Place. While in the room above

---

599 Hallam, "Women's Films: Melodrama and Women's Trauma in the Films of David Lynch," 23.

the convenience store, sitting at the green Formica table, the Man from Another Place smiles at several bowls of creamed corn, identifying them as garmonbozia. Phillip Gerard, Mike's host, accuses Bob/Leland of stealing "corn" he had "canned over the store." After killing Laura, Bob and Leland appear in the Red Room before Mike and the Man from Another Place, both of whom demanded, in unison: "Bob, I want all my garmonbozia." In response, Bob holds his hand to Leland's stomach wound, causing it to disappear, throwing blood onto the floor. Moments later, the Man from Another Place eats a spoonful of creamed corn. The strange term may come from the word *ambrosia*, the food that was said to sustain the ancient Greek gods, keeping them immortal.

Twin Peaks is all about achieving alchemical-spiritual perfection, psychological unity, signified by the White and Black Lodges. Duality transcends; we have the *nigredo*: Laura's death, the Saturn lamp, Earle, Bob, and Leland. We have the moon, the *albedo*, the sacred feminine, represented by the nocturnal orb, frequently glowing during the television show, personified by Laura, Donna, Josie, Maddy, the Log Lady, Lucy, Shelly, Nadine, Catherine, Norma, and Audrey. We have the *citrinitas*, the divine masculine, the sun, represented by Hawk, Truman, Andy, Benjamin, Pete, Cooper, Bobby, Ed, and James. Like the moon, the men are represented by the burning cinders in fireplaces we see so often, alluding to solar fire. Red saturates the town, the *rubedo*. Since the men dole out pain and suffering, such as Leo, Earle, Leland-Bob, the Renaults, and Benjamin, it is only natural that a yellow substance, creamed corn, represents their evil, alluding to alchemy. The yellow sun, and thus the creamed corn, associate with the masculine and the masculine only. In the television episode "Coma," Donna brings Mrs. Tremond (who is Mrs. Chalfont) a meal with creamed corn. Chalfont asks, "Do you see creamed corn on that plate? ... I requested no creamed corn." She doesn't want it because she personifies the silvery moon, not the diurnal orb. When she asks again if Donna sees creamed corn, the corn has vanished. Pierre is holding the yellow corn because he is a male, the *citrinitas*, the sun. The corn then disappears once more, presumably to the Black Lodge to be consumed by the Man from Another Place.

Accompanying the ring is a green Formica table in the room above the convenience store. When dealing with alchemy, green evokes one thing: the

The Man from Another Place (aka the Arm) presents the green ring in *Twin Peaks: Fire Walk with Me*.

Emerald Tablet of Hermes Trismegistus, the Threefold Sage. The Emerald Tablet is a cryptic piece of Hermeticism reputed to preserve the secret of the *prima materia* and its transmutation. European alchemists highly regarded it as the foundation of their art and the occult tradition. On its alchemical occultism, Isaac Newton writes, "Inferior and superior, fixed and volatile, Sulphur and quicksilver have a similar nature and are one thing, like man and wife. For they differ from one another only by degree of digestion and maturity. Sulphur is mature quicksilver, and quicksilver is immature Sulphur: and on account of this affinity they unite like male and female, and they act on each other, and through that action they are mutually transmuted into each other and procreate a more noble offspring to accomplish the miracles of this one thing. And just as all things were created from one Chaos by the design of one God, so in our art all things ... are born from this one thing which is our Chaos, by the design of the Artificer and the skilful [sic] adaptation of things. And the generation of this is similar to the human, truly from a father and mother."[600] Blavatsky explains, "The mysterious thing 'is the universal, magical agent, the astral light, which in the correlations of its forces furnishes the alkahest, the philosopher's stone, and the elixir of life. Hermetic philosophy names it Azoth, the soul of the world, the celestial virgin, the great Magnes, etc.' It appears to be that which gives organization ('the maze of force-correlations'), and form i.e. [sic] the perfect geometry of snowflakes."[601] The Man from Another Place holds the ring aloft, saying, "With this ring, I thee wed," representing

---

600 Hermes Trismegistus, *The Emerald Tablet of Hermes* (Merchant Books), 35.
601 Ibid, 35-36.

the alchemical treatise *The Chymical Wedding of Christian Rosenkreutz*, documenting the marriage of the sun and moon.

Suppose the green Formica table represents the Emerald Tablet. In that case, one presumes the ring is a piece of the table (or related to it), akin to the Chintamani Stone: a wish-fulfilling jewel within both Hindu and Buddhist traditions, said by some to be the equivalent of the Philosopher's Stone in Western alchemy. It is one of several Mani Jewel images found in Buddhist scripture. The Chintamani Stone was thought to be possessed by Russian mystic Nicholas Roerich (1874-1947), who had obtained the stone from Ascended Masters in Tibet, Shambala. Likewise, *Twin Peaks*' green ring has a lost, occult history. In September 1805, the Corps of Discovery contacted the Nez Perce tribe in northwestern Washington and treated with their chief, Twisted Hair. The chief told the Freemason, Meriwether Lewis (1774-1809), about a sacred grove above the nearby falls where several white men lived, giving him three bizarre artifacts, they had given to the tribe. One of these was an inscribed gold ring that Lewis sketched for President Thomas Jefferson in a dispatch. After visiting the sacred place, Lewis destroyed the map but wrote that he intended to keep the ring. Lewis further reported that Twisted Hair had allowed him to take the ring with him, but at the same time also emphatically warned him to keep the ring in a small leather pouch at all times and never to try to wear it on his fingers. After Lewis' mysterious death at Grinder's Stand in October 1809, the leather pouch which Priscilla Grinder had seen him worrying the night before his death was found in his possessions, empty. Major Garland Briggs posited that the traitor Major James Neely had a hand in Lewis' death, speculating he might have taken the ring. Briggs notes Neely had been seen by witnesses wearing some of the deceased Lewis' clothes in the days after the governor's death. Briggs also noted that Neely disappeared under mysterious circumstances shortly after these sightings were reported. With this, all traces of the ring disappeared from known history for over a century.[602]

In August 1945, L. Ron Hubbard (1911-1986) attended a Thelema gathering at the Parsonage, the Pasadena home of rocket scientist Jack Parsons, the leading disciple of Crowley in America. During a conversation between the two that Hubbard later recounted for Congressman Richard

---

[602] Frost, *Secret History*, 3-40, *passim*.

CINEMA SYMBOLISM 3

Nixon (1913-1994), Hubbard noticed the rocket man fiddling with an inscribed gold ring on his left ring finger as he expounded on the tenets of Thelema and the nature of alchemy. Following this, Colonel Douglas Milford met with Parsons on two occasions; the first time on December 3, 1949, to gather intel on him for Project Grudge. The second on June 15, 1952, just two days before Parsons' mysterious death. Posing as a journalist from a left-wing magazine, Milford got an extensive interview with Parsons both times. During both meetings, Milford noticed that Parsons was wearing a jade green ring on his right hand. Notably, when Parsons died on June 17, 1952, burning out his fuse in an unexplained explosion during an experiment he was conducting in his apartment, his right arm was by all appearances obliterated in the blast, and no trace it of it was ever found. During a private meeting with Richard Nixon, now President of the United States, on February 19, 1973, at Nixon's compound on Key Biscayne, Florida, Douglas Milford noticed Nixon wearing a green ring on the ring finger of his right hand.[603]

Although the MacGuffin wards off Bob, it is a bad omen with catastrophe descending upon those who dare to put it on their finger.

Finally, Lynch uses angels to give the White Lodge and Judeo-Christian vibe; it is the first time he uses seraphs, presenting them as guardians, or cacodemons to those who dare forsake their trust. The first mention of an angel occurs in a dialog between Donna and Laura. Donna inquires, "Do you think that if you were falling in space, you would slow down after a while or go faster and faster?" Laura has a distant look in her eye, replying, "Faster and faster. And for a long time, you wouldn't feel anything. And then you'd burst into fire, forever. And the angels wouldn't help you. Because they've all gone away." Laura sees angels as entities that will not help her, suggesting a blurry awareness of the supernatural plane she will soon join.[604]

An angel appears in a small picture decorating Laura's bedroom wall. It depicts an archetypal seraph in white robes with feathered wings, serving children a meal. She gazes at the picture for strength and inspiration, even going so far as to question it tearfully regarding Bob's relation to her father. Finally, on the night of her death, she looks to the picture, seeking divine

---

603 Ibid, 243-266, *passim*.
604 Stewart, *David Lynch Decoded*, 51.

intervention. But the angel vanishes, foreshadowing her death, reinforcing her belief they will not help her because she has abandoned virtue, choosing self-destruction instead.

Inside the train car, an angel frees Ronette from her bonds but does nothing to help Laura. In the White Lodge, an angel (Lorna MacMillan) hovers before her, signifying divine mercy. Laura, it seems, has been forgiven for her transgressions. The screen fades to luminous white, indicating she has ascended to Heaven *qua* the White Lodge. Lynch used this same dissolve in *The Elephant Man* when John Merrick dies, suggesting he has entered Heaven. He repeats this device in *Mulholland Drive*: after Diane shoots herself, we see her as Betty in the afterlife, illuminated joyously, beside her lover Rita. Laura's tormented soul is allowed to rest in peace, at least for a little while.

Fire Walk with Me's climax was the end of *Twin Peaks*. The television show was canceled, and no more movies were produced. Twenty-five years passed, just like Laura predicted.

Twin Peaks: The Return

The show's third season, known as *Twin Peaks: The Return*, is an eighteen episodes miniseries, premiering on Showtime on May 21, 2017. Developed and written by creators Lynch and Frost, the season is a continuation of the 1990-1991 ABC series, and *Fire Walk with Me*. Led by original star Kyle MacLachlan and directed by the maestro, fans rejoiced because many original cast members returned, rounded out by new characters. Many of these characters are portrayed by actors and actresses from Lynch's other cinema; there are so many this author was waiting for the Elephant Man or a Third-Stage Guild Navigator to turn up. The new series features more alchemy, fused with numbers, disclosing a vast Gnostic cosmology, with Laura embodying a fallen Sophia, and Cooper as Aeon Jesus, her redeemer, trying to bring her to fullness.

"I'll see you again in twenty-five years," Laura informed Agent Cooper while seated in the Red Room. Set twenty-five years after the events of the original *Twin Peaks*, the season follows multiple storylines, most linked to FBI Special Agent Dale Cooper and his initial 1989 investigation into the murder of Twin Peaks' homecoming queen. In addition to the fictional

Washington State town of Twin Peaks, the story extends to locations such as Las Vegas, South Dakota, Philadelphia, Montana, and New Mexico.

The plot involves two interweaving storylines: Mr. C's (MacLachlan) attempts to locate coordinates to enter the White Lodge on a specific day and time, with Agent Cooper finally exiting the Black Lodge (the Red Waiting Room) to return to Twin Peaks. Cooper must see through the darkness of future past to fulfill his destiny and observe the mysteries the magician longs to see. Possessed by Bob, Mr. C is Cooper's doppelganger, a cool and deadly crime lord overseeing a gang of eccentric grifters. Although Mr. C and Cooper never meet, their destinies are connected because they are, inherently, contrasting aspects of the Self archetype. Duality, once again, pervades *Twin Peaks*: Mr. C. is evil, Cooper is good. To avoid returning to the Black Lodge, Mr. C generates a tulpa: a concept in mysticism and the paranormal of a being, or object, created through spiritual or mental powers. Twentieth-century theosophists adapted it from Tibetan *sprul-pa*, which means *emanation* or *manifestation*. Mr. C's tulpa is his clone, a lookalike insurance salesman named Dougie Jones. And it works: Dougie, not Mr. C, returns to Black Lodge at the designated time, 2:53 pm, a number with occult significance.

From the first episode, "My Log Has a Message for You" (airdate May 21, 2017), it is evident Lynch and Frost are not only well versed in the occult but with popular conspiracy theories. Originally, Lynch and Frost's series was about another doomed blonde, Marilyn Monroe, and a Kennedy family conspiracy to silence her. Back in the mid-to-late 80s, Lynch and Frost worked on a biopic about the life of the famous actress and model, using the book *Goddess: The Secret Lives of Marilyn Monroe* (1985) by Anthony Summers as a template. But the network felt that involving the Kennedys would politicize the program, so the bombshell's tragic life inspired the life and times of Laura Palmer, her death the result of scheming dark forces.

Conjuring the occult world and conspiracy, Lynch alludes to a popular theory. Marjorie Green's (Melissa Bailey) chihuahua, Armstrong, sniffs the door to Ruth Davenport's (Mary Stofle) apartment. Marjorie notices a foul smell, so she returns to her room, numbered 218. By setting this sequence in the apartment's hallway, Lynch evokes *The Shining*; specifically, the Overlook's foreboding halls. As Danny plays with his toys, a ball rolls toward him, prompting him to rise, wearing his Apollo 11 sweater, proceeding to room 237. Within the world of conspiracy, this was Kubrick's way of informing the world that he orchestrated the moon-landing footage at the behest of NASA: Danny, with his Apollo 11 sweater, is the rocket ship traveling 237,000 miles–the distance from the earth to the moon in the late 70s–by going to room 237. Lynch alludes to Neil Armstrong (1930-2012), the first man on the moon, via the dog's name, Armstrong. After making a fuss, Marjorie takes the canine to her room, 218. Add 2+1+8 to get 11 for Apollo 11; thus, Lynch subtly places Neil Armstrong and Apollo 11 in his show. Lynch pastiches Kubrick's imagery, drawing a parallel, putting forth the same clandestine skullduggery. That is, Kubrick staged and filmed the moon landing footage here on earth, likely in a top-secret government facility. Lynch seems to be insinuating he was involved as well.

Before proceeding any further, I feel a detour is needed to briefly discuss the nexus between NASA and Kubrick. The link is well documented and not conspiratorial; for example, sometime during *2001: A Space Odyssey*'s filming, Kubrick developed an obsession for capturing an interior scene exclusively using candlelight. He got his chance in the mid-1970s while filming *Barry Lyndon* (1975), a period piece set during the 18th century. Shot for eight and a half months with a crew of 170 people moving between England and Ireland, *Barry Lyndon*'s is remembered for its sumptuous, painterly photography, its magic glow. Kubrick partnered with cinematographer John Alcott (1931-1986), who he had promoted from focus puller to lighting cameraman on *2001*, elevating him to cinematographer on *A Clockwork Orange* and *The Shining*. Kubrick demanded the interior scenes be lit by candlelight, an impossible feat at the time because there did not exist a lens fast enough to catch an acceptable exposure with such low lighting. In their quest to photograph the dark side of the moon, NASA commissioned ten Planar 50mm f/0.7 still lenses from the German optical manufacturer Carl Zeiss AG. When Kubrick learned of their existence from NASA, he purchased three for himself and a Mitchell BNC camera. Since these lenses were designed for still photography, the motion picture camera demanded a somewhat severe modification.[605]

---

[605] Brad Gullickson, "How NASA Contributed to the Cinematography of 'Barry Lyndon,'" *Film School Rejects*, May 9, 2019, https://filmschoolrejects.com/barry-lyndon-cinematography/ (accessed September 6, 2019).

Trusted technical wizard Ed DiGiulio (1927-2004) was charged with grounding down the lens mounts because of the extreme size of the rear element that needed to be positioned only 4mm from the film plane. After hacking away and removing whole chunks from the Mitchell camera, DiGulio accomplished a miracle of sorts. Then came a new problem: the NASA lenses had almost no depth of field, which meant that focus had to be exact or all figures would be blurry. Within ten feet of the camera, Alcott marked distances to the exact inch. To keep track of these measurements, focus puller Douglas Milsome used CCTV to record and monitor the distances. The video camera was positioned at a 90-degree angle to the movie camera, filming the actors in profile. On his TV screen, Milsome placed a grid in which he could document how much a performer had shifted in the scene. This method allowed a little flexibility of movement while maintaining focus. With those issues resolved, the 50mm lens was an exceptional weapon for closeups, but Kubrick naturally wanted to capture coverage with a wide shot. DiGuilio placed an adapter built to modify the throw of light in cinema projector lenses onto the 50mm, which effectively changed its focal length to 36.5mm with very little loss of light. DiGuilio also attempted a 24mm model, but Kubrick immediately discarded the option due to distortion.[606]

The final problem was that, due to such little light on the set, the Mitchell BNC's side viewfinder could not register the image. Who knew what the hell they were shooting? The part was just one more scrap of the Mitchell that needed replacing. Alcott crafted a mirror-based viewfinder from a Technicolor camera that reflected the desired frame for inspection. The last step in the process was Kubrick's insistence on having the entire film push-developed. The technique is an overdevelopment of the film using temperatures often balked at by the manufacturer, but the result atones for the underexposure that occurred in camera. Saturation and warping of color become positive aspects of the operation. Suddenly, what was once deemed impossible became gloriously achievable–for Kubrick and the filmmakers that came after him–thanks to NASA.[607]

Danny *qua* Apollo 11 goes to room 237 *qua* the moon; thus, Armstrong the dog *qua* Neil Armstrong enters room 218 *qua* Apollo 11. By citing

---
606 Ibid.
607 Ibid.

this popular conspiracy theory, Lynch pays homage to Kubrick and NASA, investing his production with an air of mystery; observe like a Sherlockian, because everything may not be what it seems. Lynch also mocks his cinematic techniques. When Detective Dave Mackey (Brent Briscoe) searches a car belonging to Bill Hastings (Matthew Lillard), a viscus is discovered in the trunk, looking like part of the liver. Mackey barks like a dog, "*woof*," after seeing it; the dog barking coming after, not before, the grisly revelation. Dog barking is not a bad omen; instead, it is now a response to something unpleasant. With tongue firmly planted in cheek, Lynch, it seems, is mocking himself by reversing the symbolism of dogs barking, turning one of the weird staples of his films on its head.

* * * * *

Lynch emphasizes repetition over duality, borrowing the technique from Kubrick's *The Shining*, although his motives are more ambiguous. The maestro uses doubles and repetition to signify the eldritch reincarnation cycle pervading the Overlook; however, Lynch's reasons are less clear. Since debuting in April 1990, *Twin Peaks* has been all about the bunnies, a traditional totem of fecundity. From a small box of chocolate rabbits found in Laura's bedroom to Jack Rabbit's Palace, the hare is an odd trope. Back in the Pilot episode, Cooper discusses rabbits before the town hall meeting. Norma advertises Rabbit Chili, and, in *Fire Walk with Me*, there is a rabbit figurine in the Hayward house next to the fireplace. Odessa, Texas, the home of Eat at Judy's coffee shop, is also the home of the world's largest Jackrabbit statue (not shown). There are two double Rs: the Double R Diner and Rancho Rosa Estates. When he is mistaken for Dougie Jones, a nearly catatonic Agent Cooper repeats back the last word spoken to him. In the episode "What Story is That, Charlie?" (airdate August 6, 2017) Sarah Palmer watches a televised boxing match that keeps repeating over and over like its glitched. From that same episode, Mr. C and Renzo (Derek Mears) arm-wrestle, echoing Laura's complaint that sometimes her arms bend back. Lynch names two characters Paige (or Page): Ben Horne's secretary, Beverly Paige (Ashley Judd), and Carrie Page (Sheryl Lee), who is Laura in another dimension.[608] The mysterious, white horse visions become a white ceramic figurine sitting on Carrie's fireplace mantel.

---

[608] *Paige* comes from Latin *págius*: a young helper of a noble, hence Beverly is Horn's secretary.

Arthurian Legend motifs repeat, evoking Glastonbury Grove, the entrance to the Black Lodge. For instance, Dougie Jones lives 25140 Lancelot Court (this is also a reference to the *citrinitas*) near to Merlin's Market. There is a picture of a nuclear blast–a mushroom cloud–behind Gordon's desk. An atomic bomb is tested on July 16, 1945, at White Sands, New Mexico, producing a mushroom cloud; the nuclear explosion is Bob's genesis, a vile archon emerging from the doomsday weapon.

In New York City, when Tracy Barberato (Madeline Zima) brings coffee to Sam Colby (Benjamin Rosenfield), the cups have the letter Z, indicating they were purchased at SZYMON'S, with the Z darkened. This shop is a franchise, from where Cooper *qua* Dougie buys the cherry pie before meeting with the Mitchum Brothers. Owls pervade the first two seasons of *Twin Peaks*, and likewise populate *The Return*, specifically outside the house of Dougie and Janey-E (Naomi Watts) on Lancelot Court, and inside Janey-E's kitchen. Diane smokes American Spirit cigarettes, a brand using a Native American for its logo, reflecting Hawk, the keeper of the White and Black Lodges' mysteries. In episode 10, "Laura is the One" (airdate July 16, 2017), Rebekah Del Rio performs "No Stars" in the Roadhouse wearing a zig-zag pattern dress recalling the carpet in the Black Lodge. The history of the green ring repeats: Wally Brando, dressing like Marlon Brando in *The Wild One* (1953), mentions Lewis and Clark's Expedition, evoking the green ring's hidden history because it was Lewis who discovered the magical bauble. "This is the water and this is the well. Drink full and descend. The horse is the white of the eyes and dark within," is repeated endlessly by a Black Lodge entity (played by Robert Brosky)–identified as a Woodsmen, an homage to the Tin Woodman (Jack Haley, 1897-1979) from *The Wizard of Oz*–in episode 8 titled "Gotta Light?"

There's a Sycamore Street in Rancho Rosa, and William Hastings and Ruth Davenport visited 2240 Sycamore Lane, traveling to another dimension, evoking the 12 sycamore trees guarding the Black Lodge's entrance. In "Beyond Life and Death" (airdate June 10, 1991), Jimmy Scott (1925-2014) performs the song "Sycamore Trees" in the Black Lodge *qua* Red Waiting Room. In episode 16, "No Knock, No Doorbell" (airdate August 27, 2017), Audrey dances to, what else, "Audrey's Dance" (1990), but in *The Return* it's played backward signaling her mental illness, dwelling in an asylum, her reality an illusion. Interestingly, back in '90, in "Zen, or the

Skill to Catch a Killer," Audrey remarks, "God, I love this music. Isn't it too dreamy?" as she dances to "Audrey's Dance" playing on the Double R Diner's jukebox. Fast-forward 25 years: in *The Return*, the music indicates her false reality; she lives in a dream, a hostage of the Demiurge.

Lynch repeats numbers ad nauseum: 10 is the sum of the time 2:53 pm (2+5+3), when Dougie returns to the Black Lodge, the precise moment when Cooper leaves it. According to Major Briggs' note, there will be riff in space-time: a portal will open on October 1 and October 2 (October is the 10th month) at 2:53 pm at Jack Rabbit's Palace; there are ten letters in *Jack Rabbit*. Cell 10 jails the corrupt deputy, Chad Broxford (John Pirruccello). Back in *Fire Walk with Me*, Phillip Jeffries materialized in the Philadelphia FBI office at 10:10 am. After leaving the Black Lodge, Cooper says 10 signifies completion: he appears to have integrated his ego with his shadow, successfully navigating the two Lodges, achieving the self, the *rubedo*. The time, 2:53, is one digit more than the magisterial number 252, which was, in both Dr. Dee and Buckminster Fuller's (1895-1983) magical mathematic formulas, the number representing *coincidentia oppositorum*, transcending duality.[609]

Lynch repeats seven, alluding to the seventh floor of FBI Headquarters back in *Fire Walk with Me*, and an even early mystery: Laura's last day on earth was February 23, 1989; February is the second (2nd) month, add 2+2+3 to get 7. An atomic bomb was tested on July 16, 1945; July is the seventh month, add 1+6 to get 7. Agent Cooper drives 430 miles to enter another dimension; add 4+3+0 to get 7. Once inside this parallel universe, Cooper travels to a hotel where he stays in room 7 with Diane, waking to become Richard and Linda. Dougie works for Lucky 7 Insurance located on the 7th floor, and Cooper gets 7s when he plays the slot machines at the Silver Mustang Casino. "Sonny Jim is in seventh heaven," Janey-E remarks, watching her son plays on a new jungle gym, as Tchaikovsky's (1840-1893) "Swan Theme" plays, giving off a somber vibe. Dr. Jacoby, now a conspiracy podcaster using the handle Dr. Amp, begins his broadcast at 7:00 pm.

A telephone pole with the number six crops up in the material world three times at three different places, designating it as 666, linking it to evil, the Black Lodge's dark dealings. In 1988, this pole was situated in (or

---

[609] James Alan Egan, *Elizabethan America: The John Dee Tower of 1583* (Newport, RI: Cosmopolitan Press, 2011), 71-108, *passim*.

Repeating cigarettes, as *Twins Peaks* pays homage to *The X-Files*, the latter influenced the former. (Left) The *X-Files'* villain, the Cigarette Smoking Man (William B. Davis), smokes Morley Cigarettes. During an *X-Files* episode, Special Agent Dana Scully (Gillian Anderson, top right) observes a pack of his cigarettes. In *Twin Peaks: The Return* episode, "Case Files," (airdate June 4, 2017), Richard Horne hides money in a pack of Morley Cigarettes (bottom right), forging a link between shows because they're both about the occult and the supernatural, using UFOs as plot devices.

just outside) the Fat Trout Trailer Park in Deer Meadow, Washington. The Arm's whooping sound emanated from the pole during a meeting above a convenience store, and Desmond and Stanley's search of Teresa Banks' trailer. When he returned to the lot that evening, Desmond got a strange feeling when he looked at the pole, hearing the same noise. In 2016, the same pole stood near an intersection in Twin Peaks. The pole emitted a buzzing sound shortly after a local boy was struck and killed in the road by Richard Horne (Eamon Farren). The pole next stood outside Carrie Page's home in Odessa, Texas. The Fireman *qua* Giant (Struycken) showed Deputy Andy Brennan this pole in a vision.

The numbers 3 and 15: after falling through the Red Room's zig-zag floor, Cooper ends up in the curious Purple Room, wherein an eyeless woman named Naido (Nae Yuuki) warns him of a wall socket numbered 15. Later, he re-enters that room, and 15 has changed to 3. The number 15 socket connects to Mr. C's cigarette lighter in his Lincoln, while the number 3 socket connects to Dougie's location. Combined, you have 315, Cooper's room number at the Great Northern Hotel. The number 3 socket links Cooper to Dougie, a tulpa of Mr. C. In contrast, socket number 15 relates Cooper to his doppelganger, Mr. C, so unifying them, *315*, designates Cooper, the genuine article, identified by his room number, 315, in the Great Northern.

When Dougie's car explodes, a junkie mom (Hailey Gates) in the house across the street repeatedly screeches "1-1-9! 1-1-9! 1-1-9!" The most reasonable explanation for her utterance is she's supposed to be screaming for help, as in *9-1-1! 9-1-1!* The junkie alludes to the Black Lodge's backwardness, foreshadowing a parallel dimension, wherein things are not what they seem, slightly off and incongruent.

"A wrong has been made right, and the sun is shining bright!" Bradley Mitchum (Jim Belushi) declares excitedly in episode 13, "What Story is That, Charlie?" If *Lizzie*'s murderous lesbians indelibly occupy the *nigredo*, and *The Neon Demon* is the *albedo's* playground, and *The Shape of Water* is the *rubedo's* magical finality, then *citrinitas* illuminates *The Return*, the golden sun, the divine masculine. The original television series was guided by luminous moonlight: Laura, Maddy, Audrey, Shelly, Donna, Lucy, Norma, Nadine, Josie, Catherine, Sarah, and the Log Lady. On the other hand, the unrelenting sun scorches *The Return*: Dougie, Gordon, Dr. Jacoby *qua* Dr. Amp, Cooper, Mr. C, Mike, Hawk, Bobby, Andy, Ed, James, Richard Horne, Ray Monroe (George Griffith), Agent Albert Rosenfield (Miguel Ferrer, 1955-2017), Anthony Sinclair (Tom Sizemore) Freddie Sykes (Jake Wardle) and the Mitchum Brothers shine a light on *Twin Peaks*' mysteries, disclosing many of its secrets. The masculine, not the feminine, defines *The Return*, their actions and reactions radiating light like a magician waving a wand, a golden bough. The *citrinitas* brings forth sunlight, magically transforming the unknown, the subconscious, into valuable consciousness, enlightening all. Solar iconography permeates *The Return*: Dougie Jones' yellow jacket, the tulpa, eventually reduced to a golden seed. His son is the sun literally, named *Sonny* Jim (Pierce Gagnon), who often wears a yellow shirt or hoodie, denoting his solar presence. The

Jones' home has a yellow telephone, and there is a ubiquitous yellow lamp in the dining room. Dr. Amp employs a golden shovel, encouraging people to dig themselves out of shit, i.e., the material world, to become conscious, thereby shedding light on false modalities accordingly. Sir Lancelot and Merlin from the Arthurian Legend turn up, a tale based on solar lore. King Arthur personifies the sun, his knights personify the zodiac, and Merlin embodies Hermes Trismegistus, the Hellenistic deity prophesying the coming of Christianity, the Son of God, Christ *qua* Logos, the Piscean Age solar Messiah.[610]

When Cooper returns to mundane reality, he is catatonic, living like he's in a dream. He does not know who he is, or where he is, yet can interact with his wife and perform his job, mainly by following and imitating others. Cooper's histrionics mirror *Being There*'s (1979) Chauncey Gardner (Peter Sellers), himself a solar avatar, becoming a messiah by dispensing wisdom via parables involving the sun and the changing seasons. By film's end, Chauncey is positioned to become the United States' President, even though he is, in reality, an idiot savant….or is he? In the concluding moments, as Ben Rand (Melvyn Douglas, 1901-1981) is placed in his Masonic-Illuminati crypt by Washington's puppet masters, Chauncey walks on water signaling his solar divinity. In remaking *Being There*, *The Return* identifies Cooper as a Christlike figure, a neo-solar deity, fulfilling his destiny when he redeems Laura. As such, Jade (Nafessa Williams) drives Cooper in a yellow jeep, becoming the chariot of the sun god Apollo *qua* Cooper. The Jeep Wrangler's seats are adorned with the model's name, Sahara, embroiled in gold letters. Jade's jewelry is also gold, including earring hoops, rings, bracelets, and a necklace. Jade takes him to the Silver Mustang Casino, wherein he saves a disheveled and malnourished elderly woman (Linda Porter, 1933-2019) by identifying winning slot machines. She nicknames him "Mr. Jackpots," using her winnings to rehabilitate herself, reconciling with her long-lost son, Denver.

What does the sun's light expose; what mysteries are solved? Hawk discovers Laura's missing diary pages, revealing that Cooper is still trapped in the Black Lodge, allowing his doppelganger to remain at large. At night, when she blathers on with James after getting off his motorcycle (*Fire Walk with Me*), we learn what caused Laura to scream, disclosed to be Agent

---

610 Yates, *Giordano Bruno*, 8.

Cooper by way of time travel. We apprehend what, precisely, Blue Rose cases are: unexplained phenomena involving tulpas and doppelgangers. Electricity is a conduit between the Black Lodge, the White Lodge, opening doors to extra dimensions. We learn Sarah Palmer hosts a pan-dimensional creature of unknown origin, corrupting her soul with a metaphysical malignancy. We finally meet Diane, who hitherto was a phantom, a linguistic creation, existing when Cooper spoke into his tape recorder. We learn garmonbozia–black corn–is toxic to humans, but sustains Black Lodge entities.

But most significantly, the sun enlightens us to *Twin Peaks'* vast Gnostic cosmology. "We are like the dreamer who dreams, and then lives inside the dream ... But who is the dreamer," Monica Bellucci asks a bemused Gordon Cole, insinuating Valentinus' hylic sphere, the illusory reality, denoting the pessimistic odor of *The Poimandres*.[611] Alchemy and Laura's mysterious murder permeate *Twin Peaks* '90-'91 and *Fire Walk with Me*; now, post *The Return*, we can apply Gnosticism when analyzing the show's dramatis personae and themes. The White Lodge–the old theater–is the pleroma, inhabited by the monad, known as Giant or the Fireman. The Black Lodge *qua* Red Waiting Room *qua* room above the convenience store designates the material world, Bob and the Woodmen are archons, toxic bums screwing around with humankind. They are fire obsessed; hence, fire walks with them, Bob, after all, was created in a fiery nuclear blast. One of them strolls around with an unlit cigarette, asking, "Gotta light?" The Log Lady, a cabalist, detests fire having bricked up her fireplace, her prophecies a positive force, her wisdom a guiding force toward illumination.

The Giant, or the Fireman, wants to extinguish the archons, to counter their destruction; upon witnessing Bob's creation, the monad emanates Sophia, Laura Palmer, cast down to the hylic world, becoming a misunderstood harlot and hellraiser. Cooper is the Aeon Jesus sent to redeem her, to bring her home. Like Biff (Thomas F. Wilson) and the sports almanac, he alters the linear timeline causing Laura to disappear from Twin Peaks, entering a parallel dimension as Carrie Page. Judy, the Demiurge, rules the archons; known initially as *Jowday* or *Joudy*, Judy is a mythological entity and powerful negative force studied by the Blue Rose Task Force. Judy is a monkey associating with the room above the convenience store; Nadio

---

[611] *Hermetica, Corpus Hermeticum, Libellus* X, 1:187-205, *passim*; Yates, ibid, 23-24.

makes monkey sounds imitating Judy upon entering the sublunary world. Judy employs electricity, usually around telephone pole 6, manipulating the material plane and the space-time continuum. Judy uses electricity as sorcery, sending Cooper to an alternative reality to locate Laura *qua* Carrie Page. Easter egg: the Woodmen look like street people, homeless bums, destroying the lives of those that cross their path, targeting most people intentionally, others randomly. One has to ask: in *Mulholland Drive*, is the bum hiding behind Winkie's, in effect, a Woodmen, one of the archons from the Black Lodge annihilating Diane Selwyn's reality? In my opinion, the answer to this question is yes.

Of course, it wouldn't be a Lynch production without duality. Major Briggs' torso is found with a severed woman's head, becoming a sickening Union of Opposites. There are two women in Dougie's life: a whore and a mother, with the former giving Dougie *qua* Cooper *two rides*. The mythical green ring, worn by Dougie on his left hand, is a negative talisman, counterbalanced by Jade, a positive force. Her necklace is a pendant displaying a downward-facing hand holding a circular ring, derived from the Hand of Fatima, or *Hamsa*.[612] In Islamic and Jewish art, the hand and the number five are prominent symbols used to ward off the evil eye.[613] With its five fingers clutching an open ring beneath it, Jade's pendant closely resembles the celebrated door knockers that flourished under Moorish occupation in Spain, later migrating to France and other neighboring countries.[614] Nineteenth-century Victorian art in England and North America popularized hand symbolism establishing trends in jewelry and decorative items that prevail today.[615] The hand's downward position suggests its meaning: the warding off bad luck and any evil influence. Initially, such doorknockers signaled the religious faith of the homeowner. Later, the same motif became a more comprehensive symbol of general protection, no longer associated with a specific spiritual practice, merging similar hand designs from Rome and Ireland, among others. The ring

---

612 Marisa C Hayes, "Jade: Ornamental Gem or Protective Talisman? A Character Study," in *The Women of David Lynch*, ed. David Bushman (Columbus, OH: Fayetteville Mafia Press, 2019), 118.
613 Ibid.
614 Ibid, 118-119.
615 Ibid, 119.

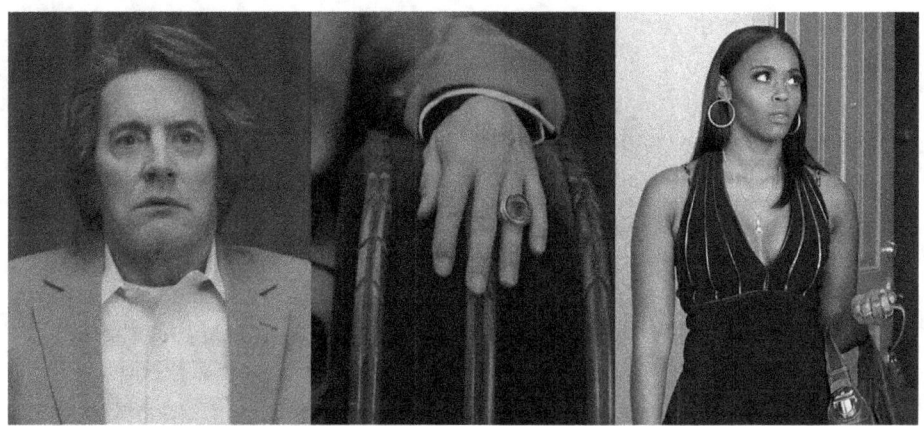

Dougie Jones (left) wears the mysterious green ring (center) while having an affair with Jade (right).

held by the hand in Jade's necklace is another critical feature of these doorknockers, offering a universal sign of completion and longevity.[616]

Jade, by wearing the doorknocker pendant, associates with portals; she discovers the green Great Northern room key in Cooper's pocket. The key opens a magical gateway, and by mailing it back to the hotel in Twin Peaks, she is helping Cooper complete his alchemical journey. Cooper has achieved the individuation of the White and Black Lodges, the alchemical *rubedo*. Aided by Phillip Jeffries, he time travels, attempting to redeem Laura *qua* Sophia. By mailing the room key back to the Great Northern, Jade has prepared Cooper for the first step of his return journey; jade the stone is linked to protection, healing, and prosperity.[617] Thus, she is Cooper's apotropaic charm; his good fortune begins as soon as he comes into contact with her. Seated beside Jade in her Wrangler, Cooper avoids assassination, guided to a good luck spot–a casino–where he receives visions, allowing him to ascertain which slot machines will win the jackpot.[618] Jade's name is also a repetitive mnemonic, recalling Jade and Emerald (twin daughters with opposite personalities, both played by Erika Anderson) from the soap opera *Invitation to Love*. A green rubber glove, worn by Freddie Sykes, gifted to him in a dream by the Fireman *qua* monad negates the green ring's negative influence. The ring is worn on the left hand, alluding to

---

616 Ibid.
617 Ibid, 116-117.
618 Ibid, 117-118.

Left-Hand Path magic, while the green rubber glove is worn on the right hand, denoting Right-Hand Path Kabbalah; by wearing the green rubber glove, Freddie will trash Bob, destroying the evil archon. Easter egg: Jade as a protective talisman: *Invitation to Love*'s Jade helps ward of disaster when her father, Jared Lancaster (Peter Michael Goetz), decides not to follow through with his plans to commit suicide, citing his daughter, Jade, as the reason for changing his mind.

Before its finale, *The Return* revives its alchemical roots. The *citrinitas* is the pervasive masculine; the *nigredo* is the Woodmen, and the *albedo* is the Silver Mustang Casino. The green ring, the Arm's green Formica table, and Jade suggest Hermes Trismegistus' Emerald Tablet. When Diane finally emerges from the Black Lodge, her hair is red, the *rubedo*, while her tulpa is reduced to a silver seed, symbolizing the moon. Cooper has successfully navigated both Lodges, White and Black, integrating his shadow, achieving individuation. Leaving the Lodges, he returns to Twin Peaks, visits Phillip Jeffries—now a giant kettle—emitting white light from its (or his) spout. Phillip is located in a chamber behind room eight at the Dutchman's Lodge, accessible from the convenience store's upper floor, the stored haunted by the Woodmen. When Cooper broaches him about time travel, Phillip produces the number eight; when turned on its side it is the lemniscate, the symbol for infinity *qua* space-time, sending Cooper back in time to February '89. Cooper unites with Laura, saving her from death, but she disappears, whereabouts unknown. The timeline is altered: Laura's dead body vanishes; Bob, an archon, is thwarted because he cannot murder her. Following the instructions of the Fireman, Cooper and Diane drive 430 miles, entering a parallel dimension, becoming people named Richard and Linda. When he wakes, Diane has disappeared, leaving behind a note identifying herself as Linda. Notice the outdated television set when Cooper looks around the room, it is not a modern flat screen but something from the '80s or '90s. However, Cooper, believing he is still Cooper as opposed to Richard, locates Laura—now working as a waitress at a diner named Eat at Judy's, a restaurant operated by the Demiurge—at her home, returning her to her house in Twin Peaks.

Only Laura is now Carrie Page, and Sarah Palmer is absent, the family home occupied by Alice Tremond (Mary Reber). Its previous owner was Mrs. Chalfont—the names are merely leftovers, bleeding through from the original reality. Cooper wonders what year it is, as Carrie *qua* Laura terrifyingly screams upon hearing "Laura!" from inside the home; again, residual from the original dimension-reality trickling through, signaling the collision of worlds. *Twin Peaks: The Return* concludes, answering many questions, but raising new ones. Easter egg: eight also repeats: Phillip is located in a chamber behind room 8, conjuring the number 8, sending Cooper back in time, and cell eight jails Freddie Sykes in the deputy's station.

    Let this author now echo Lynch's repetition: at the start of this potion, I offered a rather scathing review of *Twin Peaks*, a summary I considered revising or removing altogether. I am a fan of *Twin Peaks* and Lynch but wonder if his work would be praised if his name were removed and replaced with that of another. For example, take *Eraserhead*, a movie lauded for its surrealism, nightmarish sexual current, and Gnostic spirituality. One has to ask: if Lynch's name was taken out of the credits and replaced with Ed Wood, would it still be considered a classic, or would it be deemed crap like *Glen or Glenda* or *Plan 9 from Outer Space*? Lynch's special effects look more like an Ed Wood campy aesthetic, not something from Spielberg or Lucas' cinema. For example, in *The Return*, we see cutout heads of Major Briggs and Mr. C hovering in the White Lodge, reminiscent of *Plan 9*'s hubcap flying saucers. Likewise, the Fat Trout Trailer Park, located in Deer Meadow, Washington, has miraculously relocated to Twin Peaks, creating a huge continuity error, something not found in the cinema of Billy Wilder or Alfred Hitchcock. In a way, what makes Lynch's cinema enjoyable is the same thing that makes Wood's films entertaining. Both are intentionally incongruent, producing an air of strangeness and mystery. The difference between the filmmakers is this: Wood's movies are unintentionally bizarre, featuring bad acting fused with idiosyncratic dialog, becoming a theatre of the absurd. Lynch's films are surreal, esoteric, thought-provoking, amusingly weird paradoxes, making them classics. In this way, Lynch's media is like Wood's gimcrack cinema, but for altogether different reasons. Lynch's mysteries are tongue-in-cheek, making his work amusingly odd yet engaging; Wood's arcana takes itself too seriously, rendering his films stupid yet sublime because of their campy quirks.

    In *Cinema Symbolism 2*, I put forth the theory that *Lost Highway* and *Mulholland Drive* represented contrasting sides of Lynch's psyche, making the two films inextricable linked. Like the enigmas of *Twin Peaks*, these

Lynchian mysteries leave us wondering if we've experienced an astounding meditation on the transcendence of being or a silly avoidance of the serious.[619] We can never be sure if we are meant to cower before the sublime or laugh or heads off, or a combination of both. This sentiment is not the case when watching Wood's movies, with their stock footage, symbolic effects, and clunky narrations–we know this we are watching a freak show. Lynch's bizarre irony evokes holy images that both posit their powerful existence and dissolve before the divine as ridiculous fogs.[620] Standing before a godly pattern, we want to quake with both fear and laughter. Such is the nature of Lynch's mercurial irony; his films are enthusiastic studies in the obscure and the weird, akin to oddities at a carnival just like Wood's schlock, which is why we remember them. In his book, *David Lynch Decoded*, Mark Allyn Stewart writes, "I've always regarded Lynch's films as puzzle pieces, and each time he makes another film, it's another piece to add to the puzzle. And the more you know about the overall puzzle, the more exciting it is to watch what it ultimately reveals."[621] I could not have said it better; as for me, I hope more episodes of *Twin Peaks* are coming because we must see Cooper *qua* Richard, and Laura *qua* Carrie, return to their proper dimension.

---

619 Wilson, *Strange World*, 12.
620 Ibid, 12-13.
621 Stewart, *David Lynch Decoded*, 122.

CHAPTER XIII

Return to Middle-earth: Bilbo Baggins and the Monomyth

> Did you know that your Great-Great-Great-Great Uncle Bullroarer Took was so large he could ride a real horse? …Well he could! In the Battle of Greenfields, he charged the Goblin ranks. He swung his club so hard it knocked the Goblin King's head clean off and it sailed a hundred yards through the air and went down a rabbit hole. And thus the battle was won and the game of golf invented at the same time.
> Gandalf the Grey, *The Hobbit: An Unexpected Journey*, 2012

> He wields the Foe-Hammer! The Beater! Bright as daylight!
> The Goblin King, *The Hobbit: An Unexpected Journey*, 2012

> If he had a name, it's long since been lost.
> He would've been known only as a servant of evil.
> One of a number. One of nine.
> Gandalf the Grey, *The Hobbit: The Desolation of Smaug*, 2013

The Hobbit is a series of three high-fantasy adventure films directed by Peter Jackson. They are based on the 1937 novel *The Hobbit* by J. R. R. Tolkien, with large portions of the trilogy inspired by the appendices to *The Return of the King* (1955), as well as new material and characters written for the films. Together, they act as a prequel to Jackson's *The Lord of the Rings* film trilogy. The movies are subtitled *An Unexpected Journey* (2012), *The Desolation of Smaug* (2013), and *The Battle of the Five Armies* (2014).[622] The screenplay was written by Fran Walsh, Philippa Boyens, Jackson, and Guillermo del Toro, with the Mexican filmmaker selected to direct before he departed the project. The three films take place in the fictional world of Middle-earth seventy-seven years before the beginning of *The Lord of the Rings*. They follow the adventures of Bilbo

---

[622] The Blu-ray extended editions were viewed to write these analyses.

Baggins (Martin Freeman), a reclusive Hobbit persuaded by the mercurial wizard Gandalf the Grey (Ian McKellen) to accompany thirteen dwarves, led by Thorin Oakenshield (Richard Armitage), on a quest to reclaim the Lonely Mountain from the fierce dragon Smaug (voiced by Benedict Cumberbatch). The films also expand upon certain elements from the novel and other source material, such as Gandalf's investigation of Dol Guldur, and the pursuit by Azog (Manu Bennett) and Bolg (John Tui): two ferocious Orcs seeking vengeance against Thorin and his kindred. The Orc leaders bring to mind Gog and Magog, two unclean kings in the *Alexander Romance* (ca. 338 CE), and the nations that ally with Satan in the Book of Revelation. Like so many high-adventure stories, the monomyth is transcendent, with the Road of Trials element pervasive.

An Unexpected Journey

Approaching his 111th birthday, Bilbo Baggins (Ian Holm) begins writing down the full story of his adventure 60 years earlier for the benefit of his nephew Frodo (Elijah Wood). Bilbo tells the story of the Dwarf monarch Thrór (Jeffrey Thomas), who brought an era of prosperity for his kin under the Lonely Mountain, a kingdom known as Erebor. During his reign, deep in the mountain's bowels, a miner discovers the Arkenstone: a precious gem endowing divine kingship, investing Thrór and the line of Durin with Davidic and Solomonic qualities. The *Ark*enstone alludes to the Ark of the Covenant, a sacred relic that also signifies divine rulership, linking the Dwarves to the ancient Hebrews–more on this nexus later. Whether Tolkien named the stone after the Hebrew Ark is left to speculation, if it wasn't intentional, it was the product of the collective unconscious.

Corrupted by greed and an incessant need for gold, Thrór's kingdom declines, luring the fire-drake, Smaug, to the Lonely Mountain. Destroying the nearby town of Dale, Smaug drives the Dwarves out of their mountain, taking their gold hoard. Thrór's grandson, Thorin, sees King Thranduil (Lee Pace) and his Wood-elves on a nearby hillside, becoming dismayed when they leave rather than aid his people, resulting in Thorin's everlasting hatred of Elves.

In the Shire, the wizard Gandalf the Grey tricks 50-year-old Bilbo (now Freeman) into hosting a party for Thorin and his company of Dwarves:

Balin (Ken Scott), Dwalin (Graham McTavish), Fíli (Dean O'Gorman), Kíli (Aiden Turner), Dori (Mark Hadlow), Nori (Jeb Brophy), Ori (Adam Brown), Óin (John Callen), Glóin (Peter Hambleton), Bifur (William Kircher), Bofur (James Nesbitt), and Bombur (Stephen Hunter). Gandalf and Thorin are Threshold Guardians, initiating Bilbo into Middle-earth's mysteries. Gandalf, a Hermes Trismegistus archetype, also reflects an authentic medieval phenomenon: the freelance occultist-scholar whose stock-in-trade was useful advice as much as magical powers, often rising to the position of king's counselor. These magicians had an excellent working knowledge of metaphysics, politics, the art of war, agriculture, seafaring, economics, and the trivium and the quadrivium.[623]

The twelve Dwarves, with Thorin, their leader, signify the sun and the zodiac, Christ and the Apostle, indicating their quest is a heavenly mission against darkness, combating Smaug, the Great Dragon, Python, or the Devil. Gandalf's aims to recruit Bilbo as the company's burglar to aid them in their quest to enter the Lonely Mountain, satisfying the Call to Adventure element. At first, Bilbo is unwilling to accept (Refusal of the Call) but has a change of heart after the company leaves without him the next day. Bilbo races to join the company with a signed contract in hand, guaranteeing him 1/14 of the loot if the venture is successful. Traveling onward, Gandalf tells Bilbo there are five wizards; the fifth card of the Major Arcana is the Hierophant or Pope, making Gandalf and the other wizards divine guardians, becoming bridges between the godhead and the inhabitants of Middle-earth.[624] The Dwarves and Bilbo are soon captured by three hungry Trolls–the first test on the Road of Trials. Bilbo stalls the Trolls from eating them until dawn, when Gandalf exposes the Trolls to sunlight, turning them to stone. The company locates the Trolls' cave finding treasure and Elven blades. Thorin and Gandalf each take a weapon: Orcrist, known as the Goblin-cleaver, and Glamdring, known as the Foe-Hammer and the Beater. Gandalf also discovers an Elven dagger, giving it to Bilbo.

In the forest, the wizard Radagast the Brown (Sylvester McCoy) finds Gandalf and the company, recounting an incident at the castle-fortress Dol Guldur with a fiendish ghost and the Necromancer, a sorcerer corrupting

---

[623] *Picatrix*, Introduction, 13.
[624] Cavendish, *The Tarot*, 83; Place, *The Tarot*, 196.

Greenwood the Great with black magic. Giant spiders roam the woods, weaving webs, hence its nickname *Mirkwood*. Chased by Orcs, Gandalf leads the company through a hidden passage to Rivendell. There, Lord Elrond (Hugo Weaving), under the light of a crescent moon, examines the company's map of the Lonely Mountain, revealing a secret door that will only be visible on Durin's Day. That is, "when the last moon of Autumn and the sun are in the sky together," i.e., until sunset, on the first day of the Dwarves' New Year, which was "the first day of the last moon of Autumn on the threshold of Winter," alluding to Trismegistus' above and below. Gandalf later approaches the White Council–consisting of Elrond, the Hypatia of Alexandria-like Galadriel (Cate Blanchett), and Saruman the White (Christopher Lee). There, Gandalf presents a Morgul blade, a weapon used by the Witch-king of Angmar, which Radagast obtained at Dol Guldur as a portent that the Necromancer presages the eventual return of Sauron. While Saruman presses concern to the more present matter of the Dwarves' quest, requesting that Gandalf put an end to it, the Grey Wizard reveals to the Elven enchantress telepathically that he'd anticipated this, having the Dwarves quest on without him. Easter egg: the ghost in Dol Guldur that attacks Radagast is the Witch-king of Angmar, the same Ringwraith that stabs Frodo on Weathertop in *The Lord of the Rings: The Fellowship of the Ring* (2001).

The company journeys into the Misty Mountains, traveling a precipitous path, where they find themselves trapped amid a battle between colossal Stone Giants, so they take refuge in a cave. As they sleep, they are captured by Goblins, who bring them to their leader, the Great Goblin, also known as the Goblin King (Barry Humphries). During this time, Bilbo becomes separated from the Dwarves, falling into a fissure where he encounters Gollum (Andy Serkis), who unknowingly drops a golden ring. Pocketing the ring, Bilbo finds himself confronted by Gollum. They play a game of riddles, wagering that Bilbo will be shown the way out if he wins or eaten by Gollum if he loses. Bilbo eventually wins by asking Gollum what he has in his pocket. Noticing his ring is lost, Gollum realizes Bilbo possesses it, giving him chase. After putting the ring on by chance, Bilbo discovers the MacGuffin grants its wearer invisibility. When he has the opportunity to stab Gollum, Bilbo spares his life out of pity, escaping while the creature curses the Hobbit.

Meanwhile, the Goblin King insinuates that Azog the Defiler is still alive. Azog was the Orc war-chief that killed Thrór by beheading him, then killing Thráin, Thrór's son, and Thorin's father, during a ferocious battle outside the Dwarven subterranean kingdom of Moria.[625] In defending himself, Thorin used a piece of an oak tree for a shield, giving him the nickname *Oakenshield*. Azog lost his left forearm, suggesting the Left-Hand Path, to Thorin during the fight, leading to speculation the pale Orc died, succumbing to his wound. But the Orc survived and is pissed off, placing a bounty on Thorin's head. Gandalf arrives out of nowhere, leading the Dwarves in an escape, killing the Goblin King. Bilbo exits the mountain, rejoining the company, keeping his newly obtained ring secret. Azog and his hunting party ambush the company, so they seek sanctuary by climbing trees. Thorin charges at Azog, who overpowers and severely injures him with his ferocious Warg. Bilbo saves Thorin from the Orcs just as eagles rescue the company. They escape to the safety of the Carrock, where Gandalf revives Thorin, who renounces his previous disdain for Bilbo after being saved by him. They see the Lonely Mountain in the distance, where a thrush–a bird symbolizing persistence–awakens Smaug by knocking a snail against the mountain. Bilbo and the Dwarves are resolved: they will not stop until they reclaim Erebor. Easter egg: from primitive times to those of the Druids, the oak, strong, durable, and very long-lived, was undoubtedly the chief sacred tree of Europe and Scandinavia.[626] Hercules' club, according to legend, was made of oak, a tree sacred to Jupiter.[627] The oak is strength, signifying the divine right to rule, representing Durin's royal line. The oak is not easily broken; thus, it protects Thorin from Azog's attack, preserving his kingship.

Because it's a trilogy, other monomyth elements such as Belly of the Whale and Apotheosis, come later. Along with the components already mentioned, we Meet a Goddess, satisfied (for now) when Galadriel enters the story. Supernatural Aid is given twice: first, when Bilbo gets the Eleven blade Sting from Gandalf, glowing blue when Goblins and Orcs are near. And second, when Bilbo discovers the One Ring in Gollum's liar, granting him invisibility. The Road of Trials appears many times, starting when the

---

625 Thráin was portrayed by Thomas Robbins in *An Unexpected Journey*, and by Antony Sher in *The Desolation of Smaug*.
626 *Encyclopedia of World Mythology*, 244.
627 Cirlot, *Dictionary*, 227.

company escapes the Trolls or else be cooked alive and eaten. The Dwarves battling the Goblins, and Bilbo's riddle game with Gollum, also fulfill this element, as does their battle with Azog and his hunting party.

The Hobbits are Middle-earth's farmers, its simple folk, while the Elves its warrior-philosophers, its gentry. The world of men and women is its middle class. The Dwarves personify the Jewish people, imbued with some of the negative stereotypes associated with the Hebrews, such as being miserly, incredibly proud, and occasionally officious. Tolkien was influenced by his selective reading of medieval texts regarding the Jewish people and their history. The Dwarves' characteristics of being dispossessed of their homeland–the Lonely Mountain and Moira, their ancestral homes–while living among other groups yet retaining their culture were derived from medieval images and attitudes toward Jews. At the same time, their warlike nature stems from accounts in the Bible.[628] In medieval Europe, Jews were considered as having a propensity for making well-crafted baubles and beautiful jewelry. The dwarves of Norse mythology echoed this cultural trait; they were expert miners and metalworkers, dwelling in subterranean chambers, paralleling the Dwarves of Middle-earth.[629] Tolkien's Dwarves also employ intricate runes and glyphs as their written language, imitating Hebrew letters, Kabbalah, and Gematria's magic.

The Desolation of Smaug

The film opens with a flashback: Gandalf meets with Thorin at the Prancing Pony in Bree to lay the groundwork to retake the Lonely Mountain. Gandalf reveals there's a price on Thorn's head, while the dwarf states that he's heard rumors Thráin lives. The movie flashes forward: Azog and his Orc party pursue Thorin and his company following *An Unexpected Journey's* events. They are ushered along by Gandalf to the nearby home of Beorn, a skin-changer who takes the form of a ferocious black bear. That night, the Necromancer summons Azog to Dol Guldur, commanding him to marshal his forces for war, so Azog delegates the hunt for Thorin to his son Bolg. The following day, riding Beorn's ponies, the

---

[628] While complete details in the Biblical account of a system of fighting forms are not extant, the Midrashic, Talmudic, and Rabbinic accounts testify to fighting and combat strategies used by the ancient Israelites as well as legendary depictions of Israelite combatants.
[629] Sullivan, *Cinema Symbolism*, Chapter X.

company sets off to Mirkwood, where Gandalf discovers, near the Elven Gate, Eye of Sauron graffiti painted on a stone statue. Heeding a promise he made to Galadriel, Gandalf warns the company to remain on the path, leaving to investigate the tombs of the Nazgûl, viz. the Nine, or the Fallen Kings, in the High Fells. Upon entering the forest, the Dwarves lose their way, becoming ensnared by giant spiders–the Road of Trials continues. Bilbo sets about freeing them with his recently acquired invisibility ring and with the Elven dagger, which gets the nickname *Sting*. By wearing the ring, Bilbo can understand the spiders' language, further satisfying the Supernatural Aid component. He subsequently drops the ring, beginning to understand its dark influence after he brutally kills a creature to retrieve it. Easter egg: three rings of power were given to the Elves, seven to the Dwarf Lords, and nine rings were given to men; nine is the number of mankind because of the nine-months of pregnancy. Over time, the nine men become Ringwraiths, disciples of Sauron, because nine was looked upon as an evil number, resembling an inverted six.[630]

Wood-elves, led by Tauriel (Evangeline Lilly) and Legolas (Orlando Bloom), fend off the remaining spiders. The Road of Trial continues: the Elves imprison the company, bringing Thorin before their king, Thranduil. Thorin confronts the monarch about his neglect of the Dwarves of Erebor following Smaug's attack 60 years earlier, so he is imprisoned with the others. Bilbo, having avoided capture, arranges an escape using empty wine barrels sent downstream. Pursued by the Wood-elves, they are ambushed by Bolg and his Orc party, with Kíli wounded by a Morgul arrow. They engage in a running three-way battle down the river, but ultimately the Dwarves escape both groups of pursuers. Thranduil then seals off his kingdom when an Orc captive reveals an evil entity has returned, amassing an army in the south. Tauriel leaves to assist the Dwarves in their righteous quest, to stave off "a sleepless malice as black as the oncoming wall of night," so Legolas goes after her.

Meanwhile, Gandalf and Radagast investigate the mountain tombs of the Nazgûl, which they find to be empty. Gandalf deduces the Ringwraiths having been summoned to Dol Guldor, while Radagast speculates a human could not command such evil. Gandalf concludes Sauron has returned, placing Azog in command of a mighty army preparing for war.

---

630 Hall, *Secret Teachings*, 220.

The Road of Trials forges ahead: the company is smuggled into Esgaroth, or Lake-town, by a bargeman called Bard (Luke Evans), but are discovered raiding the town's armory for new weapons. Thorin promises the Master (Stephen Fry), his sycophantic counselor Alfrid Lickspittle (Ryan Gage), and the people of Lake-town a share of the mountain's treasure; it is revealed that Bard is a descendant of Dale's last ruler, possessing the only black arrow capable of killing Smaug. Alfrid Lickspittle is a precursor of Grima Wormtongue (Brad Dourif), the slimy chief advisor to King Théoden of Rohan, before being exposed as Saruman's spy.

Kíli is forced to remain behind, tended to by Fíli, Óin, and Bofur, as the remaining company receives a grand farewell. Next, Gandalf travels south to the ruins of Dol Guldur, while Radagast leaves to warn Galadriel of their discovery: the tombs of the Nazgûl are empty. Inside the ruins, Gandalf finds Thráin alive, but the Dwarf has been driven mad by black magic. Azog suddenly appears, so Gandalf tries to escape with Thráin, but the Necromancer overpowers them. The Necromancer kills Thráin and defeats Gandalf, revealing himself to be Sauron.

Thorin and his remaining company reach the Lonely Mountain, where Bilbo discovers the hidden entrance's keyhole, revealed by moonlight, not sunlight. The Jewish religion incorporates ancient lunar worship; their holidays, such as Yom Kippur and Rosh Hashanah, begin at nightfall when the moon shines overhead. God showed Moses the moon in its renewal, saying, "When the moon is renewed, that will be the head of the month" (Rashi's Commentary, Exodus 12:2); the other nations count by the sun, while Israel counts by the moon (Talmud, Sukkah 29a).[631] Hence, Luna's brilliance reveals the secret entrance to the Dwarves *qua* Hebrews' homeland.

Bilbo is sent into its bowels to retrieve the Arkenstone, but he accidentally awakens Smaug while negotiating the mountains of gold. While trying to find Bilbo–made invisible by the ring–Smaug divulges that he knows of Sauron's return. Back in Lake-town, Bard attempts to bring the black arrow to the town's launcher, fearing what may happen when the Dwarves enter the mountain. However, he is arrested by the Master and Alfrid in the process, leaving his son to hide the arrow. Bolg and his Orc party infiltrate

---

[631] Tzvi Freeman, "The Moon and Us," *Chabad.org*, n.d., https://www.chabad.org/library/article_cdo/aid/247861/jewish/The-Moon-and-Us.htm (accessed August 3, 2019).

the town and attack the four Dwarves but are quickly dispatched by Tauriel and Legolas. Tauriel then tends to Kíli, while Legolas leaves in pursuit of Bolg. With Galadriel absent, Tauriel satisfies the Meeting with Goddess element: her Elven healing powers and fighting abilities are second to none. As the goddess waxes, the Elf and the Dwarf are winning the boon of love. Meanwhile, a caged Gandalf helplessly watches as Azog, backed by an Orc army, march forth from Dol Guldur toward the Lonely Mountain.

The Road of Trials presses ahead: back inside the mountain, during a long chase, Bilbo and the Dwarves rekindle the mountain's forge using Smaug's flames to create and melt an enormous golden statue of Thrór, hoping to bury the fire-drake alive in the molten gold. They do so, but the dragon emerges angrily, flying out of the mountain to destroy Lake-town as Bilbo watches in horror. "I am fire. I am, death!" Smaug hisses, approaching the defenseless target.

The Battle of the Five Armies

With the Ultimate Boon–the retaking of Erebor–satisfied, and Smaug's subsequent death, one would think this is where the story ends, the adventure finished. But there is more, documenting the consequences and aftermath of the Dwarves reclaiming their homeland. Monomythic elements appear, but they are incongruous. Tolkien's storytelling is compelling, but a departure from traditional mythology, making the elements of the hero's journey a hodgepodge.

Picking up from where *The Desolation of Smaug* left off, Bilbo and the Dwarves watch from the Lonely Mountain as the Smaug sets Lake-town ablaze. Bard breaks out of prison, killing Smaug with the black arrow brought to him by his son Bain (John Bell), satisfying a late entry of Supernatural Aid. The dragon's falling carcass crushes the fleeing Master of Lake-town and his cronies, escaping on a boat laden with its gold. Again, this should be the end of the tale, but it isn't. Bard reluctantly becomes the new leader of Lake-town, with the Master's conniving servant, Alfrid, acting as Bard's reluctant servant, as they seek refuge in the ruins of Dale. Legolas and Tauriel travel to Mount Gundabad to investigate, with the female Elf bidding a heartfelt farewell to Kíli. Thorin, now struck with dragon sickness–unbridled avarice–over the vast treasure in the mountain, searches obsessively for the Arkenstone, which Bilbo had previously found but kept hidden. Upon hearing that Lake-town survivors have fled to Dale, he orders the Lonely Mountain's entrance sealed off. Erebor's halls are the Belly of the Whale, the dark place where digestion takes place, creating new energy. Inside its once mighty and magnificent passages and chambers, Thorin succumbs to the dragon sickness, his grandfather's avarice, questioning his kin's loyalty, caring only for the treasure, becoming an evil version of his former self. However, he leaves the belly a hero, emerging from Erebor to join the Battle of the Five Armies. He has seen the error of his ways, seeking redemption, demonstrating his kingship.

With the fire-drake's demise, Azog marches on Erebor with his vast Orc army, suspecting the Elves will likewise send a force to the mountain. The defiler dispatches Bolg to Gundabad to summon their second army. The Road of Trials continues when Legolas and Tauriel arrive at the Gunadabad, a northern fortress once part of the Witch-king of Angmar's kingdom, to witness Bolg's army sally forth, bolstered by giant bats. Armed confrontation is now inevitable.

The Road of Trials resumes as Galadriel, Elrond, and Saruman arrive at Dol Guldur to rescue Gandalf, sending him to safety with Radagast. They battle the Nazgûl and a formless Sauron; during the fight, Galadriel becomes an evil version of herself, banishing Sauron's spirit and the Ringwraiths to the East, satisfying the Woman as the Temptress element. The evil of Galadriel temporarily defeats the evil of Sauron–but for how long?

Thranduil, leading an Elf army, arrives in Dale to ally with Bard to reclaim a treasure once withheld by Thrór. Bard goes to the mountain to ask Thorin for the gold share that he had previously promised the people of Lake-town, but Thorin refuses. Gandalf arrives to warn Bard and Thranduil of the threat posed by Azog, but Thranduil dismisses him. Preparing for battle, Thorin gives Bilbo a Mithril shirt, which Bilbo will later give to Frodo (Elijah Wood), satisfying the Supernatural Aid requirement in *The Fellowship of the Ring*. Bilbo sneaks out of Erebor to hand the Arkenstone over to Thranduil and Bard so they can exchange it for the treasures they were promised and prevent a battle. When Bard and Thranduil's armies gather at Erebor's gates, offering to trade the Arkenstone for the promised share, Thorin angrily refuses to believe they have it until Bilbo admits giving it away, chiding the Dwarf king for letting greed cloud his judgment.

CINEMA SYMBOLISM 3

Evil against evil: appearing like a rotting corpse, Galadriel takes a turn for the worse, temporarily appearing demonic to defeat evil. The Woman as the Temptress is a metaphor for life's physical or material temptations since the hero-knight was often tempted by lust, sidelining his spiritual journey. Bilbo never encounters Galadriel or her evil incarnation; nevertheless, Galadriel's dark side serves notice that evil coexists with good, eventually becoming an omnipresent, corrupting force.

Outraged by what he sees as betrayal, Thorin nearly kills Bilbo, but Gandalf appears to shame Thorin into releasing him. Thorin's cousin, Dáin (Billy Connolly), arrives with his Dwarf army from the Iron Hills, and a battle of Dwarves against Elves and Men ensues, until Wereworms emerge from the ground, releasing Azog's detachment from their tunnels. With the Orcs outnumbering Dáin's army, Thranduil and Bard's forces, along with Gandalf and Bilbo, join the battle, fighting the Orcs. However, a second front opens when an army of Orcs, Ogres, and Trolls attack Dale, forcing Bard to withdraw his troops to defend the city, while Alfrid takes a bunch of gold and flees to his peculiar demise.

Before the conflict, inside Erebor, viz. the Belly of the Whale, Thorin suffered traumatic hallucinations before regaining his sanity, leading his company to join the battle. He rides toward Ravenhill with Dwalin, Fíli, and Kíli to kill Azog; Bilbo follows them, using his magic ring to move through the combat unseen. Tauriel and Legolas arrive to warn the Dwarves of Bolg's approaching army. Azog captures and kills Fíli as Bilbo, and the other Dwarves look on helplessly–this cycle ends the Road of Trials. Easter egg: during the Battle of the Five Armies, when all of the Dwarves are clad in armor prepped for battle, Gloin wears the same helmet worn by his son Gimli (John Rhys-Davies) in *The Lord of the Rings* trilogy.

Like father, like son: the helmet worn by Gloin (top) during the Battle of the Five Armies is later worn by his son, Gimli (bottom), in *The Lord of the Rings*.

As Thorin engages Azog in a fight to the death, Bolg knocks Bilbo unconscious, overpowers Tauriel, then kills Kíli, who had come to her aid. Legolas battles Bolg, eventually killing him. Thorin kills Azog but is fatally wounded in the process. This action satisfies the component of Apotheosis, with Thorin and the fallen Dwarves' deeds becoming folklore. "There is to be a great feast tonight. Songs will be sung, tales will be told, and Thorin Oakenshield will pass into legend," Balin later tells Bilbo, explaining divine exaltation.

The Great Eagles arrive with Radagast and Beorn to fight the newly arriving Orc army, making headway, eventually trashing the monster armies. Bilbo regains consciousness, making peace with the dying Thorin. Tauriel mourns Kili, with Thranduil acknowledging their love. Legolas then tells Thranduil he must leave, so the Elven King advises him to seek a Dunedain ranger in the north going by the *nom de guerre* Strider.

As Thorin's company begins settling back into Erebor with Dáin now King under the Mountain, Dale starts to recover and rebuild with Bard as the leader, Bilbo bids farewell to the company's remaining members, journeying home with Gandalf. As they part ways on the Shire's outskirts, Gandalf admits he knows about Bilbo's ring, warning him that they're not used without consequence. Bilbo returns to Bag End to find his belongings auctioned because he was presumed dead. He cancels the sale, but finds his home pillaged; he starts to tidy up and settle back in. Returning to the Shire with the One Ring satisfies the Magic Flight element: coming home with treasure reaped from fulfilling the Ultimate Boon. The journey is not without consequence; however, the One Ring's malevolent power remains dormant, not rearing its ugly head until many years have passed. Bilbo has changed for the better, but by returning to ordinary life, Bilbo is not a Christlike savior–Frodo will assume that mantle in *The Lord of the Rings*. As such, Bilbo does not experience monomythic elements like Refusal of the Return (on the contrary, Bilbo cannot wait to return to Bag End), Rescue from Without, Master of the Two Worlds. He is granted Freedom to Live, not fearing the future nor regretting the past, choosing to write a book detailing his adventures. Sixty years later, Bilbo receives a visit from Gandalf on his 111th birthday, thus beginning *The Fellowship of the Ring*.

One last thing remains: light, divine solar energy, thrives in the east as the rising sun, the south at midday, and the west as the setting sun. North is traditionally a place of darkness and evil, the domain of the Devil. In Middle-earth, the north is where wickedness dwells: Orcs come from the north, great serpents are from the north, Smaug is from the north, and the evil Kingdom of Angmar is in the north. Hence, the Men of the North took his body, and all that he possessed, and sealed it in the High Fells, inside a dungeon-like tomb said to be so dark that it would never come to light.[632]

The Hobbit was first published in September 1937. Its 1951 second edition (5th impression) features a significantly revised portion of Chapter V, "Riddles in the Dark," which was done to synch the storyline with its sequel, *The Lord of the Rings*, already in progress. Tolkien made some further revisions to the American edition published by Ballantine Books in February 1966 and the British paperback edition published by George Allen & Unwin that same year. Jackson's cinematic trilogy stays true to Tolkien's vision, allowing the monomyth to thrive. We have only to follow Bilbo through the classic stages of the universal adventure to see, once more, what has been revealed to us, humankind. Through the monomyth's elements, we understand the meaning and consequences of those images and themes in contemporary life, and the human spirit's singleness in its aspirations, powers, vicissitudes, and wisdom.[633] For Bilbo Baggins, like Harry Potter, Muad'Dib, Neo, and Luke Skywalker, is a hero, a mythological figure, we can attempt to emulate, bringing magic into our own lives.

---

632 The High Fells of Rhudaur are noncanonical, not appearing in Tolkien's stories.
633 Campbell, *Hero*, 28.

Campbell summarized the monomyth succinctly:

The mythological hero, setting forth from his common-day hut or castle, is lured, carried away, or else voluntarily proceeds, to the threshold of adventure. There he encounters a shadow presence that guards the passage. The hero may defeat or conciliate this power and go alive into the kingdom of the dark (brother-battle, dragon-battle; offering, charm), or be slain by the opponent and descend in death (dismemberment, crucifixion). Beyond the threshold, then, the hero journeys through a world of unfamiliar yet strangely intimate forces, some of which severely threaten him (tests), some of which give magical aid (helpers). When he arrives at die nadir of the mythological round, he undergoes a supreme ordeal and gains his reward. The triumph may be represented as the hero's sexual union with the goddess-mother of the world (sacred marriage), his recognition by the father-creator (father atonement), his own divinization (apotheosis), or again—if the powers have remained unfriendly to him—his theft of the boon he came to gain (bride-theft, fire-theft); intrinsically it is an expansion of consciousness and therewith of being (illumination; transfiguration, freedom). The final work is that of the return. If die powers have blessed the hero, he now sets forth under their protection (emissary); if not, he flees and is pursued (transformation flight, obstacle flight). At the return threshold the transcendental powers must remain behind; the hero re-emerges from the kingdom of dread (return, resurrection). The boon that he brings restores the world (elixir).[634]

Let's be honest: the monomyth, and its elements, are so universal they appear (not all of them) in just about every motion picture in some form or fashion. Where to begin: we'll start with the comedy classic, *Smokey and the Bandit* (1977). "Oh, I love your suits. It must have been a bitch getting a 68 extra fat and a 12 dwarf." – Bo "Bandit" Darville (Burt Reynolds, 1936-2018). Are not Big Enos (Pat McCormick, 1927-2005) and Little Enos Burdette (Paul Williams) Threshold Guardians, kicking off Bandit and Cledus "Snowman" Snow's (Jerry Reed, 1937-2008) "Eastbound and Down" cross-country Road of Trials? Does not the Bandit meet with the goddess, Carrie "Frog" (Sally Fields), falling in love while eluding

---
634 Ibid, 211.

the police? Could their CB Radios be construed as Supernatural Aid, the popular '70s technology allowing them to evade their pursuers, helping them complete their interstate beer run? Is not Sheriff Buford T. Justice (Jackie Gleason, 1916-1987) an ogre father archetype? Bandit and the Sheriff briefly atone at the denouement, expressing their mutual respect before continuing the chase when the outlaw races to Boston to bring back some clam chowder.

Let's turn to a movie already analyzed: *The House with a Clock in Its Walls*. Lewis is called to adventure by his uncle, who teaches him magic. Sorcery is Lewis' Supernatural Aid, and he meets with the goddess when he cultivates a friendship with Rose Rita Pottinger (Vanessa Anne Williams). Selina Izard satisfies the Woman as the Temptress, masquerading as his mother, so Lewis will use the necromantic grimoire to raise her dead husband. Defeating Isaac is Atonement with the Father; by conquering the dark wizard, Lewis saves the world from the doomsday clock.

The always popular Threshold Gaudian is pervasive in motion pictures. Glinda the Good Witch is the keeper of Oz's mysteries, instructing Dorothy in her numinous quest to attain gnosis. Doc Brown is the master of time travel; he opens the door via his DeLorean, allowing Marty to return to 1955 and alter history. *Black Swan*'s Leroy and Lily could be interpreted as Nina's wardens, instructing her in the lesser sexual mysteries to perfect alchemy: to change from White to Black Swan, finding her shadow self, becoming a masochistic Philosopher's Stone. They are more like tormentors than mentors, causing the ballerina to lose her life chasing a chimera: perfection.

Tinseltown does not use eyes in triangles to perform magic or trick us; instead, it is more devious and subtle. Through the monomyth and the archetypes, Hollywood casts its spells, mesmerizing us all, holding us captive, wanting more. This technique is one of cinema's mysteries: to present a vision of the world not as an arrangement of static stuff but as a secret spiritual river, baptizing us in unseen waters and occult forces.

CONCLUSION

> Murray, one small thing. When you bring me out,
> can you introduce me as Joker?
> Arthur Fleck/Joker, *Joker*, 2019

> Friends, we all live in the mud, in the shit!
> Shovel your way out of the shit.
> This is your shiny gold shovel. Two coats, guaranteed.
> Shovel your way out of the shit and into the truth.
> Dr. Amp/Dr. Jacoby, "Let's Rock," *Twin Peaks: The Return*, July 2017

> Damn ye! Let Neptune strike ye dead, Winslow! Hark!
> Thomas Wake, *The Lighthouse*, 2019

> It's a Celtic word. Samhain, it means the Lord of the Dead.
> The end of summer, the festival of Samhain, October 31st.
> Dr. Sam Loomis, *Halloween II*, 1981

> The music is all that matters. Nothing but the music.
> Boris Lermontov, *The Red Shoes*, 1948

"If you're good at something, never do it for free," said the Joker confidently in *The Dark Knight*. I'm sometimes asked why I do not make more videos analyzing occultism in popular culture during podcasts and interviews. As an attorney, my time is limited, so I choose to write books rather than produce YouTube videos. I love writing, and I'm more than happy to receive a guaranteed royalty payment instead of a nebulous YouTube check. Remember, there are no guarantees under the YouTube partner agreement about how much, or whether one will be paid. Thus, I write books and collect royalties, rather than filming, editing, and producing videos gratis.

As I write this conclusion in the waning days of September 2019, there are upcoming films that I would love to include in this book, but to do so would delay its publication substantially. *The Lighthouse* and *Maleficent: Mistress of Evil* are due out in a couple of weeks, and in December, we have *Star Wars: The Rise of Skywalker* hitting theaters. Due out February 2021 (moved because of the Coronavirus pandemic), *The King's Man* features an Illuminati/Carbonari-like cabal planning to kill millions by instigating a global conflict. Although I have not seen these films, the trailers and TV ads that I have viewed leave little doubt they veil esoteric undercurrents. One final Easter egg: on May 1, 2020, I watched *The Rise of Skywalker* on Blu-ray. I am, obviously, not going to analyze the film presently. However, I couldn't help notice something that I've decided to share. Note well when Rey enters Palpatine's throne room, Sith cultists chant ominously. I've heard this chant before. Specifically, in *Rosemary's Baby*, when the naked Satanists are standing around a drugged Rosemary in Roman and Minnie's apartment. The coven summons the Devil from the dark abyss to rape her to birth the Antichrist. The chant transplants the coven's Satanism to Emperor Palpatine, making him Mephistopheles incarnate.

I look forward to analyzing all of them, and many more, in *Cinema Symbolism 4*. Also, rumors recently surfaced on Twitter and Facebook about new episodes of *Twin Peaks* debuting in 2020–only time will tell if this turns out to be true or false.

Time to ring down the curtain on *Cinema Symbolism 3*; after publication, I am writing more works of occult fiction. The first is titled *Tales of the Black Flame: Belinda Taine and the Devil Door*, the first of an anthology series, and the other is the sequel to *A Pact with the Devil*. This fiction will be a nice break because writing dense books about esoteric movie symbolism and Masonic history requires much research, while works of fiction do not. Don't get me wrong, there will be a *Cinema Symbolism 4*, but these other projects must come first.

In addition to these books, I am also outlining a tome titled *Rob's Forbidden Tarot*, much like Crowley's *Book of Thoth* (1944) and *Criswell's Forbidden Predictions based in Nostradamus and the Tarot* (1972). This book will reinterpret the Tarot with brand new cards while keeping some of the classical, archetypal trumps only with unique images, adding a touch of modernity. As I've already mentioned, *A Pact with the Devil* (2017) was inspired by a vivid dream; likewise, *Rob's Forbidden Tarot* is driven by dark forces, compelling me–and even convincing me–to write the secretive book. One card from this new deck was briefly analyzed in Chapter XI of *Cinema Symbolism 2*, and, since then, I have been developing the deck for the Age of Aquarius. Tarot cards possess occult attributes and should be treated with the utmost respect. The word *Tarot* is the Druid word for *truth*, and there is nothing higher than veracity. Every person, place, or thing is openly revealed, not only to the cards' reader but to the one read. No matter how wise and proficient we may become in the Tarot's divine art, we still remain students.[635] I have long been fascinated by the seventy-eight cards; fifty-six are known as the Hall of Shadows or the Minor Arcana, the remaining twenty-two called the Grand Gallery or the Major Arcana. Hence, my interest in writing such a book, unveiling the prophetic occultism concealed within!

I am also re-editing, revising, and expanding *The Royal Arch of Enoch, Cinema Symbolism, Cinema Symbolism 2*, and *A Pact with the Devil*. *Royal Arch* will incorporate the *Path to Babylon* material, which I had intended to be a separate book, but it reads more like a series of essays. As such, I am returning the content from its source by placing it back in *The Royal Arch. Cinema Symbolism* and *CS2* will have some new information, and *Pact* will have some rewrites, tweaked scenes, and dialog. These new editions will replace the ones currently on the market and are set to hit the streets in 2021-2025.

But I digress. Cinema is the cornerstone of pop culture, a staple of modernity; it is present-day mythology. If my cinema books do anything, they prove this point beyond a shadow of a doubt. By analyzing the arcane imagery in film, we uncover the archetypes, the monomyth, numbers and numerology, folklore, Kabbalah, Freemasonry, alchemy, the supernatural, and the occult overflowing from the celluloid projected onto the silver screen. But controversy lingers, forcing us to ask: is this evidence of a Hollywood Illuminati conspiracy, the workings of a sinister unseen hand, or could it be Jungian synchronicity and the collective unconscious at play? Most Hollywood motion pictures present two different plots: a dumbed-down one for the public and a hidden one, using occult symbolism and esoteric themes to convey messages to the illuminated–this is irrefutable. By examining and uncovering the unknown, we learn higher truths,

---

635 Criswell, *Criswell's Forbidden Predictions based on Nostradamus and the Tarot* (Atlanta: Droke House/Hallux, Inc., 1972), 43.

inspiring us to meditate on the links between characters, the symbolism of the narrative, aesthetics, music, and the costuming. By investigating these cinematic mysteries and, concurrently, exploring the world of conspiracy, we discover new information, giving us a fresh perspective, allowing us to apply this wisdom to our daily lives, perhaps even gaining insights regarding the agenda of the global elites. This paradigm is happening now and forever, so beware, take care.

Rob's forbidden Tarot deck, while incorporating cards from the conventional pack, will have new cards like the Jester, the Huckster, the Forgotten Prisoner of Dark Oaks Castle, the Bookshelf, the Hand of Glory, and the Ghoul. As a teaser, here are three new cards from Rob's Forbidden Tarot; they are the Masturbator (left), the Chaos Magician (center), and the Shrunken Head (right).

FILMOGRAPHY

9 ½ Weeks. Dir. Adrian Lyne. Perfs. Kim Basinger, Mickey Rourke, Margaret Whitton, and Christine Baranski. MGM, 1986.

12 Monkeys. Dir. Terry Gilliam. Perfs. Bruce Willis, Madeleine Stowe, and Brad Pitt. Universal Pictures, 1995.

21-87. Dir. Arthur Lipsett. National Film Board of Canada, 1963.

2001: A Space Odyssey. Dir. Stanley Kubrick. Perfs. Keir Dullea, Gary Lockwood, and William Sylvester. MGM, 1968.

A bout de souffle (English: *Breathless*). Dir. Jean-Luc Godard. Perfs. Jean-Paul Belmondo and Jean Seberg. Films Around the World (USA), 1960.

The Adjustment Bureau. Dir. George Nolfi. Perfs. Matt Damon, Emily Blunt, Anthony Mackie, John Slattery, and Terence Stamp. Universal Pictures, 2011.

Alice in Wonderland. Dirs. Clyde Geronimi and Wilfred Jackson. Perfs. Kathryn Beaumont, Ed Wynn, and Richard Haydn. Walt Disney Productions, 1951.

Alice in Wonderland. Dir. Tim Burton. Perfs. Mia Wasikowska, Johnny Depp, and Helena Bonham Carter. Walt Disney Pictures, 2010.

Alice Through the Looking Glass. Dir. James Bobin. Perfs. Mia Wasikowska, Johnny Depp, and Helena Bonham Carter. Walt Disney Pictures, 2016.

Alien. Dir. Ridley Scott. Perfs. Sigourney Weaver, Tom Skerritt, and John Hurt. 20th Century Fox, 1979.

Aliens. Dir. James Cameron. Perfs. Sigourney Weaver, Michael Biehn, Paul Reiser, and Lance Henriksen. 20th Century Fox, 1986.

Alien 3. Dir. David Fincher. Perfs. Sigourney Weaver, Charles S. Dutton, and Charles Dance. 20th Century Fox, 1992.

Alien: Resurrection. Dir. Jean-Pierre Jeunet. Perfs. Sigourney Weaver, Winona Ryder, and Ron Perlman. 20th Century Fox, 1997.

All About Eve. Dir. Joseph L. Mankiewicz. Perfs. Bette Davis, Anne Baxter, George Sanders, and Celeste Holm. 20th Century Fox, 1950.

An American Werewolf in London. Dir. John Landis. Perfs. David Naughton, Jenny Agutter, and Griffin Dunne. Universal Pictures, 1981.

The Amityville Horror. Dir. Stuart Rosenberg. Perfs. James Brolin, Margot Kidder, and Rod Steiger. MGM, 1979.

Army of Darkness. Dir. Sam Raimi. Perfs. Bruce Campbell, Ian Abercrombie, and Embeth Davidtz. Universal Pictures, 1993.

Angel Heart. Dir. Alan Parker. Perfs. Mickey Rourke, Lisa Bonnet, Robert De Niro, and Charlotte Rampling. Tri-Star Pictures, 1987.

Atomic Blonde. Dir. David Leitch. Perfs. Charlize Theron, James McAvoy, John Goodman, Til Schweiger, Eddie Marsan, Sofia Boutella, Bill Skarsgård, and Toby Jones. Focus Features, 2017.

Back to the Future. Dir. Robert Zemeckis. Perfs. Michael J. Fox, Christopher Lloyd, and Lea Thompson. Universal Pictures, 1985.

Back to the Future II. Dir. Robert Zemeckis. Perfs. Michael J. Fox, Christopher Lloyd, and Lea Thompson. Universal Pictures, 1989.

Back to the Future III. Dir. Robert Zemeckis. Perfs. Michael J. Fox, Christopher Lloyd, and Lea Thompson. Universal Pictures, 1990.

Barry Lyndon. Dir. Stanley Kubrick. Perfs. Ryan O'Neal, Marisa Berenson, and Patrick Magee. Warner Bros., 1975.

Bates Motel [Television Series]. Created by Anthony Cipriano, Carlton Cuse, and Kerry Ehrin. Perfs. Vera Farmiga, Freddie Highmore, Nestor Carbonell, Olivia Cooke, and Max Thieriot. A&E Television Networks, 2013-2017.

Batman. Dir. Tim Burton. Perfs. Michael Keaton, Jack Nicholson, and Kim Basinger. Warner Brothers, 1989.

Batman Begins. Dir. Christopher Nolan. Perfs. Christian Bale, Michael Caine, and Ken Watanabe. Warner Bros., 2005.

Batman Returns. Dir. Tim Burton. Perfs. Michael Keaton, Danny DeVito, and Michelle Pfeiffer. Warner Bros., 1992.

Batman & Robin. Dir. Joel Schumacher. Perfs. Arnold Schwarzenegger, George Clooney, Uma Thurman, and Chris O'Donnell. Warner Bros., 1997.

Beauty and the Beast (French: *La Belle et la Bête*). Dir. Jean Cocteau. Perfs. Josette Day and Jean Marais. DisCine, 1946.

Beauty and the Beast. Dirs. Gary Trousdale and Kirk Wise. Perfs. Paige O'Hara, Richard White, Jerry Orbach, David Ogden Stiers, and Angela Lansbury. Buena Vista Pictures, 1991.

Beauty and the Beast. Dir. Bill Condon. Perfs. Emma Watson, Dan Stevens, Luke Evans, Kevin Kline, Josh Gad, Ewan McGregor, Stanley Tucci, Audra McDonald, Gugu Mbatha-Raw, Ian McKellen, and Emma Thompson. Walt Disney Studios, 2017.

Beavis and Butt-Head [Television Series]. Created by Mike Judge. Perfs. Mike Judge, Tracy Grandstaff, and Kristofor Brown. MTV, 1993-1997.

Being There. Dir. Hal Ashby. Perfs. Peter Sellers, Shirley MacLaine, and Melvyn Douglas. United Artists, 1979.

Bill & Ted's Bogus Journey. Dir. Pete Hewitt. Perfs. Keanu Reeves, Alex Winter, William Sadler, Joss Ackland, and George Carlin. Orion Pictures, 1991.

The Bitter Tears of Petra von Kant. Dir. Rainer Werner Fassbinder. Perfs. Margit Carstensen, Hanna Schygulla, Irm Hermann, Katrin Schaake, Eva Mattes, and Gisela Fackeldey. New Yorker Films, 1972 (Germany).

The Black Cat. Dir. Edgar G. Ulmer. Perfs. Boris Karloff, Bela Lugosi, and Harry Cording. Universal Pictures, 1934.

Black Swan. Dir. Darren Aronofsky. Perfs. Natalie Portman, Mila Kunis, and Vincent Cassel. 20th Century Fox, 2010.

Blade Runner. Dir. Ridley Scott. Perfs. Harrison Ford, Sean Young, Rutger Hauer, and Darryl Hannah. Warner Bros., 1982.

Blade Runner 2049. Dir. Denis Villeneuve. Perfs. Ryan Gosling, Harrison Ford, Ana de Armas, Sylvia Hoeks, Robin Wright, Mackenzie Davis, Carla Juri, Lennie James, Dave Bautista, and Jared Leto. Warner Bros., 2017.

The Blair Witch Project. Dirs. Daniel Myrick and Eduardo Sánchez. Perfs. Heather Donahue, Michael C. Williams, and Joshua Leonard. Artisan Entertainment, 1999.

Blue Velvet. Dir. David Lynch. Perfs. Isabella Rossellini, Kyle MacLachlan, Dennis Hopper, and Laura Dern. De Laurentiis Entertainment Group, 1986.

Brazil. Dir. Terry Gilliam. Perfs. Jonathan Pryce, Robert De Niro, Katherine Helmond, Ian Holm, and Bob Hoskins. 20th Century Fox, 1985.

The Breakfast Club. Dir. John Hughes. Perfs. Emilio Estevez, Paul Gleason, Anthony Michael Hall, Judd Nelson, Molly Ringwald, and Ally Sheedy. Universal Pictures, 1985.

Breakfast at Tiffany's. Dir. Blake Edwards. Perfs. Audrey Hepburn, George Peppard, and Patricia Neal. Paramount Pictures, 1961.

The Bride of Frankenstein. Dir. James Whale. Perfs. Boris Karloff, Colin Clive, Valerie Hobson, Elsa Lanchester, Ernest Thesiger, and E. E. Clive. Universal Pictures, 1935.

The Bridge on the River Kwai. Dir. David Lean. Perfs. William Holden, Jack Hawkins, Alec Guinness, and Sessue Hayakawa. Columbia Pictures, 1957.

Buffy the Vampire Slayer. Dir. Fran Rubel Kuzui. Perfs. Kristy Swanson, Donald Sutherland, Paul Reubens, Rutger Hauer, and Luke Perry. 20th Century Fox, 1992.

Buffy the Vampire Slayer [Television Series]. Created by Joss Whedon. Perfs. Sarah Michelle Gellar, Nicholas Brendon, and Alyson Hannigan. The WB and UPN, 1997-2003.

The Cabinet of Dr. Caligari. Dir. Robert Wiene. Perfs. Werner Krauss, Conrad Veidt, and Friedrich Feher. Decla-Bioscop, 1920.

Children of Paradise. Dir. Marcel Carné. Perfs. Arletty, Jean-Louis Barrault, Pierre Brasseur, Marcel Herrand, and Pierre Renoir. Pathé Consortium Cinéma, 1945.

The China Syndrome. Dir. James Bridges. Perfs. Jane Fonda, Jack Lemmon, and Michael Douglas. Columbia Pictures, 1979.

A Christmas Story. Dir. Bob Clark. Perfs. Melinda Dillon, Darren McGavin, and Peter Billingsley. MGM, 1983.

The Chronicles of Narnia: The Lion, the Witch and the Wardrobe. Dir. Andrew Adamson. Perfs. Tilda Swinton, Georgie Henley, and William Moseley. Walt Disney Pictures, 2005.

The Chronicles of Narnia: Prince Caspian. Dir. Andrew Adamson. Perfs. Ben Barnes, Skandar Keynes, and Georgie Henley. Walt Disney Pictures, 2008.

The Chronicles of Narnia: The Voyage of the Dawn Treader. Dir. Michael Apted. Perfs. Ben Barnes, Skandar Keynes, and Georgie Henley. 20th Century Fox, 2010.

Cinderella. Dirs. Clyde Geronimi and Wilfred Jackson. Perfs. Ilene Woods, James MacDonald, and Eleanor Audley. Walt Disney Productions, 1950.

Cinderella. Dir. Kenneth Branagh. Perfs. Cate Blanchett, Lily James, and Richard Madden. Walt Disney Studios, 2015.

"The City of New York vs. Homer Simpson." *The Simpsons*. Season 9, Episode 1. Fox Network, September 21, 1997.

Clash of the Titans. Dir. Desmond Davis. Perfs. Harry Hamlin, Laurence Olivier, Judi Bowker, Maggie Smith, Burgess Meredith, and Ursula Andress. MGM, 1981.

A Clockwork Orange. Dir. Stanley Kubrick. Perfs. Malcolm McDowell, Patrick Magee, and Adrienne Corri. Warner Bros., 1971.

Closing Gambit: 1978 Korchnoi versus Karpov and the Kremlin. Directed by Alan Byron. Cast: Boris Gelfand, Stuart Conquest, Viswanathan Anand. Content Media, 2018.

Coming to America. Dir. John Landis. Perfs. Eddie Murphy, Arsenio Hall, James Earl Jones, Shari Headley, and John Amos. Paramount Pictures, 1988.

The Conjuring. Dir. James Wan. Perfs. Patrick Wilson, Vera Farmiga, and Ron Livingston. New Line Cinema, 2013.

Creature from the Black Lagoon. Dir. Jack Arnold. Perfs. Richard Carlson, Julia Adams, Richard Denning, Antonio Moreno, and Whit Bissell. Universal Pictures, 1954.

Creepshow. Dir. George A. Romero. Perfs. Hal Holbrook, Adrienne Barbeau, Fritz Weaver, Leslie Nielsen, Carrie Nye, and E. G. Marshall. Warner Bros., 1982.

Crimson Peak. Dir. Guillermo del Toro. Perfs. Mia Wasikowska, Jessica Chastain, and Tom Hiddleston. Universal Pictures, 2015.

The Crow. Dir. Alex Proyas. Perfs. Brandon Lee, Ernie Hudson, and Michael Wincott. Miramax Films, 1994.

The Da Vinci Code. Dir. Ron Howard. Perfs. Tom Hanks, Audrey Tautou, Ian McKellen, and Alfred Molina. Sony Pictures Releasing, 2006.

Damien: Omen II. Dir. Don Taylor. Perfs. William Holden, Jonathan Scott-Taylor, and Lee Grant. 20th Century Fox, 1978.

Darkman. Dir. Sam Raimi. Perfs. Liam Neeson, Frances McDormand, Colin Friels, and Larry Drake. Universal Pictures, 1990.

Dark City. Dir. Alex Proyas. Perfs. Jennifer Connelly, Rufus Sewell, William Hurt, and Kiefer Sutherland. New Line Cinema, 1998.

The Dark Knight. Dir. Christopher Nolan. Perfs. Christian Bale, Gary Oldman, Heath Ledger, and Aaron Eckhart. Warner Bros., 2008.

The Dark Knight Rises. Dir. Christopher Nolan. Perfs. Christian Bale, Tom Hardy, and Anne Hathaway. Warner Bros., 2012.

Dark Night of the Scarecrow. Dir. Frank De Felitta. Perfs. Larry Drake, Charles Durning, Tonya Crowe, Jocelyn Brando, and Lane Smith. CBS, 1981.

The Dark Secret of Harvest Home. Dir. Leo Penn. Perfs. Bette Davis, David Ackroyd, Joanna Miles, Rosanna Arquette, and Norman Lloyd. NBC, 1978.

Dark Water. Dir. Walter Salles. Perfs. Jennifer Connelly and Tim Roth. Buena Vista Pictures, 2005.

The Day the Earth Stood Still. Dir. Robert Wise. Perfs. Michael Rennie, Patricia Neal, and Hugh Marlowe. 20th Century Fox, 1951.

Dial M for Murder. Dir. Alfred Hitchcock. Perfs. Ray Milland, Grace Kelly, and Robert Cummings. Warner Bros., 1954.

Die Hard. Dir. John McTiernan. Perfs. Bruce Willis, Alan Rickman, Alexander Godunov, and Bonnie Bedelia. 20th Century Fox, 1988.

Dirty Dancing. Dir. Emile Ardolino. Perfs. Patrick Swayze, Jennifer Grey, Jerry Orbach, and Cynthia Rhodes. Vestron Pictures, 1987.

"Donald Trump Counting Sheep, 2010 Certa Mattress Commercial," *YouTube*, 0.31, posted by "LIBERTY VIDZ," September 27, 2018, https://www.youtube.com/watch?v=ctCORNEvkCo.

Donnie Darko. Dir. Richard Kelly. Perfs. Jake Gyllenhaal, Jena Malone, Maggie Gyllenhaal, Drew Barrymore, Mary McDonnell, Katharine Ross, and Patrick Swayze. Newmarket Films, 2001.

Dr. Strangelove or: How I Learned to Stop Worrying and Love the Bomb. Dir. Stanley Kubrick. Perfs. Peter Sellers, George C. Scott, and Sterling Hayden. Columbia Pictures, 1964.

Dracula. Dirs. Tod Browning and Karl Freund (un-credited). Perfs. Bela Lugosi, Helen Chandler, and David Manners. Universal Studios, 1931.

Dune. Dir. David Lynch. Perfs. Kyle MacLachlan, Virginia Madsen, Leonardo Cimino, Brad Dourif, José Ferrer, Linda Hunt, and Francesca Annis. Universal Studios, 1984.

The Elephant Man. Dir. David Lynch. Perfs. John Hurt, Anthony Hopkins, Anne Bancroft, and John Gielgud. Paramount Pictures, 1980.

"End of Days." *Legends of Chamberlain Heights*, Season 1, Episode 8. Comedy Central, November 16, 2016.

"The End of the World." *Trackdown*. Season 1, Episode 30. CBS, May 9, 1958.

Equilibrium. Dir. Kurt Wimmer. Perfs. Christian Bale, Emily Watson, and Taye Diggs. Miramax Films, 2002.

Eraserhead. Dir. David Lynch. Perfs. Jack Nance, Charlotte Stewart, Jeanne Bates, Judith Anna Roberts, Laurel Near, and Jack Fisk. Libre Films International, 1977.

Escape from New York. Dir. John Carpenter. Perfs. Kurt Russell, Lee Van Cleef, Adrienne Barbeau, and Ernest Borgnine. AVCO Embassy Pictures, 1981.

E.T. the Extra-Terrestrial. Dir. Steven Spielberg. Perfs. Henry Thomas, Drew Barrymore, and Peter Coyote. Universal Pictures, 1982.

The Evil Dead. Dir. Sam Raimi. Perfs. Bruce Campbell, Ellen Sandweiss, Richard DeManincor, and Betsy Baker. New Line Cinema, 1981.

Evil Dead II: Dead by Dawn. Dir. Sam Raimi. Perfs. Bruce Campbell, Sarah Berry, Dan Hicks, and Kassie Wesley. Rosebud Releasing Corporation, 1987.

Excalibur. Dir. John Boorman. Perfs. Nigel Terry, Helen Mirren, Nicolas Clay, Cheri Lunghi, and Nicol Williamson. Orion Pictures Corp., 1981.

eXistenZ. Dir. David Cronenberg. Perfs. Jennifer Jason Leigh and Jude Law. Miramax Films, 1999.

The Exorcist. Dir. William Friedkin. Perfs. Linda Blair, Max von Sydow, Ellen Burstyn, Jason Miller, and Kitty Winn. Warner Bros., 1973.

Eyes Wide Shut. Dir. Stanley Kubrick. Perfs. Tom Cruise, Nicole Kidman, Sydney Pollack, and Todd Field. Warner Bros., 1999.

"Falling." *Supergirl*. Season 1, Episode 16. CBS, March 14, 2018.

Fatal Attraction. Dir. Adrian Lyne. Perfs. Michael Douglas, Glenn Close, and Anne Archer. Paramount Pictures, 1987.

The Fifth Element. Dir. Luc Besson. Perfs. Bruce Willis, Gary Oldman, and Milla Jovovich. Columbia Pictures, 1997.

Fight Club. Dir. David Fincher. Perfs. Brad Pitt, Edward Norton, and Helena Bonham Carter. 20th Century Fox, 1999.

Finding Neverland. Dir. Marc Forster. Perfs. Johnny Depp, Kate Winslet, Julie Christie, Radha Mitchell. Miramax Films, 2004.

Follow the Fleet. Dir. Mark Sandrich. Perfs. Fred Astaire, Ginger Rogers, Harriet Hilliard, and Randolph Scott. RKO Radio Pictures, 1936.

Forbidden Planet. Dir. Fred M. Wilcox. Perfs. Walter Pidgeon, Anne Francis, and Leslie Nielsen. MGM, 1956.

Fraggle Rock [Television Series]. Created by Jim Henson. Perfs. Gerry Parkes, Jerry Nelson, Dave Goelz, and Fulton Mackay. HBO, 1983-1987.

Frankenstein. Dir. James Whale. Perfs. Colin Clive, Mae Clarke, and Boris Karloff. Universal Pictures, 1931.

Frankenstein Meets the Wolfman. Dir. Roy William Neill. Perfs. Lon Chaney Jr., Ilona Massey, Patric Knowles, Lionel Atwill, Bela Lugosi, and Maria Ouspenskaya. Universal Pictures, 1943.

The Fugitive [Television Series]. Created by Roy Huggins. Perfs. David Janssen and Barry Morse. ABC, 1963-1967.

The Fugitive Kind. Dir. Sidney Lumet. Perfs. Marlon Brando, Anna Magnani, Joanne Woodward, and Maureen Stapleton. United Artists, 1960.

Full Metal Jacket. Dir. Stanley Kubrick. Perfs. Matthew Modine, Adam Baldwin, and Vincent D'Onofrio. Warner Bros., 1987.

Gangs of New York. Dir. Martin Scorsese. Perfs. Leonardo DiCaprio, Cameron Diaz, and Daniel Day-Lewis. Buena Vista Distribution, 2002.

Ghostbusters. Dir. Ivan Reitman. Perfs. Dan Aykroyd, Harold Ramis, Murray, Sigourney Weaver, Rick Moranis, Annie Potts, William Atherton, and Ernie Hudson. Columbia Pictures, 1984.

The Ghost of Frankenstein. Dir. Erle C. Kenton. Perfs. Lon Chaney Jr., Bela Lugosi, Cedric Hardwicke, Ralph Bellamy, Lionel Atwill, and Evelyn Ankers. Universal Pictures, 1942.

Glen or Glenda. Dir. Edward D. Wood, Jr. Perfs. Edward D. Wood, Jr. (as Daniel Davis), Bela Lugosi, Lyle Talbot, Delores Fuller, Conrad Brooks, and Timothy Farrell. Screen Classics, 1953.

The Good, the Bad and the Ugly. Dir. Sergio Leone. Perfs. Clint Eastwood, Eli Wallach, Lee Van Cleef. United Artists, 1965.

The Graduate. Dir. Mike Nichols. Perfs. Anne Bancroft, Dustin Hoffman, and Katharine Ross. Embassy Pictures, 1967.

The Green Mile. Dir. Frank Darabont. Perfs. Tom Hanks, Michael Clarke Duncan, and David Morse. Warner Bros., 1999.

Gremlins. Dir. Joe Dante. Perfs. Zach Galligan, Phoebe Cates, Hoyt Axton, Polly Holliday, and Frances Lee McCain. Warner Bros., 1984.

Gremlins 2: The New Batch. Dir. Joe Dante. Perfs. Zach Galligan, Phoebe Cates, Dick Miller, and Jackie Joseph. Warner Bros., 1990.

Gretel & Hansel: A Grim Fairy Tale. Dir. Oz Perkins. Pers. Sophia Lillis, Sam Leakey, Alice Krige, Jessica De Gouw and Charles Babalola. United Artist Releasing, 2020.

Groundhog Day. Dir. Harold Ramis. Perfs. Bill Murray, Andie MacDowell, and Chris Elliott. Columbia Pictures, 1993.

Hairspray. Dir. John Waters. Perfs. Ricki Lake, Divine, Debbie Harry, Sonny Bono, Jerry Stiller, Leslie Ann Powers, Colleen Fitzpatrick, and Michael St. Gerard. New Line Cinema, 1988.

Hairspray. Dir. Adam Shankman. Perfs. John Travolta, Michelle Pfeiffer, Christopher Walken, Amanda Bynes, James Marsden, Queen Latifah, Brittany Snow, Zac Efron, Elijah Kelley, Allison Janney, and Nikki Blonsky. New Line Cinema, 2007.

Halloween. Dir. John Carpenter. Perfs. Jamie Lee Curtis, Donald Pleasence, and Tony Moran. Compass International Pictures, 1978.

Halloween. Dir. David Gordon Green. Perfs. Jamie Lee Curtis, Judy Greer, Andi Matichak, Will Patton, and Virginia Gardner. Universal Pictures, 2018.

Halloween II. Dir. Rick Rosenthal. Perfs. Jamie Lee Curtis, Donald Pleasence, and Charles Cyphers. Universal Pictures, 1981.

Halloween II. Dir. Rob Zombie. Perfs. Malcolm McDowell, Tyler Mane, Sheri Moon Zombie, Brad Dourif, Danielle Harris, and Scout Taylor-Compton. Dimension Films, 2009.

Halloween III: Season of the Witch. Dir. Tommy Lee Wallace. Perfs. Tom Atkins, Stacey Nelkin, and Dan O'Herlihy. Universal Pictures, 1982.

Halloween 4: The Return of Michael Myers. Dir. Dwight H. Little. Perfs. Donald Pleasence, Ellie Cornell, and Danielle Harris. 20th Century Fox, 1988.

Halloween 5: The Revenge of Michael Myers. Dir. Dominique Othenin-Girard. Perfs. Donald Pleasence, Danielle Harris, and Ellie Cornell. Galaxy Releasing, 1989.

Halloween 6: The Curse of Michael Myers. Dir. Joe Chappelle. Perfs. Donald Pleasence, Paul Stephen Rudd, and Marianne Hagan. Dimension Films, 1995.

Halloween H20: 20 Years Later. Dir. Steve Miner. Perfs. Jamie Lee Curtis, Adam Arkin, Michelle Williams, and Adam Hann-Byrd. Dimension Films, 1998.

Halloween 8: Resurrection. Dir. Rick Rosenthal. Perfs. Busta Rhymes, Bianca Kajlich, and Thomas Ian Nicholas. Dimension Films, 2002.

Hardware Wars. Dir. Ernie Fosselius. Perfs. Scott Mathews, Cindy Furgatch, and Jeff Hale. Pyramid Films, 1978.

Harry Potter and the Sorcerer's Stone. Dir. Chris Columbus. Perfs. Daniel Radcliffe, Emma Watson, Rupert Grint, Alan Rickman, and Maggie Smith. Warner Bros., 2001.

Harry Potter and the Chamber of Secrets. Dir. Chris Columbus. Perfs. Daniel Radcliffe, Emma Watson, Rupert Grint. Warner Bros., 2002.

Harry Potter and the Prisoner of Azkaban. Directed by Alfonso Cuarón. Perfs. Daniel Radcliffe, Emma Watson, and Rupert Grint. Warner Bros., 2004.

Harry Potter and the Goblet of Fire. Dir. Mike Newell. Perfs. Daniel Radcliffe, Emma Watson, and Rupert Grint. Warner Bros., 2005.

Harry Potter and the Order of the Phoenix. Dir. David Yates. Perfs. Daniel Radcliffe, Emma Watson, and Rupert Grint. Warner Bros., 2007.

Harry Potter and the Half-Blood Prince. Dir. David Yates. Perfs. Daniel Radcliffe, Emma Watson, and Rupert Grint. Warner Bros., 2009.

Harry Potter and the Deathly Hallows Part 1. Dir. David Yates. Perfs. Daniel Radcliffe, Emma Watson, Rupert Grint, Evanna Lynch, Ralph Fiennes, Alan Rickman, and Bonnie Wright. Warner Bros., 2010.

Harry Potter and the Deathly Hallows Part 2. Dir. David Yates. Perfs. Daniel Radcliffe, Emma Watson, Rupert Grint, Evanna Lynch, Ralph Fiennes, Alan Rickman, and Bonnie Wright. Warner Bros., 2011.

Häxan: The Witches or Witchcraft Through the Ages. Dir. Benjamin Christensen. Perfs. Benjamin Christensen, Clara Pontoppidan, Oscar Stribolt, Astrid Holm, and Maren Pedersen. Skandias Filmbyrå, 1922.

Heat. Dir. Michael Mann. Perfs. Al Pacino, Robert De Niro, Val Kilmer, Tom Sizemore, Diane Venora, Amy Brenneman, and Ashley Judd. Warner Bros., 1995.

Hereditary. Dir. Ari Aster. Perfs. Toni Collette, Gabriel Byrne, Milly Shapiro, and Alex Wolff. A24, 2018.

The Hobbit: An Unexpected Journey. Dir. Peter Jackson. Perfs. Ian McKellen, Martin Freeman, and Richard Armitage. Warner Bros., 2012

The Hobbit: The Desolation of Smaug. Dir. Peter Jackson. Perfs. Ian McKellen, Martin Freeman, and Richard Armitage. Warner Bros., 2013.

The Hobbit: The Battle of the Five Armies. Dir. Peter Jackson. Perfs. Ian McKellen, Martin Freeman, and Richard Armitage. Warner Bros., 2014.

The House of Fear. Dir. Roy William Neill. Perfs. Basil Rathbone, Nigel Bruce, Aubrey Mather, and Dennis Hoey. Universal Pictures, 1945.

The House with a Clock in Its Walls. Dir. Eli Roth. Perfs. Jack Black, Cate Blanchett, Owen Vaccaro, Renée Elise Goldsberry, Sunny Suljic, and Kyle MacLachlan. Universal Pictures, 2018.

House of Frankenstein. Dir. Erle C. Kenton. Perfs. Boris Karloff, Lon Chaney Jr., John Carradine, J. Carrol Naish. Universal Studios, 1944.

The Hunger. Dir. Tony Scott. Perfs. Catherine Deneuve, David Bowie, and Susan Sarandon. MGM/UA, 1983.

The Hunchback of Notre Dame. Dir. Wallace Worsley. Perf. Lon Chaney. Universal Pictures, 1923.

The Hunchback of Notre Dame. Dir. Gary Trousdale, Kirk Wise. Perfs. Tom Hulce, Demi Moore, and Heidi Mollenhauer. Buena Vista Pictures, 1996.

"Nothing to Fear." Batman: The Animated Series. Season 1, Episode 10. Fox Kids, September 15, 1992.

Inauguration of the Pleasure Dome. Dir. Kenneth Anger. Perfs. Samson De Brier, Marjorie Cameron, Renate Druks, and Joan Whitney. 1954 (later released by Mystic Fire Video).

Inception. Dir. Christopher Nolan. Perfs. Leonardo DiCaprio, Ken Watanabe, Joseph Gordon-Levitt, Marion Cotillard, and Ellen Page. Warner Bros., 2010.

Intolerance. Dir. D.W. Griffith. Perfs. Vera Lewis, Ralph Lewis, Mae Marsh, Robert Harron, Constance Talmadge, and Lillian Gish. Triangle Distributing Corporation, 1916.

Jacob's Ladder. Dir. Adrian Lyne. Perf. Tim Robbins, Elizabeth Peña, and Danny Aiello. TriStar Pictures, 1990.

Joker. Dir. Todd Phillips. Perfs. Joaquin Phoenix, Robert De Niro, Zazie Beetz, and Francis Conroy. Warner Bros., 2019.

"The Joker Is Wild." *Batman*. Season 1, Episode 5. ABC, January 26, 1966.

Jules et Jim. Dir. François Truffaut. Perfs. Jeanne Moreau, Oskar Werner, and Henri Serre. Janus Films (USA), 1962.

Killer's Kiss. Dir. Stanley Kubrick. Perfs. Frank Silvera, Jamie Smith, Irene Kane, and Ruth Sobotka. United Artists, 1955.

The Killing. Dir. Stanly Kubrick. Perfs. Sterling Hayden, Coleen Gray, and Vince Edwards, and features Marie Windsor, Elisha Cook Jr., Jay C. Flippen, and Timothy Carey. United Artists, 1956.

The King of Comedy. Dir. Martin Scorsese. Perfs. Robert De Niro, Jerry Lewis, Sandra Bernhard, and Diahnne Abbott. 20th Century Fox, 1982.

King Kong. Dirs. Merian C. Cooper and Ernest B. Schoedsack. Perfs. Fay Wray, Robert Armstrong, and Bruce Cabot. RKO Radio Pictures, 1933.

Kings Row. Dir. Sam Wood. Perfs. Ann Sheridan, Robert Cummings, Ronald Reagan, and Betty Field. Warner Bros., 1942.

Krull. Dir. Peter Yates. Perfs. Ken Marshall, Lysette Anthony, Freddie Jones, and Francesca Annis. Columbia Pictures, 1983.

The Lair of the White Worm. Dir. Ken Russell. Perfs. Amanda Donohoe, Hugh Grant, Catherine Oxenberg, Peter Capaldi, Sammi Davis, and Stratford Johns. Vestron Pictures, 1988.

The Last Temptation of Christ. Dir. Martin Scorsese. Perfs. Willem Dafoe, Harvey Keitel, Barbara Hershey, Harry Dean Stanton, and David Bowie. Universal Pictures, 1988.

The Last Unicorn. Dirs. Arthur Rankin Jr. and Jules Bass. Perfs. Alan Arkin, Jeff Bridges, Mia Farrow, and Tammy Grimes. Jensen Farley Pictures, 1982.

Legend. Dir. Ridley Scott. Perfs. Tom Cruise, Mia Sara, Tim Curry, David Bennent, Alice Playten, Billy Barty, and Cork Hubbert. Universal Pictures, 1985.

The Lego Movie. Dirs. Phil Lord and Christopher Miller. Perfs. Chris Pratt, Will Ferrell, Elizabeth Banks, Will Arnett, Nick Offerman, Alison Brie, Charlie Day, Liam Neeson, and Morgan Freeman. Warner Bros., 2014.

Letter Never Sent. Dir. Mikhail Kalatozov. Perfs. Tatiana Samoilova, Innokenty Smoktunovsky, Galina Kozhakina, and Vasily Livanov. The Criterion Collection (DVD, 2012).

The Lighthouse. Dir. Roger Eggers. Perfs. Robert Pattinson, Willem Dafoe, and Valeriia Karaman. A24, 2019.

The Lion King. Dirs. Roger Allers and Rob Minkoff. Perfs. Matthew Broderick, Jeremy Irons, and James Earl Jones. Walt Disney Pictures, 1994.

The Little Mermaid. Dir. Ron Clements and John Musker. Perfs. Jodi Benson, Christopher Daniel Barnes, Kenneth Mars, Pat and Carroll. Buena Vista Pictures, 1989.

Lizzie. Dir. Craig William Macneill. Perfs. Chloë Sevigny, Kristen Stewart, Jay Huguley, Jamey Sheridan, Fiona Shaw, Kim Dickens, Denis O'Hare, and Jeff Perry. Saban Films, 2018.

Lolita. Dir. Stanley Kubrick. Perfs. James Mason, Sue Lyon, Shelley Winters, and Peter Sellers. MGM, 1962.

The Lord of the Rings: The Fellowship of the Ring. Dir. Peter Jackson. Perfs. Elijah Wood, Ian McKellen, Christopher Lee, Viggo Mortensen, and Orlando Bloom. New Line Cinema, 2001.

The Lord of the Rings: The Two Towers. Dir. Peter Jackson. Perfs. Elijah Wood, Ian McKellen, Christopher Lee, Viggo Mortensen, and Orlando Bloom. New Line Cinema, 2002.

The Lord of the Rings: The Return of the King. Dir. Peter Jackson. Perfs. Elijah Wood, Ian McKellen, Viggo Mortensen, and Orlando Bloom. New Line Cinema, 2003.

Lost Highway. Dir. David Lynch. Perfs. Bill Pullman, Patricia Arquette, and Robert Blake. October Films, 1997.

The Lovely Bones. Dir. Peter Jackson. Perfs. Rachel Weisz, Mark Wahlberg, Saoirse Ronan, and Stanley Tucci. Paramount Pictures, 2009.

Mac and Me. Dir. Stewart Raffill. Perfs. Christine Ebersole, Jonathan Ward, Katrina Caspary, Lauren Stanley, and Jade Calegory. Orion Pictures, 1988.

Make Mine Music. Dirs. Jack Kinney, Clyde Geronimi, Hamilton Luske, Joshua Meador, and Robert Cormack. Perfs. Nelson Eddy, Dinah Shore, Benny Goodman, the Andrews Sisters, and Jerry Colonna. RKO Radio Pictures, Inc., 1946.

Maleficent. Dir. Robert Stromberg. Perfs. Angelina Jolie, Elle Fanning, and Sharlto Copley. Walt Disney Studios, 2014.

Maleficent: Mistress of Evil. Dir. Joachim Rønning. Perfs. Angelina Jolie, Elle Fanning, Chiwetel Ejiofor, Sam Riley and Michelle Pfeiffer. Walt Disney Studios, 2019.

The Man Who Knew Too Much. Dir. Alfred Hitchcock. Perfs. James Stewart, Doris Day, Brenda de Banzie, and Bernard Miles. Paramount Pictures, 1956.

The Man Who Laughs. Dir. Paul Leni. Perfs. Mary Philbin, Conrad Veidt, and Brandon Hurst. Universal Pictures, 1928.

Maria's Lovers. Dir. Andrey Konchalovsky. Perfs. Nastassja Kinski, John Savage, and Keith Carradine. Cannon Films, 1984.

Mark of the Vampire. Dir. Tod Browning. Perfs. Lionel Barrymore, Elizabeth Allan, Bela Lugosi, and Lionel Atwill. MGM, 1935.

"The Mazarin Stone." *The Memoirs of Sherlock Holmes*, Season 1, Episode 5. ITV, April 4, 1994.

The Matrix. Dirs. the Waschowskis. Perfs. Keanu Reeves, Laurence Fishburne, Hugo Weaving, and Carrie-Anne Moss. Warner Bros., 1999.

The Matrix Reloaded. Dirs. the Waschowskis. Perfs. Keanu Reeves, Laurence Fishburne, Hugo Weaving, and Carrie-Anne Moss. Warner Bros., 2003.

The Matrix Revolutions. Dirs. the Waschowskis. Perfs. Keanu Reeves, Laurence Fishburne, Hugo Weaving, and Carrie-Anne Moss. Warner Bros., 2003.

Memento. Dir. Christopher Nolan. Perfs. Guy Pearce, Carrie-Anne Moss, and Joe Pantoliano. Newmarket Films, 2001.

Metropolis. Dir. Fritz Lang. Perfs. Brigitte Helm, Alfred Abel, and Gustav Fröhlich. Paramount Pictures (USA), 1927.

Midsommar. Dir. Ari Aster. Perfs. Florence Pugh, Jack Reynor, and William Jackson Harper. A24, 2019.

Minority Report. Dir. Steven Spielberg. Perfs. Tom Cruise, Colin Farrell, Samantha Morton, and Max von Sydow. 20th Century Fox, 2002.

Modern Times. Dir. Charlies Chaplan. Perfs. Charlie Chaplan, Paulette Goddard, and Henry Bergman. United Artists, 1936.

The Monster Squad. Dir. Fred Dekker. Perfs. André Gower, Robby Kiger, Duncan Regehr, Stephen Macht, Stan Shaw, and Tom Noonan. TriStar Pictures, 1987.

The Morton Downey Jr. Show [Talk Show]. Created by Morton Downey Jr. WWOR, 1987-1989.

Mother! Dir. Darren Aronofsky. Perfs. Jennifer Lawrence, Javier Bardem, Ed Harris, and Michelle Pfeiffer. Paramount Pictures, 2017.

Mulholland Drive. Dir. David Lynch. Perfs. Naomi Watts, Laura Harring, and Justin Theroux. Universal Pictures, 2001.

The Mummy. Dir. Karl Freund. Perfs. Boris Karloff, Zita Johann, David Manners, Edward Van Sloan, and Arthur Byron. Universal Studios, 1932.

The Mummy. Dir. Terence Fisher. Perfs. Christopher Lee and Peter Cushing. Universal International, 1959.

The Mummy. Dir. Stephen Sommers. Perfs. Brendan Fraser, Rachel Weisz, John Hannah, Kevin J. O'Connor, and Arnold Vosloo. Universal Pictures, 1999.

The Mummy's Hand. Dir. Christy Cabanne. Perfs. Dick Foran, Peggy Moran, Wallace Ford, Eduardo Ciannelli, and George Zucco. Universal Pictures, 1940.

The Mummy Returns. Dir. Stephen Sommers. Perfs. Brendan Fraser, Rachel Weisz, John Hannah, Arnold Vosloo, Oded Fehr, Patricia Velásquez, and Dwayne Johnson. Universal Pictures, 2001.

The Mummy's Tomb. Dir. Harold Young. Perfs. Lon Chaney Jr., Dick Foran, and John Hubbard. Universal Pictures, 1942.

Murders in the Rue Morgue. Dir. Robert Florey. Perfs. Bela Lugosi, Sidney Fox, and Leon Ames. Universal Pictures, 1932.

Mystery of Chessboxing. Dir. Joseph Kuo, Perfs. Mark Long, Jack Long, Lee Yi Min. Hong Hwa International Films, 1979.

National Lampoon's Vacation. Dir. Harold Ramis. Perfs. Chevy Chase, Beverly D'Angelo, and Imogene Coca. Warner Bros., 1983.

The Neon Demon. Dir. Nicolas Winding Refn. Perfs. Elle Fanning, Christina Hendricks, and Keanu Reeves. Amazon Studios, 2016.

Nerve. Dirs. Henry Joost and Ariel Schulman. Perfs. Emma Roberts, Dave Franco, and Juliette Lewis. Lionsgate, 2016.

The New York Ripper. Dir. Lucio Fulci. Perfs. Jack Hedley, Paolo Malco, Almanta Suska, and Alexandra Delli Colli. Vidmark Entertainment (USA, VHS), 1987.

Nightbreed. Dir. Clive Barker. Perfs. Craig Sheffer, David Cronenberg, and Anne Bobby. 20th Century Fox, 1990.

Night of the Creeps. Dir. Fred Dekker. Perfs. Tom Atkins, Jason Lively, Steve Marshall, and Jill Whitlow. TriStar Pictures, 1986.

Night of the Living Dead. Dir. George Romero. Perfs. Duane Jones and Judith O'Dea. Continental Distributing, 1968.

The Night Stalker. Dir. John Llewellyn Moxey. Perfs. Darren McGavin, Simon Oakland, Carol Lynley, and Barry Atwater. ABC, 1972.

The Night Strangler. Dir. Dan Curtis. Perfs. Darren McGavin, Simon Oakland, Jo Ann Pflug, and Richard Anderson. ABC, 1973.

"Nothing to Fear." *Batman: The Animated Series*. Season 1, Episode 10. Fox Kids, September 15, 1992.

Nosferatu: A Symphony of Horror. Dir. F. W. Murnau. Perfs. Max Schreck, Gustav von Wangenheim, Greta Schröder, Alexander Granach, Ruth Landshoff, and Wolfgang Heinz. Film Arts Guild, 1922.

The Old Dark House. Dir. James Whale. Perfs. Boris Karloff, Melvyn Douglas, Charles Laughton, Gloria Stuart, and Raymond Massey. Universal Pictures, 1932.

The Omen. Dir. Richard Donner. Perfs. Gregory Peck, Lee Remick, David Warner, and Billie Whitelaw. 20th Century Fox, 1976.

Omen III: The Final Conflict. Dir. Graham Baker. Perfs. Sam Neill, Rossano Brazzi, Don Gordon, and Lisa Harrow. 20th Century Fox, 1981.

One Flew Over the Cuckoo's Nest. Dir. Milos Forman. Perfs. Jack Nicholson, Louise Fletcher, and Michael Berryman. United Artists, 1975.

Open Your Eyes. Dir. Alejandro Amenábar. Perfs. Eduardo Noriega, Penélope Cruz, and Chete Lera. LIVE Entertainment, 1997.

Orgy of the Dead. Dir. A. C. Stephen. Perfs. Criswell, Fawn Silver, and Pat Barringer. Crown International Pictures, 1965.

Out of the Past. Dir. Jacques Tourneur. Perfs. Robert Mitchum, Jane Greer, Kirk Douglas, and Rhonda Fleming. RKO Radio Pictures, 1947.

Pan's Labyrinth. Dir. Guillermo del Toro. Perfs. Ivana Baquero, Sergi López, Maribel Verdú, Doug Jones, and Ariadna Gil. Warner Bros., 2006.

Paths of Glory. Dir. Stanley Kubrick. Perfs. Kirk Douglas, Ralph Meeker, Adolphe Menjou, George Macready, Wayne Morris, and Richard Anderson. United Artists, 1957.

The Patriot. Dir. Roland Emmerich. Perfs. Mel Gibson, Heath Ledger, and Joely Richardson. Sony Pictures, 2000.

Pee-wee's Big Adventure. Dir. Tim Burton. Perfs. Paul Reubens, Elizabeth Daily, Mark Holton, and Diane Salinger. Warner Bros., 1985.

The People Under the Stairs. Dir. Wes Craven. Perfs. Brandon Adams, Everett McGill, Wendy Robie, and A. J. Langer. Universal Pictures, 1991.

Plan 9 from Outer Space. Dir. Edward D. Wood, Jr. Perfs. Gregory Walcott, Vampira, Tom Keene, Conrad Brooks, Criswell, Bela Lugosi, Tor Johnson, Paul Marco, and Mona McKinnon. Valiant Pictures, 1959.

Phantasm. Dir. Don Coscarelli. Perfs. Michael Baldwin, Bill Thornbury, Reggie Bannister, and Angus Scrimm. AVCO Embassy Pictures, 1979.

Phantom of the Opera. Dir. Rupert Julian. Perfs. Lon Chaney, Norman Kerry, and Mary Philbin. Universal Pictures, 1925.

Poltergeist. Dir. obe Hooper. Perfs. JoBeth Williams, Craig T. Nelson, Heather O'Rourke, and Beatrice Straight. MGM, 1982.

Psycho. Dir. Alfred Hitchcock. Perfs. Anthony Perkins, Janet Leigh, and Vera Miles. Paramount Pictures, 1960.

Quills. Dir. Philip Kaufman. Perfs. Geoffrey Rush, Kate Winslet, Joaquin Phoenix, and Michael Caine. Fox Searchlight Pictures, 2000.

The Raven. Dir. Lew Landers. Perfs. Boris Karloff, Bela Lugosi, and Irene Ware. Universal Pictures, 1935.

Ready Player One. Dir. Steven Spielberg. Perfs. Tye Sheridan, Olivia Cooke, Ben Mendelsohn, T.J. Miller, Simon Pegg, and Mark Rylance. Warner Bros., 2018.

Rebecca. Dir. Alfred Hitchcock. Perfs. Laurence Olivier, Joan Fontaine, and George Sanders. United Artists, 1940.

Red Dawn. Dir. John Milius. Perfs. Patrick Swayze, C. Thomas Howell, Lea Thompson, and Ben Johnson. MGM/UA Entertainment Co., 1984.

Red Riding Hood. Dir. Catherine Hardwicke. Perfs. Amanda Seyfried, Gary Oldman, Billy Burke, and Shiloh Fernandez. Warner Bros., 2011.

The Red Shoes. Dirs. Michael Powell and Emeric Pressburger. Perfs. Moira Shearer, Anton Walbrook, and Marius Goring. Eagle-Lion Films, 1948.

Red River. Dir. Howard Hawks. Perfs. John Wayne, Montgomery Clift, and Walter Brennan. United Artists, 1948.

Red Sparrow. Dir. Francis Lawrence. Perfs. Jennifer Lawrence, Joel Edgerton, Matthias Schoenaerts, Charlotte Rampling, Mary-Louise Parker, and Jeremy Irons. 20th Century Fox, 2018.

Repulsion. Dir. Roman Polanski. Perfs. Catherine Deneuve, Ian Hendry, and John Fraser. Compton Films, 1965.

Road House. Dir. Rowdy Herrington. Perfs. Patrick Swayze, Ben Gazzara, Kelly Lynch, and Sam Elliott. MGM/UA Communications Co., 1989.

The Rocky Horror Picture Show. Dir. Jim Sharman. Perfs. Tim Curry, Susan Sarandon, and Barry Bostwick. 20th Century Fox, 1975.

Rogue One: A Star Wars Story. Dir. Gareth Edwards. Perfs. Felicity Jones, Diego Luna, Ben Mendelsohn, Donnie Yen, Mads Mikkelsen, Alan Tudyk, Riz Ahmed, Jiang Wen, and Forest Whitaker. Walt Disney Studios, 2016.

Rosemary's Baby. Dir. Roman Polanski. Perfs. Mia Farrow, John Cassavetes, and Ruth Gordon. Paramount Pictures, 1968.

Royal Wedding. Dir. Stanley Donen. Perfs. Fred Astaire, Jane Powell, Sarah Churchill, and Peter Lawford. MGM, 1951.

Sabrina. Dir. Billy Wilder. Perfs. Humphrey Bogart, Audrey Hepburn, and William Holden. Paramount Pictures, 1954.

Salem's Lot. Dir. Tobe Hooper. Perfs. David Soul, James Mason, and Lance Kerwin. CBS, 1979.

Satanic Panic. Dir. Chelsea Stardust. Perfs. Rebecca Romijn, Arden Myrin, Hayley Griffith, and Ruby Modine. RLJE Films, 2019.

Saving Private Ryan. Dir. Steven Spielberg. Perfs. Tom Hanks, Edward Burns, Matt Damon, and Tom Sizemore. DreamWorks Pictures, 1998.

A Scanner Darkly. Dir. Richard Linklater. Perfs. Keanu Reeves, Robert Downey Jr., Woody Harrelson, Winona Ryder. Warner Independent Pictures, 2006.

The Scarlet Claw. Dir. Roy William Neill. Perfs. Basil Rathbone, Nigel Bruce, and Gerald Hamer. Universal Studios, 1944.

Science of Star Wars [TV Documentary Miniseries]. Perfs. Anthony Daniels, Dominic Frisby, and Xing Hong Shi. The Discovery Channel, 2005.

Shadow of a Doubt. Dir. Alfred Hitchcock. Perfs. Teresa Wright, Joseph Cotten, and Macdonald Carey. Universal Pictures, 1943.

"Shadow Play." *The Twilight Zone*. Season 2, Episode 26. CBS, May 5, 1961.

Shall We Dance. Dir. Mark Sandrich. Perfs. Fred Astaire and Ginger Rogers. RKO Radio Pictures, 1937.

The Shape of Water. Dir. Guillermo del Toro, Perfs. Sally Hawkins, Michael Shannon, Richard Jenkins, Doug Jones, Michael Stuhlbarg, and Octavia Spencer. Fox Searchlight Pictures, 2017.

Sherlock Holmes Faces Death. Dir. Roy William Neill. Perfs. Basil Rathbone, Nigel Bruce, Dennis Hoey, Arthur Margetson, and Hillary Brooke. Universal Studios, 1943.

The Shining. Dir. Stanley Kubrick. Perfs. Jack Nicholson, Shelley Duvall, and Danny Lloyd. Warner Bros., 1980.

The Silence of the Lambs. Dir. Jonathan Demme. Perfs. Jodie Foster, Anthony Hopkins, Scott Glenn, and Ted Levine. Orion Pictures, 1991.

Sleeping Beauty. Dir. Clyde Geronimi. Perfs. Mary Costa, Bill Shirley, and Eleanor Audley. Walt Disney Productions, 1959.

Sleepy Hollow. Dir. Tim Burton. Perfs. Johnny Depp, Christina Ricci, Miranda Richardson, and Michael Gambon. Paramount Pictures, 1999.

Smokey and the Bandit. Dir. Hal Needham. Perfs. Burt Reynolds, Sally Field, Jerry Reed, and Jackie Gleason. Universal Pictures, 1977.

The Smurfs [Animated Television Series]. Created by Pierre "Peyo" Culliford. Perfs. Don Messick, Danny Goldman, and Lucille Bliss. NBC, 1981-1989.

The Smurfs. Dir. by Raja Gosnell. Perfs. Hank Azaria, Katy Perry, Jonathan Winters. Columbia Pictures, 2011.

The Smurfs 2. Dir. by Raja Gosnell. Perfs. Neil Patrick Harris, Jayma Mays, Katy Perry. Columbia Pictures, 2013.

Snow White and the Seven Dwarfs. Dirs. William Cottrell and David Hand. Perfs. Adriana Caselotti, Harry Stockwell, and Lucille La Verne. Walt Disney Productions, 1937.

Snowpiercer. Dir. Boon Joon-ho. Perfs. Chris Evans, Song Kang-ho, Tilda Swinton, Jamie Bell, Octavia Spencer, Go Ah-sung, John Hurt, and Ed Harris. The Weinstein Company, 2013.

Son of Dracula. Dir. Robert Siodmak. Perfs. Lon Chaney, Jr., Robert Paige, Louise Allbritton, and Evelyn Ankers. Universal Pictures, 1943.

Son of Frankenstein. Dir. Rowland V. Lee. Perfs. Basil Rathbone, Boris Karloff, Bela Lugosi, Lionel Atwill, Josephine Hutchinson, and Donnie Dunagan. Universal Pictures, 1931.

The Sound of Music. Dir. Robert Wise. Perfs. Julie Andrews and Christopher Plummer. 20th Century Fox, 1965.

Spartacus. Dir. Stanley Kubrick. Perfs. Kirk Douglas, Laurence Olivier, and Jean Simmons. Universal International, 1960.

The Spider Woman. Dir. Roy William Neill. Perfs. Basil Rathbone, Nigel Bruce, and Gale Sondergaard. Universal Pictures, 1943.

Spies Like Us. Dir. John Landis. Perfs. Chevy Chase, Dan Aykroyd, Steve Forrest, and Donna Dixon. Warner Bros., 1985.

Star Wars: The Phantom Menace. Dir. George Lucas. Perfs. Ewan McGregor, Liam Neeson, and Natalie Portman. 20th Century Fox, 1999.

Star Wars: Attack of the Clones. Dir. George Lucas. Perfs. Hayden Christensen, Natalie Portman, and Ewan McGregor. 20th Century Fox, 2002.

Star Wars: Revenge of the Sith. Dir. George Lucas. Perfs. Hayden Christensen, Natalie Portman, and Ewan McGregor. 20th Century Fox, 2005.

Star Wars: A New Hope. Dir. George Lucas. Perfs. Mark Hamill, Harrison Ford, and Carrie Fisher. 20th Century Fox, 1977.

Star Wars: The Empire Strikes Back. Dir. Irvin Kershner. Perfs. Mark Hamill, Harrison Ford, and Carrie Fisher. 20th Century Fox, 1980.

Star Wars: Return of the Jedi. Dir. Richard Marquand. Perfs. Mark Hamill, Harrison Ford, and Carrie Fisher. 20th Century Fox, 1983.

Star Wars: The Force Awakens. Dir. J.J. Abrams. Perfs. Daisy Ridley, John Boyega, and Oscar Isaac. Walt Disney Studios, 2015.

Star Wars: The Last Jedi. Dir. Rian Johnson. Perfs. Mark Hamill, Carrie Fisher, Adam Driver, Daisy Ridley, John Boyega, Oscar Isaac, Andy Serkis, Lupita Nyong'o, Domhnall Gleeson, Anthony Daniels, Gwendoline Christie, and Frank Oz. Walt Disney Studios, 2017.

Star Wars: The Rise of Skywalker. Dir. J.J. Abrams. Perfs. Mark Hamill, Carrie Fisher, Adam Driver, Daisy Ridley, John Boyega, Oscar Isaac, Andy Serkis, Lupita Nyong'o, Domhnall Gleeson, and Anthony Daniels. Walt Disney Studios, 2019.

The Stepford Wives. Dir. Bryan Forbes. Perfs. Katharine Ross, Paula Prentiss, Peter Masterson. Fadsin Cinema Associates, Columbia Pictures, 1975.

Stoker. Dir. Chan-wook Park. Perfs. Mia Wasikowska, Nicole Kidman, and Matthew Goode. Fox Searchlight Pictures, 2013.

The Story of Ruth. Dir. Henry Koster. Perfs. Stuart Whitman, Tom Tryon, and Peggy Wood. 20th Century Fox, 1960.

Sunset Boulevard. Dir. Billy Wilder. Perfs. William Holden, Gloria Swanson, and Erich von Stroheim. Paramount Pictures, 1950.

Superman. Dir. Richard Donner. Perfs. Christopher Reeve, Margot Kidder, and Gene Hackman. Warner Bros., 1978.

Superman III. Dir. Richard Lester. Perfs. Christopher Reeve, Margot Kidder, and Richard Pryor. Warner Bros., 1983.

Suspiria. Dir. Dario Argento. Perfs. Jessica Harper, Stefania Casini, and Flavio Bucci. Seda Spettacoli, 1977.

Suspiria. Dir. Luca Guadagnino. Perfs. Dakota Johnson, Tilda Swinton, Mia Goth, Elena Fokina, and Chloë Grace Moretz. Amazon Studios, 2018.

The Tales of Hoffmann. Dirs Michael Powell and Emeric Pressburger. Perfs. Moira Shearer, Robert Helpmann, and Léonide Massine. Lopert Films, 1951.

Taxi Driver. Dir. Martin Scorsese. Perfs. Robert De Niro, Jodie Foster, Albert Brooks, Harvey Keitel, Leonard Harris, Peter Boyle, and Cybill Shepherd. Columbia Pictures, 1976.

The Terminator. Dir. James Cameron. Perfs. Arnold Schwarzenegger, Linda Hamilton, and Michael Biehn. Orion Pictures, 1984.

The Terminator 2: Judgement Day. Dir. James Cameron. Perfs. Arnold Schwarzenegger, Linda Hamilton, and Robert Patrick. TriStar Pictures, 1991.

The Texas Chainsaw Massacre. Dir. Tobe Hooper. Perfs. Marilyn Burns, Gunnar Hanson, Edwin Neal, and Allen Danziger. Bryanston Distributing Company, 1974.

There Will Be Blood. Dir. Paul Thomas Anderson. Perfs. Daniel Day-Lewis, Paul Dano, and Ciarán Hinds. Paramount Vantage, 2007.

They Live. Dir. John Carpenter. Perfs. Roddy Piper, Keith David, and Meg Foster. Universal Pictures, 1988.

The Thing from Another World (aka *The Thing*). Dir. Christian Nyby. Perfs. Margaret Sheridan, Kenneth Tobey, Robert Cornthwaite, Douglas Spencer, and James Arness. RKO Radio Pictures, 1951.

The Thirteenth Floor. Dir. Josef Rusnak. Perfs. Craig Bierko, Gretchen Mol, Armin Mueller-Stahl, Vincent D'Onofrio, and Dennis Haysbert. Columbia Pictures, 1999.

Thor: Ragnarok. Dir. Taika Waititi. Perfs. Chris Hemsworth, Tom Hiddleston, Cate Blanchett, and Idris Elba. Walt Disney Studios Motion Pictures, 2017.

Three Outlaw Samurai. Dir. Hideo Gosha. Perfs. Tetsuro Tamba, Isamu Nagato, Mikijirō Hira, and Yoshiko Kayama. Janus Films, 1964.

To Kill a Mockingbird. Dir. Robert Mulligan. Perfs. Gregory Peck, Mary Badham, Phillip Alford, and John Megna. Universal Pictures, 1962.

The Tomb of Ligeia. Dir. Roger Corman. Perfs. Vincent Price, Elizabeth Shepherd, John Westbrook, and Oliver Johnston. Warner-Pathe, 1964.

Total Recall. Dir. Paul Verhoeven. Perfs. Arnold Schwarzenegger, Sharon Stone, and Michael Ironside. TriStar Pictures, 1990.

"Tricia Tanaka Is Dead." *Lost*. Season 3, Episode 10. ABC, February 28, 2007.

Trick 'r Treat. Dir. Michael Dougherty. Perfs. Anna Paquin, Brian Cox, and Dylan Baker. Warner Bros., 2007.

Trilogy of Terror. Dir. Dan Curtis. Perfs. Karen Black, Robert Burton, John Karlen, and George Gaynes. ABC, 1975.

Time Bandits. Dir. Terry Gilliam. Perfs. John Cleese, Sean Connery, Shelley Duvall, and Katherine Helmond. Avco Embassy Pictures, 1981.

The Truman Show. Dir. Peter Weir. Perfs. Jim Carrey, Laura Linney, and Ed Harris. Paramount Pictures, 1998.

Twelve O'Clock High. Dir. Henry King. Perfs. Gregory PeckHugh Marlowe, Gary Merrill, Millard Mitchell, and Dean Jagger. 20th Century Fox, 1949.

Twin Peaks [Television Series]. Created by Mark Frost and David Lynch. Perfs. Kyle MacLachlan, Michael Ontkean, Mädchen Amick, Dana Ashbrook, Ray Wise, Piper Laurie, Sheryl Lee, Richard Beymer, Lara Flynn Boyle, and Sherilyn Fenn. ABC, 1990-1991.

Twin Peaks: Fire Walk with Me. Dir. David Lynch. Perfs. Ray Wise, Sheryl Lee, Moira Kelly, David Bowie, and Chris Isaak. New Line Cinema, 1992.

Twin Peaks: The Return [Television Series]. Created by Mark Frost and David Lynch. Perfs. David Lynch, Kimmy Robertson, Sheryl Lee, and Kyle MacLachlan. Showtime, 2017.

V for Vendetta. Dir. James McTeigue. Perfs. Hugo Weaving, Natalie Portman, and Rupert Graves. Warner Bros., 2005.

Vanilla Sky. Dir. Cameron Crowe. Perfs. Tom Cruise, Penélope Cruz, Cameron Diaz, Jason Lee, and Kurt Russell. Paramount Pictures, 2001.

Vertigo. Dir. Alfred Hitchcock. Perfs. James Stewart, Kim Novak, and Barbara Bel Geddes. Paramount Pictures, 1958.

Videodrome. Dir. David Cronenberg. Perfs. James Woods, Sonja Smits, and Deborah Harry. Universal Pictures, 1983.

Wait Until Dark. Dir. Terence Young. Perfs. Audrey Hepburn, Alan Arkin, and Richard Crenna. Warner Bros.-Seven Arts, 1967.

The War of the Worlds. Dir. Byron Haskin. Perfs. Gene Barry and Ann Robinson. Paramount Pictures, 1953.

The Warriors. Dir. Walter Hill. Perfs. Michael Beck, James Remar, and Dorsey Wright. Paramount Pictures, 1979.

Watchmen. Dir. Zack Snyder. Perfs. Jackie Earle Haley, Patrick Wilson, and Carla Gugino. Warner Bros., 2009.

Watership Down. Dirs. Martin Rosen and John Hubley (uncredited). Perfs. John Hurt, Richard Briers, Michael Graham Cox, and Simon Cadell. Nepenthe Productions, 1978.

Weird Science. Dir. John Hughes. Perfs. Anthony Michael Hall, Ilan Mitchell-Smith, and Kelly LeBrock. Universal Pictures, 1985.

White Zombie. Dir. Victor Halperin. Perfs. Bela Lugosi, Madge Bellamy, and Joseph Cawthorn. United Artists, 1932.

The Wicker Man. Dir. Robin Hardy. Perfs. Edward Woodward, Christopher Lee, and Diane Cilento. British Lion Films, 1973.

The Wicker Man. Dir. Neil LaBute. Perfs. Nicolas Cage, Ellen Burstyn, Kate Beahan, Frances Conroy, Molly Parker, Leelee Sobieski, and Diane Delano. Warner Bros., 2006.

The Wild Bunch. Dir. Sam Peckinpah. Perfs. William Holden, Robert Ryan, Ernest Borgnine, Edmond O'Brien, Ben Johnson, and Warren Oates. Warner Bros., 1969.

Wild at Heart. Dir. David Lynch. Perfs. Nicolas Cage, Laura Dern, Diane Ladd, Willem Dafoe, Harry Dean Stanton, and Isabella Rossellini. The Samuel Goldwyn Company, 1990.

Willy Wonka & the Chocolate Factory. Dir. Mel Stuart. Perfs. Gene Wilder, Jack Albertson, Peter Ostrum, and Roy Kinnear. Paramount Pictures, 1971.

The Witch. Dir. Robert Eggers. Perfs. Anya Taylor-Joy, Ralph Ineson, and Kate Dickie. A24, 2015.

The Wizard of Oz. Dir. Victor Fleming. Perfs. Judy Garland, Frank Morgan, Ray Bolger, Margaret Hamilton, and Billie Burke. MGM, 1939.

Wolfen. Dir. Michael Wadleigh. Perfs. Albert Finney, Diane Venora, Edward James Olmos, Gregory Hines, and Tom Noonan. Warner Bros., 1981.

The Wolfman. Dir. George Waggner. Perfs. Claude Rains, Warren William, Ralph Bellamy, Patric Knowles, Bela Lugosi, Maria Ouspenskaya, Evelyn Ankers, and Lon Chaney Jr. Universal Pictures, 1941.

The X-Files [Television Series]. Created by Chris Carter. Perfs. David Duchovny, Gillian Anderson, and Mitch Pileggi. 20th Century Fox Television, 1993-2018.

The Zero Theorem. Dir. Terry Gilliam. Perfs. Christoph Waltz, David Thewlis, Mélanie Thierry, and Lucas Hedges. Stage 6 Films, 2013.

Zorro, The Gay Blade. Dir. Peter Medak. Perfs. George Hamilton, Lauren Hutton, Ron Leibman, and Brenda Vaccaro. 20th Century Fox, 1981.

BIBLIOGRAPHY

Adams, W.H. Davenport. *Witch, Warlock, and Magician*. London: Chatto & Windus, 1889.

Adler, Shelley R. *Sleep Paralysis: Night-mares, Nocebos, and the Mind-Body Connection*. New Brunswick, NJ: Rutgers University Press, 2011.

Alighieri, Dante. *The Divine Comedy*. Translated by C.H. Sisson. 1555. Reprint, Oxford: Oxford University Press, 1993.

Andersen, Hans Christian. *Hans Christian Andersen's Fairy Tales*. London: Constable & Co. Ltd., 1913.

Andrews, Mark, and Gary Jules. "Mad World." Recorded 2000. Track 17 on *Donnie Darko* (soundtrack). Enjoy Records, 2002, YouTube music video.

Anger, Kenneth. *Hollywood Babylon*. 1975. Reprint, New York: Bell Publishing Co., 1981.

——. *Hollywood Babylon II*. New York: E.P. Dutton & Company, Inc., 1984.

Ars Goetia: The Lesser Key of Solomon the King. Translated by Samuel Liddell MacGregor Mathers, edited by Aleister Crowley. 1904. Reprint, San Francisco: Weiser Books, 1997.

Astaire, Fred. "Slap That Bass." *Shall We Dance*, 1937, YouTube video.

Baigent, Michael, Richard Leigh and Henry Lincoln. *Holy Blood, Holy Grail*. New York: Dell Publishing Group, 1983.

Baigent, Michael and Richard Leigh. *The Temple and the Lodge*. London: Corgi Books, 1990.

The Beatles. "Sgt. Pepper's Lonely Hearts Club Band." Recorded February 1–March 6, 1967. Track 1 on *Sgt. Pepper's Lonely Hearts Club Band*, 1967, compact disc.

Belanger, Michelle. *Names of the Damned: The Dictionary of Demons*. Woodbury, MN: Llewellyn Publications, 2019.

Billington, James H. *Fire in the Minds of Men: Origins of the Revolutionary Faith*. New York: Basic Books, Inc., Publishers, 1980.

Blake, William. *William Blake: The Compete Illuminated Books*. Introduction by David Bindman. 2000. Reprint, New York: Thames and Hudson Inc., 2019.

——. *The Complete Poetry and Prose of William Blake*. Edited by David V. Erdman. 1965. Revised ed. New York: Anchor Books, 1988.

Blavatsky, Helena P. *Isis Unveiled*. 2 vols., 1877. Reprint, Middletown, Delaware: Pantianos Classics, 2018.

——. *The Secret Doctrine*. 1888. Reprint, New York: TarcherPerigee, 2016.

——. *The Theosophical Glossary*. London: The Theosophical Publishing Society, 1892.

Bloomfield, Maurice. *Cerberus, the Dog of Hades*. Chicago: The Open Court Publishing Company, 1905.

The Book of the Dead. Translated by E.A. Wallis Budge. 1894. Reprint, London: British Museum, 1920.

Bowie, David. "Underground." Recorded July-September 1985. Track 12 on *Labyrinth* (soundtrack). EMI, 1986, YouTube music video.

Braier, Natasha. "Inside the weird world of The Neon Demon." *The Guardian*, July 4, 2016. https://www.theguardian.com/global/2016/jul/04/inside-the-weird-world-of-the-neon-demon (accessed March 2, 2019).

Brown, R. *The Religion of Zoroaster Considered in Connection with Archaic Monotheism*. London: D. Bogue, 1879.

Brown, Sanger, II. *The Sex Worship and Symbolism of Primitive Races*. Boston: Richard G. Badger, 1916.

Bunce, John Thackray. *Fairy Tales: Their Origin and Meaning.* London: MacMillan and Co., 1878.

Burden, Zora. "Another Place: The Esoteric Symbolism of Twin Peaks/Agent on the Threshold: The Taoism and Alchemy of Twin Peaks." *Zora Burden: Writer, Artist, Poet*, August 2015. https://zoraburden.weebly.com/the-esoteric-symbolism-of-twin-peaks.html (accessed August 1, 2019).

Campbell, Joseph. *The Hero with a Thousand Faces.* 3rd ed. Novato, CA: New World Library, 2008.

Campbell, Joseph, and Bill Moyers. *The Power of Myth.* New York: Anchor Books, 1991.

Carabine, Deirdre. *The Unknown God, Negative Theology in the Platonic Tradition: Plato to Eriugena.* 1995. Reprint, Eugene, OR: Wipf & Stock, 2015.

Carpenter, Edward. *Pagan & Christian Creeds: Their Origin and Meaning.* New York: Harcourt, Brace and Company, 1921.

Carroll, Lewis. *The Complete Works of Lewis Carroll.* Introduction by Alexander Woollcott. Ware, Hertfordshire, England: Wordsworth Editions Ltd., 1991.

Carter, John. *Sex and Rockets: The Occult World of Jack Parsons.* Los Angeles: Feral House, 2004.

Case, George. *Here's to My Sweet Satan: How the Occult Haunted Music, Movies, and Pop Culture.* Fresno: Quill Driver Books, 2016.

Case, Paul Foster. *The Tarot: A Key to the Wisdom of the Ages.* 1947. Reprint, New York: TarcherPerigee, 2006.

——. *The True and Invisible Rosicrucian Order.* York Beach, ME: Samuel Weiser, Inc., 1985.

Cavendish, Richard. *The Black Arts.* New York: G.P. Putnam's Sons, 1967.

——. *The Tarot.* New York: Harper & Row, Publishers, 1975.

Churton, Tobias. *Aleister Crowley, the Beast in Berlin: Art, Sex, and Magick in the Weimar Republic*. Rochester, VT: Inner Traditions, 2014.

——. *The Mysteries of John the Baptist: His Legacy in Gnosticism, Paganism, and Freemasonry*. Rochester, VT: Inner Traditions, 2012.

——. *Occult Paris: The Lost Magic of the Belle Époque*. Rochester, VT: Inner Traditions, 2016.

Cicero, Chic and Sandra Tabatha Cicero. T*he New Golden Dawn Ritual Tarot: Keys to the Rituals, Symbolism, Magic and Divination*. Woodbury, MN: Llewellyn Publications, 2018.

Cielo, Astra. *Signs, Omens and Superstitions*. New York: George Sully & Company, 1918.

Cirlot, J.E. *A Dictionary of Symbols*. New York: Philosophical Library, 1962.

Coates, Jon. "Scientists find starting the day with Beach Boys instead of alarm leads to good vibrations." *Express*, April 21, 2019. https://www.express.co.uk/life-style/life/1117146/beach-boys-pop-songs-alarm-scientists-good-vibrations-sleep-ineptia (accessed February 7, 2020).

Conner, Miguel. "Alice in Wonderland and the Occult." *Cinegnose: Cinema Secreto*. December 29, 2009. http://cinegnose.blogspot.com/2009/12/alice-in-wonderland-and-sophia-gnostic.html (accessed October 22, 2018).

——. *Voices of Gnosticism: Interviews with Elaine Pagels, Marvin Meyer, Bart Ehrman, Bruce Chilton and Other Leading Scholars*. Dublin: Bardic Press, 2011.

Coverley, Merlin. *Occult London*. Harpenden, UK: Oldcastle Books, 2017.

Criswell. *Criswell's Forbidden Predictions Based on Nostradamus and the Tarot*. Atlanta: Droke House/Hallux, Inc., 1972.

Crowley, Aleister. *777 and other Qabalistic Writings of Aleister Crowley*. Edited by Israel Regardie. 1973. Reprint, San Francisco: Weiser Books, 1986.

——. *The Book of the Law*. 1938. Reprint, San Francisco: Weiser Books, 1976.

——. *The Book of Lies*. 1912. Reprint, York Beach, ME: Red Wheel/Weiser, LLC., 1981.

——. *The Book of Thoth*. 1944. Reprint, San Francisco: Weiser Books, 2011.

——. *The Confessions of Aleister Crowley*. Edited by John Symonds and Kenneth Grant. 1969. Reprint, London: Penguin/Arkana Books, 1989.

——. *Liber DCCCLX John St. John*. n.p., n.d.

——. *Liber Aleph vel CXI: The Book of Wisdom or Folly*. 1962. Reprint, York Beach, ME: Red Wheel/Weiser LLC, 2006.

——. *Magick*. Edited by John Symonds and Kenneth Grant. 1973. Reprint, London: Routledge & Kegan Paul, 1981.

——. *Magick Without Tears*. Edited and Introduction by Israel Regardie. Tempe: New Falcon Publications, 1991.

Curl, James Stevens. *The Art and Architecture of Freemasonry*. London: B.T. Batsford Ltd, 1991.

——. *A Celebration of Death: An introduction to some of the buildings, monuments, and settings of funerary architecture in the Western European tradition*. 1980. Reprint, London: B.T. Batsford Ltd, 1993.

Damrosch, Leo. *Eternity's Sunrise: The Imaginative World of William Blake*. New Haven: Yale University Press, 2015.

Daniels, Les. *Batman: The Complete History*. San Francisco: Chronicle Books, 2004.

"David Lean Lecture: David Lynch." *British Academy of Film and Television Arts*, October 27, 2007, http://www.bafta.org/media-centre/transcripts/bafta-television-lecture-david-lynch (accessed July 5, 2019).

Davidson, Gustav. *A Dictionary of Angels, Including the Fallen Angels*. 1967, Reprint, Florence, MA, 1994.

Davies, Owen. *Grimoires: A History of Magic Books*. New York: Oxford University Press, 2010.

De Plancy, Collin. *Dictionary of Demonology*. Edited and translated by Wade Baskin. 1818 published as *Dictionnaire Infernale*. Reprint, New York: Philosophical Library Inc., 1965.

De Sade, Marquis. *Juliette*. 1797. Reprint, New York: Groove Press, 1994.

De Sade, Marquis. *The 120 Days of Sodom*. 1904. Reprint, Radford, Virginia: Wilder Publications, LLC., 2009.

Devore, Nicholas. *Encyclopedia of Astrology.* New York: Philosophical Library, 1947.

Dickens, Charles, *A Christmas Carol*. 1843. Reprint, Elegant Books, n.d.

——. *A Tale of Two Cities*. 1859. Reprint, Seattle: AmazonClassics, n.d.

Dictionary of Greek and Roman Biography and Mythology. Edited by William Smith, LL.D. 3 vols. Boston: Little, Brown, and Company, 1870.

Dion, Celine, and Peabo Bryson. "Beauty and the Beast." Recorded 1991. Released as a Single. Walt Disney-Epic-Columbia, 1991, YouTube music video.

Egan, James Alan. *Elizabethan America: The John Dee Tower of 1583*. Newport, RI: Cosmopolitan Press, 2011.

Ebiri, Bilge. "'Neon Demon' Auteur Nicolas Winding Refn on his Fluorescent Narcissism." *The Village Voice*, June 27, 2016. https://www.villagevoice.com/2016/06/27/neon-demon-auteur-nicolas-winding-refn-on-his-fluorescent-narcissism (accessed April 14, 2019).

The Emerald Tablet of Hermes Trismegistus. Merchant Books, 2013.

Encyclopedia of Magic & Superstition: Alchemy, Charms, Dreams, Omens, Rituals, Talismans, Wishes. New York: Crown Publishers Inc., 1974.

Encyclopedia of World Mythology. New York: Galahad Books, 1975.

Eurythmics. "This City Never Sleeps." Recorded 1982. Track 8 on *9 1/2 Weeks* (soundtrack), Capitol Records, 1986, compact disc.

Evon, Dan. "Is 'Baron Trump's Marvelous Underground Journey' a Real Book from the 1890s?" *Snopes*, August 1, 2017. https://www.snopes.com/fact-check/baron-trumps-marvelous-underground-journey/ (accessed November 1, 2018).

"The Exorcist: CIA Script?" *Ann Arbor Sun*, June 28, 1974. https://aadl.org/node/197187 (accessed June 25, 2019).

"Exploring the Spiritual Foundation of Harry Potter: Alchemy." *Harry Potter for Seekers*, n.d. http://www.harrypotterforseekers.com/alchemy/alchemy.php (accessed September 7, 2019).

Farrar, Stewart. *What Witches Do*. New York: Coward, McCann, & Geoghegan, Inc., 1971.

Faxneld, Per. *Satanic Feminism: Lucifer as the Liberator of Woman in Nineteenth-Century Culture*. New York: Oxford University Press, 2017.

Ficino, Marsilio. "Marsilio Ficino on the alchemical art," *Liber de Arte Chemica* from *Theatrum Chemicum*, Vol 2, Geneva, 1702, 172-183. Translated by Justin von Budjoss. *The Alchemy Web Site*, n.d. http://www.levity.com/alchemy/ficino.html (accessed January 21, 2020).

Fischer, Russ. "New Details on Guillermo del Toro's Haunted House Movie 'Crimson Peak,' Plus New 'Pacific Rim' Images." *Slash Film*, February 18, 2013. https://www.slashfilm.com/new-details-on-guillermo-del-toros-haunted-house-movie-crimson-peak-plus-new-pacific-rim-images/ (accessed May 1, 2018).

Fleming, John V. *The Dark Side of the Enlightenment: Wizards, Alchemists, and Spiritual Seekers in the Age of Reason*. New York: W.W. Norton & Company, 2013.

Flowers, Stephen E. *Fire & Ice: The History, Structure, and Rituals of Germany's Most Influential Modern Magical Order: The Brotherhood of Saturn*. St. Paul, MN: Llewellyn Publications, 1994.

Ford, Clementine. "'Lizzie' Shows Us the Erotic Side of Fussy Edwardian Fashion." *Garage*, September 26, 2018. https://garage.vice.com/en_us/article/wjyxjm/lizzie-borden-costumes (accessed March 2, 2019).

Foster the People. "Pumped Up Kicks." Recorded 2010. Track 3 on *Foster the People*, Startime International, 2011, YouTube music video.

Fox, Lauren. "The Triple Goddess." In *The Women of David Lynch*, edited by David Bushman, 75-86. Columbus, OH: Fayetteville Mafia Press, 2019.

Franz, M.-L. von. "The Process of Individuation." In *Man and his Symbols*, edited by Carl G. Jung, 157-254. New York: Dell, 1968.

Frazer, J.G. *The Golden Bough: A Study in Magic and Religion*. Abridged ed. 1922. Reprint, London: Papermac, 1994.

Freeman, Tzvi. "The Moon and Us." *Chabad.org*. n.d., https://www.chabad.org/library/article_cdo/aid/247861/jewish/The-Moon-and-Us.htm (accessed August 3, 2019).

Freke, Timothy, and Peter Gandy. *The Jesus Mysteries: Was the "Original Jesus" a Pagan God?* New York: Three Rivers Press, 2001.

Friend, Hilderic. *Flowers and Flower Lore*. Troy, NY: Nims and Knight, 1889.

Frost, Mark. *The Secret History of Twin Peaks*. New York: Flatiron Books, 2016.

Freud, Sigmund. *Beyond the Pleasure Principle*. Edited and translated by James Strachey with an Introduction by Gregory Zilboorg and a Biographical Introduction by Peter Gay. New York: Norton, 1961.

Fulcanelli: Master Alchemist. *Le Mystere des Catherdrales: Esoteric Interpretation of the Hermetic Symbols of the Great Work*. Translated by Mary Sworder. 1926/1990. Reprint, Las Vegas: Brotherhood of Life, 2016.

Gardiner, Philip. *The Bond Code: The Dark World of Ian Fleming and James Bond*. Franklin Lakes, NJ: New Page Books, 2008.

Gerberth, Vernon J. *Practical Homicide Investigation: Tactics, Procedures, and Forensic Techniques*. 4th ed. New York: CRC Press, 2008.

Giammarino, Michael. "'He's Coming to Get You, Laurie!' What Dr. Dementia's Halloween Horror Movie Marathon Tells Us About Michael Myers And Laurie Strode." *Dread Central*. April 29, 2019. https://www.dreadcentral.com/editorials/293221/hes-coming-to-get-you-laurie-what-dr-dementias-halloween-horror-movie-marathon-tells-us-about-michael-myers-and-laurie-strode/ (accessed October 4, 2019).

Gibbs, Laura. "Sundial: UMBRA SUMUS." *Bestiaria Latina Blog: A round-up of what's going on at BestLatin.net*, February 7, 2013. http://bestlatin.blogspot.com/2013/02/sundial-umbra-sumus.html (accessed March 3, 2019).

Gilman, Charlotte Perkins. *The Yellow Wallpaper*. Boston: The New England Magazine, 1892.

Girard, Stephen. *The Mystic Dream Book of Stephen Girard: A Complete Guide to Wealth, Health, and Happiness; Consulted Daily by This Eminent Man, Taken From the Arabic of Mohammed Kazvini; Embracing the Mysticism, Rites, and Ceremonies of the Orient, Adapted to the Wants of All Classes and Conditions of People*. Revised ed. Philadelphia: Rufus C. Hartranft, 1886.

Gordon, Mel. *The Seven Addictions and Five Professions of Anita Berber: Weimar Berlin's Depraved Priestess of Depravity*. Port Townsend, WA: Feral House, 2006.

——. *Theatre of Fear and Horror: The Grisly Spectacle of The Grand Guignol of Paris 1897-1962*. 1988. Reprint, Port Townsend, WA: Feral House, 2016.

——. *Voluptuous Panic: The Erotic World of Weimar Berlin*. Port Townsend, WA: Feral House, 2006.

The Gospel of Judas. Translated by Mark M. Mattison. *gospels.net*, n.d. https://www.gospels.net/judas (accessed January 22, 2019).

Graceland: The Home of Elvis Presley, https://www.graceland.com.

The Grand Grimoire with the Great Clavicle of Solomon also known as the Red Dragon: or the Art of Controlling Celestial, Aerial, Terrestrial, and Infernal Spirits. Edited by Antonio Venitiana del Rabina. 1521. Reprint, Brossard, Quebec, CA: Editions Unicursal Publishers, 2019.

Greenwood, Earl and Kathleen Tracy. *Elvis: Top Secret – The Untold Story of Elvis Presley's Secret FBI Files.* New York: Signet Books, 1991.

Greer, John Michael. *The New Encyclopedia of the Occult.* St. Paul: Llewellyn Publications, 2005.

Grey, Rudolph. *Nightmare of Ecstasy: The Life and Art of Edward D. Wood, Jr.* Portland: Feral House, 1994.

Grimassi, Raven. *Encyclopedia of Wicca and Witchcraft.* 2nd ed. Woodbury, MN: Llewellyn Publications, 2019.

Grimm, Jacob and Wilhelm Grimm, *The Original Folk and Fairy Tales of the Brothers Grimm: The Complete First Edition.* Translated by Jack Zipes. Princeton: Princeton University Press, 2014.

Guiley, Rosemary Ellen. *The Encyclopedia of Witches and Witchcraft.* New York: Facts on File, Inc., 1989.

Gullickson, Brad. "How NASA Contributed to the Cinematography of 'Barry Lyndon.'" *Film School Rejects*, May 9, 2019. https://filmschoolrejects.com/barry-lyndon-cinematography/ (accessed September 6, 2019).

Hall, Manly P. *Freemasonry of the Ancient Egyptians.* 1937. Reprint, Los Angeles: The Philosophical Research Society, Inc., 1965.

——. *Lectures on Ancient Philosophy.* 1970. Reprint, New York: Tarcher/Penguin, 2005.

——. *The Lost Keys of Freemasonry.* 1923. Reprint, New York: Tarcher/Penguin, 2006.

——. *The Secret Destiny of America*. 1942. Reprint, New York: Tarcher/Penguin, 2008.

——. *The Secret Teachings of All Ages: An Encyclopedic Outline of Masonic, Hermetic, Qabbalistic and Rosicrucian Symbolic Philosophy*. 1928. Reprint, New York: Tarcher/Penguin, 2003.

——. *Twelve World Teachers*. Los Angeles: Philosophical Research Society, Inc., 1965.

Hallam, Lindsay. "Women's Films: Melodrama and Women's Trauma in the Films of David Lynch." In *The Women of David Lynch*, edited by David Bushman, 15-32. Columbus, OH: Fayetteville Mafia Press, 2019.

Hamilton, Edith. *Mythology*. 1942. Reprint, New York: Back Bay Books, 2013.

Hancock, Graham, and Robert Bauval. *Talisman: Sacred Cities, Secret Faith*. Canada: Doubleday Canada, 2004.

Hancox, Joy. *The Byrom Collection and the Globe Theatre Mystery*. London: Jonathan Cape, 1997.

Hartland, Edwin Sidney. *The Science of Fairy Tales: An Inquiry into Fairy Mythology*. London: Walter Scott, 1891.

Hayes, Britt. "Sunday Reads: SUSPIRIA – Psychoanalyzing Luca Guadagnino's Rapturous Rebirth of a Horror Classic: An investigation into the psychology of SUSPIRIA." *Birth. Movies. Death.*, November 4, 2018. https://birthmoviesdeath.com/2018/11/04/sunday-reads-suspiria-psychoanalyzing-luca-guadagninos-rapturous-rebirth-of (accessed December 3, 2018).

Hayes, Marisa C. "Jade: Ornamental Gem or Protective Talisman? A Character Study." In *The Women of David Lynch*, edited by David Bushman, 113-124. Columbus, OH: Fayetteville Mafia Press, 2019.

Heidegger, Martin. *Being and Time*. Translated by John Macquarrie and Edward Robinson. New York: Harper, 1962.

———. "What is Metaphysics?" In *Heidegger: Basic Writings*. Revised and expanded edition, edited by David Farrell Krell, 89-110. New York: Harper Collins, 1993.

Henderson, Joseph L. "Ancient Myths and Modern Man." In *Man and His Symbols*, edited by Carl G. Jung, 95-156. New York: Dell, 1968.

Henry, John. *The Scientific Revolution and the Origins of Modern Science*. New York: Palgrave Macmillan, 2008.

Hermetica: The Ancient Greek and Latin Writings Which Contain Religious or Philosophic Teachings Ascribed to Hermes Trismegistus. Edited and translated by Walter Scott. 4 vols., 1924-1936. Reprint, Boston: Shambala Publications, Inc., 1985-1993.

Hochheim, Eckhart von. *The Complete Mystical Works of Meister Eckhart*. Translated and edited by Maurice O'C Walshe. New York: The Crossroad Publishing Company, 2009.

Horton, Perry H. "An Opposition of Self: Duality and 'Twin Peaks.'" *Film School Rejects*, May 17, 2016. https://filmschoolrejects.com/an-opposition-of-self-duality-and-twin-peaks-dee93503e4e5/ (accessed July 15, 2019).

Hothersall, David. *History of Psychology*. New York: McGraw-Hill, 2003.

Hueffer, Oliver Madox. *The Book of the Witches*. New York: The John McBride Co., 1909.

Hughes, Mark. "Exclusive: Christopher Nolan Talks 'Batman Begins' 10th Anniversary." *Forbes*, July 3, 2015. https://www.forbes.com/sites/markhughes/2015/07/30/exclusive-christopher-nolan-talks-batman-begins-10th-anniversary/#57a938da8b53 (accessed March 17, 2019).

Hunter, M. Kelley. *Living Lilith: Four Dimensions of the Cosmic Feminine*. Bournemouth, UK: The Wessex Astrologer Ltd, 2009.

Hutchinson, Horace G. *Dreams and Their Meanings: With Many Accounts of Experiences Sent by Correspondents and Two Chapters Contributed Mainly from the Journals of the Psychical Research Society on Telepathic and Premonitory Dreams*. London: Longmans, Green, & Co., 1901.

Idel, Moeshe. *Golem: Jewish Magic and Mystical Traditions on the Artificial Anthropoid*. Albany: State University of New York Press, 1990.

IMDb. https://www.imdb.com.

INXS. "Never Tear Us Apart." Recorded 1987. Track 8 on *Kick*. Atlantic Records (USA), 1987, YouTube music video.

Irwin, William. *The Matrix and Philosophy: Welcome to the Desert of the Real*. Chicago: Open Court, 2002.

Jackson, Michael. "Thriller." Recorded 1982. Track 4 on *Thriller*. Epic Records, 1982. YouTube music video.

Jennings, Hargrave. *Phallicism, Celestial and Terrestrial, Heathen and Christian*. London: George Redway, 1884.

Jung, Carl G. "Approaching the Unconscious." In *Man and his Symbols*, edited by Carl G. Jung, 1-94. New York: Dell, 1968.

——. *The Portable Jung*. Edited by Joseph Campbell, translated by R.F.C. Hull. New York: Penguin Books, 1976.

Karina, Lilian, and Marion Kant. *Hitler's Dancers: German Modern Dance and the Third Reich*. Translated by Jonathan Steinberg. New York: Berghahn Books, 2004.

Kelley, Ruth E. *The Book of Hallowe'en*. Boston: Lothrop, Lee & Shepard Co., 1919.

Keramaris, Kostas. "Katy Perry I sold my soul to the devil." *YouTube* video, 0.34, February 9, 2015. https://youtu.be/SPvtGvGtOzM (accessed April 15, 2020).

Kern, Hermann. *Through the Labyrinth*. New York: Prestel, 2000.

King, C.W. *The Gnostics and Their Remains, Ancient and Medieval*. London: David Nutt, 1887.

Kolb, Leigh Kellmann. "The Uncanny Electricity of Women in David Lynch's Worlds." In *The Women of David Lynch*, edited by David Bushman, 1-12. Columbus, OH: Fayetteville Mafia Press, 2019.

Kolker, Robert P., and Nathan Abrams. *Eyes Wide Shut: Stanley Kubrick and the Masking of his Final Film*. New York: Oxford University Press, 2019.

Kuhn, Alvin Boyd. *Halloween: A Festival of Lost Meaning*. 1922. Reprint, Whitefish, MT: Kessinger Publishing, 2004.

Lagercrantz, Olof. *Epic of the Afterlife: A Literary Approach to Swedenborg*. Translated by Anders Hallengren. 1996. Reprint, West Chester, PA: The Swedenborg Foundation, 2002.

Landis, John. *Monsters in the Movies: 100 Years of Cinematic Nightmares*. New York: DK, 2011.

Lang, Andrew. *Custom and Myth*. New York: Harper & Brothers, 1885.

Langley, Travis. *Batman and Psychology: A Dark and Stormy Knight*. Hoboken: John Wiley & Sons, Inc., 2012.

Laqueur, Thomas W. *Solitary Sex: A Cultural History of Masturbation*. Brooklyn, NY: Zone Books, 2004.

LaVey, Anton Szandor. *The Compleat Witch or What to do When Virtue Fails*. New York: Dodd, Mead, & Company, 1971.

——. *The Satanic Bible*. New York: Avon Books, 1969.

——. *The Satanic Rituals*. New York: Avon Books, 1972.

Leo, Alan. *Saturn: The Reaper*. London: Modern Astrology Office, 1916.

Levi, Eliphas. *The History of Magic*. Translated by Arthur Edward Waite. 1860/1913. Reprint, Mansfield Centre, CT: Martino Publishing, 2012.

——. *The Key of the Mysteries*. Translated by Aleister Crowley. 1861. Reprint, York Beach, ME: Weiser Books, 2002.

——. *Transcendental Magic: Its Doctrine and Ritual*. Translated by Arthur Edward Waite. 1896/1958. Reprint, Mansfield Centre, CT: Martino Publishing, 2011.

Lindow, John. *Norse Mythology: A Guide to the Gods, Heroes, Rituals, and Beliefs*. New York: Oxford University Press, 2002.

Literary Wonderlands: A Journey Through the Greatest Fictional Worlds Ever Created. Edited by Laura Miller. New York: Black Dog & Leventhal Publishers, 2016.

Lockwood, Ingersoll. *Baron Trump's Marvellous Underground Journey*. Boston: Lee and Shepard Publishers, 1893.

Louv, Jason. *John Dee and the Empire of Angels: Enochian Magick, and the Occult Roots of the Modern World*. Rochester, VT: Inner Traditions, 2018.

Lucy, Margaret. *Shakespeare and the Supernatural: A Brief Study of Folklore, Superstition, and Witchcraft in Macbeth, Midsummer Night's Dream and the Tempest*. Liverpool: Shakespeare Press, Jaggard & Company, 1906.

Luijk, Ruben van. *Children of Lucifer: The Origins of Modern Religious Satanism*. New York: Oxford University Press, 2016.

——. "The Resurrection of Satan in Nineteenth-Century (Counter) Culture." In *The Devil's Party: Satanism in Modernity*, edited by Per Faxneld and Jesper Aa. Petersen, 41-52. New York: Oxford University Press, 2013.

Lynn, Heather. *Evil Archeology: Demons, Possessions, and Sinister Relics*. Newburyport, MA: Disinformation Books, 2019.

Macfarlane, Steve. "Interview: Nicholas Winding Refn on *The Neon Demon*." *Slant*, June 24, 2016. https://www.slantmagazine.com/features/interview-nicolas-winding-refn-on-the-neon-demon/ (accessed April 22, 2019).

Mackay, A.B. *The True Gnostics: A Sermon*. Montreal: W.M. Drysdale & Co., 1880.

Mackey, Albert G. *An Encyclopedia of Freemasonry and its Kindred Sciences*. 2 vols. New York: The Masonic History Company, 1921.

Macoy, Robert. *A Dictionary of Freemasonry*. 1869. Reprint, New York: Bell Publishing, 1989.

Madonna. "Material Girl." Recorded April-May 1984. Track 3 on *Like a Virgin*. Sire-Warner Bros., YouTube music video.

Maier, Bernard. *Dictionary of Celtic Religion and Culture*. Rochester, New York: Boydell Press, 1997.

Mallory, Michael. *Universal Studios Monsters: A Legacy of Horror*. New York: Universal Publishing, 2009.

Mansel, Henry Longueville. *The Gnostic Heresies of the First and Second Centuries*. London: John Murray, 1875.

Marlan, Stanton. *The Black Sun: The Alchemy and Art of Darkness*. College Station: Texas A&M University Press, 2016.

Marshall, Peter. *The Magic Circle of Rudolf II: Alchemy and Astrology in Renaissance Prague*. New York: Walker & Company, 2006.

Matthews, Philip. "Finding Love in Hell." *Werewolf*, March 25, 2015. http://werewolf.co.nz/2015/03/finding-love-in-hell/ (accessed July 15, 2019).

Melanson, Terry. *Perfectibilists: The 18th Century Bavarian Order of the Illuminati*. Walterville, OR: Trine Day, 2009.

Mercer, J.E. *Alchemy: Its Science and Romance*. New York: The Macmillan Co., 1921.

Michelet, Jules. *La Sorcière: The Witch of the Middle Ages*. Translated by L.J. Trotter. London: Simpkin, Marshall, and Co., 1863.

Miller, Frank. *The Dark Knight Returns*. Burbank, California: DC Comics, 1986

Miller, Jason. *Sex, Sorcery, and Spirit: The Secrets of Erotic Magic*. Pompton Plains, NJ: New Page Books, 2014

Miller, Julie. "*Mother!'s* Ending: What Does It All Mean?" *Vanity Fair*, September 16, 2017. https://www.vanityfair.com/hollywood/2017/09/mother-movie-meaning-explained (accessed December 2, 2017).

Miller, Steven. "It's All About the Bunnies in Twin Peaks." *Twin Peaks Blog*, April 21, 2019. https://www.twinpeaksblog.com/2019/04/21/its-all-about-the-bunnies-in-twin-peaks/ (accessed September 10, 2019).

Mills, Charles De. B. *The Tree of Mythology, It's Growth and Fruitage: Genesis of the Nursery Tale, Saws of Folk-Lore, Etc*. Syracuse: C.W. Bardeen Publishers, 1889.

Miss Carruthers. *Flower Lore: The Teachings of Flowers, Historical, Legendary, Poetical, and Symbolical*. Belfast: McCaw, Stevenson & Orr, 1879.

Miss_Jessel. "The curse of the red shoes: dancing manias of the middle ages." *Haunted Palace Blog,* April 4, 2013. https://www.hauntedpalace-blog.wordpress.com/2013/04/04/the-curse-of-the-red-shoes-dancing-manias-of-the-middle-ages/ (accessed April 24, 2019).

Mitchell, John, and John Dickie. *The Philosophy of Witchcraft*. Paisley: Murray and Stewart, 1839.

Moir, George. *Magic and Witchcraft*. London: Chapman and Hall, 1852.

Monod, Paul Kleber. *Solomon's Secret Art: The Occult in the Age of the Enlightenment*. New Haven: Yale University Press, 2013.

Moore, Alan. *The Killing Joke*. Burbank, CA: DC Comics, 1988.

Morrison, Mark S. *Modern Alchemy: Occultism and the Emergence of Atomic Theory*. New York: Oxford University Press, 2007.

Mortensen, Karl. *A Handbook of Norse Mythology*. Translated by A. Clinton Crowell. New York: Thomas E. Crowell Company, Publishers, 1913.

Muir, M.M. Pattison. *The Story of Alchemy and the Beginnings of Chemistry*. London: George Newnes, LTD., 1902.

Murray, Alexander S. *Manual of Mythology: Greek and Roman, Norse, and Old German, Hindu and Egyptian Mythology*. 2nd revised ed. New York: Charles Scribner's Sons, 1893.

Murray, Margaret. *The God of the Witches*. London: Sampson Low, Marston & Co., 1933.

Nabokov, Vladimir. *Pale Fire*. 1962. Reprint, Vintage International, 1989.

Near, Laurel. "In Heaven." *Eraserhead* (movie), 1977, YouTube music video.

Nelson, Victoria. *The Secret Life of Puppets*. Cambridge: Harvard University Press, 2002.

Nichols, Sallie. *Jung and Tarot: An Archetypal Journey*. 1984. Reprint, San Francisco: Weiser Books, 2004.

Nicolaou, Elena. "How *Midsommar's* May Queen Scene Connects To A Real Swedish Legend." *Refinery29*, July 3, 2019. https://www.refinery29.com/en-us/2019/07/236964/midsommar-real-may-queen-dance-harga-legend-devil-dark-one (accessed January 22, 2020).

Nicoll, Maurice. *Dream Psychology*. London: Henry Frowde, Hodder & Stoughton, 1917.

Olcott, William Tyler. *Star Lore: Myths, Legends, and Facts*. 1911. Reprint, Mineola, NY: Dover Publications, 2004.

——. *Sun Lore of All Ages: A Collection of Myths and Legends*. 1914. Reprint, Mineola, NY: Dover Publications, Inc., 2005.

Opie, Iona, and Peter Opie. *The Classic Fairy Tales*. New York: Oxford University Press, 1980.

Ouspensky, P.D. *The Symbolism of the Tarot: Philosophy of Occultism in Pictures and Numbers Pen-Pictures of the Twenty-Two Tarot Cards*. Translated by A.L. Pogossky. 1913. Reprint, Mansfield Centre, CT: Martino Publishing, 2013.

Pagels, Elaine. *The Gnostic Gospels.* 1979. Reprint, New York: Vintage Books, 1989.

Parker, Derek, and Julia Parker. *The Complete Astrologer.* New York: McGraw-Hill Book Company, 1971.

Pendle, George. *Strange Angel: The Otherworldly Life of Rocket Scientist John Whiteside Parsons.* Orlando: Harcourt, Inc., 2006.

Pennick, Nigel. *Witchcraft & Secret Societies in Rural England: The Magic of the Toadmen, Plough Witches, Mummers, and Bonesmen.* Rochester, VT: Destiny Books, 2019.

Pernety, Antoine-Joseph. *Treatise on the Great Art: A System of Physics According to Hermetic Philosophy and Theory and Practice of the Magisterium.* Edited by Edouard Blitz, M.D. Boston: Occult Publishing Company, 1898.

The Complete Picatrix: The Occult Classic of Astrological Magic – Liber Atratus Edition. Translated by John Michael Greer and Christopher Warnock. 1256. Reprint, Adocentyn Press, 2018.

Pietsch, Theodore W. *Trees of Life: A Visual History of Evolution.* Baltimore: Johns Hopkins University Press, 2012.

Pike, Albert. *Morals and Dogma of the Ancient and Accepted Scottish Rite of Freemasonry.* 1871. Reprint, Richmond, VA: L.H. Jenkins, Inc., 1960.

Place, Robert M. *The Tarot: History, Symbolism, and Divination.* New York: Tarcher/Penguin, 2005.

——. *The Tarot, Magic, Alchemy, Hermeticism, and Neoplatonism.* 2nd ed. Saugerties, NY: Hermes Publications, 2019.

Plummer, George W. *Rosicrucian Symbology.* New York: Macoy Publishing and Masonic Supply Co., 1916.

Porter, Darwin, and Danforth Prince. *Hollywood Babylon It's Back!* New York: Blood Moon Productions, 2009.

———. *Hollywood Babylon Strikes Again!* New York: Blood Moon Productions, 2010.

Presley, Elvis. "Suspicious Minds." Recorded January 23, 1969. Released as a Single. RCA Records, 1969, YouTube music video.

"Psycho Symbols, Allegory and Motifs." *Grade Saver*, n.d. https://www.gradesaver.com/psycho/ study-guide/symbols-allegory-motifs (accessed January 10, 2018).

Radiohead. "Everything in Its Right Place." Recorded 2000. Track 2 on *Vanilla Sky* (soundtrack). WEA/Warner Bros., 2001, YouTube music video.

Regardie, Israel. *The Complete Golden Dawn System of Magic*. Tempe, AZ: New Falcon Publications, 1994.

———. *The Philosopher's Stone*. n.p., 1938.

———. *What You Should Know About the Golden Dawn*. 1936. Reprint, Tempe, AZ: New Falcon Publications, 2006.

Remes, Pauliina. *Neoplatonism: Ancient Philosophies*. Berkeley: University of California Press, 2008.

Robertson, John M. *Pagan Christs: Studies in Comparative Hierology*. 2nd ed. London: Watts & Co., 1911.

Rogers, L.W. *The Occultism in the Shakespeare Plays*. New York: The Theosophical Book Company, 1909.

The Rolling Stones. "Paint It Black." Recorded March 1966. Track 1 on *Aftermath*. London Records, 1966, compact disk.

Rotten Tomatoes. https://www.rottentomatoes.com.

Rudolph, Kurt. *Gnosis: The Nature and History of Gnosticism*. San Francisco: Harper, 1987.

Russell, Jeffrey Burton. *The Devil: Perceptions of Evil from Antiquity to Primitive Christianity*. Ithaca: Cornell University Press, 1990.

——. *A History of Witchcraft: Sorcerers, Heretics, and Pagans*. 1980. Reprint, New York: Thames and Hudson Inc., 1991.

——. *Lucifer: The Devil in the Middle Ages*. Ithaca: Cornell University Press, 1992.

——. *Mephistopheles*: *The Devil in the Modern World*. Ithaca: Cornell University Press, 1992.

——. *The Prince of Darkness: Radical Evil and the Power of Good in History*. New York: Cornell University Press, 1993.

——. *Satan: The Early Christian Tradition*. 1981.Ithaca: Cornell University Press, 1991.

Salisbury, Mark. *Crimson Peak: The Art of Darkness*. San Rafael, CA: Insight Editions, 2015.

Saposnik, Irving S. *Robert Louis Stevenson*. New York: Twayne Publishers, 1975.

Schama, Simon. *Citizens: A Chronicle of the French Revolution*. New York: Vantage Books, 1990.

Schechter, Harold. *Deviant: The Shocking True Story of Ed Gein, the Original "Psycho."* New York: Pocket Books, 1998.

Schneider, Steven Jay. *101 Horror Movies You Must See Before You Die*. Hauppauge, New York: Barron's Educational Books, 2009.

Scholem, Gershom. *Kabbalah*. 1974. Reprint, New York: Meridian, 1978.

——. *On the Kabbalah and its Symbolism*. Translated by Ralph Manheim. 1960. Reprint, New York: Schocken Books, 1996.

Sepharial. *The Kabalah of Numbers: A Handbook of Interpretation*. London: William Rider and Son, Limited, 1911.

Shakespeare, William. *Cymbeline*. 1623. Reprint, New York: Simon & Schuster, 2003.

——. *Hamlet*. 1603. Reprint, New York: Simon & Schuster, 2012.

——. *Macbeth*. 1623. Reprint, New York: Washington Square Press, 1992.

——. *Richard III*. 1623 (First Folio). Reprint, New York: Washington Square Press, 2004.

Shelley, Mary. *Frankenstein; or, the Modern Prometheus*. 1818. Reprint, Mineola, New York: Dover Publications, 1984.

Shewfelt, Raechal. "Joaquin Phoenix's 'Joker' character was inspired by a 'Wizard of Oz' star." *Yahoo*, September 30, 2019. https://www.yahoo.com/entertainment/joaquin-phoenixs-joker-character-was-inspired-by-a-wizard-of-oz-star-204041947.html (accessed February 16, 2020).

Simek, Rudolf. *Dictionary of Norse Mythology*. Translated by Angela Hall. 1984. Reprint, Rochester, NY: D.S. Brewer, 2000.

Skal, David J., and Elias Savada. *Dark Carnival: The Secret World of Tod Browning, Hollywood's Master of the Macabre*. New York: Anchor Books, 1995.

Skal, David J. *The Monster Show: A Cultural History of Horror*. New York: Farrar, Straus and Giroux, 2001.

Sharp, Dennis. *The Picture Palace and Other Buildings for the Movies*. New York: Frederick A. Praeger, 1969.

Snuffin, Michael Osiris. *Introduction to Romantic Satanism*. Throned Eye Press, 2020.

Spelling, Ian. "Guillermo del Toro and Ivana Baquero escape from a civil war into the fairytale land of *Pan's Labyrinth*." *Science Fiction Weekly*, December 25, 2006. https://web.archive.org/web/20080609075453/http://www.scifi.com/sfw/interviews/sfw14471.html (accessed October 10, 2019).

Spence, Lewis. *Encyclopaedia of Occultism: A Compendium of Information on the Occult Sciences, Occult Personalities, Psychic Science, Magic, Demonology, Spiritism, Mysticism, and Metaphysics*. 1920. Reprint, New Hyde Park, NY: University Books, 1960.

Steinbeck, John. *Of Mice and Men*. 1937. Reprint, New York: Penguin, 1993.

Steinmetz, George. *The Royal Arch: Its Hidden Meaning*. New York: Macoy Publishing and Masonic Supply Co., 1946.

Stekel, William. *Sex and Dreams: The Language of Dreams*. Boston: Richard G. Badger, 1922.

Stewart, Mark Allyn. *David Lynch Decoded*. Bloomington, IN: AuthorHouse, 2007.

"Style Crush: Kim Basinger in 9 ½ Weeks." *Little Spree*, January 8, 2018. https://littlespree.com/brands/matches/style-crush-kim-basinger-in-9-1-2-weeks/?cn-reloaded=1 (accessed September 12, 2020).

Sullivan, Robert. *Goodbye Lizzie Borden*. Brattleboro, VT: The Stephen Greene Press, 1974.

Sullivan, Robert W., IV. *Cinema Symbolism: A Guide to Esoteric Imagery in Popular Movies*. 2nd ed. Baltimore: Deadwood Publishing, LLC, 2017.

——. *Cinema Symbolism 2: More Esoteric Imagery in Popular Movies*. Baltimore: Deadwood Publishing, LLC., 2017.

——. *The Royal Arch of Enoch: The Impact of Masonic Ritual, Philosophy, and Symbolism*. 2nd ed. Baltimore: Deadwood Publishing LLC, 2016.

Sutin, Lawrence. *Divine Invasions: A Life of Philip K. Dick*. New York: Carroll & Graf Publishers, 2005.

Swift, Taylor. "Style." Recorded February 2014. Track 3 on *1989*. Big Machine Records, 2014, YouTube music video.

Tadelis, Steven. *Game Theory: An Introduction*. Princeton: Princeton University Press, 2013.

Tauring, Kari. *The Runes: A Human Journey*. Lulu.com, 2007.

Thorsson, Edred. *Futhark: A Handbook of Rune Magic*. 1984. Reprint, York Beach, ME: Samuel Weiser, Inc., 1992.

Tears for Fears. "Head over Heels." Recorded 1985. Track 19 on *Donnie Darko* (soundtrack). Enjoy Records, 2002, YouTube music video.

Thomson, David. *Europe Since Napoleon*. 1957. Reprint, London: Penguin Books, 1990.

Thompson, Emma, and Audra McDonald. "Beauty and the Beast (Finale)." Recorded 2015-2016. Track 16 on *Beauty and the Beast* (soundtrack). Walt Disney, 2017, YouTube music video.

Tsarion, Michael. *Astro-Theology and Sidereal Mythology*. Seattle: Taroscopes, 2008.

Twyman, Tracy, and Alexander Rivera. *Baphomet: The Temple Mystery Unveiled*. n.p., 2015.

Valiente, Doreen. *An ABC of Witchcraft Past & Present*. New York: St. Martin's Press, 1973.

Valli, Frankie. "The Sun Ain't Gonna Shine (Anymore)." Recorded July 1965. Track 7 on *Solo*. Smash Records, 1967, YouTube music video.

Versluis, Arthur. *Esoteric Origins of the American Renaissance*. New York: Oxford University Press, 2001.

———. *Magic and Mysticism: An Introduction to Western Esotericism*. Lanham, MD: Rowman & Littlefield Publishers, Inc., 2007.

———. *The Secret History of Western Sexual Mysticism: Sacred Practices and Spiritual Marriage*. Rochester, VT: Destiny Books, 2008.

Vickers, Graham. *Chasing Lolita: How Popular Culture Corrupted Nabokov's Little Girl All Over Again*. Chicago: Chicago Review Press, 2008.

Waite, Arthur Edward. *The Book of Black Magic*. American ed. 1972. Reprint, San Francisco: Red Wheel/Weiser, LLC, 2008.

———. *The Pictorial Key to the Tarot*. London: W. Rider, 1911.

Waite, Robert G. L. *The Psychopathic God: Adolf Hitler*. 1977. Reprint, Boston: Da Capo Press, 1993.

Wall, O.A. *Sex and Sex Worship (Phallic Worship)*. St. Louis: C.V. Mosby Company, 1922.

Watson, Paul Joseph. "Why the WOKE Establishment Hates Joker." *YouTube* video, 9:16, October 8, 2019. https://youtu.be/MxLZv2qdlUI.

Weaver, Tom, Michael Brunas, and John Brunas. *Universal Horrors: The Studio's Classic Films, 1931-1946*. 2nd ed. Jefferson, NC: McFarland & Company, Inc., Publishers, 2017.

Welk, Lawrence. "The Moon is a Silver Dollar." Recorded 1939. Released as a Single. YouTube video.

Westcott, W. Wynn. *Christian Rosenkreuz and the Rosicrucians*. London: The Theosophical Publishing Society, 1894.

Wigston, W.F.C. *Bacon, Shakespeare, and the Rosicrucians*. London: George Redway, 1888.

Wilson, Colin, *Aleister Crowley: The Nature of the Beast*. London: Aquarian Press, 1987.

——. *The Occult: A History*. New York: Random House, 1971.

Wilson, Eric. *The Melancholy Android: On the Psychology of Sacred Machines*. Albany: State University of New York Press, 2006.

——. *Secret Cinema: Gnostic Vision in Film*. New York: Continuum International Publishing Group Inc., 2006.

——. *The Strange World of David Lynch: Transcendental Irony from Eraserhead to Mulholland Dr*. New York: Continuum International Publishing Group Inc., 2007.

Wind, Edgar. *Pagan Mysteries in the Renaissance: An Exploration of Philosophical and Mystical Sources of Iconography in Renaissance Art*. Revised ed. New York: W.W. Norton & Company, Inc., 1968.

The Witches' Dream Book and Fortune Teller. New York: Henry J. Wehman, Publisher, 1885.

Yates, Frances A. *The Art of Memory*. 1966. Reprint, London: The Bodley Head, 2014.

——. *Giordano Bruno and the Hermetic Tradition*. 1964. Reprint, Chicago: The University of Chicago Press, 1991.

——. *The Occult Philosophy in the Elizabethan Age*. 1979. Reprint, New York: Routledge Classics, 2001.

——. *The Rosicrucian Enlightenment*. 1972. Reprint, New York: Routledge Classics, 2010.

——. *Theatre of the World*. Chicago: The University of Chicago Press, 1969.

Young, Julian. *Heidegger, philosophy, Nazism*. New York: Cambridge University Press, 1998.

Young, Killian. "How an Old Jazz Song Pays Homage to Stanley Kubrick's The Shining." *Consequence of Sound*, July 31, 2014. https://consequenceofsound.net/2014/07/how-an-old-jazz-song-pays-homage-to-stanley-kubricks-the-shining/ (accessed December 11, 2018).

Yuan, Jada. "Nicolas Winding Refn and Elle Fanning on *Neon Demon*, Fanning's Physical Beauty, and a Knife-Wielding Keanu." *Vulture*, May 30, 2016. https://www.vulture.com/2016/05/elle-fanning-nicolas-winding-refn-neon-demon-sex-keanu.html (accessed April 11, 2019).

Ziegler, Andrew. "There's a 'Matrix' Reference in 'Star Wars' That'll Make You Question Everything." *Buzzfeed*, November 29, 2017. https://www.buzzfeed.com/andrewziegler/this-link-between-the-matrix-and-star-wars-will-bl (accessed April 14, 2018).

Zimmerman, Daniel. *The Plots of Father Brown Stories of Gilbert Keith Chesterton*. Lulu.com, 2014.

INDEX

Numbers in italics indicate photo or photo caption.

9 ½ Weeks, XLIII, *XLIV*, XLVIII, L-*LIII*, LV, *LVII*, LXV, *LXVII*, LXIX, 365, *370*, 372, 407, 426, *433*
2001: A Space Odyssey, 389, 399, 587
Ace Elevator Company, XXIV-XXV
The Adjustment Bureau, 20, 50
"The Adventure of the Devil's Foot," 323
Agrippa, Heinrich Cornelius, 52, 211, 271, 288-289
Alchemy, XIV, *XXXIV*, *XL*, XLIX-L, LII-*LIII*, *LVII*, *LXII*, *LXVI*, LXXVI-LXXXV, *XC-XCII*, XCVII, CVII, 48, 51, 77, 131-*133*, 136-137, 168, 201, 211, 244, 288-291, 317, 349-*350*, 355, 363-*366*, *370*, 377-385, 409-410, *413*, 422, *426*, *433*, 543, 545, 555, 567-568, 570, 578, 581, 583-585, 595, 615, 618
Alice in Wonderland, *XXXVII*- XXXVIII, 36, 38-39, 235, 237, 403, 556
Alice Through the Looking Glass, 36
The Amityville Horror, 394
An American Werewolf in London, XLVIII, LXVIII
Ancient Order of the Bonesmen, 557
Andersen, Hans Christian, 372, *375*, 377
Angel Heart, XXXIII, 134, 142-143, 161, 580

The Arch of Hysteria, 403
Ars Goetia, LVII, 108, 175, 210-211, 271
Argentium Astrum, XCVIII, *156*, *176*
Asclepius, XLVI, 19, 48, 152-153, 288-289
Back to the Future, XXX, 84, *97*, 186, 206-*207*
Back to the Future II, 186
Bael, LVII
Baphomet, XXXII-*XXXIV*, *XLVII*, 129, 132, 144, 168-169, 176, 220, 229, 230, 240, 367-368, 578
Barry Lyndon, 389, 587
Basilides, 22, 40-41, 43-44, 57, 85, 88, 90-93, 113, 303, 464, 516
Bates Motel, XLVIII, LXXXV, 1-17, 571
Batman Begins, 319-325, 336, 341
Batman Returns, XXXVIII-*XXXIX*, *45*, *371*
Baudelaire, Charles, LII
Bausch, Philippine "Pina," 158
Beauty and the Beast, LXXXVIII, 122, 123-140, 410
Beavis and Butt-Head, XXIII
Being There, 594
Bernhardt, Sarah, XIV
The Black Cat, 149, 157, 213, 246
Black Swan, XXXIX-XLI, *XLII*, LXXXVIII-LXXXIX, *XC*, 32, *133*, *167*, 177, 251, 344, 375, 377, 382, 401, 407, 410, 412-*413*, 425-*429*, 458, 491, 499, 568, 615

Blade Runner, XCII, XCIX, C, 20, 55, 79, 286, 287, 291-299, 305, 310, 317, 321

Blade Runner 2049, XCIX, C, 286, 287, 299-306

Blake, William, XVI, L, 55, 301, *364* 367, 370

Blatty, William Peter, XIX-XX

Blavatsky, Madame Helena, 469, 550, 582

Blue Oyster Cult, XLVIII

Blue Velvet, CI, 32, 66, 134-135, 247, 503, 532, 544-545, 546, 548, 552, 564, 577

Book of Thoth, XXX, 617

Borden, Lizzie, and Borden Murders see *Lizzie*

Bowie, David, 298, 305, 573

Brazil, 116, 320, 461

Breakfast at Tiffany's, LXIX, *LXXI*, 555

The Bride of Frankenstein, LI, 481

The Bridesmaid, XXVIII

The Brocken, LI, 157

Bruno, Giordano, XXVII, 211, 288

Bryant, Kobe, XVII

Buffy Summers (character), 31, 34

Buffy the Vampire Slayer, 57

Lord Byron (George Gordon), L-LI

The Cabinet of Dr. Caligari, C, 55, 149 156, 307-315, 344

Carnarvon (George Herbert), 144-145

Carter, Howard, 144-147

Central Intelligence Agency, see CIA

Children of Paradise, 160, 562

CIA, XIX, 101, 329, 336, 425-426, 428, 430-431

A Clockwork Orange, 386-387, 399-400, 58

Colors, alchemical scheme, *nigredo, albedo, citrinitas,* and *rubedo,* see Alchemy

Confraternity of the Plough, 557

Corman, Roger, XIV

Creature from the Black Lagoon, XXXVII, 410, 415, 421

Creepshow, LX

Crimson Peak, XXVIII, XXXVIII, XLI, *XLII,* LXX, 235, 238, 417

Cromwell, Oliver, XXXV

Crowley, Aleister, XV-XVI, *XXI*, XXX, *LIII,* LV, *XC,* XCV-XCVIII, 149, *156,* 160, 168, 175, *176,* 177, *213,* 235, 242, 250, *364,* 368-369, *370,* 373, *433,* 463, 468, 556, 565-566, 573, 583, 617

Da Vinci, Leonardo, *XV*, LXIV, *CVI*, 112, 260

The Da Vinci Code, XV

Dahmer, Jeffrey, *403*

Dakota Apartments, 102, 177, 362,

Dark City, 50, 55-67, 69, 85, 92, 98

The Dark Knight, LXXV, 134, 325-334, 336, 341

The Dark Knight Rises, LXIX, *LXXI*, 335-342, 616

Dark Night of the Scarecrow, XCV, XCVIII, 205, 221-227

Dark of the Moon, see *The Black Cat*

The Dark Secret of Harvest Home, 211, 245, 263

Dark Water, XXVI

Dee, John, XCVIII, 136, 211, 213-*215*, 231, 288, 591

De Guaita, Stanislas, *XXXIV*, XXXIII

Descartes, Rene, 95, 292-293

Donnie Darko, LXXXVIII, 67-85, 105, 114-115

Double Indemnity, 545

Dr. Strangelove, 386, 400

Dracula (1931 film), XXXVII-XXXVIII, 144, 146, 148, *150*-151, 410

Eckhart, Meister (Eckhart von Hochheim), XXXIII, 43, 303, 570

The Elephant Man, 510, 546-547, 585
Epstein, Jeffrey, XXII
Eraserhead, CV, 63, 504-520, 544-545, 547, 548, 556, 575, 599
The Evil Dead, 72, 79, 217
Evil Dead II, LXV, 215, 217
Excalibur, 355
eXistenZ, 67, 85-98
The Exorcist, XIX-*XX*, XXX, XXXVIII, LVIII, 142, 171, 246, 438, 442, 485, 556
Eye of the Devil, 362
Eyes Wide Shut, XXII, 9, 98, 246, 257, 320 388-389, 399-400
Ficino, Marsilio, *CVI*, 20, 37, 43, 94, 153-154,
Fight Club, *XXII*-XXIII, XLIV, LXXXVI, 20, 25, 30, 48, 67
Floyd, George, 344
Forbidden Planet, LXXII
Fortune, Dion, XCI
Frankenstein ('31 film), XXXVII, 144, 146, 149, *482*
Fraternitas Saturni, 313
Freemasonry, XIV, XLV, XCVII-XCVIII, 33, 42, 51, 168-169, 178, 212, 235, 239, 261, 318, 472, 472, 474, 476, 501, 516, 565-566, 618; influence on Hollywood, 478-479
Freud, Sigmund, LXII-LXIII, 64, 153
Full Metal Jacket, 387, 392, 400
Gacy, John Wayne, *343*-344, 354
The Ghost of Frankenstein, 376
Glen or Glenda, 24-25, 370, 493, 506, 599
Gnosticism, XIV, XLIV, LII, LXVII, LXXXV-LXXXVII, 19-122, 435, 495, 505, 516, 520, 523, 575, 595

Goat of Mendes, see Baphomet
Good, the Bad and the Ugly, 26
Green Mile, 482-483
Gretel & Hansel, 234-*235*
Hairspray, 410, 424-425
Halloween 1978, XLVIII, LXXI-LXXII, LXXIV, 178-192
Halloween 2018, XCV, XCVIII, 178-192, 32
Halloween II, LIX, LXXI-LXXIII,178-192
Halloween III: Season of the Witch, LVIII-LIX, 52, 186, 188, *555*
Halloween 4, 180, 186, 189
Harris, Eric, *XXIII*
Häxan: Witchcraft Through the Ages, *XLVII*-XLVIII, 235
Hepburn, Audrey, LXIX, *LXXI*, LXXXIX, 105
Hereditary, XLVIII, 246, 248, 259, 271
Hermes Trismegistus, XV, XXXIII, *XXXIV*, XXXVI, XLV, *XLVI*, LXXVII, LXXIX, CV, 19, 22, 48, 112, 142, 212, *261*, 263, 288,292, 318, 322, 339, 476, 567, 582, 594, 598, 603-604
Hermetic Order of the Golden Dawn, see Golden Dawn
Hero's Journey, see Monomyth
Hitler, Adolf, 44, 115, 243, 440
The Hobbit: An Unexpected Journey, 601-606
The Hobbit: The Desolation of Smaug, 601, 606-609
The Hobbit: The Battle of the Five Armies, 609-613
The House of Fear, *XXXI*, XXXII
House of Frankenstein, 239, 314

The House with a Clock in Its Walls, XCV, XCVIII, 205-220, 615
The Hunchback of Notre Dame, 48, 125, 410-*411*
Hugo, Victor, XV, L
Iamblichus of Chalcis, 43
I Love Lucy, 146
The Illuminati, XXI-XXII, XXVII, XLIII, LXXV, LXXXV, 9, 17, *33*, 169, 178, 235, 240, 257, 301, 323, *370*, 431, 469, 501, 565, 566, 569, 594, 617, 618
Jacob's Ladder, XXXIII
Joker, LXXV, C-CI, 312, 317, 319, 342-359
Jung, Carl G., XVI, XLIX, LXIII, LXXIV-LXXVII, XCI, 14, 131, 136-137, 165-166, 170, 172, 178, 193, 239, 322, *525*, 570
Kelley, Edward, XCVIII, 52, 213-*215*
The Killing, 326, *399*
The Killing Joke, 343, 345, 346, 353, 357
The King of Comedy, 344
Klebold, Dylan, *XXIII*, XXIV
Lam, Elisa, XXV-XXVI
LaVey, Anton, 231, *253*, 254
Led Zeppelin, 78, 468, 557
Legends of Chamberlain Heights, XVII
The Lego Movie, 109-115
Les Fleurs du mal, see Charles Baudelaire
Lesser Key of Solomon, see *Ars Goetia*
Levi, Eliphas, XV, *XXXIV*, L, XCVIII
The Lighthouse, 227, 617
Lilith, LIV, 32, 135, 192, 202, 204, 319, 367, 369, 371, 373, 488
The Lion King, XXXIII, 125, 481
The Lion, the Witch and the Wardrobe, *480*

Lizzie, XCV, XCVIII, 192-205, 372, 384, 401, 410, 564
Lolita, CIII, 72-*73*, 300, 363, 385-401, 432, 434
London After Midnight, XXX
Loren, Sophia, *253*, 254
Lost Highway, 44, 94, 109, 247, 463, 501, *503*, 547-548, 580, 599
Lucifer, XV, XXXII, LI, *LVII*, 32, 108, 134, 142-143, 169, 192, *213*, 234, 244, 271, 290, 293-294, 334, 377, *433*, 469, 482, 570
McDonald's, see *Mac and Me*
Mac and Me, XXXI
Maleficent, XXXII, *129*, 404
Maleficent: Mistress of Evil, XXXII, *129*, 617
The Man Who Laughs (movie), *312*, 344, 347
Mani, 34-35, 38, 318
Mansfield, Jayne, *253*, 254
Manson, Charles, 84, *362*
Maria's Lovers, LXIII
Mark of the Vampire, CIII
Masturbation, XXXIX, XL, L-*LIII*, LIV-LV, LVI-*LVII*, LXII-LXIII, LXVI, LXIX, LXXIII, LXXXIX, *XC*, *129*, 157, 160-161, 195, 200, 266, 271, 361, 363, 365, 366, 369-370, 382, 397, 406-407, 412-413, 415, 419, *433*
Mathers, Samuel Liddell MacGregor, XCVI-XCVII, 565-566, 575
The Matrix, XXII, LXVII, *LXVIII*, LXXXVI, 19, 20, 22, 26, 35, 39, 48, 50, 66-67, 70, 85, 92, 98, 109, 112, 118, 313, 521

The Matrix Reloaded, LXVII, 22, 521
The Matrix Revolutions, 22, 54, 521
Memento, 67
Mentmore Towers, 320
Metropolis, 44-55, 115, 118, 156, 311, 410, 416
Midsommar, XCV, XCVIII, 245-286
Milton, John, L, 290
Mimas, 451
Modern Times, LXXV, 352
Monomyth, LXVII, LXXXV, CIV, 210, 437, 444-449, 454-456, 464, 601-615
The Monster Squad, XXXVII-XXXVIII
Morley Cigarettes, 592
Mother!, *XLVII*, CV, 485-499
Mulholland Drive, XXXVI, 15-16, 24, 66, 77, 102, 365, 402, 502-503, 533, *543*, 545-548, 568, 570, 577, 585, 596, 599
Murders in the Rue Morgue, C, 55
The Mummy, XXXVII, XCV, 144-155
The Mummy Returns, 320
Nabokov, Vladimir, 73, 300, 385, 395, 397
Naughty Nina Carter, see *An American Werewolf in London*
The Neon Demon, CIII, 363, 401-410, 432, 434, 593
Neumann, Erich, 165
The New York Ripper, LXIX
Night of the Creeps, XXXVII
Night of the Living Dead, LXXII-LXXIII, 491
The Night Stalker, 221
The Night Strangler, 221
Nosferatu, 45, 55, *61*
Notre-Dame Cathedral, *XXV*, 125
Nude Descending a Staircase, No. 2, 309
Onanism, see Masturbation

One Flew Over the Cuckoo's Nest, 377
Ordo Templi Orientis, see OTO
OTO, XCVIII, 313, 368-369, 523
A Pact with the Devil, CVIII, 85, 433, 554, 578, 617-618
Paimon, XLVIII, *LVII*, 271
Pan's Labyrinth, XCV, XCVIII, 234-245, 409
Papus (Gérard Encausse), XIV
Parsons, Jack, 214, 583-584
Paths of Glory, 389
Péladan, Joséphin, XIV, *XV*, LVI, 372, 522
The Persistence of Memory, 215-*216*
Peter and the Wolf, 304-305
Pike, Albert, *129*, 169, 469, 495, 574
Pink Floyd, 313, 443
Plan 9 from Outer Space, XXXVII, 481, 599
Poe, Edgar Allan, C, 132, 154, 252, 397
The Poimandres, XLVI, 19, 119, 153, 595
Porphyry of Tyre, LXXXVI, 43
Presley, Elvis, LXXVI, CIV, 298, 302, 466-484, 520, 524, 526, 529, 532, 542, 544
Psycho, LXXXV, 1-17, 365, 389-390, 395, 517
Quills, 320
Ramirez, Richard, "the Night Stalker," XXVI
Ramses III, *147*
The Raven, 132
Ready Player One, 96-98, 100, 119
The Red Dragon, 235
Red River, 394
The Red Shoes, *CII*-CIII, 363, 367, 372-385, 409-410, 421, 426, 432, 434
Red Sparrow, CIII, 363, 425-434
The Revolt of Islam, L
Rites of Lucifer, see *The Black Cat*
Robespierre, 340-341, 470

Roerich, Nicholas, 583
Rogue One: A Star Wars Story, 449-456, 457
The Rolling Stones, 384
Romantic Satanism, XVI, LI-LII, LV-LVI, CIII, 37, 196, 290, 364, 372-385
Rosemary's Baby, XXV, *XCII*-XCIII, 102, 143, 159, 177, *362*, 486, *489*, 493, 552, 617
Rosicrucianism, XIV, XXVII, LXXXIII-LXXXV, XCVII, 170, 206, 430, 474
Sabrina, 105
Salem's Lot, 221
Satanic Panic, *XXI*, LXIX
Saturn Devouring His Son, *241*
A Scanner Darkly, 20
The Scarlet Claw, 3, 20
Scopes Monkey Trial, C
September 11, 2001, *XXII-XXIV*, 85, 115, 341
Sgt. Pepper's Lonely Hearts Club Band, 468
The Shape of Water, CIII, 235, 363, 409-425, 434, 593
Shadow of a Doubt (film), 365
Shelley, Mary, L, 149, 289
Shelley, Percy Bysshe, L
Sheridan Le Fanu, Joseph Thomas, L
Sherlock Holmes Faces Death, 22
The Shining, XXXVIII, LIX-*LX*, 66, *97*, 117, 120-121, 142, 171, 235, 246, 260, 264, 270, 292, 387, 394, 397, 400, 403, 486, 586-587, 589
Silver Star, see *Argentium Astrum*
The Simpsons, XXII, *XXIV*
Skull and Bones, 428-430, *431*, 557
Sleeping Beauty, 124, 127, 136, 337
Smokey and the Bandit, 614
The Smurfs, XXX-XXXI

Snowpiercer, 115-122
Sock and Buskin, 345-*346*, 354
Son of Dracula, 155
Son of Frankenstein, 263, 376
Sophia, XCIX, 27-32, 35-40, 49, 50-51, 54, 62, 64, 66, 113, 135, 348, 495-496, 505, 513, 519, 522, 558, 585, 595, 597
Sophia Serrano, 99-108
Spartacus, 389, 391
Spies Like Us, XXV
The Squaw Man, 479
Star Wars: A New Hope, XXXV, LXXXIV, 439, *440*-441, 448-449, 450-*451*, 452, 454-455, 457
Star Wars: Attack of the Clones, XVII-LXVIII
Star Wars: The Empire Strikes Back, LXIV, 394, 405, 440, 452-453, 462
Star Wars: The Force Awakens, 436-449, 450, 456, 463, 480
Star Wars: The Last Jedi: 303, 454, 456-465
Star Wars: The Phantom Menace, 438, 440
Star Wars: Return of the Jedi, 394, 436, 452, 459, 462
Star Wars: Revenge of the Sith, 193, 451, 453, 462
Star Wars: Rise of Skywalker, CIV, 442, 457, 464, 617
Stetson, Colin, XLVIII
Stoker, 7, 193, 364-*366*, 372
Stonehenge, LVIII-LIX
Sullivan IV, Robert W., 84-85
Supergirl, LXV
Superman III, LXV
Suspiria 1977, XLIII, *XLIV*, XCV, 157, 170-171, 177-178, *194*, *235*, 402

Suspiria 2018, LI, LXV, XCV, XCVI, XCVIII, 155-178, 187, 346, 568
Swedenborg, Emanuel, XVI, *366*
Swift, Taylor, LXXVIII
Tales of Hoffmann, 462
Tarot, *XXIII*, *XXXIV*, XLIV, LXXVII, LXXXIII-LXXXIV, XCV, XCVII, 133, 169, 232-*233*, 427, *429*, 496-*497*, *555*, 563, 617-*619*
Tate, Sharon, *362*
Taxi Driver, 344
The Texas Chainsaw Massacre, 189, 408
There Will Be Blood, 394
The Thing from Another World, LXXII
Time Bandits, 23
Toadmen, 557
Total Recall, 20
Trick 'r Treat, *LX*, 143
Trilogy of Terror, 221
Troubadours, 522-523, 538
The Truman Show, LXXXVI, 20, 23, 29, 34-35, 67, 92, 98
Trump, Barron, *XVII*
Trump, Donald, XVII-XVIII, 115, 134-135, 347, 349, 351
Twin Peaks (1990-91), XXXIV, CV, 1, 134 159, 247, 501-503, 506, 535, 545-572
Twin Peaks: Fire Walk with Me, CV, 501, 572-585
Twin Peaks: The Return, LXXXV, CV, *502*, 585-600
Unterweger, Johann "Jack", XXVI
The Wolfman, *XXXI*, XXXVII
Valentinus, 21, 35-40, 49, 57, 62-63, 85, 119, 318, 595

Vanilla Sky, 67, 98-109, 115
Voltaire, L, 21, 475
Wait Until Dark, LXXXIX
The Warriors, XXXV-XXXVI, 40, 482
Whale, James, XIV, 149, 290
White Zombie, 314
The Wicker Man, XXXII, XCVIII, 245, 260, 264, 266, 281-282
Wild at Heart, CV, 502, 504, 520-544, 546-547, 563
The Wild Bunch, 462
The Winter's Tale, LXXVIII-LXXXIII
The Witch (or *The VVitch*), XXXII, XCV, XCVIII, 227-235
Witches' Sabbath, 230
The Wizard of Oz, LXIX, 22, *23*, 27, 55, 235, 244-245, 256, 501-*502*, 520, 524-525, 537, 543-*543*, 544, 590, 615
Wolfen, 356
The X-Files, 571, *592*
Zorro films, 355
Zucco, George, 254

ABOUT THE AUTHOR

Robert W. Sullivan IV is a historian, philosopher, writer, antiquarian, lay theologian, mystic, jurist, radio-TV personality, showman, best-selling author, CEO, and attorney. He received his B.A. (History) from Gettysburg College in 1995 having spent his junior year studying European history and philosophy at St. Catherine's College, Oxford University. He received his J.D. from Delaware Law School–Widener University in 2000. Mr. Sullivan is a Freemason having joined Amicable-St. John's Lodge #25, Baltimore, Maryland in 1997; he became a 32nd degree (Master of the Royal Secret) Scottish Rite Mason in 1999, Valley of Baltimore, Orient of Maryland. A lifelong Marylander, he resides in Baltimore.

www.robertwsullivaniv.com

www.ingramcontent.com/pod-product-compliance
Lightning Source LLC
Chambersburg PA
CBHW071212290426
44108CB00013B/1162